Penguin Handbooks
The Parents' A to Z

Penelope Leach was educated at Cambridge University,
where she read History, and at the London School of
Economics, where she obtained a Ph.D. in Social
Psychology. She has researched into juvenile crime for the
Home Office and into the development and upbringing of
children for the Medical Research Council. As Jane Adrian,
she contributed regularly to *The Times* and to the *Sunday
Times*, and she writes under her own name for *Mother and
Baby*, *Mother*, *Family Circle* and other magazines. She has
broadcast frequently, including series for 'Woman's Hour'
and for BBC further education, as well as on many phone-in
programmes. She is a vice-president of the Pre-School
Playgroups Association and the Health Visitors' Association,
has served on the committee of the Developmental section of
the British Psychological Society and is a sponsor of the
Society of Teachers opposed to Corporal Punishment. Her
first book, *Babyhood*, was published by Penguin in 1974 and a
revised and expanded edition appeared early in 1983. Her
second book, *Baby and Child*, was published in 1977 and a
new edition, especially prepared for Penguin, appeared in
1981. In 1979 her appeal for a better deal for parents and
young children appeared as a Penguin Special called *Who
Cares?*

Penelope Leach is married to an energy specialist and they
have two children, a girl and a boy.

Penelope Leach

The Parents' A to Z

A Handbook for
Children's Health, Growth and Happiness

Penguin Books

Penguin Books Ltd, Harmondsworth, Middlesex, England
Viking Penguin Inc., 40 West 23rd Street, New York, New York 10010, U.S.A.
Penguin Books Australia Ltd, Ringwood, Victoria, Australia
Penguin Books Canada Limited, 2801 John Street, Markham, Ontario, Canada L3R 1B4
Penguin Books (N.Z.) Ltd, 182–190 Wairau Road, Auckland 10, New Zealand

First published by Allen Lane 1983
Published in Penguin Books 1985
Reprinted 1987

Copyright © Penelope Leach, 1983
All rights reserved

Reproduced, printed and bound in Great Britain by
Hazell Watson & Viney Limited,
Member of the BPCC Group,
Aylesbury, Bucks
Set in Linotron Palatino by
Rowland Phototypesetting Limited
Bury St Edmunds, Suffolk

*To the doctors, nurses and ancillary staff of the
James Wigg Practice, Kentish Town Health Centre,
who make parent/professional teamwork in child-care
a daily reality rather than just an ideal.*

This book touches on many matters which fall within the province of the general practitioner. I have naturally been concerned that information and advice concerning diagnosis and treatment should be not only accurate in content but also acceptable in tone to members of the medical profession. I am therefore extremely grateful to Dr Michael Modell, FRCGP, MRCP, DCH, for his kindness, time and care in reading and commenting on the relevant portions of the manuscript.

I must stress, however, that responsibility for the opinions and interpretations presented here remains my own.

Penelope Leach
1983

What this book is for . . .

Since the publication of *Baby and Child* many kind users have written to say that they are 'running out of book . . .' Their child is growing past the toddler stage, or they now have a schoolchild as well as a baby in the house, and they want 'something similar which deals with older children as well'.

For a long time I thought it was impossible to write anything useful concerning children whose important experiences are linked as much to school, community and friends as to home and family. After all, every person, every family and every environment is not only unique in itself but unique in its combinations and effects so that it seemed even dicier to generalize about five-, seven- or thirteen-year-olds than to generalize about babies. But gradually, through contacts with more and more families, I began to see that while all the *people* in families are of course unique, the *issues which families face* are not. There are vast differences between any single-parent family and any partnership, yet they all have to provide meals, cope with measles, choose schools and decide when to call a doctor. A family with just one young baby faces quite different risks from a family with three schoolchildren. Yet both sets of parents have to think about their children's safety and cope with any accidents or disasters which do occur. Money, employment, housing and the availability of relatives and friends all affect family life, but both the most and the least privileged families have to decide how to allocate amongst their various members whatever resources are available. Above all, however much one family may differ in every detail from another, parents all share an overriding concern for their children. We want our children to be healthy and happy. We all work to keep them so and when things go wrong we all want to be sure that we have thought of everything which might explain and improve the situation. Every baby, toddler, child and adolescent is a unique and irreplaceable human being, yet each has to follow the same broad and winding path from birth to maturity. Every parent is a unique person, too, yet each will meet some of a range of similar experiences and issues, problems and pleasures, as his or her children grow. So while this book does not try to follow a 'typical' or 'average' child through all the years he or she spends within the family, it does try to pool those common experiences and concerns and set out those issues and problems, so that any individual parent can use them in thinking about a particular child and coping with particular circumstances.

. . . and how to use it

Most of the material in this book is gathered into articles, or chapters, so that you can find everything which is relevant to a particular topic in one place and no topic has to be dealt with more than once. The chapter called **Accidents**, for example, deals with every kind of accident so that the general points which apply to them all (like coping with pain and fear) do not have to be written out again and again as they would have to be if burns, fractures and head injuries were each in separate parts of the book. In the same way, all the different types of allergic illness are dealt with in **Allergy**; all the issues, physical and emotional, which especially affect adolescents are in **Adolescence** and everything which might concern you about your child's education – from playgroup to choosing a secondary school – is in **School**.

These main chapters are all arranged alphabetically, so that **Abdominal Pain** comes before **Babysitters**, **Growth** comes before **Hospital** and **Teeth** comes before **Working Mothers**.

Wherever it makes sense that way, the material inside these long chapters is organized alphabetically too. In that chapter called **Accidents**, for example, you will find that Burns come before Choking and that Sports injuries come before Wounds. Often, though, it does not make sense to order the material alphabetically and you will find an age- or stage-ordering instead, such that **Language** starts with newborn babies and ends with fluent schoolchildren.

When you want to look up a specific topic, approach the book exactly as if it were an encyclopaedia. Think of a word which your topic might be under and flick through the pages until you find its proper place in the alphabet. There are running headlines at the top of every page so that you can easily see where you have got to. If the word you have chosen to look under is the very same word which I have chosen to write under, you will find an article on the topic you want exactly where you would expect it to be. **Measles**, for example, is between **Masturbation** and **Meatal Ulcers**. But if the two of us have chosen different words for the same topic, you will find yourself referred from your word to mine. If you go to F and look up 'Flu, for example, it will say **'Flu** *see* **Influenza**.

Sometimes the topic you are looking up will be one which I have written about as part of one of the big chapters rather than on its own. You will still find your topic-word in the alphabetical listing but it will direct you elsewhere. If you look up Punishment, for example, it will say **Punishment** *see* **Discipline, Self-discipline and Learning How to Behave**. You will find Punishment dealt with in that article and you will not have to read the whole thing if you do not want to. The running headlines will take you to the relevant pages.

If, by any chance, the word you are trying to look up simply does not appear in the book's alphabet, accept my apologies and try to think of another word which means the same thing. There is no listing for Potty Training, for example, but there is a chapter called **Toilet Training** and several words, such as **Bowel movements** and **Urine**, refer you to it.

On the very next pages of the book you will find a 'Guide to Contents', which lists every chapter and the main sub-sections of the longer ones. This is not so much designed for looking up specific topics which you already know you want to read about as for taking an overview of what is in the book and finding topics which might interest you. It does also give you a quick and easy way to find again a piece you might want to re-read or show to another member of the family and it is the fastest possible route to entries which you might want in an emergency, such as **Bleeding** or

Fits. Please don't try to use this Guide as an index, though. I should hate you to look in it for an entry called Toys and, finding none, decide that I had written nothing on the subject. Look up **Toys** in the main alphabetical listing of the book and it will tell you that they are in **Play**.

Although many of the entries are designed to help you cope with immediate problems, many more are designed to contribute to the kinds of thinking and family discussion which will help to avoid problems. I hope that you will read entries whenever they seem interesting to you, rather than only when you are frantic. **Eating**, for example, is an interesting subject for everyone and some of the material in that chapter might help you avoid the need to read the sections on eating problems or obesity. Every child has to learn to behave, at every successive stage, in the ways which his or her parents (and other people) find acceptable. Don't wait until your child is accused of theft or bullying, or stays out until 2 a.m. for the third night running, before you look at **Discipline, Self-discipline and Learning How to Behave**. That chapter raises issues which are most usefully discussed amongst you all from your children's earliest years. Hopefully there will be many periods during which your family life is smooth and problem-free. Even then you might find something fun to do or make in **Play**, some useful ammunition for family discussion in **Pets**, **Pocket Money** or **Television**, or some material in **School** or **Adolescence** which helps you to think ahead.

The whole book is aimed at supporting you while you help your children to grow from wherever they are now towards being healthy, happy adults. As they reach middle childhood – and perhaps especially once they have passed puberty – you may find that there are entries which you would like them to read for themselves. **Safety**/On wheels, for example, might help if you have reached a stalemate over bicycles or motor-cycles. **Growth**/Children who are 'too small', will inform and almost certainly comfort the child who despairs of being as big as his friends, while many of the issues raised in **Adolescence** could provide useful starting points for discussion, whether or not you agree with what is written about them.

Guide to contents

THE PARENTS' A TO Z

Abdominal Pain *see also* **Pain and Pain Control; Hospital**/Surgery: Appendectomy

Abdominal pain (or 'stomachache' or 'tummyache' as your child may call it) may be your first warning of a real emergency or it may mean nothing important at all. Experience as a parent and knowledge of your own child will help you to draw the fine line between unnecessary midnight calls on your doctor and neglect of the pain which does turn out to be due to appendicitis . . . In the meantime, or with any child who is not your own, play safe. The abdominal cavity runs from the chest (from which it is separated by the muscular wall called the diaphragm) to the pelvis. It contains all the organs concerned with digestion and excretion; not just the stomach but also the liver, gallbladder, pancreas, spleen, kidneys and bladder. It contains yards and yards of large and small intestine and, in females, it contains the uterus (womb), ovaries and fallopian tubes. With so many vital organs and processes grouped together it is often difficult for the victim to say exactly where the pain is and impossible for anyone but a skilled doctor to judge whether or not something is seriously amiss. You certainly need medical advice if:

Abdominal pain is accompanied by other signs of illness such as fever, loss of appetite/energy/interest, poor colour, vomiting and/or diarrhoea.

Pain is the only symptom but is severe enough to take the child's whole attention so that she cannot play, watch television, listen to or read a book.

Pain, even if less severe, lasts for more than a few hours at a level which keeps interrupting the child's activities; although she tries to go on with her ordinary life she cannot do so for more than a few minutes at a time.

● When you have to assess abdominal pain in your child, don't let your judgement be swayed by old wives' tales, for example, eating underripe fruit or too much ice-cream, eating too fast or drinking while eating, are *not* likely causes for the pain. If a child has eaten so unwisely that she really does 'make herself sick' she certainly needs a doctor rather than cries of 'I told you so . . .' It is more likely that she is suffering from some form of food poisoning than from sheer gluttony. 'Chills on the stomach' and 'colds in the kidneys' are folk-ailments rather than real diagnoses, while constipation does not cause pain.

● Be very cautious about the home treatment of abdominal pain. Most pain-relievers, for example, irritate the stomach-lining. If the stomach itself is the site of the pain, they may make matters worse. If the pain stems from elsewhere the drugs may simply add stomach-discomfort to the child's distress. Antacids and 'stomach medicines' should not be given without a doctor's approval either. They will probably have no effect at all but they might mask and confuse other symptoms. Laxatives and purges should *never* be given to a child with abdominal pain. If the pain were due to blockage or muscle spasm somewhere in the intestine, the increased intestinal activity caused by the medicine could be disastrous. If you feel that you must do *something* for the pain, make for the doctor's surgery or the telephone rather than for the medicine cabinet.

Babies and abdominal pain   Since your baby cannot tell you that her stomach hurts you will probably deduce it from the fact that she screams and draws her bent legs up. Remember that babies do this when they are crying from anger, too, and that a baby who cries hard for a long time may make her stomach uncomfortable by swallowing a lot of air. Unless she seems ill, it is worth trying to comfort her with your cheerful presence and cuddling before declaring an emergency.

If nothing you can do will comfort her, she probably does need help. Some babies cry more than others, but healthy ones seldom continue to cry while being held by loved adults. Refusal to be comforted is therefore a worrying symptom.

Colic   A few babies between about three and sixteen weeks of age suffer from what is usually described as 'three-month' or 'evening' colic. Each day, usually after an early evening feed, she is unable to play or settle peacefully to sleep because of what appear to be recurrent bouts of abdominal pain. Left in her cot she screams piteously; picked up she stops but starts again as you hold her. Offered more milk she sucks hard for a moment or two but then stops to yell once more. Everything you do for her seems to help a little for a little while but nothing relieves her completely or for long, until the episode is over for the day as suddenly as it began.

A severe attack of this kind of colic mimics an abdominal emergency so that you will probably call the doctor and find it difficult to believe him when he tells you that there is nothing at all the matter with the baby. You may even feel that he is implying that the whole upset was somehow your fault; that you failed to bring up the baby's wind or that you were tense and hurried when you fed her or tired at the end of a long day and distracted by the return home of other members of the family. Accept his basic reassurance for the moment, but if the pattern of distress is repeated on the next two evenings, seek an appointment at which you can discuss the colic peacefully with him. Evening colic is not an illness; it does not suggest that there is anything wrong with the baby. But it is an exceedingly distressing phenomenon both for her and for you. It is thought to be due to immaturity of the digestive system resulting in extra activity and muscular spasm in the baby's intestines. Although she will certainly 'grow out of it' during this first quarter year you are entitled to help and support while she does so. Some doctors prescribe a drug called dicyclomine hydrochloride which reduces the mobility and muscular spasms of the colon. If this medicine, given half an hour before the feed which precedes regular colic, is going to work for your baby, it will do so almost like magic, ending the whole problem. If it does not work, your doctor may feel that the baby is not suffering from evening colic after all. He may want to double-check for signs of illness and to discuss in detail her overall care and feeding.

• No other medicine is generally thought to be helpful in true evening colic. If your doctor does not wish to prescribe dicyclomine hydrochloride or if it does not help, don't dose her with anything else without his specific instructions. Particularly avoid over-the-counter remedies for colic. In some countries some of these contain undesirable sedatives including alcohol.

Small children and abdominal pain

Very small children find it even more difficult than the rest of us to localize pain. Yours may tell you that her tummy hurts when she has a middle-ear infection. Some common infections, such as tonsillitis, can produce genuine abdominal pain in the very young by affecting glands around the wall of the stomach. The child's attention may be focused on her abdomen even though the site of infection is in her throat which, in an older child, would be very painful. To make confusion worse, many small children cannot distinguish (or at least cannot report the difference) between abdominal pain and nausea. Your child may complain of tummyache when she is about to vomit.

With children in this age group it is therefore doubly important to avoid home-diagnosis in favour of immediate consultation with your doctor.

Mild but long-lasting abdominal pain

If a 'stomachache' is not severe enough to distress your child or worry you but nevertheless continues to be mentioned over several days, it is worth making an appointment for her to see the doctor because there are a variety of disorders which can present themselves in this way. She may have a mild urinary infection even if there are no obvious symptoms such as acute pain when she passes water. An older girl may have pre-menstrual pain even if she has not yet had her first period (*see* **Adolescence**/Menstruation); her body may be reacting to the hormonal preliminaries. Some mild food allergies show themselves in this way (*see* **Allergy**) and so do various forms of digestive difficulty including the excessive intestinal activity which is usually labelled the 'irritable bowel syndrome'.

Recurrent abdominal pain

Some children suffer from recurrent bouts of abdominal pain which, after proper examination and investigation by a doctor, turn out to have no abnormal *physical* cause but to be associated with stress and anxiety in the child. In some sufferers pain is the only symptom, in others the pain is associated with vomiting and occasionally with fever as well.

The causes of this kind of pain are not completely understood and probably vary from child to child. The following factors may contribute:

Small children tend to have a lot of attention focused on stomach and bowels especially if there are eating/toilet training battles going on. If she has anxious attention focused on the workings of her 'insides', the child may become unusually aware of the wave-like movements of her intestines which normally stay beneath the level of consciousness but which she may feel as pain.

Emotion always affects digestion, with stress and anxiety actually increasing the blood supply and the strength of the peristaltic waves. A 'strung-up' child therefore receives stronger signals from her stomach and bowels and may notice them as pain.

The reason for stress/abdominal pain may be specific to the child's life. Some, for example, always have the pain on Monday mornings in term-time but not in the holidays; others have their regular outings with a separated parent ruined by the pain. A few react in this way to any socially stressful occasion so that they can go out to tea quite happily but always have pain before a more formal party.

The reason for stress/abdominal pain may lie in the child's personality. A significantly large number of such children have exceedingly high standards of behaviour and performance, being 'good students', 'highly responsible children' and 'a child any parent would be proud of'. Often the parents are indeed proud and the family is apparently happy. But the stress of successfully meeting such high expectations may take a toll of the child which neither she nor her parents fully realize.

Help with recurrent abdominal pain

Obviously a doctor must see the child and only when obvious physical causes for the pain have been excluded can the diagnosis be made. When it is made though, the child will need:

An authoritative assurance from the doctor that there is nothing physically wrong with her body. This is vital. Pain is a worrying symptom (it is meant to be; it could not operate as a bodily warning system if it did not worry its victims) and a child is just as capable as an adult of brooding secretly about horrors like cancer . . .

An equally authoritative explanation of the probable mechanism by which the pain is produced. The more convinced the child can be that she is noticing peristaltic waves which go on all the time in everyone but which most people do not feel, the easier it will become for her to ignore them.

A direct and genuine acknowledgement from doctor and parents that the pain is real, in the sense that they believe that she feels it and that it is unpleasant. All too often pain of non-physical origin gets labelled 'imaginary' as if the poor victim was inventing a story to get sympathy and attention. She is not and she must be sure that nobody thinks she is.

Every possible attempt to lower the tensions she is under. How this is done must obviously depend on her exact circumstances. You cannot send a new baby back because he is causing stress in an older child's life but you may be able to help her accept him and believe that she still has your secure love and care. A child cannot stop going to school because she finds it stressful but she may need help from the teacher, help with a too-difficult journey, rescue from a subtle playground bully or even a different school. You may not want her to give up all social life just because the prospect of a party makes her throw up, but you might be able and willing to arrange more informal get-togethers with her real friends and let her off the birthday parties for a while. The point, of course, is that once you dissect the occasions which your child finds very stressful, you can usually find a way of helping her to cope rather than to opt out.

● Once you know that your child is liable to recurrent abdominal pain of non-physical origin, you obviously will not consult a doctor every time it occurs. Do be watchful, though, because such a child is not immune from physical causes. If you are too quick to assume that every stomachache is 'her nerves again' you may be dangerously slow to recognize the pain which is actually due to appendicitis. Every episode must be considered on its merits and, for a child with a pattern of recurrent pain, a pain which is different from usual should make you suspicious.

Abrasions *see* **Accidents**/Cuts and scrapes, grazes and puncture wounds.
Abscess *see* **Infection**/Types of infection: Localized infection.
Accident-prone children *see* **Depression**/In children before puberty; **Hyperactive Children**

Accidents *see also* Safety

Although many accidents are preventable many are not. Everyone will experience minor hurts in the course of everyday life; most people will occasionally experience something more serious. A child who is so well-protected that he or she never has *any* kind of accident is probably over-protected; deprived of a rightful ration of adventurous endeavour. It is important to believe this because if you are overwhelmed with guilt every time one of your children is hurt, you will not be competent to judge the seriousness of the situation, to give sensible first aid or to offer appropriate comfort. All these things need calm commonsense.

Calm is particularly important when a baby or very small child is hurt. Such a child does not have the experience or memory to measure up the pain, shock, surprise and anger he is feeling. He feels the pain and reacts to it, but he will take his cue as to the *importance* of that pain, from your reaction. If you are frightened for him, he will be frightened for himself. If your sympathy is tempered by quiet assurance that the whole matter is trivial, he will stay calmer this time and gradually learn that the pain of a banged knee is something which can be quickly shrugged off.

At around four to six or seven, many children go through a phase during which they are disproportionately alarmed by minor accidents. Such a child, newly conscious of his or her own body and its importance as 'my own self', may be fearful not so much of pain but of actual bodily *damage*. There may be fantasies of being 'broken' or 'spoilt'. During such a phase a child may be unable to forget about an injury while he can actually see blood or grazed skin. A piece of sticking plaster is often needed to restore morale even when the actual injury is too minor to require any treatment. You may also be able to give the child some direct and general reassurance by explaining the body's self-healing powers ('When that scab falls off in a day or two there'll be nice new skin underneath and you won't even be able to see where it happened.'). Try to avoid alarming statements like 'that's going to leave a nasty scar' or 'I think your poor arm is broken.'

In some communities, slightly older boys still suffer from the kind of sex-discrimination which says that 'boys don't cry' and labels them 'sissy' if they do. In public you will have to help your son to behave as *he wants* to behave – he will not thank you for fussing him in front of his friends – but in private don't encourage phoney ideas about 'manliness'.

Older children – certainly by adolescence – need to be able to cope with minor accidents, whether to themselves or to other people. Try to share with them the 'hunch' which makes you take the four-year-old to hospital for this head injury when you did not do so when he banged his head last week. Try also to let them decide whether their own strains need resting and be the ones who dress your minor cuts. This kind of competence is both practically useful and psychologically important. In a couple of years they will want to go off on camping trips and so forth without adults and they will need to be able to cope. They are far more likely to *feel* able to cope if 'squeamishness' has never been expected of them.

Coping with minor injuries

Most everyday cuts, scrapes and bumps do not need any medical treatment at all. Bodies are efficient at healing themselves and can often do so best if they are not interfered with. Antiseptic creams, for example, are usually worse than useless. They are useless because the chemicals they contain are not powerful enough to kill any harmful bacteria which might be around the wound; chemicals which were that powerful would damage the healthy tissue too. And they are worse than useless because they can prevent the formation of a scab which is the body's own, highly efficient, wound dressing.

But even if an injury does not require medical treatment, there may be something which you can do to make the sufferer more comfortable during the healing process. Wounds can be protected so that clothes do not rub them, for example. And you may be able to provide psychological comfort too: a child who has hurt himself often feels better if somebody appears to be doing something about it.

While you are doing that 'something' – even if it is only putting a graze under running water to remove the visible dirt – you can be doing the most important thing of all: making sure that the injury really *is* trivial. If a wound is going to need medical attention, it is far better that the attention should be sought immediately. If a cut needs stitching, for example, it must be done that same day. If you wait until the next day to decide that it is gaping open and will not close on its own, the edges of the wound will have begun to heal and stitching will no longer be possible.

For minor injuries, then, the questions are: Is there anything to be done to make the child more comfortable? And: am I sure that there is nothing seriously wrong here?

Coping with multiple minor injuries

Some injuries which would be trivial if they occurred singly can be quite serious if they occur all at once. A few nettle stings on a hand, for example, are nothing more than a painful nuisance, but nettle stings all over, following a fall into a nettle-filled ditch by a child wearing only a pair of shorts, can be a very different matter. In the same way, a small bruise is trivial, but bruising over a large area of the body can be extremely serious. It is important, then, to consider how much of the child's body is affected and not to assume that a bruise is a bruise is a bruise.

Coping with more serious injuries

First aid should be exactly what the term suggests: the help that you give *first* before getting the injured child to professional help. That first aid should consist only of things that you do to try to ensure that the child's injuries and his general condition do not *worsen* in the meantime. If he has a deep and obviously dirty wound, for example, it is cruel interference to clean, disinfect and bandage it before you leave for the hospital. The moment you get him there, the staff will take off all your careful handiwork and do it all again, better. He suffers the whole process twice and a delay into the bargain. Lay a clean linen or cotton handkerchief over the wound so that he need not look at it, and leave it all to them. In the same way, once you are clear that he is hurt badly enough to require a doctor's attention, it is not your business to try to discover exactly what his injuries are. If he has *either* fractured his collar-bone *or* dislocated his shoulder, your attempts to discover which – by making him wiggle his fingers, bend his elbow and so on – are pointless torment. What does it matter whether you know what is wrong? You know that something is. Diagnosis is for the professionals.

Occasionally first aid will actually save a life. You will find such dramatic events fully written out below. More often, first aid will ensure that a child reaches hospital in better shape than he would have done without it. Those events are also fully written out.

In all other circumstances your job is confined to recognizing that an injury is, or may be, serious, and getting the child to professional help as quickly and as comfortably as possible.

If a child is unconscious or semi-conscious

The 'recovery position' will ease the job of his heart and lungs, ensure that his tongue cannot drop back so as to obstruct his breathing and guard him against breathing in any blood or vomit. When you have carried out any other appropriate first aid measures, put him in this position while you wait for the ambulance or other help. If you have to go in search of help, this is the safest way to leave him.

● Although the 'recovery position' is ideal for the child's general condition you will have to adapt it to any obvious injuries. Above all, use your best judgement about moving him into it if there is any likelihood of damage to his spine (*see below* Head injuries).

Lie him on his tummy with his head well turned to one side. It should be turned far enough for his ear to be flat on the ground.

Gently bend the arm which he is facing, at the elbow. The hand should lie at about the level of his face.

Gently bend the leg on the same side, drawing it up until the foot is about level with the opposite thigh.

If a child seems to be dead

Mouth-to-mouth resuscitation, possibly with heart massage, might revive him when nothing else will do so. Even when these measures do not re-start spontaneous breathing and heartbeat, they can mechanically ensure that the heart goes on circulating blood and that the lungs go on oxygenating that blood. In this way the child's brain can be protected by minimal supplies of oxygen until expert help arrives to try full-scale resuscitation.

These techniques need to be taught and demonstrated. If you ever need to use them, on your own child or on somebody else's, you will have no time to try and follow instructions and diagrams from a book which you will not have with you, in any case.

Try to learn them before your first child passes babyhood. Your nearest Red Cross or St John Ambulance centre will have classes.

Try to have them taught to your own children before they are old enough to go adventuring without adults.

● If all parents both learned, and ensured that their children learned, these life-saving techniques, almost the whole population could become proficient within two generations. There is no doubt that some lives would be saved.

Bites and stings

Animal bites

In theory, every animal bite should be seen by a doctor; in practice, the tiny puncture made by a guinea pig or other small mammal requires no treatment other than washing. Bites from larger animals such as dogs are a different matter:

If a dog bite makes a puncture wound

Immediate medical attention is important. That dog's tooth makes a hole which is very likely to carry harmful bacteria, including tetanus (*see below* Cuts and scrapes, grazes and puncture wounds).

If more than one tooth bit deeply

The wound will probably be ragged as well as liable to infection; it will need careful dressing (and perhaps stitching) if a bad scar is to be avoided. Such a bite will also have bruised the tissues as a dog's teeth are not as sharp as a nail or knife. It will be painful. A child who has been attacked will probably also be very frightened.

First aid for animal bites

Speak extremely sharply, with downright amazement in your voice, to the animal. You want to convey to the bitten child that this attack was an extraordinary happening and not at all what he need expect from other animals. Run plenty of cold water into and over the wound. Cover with a sterile gauze dressing. Take the child to the doctor or hospital.

If there is rabies in your area

Animal bites have to be taken even more seriously. If this is a risk your family has to live with, or if you are going to travel to an area where rabies is prevalent, you must understand it (*see* **Rabies**).

Action after an animal bite

An animal which is liable to bite is not fit to be around children (*see* **Safety**/In the home: Safety and pets). Unless the attack was seriously provoked or more or less accidental, you may want to take action, whether the animal belongs to you or to someone else.

The bitten child may be nervous of animals after the accident (*see* **Anxiety, Fears and Phobias**). He should certainly not be expected to socialize with that same animal without concentrated adult supervision, but the more he can understand why things went wrong and therefore understand that all other animals need not be tarred with the same brush, the better.

Insect bites   Whether it is a mosquito or a flea which bites your child the local skin reaction will be similar: some swelling, some redness and some itching. Swelling is most dramatic where the skin is loose and/or richly supplied with blood vessels. A single mosquito bite near the eye, for example, can swell so that the eye is almost closed.

Prevention is the best treatment. Long-sleeved tee-shirts and trousers will do something to protect a child. If he is playing in long grass or a haybarn, socks will help too. Even an insect repellent, applied and renewed according to the instructions, will do something to protect him.

If you want peaceful nights on a holiday in a mosquito-prone area and season, take large pieces of fine butter muslin and drawing pins in your luggage. If insect screens are not provided they are easy to improvise.

First aid for   Cold water compresses will often reduce both swelling and itching.
insect bites   Calamine lotion will reduce itching at least for a few minutes (perhaps for long enough for the child to get back to sleep). An anti-histamine cream, sold for the purpose, may also help but should be used only occasionally and over small skin areas as otherwise enough medication may be absorbed through the skin to make the child sleepy.

Insect stings   Bee and wasp stings can be painful and usually frighten a child even more than the pain merits because she feels 'attacked'. Many children are frightened of these flying, buzzing insects anyway, even if they have never been stung.

First aid for   Calm the child explaining that the pain she feels now is the very worst she
insect stings   is going to feel. You will probably be able to see the place as a tiny puncture with a very small raised red circle around it. If you can see the sting in that central hole, remove it. Don't squeeze it or you may force extra venom out of it and into the child. Cold water or a proprietary sting-cream or spray will reduce the pain.

Larger insects – such as the hornet – can inflict a sting which is acutely painful for an hour or more. Of course you will be sorry for the child but you need not worry about her as long as the reaction to the sting is purely a local skin reaction.

Stings   A sting in the mouth of an unfortunate child who bites a wasp along with
requiring   her bread and jam *can* cause enough swelling to obstruct breathing. With
medical help   a baby or very young child it is probably wise to seek medical help for any sting in the mouth. With an older child who can cooperate by sucking an ice cube (or ice-cream) and opening her mouth to let you see what is happening, you can probably wait and see. If there is scarcely any swelling after twenty minutes, there will not be. If swelling is still increasing after twenty minutes, seek help.

A few children are allergic to the stings of bees, wasps and hornets. If yours is one, you will know at once because her reaction to the sting will not just be a local skin reaction but also a generalized reaction which makes her feel ill, short of breath and shocked. This is an emergency. Take her as fast as possible to the very nearest source of medical help, preferably getting someone to telephone ahead to say that you are bringing in a child with possible *anaphylactic shock*.

Once the shock has been successfully treated, the child will need further long-term treatment to deal with the allergy by hyposensitization (*see* **Allergy**/Principles of diagnosis and treatment in allergic conditions: Injection treatment for allergy). This is a must because after one such episode the child's reaction to a further sting will be even more severe and could be life-threatening.

If a child receives multiple stings – because she poked a wasps' nest for example – she may become shocked not because she is allergic but because the local pain and the fear is too much for her. Treat her for shock (*see below* Shock). Wrap the stung area (or her whole body if necessary) in a cold wet cloth or sheet and take her to hospital. She is in no danger but can be made much less uncomfortable.

Venomous creatures: spiders, scorpions, jellyfish, snakes, etc.	The bite or sting of a venomous creature is a very different matter from an ordinary insect sting because instead of injecting a substance which merely irritates the skin locally, it injects a poison which affects the child's whole system.

In Britain we are fortunate in having no venomous creatures at all except one snake, the adder, which is neither lethally poisonous nor at all numerous. But families who live or *travel* in other areas must make sure that they inform themselves of such hazards. Don't rely on a book about the country you are visiting: it may assume that you will stick to the tourist towns when in fact you plan to adventure. Ask local people for advice both on avoiding such hazards and on treatment if anyone is bitten. This is really important because while the advice given below for adder bites is harmless and probably adequate for most venomous bites, there are some creatures whose bite is so quickly lethal that more heroic and/or more specific first aid is called for.

Adder bites If your child is bitten by a snake in Europe (and certainly in the United Kingdom) assume it was an adder. Snake identification is far more difficult than most books would have you believe. Only *some* adders are grey with characteristic black diamond markings. They can be brick red with dark splodges . . .

The bite will leave one or two punctures – fang marks. You must assume that venom has been injected, but comfort yourself with the realization that the venom sac may have been empty or the venom deposited on the skin rather than through it. The child may be going to have no reaction at all or only a very mild, local one.

First aid for an adder bite Lie the child down at once and calm him as much as you can. Terror is common (*see* **Anxiety, Fears and Phobias**) and makes the development of shock (*see below* Shock) much more likely.

Wash the wound area or wipe with saliva, working *away* from the punctures. The idea is to remove venom which may be on the skin before it can get into the wound.

When you have cleaned the area well, flush the wound itself with plenty of water if you have it, or even with the cold drink from your picnic. You may remove some venom from the punctures before it can get into the bloodstream.

Persuade a child who is calm and old enough to cooperate to keep the bitten limb absolutely still. Any venom is injected into the tissues rather than straight into a blood vessel. The less he moves the more slowly it will be absorbed and spread. If a child will not or cannot cooperate, keep the bitten limb still by splinting one leg to the other or an arm to the child's own body. Put a plain dry dressing over the wound if you think this will help to calm the child. In fact do anything you can think of to keep him calm and still.

Get him to the nearest hospital. Travelling lying down is ideal but do not wait for an ambulance if your own car will be quicker, just ensure that he is carried to it, somehow, as walking will both exacerbate any shock and speed up the spread of venom.

If the bitten limb swells and/or begins to look bruised, some venom was certainly injected. If the victim feels sick or dizzy, sweats or loses consciousness, he is probably unusually badly affected but some, at least, of these systemic symptoms may be due to the fear and shock.

Hospital treatment for an adder bite

Do not be surprised if the hospital fails to give anti-venin to your bitten child. This does not mean that the doctors disbelieve you or that they are incompetent. In many cases the risks of anti-venin treatment are considered greater than the risk from the bite itself and therefore unwarranted. You can be quite sure that if they thought your child was in any danger from the bite they would treat it more directly.

He will almost certainly be given an anti-tetanus booster (*see* **Immunization**) unless you can assure the doctors that his immunity is right up-to-date. The risk of tetanus from an adder bite is actually worse than the risk from the venom.

Blisters

Most blisters are caused by friction, as from an ill-fitting shoe. At the centre of the rubbed area the outer layer of skin separates from the inner layer, which exudes fluid. The result is a fluid-filled 'bubble'. If a blister bursts, the raw patch underneath will be extremely sore and it will also be liable to infection. If you are shown a blister while it is still intact, do all that you can to preserve it. Over a few days the fluid will be re-absorbed and new skin will grow over the raw patch under the blister. The blister-skin, which has no blood supply, will dry up and fall off.

Dressing an intact blister

The most effective protection is given by a ring 'doughnut' of chiropody felt or lint with an ordinary adhesive dressing over the top. Make sure the circle of felt or lint is high enough to keep the centre of the adhesive dressing from touching the top of the blister.

Dressing a broken blister   Don't remove the blister-skin even if it is broken: its remains will offer at least some protection. Dress the raw area with a non-adhesive dressing.

● Burn or scald blisters require special attention; *see below*.

Bruises

A bruise is the visible result of blood vessels under the skin being crushed or broken. Blood escapes into the tissues. The area looks red at first, then bluish/black. As the escaped blood is broken down and re-absorbed the area may look greenish/yellow.

Trivial bruises   These are a normal part of life and require no treatment. If the bump is on a part of the body with an extensive nerve supply and loose skin (such as the back of the hand) it may be very painful at the time and the subsequent swelling may be painful too. If the child is in a fuss it may be worth giving him or her a piece of lint or a handkerchief soaked in very cold water or wrapped round ice, to hold over the area for a few minutes. The cooling will help the tiny blood vessels to close up more quickly and may therefore lessen the bruising.

Extensive bruising   If a child has a bad fall, say off a bicycle, so that she bruises a large area of shoulder, hip, thigh and knee, she will certainly be extremely sore and may need treating for shock (*see below*). The point is that although there is no visible bleeding from such an injury, the child is losing blood from her circulation into the tissues. In an extreme case she may be in a state similar to that following internal haemorrhage (*see below* Shock: Causes of major shock). After such a fall you will probably be having her checked over at the hospital anyway. But if she appears, and says she feels, all right, encourage her to be quiet and keep an eye on her for a few hours anyway.

'Black eyes'   A blow around the eyebrow, nose or cheekbone may lead to dramatic swelling and a fearsome-looking 'black eye'. The eye itself is seldom damaged as it is set back in a boney socket for protection. But if you are not sure where the blow landed and are therefore worried about damage to the eye itself, get the victim to a doctor quickly. Once the eye has been closed by swelling it will be difficult for him to determine its condition.

The bruising of a black eye sometimes travels downwards before all the escaped blood is re-absorbed so that the swelling is progressively lower down the face. Although this looks odd it is harmless.

'Blackened' nails   If a finger is caught in a door or the vacuum cleaner is dropped on a toe, the nail may turn black from bruising in the tissues beneath it. Such an injury is agonizingly painful because, unlike skin, the nail will not stretch to allow swelling. The bruise causes great pressure.

Although such an injury will heal of its own accord, the pain and the disability caused in either hand or foot may make a trip to the hospital worthwhile *if you can get there quickly*. A doctor can drill a tiny hole through the nail and thus let out the blood and relieve that pressure. He cannot do this effectively once the blood has coagulated.

If your child always seems to be covered with bruises for which you cannot account, you may worry in case he might have a 'bleeding disease'. By all means confide this worry to your doctor, but think, in the meantime, whether there is any other evidence to suggest that the child bleeds excessively. Does a small cut go on oozing? Do his gums bleed if he brushes his teeth adequately? Does a thorn-prick bleed more than one drop? If the answers are all negative, blood disorder is most unlikely.

You may also worry in case the child is being physically bullied, at school or at play, or even in case he is being abused by an adult. Bruises on the legs and arms are likely to be accidentally self-inflicted. Bruises on the body are the ones which might feed your suspicions.

A child who is being hurt deliberately by other people will be frightened, however anxious he may be to conceal the fact. You can probably get a clue by asking him calmly, 'how did you come by this lot?'

Do remember, though, that fair-skinned children do produce visible bruises where older children whose skins are tougher, or children whose skins are darker, do not. The legs of a healthy, happy, active blonde nine-year-old may almost always be a rainbow of new and old bruises.

Burns and scalds

Burns and scalds are almost always worse than they look because they do not merely affect the skin which you can see. The heat penetrates below the skin and damages the blood vessels. These react by widening (dilating) and letting the clear colourless part of the blood ooze out through their walls. In a minor burn this fluid will puff up the dead skin at the centre and make a blister. In a more serious burn which has removed the skin altogether you will see the fluid 'weeping' from the raw area. The fluid you can see may be only a small part of what is being lost into the tissues from deeper-lying blood vessels.

This fluid loss is a kind of bleeding. Only the clear part of the blood is being lost, but its loss is nevertheless reducing the total volume of fluid available to the circulation. This is why burns and scalds so often lead to shock (*see below*) and why intravenous fluid-replacement is such a vital and urgent part of the hospital treatment of burns.

Any burn which destroys the full thickness of the skin (third degree) may require skin to be grafted over it before the wound can heal. Even the smallest burn of this type requires immediate medical attention. Otherwise, use the *area* of a burn or scald as a rough guide to its seriousness. Any burn or scald which covers an area of skin more than half an inch square should be seen by a doctor. If the area is the size of your hand, the matter is potentially dangerous and the child should be taken rapidly to hospital. If the area involved is as much as a quarter of his skin area it is likely to be disastrous, even with immediate and expert medical attention.

Don't indulge in wishful thinking if your child is burned or scalded. If she empties the coffee pot down her front and the skin only looks red, it is a tremendous temptation to let yourself believe that 'it wasn't actually boiling; she's got away with it.' The process of fluid leakage beneath that reddened skin can be slow, but deadly. Get her to hospital *now*.

Immediate treatment for all burns

Whether the burn is a tiny one on a finger or a serious one caused by a pan of boiling oil, your first job is to arrest the burning before any further damage is done. You do this by removing clothes that are soaked in scalding fluid and then by cooling the burned area itself under cold running water. This cooling will stop the heat penetrating to deeper blood vessels; help the blood vessels which are already affected to close up again and stop oozing, and lessen the pain.

Home treatment for tiny burns

If you have quickly put your child's burned finger under the cold tap, two minutes' cooling may have reduced the pain and allowed you to see that there is nothing more than a red patch, a blister or possibly a small raw place. Pat it dry. Do not put *any* kind of grease or ointment on it, not even one which says it is for the treatment of burns. If it needs medication it needs a doctor.

Most burns will need some protection from life while they heal, but it is important not to put on either a dressing which might stick to the edges of the burned area *or* anything fluffy, like cotton wool, which might leave fibres in it. Use a non-adhesive dressing or a piece of sterile gauze. The burn will heal more quickly if the dressing is left undisturbed for a day or two and kept dry.

First aid for larger burns

Larger burns may be caused by taking hold of very hot cooking utensils or by splashes of boiling oil or accidents with kettles and so forth. They should all be treated exactly like a small one except that as soon as you have cooled the area for five minutes it should be loosely wrapped in a clean, non-fluffy cloth – such as a handkerchief or sheet – and the child taken rapidly to hospital.

A really large burn, such as might be caused by the child getting into a dangerously hot bath, or tipping a boiling pan down himself or catching his clothes alight is a case where your first aid may make a major contribution to his eventual recovery. Your exact actions will have to be dictated by the exact circumstances, but these are the principles:

First, stop further burning. Heat will be trapped in layers of hot-soaked clothing. Remove them, but go carefully as you reach the layer next to his skin and *don't pull off anything which is sticking to him*.

Flaming clothes will be burning him. The flames must be smothered but remember heat and flame *rise*. If you throw him down on the flames they will lap all around him. If you leave him standing they will rise towards his face and hair. If he rushes around in panic he will fan them. Grab him; throw him down with the flames uppermost. Smother them with anything you can grab such as a rug or towel; if there is nothing else, use your own body. Lie flat on him, fast, and the flames will go out before they can burn you.

Smouldering clothes will burn him more if you press them against him, pull them off, grasping non-burning areas.

Chemicals will go on burning as long as they are touching him. Take off clothes soaked in them.

Now, stop the burning from penetrating further. The heat of the burned skin will go on penetrating until you cool it, just as it does in a small burn. Use whatever is practical for the area burned – a running tap, a hosepipe, a shower or a cold bath. But remember, cooling which does not begin within five minutes of the accident is useless.

Protect burns during transport to hospital. Burns are very liable to infection, even from air-borne bacteria. Burned skin is also easily damaged by friction. To guard against both, cover the whole area with a clean, non-fluffy cloth, such as a handkerchief or sheet. Newly ironed items of this kind will have inner folds which are more or less sterile. If you have nothing else which is suitable, you can use cling film.

Protect the child from shock (*see below*). Keep him lying down and keep him as calm and quiet as you possibly can, both until transport arrives and during the journey. If he is wrapped in a clean sheet, cover that with a light blanket for warmth, but do not use hot water bottles. Do not give him anything to eat or drink.

Choking

If food or drink or any foreign object or irritating substance gets into the airway rather than the oesophagus (food passage) a powerful reflex tightens the muscles of the airway at about the level of the larynx (voice box) and causes coughing. The closed off airway prevents the foreign material travelling further down to the lungs while the coughing expels it back up into the mouth. The reflex is normally highly efficient, operating as soon after birth as breathing is established and working night and day, whether we are asleep or awake. Difficulties and dangers are therefore the exception rather than the rule.

Choking and breathlessness

The spasm of the muscles which blocks the air passage to further invasion by foreign material also blocks breathing. Usually this does not matter because the first violent bout of coughing, triggered by the spasm and powered by air already in the lungs when it began, serves to dislodge the foreign material.

If that coughing bout does not clear the obstruction, the victim will have difficulty in taking in air for another effective bout. He may become short of oxygen – even to the extent of looking bluey-grey in colour – not because the foreign material is completely blocking his air passage but because muscle spasm is doing so.

To make matters worse, those same muscles may actually be clamped around the foreign material making it more difficult to dislodge.

Breathlessness leads to panic; panic makes breathlessness worse

An older child or an adult who understands this reflex mechanism can help himself by deliberately relaxing and taking slow, gentle breaths rather than fighting for great gasps. A younger child or a person who believes that his air passage is totally obstructed, will panic as soon as he feels short of oxygen. Panic will both increase the muscle spasm and increase his body's demand for oxygen.

Take action before breathlessness begins

As soon as you can see that the first bout of coughing has not brought up the foreign material:

Strike the victim several times between the shoulder blades. If that does not immediately clear the air passage and allow the victim a complete breath, use gravity to help:

Position the victim with his head and shoulders below his legs. A baby can be held upside down; a child can be slung head down over your knee; an adult can be persuaded face down over a table or bed.

Repeat the blows between the shoulder blades with the victim in this position.

Complete obstruction of breathing

Very occasionally the air passage is completely blocked by a foreign body rather than closed by muscle spasm. In an adult the fatal object is usually a too-large piece of ill-chewed meat. In a child it is more likely to be an object, such as a marble, which unfortunately exactly fits the air passage.

If such a thing should occur, you will distinguish it from ordinary choking because, after perhaps one strangled gasp, the victim will not breathe at all. He will look totally terrified but make no sound; his eyes will bulge and his face will be suffused with red and then turn bluish. He will collapse. In adults, eating in restaurants, bystanders often think the victim has had a stroke.

What to do

This is a grade one emergency. The most urgent thing is to *get expert help*. Sending for an ambulance/doctor takes priority over anything else. But while waiting for help or transporting the victim to it, try:

Looking down his throat in case you can pull out the obstruction. You may be able to grip a piece of meat even if that marble is hopeless. (If you can see nothing, don't poke about blindly.)

Getting him into a head-down position and banging him repeatedly between the shoulder blades. With an older child or adult, use your clenched fist rather than your open hand to deliver real jolts. If the object is lodged high up in the throat (if you can see, but not grip, it, for example) this is very likely to dislodge it. But it is risky. If the object is lower down, your blows could shift it downwards, towards the lung, instead of up and out.

The 'Heimlich manoeuvre' in which pressure on the diaphragm, just below the breast-bone, is used to compress the air in the lungs and create an expulsive force through the whole respiratory system. With an older child, or adult, get him into a sitting or standing position, put your arms around him and use your fists to press inwards and upwards. With a baby or very young child, use one arm to support him and use just two fingers of the other hand to press on the diaphragm. This manoeuvre has saved many lives, but it too is risky. Over-enthusiastic thrusts may damage internal organs such as the liver.

Some other kinds of choking are less obvious and dramatic but can nevertheless be serious:

Inhaling small foreign objects

A small foreign body may get past that reflex defence, and lodge either in one of the smaller air passages or in the lung itself. Suspect this if your child has a violent fit of choking and then recovers without any foreign body appearing. Suspect it also if he has an intermittent cough, an unusual wheezy sound to his breathing or pain in his throat.´

He should be taken to hospital. Foreign bodies in the air passages or lungs can cause serious trouble later.

Inhaling liquids or body fluids

While almost every child will 'breathe' some water whilst swimming, from time to time, a child who is thought to have taken a lot of water into the lungs should always be observed in hospital even if he seems quite unaffected (*see below* Drowning).

It is dangerous for him to take fluids such as milk, or his own blood or vomit into his lungs. A baby should never be left lying with a bottle to suck. A child with a nosebleed should sit leaning forward so that blood does not trickle down his throat. A child who is vomiting should be held well forward over lavatory or basin. Anyone who is unconscious (or drunk or drugged) should be put in the 'recovery position' (*see above*) so that vomit, etc. run out of the mouth.

Precautions against all forms of choking

Don't leave babies to suck alone or young children to eat or drink anything alone. Be there to bang backs if necessary.

Don't allow 'foods' which might easily be inhaled. Peanuts are the worst offenders as they set up serious inflammation if they 'go the wrong way'.

Don't let children 'throw' food into their mouths – even for a joke or a game – and don't let them pour crisps, nuts or tiny sweets out of the packet into their upturned mouths.

Don't let children suck sweets in bed. Quite apart from the effect on their teeth, they may fall asleep and choke on what remains. It is best if no child ever eats anything while lying down.

Don't let them eat while rushing around and playing active games. A sudden push can lead to something 'going the wrong way' especially if the child is panting.

Guard babies and young children against things which might block throats; not only objects like marbles, but also bits of larger toys like the insecurely fastened wheels of a model car. . . .

Don't let a child hold his nose when taking nasty medicine, etc. If he is trying to breathe through his mouth while swallowing the dose he is the more likely to choke.

Don't try to give food or drink to a child who is sleepy, semi-conscious, unconscious or shocked. Be very careful about trying to give anything (such as coffee) to an older person who is drunk. Under all these circumstances, the choking-coughing reflex may be inefficient.

Don't force food into the mouth of a protesting child. Quite apart from the poor psychology involved, he is very likely to gag and choke.

Cuts and scrapes, grazes and puncture wounds

The principles for coping with all very minor cuts and scrapes are the same:

Interfere as little as possible. If you are not shown a bloody knee or cut finger until an hour after it happened, let it alone. Healing will already have started and 'first aid' will undo it.

Avoid 'antiseptics' and airtight dressings whenever you can. Antiseptic creams are largely ineffective in killing the thousands of bacteria which colonize every square inch of skin. Their greasiness can prevent the formation of the hard scab which is the body's natural protection for wounds. In combination with an airtight dressing, such a cream can actually keep a wound open (and subject to infection) for a long time.

Take action only to keep the child comfortable. That may mean an adhesive dressing (applied so that air can still get to the wound) to protect it from clothing, etc. Or it may mean applying such a dressing simply to conceal blood from a child who is frightened by it.

For quick healing, keep wounds dry. A scraped elbow will heal far more quickly if the child does not soak in a hot bath that same day.

Deeper cuts may require more attention. Their seriousness does not only depend on depth and size, however, but on the implement which made them and their exact place on the body.

Deep cuts on fingers, etc.
These are usually made by a very sharp but thin implement such as a knife or razor blade. They may be deep and they may bleed copiously but the bleeding is easy to stop and healing is quick and neat because the skin edges and the cut tissues underneath are neatly aligned.

Put the cut under gently running cold water while you fetch some sterile gauze and an adhesive dressing. Wrap gauze around the finger and apply pressure with your own. If the bleeding takes more than a minute to control you can speed up matters by holding the child's hand above his heart level while you press (*see below* Wounds and bleeding).

As soon as bleeding slows, apply the adhesive dressing. If you place it tightly round the finger, remember to loosen it within five minutes. If you place it firmly but not tightly and the wound bleeds through, add another dressing on top. Don't interfere again for an hour or so. By that time the blood will have clotted and the edges of the wound will already have begun to knit together so you can take off the bloody dressing, put on a clean, dry one to protect it and forget the whole matter (but keep an eye out for infection, *see below*).

Deep cuts into taut skin
Where skin is taut, as on the palm of the hand or over the ankle, quite a small deep cut can be tiresome because the edges gape open. The bleeding takes longer to stop and, if it heals with the edges set apart, a comparatively large scar will be left.

Sometimes you can apply adhesive tape (over gauze) in such a way that the edges of the wound are pulled together by the dressing. You can buy special adhesive tape, ready-shaped for this. You stick one end on one side of the cut, close the edge together and stick down the other end.

If this does not work, you have a choice between accepting a slow-healing wound leaving a scar and taking the child to have the wound stitched shut. You will have to weigh the importance of a scar against the importance of the unpleasantness of the medical procedure.

Deep cuts in awkward places A cut on a knuckle or other joint may not gape at the time but may be delayed in healing because movement continually re-opens it. It may be worthwhile to place a piece of impregnated gauze over the actual cut and then bandage the finger in the straight position which keeps the wound closed. Even twenty-four hours will probably allow enough healing to prevent the wound re-opening.

Cuts which raise skin flaps If a child 'slices' a finger so that there is a flap of skin or of skin and tissue, you can treat it exactly as you treat a simple cut but make sure that when you dress it you replace the flap exactly. It may heal completely in that position. If the blood supply to the cut flap does not re-establish itself, the flap will eventually dry up and fall off but it is still the best 'dressing' for the healing wound.

Jagged and dirty cuts Such a cut tends to leave a nasty scar and is, of course, very liable to infection. If it is shallow and in a place where scarring does not matter very much (such as on the knee of a nine-year-old!) you may be able to deal with it by running it under plenty of cold water and then dressing it, doing your best to bring skin edges together. But if it is at all deep and/or in a noticeable place, take the child to the doctor or hospital.

Cuts on the head or face The skin which covers the skull is tightly stretched and copiously supplied with blood vessels. Bleeding, even from a minor cut, is usually free and difficult to stop because skin edges cannot be pulled together.

Facial skin is soft and scars on the face matter. It is usually sensible to show such a cut to a doctor. Even quite trivial ones will often be stitched (*see* **Hospital**/Procedures: Suturing wounds).

Cuts with foreign bodies If a cut, anywhere on the body, has glass or any other foreign body in it, *don't interfere*. Don't, on any account, try to remove it. Take the child straight to hospital.

Grazes with grit The exception may be a graze which has grit or gravel in it. You can cope with this at home *if the surface skin has been completely removed.*

The graze will be extremely painful. Don't try to dab the dirt out (you are likely to push some into the damaged tissue as well as causing the victim to go on strike) instead, try running cold tap water over it, gently at first, then harder as the child gets used to it. If one or two pieces of grit refuse to wash off, you (or better still the child herself) may be able to encourage them with a tiny piece of gauze used in the running water.

If the surface skin has not been completely removed so that there is dirt and grit trapped in pockets of skin, the graze should be professionally cleaned. If it is not, infection is very likely. If the graze is on some visible part of the body such as the face or elbow, professional cleaning is even more important. Without it, that dirt may actually stain the tissues so that when it has healed, the scar is an ugly and noticeable colour.

Puncture wounds

Can be dangerous when they look trivial. It can be quite difficult to decide whether or not such a wound requires hospital treatment. Many authorities say that *all* puncture wounds should receive medical attention but, if cornered, would agree that to bother a doctor with a needle run into a finger or a rose thorn into the foot would be absurd. The decisions, in every case, will be yours but the relevant facts are these:

Danger of infection in puncture wounds

A puncture wound is made by a sharp object of very small diameter driving deeply into the tissues. Because it penetrates deeply, any dirt will be carried far in. Because its diameter is small, the entry hole is small. You cannot clean the bottom of the wound and it will heal over very readily. If the entry wound heals over with dirt trapped far beneath it, infection is very likely.

A deep hole made by a dirty object (such as the wound made when a child steps on a nail with bare feet) should always be shown to a doctor. A tiny hole made by a comparatively clean object (such as that needle in the finger) need not be. In between these extremes you must judge dirt and depth. A drawing pin, for example, may penetrate the sole of your child's shoe but if you compare the depth of the spike and the sole you will find that the wound cannot be very deep.

If you decide that a puncture wound is not serious enough to require medical attention, *try to make it bleed*. If you or the child can squeeze the puncture and get several drops of blood out, dirt will probably be carried out too. If squeezing does not work, the child can suck the puncture.

This is one kind of wound which you do not want to heal very quickly. Soak it well in warm water and bathe it again the next day.

Danger of tetanus from puncture wounds

If your child is fully immunized against tetanus and/or has had a booster injection within the last ten years (*see* **Immunization**), you need not worry about this. If not, you should realize that tetanus toxins (poisons) are produced by tetanus bacteria which live in soil – especially soil contaminated by animal droppings. There may be such bacteria on a rusty nail in the garden. If any get into a puncture wound and the wound closes over, they are especially liable to cause trouble as these bacteria flourish in an environment with little or no oxygen. The moral is: Keep that tetanus protection up to date. Otherwise you really will have to worry about puncture wounds because while tetanus is far less likely than other kinds of infection, it is deadly serious (*see also* **Tetanus**).

Dislocations

In theory, any part of the body where the bones of the skeleton are jointed so as to allow movement can become dislocated. At the hip, for example, the top of the thigh bone ends in a 'ball' which fits into and rotates within a 'socket' of bone at the base of the pelvis. If the 'ball' were displaced from the 'socket', the joint would be dislocated.

In practice, dislocations are rare without accompanying fractures because in most of the body's joints the muscles and ligaments which hold them in place are both stronger and more resilient than the bones themselves. If those muscles and ligaments are torn so badly that the joint no longer functions, one of the associated bones is almost certain to be broken. At the wrist, for example, a dislocation happens because the main bone above it (the radius) is fractured. This is called a Colles fracture. A dislocation of the ankle joint goes similarly with a fracture of one of the associated bones and is called a Potts fracture.

Obviously, then, there is no point in trying to establish whether your child has fractured or dislocated these parts of the body. If he has done the one he has probably done the other, too. And the less you interfere with the injury, the better (*see below* Fractures). There are two exceptions:

Dislocated shoulder

The shoulder joint is an exceptionally mobile one, designed to allow us to windmill our arms. The 'ball' at the top of the arm bone (the humerus) can rather easily be displaced from its shallow socket, especially if the arm receives a lot of weight while stretched above the head. A child who falls from a height and instinctively throws up his arms to protect his head may dislocate his shoulder.

Although you may not be certain that this is a dislocation rather than a fracture, it is important to move fast if circumstances and the child's behaviour make you even suspect it. The displaced parts of the joint press on nerves and overstretch ligaments and muscles at every movement.

The child will be in excruciating pain; there will be no question of waiting half an hour to see if he starts to use the arm again spontaneously. He will obviously require immediate medical help.

Tissues surrounding a dislocated joint quickly swell making the otherwise simple job of re-aligning the joint extremely difficult. The faster you can get the child to hospital the easier it will be and the less the likelihood of long-term after-effects.

Look at the position in which the (probably screaming) child instinctively nurses the arm. He will probably be holding it across his chest.

Support the arm in that position with a big sling around his neck.

Either send for an ambulance or drive him to hospital.

Dislocated jaw

Sometimes the lower jaw slips forwards and downwards, usually during an extra-deep yawn. A blow to the jaw seldom dislocates it; it pushes the lower jaw upwards and is more likely to fracture it.

The extreme and completely unexpected pain will probably make the child yell. Yelling sometimes causes the jaw to click back into place of its own accord.

If the child can now open and close his mouth without pain all will be well and you can regard the incident as closed.

If it does not click back immediately, take him to hospital so that it can be manipulated back into place before much swelling takes place.

Do not under-estimate a dislocation

Although we tend to think of a fracture as 'worse', a dislocation is usually more painful at the time *and* more painful for longer, afterwards. Torn ligaments and bruised tissues take a long time to heal. The joint may have to be immobilized in plaster for several weeks and the child will be far more miserable than he would be after a greenstick or simple fracture.

A bad dislocation can leave the joint liable to further dislocations because the holding ligaments and muscles do not heal back to quite their original strength and elasticity. It is therefore especially important to follow scrupulously any advice concerning later exercises or hospital physiotherapy.

Drowning

Water can kill in a number of ways. The popular image of drowning is of a victim submerged in water, drawing water into his lungs instead of air and therefore suffocating. But that unfortunate swimmer can drown without ever taking any water into his lungs at all. If he is trapped (by a rock or a wreck or a heavy growth of weed) several feet below the surface the pressure will be too great for his diaphragm to expand and contract. He will not 'breathe' any water. He will die simply for lack of air.

Many water-deaths are not due to interference with the air supply at all but to the kind of deep chilling which cools vital organs beyond their tolerance (hypothermia).

In many 'drowning' accidents, these disastrous things happen in sequence. A child who drifts out to sea on an airbed, for example, becomes increasingly chilled to a point where the onset of hypothermia makes him mentally confused and clouds his judgement. Eventually he rolls off the airbed in the mistaken idea that he can swim to safety. His attempts to swim increase his body's oxygen demand; the hypothermia deepens and as he fights the water so some is breathed into his lungs. Unless rescue comes he will become unconscious from a combination of suffocation and hypothermia and then he will drown.

Gloomy though it all is, it is worth understanding what happens in common water-accidents because the right action at the right time can save both life and health. Start by dismissing a couple of exceedingly dangerous old wives' tales.

'Human beings float.' It is true that a human body, inert in water, will remain partially on the surface but this does not mean that the victim will float in a position which enables him to breathe. He will float with his face and most of his head and his legs from the hips down submerged. Only the upper half of his back will remain above the water. The smaller a child the more certain it is that the head will be fully submerged. Babies' heads are large and heavy relative to the rest of their bodies.

'People do not drown until they have sunk three times.' This is total nonsense. A victim bobbing to the surface after being temporarily trapped under water will only take water into his lungs as he emerges but he will then take in more with every attempted 'breath' unless he knows how to float with his head up. If your child falls into deep water (perhaps off a harbour wall), he will sink deeply and then come back to the surface. You need to get him out the moment he appears. If you do so you will have saved him. If you wait while he bobs around you may be too late.

Babies, small children and shallow water

A baby or toddler can drown by falling face down in a bath, paddling pool or stream. With no experience or intention of putting his face in water, he takes a huge breath to scream his shock and outrage. The breath is water not air; that single inpouring of water into the lungs can be disastrous.

Snatch him up and turn him upside down. If he is furious and screaming all is well. If he is choking and gasping, empty all the water that will come out of him and take him immediately to hospital (*see below*).

All ages in deep water

When a child is completely immersed in water, by accident, his fate will depend on the exact circumstances. A swimmer who gets into trouble due to a strong ocean current or to cramp, for example, may nevertheless be able to keep his head above water for quite a long period. But even the strongest swimmer may not be able to help himself if the boom of a sailing boat knocked him unconscious as well as overboard, or if the water is so cold that hypothermia rapidly begins to affect him. A non-swimmer or a child who finds himself in rough sea when he is accustomed to a swimming pool, may worsen his own situation with panic-stricken thrashing which exhausts him and makes it impossible for him to coordinate in-breaths with moments when his nose and mouth are above water.

If he is still obviously breathing, whether he is fully or partly conscious, or unconscious, he will probably be all right, provided he receives the correct care:

Empty all the water out of him that will come. Hold a small child upside down; lie a heavier one on his front and then lift his lower body. Remember that he may vomit water from his stomach as well as it draining from his lungs: keep his head well turned to one side so that he does not breathe vomited water in again.

Arrest hypothermia by removing soaked clothing, replacing it with your own and protecting him from the chill wind.

Get him to hospital if any water at all was coughed, choked, vomited or drained out of him.

If he does not seem to be breathing, don't be too quick to despair even if you cannot feel a heartbeat either. People used to think that drowning victims should not be resuscitated if they had been without oxygen for more than a few minutes. It was believed that, while such a person might have his heart and breathing restarted, he was likely to remain 'a vegetable' because his brain would have been permanently damaged by oxygen starvation. Recent research has shown that there is a *diving response* to sudden immersion which, by a complicated set of physiological responses, puts the heart into extremely 'low gear' and concentrates the little blood it continues to pump on that vital brain. There are reliable reports of full recovery following long periods of complete immersion. Your child's chances are better if the water was very cold as the oxygen requirements of a cooled brain are reduced.

He needs mouth-to-mouth resuscitation and perhaps heart massage. If you are competent to do this yourself, start immediately you reach a boat or dry land. If you have never done it before nor been taught how to do it, don't waste time trying to remember the words and diagrams in a book. There is real skill involved. *Send for help.* In the meantime follow the suggestions above to get water out of him and reduce chilling. He may even start breathing again spontaneously.

Why fresh water is more dangerous than sea water

Water in the lungs does not only prevent vital oxygen from reaching the circulation, it is also dangerous to that circulation. Fresh water is rapidly absorbed. It dilutes the blood and breaks down the red blood cells which release a sudden load of potassium. Heart failure is often the result. A child who appears dead following immersion in fresh water cannot usually be revived.

In sea-water drowning, a high concentration of calcium and magnesium may enter the bloodstream and stop the heart. The child appears dead but if artificial respiration and heart massage are successfully carried out the salts may be dispersed around the circulation and diluted to a point where the heart can start again spontaneously.

Polluted or 'hygienized' water is dangerous too

Even a little water in the lungs can be dangerous so that any child who is thought to have breathed some in should always be taken to hospital. If you are tempted to ignore this precaution because your child was quickly fished out of that swimming pool or pond, remember that polluted water or extra-clean water loaded with chemicals can both irritate the lungs and cause peculiarly unpleasant types of pneumonia. He may seem perfectly all right now that he has stopped choking, but will he be perfectly all right in twelve hours' time? Let a doctor decide.

Electric shock

The severity of an electric shock varies with an enormous number of factors; a victim who happens to be wearing rubber soled shoes and standing on a dry floor, for example, may receive a trivial shock from a source which might have killed him if he had been standing in a puddle. To understand the risks, *see* **Safety**/In the home: Safe use of electricity.

If a child receives a momentary shock, by touching a live wire for example, the whole incident will be over before you have realized what is happening. He may suffer from minor shock (*see below* Shock) in which case he will need treating and comforting accordingly, but he is most unlikely to be seriously affected.

Electrical burns

Are a different matter. If a child touches a piece of wire which is acting as a short-circuit, it will probably burn his fingers. The burn may look trivial because the action of the electric current closes up the superficial blood vessels so that you may only be able to see a tiny bluish mark. Do not be deceived. There may be amazingly extensive damage to deeper tissues.

All electrical burns should be treated by a doctor.

Continuing electric shock

Very occasionally a child can neither let go of, nor be thrown free from, a wire or appliance which is sending current through him. A.C. current tends to cause muscles to contract and may clench the hand around a faulty appliance; even with D.C. current, a child can become entangled in a live wire and thus continue to receive current.

Stop the current immediately. If there is a wall-socket, switch it off or pull out the plug. If there is no socket, switch off all the mains if you can do so really quickly. If you cannot switch off in a hurry:

Move the child from the source of current but don't try to do so with your bare hands: he will be 'live' and you will receive the shock too. Use the nearest *poor conductor of electricity* you can grab: a wooden chair, a cushion, a rubber door mat, to push him clear.

The child may not be badly affected. If the current was passing only through his hand, for example, he will probably need to be treated for minor shock (*see below* Shock) but provided he is fully conscious and has not been burned, you need not worry.

Electric shock can stop both heartbeat and breathing by its effect on the nervous system. If the child is unconscious, he must be rushed to hospital.

If he appears dead, complete recovery is still possible provided resuscitation starts soon enough and goes on until the victim can receive hospital help. If you are competent to give mouth-to-mouth resuscitation and, probably, heart massage, start immediately. If you are not, get the nearest competent helper by the fastest possible means.

Foreign bodies inserted on purpose

Small children enjoy fitting objects into holes and make no exception for the 'holes' in their own bodies. Beads, buttons, fragments of food or toilet paper are often pushed experimentally into ears, noses or vaginas.

Obviously if you see this happen and can see the protruding object, you will remove it. Blunt ended tweezers may help. If you see it happen but the foreign body is not protruding, you will have to judge whether to try to remove it yourself or to take the child to a doctor. Your judgement must be based on the shape and consistency of the object and on how far in the child has pushed it. A soft, irregularly shaped object such as a piece of apple is easy to grasp with those tweezers. If it is visible in the nostril or ear, you can safely have a try. But a hard round object such as a bead, is extremely difficult to get hold of without special forceps. Even if you see it clearly, removal is better left to an expert.

The point is, of course, that while such objects do no immediate harm sitting in the outer passage of the ear or in a nostril, clumsy attempts to get them out can push them further in with disastrous results. If a bead is pushed all the way into the ear, for example, it will end up pressing on the delicate ear drum, possibly even perforating it and damaging the middle ear. Pushed all the way up a nostril, that same bead could exit into the child's air passage and cause serious choking.

If you are taking a child to the doctor or to your casualty department for removal of a foreign body, do remember not to give him anything to eat or drink in the meanwhile. He may need a general anaesthetic and the more recently he has had a meal or a snack the longer you will have to wait before it is safe to anaesthetize him.

Most foreign bodies are inserted when the child is alone – often because he is lonely and bored in his cot or bed – you may not discover what has happened for days; indeed you may never know.

An object made of an inert mineral substance, such as hard plastic, will set up no reaction in the ear, nose or vagina. It may simply stay there, unsuspected, until perhaps you notice that the child is not breathing with one side of his nose, or is not hearing well with one ear. Many such objects probably remain indefinitely until the body's natural secretions eventually carry them out.

An organic foreign body, such as a piece of food, is a different matter. In the nose it will set up an inflammatory reaction leading to a one-sided discharge of thick, purulent pus. In the ear it will eventually decompose leading to visible discharge. In the vagina it will similarly produce a smelly white discharge. In all such instances you should suspect a foreign body but leave a doctor to investigate.

Foreign bodies in the eye

When dust or a tiny insect gets onto the eyeball or under the eyelid the eye's natural reaction is to water and thus wash out the particle. Try and teach children not to rub the affected eye (which tends to wedge in the particle more firmly) but to concentrate on blinking instead. Younger children may find that permission to rub the *other* eye makes it easier to leave the affected one alone; rubbing the other one will actually help by increasing the tear-flow of both.

Watering and blinking will usually move the particle to the outer edge of the eye. If you turn down the lower lid you may be able to see it and remove it, very gently, with a tissue. If the discomfort is under the upper lid, grasping the eyelashes and lifting the lid a little may release the particle and enable it to float down.

Even after a foreign body has been removed, the eye may still be uncomfortable; indeed the child may still insist that there is something in it. This is usually because the eyeball has been very slightly scratched. Such tiny scratches settle down with amazing speed. An older child will understand that the foreign body *is* out and that if she leaves the eye alone the discomfort will vanish within an hour or so. A younger child may go on fiddling with it, searching for the speck he is sure is still there. If distraction does not work, try covering the eye with a pad of lint or a folded handkerchief, held on with a piece of bandage. If the eye, thus protected, remains uncomfortable for more than an hour, take the child to the doctor.

Foreign bodies on the pupil Although eyes are surprisingly tough, a speck which is actually lodged on the pupil, remaining despite the eye's watering, should neither be left there nor be removed by anyone but an expert. Cover the eye as above so that there is no chance of the child rubbing it and thus pushing the speck into the pupil. Take her straight to your doctor or to your nearest casualty department.

Penetrating Horrible eye injuries can be caused by arrows, or darts or by a stick or
injuries to pencil on which a child falls. Any such injury should at once be covered by
the eye a sterile, or at least a clean, pad (sterile gauze or lint are ideal but the inner
folds of any linen which has been ironed will do) and the child rushed to
hospital. If you live in a big city which has a specialist eye hospital, you
will save precious time by going directly there.

Less serious penetrating injuries can be caused by thorny branches
whipping across the child's face or even by particularly sharp pieces of
grit blown off a building site or thrown in a sandpit. Look at the eye
carefully in a good light. If you can *see* a scratch it is serious enough to
need medical attention. Protect it with a pad and take the child to hospital.

Liquids in Many household cleaners, solvents, etc. can damage the eye. If a child
the eye splashes something into his eyes and screams with pain, don't wait to
discover exactly what the liquid was. You can do no harm by getting rid of
it (even if it was something painful but fairly harmless like shampoo)
and, if it was something like bleach, quick action may save his sight.

You need running water from the cold tap. You need lots of it,
immediately, however much the child struggles and however fantastic
the flood on your bathroom floor. With his cooperation, by persuasion or
by force if necessary, position the child so that you can run water from the
cold tap directly through the affected eye. Make sure his head is turned so
that the unaffected eye is uppermost. If you do not, you will wash the
damaging liquid into that one too.

Irrigate the affected eye really thoroughly, turning the child's head a
little and parting the lids so that every millimetre of the eyeball and every
fold of the lids is rinsed again and again. If you have someone else to help
you, get him to check on the irritant substance. If it turns out to be
harmless, you can stop the water-treatment. If it turns out to be acid or
corrosive, or if you are not sure whether it is really dangerous or not, get
your helper to telephone your doctor or hospital to ask advice. However
dangerous the substance, ten minutes' really thorough irrigation will
have done all the good it can. Take child (and substance) to hospital.

Foreign bodies which are swallowed

Foreign bodies which are *successfully* swallowed seldom present serious
problems. If a coin or a button reaches the stomach, it will almost always
safely negotiate the rest of its journey and eventually appear in the faeces.
If you know that a child has swallowed a foreign body, by all means
contact your doctor and discuss it with him. There are a few traps for the
unwary such as ink cartridges which, while unlikely to cause mechanical
damage, can leak and thus poison the child.

Dangerous swallowed foreign bodies are those which the child does
indeed swallow but cannot 'get down'. Fish bones, open safety pins and
irregularly shaped, sharp parts of toys will all tend to 'get stuck' causing
acute pain on swallowing. Expert help will be needed both to locate the
foreign body and to remove it. Since the child will almost certainly need a
general anaesthetic, don't give him lumps of bread or drinks in an attempt
to push or wash it down. Take him directly to the nearest hospital.

Foreign bodies which are inhaled

We all 'breathe' foreign bodies in quite frequently, walking or cycling through a cloud of flies or taking a rash sniff at something. Usually such particles are trapped in our noses and expelled by the normal mucus flow. If it gets further it will provoke coughing and usually be successfully expelled. But a foreign body which penetrates even further still, into the tracheobronchial tree, is a different matter. An organic foreign body, such as that fly, will set up a violent inflammatory reaction so that the victim coughs up purulent material and rapidly becomes extremely ill. A mineral foreign body will set up much less reaction and may, indeed, go unsuspected. A very sudden persistent cough, breathlessness and/or wheezing in a child who is otherwise well should make you suspect a foreign body of this kind.

A child who has inhaled a foreign body will have to have it removed in hospital and the sooner it is removed the less likely it is that he will be really ill. Always consult a doctor if your child suddenly develops a cough and/or if an episode of choking shades into a cough.

Fractures

Although a simple definition of a fracture would be 'a broken bone', fractures range from minute quick-healing cracks to shattered bones requiring major reconstructive surgery. Serious fractures are rare in young children whose bones are still pliable and can absorb a lot of stress by bending (*see below* Greenstick fractures), but you cannot predict the probable seriousness or likelihood of a fracture from the nature of the accident. A child can fall many feet off a roof or take a terrifying tumble off a fast-moving bicycle without fracturing anything but she can trip down one step, fall with her arm in a particular position and fracture it.

When your child has obviously hurt herself, do remember that your job is to get her to professional help as quickly, as comfortably and in as good a general condition as you can manage. If her wrist is swollen and painful, it is not your job to find out whether it is actually fractured or simply sprained. What is the point of wiggling it to try to decide? The wiggling will hurt; if there is a fracture the movement may make it worse and whatever the results she will need to see a doctor. Non-interference is the best policy whenever you are dealing with even the possibility of a fracture. If a trip to the hospital is something you want to avoid if you possibly can, concentrate on comforting and then trying gently to distract the child. Don't particularly encourage her to move or use the hurt limb; just wait and see whether she begins to do so spontaneously. A child who moves and behaves entirely normally within half an hour of an accident has not fractured anything. A child who does not needs medical advice.

When you have to deal with a fracture which is horribly obvious from the weird shape or position of the limb and from the child's acute pain and shock, remember that the damage done to bone, ligaments and muscles as they were forced into that position has already been done but that any further movement – even movement to put it back into its usual position – may do further damage.

Leave it to the professionals. If possible, send for an ambulance and keep the child still while you wait for it to come. Concentrate on comforting her and treating her for shock (*see below*) and let ambulance personnel work out the best way to move her. If you are miles from a telephone and have to transport the child yourself *try to keep the damaged part from moving*. If an obviously broken arm is dangling at her side, for example, you can use scarves, tights, or whatever you have with you to tie it to her body, placing the ties well above and below the injury. If the arm is being held in a bent position across her body, you can fix it there with a sling around her neck. In theory a broken leg can be similarly supported by being tied to the uninjured one but in practice it will still be exceedingly difficult to move her singlehandedly without acute pain and further damage. You would probably be better advised to find somebody who will help you or send for help. If it seems at all possible to you that a child has damaged her spine, including her neck, *moving her could kill or cripple her* by injuring the spinal cord. Do what you can to make her comfortable and treat her for shock where she is, but don't try to move her. Find some way to summon professional help.

A child with a greenstick or simple fracture (*see below*) will usually be allowed home as soon as it has been X-rayed, seen by a doctor and put into a plaster cast. Remember that:

Fractures are not usually acutely painful once they have been treated. The child may have a bad night due to a combination of pain and exhaustion following minor shock and the stress of her time at the hospital, but if she continues to complain of pain for more than twenty-four hours you should consider having her checked again at the hospital. Sometimes, for example, an injured limb continues to swell after treatment so that the cast itself becomes painfully tight.

Wearing a cast is tiring and can strain other muscles. A child who is trying to do everything one-handedly will probably become irritable and frustrated; one who is walking on crutches or with a 'walking plaster' will be putting a lot of strain on the good leg and may become very tired and achey by the end of the day. The trick is to let her use her energy and effort on the things she really must do (like going to school) and the things she really wants to do (like having her birthday treat all the same) but to let her off some of the routine things (like making her bed or running her own errands) in between.

Mended bones and ligaments take time to regain full strength and disused muscles become slack. When that cast is finally removed do listen carefully to the doctor's advice about when the child should return to active sports or about any exercises which she should do either with you or in the hospital physiotherapy department. Once the drama of a fracture is over it is easy to stop bothering. Don't. If she does not give ligaments time to strengthen she may strain them and leave herself with a permanent weakness. If she demands too much of muscles which have not been used at all for several weeks she is likely to injure herself all over again.

You may hear various types of fracture mentioned in hospital:

Greenstick fractures The bone has bent and cracked like a green twig rather than snapping like a dry one. The fracture should heal easily and completely because the damaged part of the bone is held in place by the undamaged part and neither the blood nor the nerve supply has been completely cut off.

Simple fractures The bone has broken completely but the broken ends are still perfectly aligned with each other. A cast will ensure that the ends do not move apart and the bone should knit together again easily.

More serious closed fractures Sometimes the force which fractures a bone moves the broken ends out of alignment. This is far more serious than a simple fracture not only because the limb will have to be 'set' (i.e., have the bone ends manipulated back into the proper position for healing) but also because those broken ends have already moved inside the limb and will have damaged nerves, muscles and blood vessels. If a major blood vessel was cut there may be enough internal bleeding to cause severe shock (*see below*) and there will almost inevitably be severe pain which will increase her shock reaction.

Comminuted fractures are those in which a bone is not merely broken and displaced but broken in two or more places or actually shattered. Open surgery will be required to reconstruct the bone. Pins may be used to hold it together while healing takes place.

Impacted fractures are those in which the broken ends of a bone have been rammed into one another. Surgery will again be required.

Compound fractures Are fractures which are associated with an external wound. Sometimes the broken ends of the bone have moved so far that they have pierced the skin. Sometimes something has gone through the skin and flesh to fracture the bone. Whichever it is, a compound fracture is almost always more serious than a closed one because the bone is exposed to infection and the child may lose a lot of blood.

Head injuries

Every baby and small child gets a nasty bump on the head at some time or another. The younger the child, the larger and heavier his head in relation to the rest of him so the more likely it is that when he falls, his head will suffer. Older children often have better acceleration than brakes: they run into each other and into doors. Later still, contact sports, like football, take their toll as do missiles like cricket or baseballs or even rocks. Finally, of course, even the most sensible teenager can come off a bicycle or stand up under a beam which recent growth has suddenly made too low for him.

Bumps on the head often *look* serious. Parents know that they *can be* serious and therefore they cause a tremendous amount of worry. The worry is almost always unnecessary because there is no mystery about head injuries. If you know what to look for, you will always be able to tell whether your child needs help or not. If he seems all right and goes on seeming all right, he is all right.

Why bumps on the head often look serious even when they are not

The skin covering the head (the scalp) has a rich supply of blood vessels and is comparatively tightly stretched over a structure (the skull) with little 'give' in it.

Even a tiny cut or graze tends to bleed profusely so that your child may rush in with blood trickling down his face. Cuts tend to go on bleeding, too, because even the smallest nick in that stretched skin gapes open. While simple pressure, even through the hair, may stop such bleeding, a cut which would need no treatment if it were elsewhere on the body may need a stitch to hold the edges together.

Even if the scalp is not actually cut, bangs on the head, especially on the forehead, tend to make dramatically large and swollen bruises. If your one-year-old has a lump the size of a goose's egg it is hard to believe that the blow which caused it was unimportant.

Falls on the head are frightening. Your child may seem shocked (*see below*) after a bang which would scarcely have bothered him if he had taken it on the knee.

Why bumps on the head can be dangerous

The bony skull, covered by scalp and hair, protects the brain. Cuts and bumps on the scalp are no more dangerous than similar injuries elsewhere. Cracks or fractures in the skull are no more dangerous than similar injuries to other bones. What matters is what, if anything, has happened to the brain beneath.

There are three main ways in which the brain can be damaged by a blow on the head:

'Concussion'. This loosely used term means that the brain has been jarred and shaken in such a way that part of it has knocked against the inside of the skull. Such a child may lose consciousness (be 'knocked out') either momentarily or for hours. The seriousness of concussion depends on the exact area of the brain involved, but, as we shall see, any child who is obviously concussed should be seen by a doctor.

Concussion with bleeding inside the skull. If some of the tiny blood vessels between the brain and the skull are damaged, they will bleed. Such bleeding can be inside (subdural) or outside (extradural) the brain's covering membrane. Because the free blood is trapped inside the rigid skull it can form a clot which presses into the brain. The clot will almost certainly have to be surgically removed.

Since this kind of bleeding does not produce recognizable symptoms until clotting *has* taken place, a child who has sustained a heavy blow on the head will often be kept in hospital for twenty-four hours' 'observation'.

Skull fractures. Hairline fractures of the skull are common. Braced by the structure of the skull, such fractures heal themselves and are unimportant. If your child bumps his head, has an X-ray and is found to have fractured his skull, the fracture does not, in itself, mean that the head injury was serious.

But very occasionally there is a 'depressed fracture'. This means that a piece of the skull bone has been pushed inwards. Like a blood clot, a depressed skull fracture can put pressure on the brain. The bone will almost certainly have to be lifted back into line surgically.

Concussion and unconsciousness

Concussion does not always lead to unconsciousness but a child who is unconscious after a bang on the head is always concussed.

Do not move him unless he is in a really dangerous place such as a room which is on fire. Until he regains consciousness you have no way of knowing which parts of him are damaged (*see above* Fractures).

Do not try to wake him up.

Do not try to give him anything to drink.

Guard his breathing by loosening any clothing which may have pulled tight around his neck and by making sure that neither blood nor vomit gets into his windpipe. If he has fallen on his back and *is* bleeding from the nose or showing signs of vomiting, you will have a difficult judgement to make. To protect that vital breathing you should turn him onto his front so that secretions run out of his mouth. But if his spine – at any level from the neck downwards – should be damaged, turning him over could do further harm.

Send for an ambulance.

If he comes round while you are waiting, keep him lying down but reassure him (and yourself as you begin to see that it is so) that he is not seriously hurt but must stay lying down until a doctor has checked him over. Remember that he will be confused and frightened because he will not remember how he came to be lying where he finds himself and that fear and anxiety increase shock (*see below* Shock).

The child who has been unconscious

Often a concussed child is momentarily 'knocked out' but 'comes round' within seconds of the blow. If you see him lying unconscious but he is awake by the time you reach him, put him to lie down, treat him for shock and send for an ambulance.

If you are not sure whether he was unconscious or not, ask him exactly what happened to him. If he cannot remember falling down or cannot remember getting up again and coming towards you, he almost certainly was unconscious and should be treated as above.

Bleeding or discharge from the ears

Blood or clear fluid coming from within the ear does suggest quite serious head injury. The child should be treated as if he had been unconscious.

Bleeding from the nose or mouth can be due to direct local injury but can also be a sign of serious head injury. If you can see blood but cannot see a cut lip or bruised nose, play safe and treat him as if he had been knocked unconscious.

If none of the above signs are present but the child seems shocked and dazed, you can take time to comfort and observe him before sending for medical help. If a quick cuddle is enough to make him feel better enough to get on with life, let him. If he is more distressed than that or obviously 'feels funny', put him to lie down on the sofa and chat to him while you **watch for any change in his level of consciousness, any peculiarity in his behaviour or any new physical symptoms.** After about twenty minutes' rest he will probably be perfectly recovered. After this time:

You need
medical
advice if:
He is still very pale or greyish; his breathing seems noisy although he is not crying; he complains of feeling giddy or 'odd'; he seems 'odd' or irrational or unable to recognize or respond to you as he usually does; he seems unable to see clearly, makes odd noises or (assuming that he is of talking age) he talks nonsense or his speech is slurred.

You would be wise to consult your doctor, at least by telephone, if he vomits or complains of headache. Vomiting can be a simple reaction to the shock of the bump while a young child may confuse headache with the pain of the actual bruise, but since these symptoms can also be signs of concussion it is best to play safe.

If none of these symptoms appear and the child wants to get up and get going, let him. The chance that the bang on his head has affected his brain is now very remote indeed. It is still remotely possible, however, that there might be a slow seepage of blood between skull and brain or that a skull fracture is causing pressure. These traumas are rare and usually show up immediately as obvious 'concussion', but they can show up over the twelve or so hours after the accident: bleeding, for example, may produce no symptoms of disturbance until the blood clots and presses inwards.

Keeping a
watchful eye
for later effects
of head injury
You need not limit the child's ordinary activities in any way but, preferably without him being aware of any anxiety, you should be alert for the later development of any of the above signs of concussion, as well as for unusual clumsiness, irritability, jumpiness or any behaviour which makes you feel uneasy. As long as he seems entirely normal and ordinary, all is well.

If he drops off to sleep after the accident his body is probably using the best possible means of getting over the shock. Let him sleep but glance in from time to time to make sure that his colour and breathing seem just as usual. If you have any reason to think that sleep may be turning into unconsciousness, try waking him up. He may be cross at being disturbed but too bad. You want to be sure that he is normally wakeable.

If you cannot decide whether he seems ordinary or not, ring the doctor. He may see the child immediately or he may advise you to wake him a couple of times in the night to check his level of consciousness and to stay in touch by telephone. But once you have told your doctor about a possibly serious head injury you can be quite sure that he will play it super-safe so if he says 'don't worry', don't. And if he admits the child to hospital for twenty-four hours' observation, don't assume that the child is seriously affected. Such a medical watch is only a precaution which is usually unnecessary but can be life-saving.

● If an adolescent should have been drinking or taking other drugs at the time of a head injury it can be extremely difficult to distinguish between the signs of intoxication and concussion. Tragedies sometimes occur when adults, who are assumed to be only drunk, are left in a police cell to 'sober up' and are later found to have been concussed as well. Hospitals find it difficult too, but the responsibility is better left to them.

Poisoning (*see also* **Safety**/In the home: Safety from household poisons; Safety with medicines)

If a child takes something poisonous, he must be treated *quickly*. While some substances – caustic soda, for example – do damage even as they are swallowed, most do no harm until they have been in the child's stomach for long enough for the chemicals to start being absorbed into his bloodstream. If he has a handful of berries or pills in his stomach and you can get them up again more or less intact, he will come to no harm.

But although speed is vital, do slow down enough to think when you find your child in suspicious circumstances. Has he *really* eaten those aspirins or are they clutched in his hand, scattered on the floor or neatly posted down the lavatory? Treatment for poisoning is terrifying and horrible for a child (induced violent vomiting and/or stomach wash-outs). Once you rush him to hospital saying that he has taken something poisonous, the staff will have to take your word for it and proceed. It would be tragic if panic had led you to put him through all that for nothing.

Poisonous substances

A long list of different chemicals which are variously dangerous if consumed in different quantities will probably not help you or the child on the day a poisoning drama strikes. Many substances are poorly labelled so that you will not be able to tell whether or not there is something lethal in that furniture polish. Although a poison centre will be able to tell from the brand name alone, centres in many countries will only advise doctors so you have to seek medical aid before you can be sure whether your child is in danger or not. Finally, it is usually extremely difficult to tell *how much* a child has consumed of a suspicious or down-right lethal substance. Perhaps that bottle of liquid was full, but how much has soaked into his jersey and the carpet? As for those pills, do you really know how many there were? And can you estimate how many have been ground to powdery bits in his hand?

Unless you live in a country with superb labelling and a Poisons Information Centre which will directly answer parents' queries (as in the United States), it is best to play safe and assume that *any* of the following substances, in *any* quantity, may poison your child.

Pills, capsules and medicines

Whether prescribed or bought over the counter and whether intended originally for the child or an adult. The commonest causes of serious or fatal poisoning are: tricyclic antidepressants, iron, paracetamol and aspirin, but you must include vitamins, contraceptive pills, travel sickness remedies and anti-histamines, as well as liquids like cough mixtures.

Chemicals

☐ Home: including polishes, lavatory cleaners, deodorizers, etc.
☐ Garden: *especially* weedkillers, insecticides and fungicides.
☐ Garage: not forgetting petrol, oil, paraffin.

Berries

Unless you know what they are and that they are harmless.

Wild fungi

Unless you can see that they are genuine mushrooms or other edibles.

Tobacco

One whole cigarette, actually swallowed, could kill a one-year-old.

Alcohol   A good swig of neat spirits (rather than wine, beer, etc.) could kill a toddler.

Coping with poisoning   More and more authorities are coming to believe that stomach wash-outs (*see* **Hospital**/Procedures) are unnecessarily barbarous in many cases of possible poisoning; hospitals increasingly induce vomiting instead. If vomiting is the treatment of choice and speed is important, it may be sensible for you to get on with it without waiting until you can reach the hospital. In the United States this would certainly be the accepted advice to parents. In Britain and some other European countries you would be wise to ask your own doctor for his opinion *before it ever happens*.

Making the child vomit   If you are going to make a child vomit, you must get both the circumstances and the method right.

Don't induce vomiting if the suspicious substance is any kind of cleaner, polish, bleach, disinfectant, or petroleum product. In fact avoid inducing vomiting for anything in the 'chemicals' group. This is because some (though not all) such products either burn the mouth and throat when swallowed and will do so again coming up, or give out poisonous fumes which will be further inhaled during vomiting.

Do induce vomiting if the suspicious substance is a pill or medicine, a berry or fungus, tobacco or alcohol.

Don't try to make him sick with old-fashioned emetics such as salt and water or mustard and water. They are dangerous in themselves.

Don't rely on mechanical vomiting. You can make a child retch by boldly putting a finger to the back of his throat and wiggling it. If his retching produces a vomit containing the aspirin tablets he has just eaten, fine. But the retching may produce nothing at all or nothing useful.

If your doctor agrees, use syrup of ipecacuanha. This is a reliable and effective emetic which really does 'empty' the stomach. Indeed some research suggests that it removes just as much of the stomach contents as does a mechanical stomach wash-out. 10 ml of the syrup for a one-year-old, rising to 20 ml for a three-year-old, *followed by a glass of water*, will produce vomiting within twenty minutes. Use the twenty minutes to telephone your doctor or to start for the hospital. Take a plastic bag for the vomit: the hospital staff will need to see what came up.

Summary of first aid for poisoning
- ☐ Remove substance remaining in child's mouth, hands, etc.
- ☐ Check that some really has been swallowed.
- ☐ Give syrup of ipecacuanha if substance is appropriate.
- ☐ Telephone doctor/hospital; tell them you are bringing child and what it is that he has taken so that they can use the intervening time to check with a poison centre.
- ☐ Collect container and any scattered contents.
- ☐ Take child and container (plus vomit bag if appropriate) to hospital as fast as possible.
- ☐ If you are driving, strap child in sitting-up position or lie him on his side, in case he vomits and breathes it in.

Older children and poisonous substances

Accidental poisoning is, of course, much rarer in older children and it is usually easier to deal with sensibly because the child herself can tell you or show you *what* she has taken, and *how much*. She might eat one poisonous berry mistaking it for a fruit but she is unlikely to eat a handful because it will not taste good. In most such cases, ring your doctor, hospital or poison centre and take their advice.

Occasional tragedies happen when a child takes a swig out of a lemonade bottle which is being used as a container for weedkiller or turpentine . . . Of course this should never happen, but it does.

There are a few substances which are exceedingly dangerous even if only a tiny drop is swallowed. If you cannot remember exactly what that liquid is in the lemonade bottle, you *must* rush child and bottle to hospital.

- For non-accidental poisoning *see* **Suicide**.

Shock

Shock is a complicated condition whose basic cause is a sudden fall in blood pressure which reduces the efficiency with which the heart can pump blood through the circulation and therefore reduces the supply available to the brain.

The severity of shock depends on the cause and duration of that fall in pressure. When a child has a nasty fright or faints (*see* **Fainting**) reflex activity dilates the blood vessels to the internal organs so that the pressure within all the blood vessels is reduced. That child is momentarily in a state of shock but as she recovers from her start of fear or comes round from her faint, her blood pressure will return to normal and all will be well. When a child is severely injured, however, the fall in blood pressure which puts her into a state of shock will not be so simply reversible because something other than reflex activity is causing it (*see below* Major shock).

Causes of minor shock

The cause may be entirely emotional; a reaction to bad news, to finding a pet dead or to seeing a bloody accident.

Often the cause is a mixture of emotion and physical distress; the child may get slightly hurt in particularly frightening circumstances.

Continuing pain and fear increase and lengthen any shock reaction so that a minor burn may lead to more shock than a comparable, but less painful, cut and waiting to hear the worst may lead to more shock than bad news which is cut and dried.

Symptoms of minor shock

The victim's skin is pale, cold and clammy because, with the fall in blood pressure, the blood vessels supplying the skin close up as much as possible so that all possible blood is pumped to the vital organs.

She may shiver, tremble, feel giddy or faint; she may cry or vomit. Because its blood supply has been temporarily reduced, the brain's control over the body is disrupted.

Coping with minor shock

The child may recover so rapidly that you have no time to do anything and therefore no need to exercise your first aid talents, either. If not:

Lie her down on her side. Lying down assists the action of the heart and uses gravity to help ensure a maximal share of blood for the brain. Lying on her side ensures that if she should vomit it will run harmlessly out of her mouth rather than being inhaled.

Comfort and reassure her in whatever way is appropriate to the cause of the shock. Remember that pain and fear create a vicious circle.

Cover her with a light blanket, coat or whatever you have to preserve her body warmth.

Do not warm her artificially with hot water bottles, etc. If you do so, her skin colour may improve because the warmth will force the blood vessels beneath to re-open. But although she will *look* better her condition will actually be worse because that extra blood will be being supplied at the expense of the brain and other vital organs.

Do not give anything to drink. Neither that old stand by 'hot sweet tea' nor alcohol is at all a good idea. The tea (or other sugary drink) cannot be absorbed from the stomach while she is in shock and is therefore likely to be vomited. If alcohol is absorbed, its effects on her central nervous system will actually delay its return to normal.

If the shock-condition really is minor these measures will produce clear improvement within five minutes – perhaps less. You will see her colour return to normal and her skin will dry and re-warm: tension and shakiness will relax. She may drop off to sleep or get up and get on with life. Even if the cause of the shock reaction still exists as pain, grief or horror-remembered, she will no longer appear *ill*.

If there is no improvement within five minutes or recovery is not complete within half an hour reconsider the cause of the shock; it may have been more serious than you believed.

Causes of major shock Blood pressure can be seriously lowered by:

Heavy bleeding whether this is sudden – as from a severed artery or haemorrhage from the womb – or more insidious as when less dramatic bleeding is allowed to continue for so long that the blood loss eventually reaches a critical level.

Internal bleeding following injuries to internal organs, such as a crushed liver or lung damaged by broken ribs, or following abdominal crises such as a ruptured appendix.

Bleeding within the tissues such as may occasionally occur around the jagged ends of a badly fractured bone or within a very large area of deep bruising (*see above*).

Loss of plasma from the circulation as in extensive burns (*see above*).

Loss of other body fluids leading to dehydration. If violent or long-continued diarrhoea and/or vomiting reduces the fluid available to the body too far, the volume available within the circulation will eventually drop, too (*see* **Diarrhoea, Gastro-enteritis and Food Poisoning**).

Serious shock can also be caused without loss of fluid from the circulation or the body tissues by overwhelming systemic illnesses such as septicaemia, or if the brain's control over the circulation is disrupted.

Damage to the brain or central nervous system (*see above* Head injuries) can deprive the brain of blood or, through disruption of respiration, deprive it of oxygen even when an adequate supply of blood is still being pumped by the heart.

Symptoms of major shock

First symptoms will be similar to those of minor shock (*see above*) but may be more pronounced so that the victim is not only pale and clammy but covered in cold sweat; not only shaky and dizzy but collapsed and irrational.

Coping with major shock

Give first aid for obvious injuries such as stopping heavy bleeding or cooling burns.

If injuries are clearly serious, send for help. While waiting, treat exactly as outlined in coping with minor shock.

If injuries are not clear, treat exactly as you would treat for minor shock and wait a few minutes for signs of improvement.

If the shock-condition is serious in itself you will see no improvement and must send urgently for help. These measures cannot reverse major shock because the failure of blood supply to the brain is due either to shortage of blood or fluid or to failure of control in the circulation. Instead of recovery you will see progressive symptoms which, without prompt hospital help, may be fatal. For example:

Because the circulation is short of blood-volume, the heart beats faster and the pulse races.

Because the heart is working harder and harder to pump less than the optimum amount of blood it pumps less and less efficiently.

Because the heart pumps less efficiently less and less blood reaches the brain whose control circuits become increasingly disrupted.

Eventually this vicious circle affects breathing. The victim may breathe very rapidly yet be unable to get enough oxygen so that she suffers from what is termed 'air-hunger' and begins to gasp in uncoordinated breaths.

If you do not see immediate improvement in a shocked child send for help before you begin to see her condition worsen in this way.

While you are waiting for the ambulance or doctor, continue to treat her as for minor shock. Your first aid will not produce recovery but will do all that can be done to prevent her condition from worsening until the cause can be treated and the shock-condition reversed.

Sports injuries

Few sporting activities are more dangerous than other kinds of active physical exercise and few injuries received during sports are special; a fracture is a fracture whether it happens while kicking a football or climbing a tree. Nevertheless there are some particular risks of particular types of injury which the parents of sportsmad children may want to consider.

Sports and athletics are becoming increasingly popular with more and more people practising them and even more watching them do so. There is big money involved at the top for participants, backers, sponsors and associated industries. At the bottom, even at primary school level, there are high rewards in terms of self-esteem and status within the peer group. Children and young people tend to push themselves towards higher and higher levels of performance and competition and to be pushed, too. There are not only individual aspirations involved but also those of team-mates, coaches and club supporters. Physical courage is part of the ethos of most sports and certainly a requirement for any form of athletic training at any level. If a child's own desire to succeed is bolstered by pressures to succeed for other people's honour and glory, he may train, practise and compete when he is not fit to do so. A line has to be drawn between courage and folly; the child's wellbeing in the long-term has to be balanced against the team's wellbeing in tomorrow's game. Few young-sters will be able to exercise that kind of judgement for themselves when their competitive spirit is aroused. They need parents to do it for them.

General health and sports injuries

Even a child who has gone through all the appropriate training and reached an appropriate level of fitness for his sporting activities will nevertheless risk injury if he participates when unwell. A heavy head-cold, for example, partially obstructs breathing. The deliberate respira-tory stress incurred in a training session can easily become respiratory distress. Fever, whatever the underlying cause, means that heavy physi-cal activity will make him liable to heat exhaustion (*see below* Sunburn and heat illness) as well as to hypothermia if his sport involves water (*see above* Drowning). Some girls may be more liable to accidental injury at the time of their menstrual periods (*see* **Adolescence**/Menstruation) while both sexes will be vulnerable immediately after minor infections during which muscles have lost their full tone.

Over-use syndromes in sport

By definition, training for or participating in a sport involves repeated exercises affecting particular bones, tendons and muscle groups. They are stressed so that they build the strength to meet the demands of the chosen activity. But *too* many repetitions of the same movement or the slightest *change* in that movement (such as running in different training shoes or on a harder surface) can cause a minute amount of damage. The vital point in all these syndromes is that the very first symptoms are mild indicators of a very minor injury. Because the injury is mild, rest will quickly allow it to heal. But because the symptoms are minor, the child can easily override them and will often be encouraged to do so by over-enthusiastic coaches and colleagues who attribute the warning pain to 'a muscle strain' and suggest that the victim 'work it off'.

The most dramatic example of an over-use syndrome is a stress frac-ture. The affected bone (often the upper leg bone, the femur, in children or the lower leg bone, the fibula, in older joggers and runners) develops a minute crack rather as an aeroplane wing can eventually develop the minute cracks of metal fatigue. There is pain on exercise but no loss of function and, for the moment, the pain stops when exercise stops. If the exercise is avoided for a few days that bone crack (unlike the aeroplane wing) will heal itself. But if it continues, the crack will very gradually spread, the pain will increase and, eventually, that crack can turn into a full fracture.

Unfortunately an *early* stress fracture is almost impossible to see on a conventional X-ray. Only four to six weeks after the injury will a visible area of denser bony growth confirm such damage. The absence of early X-ray findings makes it even more likely that the child will try to dismiss his pain as 'only a strain' and struggle to go on with his activities.

A stress fracture which is allowed to develop into a full fracture is an obvious disaster, but there are less dramatic examples which are equally important. Symptoms in the Achilles tendon, linking heel with ankle, for example, are often attributed to tight football boots or hard ground conditions and therefore ignored. Yet acute inflammation or an incomplete rupture of this tendon can produce chronic pain and disability if it is left untreated and especially if it is abused by further exercise of the causative kind.

Guarding your child against the over-use syndromes takes a great deal of tact. If every time your child limps home you try to insist on a week's rest you will simply earn the label 'fussy mother' and he will first try to conceal pain from you and then eventually defy you. Yet if you do not react to that limp, leaving it entirely to the child to decide whether or not he is fit to train tomorrow or compete on Saturday, you leave him to the mercies of peers and coaches who may be as concerned with their team's reputation as with your child's wellbeing. Some children, at some stages in their sporting lives, may actually *want* you to forbid their participation because by doing so you allow them to take time off without having to admit to personal 'weakness'. You may find the following ideas helpful:

Make sure you are acquainted with your child's coach, whether he is a professional or simply an enthusiastic school teacher or father-helping-out-with-the-kids. You need to know how concerned he is for his young sportsmen's wellbeing and how he balances that against 'his' competitive successes. You also need to know how he handles the youngsters. If he is a 'macho' type who bullies them, your child is the more liable to be pushed beyond his limits. If he puts as high a premium on courage as on skill and tends to deride anyone who claims to be injured, that child will obviously find it the more difficult to draw a well-placed line between courage and folly.

Make it clear to your child that you are among his sporting supporters but that your parenting comes first and therefore that his long-term health will always matter more to you than his short-term successes. Make it clear that you take his courage for granted and know something of the pain and discomfort which is a necessary part of all sports and athletics training, so that he will realize that any attempts to call a halt when he is injured are not simply attempts to save him pain but rather to save him the risk of disability.

Refuse to indulge in amateur sportsmedicine yourself. Don't buy or apply support bandages and liniments. Explain that a wrongly applied bandage or a bandage applied to support muscles when an underlying bone or tendon is damaged, can do more harm than good. Explain also that any injury which requires treatment requires diagnosis first and that diagnosis can only be made by a doctor.

Use the child's doctor as the arbiter between you and the child whenever questions of fitness for sport cause trouble between you. The doctor may not be able to diagnose accurately an early stress-condition but he will certainly play safe by insisting on rest unless he is sure there is no risk in continued exercise. Remember that a doctor's edict will be far easier for your child to abide by than an edict from you. No self-respecting young-ster will go into the locker rooms saying 'My mum says I'm not to . . .' 'The doctor won't let me . . .' is far more socially acceptable.

Sprains and strains

People often use these terms interchangeably which is unfortunate as they differ in their nature, their usual severity and their recommended treatment.

Sprains A sprain properly refers to an injury caused by bending or twisting a joint suddenly and/or beyond its normal limits. The ligaments which support the joint are over-stretched or torn. There may be extensive damage to the surrounding tissue and blood vessels. Such an injury is excruciatingly painful. There will be rapid swelling of the joint area which may also appear bruised. Occasionally, especially when it is the wrist which is sprained, the damage to the ligaments allows a partial dislocation of the joint. This complication is called a subluxation. It is almost impossible to tell a severe sprain from a fracture without the help of an X-ray, so it is best not to try:

First aid *for sprains* Treat a suspected sprain exactly as you would treat a suspected green-stick fracture (*see above* Fractures).

Hospital *treatment* *for sprains* The affected joint will probably be X-rayed both to exclude the possibility of a fracture and to enable the doctor to get some idea of the severity of the damage done to the ligaments. Once he has this information, the sprain will probably be bandaged in such a way that support from the bandage provides some of the support to the joint which is normally given by the ligaments which have been damaged. Sometimes, especially if an ankle is severely sprained, plaster of Paris will be used to immobilize the joint.

After a sprain listen carefully to the doctor's instructions about what the child may/must do with the affected joint during the next days and weeks. A period of rest will be needed to give the ligaments time to heal but too long a period of immobility may lead to a stiff joint. Any suggested exercises should be performed conscientiously. Pain may be more severe and last longer than in a simple fracture.

Strains   A strain properly refers to overstretching or tearing of some of the fibres of a muscle or group of muscles, due to sudden or unusual movement. Sudden, awkward lifting, for example, can strain muscles low in the back, while strained muscles in the calves are common when active games are played on a slippery surface.

Because muscles occur in dense groups, these injuries are seldom serious. The affected muscle will heal itself and other muscles will support it and do its work during the recovery period. There is no risk of loss of function as there is when a joint is sprained. Very occasionally, though, a whole group of muscles may be torn to produce a much more dramatic injury. If a person grabs for a heavy, falling object, for example, the biceps can tear, leaving a visible 'hole' in the upper arm which rapidly turns blue from bleeding under the skin. This rare kind of strain requires immediate hospital treatment.

First aid for   No real treatment is required. The victim will be more comfortable if he
mild strains   avoids stressing the damaged muscle but he should not be encouraged to rest completely as gentle exercise will prevent stiffness and speed recovery. Strained muscles tend to be most painful first thing in the morning just because they have been at rest; the day's mobility relieves pain and stiffness.

Home treatment for strains often includes liniments rubbed into the surrounding skin. The logic for this kind of treatment is that the liniments increase the blood supply to the muscle and thus relieve pain and aid healing. In fact, especially with a deep-seated muscle, it is unlikely that the liniment can have any affect at all. The rubbing may, however, increase the blood supply as can a hot bath.

After a strain repeating the exercise which caused the strain in the first place will certainly be painful and may delay healing, so while some exercise is desirable, some limits may be desirable also. A calf-strain caused during football, for example, probably ought to mean no football for a few days or until the pain has gone. Putting a support bandage on so as to enable the victim to play despite a strain is a poor idea: it is better to allow the muscle to regain its true strength rather than providing it with artificial support.

Sunburn and heat illness

Although these things often come together to ruin a family holiday or bedevil a move to a new and hotter country, they need not be linked at all.

Sunburn is caused only by the sun's particular radiation or by 'sun-lamps' which are designed to mimic it. No other heat-source will cause sunburn but the sun may burn even when the victim feels cool. A sunny day's sailing, for example, may lead to serious sunburn. The cool sea-breeze prevents the victim from feeling hot and may indeed make it more comfortable to be in the sun than in the shade. Yet she is being doubly exposed to those rays because they are not only beating down on her but also reflecting back off the water to burn unlikely and agonizing places like the backs of her knees.

Heat illness, on the other hand, is caused by hot conditions irrespective of the source of the heat. The heat of the sun may cause it (with or without causing sunburn as well) but so may the heat from an indoor blast furnace. A long afternoon's tennis on a hot cloudy day can precipitate heat illness even though the cloud layer prevents sunburn. Without those clouds sunburn would have been a risk but heat illness would have been less likely because the victim would have found it impossible to play on in the direct sun.

Sunburn Is far easier to prevent than to treat (*see* **Safety**/On holiday). Everyone knows that unaccustomed skin should be only gradually exposed to the sun so that it can build up protective pigment ahead of burning point. Almost everyone hurries the process in search of that tan and many pay in soreness and eventually by losing the tan in peeling. Older people may choose to risk agony for the sake of beauty but babies and young children are entitled to protection:

Choose suntan oils or lotions carefully. Most now state their 'protection factor'; the higher the number, the greater the screening-effect. A young child may need a factor six or eight, but even this will only protect her if it is applied to *all* exposed skin and renewed frequently.

Remember that sunburn does not hurt at the time but only some hours after exposure. Don't ration your child's sunbathing time according to whether or not her skin feels uncomfortable *now*. It may be agonizing later.

Remember that your position relative to the sun changes as the day goes on. If you put a baby to sleep in the shade or under a sun-umbrella, make sure that the spot will stay shady until she gets up again.

First aid for sunburn **If the skin is red and sore to the touch,** cool it. Don't try a cold shower or bath: the superheated skin will over-react and she will be shivery and miserable. Use tepid water and let it cool her by evaporation. Cover with moisturizer or an 'after-sun' product.

Cover the sunburned area with the lightest, softest, smoothest fabric you can find. Even the seams on her tee-shirt may be painful. At bedtime, make sure that her bed-sheet is tightly stretched so that the skin is not irritated by ruckles. A baby may be more comfortable on a muslin nappy.

Keep her in the shade. Even a brief touch of sun will hurt very much and increase the burn. If you cannot keep her in the shade while staying around the beach you may have to reorganize your day and make an inland expedition by car.

If she is miserable a couple of hours later take her temperature. There may be some heat illness associated with the sunburn (*see below*).

If the skin blisters find a doctor. Many parents treat sunburn blisters themselves, using products such as calamine lotion. Although you may get away with it this is risky. If the blisters burst infection is likely and acute pain is certain. There will be superficial scars, too.

Heat illness   This is much rarer and much more serious than simple sunburn. It is most likely to occur when an *unaccustomed* individual meets some combination of the following conditions:

- Very high air temperatures especially if they are caused by radiant heat such as the sun, fire, etc.
- High humidity so that as well as being extremely hot the air is 'muggy' or 'stuffy'.
- Active exercise.
- Copious sweating which is not adequately replaced by drinking.
- Copious sweating without an adequate intake of salt.

● For the individual on holiday, being even slightly unwell, perhaps with a low-grade fever, much increases the risk of heat illness. The child is anxious to waste no time and therefore does not give in to the illness. She exercises vigorously but probably is not very hungry and therefore misses the salt which would be present in her normal meals. If a child is unwell on holiday, try to persuade her that it is better to lose one day in rest than several in real illness. If a day in her room seems unnecessary, try at least to arrange for a cool quiet day rather than a hot rumbustious one.

The severity of heat illness ranges from passing faintness and feelings of exhaustion to life-threatening collapse:

Heat syncope   This is simple fainting provoked by some of the above conditions. The child 'passes out' or collapses to the ground feeling dizzy. She rapidly comes round once she is lying down but even if she feels perfectly all right she should lie in cool conditions for a while.

Heat exhaustion   This is a generic term used to describe collapse in and due to hot conditions which lasts longer than momentary heat syncope.

The victim feels faint, dizzy and peculiar because the vital salt and water balance of the body is upset and this affects the efficient working of the heart and the supply of blood to the brain (*see above* Shock). The specific cause may be shortage of water or shortage of salt or a mixture of the two. Either or both will be related to inadequate replacement of what is lost through heavy sweating. Lack of water may simply be caused by the victim failing to drink enough extra fluids to compensate for her sweat loss. Children on vacation in foreign countries, for example, are sometimes sensibly forbidden to drink the water from hotel taps yet are less sensibly limited in the number of drinks they are allowed to purchase from the bar or café. Economizing on drinks is a very false economy indeed.

Shortage of salt is unlikely if the victim has been eating normally, but is possible if she has not wanted much food. It is also possible if heavy sweat loss has made her so thirsty that she *has* drunk a great deal of pure water. She may then have diluted the salt-concentration of her body fluids too far.

Anyone who is 'taken ill' in hot conditions should be put to lie down in a cool, shady, well-ventilated place and, as a first aid measure, should be given cool drinks containing a pinch of salt per glass.

If the victim does not feel very much better within half an hour and/or is not completely recovered and eager to get up and get on with life after, say, three hours at rest and two pints of drink, she should be seen by a doctor.

If there is any loss of consciousness, vomiting or fever a doctor should be sent for immediately, heat exhaustion may be turning into heat stroke.

Heat stroke   True heat stroke implies that the body has been subjected to such a heat load that its internal heat-regulating mechanism has been temporarily disrupted. Simply removing her from the heat-stress will not cure the condition.

The first signs will be similar to those of heat exhaustion: the child will feel dizzy, sick and 'peculiar'. But in addition she will shoot a sudden high fever and may rapidly become confused and delirious.

Heat stroke is a grade one emergency. The child must immediately be admitted to hospital where she can be cooled under controlled conditions and be treated for shock (*see above*) as well as having the fluid/salt balance of her body investigated and corrected.

Wounds and bleeding

Any wound which breaks the skin damages some blood vessels and therefore causes some bleeding. Some children (and adults!) are alarmed by the sight of blood. It may help if they realize that the bleeding from a cut helps to carry any dirt out of the wound and some is therefore highly desirable.

Bleeding from most wounds is trivial. It stops of its own accord as air reaches the broken edges of the little blood vessels. The blood clots and seals them.

Bleeding which shows no sign of stopping on its own is almost always easily stopped simply by pressing on the wound through a piece of gauze, a handkerchief or whatever. The pressure holds back the flow of blood to the cut edges of the blood vessels thus enabling clotting to take place. Even a cut which has been dripping all over the floor will stop in three minutes if you just hold onto it.

Bleeding does not become dangerous in itself until a *very great deal of blood has been lost*. A baby or small child can lose quarter of a pint, an older child half a pint, without danger. And half a pint of blood is a tremendous amount. If you need convincing, spill half a pint of something (preferably red to help your imagination along) into the sink and you will see.

Bleeding from a wound is only ever uncontrollable in this simple way if a large vein or an artery has been cut. Blood from a cut vein is comparatively deep red in colour because most of its oxygen has already been distributed. It pours steadily from the cut. Blood from an artery has been released before it has lost its oxygen and it is therefore a much brighter red. Because arterial blood is being pumped directly by the heart, it tends to spurt rhythmically from the wound, in time with the child's heartbeat. Don't worry if you cannot tell the two apart (in a really serious wound both may be present). First aid is the same for both.

First aid for
severe bleeding

Check that there is nothing (such as a piece of glass) sticking into the wound. Grab the cleanest piece of material that is close by and press hard on the wound through it. (In a real emergency use your bare hands rather than wasting time.) If the wound is on a limb, elevate it so that it is above heart level. This will, in itself, slightly reduce the pressure of the bleeding.

If the pressure slows or stops the bleeding, keep it up while you think what to do next. Can you send, telephone or yell for help while keeping pressure on the wound? If not, bind some piece of your clothing *tightly* around it so that your hand pressure is replaced by a 'pressure bandage'.

If simple pressure does not slow or stop the bleeding, push against the wound in such a way that it is squeezed between your hand and the nearest underlying bone. With a hand or arm wound, you will be able to compress the cut brachial artery between your hand and the arm bone. With a wound in an awkward (though improbable) place, like the groin, you may have to use your fist to press up against the pelvic girdle. Once you have found the right angle and controlled the bleeding, don't let go. A renewed gush may make it difficult to locate the right place again. I cannot tell you how to get help while maintaining this kind of pressure because it depends on your circumstances. But this is certainly a time to yell for help if there is anyone to hear. If you are completely alone, try to improvise a way of keeping pressure against that bone. A rolled up belt bandaged on with your tights or even the bowl of a wooden spoon tied on with the child's sock may work for long enough to let you telephone or get to a window from which your shouts can be heard.

Once you have improvised a pressure bandage, don't remove it even if blood soaks through; there may be *some* clotting and you will disturb it. Add more layers over the top.

Do remember that even if these heroic measures work like magic; the bleeding stops and, on inspection, you decide that perhaps the wound is not as bad as you had thought, you must take the child straight to the doctor or hospital. Your fingers, not to mention your handkerchief or his socks, may well have put dirt into a wound which you know has penetrated to large blood vessels. Infection is likely and would, in these circumstances, be serious.

● *Tourniquets.* Many older first aid books still recommend a tourniquet to control life-threatening bleeding especially from a cut artery. A tourniquet is a strap, belt or bandage which is put around the limb between the wound and the heart and is then tightened by having a stick or rod put through and twisted. Although a tourniquet will certainly stop bleeding from a wound it does so by preventing *any* blood flow rather than by preventing blood from escaping from the cut vessel. If you put a tourniquet around a child's arm to control bleeding from a cut wrist, you will be simultaneously depriving her whole hand of its blood supply. Such a tourniquet is both dangerous and agonizingly painful. Direct pressure on the wound is safer, more comfortable and usually just as effective. Consider using a tourniquet only in the very rare case of life-threatening bleeding from a wound on which you dare not press because it has a shard of glass or a knife sticking out of it.

Wounds and infection
(*see also* **Infection**/Types of infection: Localized infection)

Bacteria are everywhere in their millions. Some are beneficial; most are harmless; a few are not. You cannot sterilize a wound (although a doctor can). All you can do is to *clean* it (thus removing dirt which is liable to be bacteria-laden) and avoid introducing extra bacteria (which is the point of using sterile dressings and so forth).

Any wound, major or minor, can become infected. Surgical wounds in hospitals, made and treated under the best possible circumstances, sometimes become so. Infection in a minor wound does *not* mean that you were careless and should feel guilty. Being too 'germ-conscious' will not improve your first aid and it may easily make your children over-anxious.

Infection in any wound should always be shown to a doctor but if the wound was a trivial one the infection will usually be trivial too. A grazed knee, for example, takes the protective skin off a comparatively large area, leaving it open to infection by bacteria off that dirty road, from your child's own skin or from the air in your bathroom. But because the wound is open and shallow, the infection will start off at a superficial level. It will only become serious if you neglect it and are very unfortunate.

Recognizing infection early

The early signs of infection in any wound are pain, redness/heat and swelling.

A simple cut should not be painful after about twelve hours and should certainly not become increasingly painful after this time. If it does, inspect it carefully and you will probably see some of the other signs.

A scrape or graze, especially one which is associated with bruising, may 'stiffen up' and become more painful while as the bruise develops it may become more red and swollen. In such a case, consider the broken skin area itself. If the scab is yellowish (and especially if there is pus oozing at the edges) there is certainly some local infection although it may be entirely trivial. Show it to your doctor in case.

Later signs of infection

Sometimes a deeper wound appears to heal cleanly but is infected at a deeper level. This is both more serious and more difficult to spot at an early stage.

Suspect it if a wound which your child has forgotten about suddenly bothers him again. Be certain enough to make an immediate medical appointment if the pain is a continuous throbbing rather than a soreness to touch; if the area is hot to touch; if the surrounding skin is red and/or shiny looking; if there is pus seeping through the almost-healed place.

If there should be red streaks running up the child's limb from the wound area and/or he should have a temperature and/or the glands in the armpit or groin of the affected arm or leg are swollen or painful, then infection has spread from the locality of the wound into the bloodstream. Don't wait for a medical appointment. Take the child straight to the nearest hospital.

Acne *see* **Adolescence**/Problems with appearance and body-image.
Addiction *see* **Habits**.

Adenoids

A child's adenoids are a pair of bodies of lymphoid tissue which lie to either side of the back of the throat behind the entrance to the nasal passageways. Unlike the tonsils, they cannot be seen without a mirror but in early childhood the adenoids are large in relation to the size of the passages to the nose and to the eustachian tubes which drain the middle ear (*see* **Ears and Hearing; Ear Disorders and Deafness**). The adenoids play a useful role in trapping and destroying bacteria and viruses but when they are fighting infection in this way, they swell. Swollen adenoids in a small child can partially block the nose so that he breathes through his mouth habitually. More seriously, they may partially block the eustachian tubes so that infected material cannot drain freely from the middle ear and chronic infection may set in. It is usually because of a risk to hearing that removal of the adenoids is recommended (*see* **Hospital**/Surgery: Tonsillectomy and Adenoidectomy; Myringotomy).

Adolescence

'Adolescence' and 'puberty' are confused and confusing terms; difficult to relate exactly to each other and often impossible to relate exactly to your own child. Loosely, puberty refers to the physical changes which transform that child into a sexually mature 'adult' while adolescence refers to the social, emotional and psychological changes which accompany the physical ones and which will only be completed when the inverted commas can be taken off that word 'adult'. So puberty can be seen as being about physical growing up and adolescence as being about all the other kinds. Exactly how they mesh together for the individual depends both on his or her personal timetable and on the expectations of his or her family, community and society. Much adolescent conflict and difficulty is due to these two related aspects of the individual's life getting out of step.

Puberty

Puberty is not an event but a process. It begins when the pituitary gland, controlled by the brain, begins to release into the bloodstream increased quantities of the stimulating hormones called gonadotropins. Follicle-stimulating hormone (FSH) stimulates the development of egg-containing follicles within girls' ovaries and sperm-producing tubules in boys' testes. Luteinizing hormone (LH) stimulates the production of oestrogen by cells within the follicles in girls and the production of androgen by cells within the testes in boys.

At the beginning of the pubertal process extra gonadotropins are released only during sleep. The resulting extra stimulation is very slight and it takes time for the increase in circulating levels of oestrogen and androgen to bring about bodily changes. Later in puberty, as in adult life, the stimulating hormones circulate day and night and oestrogen and androgen levels are maintained at a sexually mature and fertile level.

Boys and puberty   During roughly the first year of increased hormonal stimulation the boy's testes (balls) enlarge but his penis and the rest of his body remain outwardly unchanged.

Once the testes have matured sufficiently for sperm-production to begin, their continuing growth is accompanied by rapid growth of the penis and by the first appearance of pubic and/or underarm hair. Around the mid-point of the pubertal process the hair increases, coarsens and becomes curly and once this stage has been reached the voice will deepen ('break') and some facial hair may begin to appear.

It should be noted that a boy's testes produce enough androgen to stimulate the development of these secondary sexual characteristics well before they produce the even greater quantity necessary to stimulate the pubertal growth spurt. Boys therefore often have to accept the sexual changes of manhood without the extra height which would make them feel 'grown up'. Many find this difficult. On the other hand, as long as a boy is only in the early stages of sexual maturation he can be fully assured that the often longed-for growth spurt is still to come (*see* **Growth**).

Girls and puberty   A girl's ovaries respond to the early increase in stimulating gonadotropins just as a boy's testes do, but because those ovaries are invisible, the first outward sign of a girl's sexual development will be early breast development. In most girls this is very gradual indeed. First the areolae around the nipples become more protuberant, then some breast tissue becomes visible beneath them and then, very slowly, the breasts fill out. Although breasts may be large and shapeless in mid-puberty, girls can be assured that greater shapeliness and elegance will certainly follow.

● In both sexes early breast development sometimes produces small lumps beneath the areolae. Although any worried adolescent is entitled to authoritative reassurance from a doctor, you may be able to prevent worry by assuring him or her that the lumps are not 'growths', but irregularly growing glandular tissue which will soon smooth out.

In most girls the appearance of first pubic hair follows some breast development with underarm hair close behind. Simultaneous or reversed orders are not unusual, however.

A notable and important difference between pubertal girls and boys is that in girls, hormonal levels high enough to stimulate sexual development are more than adequate to stimulate the overall growth spurt. A girl will be growing rapidly before any secondary sexual characteristics are apparent and her growth will have peaked and be slowing before she reaches her menarche and has her first menstrual period (*see* **Growth**).

Worries about puberty   Different societies have different ways of initiating children into adult society; an individual child's reactions to the physical changes in his or her body will, of course, be largely dictated by the attitudes with which he or she has grown up thus far. Some worries are common enough in most Western societies to merit mention:

Problems between the sexes, within families, school classes or other peer groups, are often caused by the differing growth rates of boys and girls.

Most girls begin their pubertal growth spurt at around nine to ten years; most boys grow at child-rates until eleven to twelve. Girls tend therefore to be bigger than boys during these critical years and their visible breast development adds to their more mature appearance. It is not until around fourteen to fifteen that the boys begin to catch up.

This difference in apparent maturity has obvious effects on friendship patterns and so forth but it can also have less obvious effects on boys' morale. In some social groups boys in their early teens use exaggerated physical showing off (whether of a socially acceptable kind such as sport or a less acceptable kind such as gang warfare) to try and assert themselves over those girls. Within a family, friendship, or even tolerance, between a mature-seeming eleven-year-old girl and her still childish-looking thirteen-year-old brother often becomes impossible. Unfairly, it is usually the boy who is judged to be at fault.

Problems of early or late puberty. Most young adolescents rely heavily on the support of their friends while they fight their way from childhood. The child who must undergo conspicuous physical changes before most of his or her friends, or who gets left behind as others develop, tends to feel isolated. On the whole, boys find it easier to accept early physical growth than delay. To be the largest in the class is usually a plus where to be a boy among young men is a minus. Nevertheless, it can be very uncomfortable to tower over friends and to be unable to trust one's voice not to break suddenly while answering a teacher.

For most girls early growth in height is embarrassing and alarming. Not only is she suddenly taller than her friends, she is also dramatically taller than boys of the same age and liable to feel that she will go on towering over them so that notions of romance are laughable. Early breast development can also be embarrassing, making the girl feel clumsy and heavy rather than elegant and sexy. Girls who remain child-sized and child-shaped whilst friends are changing may be equally distressed, especially as they tend to find themselves excluded from female conclaves which 'you wouldn't understand . . .'

Parents can help a little by:

Making sure children understand the wide age-range of normal development so that while they may still wish that they themselves were quicker or slower developers, they are at least spared worries about whether or not they are 'abnormal'.

Making sure each sex understands the relationship of physical growth to sexual development so that boys who are still small despite marked secondary sexual characteristics realize that they will still make up many inches while girls who are tall but undeveloped realize that secondary sexual characteristics will appear without a great deal of further growth.

Being careful to treat both sexes according to the maturity of their behaviour rather than their bodies so that the fast developer is not pitchforked into premature adulthood and the slower developer is not held back.

Helping the child to like his or her body even while it refuses to be 'just like everybody else's'. A little flattery for a suddenly-large son who can carry the suitcases or for a suddenly-developed daughter who can lend a sweater can be extremely helpful.

Consulting with the school on behalf of any child whose development is seriously out of step with his or her peers. Very occasionally a particularly bright child will have spent childhood in a class of children a year or more older and will, as they enter puberty, find a genuine gap opening up between them. If such a child is not only younger than the others but also a slower-than-average developer, he or she may face years of feeling 'out of it'. A step sideways within the school may need to be considered as a last resort which, while it may cause immediate misery, may be better than social isolation.

Menstruation

Ninety-five per cent of girls menstruate for the first time between the ages of ten and sixteen. Of the remainder, most will menstruate spontaneously between sixteen and eighteen but very few will do so thereafter. Around sixteen is therefore a sensible time to seek medical advice if menstruation has not yet occurred.

Menstruation cannot occur until a girl's ovaries are active; once they are active there will be signs of breast development and bodily hair. The menarche is usually only considered medically late if there are no signs of such secondary sexual characteristics by the age of sixteen. If a girl is well-developed – and especially if she has been developing over the past year or more – the doctor will probably simply reassure her that puberty is proceeding normally and that her first period will appear in its own good time. If she remains child-sized and child-shaped, simple medical tests can be taken to assess her hormone output.

Although menstruation occurs after other pubertal changes, it tends to be the change which has most psychological significance for a girl. Full and early information about what will happen to her and why, is obviously vital but so is the manner in which that information is given. Value-laden euphemisms such as 'the curse' or 'being unwell' are best avoided, while possible difficulties such as pre-menstrual tension or menstrual discomfort (*see below*) should be left to the girl herself to raise if she wishes. These things are by no means inevitable and expecting them certainly makes them more likely to occur.

Girls tend to find the menarche more difficult to handle than the other changes of puberty because a period is sudden whilst they are gradual. Breasts change and grow almost imperceptibly but vaginal bleeding just happens. Many girls, even those who accept the menarche quite comfortably, also find the constancy and inevitability of the menstrual cycle hard to accept. Once it begins it will go on, whether she wills it or not. Her body controls her self. By menstruating regularly it states a sexual maturity which may be out of step with her feelings. By not menstruating regularly it states a sexual immaturity which may be similarly inappropriate. While some girls will menstruate for the first time at exactly the right emotional moment, most will face conflict, unless you can spot the likely direction of anxiety and deal with it, in leisurely discussions, well in advance.

The girl who is likely to menstruate before she feels ready needs to be reminded that it takes more than a period to make a grown up; that people grow into their bodies and bodily functioning and that biological processes take time to settle down. It may comfort her to know that early periods are often irregular and that early cycles seldom include ovulation so that the menarche does not, in itself, imply even a bodily readiness for conception. She can also be reminded that even primary school lavatories usually contain sanitary towel dispensers because some girls menstruate while they are still quite definitely children.

The girl who is waiting impatiently for her menarche can be told, with equal truth, that she can merit the term 'grown up' by other means than menstruating; that other secondary sexual characteristics will develop first and allow her to see her own maturity and that there is no secret society of menstruating women from which she will be excluded until it happens to her.

In either case the most important message is probably the one which emphasizes that menstruation is only a physical process which in no way overrides the social, emotional or psychological aspects of growing up. If this easy and matter-of-fact acceptance is your aim, it is probably best not to appear emotionally involved yourself in your daughter's menarche. Regrets for the 'little girl who is gone forever' or bottles of champagne to celebrate the 'advent of a new woman' will tend to over-emphasize the significance of the whole matter.

Practicalities of periods

However accepting and matter-of-fact your daughter's attitudes to menstruation, having a period is a bore. The easier the practical aspects of coping, the more lightly she will be able to take it.

How much you will be involved in this very private aspect of her life will probably depend partly on her age at menarche. At twelve she may rely heavily on your advice and support. At fifteen she may 'know all about it' and have many friends whom she has seen coping. Whatever her age, though, it is worth giving some thought to basic questions like whether she should use sanitary pads or tampons.

Pads versus tampons. While purpose-made sanitary pads would seem heaven-sent to the many women in the world who have to manage without, they are nevertheless awkward and unreliable things. Even the best (and most expensive), specially shaped, water-proof backed, keep-dry lined and soluble, can show under tight clothes, leak onto white jeans, chafe and block up lavatories. Furthermore, they are embarrassingly bulky to carry to school or through a gauntlet of curious small boys from bedroom to bathroom at home; and, however regularly they are changed, they smell.

Why are so many young girls condemned to use pads when tampons are so much more convenient and efficient? Some mothers unthinkingly assume that tampons are only for the married or sexually active, while some may actually fear that using a tampon will 'break a girl's hymen' so that she is no longer 'a virgin'. Some girls are simply nervous at the idea of 'putting something up there'. While no girl who is reluctant to use a tampon should be pushed into doing so until she feels ready, some of the following points may help:

An 'intact hymen' very seldom covers the vaginal opening. In many, the hymen is merely a fringe of thin tissue lying around the edge of the opening; in others, the opening is partly covered. But in all, the hymen is stretchy and perfectly capable of accommodating a tampon. A girl with a hymen tight enough to make insertion of a tampon at all difficult may, in fact, do herself future good if she gently persists. A tight hymen can mean painful first intercourse. Since our society does not insist on blood-stained sheets to prove the virginity of brides on their wedding nights, this is something to be avoided if possible.

If a girl wants to use a tampon but does find any difficulty in inserting it, a tiny quantity of a sterile lubricant such as KY Jelly, placed on the end of the tampon or around the vaginal opening, can make all the difference.

There is no way in which an inserted tampon can 'go in the wrong place' or 'get lost'. A girl who is so ignorant of her own sexual anatomy that she has this fear needs proper information. The vaginal passage is completely closed by the cervix (neck of the womb) at its upper end. Once a tampon is in place there is nowhere it can go but out again.

Tampons cannot dam up the menstrual flow and thus increase cramps.

The only 'risk' in tampon use comes from their very comfort and efficiency: if a girl inserts one at the end of her period when the flow is light, she may forget that it is there. Left for days on end, tampons can give rise to odour, vaginal discharge and/or actual infection.

● A handful of reports of sudden illness associated with the use of 'scented' or 'deodorized' tampons suggests that these should be avoided. Such refinements are completely unnecessary.

Storage and accessibility of sanitary protection. Most girls are extremely shy about their early periods. Some may feel so private about them that their mothers are sworn to secrecy even within the family. Others may choose to tell friends yet dread brothers or sisters knowing when they are menstruating. Indeed, a very common anxiety in a girl's early adolescence is that somehow 'everyone can tell'.

While this emotional reaction usually settles rapidly, a girl's desire for privacy should certainly be accepted and catered for. You therefore need to work out where her sanitary protection can be stored so that it is easily available to her when she goes to the toilet and discovers that one of those unpredictable periods has begun. A bathroom drawer or place in the medicine cabinet is usually an easy answer. She will also need a way of carrying emergency protection with her when she is out and about. A tampon or two can easily fit into a special pocket of her purse. Pads may need a 'make-up bag' which will camouflage them from all but the most rudely inquisitive.

Stained bedding and clothing. Stained night-things are very common at the beginning of a period. Adolescents should have their own bedrooms if this can possibly be managed but if your daughter must share, she may be grateful for a private arrangement with you such that she can pull the bedding up, knowing that you will change the linen later.

Some girls find that underwear gets stained however regularly they change pads or tampons. Changing for sports then becomes acutely embarrassing. Dark-coloured underpants are a relief to many. Others prefer to wear a second pair for double security. On camping trips or at other times when laundry will be difficult and/or public, disposable underpants can be a worthwhile investment.

Odour. Menstrual debris does not develop an unpleasant odour until it has contact with the air. Tampons, changed before they permit leakage, virtually do away with this problem. Pads, on the other hand, can smell. Frequent changing and a quick wash with soap and water at each change is the only solution. Girls should not be encouraged to be over-sensitive about odour during their periods. The connotations of 'dirt' are psychologically unfortunate and the girl who decides she has a 'problem' may be tempted by 'feminine hygiene' products which are ineffective or downright dangerous (*see below* Problems with appearance and body-image: Body odour).

Menstrual difficulties

Irregular menstruation is very common, especially during the first year after the menarche. Many girls menstruate once and then do not do so again for months. Others menstruate several times in the first year but with no discernible pattern. Ensure that your daughter has sanitary protection (*see above*) available both at home and at school and make it clear that there is no cause for concern.

Regular menstruation which suddenly stops is termed 'secondary amenorrhea' ('primary amenorrhea' being absence of menarche). Secondary amenorrhea is caused by some disturbance in the balance between the ovaries, the pituitary gland and the hypothalamus. While, of course, the obvious reason is pregnancy (which certainly should be excluded if it is a possibility), such an imbalance is often caused by a radical change of environment (such as starting at boarding school) or by a major emotional upset (such as bereavement or other serious trouble at home). The girl can be reassured that her periods will return when she has settled down. It is reasonable to wait for at least six months before seeking medical advice to exclude the faint possibility of glandular abnormality.

Parents should be alert, however, if the girl has recently lost a great deal of weight. If she has been dieting, secondary amenorrhea suggests that she has lost too much weight too rapidly. If she has lost weight but does not admit that she is dieting, the amenorrhea may suggest that she is suffering from 'slimmer's disease' (*see* **Anorexia Nervosa**).

Pre-menstrual tension and dysmenorrhea are both unusual during early cycles. The water retention, irritability and depression of pre-menstrual tension and the heavy aching and/or sharp cramps of dysmenorrhea both appear to be linked not just to menstruation but to menstrual cycles in which ovulation (shedding of an ovum) takes place. Many girls, just past the menarche, do not ovulate. They may have periods regularly for a year or more before ovulation becomes regular also.

You can therefore confidently expect your daughter's early periods to be trouble-free and, if you do have this confidence, you will certainly help to ensure that they are. While pre-menstrual tension and period pains are real and have a real physiological basis, they are equally certainly affected by expectations and emotions. If your young daughter assumes that her periods will be unpleasant she is far more likely to experience them as such. If you, the person closest to her, assume that she will take them in her unbroken stride, she is far more likely to be able to do so. It is often said that menstrual difficulties 'run in the family'. While there may be some inherited tendency, a passing-on of attitudes and example from mother to daughter is a real factor. If you are a sufferer yourself, your young daughter will, of course, know that you are. But do be sure that she also knows that yours is a medical problem, for which you are receiving treatment. Don't let her assume that it is part of 'women's lot' and therefore of her inevitable inheritance.

If there does come a time when your daughter clearly has cyclical discomfort (whether it is headaches before menstruation or cramps during it), do try to react to the symptoms exactly as you would react if they occurred in a pre-adolescent. If the headache is a bad one it probably merits a simple analgesic such as aspirin or paracetamol. If the cramps are making her miserable a hot bath or a hot water bottle to take to bed may help. But don't let the fact that the headache or the cramps are part of menstruation lead you to assume (or let her assume) that she is going to be 'off-colour' for hours or days; that she should stay home from school or skip that outing. Above all, don't expect (or let her expect) the same discomfort to occur next month. If she can take each period calmly, as it comes, she will give her body every chance of adapting comfortably.

Disruptive menstrual difficulties are rare but merit proper attention. Pre-menstrual discomfort may take the physical form of water retention so that she not only feels 'bloated' but actually cannot fasten her jeans. Some find that restricting salt intake during the immediate pre-menstrual week prevents this. But if a teenager is to keep a careful eye on her diary and concentrate on what she eats for a week in each month, she had better do it with medical advice. If salt restriction does not work, her doctor might try her on a mild diuretic (drug to increase excretion of water).

Pre-menstrual trouble may seem entirely emotional. During the pre-menstrual week, everything is 'too much'. Parents are bossy; siblings are acutely irritating; friends are hurtful, work impossible . . . Parents can help by taking a little extra trouble not to pick fights during this time and perhaps by being a little more than usually tolerant when their daughter picks fights with them. You *may* also be able to help simply by reminding your tear-soaked daughter that she *is* in a pre-menstrual phase. Be careful, though, 'you must be going to have your period', can be as unhelpful and more maddening than 'I don't know what's the matter with you.' Choose a different time to discuss the whole matter. If she agrees that things do get on top of her and that rampant hormones do seem to be the reason, suggest that she keep a note of her cycle dates and learn to *go easy on herself*. She, after all, is the one who has to learn to manage her cyclical self.

Menstrual pains can range from a constant dull, heavy ache to inter-mittent but violent abdominal cramps. Every year thousands of girls are admitted to hospital because even a doctor is hard put to it to distinguish between really severe period pains and an abdominal emergency.

That dull, heavy aching (which is often felt most in the back) is certainly helped by simple analgesics and is equally certainly made worse by standing still for long periods.

Cramping pains are rather different. The uterus has to get rid of the debris of the rich lining it has been laying down to receive the ovum if it should be fertilized. Contractions of uterine muscles help this process but, it seems, sometimes become uncoordinated so that the muscular cramps actually dam up debris. During painful cramps a girl sometimes feels that she is 'getting rid of something' and it may be that there will be visible 'clots' in the menstrual flow. Heat can help by encouraging relaxation of the muscles, but lying down with a hot water bottle is not always the best treatment. Many girls find that active exercise, however disinclined they may feel for it at the beginning, increases the flow and relieves the cramping pains.

If the quality of a girl's life is being reduced by periodic discomfort, do encourage her to see her doctor and do make sure that he is not one who subscribes to the 'women's lot' school of thought.

All menstrual troubles are basically side-effects from the natural ebb and flow of the balance of hormones in the body, with oestrogen peaking at the time of ovulation and giving place to progesterone-dominance at the time of menstruation. Often a doctor will not want to tamper with this balance in a very young woman, preferring to give her body time to adjust itself. But he can still help with prescription analgesics and, above all, with reassurance that, should the troubles continue, treatment with artificial hormones can be given later.

Hormone treatment will take one of two forms. In a girl who would welcome contraception, birth control pills can be prescribed and, by preventing ovulation, they will banish most menstrual troubles too. In a girl who does not want to go 'on the Pill', artificial progestogen can be given which has no affect on ovulation but markedly reduces the intensity of uterine contractions during menstruation.

Adolescents and the adult world
(*see also* **Discipline, Self-discipline and Learning How to Behave**)

Adolescents are people; the children they were and the adults they will become. To get from one state to another most must live through personal turmoil and therefore will create social tumult from time to time. Unfortu-nately, the adult world makes 'adolescent difficulty' into a self-fulfilling prophecy. We expect adolescents to make trouble and by treating them accordingly we often create the very problems of which we then com-plain. We give children a bad name ('teenagers') and hang them.

Most of these prejudices and labels are as foolish as they are damaging. A 'teenager' is not a single entity to be grouped and categorized with others, but a person who is growing and changing. That person may be male or female; thirteen, fifteen or nineteen; sexually mature or immature; active or inactive; ambitious, clever and hardworking or apathetic, unintelligent and lazy. He or she may feel happy, loving and well-liked or miserable, angry and rejected. Furthermore, whatever he or she is like *now*, everything will change (for better or worse) tomorrow or next year. However changeable and therefore unpredictable and difficult an adolescent may be, parents, and other close adults, need to hang onto the fact that *this stage of life is part of a continuum of development*. This is the same person whom you nurtured as a baby and enjoyed as a child and with whom you will one day share family history. If all the adolescent years are seen as part of continuing development there will be no temptation to label and dismiss him as 'a hopeless rebel' or to label and abandon her because 'she's impossible to understand'. The less he or she is labelled, dismissed or abandoned the more easily and steadily will the maturing take place.

Unfortunately rich societies make few arrangements to suit growing adolescents. They insist, for example, that children remain home-and-education-based long after growth and sexual maturity have made them capable of working for money and starting families of their own. An extended period of education is fine in principle but often disastrous in practice. Many adolescents experience their last year or two of schooling as a compulsory irrelevancy with no bearing on the future. Many see that future in terms of a dole queue which clearly states 'society has no real place for you'. Even within their own homes many adolescents find that they no longer have a child's role as receiver of adult care yet are still not accepted into equality with those adults. If school work does not feel creative or useful and a youngster is unsure of his or her role at home, what is left? Sports and hobbies involve some; community projects involve a few. But there is a vast reservoir of creative energy left untapped within many communities because young people are not trusted to contribute. This matters not only because it is a waste but because it is our refusal to find interesting, creative and useful things for them to do which drives so many young people into doing things of which we disapprove or into doing the 'nothing much' which we also dislike. It is our refusal to like them, love them, share with them which drives many to reject adults altogether and rely exclusively on each other's company. It is our refusal to trust them to be kind, sensible or responsible which makes them doubt their own goodness as people so that they sometimes act out the anti-social roles we seem to expect of them. Adolescents have to change in order to grow; adults have to try to follow the changes and provide for each piece of new growth. The more parents can understand why many of their number find this difficult the more likely it is that they will be able to tailor and re-tailor their own child's world so that it always fits.

Friends versus family

In the course of adolescence your son or daughter has to separate off from you so as to be free to become an autonomous adult individual. You gave him or her most childhood values and opinions so your values and opinions have to be challenged. To continue to hold them would be to continue to be a child. The adolescent may come back to them, or to some of them, but can only do so maturely if they have been well-considered first. Your adolescent is standing back from you in this way at roughly the same time as his or her friends. Agreeing that their values must change is easy but deciding on new values is far more difficult. In order to shield themselves (and each other) from solitary personal indecision, they establish a kind of security with each other. The peer group agrees, so to speak, on norms for behaviour, dress, speech, entertainment, sexual behaviour and reactions to parents and other authority figures. Once these things are agreed upon, everyone who wants acceptance within that particular group must conform. Lack of conformity may be dealt with harshly because the non-conformer throws doubt on the correctness of the group's decisions and it was to protect themselves from such doubt that they grouped together in the first place. Peer-group relationships then are vitally important to most young adolescents and conformity to even quite minor conventions may truly matter to them. Parents may not share, but must accept, these feelings.

It is parents' inability to share which causes much of the trouble between the generations because many devoted parents are hurt by their exclusion. You can be very lonely for the child who, having been your faithful companion for many years, would suddenly rather be with anyone but you. Hurt adult feelings lie behind much of the criticism and nagging of which adolescents complain; nagging about 'unsuitable friends' for example. As a parent you may find it very hard to stay friendly when your child rejects your carefully-considered and mature advice and telephones another young idiot for advice instead. But for the moment, your child does not want to do what *you* think sensible but what his or her peers advise. Their opinion matters much more than yours and probably more than the quality of the advice, too.

Secrets make for adult hurt too. Parents have usually been accustomed to keep secrets (or to 'keep adult matters private') from their children. Now it is those children who keep them in the dark. Sometimes it helps to realize just how trivial most of those vital secrets are: snippets of gossip about who likes whom, items which you really do not need or even want to know. But their point is that you should not know, so every temptation to pry should be resisted. There is no quicker way to make your adolescent lie to you than to insist on being told of private matters. And there is no faster way to ruin the relationship between you than to invade privacy by picking up telephone extensions, going through pockets or reading letters and diaries.

The less critical you can be of your child's friends the better; they need each other and if yours knows that you accept this and are prepared to tolerate even the unexpected arrivals who strip the biscuit tin, he or she will probably do you the honour of letting you meet them and hearing at least some of their news. Then, if something goes really wrong and you foresee physical or moral danger, you will be in an excellent position to muster and use your still-powerful influence. Don't waste it on trying to stop your daughter going out with that boy with pink hair: you may need it later on when she meets a known drug-pusher or the much-older father of two. Don't waste that precious influence trying to be clever at the expense of your son's footballing friends either; he may move on into a group which invests its machismo in fast cars and bolsters its driving courage with alcohol.

If you can save your criticisms and, more especially, your vetoes, for the very occasional issues which are truly important, you will not often be defied, at least in the early stages of adolescence. However much he or she may bluster, your child knows that home is still an important haven and that he or she is more comfortable when you approve. When large issues do arise you will often find that your viewpoint has backing from the local community and/or the law and that you can use these impersonal forces as allies. In Britain, for example, sexual intercourse with a girl under sixteen is illegal. While it would be naive to suggest that the law alone would prevent a couple from having sex once their relationship had reached that point, the existence of that law may subtly act to prevent it from doing so. A girl of fourteen or fifteen may unthinkingly accept that she is 'too young' however strong her sexual feelings. Boys may similarly accept that 'young girls don't' or that wise young men don't let them; they may unconsciously keep relationships with them on a low sexual note.

Liquor laws, provided that you do not openly flout them yourselves, may be similarly useful. A British youngster will probably not refuse a drink in a pub just because he or she is under age but may not expect to join a group whose life is pub-based until he or she is older. In the United States, where the age limits are higher and the laws more strictly enforced, youngsters will tend to avoid bars because of the embarrassment of having their ages queried.

The point is not that good little teenagers will refrain from doing things they want to do because those things are against the law; it is that the laws may prevent them wanting to do those things quite so early in adolescence. It is not a question of individual virtue but of group expectation. Where an individual boy or girl does *not* want to do something which the group does expect he or she may be able to use this kind of external social control as a face-saver. It is far easier for a youngster to refuse to join some piece of idiocy 'because I don't want to lose my licence' or because 'it's all very well for you lot but they'll do me if I'm caught at my age' than to admit to being scared, disapproving or in any way out of tune with the group. If you are sensitive to your adolescent's feelings and known to be generally easy-going, you may even be asked to use an external veto from time to time. Your daughter asks you if she can go on a camping holiday with a mixed group of new friends. Does she really want to go or is she pleased to have been asked but alarmed at the prospect? If it is the latter she may be delighted to have you say that she is too young. She can raise Cain at home about your injustice and exact plenty of sympathy from her friends because of your unreasonableness but she will not actually have to make that trip. If you are not sure what response an adolescent is asking of you under circumstances of this kind, try something like: 'I'm not at all sure. I'll think about it but I'm probably going to say no,' his or her face will give you some clues.

The desire for acceptance by, and integration into, group life pushes many youngsters into activities and situations for which they know they are not ready. Parents who try to protect them with cries of 'you don't have to do it just because they do,' will only increase that feeling of group loyalty and leave the child to face the dilemma alone. Parents who understand and accept the need for group conformity and who realize that only the maturity of later adolescence or adulthood will enable the individual to stand on solitary principle, can subtly offer a great deal of help. If your child consistently finds that kind of help available, you may reach the delightful stage at which you can simply ask: 'Would you like to say that your ogre-father absolutely forbids it?'

If many parents' feelings are hurt when their adolescents reject them in favour of friends of the same age, even more are hurt when adolescents strike up close and confidential relationships with other adults. Your child spends more and more time in another home and gradually it becomes clear that he or she does so not just to spend time with the son or daughter but also to spend time with one or other of the parents. Why will he talk to them when he has rejected you? Why will she take their advice, quoting their every opinion as gospel, when she shrugs off everything you say? The basic answer is that those adults are more acceptable *just because they are not you*. Their values, judgements and viewpoints are different from yours and, above all, the adolescent has sought them out independently rather than having them thrust upon him or her.

Such relationships with other parents, with teachers, sports coaches or any other caring adults, can be truly valuable to an adolescent. If you do find yourself resenting them, remind yourself that the child is trying to grow up; needs knowledge and experience of adult thinking and behaviour and is better off getting it outside the family than not getting it at all. Remember also that such an adult confidante is no more likely to treat your adolescent irresponsibly than you would be if you were similarly placed with somebody else's child. It may be that eventually you will be so placed.

Adult communities tend to reject people at this age-stage of life. They shut them out and thus throw them, even more than the adolescents themselves wish, onto their own and each other's resources. The more they can all communicate with any and all available adults, the better.

The long road to independence

When your child enters adolescence he or she is still a dependent child; by the time it ends that child will be transformed into an adult who is no longer dependent on you for anything but the warm support and the friendly caring, which all human beings can expect from those who love them. That adolescent road from dependence to independence is long and if the journey is not also to be infernally bumpy it needs to be kept smooth. It is usually smoothest if changes in the limits, expectations and permissions laid down by parents are closely matched to changes in the competence of the child rather than being geared to outside factors. A birthday, for example, may seem an obvious marker for a new privilege but it is not the right moment for that privilege unless it happens to coincide with what is happening inside that person. Leaving school may seem to qualify him or her for new freedoms but they will neither be welcome nor well-used if the change in his or her way of life does not match up with changes in thinking, feeling and coping. Sudden 'freedom' can feel like a terrifying rejection: an end of caring. Equally it can be experienced as an intoxicating loss of control. To feel truly free, the adolescent has to feel able to move at his or her own pace, backed by parents who are neither pushing him or her out nor holding on. Some parents achieve this balancing act quite unconsciously, tuned to their children so that they can feel the right moments without having to think about them. Most will sometimes make a wrong decision and will need to think and re-think independence issues as they come up.

The following examples will not all be relevant to any family but some will probably be relevant to most.

Money A child is fed, clothed, housed, transported, entertained and 'treated' at his family's expense (*see* **Pocket Money**). An adult earns all these things for himself through paid work or grant qualifications. During the in-between period of adolescence, money and the goods and services it buys can be both a real facilitator and a symbolic indicator of every degree of independence.

Parents often ask 'how much money should he have now that he is thirteen or fifteen or seventeen?' but such a question begs the real issues. The important point is not how much money a child should have or the age at which he should have it but the *amount of choice and responsibility he is allowed in using what he has.* This needs careful thought and gradual alteration to suit his stage of life whether you are able and willing to provide a lot of money or only token sums.

The first step up from a child's pocket money is usually a weekly 'allowance' (*see also* **Pocket Money**) You may decide that it is time your child was responsible for all his out-of-pocket expenses incurred outside the home and therefore add up his necessary expenditure on things like fares and school lunches and then add a reasonable-seeming sum for spending-money.

As long as your child is prepared to treat that 'allowance' exactly as he treated his pocket money in the days when you simply handed out the school money as a separate transaction, all will be well. The spending money gives him a little choice over what sweets/magazines/cinema tickets he buys and that may be enough for now. But this kind of allowance is seldom satisfactory for long because soon he will want to exercise more choice than can fall within the scope of the spending money. As soon as he wants to save up for extra clothes, tickets to a pop concert or even a present for you, he will start to count in the necessaries-money, walking to school to save the bus fare or buying chips instead of a proper meal. If you are prepared to let him make this kind of decision for himself, fine, but probably you will feel that lunch money is for lunch rather than nonsense.

This is the time for the next step up, only this time, instead of adding up *necessary* expenditure and then adding spending-money you add up *regular expenditure that you want him to make* and then add the extra. Just as an adult must set aside money for things like rent and quarterly bills and treat only the money which remains as disposable income, so the adolescent must set aside the money you insist he spend on what you intend it for and treat only the remainder as his to spend as he pleases. Think carefully about the expenditure which you are keeping in your own power. This may be the time for him to take over responsibility for other personal expenditure such as haircuts and toiletries, but are these items to be within your or his area of decision-making? May he go without a haircut for weeks in order to use the money for something else or not? May he go without deodorant (or use yours) or do you insist that he keeps his own supply? He must know exactly what money is his to dispose of as he likes.

At this stage major expenditure is still in your hands. Your adolescent must accept not only your running of the household but your control over his clothes, sports equipment, holidays, etc. Gradually he will come to resent this, not simply because he cannot have this, that or the other unless you give him the money, but because your priorities in spending money on him become different from his own. You may, for example, plan a family vacation in which he is included. He may not want to come with you, but even if he still feels that he would enjoy the trip, there may be things which are far more important to him and which he knows that he could buy with his share of the holiday cost.

This is the time to give him some choice over what is spent on him. You may insist that he come on that vacation because his presence is important to the rest of the family, but you should certainly not insist on buying him an expensive winter overcoat if he would rather have a cheap duffel coat and the balance of the money for other things. Clothing should certainly now become entirely his business whether he is a person who yearns after expensive and fashionable clothes or one who does not care. Work out what you have been spending on his clothes and hand it over. If he goes to school 'unsuitably dressed' let the school authorities deal with the matter. If he gets wet and cold, let him revise his own priorities. If you get really sorry for him you can always buy a glorious/necessary garment for his birthday.

Once an adolescent handles all his money he should have a bank account or Giro account, a proper current one, not simply a savings account. Nowadays almost everybody is paid by cheque rather than in cash and it is important that he learns to handle the form-filling as well as keeping track of whether or not he is in credit.

Older adolescents will probably want to make major purchases which will actually alter their way of life, such as motor bikes or cars, guitars or stereo-equipment or fashionable hairdos with built-in weekly mainten- ance costs. If your adolescent can see that the *family* budget simply will not run to such things he is unlikely to fuss. It is when the family budget appears ample but his own is still strictly limited that he is likely to be bitter. Once again the real question is not how much money he may have but whether or not he may spend what there is in the way he chooses. How can your son accept with pleasure an expensive birthday gift he did not want when what he *does* want is money towards that car? How can your daughter be properly grateful for having her bedroom redecorated when it is her hair that she wants to make over? Money is being spent on them but it is being spent at your discretion and for your pleasure rather than at their discretion and for their pleasure.

When you refuse a heart's desire of this kind, do make sure that your reasons are valid and that you and your child both clearly understand them. For example:

Is there enough money for him to have what he wants? He may feel that you are far more comfortably off than is really the case. Purchases he notices may be being made on credit/be necessary to your job/be forced on you in order to fulfil the terms of your mortgage. He is entitled, now, to some understanding of the family's finances.

If there is enough money, are you refusing because you disapprove of the proposed purchase? Sometimes it seems easier to dismiss a boy's desire for a motor bike with 'do you think I'm made of money?' than to discuss your real objections which are probably to do with his safety. Make the effort of honesty. It will be far better for your relationship to be considered over-protective than to be thought mean or lacking in under-standing (*see* **Safety**/On wheels).

Is there enough money for the purchase but not for its maintenance? With a vehicle, or even some kinds of hairdo, maintenance can be a major expense and one for which adolescents often do not allow. Your son's mind may be so fixed on the old car which he could buy for a few pounds that he is forgetting licensing and insurance let alone fuel. Your daughter may be seeing herself with short curly bleached hair and forgetting that it will rapidly grow long, straight and dark at the roots. Do explain and discuss the sums involved. Perhaps he or she wants whatever it is enough to set aside money for maintenance instead of something else. Provided he or she can stay within budget the choice should be available.

Are you perhaps refusing this heart's desire on principle? Many people believe that adolescents are over-interested and over-indulged in worldly goods and think about nothing but getting their hands on the latest fashion in electronic gadgets, new sounds or new looks. If you feel like this and therefore feel inclined to say 'no' to anything which is neither necessary nor edifying, your adolescent has the right to know because you are using hard cash to control his or her lifestyle. Money is a powerful weapon in our society so until your child can earn his or her economic freedom you may well succeed. But if you are going to use that power, do it openly. You might even convince him or her that you are right and you will certainly provide an interesting adult viewpoint for thought and discussion instead of just another excuse for moaning about the frightful-ness of parents.

Part-time jobs   In many families, money-issues become confused with the related but separate issue of whether or not adolescents should take part-time jobs while still at school. In some societies and communities this is taken for granted. Adolescents – and indeed children – are expected to look for work before or after school and at weekends and in the holidays too. In others, such jobs are not expected and in the present economic climate may be exceedingly scarce. Whatever the position in your area, the question of whether or not you want, or will allow, your adolescent to take a part-time job needs consideration as does the effect that such a job will have on his or her position at school and at home.

A child who gets up at 6 a.m. and does a couple of hours' work before school will end up working a longer day than most adults. If she also does a few hours' work on a Saturday she will work a longer week, too, with fewer leisure hours than most unions would allow. It is possible that her concentration in school, her homework and her social life will all suffer. On the other hand, it is possible that the work itself, together with the money it earns her, will provide a new stimulus and lead to important feelings of success. If you forbid her to work you may be depriving her not only of money but of the right to make the effort for it. As soon as the issue comes up, think your priorities through; make sure that she understands them and try to act upon them consistently. The following points may be relevant:

Is academic success important to her? If it is, your message must surely be 'school work takes priority'. But if you want her to understand that you mean that it takes priority over other kinds of *work* rather than over leisure and pleasure, you may have to go further and explain that school work *is* work, just as your job is work, and that you will therefore try to see that she does not suffer by comparison with less-academic friends whose work earns them money.

If you have prevented her from taking a *paid* part-time job on these grounds, do also be very sure that you do not use her as *unpaid* labour yourself. If she is to spend the time after school at home because she is to work for her exams, don't constantly use her as a babysitter, gardener or cook.

Is job-experience more important than school work? It may be if she is less academically inclined, knows what job she wants after she leaves school and can find work during her school life which gives her some experience of it. If that is the case, do accept that she is no longer living just as a schoolgirl, but more as a worker on day-release. You may have to explain what is happening to the school, especially if teachers complain of skimped work. And you must not expect her to drop the part-time job every time it would suit you to take her away for a weekend . . . she may lose the job or her reputation for reliability.

Is the extra money badly needed? If the family as a whole is short of money, being able to make a contribution, via a part-time job, may be very valuable to the adolescent. Whether she contributes by using the money she earns to provide her own 'allowance' or by actually putting money into the family budget, do make sure that you acknowledge her contribution by treating her as a co-worker. What this means, in detail, will obviously vary from family to family, but if she is mature enough to contribute in this way she is probably mature enough to organize her own comings and goings; to be entitled to a meal at a time which suits her schedule and to be allowed to sleep late on Sundays without criticism.

Do you need to employ her at home? People who live together in a family group should, of course, all contribute to the smooth and comfortable running of their home. Adults do not expect to be paid for making their beds or doing other chores and neither should adolescents. But running a business from home and expecting your adolescent to help in it is different. You run the business to make money. If you did not have the adolescent's labour you might have to employ somebody else. Furthermore, by using her labour in this way you deprive her of the chance either of taking a part-time job or of opting for school work or leisure-time. It would seem fair that either she should be paid as you would pay a strange adolescent working for you after school, *or* that it should be reckoned that she is making a financial contribution to the family just as she would be if she was working for somebody else and putting her earnings in the family kitty. If you can make an arrangement of this kind, you may find that your adolescent is *more* contented than her friends who feel that they have no role to play in the family.

Do you need her to run the home while you work? Your adolescent's competence may be the crucial factor which enables you to hold a full-time job despite the presence of younger schoolchildren. But if she is expected to provide tea and sympathy for them and perhaps to complete the day's domestic chores and prepare an evening meal, do acknowledge that, in enabling you to do a full-time paid job, she is doing a part-time one herself. She is in exactly the same position as the adolescent who works in a family business.

While it can be very valuable for an older adolescent to feel that he or she is a necessary part of the home set-up, don't let yourself slip into dependence either on your child's earnings or labour. There will come a time when he or she wants (and needs) either to leave home altogether or to transfer to 'lodger' status while attending college or serving an apprenticeship. It is one thing for the adolescent to feel needed; quite another to know that his or her presence is literally indispensable. When he or she leaves school and finds a job, you must not ask, even silently and with your eyes, 'who is to look after the little ones until I get home from work?' That must not be the adolescent's problem because it is yours. You need to have foreseen both question and answer in advance. Leaving home is difficult enough for many youngsters without that kind of added stress.

Self-care   An adolescent will not have achieved full adulthood until he or she can take reasonable care of his or her own needs. Only when self-care is perfected can the youngster ever begin to be ready for the responsibilities of caring for others which are an integral part of adult life.

Learning to take care of oneself means different things to different people. To many families with adolescents it will mean becoming proficient at a variety of domestic chores and ceasing to expect adults to pick up discarded clothes. To others it will mean 'being sensible about money' while others again will see it in terms of adequate meals and sleep.

While every child should of course, learn to iron, to cook, to budget and to keep his or her health and energy at a reasonable level, many of these specifics are extremely difficult to practise in a family setting. You pick up his clothes because you dislike the sight of the littered bathroom. The adolescent knows that you will and furthermore never gets the chance to find out whether he minds his own litter because the picking up is always done before he next goes into the bathroom. If he picks them up himself, he does so *for you* rather than for himself. In rather the same way your daughter eats meals which she has perhaps helped to buy and prepare but for which she is not basically responsible. How can she tell whether she would have remembered to buy milk and bread and cat food had it all been up to her?

Where natural opportunities occur within the family, practice can be useful. Your adolescent may, for example, take over domestically while you are in hospital or on a trip. But artificially created practice (such as a rota for Sunday cooking) seldom does much for an adolescent's self-care. These arranged experiences are temporary where looking after oneself is permanent. And they take place in a setting which somebody else has arranged and for which somebody else is responsible. Self-care will only really be practised when the youngster is away from you.

For most adolescents living away from home is a vitally important part of final growing up. But if it is to be a success-experience, you need to be sure that your child has acquired more far-reaching competences than domestic skills. It really does not matter very much if your daughter cannot iron a blouse to her own standards. It will not take her more than a single evening to teach herself once there is no one else to help. But it does matter very much if she cannot keep herself basically safe and healthy; cannot find her way around a new community and its services and personnel; cannot communicate with other people, adults as well as peers, sufficiently to make herself a friendly place in a new community.

Make sure basic health principles are understood. Before an adolescent leaves home for the first time she should certainly be fully in charge of any medication which she takes regularly or frequently. A diabetic, for example, must understand not only her own daily insulin/carbohydrate balance but also what to do if it should go wrong. Be careful. You may always have nursed her through the times when her insulin needs changed because of fever, or vomiting. Can she confidently do it for herself?

If your son is subject to migraine, does he *understand* his medication or has he always swallowed the pills as you offered them, never troubling to grasp which was for what?

Does she understand both the use and the dangers of any headache remedies, laxatives and so forth which she is accustomed to having available? Will he know if a minor injury is infected and what to do about it? Will he make sensible decisions about whether or not he should go to work when unwell? Does he, for example, know how to take and then assess his own temperature and will it occur to him to do so if he feels 'peculiar'?

Have you and she discussed more dramatic dangers to health so that she is unlikely, for example, to experiment dangerously with drugs, including alcohol? Has he actually taken in your lectures on contraception and venereal disease so that he will behave responsibly both to himself and to other people?

Make sure he or she can cope with food for one. (*See also* **Eating**.) Few adolescents leaving home for the first time are going to eat what most adults would regard as a 'healthy diet', but yours ought at least to understand the amount of money he will need for fuel-food and some of the dietary safety-measures which will help to ensure that living on junk foods does not make him inefficient or ill. It is more important that it should occur to him to buy and drink milk and orange juice than that he should be able to cook a roast to perfection.

An adolescent who is constantly fighting obesity needs some extra help. Girls especially should be aware of the dangers of starvation. All too often, once on their own, just not eating seems much easier than eating a 'slimming diet' (*see* **Anorexia Nervosa**). Adolescents who are lonely may eat for comfort if money allows. You may not be able to prevent this at long range but you can at least make sure that they know which nibbling foods contain fewest calories.

Make sure the adolescent is competent to negotiate with the adult world. The adolescent who knows where to go for help and is able to ask for that help in a way which adults find appealing, is off to a head-start. Those who hate using the telephone, are terrified of anyone in uniform and have never learned to turn on appropriate charm, will find themselves at a major disadvantage. In this area, advance practice really can help. While your adolescent is still living at home she can make her own appointments with the dentist – and then put them off herself, too, instead of getting round you to do that bit for her. She can be encouraged to do her own 'asking' at school from an early age (why send a note when she can talk?) and she can not only shop but also return her own unsatisfactory goods and fight for refunds. If she wants to visit a friend in hospital, let her go by herself and brave the dragon ward-sister and let it sometimes be she who tries to persuade the television repair man into coming to the house on Christmas Eve . . . The point, of course, is that she will not always succeed; but she will fail while it scarcely matters (as you are still behind her) and she will learn, almost unconsciously, how to cope.

Make sure that your adolescent knows what services there are, what they are for and how to find them. Practice in guessing what head-word will be used in a telephone directory is useful. Familiarity with 'Yellow Pages' may enable her to cope with all kinds of unexpected eventualities like locking herself out of that new flat whilst knowledge of her rights as a very new citizen and the location of those whose job it is to ensure these for her, is vital.

Adolescents newly away from home need safety nets. If yours first goes to college or to a residential training establishment of some kind, he will have a built-in safety net provided by the institution and the adults who run it. They will not produce aspirin for his headache, clean shirts for his dates or a morning call to get him up in time, but they will (or should) notice if he is really ill; make themselves available to him if he needs help or step in if he is in serious trouble.

If your adolescent is going into a completely independent and unprotected environment – into a bed-sitting room in a strange town which just happens to contain a job for him, for example – you may need to provide a safety net yourself. For example, if he still likes your company you could:

Settle him in. Go to his new town with him, help him to find a place to live and scratch together the things he needs to make it tolerable. You can explore the town together and identify some of the places he will need to know. The fact that you have been there and do therefore know the environment may make it much easier for him to keep in touch with you by letter and telephone.

Arrange emergency communications. Without suggesting regular telephone calls (which might spoil his feeling of self-reliance), make sure that he has an actual fund of telephone-coins salted away somewhere. Although he can reverse the charges he will be able to telephone without feeling nearly so feeble and childish if he has the means to do so directly. A couple of pre-stamped ready addressed envelopes may not come amiss either.

Arrange emergency money. He is extremely likely to run out of money during the early weeks/months of independent life. He may simply mismanage his budget, but he may have the ill-luck to discover that he is paid in arrears and/or has to pay his rent in advance. A sum of money lodged in a deposit account at the bank or post office will see him through and also ensure that he can (and knows that he can) get home for a weekend if he suddenly needs a rest from all this adulthood.

Keep home available. Few adolescents leave their parents' home and settle at once into their own 'home'. While yours may immediately acquire a flat and make it into her home, she is more likely to spend quite a while feeling that her 'digs' are temporary and that a large chunk of herself (not to mention many of her possessions) are still with you.

Try to keep her place, especially her room or share of a room, intact during this stage. She may not come back to it as often as you would like, but knowing that it is still there is important. Sometimes a younger child is given the adolescent's room the moment she departs for her first term at college or month in a job. However welcome she is to the sitting-room sofa, she is bound to feel that her place has closed behind her; that she has not just left but been thrown out.

Problems with appearance and body-image

Most adolescents are deeply concerned with their own looks but although their concern may sometimes seem like mere vanity or slavish following of fashion, it is an important part of the search for self which is the prime task of this age-stage. An adolescent's appearance is the outward and visible-to-others sign of the inner self which he or she is trying to identify and confirm. The 'look' for which a youngster strives will change whenever the image of self he or she wants other people to see changes. Furthermore, the self an adolescent sees mirrored in other peoples' reactions to his or her appearance, may lead either to a confirmation or to a rejection of that particular style. At one time, for example, a girl may seek the protective camouflage of her social group's 'uniform' to such an extent that she cannot decide what particular garments to wear to a particular occasion until she has spent half an hour on the telephone finding out exactly what others will be wearing. At another time, though, a boy may want, above all, to assert his difference from everyone else. The 'gear' expensively collected during previous months will be abandoned and he may struggle to start a beard. If someone she cares about tells your daughter that she looks sexy in a particular outfit it may be worn constantly or never again, depending whether sexy was what she wanted to look. If his aunt tells your son that he spoils his good looks by wearing those scruffy jeans he may abandon or hang onto them depending on how he is feeling about elderly ladies considering him good looking!

In a family, these concerns are often derided. Children seldom care deeply about their appearances; middle-aged parents have become accustomed to theirs. Caught between these two comparatively unconcerned and un-fashion-conscious groups, the wretched adolescent may be misunderstood and mocked. There may be rows over the cost of fashionable clothes; rows over pierced ears, male jewellery, unsuitable hairstyles and shoes. There may be shocked reactions to rude messages on sweatshirts or underpants. Worst of all, there may be a general attitude of 'what does it matter?' 'What's wrong with those jeans anyway?' 'What are you fussing about, they're only spots, you'll grow out of it . . .' 'Why do you want to change your hair colour anyway? It's perfectly nice the way it is.'

While parents control the purse-strings (*see above* Money) they have the right to limit what the adolescent can spend on his or her appearance. While they control general health and wellbeing (*see above* Self-care) they have a right to guard against dangerous extremes. But none of this gives them the right either to tell a youngster what he or she should look like or to try and persuade him or her that appearances do not matter. When you try to tell your adolescent what to look like it feels as if you are trying to tell him or her *what and who to be*. When you refuse to care what he or she looks like you are, to some extent at least, implying that *you do not care what he or she is or wants to be*.

While the fashions in clothes and other gear which your adolescent wants to adopt or avoid will vary from place to place and from time to time, there are some problems with appearance which are common during the adolescent years and which, because they affect his or her own body-image and sense of self, always merit the greatest possible understanding, support and help.

Acne The blackheads and whiteheads, pimples and pustules of acne can leave permanent scars on a teenager's skin and, in an extreme instance, on the personality, too. Few things erode tenuous social confidence more than a continuous crop of spots. A boy who is wondering whether any pretty girl will ever want to go out with him will be quite sure that none ever will if he feels that instead of gazing into his romantic eyes she will be mesmerized by his disgusting pustules. A girl who half longs for and half dreads that disco, will have the balance tipped towards terror if she finds a crop of spots.

Acne cannot, at the moment, be completely prevented or completely cured. But acne can be controlled. The more thoroughly it is understood, the easier it will be to cope with it in the individual circumstances of your family.

What acne is   Skin contains sebaceous glands which, like many other glands, are stimulated into activity by the changes of puberty. These glands secrete an oily substance (sebum). Most of the sebum reaches the skin's surface via the hair follicles and produces nothing worse than oily skin, or hair which gets so greasy that it needs shampooing every couple of days. In acne, though, the sebum does not flow freely, but backs up in the hair follicles. Why this should happen to most, but not all, people is not known. Nor do we know why most sufferers have only a few, or occasional, dammed up follicles while a wretched few have hundreds of these minute blockages, not only on the face but on the chest and shoulders too.

Blackheads and whiteheads. When sebum is trapped in a hair follicle it thickens. A whitehead is simply an accumulation of this thickened sebum. A blackhead is not black because of 'dirt in the pores', it is also only a collection of thickened sebum but the sebum is dark because it happens to contain particles of the skin pigment (melanin). Dark-skinned people tend to mind whiteheads more than blackheads; fair skins look worse with blackheads, but neither has any connection whatsoever with dirt.

Pimples and pustules. The hair follicles, along which oily sebum should flow, contain bacteria. When the sebum accumulates, the enzymes in those bacteria break the sebum down into free fatty acids which irritate and weaken the hair-follicle walls. With sebum still flowing into the follicle, behind the blockage, this irritation eventually causes the walls of the follicle to rupture so that bacteria and sebum are released into the surrounding tissues. When this happens, there is inflammation and the typical pimples of acne form. Pustules are the next stage and, if the bacteria and inflammation are deep below the skin's surface, cysts and boils may form, too.

What acne is not   Old wives' tales about acne are numerous. For example:
- □ Blackheads are black because they are dirty.
- □ Blackheads and whiteheads form because the sufferer does not wash his/her face properly so that oil and old cosmetics 'plug the pores'.
- □ Yellow-headed pustules contain pus because the sufferer has picked at pimples or squeezed blackheads with dirty fingers.

This is all nonsense. More importantly it is all insulting nonsense, apparently designed to make the wretched teenager believe that the acne which is driving him or her into depression anyway is due to dirty habits.

Acne lesions come from inside the skin's structure and therefore cannot be prevented or cured by external washing (but *see below*). Advertisers have helped the cosmetics industry to make millions by suggesting that their products will produce 'deep down cleanliness' or 'penetrate the pores to float out the dirt you cannot see' or 'steam your skin really clean all through'. Resist such claims. Cleansing, whatever product is used, does not go beneath the skin's surface. Furthermore, despite popular belief to the contrary, the skin's pores cannot be opened and closed at will.

On a par with the 'dirt theory' is the equally insulting and inaccurate belief that acne afflicts only adolescents who eat junk foods (especially fried foods and chocolate), go short of sleep or are involved in sexual activity. While the hormones which affect sexual *development* certainly have a bearing on acne (*see above*) neither sexual activity nor sexual inactivity, nor the in-betweens such as masturbation and heavy petting, have anything to do with acne either way. While adequate sleep may be a good thing in itself, plenty will not improve acne nor will exhaustion make it worse.

Prevention and control of mild acne Acne begins with plugged hair follicles so, while they cannot be unplugged from outside, anything which helps them keep themselves clear will help prevent or control acne.

Washing with soap. Removes the grease from oily skin as well as ensuring that clogged make-up or dust is not making matters worse. Ordinary toilet soap is perfectly adequate, although if the skin is extremely oily a soap containing tar and/or sulphur may be beneficially drying.

Using sunshine. The ultra-violet rays in sunshine definitely discourage acne which may clear altogether during a sunny holiday. If so, using a sunlamp will help, too.

Shampooing hair and adjusting hairstyles. Acne is often worst on the forehead where the skin is covered by a fringe which is allowed to become greasy. Keeping hair free of grease may help and so may keeping it off the forehead. If hair is worn in a style which covers this area, face-washing must get right underneath it.

Removing blackheads and whiteheads. If a blackhead is visible then a hair follicle is blocked and liable to become the site of an acne pimplepustule. Removing blackheads therefore makes sense *provided it is done properly*. Obviously squeezing it out with dirty fingernails is liable to introduce infection and to leave a nasty mark, too. Either the pads of clean fingers should be used to squeeze *gently*, or a special blackhead extractor should be used.

Choosing cosmetics carefully. 'Medicated' cosmetics will not help acne because the anti-bacterial chemicals they contain cannot penetrate into the follicles. Heavy, clogging cosmetics should be reserved for special occasions and for covering blemishes. Everyday cosmetics should be those intended for oily skin.

Coping with pustules and scabs. Help your adolescent to resist attempts to squeeze those painful red bumps which come before a pustule. Persistent efforts may produce a tiny bit of pus but if there was no visible head he or she will have forced it up through skin which was still intact and made a tiny wound. *Many of these lumps will disperse by themselves* if left alone. If a yellow head does appear he or she should squeeze it as antiseptically as possible or more infection may be introduced from bacteria on the skin.

For *open* acne sores a 'medicated' soap or astringent skin lotion may just be worth using. It will not cure the places but it may help prevent them becoming secondarily infected by bacteria from outside.

Medical help for severe acne Unless these simple measures keep the skin almost completely clear almost all the time, medical advice is needed. There is no reason for an adolescent to be left to suffer and if he or she is thus left, the acne lesions may leave scars. Medical treatment at present takes two main forms:

Attempts to reduce secretion of sebum. Drugs are becoming available which actually block the production of sebum by the sebaceous glands. Some of these are not yet available for general prescription and some, such as cimetidine, have side-effects which might make a doctor reluctant to prescribe them except in an extremely severe case of acne.

Girls are more fortunate in this respect than boys. Low progesterone birth control pills markedly reduce sebum production. If a girl is considering 'going on the Pill' anyway, her acne may clear up as a side-effect. If not, severe acne may be a reason for considering this treatment especially if, like many girls, her acne tends to flare up with each menstrual period.

Attempts to reduce bacterial action within the hair follicle. Certain antibiotics (notably tetracycline) can inhibit the growth of bacteria within the hair follicle and thus prevent that cycle of sebum-bacterial-breakdown-inflammation-follicle-rupture-pustules.

Tetracycline works best for this purpose if it is taken in a low dosage over a long period and if the drug is taken on an empty stomach and without the calcium-containing drinks (such as milk) which may prevent it from being absorbed. Provided it is given under medical supervision and followed patiently without expectation of instant miracles, such long-term antibiotic treatment is both safe and usually effective.

Body odour The skin contains two types of sweat-producing glands. The eccrine glands are widely distributed over the body with a slight concentration in the palms, soles and forehead. Active in everyone, whatever his or her age, these glands produce watery sweat in response to heat and/or stress. The sweat moistens the skin and cools it by evaporation. Eccrine sweat alone seldom causes an unpleasant smell unless personal hygiene is very poor. The apocrine glands are a different matter. These are concentrated mainly in the underarm area and they become active only during puberty, when underarm hair begins to grow. Their activity diminishes as adult age increases. The activity of the apocrine glands may usher in a body-odour problem because although their sweat is odourless in itself, it develops an unpleasant smell when it is acted upon by the bacteria which are on everybody's skin. These bacteria concentrate and flourish in warm, moist areas such as the underarms and it is from such areas that sweat can least easily evaporate.

Dealing with underarm odour. Frequent washing with ordinary soap and water is the most effective way of keeping skin-bacteria to reasonable numbers and of removing the sweat on which they act. A combined anti-perspirant/deodorant will reduce the amount of sweat secreted under the arms and do something to mask or diminish the smell. Removing underarm hair makes it easier to keep the bacterial population down and easier to wash effectively.

Clothing which permits easy evaporation (especially during hot, humid weather and/or active exercise) also helps, so sufferers should settle for vest-shaped sports shirts which leave the underarm area naked, and for loose armholes wherever possible on other clothes. Some fabrics, usually man-made ones or fabrics with special finishes, become smelly far more quickly than others. The adolescent may have to experiment and reject a type of shirt which always leaves him embarrassed by the end of the day.

Any clothing which is allowed to become contaminated with sweat + bacteria and is then worn again without being washed is bound to become smelly. Adolescents often do not realize that washing clothing is just as important as washing themselves. Both sexes can be helped with under-arm odour if they are liberally supplied with shirts, tee-shirts, blouses, etc. so that they are able to change frequently – certainly every day and perhaps twice a day.

Girls may find that clothes requiring expensive dry cleaning are more practical if they wear dress-shields to absorb the sweat and protect the outer clothes from contact. Boys may find that a cotton undershirt (which will absorb sweat) will similarly prevent sweat reaching sweaters and jackets.

If a wardrobe has a slightly stale, unpleasant smell when first opened, the adolescent can be sure that clothes are contributing to the body-odour problem.

Dealing with odour in the genital area. This is more often a problem for girls than for boys. Unpleasant odour is usually associated either with menstruation or with a discharge from the vagina. Normal vaginal discharge, like menstrual blood, does not smell unpleasant until it is exposed to the air. Frequent washing and clean underwear should therefore deal with any odour (*see above* Menstruation). A vaginal discharge caused by infection or by a forgotten tampon may smell very nasty indeed. The presence of an offensive discharge between menstrual periods should mean a visit to the doctor.

Girls are often hypersensitive about odour from the vaginal area, confusing the slight, distinctive odour which is natural to it with abnormal body odour. While you must, of course, be honest with your daughter if you agree that she smells (a best friend may not tell her but it would be cruel of you not to do so), do try to dissuade her from 'feminine deodorants', 'deodorant towelettes', and so forth. Not only are these unnecessary if she keeps herself normally clean, they may also cause rashes and other allergic reactions. Don't allow a male advertising world to convince her that she needs special deodorants for her femaleness.

Dealing with foot odour. It is usually boys who suffer from smelly feet and they themselves usually do not suffer as much as those who must share bedrooms and changing rooms with them.

Feet smell unpleasant only if sweat is allowed to become colonized by bacteria and is then trapped for hours inside man-made-fibre socks and plastic shoes and, even when these are removed, *is not washed off*. The answers, then, are washing, cotton and/or wool socks, and leather or canvas rather than 'waterproof' plastic shoes. Clean socks every day should be as much a routine as clean underpants. Shoes which are not being worn should ideally be stored in an airy place.

A boy who really does follow a sensible routine of foot hygiene but still has trouble may find that his shoes (especially if they have absorbent insoles) are permanently smelly and therefore undermining all his efforts. He will have to start again with new ones.

Dealing with sweaty palms. Sweaty hands do not smell but may nevertheless be acutely embarrassing in all kinds of social situations where hands are shaken and/or held. Excessive palm-sweat is almost always caused by nervous excitement (although heat will not help) and therefore it bedevils adolescents on just those occasions when they want to be at their best. Some blot examination papers as well as social copy-books.

Keeping cool, calm and collected will certainly help when it is possible. Apart from this, running the hands under cold water may help a little as may an astringent. 'Clean up pads' come ready-moistened with astringent lotion and packed in pocket-sized packets so they can be kept usefully available. If sweaty palms are really reducing the quality of an adolescent's life it is worth consulting a doctor. Various topical (skin) preparations help some people.

Deformities, real and imagined

Adolescents need to be able to accept themselves, even like themselves, warts and all. Sometimes the warts (or sticking-out ears or over-large noses) come to assume enormous importance. It is as if the youngster has picked out one particular physical characteristic and used it as a peg on which to hang all his or her anxieties and discontents about him/herself. Parents need to tread warily.

Is the anxiety genuine or a try-on? Sometimes a youngster will say, casually, 'with a nose the size of mine, I can't wear sunspecs.' If she was only asking you to reassure her that her nose is entirely normal, instant sympathy may create a real problem. If in doubt, try feeding the line back: 'Your nose looks OK to me, what's supposed to be wrong with it?'

If the anxiety is genuine, can you see a reality-base for it? Of course this is a subjective judgement, but, at least at the extremes, you will probably know whether the feature complained of comes within normal limits or not. Large breasts, for example, are perfectly normal; the tormented possessor, aged fifteen, may be exceedingly proud of her lavish endowment in a year or two and should certainly not be encouraged to feel that a doctor could re-design her to fit her currently desired self-image. You may be able to help with better-fitting bras or better-chosen clothes but the best help you can offer will probably be warm acceptance of her new sexuality. On the other hand, markedly protruding teeth are not accepted as normal or attractive and it would, perhaps, have been kinder to have them dealt with by an orthodontist while she was still at an age when many of her friends wore braces. If you can honestly see why her teeth distress her, by all means facilitate her in seeking professional advice.

If the anxiety is both genuine and reality-based, is action practically possible? If your child has some real deformity (such as a poorly repaired hare-lip) your reaction to adolescent distress needs to be based on hard and up-to-date information. Could an unsightly scar be improved by plastic surgery? If so, could the surgery be appropriately performed at his or her current age or must it wait until growth is complete? What would surgical intervention mean in terms of discomfort and disruption of life? Could it be done at any time or would there be a wait of months/years for non-urgent surgery?

The point here is that if nothing can be done, you have to help your child towards acceptance, not by denying the existence of the problem but by helping him or her to see that it need not permeate all of life. If, on the other hand, action is practically possible, you have to give him or her the facts on which to decide whether or not to take any. If action involves plastic surgery, it is usually important to see to it that he or she receives expert counselling first. All too often a youngster half-believes that the surgery will transform him or her not just into a person without that blemish but into somebody beautiful.

Young people may be worried by a number of other more minor 'imperfections'. Too much adult attention to these 'problems' will tend to heighten their importance in the child's eyes while refusal to consider them at all will seem uncaring. Some, girls especially, can easily come to feel that their mothers do not want them to be beautiful. If the mother is seen to spend some time, money and attention on her own appearance yet will spend none on her daughter's, problems of sexual jealousy between the generations can be much exacerbated. Mothers perhaps need to ask themselves: 'Would *I* want to put up with that for myself?' If the answer is 'no', the girl is probably entitled to some consideration.

Birthmarks, scars, etc. Many such marks can either be removed, or can be made much less noticeable, by surgical and related techniques such as dermabrasion. Others can be better disguised by special creams containing masking agents than by cosmetic cover-creams. If your child has any problem of this kind *and expresses worry over it*, do facilitate him or her in making an appointment with a dermatologist (see **Birthmarks**).

Moles come in all shapes, sizes, places and degrees of pigmentation. Most can be surgically removed under local anaesthesia although some degree of scarring will be left. A mole which suddenly grows and/or darkens should, in any case, be seen by a doctor to ensure that it *is* just a simple mole. The possibility of having it removed can be discussed at the same appointment.

Problems with hair: 'Excess hair' The amount of facial and body hair is almost entirely a hereditary matter. While there are a few hormonal disorders which can cause sudden excess growth, the normal hormonal changes of adolescence are usually responsible for the increase. Boys will seldom be concerned by their hairiness but girls may be very bothered indeed by facial hair and/or by thick, dark hair on the arms and legs.

Many women remove hair from the legs using either a razor or a chemical depilatory. A few remove it (or have it removed) by waxing, which pulls the hairs out at root-level. Single hairs (such as those which may sprout on the chin, from a mole or around the nipples) are often simply pulled out with tweezers. But if a girl has a real problem with excess hair, none of these solutions may be very satisfactory. If, for example, she is bothered by a luxuriant growth of conspicuously dark hair on her arms and upper legs, shaving will produce an uncomfortable stubbly feeling; it will take a considerable amount of time at frequent intervals and thus continually remind her of 'the problem' and, when she leaves it one day too long, the stubbly hairs may be more conspicuous than the full growth. Using a chemical depilatory will keep the regrowth softer (since the ends of the hairs are not chopped off) but otherwise will be similar. To embark on such a programme in the early teens seems sad. It may be better to find a way in which she can come to accept the hairiness.

If she cannot accept it and would rather swelter in long sleeves and tights in summer than reveal her hairy limbs, it may be helpful if you suggest bleaching which makes even luxuriant hair far less conspicuous. It also has the advantage that it can be carried out at home, can be used in conjunction with any other temporary method of removal (from the lower legs in summer, for example) and that used repeatedly, it tends actually to weaken and reduce the growth.

Home bleach can be made by mixing six per cent hydrogen peroxide (called 20-volume peroxide) with twenty drops of ammonia to each ounce. A small amount should be made up and applied to ensure that the skin is not over-sensitive to it. If all is well, a fresh solution should be made up and applied immediately (peroxide action begins as soon as the ammonia is added). It should be left on for about half an hour and then thoroughly washed off.

Facial hair   Probably cannot be simply accepted and may therefore be best removed by the only permanent method: electrolysis. This involves the insertion of a tiny needle into the follicle of each individual hair which is then destroyed by an electric current. It must be carried out by a trained expert (home kits are neither satisfactory nor safe as inexpert use can scar surrounding tissue) and it is therefore expensive as well as time-consuming. Nevertheless, if a young girl has a dark moustache, she will have it forever if nothing is done; so, like straightening crooked teeth, it may be worth doing. In Britain, a sympathetic doctor can sometimes arrange for this kind of treatment to be given under the NHS on psychological grounds.

Scalp hair   Hairs grow for two to six years and then 'rest' for a few months during which time they are easily removed by brush or comb, and at the end of which time they will, in any case, be pushed out by the growth of a new hair. The loss of up to one hundred separate hairs in a day is nothing to worry about. Hair will only thin if loss exceeds regrowth. The normal rate of regrowth is such that it takes about two and a half months for scalp hair to grow one inch. Hormonal changes can lead to the scalp hair thinning. This sometimes happens in pregnancy or, occasionally, when a girl starts taking birth control pills.

Bald spots on the scalp may be due to ringworm (*see* **Ringworm**) or, rarely, to a little understood disease called alopecia areata. The cause of this disorder is not known, but spontaneous regrowth almost always occurs and certain medical treatments can hasten it.

The commonest cause of bald spots is, however, known as traction alopecia and is the result of continuous pulling on the hair, as when it is always worn tightly plaited. Usually hair growth will recover when the style is changed and the traction stopped, but occasionally some permanent damage to growth in the affected areas does occur. Rarely, pulling out the hair as a nervous habit can cause traction alopecia.

Generalized hair loss. Some individuals have a tendency to hair loss and will find their hair thinning after feverish illnesses or whenever their general health has been poor. The hair can be protected, to some extent, by minimizing the amount of manipulation to which it is subjected. Thorough brushing, for example, does not encourage growth but merely removes needed hairs which might have remained a little longer. Very frequent shampooing, chemical bleaches and perms and the use of hot rollers should all be discouraged. If fashion allows, a short style will both appear thicker and require less handling than a longer one.

Constant changes of colour, involving the use of harsh chemicals, may dry out and damage the hair so that it breaks off close to the scalp. The roots are still present but the appearance is of hair loss. Although such hair will regrow, a different regime will be needed.

Spectacles and contact lenses

If a child is becoming short-sighted, sight-correction often becomes necessary when the growth spurt around puberty suddenly increases the myopia. He or she therefore faces a new image of self as a spectacle-wearer just at the time in life when self-image becomes so vital.

In the past, having to wear spectacles seemed traumatic to many youngsters. Now, however, your child may feel easier about it. Many people wear non-prescription tinted lenses simply because they like the look of them. Spectacles have become virtually a fashion accessory.

If your child can accept spectacles, do not make a drama out of it. Instead, devote yourself to helping him or her to find the frames which really suit and, perhaps, the special frames which will glamourize her for parties or him for active sports. If the very idea of wearing spectacles fills the child with horror, you may want to consider contact lenses instead.

Contact lenses suit some people but not everyone. Your ophthalmologist and optician will, between them, advise on the medical suitability of various types of lens but it is up to you and your child to consider other issues. On some people, for example, contact lenses, however well they are tolerated, produce a somewhat watery appearance in the eyes which, together with the constant blinking which is necessary for contact lens wear, makes them quite conspicuous.

Daily wear lenses require careful attention to nightly hygiene and to safe overnight storage. This can be tedious and quite difficult for a youngster to manage if he or she frequently sleeps the night at friends' houses, goes camping, and so forth.

Lenses are easily lost and expensive to replace. Furthermore, the prescription needed by a young teenager is likely to change quite rapidly so that expensive new lenses will be needed.

Not all types of lens can safely be worn for all sports.

Extended wear lenses, which do not have to be removed each night, require less care and are less readily lost. When they were introduced it did seem that they might be the ideal answer for youngsters who, once settled with them, would be able to forget 'their short-sight for long periods. Such lenses are proving to have some problems, however, and your specialist may advise you against them.

Attempts to 'improve' appearance Sometimes a youngster wishes to make some dramatic change in his or her appearance which parents consider the very opposite of 'an improvement'. Quell any instinctive screams of indignation with the realization that you are honoured to have been consulted in advance. You are at least being given the opportunity to voice your opinions; do so gently or the next dramatic change will take place with the support of friends only.

How permanent is the change and what is the timing? If your son means to have his head shaved, he (and you) will only have to live with it for a few months. If you hate the idea you could point out that in order to get back to having a hairstyle he will have to live through the equivalent of a crew cut (which may, or may not, strike him as a horrendous notion). Otherwise it is probably not worth a row.

If your daughter means to have her hair bleached and then dyed in stripes, much the same applies except that if she has a summer job lined up which you know she will be banned from if she 'looks like that' you might possibly persuade her to wait (if she wants the job). Money is a consideration. Keeping the style will cost her a lot. Having the whole lot dyed in order to conceal the stripes while they grow out will cost a lot too.

If the change is permanent, will he/she be able to live with it forever? Pierced ears are permanent but their purpose – the wearing of earrings – need not be. You may dislike the idea of your son wearing one earring now, but even the most conservative later employer is unlikely to hold against him such inconspicuous evidence of youthful fashion-consciousness as one hole.

Tattooing, on the other hand, is both truly permanent and something which your child is most unlikely to want to live with later. In some places tattooists are forbidden by law to work on minors. If age or place deprives you of legal support, at least make sure that your child does really know:

That tattooing hurts and that if the tattooist is more concerned with artistry than hygiene, can be dangerous.

That while a small tattoo can later be surgically removed there will be a scar.

That larger areas cannot be dealt with surgically. There are techniques for fading them or for smudging out the actual picture/message, but none remove the tattoo completely.

That removal techniques of which he/she may have heard (such as superficial dermabrasion) rely on causing inflammation in the skin of the tattooed area, thus persuading the dye to move up towards the surface. They do not always work and they often leave the skin either hairless or a different colour from the rest.

Sex

Parents will have passed on their own attitudes to sexual matters long before their children reach puberty and become able to *feel* the issues which as children they could only *think about*. Nevertheless, it is during adolescence that the formal and informal 'sex education' of school and home is likely to face some acid tests. Some facts and factually-based opinions may be useful to parents facing new problems, unexpected questions or just the reality of sexually alive and active children.

Masturbation Is a normal activity, widely practised in childhood (*see* **Habits**) and almost universal in adolescence. Those who find it shocking usually have a puritanical belief that anything which is done entirely for selfish pleasure must be wrong and/or a fear of the strength of feelings and fantasies which combine to produce the complete loss of control which is implicit in orgasm (climax). Every adolescent has a right to specific assurances that:

Masturbation cannot damage penis or vagina.

Masturbation does not lead to insanity, blindness, illness or indeed to mental or physical damage of any kind whatsoever.

The feeling of weakness which follows orgasm is a normal resting reaction of the body after any form of sexual gratification. It is in no sense a sign that masturbation is 'weakening'.

That 'having sex with oneself' does not suggest homosexual leanings even when the accompanying fantasies are of a same-sex partner.

But this kind of assurance must be tactfully given, preferably in bits and pieces as 'right moments' arise over a long period of childhood. To deliver a prepared lecture on the harmlessness of masturbation would be to invade the privacy of your fourteen-year-old son or daughter.

Homosexuality At one time or another adolescents of both sexes will probably wonder whether they are homosexual. Each of us is bisexual, to some extent, both biologically and socially. Our eventual sexual direction is never absolute but always a question of which way the balance tips. The ambiguity is especially bothering to young adolescents because they are at a stage of life during which they are both trying to find their own inner balance and being expected to make and state an outward sexual choice.

Despite strong public stands by organizations of male and female homosexuals and by other sympathetic groups, claiming that homosexuality is normal, most adolescents can only recognize it as normal in people other than themselves. To wonder whether he or she is homosexually inclined is to worry about it although the worry is usually more acute for boys than for girls. Many pubertal girls have passionate 'crushes' on older girls or women yet most remain convinced that one day it will be males who engage their romantic attention. It may be that the prospect of childbirth – often made conscious at the menarche – makes it easier for them to take eventual heterosexual relationships for granted. In the meanwhile, most societies are kinder to females than to males in this respect. Close and exclusive friendships between girls are easily accepted and physical expressions of such friendship, such as holding hands or kissing, pass without the ribald comment which is aroused by similar behaviour between boys. In many families and communities this difference in values for boy and girl begins in infancy. Girls may dress in trousers, play with trains and be admired as 'tomboys'. Boys, on the other hand, may never wear dresses, are seldom offered dolls and quickly learn to dread being called 'sissy'.

Nobody really knows why some adults prefer to have sexual relations with their own, rather than the opposite, sex. What we do know, however, is that the preference can neither be changed at will nor prevented by exhortation in adolescence. Parental coercion will never make a heterosexual but may easily make a permanent breach within the family. Most adolescents will worry about possible homosexuality; most will become heterosexual adults. Parents should concentrate on helping with the anxiety and leave the adolescent's personal and private development to see to the eventual outcome.

Avoid sexual labelling. Caring activities, tender emotions and artistic interests are not signs of homosexuality. Don't try to make your son behave as a 'man's man'. He must become his own man. Close friendships between girls are not signs of lesbianism. Don't try to make your daughter behave as a flirt. She must be herself.

Avoid sexual teasing. Boys grow and develop later than girls and, in early adolescence, often feel disadvantaged in dawning sexual battles. Don't tease your son about his 'little girlfriend' when he is clearly unready for any such relationship. You may make him wonder if he ever will be ready. Many boys devote much of the energy of the mid-teens to sporting and other activities rather than to sexual ones. Don't tease your sixteen-year-old for never having had a date. If you suggest that he is in some way peculiar you may increase his tendency to believe that he is.

Accept hero-worship. Adolescents often worship from afar. The object of worship is often a member of the same sex and, for a boy, will often be a heroic sporting figure. Only your own hang-ups will make you prefer your son to cover his wall with pin-ups rather than action photos, or your daughter to blush for the science master rather than the head-girl.

Stay calm about mutual masturbation or homosexual approaches. Many of the close same-sex friendships of early adolescence have, at some time, an element of sexual experimentation. Probably you will never know about this but, if you do, remember that such a relationship does not suggest that your son 'is homosexual', that he may well fear that it does suggest this and that if he has problems in this area a shocked reaction from you can only do harm.

Many boys receive homosexual approaches from adults at some time in their lives (*see* **Safety**/From 'strangers'). Again, if such an incident comes to your notice, do underplay your reaction. If you express complete horror, your son may feel that he has been befouled, rather than annoyed. If he partly enjoyed the experience he will also feel extremely guilty.

'Wet dreams'
(nocturnal
emissions)

Once a boy's testes are producing sperm (*see above* Puberty) he may (or may not) have dreams from which he is suddenly awoken by orgasm and ejaculation. These 'wet dreams' are entirely normal and in no way under the boy's control. Their absence, however, does not suggest abnormality. Most boys have some; some boys have many more than others.

While the orgasm is intensely pleasurable, a 'wet dream' can be worrying. If the boy does not know in advance that it is likely, he may confuse ejaculation with bedwetting or believe that his masturbation has got out of his control so that he is 'doing it in his sleep'. He may also worry about the nature of the dream which caused the emission; it may be overtly heterosexual but it may be homosexual and/or sadistic or masochistic in content. Finally, of course, he may worry about practicalities such as how to cope with wet pyjamas and sheets. Like his menstruating sister he needs an easy and private way to cope.

Sexual activity between adolescents

Western media suggest that we live in an age of complete sexual freedom; their more sensational headlines suggest that freedom has become anarchy and back the claim by drawing attention to increases in schoolgirl pregnancies and adolescent venereal disease. Things are not quite as they are made to appear. While many adolescents do have sexual relationships with each other, many do not, at least until they are approaching adulthood. Of those who do have earlier sexual relationships, many conduct meaningful affairs in a responsible way rather than using promiscuous sex for passing entertainment.

Adults always have been, and probably always will be, quick to indict the sexual behaviour of the young because adolescent sexuality frightens them and affects relationships within families in ways which they dare not recognize, let alone accept. The sheer strength of adolescent sexual feeling, for example, is something most adults choose to ignore. Good sex education may deal with 'love' as well as with 'the facts of life' but it seldom deals with lust; with the fact that the adolescent will *want* sex. You can accept the existence of a feeling without necessarily encouraging its expression and it is better if you do.

In families which lack this kind of understanding and acceptance the effect which adolescent sexuality has on family relationships can be devastating. Many fathers and sons who continually pick on each other, for example, are interacting as herd bulls behave with immature rivals. If a father can recognize this elemental reaction in himself he will probably be able to find more appropriate ways of acknowledging his son's maturity. If he cannot recognize it he may eventually find himself behaving like a bull to a point where he throws that son right out of the family-herd. Mothers and daughters often find themselves in similarly difficult new squabbles. Many, for example, quarrel ceaselessly about the daughter's clothes, hair, make-up and general appearance. If the mother who always wants her daughter to dress less conspicuously, less 'sexily', can acknowledge to herself that she is partly trying to keep out new sexual competition, she may be able to accept her daughter's right to present whatever image of herself she pleases. Sometimes father–daughter and mother–son relationships need some thought, too. It is all too easy for an adult to behave seductively to an adolescent child, telling him or herself that 'there's nothing wrong with being cosy together/undressing together/ flirting together: he/she is my *baby*.' The adolescent is not a baby any more.

Even the closest and easiest relationships between parents and adolescents need monitoring a little. Fathers and mothers who find a new lease of life and fun in the activities of their growing children must ask themselves whether they are really watching and facilitating the adolescent's life or whether perhaps they are trying to live their own again through him or her. A close, confidante relationship can all too easily become an invasion of privacy. 'Tell me all about it, darling' must mean no more than 'I'm interested in anything you care to say.'

Sexual customs and mores vary widely from place to place and from group to group and, of course, parental reactions vary too. But whatever sexual behaviour you think you are seeing in your adolescent and/or his or her peer group, do remember that the group will itself have sexual customs and mores. If you can come to understand what these are, you may find them both comforting and surprising. Parents often look at their children's public behaviour now, in the eighties, and wrongly assume that it suggests the same private behaviour which it would have suggested when they were young. In the fifties and sixties, for example, couples did not go away on holiday alone together unless they were also sleeping together. Furthermore 'sleeping together' in the same bed or tent was a euphemism for sexual intercourse. Today, the girl who tells you that she and her boyfriend are going camping together may neither be announcing that she has made love with him nor that she intends to do so. The son whom you disturb in bed with a girl may still be a virgin and intending to remain so for the moment. Things have changed, but often the change is towards a greater freedom to be close with members of the opposite sex and therefore to make more informed choices of sexual partners.

Difficulties of very early sexual activity The difference in the rates at which girls and boys mature means that girls are often looking for romantic/sexual contacts long before their male peers are ready for them. 'Dating' (or whatever less-dated word is current in your children's community) has tremendous social significance for girls and the higher the standing of the boy who asks her out, the greater her social prestige. This combination of circumstances often means that a very young adolescent girl manoeuvres invitations from considerably older boys. They, if they are prepared to play the 'dating' game at all, seldom understand that their company is really wanted for public show rather than sexual action. Those who do understand it, not unnaturally often resent it. Where such a relationship continues at all (and usually it will not) the girl often finds that the romantic element is on her side only; that there is little mutual friendship between them and that the boy's drive towards sexual contact is far stronger and more immediate than her own. If she wants to hold onto the relationship, she may find herself 'paying' with sex for the boy's public company and trying to pretend to herself that the sexual contact proves that he loves her. Boys in this situation are often genuinely confused. If a girl clearly wants to dance the slow dances with him at the disco and clearly wants him to leave his male friends and pay attention to her, does she not also want to be kissed and fondled? If she wants to be kissed and fondled and if she will come with him to the car or private corner, does she not also feel the overwhelming lust which he comes to feel? If she does not share the lust, why does she insist on the evenings which build up to it? If she does share the lust why does she later seek assurances that the relationship is more than a passing and casual thing-of-the-moment?

The more both girls and boys can understand of each other's psychology and sexuality the less likely they will be to get into these painful muddles. In the meantime, young girls who go out with boys in their *own* age group are likely to have to 'make the running' but will be doing so with boys who, because they are themselves still anxious about sexual activity, are unlikely to allow matters to go further than either of them truly want. Eventually a boy will cease simply to be overwhelmingly interested in sex and his body's reactions to sexy sights and feelings; he will become interested in girls as people, and in one girl in particular. Then and only then will he be ready to share the kind of romantic closeness which his girl-peer has been dreaming of for so long. Then and only then do the two of them stand a chance of making a sexual relationship which is part of a whole relationship; of loving each other for however long or short a time.

Contraception   With efficient contraceptives more or less freely available, teenage pregnancies should be a tragedy of the past; instead they are on the increase. Unthinking adults tend to blame this on youthful irresponsibility. In fact, it is far more difficult for very young people to guard against unwanted pregnancies than it is for their more settled elders. Many youngsters, properly educated in the vital importance of using contraceptives whenever, wherever and with whoever they have sex, nevertheless get 'caught out' because intercourse takes place without either of them having intended it. If you really want to ensure that your adolescent neither causes nor experiences an unwanted pregnancy, you will need to be extremely hard-headed in your thinking and frank in your advice.

Girls who have full intercourse very early in adolescence are peculiarly at risk because they do not give themselves time to think about their own sexuality or contemplate the possibility/likelihood of having sex and realize that it is time to take precautions. Girls whose early sexual contacts are confined to fondling and foreplay are far more likely to make positive decisions. They decide that now, or with this partner, they may go farther and they therefore realize that the time has come to seek advice. It is best if a girl has 'boyfriends' before she has a lover.

First times are risky because even a girl who realized in advance that intercourse was possible may well feel uneasy about preparing herself for something which might never happen. In rather the same way, blind dates and mixed-sex trips are risky because most girls will not want to admit to themselves that they might consider having intercourse if the right fellow turned up, but may still do so, unprepared, if he does.

Many parents believe that for just these reasons all girls should use the contraceptive pill 'from the beginning'. But what is the beginning? To suggest that a thirteen-year-old should 'go on the Pill' may be to suggest that you not only expect but even recommend sexual activity. She may be bitterly hurt by what strikes her as a lack of caring. She may be shattered at your lack of trust. She may even be disgusted because she is so far from visualizing herself as an active sexual partner that she cannot bear to realize that you are ready to see her in that role.

There are physiological arguments against putting girls on the Pill early, too. Many authorities believe that it is dangerous to tamper with a newly established – or perhaps not yet fully established – hormonal balance. Many also believe that the number of years a woman spends on the Pill should be limited and therefore that it should be saved for the years when she is fully sexually active.

Other reasonably efficient methods of female contraception are also either contra-indicated or difficult for the very young to manage. A very young girl – even if she is not actually a virgin – is most unlikely to be suitable for an intra-uterine device. She could, of course, be fitted with a diaphragm to use with a spermicidal cream or jelly, but the chance of her having it with her when she comes to need it are negligible.

Responsibility for avoiding very early pregnancies has to lie with boys, and therefore with their parents, even though the dread of pregnancy is so much more real to girls and their parents. If boys were taught that they must use a sheath whenever they had intercourse until or unless other contraceptive arrangements had actually been discussed between them and their regular partners, pregnancies *and* venereal disease would both be much reduced. Sheaths are easily purchased and easily carried. A boy can become adept at using one by practising while masturbating. If he cannot cope with the thought or the reality of using a sheath he certainly is not mature enough to cope with a real sexual partner.

In some communities adolescent males have 'stopped bothering' about sheaths because 'all the girls are on the Pill'. Many girls feel pressurized by this attitude and some find themselves in situations where they have to rely on the boy withdrawing. This technique, especially used by the young and over-excited, does almost nothing to reduce the chance of her becoming pregnant while doing a great deal to reduce the chances of intercourse being satisfactory for either.

Both sexes should be taught that whatever the circumstances, *protection against pregnancy must be discussed in advance* of intercourse and that if neither partner has contraceptives available it cannot take place. If one or the other feels that no second chance will ever present itself ('he'll never ask me out again if I say no'; 'it's only the moon and the drink that have made her say yes . . .') the relationship was not ready for sex.

Once a girl has become sexually active, the Pill, properly prescribed and supervised, may be right for her. Try not to pressure her either way.

Don't pressure her to take the Pill just because she has had sexual intercourse once or twice. She may have been experimenting and have decided now that she is not ready to make sex part of her life. She may feel that the Pill is a sort of punishment or stigma. Don't pressure her to go on with it if she has been taking it during an early affair which has ended. She may feel that the affair was Love and that going on holding herself in readiness for intercourse with an unknown someone else cheapens it.

Make it clear to her that you are not against the Pill for adolescents so that if and when she wants to seek a prescription for it, she can do so openly, whether or not she consults or tells you first. If she must do it all in secret she may feel unable to go to the regular family doctor; find it difficult to keep follow-up appointments or even forget to take the pills on schedule because she has to keep the packet so carefully hidden.

Occasionally a girl who has had unprotected intercourse will at once take a parent into her confidence. If her cycles are still irregular or if they are regular and the intercourse took place more than a week after a period ended, it may be worthwhile to suggest that she see her doctor and consult him about the possibility of the 'morning after' pill. This is not a magic single dose but a short course of high-dose hormones with very unpleasant side-effects. Such treatment is in no way a sensible alternative to contraception but will ensure that there is no pregnancy this time.

If your doctor prefers not to prescribe these hormones he may be willing to assure the girl that if she should find herself pregnant he will discuss the question of a termination with her. If not, she can consult with a pregnancy advisory bureau. A counsellor will explain to her exactly when and how she can find out whether she is pregnant and exactly what her options are if she is. A girl who is afraid she may be pregnant should always seek advice immediately. Modern, do-it-yourself pregnancy tests, available from chemists, can give very early warning.

Many girls who have come through a false-alarm pregnancy-scare spontaneously seek contraceptive advice. If your daughter, having confided the fright to you, does not, discuss it with her. If she has been living and loving in the cloud-cuckoo land of 'it couldn't happen to me' it may be appropriate to remind her of the realities. But be tactful, even now. That sexual episode may still have been something she wants to forget rather than something she wants to repeat, safely. Try to let her work out her feelings with you, rather than telling her what she must do.

Venereal disease   Sexually transmitted diseases are something of which every adolescent should be aware before he or she has any such activity. VD is increasingly prevalent in the western world. Gonorrhea, for example, is the second most common communicable disease in the United States and the United Kingdom; having declined after the Second World War, it has been steadily increasing since the 1960s. Many people still try to believe that only prostitutes, promiscuous people, homosexuals or any group but their own get VD. They are wrong. *Anyone* who is sexually active is at risk and that includes people who are currently involved with their very first sexual partner if that partner has ever had sex with anybody else. It has even recently been shown to be possible to be infected with some venereal diseases without direct sexual contact although the adolescent who maintains that he or she 'must have caught it off a lavatory seat' is almost certainly indulging in wishful thinking.

Non-specific urethritis (NSU) is the commonest venereal disease among British youngsters. Gonorrhea is also common and is the disease discussed here. Syphilis is rarer though more destructive. Others, such as genital herpes, are seen occasionally and appear to be on the increase. An adolescent should not need to know *which* venereal disease he or she may have caught; the faintest suspicion of any should take him or her either to a doctor or, more anonymously, to a venereal diseases clinic.

The gonococcus bacterium requires moist mucosa to live on: dry it out or expose it to air and it dies. Although it is possible to infect oneself by using a freshly infected towel, the bacteria almost always pass from genitals to genitals or from genitals to mouth or, rarely, from mouth to mouth.

Boys will usually develop a discharge from the penis and/or pain on urination within 3–7 days of sexual contact with an infected person. But some may harbour the gonococcus for up to six weeks without symptoms while about ten per cent of infected boys never have symptoms at all but remain infectious to all their sexual partners thereafter.

Girls *may* develop a thick vaginal discharge and/or inflammation of the vulva within a week to a year of contact with an infected person. But *eighty per cent* of all girls infected with gonorrhea remain symptom-free but infectious to later sexual partners.

It is this ability of the gonococcus to remain infectious without causing symptoms to the carrier which makes it so difficult to control or eradicate. The use of a sheath protects both partners. Apart from this precaution the only hope lies in persuading everyone to seek medical help immediately if they have genital symptoms and, if they are found to have a venereal disease, to follow the whole course of prescribed treatment and to *cooperate fully in tracing every single other person who might possibly have been infected by them.* If the many boys and men and the few girls and women who do have symptoms did really report all their sexual contacts (many of whom will have no symptoms themselves and will therefore be blissfully unaware that they are carriers) gonorrhea – and other venereal diseases – could be controlled. Some authorities work extremely hard to make this kind of follow-up complete (and confidential) but at the moment they are failing. Adolescents should understand that, while it is unrealistic to think of venereal diseases as being confined to the sexually promiscuous, sex which takes place once only with a partner who cannot later be traced certainly helps to keep venereal disease on the increase.

Aggression *see* **Discipline, Self-discipline and Learning How to Behave**/Violence. *See also* **Jealousy; Tantrums.**
Air pollution *see* **Pollution.**
Alcohol *see* **Habits**/Which easily lead to addiction. *See also* **Adolescence**/Friends versus family.
Allergic rhinitis *see* **Allergy**/Hay fever.

Allergy

Allergy is a complicated subject: it is complex for medical scientists because the biochemistry involved in allergic reactions is by no means fully understood. It is even more complex for the rest of us because even basic biochemistry is difficult to grasp; and it is complex for sufferers and their parents because the actual symptoms and illnesses associated with allergy are so many and so varied. Parents who have to cope with a child's acute attacks of asthma may find it hard to believe that it bears any relation to their own mild hay fever or to another child's occasional nettlerash. But all these, and many other disorders, are likely to share a common basis as allergic reactions and they are therefore likely to share a family basis too. There is a strong inherited tendency in allergy.

What allergy is

The common basis for all allergic disorders lies in the hypersensitivity of the victim's immune system to proteins (antigens) in the micro-organisms which are all around us (*see* **Immune Response**).

Everything we touch, eat or breathe teems with micro-organisms. A tiny proportion of them present a definite threat to the human body; the rest do not. When a normal (non-allergic) person breathes room air which is teeming with cold viruses, for example, his immune system will start to produce protective antibodies against them. But when that same person breathes room air which is loaded with house-dust or pollen, his immune system will not react: it 'knows', so to speak, that the antigens in these substances present no threat. The immune system of the allergic person is not only jolted into producing antibodies by antigens which are a threat to everybody but also by micro-organisms which are harmless. He may react as strongly to that dust or pollen as does the normal person to cold viruses, or be as ill after drinking fresh cow's milk as the normal person would be after drinking milk which was heavily contaminated with harmful bacteria (*see* **Diarrhoea, Gastro-enteritis and Food Poisoning**). A person who has 'an allergy' or a strong allergic tendency, is therefore distinguished from others by his abnormal bodily response to antigens which cause no response in other people.

About one in every five children develop allergies very readily. Most of them can be shown to produce an excessive amount of one particular antibody which is known as igE. People who are known to produce excess igE are known as 'atopic'. Any antigen (protein foreign to the body) which produces an allergic response in an individual is, for him, an 'allergen'. Even though we usually associate the word 'protein' with food and eating, it is important to remember that, biochemically speaking, protein need not be food at all but can be a component in pollen, in animal fur and shed skin cells or in the microscopic house-mites which teem in the dust of even the cleanest houses. Those proteins do not have to be eaten to affect the body, either. They can be taken in as the victim breathes or can affect him by skin contact alone.

Allergic responses – the symptoms which the victim suffers – are the result of *an interaction between a particular allergen and the antibodies which he has manufactured against it*. First exposure to a substance may lead to the manufacture of antibodies but it will not lead to allergic symptoms. They will only appear when he is exposed again to the same substance and this time his body has antibodies ready to do battle. It is vitally important that parents understand this. Allergic reactions to common drugs, such as aspirin or penicillin, can be very serious indeed. A child may have one dose without apparent ill-effects yet manufacture antibodies in such numbers that a second dose makes him dangerously ill. In the same way a first bee sting may seem to have only normal effects on a child who will over-react disastrously when venom in a second sting interacts with the antibodies his body made ready on that first occasion.

Parents who are unaware of this two-stage development in allergic reactions are sometimes slow to recognize food-allergies in young children. A toddler may, for example, be given his first portion of strawberries and eat them with no apparent effects other than pleasure. When he is given strawberries again he becomes very unwell. Even if they know that 'not all children can tolerate strawberries' his parents may be inclined to say 'it can't be the strawberries, he had them last week and there was no trouble.' Last week his body had not met strawberries and therefore had made no antibodies against them. This week is different.

In most allergy-prone individuals allergic symptoms depend not only on the *presence* of a particular allergen and antibodies which he has manufactured to it, but also on the *'dose'*. Some children, for example, manufacture a low level of antibodies against animals during occasional and passing contacts with various neighbours' pets. They have no symptoms; nobody is aware of the allergy until a dog is brought into the family and the child faces massive exposure. In rather the same way a person can be sub-clinically allergic to, say, a particular mould spore but remain unaware of it until he spends a day helping a friend to clear out a vegetable-store. In some instances there need be no sudden massive exposure to the allergen but only a slow build-up over months and years. A few adults, for example, gradually develop hay fever in adult life. They have, in fact, been pollen-sensitive all their lives but only after years of low-level reaction does their antibody level become high enough for a reaction to be touched off by the next walk through a flower garden.

Allergic symptoms

When an allergen meets its antibodies a local reaction is set in process. Various chemical substances (such as histamines) are released and cause the dilatation of small blood vessels. Fluid leaks through the walls of the distended vessels, causing swelling. There may be spasm of smooth muscles – as in the air passages – and an outpouring of mucus secretions.

While this local inflammatory reaction is always similar, the resulting symptoms will obviously depend partly upon its location in the body. If allergen and antibodies interact in the nasal passageways, for example, the typical symptoms of hay fever will result. If the interaction is lower down, in the bronchi, the result may be the wheezy obstructed breathing of asthma. If the allergen is eaten and meets antibodies in the gastro-intestinal tract, the symptoms may be vomiting, cramps and diarrhoea. If the allergen gets into the bloodstream (by being eaten or injected) it may cause symptoms wherever it meets antibodies – producing both digestive disturbance and the skin reactions typical of atopic eczema, for example.

But the geography of the meeting place between allergen and antibody cannot provide sufficient explanation for the exact nature of allergic symptoms. Other factors such as the following clearly play a part in dictating the exact nature of the susceptible individual's sufferings.

Age: The natural history of allergic individuals suggests an age-related pattern. An infant will be most likely to suffer from atopic eczema accompanied, perhaps, by specific skin reactions to identifiable foods, such as hives in reaction to oranges.

Early in childhood the eczema tends to improve but asthma often begins now and may worsen until adolescence.

During adolescence, the asthma may gradually lessen but hay fever, if he has not previously suffered from it, may start now and remain with him into adult life.

During his adult life hay fever also tends to improve, first becoming more spasmodic and often finally disappearing altogether.

Concentration of allergens: A susceptible individual may manufacture some antibodies to certain allergens but experience no resulting symptoms until circumstances change to provide an overwhelming dose of the offending substance. An infant may, for example, be sensitive to cow's milk protein yet remain symptom-free through the early period of mixed feeding when although there is cow's milk in her cereals, she is still receiving her liquid milk from the breast. As soon as she is weaned onto a cow's milk product, she suffers from violent symptoms. Any major environmental change which brings the individual into contact with new antigens may provoke or show up a previously unsuspected allergy.

Infections: The exact nature of the relationship between allergies and infections is ill-understood. A child who is liable to asthma is very likely to have an attack (or an exacerbation) each time he has a cold. Is he allergic to the infecting organisms which cause colds? Does his cold sensitize him to allergic reactions? Do the symptoms of the cold exacerbate the symptoms of the allergy? Whatever the exact relationship, those who must cope with allergies learn to expect their symptoms to increase at these times.

Stress: Tension and high emotion – pleasant or unpleasant – also play a clear but little understood part in provoking or exacerbating allergic symptoms. A child may have an attack of eczema, asthma or hives whenever she is excited about a birthday treat or miserable about a family row. An adolescent may always have to face examinations with the added stress of acute hay fever. Longer-lasting stressful situations (such as the birth of a sibling or moving house) often usher in a period of the sufferer's life when allergic symptoms are much worsened.

This is a difficult area for parents to handle (*see below*) because attempts to shield an allergic child from stress may lead to her being treated like an invalid. Such treatment leads to a different (but often equally unfortunate) kind of stress as she reacts to feeling 'different' from other children and/or fights for independence.

Principles of diagnosis and treatment in allergic conditions

We do not yet know how to 'instruct' a human body to stop making antibodies to any but 'genuinely harmful' substances. There is therefore no overall cure for allergic tendencies. Diagnosis and treatment both have to be devoted to control of allergic symptoms.

Many mild allergies diagnose themselves: slight hay fever, occurring always and only when the pollen count is high, is an obvious example. Many more cure themselves without ever being diagnosed. Nettlerash, for example, will commonly vanish without trace long before the victim can see a doctor. If a variety of these minor troubles occur frequently, a doctor may offer medication to relieve the symptoms, but he is unlikely even to try to trace the responsible allergens. They could be a handful among hundreds and thousands of possibilities. The search would certainly cause the victim more trouble and discomfort than does that occasional runny nose in early summer or that quickly passing itchy rash.

In more serious situations, your doctor will rely on some combination of the following:

Avoidance of allergens   Some very serious allergic reactions can only be effectively dealt with by avoiding the allergen. Common examples are allergic reactions to particular drugs or foods (but *see below*). If a child has an allergic reaction to penicillin, further administration of the drug could even be fatal. Your doctor will emphasize to you (and to her) that she must never have it again. He will note the allergy in her medical records and stress it whenever he refers her to another doctor or a hospital. Strange doctors will always ask whether the new patient is sensitive to this drug. Sometimes it will be suggested that she wear a 'Medic-Alert' bracelet so that her allergy will become known to anyone who treats her in an emergency situation when she might be unconscious.

A few less serious allergic reactions can also be dealt with by avoidance of the allergen. A person who is specifically allergic to horse-hair, for example, may only discover the allergy on a rare visit to a stables. She may subsequently be easily able to avoid contact with horses and with horse-hair used in antique upholstery and so forth.

But these two examples should make it clear that for avoidance to be effective, the victim has both to know what specific allergen affects her and to be able to identify and avoid it in the environment. Sometimes one or the other is impossible.

Injection treatment for allergy   This form of treatment, properly called 'hyposensitization' or 'desensitization', may be appropriate if a specific allergen can be recognized in the environment but cannot certainly be avoided. A dramatic example is that of allergy to the stings of wasps and bees. Once the sting of one of these insects has caused a serious allergic reaction, a further sting could make the victim dangerously, even fatally, ill. The insects can be readily recognized but they cannot certainly be avoided.

A doctor will commonly start hyposensitization as soon as the victim has recovered from the effects of the sting which demonstrated her sensitivity. He knows that an insect sting was responsible but he must establish exactly which antigen in the venom provoked the symptoms. He does this by preparing extremely dilute solutions of the possible substances and then scratching through them into the child's skin. The allergen will cause a red weal at the scratch site. Antigens to which she is not sensitive will cause no such skin reaction.

Once the exact allergen has been identified, it is made up in solutions of varying strengths for a series of injections. The aim is to provoke the child's body, bit by bit, into producing a special *extra* antibody which, next time she is stung, will bind itself to the allergen and prevent it from interacting with her allergic antibodies. Injections begin with a very dilute solution and then continue (usually at weekly intervals) to inject the maximum amount which her body can tolerate without allergic symptoms. Usually a concentration which produces skin weals without a generalized reaction is enough to provoke useful antibody formation without being enough to be dangerous.

Once protective levels have been reached, regular injections will no longer be needed but skin tests will be repeated at intervals and a maintenance dose given whenever these show that her protection is fading.

Symptomatic treatment for allergy

While both avoidance and de-sensitization may be life-saving in a few cases of allergy, they are impractical in the vast majority.

Most allergic individuals produce antibodies against a wide range of extremely common antigens. If your child is sensitive to the mites in house-dust, to mould spores, to pollens, and to animals hairs, she cannot avoid all allergens while continuing to live in a normal environment. Since de-sensitization has to be specific, provoking the production of a special antibody to each separate allergen, attempting such treatment would condemn her to literally years of skin testing and injections. The treatment would almost certainly be more uncomfortable and life-disrupting for her than is her hypersensitivity.

Under these circumstances, the doctor will probably rely heavily on treating the symptoms as and when they appear. Anti-histamines, for example, counteract the effects of the histamine released during the allergic process, while a variety of ointments, nasal and eye drops may be used to quell local inflammations.

Some allergic sufferers take anti-histamines on a preventative basis: perhaps all through the 'hay-fever season' or whenever public bulletins warn of a rise in the pollen count. But for many, anti-histamines in effective doses produce undesirable side-effects such as sleepiness. The newer disodium cromoglycate appears actually to prevent certain processes in the allergic reaction and has few common side-effects. It is not taken by mouth but by inhalation.

Combining treatment approaches in allergy

Many allergic children have at least one period in their lives when no single treatment approach is adequate. The doctor must use every method at his disposal, in combination or in sequence, to keep her allergic attacks as few and as mild as possible while guarding her health and growth and allowing her to feel that she leads a normal life.

Attacks of allergic asthma, for example, may be brought on by a wide variety of antigens which are common in her environment and may be exacerbated by physical and emotional factors. No single approach will help very much and even a combined approach cannot completely protect her, but if every known factor is attacked energetically her asthma may be kept under reasonable control. Some allergens may be avoidable or at least her contact with them may be minimized. House-dust, for example, may be reduced by taking special precautions in her bedroom (*see below*). De-sensitization to one or two particular allergens – such as animals – may reduce the level of allergic insult to which she is subjected. Medication – both preventative and symptomatic – may reduce the number and severity of her attacks of asthma while early and energetic treatment of any infections will minimize their part in the disorder. Finally, the doctor will probably want to discuss environmental and emotional factors in her life with a view to helping you to achieve the best possible balance between treating her as an invalid and treating her as a normal child who is almost constantly ill.

Coping with allergic disorders

While medical treatment may be able to do a great deal for your child, most of the management of her hypersensitivity will fall to the family and, as she grows up, to her. The 'coping' involved may be no more than providing many tissues and a few nose drops during occasional hay fever, but it may sometimes be the pivot around which family life must revolve. Different symptom-complexes produce different-seeming illnesses and the notes that follow deal with the common allergic disorders in turn. But if you are the parent of an atopic child, do remember that today's problems arise from the same kind of hypersensitivity which produced last year's, and that it will probably produce problems that are different again as she gets older. If that strikes you as unduly or unkindly pessimistic, remember also that on the whole the symptoms produced by allergic responses do become milder with age.

Asthma

Not every specialist believes that asthma is mainly an allergic disorder; some believe that it is a disorder in its own right and that asthmatic children commonly have other allergic disorders, simultaneously or in sequence, together with a family history of allergy, only because the asthma makes them prone to allergy. Most, however, see asthma as at least primarily allergic even though its nature makes demonstration of the exact relationship between allergen and antibody difficult.

Asthma affects the bronchial tree. When it is stimulated by contact with an allergen or by another predisposing factor, there is an outpouring of mucus and spasm of the smooth muscles. In combination these reactions partially block the airway so that the victim must fight to get sufficient air in and out of his lungs. Breathlessness is terrifying and, of course, terror increases the need for oxygen and therefore creates a vicious circle. A child who has experienced (and a parent who has seen) an acute attack of asthma is likely to dread the next: terror of that terror may quickly become a factor in increasing the frequency of attacks.

Since asthma affects breathing, it is also likely to be brought on by anything which requires extra respiratory effort. An attack may therefore accompany strenuous exercise, disciplined singing or any kind of prolonged excitement.

Since asthma involves an outpouring of mucus within the bronchi, it is also often precipitated by upper respiratory infection. If asthmatic mucus should become infected it may precipitate such an infection.

Asthma is therefore intimately connected with the victim's daily life and activities and has both emotional stress and physical illness intimately connected with it. Nevertheless it need not be as devastating as many parents, newly faced with the diagnosis, may fear:

Nearly twenty per cent of all children have one or two 'asthmatic episodes' but only five per cent have the recurrent and/or severe attacks which constitute 'diagnosed asthma'. It is a mistake to anticipate a ruined childhood on the basis of a first, or even a second, attack especially as your worry and your anxious concern next time the child has a cough, may make a further attack more likely.

Asthma can occur at any age but usually begins in middle childhood. If it does begin at that stage in your child's life he has an excellent chance of being symptom-free by the time he reaches puberty. Children whose asthma begins much younger, perhaps especially those who start to suffer from it during infancy, may be slower to grow out of it. It may comfort you to know that:

Seventy per cent of all asthma sufferers will be free of symptoms by the time they are adult even though some of these will continue to suffer from hay fever or other allergic complaints.

Diagnosis of asthma   Wheezing is very common in small children whose airways are small and particularly liable to partial obstruction in a number of respiratory conditions. Many doctors will use the term 'wheezy bronchitis' for any wheezing child with symptoms suggesting upper respiratory infection. In fact, virus infection is the commonest factor precipitating attacks in asthmatic children under about five years. As long as the infection is treated, it does not matter what this first episode is called because it may well be a 'once-only' (*see also* **Chest Infections**/Bronchitis).

Early suspicion of asthma will be aroused by combinations of the following:
- A family history of allergic disorders.
- Clear-cut allergic disorder (such as eczema) in the child.
- Frequent (three or more in one year) wheezy illnesses.
- Night-time cough continuing well after the child recovers.
- Negative laboratory findings eliminating other causes of wheezing.
- Bronchoconstriction (showing as breathlessness but measured on a 'Wright peak-flow meter') after exercise.
- High serum immunoglobin E levels (demonstrated by a blood test).

Children with chronic asthmatic disease will have persistent wheezing, due to some degree of permanent airway obstruction.

Management of asthma

Partnership between parents and a trusted doctor is essential if the asthmatic child is to be helped to grow normally (both physically and psychologically) through his disability and therefore into normal adolescence. While consultation with a distant specialist may well be desirable at some point, the readily available support of a nearby doctor or unit specializing in asthma is vital. The asthmatic child will require that combined treatment approach (*see above*) but in addition, he and his parents may require careful education in the use of special drugs, training in simple physiotherapy techniques, assurance of immediate help in crisis and, always, careful follow-up to ensure that instructions are being followed and that the child is therefore suffering as little as possible from his tendency to asthma.

Avoidance of allergens in asthma

While a few patients over-react to single allergens which can be avoided (*see below*) most over-react to many common ones. Avoidance therefore is concentrated on removing as many as possible of the most obvious. The most obvious of all is the house-mite in house-dust. It may be that this common allergen partly explains the high incidence of asthma attacks during the night, when the child spends many hours in one room under dust-trapping bedding. Bedroom dust can be much reduced, though not eliminated.

Mattresses and pillows should either be made of (fire resistant) plastic foam or be sealed into plastic covers. Blankets should be banished and replaced by continental quilts of man-made fibres. Curtains, cushions, carpets and rugs should all be kept to a minimum and those left should be of cotton or man-made fibre for frequent washing.

Ideally all 'dust traps' (such as shelves full of books) should be removed from the room, but unless a 'playroom' can be provided, the psychological harm may outstrip the physical benefit. Sometimes less dust-trapping objects can be used to make the child's room personal and homely. Posters and so forth can be kept comparatively dust-free.

The child's bedroom should be closed off when housework is done elsewhere in the home. In the room itself furniture, etc. should be washed, rather than dusted. Vacuuming removes dust but may be counter-productive if an overfull bag is itself spraying dust.

Pet animals and their dander are also the source of a very common allergen but, since such pets may be important both to the child and to his family, their banishment should at least await demonstration that it is a real factor in his case. Skin or bronchial challenge testing may be carried out or the pet may be sent elsewhere for a few weeks in order to see whether the child is less wheezy and/or has fewer asthmatic episodes in its absence.

Allergy to pets causes real heartbreak to some asthmatic children. It is sometimes worth searching for a compromise. Certain dogs, for example, can be retrained to occupy a kennel. A beloved cat may be allowed only into the kitchen. The child's own gerbils may stay if their intimate care is undertaken by someone else . . . If all else fails, a non-furry creature such as a fish may do something to comfort the deprived pet owner (*see* **Pets**).

In some children, whose asthma is seasonal, other kinds of avoidance may be helpful. At one extreme, the installation of air-conditioning may work wonders for pollen sensitivity in spring and summer. At the other extreme, changing from an annual lakeside holiday to a seaside one may prevent his most serious attacks.

Avoidance of precipitating factors such as exercise is only desirable in a very small minority of severe cases as the psychological and social harm done may counterbalance the reduction in attacks. If he cannot tolerate the normal exercise for his age group, the matter is often better dealt with by drugs (*see below*).

De-sensitization in asthma

Although some doctors enthusiastically undertake injection treatment in asthmatic children, most find that lasting benefit is exceptional. Serial injections also much increase the unpleasantness of the disorder for the child himself; indeed 'injection phobia' is thought, by some doctors, to explain the apparent reluctance of some families to seek help when the asthmatic child has an attack.

Physiotherapy in asthma

With the help of a skilled physiotherapist, child and parents can learn techniques and exercises which help both overall and during attacks. Muscle tone and posture can both be improved; relaxed breathing can help breathlessness while, after an acute attack, postural drainage can clear plugs of mucus and thus speed recovery (*see* **Chest Infections**/ Physiotherapy in chest infections).

Medication for asthma

There are now many helpful drugs available both for the prevention of asthmatic attacks and for the treatment of acute ones. While some are given by mouth or injection, many have to be administered by inhalation. These may be in powder form for use with a 'spin-haler' or in liquid, either ready-packed in a measured dose aerosol or for use with a nebulizer as a mist. Improved methods of delivering the right dose of the drug to exactly the right place in the respiratory tract are vitally important. Recent improvements have made possible the home-use of certain drugs which were formerly for hospital use only. Others can now be safely administered to very small children by their parents where previously they could only be given by medical personnel. Your child's drug regime will, of course, be prescribed by his doctor. It may include medication to be given to him daily; medication for him to learn to take himself before energetic exercise; medication for him to take or be given under particular circumstances likely to provoke an attack, as well as medication to deal with an attack.

Effective relief when he has difficulty in breathing – especially when an attack wakes him in the night – is vital to your child's ability to live with his asthma. If he is allowed to become panic-stricken by air-hunger the panic will increase the breathlessness in a vicious circle. Thereafter his fear of his own fear may contribute to sleeping difficulties and, indeed, to all kinds of difficulties over becoming appropriately independent for his age. If your child ever has an attack during which you cannot give him instant relief by following the doctor's latest instructions, do not hesitate to send for medical help whatever the time of night. Afterwards, do discuss with your doctor the drugs you have available for emergency use at home in case he can prescribe something more effective. Finally, do remember that anyone who babysits for you at night must understand these emergency drugs and how they should be used. A child who is liable to night-time asthma attacks probably should not be left with an adolescent sibling or babysitter, unless he or she is unusually calm and competent. A panic-stricken, breathless child is an alarming sight and an alarmed attendant will certainly make him worse.

Helping the asthmatic child to feel 'ordinary'
Many children who are liable to asthma can and should be treated exactly as if they were liable to some mild, recurrent illness like tonsillitis. Nursed during attacks, they and their families can forget the asthma in between them and the children will be less scarred by it for being able to do so.

A less fortunate child may not be able to be treated so casually. If he is somewhat wheezy all the time; extremely breathless after exercise, and easily provoked by environmental factors into full-blown asthma attacks, he must be helped to avoid them. Chronic asthma can do permanent damage to the respiratory system. But unless your doctor persuades you that your asthmatic child is, for the moment at least, an invalid, do not treat him as one. With the aid of prescribed medication and so forth he should do and expect to do everything which his friends do, except when he is ill. 'Everything' must include the things he does not actually enjoy – like his homework – as well as the things he does want to do like swimming or playing football.

Within that normal life you may find that you can cushion the asthmatic child enough to reduce the number of his asthma attacks but not so much as to spoil his feeling of being just like everybody else. For example:

Physical stress can be reduced by arranging a car-ride home on swimming days rather than forbidding the swimming. In the same way once you know that lack of sleep tends to precipitate attacks you may be able to arrange for him to sleep late on some mornings rather than being forced to accept a 'baby's bedtime'. The trick is to define the physical stress and then to find a way of relieving it without making him feel over-protected and 'different'.

If excitement precipitates attacks, try new kinds of 'treat'. He may always miss birthday parties because he becomes ill at the last moment but he may be able to take a trip to the movies or an expedition to a museum in his stride.

If anger and frustration make him ill, teach him to talk it out. If he can shout and weep he is far less likely to become breathless than he is if he bottles up all that emotion.

Although you cannot interfere in his relationships with outsiders, you may be able to educate family members into realizing that 'unpleasant atmospheres' or 'the silent treatment' are peculiarly bad for this particular child. If they must quarrel with him it should be openly and fast so that the matter is quickly resolved and forgotten. Trouble with his friends is outside your control, but teachers should understand that while he should certainly be punished if he deserves it, just like any other child, punishments which keep him in suspense or single him out for public ridicule, should be avoided.

Major emotional disasters, such as the death or departure of a parent, are very likely to increase the severity of the child's asthma but, since they would cause distress in any child, you would of course avoid them if possible. If you cannot, try to remember that the asthmatic child's distress shows itself in a particularly dramatic, physical way but is no more (or less) real than the distress of the child who remains healthy while grieving. Every sad child needs special consideration but if you give the asthmatic child extra-special consideration you make it clear to him that the disorder gives him power. You will be inviting him to use his asthma as a blackmail weapon.

Eczema (atopic or 'infantile')

Although there are many types of eczema, this allergic type is the most common; it is also one of the commonest manifestations of allergy in an atopic child.

An atopic child who is going to have eczema will often show the first signs at around three months of age and will commonly have the disorder in its most active form during his first two years. It usually diminishes during the pre-school period and dies down or vanishes altogether during early childhood. Some older people retain one or two eczematous patches, which become active from time to time, but full-blown eczema in later life is usually clinically different.

Recognizing eczema

Eczema usually starts with bright red, scaly and wildly itchy patches on the cheeks. In many cases, that is all there is to it.

In some babies, however, the eczema spreads. Gradually, patches of red, inflamed skin, with small raised spots and a slightly swollen appearance, may appear on other parts of the body. Moist skin creases (such as those in the groin or behind the knees) are particularly vulnerable. When the eczema is very active, acute inflammation makes the patches moist and the skin fragile.

The main problem with eczema is that the affected skin is tremendously itchy. The infant scratches and scratches and, because that skin is already fragile, often lays its surface open. He then has soreness as well as itch to contend with. All too often those open places become infected and then there may be real pain. Altogether eczema is a miserable affliction for a baby and therefore a miserable one for his parents. A cycle of itch-scratch-cry may cease only when the baby is completely distracted by outside events. But because that cycle delays his sleeping and frequently wakes him during the night or nap, parents become less and less able to offer that distraction.

Looking for allergens in eczema

While there is no cure for eczema, your doctor may be able to help you to identify a particular allergen which has led to its first appearance in your baby. Sometimes, for example, eczema first appears when a baby starts on solid foods. One of these could be responsible and he will help you to carry out your own experiments at home, going back to milk only, perhaps, for a few days and then adding in solid foods, one at a time, to try to discover which (if any) food leads to a flare up of the eczema. Milk itself (*see below* Gastro-intestinal allergies) could be a causative factor. If eczema starts when a baby first has cow's milk formula in addition to, or instead of, breast milk, going back to breast milk may deal with it. Some babies can tolerate an ordinary mixed weaning diet (which, of course, includes cow's milk in made-up dishes) provided their liquid milk comes from the breast. If breast-feeding is impossible and investigation suggests a connection between cow's milk and the eczema, a non-cow's milk formula may be recommended. A child who is hypersensitive to cow's milk will usually be similarly affected by goat's milk but an artificial 'milk', based on soy flour, is well-tolerated by many.

Apart from new, or newly increased, food proteins, a search for specific allergens in infantile eczema is seldom useful. The baby may indeed be hypersensitive to many substances (as will probably be demonstrated if he should be subjected to extensive skin testing) but these reactions, while demonstrating that he is very liable to allergy, seldom help in immediate treatment.

Medical management of eczema

There are many skin applications and a few oral drugs which may be used to control the symptoms of eczema. It is important to realize that no one regime will be appropriate over a long period because it is in the nature of eczema to flare and die down and to do so not only over time but also in patches of varying severity over the body. Whatever ointments, drugs or instructions you are given, you must be absolutely sure that you understand them fully. Regular and frequent contact with your doctor (or practice nurse) will be essential.

For example, a coal-tar preparation might be prescribed and, if it is, you might be instructed to use an occlusive (waterproof, usually plastic) covering over it. But a corticosteroid cream (such as hydrocortisone) might be prescribed and, if it is, it must not be used under an occlusive dressing because, while reducing the inflammation of the skin, it also reduces its resistance to infection. If the affected area is closed off from the air, a crop of boils, thrush or some other secondary infection is very likely.

If you are told to use a corticosteroid preparation, you must be sure that you know how much to apply and over how big a skin-area. Some of the active drug is absorbed into the bloodstream from the skin. The dose applied is therefore just as important as the dose of an oral drug which you give your child.

You also have to control your enthusiasm for these highly effective preparations lest you apply them, without prior consultation with your doctor, to newly affected skin. A corticosteroid preparation combined with an antibiotic might well be prescribed for areas where infection is likely, such as the napkin area. If a new 'sore place' appears on your child's skin you may be tempted to use the same cream there. But you could be making a disastrous mistake. If that new patch is, in fact, a minor infection (such as a cold sore, a boil or impetigo), the use of a combined corticosteroid and antibiotic may cause it to spread disastrously.

Oral drugs, such as anti-histamines, may be prescribed both to control itching (by counteracting that allergic release of histamine) and, by their useful side-effect of drowsiness, to help the child sleep. Different anti-histamines and different dosages affect individual children differently. You should keep your doctor in touch with your child's response.

Family management of eczema

There are some practical things which you can do to minimize itching, scratching, skin damage and misery.

Avoid washing with soap and water. It often seems to make affected skin worse, probably by the drying effect of the soap. Use mineral oil or baby-lotion instead.

Avoid rough, scratchy or heavy clothes. A big sweater with a high neck will probably ensure a miserable morning. Several layers of thin, silky, roomy garments are far more comfortable. The baby may be most comfortable wearing nothing – or almost nothing. A room warm enough for naked play may save the day.

Keep his nails very short and as clean as possible. You cannot stop him scratching but you can ensure that he is rubbing the skin rather than cutting it open.

Don't (unless your doctor convinces you that it is absolutely necessary, perhaps because such a large skin area is badly infected) use physical restraint to stop the child scratching. Mittens or, worse, splints which prevent him getting his hand to the itch, are positively cruel. If you really *must* prevent him from touching a particular place, try to use the restraint of your own presence and distraction, gently removing his hand when it strays.

Try to accept that a child who is badly affected by infantile eczema is bound to need a great deal of extra entertainment and attention. He *cannot* give you the peaceful nap-times and nights to which you were looking forward. He *cannot* entertain himself.

Parents who can come to see the eczema as a challenge may actually be able to get some satisfaction out of each day passed in comparative pleasure; each night got through without loss of temper; each week which passes without any inflamed skin being scratched through. But parents who resent the normal demands of a small baby and/or are already over-committed to outside work and so forth, may find the demands of the baby with eczema close to intolerable. Most parents will probably find themselves somewhere between these extremes. The following notes might help:

Eczema which is atrocious today may have subsided somewhat tomorrow. It is an affliction which comes and goes, so that you can always hope for improvement.

Eczema which truly is making everybody's life impossible can probably be lessened by a new medical regime. Call your doctor before you reach breaking point. The simple fact that he is willing to try a different cream or ointment may give flagging morale a boost.

There is no shame in reaching breaking point under these circumstances. Occasionally a doctor will arrange hospital admission for a badly affected baby largely to give the rest of the family some rest. Short of that, don't feel that you yourself have to attend to him night and day. Try to arrange for extra help some of the time and use it for the baby so that you can turn your attention to yourself (for sleeping, studying or whatever you are missing most) or to other children. Their health and good humour may remind you that the eczema will pass; that living with your currently afflicted and impossible infant will one day be easy and fun.

Nobody can remain patient and entertaining if their sleep is always broken (*see* **Sleep**). Try to take turns with your partner or even to import somebody one or two nights a week. If you are taking turns, try a whole night on and a whole night off rather than 'you go this time and I'll go next'. The cries of distress may be so frequent that the latter is no help at all.

Distraction is a key. You are the key to distraction of a small baby. The more you can free yourself to carry him, talk to him and play with him when he is awake, the less stressed you will feel. But other things – especially as he gets older – can distract him too. You may be able to find a parent-and-baby club whose meetings entertain him while giving you a breather. If you explain what is going on to your doctor or health visitor, you may eventually be given priority for a playgroup place. Even taking your frantic baby to some busy public place, such as a department store, may distract him without his entertainment demanding much of you.

Eczema on visible places like the face may reduce your pride in your baby and may even make you feel that 'everybody is looking'. Emphasize to friends and acquaintances that it is not 'catching' (at some stages, eczema can look rather like the rash of an infectious disease) and try to enlist their sympathy for the child. That horrid woman who looks disapprovingly at him, crying and scratching in his pram at the supermarket, may react quite differently when she is encouraged to show him something interesting and he immediately cheers up.

Remember that this baby's experience of his own body is extremely unpleasant. Any bodily pleasure that you can give him is important and you will probably find that it makes you feel better, too. Don't let his ointments and dressings make you treat him as untouchable. Play physical games with him and cuddle him as you would any baby. If it starts him itching again, never mind. He was going to itch again in a minute anyway. Take a real pride in the way you look after his skin (the more careful and thorough you are in applying his various prescriptions, the fewer acute exacerbations he will have) and try to convey to the baby that you are handling him with love.

Most honest parents admit that they had moments when they 'could have been a baby-batterer'. As parents of a baby with severe eczema you have more provocation than most.

If you ever do feel that your patience has gone and that your temper might snap into physical action, do ask for help immediately. In many cities there are now telephone 'help services' for parents. A cry for help from the parents of a child with eczema would be especially readily understood and acted upon.

Gastro-intestinal allergies

If your child reacts badly to a particular food, do not assume that she is allergic to it. The food may have been contaminated with bacteria which have given her 'food poisoning' (*see* **Diarrhoea, Gastro-enteritis and Food Poisoning**) or it may have contained additives she could not tolerate (*see* **Eating**/Commonsense about family eating: Food-additives). Lack of certain enzymes in her digestive system can make her intolerant of particular food constituents, such as lactose, while a few foods produce symptoms similar to those of gastro-intestinal allergy but by a different mechanism. Strawberries, for example, contain substances which directly release histamine. The child may react as if there was an allergen in the strawberries to which she had manufactured antibodies.

Nevertheless there are some children who are actually allergic to certain food proteins. Much the most important, in a western diet, is allergy to cow's milk protein.

It is only in recent years that this sort of intolerance has been recognized as a true allergic response and experts still hotly dispute the numbers of children affected and the importance of the condition. Some doctors – especially in the United States – believe that it is widespread and that a degree of intolerance which is too slight to be demonstrated by clinical tests and whose existence cannot therefore be proved (*see below*), may nevertheless be responsible for a wide range of behavioural and other difficulties. British authorities tend to be more cautious.

While a proper clinical diagnosis of gastro-intestinal allergy may be vital to the wellbeing of a baby who is not thriving, a vague diagnosis of 'milk intolerance', unbacked by clinical signs or positive tests, should not be used as a universal explanation for infant difficulties. Withdrawing milk and substituting a variety of more or less extreme diets and dietary restrictions sometimes appears to lessen toddler tantrums or even to improve a seven-year-old's behaviour at school. But it may be doing so by subtle psychological mechanisms which are nothing to do with relieving her digestion of a substance against which she had manufactured antibodies. Such a child may, for example, receive a great deal of extra parental attention during dietary experiments; it may be this attention which changes her behaviour. The attention may indeed be good for her but if it is attention she needs it is a pity that it should be focused on her stomach and bowels.

Breast-feeding and food allergies

Gastro-intestinal allergies are very rare in babies who are fed on nothing but breast milk during their early months and who continue to take their liquid milk from the breast when mixed feeding begins. Breast milk seems to reduce allergic tendencies in two ways:

The actual breast milk protects against the formation of food allergies. This is because it contains immunoglobins of the IgA class which are often deficient in the immune systems of very young babies. These IgAs are thought to provide a sort of 'protective lining' for the intestinal mucosa which reduces the likelihood of adverse reaction and antibody formation to food proteins.

Being given breast milk protects the baby against being given any other kind. If she does not meet cow's or goat's milk protein, soy protein or the gluten of wheat flour which is so often present in baby-cereals, she cannot manufacture antibodies against them.

Eventually, of course, every baby must meet 'foreign' proteins in her diet but if she does not do so until her own immune system is likely to be able to protect her, and even then does so with the added protection of continuing breast-feeding, the chances of her tolerating all of them easily are much enhanced. Every baby should be breast-fed if possible. For babies who are obviously at high risk of allergy (such as the children of atopic parents) the definition of 'possible' should perhaps be stretched to your personal limit (*see also* **Eating**/Types of foods for babies).

Looking for allergens in foods
Dietary proteins are absorbed through the intestinal wall. If a baby has developed antibodies to a particular protein it will cause clinical signs such as vomiting and diarrhoea and it will eventually alter the mucosa of the small intestine. This can be demonstrated if tiny fragments are taken by biopsy and examined under a microscope. Any baby with acute gastro-intestinal symptoms should be seen urgently by a doctor. It is when a baby has very mild but chronic digestive symptoms that parents may find themselves reluctant to embark on medical tests yet wondering whether they are feeding her something to which she is allergic.

The probability is highest if you or other close relations are atopic; if the baby herself has other allergic symptoms such as eczema; if she was never breast-fed and is now being put on a mixed diet or if she was breast-fed but is now being weaned. However mild her present digestive symptoms, do seek medical advice quickly if you still have breast milk available to her. If she has developed a gastro-intestinal allergy – even if it is not to cow's milk protein itself – reintroducing breast-feeding may lessen her symptoms (*see above*) even though it cannot un-make antibodies which she has already made.

If both the baby's history and symptoms strongly suggest an intestinal allergy, your doctor may want to proceed immediately to a biopsy so as to clinch the diagnosis and exclude other forms of food-intolerance. If the baby's symptoms are mild, however, he may prefer to explore the possibility and identity of a food-allergen by the use of 'elimination diets'. Such diets simply eliminate suspect foodstuffs from the baby's diet, one by one and for stated periods, so that parents and doctor can see whether her digestion and other symptoms are better when she is without one or more of them. The item first excluded is usually cow's milk. A child who is allergic to cow's milk protein is very likely to react in the same way to goat's milk and either a return to breast milk or a soy-based formula will probably be recommended. For an elimination diet to work as a diagnostic test as well as an allergen-avoider, *all* milk must be excluded. This means that you will have to guard the baby from licks of her brother's ice-cream, from rusks containing milk protein and from a vast range of commercial babyfoods.

If a milk-free diet produces dramatic improvement, the doctor will probably regard the diagnosis as made and the treatment as obvious (*see below*). If it does not produce improvement but he still regards intestinal allergy as likely, other food proteins may have to be excluded one by one.

Living with
elimination
diets

Sometimes elimination diets produce quick, clear and excellent results. Sometimes they do not. If you find yourself embarking on an elimination programme either with a baby or an older child, do bear the following points in mind:

A child must eat adequately. If your baby is to have nothing but soya-formula, do ensure that you understand its comparative calorie value and that she drinks enough to meet her probable needs. She may not like the taste. If your child is to eliminate milk, dairy produce and eggs, do ensure that school alternatives are adequate and/or that you yourself offer adequate replacements for long-established high-calorie habits like that milky drink at bedtime or that breakfast egg. Orange juice and toast may leave her hungry or even under-nourished.

Diets can be psychologically damaging. The baby who does not like soya-milk is being deprived of feeding-pleasure and you are being deprived of your pleasure in that pleasure. The toddler who may have no chocolate is deprived of something she may clearly associate with people being pleased with her and/or with 'treats'; she may think she is being punished. The child who may have no gluten (wheat protein) probably cannot eat at the homes of friends nor in school or in a restaurant. Her diet makes her feel different and may actually isolate her socially.

Elimination diets prove nothing without food challenges. No elimination diet, however effective it seems to be in improving symptoms, can *prove* that your child suffers from a particular gastro-intestinal allergy or other intolerance. An apparent improvement may be due to chance, to extra attention or to natural maturation. Or the original disorder may have been due to a naturally passing infective illness like gastro-enteritis.

If eliminating a particular food brings relief of symptoms, the child's body should subsequently be 'challenged' with that foodstuff to see whether the symptoms recur immediately, within hours or within days. If they do recur, the food is then withdrawn again. If the symptoms are again relieved, the point is made. But even so, many doctors will wish to repeat the challenge (unless biopsy is undertaken and demonstrates a difference in the intestinal mucosa with, and without, that foodstuff). An apparent recurrence of symptoms on first challenge can be due to another illness.

Elimination diets are extremely fashionable, especially in the United States where it is estimated that about one-third of all bottle-fed babies receive soya-milk instead of cow's milk formula. There is, perhaps, a generalized feeling in that society that much ill-health is caused by eating too much and eating food which is too 'rich'. The corollary can easily be that a diet which rigidly excludes certain items will do no harm and may do some good. A toddler, with mild but persistent diarrhoea, may be put on such a diet when in truth she requires no treatment other than simple tests to ensure that the diarrhoea is not due to infection. Elimination diets can only properly be used to diagnose and treat the highly specific results of sensitivity to highly specific food proteins. If they are used as a cure-all, as a hunch or because they are 'healthier anyway', they are wrongly used.

Even a proven need for such a diet will have a natural end. In gastro-intestinal allergy (and in many cases of proven intestinal intolerance) the child, however severely she is affected in infancy, will almost always become able to cope with the offending dietary item as she grows up. Do treat even the most clearly necessary dietary restrictions as temporary and do make sure, with your doctor's help, that periodic food challenges are offered to the child so that her dawning ability to cope is discovered as soon as possible. While there are adults who are made uncomfortable by a high intake of milk, there are very few who cannot tolerate the quantities used in ordinary cooking and catering.

Hay fever (allergic rhinitis)

Hay fever is a misnomer as the disorder is neither a fever nor connected especially with hay. Nevertheless it is under this name that most people classify all the various allergic symptoms which are confined to the nasal passages and the eyes and are properly named allergic rhinitis. The classic symptoms are a 'blocked' or 'stuffy' nose; sneezing and nasal discharge. Sometimes there is obvious inflammation of the eyes (conjunctivitis) but often the eyes simply itch so that the child rubs them and may, or may not, thus make them red. If the eyes are much involved, the child may have 'bags' under them so that he looks perpetually tired.

Allergic rhinitis can occur at any age and seems to be self-limiting so that whenever it begins, it seldom persists for more than ten to fifteen years. It can be seasonal or perennial (depending on the allergens, *see below*). While it can be associated with any other sign of allergy, it seems particularly associated with asthma but in a way which means that asthma and allergic rhinitis are seldom both active at the same time. A child sufferer from allergic rhinitis may (but may not) go on to experience asthma. An asthma sufferer may (but may not) have allergic rhinitis in adult life once he is free of the asthma.

While allergic rhinitis is regarded as a trivial nuisance (and even sometimes scornfully termed 'psychosomatic'), it is directly responsible for many days lost at school and at work and for much discomfort. It deserves energetic treatment which can often be highly successful.

Recognizing allergic rhinitis

Hay fever is often missed in children because they themselves tend to be very tolerant of the symptoms while their parents seem ready to accept that their child 'is always having colds' or 'suffers from catarrh'.

Although your child may look as if he has a cold you can distinguish the one from the other. In a cold the nose is 'blocked' by a thick discharge. In rhinitis it is 'blocked' by swelling of the nasal passageways. When your child's nose runs in a cold, you can see that the discharge is thick and white or yellowey but when it runs in rhinitis it is watery. When you stop to think about it, that watery discharge could not block the passageways and his feeling that he 'can't blow' has to be due to swelling. Eyes do not always itch in hay fever but they very seldom do so in a cold. If your child keeps rubbing his eyes, hay fever is more likely than infection.

Seasonal allergic rhinitis

Although children's colds do often seem to run into one another so that it is impossible to remember when the last one ended and this one began, if you think carefully you may find that a long-continued 'cold' always seems to occur at a particular time of year. Pollen allergy (true 'hay fever') is probably the most common and this will produce symptoms in spring and early summer. Allergy to moulds and spores is also quite common. This will lead to symptoms in the early autumn, when plants are dying down and vegetables are brought in for storage. Many of the children whose parents remark suspiciously that they 'always have a cold when it's time to go back to school after the summer holidays' suffer from this type of allergy.

Perennial allergic rhinitis

As the name suggests, this type tends to persist (either continuously or on and off) all the year round. While it may be due, or mainly due, to a particular allergen such as the house-mite in dust, it is often due to multiple allergens.

Treatment for allergic rhinitis

Seasonal allergic rhinitis, which may be due to a few identifiable allergens, may merit de-sensitization, but finding the allergen is not always easy – especially in children – nor always worthwhile. In young children, for example, skin-prick tests may yield negative results even though the mucosa of the nasal passages is hypersensitive to the allergen being tested. Pin-prick tests are not popular with many children and neither are the injections to which successful testing will lead. Treatment designed to reduce the allergic response at mucosal level and/or to reduce exposure to the allergen may be more appropriate.

Disodium cromoglycate, administered as a powder to be sniffed up the nose, is often effective, and can be used during a period of high risk, to prevent symptoms, too.

Topical steroids are also highly effective in reducing the whole inflammatory picture, but applied to the nose they will have no effect on the eyes so that eye drops may be needed as well. This use of steroids is considered remarkably safe with almost no absorption of the drug. The only side-effect which is at all likely is occasional nose-bleeding (*see* **Nosebleeds**).

Decongestant nose drops (both prescription and over-the-counter) are widely used but their effect is fleeting and use over long periods can actually damage the nasal mucosa. While they may be valuable in providing short-term relief from the feeling of nasal obstruction, they should probably be reserved for occasional 'emergencies'. Such drops can, for example, make it possible for a child to breathe normally through a movie or allow an adolescent to enjoy a party.

The commonest oral drugs prescribed for hay fever are anti-histamines. Their effect is limited in many people or the effective dose rendered unsuitable by the side-effect of drowsiness. But if symptoms (such as a cough caused by the discharge dripping down the throat) are bothersome at night, these drugs may serve a double-purpose of symptom-relief and sleep-inducement.

Avoiding allergens in hay fever

Exposure to the allergens responsible for seasonal rhinitis can often be reduced by quite simple measures which need not adversely affect the sufferer's life. For example, by listening to the broadcast pollen count he may be able to time his use of preventative medication and avoid ill-timed country walks . . . If autumn is his worst time, heavy exposure to mould spores can be avoided by abandoning mushroom and blackberry picking and passing over chores like potato storage. Sleeping with bedroom windows closed will also help, while air-filtration will help even more. Few families can afford to instal air-conditioning for the especial benefit of a hay-fever sufferer. But those with atopic children might take the existence of an air-conditioning system as a major point in favour of a new house or flat when they are moving anyway.

In perennial rhinitis the sufferer probably over-reacts to a wide variety of allergens. Measures to cut down exposure to the obvious ones such as house-dust (*see above* Asthma) will be worthwhile.

Whether rhinitis is seasonal or perennial, any sudden flare up, with streaming nose, constant sneezing, swelling and watering of the eyes, should lead to some careful thinking back over the day. Such a flare up often results from massive exposure to an allergen which is constantly present at a lower level. Hours spent queueing for the attention of a veterinary surgeon, for example, may lead to such a flare up in a patient who had not previously suspected that he was allergic to the family cat. A day spent picking blackberries or mushrooms may provoke a similar reaction in someone who had not realized that autumn mould spores were part of his trouble.

Urticaria

This is a general term for any allergic reaction which shows itself in the skin. The actual meeting between allergen and antibody may take place locally, or the skin may react to problems elsewhere in the body.

Urticaria (nettlerash for example) often appears and vanishes again within an hour or two. Nobody has the chance to find out what has caused it and, while the white weals on reddened skin may look dramatic and the itching may be intense, the whole matter is trivial.

Calamine lotion may be effective in relieving itching. If the weals are extensive, a lukewarm bath containing half a cup of sodium bicarbonate will be even more effective and far more enjoyable.

Long-lasting or recurrent urticaria

Occasionally a child (usually one who shows other signs of being highly allergic) has an episode of urticaria in which as fast as one set of weals die down, others come up. She may be swollen and itchy for days at a time. Another child may have very frequent episodes. In either instance the doctor may want to try and hunt down specific allergens. Often this is a food or a drug which, once identified, can be avoided. But sometimes the group of allergens responsible may be the inhaled ones which often cause asthma or hay-fever. If pollens and dusts are causing urticaria as well as other allergic symptoms, the urticaria may be a factor in the decision to pursue active treatment.

Papular
urticaria
Usually presents as weals together with spots and little blisters. They are usually distributed over the buttocks and legs. Secondary infection following scratching is common. This form of urticaria is usually a reaction either to insect bites or to mite bites. Its allergic nature is demonstrated by the fact that while other family members may be bitten (as by midges at a picnic, for example), only one individual develops this extreme reaction. A hydrocortisone cream and/or anti-histamines by mouth are often prescribed.

Affected individuals may benefit from wearing close-fitting clothing when insects are active in the evening and from using an insect-repellent product. Pets should also be carefully checked for parasites and the child should avoid places (such as hay-barns) where mites abound.

Angio-neurotic
oedema
(Giant Hives)
This is a less common but far more dramatic form of urticaria in which a single large area of skin and underlying tissue suddenly puffs up into an enormous white weal. Common sites include the area around an eye, lip, throat or penis. The swelling goes down in a few hours and the allergen is seldom discovered.

Very occasionally this sudden swelling involves the soft tissues of the throat and may then cause difficulty in breathing. For this reason it is wise to consult a doctor for angio-neurotic oedema although in practice the drama will often be over before he can see it. Any actual (as opposed to anticipated) difficulty in breathing should, of course, mean an immediate trip to the nearest hospital.

Anaesthesia *see* **Hospital**/Surgery.
Anal fissure *see* **Constipation**. *See also* **Soiling**.
Angio-neurotic oedema *see* **Allergy**/Urticaria.
Animal bites *see* **Accidents**/Bites and Stings.

Anorexia Nervosa (Slimmer's Disease)

Victims of this puzzling disorder starve themselves in the midst of plenty. They starve themselves while they lose any excess weight; they go on starving themselves while they become thin; they starve themselves while they become emaciated; a few starve themselves to death. The disorder contradicts commonsense attitudes to food and eating (*see* **Eating**/First principles) because, whilst trapped in it, victims' appetites no longer operate as a guide to food intake. The 'natural' drive to eat to satisfy hunger and thus to satisfy bodily needs, is overridden.

Anorexia nervosa has been given a great deal of publicity in recent years and the increase in the number of reported cases suggests an 'epidemic'. Some studies suggest that as many as one or two in every hundred girls will suffer from it during some part of their adolescence. We do not know whether the increase in numbers is real or whether it has appeared because of people's greater readiness to recognize a condition which has always been frequent. Certainly every parent should know something about it. Your own children will, hopefully, remain unaffected but they are quite likely to meet and be puzzled and disturbed by others who are less fortunate. Furthermore, it seems likely that the disorder is one which can sometimes be averted if a girl at risk is recognized early. Ignored until it is well-established, it is extraordinarily difficult to treat.

Public understanding is not helped either by the popular or the scientific names for this illness:

'Slimmer's Disease': Refers to the fact that the self-starvation sometimes begins with 'normal dieting'. The victim (almost always female and usually adolescent) begins to 'slim', often in collaboration with friends or as part of a school craze. She may or may not be fat. Like other adolescents, her slimming may be motivated by a general dissatisfaction with her body or by a desire to alter the shape of one particular part of it: an over-large bottom or breasts, for example.

The girl goes through the usual dieting difficulties at first, but, unlike most of her friends, eventually finds that she can stick to her chosen regime. She loses weight and achieves her target, but instead of relaxing the diet so that her weight stabilizes at its new level, she goes on with it so that her weight goes on dropping.

● By no means every victim enters anorexia nervosa in this way. Don't assume that your daughter is not at risk because she has never been overweight/interested in dieting. But don't assume either that she is at risk every time she declares that she must lose weight.

Anorexia nervosa: Literally means loss (or absence) of appetite for nervous reasons. This technical name is extremely misleading because anorexic girls have not lost their *appetites* at all. Most of them are ravenously hungry most of the time. **What they have lost is the ability to allow themselves to satisfy that appetite.** The distinction is of vital importance to anyone who is trying to recognize, live with or treat anorexia nervosa.

Causes of anorexia nervosa

Nobody knows exactly why some people become anorexic when most do not. We cannot pin-point a cause as we pin-point the organisms which are responsible for infectious diseases or the muscle fault which leads to a hernia. Instead, we have to look at *what anorexia nervosa seems to be about*.

Most doctors and psychiatrists concerned with the disorder would probably agree that most of the following are relevant to the condition, but the exact significance of each aspect would be disputed. Remember, as you go through these points, that at no time can we answer the question 'why?'. Why does one girl with this, that or the other kind of difficulty become anorexic when many others, with similar difficulties, do not? Why does one girl with this, that or the other kind of conflict 'choose' anorexia nervosa as a means of coping with it when others find different coping-mechanisms? We do not know the answer and indeed we may never know it because there probably is no simple answer. Different life-factors interact in different ways with different personalities and the end-products of the interactions are different. Your daughter's anorexic illness is unique, just as she herself is a unique individual.

Anorexia nervosa is about growing up. Although a few males, children and mature women develop anorexia nervosa, a majority of victims enter the condition during the first year or two after the menarche; a few enter it at about the time of puberty and a few more after their periods have been established for some time. Early adolescence is a time of inner uncertainty and conflict for most young people (*see* **Adolescence**) but anorexia nervosa is not a way of growing through that uncertainty and conflict but of retreating from it. This is true at many levels. At the here-and-now physical level, self-starvation actually undoes many of the visible signs of maturity. The anorexic girl loses her rounded breasts and hips and calves, returning almost to the shape typical of a pre-pubertal child. She also loses her monthly periods; those regular reminders of sexual maturity which may, for her, seem a 'curse'.

It is about dependence. At a deeper psychological level the self-starvation undoes many of the social and psychological expectations which go with physical maturity. It de-sexes her so that she need neither compete for sexual partners nor be sought after by them. It makes her the subject of much care and concern from her parents and thus puts off inner or outer pressure on her to become more independent of them. It gives her a rich and endless source of conflict with that concerned family which effectively replaces the more usual and age-appropriate fight for freedom from parental control.

It is about control. Anorexia nervosa requires enormous self-control from its victim who must starve herself against the full power of her body's hunger-drive. Her ability to maintain this control is one of the main 'rewards' she gets from the illness but her *fear of loss of control* is also the stick which drives her. In retrospect, parents often realize that their now-anorexic daughter was always an over-controlled and compliant child. Such children tend to set themselves high ideals, work hard to achieve them and bask in the parental approval which therefore surrounds them. They tend to be highly intelligent and to be seen as 'extremely sensible'. It is the more of a shock when parents are forced to accept that 'good' may have been 'too good'; that success may have been achieved out of fear of failure and that this is a girl who dare not allow herself even a little kick over the traces lest she find herself running wild.

It is, therefore, about pleasure. Pleasure, especially sensual pleasures such as sex, eating, physical luxury and all forms of self-indulgence, seem very dangerous to the anorexic patient who often clothes her fear in rather puritanical attitudes. Once again, parents may remember sadly that this near-adult who cannot allow herself to be warm or to rest (*see below*), was a child who was never greedy, never 'spoiled', never demanding of treats and possessions.

Recognizing anorexia nervosa   Anorexia nervosa is not a disease which a person 'gets' or 'catches' so that she is healthy one week and definitely and diagnosably ill the next. Rather, it is a condition into which a person moves, often rather gradually, so that there may never be a recognizable line marking the beginning of the disorder. Nevertheless, the earliest possible recognition, whether it comes first from the patient herself or from those who are close to her, may be important. If she can recognize her own general dissatisfaction/unhappiness and see that her 'dieting' is not truly an answer to it (although it is beginning to feel like an answer to her), she may be able to abandon it. The deeper she moves into the condition the tighter the grip which it will have upon her and the more difficult it will be for her to give it up and find other ways of coping with herself.

The following signs and symptoms apply to an adolescent girl who is indisputably in an anorexic condition. If you are worried about your own daughter or she is worried about herself or a friend, you may like to ask yourself 'to what extent and in what ways does she resemble this anorexic patient?' She may be like or unlike this 'typical' anorexic girl in any number of irrelevant ways; it is her similarity or dissimilarity along the dimensions set out here which is crucial.

Weight loss. All anorexics lose a great deal of weight although not everyone who loses a lot of weight is anorexic. If your daughter has not lost (and is not losing) substantially, then whatever you have to worry about it is not anorexia nervosa.

Many adolescents diet to lose weight while others lose due to other forms of illness. If your daughter is losing you will need to consider her weight in relation to other factors (*see below*) because weight loss *alone* is not diagnostic of anorexia nervosa. Severe weight loss, however, whether it is due to anorexia nervosa or not, certainly requires investigation and explanation.

How much weight loss is too much? (*See* **Growth**.) As a very rough rule-of-thumb, check on a standard weight chart (as published, for example, by life insurance firms) for the average weight for a girl of her age and height and compare that figure with what she weighs now. If she is still within, say, ten per cent of that average then even if she has lost a tremendous amount, her weight alone gives no cause for alarm. She may have begun to diet while genuinely obese; she may have needed to lose three stone. Even if she was not fat to begin with, a weight loss which leaves her within ten per cent of the average is fair enough because there is normal variation of at least that amount around the average figure. You need worry only if she is still losing.

If her current weight puts her at fifteen per cent less than the average then there is reason for concern. Why is she so different from other girls of her age and height?

A current weight as much as twenty per cent below the average will already be affecting her general health. If weight loss continues it will soon cause a medical emergency.

In real terms, then, you might reckon that a girl whose 'expected weight' was 9 stone (126 lbs) should give cause for concern if her weight dropped below 8 stone (112 lbs) and would be becoming progressively iller as it dropped towards 7 stone (98 lbs).

If the 'expected weight' is 8 stone (112 lbs), the comparable figures would be around 7 stone (98 lbs) and 6 stone (84 lbs).

Amenorrhea. Normal menstruation requires an adequate bodyweight. Female anorexics do not menstruate regularly, at least until the disorder is coming to an end. Therefore if your daughter *is* menstruating normally (and is not on the Pill so that bleeding is induced) she is not, at this time, severely anorexic.

There are, of course, many reasons other than anorexia why she may not be menstruating. Worry about the possibility of self-starvation may pre-date the start of her periods or the weight loss may begin during the early months following the menarche when menstruation is often irregular anyway (*see* **Adolescence**/Menstruation). Furthermore, serious physical illness, emotional stress or pregnancy may account for her amenorrhea. But if menstruation was previously established and has now ceased in conjunction with major weight loss, anorexia nervosa is a likely cause.

Attitudes to weight and to eating. If your daughter is similar to the girl with anorexia nervosa in the sense that she has lost more than fifteen per cent of her expected bodyweight and has stopped menstruating, consider her attitudes to weight which you will probably discover most easily through her attitudes to eating and to food in general. Some or all of the following will probably seem to apply to her if she is anorexic.

Observation of her eating habits suggests that she is actively avoiding weight gain, whatever she may *say* concerning her wish to replace some of the weight she has lost. She will probably avoid carbohydrate-rich and fatty foods, will take smaller portions than those around her and will often refuse snacks, treats or extras others are having. If she announces a change in food-tastes it will invariably be a change which reduces her calorie intake. She may start to take coffee black, tea without sugar, or grapefruit in place of breakfast cereal. She will probably announce that she has 'gone off' any high-calorie foods for which she previously had a passion. Your chocolate cake will no longer be popular.

In other words, she behaves like a dedicated slimmer but can be distinguished from the 'normal' slimmer both by the fact that she is behaving like this when she is already far too thin, and by the fact that she pretends to agree that she needs to put on weight rather than take off more.

Weight is fascinating to her and she cannot resist talking and reading about it as well as privately thinking about it. She is obsessively interested in other people's figures and she will read diet sheets, weight charts and calorie guides endlessly, even those which are published in magazines and comics which would not normally be to her taste. She is probably an expert calorie-counter. She may be truly revolted by people who seem to her obese (since they represent what she fears might happen to her if she allowed herself to eat freely) and she may make it embarrassingly clear that she finds her own emaciated shape preferable to the bulges of those around her.

Food, which she cannot allow to herself, is nevertheless an obsession with her. She may spend a great deal of time cooking for others, reading recipe books and insisting on being the family expert in cake- or sweet-making. Often she will be highly possessive not only of her role as cook but also of the dishes she makes; having cooked the sweet she insists on being allowed to serve it. She may find it difficult to keep away from places where food is sold or prepared so that she wanders around supermarkets and hangs around the kitchen during the preparation of meals she is not going to eat.

Despite all this interest, the normal consumption of ordinary food may revolt her. Sometimes she will watch every mouthful taken by other family members as if asking 'are you going to eat more? And more? And still more?' She can be an embarrassing companion at the dinner table.

Some 'failures' in her control over her food intake may occur. Sometimes these take the form of occasional 'binges' so that having allowed herself a sip of milk she drains the whole container and another one and then punishes herself by even greater abstinence in the following days (*see below*). Sometimes her 'failures' are of a more frequent but more minor kind. She may pick with her fingers at left-over food in the refrigerator, surreptitiously lick cooking utensils or nibble tiny fragments off the biscuits in the tin. This kind of nibbling is secret, not only from everyone else but from herself. She is furious if it is called to her attention.

If your daughter seems, in all the above respects, to be in a state of anorexia nervosa, you will probably also notice other signs of her determination to control and discipline her body.

Attitudes to other aspects of her physical self. Many anorexics are fitness-fanatics, aspiring athletes, dancers, joggers, or simply people who take pleasure in making their bodies do their bidding. Even as your daughter's weight drops and her muscles vanish so that arms and legs are stick-like, she may actually increase the demands she puts on herself. She may, for example, insist that she is stronger than anyone else in the family and try to prove it by being the one who carries the heaviest boxes or singlehandedly pushes the stuck car. Success gives her great pleasure but she earns it at an appalling price paid in pain and effort. Easy physical pleasures are anathema to her even when they are not associated with food. She will seldom lounge in the sun, choose a comfortable chair or enjoy a luxurious lie-in on a Sunday morning.

What to do if it seems likely that your daughter is in a state of anorexia nervosa

There is no known 'cure' for anorexia nervosa in the sense of an accepted treatment which will certainly bring the condition to an end. Recommendations therefore cannot be absolute; they can only be ways in which an inevitably long and hard struggle can be begun. They are also a great deal easier to give than they are to carry out. If your daughter is anorexic neither you nor she are going to have an easy time and anyone who offers you a simple cure is a charlatan.

You may find some of the following suggestions helpful; but you may find that their principal use is to be angrily rejected thus helping you to clear your mind for your own ways of proceeding.

If she is in a state of anorexia nervosa, try to face it now rather than waiting a bit and then a little longer and then a little longer still. Anorexia is exceedingly difficult for parents to face because the disorder seems so *senseless*. The girl is underweight and hungry. The food is there. Why can't she just get on and eat it? It is also hurtful: she has always been loved, nurtured, 'fed' (both physically and emotionally), why does she now insist on starving herself and thus rejecting those who care? Often it is also shatteringly disappointing because parents have had every reason to see this as an 'ideal daughter' and to flatter themselves that they were not facing the kinds of adolescent rebellion common in the families of her peers. Now, apparently all of a sudden, all that goodness has turned itself into a crisis and not just the kind of crisis which might lead to an abortion or to dropping out of school, but a kind which might actually kill her. No wonder parents veer wildly between furious anger and guilty despair.

It is probably even more difficult for the anorexic girl herself to face the reality of her condition. While she may be able *intellectually* to agree that her starved body and absent menses are neither normal nor desirable she *feels* that they are infinitely preferable to that norm. Sometimes the satisfaction she takes in her concave stomach, flat chest and ability to feel 'full up' after eating three lettuce leaves makes her appear smug and self-satisfied. It is important to remember that her feelings are rooted in fear. Her behaviour is governed by her phobia of weight-gain and of the total loss of control which she feels will inevitably follow the smallest relaxation of her rules. Her satisfaction is not truly over being 'better than anyone else', but over avoiding being worse than anyone else.

Parents have a tendency to confuse the criteria which suggest anorexia nervosa (such as those suggested above) with criteria concerning a girl's general happiness and well-being. While the latter are obviously vitally important, they are not relevant to recognition of the disorder. Try not to let yourself beg the issue with statements like: 'She's so depressed just now we can't expect her to eat' or 'She'll be better once her exams are over' or 'She's far too intelligent/sensible/responsible to let this go on for long'. If she is truly anorexic the depression will not miraculously lift and free her, exams or no exams, and she would not have become anorexic if her intelligence and good sense could have protected her from the condition. Burying your head in the sand will buy you nothing but more misery.

Victims will almost always seize on any such excuse which is offered to them by parents because parents whose heads *are* buried in the sand offer them time. Time to lose a bit more of that dreaded weight; time in which the fearful prospect of gaining weight need not be faced.

The disorder will almost always be faced first by parents (or other close, concerned people) rather than by its victim. Once faced, it needs discussion because no 'cure' can even begin until the patient can see at least some reason for change.

Early attempts to raise the subject are usually met with hostility and denial. All too often the discussion deteriorates into a hysterical slanging match in which parents find themselves expressing their own hurt and disappointment and daughters sidestep every real issue with screams of 'you're all against me'. Nobody can tell anyone else how to avoid that kind of no-win situation but it sometimes helps parents to retain their calm if they can remember:

That she is the child of both of them and therefore that it is imperative that they remain in alliance with each other rather than allowing her disturbance to force a wedge between them.

That her behaviour and her defensive anger are driven by fear and therefore to answer it with anger is no more appropriate than it would be to deal angrily with a child in a night-terror.

That whatever charges she may lay or excuses she may produce, the facts of her weight loss, amenorrhea and attitudes to food remain abnormal. Don't be thrown off-course by being told that it is all your fault for moving house, getting divorced, or whatever. Parents are always easily thrown into guilt by their growing children but the fact remains that most children survive every kind of trauma without having to take refuge in anorexia. It makes no difference what your daughter thinks caused her trouble; the trouble remains and must remain the focus of your discussion.

At this early stage, you may need to prove your points by, for example, insisting that your daughter weigh herself/look at the weight chart you used in your thinking/go over with you what she is eating/accept evidence, such as nibbled biscuits and so forth, of her unsatisfied hunger. This kind of insistent talk feels highly intrusive and will no doubt be so categorized by the sufferer who hopes that she can thus shame you into 'letting her alone'. But someone must intrude for the sake of her health and safety. Leave her as much dignity and privacy as you can, but bolster yourself with your conviction that the situation is serious.

Usually some measure of agreement can be reached to the effect that there is a real problem. Many anorexics give in thus far rather easily because, once again, they hope that by accepting what is said to them they can be 'let alone' and thus avoid having to accept food as well as words.

If your daughter quickly admits that she has 'let it all go a bit far' and announces that she will 'do something about it', you will have to judge the genuineness of both the acceptance and the intention. If they are genuine then she is entitled (unless she is already seriously ill) to time to attempt self-cure. Success is not impossible but it is unusual. The lower her weight and the longer the condition has lasted, the less likely it is that she will succeed alone. However, unless she is already in physical danger from her low weight, it may be important for her to 'try' because finding that she cannot change (or cannot truly want to change) her behaviour may eventually help her to accept advice from an outside source.

Be prepared, though, for every kind of deception. Deceit is the rule rather than the exception in anorexia nervosa and it is often the aspect of the disorder which places the heaviest strain on family relationships. Your beloved daughter will probably lie to you about what she has eaten; hide food under the pillow, pour milk down the lavatory, lie about the reading on the scales, drink pints of water and avoid the lavatory for hours before she weighs herself in front of you, and earnestly discuss all manner of imaginary plans for gaining weight. She will betray you, if she has to, in other ways, too. If the plans for more sensible eating include a packed lunch at school because that would be 'easier to eat', she will let you get up in the morning and make it for her and then throw it away, day after day. If the plans include letting you serve her portions at meals she will let you try but fight you every teaspoon of the way. And, wherever food has important social connotations, she will let you down. Take her to a restaurant for dinner with your boss and you can be sure that there will be some kind of fuss over the food; offer the tiniest slice of her brother's birthday cake 'to wish him luck' and you can predict her refusal.

Unless you are a saint you will sometimes be angry and that does not matter; she knows how she should behave, wishes that she could and must face the reality of her failure to do so. But you may be able to stay basically on her side – which does matter – if you keep reminding yourself that she is driven not by the obstinacy and deliberate 'naughtiness' which you see, but by fear and irrational panic. *That innocent cup of milk frightens her* and when she is in a state of panic she will do almost anything to walk around her fear.

If your daughter is going to manage to work her way out of the anorexic state with only the help she can get from you and from her friends, she will probably do so fairly quickly. You can certainly give her time and space to do it her own way, however much trouble the disorder is making for her and between you all, *if her weight is rising*.

Seeking help for anorexia nervosa

Most anorexics, especially those who have been caught within the disorder for six months or more, will eventually have to seek outside help. Seek it urgently if she begins to alternate periods of eating as little as possible with periods of 'bingeing', even if the occasional over-eating means that her weight is only falling a little.

Seek it more urgently still if she 'binges' but manages to prevent this 'indulgence' from adding any weight either by making herself vomit or by taking vast doses of laxatives. Unfortunately, many anorexics manage the improbable feat of vomiting several times each day without any member of their highly concerned family being aware of it. But keep an eye out. Vomiting and/or purgation, in association with very low weight, can quickly disturb the body's biochemistry to a dangerous extent.

If her weight drops to twenty per cent or more below the average for her age and height, she is likely to be increasingly unwell and less and less able to make decisions or hold on to the sustained effort which would be necessary to break out of the condition. Help is therefore urgent from the physical point of view and urgent psychologically, too, as the longer she goes on with her internal battle without success the more helpless and despairing she will feel and the more she will need the prop of her anorexia.

A weight loss of thirty-five per cent of the average may itself be life-threatening. This means that a girl whose expected weight is around 9 stone (126 lbs) may be in real and immediate danger of death if her weight drops to 6½ stone (91 lbs) while a girl with an expected weight of 8 stone (112 lbs) will be in real danger around 5½ stone (77 lbs). You may read newspaper reports of anorexic girls admitted to hospital at bodyweights as low as 4½ stone (63 lbs) but do not let these convince you that your daughter's 6 stone (84 lbs) is 'not too bad for her condition'. How bad it is depends on what a girl of her height normally weighs.

Unfortunately there is no magic which will help every anorexic and her family, as the surgeon can help everyone with an inflamed appendix. Usually the best starting point is the family doctor, especially if he has known the girl herself since childhood. If she is willing to seek help but cannot bear to approach the family doctor, perhaps because he knows you as well as her, she might be able to make a direct approach to an adolescent counselling service or even to the casualty department at the local hospital. Her own doctor will have to be brought into any decisions about treatment, however, so persuade her to let him play his proper role from the beginning if you possibly can.

What that doctor will suggest depends on his knowledge and understanding of anorexia nervosa, his view of your daughter's immediate physical condition and the facilities which are available locally.

Treatment approaches in anorexia nervosa

The treatment of anorexia nervosa has two main aims:

The restoration of a 'safe' and eventually a 'normal' weight and therefore of an ordinarily balanced diet.

Loss of the weight-phobia and therefore psychological readjustment which will allow the victim to find alternative ways of dealing with the biological maturity which increasing weight will rekindle.

Doctors and psychiatrists vary widely in the relative emphasis which they place on these two aspects of a 'cure' as well as in the methods they use to try and bring them about, but all would agree that both are essential. It is useless, for example, to ensure that the girl regains her lost weight if nothing is done to help her lose her weight-phobia. As soon as she is freed from close supervision she will lose all that she has gained. On the other hand, it may be useless to take an entirely psychological approach to the disorder because the time taken to help the girl free herself of the weight-phobia may be longer than her body can survive without more food.

Professionals also vary in their feelings about attempting to help anorexic girls while they continue to live at home. While nobody can doubt that a girl's home situation and relationships within her family are relevant to the disorder, some doctors believe that removal from home into a hospital setting is a necessary first step even if she is not in dire physical straits. Others believe that problems within the home are best faced as they are lived, often with all members of the family being involved in the girl's treatment. Such a doctor might only admit to hospital a girl who was in need of physical treatment and he might keep her there only until her weight had increased to a point where her life was no longer at risk.

Hospital treatment for anorexia nervosa

Hospital treatment may include any, or any combination, of the following approaches:

A 'contract' between doctor and patient in which a 'target weight' is agreed; the patient agrees to stay in hospital and follow the path prescribed for her towards that target. The doctor agrees to guard her against her greatest fear: that if she starts eating normally at all she will become a glutton and obese. He guarantees that while insisting that she eat 'enough', he will neither encourage nor allow her to eat 'too much'.

Bed-rest until an agreed amount of weight has been regained.

Sedation to make enforced rest more tolerable.

A diet designed to increase her weight at a stated weekly rate or an ordinary hospital diet to accustom her to *normal* eating.

A variety of sanctions to ensure that she does in fact eat the food; these may range from close friendly supervision by trained nursing staff to a system under which the patient earns privileges (such as permission to get up, have visitors, etc.) by eating.

Individual psychotherapy in which she has regular meetings with one psychiatrist who will talk with her and help her to come to terms with her current situation/treatment and thence with the difficulties which led to her weight-phobia.

Group psychotherapy (often called Ward Meetings) in which all the patients (who may all be anorexics if the unit is a special one or who may include people with a wide range of emotional difficulties if the hospital is a general one) meet under the 'chairmanship' of a psychiatrist, often with the nursing staff as well. Discussions may be structured by the staff or left open for patients but will be designed to enable each one to use the experiences and support of all the rest.

Occupational therapy which may mainly be intended to keep patients pleasantly occupied or which may be an integral part of overall treatment. Art or drama therapy, for example, may be used to provide the anorexic with new ways to express her feelings and fears within the safety of a controlled environment.

● It is easy for parents to feel that a hospital is not doing anything positive for their anorexic daughter. If you find yourself thinking 'all they do is give her her meals; I can do that and they'd be better meals too,' do remember that the hospital staff are trying to help your daughter to live with a self which must change. Such a process is inevitably long, slow and almost invisible. The 'positive action' for which you long – injections, X-rays, transfusions, pills – is not appropriate to this kind of emotional illness. If you feel that she might do better at home by all means discuss your feelings, but she did not eat those meals you provided, did she?

● Concerned parents, who may have been closely involved for many months in their daughter's struggle with anorexia, often feel desperately cut-off when she is admitted to hospital. Sometimes the sense of isolation is increased because the girl herself and/or her doctors suggest that visits should be kept down for a while. Attempts to discuss what is happening with her doctor will often be met with a polite version of 'no comment'. Parents are often left with the feeling that nobody thinks they matter any more and/or that 'they' believe that the parents are responsible for their daughter's problems.

The psychiatrist who is treating your daughter must have her trust and therefore must guard her confidences. He cannot talk to you as well as to her unless special 'family sessions' at which she too is present, are arranged. He, in this sense, 'belongs to' your daughter so the answer is for you to have someone who belongs to you, too. If you discuss your feelings about the situation either with your own doctor or with a senior member of staff at the hospital, they will probably arrange for you to be seen at regular intervals by a member of staff, such as a social worker, who is connected with the treatment team but not actually treating your daughter.

Coping with anorexia nervosa at home   Whether your daughter is trying to reverse her condition without outside help, being treated as an out-patient or trying to maintain at home gains made in hospital, much of her struggle to eat will take place at home. Obviously you should be given every opportunity to discuss your role with those who are advising you; obviously too you will wish to behave in ways which your daughter feels will be helpful. The following may, however, be useful as discussion points or food for thought.

Your daughter's inner struggle is between her hungry body's demand for food (and her knowledge of 'normal' eating, health, menstruation and so forth), and her phobia of normal weight. She is convinced that were she to begin to let herself eat she would lose control and get fatter and fatter and fatter.

Your role is to reinforce the one and help combat the other. In playing this role you will largely take that internal struggle onto yourself so that your daughter tends to feel that it is you she is fighting.

It is an essential condition of progress that *she come to accept the battle as her own* (this is one important reason why she may require to get away from home into hospital). It is important, therefore, that whenever she can discuss matters rationally she agree to (or, better still ask for) feeding, and that all concerned remain aware that *when she eats she does so for herself and not for you*. Likewise, when she does not eat it is herself whom she attacks and when she deceives, by vomiting or hiding food, it is her own body she is depriving not her relationship with you.

This appallingly difficult role may be easier if you can remember that you will be accepted as a trustworthy ally rather than an enemy if you are seen as *a reliable controller rather than as a feeder*. Projecting her own battle onto you, she will tend to see you as someone who will produce more and more fattening and luxurious food; press it upon her; be pleased with every mouthful she eats and the more pleased the more she eats. If she does feel this about you then you *are* the enemy. She needs to feel that you are concerned only that she eat an adequate diet; that you would be as disapproving of over-eating as you are of self-starvation; as angry over a fridge raided for a binge as over a bedtime drink hidden behind the mirror; as appalled by a gain of a stone in a week (the kind of gain she may have nightmares about) as you are by a loss of yet another two or three pounds.

While nobody can tell anybody else how to convey attitudes and feelings to people they love, you might find some of the following useful:

Don't serve a special diet of either fattening foods or foods she especially likes. She is not suffering from *loss of appetite* therefore an especially delightful dish will not tempt her to eat any more than ordinary food will. On the contrary, the more delightful the food the more her hungry body will yearn for it and the more frightened she will be. Serve whatever meals are ordinary in your household and pay neither more (nor less) attention to her fads than you do to those of other family members. If she has always hated fish there is no point serving it now but don't leave the butter out of your usual recipe because she has decided that she cannot eat butter.

Expect her to eat that food normally: make sure that your expectations work both ways so that she is 'allowed' neither to eat less of one item *nor more of another*. She must have the rice, the bread or the potatoes, but at the same time she may not have more than her ordinary share of the salad.

Don't introduce special food-supplements and diet-drinks unless her doctor suggests it. A mug of a high-calorie beverage may be an easy way to get some food into her but she will be treating it like medicine and feel that she is being 'fattened'. She has to learn to treat food as food and to feel that nobody is trying to conceal extra calories in what she takes.

Discourage nibbling between meals at least until ordinary meals are being eaten. Of course little bits picked off plates or out of saucepans will increase her calorie intake and you may therefore feel that you should turn a blind eye. Don't. You have to try and help her towards normal eating patterns and normal social behaviour towards food. If you would not allow the dog to steal bits and pieces or the toddler to pick chocolate off the dessert in the refrigerator, she should not do so either.

Discourage eccentric cooking and/or eating behaviour. Unless she would normally cook this meal for everyone or eat that meal alone in her room, she should not do so now.

Keep realities firmly in view when she produces one wild theory after another about food and diet. She may, for example, suddenly announce that it is better for people not to drink at mealtimes. She probably hopes to reduce the feeling of fullness which eating gives her and which she dreads. Acknowledge that, by all means, but don't accept the basic premise, which is nonsense.

Keep realities about her in view, too. The established anorexic often has a genuinely distorted perception of her own size, for example. She may feel enormous when in fact she is emaciated. She may also find it genuinely difficult to perceive portions of food normally. She feels that her plateful is vast when in fact it is smaller than the plateful being eaten by her eight-year-old brother. Acknowledge the feelings but assert the reality.

Plan how you will cope with discussion about food, eating and diet together with arguments and scenes about meals and snacks and long serious conversations about plans for reform. If you do not, they can come to take up almost all a family's time and psychic energy. Obviously this is both abnormal and damaging to all concerned. Yet equally obviously these topics cannot simply be banned when they are of central and highly emotional interest. It sometimes helps to formalize them and to find some agreed authorities to whom points of argument can be referred. For example, discussions of food and progress over eating might, by agreement, be scheduled for after the evening meal and frowned on, for all members of the family including you, at other times. Arguments over food quantities and nutrients might, by agreement, be resolved by weighing and by reference to calorie tables. Your mutual goal, in terms of her regaining weight, might also be formalized so that her daily intake of calories is agreed with a lower and an upper limit, and her weekly weight is ascertained at a stated weighing.

Some people may feel that all this places abnormal stress on eating and weight and therefore contradicts the drive to normality. But limits and limited goals also provide reassuring evidence to the anorexic that she is not simply being 'fattened' in an open-ended progression to obesity and loss of control. Furthermore, since these topics *are* abnormally interesting to the family, a mildly abnormal acknowledgement of the fact may be less pathological than allowing them to submerge all other topics of family concern.

Danger signals
in ongoing
anorexia nervosa

Anorexia nervosa is a disorder which may last for years. Its victims commonly pursue a hilly course so that your daughter may reach a plateau on which her weight is stabilized, if low, and her fear apparently underground, only to start downhill again into a valley of crisis out of which she will again have to fight her way uphill.

Hopefully, she will be in regular contact with a doctor or psychiatrist who, even during her more stable times, will monitor her progress and take from you the responsibility for her safety. But there may well be times when she is either discharged from or reluctant to pursue such medical contact and, furthermore, when she is either not weighing herself regularly or is not telling you her weight or true weight. It may help you to know some of the common signs which suggest that anorexia nervosa is getting a renewed grip:

Increase in over-activity. While physical activity is a notable feature of anorexia nervosa, with its victims maintaining 'fitness programmes' and a falsely inflated view of their own strength and endurance even when starvation has reduced both their energy and actual muscle bulk to very low levels, a sudden increase in this phenomenon is often a danger sign. The girl may insist on taking over heavy tasks from her healthy brother; she may walk when she could ride and run when she could walk and/or she may suddenly add a new routine of formalized exercises or jogging into her day. Such behaviour is sometimes due to a sudden realization of her own increasing weakness and a typical but erroneous belief that she can overcome that weakness by sheer effort and will; by superhuman control over a body which is letting her down.

There is a kind of restlessness which may be confused with deliberate over-activity although it is actually part of the recognized syndrome of starvation. Just as a starving animal will fight to get to its feet again and again rather than lie still and conserve its draining energy, so the anorexic approaching crisis often becomes unable to rest or relax. She may stay up later; sleep less soundly, wake earlier and be unable to sit down for long enough to complete her homework or watch a television programme.

Lack of concentration goes with that kind of restlessness because nothing which the anorexic sets out to do can keep her body still or keep her mind off its compulsive thoughts about food. Many anorexics find that even school or other academic work – usually their main source of success – becomes impossible under these circumstances and the straight-A student may flunk her examinations or fail to hand in assignments to the amazement of all who know her.

Inability to make decisions. As the anorexic reaches the weight which is her personal borderline with danger, she becomes increasingly unable to cope with even the minutiae of daily life. You will probably notice this most in the difficulty she has in making even the least important decision. She may ask you whether she should have a bath, go to bed, wear that dress or go to school . . . But even having asked you she will often be unable to decide whether or not to take your advice. If you suddenly find that you have spent a large chunk of time discussing issues which are utterly trivial and entirely your daughter's personal business anyway, be alerted. If she does not ask you what she should do she may ask herself and answer in pathetic lists and timetables to cover each day. If you find a written schedule starting 'get up; clean teeth . . . etc.', worry.

Increase in sensitivity to cold. While people of very low bodyweight are almost always sensitive to cold, the anorexic approaching crisis often reaches a point where her body is almost incapable of keeping itself warm irrespective of the outside temperature. Her need to avoid any self-indulgence will probably prevent her from using an electric blanket or even from wearing the extra clothes which would help her to be comfortable, but when she reaches a point where she is obviously half-frozen even when the weather and the room are warm, beware.

Other physical phenomena. A family can become so accustomed to an anorexic daughter's emaciated appearance that it is only 'noticed' when a parent returns home after an absence or, perhaps, sees a photograph taken on last month's holiday. But apart from her extreme thinness, certain other physical developments, while unimportant in themselves, may suggest that her weight is actually dropping yet again.

Hair is a give-away. The hair on her head tends to become thin and lank while an extra growth of very fine new hair (laguna) may appear on her face, arms and body.

Poor circulation is common and therefore minor physical complaints such as chilblains are common, too. But if her hands and feet actually look bluish or become blue with cold and then remain a bad colour for hours after she is warm again, it is likely that she is reaching a physical limit.

Frequent headaches, in a girl who has not been previously liable to them, may suggest that her body's biochemistry is becoming disturbed.

Complaints of abdominal pain (sometimes severe enough to raise questions about appendicitis or some other abdominal emergency) often arise when the bodyweight drops even lower than usual. It may be that the girl's digestive system tries to 'close down' and therefore produces discomfort when food *is* put into it; it may be that in this state the girl is so conscious of food in her stomach that she perceives the feelings of digestion as pain. Whatever its cause, the phenomenon does suggest renewed trouble.

While the above events may arise as part of a repeating pattern of weight loss, weight gain, stability and renewed weight loss, certain others may appear as new developments in the disorder itself. If the girl is under even the most long-range and/or intermittent medical supervision, they must be brought to the attention of her doctor. If she is not, then it is urgent that help should be sought:

Vomiting and/or diarrhoea. These are often self-induced, with a finger in the throat or vast doses of laxatives, by anorexics who use them as a means either of getting rid of food which has been forced on them or of food which they have 'succumbed to'. Such behaviour is usually kept extremely secret but if it should come to your attention, you cannot afford to respect your daughter's privacy. Serious imbalances of body-chemistry can quickly follow. Of course, the new vomiting and/or diarrhoea may be due to an infection. But if it is, medical help is still urgent. A starved body cannot afford such loss of food and fluid.

Bingeing. Sudden *excesses* of eating may have been part of your daughter's anorexia from the beginning, but if they have not, their beginning is a serious development. Don't allow yourself to feel that three pints of milk and a loaf of bread, all taken in ten minutes, is a sign of returning health. It is not.

Fluid-restriction. Although this is rare, some anorexics reach a point where they cannot eat less than they are eating nor lose any more weight than they have lost. They realize that by not taking in fluid they can avoid the dreaded feeling of fullness which can follow even a glass of water into a starved stomach. Limiting fluids over a day or two produces a (to them) gratifying result on the scales but the resulting dehydration is exceedingly dangerous.

Recognizing recovery from anorexia nervosa

If your daughter is caught in anorexia for two or three or more years, she will not emerge from it as the same person. She will have changed, not only because of the disorder but also because the passing of time has changed her expectations of herself and her relationship with the outside world. If she became ill when she was fourteen and begins to recover when she is eighteen she will have 'lost' her adolescence by the time it is over. You have to look for a new young woman rather than for that schoolgirl.

She will be 'cured' or 'over it' when, and only when, those crucial dimensions describing anorexia nervosa (*see above*) are all reversed. She will be of normal weight (say within ten per cent below or above the average for her age and height), and she will menstruate with reasonable regularity. Her attitudes to food and to eating will be within normal limits for her chosen social group and what she eats will be dictated by appetite, habit and preference rather than by fear of weight gain.

Obviously such a 'cure' is not one which can come about suddenly. For example, even if she regains her lost weight comparatively quickly, her menstrual periods may not return immediately and may take some months to become regular. And while *some* change in her attitudes to eating must have taken place to allow the weight gain, it may take her a long time to lose all the quirks which have come to be associated with food and to discover relaxed pleasure in eating.

It is important that people close to the recovering anorexic should not expect miracles nor conformity. If she is now to be an ordinarily healthy young woman she must, above all, have the autonomy and independence which she could not use while she was ill. She must, for example, be 'allowed' to choose to stay slim, to be a vegetarian or to continue to dislike sweets. If everyone around her continues to regard any food preferences or refusals as a danger signal, she may tend to find herself wondering, all over again, whether there is a conspiracy to make her fatter than anyone has ever been before.

Once she carries enough weight to be safe and healthy and once she *wants* to take responsibility for herself, hand it to her with heartfelt thanks and the hope that her newly grown-up self will find some other way of coping with the stresses ahead.

Antibiotics *see* **Infection**/Antibiotics and sulphonamides; The pros and cons of antibiotics in undiagnosed infection.
Antibodies *see* **Immune Response; Immunization; Infection.** *See also* **Allergy.**
Anti-toxin *see* **Tetanus.**

Anxiety, Fears and Phobias *see also* **School**/School phobia

Anxiety and fears

Although anxiety and fear are unpleasant feelings, they are necessary ones. Feeling afraid warns the individual of possible danger just as feeling pain warns her of possible bodily damage (*see* **Pain and Pain Control**). But, just as a child can receive inaccurate and/or excessive pain signals, so she can receive inappropriate anxiety and fear signals. Parents cannot hope, and should not try, to rear children who never experience these horrible feelings, but they can do a great deal to ensure that children are well-equipped to interpret, understand and cope with them.

Unfortunately our society tends to admire tough, adventurous, 'fearless' children and therefore many parents try to 'teach' these qualities by teasing and jollying children who are anxious, and by laughing or scoffing at their fears. Nothing could be more likely to produce an anxious and fearful child. A better understanding of the roots of anxiety and fear may lead to the gentler handling which may truly produce a secure and confident person.

The roots of fear   Adults' basic anxieties and fears are often difficult to see and understand because we all learn to cover them up, to hide from them and even to hide them from ourselves. Babies and young children have had neither the time nor the experience to develop such defences. Their fears and anxieties are right there on the surface for all to see.

The 'basic fear' is, of course, the fear of being attacked, hurt, killed. Every baby has a strong will to live and reacts with fear to any life-threat.

Parents, knowing that nothing would ever be permitted to threaten their beloved baby and that they themselves would lay down their lives for her, often do not allow for the instinctive nature of her basic fears or for the fact that she cannot know that her world is a safe place. When your baby jumps, screams, pales and shakes because you have dropped a saucepan lid close beside her, remind yourself that she cannot know the harmless source of the sound. Remind yourself, if you like, that back in more primitive times the sound might have been that of a hungry tiger leaping through the brush. When she reacts with panic to being put down in her cot a little carelessly, so that her head falls back before her spine is fully supported by the mattress, remind yourself that her ancestors were more physically developed than she is and were carried on the backs of mothers far hairier than you. Her panicky clutching would, in those times, have enabled her to save herself, by grabbing handfuls of hair, from a fall which might otherwise have killed her. Notice, too, that while she always reacts to pain with displeasure – snatching away the part that is pricked by the doctor's needle, for example – she only sometimes reacts to pain with fear as well. She does so if the pain occurs in a violent context. If you accidentally bang her head on the doorframe as you carry her through, she will howl from fear as well as pain. If you are unlucky enough to touch her hand with a cigarette she will probably protest only briefly.

While even the youngest baby is programmed to react with instinctive fear to any obvious threat, older babies and young children need a much broader fear-reaction to protect them from the vast variety of threatening situations which they may meet as they grow up. This broader reaction is an *instinctive fear of what is strange*. When your toddler reacts with terror to her first meeting with a tortoise, it is not because she thinks that the tortoise will hurt her but because she does not, cannot, know whether it will do so or not. If you feel impatient, because you know the tortoise is harmless, remind yourself that one day she might meet a poisonous snake and save her own life by reacting to it in just the way that she is now reacting to the new pet.

Part of parents' irritation with young children's fears is often due to their own feelings being hurt by the child's reaction. You would not have taken her near that tortoise if it was going to hurt her, would you? Of course you would not, but a child dare not rely totally on the judgement and protection of adults because, after all, you are not always with her now and certainly will not be with her every minute as she grows up. She needs her personal fear of the strange to protect herself independently of her protectors. But how much she needs it does depend on how protected she feels. The more secure a child is in the total protection of her parents, the less fearful she will need to be.

The roots of anxiety

A baby's survival absolutely depends on adult care twenty-four hours a day. That care usually depends on there being love between baby and adult; it is to ensure that love that the baby is born with behaviours which seem loving and rewarding to her parents (such as those early smiles) even before she has learned to tell one person from another. Once she does know her 'special people' (whether they are, in fact, her natural parents or other caretakers) the love-relationship which she has with them becomes the most important emotional factor in her life and remains so for many years. *Basic anxiety is anxiety over separation from those loved people and therefore loss of their care and protection* and/or anxiety over loss of their love which might lead to withdrawal of that care and protection. The more certain she is of continuing love and care the less fearful she will be, but when anything happens to shake her confidence, fear will flood to the surface because without you, without your loving care, she cannot survive. You will see this difference from very early on when you watch your baby react to strange, potentially alarming events. When she is securely held in your arms she may be able to regard that strange tortoise with calm puzzlement or tolerate nearby thunderclaps. She will look at your face to see if you are afraid and, if you are not, she will trust herself to your protection. But when she is alone – or with strangers – she is far more likely to be afraid; and if she is with you physically but separated from you emotionally by a quarrel, she may be afraid, too. This is why irritated reactions to childish fears always work against fearlessness. Your irritation makes her feel less secure in your love and therefore opens her to fear.

Fear of separation and loss of love remain the childish basis for most anxiety all through our lives. When you misread a street map and find yourself quite unimportantly lost in a strange city, it is that infantile fear of losing parents which makes your heart pound and your hands go clammy. When you cannot sleep because your partner is out of town overnight, or cannot settle to work because your five-year-old has gone for the first time to all-day school, it is that same basic fear of separation from loved people which is acting upon you. Part of the desolation of bereavement is the infant-you feeling deserted and helpless. As adults, our physical survival does not depend on care by the people we love; we *can* survive without our partners, our children, our aged relations, but separations still remind us of a time when we could not (*see* **Death**).

If it seems to you fanciful to say that we are all more or less bedevilled by remaining fragments of baby separation-fears, think about the word 'goodbye'. Can you say it without a quaver, or do you, like most people, avoid the echoing sadness of the word with slang alternatives like 'bye-bye', 'ciao', 'see you' or 'cheerio'? Ask yourself also how many adults you know who can leave a party or other social occasion without endlessly hovering over the coats and on the doorstep, spinning out the farewells, repeating the plans for further meetings and promising, again and again, to 'see you again soon' or 'speak to you on the 'phone tomorrow'. Is there not a marked similarity with the toddler who puts off the nightly bedtime parting with cries for yet another drink of water, trip to the lavatory or just one more kiss?

The more secure we were in our love-relationships as children, the more we were allowed to feel dependent on and cared for by our 'special people', the less prone we shall be to this kind of anxiety and to fears of the threatening or the strange. Clearly, then, if we want to give our children security and confidence so that they grow up prone to as little anxiety and as few fears as possible, we shall not do it by scoffing, pushing and bullying, but by understanding, reassuring and loving. Above all, perhaps, we need to recognize the stages in a child's life at which she will be particularly prone to particular kinds of anxiety and fear so that we offer appropriate support at the right moments. The key is the developing child's competence: her ability to manage for herself and her confidence that she can do so. At birth she can manage nothing and will die without your constant care. As an adult she can manage everything, including the care and support of a child of her own. It is the stages in between which concern us here.

Babies and anxiety

Human babies are extremely helpless, physically, compared with most other mammals but they have an in-built drive to mature, to grow up and to become competent. Your baby will 'manage' everything that she can manage just as soon as she is physically and mentally ready to do so. Nothing whatsoever is to be gained from hurrying her and there is much to be lost.

If she wants lots of physical holding and cuddling and is frightened by being put to 'kick' on the floor, follow her cues. Putting her on the floor, protesting, will not speed up her physical development; it may actually hold it back. Cuddling her is not over-protecting her, it is giving her what she is telling you she needs and therefore giving her the context in which, at this stage, this particular baby will develop fastest.

When she reaches a phase in which she is reluctant to let you out of her sight, be with her as much as you possibly can and make sure that when you cannot be there she has an alternative beloved person on whom to depend. You cannot teach her not to need you so much by depriving her of you, because her need is real. She will learn for herself that she can manage short periods without you when, and only when, the love-relationship between you is so solid that it can serve her as a foundation to be taken for granted while she attends to other matters.

When it becomes clear that particular situations make her anxious and afraid, don't assume that surviving them will prove to her that 'there's nothing to be afraid of'. Instead, help her to find ways in which her anxiety can be kept at a tolerable level. Fear of being alone, in the dark, at night, for example, is very common towards the end of the first year. Of course, if you firmly close the door and leave her, she will eventually go to sleep. But far from teaching her that it is safe and comfortable to be left each night you will be teaching her exactly the opposite.

If it is your departure which makes her anxious, concentrate on helping her to feel that you are still available. Instead of closing the door and ignoring her cries, leave it ajar and pop back to reassure her from time to time or call to her in a friendly way as you get the supper.

If the darkness makes her room strange and therefore scarey, leave a light on. A low wattage bulb uses very little electricity. When she is a little older she can have a bedside light to turn on and off herself so that *she has control over the darkness.*

If there are comfort rituals or objects which help her to be happy in her cot encourage them (*see* **Habits**/Comfort habits). A dummy may give her something pleasant to do which masks her sadness; a special 'cuddly' may 'stand in' for you so that as long as she has that, she is able to let you go.

The point of all this is, of course, that *the less anxiety and fear your baby feels* the more confident and fearless she will be able to be. She learns to be these desirable things *through feeling safe*.

Toddlers'
anxiety
(see also
Tantrums*)*

Toddlers are particularly prone to anxiety and fears both because it is at this stage that many parents begin to demand tough, adventurous, independent behaviour and because their own developmental stage is an anxious-making one. Your toddler is at an emotional cross roads. He has reached a point where, in order to grow towards the comparative independence and autonomy of childhood, he has to assert his own individuality and start to take charge of himself and his own life. Yet he is still very immature and totally dependent upon your love, support and approval; the dependence of babyhood still feels far easier to him. Every time he allows you absolutely to control the details of his daily life, the independent bit of him protests: 'Go 'way; let me . . .' But every time he protests and rejects you, he becomes anxious lest you take him at his word; if you do indeed 'go 'way' that toddler turns instantly back into a baby, weeping bitterly because you have left the room without him.

Parents have a difficult, but infinitely satisfactory, job to do in holding the balance between these overriding toddler emotions. If you can give your toddler *all the personal independence he can take without fear* plus *all the love and protection he can take without frustration* you will be doing a copy-book job of sensitive parenting. Nobody can do that all the time but most of the time will produce both a secure and independent child and an enjoyable daily life for all of you.

If your toddler is feeling generally anxious – either because you are pressing him to be more 'grown up' than he can easily be or because he is pressing himself – you will probably see overall signs like the following:

He will be extra-clingy, choosing to follow you wherever you go rather than stay alone in a room to play; choosing to hold your hand or ride in the pushchair rather than run ahead; choosing to sit on your lap or leaning against you rather than separately on the floor.

He may seem unusually 'good' because he is feeling extra-dependent on you and, therefore, whenever he can remember how you like him to behave (which will not, of course, be all the time) he will do so.

He will not enjoy new places or people because he dare not leave you to explore.

He may have new (or extra) difficulty in going to sleep, adding to his bedtime rituals, taking more and more comforting toys into bed with him and thinking up fresh ways to persuade you to return for another goodnight.

He may enter a phase of nightmares (*see* **Sleep**).

He may lose enthusiasm for food and/or for feeding himself, preferring the more babyish items in his meals (including a bottle unless this has long been abandoned) and demanding that you feed him with a spoon even though he is competent to do so himself.

A toddler who is behaving in these ways is usually feeling anxious about your love and protection and therefore anxious about his own ability to manage what he has to manage. There are some obvious measures you can take and avoid:

A large extra measure of loving attention may work wonders. It may, for example, be a good time to take a week's holiday from work so that you can be with him and he need not make the effort which may be involved in his usual day-care arrangements. If he is at home with you anyway, it may be a good time to embark on projects he can share with you rather than being busy with your own affairs and therefore anxious that he should occupy himself. It certainly will not be a good time to arrange many social engagements for him to keep without you.

New demands will certainly make matters worse so if you were contemplating a fresh effort at toilet training/getting him off his bottle/insisting that he dress himself or tidy his own toys, go easy for a while.

Rows with you will make matters much worse and the very worst kind of row will be the kind which suggests to him that you love him less than you once did. Don't, please don't, let yourself use, even in anger, phrases like 'I'm fed up to the teeth with looking after you all day . . .' or 'It's no good coming to me for love when you're so naughty . . .' A toddler who is already feeling anxious about you may take you far more literally than you intend. He may actually *believe* that you do not love him and do not like caring for him.

Feeling competent will help, feeling helpless will increase his anxiety. Lots of praise for things he does easily and well will help him to feel that he is 'on top' of his life but taking over tasks in the middle because he is slow, or refusing to let him have a go because 'you're too little' will have the opposite effect.

Try, above all, not to use your superior strength and power to force him to do as you wish. If you reinforce the command to 'hurry up' by scooping him up and carrying him when he meant to walk, you really do make him feel helpless.

Toddler fears   Almost every toddler will have one or two specific fears at any moment in his or her life but toddlers who are feeling generally anxious may have their lives dominated by many fears all operating at the same time.

The commonest fears amongst western children up to the age of three-and-a-half are, in order: fear of dogs, darkness and its associated bogeys and ghosts, snakes and some insects, emergency sounds such as fire or ambulance bells or sirens, and assorted varieties of people such as uniformed policemen or nuns in long habits. In addition to these feared objects, children also commonly fear some of the things adults do to them or force them to do. Being pushed high on swings heads this list, followed equally by submersion in deep water (whether in swimming pool, lake or ocean), fairground rides and boat rides, and a variety of games which combine chasing with surprise – such as some kinds of 'hide-and-seek'.

Most of these fears arise unexpectedly and pass as suddenly as they began. If you will allow him to, your toddler will deal with them for himself by avoiding the things or the situations which frighten him. If you will let him steer well away from that dog, run to your arms when the ambulance passes and keep off those swings, the fear will pass as he enters a less anxious phase. If you try to force him to 'face it', to 'find out for himself that there's nothing to be frightened of' or to 'stop being such a baby', that fear may harden into a phobia (*see below*) and his general anxiety-level will rise.

Try to treat your toddler's fears with the same tolerant helpfulness you would offer to an adult. If you knew an adult friend was afraid of snakes, you would not expect her to come with you into the Reptile House at the zoo, nor tease her for preferring to wait outside. Why must the toddler come in? If you knew she was afraid of heights you would yourself climb the ladder to retrieve her scarf from that tree; why must the toddler get down from the climbing frame without help?

Every time you make your toddler experience his fear, you strengthen it. But every time you enable him to meet or do something without feeling afraid, you strengthen *him*. If you do not force him into that Reptile House today, he may see a grass snake in the pet-shop window next week and find it interesting instead of alarming. If you help him down from that climbing frame today he may find that jumping the last rungs was fun and want to climb a little way tomorrow. If you let him lead along a path which never takes him over the edge into fear, his fears will gradually recede.

Try to be clear, then, that there is a difference between 'fearlessness' and 'bravery'. A fearless child is simply one who is unafraid. He is someone to be proud of because he will be a child who is confident in your loving care and therefore confident of his ability to cope with life. But a brave child is one who does, or puts up with, things even though they frighten or hurt him. When we say to a toddler 'Oh come on, get in the water; you're not really scared; you like it really', we *pretend* that we want them to be fearless when what we are really demanding of them is that they should be brave.

Sometimes we do need to demand bravery of a child – perhaps because he must have a dental filling or a painful dressing – but when we do, we should be honest about it. The message is not 'It won't hurt,' but 'it will hurt but it will soon be over and I have to ask you to put up with it because it is necessary'. Most of the time we should not demand bravery because every time we do, we expose the child to fear and reduce his fearlessness. A toddler who is continually pushed in this way may have so much of his time and emotional energy taken up by meeting your demands for bravery that he has none left for being the tough, adventurous child you so much want. Let him find fearlessness for himself; build his own courage out of confidence and find it tested only rarely and when it is necessary.

Pre-school children's anxiety and fears

If your toddler emerges into a child who is sure that you are on his side, loving and lovable, he will also be sure of himself, and feel loving and lovable. He will be all set for what can be an enthrallingly happy couple of years spent increasingly turning his attention and affection outside the family and onto new adults and peers. Cries of 'my teacher says . . .' and 'my friend wants me to . . .' are a vote of confidence in you as parents.

Where a pre-school child is beset by much anxiety and many fears, it is usually because of the outside demands made upon him rather than because of his internal conflicts. Points to watch are:

That nobody should hurry him or her into any new growing-up experience. Try not to push the playgroup or nursery school to admit her early 'because she is so bright'. She can go on being bright at home or within the parent-and-toddler group. She will still be bright when she is emotionally ready for that next step. Try not to let him be pushed into 'big school' at four just because it has places in its brand new reception class. Let him enjoy being 'one of the big ones' in playgroup or nursery school before he must face being a very *very* little one all over again. Try not to push for lessons in dancing or drama, piano or swimming just because other children go. If your child dreams of being a ballerina or an actor, fine, try those Saturday mornings. But if he or she has no view on the matter, don't fill every moment with formal learning even if it is not of the academic kind. A child in this age period has a lot of life-learning still to do and all the time in the world for acquiring special skills.

Anxiety when starting school

Starting school is a very big step for most children and an enormous one for some. You should almost expect an upsurge of anxiety in your child because, however capable you have helped him to feel so far, he is almost certain to wonder whether he can cope without you in this new big group with its vast noisy buildings, countless children, many so much larger than he, and all these strange adults with apparently limitless authority and power (*see also* **School**/Starting school).

Steady (almost boring) home support and home routines will see most children through. But where there are real problems over going to school or fears of events within it, you must now work with the teacher because you do not have the actual power to influence what happens to him, minute by minute and day by day when you are not there. Remember that:

Fear creates fear so that even if he overcomes his anxiety and goes into school each morning, the fact that he does so *feeling anxious* is likely to make a vicious circle. If he feels sick and shaky every Monday morning, those horrible feelings will become linked in his mind with school and he will come to dread the feelings as much as the school. He may even go on having the anxiety-symptoms after he has actually come to enjoy the business of being at school. So, as before, the important consideration is that anxiety should be avoided if it possibly can be. Your aim is not just to get him there but to get him there feeling happy.

Older children and anxieties at school

As children become older and more involved in group life with others the same age, they have to find ways of concealing anxiety and fear which would be unacceptable within the group, and of coping, privately, with their own feelings. Parents sometimes have to strike a difficult balance between interference and neglect; between allowing the child her rightful autonomy and leaving her to cope when she cannot easily do so. If, for example, a child who has always loved acting refuses to join the drama club or have anything to do with school productions, you may deduce that she is anxious at the idea of performing publicly in that setting. If she seems to pick her friends always from amongst children who are shy, anxious to please and not very popular, you may deduce that she is 'playing safe' and avoiding the risks of friendship with children who might reject her. If she always aims to arrive at school just before lessons begin and to come home the moment they end, it may be clear to you that the liberty of the school playground frightens her, while the gradual development of a 'weak ankle' which keeps her off physical education and team games, may tell you something of her feelings about these activities. If a child is finding it necessary to limit her own life and experiences, do herself out of treats and generally reduce the richness of her life because of anxiety, she needs some help. If she does not get it she may project an image of herself at school which others come to believe. She may find herself valued far below her potential and suffer for it later. But if she is enjoying the life she is making for herself; if she is lively and interested and involved, it may be *your anxiety for her* which is the real issue. You may want her to shine more brightly than she feels she can. Once again, honest discussion with her teachers should give you some clues.

Handling other common fears   Older children, like adults, learn to avoid situations which make them uncomfortably anxious and to handle specific fears. Some of the 'odd' behaviours you may observe in your child are coping-devices of this kind. The child who, for example, 'prefers' to walk home the long way may, in fact, be afraid of the park he must cross on the shorter route or may have made a semi-conscious pact with himself always to count that particular set of paving stones on the way home in order to ward off evil. The child who starts singing as she leaves the living-room and sings, loudly, until she reaches her bedroom is probably frightened of a particular bogey on the stairs. The one who always seems unreasonably relieved to see you when you get home may live in terror of your being murdered on the train . . . Parents cannot protect their growing children from this mixture of rational and irrational fear (she *might* get assaulted; you *might* be murdered; the paving stones and the singing will not avert disaster but do avert the discomfort of anxiety) but they can be sensitive to it and help to keep it within bounds. Like a younger child, this one will be less anxious overall, the less anxiety and fear she experiences in her everyday life. But, unlike a younger child, she will not want to admit to you (or even perhaps to herself) that she is afraid. Tactfully, then, you have to notice the obvious sources of anxiety, the obvious fears, and offer her more effective ways out than her own chants and charms. If you know that leaving the warm bright living-room and facing the dark lonely stairs makes your hulking twelve-year-old feel anxious, you could just happen to have left on the stairs light or be going up to the bathroom yourself at the relevant moment. And if you know that about your child, you can reasonably deduce that being left alone in the house after dark will alarm her. You can see to it that if she feels too old for a 'babysitter' when you go out, she has a friend to spend the night with her instead.

Adolescent anxiety and fear

Like toddlers, adolescents *have* to achieve a dramatic spurt in growing up yet seldom feel entirely safe in doing so. At this stage most of her anxiety will be focused on the kind of person she feels herself to be/wants to be/will be when she is fully adult. Most of her fears will be of various kinds of failure, whether failure to attract the opposite sex; failure to pass her examinations; failure to 'stand up to' you or failure to be as beautiful and as popular as she would like to be. She has to work it all out for herself but she does not have to do it by herself (*see* **Adolescence**).

As well as offering her steadfast and unalterable love and support of the kind which sincerely means that you love and will help her now and would go on loving and helping her *whatever she did*, keep an eye out for high levels and degrees of anxiety and fear which may actually damage her ability to move into adult life.

Free-floating anxiety

This is the term used to describe anxious feelings which have no particular focus. The victim does not know what she is worried *about*; all she knows is that her heart pounds, her hands feel clammy, she feels shaky, perhaps nauseated, restless, disturbed and plagued by feelings of foreboding and dread. When she wakes up in the morning she feels as if something terrible has happened or something terrifying has got to be faced. Yet thinking over the prospect of a perfectly ordinary, even potentially pleasant, day ahead brings no relief. Indeed, finding no reasonable explanation for her feelings may bring fear of the feelings themselves. 'What is the *matter* with me?' she asks herself.

This kind of anxiety is a major component of many emotional disturbances and illnesses. An adolescent who remains in such a state for more than a few days or who is subject to recurrent 'panic-attacks' with no obvious cause, needs help via her doctor. It is to be hoped that he will not simply offer her tranquillizers to 'calm her down' but will help her, either himself or by referring her to a psychiatrist, *to work out what she is really feeling anxious about*. Until she can recognize the source of those feelings, they will paralyse her and produce the same old circle of anxiety, fear of anxiety, more anxiety. Helping her to see, for example, that her imminent departure for college has touched off old separation anxieties which date back to her nursery school days or earlier, will not automatically cure the anxiety but will make it possible for her to think it through and look for ways of coping better. Perhaps she is not ready to leave home so finally: perhaps her childhood room should remain available to her and plans be made for her to return at weekends until college life becomes her life. Perhaps she *is* ready but is worried that you will be lonely without her. Perhaps a seemingly commonsense suggestion by you, that she should start taking the contraceptive pill before she starts her college life, has made her feel pressured towards sexual activity for which she is not emotionally ready.

An anxious adolescent who can pin-point the source of his or her feelings will no longer feel so hopeless and helpless because he or she will be on the way towards coping with them. Feeling able to cope will, in itself, reduce his or her anxiety-level and produce a benevolent circle of confidence – competence – more confidence.

Coping with the physical effects of anxiety

People of all ages vary in the extent to which anxiety-inducing situations affect them physically. Just as pain is supposed to warn the victim of physical damage but may 'misfire' so that a trivial injury hurts more than a serious one, so anxiety is supposed to prepare the body for 'fight or flight' but may produce an over-reaction which actually reduces competence. The adolescent who goes into an examination or onto a concert platform with no anxiety or 'nerves' at all, probably will not give her best possible performance. A little extra adrenalin would produce extra effort, extra brilliance. But the adolescent who faces such a test with her hands shaking, her stomach churning, her skin clammy and her head full of the sound of her own pounding heart, will not give her best performance either. Her anxiety-reaction has gone over the top and become destructive rather than useful.

Of course the way that people face challenges and stresses is intimately concerned with their basic self-confidence, as well as with their past experiences of success and failure, of ability or inability to cope. But, in the here-and-now, a great deal can often be done to bring stress-reactions down to somewhere near the optimum level. Practice, for example, may be valuable but it is important that it be the right *kind* of practice. A child who always does poorly in examinations because of acute anxiety will not learn to stay calmer by practising having 'exam nerves' – in this as in every other area, fear breeds fear. She will only learn to stay calmer by practising *not* having 'exam nerves'. She may therefore benefit from being encouraged to practise writing her answers at home, rather than within the formality of an examination room; from practising 'writing to time' when there is nothing at stake but ordinary homework, or from practising 'mock exams' in which everything is as it will be on the big day except that the questions are easy and success more likely.

Parents cannot, of course, arrange this kind of help on their own, but any school, music teacher or sports coach should be happy to cooperate on behalf of any child whose test-performance does not measure up to his or her year-round standards. Under some circumstances it may also be sensible to consult the doctor. He may consider that the adolescent could benefit from a psychologist's help (*see below* Phobias).

Phobias

The line between an 'ordinary' fear and a phobia is blurred but important. Where a fear is usually firmly attached to its object, so that the victim only feels afraid when she has to face the thing she fears, a phobia has an existence of its own in the victim's mind and imagination. A child with a phobia of dogs, for example, is not only frightened when she meets a dog, she is also frightened when she sees one, hears about one, thinks about one. She does not only leave the park if she sees a dog, she keeps out of the park in case there might be one there. She may not be able to look at books for fear of the fear-feelings which will consume her if there is a picture of a dog; even the television advertisements may become a source of terror because of the dog-food slots.

Although phobias are common and usually insignificant in toddlers and very young children – yielding, like other fears, to a lessening of general anxiety – phobias in older people are more important. Since fear breeds fear, phobias tend to fuel themselves. The victim experiences horrible anxiety, becomes terrified of experiencing it again and therefore becomes increasingly anxious and liable to fear. Many phobias also spread and generalize themselves. That example of a phobia of dogs, for example, would, if it was left unchecked, tend gradually to confine the victim to her home: the only place where she can be quite sure no dogs will be. It is easy to see how this situation could lead to her becoming phobic of the outside world.

Behavioural psychologists have developed sophisticated techniques for dealing with phobias by a method which is known as 'de-sensitization'. Very briefly, the method involves first finding the 'psychological distance' from which the patient can view the feared object (let us stay with dogs) *without feeling afraid*. If the sight of a dog in the far distance evokes any fear at all, even greater distance will be tried, by using a picture of a dog instead of a real one or even by using a cartoon of a puppy instead of a real picture of an adult dog. Once any kind of contact with any kind of dog-stimulus can be tolerated without fear, the process of de-sensitization can be started. Day by day the psychologist increases the contact between patient and dog, making it closer and more realistic but *never allowing it to evoke anxiety*. However minute the progressive steps, the repeated experience of dogs-without-fear gradually teaches the patient not to associate dogs with fear and therefore not to be afraid. A person thus treated does not have to come to be a dog-lover. She may always prefer not to own, or even to pet, dogs. But she will eventually come to be able to tolerate/ignore them so that their existence (in reality and in her mind) no longer dictates or limits her lifestyle.

● Parents often attempt a sort of do-it-yourself de-sensitization with phobic young children. 'If only she would touch that sweet puppy,' they say 'she'd soon find out how warm and cuddly and gentle he is.' Be careful. If your attempts frighten your child, you will make matters worse. If a phobia is ruining a life, expert help is needed.

Appendix

The appendix is a very small dead-end tube leading off the large intestine. It is rich in lymphoid tissue and may play some part in the production of antibodies (*see* **Immune Response**). However, it is not a necessary organ and seldom becomes of interest to the individual unless it becomes inflamed (*see* **Hospital**/Surgery: Appendectomy).

Appetite *see* **Eating**. *See also* **Anorexia Nervosa**.
Asphyxia *see* **Accidents**/Choking; Drowning. *See also* **Safety**/In the home: From general household hazards.
Asthma *see* **Allergy**. *See also* **Chest Infections**.
Astigmatism *see* **Eyes and Seeing**; **Eye Disorders and Blindness**/Faults in vision.
Athlete's foot *see* **Ringworm and Athlete's foot**.
Audiometry *see* **Ears and Hearing**; **Ear Disorders and Deafness**. *See also* **Language**/Three to six months: Watching out for deafness; **Medical Specialities**.

Baby Alarms

A microphone placed near your baby and a speaker placed near you ensure that you will hear him if he cries or calls. Available systems range from inexpensive ones, which involve trailing wires through the house, to more luxurious built-in-systems with outlets in every room. You may prefer the first type because you can put the microphone beside the pram at the far end of the garden or take the whole thing with you when you go camping or to friends' houses.

Many families never have this kind of alarm system but those who have ever had one are seldom prepared to go back to life without it. If you know that you will hear your baby if he needs you, you can forget about him until he does. If you know the music will not drown a nightmare, you can turn the stereo as loud as you please. If you know that the wire joins the two of you, you can use any room as a nursery instead of having your arrangements constrained by the need to keep him close to where you sleep. By turning the volume control on that speaker up, you can even ensure that the smallest cry will blast a possibly neglectful or slightly deaf babysitter out of her chair.

Many baby alarms have a 'talk back' facility so that by pressing a button you can speak to him. Most babies are terrified by such a disembodied (and usually slightly distorted) voice so you probably will not use it while he is very young. It may, however, become very useful at the later stage when he calls endlessly for the drinks of water which are really requests for reassurance that you are still there.

While you will not want to 'listen in' to older children's private lives, a baby alarm which is left, wired in but switched off, can be useful all over again during later illness. You can agree with your eight-year-old that you will switch it on when you go to bed so that she need only call gently if she needs you in the night. You can agree to leave it switched on while she tries to have an afternoon sleep so that you can be sure to hear her when she wakes or gives up. It may even enable you to sink happily into your own bed when the possibility of recurring croup or a soaring fever would otherwise force you to stay awake and on watch.

Baby Bouncers *see also* **Play**

'Baby bouncer' is a generic term for any contraption of seat and harness in which a baby can be suspended, on strong elasticated cords, from the top of a doorframe or from a ceiling hook.

Most of the available ones have broad canvas straps which you buckle around the baby's waist and between her legs before hooking her onto those cords. The very best (originally made in France) consists of an actual canvas chair on elastic cords. It is very quick and easy to put a baby in and out of this type; furthermore it has a high back for good head support and a small 'tray' in front so that the baby has a place for some toys.

Whatever type of bouncer you are using, the idea is not that *you* should bounce or swing the baby but that she should do it for herself. You adjust the length of those elastic cords so that as she sits, her toes just touch the floor. Small whole-body movements move the whole bouncer; pushes with her toes produce up-and-down movements. Eventually, *in her own time*, she discovers that she can push down deliberately and set herself rhythmically bouncing; later on that she can twirl around and 'dance' too.

Baby bouncers give most babies tremendous pleasure because they free them to enjoy kinds of movement and degrees of power over their bodies which they are not yet mature enough to achieve without that elasticated aid. They also suspend the baby in an upright position from which she can see everything which is going on around her *and* change her own view by turning herself around. Successfully used, this gadget may keep her safe, active, busily occupied and in social contact with you as you get on with life, for longer periods than any other.

A couple of years ago, when the fashion for bouncers was at its peak, considerable anxiety was expressed about them in the medical and child-care press. It was thought, for example, that lengthy use might put a strain on very young backs or that mothers might leave babies confined in them for hours. Like any other gadget a bouncer needs to be used sensibly and, like any other plaything, it is intended to give pleasure and therefore should not be used at all if, after two or three experiments, your baby does not like it. You may like to check through the following points:

Type of bouncer and age of baby

A bouncer whose seat provides support for the back and for the head and neck can safely be used (for a baby who enjoys free physical play) from about three months of age. But a bouncer which requires her to keep her own back and neck straight, suspending her from the crutch and waist with no support at all above that level, should seldom be used before six months and even then should not be used for long periods at a time. In the first type a baby who is tired can simply stop moving, relax, even drop off to sleep as she might in a comfortable pushchair. In the second type she must exercise control over her muscles all the time.

Placing of the bouncer and safety

Some expensive bouncers come with their own stands. These are not recommended as they take up a lot of space and do not give enough height for older babies who, as they get heavier, need a long length of elastic for satisfactory (and now energetic) bouncing.

Some come with a clamp intended to fix the elastic cords to the top of a doorframe. These are not recommended either because doorframes are not standard and there have been accidents when clamps have failed or been improperly fixed. If you want to hang a bouncer from a doorframe it is better to use hefty screw-in hooks to hang it from. But a doorframe is only occasionally the best place for a bouncer because, ideally, the baby wants to bounce in a position from which she can see lots of people and interesting activities. If she is stuck in the doorway (unless it links kitchen and living-room, for example) most of what goes on will be round the corner and out of her view.

If you can bear to deface your ceiling, hooks screwed right into a rafter in the middle of your most-used room are usually the best. Those same hooks may stay in use all through her early childhood, for other gymnastics (*see* **Play** 'Messy' and energetic play for private homes).

The elasticated cords are carefully tested for strength but they, together with the clips which attach them to seat and ceiling hook, must be regularly inspected for wear. The easiest way to ensure daily safety is to put your own weight on the cords as you hang them up. If they will hold you for a moment they will certainly hold your baby for as long as she cares to play.

Using a bouncer

Any piece of equipment which holds a baby safely out of the way can be misused: yours can be imprisoned in her pram or highchair just as effectively as in her bouncer. While she is happy in it, you can indeed get on with otherwise dangerous jobs or take your eyes off her while you talk on the telephone, but obviously as soon as she is bored she should be taken out.

Some babies – especially in their first few months – are frightened by the very point of the bouncer: the ease with which it moves in space in response to their movements. If yours feels like this, don't persist now but don't decide that you have wasted the money either. She may love it in a couple of months, especially when she is at the almost-sitting, almost-crawling stage when she yearns to be more active than she can yet manage to be without help. She may take to her bouncer at six to eight months and use it frequently well into the toddler period.

A baby who does love her bouncer will probably take particular pleasure in using it outside. If you can find a convenient tree branch or have a climbing frame in your garden hang it there sometimes (perhaps when you are working or sitting in the garden) and let her bounce in sunbeams and tree-dapple.

● Don't confuse this kind of bouncer with the kind of canvas cradle-on-a-frame which is intended to provide babies too young to sit up with a very gentle springing motion as they kick. Although some young babies are comfortable in them, these are seldom worth buying because they only last for a few weeks before the baby prefers to do her kicking on the floor.

Babyfoods *see* **Eating**/Types of food for babies.

Babysitters *see also* Working Mothers

A baby or young child must have someone available to care for him at any moment in every twenty-four hours and that is a commitment which no single person (no, not even his mother) should be expected to fulfil for long. If you happen to live within a large family or other group, you may be able to come and go more or less as you please, knowing that there will always be somebody around to 'keep an eye on' the baby. But there are few families like that today. If you and your partner are in sole charge of that baby (or more especially if you are his only parent), it is important to get a babysitting system organized before your beloved child begins to feel like your gaoler.

Choosing a babysitter

The ideal person is not really a babysitter at all but an occasional mother-substitute who may, perhaps, be the baby's grandmother. If you are fortunate enough to have a willing one available, cultivate her. She can not only 'sit with' the sleeping baby while you go out in the evening, but also play with him or take him out while you pursue your own daytime interests or simply enjoy the luxury of being in your own home with nobody saying 'Mum'. If your baby does become accustomed to this sort of arrangement he will also have invaluable insurance against the dread day when you have to enter hospital or spend a few days away coping with a family bereavement. Although he will be upset by your absence he will be far less upset than he would be if he were cared for by someone whom he scarcely knows or by someone who had never before offered him personal and intimate care (*see* **Anxiety, Fears and Phobias**).

If you have no willing relatives nearby you may be able to share this kind of extended-babysitting with another family. It is truly idiotic that several sets of neighbour-parents should each feel trapped by their children when, with a little cooperation, all could offer each other a modicum of freedom while keeping all the children happy and secure. The trick is to be honest with yourself as well as with the other involved parents. If you have a big garden, for example, and the others have none, you are likely to find that you are the one with four toddlers around on summer afternoons. Do you mind? If you do, say so *before* you begin to feel put-upon. But perhaps you will not mind. Perhaps your own child enjoys the daytime company while you want, above all, to be freed to go out in the evening or to be relieved of the nursery school transport round.

Sometimes you will be offered daytime (as well as evening) babysitting by an adolescent who either 'adopts' your family or finds it a pleasant way to earn pocket money. Be very sure that you do not ask (or allow her to volunteer) for more than she is capable of doing. She may long to take your baby for walks but be quite oblivious to the sun in his eyes, unreliable strange dogs or unevenly loaded prams. She may love your baby when he smiles or sleeps but find him revolting when he cries or smells. She may mean to be one hundred per cent responsible ninety-nine per cent of the time but be quite unable to resist joining her gang when it passes your garden or slipping out to meet her boyfriend 'just for a minute'. Running risks of this kind is not fair to the baby, to you *or to the adolescent*. So, if she thinks she wants to replace you for short periods of that baby's life, let her do so first under your supervision so that you all have the opportunity to see how she gets on and to be sure that she really knows what she is taking on.

Daytime babysitting

Anyone who is going to care for your baby or young child during his waking hours needs to know him well. Because his memory is so short and he is changing so rapidly, that means that she needs to see him frequently. Even a devoted relation will seem like a stranger to a baby who only sees her every few weeks, while the one who coped so beautifully with him when he was pram-or-chair-bound may be quite unable to keep him safe and happy once he is crawling. If you plan on daytime relief, make sure that baby and sitter meet frequently, even if you only actually want to leave them together on rare occasions.

• A complete stranger, however well-trained, can never offer satisfactory care to a baby or young child. If you find yourself tempted by the 'creches' offered by some hospital outpatient departments, large stores or adult education institutes, acknowledge your own desire for occasional freedom from child-care and *make proper arrangements*.

Evening babysitting If your child normally sleeps soundly, an evening babysitter will not usually have to offer him any personal service. She is there *in case something goes wrong*. Since the child *could* become ill or have a nightmare, the ideal person is still somebody whom he knows and trusts. But since he probably will not wake up, you may feel that it is legitimate to gamble a little. A complete stranger (hired, perhaps, from an agency) will obviously terrify him if he should wake, but a friendly acquaintance or regular sitter who always comes in if you go out may be acceptable. These are some of the points other parents have found important:

Don't leave a mere acquaintance to put the child to bed. He will not settle. Put him to bed before you go out even if that means that you put him to bed a little earlier than usual.

If the child is old enough to understand, warn him that you will be out. Although he may still be amazed when Mrs Jones comes in instead of Mummy, he will then remember what you said and, hopefully, settle again to her assurances that you will soon be home. If you do not warn him and he does wake, he may be reluctant to settle to sleep on subsequent nights in case you slip away.

If the child is not old enough to understand, try to leave a telephone number. If you have no telephone in your house this is obviously impossible: the sitter cannot leave the child to ring you. But if you do have a telephone you can be reached, if you are needed, almost anywhere. The management of a theatre or concert hall will fetch you out if you leave your seat numbers with the sitter. A cinema will flash a message on the screen for you if the sitter convinces the management that it is an emergency. Even a pub will relay a message. Of course, leaving a number means that you cannot spend a completely spontaneous evening, wandering along the river or calling on various friends to see who feels like coming out for a drink, but it does not limit you to spending the evening in another private house.

Be absolutely certain that the sitter will not leave the house however late back you may be. You may have every intention of being home by midnight but you could have a puncture or an accident . . . you must be sure that your sitter will stay until you reappear and that she has no commitments (such as her own children once her husband departs for an early-morning shift) which could 'force' her to leave. It is often sensible to arrange that she can sleep in your house if you should be very late but do make sure that she does so within easy earshot of the baby (*see* **Baby Alarms**); remember that her ear may not be quite so tuned to infant cries as is yours.

Don't leave a child to care for a child. Only you can decide at what age your own older child is capable of babysitting for the younger one but remember that *if there is a real emergency, a ten-, twelve- or fourteen-year-old may be just as frightened as the baby*. After all, you are not only guarding him against the emotional horrors of waking alone from a nightmare but from the practical horrors of fire or intruders, too. It may be that both baby and child need the security of an adult in the house.

Babytalk *see* **Language**.

Bacteria *see* **Infection**. *See also* individual conditions.

Bad breath *see* **Teeth**/Some dental problems of adolescence.

Bad language *see* **Language**/Pre-school years: Nonsense and 'naughty nonsense'. *See also* **Discipline**, **Self-Discipline and Learning How to Behave**.

Baldness *see* **Ringworm**. *See also* **Adolescence**/Problems with appearance and body-image.

Bedwetting (Enuresis)

Staying dry during sleep is not a learned skill but a physiological development. Babies pass water involuntarily whether they are awake or asleep; older people's urination is a voluntary matter and therefore never takes place during normal sleep. In between those two stages, beds stop being wetted not because the child is 'trained' but because he matures to a point where he can concentrate his urine sufficiently for his bladder to hold a full night's complement comfortably *and* to a point where if his bladder is too full for comfort it will cause an awakening rather than a flood.

Children mature at different rates and the rate at which they become dry at night is no exception. There are some who sleep and stay dry all night by their first birthdays (even though they wet their nappies involuntarily, like any other baby, during the day). But there are equally normal children who are not reliably dry at night when they are five, even though they use the lavatory, like any other child, all day.

Sometimes parents unwittingly turn normal-but-slow development of dryness into a bedwetting problem, by being too quick to label their child 'enuretic'. A rough idea of the age-stages at which most children become dry at night may help:

During the first year. Every human infant wets himself and his bed.

During the second year. Some girls and a few boys begin to stay dry during day-time naps and may have *occasional* dry nights.

During the third year. Dry nights become more frequent and parents begin to see that a 'full' bladder sometimes awakens the child; she will call at 5 or 6 a.m. asking to go to the lavatory.

As this year advances, many toddlers stay dry for *most* of the night but not for quite all of it. If you get your child up especially early in the morning, she is more likely to be dry than she is if the day starts at its later, normal time.

By the end of this year quite a lot of girls will have become reliably dry at night. Boys tend to be behind girls. They will probably have swapped from occasional dry nights to occasional wet ones by their third birthdays.

During the fourth year. The majority of children will become reliably dry at night. There will be more boys than girls amongst those who still wet their beds frequently.

At around the fifth birthday. A child who still wets his bed may be just about to start staying dry or he may scarcely have started on the road towards dryness. It is important to work out which is the case for your child. If he is *becoming dry*, he will almost certainly get there on his own, and action from you may interrupt the process. If he is not already on his way, he could probably do with some help (*see below*).

Signs of progress towards dryness include even occasional dry nights; occasional awakenings and requests for the pot or lavatory; and a bed which stays dry for at least some hours of each night.

The child who has scarcely started towards dryness will not only wet his bed every night, he will wet it (as you will be able to see from the state of his bedding) several times during each night. If you go to him two or three hours after he fell asleep, you will probably find that he is already wet.

Handling normal bedwetting

Every child should be given every chance to mature into night-time dryness at his own pace. Attempts to hurry the process once it has begun often backfire. Restricting the nearly-dry four-year-old's evening drink, or waking him to pee at your bedtime, may only serve to focus his attention on the matter. If he realizes how much you care and becomes anxious about wetting, a problem may be created where none need have been. For the child who is *not* nearly-dry, such measures are useless. What is the point of 'lifting' a child at 11 p.m. when he was already wet at 9 p.m.?

Unfortunately, 'leave the whole matter alone' is advice which is more easily given than taken. A child who is too big, or who feels himself too grown up, for night-time nappies and plastic pants does not just make a wet patch on his sheet, he makes a flood. Parents do not just have to 'cope with the laundry', as some authorities say. They may have daily pyjamas and sheets *and* soaking blankets, pillows and (when the plastic sheet ruckles) a wet mattress too. Anything that will help you cope will help him:

Encase the mattress and pillow in waterproof material, either by sewing or by glueing it, like a large parcel. This will ensure that they do not get wet and smelly, or ruined for the future.

A washable duvet or continental quilt can be put straight into a washing machine without even removing the cover. This saves time both on unmaking and remaking the bed.

A tumble drier means that one set of bedding will do because the whole lot can be washed, dried and ready between morning and evening.

If you simply cannot afford these aids, an alternative approach is to acquire as many sets of sheets and blankets as you can – perhaps using Oxfam or searching the school jumble sale – and let the wet ones accumulate for several days in a plastic sack for a weekly wash in the large machine at the local launderette. Some British local authorities will offer hard-pressed mothers the same kind of laundry service which is available to families nursing incontinent elderly people. Your doctor or health visitor will advise about this.

While coping as matter-of-factly as you can with the practicalities of wet beds it is also important to remember that:

Your child cannot help wetting. He urinates in his sleep and, by definition, what we do in sleep is outside our conscious control. Although you will sometimes make it obvious that you are fed up with the washing, you have to try and make it clear that you are not fed up with him.

He will not like waking up wet. A soaking bed is both cold and uncomfortable and, eventually, shaming, too. Far from needing scolding, he needs your casual sympathy and, above all, your confidence that one day soon he will stay dry.

He will smell if he is not washed and, as he gets older, outsiders will notice and other children will tease him. If he can have a daily bath he should have it in the morning as long as the bedwetting continues. If that is impossible a thorough morning wash is vital.

His room will smell if urine-soaked items are left to dry there. The wrinkled noses of visiting friends or brothers and sisters can quickly make him feel an outcast.

If you can stay calm, your child may stay calm, too. If neither of you is anxious about his wetting, he may grow out of it without ever thinking of himself (or being thought of) as a 'bedwetter'. About ten per cent of all little boys – everywhere in the world where studies have been done – wet their beds frequently between the ages of five and seven. The numbers drop by half during the next couple of years.

If you cannot stay calm and/or your child is beginning to worry about his wet beds, trying to conceal his bedding, refusing to stay overnight with friends and generally feeling himself at a social disadvantage, you would probably be wise to seek help (*see below*).

There are two kinds of enuresis:

What enuresis is and why it happens

Primary enuresis simply means that a child has never developed night-time dryness. The word could be used of any two-year-old but it is usually reserved for children who could be expected to have become dry. You may despair when your child is four (perhaps because he shows absolutely no signs of progress) or when he is five (perhaps because he is worrying). Some doctors refuse to use the term for anyone under about seven.

Secondary enuresis is different. The term means that a child who *has been* reliably dry, for months or even years, has started to wet his bed. This is occasionally the result of physical illness; often the result of anxiety and stress. Since secondary enuresis is very upsetting for the child, as well as his parents, advice should usually be sought immediately (*see below*).

The causes of primary enuresis are seldom direct and clear-cut. Most of the popular explanations contain a little truth, a little nonsense and a big question mark:

Enuresis 'runs in families' but not, as far as we know, as a matter of direct inheritance. There seem to be two familial factors. Parents who were themselves late in becoming dry may have children who also reach this stage late. But if stress does not introduce emotional problems, such a child will still become dry spontaneously. He has not inherited enuresis but developmental delay in becoming dry. Parents who were enuretic may also unwittingly toilet train their children as they were trained, or otherwise subject the next generation to the same stresses they experienced. The child is not suffering from his genes but from a repeating pattern of child-care.

Enuresis is caused by emotional/psychiatric problems. Certainly wet bed are often associated with emotional stress but the cause-and-effect relationship is usually only direct in secondary enuresis where the child suddenly *starts* to wet after months or years of being reliably dry every night. In that situation advice should certainly be sought immediately unless the cause of the stress (such as a new baby/caretaker/school) is obvious and the parents can see how to soften it.

In other enuretic children it is thought that emotional stress *at the time when dryness should have been expected to develop* may prevent it emerging. The child who was acutely ill, or separated from his parents, or otherwise traumatized at two or three, may fail to become dry during the subsequent year or two. But when he reaches a clinic at five or six, it is not current emotional stress which is causing his problems but the interruption to development caused much earlier, plus the stress of still being wet. Many of the enuretic children who show signs of emotional disturbance are disturbed by the effects of their wetting rather than wet because they are disturbed.

It remains true that for any group of children studied after referral to a clinic dealing with enuresis, a higher than expected number will be found to come from unhappy or disturbed family backgrounds. While it is too easy to say 'he wets his bed because his Dad left', either failing to become dry *or* starting to wet may be part of a complex of reactions to anxiety-provoking situations. Where this is the case, parents will usually be able to see other signs of anxiety as well as the enuresis. They will be dealing with an unhappy and worried child whose unhappiness will be increased by the wetting, but whose wetting will seldom cease immediately even if circumstances can be improved.

Enuresis is often caused by 'kidney trouble'. While it is true that urinary infections are about five times more frequent in enuretic than in dry children, it does not seem likely that the infection often causes the wetting; curing the infection seldom ends the enuresis. Some doctors believe that the cause-and-effect relationship is the other way around: enuretic children being more liable to urinary infection, perhaps because instead of voiding into a receptacle they flood their beds and then lie with the urine pooled both around them and in the urethra. There are, however, certain medical conditions which do directly cause enuresis. sickle cell anaemia and diabetes mellitus, for example, are two quite different conditions each of which causes an excessive output of unconcentrated urine and thus leads directly to wet beds. Certain congenital abnormalities, such as the invisible form of spina bifida (spina bifida occulta) make continence impossible, while some rare neurological problems cause enuresis only when the child begins a growth spurt. He may therefore become dry at night as a small child but develop what looks like secondary enuresis later on.

Enuretic children sleep more deeply than others. Although many parents believe this, there is no evidence to prove it nor has it been possible to distinguish between enuretic and dry children on the basis of their sleep rhythms and patterns (*see* **Sleep**).

Enuretic children have an unusually small bladder-capacity. The question at issue here is not the actual *capacity* of the bladder but the volume of urine in the bladder which makes it necessary for the child to urinate. Research has shown that some enuretic children do feel the urge after drinking less than other children. Most authorities believe that this reflects only the general anxiety about bladder-emptying which most bedwetters come to feel. Certainly restricting fluids does not help.

Seeking help for a child who still wets his bed

Bedwetting becomes a serious problem as soon as you or your child feel that it is a real problem. When that will be depends not only on how calm you can be about his slow development, but also on whether there are *any* signs of progress and whether there are any other signs that suggest unhappiness or insecurity. A child who wets his bed every night *and* is having a lot of nightmares, is reluctant to separate from you and hates school, is rather unlikely to become dry spontaneously until life is easier for him. Similarly, the child who has just started to wet his bed, after a year of reliable dryness, may not only be upset about something in his waking life but also be exceedingly upset about his wetness.

As a rough and ready rule-of-thumb, then:

Don't hurry if your child is under five and you are both calm about his wet beds.

Seek help as early as four if bedwetting is new or part of general unhappiness.

Seek help by the time he is five even if he is neither worried by his wetness nor apparently anxious about anything else. If his wet beds are not worrying him yet, they soon will because he will become increasingly aware that 'most children my age don't . . .'

Delay after five only if you can see that dryness is around the corner. If his fifth birthday is coming up but the wet beds are getting rarer, you can afford to wait and see unless you are at the end of your tether or he is actually asking for help.

What kind of help and from whom?

Many health professionals, including family doctors, pediatricians, community nurses, psychologists and psychiatrists, work successfully to help enuretic children and their families. The particular professional background of the person you choose to consult probably does not matter as much as his interest in enuresis. Those who are genuinely interested report high success rates for a variety of treatment-approaches; those who are less personally involved report far less satisfactory results. Start, then, with whoever is most easily accessible to you – probably the child's own doctor – but do not allow yourself to be fobbed off with a 'don't worry, he'll grow out of it'. If you were not already worried you would not be there; furthermore, enuresis and worry go together and nobody can stop worrying on command. Most large children's hospitals, and many other hospitals, too, have special enuresis clinics; in these you will certainly find professionals who are making a special study of bedwetting and its problems.

Your doctor, or other professional, will probably want to explore with you all the 'causes' for enuresis outlined above. He will want to exclude physical problems, for example, and to get the fullest possible picture of any difficulties at home or at school which may be contributing. If he feels that the child's bedwetting is only part of a complex pattern of distress, he may want to refer you to a psychiatrist for advice and help. If, on the other hand, he is reasonably sure that any emotional distress is secondary to the bedwetting, he may see whether he can help the child to become dry at night by counselling you and supporting and motivating him. Even where parents have truly tried to avoid scolding or punishing a child for wetting his bed and believe that the child scarcely worries about it, there is often a vicious circle of shame and anguish which can be broken by an outsider whom the child believes in because he is 'the doctor'.

Everyone has his own way of working in this situation but he may, for example, go over your behaviour with you in detail and point out subtle ways in which your concern, even anger, is being conveyed to the child. Perhaps you do not scold for wet beds, but do you greet a dry one with remarks like, 'there you are you see; you can do it if you try!'? Perhaps you do not punish directly, but does the child get nice new pyjamas when he needs them or must he wear outgrown and washed-out ones because 'it's not worth buying new'? Perhaps you do not mean to shame him but do you check up on his washing with a good sniff when he comes down to breakfast? The professional will explain to the child, as a matter of medical fact, that his wet beds are not his fault; that many children take a long time to get dry but that *he will do so*. He may offer the child a chart on which he himself is to stick a star or draw a picture whenever he wakes in a dry bed so as to make a record to show next time he visits. Above all, he will offer the child a firm series of appointments – perhaps as often as every two weeks – and make it clear that he will not stop seeing him regularly until the problem is over.

With a child of, say, seven or older, who is desperate to get dry as soon as possible, or with a child who has not improved after some months of this kind of support more direct treatment may be suggested.

Drugs for bedwetting   Some doctors use certain anti-depressant drugs in the treatment of enuresis. Imipramine ('Tofranil'), for example, is both an anti-depressant and a smooth-muscle relaxant and it has proved helpful to some children in some reported series. It is, however, potentially highly toxic. Many doctors prefer not to prescribe it for children and regard it as a dangerous drug to have in a house where there are children as it has been responsible for many cases of accidental poisoning.

Enuresis alarms   The buzzer-alarm is a method by which some children can train themselves to wake up when they need to urinate rather than staying asleep
and wetting their beds.

Success rates as high as eighty per cent have been reported over periods
of use ranging from a few weeks to about six months. One relapse is
common but is usually quickly dealt with by a short period of further use
and thereafter there is normally no further wetting. Some professionals
report much lower success rates but studies comparing the subjects and
methods of successful and less successful use suggest that the following
points may all be important:

**The knowledge, enthusiasm and supportive follow-up of the pro-
fessional.** People who are really interested in enuresis, who use the
buzzer carefully as an adjunct to counselling and support and who see
patients using the buzzer at frequent intervals, are commonly successful
with it. Those who use the buzzer instead of personal attention are not.

The understanding and enthusiasm of both parent and child. Where the
operating mechanism is not fully understood, home conditions make its
installation difficult and/or no adult is prepared to take the considerable
trouble required in the early stages, success is unlikely. Where the child
fears or resents the buzzer success is impossible.

The (comparative) freedom of the child from associated difficulties.
Where enuresis is part of a widespread distress-syndrome the demands
made by the buzzer may actually cause stress rather than helping to
relieve it. Left to himself, the older child will abandon it as 'useless'. If it is
forced on a younger child by a parent who was intended to 'help' him
manage it, the buzzer simply becomes part of the pressures which he is
already experiencing as intolerable. His 'failure' to become dry, even with
the buzzer, then tends to fuel parental resentment.

A loud enough and/or correctly placed buzzer. The workings of the
system are briefly explained below. The commonest cause of failure is due
to the actual sound failing to awaken the child and/or parent. An
amplifier and/or extension into the parent's room is often required.

How enuresis alarms work. Although several different models are available and you should be given a careful explanation, demonstration and
practice session before you take one home, the principles of all are similar.
They are given here for use either as a reminder or for those who do not, in
fact, receive proper tuition.

The system consists of two mats which, when moisture closes the
circuit between them, cause an alarm-buzzer to sound.

The child's bed is made up with a waterproof sheet directly over the
mattress; one buzzer mat on top of it, a flannelette drawsheet on top of the
first buzzer mat and the second buzzer mat on top of the flannelette sheet.
On top of that the child can have his ordinary cotton sheet so that the bed
looks and feels normal, but it is best if he sleeps without pyjama trousers.

● It is important that the drawsheet separating the two mats should be
flannelette rather than thin cotton. Cotton can become sufficiently dam-
pened by sweat to cause 'false alarms'.

Wired to the mats is a lead which goes to a box containing the buzzer, an 'on/off' switch and, sometimes, a volume control. This must be placed so that the child cannot reach to switch it off without getting out of bed and so that the buzzer unfailingly wakes him up.

The child sets the alarm before getting into bed. If and when he starts to urinate in his sleep, the first few drops close the circuit, set off the buzzer, wake him and stop the urination. As soon as he wakes he has to get out of bed and switch the alarm off to stop the noise. He then finishes urinating (in a pot in his room or in the toilet) and resets the alarm before getting back into bed.

● At five or six few children can manage all this alone. A parent must either sleep in his room with him or have an extension buzzer in her own room so that she, too, is awoken and can go and supervise the procedure, check that the alarm is reset and resettle the child.

When all goes well, the buzzer-alarm acts instead of the body's own awakening response to a bladder which needs emptying. It wakes the child because he is urinating and, over many weeks, his body takes over the awakening itself so that he begins to wake up before urination has begun and the alarm has sounded. Interestingly, while the child may wake up and use the lavatory or pot several times each night for a while, the awakenings gradually tail off until he is sleeping through the night as well as waking dry.

● Since the alarm cannot sound until some urine has been released, there may be a patch the size of a saucer at each awakening. Dry sheets must be put on each time both to prevent 'false alarms' and because a dry bed in the morning is the biggest psychological boost the child can have.

Behaviour problems *see* **Anxiety, Fears and Phobias; Depression; Hyperactive Children; Tantrums.** *See also* specific problem areas in **Adolescence; Discipline, Self-discipline and Learning How to Behave; Habits; Jealousy; School.**
Bereavement *see* **Death.** *See also* **Suicide.**
Bilingual families *see* **Language**/Bringing up bi-lingual babies.

Birthmarks

Many babies are marked at birth, either by instruments used during delivery or by the pressures and stresses of the birth-process itself. Any such marks will vanish within a few days. Do ask the doctor who examines your newborn about any which you have noticed. He can almost certainly reassure you that they are temporary.

True birthmarks will not vanish so quickly; indeed some may not even be visible immediately after birth but show themselves later. The commonest types are described below, but do be sure that you check on their identity with the examining doctor.

'Stork's beak'
mark
    This is the commonest type of birthmark. It consists of flat red patches which may be on the eyelids and/or above the bridge of the nose or the

nape of the neck. The name comes from the idea that these are the places which the stork would have gripped with his beak when delivering the baby to his mother.

The marks on the face almost always vanish completely in the first year although they may show up for a while longer when the baby cries. Marks on the nape of the neck sometimes remain for life but are almost always covered by the hair.

'*Strawberry*' *mark*   Is so-called because it is a reddish area which is slightly raised and soft. A strawberry mark may not be visible at birth but may appear during the first few days of life.

A strawberry mark may start as small as a pin-prick but it will get steadily larger during the first six to nine months. If the mark is on your baby's face it is difficult to ignore it and you may find yourself bitterly resenting it. But *it will go away*. Signs that it is beginning to vanish are pale areas in the middle which eventually spread together so that only a red rim remains. Then the rim vanishes and the skin is left with no sign that the mark ever existed.

● Unlike most birthmarks, the skin covering strawberry marks is somewhat fragile. A hard knock can cause blood to ooze and, although the bleeding can always be easily stopped with light pressure, that surface damage may leave a slight scar which will be visible after the birthmark has vanished. If your child has a strawberry mark in a particularly vulnerable place, you may like to consult your doctor about covering it for protection.

● The *very* rare strawberry mark which does not vanish of its own accord can be removed by plastic surgery. But, because the removal will leave a scar and the scar will grow, it is seldom recommended before the child is around seven (*see* **Hospital**/Surgery: Plastic surgery).

'*Port-wine* *stain*'   This very rare type of birthmark consists of a dark red or purple mark which, while it is flat, may have a slightly knobbly surface.

An extensive port-wine stain on the face can be very disfiguring and unfortunately will not go away. Plastic surgery, although still sometimes attempted, is seldom satisfactory. Excellent covering creams are now available, however, and these are specially blended for each patient so that the skin tone is exactly matched. It is usually sensible to face the misfortune and have the cream prescribed from babyhood. A child who has always had it used will both accept it and learn to apply it for himself from an early age. By the time he is old enough for playgroup or school he may take it as much for granted as putting on his clothes.

Birthweight *see* **Growth**.
Black eye *see* **Accidents**/Bruises.
Bleeding *see* **Accidents**/Wounds and bleeding. *See also* **Adolescence**/Menstruation.
Blepharitis *see* **Eyes and Seeing; Eye Disorders and Blindness**.
Blisters *see* **Accidents**.
Blood donors *see* **Blood Groups**.

Blood Groups

Most human blood contains antigens in the red blood cells and antibodies in the plasma (*see* **Immune Response**). An individual cannot have corresponding antigens and antibodies in his blood because if he did they would interact: the red blood cells would clump together (agglutinate) and block his blood vessels instead of flowing through them. This is exactly what may happen if an individual is given a blood transfusion from an unsuitable donor. If the donated blood contains antigens to which he has antibodies it will not boost his circulation but may actually destroy it.

Modern surgery depends upon the ready-availability of donated blood while transplant surgery depends on more and more accurate 'typing' both of blood and tissue. Everyone should know his own blood group and understand what it means both in terms of what blood he can give and be given. Everyone who is able to give blood should do so while he has it to spare, against the day when his life depends on somebody else having done so.

The entire human race can be divided into four main blood groups (there are many, less vital, subdivisions) which are described in terms of the antigens contained in the red cells. These are referred to as ABO and the four possibilities are:

□ Blood group O in which there are no antigens (45 per cent of the population).
□ Blood group A in which there are 'A' antigens (40 per cent of the population).
□ Blood group B in which there are 'B' antigens (10 per cent of the population).
□ Blood group AB which has both 'A' and 'B' antigens (5 per cent of the population).

Once the blood group is known in terms of the antigens in the red cells, the presence or absence of particular antibodies in the plasma can be deduced:

□ Since 'O' blood contains no antigens it may contain both 'a' and 'b' antibodies.
□ Since 'A' blood contains 'A' antigens it cannot have 'a' antibodies but will have 'b'.
□ Since 'B' blood contains 'B' antigens it cannot have 'b' antibodies but will have 'a'.
□ Since 'AB' blood contains both 'A' and 'B' antigens it cannot contain any antibodies.

Who can give blood to, or receive it from, whom?

If a patients blood plasma contains antibodies, he must not be given a transfusion of whole blood which contains a matching antigen in its red cells. Even a small transfusion will stimulate those antibodies to attack the 'foreign' protein and cause the blood to agglutinate. Furthermore, since those antibodies are natural to him and continually being produced, there are always more available. The disastrous reaction will not be temporary.

The patient's own antigens are less important. Even if he is given blood which contains matching antibodies those transfused antibodies will not attack his red blood cells and cause agglutination. This is because the relatively small volume of transfused plasma does not contain enough antibodies to attack effectively the vast numbers of red cells in his circulation, and because those antibodies are not natural to him, no more will be produced. As the transfused blood becomes diluted by the patient's own, any slight and temporary reaction will die away. Basically, then, it does not matter what antibodies are given or received in a transfusion (which is why plasma rather than whole blood is often used) but it matters very much indeed what antigens are given or received. Logically, then,

People with group 'O' blood can give blood to anyone. They have no antigens which recipients' antibodies could attack and their antibodies, 'a' and 'b', will do no harm. Such people are known as universal donors' and their blood is invaluable to the blood banks. But,

People with group 'O' blood cannot receive blood from any but a group 'O' donor. Their blood contains both 'a' and 'b' antibodies which will attack either 'A' or 'B' antigens so only blood containing no antigens at all is safe for them. This is yet another reason why plentiful supplies of 'O' blood are essential to the blood banks. Contrariwise,

People with group 'AB' blood can receive blood from anyone. Their blood contains no antibodies and therefore cannot react against donor blood whatever antigens it contains. Such people are known as *universal recipients* and although their blood group is rare there is no special need for it in the blood banks. But,

People with 'AB' blood can only give blood to other 'AB' individuals. Recipients of any other blood group will have antibodies which will react against either the 'A' or the 'B' antigens. This is yet another reason why 'AB' blood is not especially useful to the blood banks: it is unusable for ninety-five per cent of the population while the remaining five per cent can be given any blood which happens to be available.

In between these extremes, people with group 'A' blood can donate to people with 'A' or 'AB' blood since neither will contain 'a' antibodies and can receive blood from people with 'A' or 'O' blood since neither will contain the 'B' antigens their own 'b' antibodies would attack.

People with group 'B' blood can donate to people with 'B' or 'AB' blood since neither will contain 'b' antibodies and can receive blood from people with 'B' or 'O' blood since neither will contain the 'A' antigens their own 'a' antibodies would attack. In emergency situations (such as war or local disaster) when supplies of 'O' blood may run short, supplies of both these groups may be critical. With only ten per cent of the population belonging to group 'B' this group, above all, requires regular donors.

The rhesus factor   Whatever a person's ABO blood group, her blood will also either contain the rhesus factor (she is 'rhesus positive') or have no rhesus factor (she is 'rhesus negative'). If rhesus positive blood is transfused into a rhesus negative patient, her blood plasma will produce antibodies against it and, once again, the transfusion will result in disaster. There is considerable racial variation in the numbers of people whose blood lacks the rhesus factor. For example, about fifteen per cent of British women are rhesus negative but only about one per cent of African women.

Haemolytic disease of the newborn

If a woman with rhesus negative blood has a baby with a man whose blood is wholly rhesus positive, the baby's blood will be positive too. If the father is half positive there is a fifty-fifty chance that the baby's blood will be positive.

If that baby's blood is rhesus positive there is a chance (no more than that) that during delivery heavy pressure on the placenta will squeeze some of those rhesus positive blood cells into the mother's circulation. If this happens her rhesus negative blood will be stimulated to produce antibodies against that 'foreign' rhesus factor. The present baby, now safely out in the big world, is unaffected; the mother is unaffected, but her blood now contains rhesus antibodies. If she carries a subsequent foetus with rhesus positive blood, those antibodies, carried continually around the baby's circulation via the placenta, will attack his rhesus positive red cells. He may die in the womb or he may be born suffering from severe anaemia and from the acute jaundice caused by the heavy load his liver has had to carry in breaking down his vanquished red cells.

● A mother can be stimulated to produce rhesus antibodies by an abortion or a miscarriage as well as by a first live-birth. This is why even first-time pregnant women are tested early in pregnancy for the presence of antibodies.

Severe haemolytic disease of the newborn is now a rarity because, provided a woman receives modern ante-natal and post-natal care, the problem can be averted. As soon as a rhesus negative mother delivers a rhesus positive baby, her blood is tested for the presence of red cells from the child. If any are found, she is given an injection of rhesus antibodies prepared from the blood of another person. These antibodies destroy the 'foreign' rhesus positive cells before their presence can stimulate her to produce her own antibodies. Because the injected antibodies are not her own, they quickly die out once their job is done. Because her own immune system has not been stimulated (*see* **Immune Response**) she is left as she was when the first baby was conceived: a rhesus negative woman whose blood contains no antibodies to the rhesus factor and will not therefore attack the blood of her next rhesus positive child.

If you have a rhesus negative child

It is important that he or she should come to understand information such as the above well before there is any likelihood of a partner-ship/pregnancy.

A rhesus negative girl, pregnant with her first child, must tell her doctor of any previous abortion/miscarriage so as to ensure that he will arrange for her blood to be tested for rhesus antibodies which may otherwise damage even a first baby. She must be brought up to accept that, unless she happens to marry a rhesus negative man, her children must be de-livered where there are sophisticated medical facilities. She cannot afford to have her babies delivered where blood testing and, if necessary, immediate injection of rhesus antibody (called anti-D Immunoglobin) is not available nor where expert care for an affected newborn might be lacking.

A rhesus negative boy should know that he is negative both because it makes him an invaluable blood donor and difficult recipient, and because it will eventually be information of importance to his partner.

Blood poisoning see **Accidents**/Wounds and infection. See also **Infection**/Types of infection: Localized infection which is spreading.

Blood tests see **Hospital**/Procedures.

Blood transfusions see **Hospital**/Procedures. See also **Blood Groups**.

Body odour see **Adolescence**/Problems with appearance and body-image.

Boils see **Infection**/Types of infection: Localized infection.

Bottle-feeding see **Eating**/Types of foods for babies. See also **Infection**/Preventing infection.

Botulism see **Diarrhoea, Gastro-enteritis and Food Poisoning**.

Bowel movements see **Constipation; Diarrhoea, Gastro-enteritis and Food Poisoning; Soiling; Toilet Training**.

Breast-feeding see **Eating**/Types of foods for babies. See also **Allergy**/Gastro-intestinal allergies.

Breath-holding see **Convulsions, 'Fits' and 'Funny Turns'**. See also **Tantrums**.

Bribery see **Discipline, Self-discipline and Learning How to Behave**/Some common disciplinary techniques.

Broken bones see **Accidents**/Fractures.

Bronchiolitis see **Chest Infections**.

Bronchitis see **Chest Infections**.

Bruises see **Accidents**.

Bullying see **School**/Problems over going to school. See also **Safety**/From 'strangers'; **Suicide; Tantrums**/Triggers for tantrums.

Burns and scalds see **Accidents**. See also **Safety**/In the home.

Carbohydrates see **Eating**/Types of food.

Catarrh see **Colds**. See also **Adenoids**.

Cheating see **Discipline, Self-discipline and Learning How to Behave**. See also **School**/Discipline in your child's school: Attitude to cheating.

Chest Infections

The upper respiratory tract includes the nose, throat and larynx (see **Colds; Coughs; Croup and Laryngitis**). The lower respiratory tract includes the bronchi, which are the main air passages leading down from throat to lungs, the bronchioles which are the small air passages networked through the lungs, and the alveoli which are the minute air sacs at the end of each bronchiole through whose walls oxygen passes into the bloodstream. Specific infections of these parts of the lower respiratory tract are known as bronchitis, bronchiolitis and pneumonia. They are here dealt with as a group, rather than as separate illnesses, because a parent will seldom be able to distinguish one from the other or even be certain when a child has a chest (lower respiratory) infection rather than an upper respiratory one.

Chest infections can be caused by a downward spread of cold viruses or bacteria from an infected throat. Many, however, are secondary infections following on from one of the many illnesses which affect the respiratory tract. Measles, for example, is sometimes followed by pneumonia. It is not necessarily that the measles virus spreads to the lungs; it may be that the virus can do sufficient damage to make it easy for further micro-organisms to establish themselves. Children with chronic conditions affecting the respiratory system (*see* **Allergy**/Asthma, for example) may be unusually susceptible to chest infections.

Whatever specific infection you have to deal with in your child, do remember that:

There is no evidence that a 'neglected cold' leads to pneumonia. Cold viruses will penetrate down into the chest if, and only if, the body fails to vanquish them at upper respiratory level. Keeping the child's feet dry has no bearing upon this matter.

Pneumonia is not the bogey-illness which it was in the pre-antibiotic era. Your child may be iller with bronchitis than with 'a touch of pneumonia' and he may be iller still with bronchiolitis, which sounds less alarming simply because few people have ever heard of it.

Bronchitis

Infection has caused inflammation and extra secretion of mucus in the bronchi which must carry air from the trachea to the lungs. The child who develops bronchitis was usually already suffering from a cold, or other upper respiratory infection. The very first sign may therefore be that he begins to seem worse when you expected him to be getting better. Other signs of bronchitis include:

A 'bubbly sounding' cough (perhaps replacing a dry one). If the child is old enough to cough up mucus rather than swallow it, it may be thick and yellowey-green. If he swallows the mucus he may now swallow so much that he vomits.

A rise in temperature. Bronchitis does not usually bring a very high fever, but is often heralded by some fever when the child's temperature had been normal with the preceding illness or with recovery from it.

Lack of appetite, lethargy and a general feeling of 'being unwell'. The child may not seem *very* ill but will seem iller than before.

Wheezy breathing even when he is not coughing due to the mucus in the passages vibrating as he forces air in and out.

'Wheezy bronchitis' Is a term which, loosely used, causes much misunderstanding. Parents who hear a doctor use it of their child sometimes assume that the child has asthma and become unnecessarily alarmed.

Wheezy-sounding breathing is to be expected in a child with bronchitis, if he does not wheeze it is only because the secretions are not very copious and/or he has temporarily cleared them by coughing.

Recurrent wheezy bronchitis is a different problem. A baby who has several episodes, especially if his breathing sounds wheezy even during the periods between bouts of illness, needs careful assessment by a doctor. He may or may not have a tendency to asthma but the condition will not be diagnosed on the basis of wheeziness alone (*see* **Allergy/ Asthma**).

Bronchiolitis

Infection has reached the bronchioles – the network of tiny air passages inside the lungs. In a severe case, the bronchioles swell and fill with mucus so that air which travels down the bronchi as the child breathes cannot get around the lung.

This potentially serious but unusual form of chest infection usually affects babies between about two and six months amongst whom it may occur in epidemics during the adult cold and 'flu season.

An affected baby will probably already have had signs of a 'bad cold'. Now he may wheeze, cough and fight for breath. He needs medical attention immediately.

If you should see a bluish colour around his mouth or under his fingernails, you can be certain that not enough oxygen is reaching his bloodstream through those clogged bronchioles. Unless you can reach your doctor immediately, take the baby to the nearest hospital.

Pneumonia

Is an acute inflammation of the alveoli which are the tiny air pockets at the ends of the bronchioles. Where bronchiolitis prevents oxygen from reaching the alveoli, pneumonia waterlogs them with inflammatory exudate so that even though oxygen reaches them, it cannot be passed through their delicate walls into the bloodstream.

Pneumonia can be caused by a variety of infecting micro-organisms, but it can also be caused mechanically, by inhalation of irritant substances or semi-solids such as vomit.

The severity of pneumonia depends not only on the cause but also on the proportion of the lung which is affected. If both lungs are affected over a wide area ('double pneumonia') the child's breathing will obviously be worse than if the pneumonia affects only a small patch of one lung. Curiously enough, a child may seem more dramatically ill with the 'lobar' or 'segmental' pneumonia which only affects one lung, than with broncho-pneumonia affecting both lungs. For example:

Lobar pneumonia usually starts suddenly, with high fever. The child seemed well this morning; tonight he seems extremely ill.

Broncho-pneumonia usually starts gradually as a worsening of existing illness. It may bring no fever.

● If you ever even *wonder* whether your child may be developing pneumonia, do not let absence of fever calm your fears. This is one instance where, while fever does mean illness, absence of fever does not mean lack of it (*see* **Nursing**/Fever).

Diagnosis of pneumonia

In a 'classic case' of either kind of pneumonia your doctor may be able to diagnose it from the end of the child's bed from:

Extremely rapid breathing, far faster than one would expect from the height of the child's fever if he has one.

A grunting sound accompanying the breathing, quite different from the wheezing of bronchitis or bronchial asthma, or from the 'barking' sound of the child with croup.

Flaring nostrils with each breath.

When he listens to and taps your child's chest, he may be able to identify affected patches in the lungs. He may arrange chest X-rays, either to confirm his diagnosis or to assess the extent of the pneumonia in deep areas of the lungs which are difficult to hear.

Treatment of pneumonia

The treatment given to your child will depend on his age, the type, severity and extent of the pneumonia, the certainty with which its cause can be stated and your doctor's preference. Some doctors prefer all children with pneumonia to be nursed in hospital, largely because they believe that oxygen treatment is helpful to all, as well as necessary to many. Do not assume that your doctor's decision to have the child admitted necessarily means that he is dangerously ill. Ask.

Many doctors will give the child antibiotics in case the infection is bacterial or in case bacterial infection should overlay the viral one.

Some will take specimens of sputum before starting such treatment so that the original infecting organisms can be cultured and the treatment adapted if necessary. Young children usually swallow rather than cough up sputum. Some may therefore have to be washed from his stomach for this purpose.

If your child is to be nursed at home, the doctor will give specific advice and help with his symptoms. If vomiting is a marked feature, for example, he will probably recommend frequent tiny drinks of a high-calorie liquid. If chest pain is a marked feature he may give the child something to ease it. He will certainly teach you, or send a physiotherapist to teach you, the vital manoeuvres which will help to clear his chest (*see below*).

Your doctor will certainly keep in close touch with you while you are nursing a child with pneumonia, but do remember that the diagnosis of pneumonia need not mean that your child is very ill. It is a technical name for a specific condition affecting the lung, but if only a small area is affected he may hardly seem ill at all and, with treatment, he may be completely recovered within the week.

Chest infections with pain

While a painful, aching chest is common whenever a child has a cough (*see* **Coughs**) acute pain *which occurs with deep breathing* usually means that the pleura (the lining of the chest wall and the lung) is inflamed so that as the lung expands with each breath, inflamed surfaces are rubbed. The more the lung is inflated, the more acute the pain. This kind of pain occurs quite commonly in pneumonia if the affected patches of lung tissue are close to the lung's surface. If the patches are deep within the structure of the lung there may be no chest pain. Chest pain in pneumonia does not, therefore, suggest that the illness is more serious; it merely gives a clue to the location of the affected parts.

Pleurisy   This is the name given to infection/inflammation of the pleura when there is no infection of the underlying lung tissue: no pneumonia. Pleurisy alone is unusual in young children. When it occurs in older children and adults it almost invariably arises from, or follows, a respiratory illness.

● The pain of pleurisy (or of involvement of the pleura in other chest infections) need not be felt in the chest, but may be sited at the side or under the ribs at the back. The pleura, after all, wraps the entire lung, not just the front surface.

Pleuritic pain can be difficult to distinguish from other causes of acute pain exacerbated by deep breathing (broken ribs for example). Although any such pain should lead to medical consultation, whether or not the victim is obviously ill, pressure may give you a clue to distinguishing pleuritic from traumatic pain. A fractured rib, for example, is very painful if pressed; pleuritic pain is increased only by inflation of the lung.

Where pleuritic pain is associated with pneumonia, the natural tendency of the victim to breath as shallowly as possible can delay recovery or be actually dangerous. Breathing exercises and effective coughing are an essential part of treatment (*see below* Physiotherapy). If you feel that pain is preventing your child from carrying out instructions or cooperating with you in this treatment, tell your doctor immediately. Pain relief may be important not only for humane but for therapeutic reasons.

In any form of pleurisy you should be aware that easing of the pain does not necessarily mean improvement in the condition. The affected pleura pours out fluid. This fluid lubricates the inflamed surfaces so that their rubbing together in breathing becomes much less painful. While this makes the situation more comfortable for the patient, the presence of fluid is pathological. The pain may be 'cured' but, while there is still fluid collected there, the patient is not.

Physiotherapy   Any chest infection involves the accumulation of secretions in the bron-
in chest   chi, bronchioles or alveoli. While antibiotics may clear infection they
infections   cannot remove secretions. To clear these out, the victim must cough them all the way back up the respiratory tract to the throat. At that level they can either be spat out or swallowed – the usual course in children.

'Postural drainage and percussion' is the technical term for tipping a child into a head-down position and thumping him. It is a mechanical means of clearing his chest when he cannot or will not cough effectively for himself. This manoeuvre is not only vital in established infections such as pneumonia but is also invaluable in preventing them from occurring, as with children liable to bronchial asthma. Many doctors who have overall charge of children with this kind of problem encourage parents to 'tip and thump' as a regular routine. The value of the exercise cannot be over-rated. Becoming skilful at doing it effectively and in a way to which a child does not object, is probably the major contribution a parent can make to his continued good health and/or his recovery.

● It would take a page of this book to describe how to do this; it will take your doctor or a physiotherapist two minutes to show you. Please ask.

● Swallowing his secretions, especially when your tipping and thumping gets a lot up all at one time, may well make your child vomit. While this is unpleasant for both of you, it is actually good for him. When he vomits, his stomach muscles compress his lungs and thus squeeze yet more mucus out.

Lung rupture and lung collapse

These extremely rare events are usually associated with chest infection although either can have a mechanical cause.

Lung rupture   If a part of the outer wall of the lung tears, air escapes and is then trapped in the space between the lung and the diaphragm and chest wall. This condition is called pneumothorax. A few individuals appear to have an inborn tendency to spontaneous rupture (spontaneous pneumothorax) and, of course, trauma can rupture a lung and lead to an air-leak. Most often, though, the condition is associated with acute respiratory difficulties, such as partial or complete obstruction of the airways, as might occur in pneumonia or bronchial asthma.

As long as the rupture in the lung has not healed, a little more air will leak with every breath. Fortunately a little is also being absorbed continuously. A very small leak will, therefore, keep itself in balance while the 'hole' closes. Such a leak will probably only be diagnosed by a doctor using a stethoscope.

A larger leak, leading to an increasing accumulation of air outside the lung, puts pressure on that lung and makes it increasingly difficult for it to keep on inflating. Left untreated, the lung might collapse; in an extreme case there might also be pressure on, even displacement of, the heart. Long before this, though, the patient would have extreme breathlessness and chest pain.

A large leak (or a small one in which the lung seems to be taking a long time to re-seal itself) is often treated by inserting a tiny tube between the ribs and into the air pocket. The apparatus (which may be left in place for several days) gradually drains the air out.

Lung collapse   Technically called atelectasis, this situation arises if the alveoli of any part of a lung become completely emptied of air so that they collapse in upon themselves like minute balloons. The lungs are never normally deflated to this extent. Even when you breathe out as fully as possible, some air remains in each air sac.

Anything which totally obstructs some of the breathing passages and, therefore, deprives a particular group of alveoli of air for a prolonged period, can lead to collapse of that segment of the lung. Common infective causes of this rare situation include an infective plug of mucus in bronchial pneumonia or in acute asthma.

Chickenpox and Shingles (Herpes Zoster)

Chickenpox is a virus infection which attacks mainly children and young adults and in which the virus settles mainly in the skin.

Shingles is an infection by the same virus (which has probably been lying dormant in the body) affecting mainly the elderly. The virus attacks one or more sensory nerves and the skin which those nerves supply.

Individuals who are in contact with shingles may 'catch' chickenpox. In theory the reverse is also true, although in practice it is rare for shingles to develop within a time period which suggests direct infection during contact with chickenpox.

An attack of chickenpox produces antibodies and lifelong immunity to that disease. The viruses which can re-emerge, years later, and give rise to shingles are thought to travel during that attack of chickenpox through nerve endings in the skin, eventually coming to rest in the cell bodies of sensory nerves lying just outside the central nervous system. Here the viruses are protected from circulating antibodies and it is thought that they are therefore able to lie dormant until, years later when those antibody levels are waning, they begin to multiply and spread back down the nerve fibres to infect the skin.

Chickenpox

This is a highly infectious disease. It varies widely in the severity of its effects.

Incubation period. About twelve to sixteen days.

Route of infection. Droplet infection from nose and throat to nose and throat.

First symptoms of chickenpox

Older children and adults may feel generally unwell, with fever, headache or sore throat, for one or two days before the rash appears. Younger children (the most frequent victims) often produce the rash as the first symptom of infection.

Acute stage of chickenpox

The rash usually appears first on the chest, the abdomen and the inner thighs. During the next day or so the face, scalp and upper parts of the arms and legs are affected.

Each 'spot' passes through several distinct phases so that as the rash develops there will be 'spots' at different stages all present at the same time. Each flat red patch thickens and becomes raised. It then accumulates fluid so that it becomes a tiny, delicate blister. Then the fluid within the blister thickens and becomes cloudy before drying out to form a scab. 'Spots' tend to appear in batches over several days. As soon as new ones (flat red patches) stop appearing, the worst will be over.

A mild case of chickenpox

The child may be bothered only by the fact that the rash is furiously itchy. He may never feel ill at all. It is important to help him avoid scratching as the blisters are very liable to secondary infection with bacteria leading to impetigo or boils, for example. Any secondary infection will require treatment by a doctor. Scratching can also lead to scarring which, while it is usually temporary, may last for months or even years. Keeping his nails short will prevent some damage, while frequent warm baths with bicarbonate of soda added and/or calamine lotion freely available for him to dab on the most itchy places, may help his morale.

A severe case of chickenpox

Older people are usually more severely affected by chickenpox, but the viruses themselves vary in their virulence so that some families experience a far more severe form than others. In a severe case, the rash can cover almost every square inch not only of the external skin and the scalp but of mucous membranes and other hidden surfaces, too. The wretched patient may have lesions in his ears and nostrils, mouth and throat and so closely around his eyes that they are swollen and inflamed. He may have such a close-packed rash on his body that, as the vesicles burst, he feels raw all over. With such a severe rash there may also be high fever, as well as the specific discomforts (sore throat, sore mouth, earache, etc.) which go with the awkward placing of sores and scabs.

There is no specific treatment for chickenpox, however severe, but a doctor should certainly be called for a patient suffering in this way. A check must be kept on infection in the eyes and ears as well as for superficial infection of external skin.

Possible complications of chickenpox

Very occasionally chickenpox virus invades the lungs to produce a viral pneumonia (*see* **Chest Infections**) or the central nervous system to produce a viral encephalitis (*see* **Meningitis and Encephalitis**). Both complications can occur up to ten days after the first appearance of the rash. If a child who had seemed virtually recovered from chickenpox suddenly seems to have a respiratory infection or to become drowsy with a severe headache, send for medical help and do not forget to tell the doctor, should it be a different one, about the recent attack of chickenpox.

● Although a child with chickenpox continues to be infectious as long as new 'spots' are appearing, he may be regarded as non-infectious as soon as the last crop have scabbed. There is no truth in the idea that the scabs themselves carry the infection.

Shingles (herpes zoster)

First symptoms of shingles

Sometimes the patient has a headache and fever for a few days prior to the appearance of diagnostic signs. Often the first diagnostic sign, in adolescents and older people, is acute pain in the area of the skin which is supplied by the affected nerve. In over fifty per cent of cases this will be a patch of skin on the chest or abdomen, but in a few cases the nerve affected serves the face or head in which case the eyes may be involved. Sometimes the damage to the nerve produces loss of sensation rather than pain, but this pain, called 'post-herpetic neuralgia', is the most usual and most troublesome symptom. While there is only pain, shingles is difficult to diagnose and some unfortunate patients find themselves dismissed as 'making a fuss about nothing' when in fact they are in very real and severe discomfort. The appearance of the rash does not signal the end of the pain, but it does produce an immediate and sympathetic diagnosis.

The rash **Shingles** produces a rash exactly like that of chickenpox (*see above*) except
of shingles that 'spots' appear only along the course of the nerve affected by the viruses. The patient may, therefore, have a girdle of vesicles or a single patch or a stripe running up the chest.

Treatment There is no specific treatment for shingles although many local applica-
of shingles tions are tried and anything which the patient believes to be helpful may be so. A doctor should certainly be involved in pain control. The rash and the pain commonly clear within two to three weeks although pain outlasts the rash in some cases (*see* **Pain and Pain Control**).

Childminders *see* **Working Mothers.** *See also* **Babysitters.**
Choking *see* **Accidents.** *See also* **Safety**/In the home.

Circumcision *see also* **Hospital**/Surgery

Surgical removal of the foreskin: the loose fold of skin covering the tip (glans) of a boy's penis.

Circumcision used to be an almost routine matter, taken for granted by a majority of western parents and doctors. Now fashion and opinion have changed, especially in Britain and western Europe. The procedure remains a necessary part of the ritual of certain religious groups, but most doctors will not carry it out 'routinely' as it is very seldom medically necessary and does carry some small risk of infection and/or bleeding as well as some inevitable discomfort to even the youngest baby.

Some parents, especially in the United States, still prefer to have baby boys circumcised at birth. If you are undecided, you may like to discuss some of the following points with the doctor who looks after mother and child during the birth.

Will an uncircumcised boy feel 'different'? In most communities the up-to-date answer is 'no' because those showers and changing rooms will contain both circumcised and uncircumcised penises. But there may still be pressing social reasons for infant circumcision in some families. If, for example, one of you is from a Jewish family, it is possible that even if you have no feeling one way or another about circumcision, older generations of the family will feel very differently. It would be sad if a grandmother found that your son's foreskin created a barrier between her and the baby.

Do the sexual partners of uncircumcised males have an increased risk of cervical cancer? Probably not. This belief was based on research showing very low rates of cervical cancer amongst Jewish women, partners, of course, of circumcised males. But these low rates now seem more likely to be due to racial differences in susceptibility to this form of cancer, rather than to the presence or absence of foreskins.

Does circumcision improve sexual performance by reducing the penis' sensitivity? Who knows? If the answer is 'yes' it is perhaps surprising that couples seldom choose to use condoms to achieve the same effect.

Is circumcision an aid to hygiene? Yes, in a sense. A male whose foreskin is intact will have to wash beneath it to remove the white secretion (smegma) which can otherwise collect there. But in the same sense mouths would be more hygienic if we removed all our teeth so that no plaque could collect between them.

Is it not worth having a newborn boy circumcised in case the operation becomes necessary later on? Later circumcision is *very* rarely necessary unless too-early attempts are made to retract a foreskin which is not ready (*see below*). Although later circumcision can be very upsetting for the boy (*see* **Hospital**/Surgery), this does not seem a valid reason for doing it sooner. After all, we do not remove appendixes in infancy in case of later appendicitis.

If a baby is to be circumcised, when and how should it be done? Circumcision for religious reasons will be performed at specified times and perhaps by specified rituals. Jewish boys, for example, are circumcised on the eighth day after birth while Muslim boys are not circumcised until somewhere between their third and fifteenth years.

If there are no religious considerations, the operation is probably best carried out while the newborn baby is still under hospital care, provided that the doctor considers that his condition warrants it. In Britain, most doctors feel that a general anaesthetic should be used. Being newborn does not prevent the procedure from being painful. In the United States, however, anaesthesia is rarely used.

Care of an uncircumcised penis

Your baby's uncircumcised penis requires neither more, less nor different care than any other part of his body or than his sister's vulva. The foreskin and the glans of the penis are fused together at birth and they usually remain fused together for months and often for several years. The foreskin cannot therefore be retracted, pulled back or washed underneath and about the only mistake a parent can make with this organ is to try. So the penis gets washed with its owner and should otherwise be left strictly alone (except by its owner!). Eventually, perhaps when he is two but perhaps not until later, that foreskin will separate from the glans. You will probably first realize that this is happening when you see your son with an erection and notice that the foreskin has retracted itself. When, and only when, it can retract of its own accord, it is sensible to begin retracting it so as to remove any secretions from underneath, during bathing. Even then this kind of washing is not *necessary*. If your son objects, leave it or, better still, show him how to do it himself.

● If leaving your son uncircumcised is a big decision for you, do be sure that it is one you have made wholeheartedly. If a bit of you is still worried about that bit of him and you fiddle about trying to pull back a foreskin which is still fused to the penis, you are likely to make minute tears in it. If that happens scar tissue may form which fuses the foreskin to the glans so that it actually cannot retract when it is ready to do so. This is one of the commonest reasons for later circumcision becoming medically necessary (*see* **Hospital**/Surgery).

Care of a circumcised penis

A gauze dressing will be applied to the raw tip of the penis and hospital staff will advise you on the care of the wound. There may be a few drops of blood in the hours after the operation, but any continuing bleeding should be reported to the doctor. The penis will be inflamed, but any extra swelling, heat or other signs of infection should similarly be reported. Usually, though, the little wound will heal without problems.

● Whatever his age, your baby son will be sore, especially if urine touches the raw area and stings, or when clothing rubs it as he is lifted or carried.

Meatal ulcers Lacking the protection of a foreskin, the sensitive tip of the penis sometimes gets chafed and irritated by nappies and urine. Occasionally a tiny ulcer develops on the edge of the glans and in the top of the urethra. Meatal ulcers cause acute pain whenever the baby passes urine and are stubbornly slow to heal because the urine destroys the forming scab. If your baby screams with pain when he urinates and you can see a tiny sore there, take him immediately to the doctor. He will probably prescribe an ointment to be applied on a tiny glass rod into the top of the urethra. This protects the ulcer from the urine and thus reduces pain and promotes healing.

● Don't neglect this kind of ulcer even if you are away from home and it is difficult to find a doctor. If it is neglected for several days it is just possible that scar tissue will begin to form, narrow the urethral opening and restrict the flow of urine. Immediate treatment will prevent this.

Cleft lip and cleft palate *see* **Hospital**/Surgery.

Colds

Colds cause more misery and loss of time from school or work than any other viral illness, yet no immunization is available. Why? The main reason is that while 'a cold' may be all-too-recognizable to the sufferer, its causative virus may be one of many kinds. The group of viruses which are most commonly responsible are those called rhinoviruses; more than one hundred of these have already been identified and there are certainly more to be discovered. Even if it were possible to discover all the possible cold viruses, and to make a vaccine which included every single one, we still should not have really effective and worthwhile protection because although each virus does provoke specific antibodies, these do not seem to last very long. It may never be both practical and worthwhile to produce such a complex multi-vaccine and administer it, perhaps as often as every few months, to everyone.

Colds, therefore, have to be lived with. Your doctor can neither prevent nor cure them, so unless you are really worried about your child, there is little point in bothering him each time he has one. You only need medical advice and help if the cold does not follow its normal, expected and uncomfortable course. Like all virus infections, colds make the affected parts of the body (the upper respiratory system) especially liable to invasion by bacteria. If your child's cold leads to a 'secondary infection' (*see below*) then it is worth seeking medical advice. Then, and *only* then, may the doctor want to consider giving an antibiotic.

Because the common cold is so common, old wives' tales concerning causes and cures are legion. Don't believe everything you hear and do bear in mind that the very existence of so many 'cold cures' is in itself proof that no effective cure is really known. If you buy a particular medicine over the counter at your chemist's shop because it makes you feel that you are doing something for the victim, do make sure that you know *what* you are buying, and that you really want to spend the extra money on a proprietary concoction which is mostly lemon flavouring with some aspirin thrown in.

Symptoms of an ordinary cold

A cold is a virus infection of the nasal passages. First symptoms therefore are a 'runny' nose which may also feel 'stuffy' because the membranes are slightly swollen. The child sneezes, because the discharge irritates the passages. He may cough as discharge runs down his throat and tickles.

Normal variants

Depending on the virulence of the virus and on the tissues which it infects, he may also have slightly red and watery eyes, a sore throat and hoarseness (laryngitis).

Degree of 'illness'

The symptoms in themselves are enough to make anyone feel miserable, but, in small children in particular, there may also be slight fever, loss of appetite and lassitude. The victim does not exactly feel *ill* but he does not feel on top form either.

Course of an ordinary cold

Colds usually begin abruptly, developing, for example, from a sneeze at breakfast-time to a full-blown cold by evening. The acute phase usually lasts from three to four days. By the end of that time the body has mustered its defences and stopped the viruses from multiplying further, but it may take several more days for the inflamed mucous membranes to get back to normal. A 'runny' nose and an irritating cough (especially when the victim is lying down at night) may continue for a week to ten days.

● Unless you have reason to suspect a secondary infection (*see below*), you can assume that a child has stopped being infectious to others about four days after his cold began.

Babies with colds

Young babies can react quite severely to ordinary colds. In the first month of life an older child's 'ordinary cold' may make your baby very ill indeed. If you suspect a cold and he seems unwell, don't judge his condition by the reading on the thermometer. His temperature may be high, normal or unusually low. Whichever it is, he should be seen by his doctor. An older baby may run quite a high fever at the beginning of the infection and he may vomit and go off his feeds so that you need to watch out for dehydration (*see* **Diarrhoea**, **Gastro-enteritis and Food Poisoning**/ Diarrhoea in babies and toddlers).

Because a baby's breathing passages are very small, the excess mucus produced during the cold may bother him more than it bothers an older child. Above all, having a blocked-up nose (which he cannot yet blow) makes it difficult for him to suck. This may make him frantic at feeding times and at other times too, because he cannot suck his dummy or fist or thumb when he is going to sleep. Because he has not yet acquired immunity to many of the pathogenic bacteria in his environment, a baby with a cold is rather more liable than an older child to get a secondary infection on top of it.

All in all, if your child catches his first cold in his earliest months, you would probably be sensible to consult his doctor. He will check that the illness *is* only a cold (or at least that it does not appear to be anything else) and he will check that there are no signs of secondary infection. He will also advise you on certain specific things which you can do to make the baby more comfortable. He may, for example, prescribe decongestant nose drops which you can use just before feeds (and perhaps just before you settle the baby to sleep) so that he can suck more comfortably. Or he may show you how to use a nasal aspirator (a plastic dropper with a rubber suction bulb) to suck the secretions out of the baby's nose. He may advise you to put a pillow *under* the cot mattress so that the baby sleeps with his head raised a little to lessen coughing. Above all, he will tell you what signs to look out for so that you can call him immediately if the cold should begin to turn into anything more serious.

Different doctors prefer different kinds of treatment for very young babies with colds. Once you have discussed this first one with your doctor you will know how he would like you to proceed next time.

● Do not give any kind of 'cold cure' to a baby without specific advice from a doctor.

● While you will not always succeed, it is worth trying to protect a young baby from colds. At least prevent cold-ridden older children from sneezing all over him or feeding him with virus-laden fingers.

Commonsense about children with colds

Your child will probably have around six to eight colds each year between his third and eighth birthdays. He will also have various infectious diseases, bouts of 'flu and the occasional gastric upset. If each of those colds has to be treated as an illness, he will be cooped-up at home for several weeks of each year. Obviously when a particular cold *does* make him ill, he will have to be properly nursed through it, but when a cold makes him no more than uncomfortable and unattractive, you have to decide what your policy is going to be: are you going to keep him at home (and stay at home yourself) to protect other children from catching his cold or are you going to provide handfuls of tissues and brisk sympathy and help him get on with his normal life?

Colds are highly infectious especially to babies and very young children who have not yet built up any immunity to most of the common cold viruses. Your child will be infectious before he has full-blown symptoms, but it is the virus-laden mucus which he sprays around as he coughs and sneezes and smears around when he blows his nose or wipes it on the back of his hand, which will most readily pass on the cold. If you can teach him to keep his mucus to himself, his colds will be less of a menace.

Teach him to blow his nose by closing one nostril while blowing down the other. If he can acquire early this genuinely difficult skill, he will discover that it keeps him more comfortable than sniffing and wiping.

Make sure he uses paper tissues and throws them away at once. Washable handkerchiefs should be banned (except perhaps for top-pocket show) and used paper ones stuffed up sleeves or in pockets can carry viruses for some time and then clog up your washing machine.

Teach him to cover his nose and mouth and turn away from people or food when he coughs or sneezes.

Try (gently) to persuade him not to rub his face against people when he has a cold. You may even be able to teach him not to share lollipops and viruses with his friends.

Persuade him to wash his hands as often as possible. He cannot wash every time he blows his nose if he is blowing it every two minutes, but recent research does show that cold viruses are spread almost as rapidly via the hands (touching food, etc.) as by droplet infection.

If your child is not yet old enough for school and does not attend any kind of organized pre-school group, it will probably be fairly easy for you to keep him away from most other children when he has colds. Remember that small babies are usually the worst affected by these viruses so take particular trouble to keep him away from well-baby clinics and so forth. If you share his care with a minder, discuss colds with her in advance. She will probably accept that a cold is part of a child's normal life and be perfectly prepared to look after him as usual, provided he is not ill. But she may also be in charge of a small baby or of a child who, perhaps because of asthma, needs special protection.

As soon as your child attends an organized group – whether a day nursery, nursery school or playgroup – do discuss colds with the person in charge.

If you keep your child at home with his colds but other mothers do not, he will miss more time than any of the other children while being fully exposed to all their viruses. That does not seem fair.

If you send your child with his colds but other mothers do not, you will be the one who is behaving unfairly.

Usually staff will have a clear view: either they will feel that colds just have to be accepted or they will feel that if children always stay away when they have colds, the infection rate within the group can be kept down. Whichever their point of view, if you abide by it you will be doing the best you can.

Schoolchildren and colds

You really do need the teachers' advice about when you should, or should not, keep your streaming child away. If they beg you not to send him, try not to even if it is difficult for you to take time off from work. At least you will know that other families are under the same pressure and that your child will not 'lose out' by comparison with them or be labelled 'delicate' because he is absent so much.

If they tell you that it is all right to send the child 'unless he is unwell', do so. Your child's viruses will only be added to a general pool and you have nothing to feel guilty about.

If they do not seem to have a 'cold policy', it would be sensible to raise the issue at a Parent–Teacher Association meeting.

Adolescents and colds

As your child grows up he will probably have a clear view of his own about whether or not he is fit for school on any particular occasion. Be thankful if he is somebody who always wants to go or at least always takes it for granted that he must. By this stage, colds do not spread so easily within the group because children have more immunity; those who do catch colds are seldom ill with them. It is simply not fair to expect your busy child to miss important lessons, sporting fixtures or after-school activities because of a mere cold.

If yours is one of the children who uses every cold as an excuse for a day or two off school he is probably not very happy there. Help him to face the fact that he is using his cold as an excuse. Using illness as an escape from unhappiness can become a habit and it is not a good one for later life. If he does not much enjoy school at the best of times, the misery of a cold may genuinely make it seem intolerable, so you need to tackle the unhappiness rather than just telling him off for skiving.

When you really cannot decide whether or not your child is ill enough to need to stay at home, ask yourself whether you would stay off work for a cold of the same degree.

Tips for making colds less uncomfortable

Although neither you nor anyone else can cure your child's cold, you can keep him comparatively comfortable while he lives through it.

Don't let room-air become too dry. Centrally-heated rooms, especially hermetically sealed and double-glazed ones, can be very dry indeed compared with rooms heated with gas or solid fuel fires, for example. Some moisture in the atmosphere reduces the swelling of the nasal membranes and therefore that 'stuffy' feeling. Try to combine the warmth you want with some ventilation like an old-fashioned open window.

If hot, dry air is uncomfortable, it should not be surprising that colds often feel better when the victim is outside. Unless you live in a very extreme climate there is no reason why a cold-sufferer should not go out.

If you have young children (and therefore years of colds and their disturbed nights ahead of you) consider buying a cold-air vaporizer. They are expensive but invaluable, not only in making children more comfortable when they have colds but in other upper respiratory infections too (*see* **Croup and Laryngitis**).

Encourage nose-blowing. Much of the coughing which goes on with an ordinary cold is due to mucus from the nose being sniffed up and trickling down the back of the throat. The child who gets rid of the mucus out of his nose will not cough so much. If he goes to bed with his nose clear he is much less likely to be woken (at least immediately) by coughing.

Many children resist blowing their noses when they have colds because the nostrils and upper lip become so sore. Vaseline, applied two or three times a day from the *beginning* of a cold, will protect the skin so that it never becomes sore.

Prop up the victim for sleeping. If mucus can trickle out of the nose there will be less disturbing coughing in the night. A child may like an extra pillow or two. Even a baby can have a pillow under the end of the mattress and be encouraged to sleep on his side rather than his back.

Use steam to 'unclog' dried secretions. Children are often at their most miserable when they have just woken up and noses (and sometimes eyes) are blocked with mucus which has dried. For a child, a hot drink as soon as he wakes may make all the difference. The drink is pleasant and the steam, around his face and in his nose and mouth as he sips, 'unblocks' him. A child too young to be trusted with a steamy drink can get the same benefit from a bath, from warm water play over the sink or just from having his face washed with a warm cloth.

Encourage quiet play if the child is 'streaming'. Although there is no *health* reason why a child should be kept quiet during an ordinary cold, there may be *comfort* reasons. If the cold is really streaming, violent physical exercise and rapid changes of temperature will provoke even more discharge. The child may be much more comfortable if he is encouraged to curl up with a book or to watch television or to play a quiet game with you.

Don't try to make the child stay any warmer than usual. Extra clothes and over-heated rooms will make him more uncomfortable and do nothing to combat the virus.

Don't dose him with cold cures: there are no genuine ones. He needs no medicine at all (except possibly an aspirin for a headache and/or fever) unless he has a secondary infection in which case he should see the doctor.

Don't try to suppress his cough unless it is keeping the household awake to such an extent that you are getting desperate. In this case you should, again, see the doctor. Most cough medicines are ineffective. A medicine which did stop coughing would be a bad idea because it is coughing which prevents mucus (and therefore viruses) from penetrating further down the respiratory tract and perhaps reaching his lungs (*see* **Chest Infections**).

Don't rub his chest with liniments. They do no good and will only make him uncomfortable and/or convinced that he really is ill.

Don't push food on him if he is not hungry or withhold it from him if he is. The cold may, or may not, put him off his food for a day or two. It does not matter either way provided he has plenty to drink.

Colds and secondary infections (*see also* **Chest Infections**)

Temporary damage done by cold viruses can provide an easy entry for bacteria to various parts of the upper respiratory tract and to the ears and sinuses. A bacterial secondary infection need not make the child very ill because his body's defensive system will get to work to combat it just as it worked to get rid of the original cold. Thick yellow or green nasal discharge, for example, is often the last you see of a cold. It does suggest bacterial infection but unless the child seems ill it requires no treatment. Suspect that the cold has progressed beyond a 'simple head cold' if:

He gets worse instead of better. If he had no fever and did not feel ill for the first two or three days of the cold and now shoots a fever on day four, or if he started the cold with a fever but was better by day three and worse by day five, for example, you should be suspicious. A simple cold, however horrible, gets gradually better not gradually worse.

● A child whose cold symptoms seem to be getting worse and who seems to be becoming iller and iller may not have an infection which is secondary to that cold, but one of the infectious diseases of childhood which starts out by mimicking a cold. Measles often begins in this way (*see* **Measles**).

He has earache, especially with fever. If he has earache at all he should see a doctor the same day. Earache with fever should be treated as an emergency; ask for the next available appointment (*see* **Ears and Hearing**; **Ear Disorders and Deafness**/Ear disorders).

He has a bad headache, especially with fever. This may suggest sinusitis (*see below*).

His throat is suddenly sore especially with fever. Any form of 'tonsillitis' (*see* **Tonsils**) can follow a cold. In a very young child you may have to respond to fever and general signs of illness as he may not complain that his throat is painful.

● You cannot rely on swollen glands in the child's neck as a clue to an infected throat or a worsening cold. Glands swell when the body's lymph system is involved in fighting infection (*see* **Immune Response**). In childhood some swelling may remain from illness to illness.

His cough gets worse and/or his breathing seems affected. All the common upper and lower respiratory infections (*see* **Coughs; Croup and Laryngitis; Chest Infections**) can follow an ordinary cold although unless the child is feverish and ill the chances are that the cough which sounds 'chesty' is not actually due to infection lower down than the throat.

● If you have any reason to think that your child has a secondary infection after a cold, by all means check with a doctor, but don't decide to be clever and give the child a few doses of the antibiotic you have left over from last time. You should not *have* any left over as the full course should have been given last time. But even if you have, only a doctor should decide whether an antibiotic is appropriate now and if so, which one. If it is, he will want the child to have a *full* course not just the remains of a bottle (*see* **Infection**/Infections which cause illness: Pros and cons of antibiotics in undiagnosed infections).

Sinuses and sinusitis

The sinuses are air-filled, mucous membrane-lined spaces in the facial bones which all connect with the nasal passages.

When a child has a cold, his sinuses are almost certain to be affected; they produce extra mucus to add to the cold's general 'runniness' and that mucus may drip to the back of his throat when he is lying down and produce a tickly cough. Usually the sinuses return to normal after the cold is over, but occasionally they become secondarily infected with bacteria to produce sinusitis which can be a quite severe and very unpleasant illness.

Just as the spaces between the bones of a baby's skull (the fontanelles) are slow to close up so that the whole skull is fused together, so the sinuses are slow to develop and enlarge to a point where their infection is possible. Since a child cannot have sinusitis in a sinus which he has not yet developed, the timetable is worthy of note:

Under two years: ethmoids only. The ethmoid sinuses are those to either side of the bridge of the nose and they are the only ones large enough for infection up to this age.

Acute ethmoiditis or 'infant sinusitis' is rare but requires immediate medical treatment as without it, infection can spread to the eyes or even to the brain. Suspect it if your baby or toddler, having had a cold or other upper respiratory infection, develops pain and swelling around the eyes together with fever.

By three or four: maxillary sinuses also. The maxillary sinuses are in the cheekbones.

Maxillary sinusitis can be caused not only by infection from the nasal passageways but also by infection from the root of a badly decayed tooth, so suspect it if fever and facial pain follows either a cold or an episode of acute toothache which was not treated (*see* **Teeth**/Some dental emergencies).

By ten: frontal sinuses as well. The frontal sinuses are in the forehead, just above each eyebrow. They are a common site of sinusitis but the illness is seldom serious.

Frontal sinusitis often presents as a headache, but unlike an 'ordinary headache' (*see* **Headaches**) there is tenderness when the area is pressed. There may or may not be fever and/or swelling above the eyes.

Treatment of sinusitis after infancy

Acute sinusitis requires medical attention. Your doctor will probably give the child antibiotics to control the infection but the illness may hang on for many days. Antibiotics are slow to penetrate the sinuses. Even once it is 'sterile', the thick matter can take a long time to reach the nasal passageways from which the child can get rid of it.

Sometimes, even once the acute infection is over, the pus-filled sinus fails to drain and the child continues to have uncomfortable pressure-pain especially when he bends down. Occasionally such a child may be referred to an Ear, Nose and Throat specialist for further treatment. Some recommend a minor operation to drain and wash-out the sinus but others prefer a more conservative approach. Certainly a person who is prone to sinusitis may find that drained sinuses 'refill' with the very next cold.

Cold Sores

These are caused by herpes simplex; a widespread virus which is carried by many people but produces symptoms in only a few. It is almost impossible to eradicate; so the child who has one crop of cold sores is likely to have others. However, the virus can lie dormant for years so that the child who is plagued by cold sores every few weeks for a year or two may then be free of them for the rest of her childhood.

Very occasionally, this same virus causes generalized illness, including infection of the penis and cervix. A mother whose genital tract is thus infected may have to have her baby delivered by Caesarean section to avoid the risk of her baby being infected during birth.

A typical first attack by herpes simplex

Does not take the form of cold sores but of mouth ulcers. The child – who is seldom below school age – has one or more shallow yellow ulcers on the inside of the lips or cheeks. They are surrounded by inflamed mucous membrane and are so acutely painful that she may be unable to eat or drink comfortably for several days. Fortunately, the ulcers soon clear up of their own accord. Few doctors consider that local applications hasten the healing although a little vaseline applied to the area may reduce the painful friction between ulcer and teeth (*see also* **Mouth Ulcers**).

Second and later attacks by herpes simplex

Do not cause mouth ulcers but instead produce a collection of tiny itchy blisters close to the mouth which burst and become yellow and crusty. The itching quickly subsides but the sores are unsightly and may take a week or more to disappear.

Nobody knows why cold sores appear in some people and not in others, nor why they appear when they do. Most seem to appear spontaneously. A few seem to be a reaction to stress and fatigue. Some follow minor illnesses (like colds; this is how they acquired their misleading name), while some girls develop them before menstrual periods.

● Consult your doctor about a first crop of cold sores: there are local applications which speed healing. Do not use cortisone ointments (*see* **Infection**/Treatment of external inflammation and infection). Any cold sore which is not obviously clearing within a few days should be seen again by a doctor as secondary infection (*see*, for example, **Impetigo and Staphylococcal Infections**) is a possibility.

Constipation

Contrary to popular belief, constipation has very little to do with the frequency with which stools are passed but a great deal to do with the consistency (and therefore the ease of passing) of those stools. A very hard, dry stool, which is difficult or even painful to pass, is a constipated one even if it is the second in forty-eight hours. A soft stool which is easy to pass is not a constipated one even if it is the first in seventy-two hours.

In the past, people were convinced that a normally working bowel should 'empty' every day and that if it did not, the owner would have all kinds of troubles such as headaches and bad breath. These nonsensical beliefs led parents to take a most unfortunate interest in their children's bowel movements and bred whole populations which took laxatives (*see* **Laxatives**) either as a once-weekly 'precaution' or whenever a day had passed without a stool. Regular use of laxative chemicals spoils the natural rhythm of the bowel's action and, if continued for long, can actually spoil its muscle tone so that natural action becomes increasingly difficult. Unless your child is prescribed laxatives for an organic disease or problems with soiling (*see* **Soiling**), do not give her any, ever.

Natural bowel rhythm

Waste from digested food is passed along the small intestine by rhythmic activity of the intestinal muscle wall (peristalsis). At this stage it is in the form of a thick liquid. When it passes into the large intestine, liquid is absorbed through the intestinal wall so that as the waste moves down the colon, it solidifies. When it reaches the rectum, the rich supply of nerve endings signal readiness to pass a stool. If the signals are ignored (perhaps because this is not a convenient moment to seek a lavatory), they die down. The rectum can expand enormously to accommodate more waste, but water continues to be absorbed from it. If further signals are ignored over many hours, the quantity of waste awaiting evacuation becomes greater and its consistency becomes drier.

Individuals vary widely in the frequency with which they need to pass stools. Some of this variation is certainly due to habit and some to diet (*see below*) but equally certainly the only 'ideal' frequency for every individual is 'whenever you feel the need to go'.

Ideally, if your child has taken over full responsibility for looking after herself in the lavatory, you will not even know how often she passes a stool. The less concerned you are, the less concerned she will be and the less likely it is that there will be any problems. After all, you do not enquire how often she urinates, nor rush to the lavatory to check. She may be a child who passes a stool every day. If she is, she may find it convenient to do so at home rather than at school, where lack of time, privacy, hygiene and toilet paper can all present her with difficulties. On the other hand, she may be a child who goes less frequently and/or less regularly. Accept that, too.

All you need to do, by way of assistance, is to ensure that there is a lavatory, time and privacy available for her when she needs it.

Constipation in young children

In a young child, the commonest reason for constipation is ignoring the signals for so long that the stool becomes hard and difficult to pass. At this stage the child may try to pass it but not have the time or patience to do so, abandoning the whole matter again and again so that it gets increasingly difficult. Or she may succeed in passing a stool but, because it is bulky and hard, doing so may be painful. It can even cause a minute tear in the sensitive tissue at the edge of the anus so that it really hurts and will hurt again next time a stool is passed.

If your child keeps going to the lavatory but emerging again in record time and without flushing the lavatory, you may suspect that something of this kind is happening. Ask her. Explain. Encourage her to take a book or a comic into the lavatory with her and settle down to deal with the whole matter, pointing out that once she has done so, it need not be difficult again.

If the child should have an anal tear she will probably tell you 'I can't, it hurts'. Take her to the doctor. This is one of the rare occasions when he may prescribe a stool-softening laxative. He can also prescribe an anaesthetic ointment for use while the split heals, which it will do very quickly.

Preventing constipation in all ages Make sure that everyone drinks enough fluid. Although most people do, most of the time, there are occasions when we let ourselves become mildly dehydrated. If the body is short of water it will take all it can from the faeces through the colon wall, thus making the eventual stool drier.

Try to provide all members of the family with a diet which contains plenty of 'roughage'. Highly refined and processed foods leave little residue for the bowels to work on. Fruit, raw vegetables, wholegrain cereals and breads all add bulk. Still more can be added by using wheat bran along with flour in your baking or by serving a bran breakfast cereal.

Contraception *see* **Adolescence**/Sex.
Convalescence *see* **Nursing**/Getting back to normal.

Convulsions, 'Fits' and 'Funny Turns'

The sight of someone having a 'fit' arouses a kind of superstitious terror in most people. Parents are no exception. But if your child does ever have any kind of convulsion or 'funny turn' it is important to try and keep your head. The more accurate information you can give to your doctor about the circumstances and nature of the 'fit', the more likely it is that he will be able to give you immediate reassurance that, while horrible, the matter is not serious. Furthermore, if you can stay fairly calm you will be able to ask him, directly, the questions that bother you later such as 'is he epileptic?' or 'is his brain damaged?' All too often parents dare not ask these questions for fear of the answer 'yes', while doctors do not volunteer the information for fear of 'putting ideas into' parents' heads. A conspiracy of desperate silence does nobody any good.

Febrile convulsions

By far the most common cause for convulsions in children under five is a very rapid rise in fever (*see* **Nursing**/Fever). About three per cent of all children have a convulsion of this kind so it cannot even be regarded as unusual. The tendency to react to a sudden rise in fever in this way runs in families so that an affected child may have a parent who reacted similarly. On the other hand, the fact that your first child has such a convulsion during infancy does not necessarily mean that later children will, too.

If a child is liable to febrile convulsions, he will usually have his first while he is between one and three years old. It is very unusual indeed to have a first such convulsion after the third birthday. If he does have one while he is a baby or toddler, the risk of him having another diminishes steadily between three and five. Even a child who has been very liable to these convulsions will grow through the tendency by the time he is five.

Mechanism of a febrile convulsion
A sudden, sharp rise in body temperature at an age when the body's temperature-regulating mechanisms are not as efficient as they will later become, 'irritates' the brain whose control over consciousness and movement is temporarily disturbed. Neurones in the brain suddenly discharge their impulses and this results in the 'fit' which you see (*see below*). Most febrile convulsions stop spontaneously within seconds, or at least within a minute or two, and do the brain no damage whatsoever.

Why a febrile convulsion is treated as an emergency
Even though it is extremely unlikely that a febrile convulsion will do your child any harm, any child who has such a convulsion must have immediate medical attention *just in case*.

If a major convulsion is allowed to continue for a long period such as twenty minutes or more, permanent damage to the brain is a possibility. Those neurones go on and on discharging; if they continue to do so for a long time their extreme activity may outstrip the body's ability to replenish their oxygen supply. The neurones become exhausted of oxygen and would eventually 'die'. Long-continuing and untreated febrile convulsions can lead to later epilepsy of the type known as 'temporal lobe epilepsy' (*see below*) because the brain cells in the area known to be the focus for this kind of epilepsy happen to be particularly sensitive to oxygen starvation.

If you send immediately for medical help, the chances are very high that the 'fit' will be over long before it can reach you. But if the 'fit' is still going on the doctor can immediately stop it with an injection of anti-convulsant medication. The moment the drug takes effect the child's brain ceases to be at risk just as it ceases to be at risk if the convulsion ceases of its own accord.

Your child's first febrile convulsion

Many intelligent, level-headed parents report panic and a strong impulse to get away from the convulsing child; to seek help or to find somebody, *anybody*, to whom he can be handed over. If this is your reaction, don't add to your misery with later secret guilt. You are in a majority.

If you did not already know that your child was ill, he may begin to convulse wherever he happens to be: playing on the floor or in the garden or sitting in his high chair. If you already knew that he was feverish he may well be lying down in his cot or bed or on the sofa. Quite frequently he will have been asleep; the fever will have risen sharply during his nap and the convulsion will begin when you disturb him.

The 'fit' usually has four phases although many take place so quickly that these stages are not distinguishable one from another:

The child suddenly looks 'strange' and/or terrified and may emit a guttural sound which parents often describe as 'inhuman'.

His whole body (or one side of it only) extends and becomes rigid and his eyes either look glazed, or roll up so that only the white is visible. It is at this stage that parents so often believe that the child is dead.

The rigidity gives way to more or less violent thrashing or jerking of his limbs and juddering of his body. His teeth clench; foam may drool from his mouth; he may wet himself.

The movements cease; the child's body relaxes and he either 'comes to', very anxious and confused, and then goes to sleep, or he drops into sleep without ever 'coming round'.

What to do during a febrile convulsion

Stay with him to prevent him hurting himself. If he convulses while sitting in a chair, put him on the floor; if he is on a bed or sofa, make sure he does not roll off. Wherever he is, don't try to control his thrashing limbs but concentrate on preventing them hitting against anything, and on keeping him on his side.

Watch out for vomiting/choking. Left alone he could roll onto his back and choke on his own secretions.

Don't try to prise his teeth apart to prevent him biting his tongue. If he bites his tongue, it will heal; if you break his teeth, they will not.

Don't try to shake him back to consciousness. His body is already receiving *too much* stimulation from his brain; violent action from you could make the whole episode more acute.

Look at your watch and wait with him for at least three minutes. If there is anyone else in the house, by all means call to them to telephone or go for the doctor, but if you are alone with the child don't leave him to go for help yourself. The convulsion will almost certainly end during those three minutes. If the child becomes conscious, soothe and comfort him as calmly as you possibly can. He must and will sleep almost immediately. If he does not become conscious but simply relaxes into deep sleep, check that he is out of range of any immediate hazards, like an electric fire, and then leave him for just long enough to telephone for help or shout to a neighbour to do so.

If the convulsion has not ceased in three minutes you must summon help without waiting for it to end naturally. Use your judgement: can you safely leave him while you dial 999? If he is drooling or has vomited and there is a real risk of choking, can you pick him up as he is and carry him to the telephone or front door? As with other rare emergencies, like arterial bleeding, this may be a time to drop conventional behaviour, open a window and simply yell for help.

If a convulsion has gone on for several minutes, the doctor will probably recommend admitting him to hospital anyway so it is probably quickest and easiest to get a neighbour or passing good Samaritan either to 'phone for an ambulance or to drive you and the child directly to the nearest casualty department.

After a convulsion
Most convulsions *will* have stopped within three minutes. If you can quickly reach your doctor, do so. In Britain, at least, a family doctor will usually drop everything to come to a child who has been convulsing. Your own doctor is the best person to assess the child and to reassure you. It is also better for the child to be left in peace for the sleep which always follows the nerve and muscle exhaustion of a 'fit'.

If the doctor is coming immediately, spend the waiting time doing what you can to cool the child without disturbing him. Open windows, remove blankets, fan him, and so on.

What the doctor may want to know about a convulsion
What the child was like before the convulsion. Did you already know he was unwell? If so, since when? Did he have a fever? What was his temperature and when did you last take it? If you did not know he was unwell, can you see now, looking back, any signs of coming illness? Did he eat his last meal? Was he cheerful and active?

Did anything seem to 'touch off' the convulsion?

Can you give any accurate idea of how long it lasted? Even if you did not manage to look at your watch (or cannot now remember what it said!), remembering your own actions and thoughts while the child was convulsing may give the doctor some idea as to whether the episode went on for seconds, a couple of minutes or five to ten minutes.

What the doctor may do about a convulsion
Apart from asking you for these and other details, he will examine the child. He will, of course, be looking for symptoms and signs of illness to account for the fever which led to the convulsion, but he may especially be making sure that he has not got meningitis (*see* **Meningitis and Encephalitis**). This is because meningitis, being an inflammation of the covering of the brain and spinal cord, is an illness which is particularly liable to cause convulsions and because it requires urgent (and almost always successful) treatment. If he cannot exclude the possibility of meningitis he will arrange for the child to be admitted to hospital.

Some doctors prefer to admit all children who have had a first convulsion to hospital, so if this is your doctor's recommendation, don't *assume* that he suspects meningitis or another serious illness.

If your doctor is happy for the child to be nursed at home, he may give him an injection of anti-convulsant/sedative medication. Don't assume that he does this because he thinks the child will otherwise convulse again. If he did think this, he would send him to hospital. Such an injection is sometimes given simply as a precaution and to help protect the brain from further irritation while the fever is being reduced. Often, the doctor will do only what he always does when he visits your sick child: identify (if possible) the infection; judge whether or not to prescribe antibiotics or other medicines; advise you on nursing the child.

If you are left to nurse a child who has just had his first convulsion, do try to believe the doctor's assurances that it will not happen again this time. But since you will almost certainly find yourself worried to distraction, do also consider sending for your partner or a friend to share your vigil. Once the child has woken up from his natural or sedated sleep, his fever is under control and he is his normal (if unwell) self again, the horror will recede. But for now you are entitled to the reassurance of adult support if you can get it.

● If an older child happens to have seen the convulsion, do find time to explain it to him or her. When drama focuses on one child it is easy to ignore another. If you were frightened, he or she was probably downright terrified.

When the drama of a convulsion is over

If this first convulsion was due to the fever caused by a simple infection and you nurse the child at home, you may find yourself worrying about the possibility of further convulsions next time he is ill. Do make an appointment to discuss this with your doctor. If your child was admitted to hospital, you should be given the opportunity for this kind of discussion before he is discharged, but if it is not offered, ask.

Your doctor will want to avoid further convulsions if possible, but he will not want you to live life in fear of them. Some parents get into the unfortunate habit of taking a child's temperature almost every day in case he has fever, or even of giving doses of aspirin almost routinely, just in case. The following are some of the things your doctor may suggest. If you find yourself unable to follow his advice because of your own worry, do stay in touch with him. Some parents are offered routine follow-up appointments for several months after their child has had a febrile convulsion and they find this extremely valuable.

No action until or unless the child has fever. You may be asked to forget the whole thing and just get on with life until or unless the child is unwell. When that happens you may be asked to take his temperature and to let the doctor know if it is above a specified level. He will probably ask you to start cooling the child immediately and to give aspirin (*see* **Nursing**/Fever).

Occasionally a doctor will suggest that, in addition to this, you should give the child an anti-convulsant drug, prescribed by him, by mouth, from the beginning of any fever. This will make a convulsion less likely if the fever catches you out by spiking suddenly, perhaps while the sick child is sleeping. Some doctors do not think this is useful, though. A fever which is going to rise very sharply often does so at the very beginning of an illness so that by the time you know the child is feverish it is already too late: he has either convulsed or he is not going to. Also, if you do have this medication in your medicine cupboard, you may find yourself tempted to dose the child not just when he has a fever but whenever you think he *might* be going to have one.

Investigations before deciding on any action. Sometimes a doctor will want a child who has had a convulsion to have an electro-encephalogram. This painless investigation may help him to decide whether or not further convulsions are very likely.

Preventative medication. Some doctors sometimes suggest that a child (especially one who has had more than one febrile convulsion) should have anti-convulsant medication every day while he is in the susceptible age period. Such medication does inevitably have some side-effects. It may, for example, slow the child down a little or make him irritable. The balance of likely benefit can only be decided between you and your doctor, because it depends on the individual child's reactions and on your own level of anxiety about the whole matter.

Breath-holding attacks (*see also* **Tantrums**)

A few babies and very small children have an extreme physiological reaction to shock or frustration. Instead of screaming with fear, pain or rage, they scream once, then draw in a huge breath as if to go on screaming, but hold it for so long that they become unconscious.

An attack of this kind can be almost as terrifying for parents as a febrile convulsion and even more damaging to family life. Some parents of breath-holders are so desperate to avoid attacks that they become quite unable to handle the child as they normally would, but over-protect and over-indulge him so that he actually cannot learn more appropriate ways of coping with himself or his world (*see* **Discipline, Self-discipline and Learning How to Behave**).

If your child has one breath-holding attack you will, of course, seek immediate medical help because you will probably not be able to differentiate it for certain from a febrile or other convulsion or 'fit'. Once you and your doctor are certain that the episode was due to breath-holding, try to believe the following points:

The child becomes unconscious because he has held his breath for long enough to starve his brain of oxygen. The loss of consciousness is a mechanical reaction rather than a sign of illness or neurological difficulty.

It is absolutely impossible for the child to hold his breath for long enough to kill himself or damage his brain; indeed, far from being dangerous, the loss of consciousness is a survival-mechanism. As soon as he loses consciousness he loses the will to hold his breath and reflex breathing immediately takes over.

Even in the extremely rare case of a breath-holding attack leading to an actual convulsion, there is no risk of brain damage. The short period of oxygen starvation was enough to provoke unusual discharge from neurones in the brain and therefore to produce the convulsive movements, etc., but because the stimulus of oxygen starvation immediately ceases (where the provoking fever in a febrile convulsion does not), it lasts for moments only.

If you find it difficult to believe this reassurance, consider hunger-strikers or people who martyr themselves for a cause by burning themselves to death. Would they take such lengthy and agonizing paths to death if it were physically possible to sacrifice themselves simply by refusing to breathe? Your breath-holding child *cannot do himself any lasting physical harm* but he will do himself (and all of you) lasting psychological harm unless you can truly believe this.

Coping with breath-holding

There are two types of breath-holding attack.

Pallid breath-holding

This is extremely rare. Following a sudden shock (which may be painful but may only be frightening) the child goes very white, slumps limply and is unconscious for a few seconds. Blows on the head from behind, and immunizing injections carried out 'while he's thinking about something else' are among the known triggers for a susceptible child.

As he matures, this reaction to shock will lessen both in frequency and severity, although the child may grow up to be a person who tends to marked physiological reactions to emotional shock (*see* **Accidents**/Shock: Causes of minor shock. *See also* **Fainting**).

In the meantime, some acknowledgement of his 'sensitivity' should be made by his family. Of course he should not be treated as 'delicate', but older children should be discouraged from 'jumping out' at him and some trouble should be taken to see that he knows in advance when an injection or other necessary procedure is coming up.

Cyanotic breath-holding

This is the usual form and it affects mainly toddlers, with a bias towards those who are especially active/bright *and* especially intolerant of frustration. Any situation which might evoke a tantrum in one child may evoke breath-holding in a susceptible one (*see* **Tantrums**).

The outraged child screams, but as if even screams were not enough to express his feelings, he eventually holds his breath while his face goes from bright red to dark red and from dark red to greyish blue. At this point in an uninterrupted attack, his eyes may glaze or roll up, his body becomes stiff and then he slumps unconscious.

Obviously extremes of frustration are better avoided for any child, but, equally obviously, attempts to avoid *any* frustration will seriously distort your child-rearing. It is not only you who must frustrate him in the name of safety or 'discipline', but life which must frustrate him in the name of learning. So while recognizing your child's extreme reaction to frustration and doing what you reasonably can to 'walk round trouble' (*see* **Discipline, Self-discipline and Learning How to Behave**) you have to face the fact that you neither can nor should avoid situations which may lead to breath-holding attacks.

But if you cannot avoid them all, you can cut short any attack which occurs. Your child need never reach blue unconsciousness.

He will not have a breath-holding attack when there is nobody there to see so you need not worry about what happens to him when his toys make him furious in his cot in the morning.

When you see trouble brewing, keep an eye on him. Wait just long enough to see whether this time he *is* going to scream it out.

As soon as it is clear that the breath is being held, use your forefinger to hook forward the base of his tongue. He will release that breath as a reflex. If you always abort breath-holding attacks in this way, your child will probably give them up in favour of some other form of tantrum. If, on the other hand, you resort to traditional but ineffective methods (shaking, smacking, cold water, etc.) he may not. Some children, as they reach three or four, actually learn to breath-hold as a deliberate manipulation of parents so it is worth adopting the tongue method from the very beginning while the whole pattern is subconscious.

Other 'funny turns' which do not suggest neurological disorder

Although nothing is as alarming as the sight of a child having a violent 'fit', or falling unconscious before you, any 'attack' which puts your child out of touch with reality, and therefore out of reach of your voice and touch, can be peculiarly alarming. Many children become like this when a very high fever makes them delirious (*see* **Nursing**/Fever) A few lose touch with the real world during:

Masturbation
(*see also* **Habits**)

Masturbation and other forms of repetitive pleasurable self-stimulation are entirely normal and probably universal, but a few infants and young children adopt methods which look worryingly like 'funny turns'. A baby may rock repeatedly backwards and forwards, for example, thighs held together, muscles tensed and face reddening. A toddler may adopt an odd posture (perhaps involving rubbing himself against the cot bars) and he may be so tense that his muscles judder, and so involved that he holds his breath so that his face becomes purple. While this sort of activity is going on the child is oblivious to anything which is going on around him. The episode will usually end with a sort of mini-climax, in which a moment's shaking leads to relaxation of the muscles and the child appearing to 'come to himself'.

However extreme your child's self-gratifying behaviour, you can always assure yourself that he is not 'having a fit' simply by speaking to and touching him. Masturbation can always be interrupted. A 'fit' must run its course or be stopped by sedation.

Night-terrors
(*see also* **Sleep**)

Night-terrors are terrifying to parents because the child who is involved in one often has quite a long period during which he *looks* as if he is awake but he reacts quite irrationally to them. Sometimes he will look right through you, searching for the horrors he is seeing in his mind behind your reassuring face. Sometimes, if you force him to acknowledge your existence and presence, he will take you into his terror and make you part of the horror. Instead of accepting your comforting embrace he will fight to escape you, screaming piteously at you 'don't, oh don't . . .' It is definitely eerie, but eventually this curious semi-conscious state will turn into real consciousness. The child will neither remember nor be harmed by the night-terror. Yours are the nerves which may be left jangling long after he has dropped back into contented sleep.

Paroxysmal
vertigo

This is a very rare and ill-understood complaint which is only mentioned here because it is both singularly unpleasant for the child and singularly frightening for the parents. It is, nevertheless, entirely harmless. Only children between about one and five years are ever affected so that even if yours should be one of the few who suffer from it you can all be certain that she will grow out of it comparatively quickly.

The child suddenly experiences acute and overwhelming giddiness which she may graphically describe as 'everything going round and round and round'. She may feel sick, vomit, sweat; she may clutch at the wall for support or lie pressed to the floor, desperately trying to find some feeling of solidity in a world gone mad. She behaves as if she were being forced to stay for much too long on a violent fairground ride.

The most unpleasant part of this peculiar affliction is that there is no loss of consciousness or awareness and that no drug has any effect. Attacks do not last for long. The child may like to be held closely during them, gaining some security from your supportive adult body.

'Fits' and 'funny turns' which do suggest neurological disorder

Children who are liable to 'fits' or 'funny turns' which are not due to any of the above syndromes are commonly called 'epileptic'. That label sounds as if 'epilepsy' were the name of a disease. It is not. It is simply a term used to describe people who have some disorder within the brain which makes them liable to some form of 'fit'. The nature of that underlying disorder may or may not be known. The 'fits' themselves may always be of one type or they may vary. They may be touched off by particular triggers or they may occur for no discernible reason, and they may be of any degree of severity. If your child has a problem of this kind, do remember (and make sure that other people closely concerned with him also understand) that:

The 'fits' are not the disorder but only a sign that there is one.

The label 'epileptic' conveys very little that is meaningful about the sufferer; to know anything about what he should or should not be allowed to do, for example, one needs details, not a stereotype.

A final 'cure' for epilepsy is very rarely possible, but anti-convulsant medication can usually suppress the activity of those abnormally-firing brain cells so that no actual 'fits' ever occur. With your help and the child's cooperation, doctors will try to achieve the best possible balance between over-sedating the child so that he has no fits but cannot function normally, and under-sedating him so that he functions normally but still has the occasional seizure. This may involve some trial and error, but time is on your side. Seizures usually become less frequent with age; as your child gets older his medication can usually be reduced and he may eventually be able to give it up altogether.

Your help will also be needed in identifying 'triggers' for your child's seizures. If, for example, they tend to be touched-off by flickering television images or strobe lights, avoiding badly adjusted television sets and discos may enable medication to be reduced. If a girl's seizures are related to her menstrual periods, measures to prevent fluid and salt retention during that part of her cycle may much improve the medication's effect.

If your child has 'fits' or 'funny turns' which are eventually diagnosed as epilepsy, do try not to think of him as 'an epileptic' but to think of him instead as a child with this particular tendency who, with good parental, medical and patient teamwork, can lead an entirely normal life. Such an optimistic outlook will very *very* seldom be proved wrong in the long-term, even if there are short periods during his childhood when his activities have to be curtailed for safety reasons while his drug-schedule is being adjusted.

Although seizure-disorders are rare and must always be diagnosed by a medical team rather than a parent, a brief discussion of some of the least rare is given below. This is because early recognition and treatment is important, and because failure of the adult world to recognize a mild seizure-disorder in a child sometimes leads to injustice and to unnecessary psychological damage.

Absence
epilepsy
('petit mal')

This is a comparatively rare form of epilepsy; it never occurs in children under three and is commoner thereafter in girls than boys.

In a 'simple absence', the child's awareness is suddenly shut off and as suddenly returns a mere few seconds later. There are no movements other than frequent eye-blinking. In a 'complex absence' attack there may be jerky movements or lip-smacking or grimacing.

Although children with 'petit mal' epilepsy are sometimes accused of 'wool-gathering' or 'not paying attention' any observant adult can distinguish between the two. In the epileptic attack the withdrawal of attention is sudden and total and *cannot be ended by adult stimulation*. If you speak to an 'absent' child she will not hear or answer until awareness has returned, where the day-dreaming child will 'come to' with a guilty start.

It is essential that teachers should know of a child's tendency to 'petit mal' which is not completely controlled. Many school difficulties arise if irritated teachers call attention to the condition.

'Drop attacks'

These are similar to infantile spasms (*see below*) but affect children over two years of age. The child falls, often as if violently pushed, either forwards or backwards. Sometimes there is no forward or backward impetus but he simply collapses on the floor without warning.

The child rights himself so rapidly that parents sometimes do not realize that anything other than a normal fall has taken place. Your clue, at least a second time, may be the child's failure to throw his arms up to protect his head or face. Injuries are quite common and have sometimes led to accusations of 'battering'. Innocent parents' accounts of a child 'just suddenly falling' can seem improbable to the inexperienced casualty department doctor.

'Grand mal'
epilepsy

These generalized seizures are the kind which most people think of when they hear the word 'epilepsy'. They are of the type which is usual in febrile convulsions and are described under that heading (*see above*).

Infantile spasms
('Salaam
spasms', West's
syndrome)

These affect only infants under about two years. The baby suddenly jerks forward, flexing at hips and neck. The jerks are repeated (perhaps twenty or more times) with a few seconds between them. A cry sometimes accompanies each. Occasionally these spasms are mistaken for early efforts to sit up, or as attempts in an older baby to get from sitting position to standing or crawling.

● A specific drug treatment is possible if, and only if, it is started within three weeks of the first spasm. Don't wait and hope.

Psychomotor attack   In this type of epilepsy the affected part of the brain is the temporal lobe which is responsible for the 'storage' of memories, feelings and perception of smells. The affected child commonly feels that something terrifying is about to happen to him. Alternatively, he may remember something (always the same memory) or 'smell' burning or some other (usually unpleasant) odour. His fright and confusion culminates in a momentary 'absence' similar to that of 'petit mal' attacks.

● Some 'grand mal' seizures are also preceded by similar kinds of experience. Older patients sometimes 'know' when a seizure is imminent because they experience a collection of sensations which together form their personal 'aura'.

Corporal punishment *see* **Discipline, Self-discipline and Learning How to Behave**/Punishment. *See also* **School**/Discipline in your child's school.
Cosmetic problems *see* **Adolescence**/Problems with appearance and body-image. *See also* **Birthmarks; Hospital**/Surgery: Plastic Surgery.
Cot deaths *see* **Death**/Sudden Infant Death Syndrome.

Coughs *see also* **Chest Infections; Colds; Croup and Laryngitis; Whooping Cough**

Coughs are difficult symptoms for parents to assess because, while a cough always denotes irritation in the respiratory system, the seriousness of a cough depends both on the *cause of the irritation* and on the *area of the respiratory system* which is affected. Furthermore, these two considerations interact with each other. If a child fails to swallow a crumb and coughs because it has 'gone the wrong way', the matter is trivial as long as the crumb has only reached the larynx (voice box). But if he is coughing because that same innocent little crumb has got much further down the system, the matter might be more serious (*see* **Accidents**/Choking; Foreign bodies which are inhaled).

If a child has a cough which lasts for several days without any obvious reason (such as a cold), he should certainly see a doctor, if only so that you can be reassured. If the nature or extent of a child's coughing (and the kind of breathing which accompanies it) really worries you, an emergency visit is called for. But most of the time most coughs are innocent. The following brief account of where and why they take place may save you from some nights of worry over the spectre of pneumonia (*see* **Chest Infections**).

The respiratory system starts at the nose and mouth and culminates in the lungs. On the way air travels through the throat, the larynx (voice box), the trachea (windpipe) and the bronchi (major air tubes leading into the lungs). The cough reflex protects the respiratory system by closing off the route and forcibly expelling anything which should not travel down it, back up into the throat where it can be swallowed. That 'anything' may indeed be almost anything. It may be that crumb; it may be dust; it may be air which, taken in through the mouth, is too cold to be allowed to reach the lungs without time to warm itself; above all, it may be mucus or pus, the products of infection anywhere in the system.

This protective coughing is vital because it ensures that irritants do not reach the bronchi and the lungs. When a child with a cold coughs, it is his cough which ensures that the infection stays at upper respiratory level. Without it, virus-laden mucus might reach down to the bronchi and there set up the infection we call bronchitis. Anybody who is in a state where his cough reflex is likely to be depressed or absent, has to have his respiratory system artificially guarded. The child who is unconscious, for example (see **Accidents**/Coping with more serious injuries: If a child is unconscious), must be turned into the recovery position so that the secretions or vomit which he may not be able to cough up will trickle out of his mouth rather than down into his lungs. The hospital patient under anaesthesia or in a coma will have an artificial airway inserted which can be kept clear by suction.

But while the basic function of a cough is protective and benevolent, the body does not always get it right. In some infections (see below) there is irritation of, say, the trachea, without any mucus being produced. The patient coughs and coughs, responding to that irritation when in fact there is nothing to be coughed up and therefore nothing to be prevented from going down. This kind of dry, irritating tickle-cough is one of the few kinds which it may sometimes be legitimate to quell with cough suppressants. In other infections (see **Allergy**/Asthma; **Croup and Laryngitis**; **Whooping Cough**) spasm of muscles in the respiratory passages produces coughing which is not only unproductive but so uncoordinated that it may actually interfere with breathing. Coughs of this kind will also require medical help.

Coughs with colds (see also **Colds***)*
Most colds cause coughs, especially at night. During the day the child's nose runs and he either blows or wipes the mucus out or sniffs it back up and swallows it. At night, because he is lying down, the mucus tends to run to the back of the throat, tickle and cause him to cough. Because he is asleep, his swallowing is much reduced. The mucus is coughed into his mouth but runs back down to the throat so that he coughs yet again.

The only (partial) remedies for this kind of cough are mechanical ones designed to get the mucus out of the way. Raising the head of the mattress (or providing an older child with extra pillows) may help. Starting the night with a thoroughly cleared nose will help for a while. During a night which is being badly disturbed by constant coughing it is often worthwhile to wake the child so that he can sit up, clear his nose and start all over again more comfortably.

Coughs with thick, sticky mucus
Bacterial secondary infection (following a cold or almost any viral infection of the upper respiratory tract) may make secretions thick and sticky so that however much the child coughs he cannot 'clear' himself. Under these circumstances an 'expectorant cough medicine' may be useful. These medicines do not *prevent* coughing; they act to liquify the mucus so that it can be coughed up more effectively and with less effort.

A young child should not be given such medicine without a doctor's advice. If you give one to an older child, perhaps because his colds 'always go through a thick stage', do remember that most of them contain drugs which, in larger doses, act as emetics. If you give him more than is recommended or dose him too frequently, you may add to his misery by making him vomit.

Coughs with aching chests A constant ache in the chest, or pain when coughing, tends to alarm parents whose minds instantly turn to pleurisy or pneumonia (*see* **Chest Infections**). Remember that a child who is coughing frequently is forcing the muscles of the chest wall to do a lot of unusual work. Some aching is so frequent as to be almost the rule rather than the exception. *Sharp* pain when coughing requires medical advice. Otherwise pain associated with *breathing* matters more than pain with coughing. It may mean that infection has spread downwards.

Coughs with 'chest colds' 'Chest cold' is a term which is certainly imprecise and may be nonsensical. If your baby or young child's cough sounds 'chesty' this will usually be because of his small size and anatomy. The distance from his throat to his lungs is, after all, only a matter of a few inches. His breathing passages are not only small, they are actually smaller for his overall size than are the passages of older people. If there is inflammation/mucus in his throat or larynx or trachea, causing him to cough, the sound will vibrate those tiny passages and you may well hear the sound as if it came from his chest. If he is old enough to tell you that his chest aches, your diagnosis of a 'chest cold' or a 'cold which has gone to his chest' may seem confirmed.

If you are concerned about him, you will, of course, consult your doctor. But do remember that a cold which has truly 'settled on his chest' has stopped being 'just a cold' and become a chest infection. If this has happened the child will be clearly unwell. It makes more sense to consult your doctor because the child is ill, whatever his cough sounds like, than to do so because his cough sounds 'chesty' when he seems perfectly well in himself (*see* **Chest Infections**).

Coughs with exhaustion If a cough is too frequent and/or too violent it can be exhausting, whatever its underlying cause. If your child coughs so often during the *day* that his activities are interfered with and/or he seems floppy after each bout, it is better to seek medical help in finding the cause than to try and stop the cough with cough suppressant medicines.

Coughs with difficult breathing Often a child with a cold or other minor upper respiratory infection will breathe noisily. Any mucus in those small air passages will vibrate and may cause all kinds of snoring or whistling noises. If the infection has also given him a fever, his breathing may be more rapid than usual as well.

Neither noisy nor rapid breathing *on its own* suggests that a child's existing infection has become worse. Laboured breathing, on the other hand, should be treated as an emergency and your doctor called, whatever the time of night.

Recognizing laboured breathing Difficulty in getting enough oxygen to the lungs evokes fear and panic in everyone, whatever the cause. This is why attacks of asthma are so frightening (*see* **Allergy**/Asthma). If a child wakes up 'short of breath', panics and cries, it may be up to you to deduce the problem. Equally, if he was already very unwell and is now asleep but looking worse, you may want to check that his breathing is easy. Take off his pyjama top (or unbutton it) so that you can see his bare chest. The signs of laboured breathing are:

☐ Rapid, heaving chest movements which are not entirely rhythmical.

☐ A definite sucking in of the lower end of the sternum (breast bone) with each breath.

☐ A pulling in of the lower ribs at the sides, with every breath.

These last two signs are especially useful in babies and very young children. The sternum and lower ribs are attached to the diaphragm. When the diaphragm is having to exert unusual force in order to take in breath, these bones, which are still comparatively soft in a young child, are pulled inwards by its action. Although a panic-stricken crying child will, of course, breathe more rapidly than a calm one, rapid breathing in which the air is passing in and out easily, will not produce these sucking-in movements.

● Laboured breathing does mean that the child's body is having to work unusually hard to get air in and out, so it is an emergency. On the other hand, laboured breathing does not mean that the child's body is going to give up the struggle; he can actually survive on far less air than he feels he needs. Try not to panic because the more frightened he senses that you are, the more frightened the child is likely to be. Fear actually puts up his need for oxygen (so that he will be even more 'short of breath') while crying creates a vicious circle with breathlessness. The calmer and quieter you can help him to be, the less breathless he will feel and therefore the calmer he will stay.

Cramp *see also* **Adolescence**/Menstruation: Menstrual difficulties

The word cramp refers to acute pain caused by involuntary spasms of muscles. Cramp in internal abdominal muscles is sometimes referred to as 'colic' while cramp in the muscles associated with labouring lungs is called a 'stitch'. Spasm in muscles of the neck is often referred to as a 'crick in the neck'.

The basic cause of cramp is failure of the circulation through a particular muscle or muscle group to keep it supplied with energy and to remove the waste-product of its energy-use. A build-up of this waste-product, called lactic acid, is thought to be responsible for the actual pain.

Causes of cramp
Anything which drains a muscle of energy and allows lactic acid to build up within it can cause cramp. Causes, therefore, range from serious problems of circulation (such as narrowed arteries) through temporary interference with circulation (such as the pressure of the loaded uterus on major blood vessels late in pregnancy) to the most common, over-use of a muscle such that its energy demands and waste-products outstrip the resupplying and flushing functions of its blood supply.

Coping with cramp
If your child gets cramp while exercising, he must stop at once. Trying to go on running with a stitch or cramping calf muscles is idiotic. He will not,

in fact, be able to continue and trying to do so will make the pain both worse and longer lasting.

The spasms will stop and the pain will ease as soon as rest allows the muscles to be flushed by the circulation. In the meantime, the pain may be very severe indeed. You may be able to help by:

Helping him to sit or lie still and breathe steadily so that his panic-stricken writhings do not prolong the agony.

Gently rubbing affected muscles so as to increase the blood flow to them.

● Cramp while swimming can be dangerous. Children who swim in deep water and/or alone *must* be taught how to tread water/float and be trained to a point where they can be relied upon to do so despite the pain of cramp (*see* **Safety**/In the home: By, in and on water).

Preventing cramp   Unless he exhausts muscles through over-use, a healthy child will not get cramp if he:

Always ensures that his muscles are 'warmed up' before he makes stringent demands on them. Serious dancers, athletes and sportspeople are taught warm-up exercises; you can ensure that any child understands that he must move about and get his circulation speeded up before he dashes off. Going up through the gears of a car is a useful parallel.

Avoids awkward positions which limit blood flow to a limb. Sleeping in cars, for example, quite often leads to cramp.

Avoids heavy exercise in circumstances which are likely to cut down the blood flow to important muscle groups. Swimming in icy-cold water without the precaution of wearing a wet-suit or greasing the skin can be dangerous because the body seeks to preserve the warmth of the vital organs by reducing the blood flow to the skin and increasing it internally. This leaves outer muscle layers singularly liable to cramp. In rather the same way, swimming after a heavy meal can be dangerous because rather more of the blood flow than usual is concentrated on the processes of digestion. A heavy meal *and* very cold water is a lethal combination for swimmers.

● There is no reason why children, spending a precious day beside the sea, should be deprived of going in the water for an hour after a sandwich lunch. Warmth and a light meal make cramp very unlikely.

Avoids demanding exercise in circumstances where the circulation may already be affected. Playing tennis in high temperatures after a day spent sunbathing can make him very liable to cramp as a mild degree of dehydration and salt-deprivation may already exist (*see* **Accidents**/Sunburn and heat illness).

Recurrent cramp   If a child wakes in the night with cramp he may have unwittingly deprived a muscle group of sufficient blood just by lying awkwardly. A single episode of this kind is no cause for concern. If he frequently develops cramp without obvious reason, it is worth having him checked by a doctor.

Croup and Laryngitis

Laryngitis is an inflammation of the larynx (voice box) and sometimes of the trachea below it. The inflammation is usually caused by an ordinary cold virus, though any micro-organism which causes an upper respiratory infection can lead to laryngitis if it gets down that far.

Older children (and adults) with laryngitis usually only have a hoarse (or absent) voice, a tickly cough and perhaps a sore throat. Some very young children, on the other hand, are liable to a more dramatic form of laryngitis: the kind we call croup. Croup can be mild and unimportant but, especially in a baby or toddler, it can be severe.

Croup is also an inflammation of the larynx and/or trachea but, because of the very small diameter of the young child's air passageways, the swelling which accompanies the inflammation is enough to obstruct his breathing. The severity of an attack of croup depends on the degree of that swelling. Parents should know that sufficient swelling to cut off a child's air supply altogether is *extremely* rare. But they should also realize that a little swelling, just enough to make the breathing slightly laboured, can increase if nothing is done to relieve it. So even the mildest case of croup requires quick, knowledgeable action.

Some children seem far more liable than others to have croup, either all on its own, or as part of their colds. Yours may be a child who never has a sign of croup. But if a child has one attack, he is quite likely to have another with a later upper respiratory infection. Furthermore, if one of your children is liable to croup another one is rather likely to be liable too.

A first attack of croup (or any severe attack) certainly merits an emergency visit from your doctor or a quick trip to your nearest hospital if you cannot easily reach him. But once you have nursed a child through one bout with medical advice, you may feel able to cope with later attacks yourself, only calling the doctor if the croup is not easily dealt with (*see below*). If yours turns out to be a croup-prone family, a cold-air vaporizer may be an extremely worthwhile (although expensive) purchase.

First signs of croup

Sometimes the child has a cold. Sometimes he already has some signs (such as hoarseness) which suggest that his larynx may be involved. But usually there are no warning signs of croup. It just happens, usually in the middle of the night.

In a severe case, with marked swelling, you are likely to be awoken by a loud, strange barking noise, immediately followed by terrified hoarse crying interspersed with a hacking, hard cough. The barking noise is the sound air makes as the child forces it in past those swollen vocal cords.

When you reach the child you may find him struggling between coughing, crying and breathing (still with that extraordinary sound). He will certainly look panic-stricken. He may even look a poor colour: slightly grey and pale-lipped.

Immediate action for severe croup

If there is someone else in the house, get him or her to telephone the doctor while you concentrate on the child. If you are alone, start with the child and call the doctor yourself if your first measures do not produce an immediate and dramatic improvement.

The first thing your child needs is reassurance. Struggling and crying is making everything worse. Stay calm yourself and use whatever words and gestures will best calm your child. A baby, for example, will probably react best to being picked up and cuddled but some four-year-olds will react with relief and complete obedience to authoritative instructions.

Either cold moist air or warm steam will relieve the swelling enough to improve your child's breathing.

If you have a cold-air vaporizer, switch it on and direct the stream of wet cold air at the child's face. The effect is often almost miraculous.

Failing that, pick up the child and take him straight into the bathroom:

Open the window so that he can breathe the cold night air (better still if it is raining) while you turn on the hot taps to make the whole place as steamy as possible. If you have a shower cabinet, take the child in there and turn on the hot water (don't let it burn either of you); the small space will steam up faster than the whole room.

If by any chance you have no hot water supply:

Take the child to the kitchen and stand with him by an open window or door while a kettle boils. As soon as it is steaming take him close enough to breathe the steam without getting scalded.

If the doctor is on his way, keep the child in his steam-room until he arrives. If there was no-one to telephone the doctor, assess the effectiveness of the steam after about five minutes.

If there has been no improvement, or if he is still breathing with enough difficulty to frighten him (and you), take him with you while you make a dash for the telephone and call your doctor or an ambulance. Take the child back to the steam-room while you wait for help to arrive.

If there has been a marked improvement (and there usually is) you may feel that you can wait until morning for a visit from the doctor or that you will telephone to tell him what is happening and to make sure that you can reach him in a hurry if the acute croup should recur.

If you are going to manage without an immediate visit from the doctor, stay in the steam-room with the child while you plan how to moisten the air of his bedroom. Open windows are a 'must' (if yours happen to be sealed, at least switch off the central heating). If you have the kind of electric kettle which does *not* switch itself off as soon as it boils, you can use that to make steam in the room. Failing that, a pan on a camping stove will certainly make steam but it will also give out a lot of heat which is particularly undesirable if the infection causing the croup has also made the child feverish. If you must use a stove, try simultaneously cooling the room with a fan if you have one, or with a blower-heater on its 'cold' setting.

Nursing the after-effects of severe croup   If there is anyone to help you, get the air in the child's room a little moistened while you and he stay in the steam-room. If you are alone, get organized in your mind so that you can be quick and efficient about it.

Put the child into bed and make sure that he is well propped up either with pillows or, for a baby, with the head of the cot mattress raised.

Get your steam arrangements organized and grab anything you need for your own comfort. The child must not be left alone for the rest of the night in case his breathing becomes difficult again, especially if he cries for you.

● If you are using a stove to make steam you will not be able to leave the room, even for a minute, in case of an accident.

If he is still wide awake and anxious, distraction may help. The less he thinks about breathing, and about that awful feeling of oxygen-hunger, the less likely he is to have further difficulty. Being read a story is often the best possible distraction. For a baby, a stream of talk, nonsense rhymes or just 'what we're going to do when you're better' will keep his attention on you rather than on himself.

During the next half hour you will see whether or not the emergency is now over:

The child may now drift off to sleep and wake up in the morning completely recovered.

It may become clear that, although the croup is over, the infection which caused it is making the child feverish and ill. Nurse him as you normally would and call the doctor first thing in the morning.

The croup may recur, probably soon after the child goes to sleep or if you go to sleep too and the steam dries up. If this happens, start all over again but this time don't let a rapid improvement put you off getting an emergency visit from the doctor. If you cannot reach him, either send for an ambulance or take the child to hospital yourself in your own car (don't worry about taking him out in the cold air; it will actually help that breathing).

Although the acute croup does not recur the child's breathing may remain somewhat affected and coughing fits or attempts to talk or suck a bottle may provoke short bursts of that croupy noise. Again, you need a doctor; call him now if it is still only midnight; first thing in the morning if it is now dawn.

Later attacks of croup   Two things will alter your life for the better if your child has a tendency to croup:

A cold-air vaporizer. Once you own one, you can use it as a precautionary measure whenever your child has a cold and you can use it instead of all that steam-room performance whenever he has an unheralded attack. Furthermore, cold-air vaporizers are a superb aid to nursing feverish children (*see* **Nursing**/Fever) even if they have not got croup. Some medical practices in the UK own one or more of these machines and will lend them.

An easy and reasonably comfortable way of bunking down in the child's room. Whether you make a divan part of that room's furnishings or keep a collapsible bed handy, it is a tremendous help if you do not have to think, and turn the household upside-down in the middle of the night, whenever you have to supervise him.

● A tendency to croup does *not* imply that there is anything wrong with, or any weakness in, your child's respiratory system. By the time he is five or so he will almost certainly have outgrown croup. Literally outgrown it, because his larynx will be so much larger in relation to the rest of him that there will be room for a little swelling of those vocal cords to take place without obstructing his breathing. Once he is capable of having an ordinary attack of laryngitis, croup will be a thing of the past.

'Cuddlies' (Transitional comfort objects) *see* **Habits**/Comfort habits.
Cuts *see* **Accidents**/Cuts and scrapes, grazes and puncture wounds. *See also* **Safety**/In the home: From dangerous implements.
Day-care *see* **Working Mothers**. *See also* **Babysitters**.
Day nurseries *see* **Working Mothers**. *See also* **School**/Pre-school and nursery education.
Deafness *see* **Ears and Hearing; Ear Disorders and Deafness**. *See also* **Language**/Three to six months: Watching out for deafness.

Death *see also* Suicide

Few children today are brought up in ignorance of what we call 'the facts of life' but most are still kept in ignorance of the other end of that life-cycle: death. Most parents have known bereavement and many live in fear of their own deaths or the deaths of people they love. Instead of accepting death as the one inevitable event in otherwise variegated lives, they shy away from thinking about it themselves and protect children from the very concept, until personal tragedy catches the whole family unawares.

Young children cannot anticipate tragedy and grief nor empathize with people who are thus suffering. They are therefore curious about death in exactly the same way that they are curious about other aspects of life, until they find that their parents cannot answer their questions straightforwardly: that death is still the Great Unmentionable. While it would be idiotic to pretend that a child brought up with knowledge of the facts of death will be protected from personal tragedy, such a child will at least have a realistic context in which to suffer if she must. Furthermore, if the parents of this generation were to try to remove some of the mystery and horror which surrounds the subject, there would be a chance of a next generation reared with a greater acceptance of an end which must come to all of us. Parents could do for the whole population something of what the Hospice movement is doing for the dying and their families.

Information about death, like information about sex, cannot be given in a series of staged lectures. It needs to filter into a growing child from the beginning of her life and, above all, to be a topic about which she can ask questions which will be sensibly and unemotionally answered so that she is always encouraged to go on exploring the topic in her own mind and at her own pace. Most children do ask about the following points, although few are thus answered. Some are points around which childish anxiety tends to focus when death first presents itself as a reality.

Everything which lives, dies. This is so obvious that our capacity to walk around the fact is amazing. It is not a difficult idea to get across even to the youngest child if you can be calm and accepting about it yourself. You can use plants, insects and animals as well as people. Questions like 'will I die?' and 'will you die?' obviously have to be answered factually, but the idea of death as a *natural* end to life can be comfortingly linked to other facts which distance the matter from her emotionally such as:

Different living things live on different time-scales. She will be interested, for example, to be told that some insects live (in the form which she is watching) for only a day, and to have the short gestation period and lifespan of tiny mammals contrasted with that of bigger creatures and people. She will both accept this as interesting information and have the knowledge available when her pet mouse dies of old age. Furthermore, she will then work out, with your help, that people usually live not only through the aeons that seem to her to be going to pass before she is grown up, but also until their children have children of their own . . .

That physical death is final. Whatever you wish to teach your child about a possible life-after-death, it is vital that every child understand that bodies (of whatever creature) never *ever* 'come back to life' and never *ever* have any consciousness, any feeling, any life, remaining. Nobody who has been recently bereaved can fully accept the finality of death and no young child can truly encompass the concept of 'never' or 'forever'. Nevertheless, it is important to work at this one while the matter can be impersonal, because when a child does face a death which matters to her, the feelings of the corpse and the horrors of its disposal are usually a main source of anxiety. None of us likes to think of a person enclosed in a coffin, and buried in the ground or consumed in the fires of the crematorium. The more sure we are, intellectually at least, that the body is over, finished with, the more easily we accept that shrouds, satin coffin-linings and flowers are cosmetics for *us*, the living (and perhaps statements of our love to the world at large), rather than being for the dead.

Although some people may find the idea distasteful, many school-children want to know what happens to bodies after they are buried and find a natural 'rightness' in the truthful answer:

That dead bodies disintegrate back into the natural elements that make up all living things. Even before she is taught about the 'nitrogen cycle' in her science classes, your child will find it eminently sensible that plants, animals and people are fundamentally made up of particular chemicals and that, once dead, they eventually rot down into those same chemicals and thus contribute to the building blocks of new generations.

That death is necessary for renewal. Even quite a young child can easily understand that if some pigeons/rabbits did not die, the city/field would soon be overrun by the baby ones she enjoys watching. *Of course* such an idea is not going to help her accept that Grandad had to die to make room for baby Joseph, but it helps to convey the idea of a cycle of birth and death, of renewal and replacement.

● Be careful about using flowers of which your child is fond to illustrate this point. Those daffodils do not *die* to make room for later flowers: they *die down*. Next spring they will come up again. She must know that the same does not apply to dogs, rabbits or people.

That new, young creatures are needed because old ones 'wear out'. This too is an easy and a comforting concept for quite young children. It is easy because she already knows that old *objects* wear out and are replaced and she can see that old animals and people become stiff and tired and less competent. It is comforting because it links natural death with ageing and therefore removes it from her immediate concerns about herself and her family.

● If there are elderly people who are close to your child, she will probably ask whether Granny or Mrs Jones will soon die. It is a logical and factual question. If you are shocked and/or answer it in a way which contradicts everything you have previously said, you will muddle her and probably shut her up, too. You do not have to answer 'yes' or 'no' because the truth is that you do not know. You can truthfully say something like 'well most people live to be seventy and some live to be a hundred, so we don't have to worry about that yet . . .'

That natural death is usually peaceful. Insofar as young children have any concept of death, it is usually a television-concept of violence and pain. While nobody can deny that death *can* be like that (*see below*) a child who understands that most deaths are a drifting into oblivion may be partly protected from the very common horror of the actual *moment of death*. You may be able to illustrate this, in the course of her childhood, when she sees the butterfly stop flying, sit on the flower and simply become motionless, or when she herself feeds her pet one evening and finds him dead, rather than asleep, in his nest next morning.

That violent/accidental/premature death and suffering are things all human beings strive to prevent/avoid/put right. By building up a distinction in her mind between 'natural' and 'unnatural' death, you can make it clear that reverence for life is as important as acceptance of death and that people have a duty to look after themselves and other people and creatures. You can also make it clear that however hard we (or doctors, nurses and so forth) may try, we cannot always keep things alive. She will start to think along these lines as soon as she begins to bring you the baby rabbits cats have mauled, or the baby birds which have fallen from their nests. You and she together can try to save them, but she must learn that you will not always be able to.

● Once again, this kind of knowledge will not protect the child whose father dies in hospital after a heart attack, from anger at the doctors who did not save him for her. But it will give her anger some realistic context.

When a child meets death

Sooner or later your child will face a death which means something to her personally. It may be the death of a pet, a relation she seldom sees, a neighbour who was part of her daily scene, a grandparent whom she loved or even a brother, sister or parent. While nobody can tell you how to handle your child while she is facing her personal grief, other parents, who have had to see their children through, emphasize the following points:

Don't shield the bereaved child with falsehood

'I couldn't bear to tell her that her precious guinea pig had died so I hid the body and bought another. I shall never forget the tissue of lies that began when she said how *small* he seemed this morning and which culminated in "him" having babies a couple of weeks later.'

'We said Georgie [the dog] had wandered off and we were sure he would find a lovely home. It never occurred to us that she would be frantic *in case* he got killed *and* heartbroken because he had left her when she thought he loved her.'

'We told her Mrs G had moved to another city. I wish we'd told her the truth, though, because first it was "why didn't she say goodbye?" then it was "why doesn't she send me a postcard?" and now it's "I hate Mrs G". My lie has spoilt a relationship which mattered to her.'

Don't use 'sleep' for 'death'

'I told her her brother had gone peacefully to sleep . . . that I'd been with him when he went to sleep and he was happy . . . all that. I meant it to make it all right for her but it was the worst thing I ever did. It was months before she slept herself; she panicked when her dad went to sleep in front of the television and then a friend said her cat had been put to sleep and that started it all up again. Now our doctor says to explain about the anaesthetic for her operation as a "special sleep" but there's no way I can. You wouldn't think a *word* could matter so, would you?'

Think carefully about whether a child should see the dead

'In my family it was taken for granted that you went and said "goodbye" to a dead person so my mother assumed ours would see their grandfather and I didn't like to refuse her. But I wish I had. My son just froze up and wouldn't look. He was really shocked by the whole thing. The girl had hysterics: Mum said to kiss Grandad and of course he was cold . . . she screamed and screamed. It was awful. I'd never do it again, never.'

BUT

'I said no; that I'd rather they remembered their father the way he really was. But then, that night, my boy was crying and crying and I tried to talk to him and it turned out that he thought his Dad must have been in a horrible kind of accident or something 'cause I wouldn't let him go with me to see him . . . I took him to the funeral parlour the next day and he was calmer after that. He just glanced, that's all, but he could sort of see that he wasn't, well, you know . . .'

Think carefully about children and funerals

'It's a dreadful service to me; of course I have no religion so perhaps I can't judge but it really sort of rubs your nose in it with the coffin there and everything, and the burial too; horrible if it's someone you love. I'd never take a child. Tell them, yes, but not make them go through it.'

BUT

'They wouldn't take me to the funeral and I was really angry. It was my aunt. I loved her. I'm part of the family, aren't I? Why should I be left out?

Eleven isn't too young to have the person die so how is it too young to kind of see them off?'

AND

'The funeral was horrible. Horrible. But once it was over and she was buried, well, she was really sort of gone and Mum seemed better too in a way, as if she could more sort of accept it . . .'

Let children mourn

'He was so upset about the dog we went and got another puppy that same afternoon. I thought he'd never forgive us. He looked at us as if we were mad and said "that's no good to me" and I realized just what he meant. It was selfish, really. *We* didn't want to see him without a dog to play with and take for walks. But *he* wanted his beloved Wolf . . . We took that puppy back and it was nearly a year before he asked for another dog.'

'They'd had months of me being taken up with nursing their grandfather, so when he finally died we packed them off to friends and they gave them a whale of a time. Only it didn't work out too well, really. I sort of forgot that he'd come to mean a lot to them . . .'

'Sheila was the one who suffered most when her brother was killed. You see everybody expected us to be in pieces and we were sort of trying to look after each other. She got forgotten, really. Our son, but her brother. People told her to be good because we were miserable; she got pushed out when she needed us. I think we often under-estimate how much brothers and sisters mean to each other.'

But don't expect adult grief

'At first he was upset. I mean he cried and carried on like we all did. But then it was as if he'd forgotten all about it. I mean he got up and got dressed for school the very next day and then he was wanting to be out playing and he wanted his meals and all . . . I just couldn't understand it. To tell you the truth I thought he was heartless. But his teacher talked to me; said he was being very difficult at school and all that, and that children show their feelings in different ways from us. I tried to be kind but I was so miserable myself, I just couldn't cope. That's why he went to the Child Guidance in the end . . .'

'She kept asking for her Gran. No matter how many times I told her she'd gone she kept saying things about when Gran would come back. I thought I'd go crazy. I mean she *knew* she'd gone. It was as if she just wouldn't believe it.'

'He didn't really react at all when I told him about his brother. There was I, dreading it, and you'd have thought I'd told him his brother had gone on holiday. Then he was all over us and saying things like "you'd like me to come with you, wouldn't you, 'cause you like me best." Then he gave up all the things he liked doing and sort of stayed around the house being some kind of goody-goody. It was really strange. Then my Mum told me he'd said something to her about trying to make up for what he'd done, and do you know, it sort of turned out that he thought *it was his fault*. Our doctor says kids often feel that a death is somehow their fault, even if all they've ever done is quarrel and that. Anyway, of course after that we kept telling him that it was nobody's fault, things like that do sometimes happen. He's still not the boy he was though. But he's never shed a tear.'

'Sarah was only two when her father died and truly I don't think she really *noticed* very much, perhaps because he worked such long hours he didn't have a lot to do with her directly. She asked for him lots of times but she accepted it quite cheerfully when I said he wouldn't be coming. She couldn't understand why I was so upset, though. That's what she minded. But I'm sure it was better for her to be with me through the rough bits than to be off with relations or something. I've seen that come awfully hard on kids. I even used her to cry on sometimes. Tough, I know, for such a little girl but we sort of came through together.'

'Don't get me wrong, all three were very close to their mother; of course they were shattered; we all were. But the worst thing was that their whole world, their lives, fell apart. She'd been part of every detail so nothing could ever be the same.'

From those and other experiences, recollected some time after the event by parents who have had time to get over at least the shock-element of their own grief, there seem to be some pointers for us all:

That it is easy to over-protect children because we hate to see them unhappy. A new pet may insult rather than heal. Being sent away from a house of mourning may exclude rather than relieve. Being protected from adult grief, by everyone putting on 'a brave face for the children's sake', may deprive them of support and of a feeling of mutual usefulness.

That it is easy to be so lost in personal grief that the child's is under-estimated. This is especially liable to happen when it is a brother or sister who dies. Parents feel themselves the principal mourners and those around them do too. The grief of brothers and sisters is often under-estimated; sometimes they are openly pushed out of the way to give the parents mourning-space; occasionally, it is even assumed or implied that they will welcome the chance to be the only remaining child.

That most children will feel some guilt over any death which is significant to them. Guilt is part of even adult mourning: we all regret harsh words or quarrels, failures to spot illness or jus. time wasted on not being as close as we now feel. For children, the tendency is much increased because most children find it difficult to sort out feelings from actions and may believe, or half-believe, that the anger they felt on the morning of the death actually caused or contributed to it. Brothers and sisters often wish each other dead – and then find themselves apparently monstrously all-powerful. Children often feel hate towards a parent and when that parent dies, suffer torment.

That children's grief does not always show itself in ways adults approve or can even recognize. Tears, loss of appetite and disturbed sleep, almost universal in mourning adults, may be almost or completely absent in a grief-stricken child whose distress may show up in anger, behaviour disturbances or a stalwart refusal to admit to feeling anything at all.

That the degree of upset caused by a death will usually be related to the upset it causes to daily life. Children are more or less dependent on adults, not only emotionally but for the patterning of their daily lives. A child who loses his mother often loses his way of life along with her, where the child who loses his father may lose only that special and vital person. Where other aspects of a bereaved child's life *can* be held steady (where, for instance, it is financially and practically possible for the remaining family to continue in the same house/school, etc.), mourning for the lost *person* can be more easily carried through because it is not confused with distress over the related disruption.

When a child is known to be dying

If healthy children think about death, sick ones are bound to do so too. Although both parents and medical staff often prefer to assume that young patients have no idea that they are likely to die soon, research workers brave enough to approach this taboo area have found that this is not always so. Should you, or anyone close to you, ever have to face this most extreme agony of parenthood, you might find some of the following points helpful:

Ruses like changing the beds around in a hospital ward do not prevent patients knowing when another child has died. Such deaths naturally cause great anxiety, but the anxiety is made worse by the fact that nurses and doctors (naturally upset themselves) cannot permit the other children to ask questions. A conspiracy of silence may make children who are *not* dangerously ill unnecessarily fearful, while it may make children who *are* dangerously ill feel that they cannot ask questions about their own condition. It makes all the children feel that death is an unbearable subject to the adults and this can only make it the more terrifying to them.

Children undergoing treatment need hope, but that hope can be for realistic small improvements rather than for impossible cure. Sometimes when painful or unpleasant treatments are to be undertaken, adults feel that they must tell the child that they will make him better, when in fact they know that the child can never be cured. The child then asks, 'When it's over can I go home/get up/go back to school,' or whatever, and senses that the answers he gets are uncomfortable falsehoods. Usually, such a child will readily accept much smaller and more realistic goals such as 'you will be able to breathe much more comfortably/we shall be able to take out the tube so you can have a proper drink/your legs won't hurt so much . . .'

Children who wonder if/suspect that, they are dying, usually try to ask somebody. But that somebody will often not be a parent, because even very young children sense the misery of their closest adults *and try to protect them*. Just as husband and wife often pass the last weeks of one of them with neither wanting to hurt the other by mentioning death, so the same sad loneliness often happens between parent and child. Such a child may try to ask nursing or medical staff, but will often find his questions deflected, his remarks unheard and a facade of false assurance erected around him. All those who have worked in this painful area agree that *a child who wants to know should be answered.* Anyone to whom he gives a clue, be it a relation, a member of the domestic staff, a nurse or doctor, should be able to share the child's thoughts with the whole caring team and parents, so that all concerned can decide how best to communicate with him. One five-year-old, for example, said to a junior nurse, 'I shan't be here at Christmas'. She chose to take that as meaning that the little girl hoped not to be in the hospital for Christmas and brightly replied, 'No, I hope you'll be home with Mummy and Daddy by then'. Later, the same child tried another nurse with the words, 'I won't be having Christmas'. She, too, chose to misinterpret and replied, 'Oh, but you will, we have lovely Christmases here with carol singers and a tree and everything . . .' That night her mother found her crying bitterly. Asked what hurt, she said, 'my Christmas hurts'. Fortunately, her mother found the strength to discuss the child's emotional state with the pediatrician. A conference was called, the earlier remarks came to light and it was agreed that this particular child needed honest communication which would allow her to share her worry about dying just as she had always shared all her worries with her parents.

Children who do know that they are dying commonly fear:

The moment of death itself which is often seen as a violent, painful and dramatic event. Tremendous comfort can be given by realistic assurances that there will be no pain nor knowledge of the moment of death; that it will be, so to speak, a gentle and imperceptible drifting.

The separation from parents implied by death. Nothing makes children more anxious than the prospect of being separated from the people they love; of being alone and unprotected; of having to manage themselves instead of being supported. For this reason it is easier to comfort such a child with the agnostic's view of death as a complete absence of being, than with the religious person's view of death as a passing on to God or to heaven. The young child who is told that he will go to anyone, anywhere, will take the statements literally and will not want to go without Mummy. The child who can be convinced that Mummy and Daddy will be with him always (i.e., for as long as he exists at all) will be comforted.

Answering questions honestly need not always mean volunteering the whole truth

There are many situations in which, while his parents are in terror that a child may die, the prognosis is uncertain and the child himself has not considered the possibility. If there is *any* hope, however slender, that a life-threatening operation will succeed or that the new antibiotic will control an otherwise overwhelming infection, that hope needs to be fed into the child's own 'will to live'. In situations of this kind there can be no justification for burdening him with calculating the odds of his own survival and no possible benefit to him in sharing parents' fears. Furthermore, faced with surgery or with dramatic emergency treatment, his attention and anxiety will probably not be focused on the outcome but on the procedures themselves. What could be more calculated to increase his fear of surgery than the knowledge that he may never wake from the anaesthetic?

There are other situations, too, in which a knowledge of the child's own concerns should probably dictate the kind and amount of 'truth' which he is told. If, for example, he has some form of childhood cancer and his doctors are hopeful that intensive treatment will induce a remission, his parents will remain aware that the disease will probably kill him within a few years, but *his* attention will be on that disease-free period. To tell him that he 'will not live to grow up' is to spoil for him what might have been several years of life. A sick nine-year-old is concerned with whether or not he will be back at school next term or able to join the family's summer holiday. He is not concerned with whether or not he will live to go to college, to marry or to give his parents grandchildren. If repeated treat-ment-cycles are needed and periods of remission become shorter or less complete, there may come a time when he does ask 'will I ever be quite better?' and then he may need some more truth. But in the meantime, he needs the promise of returning health, however temporary, to carry him through this bout of illness.

In a similar way, most wise doctors who specialize in the treatment of children with conditions in which slow deterioration is inevitable, agree that such a child needs to be helped to live with the here-and-now, unclouded by the dark future. Usually such a child will come to terms with each stage of a progressive illness as it occurs. At the stage when all he suffered from was muscle weakness, the idea of a wheelchair-bound future would have horrified him, but by the time he needs that wheelchair it spells liberty from the imprisonment of being scarcely able to walk; it is accepted as a friend rather than an enemy.

This ability to live in the present and therefore to accept gradual change, day by day, is one which some parents learn to share in the interests of their own survival. One put it like this:

'We had a couple of black weeks soon after his illness had been diagnosed when we were wondering how we would ever tell him that he'd have to be in a chair; that he'd never be able to be completely independent; never marry or have children. . . . But he was eight. He didn't care about all that. What he cared about was finishing the tests and getting out of hospital and then about getting back to school. After a while, we realized he was happy, it was only we who were miserable. I even had a stage when I was almost angry with him for *being* happy. But then we learned; we learned that if what really mattered to him was going fishing, we'd better get fishing too *and* find a way he'd be able to fish as long as possible. That's the way we've played it ever since. . .'

Sudden Infant Death Syndrome (SIDS) or cot death

In the western world more babies who survive the first month of life will die before their first birthday of SIDS than for any other reason. Research effort is being lavished on these tragedies yet research findings – and their interpretation by the media – are often misunderstood, both by parents who suffer a cot death and by the community at large.

Cot deaths are unexpected deaths   The essence of each tragedy is that, until the moment when he was found dead, nobody had any suspicion that the baby could be in danger. The cases which hit the headlines are of healthy babies, put to bed by their parents and found dead a few hours later. But some SIDS babies were known to be unwell (usually with 'colds') prior to their deaths; some had been seen by their doctors on the previous day; a few have even died in hospital nurseries. Whether they were thought entirely well or not, whether they had been seen by health professionals or not, these babies' deaths were completely unexpected.

Not all cot deaths remain a complete mystery

Investigations after the death sometimes reveal conditions which proved fatal although nobody knew of their existence. Some examples are septicaemia; overwhelming gastro-enteritis and a variety of rare congenital heart or kidney disorders. In a sense, these should not be regarded as cot deaths at all, but as sudden deaths which, while tragic, are not mysterious. Unfortunately they are sometimes counted in with the statistics on cot deaths. More unfortunately still, they sometimes give rise to headlines which suggest that because *this* SIDS baby died because of a heart condition, heart conditions have now been shown to be the (or a) cause of cot deaths.

Rather more often, investigations reveal conditions which are not normally serious enough to cause death but which may, nevertheless, have contributed to it. A particular virus affecting the upper respiratory tract is a common example. It is usually impossible to say whether the baby 'died of the virus', died because the viral infection made SIDS more likely, or died because he was in some way especially sensitive to the virus.

Similar puzzles are presented when conditions are found which could either have caused the death or been caused by it. Inhaled milk in the lower respiratory tract is one example. Did the baby die because he deeply inhaled some of his feed, or is the feed found in his lungs because of attempts at mouth-to-mouth resuscitation?

In the majority of cot deaths no explanation whatsoever can be found

It is with reference to this group of deaths that so many theories are propounded, ranging from undetectable cardiac abnormalities, through neurological peculiarities leading to a cessation of breathing, to subtle biochemical imbalances. From time to time one such theory receives wide publicity: allergic reactions to cow's milk protein (*see* **Allergy**/Gastro-intestinal allergies) was one which became popular recently; but no single theoretical explanation for SIDS has yet stood up to careful investigation. *It is probable that there is no single explanation* but that SIDS can result from any, or any combination, of many factors.

Until or unless we learn more, we can only combat SIDS with excellent health care

We cannot prevent deaths whose cause we cannot discover, but we can try to carry, bear and rear our babies in circumstances which seem likely to give them the best possible chance of resisting or overriding anything which threatens them. Unfortunately many misleading statements about 'social factors in cot deaths' have been widely broadcast and must have given rise to fearful guilt in families who have suffered SIDS, and to equally horrendous anxiety amongst those expecting a baby.

Many of the most misleading statements arise from a confusion between *sudden deaths for which a sufficient cause is later discovered* and the *true cot deaths which defy explanation*. It is widely believed, for example, that cot deaths are more frequent amongst families of lower socio-economic class.

Taking the whole group of babies who die unexpectedly, this is statistically true, but taking only the unexplainable cot deaths, it is not. In the most recent careful British study, for example, the numbers of completely unexplained cot deaths were almost exactly equal for families from social classes I and II and for social classes IV and V. The greater overall numbers of unexpected infant deaths in comparatively deprived families probably simply reflects the fact that, despite our National Health Service, life and health are riskier for the poor than for the rich. Mothers may be less well-nourished in pregnancy; they may make less use of ante-natal care; they may be unable to provide such good conditions for the new baby and they may possibly be slower to seek help for babies who are not thriving or are unwell.

It has also been stated that SIDS is more probable in bottle-fed than in breast-fed babies, but yet again this statement needs careful consideration. Breast-feeding is certainly better for young babies (*see* **Eating**/Breast-feeding). It offers protection against many infant ills, ranging from protection against allergy to cow's milk, through protection against the biochemical dangers of formulae which are made too concentrated, to the specific protection against various kinds of infection which mothers pass to babies in their milk. A fully breast-fed baby may therefore be less likely to succumb to sudden death from a number of identifiable causes; he may even be 'healthier' in a sense which makes him more resistant to any threat, but none of that suggests that breast-feeding will prevent a true cot death. In that same British study, forty-six per cent of the babies who died inexplicably had been breast-fed for some period.

When you read headlines such as 'Mothers who smoke risk cot death', don't leap to the conclusion that your smoking caused your recent tragedy or that you must now live in terror that your child will die. Take it instead as another reminder that anything you can do to optimize your own health in pregnancy (including giving up smoking!) will be good for the unborn baby, and that everything you can do to make sure that he is well-cared for after birth will be good for him, too. But if you take care of yourself, accept all the help you can get from medical professionals and take care of him to the best of your ability, *you are doing or have done everything that can be done to guard against SIDS.*

After a family has experienced the unexpected death of a baby

Whether the death was a true cot death which remains a mystery, or whether it is eventually explained, parents' torment is often increased by their own, or other people's failure to understand some of the feelings which are certain to be aroused.

Such a death is a bereavement just as tragic as the death of a much older child. The baby must be mourned as the unique individual which he was. His existence cannot be brushed aside just because it did not last for long, nor is it usually advisable to 'replace' him by becoming pregnant again as quickly as possible. Parents who try to sidestep grief by immediately resuming life as it was before the birth commonly become exceedingly depressed within a few months. Those who are encouraged (often by medical advisers) to have another baby at once, often have very great difficulty in keeping the dead child and the new one separate in their minds and hearts and the 'replacement child' often suffers severely as a result.

Such a death almost always leads to overwhelming parental guilt and often drives a wedge between parents because one or the other feels (rightly or wrongly) both blameworthy and blamed. Usually it is the mother who feels that her husband must hold her responsible. Occasionally, a father who happened to be in charge at the time of the death, thinks that his wife must feel that if she had been there it would not have happened. Very often mothers receive a great deal of support from other family members and friends, leaving fathers to feel excluded from what is, after all, their bereavement too. Older children tend to suffer (*see above*) because they are simultaneously emotionally neglected, refused help in mourning their own loss and made to feel guilty at being still alive.

Investigations into the death should be the principal source of practical help because it is through them that a cause for the death may be discovered and that, even if no cause can be found, freedom from any responsibility for the death can be brought home to bereaved parents. If the baby did have a fulminating fatal infection or an unsuspected abnormality, they can be assured not only that they could not have known or saved him, but also that there is no mystery and therefore no realistic fear for subsequent babies. If no cause is discovered, it can be pointed out that what cannot be diagnosed, cannot be prevented. What is intolerable is ignorance: the desperate questionings of 3 a.m., 'Why us? What did I do? How could I have known? . . .' and the 'If onlys': 'If only I had woken up; if only I had gone in sooner; if only I had had him in my bed.'

The questions need answering, not only to lessen the agony of parents bereaved *now* but to increase our knowledge of sudden infant deaths so that one day, fewer parents need face such tragedies. Unfortunately parents do not always feel supported or helped by the immediate investigations. By law, any completely unexpected and inexplicable death must involve police enquiries and a coroner's inquest. The arrival of police often makes parents feel that they are under some sort of suspicion. In some neighbourhoods police enquiries also make neighbours less than helpful. There is always a tendency for acquaintances and casual friends to shun the bereaved ('I wouldn't know what to say to her . . .'). Social isolation sometimes turns into cruel rumour-mongering because neighbours assume that the police are investigating 'baby-battering'.

In many communities organizations have now been set up within which bereaved parents can both help each other and help research workers to help them. Such groups aim to support the recently bereaved and to discover from them what kind of help is most genuinely helpful. At the same time, the first-hand accounts of these babies' deaths can provide clues which may, one day, help to prevent them. If your doctor does not know of such a group in your area, you can contact directly the Foundation for the Study of Infant Deaths, 23 St Peter's Square, London W6.

Dehydration *see* **Accidents**/Shock: Causes of major shock; Sunburn and heat illness; **Diarrhoea, Gastro-enteritis and Food Poisoning.** *See also* **Nursing**/Nursing your child at home: Fluids.
Delirium *see* **Nursing**/Side-effects of high fever. *See also* **Accidents**/Head injuries.
Dental health *see* **Teeth**.

Depression

Although we speak of being 'depressed' when we are feeling sad, disappointed, lonely, discouraged and generally miserable, *clinical* depression is something very different from a passing mood. It may amount to a major psychiatric illness and one which carries with it a very real risk of suicide (*see* **Suicide**).

Authorities vary in the lines they draw between depressive *illness* and normal mood-swings or appropriate reactions to real-life stresses. What follows is not a set of rules for do-it-yourself psychiatric diagnosis but an attempt to provide parents with some useful guidelines in deciding whether or not a child or adolescent needs help and, if she does, whether it should be practical and supportive or medical and psychiatric.

Normal depression

Everyday life is full of ups and downs. When disappointments and losses overweigh the balance, temporary depression is a normal reaction. A child may come home from school feeling depressed because she has been in trouble with a favourite teacher for poor work, has failed to be included in a team for which she tried out and has not received an invitation to a friend's party. How strongly she reacts to this collection of real but minor disasters will partly depend on her own internal and biochemical state. If she is over-tired, convalescent or pre-menstrual, for example, physiology and misfortune will, so to speak, gang up on her so that, for the moment, she cannot see that she will feel better tomorrow. If, on the other hand, she is basically well and cheerful, she will probably be able to see them as separate misfortunes which she can either take action to put right or at least take comparatively lightly. In either case, a night's sleep and a new day will have lightened her mood. Even if she still regrets that poor mark, still wishes she had made the team, is still hurt at being left out of the party, she will be ready to get on with her life.

Longer-lasting situational or reactive depression

When something more serious happens – especially if it is something which alters every aspect of the child's life – depression is again a normal response. You may see it when a beloved pet dies or when a young lover defects. In either case, the larger the part played by the love-object in the victim's life, the greater the likely response. You may also see it when a house-move takes a child away from her accustomed social setting or when separation or divorce disrupts the family. For the moment, the child cannot see how to manage herself and her life in this new and unhappy situation and she may be quite unable to accept your assurances that she will 'get over it'. Nevertheless, she will. Even the depression which accompanies real bereavement seldom develops into true clinical depression. Those heartless-sounding aphorisms such as 'time heals' are actually true; she will find herself adapting to a situation within which she honestly believed that she could never be happy again.

Cries of 'pull yourself together' are scarcely tactful when addressed to someone who is miserable, whatever the reason, but *the person whose misery is reasonable* will in fact be able to cope actively with it in her own time. In life's normal moments of depression, action is often the quickest way to a more comfortable mood. The child may be able to make the effort to telephone the friend with whom she has quarrelled, or apologize to the person she has offended, and if she does so, she will feel better. If the misery arises from a collection of circumstances confused with physical discomforts, she may be able to comfort herself with a hot bath and an early night. Even in longer-lasting situational depression she may be able to see helpful action for herself, such as swallowing her pride and going to the party even without her accustomed escort. The point is that, however unhappy she may be, she can still see that there is, has been and will be, happiness in her life, and however much of her life is involved in the misery, she can still feel that that life is under her own control. Her circumstances may be horrible but her image of herself is still intact even if it is swollen with weeping.

Clinical | People sometimes refer to true depressive illness as 'Primary depression'
depression | or 'Endogenous depression'. Both terms refer to the fact that the mental state of the victim seems to arise 'out of the blue' so that if her anguish is indeed 'about' *anything* it is about some life-event which seems comparatively unimportant to onlookers. But, of course, parents have to be careful in making such a judgement. If your son says that he is miserable this term because he is by far the smallest in his class of fourteen-year-olds, cannot compete with them in sport and has no real friends, the whole matter may seem trivial to you but be of overwhelming importance to him (*see* **Adolescence**/Puberty: Worries about puberty). In the same way, if your daughter goes into a Victorian-seeming decline over a lost boyfriend, your view of the importance of the lost relationship may be very different from hers. So while sudden depression, arising out of skies you had thought blue, should certainly alert you and make you think, you need other clues to suggest illness rather than unhappiness.

We do not know why some people are liable to clinical depression while others are not. There are certain life-stresses which are often present in people who *are* clinically depressed (such as recent bereavement, childbirth, unemployment, chronic ill-health and/or pain and so forth) but since there are millions of people who suffer these same stresses without depressive illness, the real-life events cannot actually be *causes* but must serve to 'touch off' a depressive reaction in people who are already vulnerable. Those who lost, or were deprived of, parents or other vitally important caretakers during early childhood – especially those who did not fully mourn that loss – may be amongst those vulnerable personalities. So also may children whose real-life loss was not obvious, but who nevertheless grew up without the taken-for-granted security of a completely reliable and loving caretaker (*see* **Anxiety, Fears and Phobias**/ The roots of anxiety).

The following are all accepted signs of clinical depression. Few victims, especially youthful ones, will display them all, but most will display some. You may see them suddenly or you may see them as a development of the existing unhappiness of situational depression. In either case your child will be unable to 'pull herself together', act or react in ways which might make her happier, because this is an illness which is outside her control and one whose major features concern her inability to accept, far less seek, happiness.

Mood of hopeless sadness which the victim usually cannot, and does not try to, 'justify' in terms of real events.

Loss of the ability to experience pleasure so that people, activities and treats which she normally finds fun suddenly seem hollow and empty.

Feelings of personal worthlessness. The victim tends to accept anything hurtful or unpleasant which happens to her as 'no more than I deserve'. She may actually deny previous accomplishments, denying that those excellent examination results were good or asserting that she was only included in that team, play or choir because 'there wasn't anybody else'. She will certainly be extremely pessimistic about the future because whatever challenges it offers she will be sure that she will deservedly fail to meet them.

This very low self-esteem is probably the principal sign of depression for which parents should be alert and it is also the symptom which makes it most difficult for the victim to pursue her normal life. She is robbed of motivation because there is no point in trying if you know you are going to fail. She may also rob herself of important personal relationships because there is no point in telephoning a friend who only speaks to you out of pity nor do you join a group in conversation when you know that you are not truly wanted . . .

Feelings of guilt tend to follow on from feelings of worthlessness. The depressed child may feel guilty at failing to live up to other people's expectations or guilty because she can see that her state is upsetting you. Sometimes the guilt of depression becomes more generalized. She may feel as if she has committed some crime for which she deserves punishment; she may even take upon herself the crimes of the world and feel guilty because she has been well-fed all her life while the children of the developing world are starving.

Anxiety may, or may not, be an obvious feature of clinical depression (*see* **Anxiety, Fears and Phobias**/Free-floating anxiety). If it is, the victim may be over-active; unable to sit still and unable to concentrate on any task for long. If it is not, she may feel tired and lethargic; too tired to do anything; too tired even to formulate the flow of sentences which are needed for conversation. She may sit for long periods gazing sightlessly out of windows or at the television screen, and she may spend long hours in bed, unable to rouse herself in the morning to face a new day.

Physical symptoms are very common with clinical depression and may confuse you as to whether your child is physically or mentally ill. The most usual of all is probably disturbance of sleep. The child may have difficulty in falling asleep but she is also very likely to awaken as early as 3 or 4 a.m. and be unable to get back to sleep until an hour or so before the time when she used to get up.

Headaches and backaches (*see* **Headaches**) are common, as are constipation and disturbances of the menstrual cycle. If clinical depression is left untreated for long, loss of appetite may lead to weight loss. Even in the earliest stages, pleasure in food is likely to be reduced so that even if she eats normally she is no longer enthusiastic about previous favourite foods.

Thoughts of suicide and a new and morbid interest in death in general are symptoms of depression which should always lead to an urgent response. Do not convince yourself that 'she is not the type' or that 'she wouldn't be so silly'; we do not know 'the type' nor is self-destruction 'silly' if you truly believe that you are a worthless, hopeless person, a burden on others and someone for whom there is no worthwhile future . . . Actual threats of suicide are an emergency. Do not leave her alone in the black mists of her depression. She needs professional help.

Depression in children before puberty
Is often not recognized (indeed some authorities deny that it is possible) because it tends to take different forms from those suggested above. Some of its more usual manifestations seem the very opposite of depression and may therefore lead to the child being treated in highly inappropriate ways. For example, a depressed eight- or nine-year-old may:

Appear 'hyperactive', undisciplined and unmanageable (*see* Hyperactive Children). He does not *say* that he feels unworthy of your love. He does not *say* that it is not worth trying to please you because nobody could ever be pleased with a child as wicked as him. He behaves as if he did not care for you, your feelings or your opinions, he calls down upon himself more and more disapproval and punishment and they reinforce the underlying depression and therefore the 'bad behaviour'.

Appear 'accident prone' either in the sense of being completely careless of his own safety, so that he not only climbs the tall tree but tries to fly out of it, or in the sense of constantly damaging himself while apparently leading a normal life. If your child pays more visits to Casualty, wears more plaster casts and adhesive dressings, than any other child you know and embarrasses you with his frequent black eyes and facial bruises, ask yourself why. He may just be an active and courageous child who is being offered many challenges by his daily life. But he may be a child who cannot learn to look after himself sensibly because he does not feel either cared-for or worthy of care.

With these younger children, most 'behaviour problems' relate directly to feelings of insecurity about love-relationships with parents or other caretakers. Most, therefore, are reactions to sadness and inner-pain. It does not matter whether or not you regard your troublesome child as *depressed* as long as you regard him as *troubled*. Above all:

Do not believe that he does not care about you however often he says that he hates you or however don't-careish his behaviour. He does care; the trouble is that he cannot, or dare not, let you see, or even let himself feel, that he cares. Ask yourself whether your love and support are truly unshakeable and, if they are, how you can help him towards believing it. If you cannot find and enact an answer, seek professional help via your doctor or local child guidance clinic. Far from criticizing you for producing such a 'difficult child' or scorning you for 'not being able to cope with him' they will be thankful that you have been able to distinguish between 'naughtiness' and emotional disturbance.

De-sensitization *see* **Allergy**. *See also* **Anxiety, Fears and Phobias**/Phobias.

Diarrhoea, Gastro-enteritis and Food Poisoning
see also **Infection**/Infection and home hygiene

Diarrhoea

In the last stages of digestion, the walls of the intestine absorb much of the fluid from the material which is passing through it so that when a stool is eventually passed it is fairly firm and formed. The exact texture of stools varies from person to person and from day to day in the same person. But while soft, pasty stools may be entirely normal for the individual (particularly if that individual is a baby), the person who passes semi-fluid or completely liquid stools has diarrhoea.

A diarrhoeal stool means that the intestine has not, on this occasion, absorbed the usual amount of liquid from the waste. There may be 'intestinal hurry' such that the waves of contractions (peristalsis) are moving material so rapidly through the gut that it is never in contact with the intestinal wall for long enough for absorption to take place. There may be inflammation of the intestinal wall such that it is temporarily unable to absorb fluid. If the inflammation is acute, that intestinal wall may even be leaking extra fluid back the other way, from the circulation into the waste material.

Diarrhoea need not mean that a person is ill. A baby may have diarrhoeal stools following a change in formula or the sudden addition of extra sugar to the diet. An older child may have diarrhoea after a fruit-feast while an adolescent may suffer in this way after his first wine party. An ill-judged dose of a stimulant laxative (*see* **Laxatives**) can produce intestinal hurry and diarrhoea while broad-spectrum antibiotics quite often upset the normal flora of the gut and produce diarrhoea as an unwanted side-effect.

If a child past the toddler stage seems entirely well in every other way, the fact that he is passing very loose stools instead of stools which are normal for him is no cause for concern. Except in the youngest age groups (*see below*), diarrhoea only requires consideration if there are other symptoms such as vomiting, fever, abdominal pain or cramps or if the stools are passed so frequently (and the need to pass them is so urgent) that the child's ordinary daily life is disrupted.

Diarrhoea and bowel training

Children who are adjusting from nappies to using a pot or the toilet, or those who have only recently acquired this kind of control, are often 'caught out' by diarrhoea. The urgent need to pass a liquid stool is a quite different feeling from the full-rectum sensation which they have learned to recognize. Such a child may soil his pants and be truly horrified by the mess. Of course he deserves every possible reassurance and an explanation which makes it clear to him that his loose stools are a temporary state of affairs. Even so, it may be kind to keep him close to home until the diarrhoea resolves. Even if his playgroup leader or nursery teacher is as understanding as you are yourself, his 'friends' may not be.

Diarrhoea and school

Some much older children will also find it difficult to attend school while they have diarrhoea because some schools, in an effort to confine trips to the toilet to formal breaks, make it embarrassingly difficult for children to keep dashing out during a lesson.

Diarrhoea can be inconvenient whenever circumstances make ready and instant access to a lavatory difficult. It can be tiresome, for example, on a long coach-trip and it can waste precious time (and be embarrassing) during examinations. If an older child *who does not seem ill* has diarrhoea at a time like this (and some children do react to stress with this 'gut reaction') there may be a case for using one of the many 'binding medicines' which are available over the counter.

Medicines for diarrhoea

Three types of medicine are widely available in many countries:

Kaolin mixtures. Kaolin is basically a kind of clay and these mixtures act simply by adding solidity to the diarrhoeal stool. The medicine does nothing to help the intestine absorb water or to slow up the passage of waste through it. It simply adds to what is going to be passed anyway so that the result is less liquid.

Antibiotic mixtures. Happily these are not available without a prescription in the UK, but families may be offered them for 'traveller's diarrhoea' when on holiday in some western European countries. They should not be accepted. Antibiotics are seldom indicated in diarrhoea (*see below*) and never in diarrhoea without associated illness. They are often contra-indicated.

Mixtures containing codeine or opium or morphine. Sometimes offered in combination with kaolin, these mixtures aim to calm down the peristalsis and thus slow up the rate at which waste is moved through the intestine so that more fluid may be absorbed during transit. They also ease any abdominal pain or crampiness which may accompany the diarrhoea. Such a medicine, taken only in the recommended dosage, may be extremely useful.

● Don't give any medicine for diarrhoea to children under about ten without your doctor's advice.

● Don't give these medicines, even to older children, if they have any symptoms apart from the diarrhoea. If the loose stools are due to an infection, for example, it may be a mistake to encourage the body to retain them artificially.

Diarrhoea in babies and toddlers

Whatever the cause of diarrhoea, it has to be taken far more seriously in babies and very young children than in older people. Babies have a much greater turnover of water in their bodies than the rest of us. They need to drink more water for every pound of their bodyweight to maintain the fluid balance in their bodies, and they have only a very small margin to protect that balance if fluid should become scarce.

In diarrhoea, fluid can become scarce. The baby drinks his ordinary bottle, but instead of most of its fluid (as well as its nutrients) being absorbed into his circulation, most of it is passed straight out again as a liquid stool. If his intestines are much inflamed as well as hurried, that liquid stool may contain not only the liquid from his bottle but extra fluid from earlier drinks leaked back through the walls. If he loses more water and salt than he can take in and absorb, he will rapidly become dehydrated. Untreated, dehydration can upset the chemistry of the baby's whole body and make him extremely ill, even if the original cause of the diarrhoea was trivial. Dehydration is increasingly likely if:

The baby goes off his food. Milk is both food and drink to him so if he refuses his normal formula he must have some other liquid. Plain water, sweetened water or well-diluted fruit juice will all do equally well. It is the fluid which matters. The more liquid he will take the better, since only some of it is being absorbed. He will probably find frequent small drinks more acceptable than occasional full bottles.

The baby is feverish. Fever puts up the body's need for water and therefore a nett loss will occur more easily.

The baby is vomiting. If he vomits whatever liquid he is willing to drink, his body has no chance to absorb it and furthermore each episode of vomiting may lose him more fluid than he has just taken.

Preventing
dehydration

If a baby or very young child has diarrhoea, you know that he is losing fluid. If he does not seem unwell, you can afford to wait a bit before consulting a doctor. Let him have his ordinary feeds but offer extra drinks in-between. The more often he is passing liquid stools (and the more copious they are) the more often you should offer drinks. You are trying to make sure that more goes in than comes out. Very young babies sometimes feed willingly even during a diarrhoeal illness which is serious and which is dehydrating them, so do not assume that as long as he will eat, he cannot be very ill. Unless you are quite certain that more fluid is going in than is coming out, take him to the doctor. An older baby who will feed readily and take extra drinks probably will not become dehydrated, but as soon as he refuses his normal feeds, contact your doctor. He must now be counted as 'unwell'.

While you are waiting for the doctor to see your child, keep soiled nappies (that smelly plastic bag will give the doctor some idea of the amount of fluid he has lost and enable him to take a sample for the laboratory if he wishes) and keep on offering whatever fluids he will drink. Try to get about 2 oz. of fluid per hour down a baby and about twice that amount down a toddler.

If he will not drink nearly that amount or especially if he vomits what he drinks, don't wait for that appointment. Ask your doctor to see him as an emergency. If this is impossible, take the child to your nearest hospital.

● A child under a year old should not be left for more than four hours without medical attention if he is having diarrhoea and vomiting, especially if he is refusing to drink.

If you are far from medical help or if a baby suddenly shoots a high fever with diarrhoea and vomiting, he may start to become dehydrated before you can summon help. The principal signs are:

Signs of dehydration

Lethargy. The baby seems floppy, sleepy or withdrawn and usually cannot be bothered to suck so that he does not seem at all thirsty.

● Don't be fooled into 'leaving him in peace until the morning'.

Glazed and sunken eyes. The baby's face looks drawn and ill and it is difficult to get his full attention or to make him 'sparkle'.

Inelastic skin and dry-looking tongue.

Scanty urine. Sometimes the very first alerting sign of dehydration is an unexpected dry nappy. If urine is passed there will not be much of it and what there is will probably be highly concentrated, yellow and strong-smelling. His body is fighting to retain fluid so the urine will have an unusually high ratio of waste-products to water.

● In acute diarrhoea, stools may be so watery that they cannot be distinguished from urine and the nappy appears simply wet. Do not let this fool you into thinking that the diarrhoeal stools have stopped and that the baby is passing plenty of urine.

Lack of tears. A baby old enough to cry real tears may now cry dry-eyed.

Coping with dehydration

Once the fluid and salt balance in a baby's body is disturbed, he needs hospital treatment because he needs to have the fluid and salt put directly into his bloodstream by intravenous transfusion (*see* **Hospital/Procedures**) while the cause of the diarrhoea which started the trouble is found and dealt with. You can give some immediate first aid (especially if getting him to hospital will take an hour or more).

Take one pint of water (boil it, if boiling is necessary, before you measure it out) and stir in one level tablespoonful of sugar (or glucose if you happen to have it) and one *pinch* (not more than a quarter of a level *tea*spoon) of salt. The resulting solution will be the nearest thing to the fluid the baby's body requires which you can produce at home.

If the baby will suck, but is vomiting, give him a single ounce at a time, as slowly as he will take it. If he vomits at once, give him another ounce immediately. If he keeps it down for more than a quarter-of-an-hour it will probably have done some good. Give him another ounce half an hour after the first.

If the baby will not suck, whether or not he is vomiting, try and get at least a little of your mixture down him from a small spoon. Anything is better than nothing.

● Don't reverse those sugar and salt suggestions. A very little salt will help. Too much is extremely dangerous.

● If the fluid seems to provoke vomiting, stop it and concentrate on getting to the hospital at top speed. Remember that when he vomits he probably loses more fluid than you have just given him. On the other hand, if the vomiting seems to happen anyway, you may be able to time those tiny drinks so that some is absorbed before the next vomit.

• It will help the hospital doctors to decide on immediate treatment if you can jot down the times at which the baby vomited, passed diarrhoeal stools or had something to drink.

Gastro-enteritis

Although gastro-enteritis really only means inflammation of the gastro-intestinal tract (and could therefore be applied to any kind of diarrhoea and to food poisoning), it is a term which is usually reserved for diarrhoea with or without vomiting and/or fever, due to infection. As we shall see (*see below* Food poisoning), there are many types of bacteria which can cause gastro-enteritis but these normally multiply in food to reach an infecting dose and are therefore considered as food poisoning except that infant food poisoning, due to multiplication of bacteria in milk, is referred to as gastro-enteritis. In older children and adults, an illness referred to as gastro-enteritis is usually due to infection by viruses.

Some viruses typically infect the gastro-intestinal tract but many others (including some of the common cold viruses) may infect either the respiratory or the gastro-intestinal tract depending on how they are taken into the body and on where the victim is susceptible. A family 'bug', which announced itself as your head cold, may give one child tonsillitis and another diarrhoea and vomiting.

Gastro-enteritis can be a severe illness with high fever, vomiting and copious diarrhoea. But it can also be a twenty-four-hour affair amounting to no more than a few very loose stools and some nausea. The younger the child, the more likely it is that he will be badly affected because of dehydration.

Although a doctor should always be consulted about a baby or toddler with diarrhoea associated with vomiting and/or fever, medical advice is only needed for an older child if he seems really unwell. There is little that a doctor can do to help in a mild case of gastro-enteritis. He cannot find out exactly which micro-organisms caused the infection because, as we have seen (*see* **Infection**/Types of infection: Difficulties of laboratory diagnosis of infection), culturing viruses in the laboratory is a lengthy (and expensive) business and pointless in an illness from which the patient will certainly recover long before results become available. He is very unlikely to want your child to have an antibiotic because the infection is likely to be viral and the drugs would, therefore, be useless at best and actually stressful to the already stressed bowel at worst. If the illness should turn out to be severe there will be plenty that the doctor can do to make sure that his general condition is well-maintained. But ordinary diarrhoea and vomiting in a child past toddler-age is a case for home-nursing.

Nursing gastro-enteritis

Older children can become dehydrated too, although their bodies need more cause and more time than the bodies of younger children.

Make sure that your child drinks plenty from the time he begins to vomit and/or pass diarrhoeal stools. It does not matter at all if he does not want anything to eat but he should have at least a small glassful of something every hour while he is awake. Although you do not have to be absolutely rigid about it, try to see that he drinks at least two pints during any full day during which he is not eating and is passing a lot of loose stools.

If he is nauseated or actually vomiting, as well as having diarrhoea, avoid fizzy drinks and milky ones. Plain water or fruit juice is usually the easiest to take. It often goes down best if it is iced. Small sips from a small glass are less nauseating and daunting than gulps from a tumbler.

Take his temperature. If you later have to call the doctor, he will be interested to know whether the temperature he finds is higher or lower than it was at the beginning of the illness.

Let him stay in bed if he feels like it (vomiting and diarrhoea are exhausting so he may) but he does not have to stay there if he is well enough to feel bored.

Don't give 'binding medicines' or painkillers. He may have gripey abdominal pains just before each diarrhoeal stool, but if he has continuous or severe pain then its relief is up to a doctor. Call the doctor anyway if:

The child seems collapsed, confused or ill in a way which, whether or not you can say why, really worries you.

Vomiting continues over more than twelve hours or happens more than four times in six hours. The doctor may give a medicine to stop the actual vomiting and this will be pleasanter for the child and make it far easier to keep his fluid intake up.

There is blood in the diarrhoeal stools.

There is continuous abdominal pain or intermittent pain which is severe enough to stop him in his tracks/make him cry/wake him in the night. It is just possible that some quite different kind of abdominal emergency is masquerading as gastro-enteritis (see **Abdominal Pain**); you need a doctor to check. Furthermore, if it is 'only' gastro-enteritis, your doctor may give the child medicine to reduce the painful spasms of his intestine.

He goes on feeling and seeming ill for more than forty-eight hours. The diarrhoea may continue for longer than this because it takes some time for an inflamed intestine to settle back to normal, but the child should be feeling a great deal better 'in himself' by this time.

Several members of the family become ill at the same time. If they have all shared a particular meal, the gastro-enteritis may be due to food poisoning (see below). The doctor may wish to notify the public health authorities so that any slip-up in food-hygiene arrangements can be identified and dealt with.

Preventing the spread of gastro-enteritis   Although the virus can certainly be spread from one person to another via unwashed hands, etc., it may well also be one which can be spread by droplets from the nose and mouth. You may not be any more successful in controlling gastro-enteritis than you can be in controlling ordinary colds. But where there is gastro-enteritis in the family, it is worth making strenuous efforts to avoid infecting babies. Try to keep the baby apart from his suffering sibling. Take trouble over disinfecting anything touched by diarrhoea or vomit. Make sure the patient uses only his own towel, facecloth, etc. and that you do not leave his mixed up with other people's. Above all, remember to wash your own hands between playing nurse and playing parent (*see* **Infection**/Preventing infection: Sterilants, disinfectants and antiseptics).

Food poisoning

While there are many water- or milk-borne micro-organisms and other types of irritant, which can cause gastro-enteritis, many outbreaks in western societies (with their high standards of water- and milk-hygiene) are caused by bacteria in or on food. All can therefore be loosely termed 'food poisoning' although it is not the food which is poisonous but the load of pathogenic micro-organisms which it carries. Food does not have to be 'bad' to cause illness. In fact rotten, smelly, mouldy food is rather unlikely to make people ill as, unless they are starving, few will eat it.

The food which is most likely to cause illness is not just food which contains bacteria (almost all foodstuffs do), nor even food which contains pathogenic bacteria in small numbers, (most people will cope with these without experiencing symptoms), but food in which pathogenic bacteria have been given the opportunity to multiply and which is then eaten while these vast numbers are alive and active. A recent outbreak in the UK, for example, involved large quantities of frozen minced beef cooked and distributed by the 'Meals on Wheels' service. Blocks of the mince were placed, still frozen, in a larger container and 'cooked'. The quantity was so large that the mince could not be thoroughly stirred so the centre of each block was at full boiling point for a much shorter time than the outside. The cooking did not therefore sterilize the meat completely. The mince was now left in its vast pot overnight where it cooled, very slowly, to room temperature. Any bacteria which had survived the initial cooking now had an ideal environment in which to multiply. Next day the mince was merely warmed (not brought to a full boil and kept there for several minutes) so that once again a proportion of the now much greater number of bacteria survived. The mince was served into individual portions, placed in a keep-warm trolley and distributed over a period of several hours. While that trolley would have kept boiling food at a safely high temperature, it was not designed to heat food which was merely warm, so those hours provided yet another incubation period of gentle warmth. Almost everyone who ate the mince was ill.

This warning story illustrates the fact that the prevention of food poisoning is only partially under the control of individual families. We can take responsibility for the handling, storage, preparation and serving of food in our own kitchens, but many of us eat many meals, often prepared on a vast institutional scale, in school kitchens, canteens and restaurants. Furthermore, even the food which we do serve and eat at home has been pre-prepared for sale whether it is sold raw, processed or pre-cooked. We therefore have to depend very heavily on public health measures and on the public responsibility of the food industry. Where there is a failure somewhere in this complicated chain, it is important that we work out where things went wrong. If you know that you ignored an expiry date or forgot to refrigerate Monday's casserole after cooking it on Sunday morning, you can learn by your own uncomfortable mistake. But where a product which is guaranteed 'longlife' ferments within that extended shelf-period, or where you know that your own handling of food which caused illness was impeccable, it is important that the authorities be told. In the meanwhile, a very few basic food-handling principles may help you to avoid food poisoning either from your own or from anyone else's kitchen.

Most bacteria are killed by high heat. Cooking food right through so that every bit of it is exposed to high heat will usually render it safe for immediate eating.

Most bacteria multiply fastest in food which is warm. If cooked food must be cooled for later eating, cool it covered (to prevent live bacteria getting in) and fast (so that any live bacteria have a minimal chance to multiply). Keep it cold until wanted.

If it is to be eaten cold, keep it covered to prevent cross-contamination by other (perhaps raw) food, by flies, etc.

● Reject hamburgers and other 'fast foods' served to you warm from 'keep hot' containers.

If the food is to be reheated and eaten hot, make sure that it is made really hot again right through so that any bacteria which escaped the first cooking, or were introduced after it, are now killed.

● Don't ever *warm up* cooked food for a baby to just the temperature he likes. *Reheat*, cool rapidly and feed.

● Remember that your shopping bag in your office is at 'room temperature' which is warm. Don't keep food which is to be eaten without further cooking there for hours.

● Remember that shops are at room temperature too. Don't buy ready-to-eat foods from unrefrigerated counters.

Bacteria from raw foods, flies, unwashed hands or septic lesions can contaminate ready-to-eat foods. Poultry, for example, almost invariably carry pathogenic bacteria which will be killed by thorough cooking. But if raw chicken blood gets onto your chopping board or your hands and from there onto that veal and ham pie, those who eat the pie a few hours later may suffer.

Septic cuts and so forth usually teem with bacteria. Again, if these get onto meat you are going to cook they will probably cause no harm but if they get onto the creamy pastry you are going to serve cold this evening, they may multiply to an extent which will make people ill.

● Try not to buy cooked meats from counters which also handle raw meats, especially if the same slicer is used to slice, say, that cooked ham and raw bacon.

Milk, egg and sugar is an ideal growth medium for bacteria. Items such as commercially produced custard tarts and so forth will certainly breed pathogens if any are given the opportunity to reach them. Such items are probably safest sold from the freezer and/or in sealed wrappings. If you buy them 'loose' make sure that the shop is observing proper precautions against flies and keeps its goods in cool-counters.

● While ice-cream, being frozen, is reasonably safe, the ice-cream cones sold to you from a van may not be as the melted spillage round the edge of the tub or on an ill-washed scoop may be teeming with bacteria. If you want to buy ices from such a source, choose wrapped items, preferably those which are water- rather than 'cream'-based.

Salmonella food poisoning (salmonellosis)

The most frequent food-borne disease reported in man, salmonellosis is caused by tiny gram-negative bacteria of which there are many varieties. Two of the most virulent cause typhus and paratyphoid fevers which are not usually classed as 'food poisoning' as the infection takes hold over ten days to a fortnight after the infecting dose has been taken in.

The incidence of the many more rapid and less serious types of salmonellosis is difficult to estimate because, although it is a 'notifiable disease', many attacks pass off so quickly that they are never reported to a doctor while even those seen by doctors are often simply labelled 'diarrhoea and vomiting' and the laboratory studies which would identify the bacteria are never carried out.

Features of salmonella poisoning
First symptoms usually appear twelve to twenty-four hours after eating infected food. The first sign is usually fever, quickly followed by diarrhoea and vomiting. The fever may remain high for several days so that the attack is a definite 'illness' rather than an unpleasant episode.

A recovered victim may continue to excrete salmonellae in the faeces for several months or even for longer. People who work in the food industry, or with particularly susceptible populations such as young babies in nurseries, are required to have a series of faecal specimens examined to ensure that they are clear of the infection before they return to work.

Sources of salmonellae
Many animals, including those we kill for food, and rodents, suffer salmonellae infection and may excrete the organisms in their faeces even when they appear well, thus infecting each other during transport to slaughter and so forth. The most common sources of infection to people in western communities are:

Meat, especially pork (many pigs are carriers), and pork products such as sausages; especially when these meats are eaten raw or undercooked.

Eggs and egg products such as liquid egg for catering.

● Duck eggs are often highly contaminated both inside and outside. If duck eggs are used at all, they should be kept apart from all other foods whilst in the shell and should never be used in lightly cooked dishes.

Hens' eggs are seldom contaminated inside the hen but shells may become contaminated and, *if the shell is cracked*, bacteria may penetrate. Never use cracked eggs for uncooked items such as 'egg-nog' or for lightly cooked custards, etc.

Dairy products which are safe when made (because our milk is pasteurized) but may become contaminated afterwards.

Fish, oysters and other shellfish taken from sewage-polluted water, especially dangerous when eaten raw (*see* **Pollution**).

Clostridial food poisoning

Clostridiae are *anaerobic spore forming* bacteria. Widely distributed in nature, in soil, sewage and the bowels of man and other animals, the spores are very heat-resistant, sometimes surviving four to five hours boiling. However, such potentially living spores do not multiply unless they find an environment which has no (or very little) oxygen.

Features of clostridial poisoning

First symptoms may not appear for twenty-four hours after infected food is eaten. Fever and vomiting are unusual, the illness usually being confined to about twenty-four hours of diarrhoea and colicky pain.

Sources of clostridiae

Because they are so widespread, the micro-organisms are often in raw meat and poultry before it reaches the kitchen. Poisoning can be avoided, however, if cooking methods provide high heat (roasting or pressure cooking rather than simmering, for example) and, above all, if cooked meat which may contain spores is not left to cool slowly under conditions which prevent oxygen reaching those spores. The most commonly traced sources of infection are:

Large rolled joints, pre-cooked for eating cold or for re-warming. By rolling the joint, you (or your butcher) ensure that any clostridiae on the outside of the meat are taken into the centre where there will be no oxygen and where neither heat-penetration nor cooling will be effective. Eaten immediately, such a joint will do no harm. Left even for a few hours it may teem with sufficient bacteria to make anyone who eats it ill.

● Joints, especially rolled joints, should not be larger than about 6 lb. (3 kg), should ideally be very thoroughly cooked and, *especially if preferred underdone*, should be eaten immediately after cooking. If a rare roast of rolled beef must be eaten cold, it should be cooled very rapidly, in airy conditions, and refrigerated as soon as possible.

Casseroles can also provide anaerobic conditions for clostridiae as well as often being cooked at a low temperature and in advance, for reheating.

● If you intend to prepare a casserole in advance in this way, cut-up meat is safer than meat in a piece and it is essential that it reach a full boil before being put to simmer. Frequent stirring during quick cooling will help to oxygenate the casserole as will stirring during reheating, which must again be to a high temperature.

Staphylococcal food poisoning (*see also* **Impetigo and Staphylococcal Infections**)

A few strains of staphylococcus aureus can cause food poisoning if they get from their usual habitats (skin, nose and throat) into food. A few of these micro-organisms do no harm. In order to produce enough toxin to make people ill, there must be considerable multiplication.

For multiplication to take place, temperatures must be fairly high. A normal room temperature, for example, will not produce as rapid multiplication as heat-wave, or even warming oven, temperatures. No multiplication will take place in an acid environment.

Features of staphylococcal food poisoning

Symptoms appear very soon after the food is eaten – within one to six hours. The illness begins with violent vomiting; this is followed by diarrhoea but the whole episode is often over within half a day. Fever is not a feature and, if present, suggests a different diagnosis.

Although usually trivial if unpleasant, small babies or otherwise susceptible individuals can actually die from dehydration and shock.

Sources of staphylococcae

Identified sources are almost always food-handlers. They may have staphylococcal infections of the throat, or infected wounds on their hands. They pass on the bacteria by breathing on, or touching, the food.

Since it takes both time and special conditions for bacteria introduced in this way to multiply to danger-level, infection is usually traced to pre-cooked meats and meat products (pies, sausages, ham, etc.) which has not only been infected but has then been stored without refrigeration, or kept warm for long periods.

● If in doubt about the hygienic standards of a café, roadhouse or canteen, short-order food, cooked at the time, is safer than the meat pie or sausage roll which may have spent hours in a warming-cabinet.

Botulism

'Classic' botulism occurs when people eat food which contains the toxin released by spores of clostridium botulinum after germination.

The toxin is a deadly poison affecting the nerves which control muscles. When it causes death, it usually does so by paralysing the muscles which make breathing possible.

The botulinus bacillus itself is little threat to man because it is anaerobic (unable to survive in any oxygenated environment) and highly sensitive to heat. Its spores can survive for years, dormant, even in adverse conditions, and are widely distributed in soil, dust and so forth. But in dormant form they are no threat to man, either. Millions of people take the spores in with their food and excrete them again unchanged. Trouble only arises if spores are given the opportunity to germinate in food and that food, now contaminated with toxin, is eaten (but *see below*).

Spores are destroyed by sufficient heat applied over a long enough period. They cannot germinate where there is oxygen, where the environment is acid or in the presence of nitrites. The food industry, well aware of the probable presence and particular habits of these spores, takes trouble to ensure that no germination can take place in its products. Jars and cans, for example, which provide an oxygen-free vacuum, are exposed to high heat levels. Foods which are to be preserved raw, and which might provide an oxygen-free environment for spores, are subject to other precautions. A side of bacon, for example, which cannot be subjected to lethal heat and which might be anaerobic at the centre of a large piece, will have nitrites added to its preserving solution.

Most outbreaks of botulinus poisoning are therefore due to inadequate home-preserving. Home-bottled fruit is safely acid but home-bottled vegetables, blanched rather than boiled and sealed up without vinegar, just might be risky. Botulinus poisoning is very rare but it is certainly worth making sure that you follow recipes exactly, or take expert advice, before you embark on bottling your own beans, potting your own ducks or smoking your own bacon . . .

Infant botulism

This quite different version of botulism was only discovered in 1976 and is still ill-understood. Infants, like the rest of us, are frequently exposed to botulinus *spores* but are most unlikely to be exposed to botulinus *toxin* because, in the early months of life, they are unlikely to be fed on home-potted meat or pickles with too little vinegar . . . However, it has been found that a very few infants under six months (about three hundred in the world so far) can develop the symptoms of botulinus poisoning because they have eaten the spores and *germination and toxin production have taken place in their intestines*. A search for the bowel-conditions which make this possible is being actively pursued. Since no child over eight months has yet been found to be affected, it is thought that it must be some peculiarity of the bacterial flora in the very young which makes germination within the body possible. It must, however, be emphasized that the fact that this *can* happen in the very young does not mean that it is at all *likely* to happen. Even though doctors in many countries are now interestedly watching for cases of infant botulism, and finding a minute handful, there are millions of babies taking in botulinus spores and excreting them, like older people, without ill-effects.

Why mention such a scarey and remote possibility? Because there is just one precaution which many authorities believe that parents may, even at this very early stage in our knowledge, like to take. That precaution is to avoid feeding honey to babies under about one year of age.

Honey and infant botulism

Honey quite often contains botulinus spores because bees collect nectar from plants growing in soil, and honey-production cannot involve sub-jecting it to high heats. About ten to fifteen per cent of honey samples studied so far have been shown to contain some spores.

Studies of babies known to have suffered from infant botulism have further shown that some (by no means all, but more than would be likely by chance alone) had been fed with honey during the days before they became ill, and that the type of botulinus organism which made them ill was identical with the type found in the honey they had eaten.

On the evidence so far, nobody whose baby has been eating honey need panic; nobody should even say 'honey causes infant botulism'. What one can say is that a few very young babies seem able to germinate botulinus spores in their intestines and therefore that it is sensible to avoid feeding any baby any food which is known to be likely to contain these spores, especially if that food is not a necessary part of the diet.

Diet *see* **Eating.** *See also* **Allergy**/Gastro-intestinal allergies: Living with elimination diets.

Diphtheria

Diphtheria is a bacterial infection (caused by one of three strains) which starts with local infection of the nose, throat or larynx but in which the infecting bacteria then release powerful toxins (*see* **Infection**/Bacteria) which can kill by damaging vital organs such as the heart. The infection is usually passed by droplet infection from the air. Unfortunately, healthy immune people can be 'carriers' of diphtheria and the organisms can survive for some time on dust or other contaminated articles.

Diphtheria has almost been conquered in western countries by mass immunization. But we must be careful. When mass immunization began in 1940, many parents and doctors were all too aware of the fearsome nature of the disease. They had seen it, or suffered its ravages; immunization was therefore gratefully received. Now, most people – even most doctors – have never seen a case of diphtheria. A real threat has become a theoretical one and fewer people are accepting immunization for their infants *and* ensuring that they receive the necessary boosters as they grow up (*see* **Immunization**). Occasional minor outbreaks and a few deaths each year make it clear that diphtheria *could* regain its foothold in our communities. It is up to each and every family to make sure that this does not happen.

Immunization against diphtheria

Is not by use of killed or live-but-attenuated bacteria, but by use of diphtheria toxoid which is a chemically de-activated preparation of the toxins released by diphtheria bacilli. The toxoid is no longer poisonous, but it is still capable of stimulating the body to produce anti-toxins.

Schick test

Is a simple skin test to determine whether or not an older child has diphtheria anti-toxins (whether, for example, an immunization has been successful) and/or what level of natural protection he has (whether, for example, a booster would be advisable).

If he has no anti-toxins, the injection of a minute quantity of toxin into the skin produces reddening of the area. If he has circulating anti-toxins the injected toxins are neutralized and no reddened patch develops.

● Note that the interpretation of the Schick test is the reverse of the Mantoux test for tuberculosis (*see* **Tuberculosis**). In diphtheria, no reaction means that the individual is immune. In tuberculosis, no reaction means that the individual is not immune.

Anti-toxins in the treatment of diphtheria

When diphtheria is clinically diagnosed, antibiotics which are at least partially effective against most of the infecting bacteria are given but, while these may kill or prevent the further multiplication of the bacteria, they are not effective against the toxins those bacteria have already released. Passive immunity to those toxins can be temporarily given by the administration of anti-toxins prepared from the blood of horses, stimulated to produce them by previous doses of toxoid. Anti-toxins are far safer than they used to be but some individuals are still hypersensitive to the horse serum which contains them. Furthermore, while anti-toxins may be life-saving in an individual case of diphtheria, they cannot *prevent* diphtheria. Passive immunity cannot do the job of active immunization.

Discipline, Self-discipline and Learning How to Behave

see also **School**/Discipline in your child's school

Most of us would reject the idea of trying to give our children the kind of discipline which dictionaries define as 'Teaching rules and forms of behaviour through continual repetition and drill . . .' It sounds more appropriate to a military parade ground than to a family living-room. We certainly want to produce disciplined children who will, eventually, be disciplined adults, but we do not want those disciplined people to be accurately defined as 'Those whose obedience is unquestioning . . .' If we do not want the militaristic or dictionary versions of discipline, what is it that we want?

When you are thinking about the kind of discipline you do want to use, and encourage, within your family, it sometimes helps to abandon the word itself (because it is value-laden) and free yourself to think about the whole issue in a different way. If, for example, you stop calling it 'discipline', but call it 'learning how to behave', the whole business stops being something which is imposed on children and becomes something which, with our help, they do for themselves. Changing the word and the way we think about it also stops 'discipline' from being a separate issue for serious discussion around the family conference-table, and allows it to take its proper place as part and parcel of the rest of a child's growing up within the family. There is no reason why it should be any more difficult or any grimmer for a child to learn how to behave than it is for him to learn any of the other millions of things he learns as he grows up.

How *should* children behave?

It is difficult (although not always impossible) to teach knowledge or skills which you do not have yourself, so deciding how you want your child to behave is an important first step. Of course your answers will critically depend on who you are and where you live. One society's virtues can be insignificant in another and vices in a third. The difficulty of defining 'human goodness' certainly contributes to the difficulties which the world's great powers have in understanding and communicating with each other. If you do not want a mini-cold-war in your own household, make sure that you are all on an established wavelength which your child will be able to receive without too much interference and static.

But, of course, we do not have to work out exactly how we think a person should behave in every imaginable situation. As long as you are clear about the basic general principles of behaviour which you want your child to learn, he will learn them as he learns a school subject. The do's and don'ts of daily life are simply examples of these principles. The behaviours which you prevent, correct or encourage are simply class-exercises, homework and practice along the way. Whatever your own principles of behaviour, your value-system, your child will learn it and the behaviours which are consistent with it, by the same sort of process. But your own strength of feeling on a range of issues will affect the priorities which you pass on to him. If, for example, you hold closely to a principle of non-violence, this will affect your 'messages' on a range of issues from playground fights and acceptable kinds of punishment, to the sports you encourage and even, perhaps, the television viewing you permit. If your value-system is directed towards helping your child to become a good Catholic you will be teaching him to accept the teaching of a higher authority than your own. If equality of the sexes underpins much of what you believe to be important, your belief will permeate what you teach to both sexes. You may find yourself encouraging particular kinds of behaviour, not because you see them as 'good' in themselves but because your daughter's insistence on playing school football makes a crack in a mould you want to see broken. The point is that you do not have to believe in particular ideals – certainly not the ideals implicit in these notes – to use this approach to discipline. The approach works whatever the content of the teaching.

How do children learn how to behave?

The most important part of any of a child's learning (whether of behaviour, of geography or of competitive swimming) comes from inside himself. All human children, at every age-stage, have an in-built drive to grow up, to become more mature and more competent. That generalized human drive is, if you like, his engine. It is running; the power is there; he is ready to go.

Where that power takes the child is a social matter. He *can* learn almost anything which anybody chooses to show him as soon as he is physically or mentally ready. The direction the individual child takes will be dictated by the expectations of his community and society. In ours, for example, it is confidently expected that five-to-seven-year-olds without specific handicaps will learn to read. Lo and behold they do. In another culture, reading would not be expected of a child so young but he will be expected to take responsible care of a baby or a herd of goats and he will do so. Sometimes it is interesting and surprising to abandon our own clear ideas about what children of different age-stages can and cannot do, and realize just how easily they can master a range of behaviours and skills if these are part of their particular way of life.

Parents, of course, are the instruments through which those social expectations are passed on to a child, especially to a very young one. If society sets out the direction, parents plan the route and, at the beginning at least, do the steering.

The journey involved in learning how to behave is a long one. At the beginning, with a baby or toddler, you will have to keep a tight hold on the wheel and take the whole responsibility for avoiding pot-holes and taking corners safely. While you steer, your child is watching. He learns a great deal about how to behave from seeing how you behave – towards him and towards other people – but his own behaviour is not yet his responsibility.

By the time he has acquired good control over his own body, fine coordination with his hands and eyes and the vital ability to understand and communicate in speech, he becomes ready for driving lessons. You still need dual-control but he can try himself out. It is at this stage that it becomes easy to be so involved in the everyday bumps of temper tantrums and whining, breakages and cheek, quarrels and squabbles, that the goal of the journey becomes forgotten. Each of those bumps should teach your child something about how to behave, but each is only important as a minute example. If your days seem to be filled with attempts to keep your child off the flower beds, you may sometimes need to remind yourself that the goal is not that he should learn only to run in particular places, or even that he should remember and obey your instructions. It is that he should learn to enjoy and protect places that give the whole family pleasure, and that he should reach a point where he does this himself because 'keep off the flower beds' has become part of his own control over himself. Sometimes you will actually watch this happen, stage by stage. After days and weeks of the ball-in-the-flower-bed and endless reminders and scoldings, there comes a day when, alone in the garden, he prepares to kick that ball but stops and shifts his position. 'Oh no, Mike' you may hear him mutter to himself 'mind the poor flowers . . .' Self-control is coming. He is beginning to know for himself how to behave. Soon he will be able to take charge of his own steering where the road is straight, with you to help him read the map at all the junctions.

The development of self-control is, of course, the point. However successful you may be in making a small child do as you tell him, he will not know how to behave until he can tell himself. Worthwhile discipline has to be self-discipline because the kind that keeps him safe and good when you are standing over him will not help when he is on his own. As he gets older, then, it is important not to be too hooked on obedience as a prime childish virtue. The only kind of obedience which is going to help him as an independent person is obedience to his own conscience; it is that conscience which is developing as he learns how to behave.

Some vital stages in learning how to behave

Babyhood   A baby cannot learn how to behave 'well' or 'properly' until he has learned to behave in any particular fashion, *on purpose*. At the beginning of life his behaviours are either involuntary expressions of physical need (like crying from hunger) or spontaneous reactions to your behaviour (like focusing on your eyes when you look at him and smiling and 'talking' because you do).

You may find that you can build up habit-patterns in him (so that you gradually 'teach' him to last six hours at night without a feed), but there will be no principle of behaviour underlying what he does. He will not stay asleep longer because he ought, or because he knows he should not wake you up. He will not wake and cry because he wants to drive you mad, either.

Babies and   Some parents, conscious of the importance of discipline, worry that even
'spoiling'   quite young babies may get spoiled. They see older children and adults who are selfishly concerned only with their own gratification, giving no thought to anyone else's needs or feelings, and they dread being responsible for a person like that. 'We'd better teach him that he isn't the only pebble on the beach,' they agree, or, 'Life is tough and she'd better

start finding it out right now . . .' Unfortunately, deliberate attempts not to spoil a baby have a nasty tendency to backfire.

In order to become either spoiled or the socialized opposite, a child has consciously to *want* things as well as unconsciously to need them. He has to be able to see himself as a being who is separate from a lot of other beings; to know that he has rights and that they have rights too, and to be able to plan deliberately to assert his rights to what he wants over their rights to withhold it. A baby can do none of these things. It is not that he is 'naturally good', it is that he is not intellectually capable of being 'bad'. 'If I make enough fuss can I make her stop doing that and come and play with me?' is not a question a baby is capable of asking himself. If he wants your attention it is because, for that moment, he needs it. If he needs it he will ask for it. What *you* may or may not want is irrelevant, not because he is a selfish, over-demanding spoiled brat but because he is not yet developmentally capable of putting himself in your shoes.

If you do find yourself deliberately withholding attention because your baby is 'too demanding', be warned. The slower you are to meet the needs he expresses and the more you ration your attention to him, the more he will demand, because the more anxious he will become in case those needs are not going to be met. If you leave him to cry alone in his cot because 'he has got to learn', he will not learn to play there quietly. Instead he will learn to cry hard the moment he awakens because experience of being left too long has made it impossible for him to be contented there. If his anxious demands harden your determination to resist him, the two of you will be into a vicious spiral which may create exactly what you were trying to avoid: an 'unreasonably demanding', fretful, whiny baby.

The best possible foundation for later discipline is early love: love which is as mutual, as secure, as predictable and as enjoyable (for all concerned) as you can possibly make it. Why? Because at the very beginning your baby does not know that the two of you are separate. If he experiences you as warm and loving, good and need-fulfilling, he also experiences himself as all these things. This is, if you like, the very beginning of the good self-image and self-respect which are ultimately going to be his prime adult reasons for behaving 'well' or 'badly'.

As he comes to realize his own separateness from you, that same loving care both makes him see himself as lovable and opens you to receiving love from him. By loving you he does two vital things:

He learns to behave in ways which show that he singles you out for love. All those enchanting behaviours which make it proudly clear that you are Mum are practice for the kinds of behaviour we want him to learn later. He smiles at you because he loves you; he stops crying when you come because he loves you; he strokes you because he loves you; he 'talks' to you because he loves you. He is practising friendship; practising love.

He acquires the loving feelings which will ensure that once he has the choice, he will prefer to please you. After all, everything which you are later going to show him and teach him about how to behave depends for its effectiveness on him caring about you, caring for your opinion, caring whether you approve of his behaviour or not. There are going to be many moments in his childhood when this is the only factor which weighs in the balance to persuade him to do what he ought, rather than what he wants, to do. Weight the scales your way early.

The toddler years

Toddlers do a great many things which are tiresome, messy, wasteful or destructive. They try to do things which are dangerous. They seldom do anything which is positively helpful and they most particularly seem to avoid doing what they are told. No wonder these are the years during which many parents decide that lack of discipline is the root of their troubles and that the kind in which hand meets bottom is probably best. No conventional kind of 'discipline' actually *works* with this age group, though. You need patience, humour and parent-upmanship to survive unscathed but, if you can muster them, your child will emerge, at two-and-a-half or three perhaps, *ready, willing and able to learn how* to behave.

Conflict within the toddler makes for conflict with you. He is no longer a baby who feels himself as part of you, using you as his controller, his helper, the mirror in which he views himself and his world. But he is not yet a child who feels himself a separate person, ready to take responsibility for himself and his own actions in relation to you. He is somewhere in-between and if his in-betweenish behaviour is confusing and irritating for you, it is downright painful for him. He *must* separate off from you, reject your total control, develop his own likes and dislikes and pursue his own ends even when they conflict with yours. This is a developmental imperative: the essential next step in his growing up. But he still loves you with the unrivalled passion of infancy and still depends totally on your emotional support without which he cannot manage himself, let alone anything else. So any conflict in the interests of independence feels desperately dangerous to him. Emotionally, it would be far easier for him to remain a baby. You can see the conflict within him every time he yells at you to 'Go 'way' and then dissolves into tears if you obey him. You can see how the see-saw of his emotional life goes up and down every time you try to push him into greater independence or hold him back from it. If you push him on, he is babyish and whiny. If you hold him back he rebels. Somehow you have to stand in the middle and keep that see-saw balanced for him.

The trick is in understanding that he cannot yet be 'good' or 'naughty' on purpose because he does not yet know 'right' from 'wrong' let alone know which is which in everyday life. But he wants to 'be good' because he desperately wants you to love and approve of him. If you can keep him 'good', most of the time, and above all avoid making him feel that you dislike or disapprove of him, when he reaches the stage where he can be good on purpose he will want to be so – usually.

Keeping a toddler 'good'

If you try to 'discipline' a toddler you will be faced with a lack of comprehension which looks like defiance and every battle you join will end with love lost between you. So don't try for absolute control and don't join *moral* battles. He will be 'good' if he happens to feel like doing what you want him to do and does not happen to want to do anything you would dislike. With a bit of parental cleverness you can arrange life so that most of the time he wants the same things that you want.

Suppose he has his dolls and soft toys all over the floor and you want them cleared away. If you tell him to do it he will probably refuse. If you explain that he should do it to help you, because you are so busy, because you do so many things for him, he will be completely uncomprehending and may make you feel that he doesn't care whether you are tired or busy or not. Cross, you can shout at him, punish him, threaten no ice-cream for dinner; you can reduce him to a jelly of misery *but none of that will get the toys off the floor*.

But try saying, right at the beginning, 'I bet you can't get all those toys put away before I've peeled these potatoes' and you turn the whole thing into a game. Now he *wants* to pick them up, so he will. He is not doing it because he is 'good'; because he knows he ought or 'for Mummy'; he is doing it because you have made him want to do what you wanted done.

Yes, this approach walks round trouble. But why is it wrong to steer his developmental car so that it does not keep crashing? The pay-off now is a pleasanter family life for all of you. The pay-off later is even more important.

That toddler is growing up. Soon he *will* understand your feelings and your rights; *will* remember your instructions, understand them and foresee the results of his own actions. Soon he *will* be able to behave well or badly on purpose. Which he chooses will depend largely on how he feels about you. If he reaches the next stage of growing up feeling that you are basically loving, approving and on his side, he will want, most of the time, to please you. So, with many lapses and mistakes, he will do as you wish. But if he reaches that stage feeling that you are basically hostile and disapproving; that what you want is incomprehensible and pushed upon him only by naked power, learning how to behave may be far more difficult for him. Some three- and four-year-olds feel that it is no use trying to please their parents because they never are pleased; no use minding when they are cross because they so often are; too dangerous to love them because they have so often seemed rejecting and hurtful. If the real business of learning how to behave is to take place smoothly and happily, your child must reach pre-school age wanting your approval; confident that it is easily earned; happy to cooperate with you to solve problems and absolutely sure that he loves you and that you love him.

A happy toddler is an easy toddler to 'manage' and a toddler who is kept easy now will be easy to teach happily later on.

The pre-school child If you like your child; are proud of him and really quite pleased with the job you have done as a parent so far, you will probably start showing him and teaching him how to behave as soon as he shows that he is ready to understand and without ever really having to think about it. If you do think about it, try to remember the purpose of the whole process: it is not that he should accept discipline/instructions *from you* but that he should gradually come to discipline *himself*. If you are tough enough with a three-year-old you may be able to see to it that he obeys you, tells you the truth, behaves as you say and fears your displeasure. But none of that will keep him safe, honest and good when you are not there to tell him what to do. You are not going to be with him forever. By the time he is spending hours outside your company and influence, you want to be sure that you can trust him to look after himself and his behaviour in all the ordinary situations he may meet.

All the following points are aimed in this one direction: at helping the child towards self-discipline or, if you prefer, towards the development of conscience. You will show him how to behave in countless different circumstances and situations but you will be teaching him that all those different items of behaviour add up to a few basic and vitally important principles. As he comes to understand those principles so he will become able to fit new events to them, and gradually you will be able to withdraw your constant control. He will apply the principles for himself because he has taken them in and made them part of himself.

Showing him how to behave

Do as you would be done by; your child will seldom give you (and other people) more consideration, cooperation and politeness than he gets from you. If you are always too busy to help with a construction kit and always ready to scream at him if he trips over your feet, he will not readily help you to lay the supper table nor refrain from yelling at you when the comb pulls his hair . . .

Make sure that behaving well is nicer for him than behaving badly. It is easy to fall into the trap of buying a treat to keep a ceaselessly whining child quiet while you finish your shopping, and not buying one for the child who is happily fetching and carrying for you.

Try to keep instructions positive; 'do' usually works much better than 'don't', partly because small children prefer activity to inactivity and partly because being forbidden to do things tends to arouse rebellion. 'You can't eat that in the sitting-room', makes him feel 'Oh, can't I? Just watch me . . .' 'Bring your snack and eat it here with me' will probably work better.

Try to be clear. Some instructions *sound* positive but are so vague as to be meaningless. 'Behave yourself', for example, really means 'don't do anything I wouldn't like'. Not only is that negative, it is also an impossible instruction for him to follow because he cannot possibly work out all the things he might do which you might dislike.

Whenever there is time, tell him your reasons. Apart from emergencies (*see below*) you insult your child's intelligence if you ask for unthinking obedience and you also make it impossible for him to begin to fathom those vital basic principles of behaviour. Suppose you say crossly, 'Let that telephone alone' and he says 'Why?'; there are all kinds of possible reasons for your instruction. Is it dangerous for him to touch? Is he likely to break it? Are you expecting a call which cannot come while he has the receiver off? Is it the tinging noise you are sick of? If you tell him why, he can add this snippet of behaviour into his knowledge of how to behave. If you just say 'because I say so' he learns nothing except that adults are incomprehensible.

Try to reserve a sharp 'no' for emergencies. There are many occasions when his safety will depend on instant obedience to that command, with the reasons given later. If you fill his days with cries of 'no', the word will not pull him up short as he approaches the road, the dog which looks unreliable or the motor mower which has been left running . . . If you reserve that word, in that tone, for occasions when you are protecting him from danger, he will come to see it as a protection-word rather than as something to rebel against.

Try to keep 'don't' for general rules. 'Don't . . .' works well if you want to forbid a particular action indefinitely: 'Don't fiddle with the car-locks' for example. It does not work for things like 'don't interrupt while I'm talking' because there are many times when you would actually want him to interrupt: when he saw smoke/heard the baby crying/needed to go to the lavatory, for example. 'Can you wait a minute until I've finished talking?' makes it clear that you would *rather* talk in peace but can be interrupted for legitimate reasons. Rules are extremely useful in keeping a small child safe, but they are too rigid and inflexible to be of much help in his learning how to behave.

Be consistent in your *principles* but don't worry about the details. As long as you know the kinds of behaviour you think desirable and are consistent about those, it does not matter if daily life finds you allowing an activity one day and forbidding it the next. Your child is not a circus animal, learning always to respond to the same signal with the same trick. He is a human being, being taught to respond as best he can to a vast range of signals. If you let him jump on the bed today because it is wet, he feels energetic and you feel playful, he will not necessarily expect to be allowed to do it again tomorrow. The principle is that certain activities are only allowed sometimes. Sweets ad lib at Christmas will not undo all your plans about serving them only at dinner, either. The principle is that Christmas is a special time. As to suddenly forbidding him to use the drum you gave him yourself last week, isn't your headache the reason for today's ban? Fair enough. The principle is that when people don't feel well other people have to try and adapt their behaviour so as not to make things worse.

Even inconsistency between his parents will not confuse a child at this stage if it is honestly discussed in front of him so that he cannot play one off against the other. It is only if one parent cheats, by allowing what the other forbids as soon as his or her back is turned, that the child is likely to wonder who is right.

When you are wrong or genuinely find your view changed, say so. Your small child is watching your behaviour and, to some extent, modelling himself on you. He knows he is not perfect so admitted imperfections in you make you a better model, not a less respectable one. If you accuse him wrongly and refuse to believe his truthful denials, you must apologize. By all the principles you are trying to teach, you were wrong. If you save your face you do so at the expense of his learning. If you forbid him to do something, perhaps without much thought, and he then persuades you that you could have allowed him to do it, say so. He has weighed up a question of how he should behave and come up with the right answer. If you do not acknowledge it, you make him feel that the rational persuasion which is an important part of your teaching is actually useless; that only power matters.

Trust him to mean well. The more a child feels that you are always standing over him, ready to instruct and correct him, the less he will bother to think for himself what he should and should not do. Within the limits of his age-stage, try to give him as much responsibility for his own behaviour as he can take and then let him feel that he is trusted. If you are willing to let him go out with his friends, don't send him off with cries of 'remember to do this . . . don't do that . . .' By letting him go at all you are letting him take charge of himself. Your exhortations will not make him take charge better; they will simply make him uneasy about whether he actually *can* manage.

When other children become important (see also **School**)

Your child will accept the principles of behaviour which you are trying to teach far more easily if they fit in with the behaviour he sees and shares with friends outside his home. His peers are the society for which you are trying to prepare him. If his dawning conscience must conflict with peer-group activities and loyalties, he will have a hard job abiding by it. This is why it is so much easier to cope with 'discipline' in a family which feels itself comfortably part of the neighbourhood, than in one which determinedly sets itself apart. If you want to rear your child within religious or cultural patterns which are foreign to the families of his school friends, you will certainly need to ensure that he has a second peer group of similar background amongst whom he can find support.

If, on the other hand, you simply find yourself vaguely disapproving of the value-systems and behaviour of many of your neighbours, tread carefully. Of course there is no reason for a child to be allowed to do everything that all his friends do, but if you ask him to be very different, especially if you present that difference as 'morally superior', you invite eventual conflict between the value-systems.

One way around this is to take trouble to ensure that you offer, within your value-system, genuine alternatives to replace what you force him to forgo. At its simplest, if you do not want him to play in the street with 'the rough kids from that Estate', who *is* he to play with? A peer group he must have and if you forbid the obviously available one you will have to muster another. Likewise, if you see television as both a poor influence and a waste of time for children, you may control his early viewing strictly or even refuse to have a set in the house. But when he finds that he is the only child in his class who does not watch a particular programme and cannot, therefore, share the fantasy games which spring from it, he will need to be aware of something very positive in his life which replaces that television. If he truly enjoys the activities of which you do approve – reading, playing music, growing things, keeping animals or whatever – he may accept that there is not time for everything, and that the way he spends his time is more fun than the way other children spend theirs. But if he does not enjoy those alternatives, he will feel that you deprive him of television only to make him 'different' or, more painfully still, 'better' than the other children when all he truly wants is to be one of the gang.

*The young
adolescent's
behaviour*

If your fourteen-year-old suddenly appears to have forgotten how to behave, don't make the mistake of trying to teach him, all over again, as you taught him ten years before. Being surrounded by do's and don'ts, complete with patient explanation, will certainly not improve his behaviour and may understandably increase his rebellious cries of 'you treat me like a child'.

Once a child reaches adolescence you have to accept that you have run out of time for teaching your principles of how to behave. The best that you can hope is that he will allow you to help him apply those principles to his new self and experiences. He does not leave his clothes on the floor because he has forgotten the principles of order you worked to teach him. He remembers them all right; he is just wondering whether they are his as well as yours: does he actually *mind* a muddle? He does not leave them there for you to pick up, either. He leaves them there to be left there; you pick them up because you cannot stand the sight. If you can accept that he has the right to try out his own ways of doing things and can confine yourself only to insisting on your own rights, compromise is usually possible. Perhaps he can keep his room in a muddle with the door firmly closed provided he does not spread the chaos to parts of the house you have to use, too (*see also* **Adolescence**/Adolescents and the adult world).

*The older
adolescent's
behaviour*

The question now is not whether your child knows how to behave but whether he agrees with your views of how people should behave. Before he achieves independent adulthood he has to take out all those values and look at them again in the light of his new self and his new experiences. Some he will reject: he has an adult's right, now, to disagree with you, even on matters of fundamental principle. Many he will have to adapt to fit with the ideas and circumstances of his generation. Others he will probably settle with for life (*see* **Adolescence**/Friends versus family).

Parents who cannot acknowledge an adolescent's right to question their values and to experiment with behaviour based on different value-systems, tend to condemn themselves not only to endless futile rows, but also to exclusion from the adolescent's thinking. If he believes that you are immovably certain of your own rectitude he will not bother to argue with you about anything more important than the ring around the bath . . . Parents who can stand back a little and be interested in the journey of this near-adult who is now driving his own car, may still be able to offer considerable guidance over the more complicated bits of the route.

The trick seems to lie in two kinds of honesty:

Honesty about your real concerns. Many of the issues which cause trouble between adolescents and their parents are important and basic ones poorly disguised as matters of 'discipline'. What time, for example, should your daughter come home from Saturday night dates? Whatever time you set, be it 10 p.m. or 3 a.m., eventually there will be trouble. She will be late and you will be angry because she failed to do as she was told or as she promised. If you then 'punish' her, perhaps by saying that she must stay in next weekend or accept an earlier curfew on the next occasion, the trouble will eventually intensify because you are not treating her as a near-adult but as a child-in-your-power. Since she is *not* genuinely in your power any more, you cannot ultimately win if she chooses to fight you. Deceit and defiance are both powerful weapons in the hands of a seventeen-year-old.

But, of course, that kind of row is not really about her willingness or otherwise to do as you say. It is about the anxiety you feel when her knowledge of how to behave in sexually charged situations is actually being put to the test. The late hour does not worry you because it deprives her of sleep but because *you* cannot sleep for wondering if she is in the back of a parked car or taking part in an orgy or being raped in the deserted streets . . . If these are the real issues they are clearly not going to be resolved by a curfew. If she intends, or is going to slip into, a full sexual relationship at this stage in her life, she will do so as readily at 8 p.m. as in the small hours. If she cannot make sensible arrangements for her own safety on the streets coming home from a party she will not do so coming home after school either.

Open discussion about these real issues may, or may not, comfort you, depending on whether or not her attitudes turn out to be those you would prefer, but it will at least prevent endless, pointless arguments and allow you to be certain that issues which have previously only been discussed in theory have been brought to her practical attention. Surely it is better to know if she is, in fact, going to bed with her boyfriend so that instead of refusing to speak to her because she was late again you can make sure that she knows where to get advice on contraception? Surely it is better to know if her friends live in a risky area and parties go on late so that instead of being kept in the dark you can assure her that you would rather meet her, or at least provide the money for a taxi, than have her come home alone? Even if your expressions of this kind of down-to-earth concern make her bristle that you are 'interfering', she will in fact see them as caring and she may remember them, at critical moments, when cries of 'don't be late' have become part of meaningless adult background noise.

Honesty about your convenience. Much of the trivial-but-constant friction between older adolescents and their parents arises out of the difficulties which inevitably occur when extra adults (or near-adults) share a family house. Of course it is maddening to find the bathroom messy every morning; to cook meals for people who do not come in to eat them; to take careful telephone messages for them but never to receive one's own, or to have to rescue wet raincoats and muddy boots off the hall floor. A lodger who caused this kind of inconvenience would probably find himself without a room, but one's own, rather large, child is different. If it is recognized, from early in his drive for independence, that a child's right to live his own life is balanced by his parents' right to do the same, many of these irritations can be dealt with by agreeing some ground-rules for cooperative living. Unfortunately, many parents (perhaps especially mothers) cast themselves in a self-sacrificing role and then, after months of stored resentment, blow. Of *course* your eighteen-year-old should not expect a hot meal to await him every evening when more often than not he stays out until midnight. But equally he is bound to expect it if his mother has always maintained that 'I'm cooking anyway, dear, so it makes no difference . . .' Of *course* he has no automatic right to expect his mother to launder the shirts she picks up off the floor. But if she has always picked them up, washed and ironed them and returned them to his cupboard without comment, he is likely to take the service for granted as a kind of magic and be bitterly hurt when an innocent 'Is my blue shirt ready, Mum?' suddenly brings down wrath upon his head. We need to do adolescents the honour of treating them as we would treat adult friends. We need to tell them when we are *beginning* to be irritated rather than when we reach screaming point; we need to acknowledge equal rights and work out mutual compromises.

Of course this reasonable kind of approach will not always work. Your older adolescent may refuse to accept your ground-rules; you may find life lived by any other rules intolerable. But at least if your disagreement is brought into the open, a compromise may be possible. You cannot live comfortably any more as a conventional family group, but could you still offer the cheap accommodation, occasional hot meals and background support he needs in his life if some degree of internal separation was arranged? Could he have a bed-sitting room? Become, so to speak, a young lodger? Would everything ease if he had a college room and only came home at vacation times? Could he have lodgings during the week and come home at weekends? Families often find that once the adolescent's independence is properly acknowledged and catered for, everything changes. Instead of being hurt and furious because he has been out four nights in a row, you may find yourself pleased and touched because he spent the fifth evening with the family.

If no compromise is possible it is sometimes better if the adolescent leaves home altogether. If he can no longer live within the family his energies will be better spent learning how to live outside it than in fighting it. At least if you agree to part you have a chance of remaining friends. One of the great tragedies of youth unemployment is that it condemns many youngsters who would be better away from home to remain in the only accommodation which they can afford, their parents' houses.

Some common issues in discipline

Common themes recur during many years of childhood. Often it is vitally important to tailor your reactions to 'wrongdoing' to the exact level of your child's understanding. The following notes may help:

Obedience   Instant and unquestioning obedience might keep life peaceful for some parents for a few years but it cannot produce children who think for themselves and therefore can be trusted to look after themselves from an early age. Victorian parents got that obedience from their children but they also provided a degree of protection for their young which would be unheard-of today. If you insist that your child does exactly as she is told at home, will she know what to do when nobody tells her, outside? If she must always obey grown-ups, will she know that she must *disobey* the neighbour who orders her into his house (*see* **Safety**/From 'strangers').

If you can rid yourself of the concepts of 'obedience' and 'disobedience' and think, instead, of the child cooperating, you may find that you can defuse the whole issue.

She may not do as you ask because she wants to do something different, like finish her game or stay until the end of the party. The problem is not her 'disobedience' but a genuine conflict of interests. Dealing with it as such prevents it from being an issue of naughtiness and makes it one in which compromise may be possible. The young child may, when you think about it calmly, be able to have ten more minutes' play before the family meal begins to spoil. The older girl may be able to understand why her lateness worried you, and agree to telephone next time.

She may not do as you ask because she has not understood what you meant. You told her not to go out but she did not realize you meant to ban the garden, she thought you meant out in the street.

She may not do as you ask because she forgot. Forgetting to do the shopping on the way home from school may be tiresome, careless, inconsiderate, but it is not deliberate disobedience.

She may not do as you ask because what you ask seems impossibly difficult and/or unreasonable. If you told her not to bring that friend home with her again and you catch the two of them together the very next day, you may have told her to behave in a way which she is actually unable to fit into *her* principles of how to behave. The problem is a friendship of which you disapprove, not a piece of disobedience.

She may sometimes fail to do what you ask because she is out to annoy you. She feels uncooperative and bolshy. You tell her not to touch your new book and she goes straight to it. You tell her to clear up her room and she sits and looks at the muddle until supper-time . . . These, and only these, are examples of true 'disobedience'. They are deliberate attempts to provoke and almost always best handled by refusing to rise to the bait. 'Fancy you going off and doing (not doing) the one thing I asked you not to do (to do) . . . you must be in a silly mood.' Where is the argument she was looking forward to? While she is wondering, you can wonder why she is spoiling for a fight.

Lying   Do you worry about lying as a moral issue or as a practical one? It is important to decide, because if you wish to teach truth as a basic moral virtue so that lying is one of the ways in which it is always wrong to behave, you will probably have to tailor your own behaviour (with the child and with other people) to fit. Most of us tell lies/untruths/'white lies' pretty frequently. Children hear us do it: hear us refuse an unwanted invitation on phoney grounds, agree that the heat they know we enjoy is intolerable, and thank relatives warmly for gifts they have seen us reject . . . If it is acceptable or even desirable (because we must not hurt people's feelings) for us to behave like this, why is it wrong for them? And if they are never to lie must they therefore always tell the truth, or must they learn the even more difficult lesson of finding something to say which is neither untrue nor hurtful?

Much childish lying is the denial of wrongdoing. If you want your child to confess voluntarily whenever he has done something wrong, by mistake or on purpose, you will have to show him that this is not only a virtuous but a sensible way to behave. If every confession is followed by overwhelming anger he would have to be pretty stupid to carry on with it.

If you want the child to admit to wrongdoing when he is rightly accused of it, you will have to offer in return a genuine readiness to believe him when he denies it. If you *know* he was responsible, it is kinder to tell rather than ask; if you ask whether he did it and he says 'no', you are trapped into either withdrawing that trust or pretending to believe him when you do not.

A lot more lying comes into the category of careless or exaggerated or over-dramatic talk. Small children tell 'tall stories' partly because their heads are full of Santa Claus and talking animals as well as parents who give presents and real rabbits who need feeding each day. There is room for both but the line between fantasy and reality takes a long time to solidify. Later on, your child may indeed make up elaborate stories which are in fact lies. But again, don't be too quick to moral outrage. If you want to entertain the family with the story of your day, don't you ever cheer up the tale a bit? Ask yourself whether anything is being said which *matters*. Is this amusing gossip actually hurtful? Are you being given a worrying picture of that teacher or a wrong impression of your child's prowess? If you think you may be, try accepting the story as good entertainment but then asking 'by the way what *exactly* did he say because I'm sure he can't really have been as nasty as that . . .' The child who was simply being entertaining will probably welcome some more conversation based on reality.

There are very practical reasons why people who care about each other should not lie. The story of the boy who cried wolf is still the best way I know of making it clear to little children that if they tell many falsehoods they may not be believed when it really matters. Told as part of your desire to care for and protect the child, it will probably leave a lasting impression. Older children who lie a great deal are usually either very frightened of parental disapproval or fighting off too many questions which they feel as intrusive. There are principles of how to behave at stake but they are to do with your whole relationship with each other rather than specifically to do with honesty or falsehood.

Many adolescents lie to their parents simply to keep the wheels of life oiled. If your daughter knows that you do not approve of a particular boy-friend, but means to meet him at tonight's party, she may well misinform you simply to spare both of you from a row. If your son knows that it would horrify you to know that he drank alcohol with his friends, he may well tell you that he does not. It is for you to weigh up the morals against a legitimate (and sometimes kindly) way for a budding adult to protect his or her own privacy. The principle at stake would seem to be one of communication rather than truth.

Stealing   Pre-school children are often very vague about property rights. Within the family there are lots of things that belong to everybody, some that belong to particular people but can be freely borrowed and some which are private possessions reserved for the owner's use. If you want a small child to get this straight and stick to it, you will have to spell it out *and* make sure that everybody (including her baby sister) respects her 'private' things as she is expected to respect yours.

Outside the family there are genuine complications. It is all right to bring your painting home from playgroup but not a piece of plasticine. It is all right to keep the little ball you find in the bushes in the park but not to keep the coin you find nearby. It is fine to take leaflets from the supermarket checkout but not the sweets arranged at your level close by . . .

It is important that your small child should not appear to steal because other people make such a song and dance about it. It may be a good case for a few rules which will tide her over while her understanding grows: 'Don't bring anything away from anywhere without asking a grown-up if you may' and, perhaps 'always ask a grown-up if it is all right to keep anything you find or anything another child gives you.' Try not to be especially moralistic about money because at this stage money is just treasure. She knows it is precious because she hears you talk about it and sees you swap it for nice things. But it is just like one of those tokens you put in slot machines; she has no concept of *real* money. If she takes money from your handbag, pause to ask yourself what you would have said if she had taken a lipstick. Then say the same thing about the money.

The small child who is forever pinching things – from you, from other children, from shops – may be in emotional trouble. She may be trying to take something which she does not feel she is being *given*. It will usually be love, approval or friendship of which she feels short. Sometimes, if you can use this kind of behaviour as a cue to you to *offer* what she needs, the stealing will stop overnight.

Children who steal once they clearly understand not only that they should not, but also the social importance of honesty *may* be:

Stealing as a 'dare'; a deliberately dangerous game with authority. There are sometimes outbreaks of pinching from shops, for example, which, while they need stamping out at once, are better dealt with as stupid, dangerous naughtiness than with moral outrage. Making the child return the goods to the shop may often bring it home to him that the owner could have called the police.

Stealing something truly needed. Usually this will be a one-off: an object which you refused to buy (often because you thought it a silly waste of money), not realizing that the current school craze made it, in his terms, a truly necessary item. Obviously you cannot let him keep it, but you may feel it appropriate to discuss the matter with him and perhaps re-arrange his pocket money so that he will in future have an honest way of acquiring such items (*see* **Pocket Money**).

Stealing to buy friendship. Pinching small amounts of money to buy sweets for playground distribution is often the sign of trouble at school which jolts parents into action. Once again, while you have to deal with the stealing, the underlying problem is the more important.

Stealing (as the small child does) because he feels, in some deep-seated way, deprived of something nice. Unless you can easily see the problem *and* offer the love that fills the gap (no easy matter when you are shocked to find your child is stealing from you) you might be well-advised to seek help from your local child guidance clinic. Staff will both help you to see the matter calmly and help you all to put the relationship on a more comfortable footing (*see* **Depression**/In children before puberty).

It is worth remembering that, for your child's own protection, you cannot take stealing lightly however convinced you may be that his motives are sad rather than wicked. To be branded a thief at school or to find himself in the Juvenile Court will do him no good at all.

Cheating If your child is never to cheat you will have to teach her a far-reaching honesty which will guide her in innumerable different circumstances because there are so many kinds and degrees of cheating. You may, for example, teach a small child that it is cheating ('unfair') to use her greater size to push ahead in the queue for the slide. You will certainly teach an older one that it is cheating to copy the answers to the French test from another child's paper. Hopefully, you will also make it clear, by your own example, that it is cheating, rather than clever, to ride the bus without paying the fare or to run the car without renewing the licence. But the basic idea behind your teaching about cheating has to reflect the fact that society cannot work if people are not basically honest with each other. Unfortunately, unless you are unusually scrupulous yourselves, she may learn easily that it is cheating to leave the restaurant without giving the busy waitress her tip, but have far more difficulty believing that it matters if she cheats the faceless insurance company or the tax man.

Cheating is most often an issue among schoolchildren who are in competition with each other. While of course you must make it clear to a child that copying that test paper is a kind of stealing of the other child's work and credit, you may also like to ask yourself why she needs to cheat. Is the school very competitive? Is the class working too fast for her? Is she afraid of the teachers (or you)? Would she be happier in a school where children competed only against their own previous best and where helping each other with set work was normal rather than immoral? (*See* **School**/Discipline in your child's school: Competition and shaming).

Violence All mammals will use their natural weapons – teeth, claws, feet, strength – when they are angry and/or frightened. Human children are no exception. You are doing well if your child uses words rather than blows, *almost* always, by the time he goes to school.

Babies and toddlers cannot put themselves in other people's shoes and therefore genuinely do not realize that the child they bite suffers exactly as they suffer when they are bitten. It is for this reason that 'showing a child what it is like' by biting or hitting him back, is useless. He will be hurt and horrified but he will not learn the intended lesson.

With this age group words alone are not, of course, enough. Every time you tell him not to bite/pull hair/hit/kick or otherwise hurt someone, you also have to prevent him physically from doing so. If the verbal message is always linked with direct intervention, he will eventually understand.

● A small child who goes through a stage of attacking others, apparently without provocation, can be very hard to cope with, especially as he and his mother tend to be increasingly unwelcome in the playground or parent-and-toddler group. You may find that you can get positive support from the other parents, and prevent your child becoming a social outcast, if you set yourself *never to allow his attacks to succeed*. It may mean that for months you have to follow him around whenever he is playing near others. It will certainly mean that you have to foresee violence even before he registers his own aggressive feelings. But it can be done and, if you can make your watchful care feel to him like loving interest, and simultaneously take off him some of the home-pressures which he may be feeling as overpowering, the stage will not last very long.

Schoolchildren. A sad but necessary part of learning how to behave is learning what to do when other people are horrible. To some extent your child will learn for himself on the basis of what he finds works. But you need a consistent view, too. Is he to hit back if a child hits him? Is he only to hit if that is the only way in which he can extricate himself? Is he to hit if other children tease or torment him other than physically? Is he to learn to fight so that others will respect him? Is he to take problems with violence to a teacher or other adult or is that 'telling tales'? Your ideas may be based on principles or partly on practical considerations such as your child's size or position in the neighbourhood, but he does need to know what you think is right whether or not he can always do it. All too often a child tries to steer clear of a fight only to find his parents joining with others in calling him a sissy. Or a girl may come home scraped and proud of herself for 'seeing those kids off' only to find her parents saying that she is too old to be such a tomboy . . .

If you do want your child, male or female, to follow as non-violent a path as possible, your example is important. If nobody in the family ever uses their physical strength to win a point or inflicts pain to clinch an argument, the child will accept a non-violent point of view and learn other techniques. But if physical punishment is taken for granted in the household and rows between adults commonly end with broken china, he will not take you seriously.

Television and violence

Many people blame television for the easy familiarity which today's children have with physical violence. Certainly most children of older generations would never have *seen* anyone shot, hit over the head with a brick, rammed by a car, raped or tortured. It is not yet clear how directly violent television programmes affect children's real-life behaviour but it seems likely that newscasting and documentary reporting has more effect than fiction. Children, especially rather young ones, make little connection between reality and fantasy and tend to see those Western 'deaths' in terms of the 'bang-bang you're dead' of their own games. But to see policemen dragging ordinary people through the streets by their heels, or young people hurling paving stones at each other in familiar streets, is a different matter. Children who are being reared *amidst* violence – those of Northern Ireland, for example – certainly do take violence for granted as the obvious way to express feelings or to make points. The young ones play the same violent games as other children but they play them as direct practice for a violent future and move easily from toy guns to real ones.

Whether you decide to censor your child's viewing or not, it is probably important that you view programmes you expect to be violent with him so that you can, as you watch, make the important points. 'It may look funny/serve him right but imagine what it would really be like . . .' and 'James Bond may be able to go on climbing a mountain with four bullets in him, but anyone else would be screaming, vomiting, bleeding and dying . . .' In the same, perhaps rather brutal, way, a child who does see documentary violence on television may need to be reminded that what he sees is tragedy. The simple fact that that bruised policeman has a wife who will be worried about him, or that that panic-stricken child has just seen her mother beaten, will often prevent a child from just accepting what he sees as part of the way people behave (*see also* **Television**).

Make-believe violence Some families ban toy guns and war-toys and, with hi-jacking using replicas on the increase, it may be that realistic toy weapons should be banned altogether by law. But even if you do refuse to allow your child this kind of toy you will not prevent make-believe violence. If he has no gun he will use a stick. If he may not have a toy tank he will use a car . . . Some war-toys and war-games are singularly tasteless: many people, for example, must be offended by a game which gives maximum points to the player who can produce a nuclear explosion. Ban them on the grounds that you dislike them, by all means, but don't expect your child to share your views at least until he is old enough to understand the real implications of nuclear war and is therefore too old for the game.

Probably we teach children more about the horrors of war and the virtues of non-violence by allowing the toys as toys, but using the games that he plays with them as triggers for conversation about the realities. Bans tend to produce a backlash of extra interest.

'Allowable' violence Before your child reaches his teens you will also need to decide your policy on the kinds of violence which our society does allow. Would you, for example, support your son in competitive boxing; a sport whose ultimate aim is unconsciousness in the opposing competitor? Would you allow an air-gun for vermin-shooting and if so a different weapon for shooting game? Would you see a military career as a welcome possibility? We certainly produce confusion if we express horror at the idea of shooting a deer but encourage shooting rats. Confusion is worse if nothing must be killed on purpose except people in a war . . .

Some common disciplinary techniques

Arguing and bargaining Sooner or later your child will catch onto the idea that if you want him to do something he does not want to do he has bargaining power. Instead of going meekly to change his shirt when told he says, 'If I change my shirt 'cause you want me to, will you get my paints for me?' Although this kind of thing strikes some parents as cheeky (the child should do as he is told without argument), bargaining is a very useful form of human interchange and one in which your child needs some practice before he is old enough to join a trades union.

Of course it will be boring and time-consuming if your child tries to exact a return for every single thing you ask him to do, but learning the value of his bargaining power is part of his education. You might allow him some when your request is exceptionally boring for him and you might sometimes offer this kind of bargain too: 'You really can't go out in those jeans, they're too filthy. Will you go and put on some clean ones if I get your bike out to save time?'

The same kind of approach can work well when much older children are arguing for rights you are reluctant to concede. If your adolescent argues for her right to live in a muddle behind closed doors all week, a mutual clean-up at the weekends might be a fair bargain; if your son wants you to give drinks and sandwiches to the whole team on Saturday night, he might give you Sunday breakfast in bed.

Bribes and prizes If you are shocked at the idea of bargains you will probably be even more shocked by the idea of bribes. They sound less immoral if you call them prizes.

Small children are usually clear-sighted about other people's goodwill and about justice. If you have to make a child do something he very much dislikes, a prize can both make it seem worth his while to cooperate and make him realize that you are trying to soften the blow. He is in the pool on a scorching afternoon and you realize a forgotten appointment. 'I am sorry but we will have to go home now after all. Would it help if we stopped on the way and chose some ice-cream for supper?' It is a bribe but it is also a perfectly reasonable bargain.

An actual prize sometimes makes all the difference to the child faced with real unpleasantness, such as stitches in his scalp or having a tooth out. It is not the *object* which matters: it is having something nice dangling just the other side of the nasty few minutes. Don't make the prize conditional on good behaviour, though. The prize is for getting through the ordeal. He may need to make a fuss and, if he does, a conditional prize will only make the whole thing worse for him (*see* **Hospital**/Procedures).

Personally I do not believe that prizes from parents for the traditional things (like passing examinations or getting into teams) make much sense. The child wants to succeed anyway. If he does succeed he does not need your prize to give him pleasure. It is if he fails that he might need a morale-boost. Sometimes you may actually be able to arrange this sort of back-to-front prize to good effect: 'If you don't make the team we will at least be able to go to the sea that Saturday'.

Punishment The concept of 'punishment' as something unpleasant done to a child because of something he has done wrong, really belongs with 'discipline' rather than with 'learning how to behave'. A specific punishment may show your child what you will not put up with today, or now this minute, but it tells him nothing about the behaviour you do want, now and always.

If you and your child are cooperating in this learning how to behave process, you will seldom need to think up a deliberate punishment because he will be working for your approval and your disapproval will make it clear to him when he has gone wrong. If you are not cooperating and he does not care whether you approve or not, you certainly are not going to get the cooperation back by punishing him.

Of *course* you are sometimes going to be cross. Of course you are sometimes going to lose your temper, shout, snatch away the ornament he is going to break, or the kitten he is mawling, or temporarily lock away the bike with which he was playing a dangerous game. But these are reactions rather than calculated punishments. As such they are often the most 'fitting' kind. After all, if the reason for your anger is that he is endangering himself on that bike, what more obvious result, given that you care for him, than that it should vanish until he can be more sensible with it?

Calculated punishments are different. Looked at coldly, there is little to be said for any of the usual ones:

Smacking and other kinds of physical punishment. If you clip your child on the backside in a moment of anger you will be very unlucky if it does him any harm and it may do your state of mind some good. But physical punishments which are pre-meditated have nothing to be said for them. They do not work and because they do not produce the desired effect they have a nasty tendency to escalate.

You smack your child for touching the television after six warnings. He is hurt and angry but, because the touching was all impulse, tomorrow he forgets and does it again. Logically you must smack him again, but this time, harder. He will be even more upset but he still will not remember. The next day's naughtiness seems to you like deliberate defiance. This time, you decide, you must show him once and for all . . .

Research has shown us several important things about smacking:

Children can never remember what they were smacked *for*. Smacking cannot therefore change behaviour.

Children who are smacked are never sorry for what they did, even at the time. They are so overwhelmed by pain and indignity that the reaction is pure anger, not remorse.

Children who are smacked only fail to retaliate because they are conscious of the adult's overwhelming size and power. Smacking, therefore, cuts right across any attempt at cooperation and certainly across anything you are trying to teach about using strength gently or relying on words rather than blows.

Children who are often smacked do tend to take it out on younger or smaller ones; smacking may therefore contribute to the making of a bully.

An unexpectedly large minority of smacked children eventually suffer actual injury. Examples are 'light blows' that happen to catch him off balance so that he hits his head on something; blows that accidentally land on his spine rather than his bottom and blows which hit an ear and burst its drum.

● Violently shaking a small child is always dangerous. It can cause whiplash injury to the spine and/or concussion due to the brain being knocked against the inside of the skull.

Corporal punishment at school. Home-smacking at least goes on in an overall context of love and concern. The institutionalized use of violence and pain, to control or 'teach' a child, is the cold assertion of superior power and something which most countries have long abandoned. Parents in countries where schools still maintain this right may like to ask themselves why children can be beaten when rapists and murderers may not. Sadly the answer is that teachers stand 'in loco parentis' and therefore as long as parents maintain the right to beat their own children, some teachers will insist that they have the right to beat those same children when they are in the school's charge.

Parents who would prefer to withhold this right from their children's teachers may like to know that the European Court of Human Rights supports their viewpoint and that there are societies – including many experienced teachers – working actively and successfully to bring corporal punishment in schools to an end (*see also* **School**/Discipline in your child's school).

Confining a child to his room. This is not a very sensible kind of punishment either: if he hates being there alone, the punishment may put him off his room (or bed) as a friendly place for going to sleep. Can you afford that? He may come out. Are you prepared to lock the door? If he does not mind being there, but simply plays or reads, what will you do to punish him next time? Lock him in the lavatory? Or a cupboard? There is a real danger that imprisonment will escalate, just as smacking tends to do.

If there are occasions when you feel that it is important to be apart from your child (perhaps because he is throwing a semi-deliberate tantrum or because your own temper is going) it is better if *you* go away. With a small child you obviously cannot go far, in case he gets into danger, but with an older one who is driving you out of your mind you could always take your book into the bathroom and lock the door.

Shaming him. Punishments designed to make a child feel silly will never make him behave more sensibly. If you take away his shoes because he ran away from home, or make him wear a bib because he spilt his food down his clothes, you will make him *feel* stupid and babyish: incapable of the kind of behaviour your punishment is meant to encourage.

In the course of developing the conscience which will keep on telling him how to behave once you have stopped, he will often be *ashamed of himself* but you cannot induce that inward feeling by imposing shameful punishment on him.

Discovering what happens when he gets his behaviour wrong. Life is full of 'punishments' administered not by you but by the logical consequences of your child's own actions. The more certain you are that the behaviour you are asking of him is right (practically, morally or both) the more certain you can be that you will not have to fall back on all those invented sanctions like 'no television'. If, for example, you are right in thinking that his new car will break if he uses it to play 'crashes', there is absolutely no point in punishing him for refusing to stop the game. The car will break; he will be sad; you will be proved right. So direct is the lesson that you can well afford to be quick with comfort and glue. If you are right in thinking that his gang-leadership is actually bullying, you will have no need to punish him for that either: the gang will melt away and he will not have one to play with, let alone to lead. Once again you can afford to be ready with explanations and help. If you are right in thinking that reading late in bed will make him too tired for school, you will not need to punish his disobedience by removing his bedside lamp: he will be tired the next day and that will be punishment enough. But are you right? Will he be tired? He may just fall asleep over his book when he needs to . . . maybe the reading in bed was not wrong after all, or maybe it was wrong because it wasted power by keeping the light on all night, rather than because it made him tired.

If you go on thinking of learning how to behave as a journey, involving a complicated route and difficult steering round obstructions, you will usually be able to cast yourself in a positive and helpful role rather than in a punitive one. If you can do that, you are likely to keep your child's cooperation; his desire to please, and therefore your ultimate sanction of displeasure.

Your anger is the most effective punishment of all. Parents who say that this approach to discipline is unrealistic usually assume that all this talk of 'cooperation' implies constant sweetness and light and reasonableness all round. Of course it does not. Every parent gets cross (for good and poor reasons). The whole point is that the more cooperative the two of you are being in this business of learning how to behave, the more your child will mind your crossness. Use it as gently as you can. Above all, try, when you are irritated or angry, to make it clear to the child that you are fed up with his *behaviour* rather than with him-as-a-person. If you tell a small child 'For heaven's sake, go *away*' you may hurt his feelings and you certainly do not tell him what he has done to turn you against him. If you rephrase the message 'For heaven's sake take that drum into the garden' you make it clear that it is the noise which offends.

Dislocations *see* **Accidents**.
Disobedience *see* **Discipline, Self-discipline and Learning How to Behave**. *See also*
   Adolescence/Adolescents and the adult world; Friends versus family.

Divorce, Separation and One-parent Families

The 'normal family' of the television ads still consists of two parents who are married to each other and their mutual and legitimate children. But only a very small majority of today's children will be born to, reared within and launched into adulthood from, such a family. A very large minority indeed will spend at least a part of childhood living in a different kind of family. For far too long those families have been ignored except to be condemned. 'Broken homes' have been regarded as the cause of innumerable social ills yet nobody has looked either at the severity of the breakage nor at the kinds of glue which might repair it. Unmarried or separated parents have been encouraged to feel that because they were outside the social norm, they were also beyond the social pale. Often already shattered by emotional trauma within their personal lives, they have been left to cope with guilt and without either information or practical help. Very gradually, though, information is being accumulated from research studies. Armed with at least a few value-free facts you may be able to seek, or to offer, something more useful than a sermon or a platitude.

Interpreting the divorce statistics

Divorce statistics make good shock headlines for the popular press. Currently, divorce ends about one in three marriages in the UK, Australia and the USA and almost half in South Africa.

But divorce statistics tell us very little about children. By no means every divorce affects a child: about twenty-five per cent of UK divorces, for example, are between childless couples, while some take place after children have grown up and left home. On the other hand, a great many children are affected by separations which are never formalized in the divorce court and therefore do not appear in those statistics. Even where it is known that children of dependent age are involved in a divorce, the statistics do not tell us how many children, nor how old they are now, or were when separation/proceedings began.

Figures giving the proportions of families in which one parent is absent are a little more informative, as long as it is remembered that these include families which have been single-parent from the beginning, as well as those in which one parent has died. Again, we do not have a complete breakdown by the numbers and ages of these children, but the current figures are estimated as follows:

Australia: one in six	S. Africa: one in three
Canada: one in four	UK: one in four
New Zealand: one in seven	USA: one in three

Families with an absent parent

The father is the absent parent in more than ninety per cent of single-parent families. Reasons range from the obvious ones such as the fact that there is no male equivalent to the unmarried mother, to less obvious ones such as the greater likelihood of early death amongst males.

Where there is separation/divorce, welfare workers and law-courts still tend to recommend/direct that mothers should have custody, especially when young children are involved. Even when custody is not disputed, or is allocated equally to both parents, couples themselves usually take it for granted that the mother should assume daily care and control. Of course there *are* fathers coping alone, but they are still a rarity. Those who have young children usually have some female help, employed or otherwise (*see below*). Most have charge of school-age children, usually teenagers and often sons rather than daughters.

Family changes over time

Statistics may tell us how many families were without a parent at the time they were collected, but they tell us nothing about what will happen to those families in the future. If divorce rates are rising, so are remarriage rates. If separations are frequent, so are new partnerships. A child whose father leaves the family may experience any combination of a complexity of relationships with adults in the remaining years of his childhood.

His parents may join up again, temporarily or permanently. Many couples go through several 'reconciliations' before the marriage is ended or reinstated.

He may live with only his mother, with his mother and a lover or series of lovers, with his mother and a permanent partner or with his mother and a step-father. Any of those males may, or may not, function as father-figures for him, and any of them may, or may not, also bring children of their own partially or fully into the family. At the same time, the absent father may move through a variety of relationships which may or may not bring the child an extra mother-figure and/or children who are formally or informally his step-brothers and sisters. Eventually there may be half-siblings, too.

For some children 'family' experience will not even remain linked with male–female partnership. The child may be brought up within a homo-sexual partnership, within a communal household, or by a widowed grandmother who frees his mother to work.

Stereotypes such as 'broken home' are meaningless unless we know a child's exact situation, now, and furthermore know something about how he perceives that situation.

Separation and divorce from a child's point of view

Recent British and American research, which has not only studied fami-lies in crisis but followed them up over a period of years, agrees on the following 'facts'. They may or may not be true for your children, or the children with whom you are concerned, but they are the nearest thing we have to hard information.

Separation/divorce makes children miserable. Children too young to understand what is going on commonly refuse to believe in the fact or permanency of the separation. Older children bitterly resent it. It appears that, however poor the relationship between their parents has been, children would prefer it to continue. Many dream of, and work for, reconciliation. The only exceptions researchers have found are among the few children who are physically terrified of the departing parent. They and only they may be relieved to see him go.

These findings do not, of course, mean that a marriage which is not working should be held together 'for the children's sake', but they do mean that separating parents cannot rely on children to agree that the family would be better split up than constantly quarrelling.

Children tend to take guilt upon themselves. Younger children, unable to fathom much of the reality of an adult sexual/ habitual/cooperating relationship, tend to assume that they were the cause of the break-up. It is difficult for a child who is, after all, the centre of his own life and thinking, to believe that he is not similarly the whole centre of his parents'. Furthermore, much of the friction which he has seen has often involved his own behaviour – his noise or his discipline, his mother's spoiling or his father's neglect – so he easily sees these accumulated small issues as the cause of the crash. There may be subtler reasons for guilt, too. Young children are sexually aware creatures who, in the normal course of early development, dream of partnership with the person of the opposite sex whom they love most (the parent) and therefore dream of ousting the present partner (the other parent). The little boy who has secretly dreamed of 'looking after Mummy' if only Daddy didn't get in the way, sees Daddy's departure not only as a practical disaster but as evidence of his own wicked and terrifying power: he wished him away and now he wishes he had not. The little girl whose father leaves is similarly placed: clearly her love-object has left because it was wicked of her to want to get into her mother's place. The young child who is beset by this kind of guilt will be anxious too. Because he is so wicked and has caused one parent to leave the home, will the other parent not also desert him? At its mildest, such anxiety tends to make the child cling to home and keep a too-careful eye on his mother's movements. At the other extreme, it may make him feel so totally wicked and unlovable that he becomes convinced that neither parent can love him and that total abandonment is inevitable (*see* **Depression**/In children before puberty).

Older children, who have lived through the stage of longing to replace the same-sex parent and have begun, instead, to identify themselves with him or her, are liable to a different sort of guilt. The separation makes them angry: angry, very often, with that same-sex parent. Whatever explanations they are given for the ending of the marriage they tend to feel (as do others outside the relationship) that they could have done better. A boy may feel that he could have remembered to 'phone when he was working late or could have spared one weekend day for the family; a girl may feel that she could have held her tongue and avoided nagging . . . But the anger itself leads to guilt and to anxiety. Guilt over lack of sympathy with the same-sex parent and anxiety because if those real feelings were known, surely the parent who has stayed with the family would leave, too (*see* **Depression**/Longer-lasting situational or reactive depression).

Children tend to be shut out by separation/divorce. Many parents become so involved in their own feelings that they cannot acknowledge children's mourning for the loss of the absent parent. Older children, interviewed later, say things like: 'You'd have thought she was the only one it mattered to . . .' and 'I just kept feeling: OK, but what about *me*?' To make matters worse, the parent who stays with the family is often as *emotionally* absent as the other parent is physically apart. Children feel unsupported and are aware that their own concerns are trivial, as compared with all this high adult emotion.

Split loyalties are agony. While some conflict of loyalties is probably inevitable, the children who suffer most are those for whom that conflict is made most acute. A few mothers actually try to enlist children against their fathers. Many more imply, often rather subtly, that any communication between departed father and children is disloyalty. Some of the points made by adolescents highlight the pain:

'I couldn't bear him having to skulk on the street corner when he met us, but if he came to the house she looked all pained and long-suffering.'

'I wanted to 'phone him, tell him things that had happened, you know? She never stopped me; never *said* anything, but if she came in and I was on the 'phone to him she'd sort of go out, looking peculiar . . .'

'She'd ask me to do things, jobs around the place, and sigh because he hadn't done them before. I hated that; hated her for trying to make me feel I was better than him.'

'Sometimes I'd say, "Dad would have let me do such and such" and she'd say, *very* politely, "If your father had wanted to be the one to say what you should do, I think he'd have stayed around . . ."'

'She was unhappy, OK, I know that, but she was always *sighing*: over money or how hard she was working and all that. Everything she said was sort of a dig at him . . .'

Children *worry* about the absent parent. For young children in particular, exclusion from the warmth and safety of home and family seems a horrendous exile. The fact that a man has left voluntarily is either beyond their comprehension or makes no difference to the fact that they worry about how he will manage alone. Four- to-ten-year-olds in particular ask:

'Where will Daddy sleep?'
'Who will cook his supper?'
'Who is looking after Daddy?'
'Isn't he lonely?'
'Doesn't he miss us?'
'Has he got a television? Will he watch [the favourite programme]?'

Mothers who share this kind of concern, or can find the generosity to acknowledge the reality of the child's and can offer practical reassurance that *Daddy's all right*, do the child an important service. As soon as it is possible, children should see for themselves that the father's living circumstances *are* 'all right'.

Things which help children when parents separate

Talking helps. Children whose parents discuss what is happening with them survive the immediate shock better than those who are just told, so to speak, 'he's gone and good riddance'. Two recent studies show that only twenty per cent of parents discuss the situation with children.

Knowing (seeing) that the mother is 'all right'. Children can accept grief and anger and need (*see above*) to be let in on what is happening, but they also need to know that, somewhere inside, the mother is 'solid' not smashed; not finished.

Outside support helps. The more colleagues and friends are around, the less the child will feel isolated himself or concerned for the mother's loneliness.

Grandparents can help. The more 'family' the child can feel he still has, the better. And if he used to spend time with Dad's Mum, why not now?

The structure of daily life going on as usual helps if the remains of the family can stay (at least for the first months) in the same house and therefore the same schools and neighbourhood. The child who loses a parent *plus* his familiar daily life is lost indeed (*see below* Poverty).

Different treats and special days. It is birthdays and festivals, school sports days and holidays, which bring the absent parent and the lost family most painfully to the fore. Children survive better if these can be glorious in a new way: perhaps because the family teams up with friends or invites relatives.

Brothers and sisters. 'Only' children tend to suffer most at the time of a separation/divorce. The burden of companioning the parent who stays, and of being, perhaps, her confidante or pawn, is very hard to bear alone. Where there are two or more children, they will often become very close in adversity and it may be from a brother or sister that the remaining parent finds out a particular child's immediate worries.

The children of one-parent families

Physical separation from one parent presents children with a shock-situation. Adaptation can take a long time and will usually take about two years. But *children do survive*. A 'broken home' need not be a recipe for disaster; a ticket to school-failure or a passport into adolescent delinquency. Recent research, in America and Britain, has made it clear that, where the consequences of divorce do seem to have been damaging, the damage has usually been done not solely by the divorce itself but by the social circumstances in which the child was reared after it.

British researchers carefully studied that other large group of children from single-parent families: those who are illegitimate. When matched groups of illegitimate, legitimate and adopted children were studied over many years, the illegitimate children were found to compare poorly with the others on a range of measures from physical growth through school performance to social adjustment. Interestingly, the adopted children were found to be doing even better than the legitimate group. On the face of it, the results clearly indicated that it was better for illegitimate children to be adopted than to be brought up by single mothers . . . Fortunately, the team did not accept this superficial interpretation but looked more carefully at their data to try to find out *why* the illegitimate children were so disadvantaged. The answer lay not in membership of a one-parent family but in the social/environmental circumstances of the families. The illegitimate children were living in poverty; as a group their families suffered from the lowest incomes, the worst housing and the most intractable employment problems. In stark contrast, the adoptive families, carefully selected by the adoption agencies, were a highly privileged, professional, middle-class group. The legitimate children, representing a British 'norm', were far better off than the single-parent families but not as conspicuously privileged as the adoptive ones. The children's measured performance closely followed these social differentiations. In further analysis, the workers re-examined all the child-measures *allowing for* social factors such as income and housing. Immediately the picture changed: adopted children now did no better than the children of either of the other two groups nor did the single-parent children do any worse. In fact, once these social factors were allowed for, there were no differences between any of the groups of children *except on social adjustment*. Here, and only here, that middle group of legitimate children were found to have the edge over both other groups.

Whether a child's family is single-parent because he was born illegitimate, or because he has lost a parent through separation, divorce or death, it seems that the social circumstances of the rest of his childhood are a key factor in what happens to him.

Poverty   Most families today find it difficult to keep up a standard of living which seems reasonable to them, even while the children have two adults to provide for them. In many families both parents work and there are therefore two incomes. In others, only one parent may work (because the mother takes time off to rear young children and/or because of redundancy, etc.) but the other parent is available to provide 'free' child-care and to use her or his time to ensure that the money which is coming in is stretched as far as possible in myriad minutiae from buying inexpensive food, to do-it-yourself activities around the house. A single parent loses out all the way around. She may have to accept low-paid work because of her domestic responsibilities, or hold onto a better-paid job which involves her in expensive arrangements for the children. Either way she is going to be short of both time and energy and will have to spend money to replace both. Where a divorce settlement provides her with child-maintenance, this will seldom be adequate to cover *family* expenses (rent, mortgage, rates, etc.) even if it does, in fact, cover out-of-pocket expenses such as clothing and pocket money. She may, of course, be allocated alimony by the divorce court, but a man cannot be forced to pay out money which he has not got and even two-thirds of his income (the maximum a British court will settle) will not cover what one hundred per cent of that income covered before the divorce. Everybody is going to be poorer, even before there is any question of a 'second family'.

Poverty, change   While a child can ride easily through a minor reduction in the family's
and instability   spending power, the total change in environment which is often involved when the family home must be sold and everything must alter is a different matter. When a house-move and a new school is coupled with a mother who is not only miserable but working long hours, seldom home and permanently exhausted, it is not surprising if children react badly. A small child may cling and become disorientated: an older one may, so to speak, abandon home as a bad job and turn to his peer group. If a new stability, albeit a less privileged one, can be quickly arrived at, he will settle to his new life, but if everything continues to seem strange and chaotic he will survive as best he can and that survival may not be of the kind which is socially approved.

The experience of one mother who was superbly supported by her community and thus enabled to hold life steady for her three children, may illustrate the down-to-earth needs which so often go unmet:

'Everybody was fantastic. It was little things that obviously mattered most and one way or another we sorted them all out. The little one was at playgroup and at a minder afterwards. No way could I afford that any more but the group just gave her a free place which meant I could manage the minder. All three were used to being driven about and my way of life had depended on a car. But a neighbour said car-sharing was the in-thing and took the two older ones to school with hers and we took to doing our big shop in her car on Saturdays. Weekends would have been hell but my son's scout leader caught on to that one and joined him in with a Saturday football group and it was through him that we got onto the Big Brother scheme. All right, it's not the same doing things with a Big Brother as with Dad, but it's better for a twelve-year-old than hanging around the house with Mum and sisters, isn't it? It was the middle one who was terrified we'd have to move. Her whole life goes on within walking distance of here – all her friends, everything. Her teacher asked me straight out whether I could manage and when I said I didn't know, asked if I'd thought of taking in a lodger. I hadn't but we haven't been without one since. Her rent pays a lot of the mortgage *and* she babysits too; the children like having another adult in the house. I think it makes them feel more secure . . .'

That mother was unusually fortunate in her friends and contacts, but this is the kind of help which is just beginning to be available to single-parent families through various charitable and self-help organizations such as The National Council for One-Parent Families and Gingerbread.

Children's relationship with the absent parent

The child who is suddenly pitchforked into a single-parent family, because his other parent leaves, needs the practical structure of his daily life held steady but he also needs the quaking structure of his emotional relationships steadied, too. Although, of course, every child, every parent and every relationship is unique, research does suggest that the following points are usually very important:

He will need to know, and see, that the end of mother–father love is not the end of father–child love. He needs to be helped over his immediate guilt (*see above*).

He needs to be told and shown that, whatever his parents now feel about each other, the absent parent still loves and cares about him.

He needs to be told and shown that he can love and be loved by the absent parent without risking the love of the one at home. He will, from time to time, feel disloyal, but with help, can come to believe that his mother *wants* him still to 'have' his father.

He needs to see that father often enough and regularly enough that they can stay in touch with each other's ordinary, everyday concerns. For a young child that probably means at least once a week. If the gaps are longer, he will neither remember all his 'news' nor feel it worth the effort of trying to keep his father informed of rapidly changing friendships, school successes/disasters and so forth.

He needs to be able to talk freely about his father to his mother and vice versa. That means that neither must use him as a spy in the enemy camp, nor freeze with disapproval when they hear mention of the ex-partner's new purchase, new friend or new problem . . .

● More than half of the British children whose parents divorce lose touch with the absent one within a few months. Evidence suggests that none truly wish to do so and that lifelong emotional damage may be the result.

Parents who have left their families sometimes genuinely wonder whether it would not be better for the children (especially very young ones) simply to 'forget about me'. If visits cause obvious emotional upset it may seem easier on everyone simply to drop them. It seems that this is almost invariably a serious mistake; on a par with the mistake which used to be made when young children who were upset by being visited in hospital were left unvisited because they 'settled better'. We know now that these children needed *more* time with their parents, not less, and we have moved from timed visits to rooming-in or unrestricted access. In the same way, this child needs *more* time with the absent parent, not less; the upset caused by today's visit must be tolerated in the interests of next year, rather than avoided in the interest of immediate 'peace'.

Arrangements for 'access'   The children who settle most easily to life in a split family appear to be those who can have free access, as the spirit moves them, to the absent parent. In several studies, for example, having the two households within bicycling or walking distance of each other, and having a key to both, has been the children's answer to 'what would be/is the ideal arrangement?' Of course this will be impossible for many families but it may serve as an ideal to which you can aspire. Whatever arrangements are made, the following points seem to be important:

Young children must have parents who will talk to each other, even if it is only on the doorstep or over the telephone. You cannot make pleasant plans using a three-year-old as a messenger, nor expect a five-year-old to explain for herself that she has a cold and may not swim, or that she will not be able to come out next week because of the school play . . .

There are circumstances under which children need parents to be able to be together, even if only for short periods. A child who is ill in bed, for example, should not have to wait until he is completely better before he can see his Dad. A child whose father is in hospital should not have to cope alone or go without seeing him. A child whose father is mentally ill, or otherwise in alarmingly poor shape, still needs to see him, but needs to do so with the person who can give him security and explain what he saw to him afterwards. Ideally, even older children should be able to count on both parents seeing their great moments. You cannot play a match twice so that each of the people you most care about can see it separately.

As soon as possible, children need to visit the absent parent's home. However unsuitable it seems, unless it is very temporary, they need to be able to visualize his whereabouts (*see above*).

If the absent parent is to remain a *parent* rather than a visitor he needs a base. Conducting an intimate relationship on the basis of visits to the zoo and ice-cream in cafés is almost impossible. Using the family home as this base is usually a tremendous strain to all concerned (even where the resident parent will permit it). Unless or until he has a home of his own, a friend's house may be better than nothing.

Children need to meet people who are important to the absent parent. If he is sharing his home, bed and life with somebody, it is usually a mistake to conceal the fact and keep them away.

● Contrary to popular belief, children are often much happier once they know that separated parents have new lovers, provided those lovers did not cause the breakdown of the marriage. Once the divorce is accepted, the spectre of either parent's loneliness is a horrific one to many children (*see above*).

Children who refuse visits   This happens for many reasons and at all ages. Leaving the child to decide about visits himself is not usually the right answer.

Very young children may not like being separated from the mother, especially during this period of anxious clinging. The answer may be to start again with short visits at home, walks in a familiar park and so forth.

Fathers who have had little to do with their young children may not turn into skilled child-managers overnight. While it may be tempting to 'let him see what it's like to cope with them all day', it is not fair to the children, let alone their Dad. Visits at a friend's house, where there are familiar playmates and another parent to learn from, may be the answer.

Older children, especially those who are getting used to the situation, may find routine visits a bore either because the parent does not find interesting things to do with them or because they want to be busy with their own friends and affairs. The occasional parent obviously has to find a way of life which works during visits, but the timing of the visits may have to be altered to suit the child better, too. Sometimes an after-school visit is better than a weekend day. The parent at home has to resist the temptation just to say 'well you don't have to go out with him if you don't want to', because once they are out of touch it will be far more difficult for the child to regain a relationship which is basically important to him.

Adolescents often come to resent visits which are arranged *for* them or which make them different and take them away from their friends. Being allowed to plan for themselves often helps. So does being encouraged to include the absent parent in real everyday life, rather than treating visiting times as entirely separate. It may be the absent parent who can find the time to drive him to the sports centre for those practice sessions or lend his stereo and space for that party.

Children's relationships with parents' lovers

There is little formal research on this topic: the following points come directly from involved families:

Beware of territory. Mothers with custody (and a shortage of babysitters) resent the fact that children accept women-friends whom they meet when out with their fathers much more easily than they accept men-friends who come to the family home. It is not sex-discrimination. Fathers with custody have the same problems when women visit the home. The point is that the house 'belongs to' the child and contains the ghost of the absent parent. The visitor invades privacy and may unwittingly use '*Mummy's* kitchen' or sit in '*Daddy's* chair'.

Casual affairs are probably best based on the lover's ground. If and when the relationship develops to a point where it is important that he get to know the children, this can probably best be done on expeditions out with him, and by having him to the family home as a family visitor, rather than as your private one.

Beware of authority. Few children will readily accept instructions or reproofs from a comparative stranger, but most adults find it difficult to *live with* children without giving any. This is put forward by many parents as a strong reason against having a living-in partner until or unless he or she is going to become a parent-substitute or step-parent.

If you want to try out the business of living together as a potential family group, it often works best if you all go and do it somewhere new – in a rented holiday home for example – so that nobody's territory is being invaded and everyone can work out the ground-rules for cooperative living together.

Beware of manipulation. Many children work hard to influence parents' choice of partner. Techniques vary from the blatant (spiders in shoes) to the more subtle (pretend she isn't there at all). Either can be extremely off-putting. It works the other way too. If you have a series of affairs, you may find your children making plans for next summer's holiday with the lover you are just getting tired of . . .

If you know an affair is not likely to be permanent, but want everybody to have fun, try to make it clear to the children that they need not concern themselves overmuch one way or the other. But if you think or hope that it will be long-lasting, make that clear, too. All too often step-parents say sadly, 'Her kids and I just never got on; I think we got off on the wrong foot.' That usually means 'we none of us realized at the beginning that we had to try and like each other and by the time we knew it was too late.'

Beware of repeated 'desertions'. Lovers who like children, and are trying to please you, may easily become close friends with yours, especially if the children are feeling starved for adult male (or female) company. Don't let the children come to count on the things they do together at weekends, the help he gives with homework or the glorious feasts she cooks on Fridays, unless you are pretty sure your own relationship is going to last. If you could not keep a marriage going 'for the children's sake' you certainly won't want to keep an affair going for that reason, yet repeated experiences of being left by loved people will certainly not help them to get over the divorce or to feel kindly towards you.

Children's relationships with step-parents

Many children's ideas about step-parents come from fairy stories in which they are invariably wicked and cruel. Even if your child likes the future parent-substitute, you may find that once he knows there is to be an actual marriage his attitude changes. School friends may even tell him to 'watch out for poisoned apples . . .'

Children can develop extremely close and warm relationships with step-parents. Some even maintain that despite the misery at the time, they are glad there was a divorce because 'I'm closer to my step-father than I ever would have been to my real father.' Making it work takes a lot of tact. The following hints may also help:

A house-move makes a better start than having all of you move in with him (her) or vice versa: Although children survive the trauma of one parent leaving better if other aspects of life can stay the same (*see above*), making a new family grouping usually works more easily in a new environment. Everyone shares mutual territory about which nobody feels possessive, and there can be mutual ground-rules for living in it from the beginning.

Room has to be left for the 'real' parent. That means room in the child's life – so that his regular visiting days don't suddenly become new-family days – and psychological room, too. Be careful, for example, not to push him to call the step-parent 'Mum' or 'Dad' (unless he asks, or does it spontaneously), or to assume that he will do with the new 'parent' the things he has been doing with the real but absent one.

Room has to be left for the old family, too. Don't expect the child to drop old family stories, in-jokes and so forth: tell them to the new person. Don't expect him to drop *anything*: try to make the new relationship completely extra-rather-than-instead.

Although their relationship is *because* of you, the step-parent and children cannot make it *through* you. Try not to stand in the middle, like a maypole around which everybody dances. Step-parent and children have to get to know one another as people rather than as your append-ages. However jealous a child may seem to be of the newcomer, she will enjoy your new happiness and give him credit for it; eventually she will be ready to seek a share for herself.

Try not to expect the step-parent *or* children to accept sex-stereotyped family roles too quickly (if at all). A step-father, for example, usually needs to go very easily on 'discipline', 'manners' and so forth. With adolescents he may never be permitted an authoritarian relationship but may, if he will accept it, eventually be offered friendship instead. A step-mother will probably need to hold back on personal care, however warmly she feels towards the children. She will be felt to be 'stepping beyond the bounds' if she tries to plait hair or wash necks, at least until the children spontaneously hug and kiss her.

Try to arrange for the step- and natural parent to meet, especially if you have managed to keep your relationship civil since the divorce. Children need to feel that all the adults who are closely concerned with them are on the same side. It also helps if they do not feel that they can at all easily play one off against the other or have their wilder fantasies believed . . .

Ears and Hearing; Ear Disorders and Deafness

The ears are not only the organs of hearing but also those of balance. Each ear has three main parts:

The outer ear   Is the visible ear itself (the pinna) together with the ear canal which is about one inch long and made into a dead-end by the ear drum.

The complex shape of the pinna gathers sound waves and directs them along the ear canal to vibrate the delicate membrane of the ear drum.

The middle ear   Is a tiny chamber, sealed off from the outer ear by that ear drum but connected to the back of the throat by the eustachian tube. This tube opening keeps air pressure equal on either side of the ear drum but it also provides a route up which bacteria or viruses can travel from the throat.

The inner ear   This is a complex set of structures:
The semi-circular canals are fluid-filled tubules which act (rather like a spirit level) to convey information about balance and the position of the head. Disturbances of this part of the inner ear can lead to giddiness, vertigo and nausea. This may well be a factor in motion-sickness.
The ossicles are structures which are adjacent to the ear drum and transmit its vibrations to the cochlea.
The cochlea contains the actual sound-receptors, which translate those ear-drum vibrations into nerve impulses and transmit them along the auditory nerve to the brain where they are interpreted as sounds.

Deafness

There are two main types of deafness, each of which may, of course, affect either one or both ears and be of any degree of severity.

Nerve deafness (perceptive deafness)   This type is due to malformation of, or damage to, the actual auditory nerve. Congenital deafness (such as that associated with foetal german measles) is of this type. It can also develop later due to infection or severe head injury, or gradually after years of work in an extremely noisy environment or with the degeneration of age. Nerve deafness is usually irreversible although the individual can be helped with increasingly sophisticated hearing aids.

Conduction deafness   Arises not because the actual hearing organ is defective but because something interferes with the transmission of sound waves from the outer ear to the cochlea. Many ear disorders can reduce the acuity of the affected ear but with prompt treatment permanent deafness is unusual.

● It is vital that any deafness should be detected early. A totally deaf baby will make sounds so do not wait for suspicious silence before checking that he can hear properly. Older children with even minor degrees of temporary deafness can miss a lot of what is said to them and may even be unfairly scolded for poor work at school. Make sure that ear troubles are carefully treated and schools kept informed.

Ear disorders

If a child has earache he should be seen by a doctor on that same day. If he also seems ill, is feverish and/or has discharge from the ear, he should be seen as an emergency even if it is the middle of the night. There are many causes for earache which are not urgent (the pain may, for example, be referred from an aching tooth, inflamed sinus or the general congestion of a simple head cold) but if infection is present, immediate treatment is vital.

A baby will not, of course, be able to tell you that his ear hurts; indeed he may not be able to localize the pain himself so he may not even give you signs such as rubbing at it while he cries. This is one reason why a feverish baby should always be checked by a doctor. He will examine the ear drums and satisfy himself that infection there is not the cause of the illness.

● Don't use folk-remedies for earache. However desperate you may be to do something to help the child, warmed oil in the ear is at best useless and at worst highly dangerous. If you must do something while you wait to see the doctor, give the correct dose of your chosen analgesic (see **Pain and Pain Control**).

Otitis media Infection of the middle ear is the commonest cause of acute earache. It usually arises because the child already has an upper respiratory infection and the bacteria or viruses from his throat, his tonsils or his sinuses find their way up the eustachian tubes.

● Teach the child to blow his nose by blocking one nostril while he blows down the other. Blowing both together increases the chance of matter being forced into the eustachian tubes.

Unfortunately infection reaches the middle ear more easily than it can drain from it. In small children, especially, the opening of the eustachian tubes into the throat is often partially obstructed by relatively large adenoids making the free drainage of matter difficult. If infection leads to inflammation and then to the formation of pus, pressure will build up against the ear drum. In the pre-antibiotic era, burst ear drums were commonplace as was the spread of this kind of infection into the mastoid bone behind the ear and thence into the covering of the brain (see **Meningitis and Encephalitis**). Nowadays prompt antibiotic treatment almost always controls the infection rapidly. If a lot of pus rapidly accumulates in the middle ear, the drum may burst before treatment can even be begun. The child will have discharge from the ear, sometimes referred to as 'glue ear'. With energetic treatment the infection can be controlled so that the drum heals cleanly.

Repeated middle-ear infections can leave the child with chronic scarring of the ear drum and/or a collection of fluid which will not drain. Sometimes his adenoids will be removed to reduce the number of infections/improve drainage (see **Hospital**/Surgery: Tonsillectomy and Adenoidectomy). Occasionally a surgical incision will be made in the ear drum so that the pus can be cleaned out and the drum heal cleanly (see **Hospital**/Surgery: Myringotomy).

Otitis externa   Infection of the outer ear canal can be caused by bacteria multiplying in the normal ear wax, by infected eczema, by a minute fingernail scratch which becomes infected, by a boil at the root of one of the hairs in its lining or by inflammation/infection around a foreign body which nobody knew was in the ear. Whatever the cause, otitis externa will usually be excruciatingly painful, especially when the ear is moved or the child tries to lie on that side. If the trouble is associated with eczema, the ear may not be painful, but infuriatingly itchy.

The child should be seen immediately by a doctor. Prescribed medicaments can be applied directly to the site in the form of ear drops, but the condition may nevertheless take a long and tedious time to clear up.

Mechanical blockage of the ear canal   **Excess wax,** especially wax which has become impacted due to unwise attempts to clean it out with 'Q Tips' or screws of cotton wool, can block the passageway causing hearing loss. Such wax will need to be first softened and then syringed out by a doctor.

Foreign bodies are quite often poked into the ears by bored children who then either forget the whole matter or are unwilling to admit it. Such a foreign body will interfere with the hearing of that ear and may lead to infection. If you suspect one, take the child to the doctor. If you can see a foreign body in the ear, do not try to remove it yourself. There is a real risk that you will push it not only further out of reach but also up against the ear drum which it might damage (*see also* **Accidents**/Foreign bodies inserted on purpose).

Mechanical damage to the ear drum   Although the ear drum is a very tough membrane, it can be damaged, even perforated, by a caretaker or child who pokes about in the ear with a hard object or falls on something sharp. If you even suspect such an accident, have the ear checked by a doctor. Although most perforations will heal leaving no permanent damage to the hearing, medical care is essential both to ensure that there is no damage to the middle or inner ear and to ensure that healing takes place without infection.

● Clean only the visible parts of children's ears and don't put anything into the ear canals. A child whose ears are never interfered with is less likely to poke things into his own or those of his baby sister.

Water in the ears   Water in the ear canal does no harm unless the child has otitis externa. If it feels uncomfortable after swimming, water may have become trapped behind some wax so that droplets are being pressed against the drum. Encourage the child to lie with the affected ear downwards to encourage drainage.

Occasionally water may reach the middle ear via the eustachian tubes, due, for example, to the child sneezing or laughing/choking while submerged. The child may complain of an irritating buzzing feeling. Unless it contributes to the beginning of a middle-ear infection, such water will eventually drain back harmlessly down the eustachian tube.

Dizziness/ vertigo   Dizziness and/or vertigo are signs that the sense of balance, controlled by the semi-circular canals, is disturbed. Familiar to every child who has whirled round and round on his own feet or a fairground ride, it may also come on suddenly if middle-ear infection or head injury disturbs the canal's functioning. In later life a degenerative disorder known as Meniere's disease has vertigo as one of its principal and most distressing symptoms.

In a child, dizziness or vertigo due to ear disorders are usually fleeting; they pass as soon as he has lain down for a few minutes. If they do not, decongestant *nose* drops may help, by relieving nasal congestion, opening up the eustachian tubes and thus allowing the pressure within the middle ear to equalize with outside pressure.

Dizziness or vertigo lasting for an hour or more, or occurring after head injury, should be reported to a doctor.

Eating

It ought to be easy to feed a family in the affluent west. There is enough food for everyone and enough choice for all tastes. We do not have to worry about famine and starvation; we do not even have to adjust our eating to seasonal gluts and shortages or to the geographical peculiarities of our home areas. To the millions of people in the developing world who face life-and-death problems with food, we must indeed seem to have it easy.

But feeding a family remains fraught with anxiety. An abundance of food brings anxiety about people eating too much, becoming obese and prone to all the ills associated with overweight. A vast range of foods, available courtesy of the food industry, brings anxiety over choice itself: out of all the foodstuffs available, what *should* people eat? That range of foods can only be made available with the aid of high-technology farming and food-processing methods; how harmful are those chemical fertilizers, insecticides, preservatives, colourings and flavourings? Are we feeding our children poison in their television dinners?

Bombarded as we are with information and exhortation, warnings and scare stories, opinions and prejudices about food, the simple and satisfactory business of eating to satisfy hunger and sustain life, health and growth, has come to seem complicated and worrying. The following, deliberately simplistic and middle-of-the-road, approach to family eating is intended to defuse the emotional issue of food with an infusion of ordinary commonsense in the hope that it may help some families to avoid the 'eating problems' which currently bedevil so many over so many years.

First principles: food is fuel and eating is a pleasure

Bodies need food to fuel the processes of life itself, to keep hearts beating, blood circulating, lungs functioning, the digestive system working and nerves and muscles interacting as they should. Even an individual in coma or deep sleep needs energy for this kind of maintenance. As soon as any kind of work is demanded of the body, further food-fuel is needed.

Sitting in front of a television set takes more energy than lying in bed; sedentary work in an office takes more still while heavy manual labour or a day's active play will use up even more.

The fuel-value of foods is measured by one of two systems: in calories or in joules. Either system assigns a numerical energy-value to a given weight of particular foodstuffs. When we say that an ounce of this food 'contains 200 calories' we mean that, eaten and digested, that food will make 200 calories-worth of energy available to the body.

In our concern to feed our children foods which are 'good for them' and to ensure that they are not deprived of vitamins, minerals and other vital nutrients, we sometimes forget that *the prime need is for enough fuel*. Every food contains calories and a body which is short of energy will use any food which it is given to meet immediate energy needs (*see below* Protein).

Bodies do not only need food to fuel activity. They also need it to repair and replace lost or worn-out tissue, from trimmed hair and nails to damaged organs and skin. Provided there is adequate food available, so that the body is not short of overall energy, it will select the nutrients it needs to keep itself in good shape from amongst those in its diet.

With adequate food available, bodies can also store some nutrients so that they are ready to cope with any unusual demands made upon them. If a well-fed athlete's sprint uses up the energy immediately available to his muscles, for example, his body will mobilize glucose from a short-term store in his liver. If heavy menstrual loss, or other haemorrhage, uses up the iron circulating in the bloodstream, iron reserves will be mobilized for the new red blood cells which are suddenly urgently needed. When stores have been depleted in this way they will be replenished gradually by the body, provided it is taking in food which is surplus to immediate energy requirements.

Babies, children and adolescents must meet all these needs from their food but *in addition they must grow*. Their bodies need not just the small quantities of particular nutrients taken up by repair and replacement of tissue, but the much larger quantities required for building it. Like adults, children's bodies will meet immediate energy needs first so that adequate growth will only take place when there is plenty to spare.

Since eating is a biological necessity, survival of the race depends on people recognizing their need for food (by feeling hungry) and enjoying meeting it. Without appetite and satisfaction, people might simply not bother with food. As it is, people can almost always be absolutely relied upon to eat enough for their bodies' needs, provided that adequate food is available to them. Even where emotional problems bedevil eating (*see below*) or physical problems make it painful, *people will not starve themselves in the midst of plenty*. Of course there are exceptions. A person so submerged in depression that she can no longer feel normal biological drives may indeed forget to eat. A political prisoner may override the hunger-drive with a tremendous act of will and starve himself to death as may a disturbed adolescent, using similar will-power but different motivation (*see* **Anorexia Nervosa**). But there are no exceptions which apply to healthy children. If you can believe this, believe that your child will eat enough and should enjoy doing so, he is most unlikely to have 'eating problems'.

Types of food for babies

Young babies have to have all their food – and most of their vital water – in the composite form of milk. Just as the placenta carried nourishment to the baby from the mother while he was inside the womb, so her breasts carry the nourishment intended for him once he has emerged. For generations the milk which cows produce for calves has been used as an alternative. Now, recognizing that calves' milk and babies' milk is radically different (*see below*) we have learned to adapt it more and more in fairly successful attempts to bring it closer to what human babies need.

Breast-feeding   In western societies breast-feeding is not taken for granted. Influential groups argue in its favour – and offer practical assistance to nursing mothers, too – and many individual mothers believe that it is 'the natural way' or 'a baby's birthright' and give it a try. But giving it a try is not at all the same as just accepting it. A bottle of formula is never further away than the nearest chemist or supermarket, and it is from a bottle that most young mothers have watched relatives and friends feeding babies. If you ask a child to draw a picture of a new baby being fed, the chances are that she will draw a bottle. Many mothers who are thinking about how to feed their coming baby will have friends who tried breast-feeding and 'failed', or who breast-fed for a dutiful few weeks and thankfully gave up. Some (according to recent British research) will have husbands who 'don't like the idea'. Others will have job or career plans which seem easier to arrange around bottle-feeding (*see* **Working Mothers**); others again will be in touch with health professionals whose support for breast-feeding is half-hearted. It all amounts to a situation in which *breast-feeding is a positive choice* rather than simply the way young babies are fed.

Quite a high proportion of mothers will make that positive decision and put their babies to the breast after birth. Some will enjoy the feeling; enjoy an 'easy-to-feed' baby's obvious pleasure and be motivated to stick with it. Others will meet difficulties and discomforts and, after a few days or a few weeks, turn to that bottle. One of the facts that the ardent propagandists for breast-feeding often leave out of account is that getting started with breast-feeding is not always easy. The mother whose baby is not easy to fix on the nipple, who sleeps after a few sucks and who turns his head away when she offers and re-offers the breast, is liable to feel rejected. If he is offered a bottle and sucks it more eagerly, it is easy for her to feel that 'he likes it better'. If he is also one of the many babies who not only loses weight in his first days but gains slowly thereafter (*see* **Growth**) it is easy for her also to believe that the bottle would be 'better for him'. There are major physical sensations for the mother to cope with, too. Some revel in suckling as a sensual experience but others are surprised and alarmed by it. Some have painful uterine contractions when the baby sucks. Some get sore nipples which may even crack to produce sharp pain. Many find that the early milk supply gets out of phase with the baby's feeding so that there are times when he is obviously hungry and others when she is painfully engorged. These are all *early* difficulties. Mothers who persist almost invariably find that everything settles down to a perfect and pleasurable situation of supply and demand, and mothers who have had this experience with one child seldom opt for the bottle with a second. But a great many mothers never get through the rough beginnings to reach the calm which follows.

Every mother must make her own decision because it is she, and her baby, who have to live with that decision and nobody therefore has the right to over-persuade her. Healthy, happy babies can be reared on modern formulae and a mother who is struggling to breast-feed when she does not really want to may cast a shadow over her whole relationship with her child. Every mother is nevertheless entitled to make that decision in the light of some facts, which babymilk advertisers will not stress. Product X is *not* 'the perfect food for your baby'. Only your own milk is that.

Some differences between human and (modified) cow's milk

The differences between the milk produced for calves and that produced for human babies are so great that it is infinitely quicker to list the similarities, which are water and the type of sugar called lactose. Everything else is different – either in type or concentration – and some of the differences (in the concentration of minerals such as sodium and potassium, for example) are so great that unmodified cow's milk is downright dangerous and so were the old-fashioned dried milks on which millions of babies were reared with unrecognized ill-effects.

Cow's milk contains too much of the wrong kind of protein. Modern formulae reduce the protein-concentration of a made-up feed but can do little to alter its type. There are amino-acids (*see below* Proteins) in cow's milk which are absent from human milk. It is these amino-acids which are thought to be responsible for sensitizing some infants to cow's milk protein. Exposure to these in the first six months of life is thought to be responsible for many allergic disorders later on (*see* **Allergy**/Gastro-intestinal allergies).

Cow's milk also contains much more saturated fat than breast milk. Modern manufacturers get around this by replacing the butter-fat with fats or oils of vegetable origin (*see below* Fats) but the fats in breast milk are thought to be better absorbed by babies and may therefore make it easier for them to absorb the fat-soluble vitamins (*see below* Vitamins and Minerals).

The exact nature of the minerals and vitamins in breast milk are still a vexed question, but iron, for example, although low in all milks, is far better absorbed from breast milk than from any other source so that breast-fed babies do not require extra iron from solid foods until later in their first year. Vitamin D is also readily absorbed from breast milk so that rickets (*see below*) is almost unknown amongst babies fed from the breast.

Breast milk also protects babies from various forms of infection. Few breast-fed babies get gastro-enteritis, for example (*see* **Diarrhoea, Gastro-enteritis and Food Poisoning**) and this is not only because their milk comes uncontaminated from the breast, sidestepping the hazards of unsterilized bottles or visiting flies, but also because it contains a variety of protective and anti-infective substances, together with some passive immunities (*see* **Immune Response**). We cannot yet even begin to copy these in a formula.

Finally, while most studies of breast milk are carried out using pooled samples from many mothers, so that 'breast milk' is described as if it were a single and consistent substance, there is recent evidence to suggest that any mother's milk changes substantially, not only from day to day but even within a single feed. Many authorities now believe that these changes may help the baby to control his own intake of milk according to his appetite; enabling him, so to speak, to stop wanting to suck more milk when his body has received adequate nourishment. Babies who are entirely breast-fed are far less likely than bottle-fed babies to become fat (*see below* Obesity). This may not only be because they are protected from over-concentrated formulae and too many extras (*see below*) but also because the food they do receive has an in-built appetite control.

'Babymilks'   If you decide to feed your baby on an artifical formula do consult your doctor, health visitor or other health professional about which of the many products available in your community you should use. On the whole the most 'natural' food (*see below* Commonsense about family eating: 'Natural' foods) will not be the one to choose. You will want the most highly modified milk you can find: the one which produces a feed least like cow's milk and most like breast milk. Obviously such a formula will be more expensive than dried cow's milk with some minerals taken out and some vitamins added.

Some health professionals may advise you not to use a cow's milk formula at all but a formula based on goat's milk or based on soya flour. Although some people do believe that goat's milk is in some way 'healthier', there are few differences between goat's and cow's milk which are at all likely to be important to a young and healthy baby. Soya-based milks are often prescribed for babies thought already to be allergic to cow's milk protein but whether it is worth using such a milk in the hope of *preventing later* allergy is a matter for you and your doctor to decide. You might consider it if yours is an atopic family (*see* **Allergy**).

Whatever formula you feed to your baby do make sure that you always:

Mix the formula to exactly the recommended strength which the manufacturers will have worked out so that the resulting feed is of similar concentration to breast milk. Over-concentrated feeds – even when the formula is highly modified – may at worst put a strain on your baby's kidneys, by overloading him with salt and other minerals, and at best will make him fat because he wants his normal quantity of milk-mixture but you have packed in extra calories.

Prepare it hygienically remembering that warm milk is an ideal breeding ground for bacteria and that gastro-enteritis is still dangerous to babies (*see* **Infection**/Preventing infection. *See also* **Diarrhoea, Gastro-enteritis and Food Poisoning**).

Avoid adding any extras such as sugar or spoonfuls of cereals. If your baby needs extra food-calories, give them to him from a spoon so that you can see whether he actually wants them or not. If you hide them in his beloved bottle you do not give his appetite a chance to guide his eating.

Other   Once your baby has anything to eat in addition to milk you will probably
'babyfoods'   use at least some special 'babyfoods'. Some of these are extremely useful.

The cereals especially prepared for infants, for example, have added minerals and vitamins which may be good for him (*see below*). The fruits, meats, desserts and so forth have a smooth texture and consistent taste and may be good for you because they save you trouble. But do remember that all these 'special' products are only *foods*; the only 'special' things about them are that they are prepared in a form which is easy for your baby to eat and digest and that they are energetically advertised and sold to you as 'first foods' or 'weaning foods' or whatever.

Once a baby is ready for tastes of any 'solid' foods he can have anything you normally serve at your table with the exception of hot spices, salty seasonings, drugs like alcohol or coffee and, perhaps, honey (*see* **Diarrhoea, Gastro-enteritis and Food Poisoning**/Infant botulism). If you do want to feed him family-food rather than 'babyfood', you will have first have to purée most items and sieve (to get rid of pips or very hard stalks, etc.) some others. A 'Baby-Mouli' will do both jobs at once.

If you have a freezer, you can compromise between using 'babyfoods' and fiddling about making each family meal suitable for him; you can batch-prepare your own foods and freeze them in baby portions.

• Do be careful about frozen foods – commercial or your own – when they are being fed to babies (*see* **Infection**/Preventing infection: Infection and home hygiene); thorough defrosting, etc. is really important.

One great advantage, though, of feeding a baby on family-food is that he will not be kept on specially puréed food for too long. Give him the opportunity to discover the exciting different textures of different foods during his first year. It is children who were fed exclusively on those oh-so-consistent cans and packets, month after month, who tend to gag on 'lumpy foods' and insist that they cannot chew crusts even whilst they chew their toys and books to pieces.

Types of food for everyone else

With a wide range of foodstuffs available, it is natural that parents should be concerned to offer their children an ideal selection at every age and stage. Millions of words are written every year about introducing a baby to weaning foods; about a 'good mixed diet' for toddlers, about 'healthy eating' for children and about what we should all do to avoid too much sugar/too many refined foods/too much animal fat and so forth. Providing an adequate diet for a family does not have to be so complicated.

Human beings are omnivores; that means that they can nourish themselves adequately on both animal and vegetable foods and on a vast range of combinations of these. There are essential *nutrients* (substances which human bodies need to obtain from foods) but *there are no essential foods* for anyone old enough to be weaned. So widely available are the nutrients we need that people can abandon or reject many foods and categories of foods before there is the least danger of malnutrition. People who 'don't like vegetables' or 'can't take milk' may present problems to harassed hostesses or busy mothers, but they present no problem to their own health. In a society where many foods are plentiful, nutrients missed in one food will always be available in another. Don't take too seriously the thousands of books or articles on diet which give you tables which suggest the foods your family 'requires'. Such tables will, for example, set out the numbers of calories (units of food-energy) which people of different ages, weights, heights, sexes and levels of activity, need each day. Within that overall food-requirement you will be told how many grams of protein and milli- or micro-grammes of various vitamins and minerals there should be. Calories from high-protein foods are not usually counted into the day's total (because these foods are used so inefficiently for energy) so your table will probably also say what proportion of the day's calories should come from carbohydrates or from fats.

Nutritional tables of this type represent averages of the intakes of large groups of people; the researchers who first construct them intend them for the guidance of people who are responsible for feeding large groups. The catering officer of a large residential establishment can, for example, take such a table and from it work out what he should make available, daily and over time, and how to provide needed foodstuffs most economically. But that catering officer knows that the food he provides will not be shared out equally: he does not expect each of one hundred people to eat one-hundredth of the diet. He does not even expect that everything will be eaten or that nobody will ever wish there were more of one particular item. All he knows, or cares, is that if he provides that diet, nobody need actually go unhealthily short of anything.

People are not average, they are individual. Their individual needs are not average either. If you try to provide for your family a scaled-down version of that caterer's guide, you will drive yourself mad weighing and measuring and trying to work out how much of this is in that. And all to no purpose because the nutrients your child needs today may bear no relation to what the tables say he 'ought' to need, and they may bear no relation either to what he needed last week or will need next month.

Nobody can design an ideal diet for your child. Even a skilled professional dietician can only make an educated guess and even he will not be able to ensure that the child eats it . . . So read all that literature if you want to, but remember that your only real criteria of the adequacy of your child's diet are his health, his growth (in weight *and* height), his energy and enthusiasm for life (*see* **Growth**).

In the following notes you will find the main groups of nutrients from which human diets are made up, but you will not find foods classified within these nutrient-groups in the usual way. This is because real foods – and more especially manufactured or processed foods and cooked dishes – hardly ever consist of one nutrient alone. To suggest that a child should have two portions of food from 'the protein group' and two from the 'carbohydrate group' is to ignore the fact that his meat will bring fat with it; his bread will contain some protein and that both items will contain a variety of vitamins and minerals.

Carbohydrates   These are the substances which human bodies can most quickly and easily break down into the sugars which provide them with energy. As such they are basic nutrients without which nobody could eat healthily.

There are many forms of carbohydrate and they occur in a vast range of foodstuffs. Unfortunately they are linked, in many people's minds, with foods which are widely regarded as 'empty calories' and 'fattening starch'. Sugar, for example, is pure carbohydrate. When a child eats sugar he takes in calories and nothing else: no other nutrients which his body might need; just energy. Our extensive use of pure refined sugar is certainly to be frowned upon (*see below*) but this does not mean that 'sugar is bad for you'. How can a source of calories be bad in itself? It can be well or foolishly used, but that is quite a different matter. All cereals and therefore the foods made from them, like breakfast cereals, breads and cakes, are high in carbohydrates and it is these foods which tend to be seen as 'starchy' and 'poor quality'. But cereals and cereal products bring other valuable nutrients with them, especially when they are not highly processed or when processed foods are enriched during manufacture. Furthermore, neither the bulk of food which we need for ordinary digestion and excretion (*see* **Constipation**), nor the number of calories we need for basic fuel, could easily be provided without carbohydrate-rich foods. A diet consisting *exclusively* of a refined cereal might indeed provide adequate energy without providing enough essential nutrients, but a diet rich in essential nutrients but without adequate calories would just as certainly lead to malnutrition.

Root vegetables are also high in carbohydrates but they too contain nutrients as well as energy. The humble potato, for example, is probably the best *single* food in the world. While nobody would recommend that a child be fed nothing but potatoes, a child thus fed would survive for longer, and grow better, than he would on any other single food except for unlimited quantities of milk.

Other vegetables and fruits, as well as items usually classified as 'protein foods', such as milk and nuts, also contain varying amounts of various carbohydrates. It is the ready-availability of energy within such foods which ensures that bodies can make the best possible use of the other nutrients they contain (*see below* Protein-sparing).

Proteins   Every human being needs proteins because these are the substances out of which bodies build tissue and therefore they are needed for repair and replacement. Growing children have a particular need for proteins without which they cannot grow.

Proteins are made up of amino-acids. Different foods contain various proportions of these amino-acids. Meat, fish, eggs and other animal and dairy produce happen to contain all the amino-acids needed for human growth and repair. These 'animal proteins' have therefore come to be known, somewhat misleadingly, as 'first class'.

The term is misleading because it carries with it the implication that 'second class proteins' (the various combinations of amino-acids present in vegetable foods) are somehow inferior. They are not. If a child eats one of these vegetable foods alone, his body will not be able to use those amino-acids to the full because they do not constitute 'complete protein'. But if he eats two or more vegetable foods together, the chances are that the amino-acids in one will be complemented by those in the other so that his body can use them all. Equally, if he eats one of those vegetable foods with even a minute quantity of complete animal protein, the deficiency in the vegetable food will be balanced by the complete range in the animal food and he will again be able to use both.

When you add milk to a child's cereal, grated cheese to his baked potato, or ham to his sandwich, you do not just add a small quantity of protein-rich food to a carbohydrate-rich dish, you add the completing factor which will make that cereal, potato or bread fully usable both for energy and for growth.

Protein-sparing   As we saw earlier, human bodies meet their current energy needs first, out of whatever food is available to them. Only when there is no 'energy gap' do they use specific nutrients for specific purposes, such as growth. A child who is starving, whether in the immediate short-term sense of having used up his current energy reserve, or in the long-term sense of already suffering from malnutrition, will not therefore be able to use protein for growth until or unless he also takes in enough fuel-food, calories, for his immediate needs. Feed such a child a slice of lean meat and his body will break it down, metabolize it, to release energy. The process of this breakdown is extremely inefficient; he will get fewer calories from that slice of meat than he would have obtained from the same weight of bread and he will have received no benefit at all from the fact that the food you offered was animal protein. But give him the bread (or other carbohydrate-rich food) which his body can easily process for immediate energy, *and* some meat, and his body will spare that protein for repair or growth.

This is, of course, the logic of the particular combinations of foods which are traditional in different communities. A hamburger in a bun, fish and chips, or bread and cheese all 'spare' their protein for the body's optimum use by simultaneously ensuring it is an easy source of energy.

It is also the logic behind the high-protein slimming diet. If the slimmer takes almost all his calories in the form of high-protein foods, he will be able to eat more for less weight gain, because those proteins will be processed to fill his energy gap less efficiently than would carbohydrate foods.

Worries about   While a genuine shortage of protein is disastrous to growing children, it is
proteins   exceedingly rare in the western world. Many parents nevertheless worry incessantly about whether their children are getting enough, especially as many small children dislike the most obvious sources such as butcher's meat and fish. Some will always choose to buy a baby cereal which is advertised as 'high protein' even if it is more expensive and less well-liked than another brand. Some continue to push milk down schoolchildren who are already fat, because they cannot believe that without that magic potion there could be enough protein in the diet. A good many create eating problems out of this anxiety because they are always pushing the child to eat 'high-protein' foods which he dislikes while holding back on the 'junky' foods which he prefers. It may help to remember the following points:

'First class' or 'animal' protein is no better for your child than completed protein whether this comes from combinations of cereals, vegetables, pulses and seeds or from tiny quantities of animal protein eaten with vegetable foods.

Meat, fish, eggs, cheese, etc. contain such high concentrations of amino-acids that only tiny quantities are actually needed. The portions of these foods which we commonly serve really do reflect the wealth of our society. Nobody *needs* eight, ten or more ounces of lean meat at one meal. Most of that surplus protein will be inefficiently broken down for energy.

Sausages, fish-fingers, hamburgers, canned infant foods, etc. contain animal protein padded out with cereals and vegetables but the balance of protein to carbohydrate is still entirely adequate. If your child (like many others) prefers his 'meat' in this concealed form, there is nothing nutritionally wrong with it. You may find that a 'Junior Beef Dinner' gives you rather little beef *for your money* but it will give him plenty for his growth and health.

Cheese is a particularly highly concentrated source of animal protein. Many babies and young children are passionate about it if they are given the chance.

Milk is a beautifully balanced food containing plenty of protein but the amino-acids are in the skim not the cream. Products like yogurt are therefore rich in protein while products like butter are not.

Beans, seeds and nuts contain balances of amino-acids which are almost adequate for human growth. While these foods are not always easy to use in a young child's diet (he may choke on roast peanuts and loathe soya beans), dishes which include them are almost always high-protein combinations. Even the much-derided baked bean is good food.

Your child gets protein from unexpected sources. Many widely liked staple foods, such as bread and potatoes, contain low *concentrations* of amino-acids but contribute substantially to the protein in your child's diet because they are items of which he eats a lot at one time.

Many of the items you may frown upon (like cakes and biscuits) contain 'good things' like milk and egg in their recipes. Even some 'junk foods' (*see below*) contribute to his adequate protein intake. Potato crisps, for example, contain quite large amounts of protein. In one dehydrated packetful the child gets the amino-acids from, say, two whole potatoes: a 'helping' he would not have managed if the water had not been removed.

Fats Fats provide the most concentrated source of calories in a human diet. This means that even if you eat a large slice of bread with only a small quantity of butter on it, you may get more calories from the butter than from the bread. Similarly, a fat-free sponge cake will be far lower in calories than a sandwich cake whose recipe is otherwise identical, while a given portion of potatoes will yield about twice as many calories if it is roasted in fat rather than boiled, and about three times as many if it is deep-fried as chips.

Fats do not contribute much more than energy to the diet. There are more nutrients in butter than in refined white sugar, but not many more. Apart from *minute* quantities of essential fatty acids and some fat-soluble vitamins (*see below*), human beings do not actually need any fats at all. Confusion about this sometimes arises because milk is a valuable food, dairy produce is regarded as 'good for you' and therefore butter, cream and things which are made from them are regarded as 'good' too. Apart from the calories (which may or may not be desirable) the 'goodness' of milk is in the skim.

Nevertheless some fats, sensibly used, are useful. They do a great deal to make a diet enjoyable as anyone who has had to follow a totally fat-free diet on medical advice will tell you. They are an integral part of the art of cooking. Their many calories are processed by the body to release energy more slowly than do carbohydrates. Meals which contain some of their calories in the form of fat may therefore seem more satisfying for longer. They will, in fact, produce a slower, steadier and longer-lasting rise in blood-sugar than meals containing all their energy in the form of carbohydrate. While their high concentration of calories makes them a 'fattening' item for someone wanting to eat a normal bulk of food without taking in too much energy, that same high concentration makes them extremely useful in the diet of the person who cannot get through enough bulky foods to meet his energy requirement. Babies, for example, simply could not hold enough skimmed milk to give them the calories they are likely to need. Formulae must contain fats whether they are the dairy fat in the cow's milk from which they were made, or the vegetable oils often added to skimmed milk in modern babyfoods. Athletes would have to eat an extraordinarily bulky diet if they had to meet their very large energy requirements without any fats, while arctic explorers or deep sea fishermen, whose environment and way of life imposes very high energy needs upon them, commonly rely on fats both to enable them to carry and to consume enough calories.

Fats, cholesterol and heart disease

People already suffering from atherosclerosis ('furring up' of the arteries) or known to have high levels of cholesterol in their blood and therefore thought to be especially liable to heart disease, may be put on special diets designed to minimize their intake both of cholesterol itself and of the kinds of fat which lead the body to manufacture cholesterol. Any medically prescribed diet must, of course, be carefully followed. For the rest of us, considerable confusion exists about the whole topic and it will probably continue to exist as new research produces new findings and their interpretation fuels controversy.

Fats are made up of fatty acids, just as proteins are made up of amino-acids. They are commonly classified according to their degree of saturation. 'Saturated' and 'unsaturated' refer to the chemical composition of the fat in terms of whether or not it holds as much hydrogen as it can.
□ Saturated fats tend to increase the level of blood-cholesterol.
□ Mono-unsaturated fats seem to have no effect on blood-cholesterol.
□ Polyunsaturated fats actually lower the level of blood-cholesterol.

Most fats contain various proportions of all three classifications but they are usually referred to by the predominant type. Guidance as to which type of fat should be classified within which group is difficult, because manufacturing processes can alter the balance within any one product (a margarine, for example) while the exact composition of the food offered to an animal intended for slaughter can alter the balance in its fat. Very approximately you can assume that:

Animal fats (including meat fat, egg yolk and dairy fats like butter and cream) are highly saturated. If you are not sure whether a particular cooking fat is of animal or vegetable origin, the fact that highly saturated fats are usually solid at room temperature, where unsaturated ones are not, may help you. This is not a certain guide, though. While some vegetable 'shortenings' are made solid by hydrogenation and therefore lose their polyunsaturates while being made suitable for pastry-making, more recently developed solid margarines and cooking fats are specially treated to retain these cholesterol-lowering qualities.

Vegetable oils (except coconut oil) are low in saturated fat. Peanut and olive oil are classified as mono-unsaturated: they will not add cholesterol but they will not lower the blood-levels either. Safflower, corn, soybean and cottonseed oils are classified as polyunsaturates and will lower cholesterol levels.

If you are not trying to lower blood-cholesterol levels but are simply trying to provide a sensible and healthy diet, the following points may help you both to keep cholesterol levels down and prevent unseen fat adding unwanted calories:

Meat fat is likely to be highly saturated and therefore undesirable in large quantities. Don't make children eat the visible fat they almost all dislike, whether it is the fat of bacon or ham, chops or ill-trimmed casserole meat.

Many dishes are actually improved by ridding them of excess meat fat. If you roast or grill on a rack, much surplus fat can be drained off meats or favourite items like sausages. If you make casseroles and stocks a day ahead, the fat which solidifies on the top can be lifted off before use.

If these methods become a routine part of your cooking, there is no reason to deprive children of the meat fats which they regard as a treat, such as the crispy skin of chicken or the crackling on a roast of pork.

Dairy fats tend to be important *visible* luxuries so that to ban butter, cream and so forth would be a real deprivation. You can cut your family's consumption a long way, without anyone noticing, if you keep down their concealed use in cooking. If your family does not like poly-unsaturated margarine on its bread, for example, you could continue to use butter as a spread but use margarine for cakes, pastry and so forth. Most sauces which require milk can equally well be made with skim as with whole milk, while many dishes which are finished with cream can be made successfully using yoghurt.

Many families serve a good deal of fried food whether they would admit it to a dietician or not. While food which is fried will always be higher in calories than food which is not, using a polyunsaturated vegetable oil rather than lard, margarine or butter, will substantially reduce the family intake of saturated fats and slightly reduce its calories. Vegetable oils can be heated to a higher temperature than animal fats before they burn. Frying which is carried out at a high temperature tends to seal the food rapidly and thus prevent it from absorbing so much fat. Greasy, soggy chips have usually been fried too slowly while fried bread, mushrooms or potatoes, sautéed in butter, can absord truly phenomenal amounts.

Milk is a *food* which happens to be in liquid form. While it is an excellent food, it is one which some families (especially in the United States) misuse. Instead of treating it as a food – and therefore as an integral part of, or replacement for, meals or snacks – it is treated as a *drink* to accompany meals or to quench simple thirst. If milk-drinking is a habit in your family, and you are concerned either about their intake of animal fat or their figures, encourage water or fruit juice instead.

Vitamins and minerals

A human body's use of those major groups of nutrients is largely controlled and regulated by the minute quantities of vitamins and minerals which it takes in at the same time. These essential substances act and interact at a basic biochemical level which is far more complex than most people realize. Everyone knows, for example, that children must have calcium 'for healthy bones and teeth' but few realize that the use which a child's body can make of any calcium available to it is controlled by two sub-groups of vitamin D. Everyone knows that vitamin A is needed to protect normal vision but few realize that it also plays a subtle and far-reaching role in the body's growth system and in the formation and timed release of certain hormones.

There is no shame in being ignorant of the workings of these substances within our bodies. Medical science itself has by no means completed its work, either on the list of dietary elements which are essential or on their modes of action. But it is a pity if, in our ignorance, we succumb to the blandishments of industry and dose ourselves and our children with multivitamins and mineral tonics on the grounds that if a little vitamin A is good for you, more might be better, or that if plenty of vitamin C is recommended, some vitamin E might be good, too. Deficiency diseases kill and maim millions of people every year but they do so in the developing world, where all food is short or where the only food available is an impoverished staple such as cassava or polished white rice. The point is that if people do not get enough of anything to eat they will get neither the basic food blocks nor the vitamins and trace elements which enable their bodies to use them. If they get enough food-calories but without any of those extras, they will have the food blocks but will still not be able to use them to build and maintain healthy bodies. Vitamins and trace elements come with *foods* and where there is an adequate range of foods constantly available, people do not succumb to pellagra, scurvy or beri-beri.

Western adults do not therefore have to worry about a vitamin and mineral intake which will prevent disease and would be better advised not to go looking for one which will miraculously improve good health. Those who try to discover *exactly* what they should have of *everything* are asking for a crystal ball rather than for available information.

If you do go to your doctor seeking an 'ideal' regime of vitamins and trace elements, he cannot honestly do more than suggest that you take a 'good mixed diet' (*see below*) and, should he see any clinical reason to do so, make specific tests to ensure that you have no specific deficiencies.

Take that familiar necessity, iron, as an example. Nutritional tables will tell you how much daily iron is suggested in the average diet for your nutritional group. If you decide to work out whether you are getting that much, by checking the iron content of all your foods, you may well find that your diet, *on paper*, falls short. If you chase off to the doctor for a prescription for iron, he will almost certainly tell you that you are not iron-deficient. If you demand to know how this can be, he will not be able to give you a straightforward and logical answer. It may be that you have excellent iron stores and therefore do not need that average recommendation which is for everyone's safety and, therefore, must cover exceptionally high needs in some. It may be that your calculations of the iron in your diet are wrong (did you remember that curry powder?). It may be that the traces of iron you are getting are in a form which your body can absorb efficiently whereas much dietary iron is simply excreted. If you were suffering from iron-deficiency anaemia, your general health would be affected and your doctor would quickly diagnose, and prescribe for, the trouble. But if you are not clinically short of iron there is no possible benefit in taking extra whatever your reading of the dietary calculations may suggest. Crossly sidestepping your doctor and buying yourself an 'iron-tonic' over the counter will do you no good at all.

Industries exist primarily to make money. Those which manufacture, advertise and sell vitamins, minerals, tonics and other 'health products', are no exception. In recent years public concern over health has peaked and industry has cashed in. There are thousands of products available and families spend millions on them every year. Before you join in, think:

No 'tonic' can truly give you happiness, beauty, virility or health unless it contains something your body is actually short of. While it may be less damaging to take vitamins than tranquillizers when life seems hard, either one is a pseudo-escape from mood or misfortune which would be better faced and dealt with.

Families which dose themselves tend to produce children who expect a pill for everything. We already rely too much on drugs and too little on ourselves and each other.

Belief in these 'health miracles' leads some people to ignore real symptoms which should be reported to a doctor. Men who become impotent can usually be helped, but not by vitamins. Elderly people who become senile need medical care not miracles. Children who lack energy may be physically or emotionally ill, but in neither case will a 'tonic' help.

Overdosage with certain vitamins is actually dangerous. Too much vitamin A or D, for example, is at least as bad for your child as too little. Furthermore, the more bottles of such pills you have around your house, the greater the chance that a child will accidentally overdose himself with something which can be lethal, like iron (*see* **Accidents/Poisoning**. *See also* **Safety**/In the home: Safety with medicines).

Leaving paper-calculations about quantities strictly alone, there are nevertheless a very few vitamins and minerals which may be scarce *in the particular diets of particular groups of children*. Supplementation or an improvement in diet may be sensible for these, but you should always consult your doctor or health visitor if you think that this applies to a child within your family.

Vitamins and minerals for breast-fed babies

Your milk will contain everything your baby needs for the first four to six months at least, provided that:

□ You are well.

□ Your own diet is adequate and mixed.

□ You are not a heavy smoker, drinker or regular drug-taker.

□ You are not trying to follow a slimming diet as well as losing to your baby the extra fat your body laid down during pregnancy, in order to be able to make milk.

Iron. Breast milk contains very little and some doctors will recommend iron-drops. Others believe that that trace of iron is so well-absorbed that it is enough. Follow advice.

Vitamins A, D and C. The requirement for these vital vitamins during periods of rapid growth is so high that many doctors recommend routine supplementation for all infants.

Fluoride. Fluoride has now been conclusively shown to help strengthen teeth against decay. Fluoride passes poorly into breast milk, so even in an area where the water naturally contains an adequate amount, a supplement at this stage may be advisable (*see* **Teeth**/The formation of teeth).

Vitamins and minerals for bottle-fed babies

When bottle-fed babies were given diluted and sweetened cow's milk they urgently required additional iron and vitamins A, D and C. Now every bottle-fed baby should instead be receiving a properly manufactured and carefully reconstituted formula and many of these are already fortified. It is essential that you check the *actual formula you are using* with your doctor or health visitor so that you can be properly advised on whether or not your baby requires any extras. This is especially important with respect to vitamin D (*see below*) as a fully-fortified formula plus a full dose of supplementary vitamin drops could, just possibly, amount to a dangerous overdose.

Fluoride. If formula is being made up with water in a high-fluoride area, the baby may not require any extra. Check.

Vitamins, minerals and weaning

When your baby drinks 'ordinary milk' instead of breast milk or formula he loses the perfection of the one and the fortification of the other.

Some weaning foods (such as baby cereals) are highly fortified with vitamins and minerals. These foods are extremely useful. The baby is most unlikely to eat such large quantities as to make supplementary vitamins A, D and C undesirable, but their regular consumption may well meet his needs for iron and other trace elements.

Vitamins and minerals from weaning to school age

These are years of rapid growth and often of capricious appetite and 'eating problems'. Even where a lack of vitamins A, D and C cannot be demonstrated in the diet, many people consider that their supplementation is a valuable safety-precaution which will do no child any harm, and will do the few who might otherwise suffer from deficiency, a great deal of good.

● Remember that overdosage of vitamins A and D is *dangerous*. Give only the recommended dose and lock away your supply.

Children who
may be at risk
of rickets

Rickets is a disease in which the bones do not grow and harden properly. Limb bones may be deformed because they are too soft to carry the child's weight; the bones of the skull may be slow to join up so that the fontanelles remain open for an unusually long time; the spine may be bent or twisted while the teeth may be soft and particularly liable to decay.

Such a 'classic' case of rickets would be unusual in a western country, but lesser degrees of the disorder are not nearly as rare as most people suppose.

Proper bone-formation requires that the body receive adequate amounts of minerals such as calcium and phosphorus (which usually occur together in the same foods) *together with* quantities of vitamin D which will enable it to absorb and use those minerals. If a child has adequate intakes of both, there will be no problem. If he has very inadequate supplies of either one he will be at risk. If he has just-adequate supplies of either one then other factors which can affect his body's readiness to absorb what little is available may tip the balance either way.

Calcium. The main source for most children is milk and the many dairy products and manufactured foods which contain milk. In Britain and some other western countries, flour and therefore the bread made from it, are, at present, compulsorily fortified with calcium and other minerals. A scarcity of calcium in the diet is therefore unlikely. However, that diet may make it more or less easy for the body to use the calcium it takes in. For example: wholegrains contain a substance called phytate which prevents the absorption of calcium by forming with it insoluble calcium phytate in the intestine.

Where wholegrain flour is made into a risen bread, using yeast, some of the phytate is inactivated. But where such flour is used to make un-leavened bread (such as chapattis) or where wholegrains are eaten as cereals, the phytate may hold onto enough of the otherwise-available calcium to render a rather low intake too low. It is thought that a high phytate intake may contribute to rickets in some communities which eat wholegrain chapattis to the exclusion of all white flour or risen bread. It may possibly contribute to the risk of rickets in families who eat a vegan diet (*see below*) and whose children therefore receive no calcium from milk and dairy produce. It might do so in a health-conscious family which deliberately kept 'fattening' dairy foods to a minimum, and preferred wholegrains to refined foods.

Vitamin D. The only concentrated dietary sources are fatty fish (sardine and tuna, for example) and fish oils. There are traces of the vitamin in dairy produce and some foods (such as margarine in Britain and margarine and milk in America) are fortified with it, but it would still be difficult to provide for a young child's needs from his diet alone.

Human bodies can produce vitamin D when bare skin is exposed to sunlight and it is through this process that most people obtain enough. But there can be difficulties:

Dark skin evolved to protect people from tropical sun and can 'protect' them too well from weaker northern sun. A dark-skinned child will (all other things being equal) manufacture less vitamin D during an English summer than his pale-skinned friend. When winter comes and sunshine is rare, his stores may be inadequate.

Skin cannot make vitamin D if it is not exposed to that sunshine. Regular exposure even of the face and hands may be enough, especially for a white child, but any child who is kept indoors almost all the time (perhaps because his mother is newly arrived from a society where women traditionally stay indoors) may make too little vitamin D.

The sun's rays cannot be effective through heavy atmospheric pollution. Even a fair child who spends quite a lot of time out of doors may fail to make sufficient vitamin D if he lives in the overcrowded centre of a city which is liable to smog (*see* **Pollution**: Air pollution).

A shortage of vitamin D is a more frequent cause of rickets in the western world than is a shortage of calcium. If yours is a fair-skinned child who spends a lot of time out of doors wearing minimal clothes because there is lots of sunshine, he is most unlikely to be short of the vitamin. But since none of us can lay on sunshine on demand, and few of us can induce in our children a passion for herrings, a daily supplement throughout early childhood is probably sensible.

● Too much vitamin D is exceedingly dangerous, leading to hypercalcemia in which extra bony deposits are laid down. Give only the dose prescribed by the doctor or health visitor and keep tablets safely locked away.

Children who might need extra iron

Most of the children who are at all likely to run short of iron will be under medical care already. They may include premature babies (born without adequate stores from the mother); children with certain biochemical disorders leading to abnormal loss of iron, and any child who has had severe haemorrhage.

Regular bleeding without illness sometimes leads to iron deficiency. The most usual in young children is a marked tendency to nosebleeds. Older girls whose iron stores were only just adequate at the menarche occasionally become anaemic during the first few months of menstruation, especially if this is extra-heavy (which is rare).

If you have any reason to think your child might need extra iron, seek a doctor's advice rather than buying over the counter. Many types of iron are quite unused by the body, being simply excreted. If your child is to benefit from a supplement it must be of a type his body can absorb.

● Overdosage of iron is dangerous and often fatal.

Children who might be in need of almost anything

The more severely the diet is restricted the more possible it is that some important vitamin or mineral will be lacking. The younger the child the more likely it is that such a lack will matter.

If you impose a severely limited diet on your child (*see below* When the diet is restricted) check it out with your doctor first. If, for example, you are vegetarian and prefer to exclude dairy produce and eggs as well as actual meat and fish, your child may need supplements of extra vitamins (such as B_{12}) which are thought only to come from animal sources.

If your child is placed on a severely limited diet by a doctor, make sure that his supervision of the child's disorder includes follow-up supervision of what he may eat. When the possibility of allergy is being investigated, for example, a child is sometimes limited to a very few items of food, but the limitation lasts for only a few weeks and therefore does no harm. But in biochemical disorders, a strict diet may be needed for years and therefore the implications for normal growth may be considerable.

If your young child puts himself on a severely limited diet the chances are high that it will include at least small quantities of a wide enough range of foods to supply his needs. But keep on with his regular supplement of vitamins A, D and C and, if you are worried, list what he takes and check it with your doctor.

If an older child puts herself on a severely limited diet, the chances are that it will not last for long. A few weeks' 'slimming' will do her no harm. If it should last for months and lead to major weight loss, so that the total amount of food she is taking is clearly inadequate for her body's needs, consider the possibility of slimmer's disease (*see* **Anorexia Nervosa**).

Vitamin C: the vitamin from which we might all benefit

Although a clinical deficiency of vitamin C (scurvy) is almost unheard-of in western societies it is possible that many people take in less than their bodies could use. Vitamin C does not only protect against the effects of deficiency, it also positively contributes to a variety of healthy processes, ranging from the conversion of certain carbohydrates to energy and the metabolism of some proteins, to the formation of the connective tissue through which wounds heal. Some people believe that it also contributes to the body's defence against everyday infections.

Vitamin C cannot be stored by the body so that continual supplies are needed: any normal surplus is simply excreted. While it is widely distributed in fruits and vegetables it is often destroyed by modern food processing, storage and cooking. If you are going to spend money on foods which you serve largely for their richness in vitamin C, you might as well ensure that what was in the food when it left the ground is still available when it reaches your family.

● A few years ago it became fashionable to take mega-doses of vitamin C on the grounds that it *might* help to ward off colds and that even if it did no good it could do no harm. There is now some evidence to suggest that regular overdoses of the vitamin may predispose some people to form kidney stones.

Vitamin C is water-soluble and partly destroyed by heat. Soaking a vegetable takes some away: wash and dry or merely wipe clean when possible. Every time you boil and drain a vegetable you pour most of the vitamin C down the sink. Cook rapidly in as little water as possible and try to use that in soup or gravy. Canned vegetables will still have some vitamin C after processing but most of it will be in the canning liquid: use that if you can.

Stewing fruits and serving them in their juice preserves much of the vitamin C: the fact that the fruits are acid prevents the heat from breaking so much of the vitamin down.

Most vegetables and fruits have most of the vitamin directly under the skin. The less you peel the better. Potatoes, in particular, are an unexpectedly good source if cooked in their skins. The apples which are many children's favourite fruit and only raw food, will have far more vitamin C if eaten skin and all.

Vegetables gradually lose vitamin C during storage, especially in sunlight and once cut or broken. Obviously the fresher the better, but if you have no control over harvesting, at least avoid vegetables which have been displayed in the open air; avoid buying more than you can use within a day or two and avoid chopping, etc. until you are ready to cook or eat.

Frozen vegetables and fruits are usually processed while very fresh and vitamin C is unaffected by very low temperatures. These items may therefore be better sources than 'fresh' produce which has travelled the continent and been in the shop for days.

Dried and dehydrated fruits and vegetables have usually been heat-processed and will, therefore, contain little vitamin C unless, as with potatoes, the vitamin has been added at the end.

Easy extra sources of vitamin C include:
- Oranges and other citrus fruits and their (freshly squeezed) juices. The skin protects from light and the fact that we eat them raw protects from heat and water.
- Frozen juices or 'whole fruit' or 'natural fruit' juices are just as good.
- Salads – including many other vegetables than lettuce and tomatoes – are obvious sources but may be disappointingly low in the vitamin if they have been pre-prepared and are wilting.
- Tomatoes and (freshly prepared or commercially frozen) juice.

'Sources' of vitamin C which may mislead you include:
- 'Fruit' drinks which are not actually made of fruit at all;
- Green vegetables which have been kept hot in steam tables, etc.;
- Processed items which may be somewhat misleadingly advertised such as 'vegetable soup, full of natural goodness' and 'whole-fruit jam'.

Why a 'mixed diet' is a good diet

When parents consult health professionals about food for a child after weaning, they are usually told that he should have a 'good mixed diet'. If they are brave enough to ask further what such a diet should consist of, they are likely to be told to make sure that he has meat or fish once a day, an egg or some cheese every day, plenty of green vegetables and fresh fruit, with bread, potatoes and cereal to 'fill him up'. There is nothing whatsoever the matter with such a diet except that very few small children want to eat it, not every parent wants to serve it and the implication is that unless it is complete, it will be inadequate. The moment it becomes clear that the child hates beef, refuses egg and will eat only peas as a 'green vegetable', the wretched parents begin to feel that they are doing wrong. Quite soon they also feel that the child is doing wrong. Feeding problems are then almost inevitable (*see below* Commonsense about family eating).

The real point about that 'good mixed diet' is not that it is essential but that it should be easy. If you can provide a child with a wide range of foods in different combinations and permutations, meal by meal, day by day and month by month, you will never have to worry, or even think, about whether or not he is getting the 'right' things to eat. A mixed diet ensures adequate nutrition in a number of ways:

Different foods provide different nutrients and therefore compensate for each other's deficiencies or excesses. At its simplest level this may mean that a low-calorie main course (a salad, perhaps) is balanced by the accompanying potatoes or by the pie which follows for dessert. At a more technical level, that salad will provide plenty of vitamin C so that the fact that there is none left in those well-boiled potatoes or in that processed pie-filling does not matter.

Different foods enable the body to make full use of important nutrients. Your child's body may need protein but it may also need energy-food, right now. If you served that salad with cold meat, adding neither the potatoes nor the fruit pie, he would probably process the meat for its energy. By making sure that there is enough carbohydrate and/or fat to meet his energy gap, you ensure that the protein in that meat can be used to its best effect.

You cannot know exactly what nutrients your child needs at any given moment or on any given day but by offering him a mixture you ensure that he will meet those needs, for himself. Furthermore, if he always has a sufficiency of everything available, he will retain the stores of nutrients which help him to meet particular physical demands.

Different kinds of *meal* are important, too. Working out what nutrients may be missing from, or dangerous substances added to, processed or convenience foods is exceedingly difficult (*see below*). The easy way to be sure that you neither deprive a child of anything important nor feed him damaging quantities of anything, is to mix your use of such foods into meals made from fresh ones. A diet made up entirely of take-away fast-foods and frozen television dinners might not be good for him, but as part of a mixture such meals will certainly do no harm.

Different kinds of *cooking* contribute to that mixture. If almost everything you serve is fried, for example, your family will consume a lot of fat (including oil) and whatever else the diet is like, it will be high in calories for its bulk, so the child may get fat. But if you use the same foods but sometimes fry, sometimes grill, sometimes roast, sometimes boil and sometimes bake them, there will be a far better balance. Similarly, if every vegetable you serve is boiled for ten minutes in plenty of water and then drained, very few of their vitamins will reach the child because they will have gone down the sink. Boil them sometimes, by all means, but if you sometimes stir-fry or casserole them and sometimes serve them raw, vitamin-rich meals will balance the rest.

When the diet is restricted

Some children refuse to eat a completely mixed diet (*see below* Eating problems) while others cannot be offered one. The more restricted your child's diet, the more you will have to think about the items you do serve in order to be sure that his body can find what it needs from amongst them.

Important nutrients are so widely dispersed among different foods that a child who omits particular *items* – even if they add up to a lot of items – will seldom present any nutritional problem. It is when the diet excludes whole categories of types of food that difficulty can arise. For example:

A vegetarian diet presents no problem at all

Meat, fish and the products made from them are not a large enough food category to matter. There are many other sources of protein and, with dairy produce permitted in the diet, a vegetarian need not even search for combinations of vegetable proteins which always complement each other. He can eat vegetables and cereals and, with milk and cheese and egg in the diet, you can be sure that all will be well. Many people believe that a good vegetarian diet is actually healthier than an omnivorous one. Certainly many vegetarian families do tend to serve more varied food than those who unthinkingly rely on meat-and-two-veg.

A vegan diet can be healthy but needs some thought

Once dairy produce and eggs are eliminated as well as meat and fish, the child receives no animal protein at all and must therefore obtain all the protein he needs for adequate growth from a rich mixture of cereals, pulses, nuts, vegetables and fruits. If problems do arise, this is usually because such a diet tends to be low in calories for its bulk. The child therefore has to eat a comparatively large quantity of food in order to get the energy he needs and leave enough over for growth. On the whole, research shows that such children do grow healthily but that they are lighter for their height than vegetarian or omnivorous children: they can seldom eat enough to lay down a surplus as fat.

The possibility of protein shortage during that critical first year, when the baby will not eat/digest large quantities of bulky vegetable foods, can be averted by lengthy breast-feeding. Thereafter, you may find that soya beans or products made from textured soya protein are a great help.

A diet containing no animal food is likely to be low in vitamins A, D and B_{12}. Unless supplementation is against your principles, the child should receive these vitamins throughout his early life. If it is against your principles you will need to discuss the matter with your doctor or health visitor.

A fruitarian diet cannot support adequate growth

Some vegan families wish to restrict their diet even further by omitting cooked vegetable and cereal foods, relying entirely on raw fruits. Even if there is sufficient money available to buy a wide range of fruits both in and out of season, such a diet is not suitable for growing children. Fruits contain such low concentrations of proteins that impossibly large quantities would have to be consumed for a child to obtain his needs. If some nuts and seeds are permitted the proteins available to him will be increased, but his needs will still not be met because such foods are comparatively indigestible in the raw state.

Zen macro-biotic diets are unsuitable for children

Although the exact diets vary, these all share in a deliberate attempt to reduce the body's intake of foodstuffs to a bare minimum necessary for continued activity and survival. A child has to do more than survive: he also has to grow and he will not do so on brown rice alone.

• Parents whose beliefs lead them to offer an unusually restricted diet to their children should consult a health professional at the earliest possible moment; preferably as soon as the pregnancy is recognized and certainly before any attempt to wean the child from the breast is considered. Early consultation will almost always mean that the child's healthy growth can be ensured within the framework of his parents' beliefs and that professionals will take a great deal of trouble to find ways in which this can be done. It is when a child has already had his health impaired by an unsuitable diet that doctors sometimes have to suggest dietary additions which the parents find unacceptable, and it is when they are faced with a child who is suffering that such professionals may tend to seem less than respectful of the parents' convictions.

If a restricted diet is medically prescribed

The prescribing doctor or dietician should certainly work out with you the full implications. A diet designed to maintain a careful balance between carbohydrates and insulin in diabetes, for example, should present no additional problems provided you fully understand the freedom with which one carbohydrate-rich food may be exchanged with another. A diet to exclude the gluten in wheat and its flour may be rather more difficult because so many manufactured foods contain wheat flour. But again, full information should make it clear that the child still has available to him a very wide range of foods. In all such circumstances, it is important that you find and stay in contact with a professional whom you both trust and find it easy to get along with. The problems presented by the diet will change as the child grows and changes, and the information you will need will be extremely down-to-earth. You do not only need lectures on the nature of carbohydrate metabolism: you need to know 'what else can I give him for supper?' and 'what shall I do about school meals?' and 'can he have his favourite breakfast cereal?' . . .

If money is very short

Remember that a diet can be restricted in the sense of excluding luxury or 'treat' foods without being at all restricted in the dietary sense. Your child may yearn for iced biscuits, bought pies, fun snacks and canned fruits, but while his morale may suffer if he cannot have them, his diet need not. Feeding a family adequately on very little money is most difficult when poverty goes (as it so often does) with lack of time and lack of decent cooking facilities. If you are living in one room and working all the hours the nursery will keep your child, you *need* the convenience of convenience foods and you cannot search the street markets for cheap foods nor undertake the long, slow cooking which will turn them into highly nutritious dishes.

Perhaps the most useful point to remember is that *enough calories are the prime essential* because without them the child's body will not use the meat you can ill-afford. Do remember, too, that *western staples, like bread and potatoes, are good foods* much maligned by those with their minds on slimming rather than eating. Your child will be better off with enough of these to satisfy his appetite, together with small quantities of cheese, milk and so forth, than with small portions of 'better quality' foods which leave him perpetually hungry.

Commonsense about family eating

It is easy to write about food and eating in an easygoing and objective way. It is far more difficult to behave that way when faced with the realities of feeding a family. Food is not only a biological necessity and a physical pleasure, it is also highly emotional stuff; a symbol of love from the mother who prepares it; a symbol of acceptance or rejection of that love by the child who eats it or spits it out; a symbol of the unity of the family gathered round the meal table or of rejection of that unity by the adolescent who leaves a vacant place. But while it is often helpful to recognize these emotional aspects of family eating, it is vital to keep them under control: to keep the practical business of eating as separate as you can from more complex concerns. The more you can do so, the less likely it is that yours will be a family which is beset by 'eating problems'.

Keep eating separate from morals and ethics

Everyone has a right to their own moral and ethical convictions. If you are convinced vegetarians you will obviously feed your family a vegetarian diet and you may try to convert your omnivorous friends from their meat-eating. But when you do so, be clear that you are arguing with them about ethics rather than about diet. They are not poisoning their children's bodies by giving them fish-fingers, whatever you may think they are doing to their minds.

This kind of confusion between ethics and nutrition bedevils us at many levels and makes it difficult to see the wood of real issues for the lobbyists' trees. Confusion exists, for example about:

'Natural' foods. There is a great deal to be said for foods which are 'natural' in the sense that they are grown in their own time and place and sold to us with nothing added and nothing taken away. Some such foods are nutritionally superior to their processed counterparts. Rice, for example, loses its B vitamins when it is polished and gains nothing. Some foods are different in the natural form but the loss or gain is not absolute: whether you want the natural or the refined/processed form depends on what you want from that food. Flour is the obvious example. The most 'natural' flour is simply ground wholewheat. It contains more B vitamins and more roughage than refined white flour, but the white provides more usable calcium. Wholewheat flour can be cooked in some very interesting ways but will not make a good sponge cake. White flour makes boring, cottonwool bread but will rise to the occasion of that sponge. The choice is yours; the variety is available but to state, as a matter of conviction, that one kind of flour is superior to another is idiotic.

Most of the foodstuffs which are available in 'natural' as well as processed forms differ only in taste and not at all in nutritional value. War-time dried egg, for example, contained all the nutrients of real eggs yet nobody could be blamed for preferring the 'natural' thing. Most people would similarly rather eat a real potato than a helping of dried mashed (even if it does have added vitamin C), and most of us would select a locally grown strawberry rather than a squashy bright pink thing out of a can. Since eating is meant to be pleasurable, taste is an excellent reason for buying one kind of food rather than another, provided we admit that we buy for the taste rather than because 'natural' food is, in some vaguely moralistic way, 'better'.

Naturalness-for-its-own-sake, divorced from nutritional superiority or more enjoyable taste, makes the arguments silly. Some people will tell you, for example, that you should use only coarse brown sugar, never refined white. Why? There are plenty of arguments against using too much sugar of any kind but if you are going to use sugar, you might as well use the kind you prefer. The minute traces of minerals left in brown sugar and removed in the final refining which whitens it, make no useful contribution to diet, nor is that brown sugar any more 'natural' than sugar which has been processed through just that final stage.

Sometimes the arguments about 'natural' foods get confused with morals in a different way. People will try to persuade you to spend extra money to buy free-range rather than battery-produced eggs. Fine if you think they taste different; the nutrient value is the same. The persuaders are probably really thinking about the miserable lifestyle of those battery hens but if they are, they should say so. It is for you to decide whether or not to operate a personal ban on intensive farming.

Try not to let the slogans of the health food industry convince you that anything bought in their stores will be 'good for you' and that anything bought in a supermarket will not. You will find manufactured goods on those shelves which are just as elaborately processed as anything in the supermarket and a great deal more expensive. If your baby *likes* 'natural muesli' (and you can afford it) fine, if not, remember that it is only food and there are plenty of other enriched and nourishing cereals available.

Organically grown foods. Since there is no non-organic way to grow anything this is a pretty silly phrase, but it is usually taken to mean that the plant concerned has been grown without artificial fertilizers or insecticides or fungicides. It is supposed to taste like the food you might pick from your garden and it may. Once again, if you like the organically grown vegetables which are available to you, can afford the higher prices and the time it takes to remove those natural blemishes, fine. If none are available or you cannot, your family's diet will not be nutritionally affected in any measurable way. You may bitterly regret our society's use of highly dangerous pesticides and long to ban all such substances from your family's diet, but unless you really can grow *all* your own food you do not have that option. However many organically grown cauliflowers you buy, the family will still be eating mass produced and imported items in all their other foods.

Some people feel very strongly about the risks which intensive methods of agriculture impose upon us all. Lists of pesticides in current use make terrifying reading and, when one realizes that some of the most dangerous are used because they make it possible for manufacturers to increase already vast profit margins, it is easy to become morally outraged. But there is another side to the story. Without methods of this kind, the world would be even shorter of food than it already is. There are already too many people on this planet for Nature to provide without help from Technology. If we must have a moral dimension to this argument at all, world hunger must surely be the overriding one.

Food-additives. Some of the chemicals which are added to manufactured and processed foods are valuable additions to a family's diet. The fortification of flour, for example, much increases the nutrient value of the bread which is our staple food. The addition of vitamins to margarine makes some 'difficult' ones easy to provide, while the vitamin C which is added to many commercially prepared 'fruit drinks' makes a cheaper product nutritionally equivalent to the fresh juices which many families cannot afford. We cannot legitimately scorn all additives if we are considering nutrition rather than principle.

Many types of food-additives are certainly undesirable but even these usually have something to be said for, as well as against, them. Some of the most obviously worrying are:

Drugs given to animals to speed up growth, weight gain, egg laying . . . so that they reach marketable size faster and for less expenditure on their food, housing, etc. or so that hens come into lay or turkeys reach marketable sizes at convenient times, such as just before Christmas. The use of hormones and antibiotics, for example, is highly controversial and almost certainly damaging (*see* **Infection**/Treatment of infections which cause illness: Problems in antibiotic use).

Preservatives used to increase the shelf-life of a vast range of manufactured foods. Without some preservatives modern food production would be impossible – those 'sell by' dates would have to be today or tomorrow; there could be no 'long-life' products and items ranging from packet soups to custards and jams could no longer be stocked weeks ahead either in shops or homes. Some items of food, such as sausages, bacon and cooked ham, which are now safe if they are handled properly, would become very risky, too. The nitrites which are added to preserve them may be risky, but they prevent the growth of some extremely dangerous food-poisoning organisms (*see* **Diarrhoea, Gastro-enteritis and Food Poisoning**/Botulism). The risks of food which has 'gone bad' have to be balanced against the risks of the chemicals which stop it deteriorating. There are three parties to any argument. Manufacturers, while it would clearly not be in their interests to poison us all, are primarily concerned to maximize their profits and will therefore tend to use as much of the most effective cheap preservative as their product needs, to take a good share of the market. Consumers want their food to be safe and well-preserved and as cheap as possible. Public health watchdogs want to strike a proper balance. Perhaps it should be their role to educate consumers as well as to control manufacturers. If we want food in which fewer and safer preservatives are used, we shall have to be prepared to shop more frequently, to refrigerate more food items and to pay more.

Colourings and flavourings are used in an extraordinarily wide range of foods and there is no doubt that some are dangerous. Rows blow up from time to time in one country or another when yet another such chemical is shown to cause cancer in laboratory animals or skin rashes in human consumers. Unfortunately there is seldom agreement amongst the experts as to the balance of risks surrounding one particular chemical. Saccharin, for example, has come under fire in the United States but is still permitted in British foods and for open sale as a sugar-substitute. Too much sugar is fattening/bad for teeth and dangerous to certain groups of people such as diabetics, so some artificial sweeteners are perhaps needed. On the other hand, nobody would want to use a sweetener they knew to be dangerous: it would be better to go without the sweetness. The point is that the balance is one which should be struck with regard only to human health and welfare; it is worrying when such decisions are clearly made with an eye to the commercial world.

Many colourings and flavourings seem completely unnecessary. But are they? Would we, the consumers, really buy and eat canned strawberries if they were not dyed that rich pink colour but were left the sickly cream shade they naturally become after canning? Would we pay for our orange jelly the kind of money that it would cost if it contained only the flavour of real orange juice? Would we settle for canned soups which all tended to be mud-coloured whether they were called 'tomato' or 'mixed vegetable' and what would your children say about pale baked beans? Most natural colours and flavours *could* be intensified in such products by using concentrates of the actual foodstuff, but they would be very, very much more expensive. Part of the problem is that we have become accustomed to brightly coloured food and have allowed our children to expect brilliant iced biscuits and lurid soft drinks. Part of it is that we expect to eat cheaply foods which are out of season and/or native to quite another country and/or not really suitable for the purposes to which they are put. Banana custard, for example, takes a lot of fresh bananas if it is to have much taste; its natural colour is greyish. If we want strongly flavoured yellow custard we invite synthetics . . . Commonsense about family eating suggests some middle-of-the-road ways in which individuals can cope with the nutritional aspects of this kind of dilemma:

Concentrate on that *mixed* diet so that children do not consume daily portions of anything except basic foods. If there are antibiotics in veal, dangerous pesticides in fruits and a clutch of risky colours and flavours in soft drinks, they are far less likely to harm the child who only eats each occasionally, than the child who drinks the same fizzy potion twice a day for months on end.

Look carefully at the diet of a child who *is* hooked on a few particular food items to the exclusion of all else. Fizzy drinks are, perhaps, an unnecessary indulgence. You could stop buying them or try using simple soda water with fresh fruit juice. The child who eats baked beans twice a day will certainly be getting more of whatever is in those cans than the manufacturers *or* health officials expect, so, if you cannot wean him off them, it might be worth trying him with your own home-made version or at least ringing the changes among brand names.

Try, perhaps, to bring up children with some knowledge of what foods *really* look like and taste like so that without being moralistic about it you discourage the view that a cereal which is not rainbow coloured must be boring. A child who has eaten locally grown asparagus with pleasure will not expect all asparagus to be bright green while a child who has been allowed to be a connoisseur of fresh apples will find many commercially produced 'apple juices' and 'apple pie fillings' unnaturally strong.

Leave artificial flavours and colours out of foods you prepare at home so that your gravies taste of the meat they are to accompany rather than of 'stock cubes' and your coffee pudding tastes of coffee rather than of coffee-concentrate.

Where you really must have artificial aids – in icing a birthday cake, for example – use vegetable food colourings rather than artificial ones.

If you want to campaign about these issues, remember that your lobbying will be far more effective if it is directed towards strengthening the power of the public health authorities, so that they can be as free as possible of commercial or political interference, than if it takes the form of a private family ban on this, that or the other food item of which you have become suspicious. This is true of all the above issues: your local producer of battery hens and eggs is not even going to *know* if you refuse to buy his goods and he certainly is not going to care whether you do or not provided that other people go on doing so. He may care, he may even change some of his ways, if you join in a public fuss (*see also* **Pollution**).

Keep eating separate from family discipline

The more relaxed you can be about the food you serve to your family, the more pleasure and the fewer problems you are likely to have over children's eating. Of course this does not mean that children should be given anything they like to eat. A baby or toddler does not even know what he will like because he does not know what there is. Children have to be introduced to, and offered, a range of foods out of which they can make a diet which they will enjoy with good appetite to the benefit of their bodies. The point is that you offer it and let them, as far as possible, select amongst it. You reserve the right to buy, cook and serve what you think fit, but you allow them the right to eat it or not as they think fit.

The basis of most common 'eating problems' is again that we tend to confuse moral issues with nutritional ones; the pleasant need-fulfilling business of eating food with the less-pleasant and entirely social business of table-manners, general behaviour and 'doing what he is told'. Your child must 'learn how to behave' (*see* **Discipline**, **Self-discipline and Learning How to Behave**) and he must nourish his body; he will do each more easily, and with less wear and tear on you, if you keep the two endeavours entirely separate in your mind. The following examples of common meal-time rules and exhortations may help to make the point. A child should:

Eat everything which is put before him

Why? It may be more than he feels like eating; if you push him, you try to make him obey you, rather than his own appetite. Success will not make him more obedient, just fatter. Failure will make a completely unnecessary row and a sadness to replace the pleasure of eating.

It may be food that he dislikes; if you push him you will certainly confirm the dislike so the more 'important' the food, the more unfortunate the pressure.

Taste in food is something to be encouraged: he will broaden his tastes only if he is confident that 'trying a bit' will *not* lead to a row if he then leaves it.

Do you eat food you dislike?

Food is certainly too valuable to waste but it is no less wasteful to throw it away or feed it to the cat *after* a long wrangle than before, and it is surely more wasteful to feed it to a child who does not want it than to pass it on to the teenage sister who is always hungry.

Finish his meat course before being allowed any sweet

Why? That meat course may, or may not, have more food-value than the sweet course; that depends both on what dishes you are offering and what nutrients his body needs. But certainly there is no surer way of making the sweet more desirable than the meat, than pressing him to earn the one he does want by eating what he does not.

Eat green vegetables

Why? There is nothing valuable in green vegetables that is not also available in other foods (*see above*).

Drink milk

Why? After early infancy there is no reason whatsoever why a child should drink milk if he does not like it. Admittedly it is a very convenient item for a child to like, but your convenience and his nutrition are different matters. Nutritionally he can get the same nutrients from things he may like very much indeed, such as yogurt, cheese, puddings and so on.

These are all unnecessary no-win battles. You will not often manage to make him eat what he does not want and when you do, you should not. Trying will make nothing but misery for all. Some other common rules about family eating have rather more sense to them but still need tactful administration and separation from discipline:

Children should eat regular meals

Eating is largely patterned by habit. The child who is accustomed to three meals a day will probably feel hungry at roughly the usual times, but there is no physical necessity for one daily eating pattern rather than another, or for sticking to a pre-arranged schedule if appetite dictates otherwise. Dietetically there is nothing wrong with dividing a day's food intake into two or six parts rather than three.

Eat a good breakfast

This is a difficult one. Studies have clearly shown that children who go to school without having had any breakfast at all tend to flag by mid-morning. Energy-levels and concentration may drop and, if tests are carried out, children's blood-sugar levels (a measure of immediately available calories) are found to be very low. But studies also show that there are many children (and older people, too) who cannot feel hungry within an hour of waking up.

If yours is one of these, try for a compromise rather than for daily rows over the cereals and eggs. Many children will be positively hungry by the time they have made the journey (and the effort) which gets them to school. A cheese sandwich to eat on arrival may be an unconventional 'breakfast' but we are trying to think about diet not convention . . . Some children can comfortably accept plenty to *drink* first thing in the morning even though they cannot comfortably eat. An egg beaten into milk and fruit juice is nutritionally just as good as the breakfast of juice, egg and milk you wanted him to have in the first place.

Avoid eating between meals

Obviously the child who takes in small quantities of food at frequent intervals all through the day is not going to want full-sized meals as well: if he does want them the combination will probably provide more total food than his body needs and therefore make him fat. Apart from this risk, there is nothing dietetically wrong with 'little and often'. Babies often thrive better on such a feeding pattern (as many exhausted parents know!); some toddlers prefer it and some sick children can only keep themselves properly nourished and hydrated on this basis.

Parents who feel morally outraged when a child begs for food between meals are usually worried about him being 'greedy', and concerned that his snacks will consist of 'junk foods' which will fill him up so that he is not hungry for proper, nourishing food.

Greed is a nasty word which we all associate with fat children with sticky mouths and whiny voices. But greed can also be part of hunger and an entirely desirable anticipation of the pleasure of satisfying that hunger with food. If he is hungry, he should feel a little greedy. Greed is only undesirable if the child is not hungry but simply craving for sweets and/or trying to bully you.

Many children do get genuinely hungry between meals. It is a long time from lunch until supper especially if the one was a school meal you disliked or a simple sandwich, and the other is on the late side because both parents work long hours. Adults who feel hungry before a meal is due or ready, think nothing of having a snack to keep them going. You yourself, even as you insist that your child wait until supper-time, may well have been tasting and nibbling this and that as you prepared the meal.

If you accept that your child may be hungry between meals (rather than 'just greedy') and if you also accept that if he is hungry it is right that he should have something to eat, you can easily steer a path between indulging greed and satisfying appetite.

Some common-sense 'snack policies'

Accept that your child is usually hungry at this particular time of day (mid-morning, perhaps, or immediately he comes home from school) and cater for him. A planned snack remains in your hands so that it can be anything from a mini-meal to a token gesture. The child who has such a snack is unlikely to keep begging for bits and pieces.

Realize that most of your child's begging comes from a desire for particular things which he only gets between meals – sweets and potato crisps, for example. Control the intake of these (especially if he is getting fat) while still allowing for real hunger, by offering those treat foods as part of *meals* and offering the simpler foods, like bread and butter, milk and apples, when he wants something in between (*see below* Commonsense about 'junk foods'; sweets).

Decide which foods any member of the family may have whenever he is hungry and keep them available. This often works well with older children who are unlikely to raid the fridge for food you were planning to serve tonight, if they know they can help themselves from the biscuit barrel, fruit bowl, or milk supply.

Commonsense about 'junk foods'

Leaving sweets aside for a moment (*see below*), commercially prepared and energetically marketed snack foods cause more trouble than they need in many families. The trouble is again largely due to a confusion between nutrition and morals.

A food is usually regarded as 'junk' when it contains nothing that is nutritionally useful. But be careful. That food will yield calories even if it does not bring with them any useful proteins, minerals or vitamins. 'Empty' calories may not be useless to a body which only requires a quick renewal of its energy supplies. Of course, the child who eats so many of these foods that they fulfil his energy requirement completely will then not want the foods whose calories come with other nutrients; in the long run his diet would suffer. But the child who is just plain hungry, hours before lunch, may be just as well off with 'empty' calories as with more complex nourishment.

By no means all the foods which people call 'junk' do consist of empty calories anyway. That packet of potato crisps has quite a high protein content for its calorie count. That dairy ice-cream may be quite as valuable to the diet as a milk pudding, while a commercially prepared hamburger, complete with all the trimmings, can be a meal in itself. These are *foods*. Most parental dislike of them is really to do with discipline rather than nutrition. Small children beg for them and make us wonder if they are getting spoiled. Schoolchildren spend money on them that was intended for bus fares or the charity collection. Adolescents go in search of them instead of coming home in time for supper . . .

The real indictments of such foods are:

□ That so much money is spent on glamorous packaging and advertising that they are made both more attractive and more expensive than equivalent ordinary foods.

□ That if this leads to them being eaten *as well as* 'ordinary' food they may contribute to obesity.

□ That if they were eaten to the *exclusion of all fresh and raw foods*, they would probably constitute a diet which was high in fats and low in vitamins – especially vitamin C.

□ That this group of foods, probably more than any other group, tends to be loaded with artificial colourings and flavourings.

But none of this makes these foods something to be avoided at all costs; something which it is somehow morally wrong to eat. It just makes them foods which, like all other foods, should be eaten in sensible moderation well mixed in with a varied diet.

Commonsense about sweets

If people never ate sweets they would have fewer holes in their teeth (*see* **Teeth**). There is no doubt about this. From the point of view of dental health it is a great pity that any clever manufacturer ever thought of marketing refined sugar made into pretty coloured, flavoured shapes. But manufacturers did think, and now families have to think for themselves about how to manage the existence of sweets. You certainly cannot get rid of them. Clearing up some factual points may make a good start:

Sweets are more or less pure refined sugar. Some (real chocolate, not chocolate-flavoured candy, for example) have a few nutrients in them, but basically they are calories with additives. From the dietetic point of view they can be regarded as just the same as other 'junk' foods. Apart from their effect on teeth, they are neither better nor worse.

Refined sugar produces acid in the mouth and makes the ideal environment for breeding of the bacteria which are in the plaque on teeth. These bacteria are the cause of dental decay.

All **refined sugar products have this effect.** Sweets are worse for your child's teeth than cake or sweetened cereal only to the extent that the sugar clings more closely to the teeth and remains longer in the mouth. Plain cake, washed down with a glass of milk, may leave less sugar around than a sweet, but a slice of sticky parkin may be just as bad as the sweet.

Bacteria do not care where sugar comes from. The sugar in a healthy apple feeds them as sugar from the bowl of sweets does. But the sugar in the apple is less concentrated and the friction it exerts as the child chews will tend to remove most of it quite quickly. Don't make the mistake, though, of banning sweets by replacing them with raisins . . . sweet and sticky, they will not improve dental health.

It follows from all this that some types of sweet will be far worse for your child's teeth than others. Toffees, for example, take a long time to chew and are well worked into the spaces between the teeth in the process. Must he have toffees? Boiled sweets take a long, long time to suck and will be creating that acid environment all the time. Must he have them? He will be better off with Smarties or tiny jelly sweets or anything which is rapidly melted and gone.

Most human beings seem to have an in-built desire for sweet things. New babies, for example, suck harder and for longer on bottles of sugared water than they do on plain water; children doing 'taste tests' usually put the sweetest tastes at the 'best-liked' end of the scale, while our historical ancestors risked a great deal to rob wild bees of the only concentrated sugar then available. The chances are that your child will like sweets, but even if he is not an especially 'sweet-toothed' person, he will almost certainly want sweets because:

Millions of pounds' worth of advertising is devoted each year to ensuring that he does want them. Within those advertising campaigns every trick of the trade is used, from linking sweets with sexy holidays on palm-fringed beaches, to presenting them as symbols of parental love or peer-group popularity. For the youngest age groups, sweets are made into objects which are desirable to look at and to play with as well as to eat. What self-respecting two-year-old will *not* want a dispenser shaped like his favourite television character, even if he does not particularly like the little sweets it pops out?

Distributors ensure that sweets are on show everywhere and especially where young children go with adults and are bored. It is not chance which places the sweet display next to the supermarket queue or the train platform.

Adults use sweets as part of the emotional currency of family life. We give sweets to console disappointed children, to comfort the hurt, reward the brave and praise the successful. We buy them to convey pleasant messages like 'thank you for having me' or 'happy birthday'. We make them an integral part of our festivities and our treats.

If you doubt that this is an important part of 'the sweet problem', ask yourself whether you ever see children whining, begging and bullying for any other kind of food they particularly like. Many children have a passion for strawberries, for example, yet they do not behave over strawberries as they behave over sweets. The fruits just do not have the same emotional importance.

While the very existence of sweets may pose a problem for all of us, they need not create particular problems within your family if you find commonsense ways of handling them. Various families have managed using each of these approaches:

Putting off the time when each child became aware of sweets. You may be able to manage this for two or three years with a first child; probably not so long with a later one. Any length of time is worthwhile for the protection it gives to those first teeth.

Studiously avoiding any emotional loading. Don't give sweets to a toddler who has been 'good' about something; indeed don't give food for this reason at all. Remember the food-is-for-satisfying-appetite approach. You may have to ask other people not to bring sweets as presents and so forth, and of course you will have to make sure that sweets are not playing a part in your adult emotional life. If your child sees his father bringing home chocolates because he is late, you do not stand a chance.

Buying the first sweets which are demanded without obvious reluctance but with the same casual air you would use if he begged to try a new vegetable.

Not keeping sweets in the house – ever – but instead assuming (as you do with other foods) that whatever is bought will be eaten and that there will be no more until the next purchase. This prevents the one-sweet-every-three-minutes-all-evening which is terrible for teeth.

Choosing the least damaging kinds of sweets and giving them neither as extras nor as enormous treats but as part of meals. Try to choose meals after which the child will brush his teeth.

Remembering that for many children *buying* sweets is part of the fun of having them. If he wants to go shopping with his pocket money, suggest some other things (fun-foods and non-foods) which he could buy.

Eating problems

While a commonsense approach to family eating will hopefully prevent most 'feeding problems' amongst those who have plenty of food available, it will not prevent them all. Feeding children is an important part of caring for their physical needs, and physical caring is all mixed up with love so it will never be as easy to be rational about food as the cold print of a book suggests. But if you *are* worried and know that problems are therefore looming, or even if you *have* worried and have therefore allowed problems to begin, it is still worth making the effort to reverse the trend.

Babies and eating problems

Many parents worry ceaselessly about babies' refusal to eat enough or enough of the 'right' things. If you are worried about your baby it is sensible to consult your doctor or clinic immediately. If your worry has any physical foundation it should be identified as soon as possible; but it cannot be emphasized too strongly that the problem is probably yours, not the baby's. If your baby is found to be gaining weight within the (wide) normal limits for his age and physical type and to be normally healthy, energetic and contented, *the food he willingly takes is adequate for him*. Try to accept authoritative reassurance before attempts to push down more food than he wants produces real trouble. Once you have seen your doctor, it may help you to go over the following points.

Most babies whose parents worry over their eating are far from thin; many of them are actually fat. A baby who is neither thin nor failing to gain weight cannot be under-nourished.

Some babies who *are* at the lower end of the normal weight-range or who are gaining weight rather slowly, are particularly active types. Provided your baby is well, this is a positive rather than a negative characteristic.

Many babies who are 'difficult' to feed are being asked to conform to patterns for which they are not ready. Some common ones are:

'Solid' foods in addition to breast milk/formula in the first three to four months of life. Some babies will accept these additions but many will not. No baby (unless your doctor advises you otherwise) *needs* anything but milk in this period.

Feeding times which do not fit in with his own developing patterns of digestion and hunger. Making a small baby wait for feeding, for example, can lead not to increased appetite once the milk is offered, but to so much angry miserable crying that he is too tired to do more than quell his first hunger-pains before he falls into exhausted sleep. Inevitably, a very small feed makes him likely to ask for the next one early, too, and the pattern can become a vicious circle.

Attempts at early weaning and/or early introduction of a cup. Sucking is not only a small baby's natural feeding method, it is also his greatest pleasure. If he is not allowed to suck milk from breast or bottle he will sometimes refuse to drink it at all.

Later in the first year difficulties may be due to adult attempts to make the baby eat their way rather than his. Some examples include:

Not being allowed to partake in the feeding process, by holding onto his own bottle, clutching at the spoon or dabbling in the food. Tidy-feeding often feels like forced-feeding.

Not having his dawning likes and dislikes noted. If he clearly hates spinach or egg yolk, trying to force it down him may lead to a rejection of all solid foods. Sometimes it is texture rather than taste to which the baby objects. Some find the transition from creamy-smooth babyfoods to lumpy toddler-foods very difficult. A few always gag on lumps and enjoy food more if it is *either* smooth *or* finely cut up; never carelessly mashed.

Not having the variability of his appetite from meal to meal or day to day accepted.

Toddlers and eating problems

In the rich west, problems with eating in this age group are closer to the rule than the exception. The basic reason seems to be implicit in the child's stage of development and the effect which the development has on many parents. Toddlers are still highly dependent on adults both for physical and emotional care, yet they have reached a point where that dependence begins to conflict with their drive to grow up and become independent people in their own right. The toddler tends to alternate clinging with demands that the parent should 'Go 'way' or 'let me'. If he is pushed in the direction of independence, he hangs on ever more tightly, but if he is kept too much in the parents' power he fights for his freedom.

Natural functions such as eating, sleeping and excreting, provide the toddler with perfect battlegrounds on which to work out this sort of conflict. The ground is perfect for the toddler both because it is one which no parent can completely ignore (natural functions have to be socialized) and because it is one on which no parent can actually win. You can put your toddler to bed but you cannot force him to sleep. You can put him on a pot or lavatory but you cannot force him either to perform or to tell you when he is going to. You can sit him in front of a meal but you cannot make him eat it.

Since you cannot win it is almost always best for everyone if you do not join battle. But avoiding battles does not just mean not allowing yourself to get angry, and it certainly does not mean 'giving in'. It means resolutely refusing to allow these no-win situations to become issues between you and your toddler. You can teach him to 'do as he is told' however you like (*see* **Discipline, Self-discipline and Learning How to Behave**) but it is disastrous to try and teach this sort of lesson in a situation where it is easily possible for him to defy you.

Unfortunately, refusing to be drawn into battle is far more easily said than done because these issues are important to daily life and therefore you will care about them. A toddler who is spoiling for a fight about something will not be slow to realize that you care, and to exploit the fact. All you have going for you is your much greater cleverness and experience. By using these you may be able to prevent your toddler from spotting the fight-potential of the meal-table.

Try, from the very beginning, to treat his eating as a pleasure. That means, for example, glorying in the greedy sucking of his early months, offering first tastes of solid foods but being quick to stop if he does not like them, being far more concerned with his enjoyment than his mess and being pleased to help him take over responsibility for feeding himself as soon as he wants to. If he has never been forced, as an infant, to have more than he wants, or anything he dislikes, he will not enter the toddler period with any but positive feelings about food and the business of eating it.

Encourage meal-time independence even at the expense of 'manners'. If your toddler eats potatoes dipped in his juice, with pleasure, don't be too quick to make him separate them or he may refuse both. If he enjoys eating fish with his fingers don't insist on a spoon or he may reject the fish. If he likes eating but hates staying in his chair until others have finished, don't keep him imprisoned for long or the next meal may not seem worth it to him. Above all, once he can feed himself, *don't feed him*. It is the 'one more for Mummy' or 'just a bit more or you'll be hungry later' approach which so quickly tells him that you care whether he eats or not.

Don't force him to eat (or even try) anything he does not want. If you are feeding him on his own, tell him what is available and let him say (or point to) what he wants. If he is eating with the family, ask him what he wants as you serve the food, just as you would ask an adult, or let him serve himself when he is able. There may be meals or days when he selects a very unbalanced plateful – perhaps only the meat or only the potato – but pressure from you will only make problems, where his own selection will balance itself out in time. Above all, don't ever make him 'buy' the items he enjoys, by eating the items he does not want. You want him to feel that *he should not have food he does not want*. In this way food can remain the pleasure and privilege which it really is, rather than the miserable duty it can so easily become.

Stick to this principle even if what he wants is nothing. No basically healthy child will starve himself if offered foods which he normally eats, so if he does not want to eat today, refusal should be his right. He may be unwell (in which case he is probably better off without the meal); he may be 'trying it on' in which case the less reaction he gets the better, or he may just not be hungry, in which case he will be very ready for the next meal. Be careful, though. If, when he says he does not want any lunch, you offer quite a different dish, he is bound to realize that you can be pressured into providing not just pleasant food but any particular item he happens to fancy. Equally, if having refused any lunch, he finds himself offered an extra snack 'because you must be hungry', he is bound to realize that you cared about the lunch really however casual you seemed about it at the time. If he asks for something to eat before the next meal-time, by all means give him whatever simple snack is routine in your house. But don't make an issue of it or take more trouble than usual.

If you have allowed eating to become a battleground between you and your child you may need an actual campaign to end the war. The tactics are much the same as those outlined above but the following points may be useful to your planning.

Start by convincing yourself that your child is healthy and adequately nourished. If just looking at him is not enough, ask the doctor to check him over and explain why you want this. You will never convince your child that there is no more mileage to be got out of meal-time battles while you remain anxious about his eating.

Ask yourself what he likes to eat and when he usually does eat. If you find yourself answering 'nothing and never' then you *are* still anxious. If necessary, make yourself a list. Those odd sips of milk, biscuits, bites of apple and wheedled sweets cannot be adding up to nothing or he would not be adequately nourished.

If what he likes is plain bread at breakfast, ham for lunch and milk and biscuits for supper, include those items in the meals being served to the family and let him choose and eat them. No comment; no pressure; no wheedling; no spoonfeeding.

If he is obviously surprised by your new tactics, or hurt by your apparent sudden lack of concern, find a way of talking to him about it. Something along the lines of 'I think we've been getting in a muddle about meals; you're quite a big boy now and it's up to you to eat what you want so I'm not going to fuss you about it any more . . .' may be about right. Do remember, though, that if major fusses over food have recurred at regular intervals every day for months, those fusses may have accounted for the bulk of the personal attention you have been paying to him. Withdraw the fusses and he may badly miss the attention and feel that he is being in some way punished. Try to use some of the time and energy you save on caring about *what he eats* in making it clear that *you still care about him*. If a non-lunch only takes two minutes, maybe it will leave time for an extra game, a story or a walk.

Make sure that your partner and other family members are in on your new policy. A casual remark such as 'Don't let Mummy see you pushing that food around' can set back the whole campaign by days.

With misery removed from the family table, let him see that the rest of you *enjoy* food. He probably will not risk it at once, but sooner or later he will ask to try the new food that his sister is greeting with such pleasure.

Older children and eating problems

Somewhere around four or five most children, even those who have had feeding problems as toddlers, begin to eat much more enthusiastically. This is a highly imitative stage so eating in company – both at school and at home – often leads children into trying items and dishes they have previously rejected. On the other hand, this is also the age when children are liable to notice and resent any dietary restrictions which set them apart from their peers, so it is a time to be tactful about sending an apple if the others all have glamorous junk foods.

Most schoolchildren are 'faddy' about what they eat. But the truth is that most *people* are 'faddy' whatever their ages. The difference is that, as adults, we are free to buy, cook and serve what we like, whereas children are in the hands of others.

Children's fads need seldom present a real problem if they are tactfully and sensibly handled. Perhaps the first tactful step is to stop calling them 'fads' and call them dislikes instead. Handling dislikes with a minimum of trouble usually depends on accepting that the child's diet will not suffer if he leaves out certain items which you regularly serve. Suppose, for example, that he hates eggs. What does it matter? If it is breakfast which is in question he can have the bacon without the egg. If it is egg dishes at lunch or supper, it is usually easy to substitute some cheese . . . If he is anti-vegetables he can leave those out too. He probably eats potatoes and might eat some other vegetables as well if you gave them to him raw. But even if he eats none at all he will come to no harm. His plate may look rather empty compared to those of other family members, but if it is empty of items he dislikes, he will not mind; the problem, as usual, is yours not his.

Unless you are prepared to cook several different versions of each meal, often over a period of years, it is probably wise to couple willingness to let him leave out the items he dislikes with unwillingness to cook something different just for him. Eggs and bacon, or just eggs, or just bacon, is one thing, but eggs and bacon or baked beans on toast, is quite another on a busy morning.

Obesity: the problem of eating too much

It is ironical that parents who have worried ceaselessly because their young children did not appear to eat enough often face later worries because those children become fat.

Unless you are authoritatively assured otherwise by a doctor who has carried out appropriate investigations, you must assume that any member of the family who becomes obese *has* been eating too much. Phrases like 'it's her glands . . .' may sound comforting but they are very seldom meaningful.

How much food is too much? Nobody can answer that question honestly in terms of food intake; it can only be answered in terms of the *results* of the food intake: the individual's weight or weight-trend. Human beings are so variable in the efficiency with which their bodies use food-fuel and in the activities which they ask of those bodies, that a diet which is just right for one may make another lose weight and a third become obese. The right amount of food is the amount which keeps an individual's energy intake and expenditure balanced *over time*. Anyone can put on a little over a period of Christmas celebration or take off a little during an energetic summer holiday, but if the everyday diet is right, such temporary changes will soon correct themselves. On the other hand, even a few more calories than the body can use, eaten regularly over weeks and months, will gradually be laid down as body-fat.

The complication of growth. Children do not only need food-fuel for their bodies' current activities but for growth, too. Where a weight which is both appropriate and stable is the ideal for adults, a weight which increases in direct ratio to growth in height is the ideal for children. But don't expect a day-to-day match. While growth-curves (*see* **Growth**) are remarkably steady over long periods of time, they often have marked short-term steps in them. Some of these are caused by short-term, but acute, illnesses which slow down weight gain without affecting growth in height. But many are simply part of the child's overall growth pattern. A baby's weight may increase to a point where he looks chubby, but then a growth spurt increases his height to a point where his weight is appropriate again. A child approaching school age may suddenly grow so rapidly that for a while he looks positively thin and 'leggy', but then the height increase slows, the weight increase continues and the two get back into balance. Although it is an unkind mistake to assume that every child goes through a 'puppy-fat stage' near to puberty, it is true that a relative gain in weight often precedes a spurt of growth in a boy's height and that a similar kind of weight gain is a necessary trigger for a girl's menarche (*see* **Adolescence**/Puberty).

Avoiding obesity. It is much easier to avoid accumulating body-fat than it is to persuade the body to use up fat that has already formed. It is also far easier to avoid the eating habits which are likely to lead to obesity than it is to change habits which are firmly entrenched. Parents who can help their children not to become overweight may save themselves and those children a lot of later misery.

Only experience of your own child, from earliest infancy onwards, will tell you whether he is a person who uses food so efficiently that he seems able to grow and gain weight on very little, or one who uses it less efficiently and/or uses up calories in greater activity, so that however much he eats he gains weight slowly. In our society it is certainly more fun to be the latter. For the former, the greatest help comes from keeping food out of the emotional arena (*see above*) so that as far as possible he grows up treating it *only* as the pleasurable satisfaction of physical need; never as anything to do with love. He is going to want sweets and ice-creams, milk-shakes and pies. You cannot prevent him wanting them but you may be able to prevent him wanting them particularly when he is sad or lonely (to stand in for love) or when he is having a particularly nice time (to complete it) or when he has had a quarrel (to show that all is forgiven).

Coping with children's obesity

A fat adult knows that if he can reduce his calorie intake to a point where the energy he expends each day exceeds the fuel he is taking in, he will lose weight. This simple balancing act is the basis for all the thousands of 'reducing diets' which are produced each year. There is no magic in 'bananas and milk' or in 'slimmers' meals' either. Each different formula is just a different way for people to eat less while feeling satisfied and paying manufacturers for the privilege.

Children, however, should not reduce their calories so as to produce a 'nett energy debt'. If they do there is a chance that their bodies will be deprived of the food elements they need for growth.

Unless you are working under the direct supervision of a doctor, don't try to make a growing child *lose* weight. Instead, aim to **keep his weight where it is while his height goes on increasing.**

Young children. A diet which will stop a fat child gaining weight while his increasing height makes him slimmer, will obviously be a long-term affair. Ideally, it should be one which he barely notices. If his diet becomes a focus for your concern you will find yourself coping not just with his weight but with all the emotional problems touched on above as well.

You may like to consult your doctor about a suitable diet for him, but try to use any such diet only as a general guide to types and quantities of food. There is absolutely no reason why he should stick to any diet, item by item and meal by meal. All that matters is that he should continue to get adequate nutrition while taking in fewer overall calories than before. The following hints may be helpful.

Cut down on fats. Fats like butter and margarine, cooking oils, cream and all the things which are made with, cooked in or topped by them, are the most concentrated source of calories in the diet. Often that slice of bread and butter has more calories in the butter than the bread just as those potatoes treble their energy-value when they are made into chips.

You can cut a child's calories substantially without him noticing any difference in his food if you change his fat intake. Even the 'treat' foods which are high in fats usually have an acceptable substitute, such as water-ice or sorbet instead of ice-cream; yoghurt (if he likes it) instead of cream with his fruit; fatless sponges instead of his usual cake and dry-fried or grilled foods instead of deep-fried ones.

● Remember that full-cream milk (especially the first glass out of an unshaken bottle) contains a lot of fat but that the things you *want* from that milk (such as protein and calcium) are in the skimmed part. You may like to buy skimmed milk for him. If not, at least make sure that you pour off the top before you give it to him. Children past infancy do not need milk as a regular drink so if two or three glassfuls each day are a family habit, see whether he would be happy to cut them out and drink water or fruit juice or 'squash'.

Look at his sugar-intake. There is no reason why he should not go on having the sugar which he notices and which may make the difference between food he likes and food he will not, but he may be taking in a lot of calories from sugar without even noticing it. Many commercially produced soft drinks, for example, contain a lot of sugar. He might actually prefer an unsweetened fruit juice. Jams are rich in sugar; he might like yeast extract or fish-paste instead. Canned fruits in syrup are sugar-rich; you can buy the same fruits without the syrup, drain off the syrup or serve your own, far less sugared, stewed fruits.

● The trick here is to consider the sugary items your child has routinely, every day, and try to substitute for them. If you do this there is no need to upset him by banning occasional sugary *treats* whether they are actual sweets or slices of birthday cake.

Look at his other snacks. If he is eating a lot of calorie-rich snacks *and* all his meals then you may want to see whether you can convert him to less fattening nibbles. Sometimes children's casual eating is more a matter of habit and availability than actual choice. Must he always have potato crisps or would he substitute an apple if there were no crisps in the house? Are bananas the only fruits he likes or simply the only fruits you buy routinely? Would he perhaps be actually pleased to find oranges instead? Does he raid the biscuit tin for whatever you have put there or does he actually insist that it contain those chocolate ones . . . ?

● Trying to ban snacks altogether is usually a mistake because it makes a noticeable difference not only to the child's food intake but also to the expected routine of his day. You will avoid making your 'slimming drive' noticeable if you manipulate the snacks instead of banning them. Sometimes a child who nibbles all day will actually eat less if you positively offer a formalized snack than if you leave him to help himself.

Look at your own shopping and cooking. With a young child in particular, what he eats is largely dictated by what is available in the house. You may be buying, as part of your routine weekly housekeeping, a number of high-calorie items which he would not miss if they were not there. You may not be buying low-calorie items which he would much enjoy.

In the same way, you may be cooking, because you have always cooked, meals within which a great many calories are concealed. It may be better to put a little bit of butter *on* those mashed potatoes, to make them look luxurious, than to beat in a much larger amount earlier on.

Adolescents. Many adolescents, especially girls, diet as part of their general desire to improve themselves and their appearance, not only in the eyes of other people but in their own eyes, too. A teenager who has actually become obese certainly needs all your support in losing weight. It is very difficult to be fat and happy in today's teenage society. A boy who has made his growth spurt, or a girl whose menstruation is established, will probably do well on an adult reducing diet, but if you are in doubt about the possible effects on growth or general health, suggest a preliminary check-up with the doctor.

If your child is facing the fact that she is fat, try to use this new decision to get slimmer as a time for education about food and eating. If she can learn, now, to eat a low-calorie diet which is sensibly balanced, there is a good chance that she will form new eating habits which will enable her to stay somewhere near her preferred weight indefinitely. If she just goes on a crash starvation diet she will not stick to it, while if she adopts one of the commercial schemes or crank ideas, she will never learn to balance ordinary food intake against her own body's energy-needs. It is really sad to watch a fourteen-year-old, who is trying to slim, choose a milk-shake to accompany her hamburger. Fruit juice and coffee are both available but nobody has taught her that milk-shakes are among the unnecessary extras which contribute to unwanted pounds.

● Some adolescent girls begin to diet when nobody but themselves would consider them overweight. Often this kind of dieting is part of a school craze, but it is also often part of a girl's expression of general discontent with herself and with her burgeoning body. Try to be aware of these added emotional implications. Telling her not to be so daft will not help, but offering additional ways for her to look as she wants to look, together with assurances that you consider her attractive and lovable, may help very much indeed (*see* **Anorexia Nervosa**).

Eczema *see* **Allergy**.
Electric shock *see* **Accidents**. *See also* **Safety**/In the home: Safe use of electricity.
Enemas *see* **Nursing**/Medicines: Medicines which are not to be swallowed. *See also* **Soiling**.
Enuresis *see* **Bedwetting**.
Epilepsy *see* **Convulsions, 'Fits' and 'Funny Turns'**/'Fits' and 'funny turns' which do suggest neurological disorder.
Eye drops and eye ointment *see* **Nursing**/Medicines: Medicines which are not to be swallowed. *See also* **Eyes and Seeing; Eye Disorders and Blindness**.
Eye injuries *see* **Accidents**/Bruises: 'Black eye'; Foreign bodies in the eye. *See also* **Eyes and Seeing; Eye Disorders and Blindness**.

Eyes and Seeing; Eye Disorders and Blindness

Each eye is an almost-perfect sphere embedded for protection in bony sockets in the skull. The anatomy of the eye is complicated and probably easiest to understand in terms of three layers, each of which has separate functions:

The outermost layer – the cornea. The whole eyeball is encased in this tough fibrous layer which is called the sclera. At the front of the eye it forms the transparent cornea. Reflected light must pass through the cornea which focuses it to give us vision. If injury or disease scars or clouds its transparency, vision will be affected. Modern techniques have made corneal grafting highly successful.

The middle layer – the iris. This layer of rich blood vessels has the coloured part of the eye – the iris – in front, beneath the cornea. The dark spot in the centre of the iris is the pupil – an opening whose size, moment by moment, is controlled by the iris which opens it to let the maximum amount of light through when lighting is poor, and closes it up to control the amount of light when lighting is good. This is what is happening when our eyes take time to adjust to sudden darkness or dazzle.

The innermost layer – lens and retina. The reflected light allowed through the pupil by the iris travels through the jelly-like substance which fills the eyeball to meet the lens which focuses it on the retina. In the retina, the light triggers highly specialized nerve cells which pass the light-messages, now in the form of nerve impulses, along the optic nerve to the brain which then interprets them as images.

Detachment of the retina sometimes occurs spontaneously or due to injury or disease. Modern ophthalmic surgeons have developed techniques by which detached retinas can often be 'welded' back into place with laser beams.

Coordination of the eyes

Human beings are fortunate in that, unlike most other animals, they have binocular vision with the two eyes working together, viewing overlapping fields and therefore giving a very wide range of vision in depth.

Six muscles per eye, attached to the bones of the face, contract and relax constantly so that our eyes move all the time that we are looking at anything, and do so far more rapidly and accurately than we could move our whole heads. Any derangement of the action of these tiny muscles means that eye-coordination is less than perfect (*see below* Squint.)

Protection of the eyes

Apart from their protectively recessed position in the skull, the eyes are also protected by the eyelids – double folds of skin lined on the inside with a lubricated layer which also covers the sclera. This lubricated layer, called the conjunctiva, ensures that the surface of the eye is not scratched by dust or other particles when the eyelids blink.

Blinking is a further protection. Like a car's windscreen wipers, our eyelids flick down over the eyeballs and back again to ensure that foreign bodies are moved off the eye's surface and the cornea is kept clear. Fluid for washing is constantly supplied by the tear glands which are in the bony socket above the eyeball itself. Surplus fluid drains through tiny tear ducts in the inner corners of the eye which carry it into the nose (*see below* Watery eye).

Faults in vision

Perfect vision depends on each part of the eye being correctly shaped and functioning in proper relation to each other part. The commonest visual deficiencies, corrected by spectacles or contact lenses, are:

Short-sight
(Myopia)
Usually due to an unusually long eyeball whose cornea cannot focus the reflected light rays passing through it so that the image of what the child is looking at appears exactly on the retina. Instead, the image appears in front of the retina.

The child can focus clearly on objects which are close to him, using the final focusing power of the lens of his eye, but he cannot focus clearly on objects which are at a distance. His far-sight is therefore blurred.

Spectacles with concave lenses move the light rays back so that they do focus exactly on the retina.

Some degree of short-sight is very common but is often missed in early childhood. It is only when a child is old enough to read (or find himself unable to read) distant advertisements, bus numbers and so forth, that short-sight becomes obvious. He himself is unlikely to be aware of mild myopia until correction by spectacles reveals to him a whole new world of distant clarity. Obviously it is a pity if young children miss any of the sights of the world they are exploring, or if older ones are scolded for poor copying off a blackboard they cannot see. Parents can help to ensure that myopic children get spectacles early by:

Being alert to the possibility of short-sight in any child and having a particularly high index of suspicion if other members of the family are myopic.

Making sure that the child's eyes are regularly tested from about three years. Although routine testing, such as that carried out at a well-baby clinic, should detect marked myopia, milder degrees are quite difficult to establish in a child too young to use the standard test equipment or, even given stimuli designed for his age group, not certain to respond reliably. A skilful optician or ophthalmologist is needed.

Watching the child for signs of difficulty with far-vision. In a young child the most usual sign is that he screws up his eyes when he is trying to see distant objects. By doing so he can actually improve his focus by compressing the cornea.

Whether or not he screws up his eyes, parents on the watch for short-sight can usually compare the child's ability to identify distant objects with their own. If you can see that those are sheep rather than cows (wearing your glasses, if you require them) then he should be able to recognize the sheep, too. You, and only you, will know whether he calls them cows because he cannot see them clearly or because he is confused about animals' names. In the same way, remember that when you meet him coming down the street, he should be able to recognize you at very much the moment that you can recognize him. If his face remains blank or searching until you are nearly at your meeting point, you will have to decide whether he failed to see you because of his vision or because he was thinking about something else.

Long-sight
(hypermetropia)

In children (as opposed to the elderly) this is usually due to the eyeball being unusually short so that the cornea and lens cannot prevent the focused image falling behind the retina. Although much rarer than myopia, far-sightedness is potentially more serious. Where the short-sighted child may simply ignore objects outside the immediate surroundings within which he can see clearly, the long-sighted child must continually fight to see the people and objects which are of most importance to him. He may be effectively partially blind. Continual accommodation of the lens may also lead to tiredness or even pain in the eyes. Convex lenses move the light rays forward so that they do focus exactly on the retina.

Important degrees of hypermetropia are comparatively easy to spot, even in very young children. Typical signs include:

'Backing off' from faces or objects so as to see them more easily. Instead of talking to you most concentratedly and responsively when sitting on your lap, the child may respond most socially from across the room.

'Losing' things that are close to him. The child may see the toy he wants on a high shelf but be quite unable to find it amongst the others when held up within reach. He may similarly become confused by food on his plate and so forth.

Lack of interest in sitting-down play. The very hypermetropic child will probably be comparatively uninterested in picture books, construction kits and so forth because 'seeing what he is doing' is at least effortful and may be impossible for him.

Clumsiness. A somewhat older child may be thought clumsy or 'not good with his hands' because his arms are not long enough to enable him to carry out fine tasks at a distance from which he can see fine detail comfortably.

Astigmatism

Is due to irregularity in the shape of the eyeball and therefore some distortion in the normal curvature of the cornea and lens. The most usual result is that the affected individual cannot focus on both vertical and horizontal objects at the same time: if one is in focus, the other is blurred.

Astigmatism may be present with or without short- or long-sight. It can be completely corrected by correctly prescribed spectacles.

Starting to wear spectacles

Few children actually *welcome* the need for spectacles but the ease with which a child accepts them is usually directly related to the benefit he feels. The child who has never before seen a movie clearly, or been able to field a ball competently, will not readily return to his myopic world. It is the child whose vision is only mildly affected – especially if the main problem is an astigmatism which does not much bother him – who may fight against wearing what is prescribed. Occasionally your optician, after consultation with an ophthalmic surgeon, will decide that if such a child really resents his spectacles he need not wear them. It will probably be suggested that you bring him for regular reassessment, especially if there is any question of the condition worsening. Usually, though, a child who needs spectacles has to be helped to accept them as a necessity. A very young child will seldom mind provided his spectacles can be made easily comfortable for him. A variety of types of frame can be tried with the aim of finding one which enables him to have his spectacles put on and then to forget all about them. Sometimes elasticized frames are the answer.

● While vanity does not usually put a pre-school child off his spectacles, *your vanity on his behalf* may easily do so. It is important not to allow your very natural regret at the sight of him in spectacles at such a young age to suggest to him that you prefer him without them.

Older children may dislike both the idea and the appearance of spectacles. Boys often feel that they ruin a 'macho' or 'sporting' image; girls that they make them less pretty. There are a variety of ways in which, depending on the child's age and exact visual difficulty, you may be able to help him:

Explode the myths about spectacles meaning 'bookishness' or lack of sexual attractiveness by pointing out the many hero and heroine figures in your child's life who wear them.

Stress the advantages of better sight by playing up the new ability to catch a ball, pick a friend out of a crowd, recognize an eagle on the wing or whatever is relevant to your child's life.

Help him organize occasional wear if this is appropriate. A slightly myopic child, for example, may prefer to reserve his glasses for long-distance activities, reading the blackboard and so forth. An astigmatic child may accept their wear only for visually complex tasks. The kind of case which will readily slip into (but not out of) clothing with a suitable top pocket, makes this kind of use far easier. So does the provision of an extra pair of spectacles to be kept safely against the time when the others are mislaid.

If you must insist that he wears them all the time, balance firmness on the matter with real trouble taken to find spectacles he likes. Constant wear *is* going to change his appearance. Once he will accept that change at all, he has the right to make it as acceptable a change as possible. Spectacle frames are expensive but give him the widest choice you can possibly afford and the most honest advice you can muster.

If expense is not an obstacle, special frames for special occasions may produce miracles of acceptance. For example, some boys positively like prescription goggles for sports; both sexes often welcome prescription sunglasses which can then pass as a fashion accessory, while some girls are comforted by different spectacles for party-wear.

● Although every child should have at least two pairs of spectacles in case one gets lost or broken, buying two which are very different with a view to the child choosing each day as he chooses his sweater, is usually a waste of money. Spectacles which are worn all day and every day become comfortable and the wearer becomes accustomed to the way they sit on the nose and so forth. Changing to a different pair produces a noticeable change in comfort and focus, as well as a change in what has now become a familiar self-image. Most children will only wear that second pair when the first *is* lost or broken and will prefer the replacements to be the same.

Consider contact lenses. For most children (though by no means all adolescents) the trouble of caring for lenses and the stresses associated with putting them in and out, dropping them and so forth, over-balance their advantages over spectacles. But for some, contact lenses prove trouble-free and are very much preferred, while for many others your *willingness to consider* this comparatively expensive alternative is a morale-boost in itself.

● Don't offer contact lenses without checking with the child's ophthalmic surgeon. They may be unsuitable for his visual needs (*see also* **Adolescence**/Problems with appearance and body-image).

● Budget not only for providing the original lenses and replacing (or insuring) any that get lost, but also for the new ones you will have to buy as his myopia alters with age and growth. He might need as many as six new prescriptions between the ages of ten and sixteen.

Squint (strabismus)

Human beings have two eyes which are set apart from each other. The two should focus together so that the image the brain receives from the left eye merges perfectly with the image it receives from the slightly different vantage point of the right. In strabismus this perfect alignment does not take place. While one eye (let's call it the 'good' eye) sends the brain an image of the object the child is trying to look at, the 'bad' eye is looking elsewhere and therefore sending the brain a different image. The resulting 'double vision' would be quite intolerable to the child if he did not immediately deal with the situation by accepting only the image from the 'good' eye. Because his brain is able to 'ignore' the unwanted extra image from the squinting eye, the child can see perfectly adequately. Parents with a child with mild strabismus may therefore not realize that there is any problem. With a more obvious squint they may see the problem as merely cosmetic. In fact *any degree of strabismus presents a real threat to the vision.*

How a squint threatens sight

Eyes only continue to see if the images they produce are accepted by the brain. If a child is allowed to go on, for months or years, using only the images he receives from his 'good' eye, the 'bad' eye will progressively lose its sight and eventually become blind. While people can and do manage life perfectly well with only the sight of one eye, this is a handicap, and it is also a risk in that if any accident should befall that one sighted eye the child will be left with no vision at all. *Squints must be diagnosed early and treated.*

● If you wonder how a squinting child can possibly ignore the errant half of what would otherwise be double vision, try looking through a microscope or telescope without shutting or covering the other eye. You will find that because your attention is on the eye you are using, the different and unmagnified image which is being seen by your other eye fades out of your consciousness altogether.

Recognizing
strabismus

Recognizing a marked squint, in a child or adult who has not been adequately treated, is all too easy. One eye looks at you as she speaks; the other 'looks' away to the other side of the room. But such a squint has already been neglected for far too long. The ideal is that even very mild degrees of strabismus should be recognized as soon as they begin. They may occur from birth; they may develop during the early months or years or they may occur only when the victim is tired.

If you think that your child's eyes do not always move exactly together; if one sometimes 'wanders' away from the focus of the other or takes longer to arrive at the focusing angle, seek advice from your doctor or ophthalmologist.

● Don't let terms like 'wandering eye' or 'lazy eye' lull you into believing that this is not a 'real squint'. Such a child's strabismus may or may not be serious but it definitely needs professional supervision.

Small babies can have 'pseudo-strabismus'. If it is a baby under six months about whom you are concerned, you may get a pleasant surprise when you ask a professional to check her eyes. Firstly, very new babies often do have trouble in holding both eyes in steady focus. Practice and strengthening muscles may enable her to gaze into your eyes without a waver by the time she is a couple of months old. Unless one eye is *fixed* so that it never moves with the other, there is no need to concern yourself until she is around three months old.

Even at this period, a slight strabismus which you think you are noticing may not be real. Small babies have relatively less white in proportion to the coloured part of the eye. They also often have marked folds of skin lying vertically down the inner corner of the eye. When such a baby looks off to one side, one eye moves to the outer side of the eye, exposing a lot of white between the inner corner and the pupil and still leaving a crescent of white between the outer corner and the pupil. The other eye, moving correctly with it, moves to the inner side where the coloured part tucks itself under that fold of skin so that no white can be seen; it looks as if the two eyes are misaligned.

● The more marked the folds of skin at the inner corners of your baby's eyes the more likely you are to notice this phenomenon: oriental babies are especially prone to it.

Treatment for
strabismus

There is a variety of treatments for different kinds and degrees of strabismus in different ages of child, but all are primarily directed at preserving the sight of the 'bad' eye. They are only secondarily concerned with cosmetics.

To preserve that sight the child has to be prevented from using only the images from her 'good' eye and her brain forced to accept images from the 'bad' eye. To this end the 'good eye' may be covered (with a patch or spectacles with one blanked out lens, for example). In addition, the child may be taught various exercises designed to improve the functioning of the muscles which control eye movements and, of course, spectacles may be prescribed to correct any concomitant faults in her vision.

● If a mild strabismus is picked up early, while the sight of the 'bad' eye is still adequate, having the 'good' eye covered may not present much hardship. But if the sight of that 'bad' eye is already reduced, this vital treatment may be bitterly resented. The child feels that she is being forced to see poorly when without those glasses (or that pad or whatever) she can see perfectly well. Proper treatment of strabismus can require very great patience, especially in a child who is not old enough fully to understand or cooperate.

Surgery for strabismus   Sometimes the eyes fail to align properly with each other because the controlling muscles are of unequal lengths. An ophthalmic surgeon may, in one or two operations, be able to correct the squint (*see* **Hospital/ Surgery: Squint**).

Colour blindness

Some degree of colour blindness is far more common in boys (about 8%) than in girls (about 0.5%). The resulting colour-confusion is seldom complete, though. Mild colour blindness may present no difficulty at all. The following notes will be relevant only to severely affected children.

The most usual difficulty is in distinguishing red from green and it is unfortunate that these particular colours often stand respectively for 'danger' and 'safety' in our mechanized society.

Colour blindness is often not recognized before a child goes to school because many children confuse the *name labels* for colours during the pre-school years and parents may not realize that their child's confusion is visual rather than verbal. Often the colour blindness is first recognized when the child is introduced to colour-coded educational apparatus. Sadly, recognition may follow only after he has already been labelled 'stupid' or 'obstinate'.

For psychological reasons early recognition of colour blindness is important, and once it is demonstrated you should take care not only to tell teachers and others concerned with your child, but to keep reminding them, too. It is easy for a teacher to forget to tell a new colleague about such a minor handicap but it is not easy for your child to forgive an adult who bawls him out for putting on the other team's red band instead of his team's green one.

During childhood it is important to allow for the colour blindness in all your safety-teaching and to communicate freely with the child about it so that you know in what respects he is at risk. For example, kitchen appliances often have red lights to indicate that they are 'on'. Can the child clearly see the indicator even though he does not see it as 'red'? Traffic lights use colours but they also use positional cues. Instead of teaching your child 'green for go' you have to teach him the relative positions of the 'stop' and 'go' lights. Electrical wiring is colour-coded, too, but in most countries the red–green dichotomy has been abandoned. Check up on cheap imports, though, and make sure that your child really *can* differentiate the 'live' wire from the 'earth' before he starts working with them.

In adult life a few careers will be closed to your child – that of airline pilot or engine driver, for example. Some other jobs will be made far more difficult for him by his colour blindness and it may be a kindness to keep open discussion going. He could, for example, train as a civil engineer or as a nurse, but if he does so, he should think carefully before taking jobs within his profession which involve much use of equipment such as colour-coded plans or biochemical tests.

Most colour blind adults, however, lead entirely normal lives with only their intimates ever being aware of the problem. Many become extremely skilful at deducing the colours which are difficult for them from variations in shade and hue.

Eye disorders

'Bloodshot' eyes (conjunctivitis)

When the conjunctiva (the lining inside the eyelids and over the outside of the eyeball) becomes inflamed, the white of the eye looks red and the edges and lids may be puffy and unusually pink. This kind of inflammation is called conjunctivitis whatever caused it. Common types are:

Conjunctivitis as part of another illness. It is usual in measles, for example, and may occur with a cold or other virus infection.

'Pink eye' or infectious conjunctivitis tends to occur in epidemics, especially in schools. The child should see a doctor who will probably prescribe an antibiotic ointment or antibiotic drops which will clear the infection rapidly.

● Do not *ever* keep such ophthalmic ointments or drops from one episode of conjunctivitis for use in another. Most have a very short shelf-life and will therefore be useless another time; furthermore, the tube or dropper is very likely to have become infected. Only sterile substances must be used to treat eyes (*see* **Nursing**/Medicines: Medicines which are not to be swallowed).

Conjunctivitis due to a foreign body in the eye. Obviously the first essential is to try to find and remove the cause of the irritation (*see below*) but the child should also see the doctor because if visible irritation has been caused, infection is likely unless the eye is treated.

Foreign bodies in eyes

When a speck of dust or other foreign body gets onto the eyeball or onto the underside of the eyelid, the eye's normal reaction is to water and thus float it out again. If you can possibly persuade your child not to rub the eye (and therefore embed the foreign body more firmly) the whole matter will probably right itself. A good trick to teach a child is to rub the *other* eye. This both fulfils his need to do something about his discomfort and helps to produce the needed watering.

If watering does not work, take the child into a good light and inspect the eyeball carefully. If a speck is stuck to it, take him to your doctor or casualty department to have it removed. It is not safe either to leave it there or to try and remove it yourself. You might worsen the scratch it will have made already.

If you can see nothing adhering to the eyeball, try lifting the top lid to give anything stuck there the chance to float down; then turn down the lower lid. If you can see a speck on either lid you should be able to remove it using the corner of a handkerchief or a piece of tissue. Even if you can see nothing, these manoeuvres may allow the foreign body to move into a position where it ceases to be uncomfortable.

Even after you have successfully removed a foreign body the child may continue to complain of discomfort in the eye. It may have been slightly scratched. If he has still not forgotten the discomfort after an hour or so, show the eye to a doctor (*see also* **Accidents**/Foreign bodies in the eye).

Sticky eye   An eye which is sticky with mucus is very common in the first days of life. The hospital staff will bathe the matter away and may take swabs for the laboratory to make sure there is no bacterial infection.

In later infancy such a sticky eye usually is due to infection. The baby should be seen by a doctor who will probably prescribe antibiotic ointment and will show you how to bathe the eyes to remove all crusts and stickiness. The important points are:

Use boiled cooled water and cotton wool swabs.

Wipe the affected eye from the inner corner outwards so that any drips of (infected) water are unlikely to reach the other, unaffected, eye.

Put the baby to lie with the affected eye downwards so that watering from the affected eye does not run into the other.

Repeated sticky eyes are a nuisance but they can always be treated successfully and, however bad they may look, they never harm the eyes.

Watery eye   If one eye keeps on watering and/or is often sticky, the baby may have a blocked tear duct so that surplus tears are not carried away into the nose but accumulate and drip out of the eye.

Blocked tear ducts usually clear themselves during the first year, so your doctor will probably advise patience. If the problem persists, an ophthalmic surgeon can open up the duct by passing a very fine probe along it while the baby is under a general anaesthetic (*see* **Hospital**/ Surgery: Blocked tear duct).

'Black eye'   If you are afraid that a fall or a blow to the eye may have damaged the eye itself, take the child to a doctor quickly because if you delay, swelling may close the eye and make examination impossible.

Usually, though, a 'black eye' is a misnomer because the eye itself is unaffected. Bruising is to the surrounding tissues only and although the injury may look dramatic and remain visible for some days, it is not at all serious.

● If you happen to be present *and* within reach of cold water when the blow falls, an instant cold compress laid over the area may reduce the eventual swelling. The coldness reduces the dilatation and leakage from the tiny blood vessels under the skin. Once the bruise has formed, however, there is no point in this treatment. Folk-remedies, such as raw steak held to the area, have no value.

Over a few days the swelling and discoloration may move downwards. The eye re-opens but the child's cheek is oddly-shaped.

Styes A stye is a tiny boil on the eyelid due to infection in the hair follicle of an eyelash. Some children never have styes; some have occasional ones; a few seem prone to repeated styes. A child who has several in as many months should see his doctor; some other condition, such as dandruff, may be associated with them.

Styes are not serious and never affect the sight or do real harm to the eye but they are painful, unsightly and infectious. The child with a stye should use only his own facecloth and towel and should try not to put his hands to his eyes because he may carry infection from the stye to the other eye. Home treatment is usually adequate for styes:

Increase the blood supply to the area by applying warmth. This will help the infection to 'come to a head' and clear more easily. A piece of lint or cotton wool should be wrung out in hot boiled water and, as soon as it has cooled to a bearable temperature, be held over the area. If the stye is at an awkward angle or you want to avoid any chance of spreading matter from it to another part of the eye, wrap the soaked material around something like the handle of a wooden spoon so that you can touch it to the stye only.

Remove the eyelash whose root is the source of the infection. If you look carefully in a good light, you may be able to see that one particular eyelash is embedded in the stye. If you remove it, using tweezers, pus will be able to drain away, pain will be almost completely relieved and healing will be hastened.

● It is not always possible to identify the affected eyelash. If in doubt, pull *very* gently. If you have the right one, it will come out extremely easily due to its infected root.

Blepharitis Is a more generalized inflammation of the edges of the eyelids. It may be associated with a sticky eye and/or with a stye, but usually the whole margin of the eye (or perhaps both) is red and sticky and there may be pus visible in the corners and crusted all round the eye each morning.

Blepharitis is often associated with dandruff or with other skin problems, especially those with an allergic component. Although one particular member of the family may seem to be susceptible, many types of blepharitis are, in fact, infectious, so care should be taken with facecloths and towels.

If blepharitis is due to infection, your doctor can treat it with antibiotic ointment. If it is not, he will advise you on a search for other causes and cures. Do not leave it untreated as, although it is not serious and will do no lasting harm, it can last for a long time and leave the child, for a period at least, lacking eyelashes and/or with scaly scarring around the edges of his eyelids.

Fainting

A faint (or syncope as it is called in medical terminology) is possible whenever the brain is starved of oxygen – usually because something interferes with an adequate supply of oxygenated blood.

Many people never faint. Some seem prone to do so. The most usual victim is an older schoolgirl or adolescent. People who faint once or twice seem liable to do so again, but whether this is because they have a tendency to inadequate perfusion of the brain with blood, or because the experience of fainting produces fear of fainting which in itself makes fainting more likely, nobody knows. Certainly fear and anxiety play a part both in causing individual faints (as when someone faints while watching a bloody accident or after an emotional shock) and in causing the 'epidemics' of fainting which occasionally affect school assemblies or military parade grounds. Under these circumstances, the sight of one person fainting is often enough to start a chain-reaction.

Common causes of fainting

Brains are likely to become deprived of adequate oxygen when:

Environmental conditions are stuffy and 'airless' as in a crowded and ill-ventilated room: less oxygen than usual is taken in with each breath.

Environmental conditions are very hot, whether outdoors in sunshine or in overheated rooms. Under these conditions an unusually large blood flow may be diverted to the skin in the body's efforts to cool itself, slightly less is therefore available for the brain.

The individual must stand still for a long period. Standing up means that the heart must work against gravity to keep the brain well-supplied with blood. When there is physical movement – as in walking about or even in fidgeting – the pumping action in the blood vessels of the legs assists the heart, but when movement is forbidden – especially when a particular posture such as 'attention' must be maintained – there can be some pooling of blood in the veins of the legs so that the blood returns sluggishly through the circulation for re-oxygenation and the brain may therefore gradually become deprived.

A large meal has recently been eaten so that a larger-than-normal proportion of blood flow is being used in digestion.

Preventing faints

Institutions, such as schools, could minimize fainting if they would arrange for young people to be able to sit (even if only on the floor) during assemblies and so forth. Where emphasis must be put on standing – as in parades or for inspections – arrangements should be made for frequent short breaks during which everyone is encouraged to move around freely.

If you have a child who faints several times, or who faints only once but in acutely embarrassing and alarming circumstances, her own fear of fainting may make further episodes much more likely. Every time she faints – or feels that she may be going to do so – her anxiety and therefore her proneness to fainting will be increased.

Under these circumstances it may be important to help her *not to feel faint,* even though fainting is not, in itself, at all dangerous. Her school should certainly be sympathetic to a special request that she be allowed to sit close to an open window or exit. The child herself should be encouraged to avoid 'faint-prone' circumstances. She should realize, for example, that it is better to avoid extremely crowded, hot, emotionally-charged situations (such as pop concerts or demonstrations) than to risk fainting in circumstances from which she cannot easily either escape or be rescued. She should, of course, be encouraged to sit in the corridor of an over-crowded train rather than stand throughout a long journey, even if her clothes do get dirty.

Coping with faints

The victim of a faint almost always gets some warning:

She will go very pale.

She may feel sick and/or dizzy or 'odd'.

She may come out in cold sweat, especially on her hands and face.

At this stage, she can rescue herself (unless she is hemmed in by a crowd). If she sits down and puts her head below the level of her heart, extra blood, bearing the needed oxygen, will reach her brain and she will recover. Alternatively, if she can force herself to walk out of the overheated hall and into fresh air, the combination of movement with more environmental oxygen will probably serve the same purpose.

● It is important to emphasize these early signs to a girl who worries about fainting. Suddenly 'falling unconscious' is what she dreads; if she knows that she will always have time to escape the situation, her anxiety will lessen and with it the likelihood of a faint.

If she faints completely she will fall and, by doing so, she will start her own recovery because once she is lying down sufficient blood will reach her brain. You can help by:

Persuading other people to stand back so that she gets as much air as possible. If she is in a very hot, crowded, airless place, it may be worth carrying her outside.

Loosening anything which may restrict her breathing such as a tie.

Turning her on her side so that if she should vomit she will not choke.

Unconsciousness from an ordinary faint is usually only momentary – her eyes will probably be opening by the time you reach her side – but she should lie down until she ceases to feel giddy or odd and she should then get up slowly and sit in a cool airy place until she feels normal again.

Feet *see also* **Ringworm and Athlete's Foot; Warts and Veruccae**

Your child's feet are vitally important. They have got to carry her full weight throughout a long life. Pain, deformity and loss of function in the feet is one of the commonest causes of loss of mobility and independence in otherwise healthy elderly people. If you can keep your child's feet healthy *throughout their period of growth* you will have made a real, if unglamorous, contribution to her future health and happiness. Remember that ill-fitting shoes and socks can damage soft young bones without causing pain.

First shoes and socks

In cultures where everyone goes barefoot there are few deformed feet and no corns or bunions; instead there are toes squashed by cattle and soles ripped by thorns and stones . . . You have to steer between these two extremes, recognizing that shoes are needed for protection but that feet stay strong and healthy if they are left bare as much as is safe.

Healthy feet do not need support; they provide their own support through well-developed, well-exercised muscles. Only in special circumstances, such as athletic training or sports, are shoes needed which give 'proper ankle support'.

Babies are best without shoes or socks until they can walk well enough to do it outside where their feet will need protection. If you think your baby's feet will get cold, use sleeping bags or sleeping suits with big, roomy feet.

● Cool feet do not suggest that a baby is chilly. Check her bare stomach or thighs instead. If they feel warm then she is warm enough.

Have first shoes fitted by a trained fitter in a specialist shop. She should measure the length and breadth of *each* foot with the child standing up, and she should only offer you a shoe which is exactly the right fitting. Never accept a 'D' instead of an 'E' because it happens to be the colour your child prefers. And never accept 'extra room for growth' either. Trained fitters are taught to make a proper growth allowance; too much is as bad as not enough.

Whenever she wears shoes she should wear socks to prevent rubbing. Endlessly rubbed places and repeated blistering can lead to the formation of callouses on the feet.

Choose socks as carefully as shoes. Nylon stretch socks are a great help to parents but they can be disastrous for children. If you buy a sock advertised for a range of sizes such as 5–7 and your child is a size 7, buy the next size up, the 8–11. If you buy cotton or wool socks, do check, after the first washing, to be sure that they have not shrunk. The best way is to buy two pairs, wash one pair and then compare them.

Take child and shoes for re-measuring at least every three months. That specialist shop should be happy to check the old shoes for you and tell you honestly if they still fit your child. If she needs new ones, do remember to make a clean sweep of *all* footwear. If those shoes are now too small so will be the boots and the socks you bought at the same time. As she gets older you will need to remember sports shoes and dancing shoes as well as tights and those spangled socks she likes for parties.

Don't pass shoes down from child to child even if the size and fitting seems appropriate. Each wears a shoe to her own particular shape which cannot be the right shape for anyone else. You may be able to make an exception for wellingtons (rubber boots) which hold their own shape.

Shoes for schoolchildren As your child gets older you may have to fight fearful battles to persuade her to accept shoes which fit, rather than shoes which look fashionable. Shoe manufacturers are gradually beginning to realize that both these ideals should be available in one pair of shoes, but it can still be difficult. Some families find that the following tips help to avoid both battles *and* damaged feet . . .

Willingness to buy fashionable shoes for best in return for cooperation over wearing 'sensible' shoes for school and everyday.

● Although short periods in high heels, wedgies or pointed toes will do less harm than longer periods, do keep an eye on the fit of these shoes which, little worn, may go on looking new long after they have become too small.

Willingness to spend the money for good sports shoes so that the child has properly fitted 'trainers' of which she can be proud rather than ill-fitting plimsolls.

Acceptance of sloppy summer casuals balanced by encouragement to abandon them in favour of bare feet whenever possible.

● A soft canvas shoe will probably do little harm unless it is so loose and 'comfortable' that the child actually screws up her toes and/or shuffles to keep it on.

Special shoes for 'foot problems' A generation ago many children were compelled to wear special shoes designed to correct 'flat feet' or to stop them 'toeing in'. Now most authorities believe that time and growth will correct most of these 'problems' anyway. Almost every toddler walks flat-footedly and appears bandy legged due to nappies and a straddle-legged stance designed to help her balance. Many older children go through phases when they walk oddly and here again there is no substitute for growth and natural muscular development. If you are really concerned about your child's feet or limbs, by all means have her checked by a doctor. He will probably suggest as much free active play, barefoot, as possible.

Toes and toenails Injuries to toes and toenails are excruciatingly painful because of the rich nerve supply. Furthermore, a fractured toe or a nail so badly bruised that it eventually comes off, can leave permanent slight deformities. Do make sure that your child has shoes which offer adequate protection for her chosen activities. Mowing the lawn in open sandals, or handling iron-shod horses in bare feet, is asking for trouble.

'Ingrown' toenails, in which the outer edge of the growing nail presses increasingly into the flesh, can be very painful and can become a chronic problem. You can avoid it by always cutting toenails straight across (rather than in a curve) and by teaching her to do the same. If an ingrown toenail does develop, take the child either to the doctor or to a chiropodist. Home treatment, such as digging out the offending corner of the nail, will only deal with the problem temporarily.

Fever *see* **Nursing**/Fever. *See also* **Infection**/Types of infection: Infections which cause illness.
Fireguards *see* **Safety**/In the home.
First aid *see* **Accidents**.
Fits *see* **Convulsions, 'Fits' and 'Funny Turns'**.
Flat feet *see* **Feet**.
'Flu *see* **Influenza**.
Fluoride *see* **Teeth**. *See also* **Eating**/Types of food: Vitamins and minerals.
Food *see* **Eating**.
Food allergies *see* **Allergy**.
Food poisoning *see* **Diarrhoea, Gastro-enteritis and Food Poisoning**. *See also* **Infection**/ Preventing infection: Infection and home hygiene.
Food refusal *see* **Eating**/Eating problems. *See also* **Anorexia Nervosa**.
Foreign bodies *see* **Accidents**.
Foreskin *see* **Circumcision**.
Fractures *see* **Accidents**.
Frustration *see* **Tantrums**.
Fungus infections *see* **Infection**/Fungi: Fungi as 'germs'. *See also* individual conditions.
Gastro-enteritis *see* **Diarrhoea, Gastro-enteritis and Food Poisoning**. *See also* **Infection**/ Preventing infection: Infection and home hygiene.

German Measles (Rubella)

Rubella is a virus infection which usually produces an illness so brief and mild that it may never be seen by a doctor or may be wrongly diagnosed when some other disorder is causing a rash.

Rubella would be an unimportant illness, and one which would certainly not merit mass immunization, if it were not for its potentially disastrous effects in the earliest stages of foetal life. 'Congenital Rubella Syndrome' is most likely to affect the infants of mothers who contract rubella when they are not yet even sure that they are pregnant. Sixty per cent of such mothers may have babies with a variety of defects, including deafness, cataracts in the eyes and damaged heart valves. By the fourth month of pregnancy the risk has already dropped: only about five per cent of such babies are likely to be affected if the mother contracts rubella.

If a woman has had rubella in childhood or before she became pregnant, then she and her foetus will be protected. Unfortunately, many women who believe that they did have the disease in childhood, turn out to have no antibodies against it. Their 'german measles' was wrongly diagnosed, assumed when a transient rash occurred during a rubella epidemic, or simply misremembered. There are so many virus infections which can produce mild fever and rash that definite diagnosis is usually impossible.

Public health authorities now offer rubella immunization to all girls during childhood, whether or not they are thought to have had the disease. The vaccine does no harm even when given to an individual who already has adequate antibodies of her own. Unfortunately, the acceptance rate is nowhere near one hundred per cent and the immunization programme is so recent that there are many adult women of child-bearing age who were out of school before it was available. There will continue to be a risk to foetuses as long as any girls reach puberty unimmunized.

Parents, therefore, have a heavy, double responsibility in rubella.

Make sure your own daughters are immunized

Unless your doctor advises against the injection for a particular reason (allergy to the traces of antibiotics used in the manufacture of the vaccine is the most likely), every girl should be immunized before puberty or while there is no possibility that she could be pregnant or could become so in the three months after immunization.

By ensuring this you ensure the safety from rubella of *your own daughters' children.*

Make sure your family does not infect anyone else

If immunization is available in your community to anyone who requests it, making sure that you all receive the injection is the surest way. If it is not available to boys or to younger girls, one of them may become infected and pass the infection on before you know that they have rubella. Nevertheless, you can responsibly minimize that chance:

If you know there is a local epidemic of rubella, watch out for the signs (*see below*).

If you suspect rubella, have a diagnosis attempted by a doctor whether the child is 'ill' or not. He will often be able to tell you if the child has *not* got rubella even though he probably cannot categorically state that this infection is rubella.

If rubella is likely, warn any women of reproductive age who have had contact with the child in the past *three weeks* (*see below* Incubation period). Don't only warn women you know to be pregnant; it is the women who did not know, or were not sure, three weeks ago who are likely to be at greatest risk.

Isolate the infected child not only from pregnant women or even from all women who might be pregnant, but from anyone who has not definitely had the disease/been immunized. Otherwise your child may give it to another little boy who may give it to the aunt who forgot to take her contraceptive pills last weekend . . . Isolation only needs to last for a week. Don't listen to the people who say, 'Oh, send him to school. The sooner they all get it the better.' In this disease, every child who 'gets it' will be a risk to newly pregnant women. Better immunity by injection than by infection.

Side effects of rubella immunization

There are usually no side-effects in children. In adults there may be a reaction, one to two weeks after the injection, resembling a very mild form of the disease itself (*see below*).

Having rubella **Incubation period.** Up to twenty-one days (longer periods have been recorded).

Route of infection. Droplet infection from nose and throat to nose and throat.

First symptoms of rubella Possibly a mild sore throat and mildly runny nose. Always (if the victim searches because he/she feels unwell which is often not the case) swollen glands in the neck, directly behind the ears and at the nape of the neck.

A day or so later (but often the first and only symptom to be noticed) rash starts on the forehead and spreads down. The rash, which may itch slightly, consists of flat (unraised) small pink areas which quickly merge together so that the skin looks flushed all over. At this stage scarlet fever is sometimes wrongly diagnosed. The rash fades, often within a day. It is not unusual for these rash-stages to come and go so rapidly that they are missed altogether, or that a child goes to bed one night with a rash which her parents intend to show to a doctor the next day, but which the doctor never sees because it has vanished overnight.

Treatment of rubella None, except in very rare complications such as middle-ear infection.

● Although for most families german measles is a non-illness, with the child up and around (although isolated for a week), some older girls may suffer from pain in, or even swelling of, some joints. This may last for up to a fortnight and, while unpleasant, leaves no after-effects. Aspirin and rest are usually helpful.

'Germs' *see* **Infection**/What 'germs' are: Bacteria; Viruses; Fungi; Protozoa.
Giddiness *see* **Convulsions, 'Fits' and 'Funny Turns'**/Paroxysmal vertigo; **Fainting.** *See also* **Ears and Hearing; Ear Disorders and Deafness**.
Gingivitis *see* **Teeth**/Some dental problems of adolescence.
Glands *see* **Immune Response; Infection**/Types of infection. *See also* **Adolescence**/Puberty.
Glandular Fever *see* **Infection**/Types of infection: When the laboratory may help in diagnosis.
Glue-sniffing *see* **Habits**/Habits which easily lead to addiction.
Grazes *see* **Accidents**/Cuts and scrapes, grazes and puncture wounds.

Growing Pains

As far as we know, growth is never a painful process so the sharp aching pains which afflict some children's legs cannot actually be due to growth or even to a 'growth spurt'. However, these pains are certainly real. They afflict particular children at particular age-stages and may be acute enough to stop a child playing or to wake him or her in the night.

Most authorities believe that these pains must be due to mild muscular strains which arise because the child is currently spending a lot of time at one particular physical activity – whether football or hopscotch – and neither rests nor changes activities often enough to allow the affected muscles to recover.

If pains of this kind really trouble your child you may prefer, for both your sakes, to have a doctor check on them. In the meanwhile reassurance, casual sympathy, perhaps a rest or hot bath, are all that is required.

Growth *see also* **Adolescence**/Puberty: Worries about puberty

The rate at which any child grows and her eventual adult size, shape and proportions, are determined by a complicated mixture of genetic and environmental influences. A girl's 'growth plan' is laid down in her genes, rather as a rocket's flight plan is laid down on the drawing board. All other things being equal, she will grow to that target just as the rocket will travel to its destination. But it is a long journey from fertilization of the ovum to the resulting child's menarche at exactly fourteen years one month, or final adult height of 5ft 3in. or 5ft 7in. Like that rocket, your child needs fuel for the journey (in the form of food and care) and, like that rocket again, deviations from the planned course can be caused by environmental disturbances like serious illness or long-term emotional upset. Many of these are self-righting (*see below* The phenomenon of 'catch-up growth'), but a few, such as failure of the supply of growth hormone (*see below* Children who are 'too small'), may throw her growth permanently off its track.

Thinking about your child's growth

The whole of a child's body grows. You cannot measure her bones or internal organs, but you must, at least, take account of weight *and* height. A baby's weight gain alone, may assure you that she is getting enough milk and not too many cereals, but this is using weight as a clue to nutrition rather than growth. Weight gain without matching height gain may mean that she is getting fat rather than large.

Even weight and height together need looking at over time. Present measurements only tell you how *much* she has grown. You also need to know how *fast* growth has been (her growth-rate) and the timing of growth-phases such as the adolescent spurt. To call her 'small for twelve' is meaningless; how much and how rapid growth is still to come?

Growth charts for children

Instead of a chart giving 'average' heights and weights for children of particular ages, a child's growth needs to be considered against standard-ized 'centile' graphs which, by extensive research and elaborate statistical techniques, are constructed to give the expected upward curves for height and weight throughout children's growing time. Very briefly, such curves are produced by weighing and measuring thousands of children, at many different age-points, and dividing up the resulting measure-ments so that a given number of sample children were above and below a particular point at a particular age. The divisions can be as fine as you please, but the fiftieth centile will always have half the children above and below it. The twenty-fifth centile will always have three-quarters of the children above and a quarter below. The seventy-fifth centile will always have a quarter of the children above and three-quarters below, and so on. At any age, the ninety-seventh centile will represent large children (only three in every hundred will be bigger) and the third centile will represent small children (only three in every hundred will be smaller). These centile points are still static points. They cannot tell you what happened to growth in between them. Further work is done following the actual growth, week by week, of yet more children, in order to see at what rate they gained the pounds or inches that separate two age-measurements.

Centile charts
for your use

The result of all that research into children's growth is put together to produce a series of curves like those on the charts overleaf. They give a background picture of normal growth. The first pair of charts show the weight increases and the height increases of girls: small girls, larger girls, big girls; girls growing at a steady rate through the middle years of childhood and girls growing rapidly towards puberty. The second pair of charts does the same for boys. The middle lines, labelled '50' are the fiftieth centile lines, with half of all children either side of it. Heavier or taller children are above this – and the seventy-fifth, ninetieth and ninety-seventh centile curves are drawn in. Lighter or shorter children are below and the matching twenty-fifth, tenth and third centile lines are also drawn in. Notice that although the children's actual measurements vary, with two-year-old girls weighing anything from ten to fifteen kilos, for example, all the children's growth-curves are similar in shape. Whatever your child's actual weight and height now – wherever it places her, on or between the illustrated centile lines – if you record her measurements from time to time and join your marks together, her growth will also make a curve which is this shape. Of course, there will be 'jiggles' in the curve where she gained little weight during a hot and active summer, or put on extra during a greedy Christmas holiday, but, if her growth is proceeding normally, this is what her curve will look like over time.

Starting to use
the charts

Although it is fun to record growth from birth onwards, you can usefully start these charts for a child of any age. They are often most useful later on, especially around puberty (*see below*).

If you are starting in infancy, do remember that a very small baby, one whose birthweight and length enter her right at the bottom of the chart, may be *meant* to be small. You are probably small, too, and there is nothing the matter with being a person who is smaller than most. If she is just the size she is meant to be and her early measurements put her around the third centile, her growth is likely to continue around that curve. However, if she was small because she was premature or 'small-for-dates', early ejection from the womb, or lack of nourishment in it, may mean that she did not grow the optimum amount before birth. You may see a lot of 'catch-up growth' (*see below*) and within a year or two her personal growth-curve may have moved up from near the bottom to nearer the middle centiles. Remember also that these charts are not intended to record weekly, or even fortnightly weight gains; they are meant to provide an overall growth record not constant reassurance about feeding. You may want to keep more detailed records as well at the beginning of a baby's life. Weighing, and more especially measuring, a baby who cannot stand is difficult without proper equipment. If you attend a clinic regularly, staff will weigh and measure and you can copy their figures onto these charts. Later on you might take the baby to the clinic every three months or so for this purpose.

When you weigh toddlers and older children, try to use the same scales each time to minimize inaccuracy. Measure height by standing the child against a door, heels against it, eyes straight ahead and with a book on her head, at right angles. If you mark where book and door meet, the child can move away while you measure from floor to mark with a tape.

Before you start keeping a record for either sex, decide whether you will use kilos and centimetres or pounds and inches. Metric measures are up the left-hand sides of the charts and are the most accurate. Imperial measures are up the right-hand sides of the charts and are quite accurate enough. You can use each chart for more than one child if you use different colours.

WEIGHT RECORD FOR GIRLS

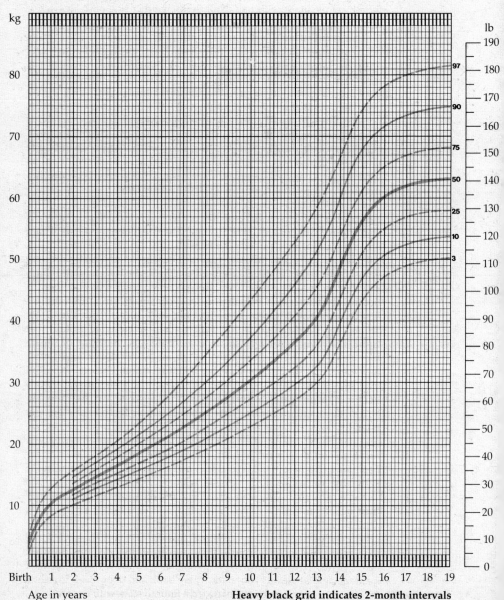

Age in years   **Heavy black grid indicates 2-month intervals**

Each time you want to enter a weight or height, find your child's age along the scale at the bottom of the chart and her weight or height up the side. You make your mark where a line straight up from her age meets a line straight across from her weight or height. You may find it easier to follow the lines accurately if you use two rulers or postcards.

HEIGHT RECORD FOR GIRLS

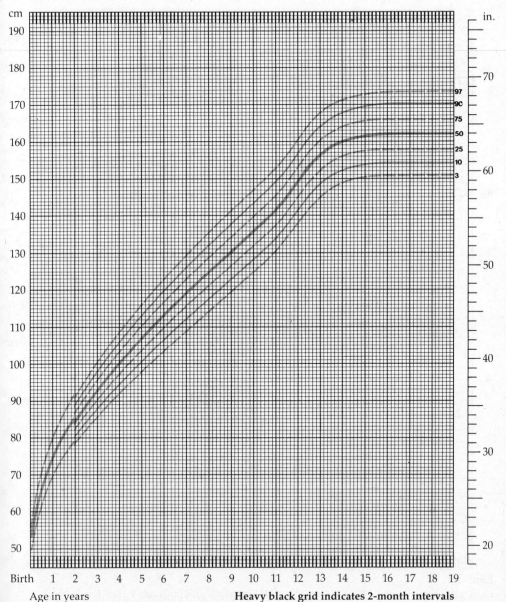

Age in years   **Heavy black grid indicates 2-month intervals**

Weight changes rapidly so people sometimes weigh frequently, especially if they are slimming. There is no point in weighing very often for these records, though. If you try to record gains of less than half a kilo or one pound, your marks on the chart will not be accurate. All you are interested in is the trend over time. Three-monthly weighing would be ample.

WEIGHT RECORD FOR BOYS

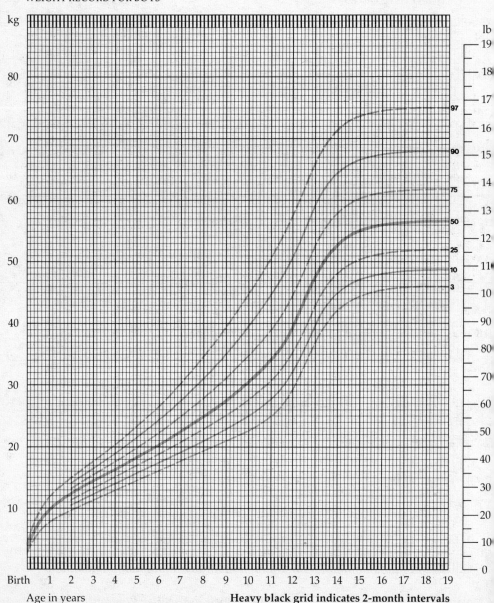

Age in years   **Heavy black grid indicates 2-month intervals**

Height increases even more gradually than weight and accurate measurement is more difficult, too. If you measure often you will sometimes think your child has shrunk! Three-monthly measuring would again be ample and six-monthly would be adequate. Your teenage son may enjoy being measured more often when he reaches the stage where he is growing half an inch each month.

HEIGHT RECORD FOR BOYS

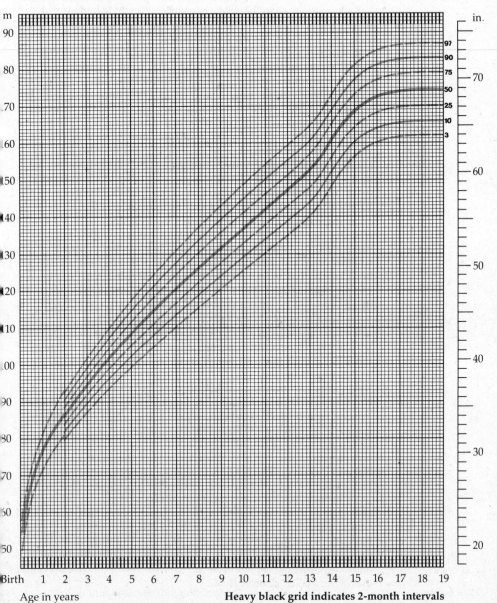

Age in years   **Heavy black grid indicates 2-month intervals**

Irregularities of growth

The phenomenon of 'catch-up growth'

Every child has a 'natural' growth trajectory, but if the supply of fuel from the environment is inadequate, her growth may be pushed off that curve so that she does not grow as much as she could, as fast as she should. She will not *stop* growing; you will still see increases in weight and height, but she will slow up so that other children, growing more and faster, overtake her. On a growth chart the child's personal line might flatten so much that the curves beneath hers – curves which are right for naturally smaller children – cross hers in their upward paths.

Research has shown that if starvation, illness or emotional neglect are short-lived, even if they are acute, their effect on growth is temporary. As soon as conditions improve, the child grows extra-fast. A baby, born weighing only 5½lb because she was inadequately nourished for the last few weeks in the womb, for example, may gain almost twice as much weight each week as is expected and will go on gaining very fast until she has reached the weight she would have been if her pre-birth diet had been adequate. But she does not go on growing at that rate. If her birthweight put her around the third centile when she was genetically programmed to be a fiftieth-centile baby, the rapid gain will continue until her weight-curve reaches the fiftieth-centile curve. Then it will slow down until she is gaining the amount which keeps her upward curve at that level.

Longer-term starvation or deprivation is a different matter. If a child's growth is slowed down for a long time, so that for months her personal curve is much flatter than the normal growth curves, a change in circumstances may indeed enable her to start a period of 'catch-up growth' but it may be too late for her to catch up to her ideal and intended size. She grows at least as fast as other children, maybe faster, but the field has left her behind; her new gains are being built onto such a reduced starting point that she will always be rather small.

If your child *loses* a lot of weight, perhaps due to an acute illness coupled with pining for you from a hospital bed, you can confidently assume that 'catch-up growth' will start as soon as she is home and happy and that it will put her back on track. All that her chart will show is a dip in the weight line. But if your child fails to grow and thrive over a period of months, it is important that your doctor should investigate possible reasons such as malabsorption syndromes. The longer she continues to grow very slowly, the less likely it is that her growth will eventually catch itself up.

Although failure to thrive, or deliberate self-starvation (*see* **Anorexia Nervosa**) show themselves first in failure of *weight* gain (or major and long-continued weight loss), less-visible effects on *height* may be even more serious. Bodies which are short of nourishment use whatever is available to them for immediate energy (*see* **Eating**/First principles). Children grow only when there are nutrients to spare from the immediate business of staying alive. This is why no growing child, however fat, should ever be put on a diet designed to make her lose weight, but only on one which will hold her rate of weight gain down while increasing height makes her a taller, slimmer child.

Children who are 'too small'

Parents sometimes become concerned about a child's height when they first see her stand beside other toddlers, or when she enters a new school class and finds herself the smallest, or when a younger brother or sister overtakes her in height. Ask yourself the question 'Too small for whom?'

There is nothing wrong with being small if small is what she is meant to be. *Somebody* has to be the smallest in any group and greater size is no indication of greater health or stamina.

If she is, and always has been, healthy, she is probably a small child of small parents. Even if you have never charted her growth, you can use the centile charts to check on this, by comparing her centile position, now, with what is called a 'sex-adjusted parental height':

Measure each other carefully, add your two heights together, add 10cm if the child is a boy or subtract 10cm for a girl and divide the resulting figure by two. If you now enter that combined height at the nineteen year point on the height chart for the child's sex, you will probably find that it falls on, or very nearly on, the same centile curve as the child's height. In other words, you will find that if, at nine years, she is of a height which puts her just below the tenth centile, the two of you together add up to 'tenth-centile parents'.

● That sex-adjusted parental height is also a reasonably good predictor of the child's eventual adult height.

If that sex-adjusted parental height lies on a much higher centile than hers then you are right in thinking that she is unexpectedly small. Is she growing at a normal *rate*, but doing so from a much reduced starting point caused by earlier illness or trauma? Or was her growth normal earlier on but is it now proceeding very slowly? This is a question which, failing obvious signs of illness or despair, can only be answered by growth records. If you have been keeping them, you will be able to see whether a normal upward curve has recently flattened off, or whether a curve very low down the graph is proceeding normally. If you have kept no records and you take the child to a doctor because you are worried about her smallness, he will be able to tell you little until he himself has recorded all your present heights and her height gains over several months.

If a doctor finds that although your child is small, her growth-rate is normal, there will be little he can do apart from reassuring and advising you. Medicine cannot improve on a normal *rate* of growth. Something delayed her earlier growth but it is over now.

If a doctor finds that your small child is growing very slowly or not at all, investigations may be appropriate and treatment may be possible. Apart from obvious illnesses and upsets, there are a few conditions (such as Turner's syndrome and certain thyroid deficiencies) which can interfere with growth for a long period before they produce other symptoms.

Children who, for whatever reason, lack naturally produced growth hormone, can now be given it artificially. Growth which is re-started in this way may never make up for the growing time the child has lost, but may be sufficient to turn an abnormally small person into a normal one who is not tall.

Small children with delayed puberty

Some children are larger than others and some children reach puberty (and therefore start their growth spurt) earlier than others. The child who is both comparatively small *and* has a comparatively late puberty may become very small indeed compared to others, and at just the time in life when comparisons with others become agonizingly important (*see* **Adolescence**/Worries about puberty).

A girl may find herself not only yearning for the bras and tampons which signal her friends' maturity, but also shut out of their fashions and pursuits. At fourteen she may be the size and shape of most ten-year-olds. She may have to buy most of her clothes from children's shops and be bitterly aware that she looks absurd in make-up or the latest hairstyle. Because she looks like a child the adult world will tend to treat her as a child; her friends can sneak into adult movies, discos or bars; when she tries to join them she is stopped.

A boy of similar age may be equally distressed, especially if his is a social group which categorizes people by their strength, their physical toughness and their sporting prowess.

Sometimes children in this situation are rejected by their peers. More often they themselves provoke dislike by trying to compensate for feelings of bodily inadequacy with self-assertive aggression. Where a child continues to mingle happily with the group it may be because other girls or boys treat the still-childish one as something of a mascot. It is more comfortable to be a mascot than to be rejected, but it is important that the child be helped to see her/himself as a full person-among-young-persons rather than as a junior who is grateful for patronage.

Parents and teachers can often help a child in this situation by encouraging abilities and accomplishments which are respected by the peer group but in which small size is no disadvantage. It is no use encouraging that small teenager to improve his drawing and painting. His group will not join the art master in giving him credit. He needs something which they would all like to do well. One such boy returned to school one autumn to find himself the very last child-sized bloke in the class. He suffered on the playing fields, and provoked suffering in the changing rooms, until he was invited by the sports master to try out for the newly formed rowing club. He became the boat's cox and was happy to relinquish the honour three years later when he was too big and heavy for the job. A girl in a similar situation found her own solution. She got through what might have been a sad two years on the strength of a talent for guitar-playing. She put it like this: 'I felt a fool dancing at parties; like a kid at big sister's birthday-do. I nearly stopped going, but someone's record player broke and somebody said I could play and I did. I don't feel a fool playing for them to sing . . .' Folk-singing 'caught on' in her group and she became a popular leader while she did her growing.

For many such children there will be no magic solutions, but all will fare better if adults will grant them the maturity they feel rather than treating them as the children they still appear to be.

Ultimately, of course, small children with delayed puberty do have to accept their own biological clocks and wait for the growth spurt and the secondary sexual characteristics for which they long. Most can be helped to do so if they are assured that *they are going to grow*.

Once again, a personal record on a centile chart can be tremendously useful. The child can be shown his or her personal line on the graph and can be shown what happens to that line (or to the centile lines on either side of it) when the adolescent growth spurt begins. If he or she can see that growth has always followed that curve and therefore always will, that sharp and continuing rise will be comforting even if it is still in the future. Furthermore you can point out, from the graph, that a growth spurt which starts late also finishes late. If most of his friends are already enormous, their growth is slowing while his fastest rate is still to come. If most of her friends are menstruating, their fastest growth spurt is already over and she will catch up at least some of them. If the child would like further reassurance, it may be worth checking on probable adult height by working out your sex-adjusted parental height (*see above*). If there is not enough reassurance to be derived from looking at a height chart, a doctor can arrange for more accurate predictions of eventual adult height, using X-rays of the hand-bones. From these a growth specialist can relate a child's present height to his bone-age (skeletal maturity) rather than to his chronological age. If his bones are 'younger' than he is, there may be even more growth still to come.

What a doctor will not, and should not, do is to go along with any desperate requests to give the child 'hormone treatment' to provoke an earlier puberty. The normal adolescent growth spurt adds a predetermined number of centimetres to every child's height. Therefore the child's adult height depends on the height to which those centimetres are added. If puberty were artificially induced in a girl who was 4ft 3in. tall, she would finish her growth spurt at a lower height than would be the case if the spurt starts later on when she has reached 4ft 7in. . . .

Children who are 'too tall'
In most communities even exceptional tallness is admired throughout childhood and continues to be admired in adolescent boys and men. It is only girls and women who are often considered 'too tall'.

A girl with very tall parents may indeed grow up to be a tall woman. And why not? Ideally she should be able to live with, and enjoy, this image of herself from earliest childhood. If her tallness happens to be coupled with an early adolescent growth spurt, she may have an embarrassing couple of years when she towers over her peers of both sexes. Like the 'too small' child she should be shown a centile chart and made to understand that her growth will slow as others speed up and they will therefore all end up in the same league. Real worry can again be allayed by X-ray studies. They may show a degree of skeletal maturity suggesting that she is further into the growth spurt than her age implies.

Occasionally a doctor may suggest hormonally inducing an early puberty so that the growth spurt builds on a lesser height. Think carefully about such treatment. An exceptionally tall girl may have problems with her self-image, but a girl who menstruates at nine years may have problems too.

Gum boils *see* **Teeth**/Some dental emergencies.

Habits

Habits are repetitive activities which start because they are useful or rewarding to the individual but which become semi-automatic. We all have habits; indeed most people get through the most tediously repetitive activities of daily life by carrying them out habitually. If you always put on your clothes in the same order, you never have to think about which garment to put on first; your mind is free for other matters or for drifting and dreaming.

Although most habits are harmless and some are actually useful, their very repetitiveness means that they can irritate other people and thus be a source of social stress. When a relationship begins to break down, it is often the harmless but hateful minutiae, like leaving the caps off toothpaste tubes, which become the focus for discord.

Some people are more 'creatures of habit' than others. People whose calm and efficiency depends on being able to do everything in exactly the usual way and at exactly the usual time may find it difficult to adapt flexibly to unusual circumstances. If your morning's work is ruined because you could not have your habitual seat on the commuter-train, rigidity may be making you rather vulnerable to stress.

Many people confuse the term 'habit' with 'addiction' (not least because the words are interchanged in the drug-underworld of fiction) but there are some important differences. In a true addiction – whether to drugs, to gambling or to a high-risk sport like skiing – the individual develops 'tolerance' to his chosen stimulus so that the dose of heroin, size of stake or steepness of mountain which satisfies him today will not do so tomorrow. He will have to seek more stimulation for the same thrill. This is quite different from an ordinary habit in which there is no conscious thrill, the original pleasure or benefit having been long-buried. A true addict is probably also a compulsive. Not only must he gamble for higher and higher stakes when he gambles, he cannot resist gambling even though the habit has taken his house and his car, and threatens his job and his marriage.

Almost every child or adolescent will develop 'bad habits' from time to time. When you find yourself worrying over one, it can be helpful to put aside your personal irritation and ask yourself exactly what place the repetitive behaviour is playing in her life and just exactly why you find it worrying. For example:

☐ Might the habit do her actual physical harm?
☐ Does it suggest to you (or to others) that she is anxious or 'neurotic'?
☐ Is the habitual activity taking over her life, squashing out others?
☐ Does she herself long to give it up but find doing so impossible?
☐ Is the habit harmless to her but absolutely infuriating to you or other people?

Sometimes asking yourself that kind of question will put your worry into perspective and allow you to stop nagging the child about it. Sometimes it will show you that you do indeed have cause for concern, but about the child's life and happiness rather than specifically about her 'bad habits'.

Comfort habits

Thumb-finger-
sucking

Very young babies. Some babies are known to suck their thumbs in the womb and they go on being able to do so from birth. Others take weeks to 'find' their thumbs or fingers although they suck eagerly if helped, or offered someone else's. This kind of sucking is part of an infant's exploration and learning (*see* **Play**) as well as an obviously enjoyable sensual experience and pastime. It is truly sad to discourage it.

● If you still wish she would not do it, remember that physiotherapists dealing with paralysed babies take pains to *help* them suck their thumbs, lest their disability deprive them of this important stage.

Older babies. Many (perhaps most) babies go on sucking their thumbs or fingers but gradually show that the sucking has become a relaxer and comforter rather than a pure pleasure. Unless the sucking takes almost all her waking time (*see below*), it remains a positive benefit. All other forms of comfort (your arms, the dummy you may or may not offer, her bottle or the breast) are under someone else's control so that she can never be sure of getting them when she needs them. But her own precious thumb is hers and always available. She will probably suck it whenever she is tired, uncertain or shy. It helps her to be confident. It may enable her to let you leave her at sleep-times and to tolerate being spoken to by a stranger . . .

Children. Many babies give up thumb-sucking spontaneously during the second year. Although parents often believe that a child would not have gone on thumb-sucking if she had been allowed to go on sucking a bottle, many in fact give up both kinds of sucking at about the same time as if they had simply outgrown the need or the satisfaction.

If your child does not give it up of her own accord, don't try to make her. Nothing you can do (within the bounds of humanity) will 'break the habit'; trying will cause endless friction between you and the thumb-sucking will do no harm anyway. You do not have to worry lest it damage the position of her teeth until she is at least six years old (*see* **Teeth**). Even then, a private thumb-sucking session when she is settling down to sleep is neither harmful nor anyone's business but her own.

'Cuddlies':
(transitional
comfort objects)

Somewhere around his first birthday your child may adopt an old nappy, scarf or cot blanket; a teddy bear or one of his father's ties. Psychoanalysts call these beloved objects 'transitional comfort objects' because children seem to use them to stand in for absent mothers as a sort of talisman of security, safety and affection.

If your child uses a cuddly, it will probably be his most emotionally important possession; the one object you must not lose, leave behind or ever, *ever*, throw away. He may simply hold and finger it; he may wind it round his hand while he sucks his thumb, or he may use it in all kinds of elaborate ways with, or without, other comfort habits. Whatever he does with it, he will probably need it whenever he is to go to sleep, whenever you leave him, whenever he is over-tired, upset or hurt and, above all, at any time when he is under stress and cannot have you. It must therefore go with him to the minder or to hospital.

Most authorities believe that cuddlies are beneficial for a young child. None believe that their use is a sign of insecurity or any other difficulty.

● The grubby look and strange smell of his cuddly is part of its benevolent nature to your child. However ashamed you may be of it, don't wash it more often than you can possibly help.

● The accidental loss of a cuddly can traumatize a whole family for weeks. As soon as your child adopts one, see whether you can find or buy another – or even two more – or, if it is a unique shawl or blanket, cut it in half before he has really learned its details and keep the other half against disaster. A new one will not smell right but is better than nothing.

Other comfort
habits

Babies find a variety of rhythmical physical activities pleasing and relaxing from the early months of life. Some learn to rock themselves (and their cots!) on hands and knees; some roll their heads from side to side; a few pull their ears or rhythmically thrust their tongues in and out . . . Some babies combine a habit of this kind with thumb-sucking and/or using a cuddly so that the whole complex of behaviour becomes their own personal comfort-ritual.

If your child only falls back on these repetitive physical activities when he has got nothing else to do – as when you leave him for the night before he is sleepy, or refuse to get him up from a nap – they, like sucking, can be seen as positive behaviours and the habit will almost certainly cease when he finds other ways to entertain himself. But habits of this kind *can* suggest stress or emotional disturbance, and *can* harm the child in the sense of taking his time, energy and attention from other, more varied, experiences. You may want to think rather hard about him, his relationship with you and the general satisfactions of his life if:

He prefers comfort habits to people. If he prefers to rock in a corner by himself rather than play with you, has something gone wrong between you? If he frequently needs comfort, why is that?

He will not interrupt the habit-activity to respond to you. Occasionally a child uses a habit like rocking to block out the outside world, almost as a kind of self-hypnosis. Why does he need to block it out?

He often breaks off to indulge his habit in the middle of other activities. Any child can take a quick thumb-sucking, hair-twiddling rest in the middle of a game, but if you often look up to find that he has stopped crawling around with his toys and is rocking instead, then the real world is not holding his attention. He may be overwhelmed with anxiety or anger which only his comfort habit can make tolerable.

His particular habit actually causes (must cause) physical pain. The most common such habit is head-banging, in which the child typically bangs his head rhythmically against the end of his cot as he rocks on hands and knees, or against a wall or piece of furniture as he sits and sways. Some head-bangers cause bruises and grazes on their heads and appear frustrated when padding the end of the cot makes it impossible for them actually to hurt themselves.

Your child might be head-banging because he is frustrated, bored and lonely. Masses of extra loving attention and interesting play, together with a drastic reduction of the time he is expected to spend alone in his cot, may end the habit immediately. If it does not, seek professional advice quickly as habits tend to strengthen with use.

Other common and less common habits

Dirt-eating
(pica)

All exploring crawlers and toddlers occasionally put a lump of mud, piece of coal or other unsuitable object in their mouths. A very few children, usually between about two and four years, develop an actual appetite for the inedible. The habit is commoner amongst emotionally disturbed or mentally handicapped children than amongst healthy ones, although it can be related to anaemia in an otherwise healthy child. If your child appears to seek out faeces, earth, sticks and other 'dirty' substances to eat, seek medical advice. In the meantime, guard him carefully against the high risk that he will poison himself (*see* **Safety**/In the home).

● Many people believe that pica is caused by a child having worms. This is untrue although the child with pica is more likely than other children to become infested.

Nail-biting

Nail-biting is almost unknown in babies but may begin in a pre-school child and is extremely common in schoolchildren. It sometimes starts in direct imitation of another child, but it usually begins by chance when a long nail tempts her and she then finds biting it enjoyable.

Nail-biting is so common that it is difficult to classify it as a sign of anxiety. But the true nail-biter gives herself so much pain – not only at the time but afterwards when she must use a finger whose quick is exposed – that it is equally hard to regard it as normal. Certainly most children who bite their nails do so when they are under stress – during a difficult lesson or while waiting for an activity which makes them nervous – and can often let their nails grow when they are happy and relaxed.

Neither scolding, punishment nor supposedly 'helpful' actions like painting bitter-tasting substances on the nails, will help. They will only make an anxious child more anxious, and defiant as well. Appeals to vanity, backed by clear nail varnish, may help a little, but the habit will probably only cease when she is more relaxed and at ease with herself. Even then it may return whenever she feels insecure.

Nose-picking

All children pick their noses from time to time *and* eat the product. Nothing you can do will stop your child altogether because if a dried bit of mucus is tickling the inside of his nostril or obstructing his breathing, his hand will go to it quite unconsciously.

If you are tactful, you may be able to teach him *not to do it in public*. It is, after all, a question of manners rather than morals and 'I don't like to see you picking your nose' is far more likely to get a three-year-old's cooperation than 'you are not to pick your nose'. Whose nose is it anyway?

Some children (perhaps especially those who have been nagged about it) pick their noses as a nervous habit rather than just as a quick way to get comfortable. Constant picking eventually makes scabs and scabs make the picking ever-more irresistible. Looking despairingly at your six-year-old's nose, you may wonder how it can ever heal. Amazingly, it will.

You can help to prevent scabs forming, and help them heal, by keeping the child's nails short. But don't cut his nails as a punishment or you will increase the emotion attached to the nose-picking business. Let him assume that you are simply cutting his nails because they need cutting (perhaps because cleaning them is otherwise so tiresome for him). Make no connection between nails and nose.

An older child may be self-conscious about visible scabs and actually enlist your help in stopping this habit. If so, as well as short nails, you can offer some vaseline which will keep the scabbed area soft and therefore less irritating/tempting. The child may like to keep his own pot of vaseline beside his bed to put on at night when nose-picking is most tempting.

Rituals and compulsions
Rituals serve us all as magical insurance policies against some undefined danger or ill-fortune. We all use at least a few. Some people feel uncomfortable if they walk under a ladder and it is not the practical possibility of a dropped can of paint which makes them take trouble to go around. Many throw some spilled salt over a shoulder even in the most formal company and not really because they believe it will foil the devil by stinging his eyes. Almost all of us have certain ritualized actions – like kissing partners before we leave for work or looking into our children's rooms just before we go to bed – which we carry out simply because we feel uncomfortable if we do not.

Many children, especially between the ages of about seven and ten, develop rituals which are of this kind even though they may seem especially conspicuous and silly to adults. Yours may avoid the cracks in the pavement, touch every railing, bang the other elbow if one gets knocked or chew his food a certain number of times . . .

Rituals of this kind can be highly irritating, especially if they make a child who is already at 'the dawdling stage' slower than ever to finish his meal or get ready for school. But they are not harmful nor do they suggest unusual anxiety *unless they appear to be taking over the child's life.* If you are worried, quell your irritation for a few days and watch:

Does he just run along the pavement, cracks and all, if he is in a big hurry, or will he miss the bus rather than tread on a crack?

Does he chew each mouthful in a ritualized way even if he is involved in conversation with friends or bolting a hamburger before the movie?

If his rituals are so necessary to him that he lets them get in his way, they may be turning into compulsions.

A child with a compulsion really *has* to go through his self-imposed ritual, whatever it may cost him in missed buses or ridicule. It is not just that he feels safer passing those railings if he touches each one, but that he will walk the long way around *in order to touch them.*

Compulsions are common, too, but a little more worrying than ordinary rituals, both because they may actually alter the child's life and take up time and energy better spent on other things, and because they suggest that he does not feel sufficiently in control of himself and his own life to be able to manage without these spurious external 'controls'. A child with a compulsion to wash his hands whenever they even might have become dirty, and who therefore cannot bear to play out in the country where there is no washbasin to which he can keep returning, is an extreme but not uncommon example. Such a child may be having trouble with feelings of 'dirtiness' perhaps to do with thoughts or dreams which shock him, or with masturbation of which he is ashamed (*see below*).

If your child has a compulsion of this kind, it is often helpful to find an opportunity to talk to him, in general rather than embarrassingly personal terms, about whatever aspect of himself you think is worrying him. You might, for example, be able to introduce the subject by talking about the different ways we use the word 'dirt' and the fact that earth, paint and so forth are not really 'dirty' at all. You can then move on to the other meanings: the 'dirty thoughts' or actions, and muse with him about the fact that to call them 'dirty' is really absurd since every boy in the world shares them . . .

Whether you can find a way to talk usefully or not, it is important to find *some* way to help such a child accept himself in a more relaxed way. If he continues for long with a compulsion like washing, he will very quickly be labelled 'odd' by his peers; he may abandon games and activities which prevent him washing so that he becomes known as the 'sissy' who will not rough-house or go fishing, and, of course, as his compulsion affects other people's view of him, their view will affect his image of himself. Your child guidance clinic may be able to help him and help you to do so.

Tics and other habit spasms
Tics are among the most irritating but least worrying of childish habits. The tic may be any repetitive gesture such as tossing the head, sniffing, rubbing a particular place on the face, or touching the nose or an ear . . . other types include a variety of grimaces, blinking, screwing up the eyes and so forth.

Most tics – like other habits – start with a real purpose. The head tossing may have been effective in getting her fringe out of her eyes; the sniffing may have been part of long-continued catarrh. But the habit does not stop when the hair is cut or the catarrh cured and it does not stop because you nag about it, either.

If you can manage not to make the child feel permanently 'got at' and self-conscious about it, the tic will fade out on its own, but it may be replaced by some other, equally annoying, habit. Children who are liable to tics and habit spasms often have one after another and may be children who are under some kind of stress or strain. If the current habit fades during a relaxed family holiday and returns with the new school term, a visit to a separated parent or the approach of an examination, you can be fairly sure this is the case. A complete 'cure' will then depend on either reducing the stress or increasing the child's ability to cope with it.

Masturbation

Small babies touch their genitals because they are there. Baby boys do so more than baby girls because there is more to get hold of. Older babies, young children, older children, adolescents and adults deliberately stimulate their genitals (masturbate) because it is exciting and enjoyable.

Although most parents probably do now accept that masturbation is both universal and harmless, many still find it extraordinarily difficult to tolerate in very small children whom they would prefer to think of as innocent of sexual feelings.

Most childhood masturbation is not a 'habit' but a conscious seeking for a particular kind of pleasure. Nobody has the right to try to deprive him or her of that pleasure but equally no child has the right acutely to embarrass Great Aunt Sophie. If you are clever, most masturbation can be handled as a matter of manners rather than morals.

Babies and touching

If you do not like your infant fingering himself in public, don't take his nappies off. If he is naked on the beach and discovers his penis, he can be easily distracted (*not* reproved) as long as you interrupt before he has actually started deliberately to stimulate himself.

Babies and masturbation

At somewhere between a few months and one-and-a-half years, he will discover that rubbing his genitals against something hard (perhaps against the cot bars while he rocks backwards and forwards) or rubbing himself with his hand, is exciting. Some babies become abstracted, turn red in the face, pant and appear to be working themselves up to a climax. Left to themselves they eventually relax and go to sleep. If he is on his own (or was until you came in) leave him to it. Who is he harming? If you are on a crowded bus and you can't stand it, distract him as soon as he begins, perhaps using words like 'not now darling . . .'

Toddlers, pre-school children and masturbation

A toddler who has not been made to feel shamed and furtive about masturbation will often confide to you that 'I like doing that; it feels nice.' This is your opportunity. Acknowledge that it does indeed feel nice to everybody, but point out that most people like to keep their genitals private from all but very close people and that playing with them is something for him to do when he is by himself. You may find the phrase 'private parts' a useful one. Try to keep the whole thing on a par with what you teach him about picking his nose.

You are trying to teach him to be discreet but not to feel furtive. It follows, therefore, that if you go into his room and find him masturbating, you should ignore it. If you react with shock, even amused shock, you are contradicting that message. After all he *was* being discreet until you invaded his privacy.

● Some children discover the pleasures of masturbation much earlier than others and do it more often, or more often to your knowledge. This does *not mean that the child is 'oversexed'; it does not mean that he will start other sexual interests or activities early; it does not mean that he needs circumcision/she has worms . . .*

Older children and masturbation

However hard you have tried not to make masturbation into a furtive activity, your child will certainly have picked up strong messages about your disapproval of it when you are around by the time he reaches school age. *Public* masturbation after, say, four or five, may well be a sign of emotional insecurity/disturbance.

Compulsive masturbation

In which the masturbation *has* become either a habit of which the child is not aware *or* a compulsion over which he has no control may suggest:

That a boy is unconsciously worried lest he lose his precious penis. Such a child will clutch himself defensively whenever he is upset, particularly if an adult is scolding him. He may sit through a scarey television programme stroking himself for reassurance. He may, or may not, have been told that Mummy will 'cut that off if you don't leave it alone'; equally he may or may not have been horrified to discover that there are children (girls!) without penises, and therefore worked out for himself the possibility of losing his own. Directly assure him that his equipment is his own forever; a gentle reminder, 'you don't have to hold onto it, love', from time to time may help him to be aware of the habit and to drop it.

That he is out to shock. A child who masturbates openly, and increases his tempo when he sees you have noticed, is often seriously angry with you. On an unconscious level he is feeling that you are an enemy; a killer of his pleasure. He flaunts the one pleasure which you cannot take away and which he knows you most dislike.

That the pleasure and relaxation he can get from masturbation has become compulsive because other aspects of his life are intolerable to him. Like a true addict, he must masturbate more and more and by doing so he increasingly cuts himself off from alternative pleasures.

Under circumstances like these it is almost always best to seek professional help quickly. Public masturbation *is* taboo in our society and a child who breaks that taboo will be made to suffer for it. Don't tell him that you are taking him to see a doctor who will stop him playing with himself. Tell him something to the effect that you think he is unhappy and worried and that the two of you together are going to talk to someone who is very good at sorting out children's worries.

Habits which easily lead to addiction

If your child or adolescent *habitually* smokes, drinks alcohol, sniffs certain solvents or glues, or takes mind-affecting drugs, there is a real chance that she will become addicted. While it is important that parents *and children* understand and recognize the risk – because avoiding addiction is infinitely easier than shedding it – it is also important that parents do not over-react to casual social experimentation with potentially addictive substances. A cigarette behind the pavilion is more likely to turn your child green than turn her into an addict, while getting drunk at a party may put her off alcohol for months.

The easiest way to understand why habits of this kind are more likely than habits like nail-biting or facial tics to turn into addictions, is to compare them in terms of what they mean to the individual:

Addictive habits are pleasurable. The child who bites her nails gets no real pleasure at the time and the results are painful. The child who drinks alcohol, on the other hand, gets a feeling of relaxed lack of inhibition; of being more confident, wittier and generally 'heightened'. The fact that she may be making an idiot of herself is irrelevant. She *feels* good.

Next time this child goes to bite her nails she probably does so unconsciously and later wishes she had not. But the next time she has a drink she consciously looks forward to those pleasant feelings.

Addictive habits are usually sociable. Biting one's nails is a solitary pastime and one which peers are most unlikely to admire. Drinking alcohol or smoking 'pot', on the other hand, is usually part of in-group social life and, furthermore, for the child or young adolescent it usually stands as proof of readiness to join the gang.

Addictive habits directly affect body-chemistry and the body may develop tolerance. Nail-biting affects fingers but it does not affect body-chemistry so the body does not come to 'look forward' to the next nibble. Alcohol and other drugs do have direct physical effects and the body may become accustomed to one level of intake so that it ceases to react so markedly. At this point some tolerance has been established and, if the child is addicted to the sensations she used to get from two drinks or one pill, she is likely now to want four drinks or two pills . . . The addictive habits, therefore, have a built-in tendency to escalate.

The compulsion to go on with addictive habits may be increased by withdrawal symptoms. Nail-biting may be a compulsion in the sense that the child cannot stop herself doing it even if her bleeding fingertips are ruining her piano-playing and/or making her feel hideous. But at least if she manages to resist the compulsion, her body will not urge her to give in. If she is truly addicted to certain drugs, her compulsion to go on taking them may be very strongly reinforced by the fact that when she resists, or cannot get hold of them, she experiences extremely unpleasant symptoms from a body which can no longer function normally without them.

Withdrawal symptoms are usually associated in people's minds with lurid pictures of sweating, shaking, vomiting heroin addicts. In fact, many people who do not consider themselves 'addicts' at all suffer from withdrawal symptoms if they run out of cigarettes in the middle of the night or cannot have their usual ration of strong coffee . . .

Minimizing the chances of your child developing a dangerous addiction

Nobody really knows why some children and adolescents develop addictions while others, exposed to the same sub-culture, do not. It does seem clear, however, that the happier your child is with herself and her growing up, the less risk there is. It is children with the most desperate need to change themselves, or prop themselves up, who seem most likely to adopt a chemical support-system which may eventually destroy them. As well as taking any marked signs of insecurity, anxiety and distress in your child seriously, you may like to consider some of the following suggestions culled from parents who have, and have not, successfully steered their families around this particular hazard:

Give every child realistic information. That means ensuring that growing children understand both the compulsive nature of habits like drug-taking *and* their destructive effects. But it also means discussing with them the (sad) fact that almost everybody in our society is at least mildly addicted to something which is at least a little damaging to their health. Your child is more likely to take seriously your diatribe against heroin if you are willing to acknowledge that you cannot start the day without coffee. And she is more likely to avoid starting to smoke cigarettes herself if you can admit that you are an addict and wish that you were not than if you try to dismiss all anti-smoking propaganda as nonsense.

Try not to force your child to choose between you and her peer group. If you deeply disapprove of your child's friends and try to emphasize the distinction between her 'nice' family and her chosen group, you will not persuade her to give up that group but you may edge her into a position where she keeps her peer-group activities secret from you (*see* **Adolescence**/Friends versus family). If secrets and falsehoods then come to light and there are rows, you will be inviting greater and greater rebellion; the child who might have had one drink in the pub with the others (instead of none) and come home at midnight (instead of 10 p.m.) now determinedly shocks you by coming home drunk at 3 a.m. . . . Staying on her side and understanding that her friends are important to her gives you the best chance of being a moderating influence if one should be necessary. And it may be. Many youngsters drink or take drugs first to be 'one of the gang'. She may need help in finding ways of keeping her end up in such a group without getting into the habit of relying on alcohol, or she may even need help one day in extricating herself from a group whose habits she knows to be risky. If you are against her and them, yours will not be help she can accept.

Don't over-react to experiments. She may have to try the glamorous and grown-up habits she sees all around her. A true shock reaction from you is liable to hand her an irresistible weapon in any rebellion which is coming.

Differentiate honestly between types of addiction. Although most parents would prefer their children to grow up as non-smokers and only occasional social drinkers, many find that throwing too much weight against these 'socially accepted' addictions lessens the force they can throw against the ones which matter even more – such as the use of hard drugs. One put it like this:

'I tell them they'd be fools to start smoking; filthy, expensive and bad for them. I tell them that their own minds and bodies can give them all the kicks they need without messing themselves up with alcohol all the time. I tell them that marihuana is illegal and I won't have it in the house whoever brings it; that I've never smoked it myself and don't want to. Then I tell them that hallucinatory drugs like LSD, and hard ones like heroin, are killers; that if they want to bump themselves off there are easier ways and that I will do *anything*, including moving to another country or getting help from the authorities, to prevent them even trying them out . . .'

Haemolytic disease of the newborn *see* **Blood Groups**.
Halitosis *see* **Teeth**/Looking after teeth; Some dental problems of adolescence.
Hay fever *see* **Allergy**.

Headaches *see also* **Migraine; Pain and Pain Control; Hospital**/Procedures: Lumbar Puncture

The covering of the brain itself (the meninges), the inside of the skull, the spaces within the facial bones (the sinuses), the scalp and the neck are all richly supplied with nerves and with blood vessels. Almost any stimulus to those nerves may cause pain fibres to react and send 'messages' to the brain which may construe them as the pain we call headache. Many authorities believe that this kind of stimulation is going on all the time but being prevented, most of the time, from reaching conscious pain-levels by the brain's own pain-control mechanisms (*see* **Pain and Pain Control**). It is when the control-mechanisms are operating least effectively that headaches are most likely to be experienced. This does not, of course, mean that headaches are not real: the pain is certainly real and often distressing. But it does mean that headaches very seldom signal real bodily disease or damage, but are usually an over-reaction by the brain to trivial stimuli. Long-continued muscular tension in the upper shoulders and neck, for example, can set up pressures which are perceived as head-pain. Changes in blood pressure, dilating or restricting those large arteries, can be felt as painful. Over-stimulation of the optic and auditory nerves can produce a painful spin-off effect on other nerves, while pressure-changes within even healthy sinuses (*see* **Colds**/Sinuses and Sinusitis) can produce headache.

The efficiency of the brain's own pain-control mechanisms and therefore the readiness of the brain to perceive pain are, as we have seen, associated not only with the body's general physical condition but also with mood. This seems to be peculiarly so in the case of head-pain. A child is most likely to experience a headache when she is tired/stressed/anxious. The child who has very frequent headaches, or a low-level headache which seems to last for days at a time, is usually one who is depressed (*see* **Depression**).

Most headaches, then, are of no physical significance whatsoever, but may be of some emotional significance. Head-pain which is noticed by a child who is already fed-up or miserable is liable to lower her mood still further and thus prolong itself. There is, therefore, an argument for interrupting the pain with simple painkillers. This can give her mood a chance to lift so that she is protected against the return of pain when the drug wears off. On the other hand, repeated doses for a continuing headache are seldom sensible. If the headache will not lift, attention needs to be paid to the child's general mood and state. If, for example, she feels the headache as part of Monday-morning-school-miseries, a dose of analgesic may help her get to school and through the bad patch. But if the headache recurs as part of global tension about school, it is the tension which must be relieved (*see* **School**/Problems over going to school).

Of course, not every headache is an over-reaction to unimportant stimuli: there are serious illnesses of which headache is a symptom, while headache forms part of the picture in many minor infections. The following notes are intended to help you in your thinking about your child's headaches and to sort out the few which may signal a need for medical attention from the rest.

Headaches in babies and toddlers

These are unusual, partly because the very young either cannot communicate, or cannot distinguish, the source of their pain, but also partly because they are less prone to perceiving head-pain.

If a baby seems to have a headache consult a doctor. If the pain really is a headache, a cause needs to be sought; if in fact it is earache, treatment is urgent (*see* **Ears and Hearing; Ear Disorders and Deafness**/Ear disorders).

If a toddler or pre-school child has a headache she may tell you that her eyes hurt or that her hair hurts. If the pain is sufficient to distract her from her normal activities – whether or not she has any other symptoms – consult your doctor.

Headache which is unusual for your particular child

Some people are far more headache-prone than others. A child who has rather frequent headaches will manage them and her life better if you do not over-react, but the child who suddenly produces a severe first headache, or a type of headache which surprises and frightens her, needs to be taken more seriously. If she has other symptoms you will probably be consulting your doctor anyway. If she has no other symptoms, try one period of quiet rest – lying down or sitting quietly, whichever she prefers, – and then telephone your doctor for advice.

A child who is really distressed by head-pain needs a doctor. The chances are against any serious cause for the pain, but she is entitled to authoritative reassurance, proper analgesia and a checkover to see whether, in fact, she is brewing an infection which is not yet producing other symptoms.

Headaches associated with menstruation

Hormonal changes and associated water retention towards the end of the menstrual cycle often lead to headaches. It is important that your daughter learn confidently to cope with her own feelings during these regularly recurring days, so if headaches are a regular feature, a consultation with her doctor is probably worthwhile. The point of the visit is not treatment for the headaches, but an opportunity for her to receive authoritative reassurance that all is well (*see* **Adolescence**/Menstruation: Menstrual difficulties).

*Headaches associated with head injury (see **Accidents**/ Head injuries*

Any child may complain of headache after a bump on the head. Usually this is no more than the pain she feels from the actual bruise. Sometimes this trivial pain alarms her because it keeps reminding her of the fright the fall gave her. Reassurance and distraction will usually deal with the matter.

Severe headache, which prevents distraction and/or makes the child want to lie down, usually means that a medical check would be advisable.

Headache occurring an hour or more after the accident and after the child has gone back to her normal activities, requires medical attention because of the remote possibility that the bump has led to bleeding and pressure inside the skull.

Recurring headaches, after a head injury which was severe enough to require medical attention, should be discussed with the doctor who attended to her. Headaches of this type are often more emotional than physical in origin but can delay full recovery after a concussion.

Headaches associated with other symptoms

Many infectious diseases and viral illnesses have headache as one early symptom. If your child has a headache for which you cannot account and which you feel is unusual for her and therefore worrying, take her temperature (*see* **Nursing**/Fever). You will probably find that it is raised. The mild dehydration which often accompanies a rising fever can affect the blood vessels of the head and cause the headache. Some illnesses are famous for their continued 'headacheiness' (*see* **Influenza**) while some ordinary head colds lead to secondary inflammation of the sinuses which causes its own unpleasant kind of headache (*see* **Colds**/Sinuses and Sinusitis). In cases of this kind it is the general picture which is of interest rather than the headache itself.

Panic-stations headaches

If you should find yourself really worried by your child's headache, it will probably be the possibility of either meningitis or a brain tumour which is panicking you. While both these conditions do occur, it is important to remember (even at 3 a.m.!) that they are exceedingly rare and that if either does occur the child will not only have a bad headache, she will also be obviously ill. Of course, if you are worried that is reason enough to seek your doctor's help, but in the meantime the following notes may help.

Headache is not the only symptom of meningitis (*see* **Meningitis and Encephalitis**), indeed, in the very young children who are most prone to these illnesses, headache may not even be the most notable feature. A child of any age who has meningitis will almost certainly also show some of the following signs:

□ Unusual mood or behaviour, ranging from sudden acute irritability and tearfulness, to marked sleepiness and lethargy. Babies will often seem withdrawn, refusing to make eye-contact with their mothers, lying gazing into space or suddenly fretfully crying.

□ Vomiting, often sudden and not preceded by nausea.

□ Dislike of light such that she turns away if you switch on a light, seeks a dark place to lie down or buries her head under the bedclothes.

□ Fever – although this is often not nearly as high as people expect.

□ Stiff neck which prevents her putting chin on chest while sitting up.

The headache of a brain tumour develops as pressure builds up so that a sudden and severe headache is most unlikely to be due to a tumour. The child who really does have a brain tumour will probably gradually develop a tendency to experience head-pain when she first gets moving in the morning and when she changes position or gets up suddenly after a long period of sitting still. If you should see such a pattern developing in your child, so that she complains of headache each day for several days, she should certainly see the doctor. The chances are still that the headache is of emotional origin (*see above*) but a tumour is certainly something for which your doctor will check before reassuring you both and turning his attention to whatever life-stresses seem likely to be contributing to the chronic headache.

● If a child whose recurring headaches had been considered to be of emotional origin should develop an unsteady gait, or begin to use a limb awkwardly, seek medical advice immediately. These signs do suggest that there may be some untoward pressure on the brain.

Head-banging *see* **Habits**/Other comfort habits.
Head injuries *see* **Accidents**.
Hearing *see* **Ears and Hearing; Ear Disorders and Deafness**. *See also* **Language**/Three to six
    months: Watching out for deafness.
Heat stroke *see* **Accidents**/Sunburn and heat illness.
Height *see* **Growth**.
Hepatitis *see* **Jaundice**.

Hernia

A hernia (sometimes called a 'rupture') is a protruding pouch of skin containing intestine which has passed through a gap in the muscular wall of the abdomen. There are two common kinds affecting babies and young children: an umbilical hernia in which the fault is close to the navel, and an inguinal hernia in the groin. In boys an inguinal hernia may involve the scrotum.

Umbilical hernias

In the foetus, the umbilical cord, with its blood vessels, comes through a gap in the abdominal muscles called the 'umbilical ring'. Sometimes after birth and separation of the cord-stump, there is a delay in the closing of that umbilical ring in which case a portion of the intestine may bulge through.

These very common hernias, which are especially frequent amongst West Indian babies, vary in size and may balloon alarmingly when the baby cries, but they are harmless and self-righting. In the past, strapping was sometimes applied to hold the intestine back, but it is now thought that natural healing of the fault occurs more rapidly if it is left completely alone. The hernia will be gone by the time the child is five. Surgery is almost never required.

• A prominent navel does not mean that a new baby has a hernia. His navel probably sticks out because he has not yet much fat covering his abdomen. By six months or so he will have acquired a layer of fat which will put his navel at the bottom of a valley rather than at the top of a mountain.

Inguinal hernias

Are less common than umbilical ones although still not unusual. They occur more often in boys than in girls. In a baby boy such a hernia may involve the scrotum and may sometimes be associated with an undescended testicle on that side (*see* **Undescended Testicle**).

During foetal development, the testicles move from inside the abdomen down an opening through the abdominal muscle wall called the inguinal canal. Usually this canal closes before birth but if it does not, a loop of intestine may later be pushed through the opening. At birth, even if the canal is open, there will seldom be any intestine in it and therefore there will be no hernia. Such a hernia can occur at any time while the inguinal canal remains open but most usually appears in the first year of life. The swelling often vanishes when the child is lying down because in that position the loop of intestine slips back into the abdomen; if you are in doubt, consider the groin area when the child is in an upright position (*see* **Hospital**/Surgery: Hernia).

Herpes simplex *see* **Cold Sores**.
Herpes zoster *see* **Chickenpox and Shingles**.
Hives *see* **Allergy**/Urticana.
Homosexuality *see* **Adolescence**/Sex. *See also* **Safety**/From 'strangers'.
Hormones *see* **Adolescence**/Puberty; Sex. *See also* **Growth**/Children who are 'too small'; children who are 'too tall'.

Hospital

If a child is hurt or ill or has some condition which needs investigation or surgical intervention, the drama surrounding those physical needs often masks all others. It is easy for frantic parents, as well as busy hospital staff, to forget that Johnny with appendicitis is still Johnny. The fact that he has a bellyache requiring expert attention does not stop him being the child he has always been, requiring all the kinds of attention he always needs. The more parents can help staff to deal with the person-who-is-Johnny, the more easily they will be able to cope with his body's crisis and the more 'like himself' he will be when he comes home again.

If a hospital admission is planned in advance (perhaps for an elective operation like tonsillectomy (*see below*)) there is a great deal which parents can do to help it go smoothly. You may, for example, be able to choose among available hospitals and medical personnel; find out in detail what your child's life and treatment there will be like, and prepare him for it. If the admission is at short notice or as an emergency, this kind of advance planning is obviously impossible, but there will still be a great deal that you can do to minimize the child's distress.

Babies and small children in hospital

Parents and other familiar and loved caretakers lend small children not only their security but also some part of their identity. At three months your baby literally will not know where she ends and you begin; at six months she will perceive herself-and-you as a unit and be unable to function as she usually does if she is deprived of your normal care and expected presence. At nine months she will know all too clearly and often protest if the space between you becomes too great. At eighteen months or two years she will be struggling to be a person in her own separate right, but able to maintain that vital effort only if she can voyage from a port of your making. At three or four she may be proud of her ability to manage herself in her own everyday world, yet still be thrown into incoherent panic if she must face the unfamiliar without your familiar support. She can cope with her usual routine (including, perhaps, going without you to a pre-school group and to friends' houses) but if she finds herself removed from everything and everybody she has ever known, *and* in a place which is strange and frightening, *and* faced with unpleasant, or even terrifying procedures at a time when she is in pain or feeling ill, she will be as panic-stricken as you might be if you were sent into space without warning or training.

It is hard for any adult to imagine the total dependence of babies and small children. Often those of us who are parents actually try not to imagine it, because being totally responsible for another human being's stability and happiness is a terrifyingly heavy responsibility at the best of times. When circumstances make it impossible to protect a child from fear or pain, the burden can be almost intolerable because, if you let yourself realize her feelings, you will have to share them; to feel for her what she is feeling for herself. But if a child in the vulnerable age group must go into hospital, the degree of her dependence has to be faced and met, just as it has to be met when parents are considering day-care (*see* **Working Mothers**). *If it can possibly be managed, that child should have a parent or other familiar adult with her all the time she is in the hospital.* If she does, she will face all the strangers and the strangeness from a secure groundbase and ride through actual discomforts better, too.

Rooming-in with your child in hospital

In Britain and the United States and in other western countries it is officially accepted that very young children do better in hospital if they have a familiar adult with them to keep up their ordinary daily care/love/support while medical personnel deal with their physical condition. Unfortunately, official support does not mean that every consultant or ward sister approves of parents staying, nor does it mean that money has been made available for every children's unit to provide facilities for parents.

Your local hospital belongs to your community. It may be sensible to acquaint yourself with its policies and facilities before you need them. If one hospital restricts parental access to sick children, there may be another which does not. If you know which is which you may, even in an emergency, be able to pick the one which is better for you. It may be a good idea to make your position clear to your doctor too. If he knows, from the time of your child's birth, that if she ever had to go into hospital you would wish to go too, he can avoid, for example, referring you to a specialist who does not approve.

Within your community you may find:

A special purpose-built parent–child unit with separate rooms or cubicles for each adult/child pair, plus varying extra facilities like kitchenettes and sitting-rooms for the caring adults.

Wards adapted for parents and children, perhaps with some isolation cubicles equipped with adult beds as well as cots, or with a few single rooms or side-wards which are used in this way when necessary. Sometimes parents will be made very welcome in this kind of situation.

Ad hoc arrangements which usually reflect the enthusiasm of a particular sister, or perhaps consultant, for parents staying if they wish, despite an absence of official money for facilities. There may be camp beds which can be put up beside the child's bed or even simply garden-loungers and a welcome . . .

The trouble with ad hoc arrangements is that you do tend to get in the way of the staff. If, for example, there are no lavatories for parents, you will have to use either those intended for the child-patients or those intended for the staff. It is worth remembering that nurses who are prepared to let you stay under difficult circumstances of this kind must truly believe in your importance to your child so, even if they cannot make your stay at all comfortable, they will almost certainly ensure that it really does benefit her.

The role of a parent rooming-in with a child

The role staff expect you to play will vary, not only from hospital to hospital, but from senior nurse to senior nurse and, of course, from child to child too. The important thing is to *ask*, as soon after your arrival as possible, exactly what staff would *like* you to do. If you can manage to have a conversation with the nurse in charge of the ward, you can make it clear that *you only want to help them to help your child*. You need, for example, to make it clear that you will not give the child sweets if you are told not to; give her the drink she is crying for during the hours before an operation when fluids must be banned; get her out of bed for a cuddle if you are told to keep her still, and so on. You also have to make it clear (by your behaviour more than words) that *you can stand what is to happen to her*. Nursing a child who is in pain from serious burns, for example, is harrowing enough for the nursing staff without having to cope with a parent who is continually in tears.

Once staff accept that you are not going to behave in a way which makes things worse for the child (or for them), they will usually leave all her ordinary everyday care and entertainment to you, and confine themselves to actual nursing. You may like to bear in mind that this is something of a sacrifice for the staff because it does mean that you get the child's smiles, leaving them the tears. It often helps everyone if you can encourage your child to be friendly to the nurses.

Good children's nurses say that they learn a great deal from watching children with their parents in hospital; you can probably learn a great deal from watching them with your child, too.

If the hospital will not let you stay

If the admission was planned in advance (say for a tonsillectomy), this should not arise. Make it clear to your doctor when the operation is first discussed that you will want to be with the child. He will then refer you to a hospital with suitable arrangements. If he does not know of one, get in touch with the National Association for the Welfare of Children in Hospital. They keep up-to-date lists of hospitals with rooming-in facilities/policies and will sometimes speak on your behalf, too.

If your child is admitted to hospital as an emergency, perhaps following a febrile convulsion (*see* **Convulsions, 'Fits' and 'Funny Turns'**) or an accident, you probably will not be able to choose where she is taken. But stay close. Nobody has the right to insist that you leave the side of a very sick or injured child at least until her condition is stable and doctors have talked to you about what they propose to do for her. If a nurse asks you to leave, just say politely that you prefer to stay 'until we know more'. (It is often a mistake to start off by saying that you are determined to remain indefinitely!) If you sit quietly by the bed or cot and talk sensibly to anyone who comes to examine the child, they are most unlikely to quarrel with you about leaving.

You may have to sit up on a hard chair all night, but by the next day the drama will be over; this is the time to discuss the doctors' plans for the child and your wish to stay. At the very least, they should be prepared to allow you the compromise of open access.

*Open access
to your child
in hospital*

If a small child cannot have you with her all the time in hospital, either because the hospital will not allow it or because you cannot manage it, open access is much better than nothing.

Taken literally, as it should be, the phrase means that you can spend as much time as you wish with your child and at whatever hours suit you. The only difference from rooming-in is that you do not actually live on the ward.

In some open-access wards, parents are positively encouraged to arrive in the morning before their children have breakfast and to stay until they are actually asleep at night. Although some small children will be appalled if they wake in the night in a shadowy ward, perhaps with another child crying and a uniformed nurse to offer comfort, a surprisingly large number either sleep right through or accept this night-time 'babysitting'.

If you are offered open access and your child does wake and is very upset, the sister may allow you to sit up with her for the first night or two. She may wake, for example, during the first painful twenty-four hours after an operation, or during the acute stage of an illness when she must have drips changed and so forth. When she is a little better she may be easily able to accept that you will go home when she is asleep and come back when she wakes up in the morning.

*Extended
visiting*

Some hospitals offer only extra visiting time as a concession to very young patients. Although it is better to be allowed to stay with your child every afternoon and return for an hour every evening, than to be confined to one or the other, even this amount of visiting is nothing like as good as rooming-in or open access.

Procedures will be carried out when you are not there so your child will have to get through them without your support and you will seldom know exactly what has been happening to her.

You will not be expected to undertake any of her care so you will lose your role as her personal person and she will have to put up with the nurses' ideas about brushing her hair or reading bedtime stories.

If you are to use every possible visiting moment you will be constantly travelling which may be impossible and/or prohibitively expensive.

*Deciding
whether you
can/should stay
with your child
in hospital*

If you are able to drop everything and everybody and devote yourself to the child who is in hospital, fine. But can you and should you? What about other children at home? This is one of the many occasions in family life when it would be convenient to be able to divide oneself in half . . .

Nobody can make the decision for you, but you might find the following questions useful to your own thinking:

Can the sick child cope in hospital without you? If the answer is not clear, try asking yourself whether you would be happy to send her alone to a residential nursery if she was well. If you genuinely think that she might enjoy staying away from home for a holiday, then she might manage in hospital. If the idea of sending her away without her family strikes you as absurd or horrific, then she will not. A good children's ward will do its best to make life pleasant, even fun, just as that residential holiday home would do. But here there is the added stress of illness and the procedures associated with it.

Can children at home cope without you? Obviously this depends on your partner, extended family, social network or other possible caretakers, but it is worth remembering that even a toddler (who will miss you and be furious with you for going away) will cope better than the hospitalized child just because he is not ill and is not in a strange place.

Can you cope? People often concentrate on the needs of children in hospital to the exclusion of their rooming-in parents. Rooming-in with a sick child can be a devastatingly boring and claustrophobic experience, especially if there are no other parents in residence and/or the child is in isolation (with you) and/or asleep most of the time. Take *things to do*. Arrange for people to *come and visit you* and try to persuade staff to keep you busy. Sometimes you can be enormously valuable to other children, whose parents are not staying, as well as to your own.

Many hospitals assume that if anyone stays with a child it will be the mother. But things may work out better for everyone if you can all share all the caring. See whether Sister will accept your partner, your mother or your minder to stay with the child some of the time so that you can go home. If she will not, try at least to have someone the child knows well come to the hospital for an hour or two each day so that you can get out, even if it is only to walk the streets.

Older children in hospital

If a child is to manage the experience of hospital without your constant, or almost-constant, presence, he needs to be armed with information. If the admission is planned in advance, do try to find out something about most of the following points and then pass it on to him. With a child of, say, six or eight, it is no use waiting for him to ask questions and then answering them, because he will not know what questions to ask. Worse still, he may have *mis*information (perhaps from television or tall-tale-telling friends). He will not ask because he thinks he knows, but what he knows may be horrendously wrong.

The child who must go to hospital may need to know:

Why he needs to go to hospital. This is not the same as knowing what is to be done to him. For example, a child can know that he is to have his tonsils removed without understanding that the operation is intended to reduce the frequency or severity of his bouts of tonsillitis.

● If that 'why' is not very clearly spelled out, often again and again, many children tend to feel that the hospital experience is some kind of punishment. Adult phrases like 'to make you better . . .' are ambiguous: what kind of better? – healthier, happier or 'gooder'? Missing school is often seen as 'naughty' (especially by children who secretly dislike going and may have 'swung the lead' from time to time) so a 'cure' can easily turn into a punishment. Furthermore, many children who have been ill a good deal have heard parents grumbling about having to take time off work and so forth so that they already feel that they are disapproved of for being unwell. Sometimes the guilt is more subtle. A child with appendicitis, for example, might be expected to accept hospitalization 'to make your poor tummyache better', but he may already be seeing that tummyache as punishment for having angry thoughts about his Dad . . . Sometimes it is helpful to ask the child why *he* thinks he has to go into hospital. His answer may give clues to this kind of thinking. Sometimes even the most sensitive parent will not be able to rid a child of this haunting feeling of guilt, but it will help, at least a little, if it is made clear to him that his parents wish it were not necessary and will miss him while he is away.

What is to be done to him. Many children get very confused about their bodies and where different bits are. It is important to be sure that your child knows where his tonsils are (he can look, in a mirror) or where the 'middle ear' which is to be drained is (you can relate his own ear to a simple diagram). One little boy, for example, was convinced that his tonsils were in his belly (glands in his abdomen always hurt when he had tonsillitis) so he was convinced he was to have major abdominal surgery. After the event, instead of being relieved to find he was wrong, he was horrified to find that his throat was bleeding.

● For many children, any kind of surgery or medical intervention is so horrific an idea that their own fantasies about it are unbounded. If you describe that middle-ear operation, be sure to *say* that nothing will go inside his head; he may well imagine that his skull is to be cut open. If you describe that circumcision, remember to *say* that his actual penis will not be touched: he may well imagine that it is to be cut off, perhaps to turn him into a 'good girl like my sister . . .'

How it is to be done. Including anaesthesia, etc. Be a bit careful what words you use here. Phrases like 'they will put you to sleep' may make him remember what the vet did to that poor dog . . . (*see below*).

● Remember that the child's view of what is horrific may not be the same as yours. You may welcome a pre-med before an anaesthetic, but the fact that it is to be given by injection may worry him. Remember, too, that he will not take for granted minor discomforts that adults expect. If he knows that he will not be allowed to drink freely after the operation, for example, he will still want the drink but he will at least know that he is not being kept thirsty out of sheer brutality.

When you will be there.

What state his body will be in afterwards. He has a right to know if he is going to be in pain – and a right to know that he can have medication for it. He also needs to know if any bit of him is going to look peculiar (as a leg in a plaster cast or an arm with an intravenous drip in it will look odd to him) or if any bit of him is not going to work normally, or if there will be blood.

How (if) he can contact you, by trolley-telephone for example.

Something about ward life such as whether he will be in a big room with lots of children, or a small one with just one other; whether he will be allowed his own pyjamas or hospital ones; whether he will have to stay in bed or not; whether there will be ordinary lavatories, or commodes, or bed-pans for a while; whether there is television/a playroom/a teacher/a trolley-shop, etc.

Obviously, if your child is admitted to hospital as an emergency, you will not be able to give him all this information because you will not have much of it yourself. It can be a useful rule of thumb *not to leave him until you do have it*. In practice this will usually mean that you and he together go through examinations in the casualty department and wait it out while a place is found for him in a ward. You go to the ward with him and are there while he is being 'settled'. Sticking close, you wait until you have had sufficient opportunity to talk to the nurse in charge and to the doctor who is taking over the child's care, *and* until you have been able to pass everything you have discovered on to the child himself, before you even consider leaving him.

Adolescents in hospital

Some hospitalized adolescents are in a similar position to full adults: subject to their fears and fantasies but free from particular age-related problems. But some are not. If your adolescent faces a planned admission, or must unexpectedly go into hospital, it may be worth considering some of the following points:

Placement in an adult or children's ward   He may be misplaced in either. Children's wards tend to contain, and be run predominantly for, very young children. Food, meal service and 'lights out' times may all be inappropriate for a fourteen- or fifteen-year-old and he may also be driven out of his mind by the demands of the young children to 'read to me' and to 'see what I've got . . .' Adult wards, on the other hand, often contain many patients who are very sick and/or very elderly. Many adolescents are disturbed and depressed by what they see, hear and are told, in such a setting.

Some hospitals do recognize that adolescents are usually better off if they can be nursed with their peers. There may be an adolescent unit; an 'older children's ward' or at least some attempt at age-grouping within the available space. If there is not, *most* adolescents will be better off placed with children than with adults, especially if they can be helped (by you and by the staff) towards a helpful 'adult' role there. It is usually more comfortable to be a 'helper' (however reluctant), than a fish out of water.

Privacy   Unless your adolescent is accustomed to boarding school, camp or other forms of communal living, he or she may find the lack of general privacy on a ward very distressing, and the invasion of personal bodily privacy involved in using a bed-pan or being bathed, positively agonizing. There is only a limited amount which you can do to spare him or her necessary medical or nursing procedures, but you can at least make sure:

That you provide 'modest' nightwear and an easy all-covering dressing gown. Girls who dislike pyjamas may be happier, once they are walking around, if they have underpants to wear under a nightdress and a bed-jacket to wear over the top. They may also need help from you in coping with menstruation if it occurs during the hospitalization.

That you do not tell his or her friends anything without permission. Some adolescents feel extremely private about their physical ills and would rather spend five days in hospital visited only by their families, than have their peers told intimate details and encouraged to visit them in the hospital setting.

Sexual problems If the hospital admission involves specific attention to sexual parts, even the most sophisticated-seeming adolescent may be prey to worries and fantasies with which you, or the doctor prompted by you, may be able to help. A boy requiring late circumcision, for example, may worry that the infection under his foreskin was caused by venereal disease or by masturbation or that the doctors may think something of the kind. A girl being investigated for late menses, may wonder whether an examining doctor can tell anything about her sexual life. Either sex may worry about future potency or fertility and find it difficult to ask.

● Adolescents with sexually related difficulties are often more at ease with a doctor of the same sex.

Hospital procedures

Whether your child goes to hospital for planned investigations or surgery, or for emergency care after an accident or sudden illness, there are various procedures which you are likely to have to face together.

If he is an in-patient, he will probably be in a children's ward and senior staff, at least, will have experience of children and a special interest in them. But if he is treated in a casualty department, or even in some out-patient clinics, you cannot assume that all the staff will be especially child (or parent) orientated. In a casualty department in particular, he may be rather an unwelcome patient. Staff are often young and inexperienced so that they may be as nervous of carrying out certain procedures as you are of having them done. They are usually trying hard to impress their superiors so that any 'fuss' made by the child may upset them because it seems to reflect poorly on their skill. They are often over-worked and over-tired – which reduces anyone's patience – and they may have life-and-death problems to cope with which rightly matter even more to them than does the less critical problem which is taking all your attention. Furthermore, some staff will be genuinely unaware of the distress which many, to them 'routine', procedures can cause to a child. Of course everybody knows that pain hurts, but not everyone understands the interaction between fear and pain, or the extent to which the strangeness of the hospital setting makes a child liable to fear.

If you can see medical personnel as highly trained and caring human beings, rather than gods in whom feet of clay are intolerable, you will probably be able to work in partnership with them so that your child gets through whatever procedures are necessary with minimum trauma. Whether you find yourself beautifully supported by staff who largely relieve you of the burden of supporting your child, or completely unsupported in your solitary efforts to persuade a screaming child to keep still, there are a few techniques, hints and pieces of information which may help you all.

Supporting your child during hospital procedures

Babies, toddlers and hospital procedures

Very young children are often more upset at being separated from parents and handled by strangers than they are by the procedures those strangers carry out. If hospital staff will allow you to stay with your child whatever is done to him, do.

If he is an out-patient or emergency, staff will seldom try to dissuade you from staying close. If he is an in-patient, certain procedures may be carried out at times when you just do not happen to be in the ward. Since doctors cannot really be expected to organize their day's work around your visits, this is one good reason for living-in if possible (*see above*).

If you want to stay with your child and be the one to hold him, don't let fear that blood, needles, etc. will be too much for you, put you off. You do not have to watch what is being done to your child's body. Let the professionals get on with that while you concentrate on keeping in eye-contact with the child and providing a safe focus for him-as-a-person.

Older children and hospital procedures

School-age children, or even pre-school children are usually better able to cope with strangers and may be able to make instant friends with medical personnel. A child who is an in-patient may be well able to get through routine procedures without you but will probably still manage emergency procedures better if you stay with him. Your presence can give all kinds of unspoken but nevertheless vital assurances.

You are there, so *you know what is being done to him.* Any fantasies about mad doctors and torture are kept under control and the fact that you *accept what is done as necessary* makes it easier for him to accept it too. If things should get bad, you will obviously be sympathetic (which the staff may be too busy to be), but just by being there while they do the unpleasant things, you make it clear that you *expect the child to put up with it.* Since he knows that you do not usually demand the impossible, this also helps him to believe (and discover) that he can manage.

You are there as a person not as an operator and you know the child as the medical personnel cannot. You can therefore *talk him through,* and spot extra agonies like embarrassment.

If he wants to cooperate or be 'good' or 'brave' you can bolster his self-esteem whatever happens. After all it *is* brave to *try* not to cry, even if the effort does not succeed. If he should feel that he has made a shaming exhibition of himself (perhaps partly because of unfortunate exhortations from staff), you will be in a position not only to help him survive at the time but also to help him approve of himself afterwards.

Adolescents and hospital procedures

Adolescents may prefer to face unpleasant episodes on their own, especially if having you there makes them feel that they must put a good face on everything to protect your feelings. Older children and adolescents should, perhaps, have the choice, but a real choice does need to be based on real information about what is to happen to them.

The vexed question of keeping still for hospital procedures

A lot of hospital procedures either require the child to keep perfectly still or are very much easier/less uncomfortable if he can do so. There are a few tricks which can help with different children in different circumstances.

Holding babies still

If a baby is to be hurt, or even if anything which will feel strange is to be done, he will have to be held. Make sure that you hold him completely immobilized. If you half-hold him he will probably feel just restricted enough to be irritated and therefore even more inclined to wriggle than if he had not been held at all.

Depending which part of his body is to be manipulated, wrapping the whole baby tightly in a blanket is often effective. Swaddled efficiently, you can control the whole child with one arm, leaving your other hand free either to hold the relevant part or to stroke him.

If he is not going to be hurt, or even actually touched, but is to have an X-ray or something of the kind, you may be able to keep him still without physically holding him at all. Attracting his attention will often 'freeze' him for the necessary seconds.

Keeping toddlers still

It is well worth preparing for procedures which do not hurt, by actually teaching toddlers and pre-school children to keep still on command. Games like 'Grandmother's Footsteps' or 'Statues' are usually very popular and can easily be evoked when needed for that X-ray.

If a toddler is to be hurt, he too will have to be held by force and may be too heavy and strong for the blanket-method. Provided that the doctor can still get at the area he needs to reach, it is often easiest if you sit down yourself and stand the child between your thighs. Thrashing legs are thus isolated from the rest of him and you have both hands free for his arms.

Helping older children to keep still

Older children who *intend* to cooperate should not be held by force until or unless it becomes clear that their self-control is not up to the task. Often such a child cannot actually keep the arm that is having a needle put in it still, but can keep the rest of his body still, especially if it is up against yours. It often helps if he can sit on your lap, with one of your arms holding him against you while the other holds that arm steady.

Movement is a more or less instinctive reaction away from pain, but the energy which a child's body tells him to put into flight can often be vented in a different way. A child who is having a rectal examination, for example, can often leave the lower half of his body passively in the hands of the doctor if he is encouraged to ba·g his hands and arms on the couch. A child who must keep his arm still while it is stitched may manage to keep stiller if he is encouraged to shout, loudly, with each prick.

Sedation and anaesthesia for hospital procedures

Doctors, and the hospitals in which they work, vary greatly in the relative importance they attach to children's distress and to the side-effects or risks of sedative drugs or anaesthetics. Some take great pride in making full use of such chemical aids for children, while others use the same criteria (also very variable) as they use for adult patients. In Britain, for example, some doctors use self-administered gas-and-air (exactly like that used in childbirth) for children undergoing a range of procedures from having stitches removed to having burns dressed. Others will prescribe a sedative for parents to give a child prior to procedures, such as complex kinds of X-rays, which are liable to be frightening even though they are not painful. Some use local anaesthetics freely for such procedures as excision of abscesses others reckon that the pain of injecting the local anaesthetic is greater than the discomfort of the procedure itself.

Obviously you (or rather your child) are largely in the hands of your doctors. But it may sometimes be worth your while to ask, very politely, whether any extra relief can be given. In a busy casualty department, for example, it may simply not have occurred to the doctor that you would rather sit quietly with your child for half an hour while a sedative takes effect than have him dealt with now, fully awake and frightened. Remember also that the doctor who is dealing with your child in this present situation cannot know, unless you tell him, about any previous experiences which may have made that child especially sensitive. If he knew about the unpleasant treatment your child had had following an accident only a month ago, he might well agree that a general anaesthetic should be given this time, even if it does mean that the child must wait several hours until his stomach is empty.

If your child should require a *series* of procedures (such as twice-weekly dressings) and you find that he is becoming increasingly afraid of them, do make an appointment and discuss it, either with the hospital consultant or through your own doctor. Nobody wants a young child to emerge from any condition with an acute and lasting fear of hospitals and medical personnel, but the staff who actually carry out the procedure will probably not have the authority to change it on the spot if you raise the matter while they are poised and ready to proceed. You need a discussion in between appointments.

Some common hospital procedures: blood tests

A sample of your child's blood will be needed in many different circumstances ranging from diagnosis of an illness (*see* **Infection**/Infections which cause illness: When the laboratory may help in diagnosis) to establishment of his blood group in order to have cross-matched blood available to him if he should require transfusion after surgery (*see* **Blood Groups**). Always ask, though, why blood is needed. Very occasionally samples are taken 'routinely'. You may prefer not to have blood taken from your child unless it really is necessary.

Heel or thumb prick   If only a small quantity of blood is needed, the doctor may take it from the heel of a young baby or the thumb of an older child, by 'pricking' the cleaned skin with a small lancet and then squeezing out a drop or two of blood.

The 'prick' hurts, of course, but this method has two great advantages: it is over so quickly that the child has no time to be afraid and, especially if he is very young, quickly forgets the whole thing; and it is not critical that he be kept absolutely still.

● If the thumb is used, be sure to tell the doctor if the child is left-handed or happens to need one particular thumb for comfort-sucking. It will need an adhesive plaster for a few hours and may be sore for a day or two.

Venepuncture
(taking blood
from a vein)

In older children (and adults) blood is usually taken from a vein on the inner side of the elbow, but in babies a variety of veins which come close to the surface of the skin may be used. The chosen site will depend on the size of the veins. Taking blood from the tiny veins of a small baby is a difficult task.

If a venepuncture goes smoothly at the first attempt it may scarcely bother the child, but if repeated attempts are needed it can be exceedingly traumatic. First-time success certainly requires a skilled operator and a 'good vein', but a perfectly still child helps too. Don't be surprised if the blood is taken by a technician rather than a doctor: this is a skill learned and kept up by constant practice: that technician will probably be far more expert in this particular respect than the grandest consultant.

Once a vein has been chosen, she will persuade it to stand out, either by squeezing the child's arm above the chosen spot or, in an older child, by putting a rubber strap tightly around for a few moments. She will clean the skin at the point where the needle is to go in. The needle now has to go through the skin and then be persuaded into the vein itself. If you are fortunate, these two stages will both take place as one and, once the needle is in the vein, the blood will be withdrawn without further discomfort. If you are less fortunate, the needle will go through the skin but the vein will slip away from its point which will then have to be moved in pursuit. It is movement of the needle under the skin which is most painful. If the vein continues to escape, the technician may withdraw the needle altogether and start again, possibly at a new site.

● Many small children are frightened by the sight of their own veins standing out. It is often best to position the child so that he cannot see, or persuade an older one not to look.

● Once the needle is in the vein (ask the operator) there will be no more pain. You can safely assure the child that 'it won't hurt any more' but he must still keep still until the needle has been withdrawn. An older child who is interested may enjoy watching his own blood being drawn up into the syringe.

● Very occasionally an inexperienced person has real difficulty puncturing a child's vein. While she will probably seek help from someone else when she thinks the child has 'had enough', you may feel entitled to ask her to do so if she wants to go on trying for longer than you consider the child can stand. If you ask whether the child may have a rest before any more is done, she will probably take the hint without taking offence.

Blood and other transfusions

Transfusions, not only of blood but of fluids to a dehydrated baby or child, or drugs to a very sick one, can be life-saving. If your child needs any kind of transfusion he will certainly be admitted as an in-patient, but the transfusion may be set up and started in the casualty department.

From the child's point of view, having a vein punctured to receive something into the bloodstream is very similar to having one punctured to take blood out. There are some differences which you may like to know:

☐ The very sharp needle with which the puncture is performed is not left in the vein. It is used to introduce a very fine plastic tube and is then withdrawn, leaving the tube to carry the transfusion.

☐ Too much movement can dislodge the tube. Veins inside the elbow are, of course, subject to a lot of arm-movement so a vein on the back of the hand, wrist or forearm is a more likely choice.

☐ Whichever vein is selected, the hand/arm will be kept still (often with a splint) and the tubing will be taped to it. Your child will not be able to use that limb freely.

● Remember to tell the doctor if he is left-handed.

☐ As well as choosing a vein which is not subject to too much movement, the doctor has to find one which is large enough to carry the transfused fluid into the circulation and go on doing so for hours or even for days. In a baby, the 'best vein', from both these points of view, may be one on the scalp. If a scalp vein is used, a small patch of hair will have to be shaved but this will quickly grow back. Parents watching the insertion of an intravenous needle into the scalp sometimes have the horrors because it looks as if it is going into the baby's head. It is not and, of course, it could not; there is solid skull under that scalp.

Injections into a vein   If a child is going to need several doses of drugs put directly into his circulation via a vein, a transfusion set will usually be set up so that each subsequent dose can be 'injected' into the equipment and dripped painlessly into the child. Occasionally, though, drugs will be given by direct injection into the vein, in which case, from the child's point of view, each dose will be similar to venepuncture for a blood test. Anaesthetics given into a vein produce unconsciousness very rapidly and usually prevent the child remembering the venepuncture.

Some types of X-ray are carried out following the intravenous injection of chemicals which will show up on the X-ray film and therefore enable the doctor to see, for example, the child's kidneys or other soft tissues. When an elaborate X-ray is planned for your child, do ask your doctor whether any such injection is involved. It is a pity to assure an older child that 'it'll only be an X-ray and you know they don't hurt' if, in fact, there are painful preliminaries.

Other injections

You (and your child) will probably be accustomed to intra-muscular and sub-cutaneous injections because he will have met needles during routine immunizations, if not for any other reason. Such injections are painless, or almost so, both because they are put into ideal sites (such as the top of the buttock or upper arm) and because such a small quantity of fluid is injected.

In hospital, you may meet some types of injection which are less quick and easy. Examples are mentioned here so that you can decide whether or not your child should be warned. If you do not warn him, he will be 'good' here and now, but may be so dismayed that there is a risk of him being 'needle-shy' next time he is due for a routine injection. On the other hand, if you do warn him that this one is different, fear and tension may make it worse for him . . .

Injections into unusual sites   The most common example is local anaesthesia in which the drug must be placed where it will effectively deaden the nerves serving the area which would otherwise be painful. This may mean a needle passing between knuckle bones to deaden a finger, or beneath the skin of the temple to deaden the area of a face-wound which is to be stitched.

The fluid has to be injected slowly so that the procedure may be rather lengthy, giving the child plenty of time to get in a panic. Furthermore, although the operator will try to keep the anaesthetic moving into the tissues ahead of the needle point, so that he deadens them as he goes, he is, by definition, injecting an area which is rich in nerves; there may be considerable pain.

Injections of large volume, or viscous liquids   If a large volume of a thickish fluid is required (as in some forms of penicillin and in gamma globulin (*see* **Infection**/Treatment of infections which cause illness: Anti-viral drugs)) the injection will be slow and comparatively painful. The fluid is pushed in gradually so as to give the tissues every opportunity to absorb it as it is given. But, inevitably, the receiving tissues become distended and this is what hurts.

● If a child goes on complaining of pain after an injection of this kind, rubbing the area (or encouraging him to do so) will speed up the dispersal of the fluid as well as giving him something to do which distracts from the discomfort.

Lumbar puncture and other 'needles'

Just as needles can be put into veins to take out blood as well as to put in fluids, so needles may sometimes be used to take sample-fluids from various parts of a child's body.

Although it is not pleasant to think about a needle being put through your child's chest-wall to remove fluid from around a lung, or through the wall of his abdomen to remove urine from his bladder, many such procedures are far worse to think about and watch than they are to experience. It may help you to remember that internal organs do not have the same kind of pain-sensitivity as other body-structures. Most are highly sensitive to stretching, for example, but not to being cut or punctured. If your child should have to have a procedure of this kind carried out, local anaesthesia will be used to deaden the skin and under-lying muscle layer, but once that injection is over the procedure will be painless although it may 'feel funny'.

Lumbar
puncture

A lumbar puncture is performed for two purposes: to enable the doctor to measure the pressure of the spinal fluid and to enable him to take a small sample of the fluid for microscopic examination and the culture of any bacteria.

Lumbar punctures are needed relatively more often in babies and young children than in older children and adults. The very young are more liable to types of infection which may affect the brain or nervous system (*see*, for example, **Meningitis and Encephalitis**), and clinical diag-nosis is much more difficult in a child too young to describe his symptoms and feelings.

Doctors and patients both vary in their views of how unpleasant lumbar puncture is and this probably reflects the fact that its unpleasantness varies. An expert operator can carry out a lumbar puncture on a relaxed child and leave him agreeing that it was 'only a prick in the back'. Other children find the whole procedure terrifying and are therefore far more difficult to work with. Furthermore, even the most expert operator can fail to get the needle into exactly the right place at the first attempt and further attempts can become more and more of a traumatic struggle.

A lumbar puncture will not be carried out on your child unless it is thought at least possible that he is seriously ill. That being so, it has to be accepted and got through somehow.

Some doctors very much dislike carrying out this procedure with a parent present and some experienced children's nurses maintain that if the child has to be held by force, against all the will that he can muster, it is psychologically better if it is not a parent who imprisons him. You will have to decide, in consultation with medical personnel and considering your own child. Sometimes the doctor will give him a preliminary sedative which, while it will not keep him asleep throughout the lumbar puncture, may prevent him being frightened by being taken away from you and may also mean that he remembers nothing about it later.

Whether you are to be present or not, you may find the following information helpful:

The child's physical position is critical to a successful lumbar puncture. He will be put on his side with his back parallel to the edge of the couch and then his knees will be curled up towards his chest so that his vertebrae separate. A pillow may be placed between his bent knees to keep his spine horizontal.

The spinal fluid is taken from the part of the spinal canal which carries on *below the level of the spinal cord itself*. There is, therefore, no risk of the needle going into the cord.

A local anaesthetic is injected into the skin and deeper tissues first.

Once the lumbar puncture needle has been inserted and its position checked, there is no more painful manipulation: necessary pressure gauges and collecting vessels are attached to that needle.

After the procedure is over, the child will be nursed lying flat (possibly on his face for as long as he will tolerate this) for about twenty-four hours. This is to avoid the headache which can follow the removal of even a small sample of spinal fluid.

If you are with the child, persuading him to remain lying down is the most useful role you can fulfil. Picking him up, however much you/he want a cuddle, is unhelpful.

Headache, although a notorious result of lumbar puncture, only affects about half the patients on whom the procedure is performed and is severe only in about half of those. Painkilling drugs will be given if your child is one of these.

Plaster casts for fractures

If your child sustains a fracture (*see* **Accidents**) she may have the affected part encased in plaster so that the bone is held in exactly the correct position while it heals.

A serious fracture may be dealt with under general anaesthesia. It may even involve surgical procedures such as 'pinning' the fractured bone. A simpler fracture may not require general anaesthesia so that the child watches the plaster being applied, usually in the form of a bandage, saturated in a solution which hardens as it air-dries.

Having plaster applied while conscious
In most hospitals, plastering fractures is a technician's task and not every such technician is accustomed to handling small children – especially shocked ones. There can be pain involved as the limb is moved during the procedure. There can also be fear. The child watches as her limb vanishes under layer upon layer of cold, wet material which gradually becomes stiffer and heavier until it ceases to feel like her own limb at all.

Help a small child to say a temporary farewell to her arm or leg. If you explain that it is going to be 'packed up safely' so that nothing can knock it or hurt it while it gets better, you may make it easier for her to accept the cast. If you keep reminding her that the arm or leg is just as it has always been but that nobody will be able to see it again until the plaster is taken off, you may be able to help her see it as a 'secret place'. Don't take it for granted that she, like you, realizes that this stiff, heavy white limb is only a temporary 'replacement' for her own. Some children do actually believe either that the plastered limb is an artifical replacement for their own which is somehow 'lost', or that the natural limb is still there but will always have to have the plaster on it.

Coming round from anaesthesia to discover a plaster cast
If your child is to have a cast applied under general anaesthesia, do warn her and discuss it with her in advance if circumstances allow. Sometimes parents are so concerned with the injury, and with seeing their child through the preparations for surgery, that they forget what a shock it may be if she wakes up and finds her body changed.

Whether you have managed to warn her or not, when she does come round it may be important to emphasize that:

The hurt limb is still there, under the cast.

That the cast will be removed, using some time-scale which she can understand such as 'before we go on holiday' or even 'when there have been six Mondays and six Tuesdays and six Wednesdays . . .

That when it is removed the limb will look and behave quite normally.

● This last will probably not be exactly accurate as limbs which have been in a cast usually lose both muscle bulk and tone so that they look comparatively thin and feel rather weak. But with a young child it is usually better to deal with that aspect of the matter later on, when she has adapted to having the cast and is beginning to anticipate having it off again.

● Children who attend a playgroup or go to school are often much cheered if they are reminded of the peer-group status a cast confers and of the chance of getting their friends to write on it . . . If crutches are necessary, they, too, may be regarded with pleasure (rather like a new version of stilts) while if it is an arm which is plastered, having to have help with getting dressed, etc. may seem fun – for a while (but *see* **Accidents**/Fractures).

Stomach wash-outs

If a child eats or drinks something poisonous or something which may be poisonous if enough has been taken, or deliberately takes 'an overdose', the doctor may think it necessary to wash out her stomach in order to remove as much as possible of the offending substance before it can be absorbed into her bloodstream (*see* **Accidents**/Poisoning). The procedure involves threading a tube up one of the child's nostrils and then working it very carefully down the throat, always making sure that it goes down her food passageway and not down her breathing passageway instead.

Most people find the placing of the tube extremely unpleasant, mainly because as soon as it touches, and moves across, the back of the throat, it makes the victim gag. Gagging and retching keeps closing the throat so that working the tube further and further down is a slow business. The back of the throat is usually sprayed with a local anaesthetic to reduce its sensitivity and lessen gagging. Medical personnel will try to persuade your child to keep on swallowing that tube, rather than fighting it. If she can do this, her swallowing will not only help the tube to go down but also give her something positive to do to help herself.

Once the end of the tube has completed its journey and is known to be safely in the stomach, liquid is poured down it and then suction is applied to bring that liquid – together with the poison – back out again. This siphoning-procedure will be repeated until medical personnel are sure that all the poison which can be removed has been washed out.

Gagging usually stops once the tube is in place, but the child may still be panicky because having one nostril blocked makes her feel that she cannot breathe freely. Try to help her to breathe gently and *not to fight*. If she struggles so much that she dislodges the tube she will have the whole horrible business to go through again. Even if she does not actually dislodge it, placing it by force will leave her with a very sore throat.

Suturing wounds

Suturing a wound simply means holding the edges together mechanically while it heals. Sutures may be stitches or various kinds of clip or clamp.

Some wounds have to be sutured if they are to heal cleanly, quickly and satisfactorily. A long gash, which has penetrated further than the skin into the underlying tissues and is gaping open, for example, might cause real trouble if it was not sutured. It would have to heal from the bottom up, like a hole. Before it began to heal it might be difficult to control bleeding. While it healed in this way it would be very liable to infection. After it had healed there might well be some loss of sensation and/or function in the area because severed muscles and nerves had not been given the chance to come together. There would probably be a large scar, too. A wound as serious as this will probably be dealt with like a minor operation and the child may be given a general anaesthetic. If he is going to be unconscious while medical personnel deal with his wound, he will not care what they do. But with less serious wounds there may be an element of choice in treatment.

Decisions on whether or not a wound should be sutured sometimes depend partly on its position on the body. If a wound is not going to be subject to very much wound-opening movement, it may be dealt with by compromise measures. There are various types of skin-closure, for example, which work on the same principles as the method recommended for home use (*see* **Accidents**/Cuts and scrapes, grazes and puncture wounds). One usual type consists of very adhesive plasters which are butterfly-shaped. One 'wing' is stuck to the skin on one side of the cut: the edges are drawn together and the other 'wing' is pressed to the other side so that they are held together. Another commonly used type is called a 'steristrip' and has adhesive strength great enough to hold even some gaping wound-edges together.

Stitches The doctor has to decide whether or not to use a local anaesthetic. If he decides not to, it will not be because he is a brute but because he does not believe that the stitches will hurt much more than would the local anaesthetic. This may be because the local would have to be put into a particularly uncomfortable place in order to be effective, and/or because only one or two stitches are needed, and/or because wherever the anaesthetic is injected, he knows it cannot be wholly effective.

Wounds are stitched much as material is sewn. A special curved needle is threaded with a short length of suture-material with a knot at the end. Holding the needle with forceps, the doctor pushes it through one edge of the cut, pulls it through so that the knot is against the skin and then pushes the needle through the other edge. When he has pulled it through so that the wound is held closed, a knot is put in that end of the suture, too, so that there is a knot at either side of the wound-line.

Obviously having the needle pushed through the skin is painful unless an anaesthetic has been used and it may be felt even if one has been given, but a skilled operator can complete both sides of one stitch almost as a single movement so that the pain is very brief even though there is some fiddling about while knots are made. Most children tolerate one or two stitches well. A series of four or more is rather a different matter. Babies tend to get into a lather of despair while older children find their courage ebbing with every new needle.

● With a child who is trying to cooperate and will communicate during suturing, you may be able to offer a great deal of help by giving him constant progress-reports. If he knows that you will warn him when the actual pricks are coming, for example, he may be able to relax during the in-between bits while knots are being tied or fresh needles prepared, and he may be able to avoid watching the procedure, leaving you to do so instead. If his courage is flagging you can also remind him that 'that's more than half' or 'only one more . . .'

Cuts on the face Comparatively minor cuts on the face may have to be stitched. Vulnerable areas – such as the forehead – have tightly stretched skin so that cuts tend to gape and go on bleeding. Furthermore, it is of course important to minimize facial scarring.

Unfortunately the face is not the pleasantest area to have stitches put in. The child will have to lie on a couch, rather than sit on your lap, and this deprives him of some comfort and comfortable holding. Local anaesthesia in this area is often rather ineffective but the skin is nevertheless highly sensitive. Having needles and forceps close to the eyes is frightening, too.

If you are faced with this situation you may like to try and be sure that the doctor attending to your child really is experienced. A combination of inexperience and a really frenzied wriggling child *could* result in nightmares and an unnecessarily untidy scar. Try confiding to the doctor that your child (perhaps already upset by the actual accident) is going to be 'a bit difficult' and asking him whether he does not think that some sedation, or even an anaesthetic, might be worthwhile. If he is unsure of himself (or if he is absolutely confident but sorry for you and the child) he may greet the suggestion with relief.

If he is certain that he can do a satisfactory job in the way he always intended to do it, believe him and do all you can to help.

Traction

Very occasionally a child with a serious fracture or other accidental injury requires to have part of her body put under traction during healing. Traction simply means that the affected part is pulled into the desired position and then held there by a system of pulleys and weights. A badly fractured thigh, for example, might require the leg to be raised on a cradle at the end of the bed with a specific weight attached to the ankle.

Being 'in traction' is unpleasant for anyone. It is intensely boring to be fixed to a bed, perhaps for several weeks. It is extremely frustrating to have movement within the bed so much restricted and a variety of minor discomforts are liable to arise, too. Bottoms get sore because patients cannot roll onto their sides; itches develop in places which cannot be reached and so forth.

For children, being in traction may also be terrifying. Always rather helpless in the ill-understood hands of the adult world, such a child is now completely helpless. Various instinctive escape routes (such as hiding under the bedclothes or running away) are physically impossible for her. Comfort-rituals may be unusable because of her unnatural and imposed position. Furthermore, she may be prey to fantasies ranging from a conviction that she is being punished by this cruel confinement for some fearful private crime, to a secret belief that she has been made part of the machinery of pulleys and weights . . .

Obviously your child's reactions will depend on her age, her maturity and her personality; obviously, too, they will depend on the kindliness of the nursing staff and the entertainment which she finds in the ward. But for most children, especially those who are too young fully to understand what is being done to them and why, and too young also to occupy themselves in reading, listening to the radio and so forth, the constant presence of a parent or other loved adult will be vitally important.

Being with a child in traction

Rooming-in may be difficult or impossible. Even if the hospital has rooms or side-wards for children with their mothers, the staff are likely to want your child in the main ward so that they can see her from the Nurses' Station. After all, she cannot get up to fetch what she needs or go to the lavatory; if she were out of sight she might get neglected.

Once any operation is over, the child is not acutely ill so you may find it difficult to justify absenting yourself and thus disrupting the lives of other family members, employers, etc. The disruption is likely to go on not for several days but for several weeks. Some kind of 'open access' (*see above*) is probably your best option and, within it, some compromise.

Try to stay with her throughout her waking hours until it is clear that she has accepted her situation. With a parent's help, most children, even at three or four, once they have been in enforced residence for two or three days, will come to realize that nobody is going to do anything else which is horrible to them and that the nurses *are* friendly. During that time you will probably have been able to deal (so far as this is possible) with her fears and fantasies, too.

Once she has 'settled', help her to begin to use what the ward offers. A child confined in this way usually attracts a good deal of sympathy and attention. There may be a play-leader or teacher on the ward for part of the day and, if your child will make friends with her, this may be a time when you can leave her. There may also be older and more mobile children who will read to her or at least play their own games where she can watch them.

Help her to enjoy other visitors. With your help any but the smallest child will come to realize that, immobilized in bed, just playing with you will come to be positively boring. This is the time to enlist outside friends, child and adult, who can bring her fresh stories, jokes or gossip.

Use every trick you can think of to mark off the hours for her so that they seem to pass faster. Help her, for example, to learn the ward routine so that the arrival of the drinks trolley marks off the first part of the morning, or the arrival of doctors on their rounds tells her that it will soon be lunch-time. If she is old enough and a visible television set is available, choosing programmes, and waiting for them, can pass almost as much time as the programmes themselves. Things which change as the days pass help, too. A budding pot-plant will mark off the days it takes to open, while sprouting seeds grow almost visibly towards edibility.

Help her use the enforced confinement to learn something new. An active four-year-old would probably not have sat still for long enough to learn to knit or crochet, but if you teach her now, she may acquire enough skill to be proud of herself. If she is a child who enjoys being shown how to do things, you may find your hours with her less boring if you teach her, too. There are a lot of skills with which we might not bother mobile children but which those who must stay still might enjoy. The range is almost limitless: from reading to changing electric plugs.

Urine specimens

A specimen of your child's urine will commonly be needed not only if the possibility of kidney disease is being investigated, but also if the reasons for an unexplained fever or other symptoms are being sought.

If urine is to be cultured to see how many micro-organisms it contains it is obviously important that extra micro-organisms should not contaminate the specimen while the child is passing it. The hospital will probably use a version of the 'clean-catch' method described below. There is nothing painful about it, but babies and toddlers may resent being handled by strangers and older children may be embarrassed. In either case you may be able to help by collecting the specimen yourself, following exactly the instructions you are given.

It is worth taking a lot of trouble about this because if a satisfactory specimen cannot be obtained in this way the doctor may feel that a specimen should be taken straight from the child's bladder by suprapubic bladder puncture (*see above* Lumbar puncture and other 'needles'). Obviously it is kinder to the child to avoid this procedure if possible.

A 'clean-catch' technique for babies   A baby does not know when he is going to urinate and neither do you. To get round this problem there are special plastic bags, designed for both boys and girls, which stick, with a special adhesive, around the vulva or above the scrotum. Properly applied, these bags make a tight seal to the skin so that once the genitals have been cleaned with the antiseptic provided and the bag has been applied, the urine, when eventually it arrives, will be 'clean' (uncontaminated). It may be your job to watch the baby and his bag and to alert medical personnel as soon as urine is produced. The weight and wetness will quickly lead to it becoming dislodged so that the specimen is lost or contaminated.

A 'clean-catch' technique for older children   The genital area has to be cleaned. You may be told to retract a boy's foreskin (if it retracts easily) and wash beneath it. For a girl, you may be told to part the labia and make sure that you swab between them.

In some cases, once cleaning is completed the child is simply asked to urinate into a sterile container, but in other cases you will be asked to have two containers ready. The beginning of the urination is discarded and only the second half caught in the container which will be used for testing. This is to ensure that any remaining micro-organisms in the genital tract are washed out by the first urine so that what is caught can be regarded as representative of the urine as it was in the child's bladder.

Many schoolchildren will prefer, and be fully able, to carry out the preliminary cleansing for themselves provided you supervise. An adolescent should, of course, carry out the whole procedure for himself and may much prefer to take his instructions directly from a nurse.

X-rays

A very large number of diagnostic techniques come under the general heading of 'X-rays'. Some involve unpleasant preliminaries, such as the intravenous injection of contrast-media (*see above*), but otherwise they are entirely painless. Because everybody knows that X-rays do not hurt, parents and hospital staff sometimes do not allow for the fact that they can frighten the very young. Familiarity with the idea of an X-ray helps a little, so do try to ensure that as soon as your child is old enough to understand about any kind of photograph he knows about this kind, too.

Helping your child in the X-ray department

If an adequate X-ray is to be taken your child will have to keep the relevant part still. He may also have to keep still in a difficult position. A chest X-ray, for example, may require him to hold his breath for a couple of seconds. An X-ray of a damaged arm may require him to keep it in a position which hurts.

Unfortunately you cannot usually *hold* your child still for an X-ray and you may not even be able to hold the rest of him for comfort while his arm is being X-rayed. Most hospitals have very strict rules which forbid anybody but the patient from being subjected to the machine's radiation (even though this is minute). Furthermore, if you were holding your child, the eventual 'picture' which has to be interpreted would be confused by the mix-up between bits of you and bits of the child. He is probably, therefore, going to have to stand, sit or lie alone in front of the machine.

X-ray machinery is large and formidable. Just being near it may frighten your child. Sometimes bits of that machinery move towards and away from him as the technician adjusts distances and so forth. To a small child that movement is often the last straw that evokes panic and flight.

Try and enlist the sympathy of the operator so that the child is given time to look around. If he or she will explain a little of how it all works to a toddler or pre-school child, or show a baby the lights and their reflection off all that shiny metal, he may be able to be interested rather than afraid.

Show the child where he is going to stand or lie and which bit of the machinery is going to take 'the picture'. Try and get the operator to move any bits which will move later, so that the child can see, while you are still with him, that he is not going to be devoured or squashed.

Get him to practise anything he will have to do like holding his breath while you and the operator count to three.

If the child has a painful place to be X-rayed, make sure the operator knows that it is painful and ask her, in front of the child, what position she will need it in. She will have a variety of foam-blocks and wedges which can be used to help keep a limb still or a child in a particular position; your aim is to get her to arrange the child to her technical satisfaction before she sends you out of the way.

Ask if you may stay in the screened cubicle used by the operators themselves. There is no reason why you should be sent right out of the room if your leaving will distress the child. If you are allowed to stay, *keep talking* to the child.

Surgery

While the full range of surgical techniques may be applied to babies and children, these brief notes on some of the more common childhood operations may be useful. They are intended to give parents a starting point for asking questions and to suggest some of the aspects of surgery which a child may find unnecessarily alarming unless he is well-prepared.

Preparations for surgery

Except in an emergency, a child will usually be admitted to hospital at least twenty-four hours before any operation. If preliminary investigations or treatment are required he may be admitted sooner. There are several reasons for this:

Members of the surgical team will want to examine him.

The anaesthetist will examine him to make sure that he is fit to receive an anaesthetic. Occasionally a non-urgent operation will be delayed if a child has a respiratory infection, for example.

Nursing staff hope to 'settle' the child so that he has some familiarity with the ward and the people who will be caring for him. If he is very young, they will want to establish his level of communication; the words he uses for things he wants and so forth. This is the time to make sure that everyone realizes the importance of that rag (*see* **Habits**/Comfort habits: 'Cuddlies') or those spectacles.

He will have to be deprived of food and drink for a period before the operation. The risks of anaesthesia when the stomach is not 'empty' are very great. Hospitals usually prefer patients to be under professional care in case somebody feels that 'just a little drink' does not matter, or the child helps himself.

● Although, of course, not every operation can take place first thing in the morning, this is the best time from a young child's point of view because he will then scarcely notice that he is missing meals and not being allowed a drink.

There may be specific preparations for this particular operation. Sometimes, for example, hair is shaved from an operation site, or a course of antibiotics may be started before the operation to help prevent infection afterwards.

● It is always worth asking in advance about specific preparations. Some children are more upset by non-painful procedures which they were not expecting than by the operation itself.

Anaesthesia   The anaesthetist is an extremely highly trained and skilled professional with a wide range of techniques at his disposal. From the child's point of view, it does not matter exactly what happens while he is unconscious. It is the 'going to sleep' and the 'waking up' which are important. These are some of the fears commonly expressed by toddlers and pre-school (or older) children:

'Being put to sleep' is the same as being killed. Even a child who has little understanding of the nature of death may equate anaesthesia with the end of a beloved pet who was 'put to sleep' by a vet.

If anaesthesia is 'sleep', going to sleep is dangerous. Some children specifically fear that 'they' might 'cut him open' while he is normally asleep at night; others fear that they might wake up in the middle of the operation or that the operation might begin before they are fully asleep.

● The words parents use to explain anaesthesia are obviously critical and equally obviously have to be chosen for the individual child. Some find that 'special sleep' or 'magic sleep' are useful phrases. Whatever words you choose, the important thing is to make it clear to the child that anaesthesia is *different* from ordinary sleep; that it *only* occurs when a doctor says it is going to and that doctors and nurses can *always tell* the difference.

Once convinced of the above, some children are terrified of the idea of being moved away from the ward whilst 'asleep', often because they do not know where they will be taken and they therefore feel that their parents will not be able to find them.

● Depending on the child's age and condition and the hospital's policy and geography, it can be helpful if you can accompany the child to the operating theatre or anaesthetic induction room to show him, in advance, where it is in relation to the ward. If this is impossible, try at least to ensure that you are with the child until he is taken from the ward (he will be sleepy, *see below*) and that you are there waiting for his return.

Children are usually given pre-medication before an anaesthetic. The drugs given will have the double effect of drying the child's respiratory tract (which will make his mouth feel dry but also lessens the chance of his choking during the anaesthetic) and making him feel sleepy and don't-careish. The 'pre-med' is usually given about an hour before the operation. It may be given by mouth, by injection or in the form of a small enema ('per rectum').

● The anaesthetist will tell you which method he has ordered. If you are not there when he visits the child, he will have left orders with the nursing staff. Ask the senior nurse.

● If you are allowed to stay with your child once he has had his 'pre-med', do encourage him to drift peacefully off to sleep. The less he fights these sedative drugs the more effective they will be, and the more effectively they work for him the less he will even realize, let alone be afraid, when he is fetched from the ward for surgery.

Recovery from anaesthesia

The after-effects of anaesthesia vary widely not only according to the depth of anaesthesia and the length of time for which it was required, but also from child to child. Yours may recover rapidly and smoothly, but on the whole we all tend to underestimate the length of time it takes bodies to rid themselves of anaesthetic drugs. Be prepared for any of the following:

In most hospitals, the child will be taken from the operating theatre to a 'recovery room' rather than straight back to the ward. He may be kept there until specially trained staff are satisfied that his breathing, cough reflexes, blood pressure and so forth, are all back to normal.

● If you are waiting in the ward, don't assume that because your child is gone for several hours the operation has lasted for hours or has gone wrong in any way.

He may be returned to the ward looking unexpectedly (to you) ill. Anaesthesia often leaves children a very bad colour for a while.

Many children vomit after anaesthesia. Some vomit frequently over several hours.

It is possible that he will be returned to the ward with a drain in the surgical wound, a catheter in his bladder or a drip going into a vein. Even if you have not been warned and therefore were not expecting anything of this kind, don't assume that anything has gone wrong. The surgical team aims to keep him in the best possible condition for recovery. That drip, for example, does not necessarily mean that he lost a lot of blood. It may simply be intended to ensure optimum fluids until he can drink.

While he comes round, the child may seem very distressed and/or 'wild'. Remember that, while there may be pain, he will over-react to *any* discomfort while he is still semi-conscious. Screams need not mean agony. His state is likely to be similar to that of delirium. It will settle as his body rids itself of the anaesthetic drugs.

● If staff will allow you to be with the child while he recovers, your best role is that of familiar comforter. The more you can soothe the child and persuade him to let himself sleep, the less he will know about this unpleasant period and the sooner it will be over. When he stirs or cries, tell him that you are there and that it is 'all over', but then stroke him back to sleep again. Don't try to make him sit up and take notice. You may need to repeat your reassurances several times as his first 'awakenings' will be brief and forgotten.

● However unpleasant this period *looks*, take comfort from the fact that the child will not remember much about it afterwards.

Even once the child is definitely awake and apparently 'over' the anaesthetic, he may be depressed, irritable and miserable for hours or even for a day or two.

Staff may seem brutally insistent that the child get out of bed and/or do breathing and other exercises with a physiotherapist very soon after the operation. It is vitally important that his muscle tone and efficient circulation be maintained and that, even if it hurts, he breathe deeply and cough efficiently so as to keep his respiratory tract clear of mucus.

● Your role will depend on whether staff do want to encourage activity or whether the operation was one after which they want him kept quiet. Since you are probably the person best able *either* to encourage him out of bed and into taking an interest in the other children, *or* into resting quietly while you read that favourite book aloud, do ask.

Some children, after some operations, are haunted by dressings which, they feel, may cover some horrible mutilation. Since a surgical wound is almost always less horrific than imagination suggests, your child may feel better if he is encouraged to look at his scar the first time the dressings are changed.

● Remember, though, that he does not have your experience of the healing process. Having discovered that his belly is still *there* after removal of his appendix, he may be convinced that the wound and stitches which he can see will remain forever. If you react favourably ('that's beautifully neat. Once those stitches are out and the skin has all healed it will hardly show . . .') he may believe you. If you happen to have a nicely inconspicuous surgical scar in the family, show it to him.

Appendectomy

Removal of the appendix, performed, as a matter of urgency, when a child has, or is thought to have, appendicitis.

The appendix is a small dead-end tube leading off the large intestine. Because it is a dead end, this tube can only discharge anything which gets into it from the intestine back the way it came and it is therefore rather liable to inflammation. Opinions about appendicitis have changed radically in recent years. It used to be thought that the appendix became inflamed when something small and hard, like a fruit pip, became wedged in it. Now it is thought that blockage of that single opening by small hard pellets of waste-matter is a more frequent cause. Certainly there is no need to worry about the possibility of appendicitis just because your child swallows grape pips or a cherry stone. For many years the appendix was regarded as a completely useless, obsolete addition to the intestine. Occasionally explorers would have their appendixes removed prior to their travels in case of appendicitis while they were far from civilization. Now it is known that the walls of the appendix are rich in lymphoid tissue (*see* **Immune Response**) which might play a role in the production of antibodies. While people can manage perfectly well without their appendixes, nobody would have one removed unnecessarily.

It used to be thought that an appendix could 'grumble', causing bouts of abdominal pain which then receded. Now most doctors believe that recurrent abdominal pain must have some other cause (*see* **Abdominal Pain**). Appendicitis gets worse and worse until the appendix either bursts (causing peritonitis) or is removed.

Diagnosing
appendicitis

There are many causes for abdominal pain with or without associated symptoms such as vomiting, constipation, diarrhoea and fever (*see* **Abdominal Pain**). A skilled surgeon can examine the child's abdomen, assess the pain which particular manoeuvres (often including a rectal examination) do or do not provoke, and make a highly educated guess as to the cause. But even he cannot always be certain of a diagnosis of appendicitis. If he is in doubt, but on balance thinks appendicitis *unlikely*, he may keep the child in hospital for observation. All preparations for surgery (including withholding food and drink) will probably be made so that the operation can be performed immediately if the condition becomes clear. If he is in doubt but on balance considers appendicitis *likely*, he will probably operate. The risks of an unnecessary appendectomy are far less than the risks of waiting too long.

If an inflamed appendix is not removed quickly (usually within twenty-four hours of the first symptoms) it is likely to fill with pus and eventually burst. This is the situation which most often gives rise to the condition known as peritonitis, in which infected material spreads through the abdomen causing widespread inflammation and infection. Instead of the very simple operation involved in removing the appendix, the surgeon then has to repair the rupture and deal with the infection. Peritonitis, even today, is dangerous.

Removing the
appendix

Appendectomy is a routine operation for the hospital even if it is a once-in-a-lifetime experience for your child. No special preparations are usually needed. Pre-medication and anaesthesia will be given.

The appendix is removed through a small incision low down on the right of the abdomen. Many surgeons pride themselves on leaving a scar not more than a couple of inches long and below the 'bikini line'.

The child will probably be allowed home as soon as the stitches are removed: often about day seven.

Blocked tear (lacrimal) duct

Lacrimal ducts carry surplus tears from the eye into the nose from which they drain. When a child cries, the surplus fluid appears as external tears, but the rest of the time the ducts ensure that the eyes have enough bathing fluid but not too much.

Many newborn babies have runny or 'sticky' eyes. The maternity hospital may take swabs in order to check for infection, but often the condition is simply due to debris, such as amniotic fluid or blood, getting into the eye during birth (*see* **Eyes and Seeing; Eye Disorders and Blindness**/Eye disorders).

Diagnosing
a blocked
tear duct

A baby who, during his first few months, has an eye which constantly runs clear fluid or which recurrently becomes 'sticky', may have a blocked tear duct. The ducts usually clear themselves by six months of age so each episode of 'sticky eye' will be treated symptomatically to begin with.

If there is continual running or frequent stickiness in the second half of the first year, your doctor may advise that the duct be cleared by an ophthalmic surgeon under general anaesthesia.

Clearing a
tear duct
Parents will often be given some choice about the timing of this very minor operation. If you feel strongly that you would prefer to wait a further three months, hoping that the tear duct will clear itself, your doctor will probably accept this. But unless you have strong reasons for waiting it is probably better to accept the earliest appointment you can be given; the whole hospital experience is likely to be more upsetting to a one-year-old than to a child of eight or nine months.

The operation only involves passing a very fine probe along the tear duct. Anaesthesia is very brief; since there is no cutting involved there should be no pain, and there will be no stitches to be removed nor any scarring. You may be allowed to take the baby home on the same day.

Circumcision

Circumcision is a minor operation but one which, in a child past early infancy, can cause major upset. A toddler is likely to be uncomprehendingly furious at this assault on his precious self. A four-year-old may suffer agonies (sometimes amounting almost to an identity-crisis) concerning what he may see as a punishment for his sexuality or the secret sensuality of his love for his mother. Even an eight- or nine-year-old, well able to understand why the operation is needed and allowed to share in the decision to have it performed, may find the whole procedure deeply embarrassing and depressing. If a baby is left uncircumcised, the procedure is seldom needed later unless over-enthusiastic attempts have been made to retract his foreskin (*see* **Circumcision**). Some of the reasons for the operation include:

Diagnosing a
need for late
circumcision
Persistent or recurrent soreness/infection under the foreskin (balanitis). This can often be dealt with by a combination of drugs and improved hygiene, but occasionally the frequency of the bouts, or the scarring they are causing, does make surgery necessary.

Tightness of the foreskin (phimosis) so great that the flow of urine is obstructed or slowed down.

Failure of the foreskin to roll back easily when the penis is erect. While this may go with phimosis it does occasionally occur separately. The foreskin is not tight; it can easily be retracted with the hands, but it does not retract itself as erection takes place.

Removing the
foreskin
Unlike infant circumcision, the operation is always carried out under a general anaesthetic. A 'cuff' of foreskin is removed and the edges of the cut are stitched together (another difference from the infant procedure which requires no stitches). The patient is often allowed home later the same day, as soon as he has recovered from the anaesthetic. If you are offered this 'day surgery' for your child, do accept it as not having to stay in the hospital will probably much reduce his distress.

Stitches are usually removed about a week later and the soreness should be over within two weeks.

● If erection occurs in the few days following circumcision it is likely to be very painful. This can add to the distress of a very small boy who feels that his own organ is attacking him, or to that of an older boy whose erections may be a very private pleasure. Difficulty in getting to sleep after circumcision is sometimes due not only to the general upset but to the fact that the boy cannot settle down with his hand on his penis for comfort.

● While the hospital will instruct you in caring for the surgical wound, there is quite a lot you can do to make the first few days at home more comfortable. A protective 'box', for example, as worn by many sportsmen, may help an older boy; a toddler's equivalent can be quickly produced if you cut a hard but hollow rubber ball in half.

● If a school-aged boy has to have this operation, do try to arrange it during the holidays and help him to keep the whole matter entirely private from his peers if he prefers. If he must return to school before the wound has healed to a point where his penis looks normal (though now circumcised) it may be a kindness to get him temporarily excused from games or any other circumstances which demand that he strip in public.

Cleft lip

A baby's upper lip develops in two parts while she is in the womb and normally joins up before birth. If this joining fails to take place, she will be born with it still separated in the middle.

Facing a cleft lip   The first sight of their new baby with a cleft lip usually gives parents a shock which is out of proportion to the real seriousness of the condition. It looks dreadful, but it has no implications for the baby's health (unless the palate is also cleft, *see below*) and only short-term implications for her appearance. Ideally, you should be shown photographs of babies whose cleft lips have been repaired, within minutes of seeing your own affected child. If nobody offers you such photographs, do ask to see some. Such babies look (and are) perfectly normal. The scars, even at the beginning, are scarcely visible. What you have to cope with is your own shock and misery – perhaps even amounting to a feeling that you cannot love a baby who looks like that – and a wait of approximately three months before surgery can put the matter right.

Repairing a   Repair of a cleft lip is usually undertaken when the baby is about three
cleft lip   months old. It should be (and almost always is) undertaken by a plastic surgeon. Some such surgeons specialize in this condition and it is certainly worthwhile to seek out such a professional if possible. The operation is not serious but it is lengthy as the finest and most careful stitching is used to bring the two parts of the lip into perfect alignment.

The baby will probably be kept in hospital for several days as you may need help with feeding her, and with ensuring that her questing hands do not ruin the plastic surgeon's work.

Cleft palate

The 'roof' of the mouth also develops in two parts and, like the upper lip, occasionally fails to close up before birth. The two conditions often, but not invariably, go together.

Facing a cleft palate

If the lip is intact, a cleft palate is not immediately obvious and therefore the shock to new parents is far less. The condition is far more serious, however. The space between the two halves of the palate mean that when the baby sucks milk, it is free to go up into her nasal passages and choke her. She will not be able to feed normally.

Preparing for repair of a cleft palate

The two halves of the cleft palate cannot be finally joined together until they are of approximately the same size, and until growth within the mouth has reached a suitable point. The final operation commonly has to wait until the baby is about eighteen months old. In the meantime she has to be fed. Very early feeds may be accomplished by using a special bottle-teat with a wide flat guard on the top which effectively prevents milk escaping to the absent roof of the mouth. Within days, minor surgery will probably be carried out to fit a plate to the palate. This first operation serves the double purpose of blocking off that opening and encouraging the smaller half of the palate to grow relatively faster than the larger half.

These plates may need frequent changing to allow for the child's growth, to keep feeding as easy as possible for you both, and to make sure that she has the greatest possible freedom to make early sounds. If you can come to terms with this difficult period, believe that your child's difficulties really will be finally solved before she reaches kindergarten age, and work with the hospital team throughout her infancy, you will all be ideally placed to ride through the final operation when the time comes.

Repairing a cleft palate

The ease or difficulty with which the final repair of a cleft palate can be accomplished depends on all that early preparation. Being a toddler, your child is rather likely to be upset by the hospital admission, but being accustomed to hospital appointments, she may cope rather better than a child who is admitted as an emergency. The surgery itself is not dangerous but there is likely to be considerable pain and difficulty in feeding afterwards. She may be in hospital for some days and will certainly survive better if you can be with her.

● If you know an adult whose cleft lip/palate was poorly repaired many years ago, you may find it difficult to believe that your child will ever look normal. But she will. The techniques of plastic surgery have improved and so has our knowledge of the correct timing for these operations. Once again, when you find yourself in despair, do ask for 'before and after' photographs.

Hernia (inguinal)

Diagnosing an inguinal hernia

If you should notice a 'swelling' low down on your baby's abdomen, in the groin area or over the scrotum, a loop of intestine may have found its way through the inguinal canal to form a hernia (*see* **Hernia**).

As we have seen, the inguinal canal usually closes up when the testicles have travelled down it to take up their permanent position in the scrotum. But sometimes the canal remains open which is why inguinal hernias are frequently associated with undescended or retractile testicles (*see below* Undescended testicles).

The appearance of such a hernia is not an emergency in itself but it can become an emergency if that loop of intestine should become trapped outside the body and thus lose its full blood supply. If you lie the baby down, the hernia will probably vanish and this will show that the intestine has slipped back into its proper place. If lying him down does not produce this effect and the bulge remains visible, you would probably be wise to take the baby directly to your nearest casualty department.

If the hernia does vanish when the baby is lying down, make an appointment to see your doctor as soon as it is convenient. The hernia may, or may not, reappear whenever the baby is in an upright position, but as long as it continues to slip freely in and out of the abdomen there is nothing to worry about. Your doctor will probably refer you to a surgeon and the operation will be carried out as soon as it can be arranged, but not as an emergency.

Correcting an inguinal hernia   If an inguinal hernia is operated upon within days, or a few weeks, of its first appearance, the procedure is very quick and simple. All the surgeon has to do is to ensure that the testicles are in the scrotum and that the intestine is in its rightful place, and then tie the ring of muscles around the inguinal canal so that a retractile testicle can no longer go up, nor any intestine come down, it.

If surgery is long-delayed, the affected muscles may become stretched and weakened so that a far more elaborate repair is needed.

Hydrocele

A hydrocele is a collection of fluid around the testicle which makes the scrotum look enlarged and swollen. If a hydrocele is present on one side only, parents sometimes mistake it for an inguinal hernia (*see above*). Often, though, both sides of the scrotum are affected. The hydrocele is often present at birth.

A hydrocele almost always resolves itself without any treatment at all. The fluid absorbs, leaving the testicle entirely undamaged. Only in the extremely rare case of a hydrocele persisting after the first year is surgery considered.

That rarely needed surgery for hydrocele is simple in itself, but the age at which it must be carried out is unfortunate. Toddlers tend to react badly to hospital admission, while little boys are usually extremely concerned about their genitals and may react very badly to any surgical interference in that area.

Intussusception

Although this is not at all a common condition, it is mentioned here because immediate recognition and surgery are vitally important.

Acute intussusception occurs when a portion of the intestine telescopes into the portion immediately ahead of it, causing a concertina-like bowel obstruction. This rare abdominal emergency is least uncommon in babies between about three months and one year. It can usually be differentiated from other forms of 'colic' by the following signs:

Diagnosing intussusception

Excruciating pain causes the baby not only to scream and draw up his legs, but to go very pale or greyish and sometimes to become soaked in sweat so that his hair is plastered to his desperately thrashing head.

The pain occurs in distinct bouts geared to the rhythmical contractions of the bowel. As these peristaltic movements force the telescoped bowel forward, pain occurs. As the wave of intestinal movement passes, the pain stops. A baby who has had one or two bouts of pain of this intensity will commonly drop off to sleep from sheer exhaustion, but will be woken within a minute or two by the next bout.

The baby is very likely to vomit and to bleed from his rectum so that any stool he passes looks like redcurrant jelly. But if you suspect this emergency, don't assume that because he has not vomited or passed a 'redcurrant jelly' stool, you must be wrong: seek medical advice immediately.

Correcting an intussusception

If an intussusception is operated upon early, the surgery involved is comparatively simple. An incision is made through the abdominal wall and the intestine pulled back into shape. If surgery is delayed, the affected part of the intestine may be squeezed tightly for so long that lack of blood causes it to become gangrenous. The damaged part has to be removed and the operation becomes a very serious procedure.

Myringotomy (drainage of the middle ear)
(*see* **Ears and Hearing; Ear Disorders and Deafness**/Ear disorders)

Repeated infections in the middle ear, especially if these are combined with much-enlarged adenoids, can lead to the accumulation of matter which will not drain freely down the eustachian tubes and into the throat. Matter or fluid in the middle ear immediately affects hearing; repeated infection can cause scarring which will reduce hearing permanently.

Draining the middle ear

A tiny incision is made in the eardrum so that the middle ear can be drained from the outer ear. On its own, this is a very minor surgical procedure. Your child will be given a general anaesthetic but will usually be allowed home as soon as he has recovered from it.

Sometimes a tiny plastic or metal 'button' (called a grommet) is left in the surgeon's incision so that any further accumulations of fluid can continue to drain out. You may have to ban swimming, and take care that no water gets into the child's ear during bathing. The grommet usually comes out by itself as healing proceeds.

Myringotomy is sometimes combined with removal of the adenoids if these are thought to have been contributing to the ear problems. In that case, of course, your child will be kept in hospital for a few days (*see below* Tonsillectomy and Adenoidectomy).

Plastic surgery

While the work of a plastic surgeon may be vital – and almost miraculous – to a child born with a cleft lip or seriously scarred in an accident, its use to correct minor blemishes and deformities is, and should be, strictly limited. Plastic surgery involves cutting; cutting makes scars and scars grow as a child grows. If your child should be born with a strawberry mark on her face (*see* **Birthmarks**) she *will* be able to have it removed surgically if it should be one of the rare ones which does not vanish of its own accord, but you and she will both have to accept it for several years first. If she should have a dark and ill-placed mole, this too can be removed one day but that day is so far into the future that it is a pity if she has to go through most of her childhood waiting to change herself. On the whole, characteristics like sticking-out ears or 'odd' noses are better accepted as part of the individuality of the individual child. If you can accept and love her as she is, she will probably be able to do so too.

Appearance usually becomes vitally important to adolescents and at this stage plastic surgery is more likely to be satisfactory because growth is almost complete. If the blemish is real – in the sense of being not only clearly visible but also ugly to everyone who sees her – its removal may do a great deal to boost her confidence and to help her approve of her nearly-grown-up self. Be cautious, though. Some adolescents pick on a particular physical characteristic and use it as a focus for discontent which is really far more deep-seated. A 'nose-job', however expertly performed, may cast your daughter even farther into a depression which was not really about her face but about her identity as a person (*see* **Adolescence/**Problems with appearance and body-image).

If ever you contemplate seeking plastic surgery for a child of any age, do start by consulting the doctor who knows her best. In some communities there are plastic surgeons whose practice is almost entirely 'cosmetic', rather than medical, and who will strive to give the patient what she says she wants without a full assessment designed to ensure that the procedure is in her best interests. The recent example of a fifteen-year-old who responded to an advertisement and had her breasts 'augmented' is a salutary case in point. Nobody pointed out to her that, even if the procedure was entirely 'successful', it was likely to cause difficulties if she ever wanted to breast-feed a baby.

Pyloric stenosis

The pylorus is the muscular valve which controls the flow of food and gastric juices from the stomach into the duodenum and thence into the intestines. In pyloric stenosis, the muscles thicken so that the valve does not function correctly. Food-flow is either partially or completely blocked. The condition is far commoner in boys than in girls but is also commoner in first-born than in later children. If your first son has it, the chances of later boys in your family having it too are only a little greater than the chances for an unaffected family.

Signs of pyloric stenosis   If milk is taken into the stomach but cannot reach the duodenum, there is only one place for it to go: back up again. The principal sign of pyloric stenosis, then, is vomiting. It may take place during feeding or soon afterwards. While the first episodes may seem like ordinary 'spitting up', the vomiting becomes extremely forceful as the degree of obstruction increases. Milk is often ejected several feet, perhaps hitting the wall behind you. It is accurately named 'projectile vomiting'.

Left untreated, pyloric stenosis deprives a baby of nourishment and, more importantly, of fluid. He will therefore lose weight and become dehydrated. He will produce very little waste-matter as his food is not reaching the intestine.

Recognizing pyloric stenosis early

Ideally pyloric stenosis should be recognized before the obstruction has become great enough to deprive the baby of fluid and food. You will probably distinguish between the vomiting of early pyloric stenosis and vomiting due to any other cause, such as infection, if you notice that although he vomits whenever he is fed *the baby is hungry*. He is not ill. He wants the food and this is your clue to the fact that the vomiting is mechanical.

● It takes that muscular valve a week or two to thicken enough to cause trouble, so any vomiting in the very first week or two of life is unlikely to be from this cause. On the other hand, if the pylorus is going to cause obstruction it will certainly have begun to do so by the time the baby is around six weeks. Vomiting which *begins* later must have another cause.

Diagnosis of pyloric stenosis

Your doctor or health visitor can confirm your suspicions by watching the baby during a feed. Forceful contractions of the distended stomach can be seen against the obstruction outlined under the baby's skin. Even without watching a feed, your doctor may be able to feel the thickened muscular valve through the skin of the abdomen.

Treatment of pyloric stenosis

In some countries such babies are treated with special feedings and antispasmodic drugs in the expectation that the condition will right itself. But in most western countries, and certainly in Britain and the United States, definitive surgery is undertaken as soon as possible. Should you have to wait a few days for surgery, dietary and drug treatment may be prescribed in the meantime.

Relieving the obstruction of pyloric stenosis

The operation is simple and quick, involving only a short general anaesthetic while the surgeon makes an incision through the abdominal wall and pylorus so as to relieve the obstruction. The baby can usually be fed normally within a few hours (although he may vomit at the first couple of feedings) and normal digestion begins immediately and continues thereafter. No further problems need be anticipated.

Squint (strabismus; 'cross-eyes' 'lazy eye')
(*see* **Eyes and Seeing; Eye Disorders and Blindness**)

Not all squints can be cured by surgery, but some, especially the types which are present from birth or noted in the first year, are largely due to an imbalance in the lengths of the muscles controlling the movements of the two eyes. An ophthalmic surgeon can readjust the muscles so that the eyes work together.

Although eye surgery on a baby or small child is neither pleasant to think about nor to undergo, a surgical solution is a far happier option than the long drawn-out treatments which may otherwise be needed.

● If your child is to have surgery for strabismus do make every effort to stay with him. There are several reasons why this is especially important.

Eyes may or may not 'window the soul' but they are certainly very personal-feeling, even to a baby. The many eye-examinations he will undergo will upset him more than examinations of, say, a hernia.

If he needs one operation he may well need a second later on. The less traumatic the first, the more easily he will ride through the next.

Eye surgery probably means quite a lot of other procedures, such as eye drops and so forth, before and after the operation. He will tolerate these better if you are there.

He will probably have to have one or both eyes covered for a period. Busy nurses may be unable to watch him every moment so if he pulls the bandages off when left alone they may even resort to tying his hands to the sides of the cot . . . If you are there you can protect him from all that. Even if he is old enough to cooperate in leaving the bandages alone, being unable to see is very frightening for anyone and positively terrifying for a small child in a strange place. He needs to be able to hear you and feel your touch.

Tonsillectomy and adenoidectomy

Children under five tend to have rapidly growing tonsils and adenoids and to be prone to tonsillitis, middle-ear infections and catarrhal problems. A couple of generations ago it was thought that the tonsils and adenoids *caused* these childish illnesses and they were therefore removed, almost as a matter of routine, from many children. Now, both knowledge and attitudes have changed and the operations have become much less frequent.

A five-year-old who has three or four bouts of tonsillitis and several colds in one year, looks rather pale, has a poor appetite and breathes through his mouth, will probably be found to have enlarged adenoids and big, wobbly tonsils which almost meet in the middle. During his illnesses, those tonsils may have white or yellowey flecks on them. It is easy to see why people believed that the tonsils were harbouring the infection and that taking them out would produce a healthier child. In fact those tonsils are *reacting to* infection, rather than causing it. Since it is their prime function to react to infection by instigating the production of antibodies, the child may well be better off with than without them. Some research comparing the later health of children who have, and have not, had tonsillectomies/adenoidectomies shows no significant difference in the number or severity of later infections. All tend to 'grow out of' the tendency to frequent upper respiratory infections by the age of about seven, while the tonsils and adenoids shrink significantly during the early school years.

When tonsillectomy may be advisable   Some authorities believe that tonsils which have been infected again and again may have pockets of pus trapped within them which can act as a reservoir of infection which flares up to cause recurrent symptoms.

Whether or not tonsils ever actually cause infection, most authorities would agree that their removal should be considered if a school-aged child has had three or four bouts of acute tonsillitis a year for at least the last two years. If a child's tonsils are removed his adenoids will probably be removed at the same time.

When adenoidectomy may be advisable

If enlarged adenoids are contributing to frequent middle-ear infections, by obstructing free drainage through the eustachian tubes (*see above* Myringotomy) their removal may be urgent.

● Mouth-breathing, snoring and so forth are not in themselves sufficient reasons for this operation because they will resolve spontaneously as the adenoids shrink during childhood.

An adenoidectomy which is undertaken to protect a child's ears and hearing may be carried out when he is only two or three years old. The tonsils will seldom be removed at the same time because they still have years of useful work ahead of them.

When tonsils and adenoids are removed

Although 'T and A' is now a very safe operation, the immediate post-operative period may be unpleasant for the child and alarming for parents.
    The child's throat is naturally extremely sore (although the raw patches heal surprisingly quickly). If he vomits because of the anaesthetic, there may be bleeding. If he cries because of the pain, the blood and the vomiting, he will increase all three and may get himself into a horrible vicious circle. It is as well that you should be warned because, provided that the hospital will allow you to be with the child while he recovers, and provided you do not panic, you have a vital role to play.

Keep the child as quiet and calm as you possibly can. The stiller he keeps and the more he allows himself to sleep off the anaesthetic, the less likely it is that he will vomit. The less panicky he gets because of pain and blood the less there will be of either.

● A few hospitals still try to prevent parents from sitting with children while they recover from 'T and A' anaesthetics because they do not trust those parents not to get upset. Try to select a hospital which cooperates with parents, and prove to the staff that you can help, rather than hinder, them and the child.

Undescended testicles
(for recognition of the condition *see* **Undescended Testicle**)

A testicle which has not descended by the time a boy is around three or four must be brought down into the scrotum and fixed there. The operation is not physically serious but its nature and timing are psychologically unfortunate. Whether your son can voice these feelings or not, he is very likely to see this interference with his sexual parts as some kind of attack on his maleness.
    Some doctors and surgeons may agree to leave the operation until a little later in a boy's life, but any such decision should be reached very carefully. Early descent of the testicle is thought to optimize its chances of

absolutely normal sperm production later. The abdomen is too warm for testicles which have evolved into their scrotal position largely because they function best if kept a few degrees cooler than the rest of the body. Perhaps slightly reduced sperm production in one testicle would not matter very much to your son – many men father plenty of children with only one – but there is always the slight risk of the 'good' one getting damaged . . . Furthermore, delaying the operation until, say, seven or eight, may help the boy to accept explanations about the surgery but may have left him vulnerable to feeling 'different' when boys at school first compared sexual parts.

On the whole it is probably best to accept the earliest possible operation and to concentrate on seeing your child through it as best you can. This is another occasion when having a parent room-in will certainly help.

Visiting by children

Hospitals vary in their attitudes to visiting children: some pride themselves on making them welcome, others ban them altogether or tolerate only those above a certain age.

If you are considering taking a young child to visit, say, a parent who is in hospital, do consider the following points before you do so:

A child who wants Mummy wants her as she usually is

However much he is missing her, a mother who, because of her physical state, neither looks nor can behave as he expects, can be extremely frightening. Before you take him to visit her, go by yourself and try to consider her through his inexperienced eyes. It may be better to delay the visit if, for example:

Her colour is bad, eyes puffy, hair stringy . . . The child will look mostly at her face. Does it look worse than he has seen it first thing in the morning after she has had an especially bad night?

She has anything attached to her such as an oxygen mask, nasal tube, intravenous drip. A young child, who will inevitably feel that his mother has been 'taken over' by the hospital, may have terrifying fantasies about her having become 'part of those machines . . .'

She is in pain. A young child probably will not recognize pain as pain, but he will register it as distress and be very distressed himself.

She is obviously sedated. Again the child will not recognize sedation for what it is, but will sense his mother's strange detachment from reality (which for him means himself) and may feel that she rejects him.

● The sick parent may long to see the child and be convinced that he or she can put on an act sufficient to reassure him. Use *your* judgement; the patient cannot see him/herself.

If the child saw an accident, or drama, a glimpse may reassure

If the whole family was in a car crash and the father was badly hurt, children who saw him carried, covered in blood and unconscious, into the ambulance, may desperately need to glimpse him in his hospital bed just to see that he is actually alive. Under those circumstances, a quick wave from the doorway of the ward may be a good compromise.

If a brother or sister got hurt or fell dramatically ill (as with a febrile convulsion, for example) in front of the child, she may be convinced that the whole thing was her fault and that everybody (especially the sick sibling) now hates her. Again, a visit may be important, even if the patient is in a bad way, but be sure that everything the child sees is carefully explained.

If a parent has elective surgery a child may feel the hospital made him/her ill It is extremely difficult for a young child to understand why a parent, who appeared perfectly well, should choose to enter a hospital and have an operation which appears to make her ill. If the procedure only involves a short stay, it may be better if the absence is carefully explained but the child does not visit. If the hospital admission is for a week or more you will have to explain very carefully, using any parallels in the child's experience which you can think of. Has he, for example, ever had a tooth extracted? If so, you may be able to point out that, just as the dentist had to pull the tooth out, leaving a sore hole, because otherwise it would not stop aching, so the doctor has had to make Mum's leg sore to deal with the varicose veins which would not stop aching.

Hydrocele

A hydrocele is a collection of fluid swelling the scrotum around one or both testicles. For further discussion *see* **Hospital**/Surgery.

Hygiene *see* **Infection**/Preventing infection: Infection and home hygiene: Sterilants, disinfectants and antiseptics. *See also* **Diarrhoea, Gastro-enteritis and Food Poisoning; Nursing**.

Hyperactive Children (The Hyperkinetic Syndrome)

Does your child have a very short attention span so that, left to himself, he darts from one thing to another and, even given attention, finds it difficult to concentrate for more than a minute or two? Does his supply of energy seem to be inexhaustible so that he rushes around all day; finds himself physical activities even in the most unsuitable circumstances and wears out everyone except himself? Is he so impulsive that he seems to have no thought for his own safety or anyone else's, so that he is courageous to the point of recklessness and boisterous to the point of violence? If so, he may be a perfectly normal toddler or pre-school child; a somewhat anxious and unhappy schoolchild, or a 'hyperactive' child.

Which he is depends not so much on his behaviour, or even on whether or not he is past the age when this kind of behaviour is universal, but on what you, and other adults who are significant to him, think of that behaviour.

If he is loved, accepted and 'managed' without undue stress, the question of whether his behaviour is 'normal' will not arise. You and the rest of the family accommodate him as the individual he is and, while you may sometimes moan about the sheer hard work involved in parenthood, it will probably not occur to you that he could be altered by anything but the normal processes of socialization: his own maturing and the influences around him. But if you, and the rest of the family, are having your lives disrupted by this child, the havoc he wreaks, the supervision he needs, his noise, his refusal to pay attention to you or to respond to what seems to you to be ordinary discipline, you may begin to wonder whether there is something wrong which could be righted. Once you begin to wonder, the reactions of outsiders will begin to have an impact too, especially if reciprocal child-visiting arrangements break down because your neighbours do not want him in the house; minders refuse to care for him because he is so disruptive and grandparents stop suggesting family Sundays because they find him intolerable.

Pre-school or infant school teachers are probably the most influential outsiders in a child's life and it is often they who first *alarm* parents about a child's overactivity. A teacher has responsibility not just for your child but for a group. She has expectations as to the limits within which all those children should behave, and she has planned activities and learning processes which the group is to undertake. There is no doubt that one child who is, for whatever reason, unable, unready or unwilling to cooperate can make her job far more difficult – even impossible. If the child's impulsive behaviour includes overturning furniture onto other children's toes, blipping them over the head with toys and/or physically attacking them, she may have complaints from other parents to deal with as well as her own sense of inadequacy in not being able to hold your child's attention or peacefully to pursue her group's education.

Once criticism and complaint from the school is added to your own exhaustion and stress in dealing with the very active, distractable, impulsive child at home, you may well feel that you need some help.

You can seek help and advice from your doctor, health visitor or, if the child is of school age, from the school medical officer. But the help and advice you are offered will depend on where you live and on the attitudes of those you consult. Broadly speaking, in most parts of Britain, problems concerning a child's behaviour and management will be regarded as social/psychological issues; but in most of the United States and in a few places in Britain, these particular problems of 'hyperactivity' will be regarded as medical. The difference may be crucially important to the whole family and particularly to the child himself. They may, indeed, be important to society as a whole.

The socio-psychological approach to 'hyperactivity'

All behaviour results from an interaction between the child's unique self and the people who care for him in the environment they all share. A child emerges from the womb. He is already partly shaped by a combination of his genetic make-up and his experiences before and during birth. He is born to parents who already have an infinite complexity of personality, and of aspirations and expectations about him. As they meet they begin to affect each other's behaviour in an endless feedback loop. Perhaps the newborn is jumpy and irritable. His parents may react to his behaviour with soothing comfort, with impatience or with inept anxiety. Whatever their reaction, it will influence the handling they offer the baby, and that handling will affect the next stages of his development and, therefore, the feedback which they get from him . . . Sometimes a child 'fits' so perfectly with his parents that all seem to dance, all through his childhood, to the same familiar melody. More often there are periods in a child's life when he seems to dance to a different rhythm. Occasionally child and parents find each other 'difficult' from the beginning so that the band spends more time in discord and re-tuning than in music.

This sort of approach recognizes that a parent's power to *change* a child's current behaviour is always limited by that child's personal growth and maturity. However strong and mutual the theme, you cannot teach a two-year-old to behave as we expect eight-year-olds to behave. But it also recognizes that the stronger that mutual theme has been and, therefore, the more confident all parties are that they both love each other and are loved, the greater will be their fundamental desire to cooperate with each other. Parents who have enjoyed a child's infancy and reached the toddler-phase able to respect themselves as 'good parents' and the child as a 'smashing fella', will usually ride through two-year-old tantrums and teases easily. That same child, sure that he is loved and approved of by parents whom he trusts, will not usually have to put up too big a fight about growing up. The longer such a mutually beneficial circle goes on being traced and re-traced, the solider the base it makes for the increasing complexities and stresses offered to the growing child by the outside world. But there are vicious circles too. Diverse forces may act to put parents and child out of step with each other. A new baby can change a mother's view of her toddler, from 'healthily active' to 'a pain in the neck', almost overnight, and more gradually change his confidence and his image of himself, too (*see* **Depression**/In children before puberty). A house-move – perhaps from the casual informality and open spaces of a rural setting to the tight-scheduling and restrictions of life in a city apartment – can change a four-year-old's way of life so radically that the *joie-de-vivre* which formerly made his parents laugh at most of his antics turns to a sulky anxious whining which makes them notice and reprove him for every infraction of a new set of rules. The point is that anything which acts strongly on either parents or child will act also on the rest of the family – to good effect or to bad.

Seeking help if your child is 'hyperactive'

If your child seems to you to be unmanageable, whether or not teachers and other adults are complaining of him, discuss the matter with your doctor or health visitor. Unless one of them can help you directly, you will be referred on, probably to a child guidance clinic. The professional who actually talks to you will probably be a member of a team which includes medical doctors, psychiatrists, psychologists, neurologists, teachers and health visitors.

She will be acutely aware that the behaviours which lead to some children being labelled 'hyperactive' are normal behaviours for most children some of the time. We cannot say 'this child is hyperactive: look, he threw a chair through the window and then rushed off for no reason and pushed over the baby and when I called him for supper he took ten minutes to come and then only sat up for three seconds . . .' That could be any strong, unsupervised toddler, or any four-year-old who was having a really bad day. The professional accepts that you believe your child's behaviour is at least exceptional, if not abnormal. But she has to call on all the team's knowledge of the vast variety of normal behaviours in children of whom nobody is complaining, in order to assess your child's for herself. It is important not to be offended if she appears to doubt, or minimize, the incidents you report to her. She does not doubt your stress and distress, nor the accuracy of your reports, but she has to put them into a developmental context. It may help, amuse or shock you to learn that two big surveys in the United States showed that *forty-nine per cent of all parents thought their children were overactive* while teachers classified *fifty per cent of children as restless and unable to sit still and thirty per cent as definitely hyperactive*. Figures like these make it clear that many adults would like children to behave differently from the way most of them actually do behave. Many parents and teachers obviously fall into the trap of assuming that most other children behave 'better' than the ones they have to deal with, and therefore that it is the 'good' and 'easy to manage' children who are the norm. It is not.

The team will want to discover whether the child's behaviour *always* seems hyperactive or whether there are circumstances in which he does not single himself out from other children. The mother who said 'He's not hyperactive this year. He's got a good teacher,' put her finger squarely on an important variable. The child's behaviour will seem aberrant to adults who cannot cope with it, but you need to know whether the relevant factor is his behaviour or that of the adults. Children who are wildly hyperactive at school but not at home, or vice versa, are usually reacting to an environment which they find impossibly stressful/boring. Environmental changes will usually improve the behaviour.

If the professional discovers that the child's behaviour is hyperactive under all circumstances, to a degree which renders his behaviour quite inappropriate to his age and developmental stage, she will want, with her colleagues, to exclude the possibility that he has any medical or neurological condition which is either causing the behaviour or being associated with it in his interaction with other people. Epilepsy, for example, is sometimes directly associated with hyperactive behaviour (*see* **Convulsions, 'Fits' and 'Funny Turns'**), while some hyperactive children have associated handicaps such as mental subnormality or undiagnosed deafness. Usually, though, no physical problems are found (but *see below* The medical approach to 'hyperactivity').

Many 'hyperactive' children are unhappy, anxious children; the professional will want to explore both the present and past interaction between the child and yourselves and any key changes or events which may *either* have caused him to become distractable and wild *or* caused you to begin to react differently to such behaviour. This kind of discussion can be very threatening to parents who probably already feel both deeply angry at the disruptive child and extremely guilty at not being able to accept, love and manage him. It sometimes helps to remember that the professional is far from seeking a place to put the blame. It is the essence of her approach that the child's behaviour and yours is the music which results from you playing upon each other. It is not your fault that you are as you are; it is not the child's fault that he is as he is, nor are any of you directly responsible for all of you being as you are. She wants to see whether you can all be helped to rewrite the score so that there is music rather than discord.

There is seldom any magic in this kind of work. Very occasionally a third party can spot a flaw in the warp of family life which those who are knitted into it cannot see, and it may be possible to go back and pick up the dropped stitches. In one family, for example, the mother was deep in grief for a miscarried baby of whom the two-year-old had had no knowledge. Since she knew he could not be grieving for the baby and it never occurred to her that he could be grieving for the loss of the happy mother she had been, she reacted to his increasingly uncontrolled behaviour more and more strictly. Furious that he should become so 'difficult' just when she needed peace, she first took away all his most 'grown-up' toys because he kept breaking them, and then confined him for hours at a time to his cot because she did not feel energetic enough to keep him safe in any other way. Over the next few months a vicious circle of depression and anger was established between them. The father, desperate for them both but seldom at home, maintained some kind of relationship with the little boy whom he found 'just about manageable if you kept on the go with him all the time, but quite impossible to settle to playing on his own or even to any kind of mutual play he found at all difficult'. When he was three he was sent to nursery school. A month later he was excluded as 'totally disruptive and violent to the other children' and he was referred to the clinic. It did not take long for that mother to see where life had gone wrong for her child. It took longer for her to forgive herself on the grounds that life had, at that point, gone tragically wrong for her too. It will probably take longer still for the child to regain confidence in her love and approval and become able to feel valued enough to try the next tentative stages in growing up. But a start has been made.

Much more usually, though, no specific event can be pin-pointed. The interaction between child and parents may always have been off-key and successive events, changes and developments in all family members may simply have driven this child further and further into what has become a self-fulfilling prophecy of doom. Under these circumstances the whole team will be involved in offering help on several fronts at once. A counsellor may work with you for greater understanding of the child's feelings *and* for decisions about what behaviours should be tolerated, even provided for, and which should be firmly controlled or banned. A place may be offered in a particular nursery or kindergarten where teachers will strive to enable your child to listen and play for long enough to discover pleasure in doing so. A health visitor may come regularly to the house to help you work out and implement structured ways of playing with the child and to give you support. All concerned will try to keep it clear that *you cannot be expected to tolerate the intolerable* but that *your child cannot flourish where he is rejected*. What helps one of you will therefore help you all.

Most professionals, even in Great Britain, acknowledge that there remains a small percentage (perhaps around one per cent of *children who are referred to psychiatric clinics*) whose hyperkinesis is marked, all-pervasive and unresponsive to the kinds of help outlined here. Such children may indeed be best helped within the medical model outlined below.

The medical approach to 'hyperactivity'

Lack of attention, concentration and forethought, together with marked physical restlessness, impulsiveness and rashness are occasionally symptomatic of brain damage – either congenital or accidental. Similar behaviour, observed in children in whom no brain damage can be demonstrated, is assumed, in the medical model, to be due to some undiagnosable disturbance or dysfunction in the brain or in its complex biochemical feedback with the central nervous system. The assumption is attractive because:

If the child has a 'disorder', parents need blame neither themselves nor the child. They are relieved of personal guilt and of much of their anger at the child and, thus relieved, they can face critical relatives, neighbours or teachers with open demands for support and assistance.

If the child is a 'patient', that role can break the vicious circle his behaviour was creating with his family and moods and relationships can become warmer. This is true even if the medical diagnosis does not immediately change the disruptive behaviour. If a bedwetting child is found to have a kidney disorder, everyone's attitudes to him and his problem will alter even if the bed is still wet every night. In the same way, a diagnosis of minimal brain dysfunction or hyperkinetic syndrome changes the attitudes of the adult world, even if mother still gets little sleep and no relaxation, and the classroom remains in daily turmoil.

If the child is 'under the doctor' his 'condition' can be 'treated' whether the treatment is unpleasant for him or not. Instead of worrying about whether they are being too harsh with him for bad behaviour, parents can accept doctor's orders and sympathetically support the child through whatever is prescribed.

Medical help in 'hyperactivity'   Medical treatment usually consists of the long-term administration of stimulant drugs which, paradoxically, while stimulating the heart rate and the whole metabolism, exert a calming effect on the child's behaviour. The drug most often prescribed for this purpose is called ritalin. The main reported effects are:

A generally calming effect and reduction of frenetic activity. This is so marked, in at least some children, that parents and teachers maintain that they know immediately if a child forgets even a single dose of the drug.

Increased concentration and improved performance on cognitive tasks carried out in laboratory or 'test' situations. Teachers especially notice these effects but, while they hold for normal as well as hyperactive children, they do not seem to carry over from test situations to general levels of performance. Teachers expect children on the drug to get better grades and believe that they are doing better work. But when that work is looked at over time, there is usually no significant effect.

Changes in mood such that the child becomes much more open to adult suggestion/control; much less defiant and 'don't careish'; much more the kind of child adults find acceptable. Unfortunately this effect, welcome though it is to those who must keep the child safe and try to love and teach him, has a less pretty side. The child may become depressed and weepy and lose his joy in life, his ebullience.

Increase in heart rate, loss of appetite and disturbance to growth. Ritalin speeds up the metabolism. In the child's everyday life, it may keep him awake if given too late in the day and cause him to lose weight because he does not feel hungry for sufficient food. In the longer term, it may slow up his growth or even permanently retard it. 'Drug holidays' are often recommended for this reason, but there is evidence that parents often do not follow this advice because, having established the child on the drug, they cannot face the possibility of him returning to his former behaviour patterns, even for a couple of weeks.

Implications of medical treatment for 'hyperactivity'

A hyperkinetic child can bring intolerable stress and even danger to himself and his family and to other people. The strain of trying to keep him safe, and to protect other people and places from his impulsive outbursts or wild exploits, is appalling and often unsuccessful. He will probably both suffer and cause many accidents, and leave a trail of less important destruction in his daily wake. Although his behaviour is likely to calm down as he matures (the peak of complaints is at around six; adolescents usually appear 'normal' although they may still be impulsive and accident-prone) his current behaviour may cut him off from most of the important experiences of childhood. He does not sit and concentrate for long enough to learn either academic or manual skills, and few other children will want to be his friends. Furthermore, the longer he continues to behave in ways which the people around him find intolerable/'mad', the more likely it is that he will come to see himself as 'mad', 'bad' or both. Additional emotional disorder is therefore likely.

Given that picture, and given a drug which changes it, almost always, for the better, the argument for the use of ritalin or a similar substance seems very strong indeed. But there are real problems. Perhaps they are not problems which should torment the parent who, perhaps after years of misery, is at last able to communicate with and love her child and to see him playing and learning with others. But they are certainly problems which should concern the rest of us.

Is it ethically acceptable to use drugs to force changes in behaviour? Adults do not like the way the hyperactive child behaves. By giving him ritalin they can make him behave 'better', but perhaps he does not want to behave differently. Perhaps he has a right to be himself, however inconvenient that self may be for other people. Perhaps the drug forces him into a mould when in fact it is the mould, rather than the child's behaviour, which should be broken.

Questions of this kind apply to the use of all psycho-active (mood- and behaviour-modifying) drugs; they need to be considered particularly carefully when they are to be administered to people who are not free to accept or reject them. Many people decry the widespread use of anti-depressant and tranquillizing drugs such as valium, for example. But at least the millions of people who take these do so largely of their own volition; because they do not want to live with the depression, anxiety and pain which the drugs help to modify. The use of drugs to reduce aggression or aberrant sexual drives in prisoners or mental hospital patients is widely decried because such drugs are either given without consent, or under a forced consent which is really blackmail concerning possible release. The use of ritalin in children falls, perhaps, somewhere between these two and the ethical decisions have to be made with the greatest care *for every individual case.*

If we argue that it is ever ethically acceptable to use drugs to change a child's behaviour, why should we stop at hyperactivity? There are many other kinds of childish behaviour which the adult world finds distressing. Would it be legitimate to give sleeping drugs *routinely* to the many babies and young children whose parents are desperate for unbroken nights? It would be as easy to argue that well-rested parents can give a child a better life as it is to argue that the adult world can be pleasanter to children restrained from hyperactivity, yet most of us would probably maintain that, with the exception of occasional crises, infant wakefulness must be lived with rather than overridden.

Is it ethically acceptable to use drugs to improve performance? Stimulant drugs reliably improve some aspects of performance on some intellectual tasks and while this effect was once thought to be specific to (and therefore diagnostic of) hyperactivity, it is now clear that it is universal. An effective chemical performance-enhancer raises ethical problems as great as those raised by a chemical behaviour-modifier. Although some individuals have always used chemicals in attempts to 'improve' their performances, drugs which *reliably* had the desired effect have not previously been available and widely distributed. A few students sniffed amphetamine inhalers but as many experienced a disastrous 'high' or mistimed 'low' as felt real benefit during their examinations. People take alcohol to make them feel happy but as often find themselves maudlin as cheered.

If effective and specific drugs which would enhance our performances in a variety of spheres were readily available, would we, competitive as we are for our children or our nation if not for ourselves, really resist them? At present society is against the idea, as the strict regulations concerning the use of drugs in competitive sport show. Such drugs are unfair when only a few use them but what if they were available to all? Many people would say that fear of addiction and of side-effects would put the brakes on non-or-quasi-medical drug use, but the evidence is against them. The non-specific and unreliable drugs almost all of us use, like alcohol, caffeine and nicotine, are highly addictive and have devastating side-effects. The specific and reliable stimulants we are giving to children have side-effects which we certainly should not tolerate in a cold cure let alone a food. We use all these and, if the vast drug industry, spurred by its success and profit in this area, were actually to produce 'harmless' pink pills which would improve the home team's game; green

ones to help us through that examination and blue ones for the performance of a Casanova, we should probably accept them all.

Most doctors would probably answer points of this kind in terms of
their overriding duty to act only in the best interests of their own
individual patients. Certainly the prescription of a drug like ritalin can be
legitimate under the kinds of exceptional circumstances described above.
Unfortunately experience in the United States suggests that such carefully limited use of drugs which are effective in altering behaviour is
exceedingly difficult to maintain, if only because it is impossible to keep
such drugs entirely within the *medical* domain.

Hyperactivity, or minimal brain dysfunction as it was termed until
recently, is not a 'disease' or 'disorder' with physical signs which can be
demonstrated by medical tests. It is not even a collection of symptoms
described by a patient seeking relief. It is a (widely varying) collection of
behaviours which *somebody else wants the doctor to change*. That doctor may
decide to assume that those behaviours are symptoms of a disorder or
dysfunction which is present even though he cannot demonstrate it, but
his usual clinical role is already distorted by the lack of objective diagnosis
and by the intervention of third parties between himself and the patient.
He believes that a prescription for the drug is in that patient's best
interests, because others tell him so rather than because he clinically
judges that it is so. If doubts beset him and he refuses to prescribe the
drug then it may be made clear to him that he is acting against the
patient's interests, because, unless that child's behaviour improves, he
will be excluded from school/locked in his room/knocked down by a car.

In the United States, despite strenuous efforts by many doctors and
medical authorities, MBD or just LD for Learning Disorder, has been
taken over as a diagnosis by teachers and parents often acting with each
other through Parent–Teacher Associations or community groups. It has
been used as a label for hundreds of thousands of children who fall foul of
the adult world. The single unifying point in the thousands of descrip-
tions given of these children is that parents and teachers find them
'difficult'. Far from all being the dangerously impulsive and disruptive
children who might, after lengthy consideration, be prescribed drugs in
Britain, many of these American patients are 'restless and a poor reader'
or 'slow to respond to authority and unpopular with peers' . . . While
everyone must sympathize with the teacher whose classroom is continually violently disrupted, many of the teachers who attach this label to
children are not seeking to have impossible behaviour modified but to
have less-than-perfect behaviour perfected. As one put it: 'OK, he's not
too bad. But I just *know* he'd learn better if he was on medication. Isn't it
right that he should have what will make it easy on him?'

As the effectiveness of stimulant drugs became known in the United
States (and a vast advertising campaign for Ritalin, much of it aimed
directly at parents and teachers, certainly played its part) children began
to come home from school with notes containing messages like 'John is
not concentrating. Please see your physician' or 'Jake is still restless in
school, please arrange medication before he returns from vacation'. For
how long could doctors be expected to go on saying 'whatever for?'
against this growing tide?

The medical authorities of the United States eventually banned the use of minimal brain dysfunction as a diagnosis, recognizing that it was too vague to describe a medical entity. But doctors were still allowed to prescribe for the separate 'manifestations' of MBD such as 'restlessness'. They acted against direct advertising, too, insisting that ritalin and similar drugs be advertised only in 'ethical' (medical) journals and pamphlets. But they were largely too late. So many families were using the drugs that every family could find out about them. They also placed these drugs on the index which restricted repeat prescriptions, so that instead of taking the same prescription back to the chemist for a refill, parents had to seek a new one each time. But while that may have helped to limit the use of a child's stimulants by drug-abusing older people, it did not limit their availability to the child 'patients'. Instead of prescribing for a month and then seeing the children again, doctors gave hundreds (in some instances, a thousand or more) pills on one prescription.

Doctors cannot be blamed, teachers cannot be blamed, parents cannot be blamed. Ritalin makes children 'easier' and it is easier to be kind to less bothersome children. Ritalin makes children accept school teaching more easily and it is easier to teach children who accept the process. Everyone involved has the welfare of those children at heart, but whether this overwhelming American tide of drug use to modify socially unacceptable behaviour is socially desirable, people must decide for themselves.

Hyperkinetic syndrome *see* **Hyperactive Children**.
Illness *see* **Infection**/Types of infection: Infections which cause illness. *See also* **Nursing;** *and also* individual conditions.

Immune Response

Although human bodies are well-designed both to keep out and to deal with potentially harmful micro-organisms (*see* **Infection**/Defences against infection) some do get through these early lines of defence. Their arrival in the tissues or the bloodstream stimulates the next line of defence: the immune response.

Every micro-organism contains proteins. The proteins of, say, a diphtheria bacillus or a polio virus are recognized by the body as antigens. While increasing numbers of certain types of white blood cell strive to engulf the dangerous micro-organisms, fragments of them, or of their toxic products, are carried by other white cells either through the bloodstream or through the lymph system, to the liver, the spleen or to nearby lymph nodes ('glands'). Here, plasma cells perform a 'chemical analysis' on the foreign proteins (the antigens) and produce exactly corresponding proteins called antibodies. These antibodies combine with, and neutralize, the antigens and, in doing so, destroy the micro-organisms.

Obviously it takes time for plasma cells both to perform their 'chemical analysis' and to produce sufficient quantities of antibodies to deal with the numbers of invading micro-organisms. If and when they have done so, the current 'illness' will be over, but the role of those plasma cells continues. Plasma cells which carry a 'memory' of that particular antigen–

antibody will remain in the gamma-globulin fragment of the blood. It is rather as if a secret force, having produced the weapon which turned the tide of a battle, filed its blueprints and components so that the weapon could be produced instantly should the invader return. If the body is challenged again at a later date *by those same infective micro-organisms*, large numbers of antibodies will be released with no delay and there will therefore be no illness. The body has 'learned' how to combat those particular micro-organisms. The individual has made his own active immunity to that disease.

It is important to understand that immunity is not due only to actual antibodies continuing to circulate in the bloodstream once the immediate need for them is over, but to that 'memory trace' remaining in the plasma cells. It is that 'memory' which explains the vital difference between the *active immunity* which an individual makes for himself and the *passive immunity* which can be passed onto him by somebody else.

Newborn infants acquire passive immunity to many virus diseases because antibodies to viral antigens are small enough to pass through the placenta from the mother's bloodstream to that of the foetus. Antibodies to bacteria (especially gram-negative bacteria) are too large for such transfusion. The placenta filters them and the infant is born without passive immunity to those diseases.

Passive immunity to diseases such as measles is, of course, extremely valuable, but, like all such immunity, it is short-lived in comparison with active immunity. The infant receives antibodies to measles antigen in his circulation from his mother's blood. But he has no 'memory trace' of that antigen in his plasma cells. For a while, those ready-made antibodies will protect him if measles infection threatens, but as the level of antibodies drops, he will be less protected and, unless active immunity is provoked by immunization (*see* **Immunization**) his body may eventually have to fight the measles bacillus without the benefit of that 'secret weapon'.

Passive immunity can be, and often is, conferred on people without active immunity who are at some special risk. Techniques for doing this are extremely valuable but it is vital that everyone understand that passive immunity is temporary and that although it may be life-saving today, it cannot replace active immunity next year.

Confusion is still sadly common in the case of tetanus. An individual who has not received primary tetanus immunization or has not kept it up-to-date with boosters, suffers an injury which hospital staff consider susceptible to tetanus infection. He may be given anti-tetanus serum: a concentration of tetanus antibodies. If tetanus infection should threaten in this wound, those antibodies will combat it, but they will not provoke his body into producing its own antibodies. He is protected against contracting the disease this time but he is no more immune for the future than he was before. As long as he realizes this, all will be well. He can now seek active immunization and, even if he does not, anti-tetanus serum can be given to him again on another occasion. The danger is in confusion. At the time of a further injury he will again be asked about tetanus shots and whether his immunization is up-to-date. If he has never understood the difference between active and passive immunization he may reply that he received 'tetanus shots' only last year . . . (*see* **Tetanus**).

Similar confusion sometimes arises when gamma globulin, rich in antibodies, is given to a child who is exposed, for example, to measles, at an age when his passive immunity from his mother is likely to be waning, but active immunization has not been carried out. Told that this injection will 'probably stop him getting it and anyway will make the illness much milder if he does', the mother is relieved that the child stays well and puts the whole question of measles out of her mind. That child still requires his measles jab and should have it as soon as the temporary passive immunity conferred by the gamma globulin has worn off.

The message is simple but important: only having a disease or being actively immunized against it gives lasting protection by stimulating the individual's own immune response.

Immunization *see also* **Diphtheria; German Measles; Measles; Mumps; Rabies; Tetanus; Tuberculosis; Whooping Cough**

The body's immune system cannot provide perfect protection from all disease. Sometimes the 'invading' micro-organisms may be so numerous that plasma cells cannot produce enough antibodies quickly enough to combat them. Sometimes the bacteria or viruses multiply so rapidly that they outstrip the rate of antibody production. Sometimes those 'invaders' cause so much harm within the body that the whole system is overwhelmed. But, above all, that immune system cannot, by definition, protect the body against the *beginning of the first* episode of any particular illness. It is only the presence of the antigens of those 'germs' which stimulates the production of antibodies so that, in the natural course of events, the individual must suffer from the illness before he or she can generate specific protection against it.

Fortunately, during the last century, we have learned to interfere with that natural course of events and stimulate the body into producing antibodies without first experiencing active infection. This is the process called immunization.

When a person is immunized, dead or weakened strains of the bacteria or viruses responsible for causing specific diseases are injected or, in the case of polio vaccine for example, taken by mouth. Although the 'germs' in these vaccines are not capable of causing the full-blown illness for which they would be responsible in their fully active state, they still contain the antigens which will stimulate antibody production. Vaccine preparation and the schedule of administration are both vitally important. Too active a vaccine could make the recipient ill. Too weak a vaccine could fail to evoke that antibody response. In many cases ample antibody production without illness is best achieved by a series of injections given at carefully worked out intervals.

We cannot immunize against every infecting organism, largely because some common illnesses (such as 'influenza' or the 'common cold') are not really individual illnesses at all but collections of symptoms which may be caused by a vast range of micro-organisms which, to complicate matters further, are constantly changing (mutating). We can isolate one particular strain of 'flu, for example, make a vaccine and use it. But the people who receive it are still at risk from many, many other strains of 'flu, and even the protection which they received against that first strain may not last for very long. This is why ''flu jabs' are usually given only to people who are at very special risk, either because their health is already so poor and/or because their work is among the sick and/or because there is a current epidemic of a known strain.

Immunization programmes are not developed only by the criteria of what is scientifically possible, but also according to social and economic criteria. Clearly, immunization against a particular disease is impossible if a safe vaccine is not technically possible. But possession of a safe vaccine may not lead to a mass immunization programme. Those who administer public health programmes have to ask (and answer) questions such as: 'Will the cost of mass immunization be repaid, either monetarily (in terms of fewer work-days lost and lower medical costs) or in social terms such as less human misery?' Such questions can only be answered in terms of yet other questions such as: 'How serious and how frequent is this disease in an unimmunized population? What degree of protection will the vaccine give to how many people and for how long? What are the risks of vaccination itself and how do those risks balance against the probable benefits for vaccinated individuals?' By building up cost–benefit equations for questions of this kind, the medical administrators must decide, for each possible vaccine and for every different population, whether mass immunization is worthwhile. An interesting example is that of immunization against smallpox, the scourge of our immediate ancestors and part of every civilized country's public health programme until very recently. Some years ago, as the incidence of smallpox around the world declined, more and more exceptions to the general rule of immunization for everyone were made. Doctors exempted more and more infants on slighter grounds; countries relaxed their rules about the entry of unimmunized travellers and, eventually, the picture changed to one in which smallpox immunization was recommended only for those who actually intended to travel to and from the few remaining areas where the disease remained active. Now, smallpox has been officially eradicated and mass-immunization has ceased. There remain a handful of individuals (such as those who work in laboratories handling the infecting organisms of smallpox) for whom immunization in still 'worthwhile', but for the rest of us, the cost (monetary and health) of immunization now outweighs a benefit which has become infinitesimal as has the risk of infection.

Disease patterns change and are changed by our interference. The immunization programme which is right for one population at one time will not necessarily be the best for other populations at other times. But individuals, wherever they live, can be sure that the programme which is recommended to them by their medical personnel has been extremely carefully worked out and weighed. Those who reject or ignore such a programme not only do so at their own peril but to the peril of others, too. Smallpox would not have been 'eradicated' from our lives if we had not all followed the programme of immunization against it, and thus gradually bred generations of people whose resistance was such that the infecting organisms could find no breeding ground. Nevertheless, while accepting the immunization programme of your community, it is important to remember that, like those smallpox laboratory scientists, there will always be people whose individual needs differ from those of the population around them. When it is time for the immunization of your child, his special needs must be conveyed to, and discussed with, a doctor. If he has had febrile convulsions, for example, whooping cough immunization may carry an increased risk of side-effects. It may be better to exempt him. On the other hand, if that child is to travel to certain areas of the world where whooping cough is very prevalent, or if there is currently an epidemic of the disease in his community, it may be appropriate to vaccinate him all the same. Now an individual doctor (rather than a public health authority) is weighing the balance of risks and benefits for your individual child rather than for the population of which he is a member. How likely is he to 'catch' the disease? How much will it matter if he does? How probable and how serious are the side-effects of vaccination likely to be? (*see* **Whooping Cough**).

Your family's immunizations

Follow your community's programme, with each member's individual needs discussed with the doctor beforehand. Above all, do remember that while immunization begins in infancy, these are not only 'baby injections'. Boosters to keep the antibody level effectively high are almost as important as those primary doses. Keeping records for every family member, after infancy, is important; five years is a long time and you will forget/lose that notebook or diary. A big book like this one may be difficult to lose so there is a record page here for you, both for your children and yourselves, to use if you wish (*see pages* 396–7).

Although the timing of these immunizations will vary, your child will almost certainly receive the following:

Diphtheria, whooping cough (pertussis), tetanus

These three are usually combined into one 'triple vaccine' (DPT) and given as an injection into the buttock, thigh, or upper arm.

Three of these 'triples' are needed to build an infant's basic immunity. Different communities space them differently but it is usual for the first to be given in the first three months and the third late in the year. Where the third dose is given early, a booster may be recommended in the second year. Where the third dose is given later there may be no need for a booster until the child is ready to start school. A further booster, omitting pertussis, is given before the child leaves school.

The interval between injections is important but not critical. If your child is two weeks late he will not need to start the series all over again but if you forget for several months he might have to. Consult your doctor.

Side-effects are uncommon and mild. Your baby might be irritable and possibly slightly feverish twelve to twenty-four hours after an injection and there might be a red lump at the needle prick site which will soon disperse. Marked reactions should be seen by, or at least reported to, the doctor who might reduce, or leave out, the pertussis component of the next dose (but *see* **Whooping Cough**).

Polio (Trivalent vaccine against three main strains.) This is given as drops of syrup on the same schedule as the above. There are no side-effects.

Measles A single injection produces adequate lifelong immunity. This is not usually given until the second year. Earlier administration may fail while the infant remains protected by antibodies passed onto him by his mother (*see* **Immune Response**).

A low-grade fever about a week after the injection is fairly common but short-lived. A very few children who have fever also have a very mild version of a measles rash (*see* **Measles**).

Mumps and german measles (rubella) These are both mild infections in childhood but illnesses we want children to have early, if at all, because they are more serious in adult life. Mumps in an adult male can cause orchitis, a painful and occasionally damaging inflammation of the testicles. Rubella, of course, can disastrously damage the foetus if acquired by a pregnant woman. Societies vary widely in their immunization programmes for these two diseases. Some immunize against both at the same time as measles so as to minimize not only illness among children themselves but the likelihood of infection by those children to at-risk adults. Others withhold these vaccines until just before puberty (*see* **German Measles**; **Mumps**).

Tuberculosis (BCG) Is usually carried out before puberty in children whom a skin test show to lack immunity. Earlier testing/immunization may be recommended within a community (or within an individual institution) if an active carrier of infection is found (*see* **Tuberculosis**).

Yellow fever, cholera, typhoid fever, rabies Immunizations will be routine in some areas of the world and required for western children travelling to them. It is essential that public health experts be consulted before travel is undertaken to areas where diseases virtually unknown in the parent-country are endemic. Occasionally the immunization requirements will make holiday trips inadvisable as only necessity will balance the discomfort of likely side-effects.

Tetanus ● Because primary immunization with tetanus toxoid is included in the triple vaccine given in infancy and early childhood (*see above*), many people forget, or never realize, that protection against this peculiarly unpleasant and dangerous disease is *not complete and lifelong* when the prescribed series of those triple injections has been completed.

A tetanus booster is required every ten years throughout life if antibody levels adequate to protect against this infection in susceptible wounds is to be maintained (*see* **Tetanus**).

Diphtheria ● While contact with a diphtheria patient is much rarer than are wounds which might be susceptible to tetanus, diphtheria does still exist, as a recent small-scale epidemic in the United States and a recent death in Britain, have painfully demonstrated. Theoretically, lifelong protection requires ten-yearly boosters but, because the side-effects in school-age children and adults can be severe, boosters after infancy are not a routine matter. If diphtheria should make a come-back, this policy may change. Until that time, consult your doctor if an older member of the family is at special risk of contact with the disease.

IMMUNIZATION RECORD FOR CHILDREN: BIRTH TO SIXTEEN YEARS

Name:				Date of birth:		
	1st year			Pre-school	16th year	
Diphtheria					✕	—
Whooping cough (Pertussis)					✕	—
Tetanus						Repeat 10-yearly
Polio						Repeat 10-yearly

	2nd year		Date of infection *or* immunization			
Measles		**Mumps**				One or the other before puberty
Other immunizations e.g. cholera, typhoid, etc.		**German measles (Rubella)**				One or the other before puberty
Name of disease	Date		Date of Mantoux test	Result of test	Date of immunization (if any)	
		Tuberculosis				By puberty if not recommended earlier

Name:				Date of birth:		
	1st year			Pre-school	16th year	
Diphtheria					✕	—
Whooping cough (Pertussis)					✕	—
Tetanus						Repeat 10-yearly
Polio						Repeat 10-yearly

	2nd year		Date of infection *or* immunization			
Measles		**Mumps**				One or the other before puberty
Other immunizations e.g. cholera, typhoid, etc.		**German measles (Rubella)**				One or the other before puberty
Name of disease	Date		Date of Mantoux test	Result of test	Date of immunization (if any)	
		Tuberculosis				By puberty if not recommended earlier

IMMUNIZATION RECORD FOR CHILDREN: BIRTH TO SIXTEEN YEARS

Name:				Date of birth:			
	1st year			Pre-school	16th year		
Diphtheria						✕	—
Whooping cough (Pertussis)						✕	—
Tetanus							Repeat 10-yearly
Polio							Repeat 10-yearly

	2nd year		Date of infection *or* immunization				
Measles		Mumps					One or the other before puberty
Other immunizations e.g. cholera, typhoid, etc.		German measles (Rubella)					One or the other before puberty
Name of disease	Date		Date of Mantoux test	Result of test	Date of immunization (if any)		
		Tuberculosis					By puberty if not recommended earlier

ONGOING IMMUNIZATION RECORD FOR ADULTS

Name:					(Give dates of immunization below)		
Diphtheria							—
Tetanus							10-yearly boosters
Polio							
Other immunizations i.e. recommended due to occupational hazards, travel, etc.							
Name of disease							
Date							

Name:					(Give dates of immunization below)		
Diphtheria							—
Tetanus							10-yearly boosters
Polio							
Other immunizations i.e. recommended due to occupational hazards, travel, etc.							
Name of disease							
Date							

Impetigo and Staphylococcal Infections

Impetigo is a superficial infection of the skin caused either by streptococci or by staphylococci. These bacteria can infect healthy skin, but infection is especially likely when it is already damaged by eczema, etc.

At the sites of infection there is oozing of pus or the formation of pus-filled blisters which burst. The pus dries to form thick, yellowish crusts. The infection often starts around the nose or mouth but rapidly spreads to other parts of the body. It is extremely contagious: if unchecked it spreads rapidly through schools, nurseries or other institutions.

Although merely tiresome in children, who are quickly and easily treated with local and/or systemic antibiotics, impetigo, especially if caused by staphylococci, can be extremely serious in babies (*see below*).

Staphylococcal infections (*see also* **Diarrhoea, Gastro-enteritis and Food Poisoning**)

Apart from the strains of these bacteria which can cause food poisoning, there are many pathogenic strains, often spread by symptom-free 'carriers', which cause a variety of skin infections such as boils and carbuncles. In hospitals, these bacteria cause much post-operative infection.

While boils and so forth are usually trivial infections, easily dealt with by antibiotics, various strains of staphylococci can cause serious trouble:

Bloodstream infection by staphylococci

Rarely in children and adults, but more often in young babies, superficial infection with staphylococci may lead to septicemia. Infection may settle in an internal organ, such as a bone, and produce an abscess there. Or infection may settle in the lung and cause a serious form of pneumonia. This type of pneumonia is a leading cause of death among the few young adults who die from complications following influenza.

Antibiotic resistance: 'hospital staph'

Staphylococci in hospitals, often spread by 'carriers' among the staff, are often of strains which have developed resistance to many common antibiotics as well as high levels of virulence. Infection with these micro-organisms can spread through successive intakes of patients (sometimes reaching infection rates as high as forty per cent in a newborns' nursery) and can prove extremely difficult to treat. Attempts have been made to reserve particular antibiotics for this purpose and to use them only on isolated patients so as to minimize the likelihood of resistance developing (*see* **Infection**/Treatment of infections which cause illness/Antibiotics). Unfortunately, overcrowding in hospitals, with limited facilities for isolation, have led to the failure of this policy. Now, strenuous attempts are being made in many hospitals to limit the invasion and spread of these bacteria. Such efforts include measures to detect 'carriers' among both professional and domestic staff; avoidance of overcrowding; isolation and 'barrier-nursing' of any infected patient and the establishment of 'ultra-clean' areas (including newborn nurseries) where patients at special risk can be nursed.

One infection with staphylococci does not appear to lead to immunity, even from infection by the identical strain. Research is nevertheless going on to try to find artificial means of producing at least some immunity.

Infant Development and Care

Since this book concerns all dependent children in families, the nature and needs of babies and very young children are dealt with wherever they are relevant which is, of course, in a majority of its entries. Parents who are especially interested in this youngest age group may nevertheless find the following guidance useful:

Emotional development and needs

See **Anxiety, Fears and Phobias**, especially The roots of fear and The roots of anxiety, which deal with the importance of a baby's security with a loved caretaker.

This topic is further dealt with in **Working Mothers** and extended to issues such as 'spoiling' in **Discipline, Self-discipline and Learning How to Behave**. Problems related to this security–insecurity dimension are dealt with under headings such as **Jealousy**/Of a new baby; **Hyperactive Children** and **Depression**.

Overall development: emotional, mental and physical

See **Play**, especially Playthings for babies, which includes a chart of pointers within the baby's development suggesting activities and social interactions which he or she is likely to enjoy. A similar approach to general development in the second and third years will be found in **School**/Pre-school and nursery education.

Physical growth

See **Growth** which includes a chart, both for reference and use, of 'expected' weight and height gains from birth to age nineteen. **Eating**/Types of food for babies, deals with breast-feeding and bottle-feeding, with the shift towards an ordinary diet and, later, with feeding problems.

Specific developments and problems

Will be found under their topic-headings. **Language**, for example, deals both with the normal development of language and with such issues as stammering. **Toilet Training** includes an account of the physiological developments which must precede bladder and bowel control and of common problems. **Sleep** similarly covers both general and problem-orientated information while **Safety**/In the home, puts the safety-precautions needed for babies at different age-stages into the context of their overall development.

Specific issues in early child-care

Will be found by looking up the particular issue with which you are concerned. If you are thinking about whether or not a toddler should watch television, turn to **Television**; if you are worrying about how to break the news of a death or a divorce, turn to **Death** or **Divorce, Separation and One-parent Families**. If there is no entry on the topic you are looking for, the topic-word should nevertheless direct you to a relevant article. Smacking, for example will take you to **Discipline, Self-discipline and Learning How to Behave**/Punishment, while thumb-sucking will take you to **Habits**/Comfort habits and also to **Teeth**.

'Infantile' eczema *see* **Allergy**.
Infantile paralysis *see* **Immunization**/Polio.

Infection (for further information on infections mentioned, *see* individual conditions)

It is impossible to understand (even a little) about the nature, prevention and cure of infection without understanding at least some science. Most people do not and, as a result, old wives' tales (often out-dated, sometimes downright harmful) stand in for even a version of the facts.

The following is indeed only 'a version'; a vastly compressed and simplified account of a huge topic. But people who will follow it through may find it worthwhile. Not only will you be better able to understand what your doctor is talking about next time a member of your family is hurt or ill, you will also find that you can simultaneously increase the efficiency *and* the simplicity of your everyday hygiene, nursing and first aid. You may even save money by becoming able to ignore advertising pressures to 'disinfect' your kitchen with one product and your skin with another and to 'sterilize' everything from your lavatory to your dustbin.

What 'germs' are Everyone knows that infection is caused by germs; but what are they? The organisms which can infect people are so diverse that that term is not really very useful. We need to know *what kind of germ* we are talking about.

Our world has three life-forms: animals (including us, of course), plants and protists. It has one more semi-life-form, too: the virus, which is not included in any of those categories but must certainly have an important place in any discussion of infection.

We can quickly get rid of the animals and the vegetables because while members of either life-form can certainly harm us, neither infects us in the 'germ' sense. A nettle may 'sting', poison ivy may cause a rash, but in both cases chemicals, acting as poisons, are responsible, not 'germs'.

With animals, we must be more careful. Many species play a vital part in the *spread of infection*. The mosquito which spreads malaria from person to person or the flea which colonizes plague-carrying rats are obvious examples of these 'animal vectors'. But again it is not the animals themselves which infect us but the 'germs' they carry. Other animals can cause damage themselves, rather than bringing us their damaging 'germs', but they do so by living as parasites on or in us – like the mite which lives around hair follicles or the many varieties of worm which may inhabit the intestines. Their presence or habits cause mechanical damage; it may be invasive but it is not infective.

'Germs' are The group biologists classify as 'protists' include bacteria, fungi, protozoa
protists unless and algae. We can forget the algae which are innocent of causing infec-
they are viruses tion. Bacteria, fungi and protozoa can all infect man, although, of course, bacteria are the most important in infection, especially in people in the western world.

How protists All living things are made up of cells and all cells (whether of an onion
differ from skin, your skin or a bacterium) have a similar chemical composition of
animals and three molecules. They all carry out similar chemical activities, collectively
plants known as metabolism and including taking in and excreting of foodstuffs, converting chemicals from foodstuffs into energy for other activities, respiration and reproduction. We usually think of 'metabolism' as a

characteristic of a whole creature (and do not think of a plant as having a metabolism at all) but in fact all the metabolic processes go on in each cell.

The vital difference between animals and plants and the protists is in the degree of differentiation and specialization of their cells. Animals and plants both have specialized cells grouped into tissues: stems, flowers, livers and so forth. Animals not only have specialized tissues but complex organs in which tissues of different specializations are grouped together to perform complex tasks. The heart, for example, combines muscle, nerve and connective tissue to perform the task of pumping blood.

Protists, in contrast, consist of independent, unrelated cells. Usually the whole protist organism is one single cell, but even where many are joined together (as in many algae; seaweed, for example) each cell is the same; none are specialized for different functions as in a true land plant.

The hard-to-classify virus   Whether or not a virus is a 'living' thing is a philosophical question, but certainly it has very different characteristics from all other living things.

Viruses are smaller than microscopic: that is literally true. They are so small that a large majority cannot be seen through an ordinary microscope. They are only visible with the far higher magnification of an electron-microscope. Until sufficiently powerful instruments had been invented, nobody knew that viruses existed. Even today, when we not only have the instruments with which viruses can be examined, but know that there are still many to be discovered and identified, their size remains one (but only one) difficulty in studying them.

Viruses are not 'cells' in the usual three-molecule sense. Instead they consist only of an outer coating of a protein substance which contains an inner core of nucleic acid. Each is distinct. Not being cells, viruses have no independent life-processes. They do not convert chemicals to provide themselves with energy in order to keep themselves 'alive'. They have no metabolism of their own and therefore they cannot reproduce themselves. Their only 'function' is the invasion of other cells. Once a virus has taken over a cell, it uses that cell's life-functions for its own propagation.

This necessity to invade, to take over actual *cells*, is a vitally important difference between viruses and any other infecting organism – a bacterium for example. That bacterium may exist in your intestine, taking in nutrients from your waste-products and generally using *for its own life-cycle* the environment provided by your body. But the virus which finds itself in your intestine must either lie dormant, or must invade one of of your body cells and take it over, imposing its reproductive function on the natural function of that cell, which is thereby destroyed.

This, of course, is the major reason why the identification and study of viruses was so difficult, and it is why the treatment of virus infections remains so difficult today. Scientists could not breed viruses on a petrie-dish filled with suitable nutrients, as they grow bacteria. They had to learn to breed them inside living cells, in white mice and chick embryos for example. Even today, when antibiotics (*see below*) can so effectively destroy a wide range of harmful bacteria, we cannot produce a similar *kind* of anti-viral agent because the viruses we want to destroy are inside the living cells of the host we are trying to cure. Destroy the virus and you destroy the cell (but *see below*).

Bacteria

Many 'germs' are bacteria but only an infinitesimal proportion of bacteria are 'germs'.

If it were possible to calculate the mass of all the animal life on earth, and compare it with all the bacterial life, scientists reckon that the mass of bacteria would be twenty times greater than all the rest put together. You cannot see them but they are (almost) everywhere.

One of the most widespread and unfortunate old wives' tales in daily life is that bacteria are dangerous things humans should avoid. Humans cannot nor should they wish to. The whole of life as we know it depends upon bacterial action. Bacteria process all types of once-living-now-dead matter, breaking it down into its component chemical parts. When they have done so, they have made those basic chemicals available to be used all over again by the living and the living-still-to-come. A cow dies. Its body was built from nutrients it obtained by eating grass. The grass was nourished by nutrients in the soil. By bacterial action its body will be broken down again into the chemical elements it obtained from the grass and made available in the soil so that more grass will grow to nourish another animal . . . Without bacteria, the 'life-cycles' familiar to all of us from school lessons, could not continue. Instead of being able to use our planet's natural organic resources knowing that once our bodies had had what they needed from them, they would be returned to replenish the natural stock, we should *use them up*, just as we use up resources such as oil, which, made into plastics or burned as petrol, is not recycled to keep the oil-wells full.

There are, of course, millions of kinds of bacteria. Some can flourish wherever there is dead organic matter to be broken down; some require more specialized living conditions. There are, for example, many types which are found in soil, but some of these seek well-oxygenated earth while others flourish where there is little oxygen, deep beneath the surface. There are several types which flourish on normal human skin. Recent research suggests that a normal adult male armpit will carry about 200 million per square centimetre while there may be as many as 500 million bacteria in every gramme of scurf from the scalp. There are bacteria which flourish in animal intestines and others which concentrate where there are dead particles in water . . .

Bacteria which are normal inhabitants of the bodies of animals are called their 'normal flora' (nothing to do with flowers!). Their presence is an integral part of the body's functioning; a sort of peaceful co-existence. The bacteria find the right environment for nourishing and reproducing themselves within the animal's body; their presence does no harm and is often positively useful. Sometimes their presence is actually essential to the animal-host's life. Ruminants like cows, for example, depend upon bacterial action in their multiple-stomach system to break down the cellulose in their grass-diet and release its nutrients for their use. If you were able to sterilize that cow's stomach, she would die of starvation. She has no intrinsic ability to use cellulose. Humans also have valuable normal flora in their guts. It is bacteria, for example, which, while using our eventual wastes for their own nutrition, release the chemical we call vitamin K.

Bacteria as germs

It is from among this vast and essential population of bacteria that the ones which can and do damage man come. Such bacteria are certainly 'germs' but it is so easy to tar all other bacteria with the same value-laden brush that it may be better to stick to the more scientific term 'pathogenic bacteria' or pathogens. A bacterium may become a pathogen in a number of ways:

It may be a member of a species which is always pathogenic to man, meaning that it is never part of 'normal flora' but, should it gain entry to the body, will always cause more or less trouble (for how much trouble it may cause, *see below*).

Many of the most pathogenic species of bacteria are those which produce toxins (poisons) in the body. The tetanus bacilli, for example, need multiply only at one local site (such as a puncture wound) in the body to produce toxins which then circulate around the body to produce severe illness and often death. In contrast, most of the pathogenic bacteria which can infect wounds cause only local infection (*see below*). In order to produce an infection involving the whole body, these bacteria have to multiply enormously and penetrate into the bloodstream.

It may be a member of a pathogenic strain of an otherwise harmless species. B. coli, for example, is a normal and normally harmless inhabitant of the human bowel, yet there are strains of B. coli which are pathogenic and it is these which often cause epidemics of gastro-enteritis in infants.

It may evolve from a harmless parent-species. Many of the virulent intestinal infections, such as typhoid and para-typhoid, are caused by bacteria thought to have evolved from B. coli.

It may be a harmless inhabitant of one area of the body which is pathogenic when it reaches another. Clostridium tetani, for example, is a strain of B. coli and is itself a normal and harmless inhabitant of the bowel. But in deep wounds which provide the comparatively airless conditions which it requires, it is highly pathogenic.

It may be a normally harmless inhabitant of the body which behaves as a pathogen when the condition of that body 'invites' virulent invasion rather than continued peaceful co-existence. Perhaps the best-known example is that of the pneumococcus, many strains of which colonize the mouth and throat. If a viral cold alters that normal environment (and lowers the body's general resistance, *see below*) the pneumococcus may behave as a virulent pathogen, invading the respiratory system and producing bronchitis.

It may be a member of a species or strain of bacteria which some people can carry, without ill-effects, almost all the time, but which act as virulent pathogens in other people. All human skin, for example, is colonized by staphylococci whose strains range from harmless to highly virulent. Some 'carriers' can carry the most virulent strains (often in the nostrils) without ill-effects to themselves; unsuspecting and symptom-free, such a carrier is often the source of epidemics of staphylococcal infection in hospitals or amongst the infants in a nursery.

Viruses

All the viruses which you hear about are likely to act as germs either in animals or in plants. This is not to say that there are *no* viruses which are not germs, but that viruses are only discovered when plant or animal symptoms lead to scientific research. In general, we recognize viruses only by the diseases they cause.

Viruses as germs

Infection by viruses is rather different from infection by pathogenic bacteria, even though the resulting symptoms may be distinguishable only with laboratory help. The differences are due to differences in the nature and behaviour of the two types of micro-organism.

Viruses that are not in a host cell are not active. Some are able to exist (though not to reproduce) for quite long periods without a host cell. The smallpox virus, for example, can exist for a long time in a completely dry environment. Dust from the clothing or bedding of an infected person can infect others if it is inhaled.

Most viral illnesses, however, are contracted by a route which passes virally-infected cells directly from one living creature to another. The most common route of all is probably 'droplet infection' by which viruses, such as those of colds, influenzas and measles, are sneezed or coughed or otherwise sprayed out by one person and inhaled by another. There is probably some sense, therefore, to the belief that children will not 'catch' each other's colds if they play together outside. Air currents will carry droplets away unless the two have their heads together.

Many viruses are eaten. Food which is contaminated with faeces, for example, may pass on the enteroviruses that cause such illnesses as gastro-enteritis (echo and coxsackie viruses) and the virus of infectious hepatitis.

Viruses seldom seem to penetrate normal skin (although the spread of verruccae, certainly viral in origin, remains a puzzle). Nor do viruses in the quiescent, perhaps dust-borne, state, appear to lodge in wounds or otherwise damaged skin. But many are transmitted *through* the skin by the bites of infected animals. Rabies is the most dramatic example, but there are also many 'arthropod-borne', or arboviruses, which flourish either in blood-sucking arthropods such as mosquitoes, ticks and lice or in susceptible vertebrates bitten by those arthropods. Malaria and yellow fever, for example, are spread by mosquitoes, while several kinds of viral encephalitis are spread by ticks. In a rather similar way, serum hepatitis is passed on when injections are carried out with improperly sterilized hypodermic needles so that the virus is injected directly into the victim's bloodstream, or where even the minutest droplet of blood containing the virus gets into a cut on the skin of a new victim.

With their minute size, virus particles can also pass through the placenta to infect the foetus. German measles (rubella) virus is a grim case in point (*see* **German Measles**). Fortunately, if viruses are of a size readily to pass through the placenta (which most bacteria cannot do) virus antibodies can and do pass also (which bacterial antibodies cannot do). This is why babies are born with immunity to viral diseases much greater than their immunity to bacterial diseases (*see* **Immune Response**).

Spread of viruses within the body

Where viruses attack sheets of cells – as on the skin or mucous membranes – spread may be directly from cell to cell with the film of moisture moving over mucous membranes assisting the process.

Within the body, spread takes place along various routes depending on whether the infection is a localized or a generalized one. A generalized infection (viremia), usual in most virus diseases, means that viruses are being transported to target cells in the bloodstream or through the lymph system. Some viruses reach susceptible cells by specific routes, however. The rabies virus, for example, travels along the nerves, from the skin at the site of infection, to the brain. When chickenpox (varicella) virus causes herpes zoster (shingles), it too travels along the nerves.

Many viruses undergo their multiplication in specific types of cell within the body. We do not fully understand this viral 'targeting' of specific organs but it is certainly an important factor in any particular viral disease. For example, the viruses responsible for the familiar 'infectious diseases of childhood', such as chickenpox and measles, have a preference for skin cells, hence rash is a predominant feature of these infections. Other viruses, such as poliomyelitis and certain arboviruses, have an affinity for nerve cells and the symptoms of the disease depend upon which particular kinds of nerve cell are affected. In infectious hepatitis the cells of the liver appear to be especially susceptible, hence liver damage and jaundice are the recognizable features of this infection.

Viruses and cancer

Certain viruses invade host cells but, rather than instigating reproduction of themselves within those cells, may instead 'transform' them, 'switching off' the mechanism by which cell division is normally controlled and thereby inducing abnormally rapid and crowded cell multiplication. This process, and therefore certain viruses known to be associated with it, has been shown to occur in various forms of cancer. Burkitt's lymphoma, for example, may be due to an arbovirus. The possibility of a viral origin of at least some forms of cancer has stimulated a tremendous spate of biomedical research. It raises the possibility of cancer control.

How invasion by virus causes disease

Where the invading virus multiplies within specific types of cell, the resulting disease can usually be simply explained in terms of the massive damage done to those host cells. If a virus establishes itself in nerve cells in the brain, for example, the resulting encephalitis or paralysis is not surprising. But in these diseases, as well as in general virus diseases such as influenza, symptoms arise which do not seem to be due to specific cell-damage by the multiplying viruses. In polio, for example, while the paralysis is easily explained by the viruses' affinity for cells in the nerves which control voluntary movement, the early symptoms are much less specific. What produces the sore throat, the headache, the fever and nausea which are the typical first symptoms not only of polio but also of 'flu and almost every generalized virus disease? Such symptoms in a *bacterial* disease are thought to be related to the body's reaction to foreign proteins and/or to the release of bacterial toxins. Similar, though as yet ill-understood, mechanisms may be at work in viral infections. There is still an enormous amount to be learned.

Fungi

Fungi affect human beings far more as 'plant germs' than as direct causers of human illness. Indeed, these fungal plant diseases have several times altered the course of human history, as in the nineteenth century when fungus wiped out the Irish potato crop, killed millions, led to the emigration of more than a million to the United States and profoundly influenced English political life. Even today, fungal diseases require constant vigilance and continual new research if acceptable crop yields are to be maintained. Several groups of fungi can, however, directly disturb human health:

Fungi as 'germs' **Dermatophytes.** These fungi are not normal inhabitants of the human body but are common in nature and tend to proliferate on the skin, hair or nails of individuals who are for some reason temporarily susceptible (*see*, for example, **Ringworm and Athlete's Foot**).

Yeasts. These fungi are normal inhabitants of the human body and yeast infections arise only when the local conditions of a particular body-part change so as to provide an environment which leads to their explosive multiplication. For example:

Candida albicans is the fungus which produces 'thrush' which can cause inflammation overlain by the typical white patches seen especially in the vagina and the mouth. Thrush infection of the mouth is common in newborn infants who become infected during their passage through an infected vagina.

Aspergillus is very widespread in nature and therefore in dusts from hay, bird seed, animal housing and so forth. Spores can be found in the sputum of normal individuals.

The disease called aspergillosis arises when the fungi find a foothold in lungs or respiratory tracts already damaged by disease. The more serious disease known as 'farmer's lung' is a hypersensitive reaction to these spores (*see* **Allergy**).

'Systemic mycoses'. These are fungi which 'choose' internal organs as their first target. While the first attack is usually self-limiting, further invasion can, in some susceptible individuals, produce widespread systemic disease with a high mortality rate in the untreated.

Such fungus diseases are almost unknown in Britain. Some, such as 'San Joaqum fever', are common in particular areas of the United States, and are a common cause of disability and death in many underdeveloped areas of the world.

Fungal food poisoning. Fungus activity is responsible for an enormous amount of food *spoilage* but it can also be responsible for serious forms of food *poisoning* due to the release of toxins by the fungus interacting with the foodstuff.

Called mycotoxicoses, these diseases include the first-discovered, 'St Anthony's Fire', now known as ergotism. This is the result of eating rye or other grain contaminated with the ergot fungus. More and more fungal toxins are being identified as serious health hazards. A fungal toxin in peanut meal (aflatoxin) for example, is being indicted as a possible factor in cancer of the liver, while many others are under suspicion as causative factors in a variety of serious human disorders.

Strenuous attempts are being made to improve harvesting and storage practices in agriculture, so as to reduce fungus attack on foodstuffs and also so as to exclude affected products from the category of 'fit for human consumption'. In the meantime, the eating of mouldy food should certainly be avoided despite the common belief that the mould is 'probably penicillin'.

● Never allow children to eat foodstuffs marketed for animals, even if the pet shop's whole peanuts do appear equally suitable for people and parrots. Importation regulations and quality/hygiene checks may be dangerously inadequate.

Protozoa

Protozoa as germs

Protozoa are minute single-celled creatures who live as parasites within animal hosts. Their life-cycles are invariably complex. They often involve two hosts which may be of different species so that, for example, the sporozoites of malaria can multiply only through some of their life-forms while in a human host. Their further development and the eventual production of more infective sporozoites, is dependent on their being taken into a new host; a mosquito. Thus certain species of mosquito are not only vectors for malaria but also a necessary part of the sporozoites' life-cycle. In a similar way (although the life-cycle is different), the trypanosome, which causes sleeping sickness, requires not only a human host but also a tsetse fly which first nurtures certain stages of its development and then serves as a vector to pass on the infection.

Not all protozoan infections thus require multiple hosting. Indeed, some of these parasites appear to be normal (or at least often harmless) parasites in man. Various kinds of amoeba, for example, live in the human bowel, causing no symptoms. One such is called entamoeba Histolytica. For reasons which are not fully understood, this amoeba, carried without knowledge or harm in many individuals, can suddenly become a virulent agent in another. Instead of floating freely in the bowel, it attaches itself to the bowel wall, feeding on the tissues and red blood cells and producing ulceration and the disease we call amoebic dysentery. In certain cases, amoebae are released into the blood circulation and are transported to various organs (including the liver and the brain) where they cause amoebic abscesses.

Amoebic dysentery can be passed on only by faecal contamination. A victim or carrier excretes the amoebae which, either directly or via flies, contaminate water, vegetables or other foods which are then eaten by a new victim within whose body the amoebae can start a new life-cycle. The disease used to be thought of only as a 'tropical disease' but we now know that it can (and does) occur whenever sanitary conditions, especially public health sanitation such as control of drinking water and food production, is poor. Its true incidence is difficult to assess as many other bowel infections can produce similar symptoms and the amoebic nature of the infection can be proven only by complex laboratory identification procedures. While the disease is certainly extremely rare in Britain and, when it occurs, likely to have been brought in from abroad, some estimates put the incidence in certain areas of the United States as high as twenty per cent.

Defences against infection (*see also* **Immune Response**)

Sharing an environment with countless millions of micro-organisms, human bodies have many defences against those which are, or might become, harmful.

Resistance to infection

Micro-organisms have no 'intent'. They do not 'mean' to do an individual good or harm. Their sole 'purpose' is survival and multiplication and they will therefore colonize human bodies *if and when those bodies offer a suitable environment*.

An individual may be highly resistant to a *specific* infection, perhaps because he has a high level of antibodies to that micro-organism and therefore it has no chance of gaining a foothold (*see* **Immune Response** and **Immunization**). But that individual may also be resistant to infection in a more general sense. He may be able to maintain an optimum balance between his own body and the various micro-organisms which share it with him or with which he has contact in their mutual environment. 'Perfect health' is something which we cannot even define, let alone achieve, but there is no doubt that general health and resistance to disease are related. The relationship is not easy to see at the positive pole because even when we live with someone who 'never seems to get ill' and 'always heals quickly' and 'has an iron stomach', we cannot know what threats to health were offered and shrugged off: what would have happened to him if he had been less robust. But the relationship is easy to see at the negative pole. People who are under-nourished, poorly sheltered, chronically sick, old or newly born and frail, acquire more infections than other people and their bodies combat them less efficiently so that they suffer more from each. People who insult their bodies in particular ways – by heavy smoking, for example – do not only render themselves more liable to infection of the affected body-parts, but also make it far more difficult for the body's own defences to function efficiently when they are needed. If the respiratory tract is chronically irritated by the thousands of cigarettes smoked over many years, it will probably offer a hospitable environment to a variety of 'germs'. When germs gain a foothold, the reduced activity of the protective mucus blanket covering that respiratory tract may enable them to multiply and spread.

Sometimes attempts to improve general health and hygiene actually misfire because they upset the delicate balances between one body system and another, or between one part of the body and its micro-organisms. An important example is our use and misuse of antibiotics to which we shall return (*see below*), but there are other everyday examples too. In the vagina, the normal flora feed on shed cells from which they release sugars which ferment. The fermentation produces a slightly acid vaginal environment which discourages the growth of pathogens. When a woman uses 'feminine sprays' or douches, in a misguided attempt to keep the area extra-clean or 'germ-free', she upsets the balance, reduces the acidity and actually encourages exactly the kind of bacterial invasion she intended to prevent. The lesson is that under ordinary circumstances of 'good health' (i.e., absence of symptoms) bodies resist infection best if they are left to do so for themselves.

Mechanical barriers against infection: skin

Skin is a tough envelope consisting of several layers of cells with an outermost layer of dead, horny ones. As long as all those layers are intact, skin cannot be penetrated by micro-organisms.

But skin is not only a vital mechanical barrier to infection; it also has in-built decontamination properties. Its resident population of harmless bacteria, together with its own excretion of chemical substances (such as sebum), combine to discourage the growth *on* the skin of micro-organisms which might land there.

● Removing intact skin – from an unbroken blister, for example – often increases the likelihood of infection in the exposed raw tissue. Similarly, an over-enthusiastic use of man-made decontaminants (such as disinfectants, *see below*) can remove the normal flora and secretions and leave the artificially cleaned skin more vulnerable than it would have been in its natural state.

Specialized 'skin': mucous membrane

Routes from the outside world into the body, such as the nose and respiratory system, the mouth and alimentary tract, the vagina, the anus and the outer surface of the eye, all have specialized protection. The nose and respiratory tract can serve as an example.

The tract is covered by a fine mucus blanket which offers both mechanical and biological protection. First defences are concentrated in the nose, where hairs in the mucus blanket may trap as much as ninety per cent of inhaled foreign material. Trapped particles are conveyed, by the constant movement of the mucus blanket, either towards the nostrils or backwards down the throat. Particles and mucus together either drip out of the body or are swallowed for excretion via the stomach and intestines. The mucus blanket is also impregnated with various anti-bacterial substances (an enzyme called lysozyme, for example).

Particles which get through these nasally-based barriers (which they may do when breathing is through the mouth, for example) are similarly dealt with in the trachea and the bronchi. From this area, particles are conveyed, by the moving mucus, to the larynx to be coughed into the pharynx and swallowed (*see* **Colds**; **Coughs**; **Croup and Laryngitis**).

Only the minutest particles reach the end-structure of the air passages, the alveoli. Here there are special cells called alveolar macrophages which can engulf and kill bacteria (*see* **Chest Infections**).

Most of the normal secretions of these body areas have self-cleansing and/or decontaminating properties. Both saliva and tears, for example, destroy some bacteria and inhibit the multiplication of others. Once again, attempts to prevent such normal secretions or to substitute artificial ones often make it more difficult for the body to care for itself. Tears are better for eyes than most 'soothing' eye-lotions while a running nose is usually serving a purpose which is better not halted by 'nose drops to dry it up'.

The second line of defence: inflammation

Whenever that first line of defence, the enclosing skin, is breached in any way, the immediate response is inflammation. The injury can be to any type of skin; the skin of your finger, the skin (mucous membrane) which lines your throat or the membrane which encases your liver.

The injury can be of any type. That finger may be cut or burned; that throat may be irritated by chemicals in dust or attacked by viruses; the liver can be invaded by bacteria. We call inflammation in different parts of the body by different names (internal ones have the suffix 'itis' as in meningitis, appendicitis, laryngitis) but the process by which the body reacts to insult or injury and takes the first steps towards repairing the damage is always the same. Signs of inflammation are:

Redness (and sometimes heat). The small vessels supplying the damaged area (the arterioles) dilate so that more blood can reach the site. The minute capillaries also dilate so that the extra blood is not carried away too rapidly. The result is the red flush you see around, say, a bad graze or in a sore throat or an irritated eye.

Swelling and pain. Capillary walls become more 'leaky' when dilated, so plasma (the clear part of the blood) loaded with many kinds of white blood cell (polymorphs) which travel to the area of injury, ooze through the walls and accumulate in the tissue. This fluid is the exudate which you can see from that graze; it is the cause of the swelling in a sprained ankle or internal inflammation. Pain arises not only from nerve endings damaged in whatever accident caused the inflammation, but also by this swelling which causes pressure, and, probably, by substances, such as histamines, released from the cells. The functions of this exudate include:

Dilution of any irritants which may have been introduced as, for example, in an insect sting.

Concentration of a protein substance (fibrin) which helps to clot blood in an open wound, but which also produces minute 'internal clots'. These act as partial two-way barriers. They make it more difficult for invading bacteria to penetrate further and they also make it more difficult for the exudate to be carried away from the damaged area with the lymph flow. Obstruction of the lymph flow minimizes the risk of bacteria being carried with it, deeper into the body. It also ensures that the polymorphs (*see below*) remain in the area to perform their functions.

Concentration of polymorphs which perform elaborate scavenging tasks, engulfing bacteria, cell debris, etc. so that they can be destroyed by enzyme activity.

If tissue damage is slight and this first burst of polymorph activity succeeds in 'clearing up' the area, inflammation simply resolves; blood vessels return to normal and the exudate is re-absorbed.

If tissue damage is considerable, polymorphs clear dead cells to allow healing. Continued inflammation and exudate shows that their activity has not been successfully completed. When a clean wound stops oozing, or the swelling of an internal or joint injury goes down, healing will begin.

Types of infection

Localized infection

Some bacterial contamination of external wounds is very common. The bacteria which are 'normal flora' for the *outside* surface of the skin are 'foreign' to the polymorphs in that exudate. They must therefore be engulfed and prevented from getting further into the body via the lymph system or the bloodstream.

Pus is inflammatory exudate, packed with the dead and dying cells of polymorphs and bacteria, both being broken down by enzyme activity.

Pus from a wound certainly means that some micro-organisms got in, but it also means that some, at least, are being dealt with by the white cells. A few droplets of pus from an open wound suggests the successful end to a minor battle *if other signs of inflammation have gone.* Pus oozes from a wound, or dries into a scab. The tissue can then heal cleanly behind it.

If there is pus and inflammation continues, it is clear that the battle between polymorphs and bacteria is not over. It may still be successfully resolved (i.e., healing may take place without spread of infection) but 'back-up troops' within the body will be being mobilized (*see below*).

● If there is visible pus in, on or coming from a wound, check whether there is still redness, heat, swelling and pain around it. If there is none, healing is underway. If there is inflammation, watch carefully to make sure it is diminishing rather than increasing. Seek medical help, even for a small injury, if inflammation increases.

Pus

Since pus contains the protein of cells 'foreign' to the body, it must be ejected before healing can take place. In a superficial wound this is no problem – the pus oozes out. But in a deep or jagged wound, or when infection is internal, in an appendix for example, it can be a problem.

When the polymorphs have controlled the bacterial enemy, destroying bacteria at least as fast as they are increasing, and preventing spread via blood or lymph, healing will commence *around* the area but cannot take place *within* the pus-laden tissues. The body has controlled the infection but cannot eliminate it. The result is an abscess.

Abscesses

There are many kinds of abscess ranging from the kinds which occur when pus collects just beneath the skin (boils, carbuncles, styes, etc.) through the kinds which are fairly superficial but out of reach (tooth and ear abscesses) to the internal ones like acute appendicitis. All abscesses are painful because the accumulated pocket of pus puts pressure on surrounding tissue and nerves. The less room an abscess has for expansion, the greater will be the pressure and the agony. Hence the sleepless nights of tooth and ear abscesses. Wherever the abscess, pus has to be got rid of before healing can take place. A superficial abscess, like a boil, will eventually 'burst' and let out its own pus. Abscesses which are buried within body tissues or in internal organs will burst, too, if they are allowed to go on accumulating pus. But if that pus can find no direct route out of the body, the bursting of the abscess will spread it through surrounding tissues, often causing more generalized infection. This is why medical and/or surgical treatment is usually preferred.

If the root of a tooth is abscessed, for example, your dentist may refuse to take out the tooth and thus relieve the intense pain until he can be sure that your body's defences will be able to cope with the consequent leakage of pus from the socket. He will often insist on giving a course of antibiotics to boost those defences before the extraction (*see* **Teeth**/Some dental emergencies).

If an appendix is inflamed and therefore likely to begin to accumulate pus, its surgical removal is urgent (*see* **Hospital**/Surgery: Appendectomy). If it is permitted to build up pressure and burst, infected material will be spread through the abdomen to produce the very serious condition called peritonitis.

● When a collection of pus *can* find its own way out, it will do so. Don't be in a hurry to squeeze a hot, red, painful boil which has not yet made a 'head'. The body's defences may yet deal with the infection so that the lump vanishes without ever draining pus. If it does not, forcing pus up through skin which is still intact may also force it down, breaking down the fibrin clots which are preventing infection spreading inwards.

Localized infection which is spreading

Local infection cannot always be dealt with, or even contained, by the defensive tactics of the body's general inflammatory response. The child himself may be in a state where that response is comparatively inefficient (*see above* Resistance). The infecting organism may have been introduced in great numbers, be highly virulent and/or have found an ideal site for multiplication. When infection threatens to spread, the body's next line of defences is mobilized (*see* **Immune Response**). It is important, though, that you should recognize spreading infection early so that medical and/or surgical treatment can intervene before local trouble turns into generalized illness. Seek a medical opinion if:

Inflammation (including pain, swelling, redness, etc.) continues or increases.

Pus forms or continues to be formed after being carefully cleaned away on the first occasion that it was visible.

Inflammation spreads away from the site of the wound. This shows that 'battle' is being waged in tissues other than those originally involved in the injury. The classic sign is red streaks under the skin running from the wound towards the nearest lymph nodes, but a spreading patch of dull-red skin around or near to the wound is a common sign, too.

Lymph nodes swell. If an injury is to the hand or arm and infection is spreading, the lymph nodes in the armpit will eventually swell. In a foot or leg injury it will be the lymph nodes in the groin which are affected. If the jaw or face is the site of injury, there may be swelling of lymph nodes in the angle of the jaw. Swollen lymph nodes are a clear sign that the body's immune system is involved in fighting the infection. By this stage there may be further signs of whole-body involvement such as fever.

● Although it is obviously better to prevent localized infection from spreading, don't let 'blood poisoning' be a spectre which haunts you. Even if infection in a small wound has given rise to enlarged lymph nodes and perhaps fever, antibiotics prescribed by your doctor will quickly resolve the infection.

Infections which cause illness When micro-organisms invade the body without an obvious wound as entry-point or an obvious injury as their site of multiplication, the body's infection can only be recognized by the symptoms which it causes. We therefore tend to feel that 'being unwell' is quite different from 'being hurt' but, from the point of view of the body's reactions, both conditions are similar. Some pathogenic micro-organisms do eventually produce specific and recognizable symptoms (such as the various skin rashes of the infectious diseases of childhood), but most of them first produce the vague and general symptoms which might be the beginning of almost any infection and may indeed be dealt with by the body before they turn into anything 'diagnosable'. The very first signs of infection may, in fact, not be signs of illness at all but of the very fact that the body *is coping with a threat*. A sore throat, for example, means that something has irritated that mucous membrane. The irritation could be from dust and nothing to do with infection by 'germs'. But if it is a reaction to 'germs', the sore throat may never 'turn into' the cold, the tonsillitis or the measles which you find yourself expecting. Local inflammatory reaction may deal with the threatened invasion and the throat will return to normal.

The more types of bacteria and viruses an individual's body has battled with, the more readily will it cope, at this quick, local level, with further contacts with them (*see* **Immune Response** and **Immunization**). Many older people, for example, quite frequently think they are going to have colds, judging by first symptoms of blocked-feeling noses and perhaps soreness at the very top of the throat. Yet most of the time the expected cold does not develop. It has been 'shrugged off' by primed defenders.

Unfortunately that well-protected adult can, and often does, pass on the cold he himself is not going to suffer to someone who is less well-protected. When a particular infection is going round a family, some members will avoid illness altogether, some will have mild symptoms and others may have very marked ones (*see below* Preventing the spread of 'infectious' illnesses). The nature of the symptoms experienced by people exposed to the same infection may vary, as well as their severity. That resistant father's body may stop the invasion of viruses within the nasal passages so that he only ever has a blocked and runny nose. The viruses he passes on may cause a middle-ear infection in one child, croup in another and a humdinger of a head cold in another.

With everyday (or at least every-year) infections, then, parents usually have to wait and see. Your child reports a stuffed-up nose and you wait and see whether it will 'just go' or whether it will 'develop'. If it just goes, well and good; if it develops, you have to see what it develops into. On the whole your best overall indication that an infection is *not yet* being adequately dealt with by the body's own defences is fever (*see* **Nursing/ Fever**). While an individual can be seriously, even fatally, ill, without ever having fever at all, most infections which are more than local do have fever associated with them; furthermore, while the body's normal temperature is more variable than many people believe, high fever does mean that the body is under stress, is fighting something.

Apart from the presence or absence of fever, the number of symptoms or the number of parts of the body affected is also a useful rough and ready guide to the progress of infection. A child may be nauseated (feel sick) for many reasons, many of them trivial and/or nothing to do with infection. But if she also has diarrhoea, infection is probable. If she has fever as well as nausea and diarrhoea, some kind of infection which her body is having trouble eliminating, is almost certain. In the same way, a child with a headache can have (or be starting) almost anything or nothing physical or nothing diagnosable. Add in fever and it becomes likely that the headache is part of a physical illness. Add in a generalized achiness of her muscles and you can be sure that she has 'got something'.

Multiple infections

If this all sounds very vague, that is because recognizing infections, especially early on, is a vague business. On the whole, vague and general symptoms either declare themselves by developing into more specific ones or they go away. When symptoms do develop and become more specific, it is often not the *original* infection which is responsible but the joining in of a second 'germ' along a path paved by the first. A mild 'flu suddenly 'turns into' a serious attack of bronchitis with thick sputum, yellow with pus, being coughed up. Parents may feel that they did not take the original 'flu seriously enough and that it is their fault that the child is now really ill. But it is nobody's 'fault'. 'Flu virus damages the lining of the bronchi and bronchioles. The body was in the process of dealing with the virus invasion but that throat was open to further invasion by some of the many bacteria which commonly live harmlessly there (*see above*). The mild viral illness has been followed by a more serious bacterial one.

Secondary infections, following, or occurring simultaneously with, the first infection, are often much more serious than one on its own. The marked tendency of the measles virus to pave the way for bacterial infections of the middle ear, throat and bronchial tree, is one excellent reason for mass immunization against measles.

Difficulties of medical diagnosis of infection

Parents of an undeniably ill child often want their doctor to perform not only as a skilled diagnostician but also as a magician. They want to know 'what has she got?' It is important to the parent–doctor partnership to understand that that question is often unanswerable.

Doctors, like parents, can only see symptoms. They can look for signs hidden from lay eyes (respiratory signs, for example, detectable only by a stethoscope used by a skilled ear) and they can relate to each other symptoms which lay-people tend to regard as separate (abdominal pain as part of tonsillitis, for example). By these means they can often establish *what kind* of illness the child has – an upper respiratory infection, for example – but still be unable to say what 'germ' has caused it or what, if anything, is likely to follow. The most valuable result of a careful physical examination is often entirely negative. The doctor assures himself (and the parents) that the child's symptoms and signs are *not* suggestive of particular kinds of illness. He may, for example, tell you that her 'lungs are clear' meaning that whatever infective organism has made her ill, she has not, at the moment, 'got pneumonia'.

Quite often such a physical examination reveals no signs or symptoms at all except those (such as a quickened pulse and breathing rate) which go with fever, whatever that fever's cause. Then the doctor himself has to take a wait-and-see approach unless the child is so ill (and/or the parents so frantically worried) that he considers that she should be admitted to hospital.

Wait-and-see means that the doctor believes that the child will either produce some more symptoms (which will give him some new data to work on) or get better. It works best for parents if they know how long he plans to wait (i.e., when will he see the child again and/or how can they reach him if they get worried again) and the kind of sign or symptom he is waiting for. If those points are not volunteered, it is often worth asking the doctor what you should look out for and under what circumstances you should call him again.

Difficulties of laboratory diagnosis of infection

Wait-and-see also means that, given the present symptoms and lack of signs, the doctor does not consider that laboratory work to try and discover the infecting organism is possible or worthwhile. Again, it can help the partnership if parents understand why the doctor makes this decision.

If there are no special symptoms *the doctor and his back-up laboratory staff have no starting point.* They have no way of knowing what kind of organism they are looking for nor which body system it is most likely to be in. It may seem that one could take a sample of blood, of urine, of faeces and tell the lab staff to 'look for pathogens'. But that search would be not just difficult, expensive, time-consuming, but actually impossible. Of the hundreds of thousands of organisms which can cause trouble, many would be found because many live in the body anyway. Just finding them would tell one nothing. Each organism found would have to be counted; only an excess far above normal populations would even suggest infection. Then again one cannot just look and count. It is tempting to think of putting a drop of urine under a microscope and seeing and counting micro-organisms, but it is not possible. Micro-organisms have to be cultured (grown) and different kinds require different culture-environments. Without some idea of what is being sought, the search cannot even begin.

If there are some special symptoms the doctor may know which body system he would be searching and therefore what kind of specimen to take, but the search may still be inappropriate.

Suppose, for example, that the ill child has upper respiratory symptoms. The doctor could take a swab from her throat or nose and ask his laboratory to make cultures from it. But the chances are high that the causative organism will be a virus not a bacterium and virus-culture is a technique which is still so new and difficult that facilities for it do not even exist in many places. He could tell the lab to culture for bacteria (on the grounds that if they found no infecting bacteria he could then assume that the illness was viral), but why should he bother? If there is a bacterial cause for the illness then an antibiotic will probably be appropriate; if it is viral then an antibiotic will not. If he thinks that an antibiotic is a reasonable prescription he will want to prescribe it now, not wait several days for cultures. If he is not going to prescribe one now, the chances are that by the time he gets the lab results which suggest that an antibiotic would have helped, the child will be better.

The pros and cons of antibiotics in undiagnosed infection

Your doctor's clinical judgement is on the line every time he has to decide whether or not to prescribe antibiotics for an ill child with indefinite symptoms. Parents tend to be unhelpful because, even when they understand that under most circumstances a laboratory hunt for a bacterium takes too long to be useful, they cannot understand why the doctor does not prescribe one *just in case* the cause of the illness is bacterial rather than viral. The answer to that is as simple as it is vital: bacteria change and evolve very readily. One of the aspects of themselves which they change most readily is their own resistance to antibiotics. If your child is given an antibiotic whenever she is ill, it will sometimes help her body deal with an infection, but all the other times it will simply encourage her normal bacteria to become antibiotic-resistant. Then, when she does suffer an invasion by bacteria (perhaps by those usually-harmless residents, after she has had a virus infection) the antibiotics which should have cured her will have no effect. If your doctor does prescribe an antibiotic for your child at the beginning of a particular illness, it will probably be for one or more of the following reasons:

That her symptoms and condition make him suspect a bacterial cause. His suspicion may be based on long experience and clinical judgement so that he could only describe it by saying something like 'throats that look like this, as part of this clinical picture, often are bacterial . . .', or it may be based on harder data which he can more easily explain to you. The child may, for example, have had measles which is a viral infection. She was recovering but is now severely ill with high fever and acute ear-pain. The chances are high that a bacterial secondary infection has moved in.

That an outbreak or epidemic of bacterial infection is taking place. If this child is the third member of a family, or the thirtieth member of a school, to come down with a similar symptom-pattern which has been shown to be of bacterial origin in other people, the chances that there is a bacterial cause in her case are obviously high.

That previous and similar illnesses in this child have cleared much faster when he did prescribe antibiotics than when he did not. Recurrent tonsillitis is a good example. Many children have several bouts each winter for two or three years. The infection may be bacterial or viral and, during the first few episodes, the doctor will have to use his clinical judgement to inspire guesswork. If antibiotics always 'work', he will probably decide that the *probability is that this new bout is bacterial too*. It may not be, but on balance he may feel that antibiotics should be given.

That the severity of the illness and/or condition of the child is such that every possible precaution against secondary infection must be taken even if the current infection is of viral origin. Antibiotics are often given to babies, for example, because even though their current infections may be viral, their in-built protection against secondary invasion by bacteria is very poor (*see* **Immune Response**). They might be given to a young child who was exceedingly ill with measles because that illness had reduced her general resistance to a low level. They might even be prescribed for an adolescent who, while not very ill now, faces important examinations in a week's time and therefore implores the doctor to use every tool at his disposal to 'get me better'.

That you will give him no peace and/or will consider him uncaring if he does not. Of course, no parent would like to admit that she bullied (or could bully) a doctor into giving treatment he considered inappropriate, and certainly no doctor would like to admit that he would allow such a thing to happen. But practising medicine is an art as well as a science; human relations matter as well as symptoms and their relief. If the doctor must toss up whether or not to prescribe that antibiotic (because there are insufficient clinical signs to give him clear guidance) and you are putting heavy pressure on him to do so, that pressure may, in fact, tip the balance.

When the laboratory may help in diagnosis

Different doctors have different kinds of laboratory help more or less readily available to them, as well as varying in the extent to which they like to rely on clinical judgement or have that judgement backed by evidence. Some therefore order the culture of throat swabs, or blood or urine tests (*see* **Hospital**/Procedures) much more readily than others.

Some doctors also take a great interest in public health and in the pattern of disease occurring in their own practices. They may sometimes seek a laboratory finding not only to assist in their management of this particular patient's current illness, but also to fill in another tiny piece in the jigsaw puzzle of an epidemic.

For most families, laboratory help for a patient who is being nursed at home will most commonly be sought under some of the following sets of circumstances:

Ill-defined illness such as a mild or early attack of glandular fever. Although a virulent attack produces fever, sore throat and swollen glands as well as extreme lethargy and depression, a milder attack may only make the patient feel miserably 'under par'. If the doctor suspects GF, a specific blood test (Monospot or Paul-Bunnell) will confirm or refute his diagnosis. If he is unsure whether the patient is clinically ill or suffering from some emotional upset, a simple blood-count will show whether or not an increase in the numbers of white cells suggests *any* infection. If it does, the doctor can proceed to specific tests for GF and other infections. A diagnosis of GF cannot lead to cure (there is none) but may comfort the patient by explaining her unpleasant feelings. Negative findings may also be important as many parents wrongly assume that any vague illness is GF and that GF is a far more serious and long-lasting illness than is usually the case.

Recurrent illness such as repeated attacks of urinary infection. The doctor may decide that symptomatic treatment, with or without antibiotics, is no longer satisfactory. He may order a full urinalysis in order to establish just how many of which bacteria are present during an attack and which antibiotics they are sensitive to. He may also order tests of kidney function in order to ensure that there is no kidney damage, or inadequate function, which might be increasing the tendency to infection.

Epidemic or potentially epidemic illness. A few illnesses must, by law, be notified to the public health authorities. Those authorities also sometimes request all doctors to be on the alert for cases of a particular illness of which an epidemic seems likely. If your child suffers from 'food poisoning' when her doctor has been thus requested to be extra-alert, he may order laboratory tests of her faeces.

Special risks. Some serious illnesses are easy to diagnose through laboratory testing and worth testing for, even on suspicion, because early treatment is important. If your doctor even suspects meningitis, for example, he will order a lumbar puncture (*see* **Hospital**/Procedures) so that the spinal fluid can be examined (*see* **Meningitis and Encephalitis**).

Some conditions – heart conditions for example – make any infection a special risk. Most doctors will make unusually heavy calls on laboratory help for such a patient.

Travelling or working in far away places make diseases which are rare and exotic for your home area into possibilities. Doctors will often seek laboratory help in diagnosing conditions which they seldom, if ever, meet, but which seem possible in these particular circumstances.

Treatment of infections which cause illness

Until the Second World War we could not directly treat infections in the sense of destroying 'germs' which were causing illness within the body. Within two generations we have come to take such treatment for granted. Our grandparents will probably have nursed relatives dying from unchecked pneumonia, yet we no longer quite believe that people can die from simple *illness* in places where the full range of medical might is available to them. Death from accidents, from mechanical problems within the body and/or from surgical attempts to put them right, we can still accept; cancer is a special case: a kind of horror story of the modern world. But ordinary illness . . . surely there is a pill, an injection, a medicine? Surely there is a cure?

Antibiotics are the drugs which produced that miracle of forgetting; the drugs which seemed to give man control over infection. They are amazingly effective; they do cure many infections. But, as we shall see, they are not cure-alls. Virus infections remain largely untouched by modern treatments, their control being almost entirely a matter of prevention by immunization. Only some stages of some protozoan infections are directly 'curable' in man; their control still has to depend on public health measures and on the control of animal vectors. Fungus infection of foodstuffs produces poisons which we still cannot 'cure', so that attention must be focused on preventing such foods from being eaten in the first place. Insofar as man has defeated infection, then, he has still done more by prevention than by cure and will have to continue to do so. Public health measures may not help your family *when members are ill*, but it is those measures which ensure that they are not ill more often.

Antibiotics and
sulphonamides

Sulphonamides were the first anti-bacterial chemicals to be used in medicine. Their role has been largely usurped by antibiotics, mainly because of problems of bacterial resistance to sulphonamides (*see below*).

Antibiotics are chemicals produced by bacteria and fungi which interfere with the life-cycle of other bacteria and fungi. Those which interfere to *prevent the multiplication* of pathogenic micro-organisms are called 'bacteriostatic' drugs. They can halt the spread of infection and thus give the body's own defences the chance to overwhelm the already-present 'germs', but they do not kill them. 'Bactericidal' drugs actually destroy the 'germs'. The difference can be extremely important where the victim's own defences are poor (due, perhaps, to immuno-suppressive drug treatment) or where infection has taken place in a part of the body which always lacks defence because (like nerve cells in the brain or the central nervous system) it is sealed off from normal blood flow.

Antibiotics may be the isolated and purified chemicals from cultured moulds ('natural antibiotics'); they may be 'natural antibiotics' which have been chemically modified ('semi-synthetic antibiotics'); or they may increasingly be 'synthetic antibiotics' which have been, so to speak, chemically constructed from component parts. It is by tampering, in a variety of highly sophisticated ways, with these chemicals that medical scientists are able to alter and control antibiotic action. Some naturally occurring ones, for example, cannot be absorbed from the digestive tract and are therefore active only when given by injection. Some are active only against certain specific types of pathogenic bacteria. Some are very rapidly processed by the body so that frequent doses are necessary to keep up adequate blood-levels. The original penicillin G, for example, had to be injected and was mainly active against pathogens of the cocci group. By isolating the penicillin molecule's nucleus, scientists made it possible to add to it other chemical groups and thus to produce the wide range of penicillins which are in use today.

Problems in
antibiotic use:
bacterial
resistance to
antibiotics

Pathogenic bacteria can become resistant to the action of a particular antibiotic in a number of complicated ways, the most important of which is called 'transformation'. This process involves a population of bacteria (say in a wound) taking up fragments of genetic material (DNA) released by dead bacteria, using that 'genetic information' and consequently reproducing themselves with the ability to resist that antibiotic.

For example, if there is an epidemic of dysentery, victims will have both harmless and pathogenic bacteria in their guts. Given an antibiotic, the pathogenic bacteria (along with plenty of harmless ones, *see below*) will be destroyed, but the surviving harmless inhabitants may acquire resistance to that antibiotic. This does not matter *at the time* because the resistant bacteria are not virulent pathogens. But if and when the patient's gut is invaded by another virulent strain, those bacteria will acquire antibiotic resistance from the harmless but resistant bacteria occupying the gut. The new infection will prove far more difficult to treat. Antibiotic resistance does not just affect the bacteria involved in one illness, person or epidemic, but may be passed on, via other pathogenic or harmless organisms, so that whole bacterial populations acquire it.

It was this problem of resistance which brought the extensive use of the first 'magic drugs', the sulphonamides, to an end. And it is still this problem which bedevils antibiotic treatment. The chemical industry is involved in a non-stop race to evolve new antibiotics, or adaptations of existing ones, more quickly than bacteria can evolve resistance to them. Already there are some groups of bacterial infections (especially bowel infections) which respond so poorly to existing antibiotics that many doctors consider their use inadvisable. The antibiotic may not help the individual (whose 'germs' are probably resistant to it) and it will certainly lead to yet more resistant strains developing via his normal bowel flora.

Fortunately some pathogens show no sign of developing resistance to commonly used and safe antibiotics. Syphilis, for example, remains sensitive to the original penicillin after almost two generations of frequent use (*see* **Adolescence**/Sex: Venereal disease).

● The more antibiotics are introduced into our bodies, the more opportunity there is for resistant bacteria to develop and the more difficult it will become to find safe antibiotics to which pathogenic bacteria are sensitive. This is why the temptation to take an antibiotic in every illness 'just in case' must be avoided. It is also why the non-medical use of antibiotics (in the fattening of animals for meat, for example) is to be deplored. If we cannot use antibiotics responsibly, our grandchildren may find themselves in a world where the 'miracle drugs' are no longer miraculous.

Side-effects of antibiotics

Since pathogenic bacteria live and breed outside the cells of the infected patient, antibiotics can attack them without damaging the host cells. Nevertheless, there are side-effects, varying from antibiotic to antibiotic and from individual to individual, but ranging from skin rashes to allergic shock reactions which can cause death.

Most minor side-effects result from the fact that, while no antibiotic attacks all bacteria, many attack quite a wide range. While killing pathogens, they also kill harmless bacteria of the individual's 'normal flora' and by doing so they can upset the balance of various body systems. An upset in the normal flora of the bowel, for example, often leads to diarrhoea in a patient taking oral antibiotics for an upper respiratory infection.

Antibiotics which are active against bacteria are inactive against fungi (and vice versa). Antibiotic treatment for a bacterial infection can therefore lead to an upsurge in resident fungi and to consequent infection by yeasts and so forth (*see above*). 'Thrush' infections of the vagina, for example, are a frequent accompaniment to treatment with broad-spectrum antibiotics.

● Ill-effects from an antibiotic should always be reported to a doctor and, if there is any question of allergy, carefully noted. A child who is allergic can (and must) be taught that he 'must not have penicillin'. This information could be vital if he should be ill when away from home.

● Children on long-term antibiotics (perhaps because of recurrent infections of the urinary tract) will inevitably be suffering some upset of body-chemistry, and some likelihood of resistance to antibiotics if an acute bacterial illness should occur. You, with your doctor, must allow for this when deciding the pros and cons of prolonged antibiotic administration.

Choice of antibiotic and method of administration

As we have already seen (*see above*) a doctor who has decided to prescribe an antibiotic to a patient will usually want to begin the treatment immediately. While he may take swabs or specimens for laboratory culture, so that the treatment can be altered later if necessary, he will prescribe his 'best guess' in the meantime.

That 'best guess' may be easy: most bacterial tonsillitis, for example, involves a bacterium known to be sensitive to particular penicillins which are safe (except if the patient is allergic to them), comparatively cheap, and effective by mouth. Most bacterial urinary infections are associated with gram-negative bacteria and the doctor's 'best guess' would therefore probably be different but equally easy.

Sometimes the choice is more difficult. If the doctor is puzzled, he may want to cover many options by prescribing a 'broad-spectrum' antibiotic; one which is effective against a wide range of bacteria. If a present infection seems likely to be the continuation (or flaring up) of one which has already been treated with an antibiotic, he may think it likely that the bacteria infecting the patient now, are, or have become, resistant to the first drug. He may therefore prescribe an antibiotic from a different group. In a hospital, especially, a doctor may have knowledge of particular resistances in the local bacterial population. His prescribing of antibiotics may be carefully tailored both to fit remaining bacterial sensitivities and to avoid creating yet more resistance.

Sometimes a doctor will prescribe an antibiotic which must be given by injection. This may be because the drug he wants the patient to have is only effective by this route, or because it can be given either by injection or orally but works more rapidly by this method.

Some antibiotics (especially antibiotics against fungal infections of the skin or mucous membranes) are prescribed as a cream, lotion, ointment or drops. They are not absorbed from the gut and cannot therefore be taken as tablets.

In more serious illnesses, antibiotics may be given by intravenous injection or by being added to an intravenous drip (*see* **Hospital**/Procedures: Blood and other transfusions). This may be for maximum speed of action and/or for most effective distribution especially to areas of the body with limited blood flow, and/or to ensure a constant level of the drug in the bloodstream rather than the highs and lows which are the inevitable result of periodic administration.

● Trust your doctor. If you do not, you should have found another long ago and should do so now. Ask why he prescribes this drug by that route, by all means, but try not to imply that it is his job to give you what you want. His job is to give your child what her body needs and it may need the injections she hates.

● Do as he says and therefore do make sure that you have understood his instructions. Does a prescription which says 'every six hours' mean that the patient should be woken for the drug once in the night or does it mean 'four times a day'? (*see* **Nursing**/Medicines).

● If you cannot follow the instructions exactly, do consult the prescribing doctor, at least by telephone. If a drug says 'with food' for example, it may, or may not matter very much if your ill and unhungry child takes it on an empty stomach. You could try a compromise glass of milk but if that is refused or vomited, you must ask.

● Following your doctor's instructions means that *every single prescribed dose should be taken*. Stopping a medicine which a child dislikes as soon as she seems better is a temptation, but do resist it. A half-course of an antibiotic may quell the infection without eliminating it. She might quickly relapse. There is even a possibility that those pathogens will now have mutated so that they are resistant to the antibiotic which would have killed them if she had taken the full course. If you want to stop before the prescribed course of antibiotic has been given, ask your doctor first.

Anti-viral drugs   Viruses live and multiply *within* living cells, using the chemistry of those cells for their own purposes. Drugs which could attack viruses would therefore have to do so by attacking the host cells. Indeed, it is difficult to see how they could avoid attacking the healthy cells of the body as well. For all practical purposes it is true to say that we have no drugs for the cure of established virus infections. Several chemicals are being developed experimentally however. One (idoxuridine) is in use for the treatment of virus eye ulcers, cold sores (herpes simplex) and shingles (herpes zoster).

Interferon is the name given to a substance, discovered in the fifties, which is produced by cells when they are invaded by viruses. Its action is to prevent the multiplication of a virus within the cell and therefore its ability to spread to further cells.

Experimental work on the manufacture and administration of interferon raised high hopes which have not yet been realized. The substance is species-specific, so that people must have interferon manufactured by human cells. This means that it is both costly and difficult to produce. When injected, it acts for only a very short time.

Much scientific effort is now being devoted to finding substances which will stimulate the body itself to produce extra interferon.

Gamma globulin. Since viral vaccines produce antibodies and antibodies remain in the gamma-globulin fraction of the blood plasma, it seems logical to use human gamma globulin in the prevention and treatment of virus infections.

Gamma globulin used in this way cannot 'cure' existing infection because antibodies act by combining with the virus and thus preventing it from penetrating a new cell. Viruses which are already within cells are therefore immune from antibody attack until they have multiplied to a point where they are ready to leave that dead or damaged cell and enter new ones. In theory, though, gamma globulin should help to protect an individual from viral infection and should slow down or limit the spread of viral infection within him.

Immunoglobulin is prepared so that it contains ten to twenty times the concentration of all the antibodies which are normally present in an adult's plasma.

Hyper-immune immunoglobulin is a similar preparation except that it is made from the blood of patients convalescing from particular viral infections and should therefore contain much higher quantities of antibody to that particular infection.

Despite some outstanding successes in protecting populations newly exposed to virus diseases against which they had no immunity, gamma globulin has proved disappointing as a means of protecting individuals. It cannot, for example, be relied upon to protect the foetus of a pregnant woman who has been in contact with german measles (rubella virus). It is, and will remain, a scarce and expensive commodity and will therefore probably continue to be used only in a limited way. Its greatest application, currently, is the protection of contacts of infectious hepatitis within closed communities such as nurseries.

Treatment of external infection and inflammation

The skin and mucus membranes are, as we have seen, the body's first line of defence against infection; a defence which is frequently breached. There are many highly effective drugs which can be applied to the skin to combat local infection, but it is unfortunate that our attitudes to these drugs tend to be less respectful and responsible than our attitudes to similar drugs taken internally. People who would not be so foolish as to give one child's 'tonsillitis medicine' to another sore throat sufferer, will casually apply the cream prescribed for one to another. These casual attitudes are often reflected in the difference between the control of sales of internal and external drugs. Many countries which allow the sale of oral antibiotics only on prescription, nevertheless allow them to be freely available in creams, ointments and lotions.

Skin applications containing active drugs (as opposed to palliatives, such as softening agents for skin-chapping and so forth) should be treated with just as much respect as oral drugs. That means that before using any such application you will often need a doctor's advice, especially as skin infections are often extremely difficult to diagnose and/or to differentiate one from another.

The 'base' in which the drug is contained is often as important as the active drug. Applications to be used in or on the eye, for example, *must* be sterile. The use of an antibiotic cream, intended for application elsewhere, on a stye or other eyelid infection could be disastrous. The same applies, of course, to appropriate bases for drugs applied to mucus membranes. The base for a skin antibiotic may be damaging, even poisonous, if applied to a mouth ulcer. Even where such obvious follies are avoided, bases remain important. Some infections of the skin require an application which dries up the affected skin; others require the very opposite. Some skins are allergic to some bases but not to others. Some bases are suitable for application to open wounds, some must not be applied if the skin is damaged.

The 'shelf-life' of many skin applications is comparatively short. An out-dated application may be useless; worse, if the shelf-life of the chemicals used to prevent it from becoming contaminated is over, the ointment may actually be harbouring 'germs'. Even if there is an indication of shelf-life on the tube or jar (and you can understand it), the date it suggests may apply to its *unopened* shelf-life.

Many skin applications contain more than one drug or chemical. While one of these ingredients may be appropriate to the condition you are considering treating, the other(s) may be contra-indicated (*see below*, Applications for inflammations).

Some drugs are absorbed through the skin into the underlying tissues and thence into the circulation. An application which is safe for its prescribed use on a prescribed skin area, may amount to overdosage if it is applied to a larger skin area. So even where you are using the application prescribed by a doctor for this particular skin infection, it is important to check back with him before you extend that treatment. Ideally, any skin infection which is getting worse or more widespread, despite prescribed treatment, should be seen again by the doctor.

The following types of skin application may serve as examples both of the kinds of treatment available and of the treatment-errors which may easily be made at home.

Applications for bacterial infections   Certain bacterial infections of the skin itself can be almost-magically treated with antibiotic applications. Impetigo, for example, may clear almost overnight.

Where superficial wounds are becoming infected, antibiotic ointment or impregnated dressings may be effective in helping the body to clear up the infection and thus may promote healing. Doctors try not to prescribe for local application antibiotics which are also widely used internally, because such use on the skin increases the antibiotic-resistant population of bacteria and may act as a sensitizing dose of antibiotic to those who are allergic. For these reasons, antibiotics such as penicillin are usually avoided in favour of chlortetracycline, bacitracin and/or neomycin.

● Infections *under* the skin, even when pus is clearly going to break through, as in a boil, are unaffected by external applications of antibiotics. If an antibiotic is needed at all, it will be needed in the bloodstream (by mouth or by injection).

● Crops of pustules or patches of skin which are 'weepy' *may* be due to bacterial infection but they may not. Skin infections are difficult to diagnose so this is a task for a doctor. Self-treatment (with that antibiotic wound-cream, for example) could be totally inappropriate.

Infections of the eye and external ear may be bacterial and, if they are, drops containing an antibiotic such as aureomycin may be prescribed.

● Never put anything in an eye or ear without medical advice. The cost of 'getting it wrong' can be too high.

Vaginal infections are seldom bacterial (*see below*) and if they are, medical advice is certainly needed. Male genital infections must be diagnosed by a doctor. In a sexually active individual, genital symptoms may be due to a venereal disease (*see* **Adolescence**/Sex: Venereal disease) and medical treatment is urgent and essential not only for the individual's health but for everybody's.

Applications for fungal infections

Infections such as ringworm and thrush (some variety of which is the most common vaginal infection) can be very successfully treated with those antibiotics which are active against these particular micro-organisms (*see above*).

● Most antibiotics are active *either* against bacteria *or* against fungi but not both. Selecting the right drug therefore depends on the right diagnosis of the skin infection you can see.

Applications for inflammations

Many of the most annoying skin disorders are characterized by signs of inflammation such as redness, swelling, soreness or itching. Inflammation which is 'inappropriate' (such as nettlerash, nappy rash, contact dermatitis and so forth) can often be effectively relieved by skin applications containing one of the many corticosteroid drugs. But these, perhaps above all other skin applications, should be treated with the greatest care. It must always be remembered that steroid (and derivative) applications *suppress* inflammation and that inflammation is the skin's normal first reaction to injury or infection. If infection is causing the inflammation, such a cream will *suppress the reaction but not the cause*. Indeed, the body's ability to deal with that infective cause will be much reduced because the drug has disarmed it.

● Never, ever, use a corticosteroid application on a skin inflammation which even *might be* infective. If you are dealing with what you think is an infective skin disorder, be careful not to use a combined antibiotic/steroid cream (*see below*). If you put such a cream on a patch of impetigo, for example, wanting the antibiotic effect, you may provoke a widespread and serious septic rash because the anti-inflammatory effect of the steroid will be much greater than the bactericidal effect of the antibiotic, and the skin will be unable to prevent the infection spreading. Put such a combination on a cold sore (herpes simplex virus) and the antibiotic will, of course, be ineffective while the anti-inflammatory will allow the virus infection to lead to a nasty ulcer. Even athlete's foot may spread over a large area if treated in this way (*see* **Ringworm and Athlete's Foot**).

● Corticosteroid/antibiotic combinations can be extremely useful if they are used for skin conditions which are *primarily allergic* but where there is (or is likely to be) superimposed infection. They may be prescribed for eczema which a child has infected by scratching (*see* **Allergy**/Eczema), or for severe nappy rash which is liable to infection every time he passes a stool.

● Because these conditions are difficult to diagnose and because corticosteroids can do so much good when used appropriately and so much harm when used wrongly, it is best never to use them without a doctor's prescription (even if they are on open sale in your country), and *never* to use one which has been prescribed for another occasion or person.

● Even prescribed corticosteroid preparations on appropriate skin disorders can lead to secondary infection because they reduce the skin's natural inflammatory response and therefore provide an excellent hold for bacteria or fungi. If boils, thrush, etc. should develop, stop the treatment immediately and see your doctor.

Preventing infection

In the western world, public health authorities do more to protect families from serious and/or epidemic infections than those families can ever do for themselves. Clean water, efficient sewage disposal, hygienic production, handling and distribution of milk and other foodstuffs, the disinfection of public places, immunization programmes and the compulsory notification of particular diseases, all combine to let most of us take freedom from infection for granted, most of the time. It has not always been so and it is still not so in many parts of the world. Reasonable cooperation with such authorities is still probably the main contribution which each family can make both to its own and to every other family's health. However overburdened we may be by bureaucracy, health rules, regulations and exhortations are not appropriate ones at which to sneer or to encourage children to sneer. If they swim in that forbidden reservoir they may introduce infection which could affect thousands. If they cleverly avoid the disinfectant footbath at the swimming pool they are negating public efforts to keep down fungus diseases like athlete's foot. If they manage to skip school on the day those tuberculosis tests are due they defeat public efforts to ensure that the whole population is either naturally immune or immunized . . . If children can be brought up to understand the purpose of regulations of this kind and, perhaps through foreign travel and television documentaries, to see something of what life is like where basic public health measures are still not realized and crippling diseases are still endemic, they may reach adolescence with a sense of responsibility both for their own health and for other people's. The adolescent who spreads venereal disease through a wide circle of contacts does not *mean* to be a public menace. He simply does not realize that it can have happened to him. The girl who serves at the cooked meat counter and does not report the septic spot on her hand does not *mean* to poison her customers. She does not take hygiene instructions seriously.

Infection and home hygiene

There are bacteria everywhere and nothing that you can do will rid your home, or even your body, of them. But those bacteria are not a constant threat. Most of them are harmless anyway. A few are pathogenic but when they get into the body in small numbers the body's own defences deal with them without signs of clinical illness. It is only if a large number of virulent micro-organisms find a way into the body of a susceptible person, that infection will take place.

Numbers are critical. There are bacteria on the surface of that table, but there will not be many and they will not be there for long because, in the absence of food, they cannot multiply. If there are crumbs on the table, bacteria may be breeding. But they will not breed for long. Either the crumbs will be wiped away or that small food source will run out. Colonies of bacteria can only establish themselves and breed in rapid millions where they have a source of food – and other facilities such as warmth and moisture – and where they are left undisturbed.

If a colony of potentially pathogenic bacteria does establish itself in the home, it does theoretically present a threat to human health. But no infection will take place unless those bacteria get into a human body.

Home hygiene against infection is therefore twofold. It should aim to discourage the undisturbed growth of vast colonies of bacteria, some of which may be pathogenic. And it should aim to prevent colonies which may grow from being eaten, introduced into wounds and so forth.

Bacterial breeding grounds   Food for bacteria is living matter which is now dead. Much household 'dirt' is not, in this sense, 'dirty' at all. You may dislike the look of city dust on your windowsill but it probably will not breed many bacteria. Your child's room, littered with books, models, toys and spilled paint may look 'filthy' but its condition is not a threat to health. The kind of 'dirt' which will breed bacteria if it is left to do so is:

□ Faeces, human or animal.
□ Blood, scurf and hair, human or animal.
□ Dead rodents, insects, etc.
□ Food, human or animal.

Faeces are largely made up of bacteria and, as we have seen, while most are harmless to their host, a few which are harmless to one person can behave as pathogens in another. Standard hygienic measures, such as handwashing after using the lavatory, are therefore sensible. Even more important, perhaps, are measures to prevent animal faeces from contaminating food or hands which will then go to the mouth. Animal 'accidents' in the home require careful clearing up and disinfection of the area (*see below*). Animal toilet trays need regular cleaning and disinfection and crawling babies and small children should, as far as possible, play where the ground is not fouled by dogs and cats.

Blood is a good growth medium for many bacteria but it is seldom a contaminant in the home because we do tend to wipe it away wherever it is shed. Sanitary pads should never be allowed to accumulate, even in a closed container. If they cannot be flushed down the lavatory they should be burnt. If a wound dressing becomes blood-soaked, so that there is blood exposed to bacterial contamination from the air or from things the victim touches, it should be changed.

Scurf and other shed skin cells certainly provide a breeding ground for bacteria but quantities are so small that there is seldom a practical problem unless one family member has a skin infection (which might be passed on), or any kind of skin inflammation (which might render their own skin liable to bacterial infection). Ideally, of course, brushes, combs, facecloths and towels should be kept for individual family members as well as being frequently washed. In practice, a good deal of sharing goes on in many families without ill-effects. Animal scurf and shed hair may harbour bacteria to which human members of the family are less resistant. It is sensible to keep small children away from pets' bedding and to vacuum more than usually carefully during the moulting season.

Dead rodents, insects, etc. The mouse which your cat kills, re-discovers three days later and brings into the kitchen, will teem with bacteria. Flies and other insects are not only a threat to hygiene while they are buzzing around the kitchen, inoculating food with bacteria from outside, but also when they are dead and floating in the mayonnaise.

Food. Although most of the food you buy will contain bacteria or acquire bacteria as you prepare it, large colonies will have little chance to grow if you avoid giving them ideal circumstances. If you are unfortunate enough to buy food containing really virulent micro-organisms, kitchen hygiene will not help you. 'Food poisoning' is by no means always the cook's fault (*see* **Diarrhoea, Gastro-enteritis and Food Poisoning**).

Hygienic reminders

Cold discourages bacterial growth. A refrigerator will slow up growth; a freezer will halt it.

High temperatures kill most common bacteria. Cooking will render most food safe.

Gentle warmth – like that in the open kitchen – is ideal for many bacteria. Food standing in the open may have bacteria rapidly multiplying in it as well as being liable to acquire further bacteria from the air, from flies and so forth. Watch out for:

Frozen food which is inadequately defrosted before cooking. Heat inside a chicken or turkey, for example, may never reach bactericidal levels but only encouraging warmth.

Frozen food which is to be eaten cold. Defrosting and then reaching room temperature may provide ideal bacterial breeding conditions.

Cooked dishes or left-overs, whether frozen or not, which are to be eaten hot. If these are merely *warmed* (as is often done for babies) bacteria may find a superb breeding environment. Make sure such dishes are re-cooked or at least made boiling hot all the way through.

Milk, especially for babies (*see below*). For many bacteria, milk is a superb growth medium and milk at room temperature can produce vast colonies very rapidly. Don't leave opened milk bottles standing around the kitchen, babies' bottles waiting until they are wanted or children's milk drinks by their beds . . .

Cross contamination in cooking. Blood from raw meat or poultry, for example, can get onto your hands and/or working surfaces and from there onto foods which are then eaten raw. Try to deal with these foods separately and wash and clear up carefully in between.

Wounds and other skin lesions. If you have a septic wound on your finger you may contaminate foods in which bacteria can actively breed until they are eaten; a bowl of whipped cream, for example. Equally, if you have a clean but open wound on your finger, bacteria from that raw meat may contaminate it, unless you wash, frequently, as you cook.

Cook's wounds should be carefully covered. If you have a septic place, a boil or whatever, use a waterproof dressing and finger stall while you are preparing food.

Some of the implements we use in the kitchen are positively revolting if looked at through a microscope. Some of the worst are:

Wall tin openers which dip their points into the cat food and then the sardines and then the baby's dinner, but which are seldom washed.

Cloths used for drying up. They accumulate food particles suspended in warm water and often do not even dry out completely between uses. Dish-washer or air-drying is certainly more hygienic. So are paper or disposable cloths, provided they really are disposed of.

Washing-up brushes (and lavatory brushes). They all tend to trap and retain solid matter between the bristles.

Babies need some special hygiene

Babies are more likely than most people to be susceptible to bacterial infection because they have not been around long enough to develop wide-ranging immunity from constant low levels of exposure to various pathogens, and their bodies' own defence mechanisms are less efficient. Furthermore, if they are not breast-fed, they are fed instead with that ideal bacterial breeding substance, warm milk, and they spend considerable periods in intimate contact with their own faeces. Gastro-enteritis kills thousands of babies every year in less hygiene-conscious parts of the world, and it still makes many western babies ill, too. Various forms of infected nappy rash are as common as they are uncomfortable. Sensible precautions in the early months include:

Careful washing of bottles, teats and any equipment used to prepare feeds with detergent and water (to remove milk traces) **followed by sterilizing** either with a chemical, sold for the purpose, or by boiling.

Careful washing and sterilizing or boiling of nappies, one-way liners or any non-disposables.

Frequent changing of soiled nappies and washing of the baby's bottom with soap and water to remove all traces of faeces.

Extravagance with formula and/or solid foods so that milk which has been out of the refrigerator is never saved for another feed, and solid foods are never reheated more than once, if at all.

Care over washing hands before preparing babyfood or at least between visits to the lavatory/nappy changing and preparing babyfoods.

Washing of dummies which, while they provide no food for bacterial growth, may collect bacteria when dropped on the floor or in the park.

Small children need special hygiene too

Although older babies and toddlers are rapidly developing the ability to cope with the 'family germs', they expose themselves to bacterial infection more than most older people do because they naturally tend to explore things with their mouths and they are seldom held back from doing so by the revulsion which comes with age!

If anybody is going to explore the kitchen waste-bin it will be a young child. If anyone is going to smear faeces around and then suck their fingers it will be a young child. If anyone is going to suck that dishcloth or the lavatory brush it will be a young child. And, of course, if anybody is going to drop a piece of doughnut on the living-room floor and then discover and eat it two days later, it is going to be a young child . . .

You cannot stop babies and toddlers from sucking objects and their fingers, indeed it is a great mistake to try. With this age group in the house you have to make doubly sure that 'dirty dirt' is kept out of reach.

*Sterilants,
disinfectants
and antiseptics*

Germ-killing chemicals are the subject of massive advertising campaigns and much public confusion. There are many chemicals available and attempts to use exactly the right one for each and every purpose will lead to the spending of a great deal of unnecessary money, and probably eventually to the wrongful use of one or the other when an overstocked cupboard confuses you in a crisis. If you understand how these chemicals do and do not work, you can then choose one or two which will meet every ordinary household and first aid requirement. Whatever those advertisements may imply, neither 'good hygiene' nor being a 'good parent' depends on the use of miracle products.

Sterilization

Properly refers to the destruction or removal of *all* micro-organisms. Although we talk of 'chemical sterilants' (*see below*) the phrase is inaccurate. There will be some micro-organisms (especially the spores of some bacteria and fungi) which survive almost any chemical treatment. True sterilization can only reliably be carried out by physical rather than chemical means, and even then the method of sterilization has to be matched to the material to be sterilized. Heat, as in boiling or autoclaving, for example, is used to sterilize canned foods and surgical instruments. Filtration, in which air or liquid is forced through mesh fine enough to trap the relevant micro-organisms, is used to sterilize the air in operating rooms or liquids for injection. Various forms of radiation and toxic gases are used to sterilize materials, such as plastics, which are not heat-proof.

In the home, there are very few occasions when sterilization, as opposed to disinfection, is needed.

Home 'surgery'. Needles for removing splinters, etc. can be sterilized by heating the tip in a match-flame until it is red-hot. Tweezers, scissors, etc. can be sterilized after use around a septic wound by boiling for ten minutes in a covered pot.

Home emergencies. If you need a near-sterile pad or bandage in a hurry, choose something which has been ironed with a hot iron. The inner folds of a sheet or handkerchief, for example, will be very nearly sterile unless, of course, they were drip-dried.

Skin infections. As we shall see, normal disinfection of babies' nappies and so forth does not always kill all 'germs'. If a baby or child has a skin infection and you want to sterilize everything and, so to speak, start again, nappies, sheets, towels, facecloths, etc. can all be boiled. If you are relying on the 'boiling programme' of a washing machine, make sure that it does take the water to full boiling point and keep it there for at least ten minutes. If it does not, old-fashioned boiling on your cooker (perhaps in a preserving pan) will be more effective.

*Disinfectants
and antiseptics*

These are chemicals which, used in an adequate concentration and for a sufficient time, destroy most micro-organisms: bacteria, viruses, fungi, yeasts and at least some resistant spores. The term 'disinfectant' is used when a chemical is applied to inanimate objects – working surfaces, drains, nappies – the term 'antiseptic' is used when the chemical is applied to living skin or mucous membranes. Sometimes disinfectants and antiseptics are different concentrations or formulations of the same chemical, but do not use them interchangeably unless you are very sure of your own chemical/medical knowledge. A disinfectant used on the skin could be exceedingly dangerous. An antiseptic used down the lavatory would probably be ineffective.

Disinfectant action

For a disinfectant to kill 'germs', a particular concentration of the chemical must both reach the micro-organisms and stay in contact with them for a particular length of time.

If you pour disinfectant down the drains it will immediately be diluted by the standing water in the pipes and any which remains on the sides of those pipes will be washed away the moment anybody turns on a tap or flushes the lavatory.

If you wipe the lavatory bowl or your kitchen working surfaces with disinfectant, you may indeed use the right dilution and leave it there for the right length of time, but 'germs' will only be killed by most disinfectants if you have first removed all solid matter, and any grease, by thoroughly washing it with detergent and water. Applied without prior washing, the disinfectant chemicals cannot reach the cells of the micro-organisms. If thorough washing was carried out there will be very few micro-organisms left for them to kill. Ordinary cleanliness must precede disinfection and, in most cases, ordinary cleanliness is quite enough.

Snags to disinfectant use

Most efficient disinfectants (chlorine-releasing hypochlorites, for example, such as Domestos or Milton) are dangerous to people as well as to 'germs'. Those named here, for example, are powerful acids. If a child swallows them or gets them in her eyes, they will do serious damage. The chlorine gas they release is also dangerous if it comes into contact with other chemicals, so absentmindedly using such a disinfectant along with another lavatory product (a 'deodorizer', for example) can cause poisonous fumes or even an explosion. Even used carefully, such products are not without snags. They are powerful bleaches, for example, and while they may make your bath look beautifully white they will also ruin your carpet or your clothes.

Choosing and using a disinfectant

If you have a baby in the house, a hypochlorite disinfectant intended for babies' bottles (and therefore sold in a much safer and more diluted form) can safely be used to soak and store those bottles. When you change the bottle-solution, the used solution can then be used to disinfect and mildly bleach nappies and so forth. You can use the same dilution of the same product occasionally to disinfect toys or dummies if they have fallen on dog-fouled ground, or to disinfect pots or the lavatory if someone has been having diarrhoea. If you want to disinfect everything you can think of, perhaps including cutlery, china and bedding, because of illness in the house, the same product will do the job safely and efficiently. You will not kill 'all known germs' at this sort of concentration, but you will not kill anything else either.

While you are nursing an illness, it is sensible to disinfect thermometers between uses. Your thermometer can stand in Milton solution which should be changed daily.

If you have no very small children in the house you will have no prior need for Milton. You may, of course, want to use a full-strength domestic hypochlorite solution because you want its bleaching action on your laundry or your bath. But if you want a safe general disinfectant which, diluted according to the instructions, can be used for anything from disinfecting the carpet when the dog has been sick to disinfecting vomit bowls or thermometers, you may do better with a preparation containing cetrimide. These products include widely known brand names such as Savlon and Cetavlon. Although they are not as lethal to as wide a range of 'germs' as are the hypochlorite preparations, they are quite lethal enough to common household ones and infinitely safer and easier to use. They have the great advantage of being intrinsically detergent as well as disinfectant, so you can wash things with them instead of washing first and then disinfecting. These chemicals are inactivated by many soaps, so if you are trying to disinfect your hands before or after dealing with a wound, for example, use your chosen product to *wash* with or make sure you rinse off your toilet soap first.

Antiseptic action
Antiseptics are also widely misused. People use antiseptic mouthwashes and gargles 'for sore throats', never stopping to think that the sore throat is probably caused by viruses and that since viruses are inside their own cells, no antiseptic can kill the viruses without destroying the cells, too. Antiseptics are also applied to wounds which, if they are clean, require none, and which, if they are infected, probably require medical attention. Antiseptics are further used, in an even vaguer fashion, for 'personal hygiene' ranging from washing armpits with 'antiseptic' soaps to douching vaginas. Skin does not require artifical help in holding a balance between normal and pathogenic bacteria. If it is healthy and intact, such 'aids' may actually interfere with the balance. If it is not healthy and intact, it probably requires a specific chemical prescribed by a doctor.

Choosing and using an antiseptic
If the skin, damaged or undamaged, does require an antiseptic then it certainly needs to be cleaned in the ordinary sense of having dirt and grease removed. Ordinary washing with soap and water is far more effective than an antiseptic cream if either is to be used alone. If ordinary washing does not satisfy your need to 'do something', wash with a suitable dilution of detergent/antiseptic: the same cetrimide product suggested for general disinfection (Savlon or Cetavlon liquid), is satisfactory for this and has the advantage of giving you only one product for use in all circumstances where you want to disinfect either something or someone.

The same types of antiseptic are often applied, in cream or ointment form, to wounds where people want the antiseptic action to persist for longer than a diluted liquid will remain active on the skin. Remember, though, that the cream-vehicle may in itself delay wound healing by keeping the skin from the hardening effect of air. Furthermore, if an antiseptic-cream-and-dressing combination is left on a wound for too long, that cream, combined with exudate from the wound, may provide an actual growth-medium for the bacteria you are trying to kill or keep out.

Preventing the spread of 'infectious' illnesses
(*see also* individual conditions)

Although that phrase 'infectious illness' makes most people think of the common infectious diseases of childhood, like measles or mumps, any infection can, of course, be spread from one person to another. Some infections (like those childhood ones) will always produce similar symptoms in susceptible individuals (although their severity and any complications will vary) but others will, as we have seen, produce different symptoms depending on the nature of the 'germs' being passed on, the route they take into the next person's body, and the 'reception' they get there. Even while you think about preventing the spread of chickenpox or the common cold around your family, remember that your baby's septic nappy rash *could* infect the cut on your finger and a trace of the resulting pus in her food *could* give her an intestinal infection.

Many illnesses are infectious to other susceptible people even before the first victim has any symptoms. There is an 'incubation period' during which viruses are multiplying in her body. Their concentration is not yet great enough for her to show clinical symptoms of the disease, yet she is excreting or spraying out quite enough to infect somebody else.

Old-fashioned quarantine regulations were intended to control the spread of infection by isolating not only those who were sick but also any close contacts who might therefore be incubating the illness. As soon as one child in a family developed chickenpox, all other children in the family were sent home, too. There they were to stay until either they had suffered and recovered from the disease or the incubation period had passed and it was clear that the infection had missed them. At some times and in some communities, quarantine was taken so seriously that schools and other institutions were closed down and families lived in self-imposed purdah. Yet, little by little, it became clear that even extreme quarantine measures do little to limit the spread of most infections. In chickenpox, for example, the child is highly infectious for several days before symptoms appear. During that period she may pass the disease to her brothers, sisters and friends, and any of those children who acquire the infection will do the same. By the time that first child has diagnosable chickenpox, her contacts are only a few among many people, networked through the community, who may be incubating the disease.

Quarantine regulations for most diseases have been relaxed in most communities as knowledge of the natural history of various infections, together with immunizations against them and treatments for them, have been developed. Every family needs to know the regulations for its own schools and so forth but, on the whole, while quarantine of the sick is still normal practice, and usually commonsense, quarantine of healthy contacts is reserved for exceptionally dangerous diseases and especially vulnerable communities. If your child suffers from measles, for example, other members of her family will be allowed to pursue their ordinary lives until or unless they become sick. If she has diphtheria, on the other hand, quarantine may well be required for the whole family. If a child in a residential nursery suffers from measles she will certainly be nursed in isolation from the other children, and her close contacts, including staff, may also be separated from children who scarcely knew her.

For some diseases 'surveillance' has replaced the quarantine of healthy contacts. The family and friends of a patient are allowed to lead their normal lives during the incubation period of the disease, but they are regularly checked by a doctor so that they can be isolated and treated at the very first signs of disease.

Schools and other institutions themselves play a part in the control of a few diseases and infestations which are mild yet quick to spread in a closed community. If your child has ringworm, for example, her close contacts may be inspected and treated by the school doctor. If one child in a class is found to be infested with head lice, every child in the school may be inspected and either treated or sent home with instructions for treatment which must be carried out before they will be re-admitted.

Public health measures control the spread of most common infections within the community; your own hygienic precautions minimize the hold which pathogens are likely to achieve within the house (*see above*). It is your children's own bodily defences which will play the largest remaining part in keeping them healthy. As they grow up they will meet most of the 'germs' which are common within the family/community and they will develop immunity to them. Even if you feel that your adolescent children suffer from all-too-many colds and other minor infections, you can be sure that their bodies encounter hundreds more which they are able to resist or 'shake-off' with only the mildest and most transient symptoms.

Infection is most likely when a susceptible individual meets a 'new germ'. That 'new germ' may be fresh to the whole community (as when a new strain of 'flu sweeps through a population); new to your family (as when a holiday abroad is ruined by a 'tummy bug' which causes local residents no problems); or it may simply be new to the individual, either because she has chanced to miss out on previous contacts or because she herself is newly born.

A new baby has met no 'germs', so every pathogen with which she has contact is a potential threat. For a few months she will have passive immunity to virus infections passed to her across the placenta from her mother's bloodstream but, as we have seen, passive immunity is short-lived (*see* **Immune Response**). Against bacterial infections she does not even have that passive immunity: antibodies to bacteria are too large to pass the placental barrier. During her early months and years, that baby must meet and overcome all the infections which are common in her environment, building her own internal protection against them as she goes. Against a few specific infections we can immunize her (*see* **Immunization**) but against the many, many others, she must immunize herself.

In many families minor illnesses are most frequent amongst two- to seven-year-olds. Passive immunity has waned and the child is exposed to 'germs' brought into the home by older family members and by visiting children. When she first attends a playgroup or nursery school, whole classes will pass infections back and forth amongst themselves. There may seldom be a day when every pupil is present. Once she is old enough for real school she will have built some immunity to some 'germs', but her big new world will expose her to more which are new to her.

An apparently endless series of infections can be almost as hard on parents as on the child herself; it may comfort you a little to realize that she will 'grow out of it' because her body will gradually learn to cope, shrugging off some invaders altogether and limiting the growth and spread of others. As the frequency of her illnesses begins to drop, so will the severity of most of them. A baby is often ill with an ordinary cold: a child is rarely more than uncomfortable (*see* **Colds**).

It is arguable that there is so little you can do to limit the spread of minor infections within the family that it is not worthwhile to try. But while it is true that a child who has a cold today may well have passed it to his sister yesterday, it is also true that he is more infectious today, with this streaming nose and cough, than he was while he was merely incubating the viruses. Some degree of exposure is probably inevitable for every family member every time one is unwell, but that need not mean that it is always sensible to allow everyone to be exposed to the limit.

Whatever infection you are considering, that question of degree of exposure will apply. The child with a cold sprays virus-laden particles around every time she coughs or sneezes. Another child is most likely to breathe them in if the two faces happen to be close together when that sneeze happens. The child with an intestinal infection excretes viruses in her liquid stools; another child is most likely to acquire the 'germs' if traces of those faeces get from the patient's or your hands onto the family's food. Taking trouble not to pass on infection in the most obvious ways *may not* protect anyone, but it reduces the likelihood of spread.

If your child has some underlying condition, such as severe asthma (*see* **Allergy**), which makes everyday infections pose a real threat to his health, he will be under a doctor's care and you will be given detailed guidance. Basically healthy children neither require nor benefit from being wrapped in cotton wool, but even for them there are times when one more infection can be one too many.

Protecting very young babies from infection

A simple head cold can make a young baby quite ill and, by blocking his nose, make feeding sufficiently awkward to slow up his weight gain. A superficial bacterial skin infection in an older child (impetigo, for example) may take the form of a serious bloodstream infection in a small baby. Whooping cough, fortunately less common than it was, thanks to immunization, can still kill if it strikes a baby before his own course of injections has protected him.

Protecting such a young child from infection is not as difficult as protecting older ones; you can keep him semi-isolated without him noticing, while anti-infective hygiene measures are simply an unusually careful version of normal babycare.

Keep infectious visitors away: out of the house if possible, out of the baby's room anyway.

Don't let your own children cuddle him while they are obviously infectious.

Don't take him to crowded places in winter unless it is unavoidable.

If you must nurse an older child while caring for a baby, try to put the baby's pram in a next door room and divide your time and attention between the two rather than having them in the same room together.

Whatever the particular infection which is in the family, washing your hands carefully before you handle the baby or his food or drink will probably help.

If it is you who is ill, the baby was almost certainly thoroughly exposed to your 'germs' before you had any symptoms, so if he is going to 'catch' them he will already have done so. Handing him over to someone else, and isolating yourself, will almost certainly do more harm than it can do good. It is worth taking extra care not to let him suck your streaming nose, though. Some people recommend masks as a way of cutting down a baby's exposure to parental 'germs', but inexpertly used, such a mask can do more harm than good. It will not trap all viruses. Those which it has accumulated will be positively showered on the baby if he grabs at the mask as you bend over him, or if you rip it off impatiently to answer the telephone with him on your hip.

Protecting ill children and convalescents from infection

As we have seen, a secondary infection with bacteria sometimes follows viral infection and the result is usually more severe than the first illness. If a child has an upper respiratory infection which the doctor is treating as viral, don't assume that the next family member to become ill is 'bound to have the same'. Nursing two together may be easier for you and more cheerful for them but, unless you are sure that they both have one, clearly identified illness, it may be a mistake. For the same reason it is sensible not to hurry a child who has been ill back into his normal activities, especially if these involve school or playgroup where there will be various 'germs' around. Such a child often appears to recover, goes back to school and becomes ill again within a couple of days. It is not that his original illness has recurred but that it has made him especially liable to a new one.

Remember the possible side-effects of any treatment the child may have had for the first illness. If he has had a course of antibiotics for that upper respiratory infection, for example, his normal gut flora will be disturbed and he may be especially liable to intestinal infections for a while.

Sometimes a child who acquires one infection after another so that he never seems to be completely well can have a vicious circle of infection and re-infection broken if you can arrange for him to have a couple of weeks to get right back to normal. In the past such children were sometimes sent away to 'convalescent homes' but we now know that stress increases the liability to infection and that institutions tend to be hotbeds for 'germs'. Having a holiday at home, with plenty of outdoor activity and as little time as possible in crowded places, can give the child a chance to cope with all remaining infection before he has to face any more. While it may be difficult for you to arrange to stay at home for such an extended period, it may save you many days off work in the end.

Infectious diseases *see* individual conditions. *See also* **Immunization**; **Infection**/Preventing the spread of 'infectious' illnesses; **Nursing**.

Inflammation *see* **Infection**/Defences against infection: The second line of defence; Treatment of external infection and inflammation. *See also* individual conditions *and also* **Accidents**.

Influenza ('flu)

For many people 'flu is a catch-all term used to describe any otherwise indefinable illness with fever, usually headache, often head-cold symptoms and sometimes exhaustion or depression. Often an individual who is ill but in whom no specific symptoms leading to a different diagnosis emerge, is assumed to be suffering from 'flu.

Often he will be infected with a 'flu virus, even if the illness he is describing is quite different from the 'flu from which his neighbour is suffering. 'Flu viruses are specific infectious agents, but not only are there many strains in the community at any one time, there are also new strains cropping up in various parts of the world. It is the tendency of influenza viruses to develop and change which has so far foiled man's attempts at controlling them. Vaccines produce antibodies but they produce them only to those known strains which could be included in the injection. The next local, national or worldwide 'flu epidemic is often of a strain against which those antibodies provide no protection. Given that protection against the known strains only lasts for around one year, so that annual re-immunization is necessary, it is not surprising that, at present, immunization is reserved for those individuals or groups who are especially at risk and/or whose illness during a 'flu epidemic would cause particular disruption. People with heart defects or chronic lung conditions may be offered immunization; doctors, nurses and ambulance drivers may be given it, either routinely or when an epidemic threatens.

In 1968 the variant known as Hong-Kong 'flu spread rapidly across the world. In Britain, for example, during 1968–9 about one quarter of the entire population was affected with about 13,000 'extra' deaths attributable to the infection or its side-effects. Yet even this did not produce enough immunity in the population to prevent a further explosive outburst of the same strain in 1969–70.

Having 'flu   **Incubation period.** About two days.

Mode of infection. Droplet infection from nose and throat to nose and throat.

First symptoms of 'flu   Almost always some sore throat/nasal congestion, as the infection takes place locally. These 'cold' symptoms may, however, seem minor, as they often occur simultaneously with a rapid rise in temperature and severe headache. There may also be backache, restless aching limbs and attacks of shivering.

Acute phase of 'flu   'Flu usually develops very quickly so that the first day's symptoms are the most severe. In most patients the whole infection is brief, being over in three to four days. Cough is often a troublesome remaining symptom.

Convalescence from 'flu   While most children and healthy young people will recover rapidly and be ready to return to their normal activities two to three days after the fever has gone, prolonged lassitude and/or depression is not uncommon, especially in the elderly.

*Complications
of 'flu*

'Flu is an infection of, or via, the upper respiratory tract. Its common complications are those which arise either when the 'flu virus damages the lower respiratory tract (virus pneumonia, for example) or when bacterial secondary infection takes place (staphylococcal pneumonia, for example). Other common complications include sinus or middle-ear infections. Certain strains of 'flu can occasionally lead to central nervous system symptoms, such as meningitis (*see* **Meningitis and Encephalitis**).

● If a child has a 'feverish cold' or 'some kind of 'fluey bug' it really is not important to know whether she actually has influenza or not; whatever infection she is suffering from, symptomatic nursing (*see* **Nursing**) is all that she requires until or unless more specific symptoms develop. On the other hand, if a child seems really ill, the fact that it is 'probably only the 'flu' should not prevent you from calling a doctor. Even though he can do nothing to cure 'flu, he can make sure that nothing more sinister is involved and that there are no signs of complications.

● If there appears to be a 'flu epidemic in your community or within a school or other institution, and you have a child for whom infection might be especially unfortunate, do consult your doctor about the possibility of immunization.

Ingrown toenails *see* **Feet.**
Injections *see* **Hospital**/Procedures. *See also* **Immunization**.
Insect stings *see* **Accidents**/Bites and stings.
Intelligence *see* **Language; Learning Difficulties and Disabilities**. *See also* **Play; School/** Children with special needs.

Intussusception

This is an acute abdominal emergency in young babies caused by the telescoping of a portion of the intestine into the portion ahead of it. *See* **Hospital**/Surgery.

Jaundice

Describes a state in which the individual's skin, the whites of her eyes and other less visible body tissues are stained a yellow colour.

The yellow staining comes from a substance called bilirubin which is formed when red cells which have reached the end of their lifespan are broken down in the liver. The normal lifespan of red cells in the blood is about three months. A normal liver, working at full capacity, dissolves them when they are finished with, liberates the haemoglobin they contain, converts it into bile and passes the bile (which contains other substances also) into the intestine for excretion. If the liver is not working normally this process does not work smoothly. Broken down and partly broken down red cells accumulate and there is a build up of the resulting bilirubin which, instead of being excreted, gets back into the circulation and produces the typical yellow skin and eyes.

Jaundice, therefore, always suggests malfunction in the liver but the reasons for, and the seriousness of, the malfunction are various. The most common are:

'Physiological' jaundice of the newborn

Which may affect any baby whose liver is working at less than full capacity; it is commonest in babies born prematurely. It is termed 'physiological' because this type of jaundice reflects the temporary inability of the newborn baby's liver efficiently to cope with a task formerly supported by the mother's circulation. It does not suggest liver disease or abnormality and it usually clears within a few days, with or without treatment.

Jaundice due to excessive breakdown of red cells

Such as may occur when red cells which have not completed their normal lifespan are being 'attacked' by antibodies in, for example, rhesus incompatibility, or following the transfusion of ill-matched blood (*see* **Blood Groups**).

Jaundice due to obstruction of the bile-flow

Such as may occur if there are deformities of the bile-ducts or if there are gallstones. This last kind of obstruction, a common cause of jaundice in adults, is increasingly common amongst adolescents.

Jaundice due to infection

A variety of viruses can cause liver infection in babies, children, adolescents and adults. Two common types are:

Infectious (or epidemic) hepatitis which is usually spread from person to person by faecal contamination of food or drink. Mothers with this type of hepatitis used to be separated from their babies and small children. Now we realize that, although the illness is both infectious and potentially serious, this added misery is pointless. The incubation period is between fourteen and forty days so that anyone who is going to have the disease will have had countless opportunities to infect others long before she is ill herself and therefore able to appreciate the risk to her children.

Serum hepatitis which is usually spread by the use of contaminated needles or syringes and has an incubation period which is normally about three months but can be as long as twenty months. Tragically common amongst people who are addicted to injectable drugs, this type is also a risk to the many other people who give or receive many injections, from the staff in kidney dialysis units to the diabetic children who must inject themselves with insulin.

There is no cross-immunity between these two types of hepatitis: in theory one wretched individual could have first one and then the other. Both, however, follow a similar illness pattern.

The first symptom is often loss of appetite which, during two or three days, is coupled with general feelings of lethargy, nausea and, sometimes, abdominal pain.

Eventually the urine becomes conspicuously dark – the colour of tea without milk rather than the usual lemonade-range of colours, and the **stools** become putty-coloured.

On about days five to seven, yellow jaundice may appear. If it does, the diagnosis is easily confirmed but in some instances the child or adolescent has infectious or serum hepatitis without ever 'turning yellow'. Under these circumstances the diagnosis can be difficult.

Once he is jaundiced, he may feel better although he looks worse. He is likely to remain visibly yellow for two to four weeks but may be well enough to start convalescing before his colour is normal.

Hepatitis is always unpleasant, can be serious, requires medical attention, bed-rest in the acute phase and perhaps weeks of convalescence. Your doctor will do everything he can to minimize the possibility of any permanent damage to the liver. Bed-rest may be imposed on the victim even if he feels well enough to be up. Various types of diet may be recommended to minimize the liver's work. Alcohol is likely to be banned for quite a long period.

● Always seek medical advice if your child, whatever his age, looks yellow, whether or not you knew that he was ill.

● If hepatitis is diagnosed, be prepared for a long illness and for a very miserable, and possibly depressed, child or young person. It is usually better for an adolescent if he or she can accept, from the beginning, that this illness will put paid to imminent examinations or to social/vacation plans in the immediate couple of months. Struggling to get going again before the liver has returned to normal is not advisable.

Jealousy

Jealousy is a painful emotion and one which, instead of stimulating healthy action, as can anger, for example, tends to paralyse the victim and feed upon itself. Within many families there will be phases when somebody suffers from the green-eyed monster, but more can be done to keep him at bay than many people realize.

Jealousy and envy

Although these two words are often used interchangeably, they are not at all the same thing. Envy is a comparatively outward-looking and simple matter of wishing that one had for oneself something which somebody else has. A child may envy his friend's bicycle; an adolescent may envy her friend's figure, yet neither child need feel jealous on that account.

Jealousy is not about wanting what someone else has but about being anxious about what one lacks. If that child *is* jealous of the friend with the bicycle it will not just be because he wants a bicycle like that for himself, but because he feels that it is a love-cycle, a symbol of some love and security which the other boy enjoys and he does not. If that girl *is* jealous of the friend with the enviable figure it will be because her physical shape represents, for the monster's victim, a kind of adolescent happiness and self-acceptance which she cannot feel for herself.

Jealousy, then, is about not loving and being loved enough and, therefore, about feeling insecure and anxious about oneself in relation to the people who are important to one. Every human being has cause for envy from time to time. Life is not 'fair'. But to be able to envy someone without acute pain is healthy and realistic. It is only when the envy of superficial events or objects or achievements becomes muddled up with deep-seated anxieties that there is cause for concern.

The roots of anxiety lie in infancy; in a baby's need for absolutely dependable protection and loving care (*see* **Anxiety, Fears and Phobias**/ The roots of anxiety). The more securely loved, loving and lovable a baby and young child can feel himself, the less liable to jealousy, then or later, he will be. If you can rear a child who has a basic faith in your unshakeable love and who, because of it, can approve of and accept himself, you will have reared one who can say 'isn't he lucky?' without meaning 'aren't I a poor unworthy worm?' If you cannot, no amount of 'treating all the children exactly alike' or 'trying to give him everything he wants' will prevent him from feeling jealous because there are not enough possessions and treats in the whole world to cover the pain of basic anxiety.

Jealousy of a new baby

Many families have a second or later child when the older one is somewhere between one and three years old. At this age – especially in the second year – even the most securely loved and accepted toddler is liable to be going through an insecure patch because he is having to assert his independence of you in outward ways, while still feeling totally dependent inside. It will take him a while to discover that you do not only love and care for dependent babies who do as they are told, but also tough little children who do as they wish. When (and if) he has discovered this, he will be able to stop being so bolshy (because once he feels that there are no limits to love there is no longer any compulsion to try and discover them) and he will also be able to see himself, reflected in you, as a good and lovable person. He will not be totally insulated against jealousy; no human being's security can ever be total, but he will be very well protected.

If a new baby arrives before this vital point in an older child's personal growth he is almost certain to be made deeply anxious. An important first step in handling the situation appropriately is simply realizing that this is so. Many parents, loving their first child and looking forward to the second, find the idea of the older child being jealous almost unbearable. They are pleased and they want him to be pleased, too. Unfortunately, wishing will not make it so and to try to pretend to yourselves that the toddler looks forward to, and will love, the coming baby is often a bad mistake. Looking at it from his point of view you are asking him to put up with being supplanted as your baby; your only child; the third member of a three-person unit, and he is going to mind. However hard you try to make him feel good about it in advance (always supposing that he has any idea of your real meaning), the whole thing is going to make him feel hurt. The point is that he loves you and needs to be sure that you love him. When we love people, we want to be 'enough' for them. The new baby is a usurper of love. Put the kinds of phrase you might use to break this news to a toddler alongside your husband's attempts to get you to welcome a second wife; you can see that both are doomed to failure!

Parent to toddler	Husband to wife
'We're going to have a new baby, darling, because we thought it would be so nice for you to have a little brother or sister to play with.'	'I'm going to marry a second wife, darling, because I thought it would be so nice for you to have some company and help with the work.'
'We love you so much we just can't wait to have another gorgeous baby.'	'I love you so much I just can't wait to have another gorgeous wife.'
'It'll be *our* baby; it will be part of our family; belong to all the three of us and we'll all look after it together.'	'She'll be *our* wife; she will be part of our family; belong to both of us and we'll both look after her together.'
'Of course we shan't love you any less. There's plenty of loving for everybody and we'll all love each other.'	'Of course I shan't love you any less; there's plenty of loving for everybody and we'll all love each other.'
'I shall really need my big boy/girl now, to help me look after the tiny new baby.'	'I shall really need my reliable old wife now, to help me look after this young new one.'

Don't you think that you might be just as liable to hit first your husband and then that dear little wife over their heads with a frying pan, as your toddler is to hit first you and then that baby with the nearest brick?

Minimizing jealousy of the new baby

If you can accept that this is a truly difficult situation for him you will not fall into the trap of trying to make him share your pleasurable anticipation. The new baby is something you want and are entitled to. But it is not something your toddler wants but simply a life-development he will have to put up with. Instead, hold back for a while on telling him and concentrate on making him as secure with you, and content with himself, as you possibly can. How you do this obviously depends on his age, stage and circumstances but it might include:

Resolving current conflicts quickly one way or another. If you are in the middle of a toilet training or eating battle (*see* **Toilet Training** *and* **Eating/** Eating problems) solve them if you can do so within the next month or so, but if you know that you cannot, drop them so that the child does not feel in any way disapproved of or attacked when he comes to know of your pregnancy.

Giving him as much of you as he seems able to use. He may, of course, have this already, but if he is going *reluctantly* to a day-minder (*see* **Working Mothers**) while you do a job which you are going to have to give up in late pregnancy, it will be far better for him if you can give it up much sooner. If you work for as long as you can, stopping at home only for a couple of weeks before the birth, that toddler is going to feel that you did not love him enough to stay home with him but that you do love the new person enough to do so. All those reassuring things you have said to him in the past, about Mummies and Daddies having to work for money and so forth, will then seem to him like lies: you left him because you did not care; you stay with the baby because you do care.

Within the limits of his age-stage, finding him some other people who are important to, and fun for, him. Once the baby comes and you *are* tired, abstracted and busy, it will be far easier for him to sail through his days if he does not always even want your attention. If he is very young you may only be able to engineer Saturday outings with his father or visits to another relative's house or occasional play sessions with another toddler who lives nearby. If he is old enough, or nearly old enough, for playgroup, the leader might allow you to start settling him in immediately so that by the time the baby comes, 'my group' is a grand and important aspect of his life. Don't, whatever you do, plan to start him at such a group or at a nursery school just before or just after the baby's birth. He will certainly see it as being 'sent out of the way' and this will both increase his jealousy and possibly make it difficult for him to settle in (*see* **School/ Pre-school and nursery education**).

Trying to get him used to the idea that families have more than one child. Point out the brothers and sisters of his friends and try to find a toddler whom he knows who has a baby in the house. If he can come to accept the *idea*, the *actuality* will not be so likely to seem to him like a particular tragedy or punishment for which he alone has been singled out. It is in this general context that you can best introduce the positive aspects of having a brother or sister. 'Somebody always there to play with', for example, is indeed an appealing notion, but if you link it directly to your own coming baby you are being unfair and misleading because that baby will not be a playmate for a long time.

Start early to get him used both to the arrangements you plan for him at the time of the birth and practical changes afterwards. If he will stay with his aunt while you are in the hospital, let him pay a few visits during these next months and make sure that they are treats. If his father will take charge of him make sure that he gets some practice, not just at the things he always does but at any aspects of the toddler's routine with which he is not familiar. Minute details – such as the exact degree of the bacon's crispness – will seem overwhelmingly important to the toddler once he is stressed by your absence. If Daddy is not normally there for breakfast he may simply not know how to cook it 'so it's *nice*'.

Changes after the birth may include a change of room or promotion from a cot to a real bed. If you introduce these early enough you can probably make them seem like privileges. If you introduce them just before or after the birth they will probably seem like deprivation.

If you can trust other people not to let the news out, wait to tell the toddler until you are about six months pregnant. There are a lot of different reasons for delaying this long:

By six months a miscarriage is unlikely. The miscarriage of a baby he knew about is an extremely difficult and painful thing to try and explain to a toddler, and if he does have to know he will make it far more difficult for you to get through the days because he will keep asking about the baby.

Once he knows that a baby is coming at all it is easier for him if he can see some evidence that she is real. By six months he will be able to see the bump she makes (although he will not notice your change in shape until it is pointed out to him), and he will be able to feel her moving around and see the sharp little bumps her feet or elbows make as she kicks. Given that physical reality, you can begin to help him to think of her realistically, not as a playmate but as someone who will be helpless and wet both ends. Aim to inculcate an attitude of tolerant and amused superiority in the toddler, by telling him ruefully about the things that babies do (like sicking-up on people's shoulders) and by thinking up some funny stories about the things he did when he was a tiny baby, like the time he peed on Granny's dress or bit the doctor . . .

With only two or three months to go and all this talk going on, the toddler may be able to remember about the coming baby so that, by the time she is born, he really is expecting her. If a toddler is 'told the news' when mother first has the pregnancy confirmed, and life then goes on just as usual for nearly a quarter of his life so far before anything happens, he has usually forgotten all about it.

About two weeks before the expected date, tell him your plans for the actual birth but be very careful not to make any promises you might not be able to keep. If you hope, for example, for a twenty-four-hour stay in hospital, tell him that 'Daddy [or whoever it is] will be here with you and I shall be back with the baby very soon . . .' If you stress that you will only be away for 'one bedtime, one breakfast, etc.' and then either your condition or the baby's keeps you away for several days, he will be angry/sad and that will not help him to tolerate the baby when the two of you do get home.

When you go into the hospital, say goodbye whatever the time. It is better for him to face the parting he has to face, than to wake up one morning and find you gone and the household in drama.

When you come home with the baby, remember that it is you, not the baby, he wants to see. Of course he has to accept the baby's existence and presence and all the care which you give her, but he does not have to accept it all at once. In the first couple of days, give him as much time as you can and discourage whoever is helping you from cries of 'let's leave Mummy in peace now'. It will not hurt the new baby if, just for these first days, you pay her your most wholehearted and soppy attention during her evening and nightwaking times (*see* **Play**). It may be tactful to avoid breast-feeding in front of the toddler, too, by briefing your helper to lure him subtly away to do something fascinating. When you do feed in front of him, explain that this is how new babies feed; that this is how he fed when he was tiny. If he asks to try your milk try not to look shocked; you can always let him taste off your finger so as to be sure that the baby is not getting something better than the best of milkshakes.

Later on, accept any offers of help but don't ask him to be your 'big boy'. He may not be feeling at all big; or rather he may be feeling that his bigness is his whole problem; if he were tiny he would get as much cuddling and loving as that beastly baby. Don't make him feel that he has to help you, now, to get your approval, or that the more he appears to 'love' the baby the more you will love him. The opposite approach works better.

Offer him chances to be extra-babyish for a while. You might let him sit in the baby bath and have a sprinkle of talcum powder afterwards; you can cuddle him, pat his back and sing him a song. It may sound absurd but it is not. You want him to feel that the new baby is *not getting anything he cannot have* but only *things he has grown out of*. The sooner he can assure himself that the big bath is better or that he prefers his juice from a cup to milk out of that stupid bottle, the better.

Try to find some practical advantages to suddenly being 'eldest' to balance the inevitable disadvantages. This may be the moment for Saturday money or a later bedtime. It is certainly the moment for some special expeditions with Dad (and without the baby).

His father can make all the difference to this period if he will take a full part in caring for and companioning both children. If he will do exciting things with the toddler while you cope with the baby, or cope himself while you do things with the toddler, the pull between infant- and toddler-needs will be much less painful. Many fathers find that they cement their relationship with the older child now. He is under stress; needs his father and turns to him because he is somewhat hurt with his mother. Getting a warm response, he comes eventually to see a balance in *two* parents and *two* children.

Acknowledge jealous *feelings* while guarding against jealous *acts*. Don't ask the toddler to love the baby or ever let him feel that if you knew his real feelings you would hate him. Instead, acknowledge that she is a considerable nuisance to him just now while assuring him that one day they will be friends and companions. But don't let him hurt the baby, for his sake as well as hers. He will be dreadfully guilty, however hard you try to pretend that it was an accident. If necessary, use a cat-net to protect her against those toys thrown accidentally-on-purpose, and don't tempt him and providence by leaving him in charge of the pram outside shops.

Work to make the toddler feel that the baby likes him. We all find it easier to like people who seem to like us; your child will find it much more possible to accept his new sister if he feels that she makes affectionate advances. Arranging it is an easy piece of parent-upmanship: if the toddler puts his face close to the baby's and smiles and makes noises, she will smile at him. Once she smiles, you can play it up a little: 'He's the one she really likes' you say to the admiring visitor who had been ignoring him.

If you can reach a point when the older child says something like 'I'll keep her quiet for you, Mummy, she'll stop crying for *me* . . .' you will know that the worst is over.

With some luck and a lot of tact, two or three months will see you through to a point where he can be amusedly patronizing about the baby most of the time. Try to get there before she becomes mobile anyway. While she lies where she is put she is only a nuisance to him in the emotional sense of taking up your time and attention. Once she crawls into games and snatches and chews his toys, she will be a major practical nuisance too. If he can say resignedly 'Oh, isn't she *silly*' or 'I s'pose she's trying to copy me again', their relationship is building. If he simply dislikes her, you are all in for a difficult couple of years.

Coping with later jealousies Jealousy between brothers and sisters seldom ends just because the older child forgets what life as an 'only' was like. Balancing the emotional needs of two or more children of different age-stages continues to need thought. If, for example, one starts at school and the other at nursery school, both in the same term, both will need your full support and you will have to share it out. There will be problems over suiting everyone in treats, expeditions and holidays; problems over nursing a sick one without neglecting the other and problems over coping fairly when one gets her own way with charm and the other fails to get it by bullying.

Remember, always, that jealousy is about feelings, not objects or events. If one child feels that you care more about the other (perhaps represented by his birthday celebration) than you do about her, the fact that you take just as much (or even a little more) trouble about her birthday when it comes around, will not do a bit of good.

Remember, also, that there may be jealousy *both ways around*. While older children certainly suffer when later ones arrive, younger children are often bitterly jealous of older brothers and sisters, especially if parents go on and on emphasizing the first child's superiority in the family. Behaviour which is tactful in the first six months of a baby's life can become downright insensitive in the second year.

Try not to assume that brothers and sisters love each other. Some parents continue to insist that 'they're very close really' even when constant squabbles and complaints suggest otherwise. They are individual people. They may or may not get on well together. They have to tolerate and behave decently to each other but that is all. If you can avoid forcing them into each other's company, forcing them to share every friend and activity, they may eventually surprise you with their fierce loyalty.

Respect each child's individual dignity. If you can make it clear that you love each one individually and will never make them look small either to each other or to outsiders, you will not go far wrong. That means that you will never compare them with each other. There is no more point than there would be in comparing an orange with an apple. And it means that you will never hold one up as an example to the other, either. The charming manners and neat habits which come so easily to one may be truly difficult for the other to acquire: you will not help her by suggesting that she 'look at your brother; he doesn't leave a mess for me to clear up.'

Language *see also* **Play**

Language is the basic tool of human beings. If rising onto their hind legs, freeing their front ones to become tool-using hands, gave developing people an advantage over other animals, developing speech gave an even greater one. By using language we can communicate about things which are not physically present and about ideas which do not physically exist. We can say anything that we can do; say what we cannot do; say what no person has ever done. We can discuss possibilities, probabilities, projects and ideas which are truly 'new' in the sense of being as yet outside human experience. With this vital tool, one generation can pass on its experiences to the next so that children can build onwards without having to waste time finding out everything for themselves. The saving of time and effort and the creative possibilities which all this opens up are immeasurable: they add up to what we call 'culture'.

Children do not have to be 'taught' to speak any more than they have to be taught to walk, but they can certainly be helped to acquire and use rich and rewarding speech. A child who does acquire the 'best' language of which she is capable will also make the best possible use of her intelligence. The relationship between language and intelligence, language and thinking, is two-way. People need intelligence to learn to understand and to use language fluently and meaningfully; they also need fluent and meaningful language for their intelligence to work on. If high intelligence helps us to find the words to say what we think, so the words we know help us to decide what to think. Providing an enriched verbal environment for a child is just as important to her developing intellect as is a good diet to her developing body.

Research into language is highly complicated and controversial. No attempt will be made here to review the theories or to prove and disprove them with summaries of the studies. Interested readers can find all that in many excellent specialist books. Instead, an attempt will be made to answer the question: 'What can I do to help my child acquire and use language well?'

The biggest single step is a negative one: to get rid of the common notion that language means talking; that talking means using words and that therefore the whole process of language-learning is delayed until a baby is nearly a year old. Language is communication between one person and another. It starts as soon as a new person meets her mother in the first contact after birth. Actual *speech* is the formalized culmination of an ongoing process rather than the beginning of anything, so if you wait to interest yourself in your child's language until she can speak, you will have missed a great deal of the fun.

The other important step is to realize that children eventually use words because they want to, rather than because they have to, or need to. A baby gets everything she needs from the adults who care for her without words. She uses crying, other sounds, facial expressions, gestures, body-language . . . her needs would go on being met even if she never learned to use words. Furthermore, as we shall see, early words have nothing to do with 'need': they do not help the baby to manage her parents or her environment as a whole. Her motivation is pleasure: fun in communicating with loved people; pleasure in play, in cooperation, in sharing. This is important because you will never *ever* be able to force or stress a young child into speech. If you make her unhappy she will not talk, she will cry. Everything you do which extends her communication/speech will be pleasurable for her and therefore probably fun for you, too.

New babies' 'conversations'

Every mother knows that she studies her new baby, talks to her, jiggles her about and makes faces at her. But few mothers realize that, far from being passive receivers of such attention, even the newest babies are active partners in the interplay. Careful video-taped studies of mother–baby pairs have shown that, from the very beginning, these social sessions have all the qualities of 'conversation' except that they do not employ words. Furthermore, most of the 'conversations' are in fact started, conducted and ended by the babies rather than by the adults. Settled together after a feed for example, the baby focuses her eyes on the mother's. The mother smiles at her. The baby, still looking at the mother, changes her facial expression: perhaps she wrinkles her brow. The mother reacts: perhaps she says 'you're getting tired, aren't you?' The baby makes a small sound and moves her arms and again the mother answers, perhaps by making that same face back and tightening her arms in a cuddle. As long as the baby goes on gazing into the mother's eyes and interacting with her, it will take a major domestic crisis or crass interruption to make the mother break off the 'conversation'. It will end when the baby breaks the eye-contact by closing her eyes, turning her head or simply ceasing to focus.

In these early interactions mothers imitate babies far more than babies imitate mothers. Many charming pictures of mother–baby pairs have been published with captions suggesting that the baby is copying mother's grimaces. Careful study of video-tapes shows that it is usually the baby who puts her tongue out first and the mother who follows. She is mirroring the baby's actions for her; showing her what she is doing; lending gradual meaning to what may at first be randomly 'social' activity. This mirroring and lending of meaning is vitally important and goes on all through early childhood. When a baby's face wrinkles into the sad expression which comes before crying, the mother will imitate the face and will probably *say* 'Oh dear . . .' in sad/sympathetic tones. Quite unthinkingly she tells the baby 'this is what that face looks like and this is the feeling-meaning it conveys.'

While the very earliest 'conversations' may contain few sounds from the baby, her sound-making increases rapidly so that by three to four months she is seldom silent during a social situation (except when it is the adult's turn to answer her) and uses expressive and varied voice tones. The tones are high-pitched and lilting when compared to later speech (we usually call the whole lot 'cooing') and the mother adopts similar tones and rhythms in her replies. The mother who 'feels silly' when she makes noises at her baby, or is told by a third party that she sounds idiotic, may like to know that *adult* speech tones will immediately silence her baby. It has been tried experimentally. Even at this very early age the baby has expectations of her conversations with mother and if she gets no answer, or an unexpected or inappropriate one, she will come to a full stop; look worried and probably cry. So coo away. As is so often the case with young babies, the thing which comes naturally and feels right *is* right.

The more concentrated one-to-one attention a young baby gets, the more readily she will 'talk', and the more sensitively her communications are noticed and mirrored, the more she will vary them. Most mothers are familiar with the saying that the more an infant is *talked to* the more she will talk, but it is more accurate and useful to rephrase it in terms of being talked *with*. Chatting to your baby as you move around the room or cuddling her while you talk to her toddler-brother is fine, but the kind of talk which will increase her language-capacity is the kind that involves you totally and leaves no room for anyone else nor space between you.

Three to six months: 'talking' about talking

By around three months, you and your baby will have fallen into a conversational rhythm such that whoever starts the interaction (perhaps by catching the other's eye and smiling) each of you will then take turns so that the sounds, smiles, expressions and movements of each of you mesh together as if you were dancing to the same tune.

By around the middle of this first year, your baby will have done a great deal of sorting out, in preparation for the recognition and use of sounds, separated from physical contact, facial expressions and gestures. At three months, for example, she will differentiate between a human voice and any other sound, so that a human 'reply' keeps her 'talking' where ringing a little bell whenever she pauses does not. But by six months she will differentiate between voices; knowing yours from her father's and all familiar ones from the voices of strangers. She will sort out her listening and her looking, too, so that instead of looking at *something* when she hears a human voice, she learns to search for the face of the person who spoke. Soon she will learn also to respond to stimuli which are applied only to one sense at a time. She will learn, for example, to smile because you smile, rather than smiling-and-talking because you smile-and-talk. And she will learn to babble in reply to voices which she hears from a tape-recorder or unseen person, without the added cues given by looking. These are all important signs of her growing up. If she continued only to respond to the global social cues which stimulated her first social interactions, she would never be able to recognize an unheard friend across the street nor talk to an unseen one on the telephone.

Watching out for deafness   While a baby is learning to make these differentiations and to sort out her sensory reactions, it is tragically easy to miss the fact that she is deaf.

Because early communication is social, and because early social stimuli are a mixture of sensory impressions, a totally deaf baby, who is neither hearing sounds from other people nor from herself, will appear to react normally to you *and* will continue, perhaps for the first half-year, to make a normal range of cooing and babbling sounds. It is only at the stage when hearing and sound-making are separated off from sociable sights and feelings, that her handicap will become obvious.

If she should be deaf, early recognition and expert help are important. Parents cannot assure themselves that a baby hears normally over the full range of sounds by home-testing; nor can a well-baby clinic doctor. Complete assessment of hearing requires the expertise of an audiologist and the use of techniques such as pure-tone audiology. If you have any reason to suspect that your baby's hearing is anything other than normal, or any reason (such as a family history of deafness) to worry especially about it, consult your doctor or clinic and do not be surprised or further worried if you are referred on to a specialist. But if you have no reason for suspicion, it is nevertheless sensible to assure yourselves that the baby is hearing voices and ordinary everyday sounds.

'Testing' a baby will take two of you (or you and a member of the clinic staff). With the baby sitting in her chair, one adult makes the 'test sounds' at about eighteen inches from her ear but from just behind her so that she cannot see the object or person. The other watches her eyes or, if she is coming up to six months, the movements of her head. If she hears the sound she will move her eyes or whole head towards it. To ensure that any movements seen do not happen by chance, it is sensible to make a second sound about eighteen inches from the other ear. As she moves or looks towards that sound it is stopped and the 'test' sound is made. An abrupt change in the direction of her eye or head movements shows that she has heard it.

Suitable sounds are made by crumpling hard toilet paper, ringing a small bell, shaking a light rattle and stroking a spoon gently round the inside of a cup. Voice sounds should be tried, too, using a Psss for high tones and a gentle Oooo for low ones. Ideally, each sound should be tried for each ear but remember:

Failure to respond is usually due to distraction, boredom or tiredness. Don't panic; don't decide she *is* deaf. Try again later in the day and/or take her to the clinic for a check-up.

The fact that she responds to a whisper does not mean that her hearing is perfect. Parents have made the tragic mistake of trying the quietest whisper they could manage, from just behind the baby, and then believing that if she responded to such a quiet sound she must be able to hear all other louder ones. It need not be so. A whisper uses very high frequencies. Although it is *quiet* it may nevertheless be detected by a baby who has serious hearing loss for lower frequency-ranges.

Talking games and playing talk

The baby who is talking-about-talking and sorting out verbal talking from all the other kinds of communication, is the person all those nursery-games like 'This little piggy went to market' or 'Round and round the garden like a teddy bear' are made for. Your everyday conversations can share in the characteristics which make them perfect:

They are played in a fun-context, meant to give pleasure, and they usually end in laughter.

They have rhythm which matches her rhythms and helps her to know what to expect and what will happen next.

Their rhythm usually builds into some kind of climax (the final poke in the tummy or tickle of the ribs) and that fits with the natural ending of one 'paragraph' and the start of another piece of 'conversation'.

They have repetition which is again important in giving the baby time to foresee what is coming next and to organize her responses.

They involve only the baby and her partner. They do not require the two of them to talk about anything else than the conversation.

Six to twelve months: 'talking' about other things

In the second half of her first year the baby begins to sit up and play with objects and to move around looking at things, finding things and generally experimenting with what the environment has to offer. Now she will begin to want to talk about those things rather than just talking for its own sociable sake. She learns to use her voice for more and more complex sound-making, stringing together syllables of babble and using expression and inflection until her sounds (now usually called 'jargoning') really do sound like real speech, although there are still no words.

Using this newly enriched repertoire, she learns to call attention to things she has seen and to indicate things that she wants; she learns to ask questions and make exclamations; she learns, most touchingly of all, to make jokes and laugh at them herself. Listening to a child at this stage, it really does seem that language is just around the corner but that when it comes it will be fully-fledged fluent *talking* rather than the few, stilted single words with which she must begin.

Although those nursery word-games will probably still be popular, a new type takes first place. These are the games in which objects come and go, get passed from one to the other or get posted into boxes. She will play 'peek-a-boo' in any version you please (from all of you behind the curtains, to your face covered with your hand) for minutes on end and she will punctuate each new round with sounds meaning 'Where's it gone? There it is . . .' She will play ball, too, either rolling the ball to you and fetching it when you roll it back, or simply passing it from her hand to yours. Again she will punctuate, with her version of 'your turn; my turn . . .' Just as her very earliest communications with you had all the features of proper 'conversation', so these have all the features of the cooperative and problem-solving behaviour for which human speech is uniquely valuable.

This is the kind of play which will now contribute most to her general language development and the more she has of it the better. But there is more specific learning going on now, too: the learning of actual words. She is not quite ready to *use* words herself, but she is ready to pick out some of the words you use and begin to understand them; to discover what they refer to and therefore to work out some of what you mean.

Learning what words mean

Babies of eight or nine months commonly become highly imitative and will imitate sounds as well as funny faces, gestures and so on. Parents sometimes spend a lot of time holding up objects and saying, 'Cup. Say cup, darling. Cup, cup, come on, say cup'. And sometimes the baby will respond with a passable imitation of the sound so that the parent becomes convinced that he or she is 'teaching her to talk'.

While such a game is harmless, provided the baby enjoys it as just another play-conversation, it will not actually help her to learn language. Your conviction that it does may prevent you from offering more useful kinds of talk, or even make you irritated when she refuses to 'say again' something she imitated earlier.

A baby does not learn to say words for their own sake (or yours). She learns to say words in order to communicate more, or more meaningfully, with you. That means that she will have no interest in *saying* a word until she knows what it *means* and that even once she does know what it means, she will not bother saying it until or unless she has something she wants to communicate about it. It seems to work something like this:

The baby hears a word like 'cup' over and over again as the one constant sound in a large variety of sound-strings (sentences) which you utter. She hears, 'I'll just get your cup'; 'Let's put some in this cup'; 'Would you like this cup?'; 'I need a cup of coffee' . . . That one word 'cup' is the sound which is common to all those utterances and it is always associated with something to drink. Over days and weeks the baby comes to see that the sound and the object always go together. When she has made the association 'cup' = what the drink is in, she will know what 'cup' means.

Helping her to listen and understand words

She still cannot pick words or meanings out of a general blur of family conversation, with half-finished sentences, expressive shrugs and the television turned on. She still needs face to face conversation, or talk directed only at her and in a reasonably quiet room. And she still needs it from you, or from very familiar and beloved people. She must find word-meanings by discovering constant sounds despite changes in expression and inflection; she cannot also cope with a stranger's voice.

When you are talking to her, it is worthwhile to remember to use the key labelling-words that she will be picking up, like that label-word 'cup'. If you say, 'Here's your cup; I'll just pour some milk for you' you give her yet another opportunity. If you say 'Here it is; I'll just pour some milk for you', you do not. So when the door needs shutting, make sure you say 'I'll just shut the door' rather than 'I'll just shut it' and make sure you lead a search for the dog (or 'Jack' or whatever his name is) rather than 'that dratted animal'.

Name-labels are vital for her, especially her own. At this stage she cannot possibly think of herself as 'I' or 'me' especially as, in English at least, the correct word for oneself depends on who is speaking. I am 'me' to myself but I am 'she' or 'you' to you. So use her name and don't let 'does Mary want a biscuit?' embarrass you because it is 'babytalk'. It is her talk and she is the one doing the learning.

She will not learn name-labels for things which are not physically present, so the most useful kind of talk relates an object which is there to its name-word. The only exception is looking for things together. If you search for that dog, she may or may not know what you were both looking for to start with, but once you find him, the excitement of the successful climax to the 'game' will give its name-word extra significance for her. Name-labels which you know she understands (even if she is not using them yet) will begin to mean something to her if she sees a picture of the object, so books with realistic pictures of everyday objects can begin to provide an ever-ready version of the looking-for-something game ('Where's the cup? . . . See, here it is, on the table. And down here there's a chair just like Mary's chair . . .') Later still, such understood words will make interesting conversation or stories for her, though her father's account of his day at 'the office' (which she has never seen and therefore cannot visualize) still means nothing to her.

Talent as an actress (or a ham) is very useful at this stage. Babies with outgoing, dramatizing parents sometimes learn to understand first of all the emphatic exclamations they hear excitedly repeated. 'Oh dear!' she may hear as you pick her up from every tumble and 'Up you come!' each time you lift her from her cot.

But as well as giving her as many interesting words as you can in easy-to-understand situations, you also need to give her the greatest possible rewards for her own speech-efforts. This is where it is important to remember yet again that she is not trying to learn to *say words* but to *communicate with you*. The more you can show her that you are listening, understanding, and sharing her pleasure when you get it right, the more she will be stimulated to try. If she gestures vaguely towards a kitchen counter and makes an obviously 'wanting' sound, you might look where she is indicating and list for her the various things for which she might be asking. It does not matter whether or not her sound bears any relation to the 'proper' name for the object you eventually find. What matters is that she communicated with you; used an 'own-word' and made you understand it.

As she approaches real word-use she will use more and more 'own-words'. Don't ever correct or pretend not to understand them. Correction will only bore her because she does not want to say the same thing again, better, she wants to say something else now. The correction will not even help because if she is using an own-word it is because it is the best she has to offer at the moment. The 'proper' word will evolve when, and only when, she is ready. If you pretend not to understand her when you do, you are cheating her out of successful communication and therefore making her feel that the whole business is more difficult than it is. It will not work, either. If you refuse to hand her her bottle until she says 'bottle' instead of 'bah-boo', you are cutting across that vital pleasure-principle in language-learning. You will make her feel frustrated and cross and you are more likely to get tears than a word.

First words   Your child will probably understand dozens of words before it occurs to her that she can use one particular sound to refer to one particular person or object. Up to now her language has been all to do with action and relationships: with what she and her adult partner are doing and feeling. That jargoning, which sounded so like fluent talk, was doing-feeling-talk. But now she has sorted out enough words to start trying word-language for herself. She starts with name-labels and, since her language is still tied up with pleasure not need, they are labels for people or things she finds exciting, pleasurable or loving. Although some families report 'No!' as a first word, most children will name the cat, a parent, a favourite food or a first pair of bright red shoes . . .

Average ages for acquiring words are dangerous things to set out because children acquire words at widely varying ages and rates, and the words themselves, despite parents' anxiety, are poor indicators of language-development since understanding matters so much more than word-production. Still, most babies will have one or two labels (which may be real words or own-words but will be proper labels in the sense that they are used consistently for one and only one thing) by ten or eleven months and a dozen or so by a year. Most will be using a lot of single words and some two-word phrases (*see below*) by their second birthdays.

Later talkers   Many babies will not produce any recognizable words at all before their second birthdays, while a lot more will acquire two or three words during the second year but add no more for months. The most usual 'reasons' (if you need a reason for delay which is part of normal variation) are:

That the baby is a boy. We do not actually know why the sexes differ in this respect (although recent research suggests that there are neurological differences which may explain differential rates of development in many areas) but they certainly do. Most boys speak later than most girls, although there is some overlap in the middle so that a boy who speaks early may speak sooner than a girl who speaks late.

That the baby always has to share, and compete for, attention from her special adults. It is this element of competition and distraction which sometimes delays speech in twins. If 'private language' develops between them, it is usually because they are short of adult one-to-one talk rather than because they choose to talk to each other instead. Last children in large families sometimes share this disadvantage, as do babies who follow closely after a brother or sister who is therefore at his most demanding toddler stage during the baby's critical language-learning months.

That the baby is cared for by a succession of caretakers so that it is difficult for her ever to build up the easy loving familiarity which accelerates language-development.

That she is cared for by very silent or non-verbal people. The child of totally deaf parents is likely to be very slow to acquire language even if her own hearing is perfect. The child of a mother who was very depressed and withdrawn over many months may similarly be slowed up unless she also has more reactive caretakers available. The child who is cared for by foreign-speaking 'au pairs' or nannies may be delayed if they can neither offer adequate English nor allow her to speak in their mother-tongues (*see below* Bringing up bi-lingual babies).

That she spends her days in group care from a very early age. Children do not learn language from each other until word-talking is firmly entrenched in them. Unless a group provides a very high adult–child ratio, and an approach to care which provides each child with a mother-substitute, group membership may slow up her speech.

The second (or third) year and the importance of 'motherese'

Whether your child's single label-words start to come early or late and arrive one at a time or by the dozen, they will come unless she has some major handicap such as deafness. As long as she is of an age where you think at all about her talking, it goes on being more useful to think about her interest in, and understanding of, language than about her production of it. You cannot squeeze words out of her. She is not a parrot. Nor are unmeaningful words useful language. If you are in a foreign city, will it be useful to you to learn by heart how to ask 'where is the railway station?' No; the question is useless unless you can understand the answer.

Most parents automatically adopt, at this stage, a particular form of language which has been christened 'motherese'. It is not babytalk in the sense of using to the child her own words or phrases. It is baby-adapted talk which, whether you use it deliberately or not, makes it easy for the child to find, recognize and understand your words.

Motherese uses short simple sentences which are highly inflected and often repeated. The actual speech is rather high-pitched and musical and contains a lot of question marks. It is used with much gesture and action, can sound *daft* to childless friends, but is both vital and natural to the mother–child pair. If your work colleagues curl their lips to hear you say: 'Mary want Teddy? Want Teddy darling? Mummy will get Teddy for Mary. Here's Teddy for Mary. Yes . . . Mary's Teddy . . .' they had better visit after Mary's bedtime in future. But maybe you can remind them that while Mary is certainly not a moron, she *is* a beginner. A piano teacher offers beginners a tuneful series of easy single notes rather than a concerto. Motherese does the same.

Through motherese, you go on offering your child a wide variety of relevant single word-labels for her to select among, and pick up when she wants to. Through her extraordinary *use* of those single words she makes them do the work of your sentences. 'Up?' she pleads, holding onto your leg and gazing into your face. 'Up-up' she comments happily, copying, as you lift her, the tone in which you say 'up you come'. 'Up!' she announces with enormous satisfaction, comfortably settled on your hip.

There can be few single words more variously communicative than those of a child who is learning to talk. Your job is to give her the pleasure of knowing her communications are succeeding and, by doing so, to provide her with a bridge from single words to phrases. When she says 'Dog!' in obvious alarm as a Great Dane bounds towards you, feed back her meaning with something like 'Yes, isn't it a *big* dog?'

When she does start to string words together, first in pairs and then in longer phrases, it will be descriptive or action-words which she adds to those name-labels. She will not bother to say '*the* dog' because the second word adds nothing to the communication. 'Big dog' is much more useful. Don't look for grammar, then, look for content and colour. Every language studied contains among its earliest word-combinations the phrase which translates as 'hit ball'. It is ungrammatical. No adult would say it, but it expresses something clearly desirable to children of every nationality.

Struggling with grammar

Between about two and about five children have to master the particular rules of the grammar of their own language. They do not acquire these by direct imitation (when did you last say 'hit ball'?) because they are not interested in saying what you say but in saying what they mean. They try to ascertain grammatical rules by picking out the constants from other people's speech. The results can be comical but are almost always logical. If there are two dogs why isn't that a flock of sheeps?

Correcting own-grammar is just as futile and saddening as correcting own-words, but new motherese-techniques will lead you to offer the child a correct model in your answers to her incorrect tries. The trick (which comes naturally to all but very anxious parents) is to keep her interested in communicating with you by giving her a quick and understanding response to her speech, but to keep a correct model always available for her by answering in your own adult speech. When she rushes into the kitchen saying 'Baba cry. Quick . . .' you know that she means to tell you that the baby is crying and you should go to him at once. You show that you understand her language but you answer in your own, 'Oh, is Billy crying? Thank you. I'll come and see to him at once'. You let her tell you that she has 'eated dat biccit' but you ask her whether she has 'eaten that biscuit'. You let her talk her way but you talk yours. As long as you both understand each other, and you both say plenty to each other, the grammar will come.

Pre-school years: talking about ideas and feelings

Three- and four-year-olds who talk all the time still have not finished with language-learning. They have learned to use words in communication, but still largely in situations where action and gesture would do, or almost do, instead. Now they have to learn to use those words for that most important purpose: communicating about things which are not in the room but in their heads and for expressing ideas which are theirs alone.

The child still needs most of all your interested listening and your interesting talk. But gradually you will find that she is picking out words and phrases which allow her to talk about increasingly abstract ideas. The more idea-words you can feed in, the sooner she will be able to use them in her thinking and her play, and the more ideas she will be able to produce. She is going to learn about ideas like weight and volume and shape. Before she can really use the idea of roundness, for example, she will need the use of the word so as to be able to label for herself the difference between round and square. She is going to notice colour and begin to categorize objects by it, but before she can think and talk about colour, she needs the words. She is going to need value-abstracts like good and bad, pretty and ugly, but she will not be able to tell you her views until she can sort out those words, too.

As the child sorts out the characteristics of people, animals and objects, you will see a burgeoning of imaginary and dramatic play and hear it reflected in her language. She cannot pretend to be a horse until she has recognized some characteristics which differentiate horses from other things, but she cannot let you know that she is a horse until she can use words either to tell you or to express those characteristics in pretend-neighing or clip-clopping. Much of her most important language-learning will still be directly associated with her play, so that even though she has reached an age when play with other children is important, it is a pity if she no longer also gets the chance to play both alone and with you. It is by joining her games, active, constructive and imaginative, that you will most easily see where she has got to with words and what kinds of words she currently needs.

Asking 'what's that?' and 'why?' Fortunately the child will reach a point where she asks you directly for the word-ideas she needs. At first, often at around three, she collects name-words by continually asking you 'what's that?' It is usually a *name* she is looking for rather than an elaborate explanation, so when she points to a parcel and asks what it is, give her the simple answer 'a parcel'. If she actually wants to know what is inside it, she will find a different way of asking; if you volunteer information for which she has not actually asked you may muddle her.

'Why?' comes next and usually does mean that she wants something more or something different from the name. She may indeed start a why-session with a 'what's that?' and go straight on to 'why?':

'What's that?'
'It's thunder.'
'Why?' . . .

When 'why?' is unanswerable because it is not the right question, you can sometimes give the child what she *is* asking for, and save yourself from cloud cuckoo land, if you treat it as meaning 'tell me more about it . . .'

Desirable and less desirable talking During these pre- and early school years you will hear her use words for many different purposes and some will probably strike you as less desirable than others. She will use them, for example, to tell *herself* what to do, scolding herself in private games, instructing herself, 'careful, Sarah . . .' but she will use them to instruct others, too. Four-year-olds can be very bossy. You will hear her boasting too and spinning fantasies about herself and her family, and you will hear her using her new words-for-ideas in smug assertions of her own 'goodness' or 'prettyness'. Above all, you may moan that she seems never to *stop* talking. She may utter 20,000 words in a day with only 500 in her vocabulary and that is a lot of repetitions to listen to. She *must* talk; she must practise the sounds, the inflections and the effects of her words. You will find it less boring if you actually join in, rather than trying to tune her out and responding with only the occasional 'Uh-huh'. Keeping her talking, freely and with pleasure, is what really matters. If she is to go as far as she can in the later world of education, she needs to feel that words are always her friends and that people can always be reached by talking.

Stuttering or stammering Her ideas are usually ahead of her vocabulary so that she still finds it difficult to express a flow of thought smoothly. When she is excited, or hurried, searching for the right word holds her up so that her talk keeps hiccuping.

Jerky and uneven speech happens to almost every pre-school child from time to time but it only rarely turns into a real stutter. It is most likely to become a 'speech-problem' if you react to it anxiously; correct her; try to make her speak slowly. If you can accept her talk calmly, so that it never occurs to her that it is in any way inadequate and so that she never has to *think* about how she is speaking, it will all smooth out with practice. Being calm and accepting really is important. To see why, try consciously controlling your own breathing for a minute. It at once becomes laboured and peculiar. The same thing happens to speech if you insist that a child be conscious of it.

Babytalk   Children who insist on using babytalk, long after they are capable of expressing themselves in ordinary words, have usually discovered that adults find it appealing. When you suddenly decide that it is ridiculous, don't clamp down abruptly on talk you have previously seemed to welcome, or you may hurt her feelings and shut her up. Instead, vow that never again will your face soften to babytalk and that never again will you use it to her. Translate everything she says into proper English so that you put an adult version beside hers and, without further comment from you, she will drop it over a few months.

Some kinds of babytalk are positively useful, though. If a child does not know the word for something and can coin one which communicates her meaning, she is making language work for her in a creative way. One child, for example, enquired anxiously about the 'bell-van' because she did not know the word for ambulance. Everybody knew what she meant and she discovered, with pleasure, that she could make meaningful words of her own. If such words pass into the family vocabulary for a while that is a compliment to her and she will learn the 'proper' name while enjoying her personal one.

Nonsense and   Words are powerful; their power over other people is one of the things the
'naughty   child must discover and learn to manipulate. Along the way she may
nonsense'   discover some which evoke a particularly strong reaction from adults. If she does she will use them again and again. 'Pee-pee,' she shouts. If everyone shushes her she will certainly say it again and probably add in 'wee-wee' and 'piss-piss-piss' for good measure.

If you scold you will get into deep water. What are you scolding for? A word? Can a word be naughty? Surely not, words are just tools for her to use. If you ignore this kind of nonsense, so that the words you dislike do not have any special power, she will probably get bored with them. But you can do something more positive, too. All children love repetitive non-sense rhymes and chants. Introduce some that you *do* like and take the opportunity to start her with the sounds and rhythms of poetry, too. She may not understand all the words in 'Hiawatha' but her enjoyment of its regular beat and lovely word-sounds will help her to listen, to think and to enjoy language.

Insults   When a furious child screams that she will kill you it is easy to react with anger. But it is not fair to do so. She is using enormous self-control in sticking to words rather than physical attack and since her anger is probably already frightening her, an angry response from you will not help. Try to acknowledge the *feeling* and help her to carry on using words to tell you more – 'I'm sorry you're feeling so cross; what is it about do you think?'

Lesser insults of the 'silly old cow' variety can usually be defused if you can remember that it is a *child* who is insulting you and that you do not therefore have to be deeply offended. 'If I'm a silly old cow you are a cross little calf' will probably end the whole episode in giggles.

The point, of course, is that as she grows up you *want* her to be able to use words for feelings, words for attack or defence, because words do less harm than actions and because being able to express herself verbally is her best assurance of good communication with other people all through her life. It is the teenager who finds himself silenced by the sarcasm of the school teacher who is liable to slash her car tyres. The one who can 'answer back' has far less need to be violent.

Bringing up bi-lingual babies

Parents often ask whether it will be a good or a bad thing to bring up their child in two languages. There is surprisingly little research on the topic but some inferences can be drawn from what is known about speech development in general.

Very young babies start out by differentiating the sounds of human speech from all other sounds rather than the sounds of the speech of one language from those of another. They also make sounds which occur in all languages. It is impossible to tell the nationality of a baby by listening to her cooing or babbling. Differentiation between languages does not begin until the baby discovers that some sounds communicate while others do not. It is feed-back from adults who pick up 'English-sounding' babble and ignore 'Japanese-sounding' sounds which biases a baby gradually towards the production of his family's language sounds. It follows then that any sounds, from any language, can and will be used by the baby if they do in fact communicate and are in fact fed back to her. She learns language in the communication of shared play with loved adults. There-fore, if she experiences this kind of communication in two languages from the beginning of her life, she will come to use them both. Parents who are themselves truly bi-lingual can therefore be assured that if they continue to use both their languages in whatever balance is natural to them, the baby will come to adopt a similar language-pattern at least until the influence of outside people strengthens. There is no reason to suppose that learning two languages in this way is any more difficult for her than learning one. She is selecting out effectively communicative sounds from all the sounds she hears around her. If she learns only English, she will come to know that the dog can be 'dog', 'pup' or 'Jack'. If she learns English and French, she will discover that that same dog can also be 'chien' or 'Jacques'. Such a child will certainly go through phases in which her two languages are intermingled but this is no different from the phase in which the single-language child intermingles 'real' words with 'own' words. The child in a bi-lingual family will sort them out in exactly the same way.

But there are often complications which are usually to do with the nature of the parents' bi-linguality. The following are the most common:

Deliberate rather than spontaneous bi-linguality

If two languages are to become natural to the child both must give her equal pleasure, feed-back and reward. For this to come about the parents need not only to be equally competent in both but to use them with equal spontaneity. Often this is not the case. Italian parents, for example, may have been long resident in Britain and long-accustomed to conduct their lives and relationships in English. Yet they may have retained complete fluency in Italian and have continued to use (and think in) that language when visiting their families and so forth. When a child is expected they may decide to give her the benefit of her mother-tongue and therefore make it a matter of policy to speak to her some of the time in Italian and to encourage her to produce sounds and then words in both languages.

Under these circumstances policy is often the enemy of fluency. Because English is the language she hears most and in which she hears her parents talking to each other as well as in most of their conversations with her, English is the language in which spontaneous first words will be produced. But because they want her to produce Italian as well her parents now begin to pressure her. When she says 'Bus!' excitedly to her mother, she does not always get a rewarding 'yes, isn't it a big bus?' Sometimes her mother ignores the content of her communication and instead tells her to say 'Autobus . . .' This kind of behaviour contradicts every principle of early language-learning by removing the element of pleasurably shared communication and substituting deliberate attempts to teach. Such a child is likely to become confused; not so much confused between the two languages but confused about communication/language itself. She may become a two-year-old who says very little in any language other than the tantrum-language of frustration. If you do not live bi-lingually, you cannot successfully rear a bi-lingual child.

Multi-lingual families

Sometimes parents do not themselves share a mother-tongue but communicate with each other in a third language which both are struggling to acquire. A Polish woman may marry a German man, for example, and the two of them may produce a child while they are still far from fluent in the English of their adopted country. This is a difficult situation because if the child is brought up to be bi-lingual in Polish and German and to acquire English later and from outside the family, one or the other parent will be unable to respond to her communications whichever language they are in. Since it is vitally important that she be understood, it is probably better to rear her in English – even if that English is not fluent – so that the whole family goes on learning together. Such a child may pick up peculiar phrases or idiosyncratic inflections from her parents, but these will soon right themselves when she is mixing with other children and their families. Families which have adopted this approach say that their own English rapidly improves once their child can serve as a model for them.

Families with one 'foreign' parent

A more usual situation is that in which a parent of another nationality marries a native and, while using his language for daily life, retains her own for more private moments. Children in such families often seem able to acquire both languages but do not acquire the 'foreign' one as a bi-lingual child does, but as a private language especially linked to intimacy with that parent. Others do not actually learn to *speak* the 'foreign' language but nevertheless come to understand it, especially where it has been experienced as part of especially affectionate and rewarding situations such as bedtime lullabies . . . When such a child reaches school age she may not be *aware* that she 'knows French' but she may nevertheless find that language extraordinarily easy to learn.

Laryngitis *see* **Croup and Laryngitis.**
'Latch-key children' *see* **Working Mothers.**

Laxatives *see also* **Constipation**

Due to the mistaken belief that there is some relationship between good health and a regular daily bowel movement, these drugs are extensively misused.

Their purpose is to produce a soft, formed, easy-to-pass stool but, given adequate fluids, a diet containing plenty of roughage from fruit, vegetables, wholegrains and/or bran, and normal health and activity, the individual's bowels will produce such stools without chemical assistance. While an occasional laxative is not harmful, regular laxatives can so upset the bowel's natural rhythm that normal evacuation becomes almost impossible.

The laxative habit

Occasional laxative use easily turns into habitual use. If a person has gone, say, three days without passing a stool and becomes concerned and takes a laxative, the medicine will lead to a large stool which leaves the rectum empty. Because it is empty, it may take several days before enough faeces accumulate to give her the natural signals to go. If the original three days caused her concern, it is likely that this 'pause' will lead to further anxiety. She may well take another dose of laxative and thus enter into a vicious circle.

In extreme cases, the laxative habit can lead to loss of tone in the bowel wall or even to its chronic inflammation. If the dose is built up to a point where it provokes diarrhoea, there may be too much loss of fluid and of salt and, because food is hurried through the bowels, there may be loss of certain nutrients too.

Laxatives may be desirable for a short period whenever passing a stool may be painful, or straining to pass a hard stool dangerous. Adult conditions of this kind include the post-partum period; piles; rectal surgery and so forth. Conditions which may affect children or young people include anal fissures (*see* **Constipation**), chronic constipation (*see* **Soiling**) and abdominal surgery.

A laxative may also be useful if constipation arises after an illness, due to the combination of little food and no exercise. Certain drugs, such as codeine, also tend to cause constipation.

A single dose of a laxative will do no harm if a child or young person complains that her stools have become uncomfortably hard and difficult to pass. But having taken one dose, the possibility that a thorough emptying of the rectum will lead to a delay before she next passes a stool should be explained to her. Further doses should be withheld (from a child) or discouraged in a teenager.

When laxatives are dangerous

No laxative should ever be taken by a person with abdominal pain (*see* **Abdominal Pain**), colic, nausea and/or vomiting. The sufferer may have some acute abdominal condition. Artificial stimulation of the bowel could make it much worse.

Learning Difficulties and Disabilities *see also* **Hyperactive Children; School**

In most western societies every child has a theoretical right to the education 'best suited to his age, abilities and aptitudes'. School programmes would ideally be tailor-made (or custom-altered) to fit each customer, and aim both to help children with special talents to use them to best advantage, and to help those with general or specific handicaps to overcome them as far as possible. In practice, of course, this is largely impossible. An individual family finds it difficult enough to meet the needs of two or three children, spaced a couple of years apart. A school cannot possibly individualize its offering to every pupil. Most educational programmes are therefore necessarily set up and run to suit some theoretical 'average' child of a given age, which inevitably leaves a high proportion of children floundering or bored, in at least some areas at some stages in their lives. By no means all difficulties with the learning aspects of school are due to learning disabilities. Many are due to a (usually temporary) mismatch between the expectations of the school/class and the child's particular stage/interests. A great many more 'learning difficulties' reflect not intellectual or cognitive problems, but emotional or social ones which hamper the learning process. A child who is unhappy, anxious or depressed cannot learn easily or with pleasure, whether the cause of the upset is based within the school or at home. Sometimes apparently minor social problems have a disproportionate effect on a child's learning. A long journey to school (often associated with an inadequate breakfast before leaving home) has been shown to reduce a child's day-to-day performance and overall term grades (*see* **Eating**/ Commonsense about family eating). Door-to-door transport and a substantial morning snack at school produce major improvement under such circumstances. It has also been shown that a teacher whom the child really dislikes (usually because she 'makes him feel small' or 'doesn't like me whatever I do' or 'shouts and bangs about') is a sadly good predictor of learning difficulty for that child in that subject. In the early stages of school life such personal animosity between teacher and pupil can, in the course of a school year, convince the child that he is 'no good at maths' and the feeling – and consequent poor results – can be extremely hard for the next teacher to overturn.

It is important, for all these reasons, that all the adults concerned with an individual child should keep 'learning difficulties' separate in their minds from 'school difficulties'. To attach a learning-difficulty label to a child is to *convince him that he cannot be expected, or expect himself, to perform well in a particular subject or area*. Such a conviction can be a great relief to a child who has genuinely been struggling to learn to read and whose best efforts have only served to earn him the name 'Thicko'. But it can be exceedingly damaging to the child who simply does not like school/this school/this teacher, or who is not ready to read or willing to try.

Intelligence and learning difficulties

While nobody can doubt that general 'intelligence' goes with ability to learn, so that those of lower intelligence will find learning more difficult, research suggests that we are far too ready to ascribe early difficulties in school to tested IQ levels. In Britain, for example, a child whose tested IQ is found to be below eighty-five may well be considered more suitable for a special school than the community school, and one major reason is that he is thought likely to have difficulty in learning to read and write. In fact becoming literate does not require above-normal or even normal intelligence. Given the normal opportunities, that child will probably read and write just as early and as well as peers with higher IQs. *What* he writes, later on, is more likely to be affected by his lower intellectual capacity than the sheer ability to do so. Sadly, 'special schools' are often used as rag-bags for the many children who for countless different reasons do not 'fit' ordinary school provision. No parent should readily accept that such a school will offer the child 'the special help he needs' unless satisfied both that special help *is* needed and that the school will demonstrably provide it (*see* **School**/Children with special needs).

Specific learning difficulties

Just as hot debate rages not only about the nature but also about the very existence of the hyperkinetic syndrome (*see* **Hyperactive Children**) so there is ongoing debate about the nature and existence of specific learning difficulties.

Nobody doubts that some children find some kinds of learning more difficult than other kinds. Every family knows that a child may struggle with foreign languages but flourish in the science laboratories; fear and hate mathematics but excel in literary subjects. But skill in a *subject* is the end-product of the complex processes, the mental skills, required to handle it. The debate is about whether or not there are specific neurological variations or abnormalities which handicap affected individuals in acquiring those mental skills.

The brain is enormously complex; so complex that we are only just beginning to identify the structural areas which are responsible for some different human functions. Although a little is known about the interlinking of various parts of the brain and central nervous system and its biochemical controls and feed-back mechanisms, we are a very long way away from a full understanding of 'how the brain works'. While it is reasonable to guess that a system so complicated might have parts which functioned better, or more smoothly, than other parts, and that people might vary in which functioned best, we are still a long way from being able to prove it. It can crudely be shown, for example, that an individual who has a certain part of his brain destroyed, by accident or surgery, loses certain functions, or that the individual, a part of whose brain is directly stimulated by electric current, will react in certain ways. But it cannot be shown that this individual's brain structure or biochemistry is better or worse for this, that or the other kind of mental activity.

Just as hyperkinesis or minimal brain dysfunction is deduced from behaviour (it must be there even though it cannot be demonstrated), so a neurological foundation for specific learning disabilities is deduced. A medical model for a child's learning difficulties has the same advantages and disadvantages as does the medical model in hyperactivity and needs treating with similar caution. At present, though, the medical model in learning seldom includes the prescription of drugs except where the learning disability appears alongside unacceptable behaviour and is therefore liable to be classified as part of MBD. It may, indeed, be through professionals working to a medical model that your child will receive highly skilled and specialized teaching rather than consignment to a special school or 'slow-learners class'.

Many different kinds of learning disability are postulated to account for a wide range of difficulties. The best known is usually referred to as dyslexia (congenital dyslexia; developmental dyslexia; 'word blindness') which can stand as an example.

Congenital dyslexia

Dyslexia is usually considered to be a congenital disturbance of brain function which gives rise to a variety of learning difficulties, especially relating to reading and spelling. It affects more boys than girls but numbers are not known as referral varies so widely from place to place. A family history of similar difficulties (or of poor literacy now) is common.

Recognizing dyslexia

A child is inappropriately described as dyslexic unless he is:

Of normal, or greater than average, intelligence. A child with a low IQ would be assumed to have a general, rather than a specific, learning disability.

Normally hearing and sighted. Auditory and visual handicaps would be thought to override, or certainly confuse, a diagnosis of dyslexia.

Not demonstrably brain damaged either congenitally or accidentally.

Appropriately educated throughout his life thus far, so that he has been offered the kind of care and stimulation as well as teaching which is normal for his age in his community.

Without a 'primary emotional disturbance'. This last is a tricky point because, as we shall see, many children who are diagnosed as dyslexic are certainly disturbed, but may have become so because of the distress associated with the learning disability. An attempt must be made, however, to be sure that the cause and effect is indeed in that direction.

Those negative points exclude the most usual non-dyslexic causes for serious difficulty in learning to read and write. The professional then looks for certain aspects of the difficulty and, if most of them are present, regards the diagnosis as confirmed:

He is having major difficulty with reading and writing at about the age of seven. This age is singled out because while almost every five- to six-year-old has difficulties, the majority of seven-year-olds are making steady and rapid progress. Professionals point out that learning to read is a comparatively easy skill which most children, even those of below average intelligence, readily acquire. It is when others are succeeding and the averagely or highly intelligent child is failing by comparison, that he should be noticed and watched with care.

He can probably read words with which he has been familiar for some time but cannot read even the simplest new word. If early teaching has been by the 'look and say' method, the child may have quite a lot of words he can 'read'. But he recognizes them by their whole shape and cannot generalize the rote-learning.

He cannot use individual letters as the building blocks of words. Extremely affected children may actually be unable to recognize or differentiate individual letters. Moderately affected children may recognize them individually but still be unable to put them together as words. This is why the dyslexic child who can read (by shape-recognition) the word 'man' and the word 'cat' may still be unable to read the new word 'mat'. Phonetic reading schemes teach children partly by means of the sounds individual letters make. But it is useless to say to the dyslexic child 'what does m say?' It says nothing at all to him.

Since the child cannot use individual letters as building blocks, he cannot spell either. How can he work out the letters which will make a word when to him the only comprehensible words are ones which, over and over again, he sees complete?

He may be able to write words he has learned by shape-recognition but as long as the overall shape looks right he will not know if he is wrong. Reversals of letters (mirror writing) and reversal of letter-order are therefore common. If he is asked to write down a word which he has not learned to recognize by shape, he may have literally no idea how to proceed. Hearing the word does not help him translate it into letters on a page, nor does he have clues such as the number of letter sounds in the word the teacher dictates. His attempts at 'taking dictation' may therefore be extremely wild.

His actual letter-formation, even when copying, is usually very poor. Since the individual letters are meaningless to him they have no integrity of shape and he cannot therefore learn to 'make a nice m'. If he is making any kind of m it will be as part of an attempt to 'draw' the shape of a whole word or to copy something totally meaningless to him.

He is probably confused about 'right' and 'left'. Although all small children have to learn which is which, most children do so through their own growing awareness of their bodies. The child learns that this is one of her hands and that it is *called* Right and that everything to that side of something else is therefore right rather than left. The dyslexic child, with right–left disorientation, may be actually unable to distinguish his own right and left arms. Other signs of this disorientation include:

Difficulty in telling the time because he cannot tell whether clock-hands are pointing *to* or *past* the hour.

Difficulty with tying bows or any manual skill involving right-to-left.

Difficulty with arithmetic where, although most of us seldom give it much thought, right–left is vital. Multiplication, for example, becomes a nightmare if the numbers appear random.

He may have varying difficulties with other forms of symbolism. Plus, minus, multiply and divide signs are often confused as are the symbols for points of the compass.

He may be left-handed, mixed-handed or come from a mixed-handed family. This is by no means always the case so nobody should fear dyslexia just because a child happens to be left-handed, or be afraid of producing a dyslexic child because there is a mixture in the family. However, once dyslexia has been diagnosed, it is often found that this is a child or family in whom right–left dominance is not firmly established. The child himself, or other family members, may prefer the right hand for some activities, the left for others, or may prefer to kick a ball with the right foot even though he is left-handed.

Most people are firmly one-sided for all activities – having a complete preference for either the right or the left hand, eye, foot and so forth. It is thought that one hemisphere of the brain dominates the other to produce this effect. It is possible that the brains of mixed-handed individuals fail to develop in this one-sided way but instead develop both hemispheres equally. Instead of being an advantage, as commonsense might suggest, it is thought that this could lead to confusion between the functions of the two sides and therefore contribute to the symptoms of dyslexia.

Helping the dyslexic child

A fine line has to be drawn between over-readiness to diagnose an educational handicap of this kind and lateness in doing so. A child who has watched his peers easily acquire reading and writing skills which remain impossible for him, has experienced a gradual sinking of his position in class as they improved and he did not, who may even have been teased, scolded or patronized for his stupidity or punished for his refusal to try, will expérience tremendous relief once both he and the adults around him understand that there is a reason for his difficulties. On the other hand, a child who might have overcome mild difficulties for himself, or whose learning problems are due to emotional causes, may actually suffer loss of motivation and a distortion of his self-image if the 'dyslexic' label is attached to him. Although helping the dyslexic child is a professional matter, deciding how much emphasis should be put on his disability, and at what point in his development, is very much a job for parents.

Teaching approaches in dyslexia

The aim of any teaching programme for a dyslexic child (as for a child with any other kind of handicap) should be to try both to enable him to keep up, as far as possible, with the education of his peers *and* to help him to develop any special talents or skills which come easily to him so as to ensure that there are areas of his daily life in which he can have the satisfaction of shining.

Dyslexic children have to be helped to overcome the basic hurdle of becoming literate. In our society, people who cannot read and write are seriously disadvantaged, however intelligent they may be. It is thought that some of the thousands of illiterate and semi-illiterate adults in highly developed countries may in fact have been dyslexic children whom nobody recognized or helped.

Remedial teaching in reading and writing (and perhaps in arithmetic too) will certainly be needed, but the school's programme for slow-learners may not be helpful. The dyslexic child cannot learn to read and write by phonic methods, however slowly and individually these are taught. Instead, he has to learn by boring rote and prodigious feats of memory.

He has to learn the letters of the alphabet one by one by pure repetition.

He has to learn words by rote, too, being presented with very very simple groups of letters-which-make-words, again and again, until he knows that that is 'cat' and that is 'man', by memory, rather than by the mixture of memory-and-phonics which most children use.

This kind of learning has to be a 'drill', with constant testing of recent learning and practice of past learning, because the dyslexic child finds this kind of remembering desperately difficult. In this respect the old-fashioned term 'word blindness' is descriptive. Just learning the word 'cat' will not put 'cat' into his memory forever: it will only become imprinted if it is repeated endlessly.

Tricks have to be devised to tell him which is right and which is left. Reliable access to this information will help him to keep his learned letters in the right order, and the right way up, as well as helping him to decode the many other directional cues we all use. Sometimes a child has a mark (perhaps a scar or a mole) on one side of his body and not on the other and he can be taught that that mark is the right (or left) and therefore that the other side is the opposite. Often a more readily visible mark helps: some teachers put an indelible star on the right hand or ask parents to sew a thread to every right pocket, and so on.

● Don't be trapped by shoes or boots with 'Right' and 'Left' written on the toes. The dyslexic child will certainly put them on the wrong feet from time to time and confuse himself further. The mark that he uses must be *part of his body* so that it can serve to replace other children's consciousness of which is their own right hand or foot.

The child has to learn to write and to spell and this may present an even more difficult problem than reading. His letter-formation will be spidery and immature and he will probably never acquire an easy and personal handwriting. His spelling will be bizarre and he will always lack the 'knowledge of letters' which the rest of us use to work out how to spell a word which is unfamiliar or which we have forgotten. He will have to acquire a written vocabulary by rote/practice.

Most dyslexic children, given appropriate help early enough, can learn to read well enough to be 'literate', but writing is not only technically difficult for them but remains a poor method of communicating. However large his spoken vocabulary, however vivid his imagination and high his intelligence, the dyslexic child will never, even in adult life, do justice to himself on paper. So, while he must learn to write as well as he possibly can, other methods of verbal communication must also be opened up for him. Eventually he must be 'tested' and 'examined' by methods which give him a reasonable chance of doing himself justice.

He can learn, even at six or seven, to use a typewriter which will eventually relieve him of the necessity to go through the mechanics of handwriting. In some schools arrangements can be made for dyslexic people to take examinations using typewriters. It is not unrealistic to expect that word-processors will soon become available within schools: properly programmed, such an aid can correct the dyslexic's spelling, too.

He can learn to use a tape-recorder or dictating machine. Every dyslexic should have one of these and even the youngest should be allowed to speak their stories and essays onto them so that their ideas can flow freely. Some schools allow children to dictate their work if parents will then write it out. Others will accept a tape-cassette rather than an exercise book.

Help in dyslexia at, and from, home If a child has real problems of this kind and it is decided that he should understand as much as possible about the condition so as to realize that he is not stupid, compared with others, but faced with a much more difficult learning process, home support will be vital:

He is probably of normal or better than normal intelligence and must know it. Every effort must be made not to allow his handicap to make him feel stupid. He need not have 'happy birthday' written on his party-cake; menus can be read to him without comment; the whole family can leave taped messages for him and each other rather than writing notes . . . At the same time, this sort of tact needs to be balanced with encouragement in those areas where he can shine, whether these are drama, painting or sports, and by careful provision of information in non-written form, by television, and reading aloud, for example.

His basic learning cannot be a pleasure to him so motivation is vital. Even the most skilled of specialist teachers cannot make the drill of literacy truly interesting for the dyslexic child. It demands effort and concentration far beyond that which other children must give. A good relationship with that teacher is vital, but so is family support which honestly acknowledges the boredom.

He cannot compete with a normal class in reading and writing but needs normality where he is not handicapped and the stimulus of others where he is. This often means that he is best served by membership of an ordinary school class, supplemented by attendance at a special group. Although this may involve parents in a demanding schedule of driving him from place to place, and may even involve them in moving house so as to come within reach of specialists, it is worth it. Neither full-time membership of a generalized 'special school', nor membership of an ordinary school with individual help-sessions, will be as good.

If the handicap is marked, course and career choices may need steering. It is probably better that he should be steered towards a kind of education and job which he will be able to fulfil at his true intellectual level, than that he should choose as others do, but condemn himself to remaining always at a level below his true capability. Parents need to seek not only career advice but advice directly from examination boards and training establishments as to what allowances/special arrangements they may be prepared to make. One such child, for example, has made an excellent career in forestry. The authorities felt that the job would be suitable and were prepared to give every assistance to him in getting over the preliminary examination hurdles. Another fought his way into the Civil Service but, good though he is at his present lowly job, finds himself barred from promotion by examinations. The important point is that, in many jobs, it is the *getting there* which presents the worst problems. Once he can achieve a certain status and seniority, the affected individual can use a dictating-machine/secretary and be scarcely affected by his handicap.

Leaving home *see* **Adolescence**/The long road to independence.

Lice

Lice are insects, about 2 mm long, which feed on blood and lay their eggs (nits) on hairs. The nits are tiny white cigar-shaped objects and each one is firmly glued to an individual hair. They hatch in two to three weeks. The bites of the adult lice cause itching so your first clue to infestation in your child may be continual scratching of her head.

Infestation is becoming increasingly common amongst schoolchildren and, whilst some people believe that adult lice are more likely to move onto dirty greasy hair than onto freshly shampooed hair, it is simply not true that 'only dirty neglected children get lice'. Any child who plays and rough-houses with lots of others and/or uses their hairbrushes, can find herself playing hostess. If you examine her hair (as the school nurse will probably do once or twice each term) and see either dark coloured moving creatures on her scalp, or the little nits on the hair shafts, try not to react with horror or you will horrify her too.

Getting rid of head lice
Some of the old standard treatments for head lice are becoming ineffective because the lice are resistant to them. Your child's school, health visitor or local pharmacist will advise you as to which chemical is currently being used in your district. It will probably be a lotion containing the chemical malathion.

● Follow instructions very carefully and keep this poison locked away.

The usual treatment is to comb the lotion carefully all through the child's hair, making sure that the whole scalp is covered and using a special 'nit comb' (which has very fine teeth) to dislodge as many nits as possible. The lotion is left on overnight, shampooed out in the morning and the treatment repeated (in case a few nits have survived) a week later.

It is sensible to check the heads of all other family members, especially other children. You should also wash all brushes and combs – dipping them in the lotion if you wish – and you may like to launder the affected child's pillowcases and so forth.

● There is no point in disinfecting the entire house: lice cannot live without blood nor will they lay eggs where there are no hairs. So only objects on which there may be hairs need concern you.

● Since nits are laid close to the scalp and hairs grow about 15 cm per year, you can work out how long your child has been infested. If there are nits even one centimetre up the hair shafts, she must have been harbouring them for nearly a month.

Life-saving *see* **Accidents; Safety.**
Long-sight *see* **Eyes and Seeing; Eye Disorders and Blindness**/Faults in vision.
Lost child *see* **Safety**/From 'strangers'.
Lumbar puncture *see* **Hospital**/Procedures. *See also* **Meningitis and Encephalitis.**
Lungs and lung disorders *see* **Chest Infections.**
Lying *see* **Discipline, Self-discipline and Learning How to Behave.**
Masturbation *see* **Habits.** *See also* **Adolescence**/Sex.

Measles

Unlike some other 'infectious diseases of childhood' measles is an acute and exceedingly unpleasant illness. In the western world the infection, with its complications, still causes several hundred deaths each year. In the less-developed world it is responsible for as many as half of all childhood deaths from infection.

Measles is a virus infection. Although it is always present in the community, it tends to flare up into epidemics in alternate years.

Babies are born with some passive immunity from their mothers to this as to other common viruses. Immunization against the disease cannot be effective if it is given while passive immunity still exists, but if immunization is delayed for too long the baby will be at risk of catching the disease at just the age-stage when it is most likely to affect him severely.

Immunization against measles The exact timing of immunization must be discussed with your doctor or the staff of your health clinic. Discussion should take account of the following points:

It is usual to defer immunization at least until the end of the first year both to ensure that passive immunity no longer exists and to protect young babies against the possibility of side-effects (*see below*). But if an epidemic is brewing in the neighbourhood your doctor may advise protecting the child sooner.

Your doctor may prefer not to immunize a child who has suffered any central nervous system infection (such as meningitis) or one who is liable to febrile convulsions. But if your doctor does decide to leave your child un-immunized, it may be because he is relying on a high level of immunity within the neighbourhood to make it unlikely that he will meet the disease. If an epidemic occurs, or if the child actually has contact with a measles-sufferer, check with the doctor again. He might wish to reconsider.

Immunization can sometimes produce worthwhile levels of antibody even in a child who is already incubating the disease. A doctor will therefore sometimes carry out a crisis-immunization to try to protect the youngest member of a measles-ridden family.

Measles vaccine is cultured in an egg-medium and therefore must not be given to a child who is allergic to eggs. It is important to mention any such allergy to any doctor who is considering immunizing your child. If a child who cannot be protected for this reason has contact with the disease, your doctor may wish to give him an injection of gamma globulin (*see* **Infection**/Treatment of infections which cause illness: Anti-viral drugs) in the hope of reducing its severity.

Measles vaccine contains live (though attenuated) measles virus and therefore causes a very mild version of the disease in some children. About thirty per cent will be feverish after a week to ten days; some of those will also develop a measles-like rash. About one child in every one thousand immunized may have a convulsion as a result of this fever but since about seven in every one thousand children who have real measles have a convulsion, immunization is still a good swap for the disease (*see* **Convulsions, 'Fits' and 'Funny Turns'**).

Having measles   **Incubation period.** Ten to fourteen days.

Route of infection. Droplet infection from nose and throat to nose and throat.

First symptoms of measles   Look like a bad cold, usually with slight to moderate fever, a cough and often with puffy, reddened and watery eyes. Unlike a normal cold, the illness worsens over the first one to three days. Inside the mouth the mucous membranes are inflamed and 'Koplik's spots' may be seen, especially inside the cheeks at about the level of the molars. These spots (for which a doctor will search as they are diagnostic of an early case of measles) look like little white grains of rice, standing out against a red background.

Acute stage of measles   Around the third day the child may become irritable and unusually sensitive to bright light and to loud noises. He seems much iller and his fever suddenly runs very high – often to around 104°F (40°C). It is at this stage that the child who is liable to react to high fever with convulsions is liable to have one. Convulsions, however, are not a special feature of measles but only of the high fever which this disease has in common with many others (*see* **Nursing**/Fever).

Soon after the fever reaches its height, the typical rash begins to appear, starting behind the ears and along the hairline and working down the body. The individual 'spots' are quite small, red and scarcely raised. However, so many 'spots' characteristically appear that they may join up to produce dusky red 'blotches'. The rash is not itchy.

By the time the rash has spread to the chest, the worst (barring complications) of the illness is over. By the time the rash has reached the legs and feet the fever will probably be dropping. Once the rash has finished appearing the child can be expected to be recovered within a day or two. In an uncomplicated case the whole acute stage seldom lasts for more than a week, with the child at his illest in the middle of it.

Treatment of measles   Although measles is a virus infection, the damage to the respiratory tract lays the victim open to secondary infection by pathogenic bacteria sometimes resulting, for example, in complications such as bronchopneumonia, middle-ear infection or infection of the inflamed eyes (conjunctivitis). Occasionally a doctor may give antibiotics from an early stage to prevent these possibilities. If he does not, he will certainly keep a careful eye on the child in order to start such treatment at the first signs of such secondary infection. He may advise you to sponge the eyes and mouth with prescribed antiseptics.

● The child will probably feel extremely miserable and ill and will require careful symptomatic nursing (*see* **Nursing**). You should also keep a watchful eye, especially in the very young child, for two rare but potentially serious complications.

Post-infectious encephalo-myelitis   Very occasionally, measles infection can cause inflammation within the central nervous system which will usually first show itself either in extreme drowsiness or coma, or in convulsions after the initial high fever has begun to drop. Although any very feverish child may have periods when he is delirious, hard to awaken and/or juddery and shaky when woken, you are certainly entitled to a doctor's help in distinguishing such fever-reactions from early signs of this complication.

Inflammation of the vocal cords   Swelling of this area of the throat can occasionally occur and lead to partial obstruction of the breathing, with harsh crowing sounds as the child breathes out and obvious effort (including a sucking in of the ribcage) as he breathes in. If the child appears to be having any difficulty with his breathing, send for medical help.

Convalescence from measles   Unless there have been complications, measles may be over in a week and the child completely recovered within a day or two more.

Meatal ulcers *see* **Circumcision**.

Medical Specialities

Your family's doctor   Few people think of their family doctor or general practitioner as a specialist in medicine but, while he is not a consultant with a team of less senior doctors working under him in a hospital, a specialist he certainly is and invariably the most important one to any family. Don't make the mistake of thinking of him as less well-qualified than those who undertook special training in the specialities described below; he undertook special training too, but training in how to cope with people of all ages and all their ills rather than with particular groups of people or ailments.

Different family doctors choose to practise in different settings and different ways. Yours may work with only a receptionist to help him or as part of a big health centre which is almost like a mini-day-hospital. He may pride himself on being personally accessible to you at almost any time or he may rely heavily on appointment, rota and relief-systems. Like any other professional he is bound to enjoy certain aspects of his work more than other aspects and this may affect the services he offers. In Britain, for example, he may or may not undertake ante-natal care and operate his own well-baby clinic. All British family doctors (unlike those in other parts of the western world) make at least some home visits to patients, but even in Britain the readiness with which a doctor will come to your child, rather than always asking you to take her to him, will depend largely on his own attitudes. He may feel that the personal contact and view of his patients' backgrounds which such visits give him are worth their enormous drain on his time and energy. But he may feel that they take so much time from other patients that they should be kept to an absolute minimum.

However healthy your family, a doctor whom you (all) like, trust and feel easy with, is absolutely essential. It is he on whom you will rely in those occasional but terrifying crises – like a first febrile convulsion (*see* **Convulsions, 'Fits' and 'Funny Turns'**). It is to him that you will take those embarrassingly vague questions like: 'She doesn't seem quite herself . . . nothing special really, but I'm not happy about her . . . am I being silly?' And you will have to rely on him not to be irritated when two children manage, between them, to produce symptoms needing medical advice eight times in six weeks . . .

If you have a child who is, for the moment and in some respects, less than healthy, your family doctor will be even more important to you, however grand the hospital specialist who oversees her case. A child with severe asthma (*see* **Allergy**/Asthma) for example, will certainly be 'under the hospital' but her day-to-day care and the implementation of any special treatment recommended will be between you and that doctor.

Should any of you ever develop a mysterious and/or serious condition, it is your family doctor who will diagnose it, or at least recognize the difficulty of diagnosis and steer you in the right direction for specialist help. He knows a very great deal, but not the least important thing he knows is who *will* know when he does not.

Although you cannot, so to speak, go shopping for the right doctor, you do have some choice, at least in the sense of being entitled to change doctors if you are not happy with the one with whom you are registered. Do remember, though, that most family doctors feel that they can do their best work with families whom they get to know well, and with children whom they have seen through infancy and the infectious diseases of childhood before they are faced with worries about puberty or with adolescent depression. Try to see your relationship with him as two-way because how well he can fill his role as your family doctor depends at least as much on you as on him. Perhaps he 'won't explain', but perhaps you did not ask him or only thought afterwards of the questions you wanted answered and were then too shy to telephone and say so? Perhaps he 'won't come when he's asked' but perhaps your requests are not always reasonable. Parents have been known to summon doctors to sick children at 2 a.m. only to refuse to go out for prescribed drugs because 'It's too late tonight, I'll get them in the morning . . .' Most of the common dissatisfactions between doctors and parents can be sorted out by sensible communication (*see* **Nursing**/Contact with the doctor).

Your child may be referred by your doctor to a consultant or to a specialist hospital clinic which will be under the overall charge of a consultant. Occasionally you may want to ask for consultation with a specialist. The names and functions of different specialities can be somewhat confusing so the following notes on those you might meet may help:

Audiologist (audiology)

A specialist in the diagnosis and management of every type and degree of deafness (*see* **Ears and Hearing; Ear Disorders and Deafness**). *See also* ENT surgeon (*below*).

Dermatologist (dermatology)

Specialist in skin diseases and disorders. A dermatologist might help your doctor to manage a child with acute infantile eczema (*see* **Allergy/Eczema**).

ENT surgeon (otolaryngologist: specialist in otolaryngology)

Specialist in ear, nose and throat disorders: this will be the speciality to which your child will be referred if there is any question of tonsillectomy, adenoidectomy, or surgery to relieve deafness caused by infection (*see* **Hospital**/Surgery: Myringotomy).

If a child is partly, or wholly deaf, his *medical* condition and needs will be the province of this speciality, but any remaining hearing difficulty will be dealt with under the supervision of an audiologist who will be responsible, for example, for prescribing hearing aids and arranging for speech training.

Gynaecologist (gynaecology)

Specialist in female health and illness, especially concerned with the genital organs and reproductive tract.

It is to this speciality that your daughter might be referred for advice concerning delayed menarche or menstrual problems (*see* **Adolescence/Menstruation**).

Neurologist (neurology)

Specialist in diseases/disorders/dysfunctions of the brain and nervous system.

Your child might be referred to a neurologist following a head injury (*see* **Accidents**/Head injury); for assessment of the significance of convulsions (*see* **Convulsions, 'Fits' and 'Funny Turns'**) or if he developed any form of paralysis. Neurologists do not deal with 'nerves' in the sense of *nervousness*. This is the province of Psychiatry (*see below*).

Obstetrician (obstetrics)

Specialist in the management of childbirth. The role may overlap with that of the gynaecologist (*see above*).

Oculist

General term for a medical specialist in eye disorders. The term has an identical meaning to ophthalmologist (*see below*) which is the one which is more often used. Do not confuse oculist with optician (*see below*).

Oncologist (oncology)

A specialist in the study and treatment of tumours. Although this term is obviously associated with the treatment of cancer, benign tumours, 'lumps' and 'growths' of all kinds are also the province of this speciality. Referral to an oncology clinic is not, in itself, reason to assume that cancer is suspected.

Ophthalmologist/
ophthalmic
surgeon
(ophthalmology
'eye doctor';
'eye clinic'),

A medical doctor specializing in the prevention, diagnosis, treatment and cure of disorders of the eye. If a child is referred because of an injury to the eye or because, for example, of recurrent infection (*see* **Eyes and Seeing; Eye Disorders and Blindness**), he will be under the care of an ophthalmologist. If he has problems with vision, his overall *medical* care (including any possible surgery, as for a squint) will remain the ophthalmologist's responsibility, although in simple sight-problems such as short-sight, his *practical* management may be delegated to an optician (*see below*).

Optician
-(optics)

The word really means a designer/maker of optical instruments, especially spectacles.

An optician is not a medical doctor and cannot deal with, or prescribe for, eye injuries or disorders. With a bewildering variety of other qualifications, however, he may assume responsibility for prescribing and supplying a wide range of aids to vision. The important distinction between one type of optician and another is that:

A dispensing optician only makes spectacle lenses to the prescription of an ophthalmologist. He cannot test your child's sight and prescribe for him himself.

A 'sight testing' or 'ophthalmic' optician (also sometimes called an optometrist) can both test sight and prescribe for sight defects, as well as actually providing the spectacles. These specialists may also prescribe and supply contact lenses, and may prescribe and teach exercises to assist with certain vision problems such as squints.

● Many ophthalmic opticians or optometrists work in a commercial setting. While it is usually convenient to buy spectacles for a child in the same place where his need for them was established and the prescription given and made up, you do not have to do so. When you have a child's sight tested you are paying for a professional service. You have every right to purchase the spectacles elsewhere if you prefer.

Orthodontist
(orthodontics)

A dentist who specializes in preventing, or curing, crooked, overcrowded or otherwise misaligned teeth. If your child's teeth need attention of this kind, your own dentist may be qualified to carry out the work or may refer you to an orthodontist.

Orthopaedic
surgeon;
(fracture clinic)

Specializes in abnormalities of bones, joints and their associated muscles and ligaments. A *pediatric orthopaedic* surgeon or clinic will be one who further specializes in the orthopaedic problems of children which are different from those of adults because of continuing growth.

All fractures are dealt with by this speciality. Your child may also be referred to an orthopaedic surgeon following a sprain or sports injury (*see* **Accidents**).

Pediatrician
(pediatrics)

A doctor specializing in children's problems. Many pediatricians specialize further (*see above* Orthopaedic). Hence, the pediatrician who supervises the care of a newborn baby will be specially trained in neo-natal medicine, while the psychiatrist (*see below*) who sees a troubled ten-year-old will be specially trained in child psychiatry.

Physiotherapist
(physiotherapy;
'physio' clinic)

A term used to cover a wide range of treatments – such as massage, heat, exercise and so forth – given to cure, or to prevent, an even wider range of illnesses and disabilities.

Physiotherapists are trained in the normal functioning of the body and in the ways in which it can be assisted in curing or strengthening itself or in overcoming and compensating for its weaknesses. The physiotherapist who makes your child do breathing exercises and tips him up while she taps his chest so that he coughs up secretions (*see* **Chest Infections**/ Physiotherapy) may be doing as much to help him over his chest infection as the doctors themselves. The one who shows another child how to exercise the muscles of a leg, wasted after weeks in plaster, is ensuring that the leg will quickly regain its normal strength and shape. The one who teaches you how to handle your asthmatic or spastic child is minimizing the risk of deformities developing because of her existing disability . . .

Almost all physiotherapy depends, however, on real patient-cooperation. What the physiotherapist herself does *to* your child during a session cannot be as valuable as what you and the child continue to do in between sessions. Hers is a vital role, but if you do not take her advice seriously and work according to her recommendations, her skills cannot work for you as they should.

Psychiatrist
(psychiatry;
psychiatric
hospital or
clinic)

A medical doctor who specializes in the prevention, diagnosis and treatment of emotional and mental disorder.

Psychiatry is the medical branch of psychology (*see below*). Where the psychological *treatment of patients* is undertaken, the psychiatrist will normally be the senior consultant with overall responsibility for those patients.

● Referral to a psychiatrist does not mean that a person is 'mad' or 'crazy'. The fully-fledged mental disorders to which these slang terms refer (such as schizophrenia and other psychoses) form only a small part of the psychiatrist's work and occupy only a small number of beds in psychiatric hospitals and units. The larger part of psychiatric resources are devoted to the emotional upsets and neuroses to which every human being is subject (*see* **Anxiety, Fears and Phobias** and **Depression**, for examples).

Psychoanalyst
(psycho-
analysis)

Psychoanalysis stems from the pioneering work of Freud, but psycho-analytic theory and practice have developed and diversified so that one analyst may differ widely from another, both in his ideas and in his ways of working with patients. In general, though, psychoanalysis may be regarded as a process of assisted self-discovery. The patient may not be 'ill' in the medical sense but will be unhappy about himself, dissatisfied with his own life and relationships and generally unable to be the person he feels he would like/ought to be.

Psychoanalysts believe that the roots of present emotional difficulties lie in unconscious conflicts. The patient can see the tangled vines which are dogging his every footstep but he cannot see their source and therefore cannot uproot them. Through one-to-one work with the analyst (five times weekly in classical psychoanalysis but sometimes two or three times weekly in modern practice) these unconscious forces and motivations can be brought into conscious view where they can eventually be dealt with rationally; the individual's life and relationships need no longer be bedevilled by his personal past.

A psychoanalyst need not be a medical doctor but if he is not he will work in collaboration with one; usually with a psychiatrist. He himself must have undergone one of a very few, highly demanding, training courses.

Psychoanalysis is an extremely time-consuming and therefore expensive form of therapy. It is seldom available either under the British National Health Service or under health insurance schemes. Reduced fees are, however, sometimes available to individuals who seek help from recognized training institutes, where trainee-analysts work with them under the supervision of experienced therapists.

● In some communities it sometimes becomes fashionable to seek psychoanalytic treatment. It cannot be too strongly emphasized that such treatment is an enormous personal commitment which should never be entered into lightly.

It must also be emphasized that, while stringent professional rules govern the registration of psychoanalysts in Britain, this is not true of all countries. Be careful. This kind of 'treatment' given by an ill-qualified 'therapist' can be highly destructive.

Psychologist (psychology; psychological)   Psychology as a subject deals with the study of the mind and therefore of every aspect of human behaviour, emotion, thinking, learning, interacting. Some psychologists devote their professional lives to studying the structure and function of the brain and central nervous system. Others study whole populations of people, compiling, for example, the statistics from which we derive 'norms' for everything from 'intelligence' to voting behaviour. Some work with organizations and institutions ranging from advertising agencies to prisons. Others work directly with individual patients/clients in a wide range of counselling and helping roles. Your child will have considerable indirect contact with psychologists via, for example, the assessment tests which he does at school. He may have direct contact with a psychologist whenever he is thought to need help with emotional or learning difficulties or whenever you, his school and/or his doctor are trying to decide whether or not he does need help (*see*, for example, **Hyperactive Children**).

Psychotherapist (psychotherapy; psycho-therapeutic)   The concept of psychotherapy began with Freud (*see above* Psychoanalysis). Since then, the term has been extended and diffused so that it may be used to describe almost any attempt to alleviate emotional or mental disorder or maladjustment *through talking*. At one extreme, psychoanalysis itself is a form of psychotherapy, but at the other extreme a brief series of counselling appointments may be described in the same way.

Group therapy is the term used to describe a situation in which a carefully selected group of patients meets regularly, under the leadership of a psychiatrist or psychologist, to share, discuss and, hopefully, to illuminate, each other's problems. This method enables one trained professional to attend to several patients simultaneously, but the benefits of group membership are intended to be greater than mere economy.

Child psychotherapy ('play therapy') is the term often used to describe psychotherapy with children who are not sufficiently mature to use purely verbal help. The therapist obtains many clues to the child's thinking, and to his inner reality, both by watching his play and by playing with him in the roles which he assigns to her.

A psychotherapist need not be a medical doctor but should be trained in psychotherapeutic techniques. Some medical doctors, some psychiatrists and some psychologists undertake this further training. There are also a few (pitifully few) trained lay psychotherapists.

● Anyone can talk to a child about his feelings and his problems. In this basic sense you yourselves act as psychotherapists when you try to relieve particular anxieties or find the underlying reasons for particular behaviours. In this sense, also, many members of the helping professions, doctors, social workers, teachers, counsellors, may offer a child psychological support in the course of their contacts with him. Do remember, though, that psychotherapy in the professional sense is something different, and that the selection of a therapist is vitally important. If you are worried about your child, ignore advertisements by 'cowboy therapists' (no properly trained psychotherapist would ever advertise for business nor, given the present shortage, ever be tempted to do so). Seek such help only via your doctor, the child's school, a psychiatric training institute or an established youth guidance clinic or similar facility.

Medicines *see* **Infection**/Treatment of infections which cause illness; **Nursing**/Medicines; **Pain and Pain Control.** *See also* **Safety**/In the home.

Meningitis and Encephalitis

Meningitis refers to inflammation of the meninges: the membrane which encases the brain and spinal cord. Encephalitis refers to inflammation of the brain itself inside the meninges.

Although this kind of inflammation can be caused by accidental injury, the usual cause is infection. Bacteria, viruses or even fungi can multiply in, say, the throat or the intestine; reach the bloodstream and attack the nervous system by that route. Some 'germs' are more prone than others to behave in this way. The meningococcus, for example, seems to have a real affinity for the meninges from which it takes its name. It can cause actual epidemics of meningitis. Other bacteria are far less likely to attack the nervous system and, even where they cause meningitis in one patient, will usually only cause a simple throat or other 'ordinary' infection in anyone whom that patient infects. Most of the viruses which cause the infectious diseases of childhood *can* attack the nervous system but again, some do so more readily than others. The measles virus, for example, is a more frequent cause of meningitis than is the chickenpox virus, while mumps is more likely than german measles to lead to encephalitis.

Meningitis and encephalitis are scarey illnesses not only because they can threaten a child's life but also because they can leave a recovered child with a damaged brain or nervous system. Fortunately, the chances of your child ever contracting this kind of nervous system inflammation are very small and the chances of successful early treatment are very high.

Early treatment is vitally important so, far from trying to diagnose meningitis or encephalitis yourself, you should simply be quick to be suspicious and send for a doctor to check.

● If you ever do suspect that your child's symptoms might be those of nervous system inflammation, don't put off calling the doctor because it is 2 a.m. 'and I'm bound to be wrong . . .' The doctor himself will act on nothing more than his own suspicions: he will admit the child to hospital for tests unless he can be quite certain that there is no nervous system involvement in the illness.

Signs which MIGHT suggest meningitis/ encephalitis

Contrary to popular belief there are no absolutely certain signs and symptoms of these illnesses which are diagnostic of all types in all age groups. Any of the following might be reasonable cause for suspicion. The more of these signs and symptoms your child shows, the more suspicious you should be:

Fever with delirium, marked sleepiness or altered consciousness. Although fever can be very high in these illnesses, it need not be. Even a low fever affects consciousness, though, when the site of inflammation is the brain or nervous system. Meningitis or encephalitis is therefore more likely in a child whose temperature is only 100°F(38°C) but who is behaving as if it were 104°F(40°C), than it is in a child whose fever really is so high that delirium is to be expected.

Acute irritability in a baby or toddler who may seem positively maddened by anything and everything, and quite impossible to comfort, cheer or calm by any of your usual methods.

● In a young baby, apathetic withdrawal, such that he will not make eye-contact with you or join in any kind of social interaction, should arouse your suspicions. The apathy may alternate with irritable crying and the lack of response means that he is not comforted when you pick him up. If your baby suddenly seems *not to care* whether or not you are there and whether or not you are paying attention to him, don't assume that he has 'gone off you'; seek medical advice quickly.

Acute headache in an older child. This, the most famous of all symptoms of meningitis, is actually rather an unreliable one. The very young children who are most prone to the illness often do not appear to have headache with it at all or, if they do, they do not localize the pain but react instead with general irritability and misery. Older children, who certainly will have headache with meningitis, may, of course, have head-pain for many other reasons (*see* **Headaches**).

Neck-stiffness. This symptom is also famous but unreliable. A child whose spinal cord is inflamed will not be able to drop his chin comfortably onto his chest. His inability to do so is certainly one sign which will increase an examining doctor's suspicions. But *most* stiff necks are caused by muscular strains or by simple throat infections.

Dislike of light which may lead the child to cry and burrow under the bedding when you open the curtains, or to beg you to switch off the light beside the bed.

A convulsion (*see* **Convulsions, 'Fits' and 'Funny Turns'**). Any illness in which a child suddenly shoots a high fever may lead to a febrile convulsion, but these nervous system infections may lead to convulsions even when fever is not very high, or when the victim is past the age for ordinary febrile convulsions.

Treatment of
meningitis/
encephalitis

If your doctor suspects meningitis or encephalitis he will immediately have the child admitted to hospital.

A spinal tap (*see* **Hospital**/Procedures: Lumbar puncture) will probably be done at once. The pressure of the spinal fluid will be tested; it will be inspected for unusual cloudiness and a sample will be sent to the laboratory for microscopic examination and culture. The doctor who carries out the test may be able to tell you immediately whether or not any central nervous system infection is *likely*, but there may be a wait for laboratory results before you can know the exact situation.

If the child does have either meningitis or encephalitis but no bacteria are found in the spinal fluid or blood, it will be assumed to be caused by a virus and no definitive drug treatment will be possible. But be comforted. Viral versions of these illnesses are far less dangerous than bacterial ones.

If there is bacterial meningitis or encephalitis, treatment will probably be by antibiotics given into a vein for maximum and most rapid effect. The child may be nursed in isolation (where you should be encouraged to stay with him). Energetic attempts to get his fever down may include packing him in ice and/or using an electric fan on bare skin. Drugs will also be given for acute headache or to sedate him if he is very confused and afraid.

● Try not to be too alarmed by all this. Your child may be more or less unconscious (due to illness and drugs) for a day or two; he may obviously be dangerously ill yet *still* will almost certainly recover fully. As he begins to get better, don't allow the fact that he is weak and babyish to convince you that his brain is damaged. It takes time for both muscles and spirits to recover from this sort of illness. Consult the doctor in charge of him: he has seen many children recovering from nervous system illnesses and will probably know, even before formal tests are carried out, whether yours is, or is not, one of the few who is permanently damaged.

● A small child, even once he has fully recovered physically, may be extremely disturbed and clingy after this sort of illness. Try to arrange for him to have plenty of your time and attention for the first weeks at home.

Menstruation *see* **Adolescence**.

Migraine *see also* **Headaches**; **Abdominal Pain**/Recurrent abdominal pain

There are many types and degrees of migraine and many suggested causes and methods of relief. This is probably because migraine is not a single disorder but a more generalized tendency to periodic headaches with other associated symptoms.

The following is a brief description of a 'classic' migraine, together with the most commonly accepted explanations for it. Do realize, though, that while one person may lose two working days a fortnight with attacks of this kind throughout youth and middle age, another can have occasional attacks which are much milder and over within a few hours, while yet another may be somewhat prone to ordinary headaches yet experience only two or three full-blown migraine attacks in a lifetime.

Migraine sufferers
Include equal numbers of boys and girls and more usually those with a family history of similar attacks. Some children who are going to be subject to migraine suffer from recurrent abdominal pain or periodic vomiting during early or middle childhood.

Migraine can begin during infancy (although it is seldom recognized as such). Typically it begins during pre-adolescence; may peak during the adolescent years; settle to a pattern during young adulthood and gradually subside with increasing age.

The beginning of a 'classic' migraine
Migraine often begins with a short-lived phase known as the 'aura'. This is a varying sensory disturbance during which the victim may see zig-zag lines or flashes of light or lines of black dots across his visual field; may feel giddy and generally 'peculiar' and may smell 'phantom odours' or hear peculiar noises.

The migraine headache typically comes on after the aura is established and, once the pain begins, the aura gives way to nausea. There may or may not be vomiting.

The 'classic migraine pain' is one-sided and to the front of the head; it is a throbbing pain and may be very acute. It is usually relieved a little by lying down and, intense though it is, does not usually prevent sleep. Indeed many migraine victims quickly learn that to go to sleep is the best way to survive an attack as well as offering the best chance of a quick ending to it.

Duration of a migraine
Some children can sleep off even a bad attack in a few hours, emerging completely recovered. Others can rid themselves of the acute pain yet remain pale and unwell for hours more. Yet others have attacks lasting as long as twenty-four hours.

Precipitating factors in migraine
The most usual explanation is stress, but while most migraine attacks do occur when the victim has been under stress, the same people survive apparently equal amounts of stress on other occasions without having migraine. Many people believe that particular foods (such as wheat, chocolate, milk and alcohol) are associated with migraine (*see* **Allergy**/Gastro-intestinal allergies) while others blame noise, climatic conditions and a wide range of other factors.

Possible physical basis for migraine

It is thought that the 'aura' may be caused by abnormal constriction of arteries within the brain, causing lack of oxygen to the particular parts affected. The pain is thought to be due to dilatation of arteries in the scalp (and perhaps within the skull, too); some people believe that this extra pressure from the blood vessels stimulates pain fibres in the artery walls themselves.

Coping with migraine

Migraine tends to run in families and the lives of some adult sufferers are dominated by the affliction. When the child of such a family first shows signs of migraine, everyone naturally assumes that he too must face the worst that they face, both in terms of the frequency of attacks and of their severity. Difficult as it is to avoid it, it is vitally important not to jump to this conclusion. If you do, the child will come to see himself as a 'sufferer'; come to expect two days off school with every headache just as you have to take two days off work; come to see himself as different from his fellows. Attitudes and expectations affect pain (*see* **Pain and Pain Control**) and tension especially affects the severity of headaches. It is easy to create a situation in which migraine is a more severe problem than it need have been. If yours is a migrainous family, or if your child produces a definite first migraine, remember:

Although migraine runs in families not by any means every member suffers from it. Migraine is certainly not something to expect, look out for, or even mention as a possibility to a child.

Not every headache is a migraine. The child of migrainous parents is just as liable to 'ordinary' kinds of headache as any other child.

One full-blown migraine need not predict frequent attacks. Even a headache-prone child or adolescent may only very occasionally (perhaps only once or twice in a lifetime) have another classic migraine. Many migraine sufferers have attacks only a couple of times a year.

Migraine, even if frequent, need not be disabling. By no means every sufferer follows the 'classic' pattern (*see above*). Many, for example, never experience any 'aura' but simply start their attacks with headache, while a few sometimes experience the aura without any head-pain. Many others never vomit during their migraines and quite a few do not usually even feel sick. While most will feel a need to lie down and sleep during an attack, a great many can be rid of the episode after a two-hour nap.

Seeking medical advice for migraine

If a child has two or three really bad headaches which make him seem unwell, prevent him from getting on with life and probably only resolve completely when he has slept, you may want to consider getting a doctor's advice. In the case of a pre-adolescent, it may be better to have a preliminary talk with the doctor on your own so that the child does not hear you 'making too much of' his headaches. Eventually, the doctor will probably want to see the child to exclude the rare physical causes of acute headache (*see* **Headaches**). Once he has convinced himself, you and the child that he does not have a brain tumour/need spectacles, his attention will probably turn to methods of preventing the migraines and/or hastening the end of attacks.

Allergy is a possible cause of migraine and some doctors pursue this line energetically, especially if the child and/or his family have known allergic tendencies. Unfortunately, discovering the allergic trigger for migraine attacks can be a long process because the attacks themselves are so infrequent. If milk, for example, is eliminated, on a trial basis, from the child's diet, it may be many months before you can be certain that the diet has lessened the frequency of his migraine.

Stress can be either a cause or an exacerbation of migraine and some doctors take extremely detailed histories of recent attacks in order to try and identify particular stress factors. Migraine which begins, or becomes much worse, when the victim is in the twelve-to-fourteen age bracket, for example, is sometimes related to tensions over puberty; to hormonal changes associated with menstruation (*see* **Adolescence**/Puberty) and/or to stress associated with promotion to secondary school or the start of public examination courses.

When frequent migraines are ruining a child's life, preventative medication can help although nobody should embark on it lightly as side-effects are quite frequent. If it is thought necessary, your doctor may refer the child to a special migraine clinic where doctors, with many years' experience of the condition and the drugs, are ideally placed both to prescribe for him and to monitor his response.

Medication during attacks can certainly shorten them. 'Ordinary painkillers' (*see* **Pain and Pain Control**) are often ineffective and are sometimes vomited. Your child may need a painkiller given with an anti-vomiting drug. He may also benefit from medication which acts on the constricted or dilated arteries (*see above*).

● Once you have any suspicion that a child is suffering from migraines, don't just dose him each time with larger and larger doses of whatever painkillers you have in the house. Prescribing for migraine is a specialized business.

Early treatment means shorter attacks. Once it is clear that migraine attacks are to be a regular, even if occasional, part of your child's life, he needs to be helped to learn to react quickly and effectively to them. If they lift when he lies down and goes to sleep, he should not struggle to complete the school day. Four hours' courage may turn what would have been a half-day's migraine into a much longer one. If prescribed drugs abort the attacks, he should learn always to carry a small quantity when he is away from home so that he can take them at the first sign.

● If a child starts to have migraine when he is very young, you and his teachers will, of course, have to manage them for him. But however young he is, he should learn to take charge of his migraine for himself at the first possible moment. If he feels confident that he can cope independently whenever a migraine strikes him, he will not feel unable to go to camp or stay over with friends just in case . . .

Mouth Ulcers *see also* **Cold Sores**

Although a crop of painful ulcers inside the lips or cheeks of a small child can be due to infection by the herpes simplex virus and therefore suggest that he or she may be prone to later cold sores, most mouth ulcers occur singly and for reasons which we do not understand.

The ulcer may be inside the cheek, inside the lip or on the gum. Wherever it is there will be an inflamed red area with a shallow, yellowish-white ulcer in the centre. It will be exceedingly painful.

Mouth ulcers clear up of their own accord in about a week to ten days but, in the meantime, they may make your child's life a misery. Food creates painful friction; fruit drinks sting; and, if the ulcer is in a place where it is constantly rubbed by the tongue or against the teeth, she may be conscious of the pain almost all the time.

You may be able to help a little by applying vaseline to the area so as to reduce that painful friction. Your doctor may be able to help much more if he considers it appropriate to treat the ulcer with a cortisone ointment.

If your child is one of the unfortunates who gets these ulcers frequently, do mention them to your dentist as they are sometimes provoked by dental troubles. Otherwise there is little you can do except to assure her that, while many children never suffer from this kind of ulcer at all, even those who do so frequently usually seem to 'grow out of' the tendency. Even if she has had several this year, she may never have one again.

Mumps

Mumps is a moderately infectious virus disease. It varies widely in its severity and effects. Most known cases are mild but unpleasant illnesses in older children and young adults. A few cases, especially in males past puberty, suffer serious complications (*see below* Possible complications in mumps). A larger group than both these put together consists of children who are infected so mildly that they acquire mumps antibodies without ever being clinically ill.

A safe and effective vaccine against mumps does exist, although it is too recent for anyone yet to be sure whether its protection is lifelong. The use of this vaccine varies widely from country to country. It is males past puberty for whom protection is most important yet, by this age, most boys will already be immune to the disease either because they have suffered the illness or because they have been sub-clinically infected. A public health programme to test boys for antibodies when they entered their teens, and to immunize those few who had none, would be extremely expensive, yet a programme to immunize all such boys except those known to have had the full-blown illness involves many unnecessary injections. It may be that mumps will eventually be included among the routine immunizations offered in early childhood. In the meantime, it is comforting to realize that even if you do not think anyone in your family has ever had mumps, they may well be among the many who are immune following sub-clinical infection; even if they are not, the chances of them 'catching' mumps during an epidemic is far less than the chance of them 'catching' other epidemic illnesses such as measles or chickenpox.

Having mumps
Incubation period. Two to three weeks

Route of infection. First droplet infection from nose and throat to nose and throat but the virus is then carried in the bloodstream to produce a generalized infection which may affect various organs and be passed on by various routes.

First symptoms of mumps
Older children and adults may feel generally unwell, with slight fever, headache and stiff neck. Younger children often miss out this stage.

Acute stage of mumps
The virus tends to settle in the salivary glands, especially the parotid gland which is located in *front* of the ear. The typical swelling of mumps – often the first sign of the disease in children – runs from in front of and below the ear down to the jaw line. Swelling may extend in both directions so that the child's face is misshapen from temple to neck. Usually the first swelling is one-sided. Often the other side will swell in its turn, sometimes several days after the first.

The swelling makes eating and talking painful and the affected salivary glands cease to function properly so that the mouth tends to be very dry.

A mild case of mumps
A child with mumps may not feel ill at all, although her swollen and painful face and neck will probably bother her. Eating is virtually impossible and good nursing therefore involves offering plenty of drinks, perhaps including milkshakes and other nourishing liquids. A straw makes these easier to take.

The swelling will probably go down in three to seven days, depending whether both sides are affected together or in sequence, or whether only one side ever swells.

● *Avoid acid drinks.* Many children remember for the rest of their lives the blackcurrant juice or lemonade offered them when they had mumps. Such drinks will stimulate the inflamed salivary glands and will cause extreme pain.

● *Avoid mockery.* Most affected children are of school age and can be really upset if their deformed faces cause rude mirth.

Possible Mumps is the infectious disease most likely to cause meningitis or
complications encephalitis (*see* **Meningitis and Encephalitis**). Some studies have sug-
of mumps gested that as many as ten per cent of children with mumps may have
central nervous system symptoms. Involvement of the central nervous
system can occur even before the diagnostic swelling, or it can occur later
in the illness. Any high fever, drowsiness, severe headache, vomiting
and/or delirium should be reported to your doctor. There are seldom any
lasting ill-effects.

In boys past puberty or in young men, inflammation of the testes
(orchitis) occurs in about twenty per cent of cases. Like the salivary gland,
the testis becomes inflamed, swollen and painful. Although extremely
unpleasant, orchitis very seldom affects fertility. Often the affected testis
recovers completely. Even if it does not, both testes are very seldom
involved.

Older girls and young women may suffer similar inflammation of the
ovaries (oophoritis) indicated by abdominal pain and tenderness. This is
seldom as troublesome as orchitis.

Inflammation of these kinds, caused by the mumps virus, usually
respond well to anti-inflammatory drugs. Contact your doctor immediately if a mumps patient complains of pain and tenderness other
than in his salivary glands.

Nail-biting *see* **Habits.**
'Nerves' *see* **Anxiety, Fears and Phobias; Depression.**
Nettlerash *see* **Allergy/Urticaria.**
New baby in the family *see* **Jealousy.**
Nightmares and night-terrors *see* **Sleep.**
Nits *see* **Lice.**

Nosebleeds

Nosebleeds are common and, in a child or young person, almost always
unimportant. Often the cause of the bleeding is unknown, but sometimes
it starts following nose-blowing or violent sneezing. Picking the nose is
more usually the result than the cause of a nosebleed. A child picks his
nose if there are uncomfortable traces of dried blood there.

Whatever causes the bleeding to begin, a nosebleed in a child or young
person almost always comes from a tiny vein in the nose.

First aid Sit the child up as soon as bleeding begins. This has the double effect of
for nosebleeds lowering the venous pressure (and thus making it more likely that the
bleeding will stop) and preventing her from swallowing the blood which
will probably make her feel sick. If she sits leaning over the washbasin, a
tap can be left running so that the blood is washed away as it drips; the
child need not therefore see what can seem an alarming quantity of gore.

Tell the child to breathe through her mouth and to avoid sniffing or
swallowing. The idea is to avoid disturbing any clot which may be
forming in the nose.

The bleeding may stop as abruptly as it began, in which case nothing further need be done except to watch and/or distract a younger child so that she does not disturb the coagulating blood in the nostril until the clot farther up has had time to become firm.

If the bleeding does not stop quickly, get the child to pinch her own nostrils firmly between thumb and finger, or, if she is too young or frightened to cooperate, do it for her. Keep pressing firmly for ten minutes.

If this does not stop the bleeding, or if it starts again, repinch the nostrils, but this time apply a very cold wet cloth or, better still, a couple of ice cubes well wrapped up, to the bridge of the nose.

Persistent nosebleeding

Very occasionally a nosebleed is so copious that a significant amount of blood can be lost in a short time. If such an outpouring continues, or re-starts after, say, fifteen minutes of the above measures, the child should be taken to the doctor or local hospital. More often, although still rarely, a gentler nosebleed continues despite first aid measures. This usually means that the affected vein is so placed that pinching the nostrils does not put effective pressure on it. A gentle dripping would take many hours to amount to dangerous blood loss, but it must nevertheless be stopped, for convenience as well as safety. Take the child to the doctor.

Repeated nosebleeds

If a child's nose bleeds frequently – perhaps weekly or more often over a period of months – the inconvenience will merit medical attention. The doctor will probably spray the inside of the nose with a chemical which both shrinks the mucosa to give him a better view and anaesthetizes it. He will then look for a weak spot in a nasal vein and, if he finds one, he will probably cauterize it. The doctor's task may be easier if the child is having, or has very recently had, a nosebleed when he is first consulted. Once you have decided that one more nosebleed will be one too many, visit the doctor as soon as it occurs.

Nose-blowing *see also* **Habits**/Nose-picking

Blowing his nose is a difficult technique for a small child to learn and one which will probably seem pointless to yours as he will have no objection to a runny nose, periodically wiped on the nearest sleeve. You will be doing well if your child can blow his own nose efficiently *and discreetly* by the time he goes to school.

You can teach him to blow his nose efficiently at an earlier age if you do not bother about discretion. Show him how to block one side of his nose with his finger and then to blow down the other. The results will not be any more revolting than a continually runny nose and, if other people are present, you can hold a tissue ready to wipe the immediate results. Once he has got the idea he will soon learn to muffle the whole performance in a tissue, by himself.

If you introduce the tissue too soon, the child will probably try to snort down both nostrils at once. Not only is this inefficient, it is also undesirable as mucus may be forced into the eustachian tubes and can cause middle-ear infection (*see* **Ears and Hearing; Ear Disorders and Deafness**).

Do accustom your children to paper handkerchiefs from the very beginning, and encourage them to throw away each one immediately after use rather than squirrelling them up a sleeve for another time. Linen or cotton handkerchiefs are extremely unhygienic (as well as horrible to launder). They must have been directly responsible for the spread of millions of colds.

Nursery schools *see* **School**/Pre-school and nursery education.

Nursing *see also* **Accidents**; individual conditions

Nursing your child at home

Most of the nursing you will do at home is more a matter of commonsense than of particular skills: it is ordinary child-care writ rather larger than usual. But there are times in the lives of most families when competence and confidence in nursing a child may make a big difference. For example, going to hospital is always upsetting for a baby or young child. The more confident you can become in nursing her through illnesses, the more likely it is that she will be able to stay at home. If the doctor can see that you are panic-stricken by her croup or her raging fever, he may send her to hospital as much for your sake as for hers; equally, if he is not at all sure that you are capable of taking her temperature accurately or getting the right amount of medicine down her, he may send her to hospital even though she does not really require *professional* nursing.

Almost all illnesses will get better (with or without medicine) without any special nursing, but your skill may sometimes speed up the recovery or at least make a relapse less likely. And it can almost always make being ill a less uncomfortable experience for your child.

Finally, while you may reject all the specific suggestions made here, preferring your own ways of doing things, working out how you *are* going to cope with your children when they are ill can make those deadly winters of recurrent 'bugs' much less unpleasant for you.

Basic needs of sick children
A sick child needs all the things a well one needs only she needs them adapted to her physical condition and brought into line with any instructions from the doctor. They are summarized here only because some of them are the subject of misleading myths.

Food: unless the doctor orders otherwise (for example, *see* **Diarrhoea, Gastro-enteritis and Food Poisoning**), the child can have anything she wants to eat and need have nothing that she does not want. All those sayings like 'feed a cold and starve a fever' are nonsense unless they happen to fit with the child's appetite.

Fluids are always more important than food and especially so if a child is vomiting and/or having diarrhoea and when she is feverish. She need not eat if she does not want to, but she must drink. If she will not, cannot, or drinks and then vomits, you need a doctor's advice.

● An almost weaned baby will often drink more if she is given her bottle instead of that cup. A bottle-fed baby who will not take her ordinary formula will often take plain water or diluted juice instead. Breast-fed babies seldom refuse to suck at all (two feeds refused is certainly reason to consult a doctor) but may take less than usual at each feed. It is sensible to offer the breast more often and to offer water or juice from a bottle in between.

Older children are often put off by a large glass of something boring. They drink three sips and then leave it to get warm and dusty by the bed. Gimmicks like a *tiny* glass, a curly straw or a jug out of which to help themselves, often help. So does ringing the changes between drinks, or indulging them with frozen juice cubes or pink (strawberry jam? cochineal?) milk.

Warmth: people often believe that sick children should be 'kept warm' but if your child has a fever (*see below*) this is not only nonsense but may be dangerous nonsense.

Sick children (especially babies) need to be able to use all their energy for fighting infection and getting well. So they need to be kept at a temperature which saves them having to use any energy for keeping warm *or* getting cool. That does not mean keeping them extra-warm but keeping them, as far as is reasonably possible, at a *steady* temperature. If your home is centrally heated, most rooms are probably within a few degrees of each other anyway. If your bathroom is icy you may want to let her wash at the kitchen sink. If she is in bed, the pyjamas that keep her comfortable when she is well will be right now, too. If she is up, ordinary indoor clothes will be fine. If she is in and out of bed she may need a compromise, like pyjamas with a light jersey and slipper-socks.

● Children with upper respiratory infections (colds, coughs, etc.) will be far more comfortable if you can keep rooms normally warm but airy and not too dry. Room-heater on and window open may seem extravagant of energy (and impossible if you have sealed windows and air-conditioning) but it is probably the ideal.

The question of staying in bed

Once upon a time anyone who was sick stayed in bed, often for days at a time. Then doctors realized that lying still can cause all kinds of problems, ranging from serious ones like thromboses in adults to loss of muscle tone in anyone. They also realized that children, bored with being in bed, often use more energy leaping about there than they use if they are allowed up. The pendulum of opinion swung so that now you will only very seldom be told to keep your child in bed. But not *having* to keep her there does not mean that she may not choose, and should not be allowed, to stay in bed. Older children (like adults) often retreat to bed as a comfortable and private place of safety when they are ill. Younger children may feel unwell enough to welcome having at least a version of bed available to them.

A baby's ideal version of bed is probably your arms. She will welcome as much cuddling and carrying and sitting on laps as you can offer. When she cannot be cuddled by you, she can *feel* cuddled if you bring her pram close to where you will be and settle her in that. She probably will not want to be put right away in her cot in her bedroom (but *see below* Handling and routines).

An older child's version of bed: If an older child stays in bed in her room, you will probably spend half the time running up and down stairs and she will spend the other half feeling bored and miserable. The answer is to provide her with some kind of nest in a central area. You may have an ideal sofa in your living-room, but a portable nest has advantages. A bean-bag chair with a couple of pillows may do for a toddler but for a bigger child a fold-up 'guest bed' is more comfortable. It can be erected anywhere you please and is just the right height for her to get in and out of freely. If she is ill enough to confine herself there, you can move bed and child to make a change of scene or to give her access to the television. If the weather is right she can even have it in the garden.

Handling and routines

Like the rest of us, children who feel unwell are usually irritable and easily frustrated. Being totally indulgent is not usually a solution. Having you at her beck and call and indulging her every whim will not actually make her feel any happier for more than a minute per treat and, by the end of a day or two, she will be bewildered by your unusual behaviour and you will probably be beginning to see her as a tyrant rather than a poor little girl. Total indulgence during illness is not good in the long run either. You do not really want her to grow up believing that whenever she can persuade you that she is ill, she can do exactly as she pleases and have your undivided attention.

Of course it is no good expecting a child's most reasonable and mature behaviour when she is ill because you will not get it. A happy medium between total indulgence and unrealistic expectations often means treating the child as if she were one stage younger than she really is. You will probably get it about right if you treat a primary school child as you did when she was at kindergarten; a pre-school child like a toddler; a toddler like a crawler and a crawler like a baby. A sick baby will simply need to drop her most independent veneer and have as much of you as you can offer her.

If you do agree with yourself to accept rather unusually 'babyish' behaviour during the illness, there will probably be some top-level demands which you will therefore want to drop until she is better. An eight-year-old might be let off the new effort of plaiting her own hair. A four-year-old might be given some help with her buttons. A two-year-old might be allowed to use fingers instead of a spoon while a one-year-old might get her bottle during the day instead of only at night. But having softened your demands in this sort of way, do ask for (or, better, behave as if you take for granted) ordinarily civil behaviour at this temporary new level. That eight-year-old gets her hair plaited for her, but that does not mean that she is not expected to be pleasant about it. That four-year-old gets her buttons done up but can still say 'thank you'. The toddler may use her fingers but you are still entitled to be cross if she deliberately chucks the food at you.

Expecting ordinarily civil behaviour will usually keep a child behaving (fairly) civilly. In the same way, keeping to at least a version of her ordinary daily routines will usually keep her feeling as normal as her illness allows. She can 'get up' in the morning even if it is only into fresh pyjamas. She can have meals at the ordinary times even if they consist only of soup or a juice which is different from the one she has been sipping all afternoon. She can be settled for her usual naps/bedtime even if she has been resting for most of the day. Routines of this kind provide punctuation marks in the child's day and may make it easier for you to get through the time, too.

Difficulty (or renewed difficulty) over going to bed is a common sequel to a small child's illness. Using a 'nest' or day-bed during the day (*see above*) helps to avoid this. If she has not been in her real bed and room during the daytime, going there at night provides a change of scene, a return to normality and a different kind of comfort (*see* **Sleep**/Varying sleep needs: Making bed a pleasant place).

Passing the time

Nothing is more boring than being a child who is ill unless it is being that bored child's mother. If the illness is brief – a very bad cold, for example – you can probably keep her happy and stay sane yourself if you resign yourself to a couple of days of reading aloud, board games or whatever the current passion may be. But if she is likely to be ill for much longer – with a bad bout of measles, for example – it is worth getting organized.

For your own sake, cancel any engagements/work plans that are coming up. The more it matters to you that she should be better enough to go to her minder/school by Wednesday week, the more the intervening days will drag. Try and arrange for somebody either to lay in food for easy meals or, even better, to keep her company while you get out and shop. Try also to think of some things to do which will amuse you (or at least give you a sense of accomplishment) and amuse her, too. She may enjoy you practising the guitar or Yoga, but she will not enjoy you reading or talking endlessly on the telephone. Some mothers re-stock freezers with home-made bread, turn out junk cupboards or re-decorate rooms while companioning sick children. If most of your usual adult company is at your work place, try and arrange a few visits from friends, too, so that you remember there is an adult world out there.

Apart from obvious occupations for your child, like being read to or watching television, some of the following may occupy her happily enough to give you some peace:

A 'being-ill' box   This is a Treasure Trove brought out whenever (but only when) the child is ill. She is allowed to know that it exists but she never knows (unless she is ill three times in as many weeks in which case she may catch you out) exactly what is in it. If you are clever, such a box can become appropriate when a child is around eighteen months and stay much-loved until she is old enough to occupy herself with a new library book. Obviously the box can contain anything you (or your child) like, but the basic idea is that it should contain a large number of items (so that just looking through it takes pleasant time) of sufficient variety that at least a few are likely to take her fancy at this particular moment. With a small child in particular, the items need not all be new – even to her – as forgotten objects, or seldom-seen old friends, will often give just as much pleasure.

Put in all the surplus objects your children acquire like the second and identical painting book one received at his birthday party or the packet of felt-tip pens this one was given when she was not yet interested in drawing.

Add all the fairground/lucky dip junk the family has acquired. 'Winning' that cardboard doll gave her pleasure at the time, but in the excitement of the moment it was probably scarcely looked at.

Save for the box any pretty things which come your way such as wrapping paper which could be cut up to be used in a scrap book; tinsel which could make collage or a head-dress; little boxes, jars and other attractive packagings. You can also save things which are particularly appropriate for your own child's interests: that Sunday supplement full of photographs of cars or horses, for example.

Spice the collection with small items which you buy whenever they catch your eye and/or you are feeling generous: new plasticine, pencils, gummed paper shapes, coloured drawing paper, miniature playing cards, etc. Each of these will be new to the child once, and still welcome on other occasions when there will be some other small item which is new.

If you want to make the box more elaborate, buy wholesale 'tiny toys'. If you look in a publication like *Exchange and Mart* you will find advertisements for, say, 'One hundred items suitable for boys and girls from two to seven'. They are intended for corner shops to sell as 'pocket-money toys' at a hefty mark-up, but if you buy the collection they work out at only a few pence each. The toys are mostly junk, of course, and they may not be safely suitable for the youngest children, but the novelty of, say, ten new things all at once is irresistible to a bored, miserable child.

Add any larger toys which your normally active child will not bother with. This, for example, may be the place for that construction set to which she has never settled because she is at a rushing-about-stage. If you leave it in her toy cupboard, familiarity will breed contempt and it will probably never be used; but put it in the being-ill box and it may transform a bad day or even a whole bout of tonsillitis.

Surprise her with any plaything she is not normally allowed. Some families, for example, will not permit battery-operated items in daily play because batteries are now so expensive. The price of a battery may be worthwhile when she is having 'flu. Others ban noisy toys like mouth-organs or drums, but will willingly pay the noise-price for the child's pleasure while she is ill.

If you are running a box like this, do try to remember to sort it out after each bout of illness because otherwise it will be an unattractive jumble next time it is wanted. Remember to keep it stocked, too, preferably by adding bits and pieces to it during the summer months when (hopefully) it is little used.

A 'being-ill friend'

This can be any soft toy or cuddly person which does not happen to have become part of your child's permanent family. He emerges whenever she needs him because she is ill, and he goes away again to celebrate her being better. Such 'friends' often become important mascots to children who are 'too grown up for dolls' when they are well.

Finger or glove puppets can serve as 'being-ill friends' and fill a useful role in communication, too. Your child may confide worries about injections, medicines and so forth to a puppet. A puppet on her hand may answer questions from another on yours, too. If you cannot get a direct answer to questions like 'where does it hurt?' you might like to try working through puppet-intermediaries.

Other 'being-ill' toys

Possessions of yours which your child yearns for, but is not usually allowed to touch, can be lent to good effect when she is ill. Costume jewellery and discarded make-up (and a mirror to see the effect) are usually especially popular with both sexes. Ill children get tired and when yours is too tired to play she will need interesting things to look at and fiddle with. A mobile (you might make it together first) hung in a draught, the family goldfish bowl, a string of beads, a squeaky toy or fiendishly fiddly puzzle may all pass the boring minutes which sandwich bouts of your attention.

If a child is in bed, or immobilized by a plaster cast, for some time, she must have a proper play surface. A tray on her knees is better than nothing but a swing-across bed table is far better because she need not keep still. With a large plastic tablecloth (not a thin plastic sheet, of course) right over the bed, sofa or 'nest', she can do almost anything she normally does. Special adaptations of play for bed include:

Sugar for sand. A large mixing bowl with a couple of pounds of sugar, spoons, little pots, etc. stands in well for sand-play as long as the child is old or ill enough not to eat it (much).

Marbles in a bowl. Provided she will not put them in her mouth, marbles whizz deliciously round and round a big salad or mixing bowl. A simple game, few can resist this one whatever their age, you may enjoy it, too.

Cars and a tray for crashes, parking arrangements, etc.

Pastry for clay. However grey it becomes you can probably bake the final result as 'jam tarts' – you do not have to eat them.

'Magic' for painting. If you cannot cope with real paint while she is in bed, the kind of book in which colours appear when she paints with plain water is irresistible. It will not stunt her imagination in a few days.

'Fishing'. A magnet on a string and anything safe which it will collect can be used for 'fishing' over the edge of a bed or couch.

Being confined in bed is a time when a child may take to 'educational' activities which she could not be bothered with while she was active. Try her with new activities that involve sitting still. She might like to try cutting out or knitting for the first time at one stage, or looking up things in an encyclopedia at another.

When she is bored and you really need to do something else, try starting her off on something and then leaving her to do the next bit until you come back:

Photograph albums can be used for various activities of this kind. A young child could be asked to find all the pictures of herself; an older one might sort last year's holiday pictures and stick them in.

Magazines can be used for all kinds of identification games. You might help a young child find all the cars and then ask her to cut them out. A slightly older child might like to design a scrap book.

Beads: if she is old enough to handle beads you might start a necklace for her to finish.

Making books, etc. If you can cut out paper dolls she might go on and colour them; if you can tell a story and write it down she might illustrate it.

Although a young child probably will not know that she cares about a muddle, most children will stay happier and feel more occupied if you can keep things sorted out, and put away what is not being used. A big cardboard box that everything can be bundled into is quicker than proper putting away, and tidier and more comfortable than having everything strewn around. Ideally, use the time when she is napping or in bed in her own room to clear up her daytime 'nest' so that she can start again.

Contact with the doctor (*see also* **Medical Specialities**/Your family's doctor)

When an illness begins It is up to you to decide whether or not your child needs to be seen by the doctor. If you telephone, recite her symptoms and then say 'do you think you ought to see her doctor X, or will she be all right?' you are putting the doctor in an impossible position. He may think, from what you have told him, that the illness is probably trivial, but how can he be sure that you have reported fully and accurately? How can he, a responsible person, risk *not* seeing a child who might later on turn out to have needed him? Such a call from a parent is tantamount to a request for an appointment and it will save everybody's time if you simply make one.

Occasionally, though, it is worth making this sort of call if an illness begins late in the day or at the beginning of a weekend or holiday. In that case, you are not making an appointment because there are no normal appointments available. Instead you are warning the doctor that, if things should get worse, you might have to ask for out-of-hours attention. The doctor can leave a note for his deputizing service if he wishes, or tell you where to reach him later if you do need him.

Taking the child to the doctor's surgery In Britain, parents are exceedingly fortunate in that home visits from general practitioners are still accepted as part of ordinary family medicine. But however kindly your own doctor may be about such visits, do try not to abuse them. In most of Europe and all over America, home visits are rare or non-existent. There is a lot to be said for taking your child to the doctor if you can, rather than bringing the doctor to her.

Home visits inevitably use up a lot of a doctor's time and while you may resent the implication that his time is any more valuable than yours, you probably also resent having to wait for hours in his surgery if he has been called out by somebody else.

Facilities for examining your child are likely to be better at the surgery than at home.

These days many surgeries have facilities for performing a variety of simple diagnostic tests on the spot. Using these may enable the doctor to start treatment sooner.

On the other hand, of course, the doctor who visits your child at home will probably see her more relaxed and at ease, and will gain insight into the family background which may be useful to him on another occasion even if it is not relevant this time. He may also be able to give you better guidance about nursing her: 'this room is much too hot' is more effective than 'keep her room cool won't you?'

If you cannot decide whether to take the child to surgery or ask for a home visit, it is often sensible to leave *that* decision to the doctor. Telephone; tell the receptionist that you would like the doctor to see your child for this this and this reason and ask whether you should bring her to the doctor or whether he will come to her. If you are to take her in, you will be given an appointment so that you do not have to keep her hanging around a waiting-room passing on her infection to other people.

When a doctor visits

You are in a position similar to that of the nurses he works with elsewhere: your job is to help him do his job for your child efficiently.

DON'T:

Take the opportunity to tell him all your troubles or all your partner's symptoms.

Insist that he accept coffee or other hospitality (offer by all means but don't make him feel it would be rude to refuse).

DO:

Take him straight to the child unless there is some real reason for telling him about her symptoms in private first.

Tell him, or let her tell him, or help her tell him (depending on her age and shyness) what her symptoms are. Long stories about the amount of 'flu in the neighbourhood will not help him. He needs to know what she feels not what you deduce that she has 'caught'.

Help him set up any examination he wants to make. For example, he cannot listen to the chest of a fully clothed child or of a toddler who is sitting on the floor. He cannot work without a reasonable light either.

Keep quiet while he is using a stethoscope. He cannot hear you properly if you speak to him, nor hear the child's breath sounds if she talks to you.

Give the child, however young, a good chance to answer his questions herself. If he asks 'does that hurt?' he wants the child's answer (in words or behaviour or facial expression) rather than yours. If the child gives what seems to you a completely misleading answer (like 'no' when she had just told you that it hurt badly) it is fair enough to point out the discrepancy. Maybe the pain has stopped; that could be useful information.

Supervise the child so that she does not, for example, empty the doctor's case while he is writing a prescription.

Tell him the form of medicine the child prefers (*see below* Problems of administering medicines) **before** he has written out the prescription.

Ask for exact information/instructions.

Ask if he would like to wash his hands and give him a clean towel if he does want to.

Ask when/if/under what circumstances he will come again/want to see the child at surgery/want a progress report by telephone.

Telephone contact with the doctor   Once a doctor has seen your child, telephone contact can save time and effort for all of you because the doctor will have a picture of the child's condition and a view of how the illness is likely to progress. Whether you telephone because he asked you to do so or because you are worried by new developments or slow progress, do try to have clear in your mind the changes which have taken place since he saw her.

If he is not expecting you to telephone, it is usually best to ring through and tell the receptionist that you would like to speak to him when it is convenient. Often she will arrange to call back later on. The point is not only to avoid interrupting him in the middle of examining another patient, but also to give him a chance to have your child's notes in front of him. Her illness may be uppermost in *your* mind but *he* has probably seen dozens of patients since.

Coping with miscellaneous discomforts

Aches and pains   While a child whose illness has *acute* pain as one of its symptoms should always be seen by a doctor before any attempt is made to deal with that pain with over-the-counter remedies, many minor feverish illnesses are made miserable by headache and/or restlessly aching limbs.

If you are giving aspirin to control fever (*see below*) it will help these discomforts, too. Even if fever is not a problem, aspirin or paracetamol may make the child more comfortable. An older child or adolescent who has severe headache may find that a painkiller containing codeine is more effective. It is sensible, early in your career as a parent-nurse, to choose an over-the-counter pain remedy and check it out with your doctor (*see* **Pain and Pain Control**). If you have not done this in advance, bear the following points in mind:

A baby who is feverish enough to need medication, or in enough discomfort to need relief, should always be seen by a doctor. She cannot tell you what is wrong nor can you accurately and safely deduce anything from her behaviour, other than that she is unwell.

Toddlers and pre-school children must receive doses of medicine which are correct for their *weight* rather than their *age*. It is all too easy to overdose a lightweight three-year-old by giving her the recommended amount for 'Children from three to five'.

It is always better to use a pediatric (children's) medicine than a smaller dose of one intended for adults. Breaking tablets in halves and quarters leads to inaccuracy.

Most such medicines can be given every four hours, but that does not mean that the child should have a dose every four hours indefinitely. Some containers will tell you the maximum number of doses which it is safe to give within a twenty-four-hour period, but if your child even comes close to needing that much medication, check with your doctor.

Fevers tend to rise towards evening and sick children become tired and fretful then, too. A dose in the early evening may enable her to pass a more relaxed and cheerful time and thus settle better for the night, so try to 'save' a permitted dose from earlier in the day.

Aspirin (and some other over-the-counter pain remedies) tend to inflame the lining of the stomach especially if it is empty. Give them after a meal and always with a copious drink. If the child is eating very little, try giving the medicine with a glass of milk.

Itching   Some of the infectious diseases bring skin rashes which are intolerably itchy. A warm bath with a handful of bicarbonate of soda dissolved in the water often helps. If the child feels well enough, it may also provide a good opportunity for water-play.

Cooling lotions (such as calamine) help too, but the cool wetness and the psychological effect of doing something about the itching other than scratch, are as important as the medication. A child may scratch and moan less if she has her own supply to dab on where and when she feels the need. If you are worried about spills, measure out a 'ration' into a small plastic container.

A child with a limb in a plaster cast may be tormented by itching skin inside it, where she cannot reach to scratch. A 'back-scratcher' may enable her to reach down to the itchy place. If not, find a ruler or other long thin object which she can poke inside the cast.

Sore skin   Constant nose-blowing, or the inflammatory effects of infected mucus running from the nose, can make the skin miserably sore. Protect it, from the beginning of the illness. Some 'barrier creams' are safe, even though the child may lick it. Check. Simple vaseline or petroleum jelly will keep the skin lubricated. An older girl may prefer a 'night cream'.

High fever can lead to dry lips which then crack. Again, lubrication with petroleum jelly will prevent this although a lipstick-shaped and flavoured lip gloss may be more amusing.

If a feverish child is in bed for a few days 'pressure areas' such as her shoulders, buttocks and heels may begin to feel sore. Tightly tucked sheets which are not allowed to get crumbs on them will help. So will a good quality bath-powder applied to the carefully-dried skin; it reduces the friction. A child who is still in nappies is often especially liable to nappy rash during fever because the body, requiring extra water, concentrates the urine more than usual. As well as keeping up her fluid intake it is sensible to apply a preventative cream (such as castor oil cream) during this time, even if you do not normally use one.

Sore throats   Whatever the cause of a sore throat it is usually most sore when it is least lubricated, and least lubricated when the child has been sleeping and breathing through her mouth. A drink on waking helps, so wake a baby with breast at the ready or bottle in hand, and wake an older child with a glass of something or the treat of 'early morning tea'.

Throat pastilles/lozenges may help the older child's sore throat, but if they do, it will be more because sucking produces lubricating saliva than because of the medication they contain. If buying lozenges from a chemist gets around a family ban on sweets, fine. If there is no such ban, an occasional jelly-sweet to suck may be just as effective and more popular.

Medicines

Your doctor will only prescribe medicines if your sick child needs them. If she needs them at all, she needs exactly the amount and at exactly the intervals the doctor and/or the instructions on the container, suggests. Never alter the quantity or dosage schedule of a drug without asking your doctor first, unless you were told, from the beginning, that she should take it 'as required':

Drugs to be   If your child has an uncomfortable symptom, the doctor may prescribe a
given 'as   drug to ease it and the instructions may say something like 'four-hourly as
required'   required'. That would probably mean that she could have as much as one dose every four hours but not more. It would also mean that she did not *have* to have it at all, or go on having it once the symptom was better.

Medicines prescribed in this way might be for pain, for an irritating cough or for crampy diarrhoea (*see* **Diarrhoea, Gastro-enteritis and Food Poisoning**).

Do make sure that you know what the medicine is *called* (even if the name means nothing to you, knowing it will enable you to discuss it, if necessary, over the telephone with the doctor); what it is *for* and *what the instructions imply*. Would he prefer her to have it regularly if taking it is no problem, or will he be better pleased if she can manage without it? If it is going to be helpful, will the help be apparent from the first dose or can no difference be expected until she has had several?

Over-the-   As well as prescribing medicine 'as required' your doctor may agree to
counter   you giving the child an over-the-counter medicine such as aspirin for
medicines 'as   fever (*see below*). If you want to give the child anything out of your
required'   medicine cupboard do make sure that you mention it to the doctor who is prescribing for her. Drugs can interact with each other in peculiar ways and there is also a risk of overdosage if he does not know exactly what she is having. As an example, Codis is often given to older children for

feverish illnesses with aches and pains. If you dose your child with Codis, and the doctor has prescribed a cough medicine which also contains codeine, she may have far too much.

With all 'as required' medicines, prescribed or otherwise, be sure to ask how long you may go on with regular doses. The doctor may expect the fever to be down within twenty-four hours and suggest aspirin four-hourly. But if the child is still feverish in thirty-six hours, are you to continue the aspirin, telephone him or stop?

Medicines to be given on schedule

Many drugs – especially antibiotics – work best if they are given very regularly indeed, so that the level of the drug in the child's bloodstream stays at a steady and effective level. But children – even sick ones – commonly sleep at night and parents prefer to do so too. Your doctor may, or may not, want you to get up and wake the child to take a night-time dose. His instructions to you should make this point clear but if they do not, ask. If he says that she is to have the drug 'morning and evening', for example, you can obviously give it to her when she wakes up and before she settles for the night. But if the instructions are 'four times per day' is it all right to fit four doses into waking hours or not? 'Four-hourly' or 'six-hourly' ought to mean that you are to wake her, but it is still worth checking in case you need not. Your doctor will some-times say 'give it to her if she wakes up, which she probably will with that cough, but don't actually wake her up for it.'

It is easy to get muddled about a drug schedule, especially if you *are* allowed some lee-way within it; it is even easier if you are giving one drug on schedule and another 'as required'.

It may be worth your while to write down the times she takes the medicine. If you do, you may like to use the same sheet to note other aspects of your nursing/her illness, such as her temperature, fluid-intake or anything else which is of particular concern, in this particular illness.

Medicines to be given on a full or empty stomach

Some drugs are not well absorbed from a stomach containing a recent meal which is being digested; others can irritate the stomach unless it also contains food. When a child is ill it is not usually difficult to arrange for her to be 'empty' but it may be quite impossible to give medicine 'after meals' because she is not having any. Check with your doctor: he may suggest a glass (or even half a glass) of milk as a replacement for that meal.

Problems of administering medicines

Some doctors do not seem to realize just how difficult it can be to get medicine down a baby or small child. Your doctor may even seem a bit scornful if you express doubt about it. But if you cannot get the right amount down, you must tell him. A different formulation of the same drug might be easier for her to take. If all else fails he might want to give her the drug by injection. Don't use that as a threat to an uncooperative child, though. Most of them dislike injections very much indeed but occasionally have to have them. Making them sound like a punishment for spitting out medicine is not helpful.

Very occasionally a child will vomit medicine, either because vomiting is part of her illness or because fever makes her inclined to vomit and medicine-by-force makes her retch. If this happens more than once you must tell the doctor because it is very difficult to be certain whether she will have absorbed none, some or all of the dose before vomiting.

Having said all that, some babies and small children are completely cooperative – even enthusiastic – about most medicines. Don't make any kind of drama (or bother with the next paragraphs) until you are sure you have trouble. An attitude which simply assumes that the child will take what you offer her often works beautifully.

Liquid medicines

These are usually prescribed for children in preference to pills or capsules because they are thought easier to take. Unfortunately many children dislike the synthetic fruit flavours which ill-conceal bitter drugs. Fortunately, *babies* may not connect the first pleasant taste with the nasty after-taste and may therefore accept the dose and cry afterwards . . . older children catch on quickly, though.

Giving the correct dose. Your chemist should give you a 5 ml plastic spoon with the medicine. If he does not, ask for one. Domestic teaspoons vary in size. Use this 'standard' spoon for measuring, but not for administering, the medicine. A full spoon will almost certainly get spilled and anyway children have been known to bite these plastic spoons into lethally sharp pieces.

Measure the correct dose into a larger spoon, or make life easy for yourself by buying a special one which is like an icing-syringe with a spoon instead of a nozzle. These have the great advantage that you can stand them up, with the correct dose safely in the bottom, while you organize the child.

Sit the child up (never give medicine to a child who is lying down; she might choke), put a glass (or bottle) containing some of her favourite drink beside her ready to wash away the taste. Get her to open her mouth and then pour the medicine, all at once, as far back as you can. The further back it goes the less she will taste it.

If you do use one of these special non-spill medicine containers, even a toddler may accept the medicine more easily if she is allowed to 'do it herself'. Schoolchildren may prefer to do it themselves, too, but may find medicine easier to take from a small glass than from any kind of spoon.

Trouble with liquids

Don't mix the medicine with a drink. It will either sink to the bottom or stick to the sides. The child will probably only drink half the 'juice' and even if she empties the glass you will not know how much she has had. Effervescent tablets, such as some forms of junior aspirin, are the exception to this. They are meant to be mixed into liquids and will dissolve completely if you stir them well. You may still get stuck with a half-full glass but if the child will empty it she will have had it all.

Try concealing liquid medicine in a spoonful (no more) of something soft and strong-tasting that she really likes. Apple sauce, chocolate mousse or ice-cream are good ones to try. Tell her it is medicine but does not taste nasty this way; proceed on the assumption that she will take it.

● If you pretend it is *only* apple sauce, the peculiar taste of the spoonful may put her off apple sauce as well as medicine.

Force sometimes works, is sometimes necessary and is not as psychologically unfortunate here as in most situations. The fact that you will *make* her take it makes it clear to the child that the medicine really matters. While that may not stop her fighting you, it is not a bad attitude to implant.

Wrap a baby or toddler in a blanket so that she cannot bat the spoon out of your hand and then just sit there, with her on your lap and the medicine in your hand, and wait her out.

As soon as she opens her mouth (to cooperate, speak or yell) pop it in.

Emphasize the speed with which it was 'all over' in the hope that it will not seem to her worth such a performance next time.

Bribery. With a pre-school or older child you can often strike a bargain about medicine. A sweet afterwards is traditional (if she does not feel too ill), but a new comic or the promise that you are ready for a game or a story the moment the medicine has gone, may work just as well.

Capsules or sugar-coated pills

By no means every drug commonly prescribed for children is made in either of these forms *in children's dosages*, but if the medicine you need is available in these forms they can be especially helpful to children who want to cooperate but truly find it impossible to get down the liquid without gagging. Don't use them with an uncooperative child, though. Capsules must never be opened or crushed and if you crush a sugar-coated pill there is no point to the sugar-coating.

Moisten the gelatin coating of a capsule slightly so that it is slippery and easier to swallow. Explain to the child that either the gelatin or the sugar-coating will stop her tasting anything nasty if she gets it down quickly. Either get her to open her mouth while you pop it in, well back, for her, or let her do it herself.

Some children take these forms of medicine very efficiently and happily even as early as three years or thereabouts. If yours learns to do so, she will probably be able to take ordinary tablets similarly and then she will seldom have to face nasty-tasting liquids.

Ordinary tablets

If your child cannot just swallow a tablet with a drink, it can be crushed to a really fine powder and the powder may be easier to 'cover-up' than a disliked liquid. Not every doctor realizes this, so you will probably have to ask for tablets specially. It will not occur to him to prescribe tablets for a one-year-old unless you explain.

● When you crush a tablet, be extremely careful that you do not lose even a grain of powder. It is usually easiest to put it into a small plastic bag (or between two layers of foil), crush it with a wooden spoon and then tap out the powder.

Put a layer of anything strong tasting and slippery that your child likes into the bottom of a small spoon (jam? chocolate spread?). Put the powder on top, all in one place, and cover it completely with another delicious layer. The whole spoonful should now slide down the child's throat without her ever tasting the powder at all.

If you cannot think of anything the child will manage a whole spoonful of just now, you can, for a toddler or older child, try *mixing* the powder into a tiny quantity of something with a really strong cover-up taste like yeast extract. The result of your mixing should be a pellet, certainly no larger than a pea, which she can swallow easily. The surprise of the saltiness helps to conceal the powder.

● Remember that extra salt, especially this comparatively large 'dose' of salt, is not desirable for a baby.

If you are still stuck, there is one more trick you could try with an older child and a whole tablet.

Break off the tiniest piece of banana which will contain the pill. Push it in to make a 'banana pill' and get the child to swallow it straight down.

● Don't try this method with a grape or cherry even though the pill will neatly replace its stone. The child might choke.

Medicines which are not to be swallowed

Sometimes your doctor will prescribe (or suggest) drugs for your child which she is not to swallow but to have applied to various parts of her body by various means. Do remember that a drug which is to be dropped up her nose, or spread on a particular patch of skin, is still a drug. You need to be just as careful to understand the instructions as to dosage and frequency, and just as careful to lock away such medicines after use, as you are with oral drugs (*see* **Infection**/Treatment of external infection and inflammation).

Ear drops   The middle ear is the most usual site of ear infections but, because it is sealed off from the outer ear passage by the ear drum, drops instilled into the ear cannot reach it. If a doctor wants medication to reach the middle ear in the form of drops, these will be instilled into the nose (*see below*).

Ear drops are sometimes given to a child with an infection in the outer ear canal. Such infections are often extremely painful, especially when the ear itself is moved. If you are giving drops for this reason you will have to get the child into position without touching the ear; if you try to hold onto her ear-lobe, for example, you will probably have a screaming fight on your hands.

Ear drops are also sometimes given to soften wax which has become impacted in the ear canal. Often a doctor will do this himself but occasionally he may ask you to repeat the dose once or twice and then bring the child back to see him.

Don't put *anything* into a child's ear without specific orders from a doctor. All home remedies – such as warmed oil for earache – are at best useless and at worst dangerous.

To give
ear drops
to an infant   Draw up the correct number of drops into the dropper. Settle the baby on your lap with her head low and well turned to one side. Drop the drops into the uppermost ear and *keep her still*. If she turns over or sits up, the solution will simply run out again as the passage is a dead-end.

Enemas (and suppositories)   Enemas are liquids injected into the rectum (back passage); suppositories are meltable solids – usually bullet-shaped – which are pushed into the rectum. The best-known are intended to induce a bowel movement or to soften impacted faeces so that a bowel movement is possible, but these methods can also be used to give a variety of medicines. Anaesthetics are sometimes given to babies and young children in the form of enemas, to spare them the trauma of intravenous injection (*see* **Hospital**/ Surgery). Other medicines may be given 'per rectum' to a child who vomits if medicine is given by mouth. The drugs are absorbed into the bloodstream through the mucous membrane of the bowel instead of being absorbed from the stomach or upper intestine.

In some countries enemas and suppositories are still widely used but in most of the western world they are not. *Never give an enema or suppository without specific instructions from your doctor*. If he does tell you to do so, ask him to show you the best method, because this will depend both on *why* medication is being given by this route, and on the age of your child. If you are told to give enemas as part of the treatment for a child who soils due to long-standing constipation, for example, you will already be dealing with an emotionally charged situation (*see* **Soiling**) and it is important that you, the doctor and the child are all aware of the implications.

Eye drops   May be prescribed by your doctor for a variety of irritations/infections. If you find them very difficult to administer, he may be willing to prescribe an eye ointment instead.

● Eye drops and ointments are sold *sterile*. Their shelf-life, once the container is opened, is often very short so they should never be kept in the medicine cupboard for use another time. Furthermore one batch of drops or ointment should never be used for more than one child; there is a real risk of cross-infection.

To give eye drops to an infant   Draw up the correct number of drops into the dropper, being careful not to touch the end with your (unsterile) fingers.

Wrap a shawl or blanket around the baby so that her arms are tactfully confined. Settle her on your lap with her head back against your upper arm. Now put that wrist around the back of her head so that your hand can reach her face. Gently open her lids with your thumb and forefinger, poise the dropper and wait. Despite your fingers, she will blink. As she does so, drop the drops into the inner corner of the eye. If you get your timing right, the solution will land during the second that the eye is open between blinks. Release her lids and keep her lying still for a second while the solution is spread by her blinking.

● An older child can be given eye drops lying across a bed but, however much she means to cooperate, will still need your hand around her head to hold the eye open. Blinking or turning away is a protective reflex which she will not be able to control without your help.

Nose drops   Are sometimes prescribed in an attempt to reach the middle ear with medication. 'Attempt' is the right word because in order to reach the middle ear the liquid you instil in her nostrils must run down to her throat and then find its way up the eustachian tubes. However, drops which do not penetrate all the way to an affected middle ear may still be useful if infected adenoids (which the nose drops will reach) are contributing to the problem. Nose drops which you can buy over the counter under the general heading of 'decongestant' may be useful if a child has a badly 'stuffed up' nose because of a cold or a sinus infection. They can be invaluable to a baby who *must* breathe through her nose in order to suck her food; important to an older child who cannot settle to sleep without sucking her thumb and occasionally useful to an adolescent who must partake in a school play or get through a party. Use them with discretion and your doctor's blessing, though. Used frequently or for more than a day or two, they can produce so much artificial 'dryness' in the mucous membranes of the nasal passages that those passages produce extra secretions to compensate. The child may end up feeling even more 'blocked up' than before.

To give nose drops to an infant   If the dropper is made of glass or rigid plastic, buy a separate soft rubber dropper, which cannot damage her nose.

Use the dropper provided to draw up the correct number of drops and drop them into a clean spoon. Then suck the liquid into the soft dropper.

Lie the baby over your lap with her head slightly lowered. Turn her head a little to one side with one hand and use your other hand to put the drops up her upper nostril. Hold her still for a few seconds and then turn her head a little the other way and repeat the process for the other nostril.

● Some nasal drops sting a little if the mucous membranes are inflamed. If there is a real struggle it may be kinder to have someone else to hold her head still so that you can get the whole thing over more quickly.

● With a child too big to lie across your lap, but old enough to cooperate, lying across a bed is usually the best position. Don't let her sit up too quickly after the drops are in. If she does, some of the bitter medication may run forward in her throat to reach her taste buds.

Fever

Fever means that a child's body temperature is abnormally high. It is a very common response to infection but not an infallible sign. Neither the presence, absence nor height of a fever is a reliable guide to the presence, absence or severity of any illness. Every family should own a clinical thermometer and know how to use it, but it will not be helpful to you if you do not interpret its readings sensibly. For example:

Absence of fever   Your child can be ill, even dangerously ill, without having any fever at all. Babies in particular (and newborn ones especially), sometimes have subnormal (abnormally *low*) temperatures when, far from being well, their bodies are actually being overwhelmed by infection to such an extent that their bodies have given up fighting it. So don't ever let the fact that a child 'has no fever' convince you that she is well. If she *says* she feels ill and cannot go to school and you suspect that she is skiving because she has not done her homework, take her temperature if you want to, just to be sure it is not high, but don't base your decision to send her to school on just the fact that that temperature is normal. Base it on more general criteria like her appetite, energy and general good cheer at home, if not at school.

'Slight' fever   Although 'normal' is marked on clinical thermometers as a single point (*see below*) there is quite a wide range. Your child's body temperature will rise a little when she generates heat through active play; it will drop a little if she gets very cold while sitting still watching a parade; it will, in any case, tend to rise a little during the late afternoon and evening and be at its lowest in the small hours and early morning.

Because of this entirely normal variation, it is almost always a mistake to take the temperature of a child who seems entirely well, because if you do take it and you do find it a couple of points above normal, what are you going to do with that piece of information? Are you going to decide that, contrary to all appearances, she must be unwell? That would be a great mistake because the chances are that she is as she seems. If you are going to disregard that 'slight' fever reading, why did you take her temperature in the first place? The point is, of course, that a 'slight' fever is only one tiny piece of indefinite data to add to other pieces of data about the child's state. If you have such other data (she looks ill, feels ill, has vomited, cannot eat, does not want to play . . .) then take her temperature by all means. But if there is nothing to suggest that she is unwell, leave the thermometer in the cupboard.

'Real' fever   Barring the recent consumption of a hot drink or a furtive touch of thermometer to hot water bottle or light bulb, a temperature which is a whole degree (Fahrenheit) or more above normal probably does suggest that the child is unwell. This can be useful information for decision-making. For example, her grumpiness probably is more than 'teething' or 'Monday-morning blues'; she probably ought not to go to nursery/school/ or on that trip; you probably should keep an eye on her and take her temperature again, in a few hours, to see if it is rising or falling. But even so, the fever itself will not tell you how to handle the child. If she feels well, the fever does not mean that she must go to bed and adopt a 'sick role' unless she feels like it. The fact that it is very high does not necessarily mean that what you thought was 'only a cold' is something worse.

Finding out if a child is feverish

Some families rely on touching a child's forehead with the back of the adult hand to see if she feels extra-hot. Some reckon that they can tell, just by looking at her, whether their own child has a fever. While both methods used together have the advantage of being part of a general consideration of the child, they are pretty inaccurate and certainly will not provide useful information to the doctor if he is consulted.

Fever-testers   Modern technology has provided a more accurate version of that back-of-the-hand method in the form of special strips with heat-sensitive symbols. You place the fever-testing strip on the child's forehead and colour-coded symbols will rapidly appear. One, for example, produces a brown N if the temperature is within a normal range; a browney-blue NF if it is slightly above normal and a blue F for definite fever. The more sophisticated testers may show you how to interpret changing colour for that F which may, for example, get less blue and more green as it gets hotter.

Testers may be useful for finding out whether a child is feverish at all (when you are making one of those difficult decisions, for instance) and for babies and toddlers who cannot be trusted with a clinical thermometer in their mouths (*see below*). But they are not as reliable as thermometers and most kinds cannot tell you the exact height of a fever; once you have discovered that an older child is feverish you may want to switch to a real thermometer.

Clinical thermometers   Consist of a glass rod with a mercury-filled bulb at one end. When this mercury-filled bulb heats up, a thin thread of mercury is forced up the tube which is marked off in degrees of temperature. The mercury will stop at the level of the child's body temperature and it will stay there, even when the thermometer cools down again. The mercury will only go back down towards the bulb (so that you can start again) if it is shaken, with a flick of the wrist.

You can record a child's temperature by putting that mercury bulb anywhere where you can seal the child's skin or mucous membrane around it, excluding outside air as much as possible.

The usual technique with older children and adults is to put the bulb end of the thermometer under the tongue and leave it there with the mouth closed for a whole minute or more.

Babies and toddlers obviously cannot be trusted with a breakable glass rod containing poisonous mercury in their mouths. Their temperatures used to be taken by inserting the lubricated thermometer an inch or so up the rectum (back passage) and holding it there for two minutes. Although this is still usual in many hospitals and some homes, it is seldom either necessary or desirable. A wriggling baby may get delicate membranes bruised by the thermometer. A toddler will probably be highly affronted by the procedure. Unless your doctor tells you to use this method (perhaps because he wants accurate records of a fluctuating fever), don't.

Use a fever-tester to establish that a fever is present. If the illness requires you to keep an eye on the height of the fever, you can then use a clinical thermometer under the child's arm or in her groin. Extend the arm or leg fully; put the bulb in the centre, where the skin folds will come, and then fold the arm or leg across the chest or abdomen so that the bulb is completely covered but you can still hold on to the other end. By this method, the mercury may take a full two minutes to reach its full height so you will have to keep the child still.

• When reporting to a doctor, tell him where you put that thermometer. Rectal temperature will be a couple of points higher than oral which will be higher than armpit or groin.

Reading the thermometer   You can take your time over reading it because the mercury will not slip back down the tube until it is shaken down.

Hold the thermometer at either end. You will see that it is marked off, rather like a ruler, with big dashes for whole degrees and smaller dashes for points of a degree. The marks may be Fahrenheit, Centigrade or both.

Fahrenheit markings will probably start at 94° towards the bulb end and stop at about 108° at the other end. There will be an arrow or indicator at either 98.4° or 98.6° and this is your guide to 'normal'. The matching Centigrade markings will be about 35° and 42° with that normal indicator at 37°.

If you turn the thermometer slowly between your fingers so that the numbers face you, a thick line of mercury will appear. Look at the end of that line furthest away from the bulb. The number that its end is opposite is your child's temperature. If it is in between two numbered whole-degree markings, you will have to count the smaller markings. In Fahrenheit, tenths of a degree are only marked in pairs, so one marking above 101°F will mean that her temperature is 101.2°F. In Centigrade, the points of a degree are marked individually so the equivalent would be about 38.5°C.

As a *very* rough rule-of-thumb you might want to disregard anything below 99°F or 37.2°C and regard as fever anything at or over 100°F or 37.8°C. In between is suspicious/dubious.

Looking after the thermometer Shaking it down for re-use is an acquired skill. Hold it between thumb and finger by the non-bulb end and then flick your wrist. Practise over a bed. You will probably drop it a few times before you acquire the technique.

● Always check that the thermometer is reading well under normal before you use it. If you do not, it may not tell you what your child's temperature is now but what it was last time you measured it. The point is that the mercury cannot go *down* (without being shaken down) but only up. If it is reading 103°F (39.5°C) (from last month) when your child's present temperature is only 100°F (37.8°C), it will mislead you.

Clinical thermometers are extremely carefully tested and you can assume that they are accurate. They are easily broken, however, by being dropped on a hard surface or knocked against something. If the bulb of a thermometer is brought into contact with something *much* hotter than a human body ever could be (boiling water, for example) the column of mercury will shoot right to the top of the tube and may jam there so that it cannot be shaken down.

Keep it in its protective case where children cannot get at it and never leave it, uncased, on a bedside table or anywhere where it could get knocked off or otherwise smashed.

Stand it, bulb end downwards, in a mild disinfectant such as Milton if you are using it for more than one patient at the same time. While 'germs' will not readily survive on clean glass, you could transfer virus-laden saliva directly from a child with measles to another with a cold.

Coping with fever

A lot of children run major fevers for minor reasons like the beginning of an ordinary cold. On the whole, the younger the child the higher her temperature may go without it indicating anything serious. While this is by no means an invariable rule, it is *likely* that a twelve-year-old with a temperature of 102°F (38.8°C) is iller than her three-year-old brother whose temperature is the same.

While many children can run quite high temperatures without seeming especially affected by them, many have a sort of personal 'critical level' above which the fever itself, whatever its cause, seems to make them very unwell. Unless your children are lucky enough to avoid the usual run of infections, you will learn each one's 'critical level' and you may watch it change, too, as he or she gets older. It is always worthwhile to try and spot *high* fever early, and work to keep it under that critical level, because while fever itself will not harm your child, the side-effects of fever which has gone 'too high' are both unpleasant and alarming (*see below*).

As a very rough rule-of-thumb, you might expect that 103°F (39.5°C) was likely to be 'too high' for a baby or toddler; that 102.4°F (39°C) might be 'too high' for a pre-school child and 102°F (38.8°C) 'too high' for a young schoolchild. Older children and adolescents are less liable to the side-effects of high fever but will often feel very unwell indeed with temperatures of 101°F (38.3°C) or above.

If you know that a child is unwell and use a thermometer sensibly, you can usually keep the fever to reasonable levels by adapting the heroic measures suggested for reducing fever (*see below*). But quite often you will have no advance warning. Either the child's temperature will go up very rapidly, or she will return home from school, or wake up in the morning, already very feverish. A very sudden and sharp rise (such that your toddler is perfectly well at breakfast-time but has a temperature of 103°F and a bit (39.5°+C) by mid-morning for example) is the most likely to provoke side-effects. These are all due to the effect of the fever on the child's nervous system; the more sudden the rise the less chance her body has to adapt.

Side-effects of high fever

High fever, especially one which is rising very rapidly, naturally affects a child's brain and central nervous system as well as the rest of her body. The most extreme effect is the kind of 'fit' known as a febrile (feverish) convulsion. Only about three per cent of children are liable to those, and only between the ages of about one and three years, so you will find them dealt with separately (*see* **Convulsions, 'Fits' and 'Funny Turns'**). Other 'nervous system effects' are common:

Shivering and trembling in high fever   Healthy bodies shiver in order to warm themselves when they are cold, but a quickly rising fever upsets the body's smooth regulation of its own temperature-mechanisms. A feverish child may shiver although she *is* very hot, and may be very confused as to whether she *feels* hot or cold. A 'shivery feeling' is often the first symptom of fever which a verbal child will report. Your first clues to fever in a younger child may be that she cuddles by the heater in a room which to you feels comfortably warm, or fight to rid herself of a sweater in a room which feels cool.

Once a feverish child is resting and her body is adapting, the hot-and-cold feelings usually settle down, but she may go on being definitely trembly until the fever drops a little. If you pull back the bedding you can see little movements of the thigh muscles, for example.

Nausea and vomiting in high fever

Some of the illnesses which cause fever also cause gastric upset, but fever which has nothing to do with gastric infection may make your child feel sick. Nausea can make it difficult to persuade her to drink enough fluids. For a child who is old enough, cracked ice, or ice cubes to suck, often serve the double purpose of helping the nausea and providing water.

Of course any child who is nauseated may vomit, but if fever upsets the vomiting centre in the brain, your child may suddenly vomit without having any warning of nausea first.

Sudden vomiting is always something to watch out for in a very young child who is feverish because of the risk of her breathing vomit into her lungs. It is also a risk in much older children if their level of consciousness is affected by the fever (*see below*).

General hypersensitivity in high fever

The child's whole nervous system may over-react to high fever, so that her skin is hypersensitive to touch, she covers her ears at loud noises and cannot bear to be moved around. A baby may cry when you pick her up and try to cuddle her; an older child may shrink as if in pain when you try to sponge her face or brush her hair. Apart from working to get the fever down to her tolerance-level, leave her as much in peace as you can. It is better just to stay quietly with her, than to fuss with her pillows or insist on reading to her if she can doze.

Effects of high fever on consciousness

Sometimes a child with very high fever seems 'off her head' or delirious. She may talk, sometimes loudly and excitedly, but although she looks awake, what she says makes no sense and, after a few attempts to answer, as in an ordinary conversation, you realize that she is not really talking to you; indeed that she is not really 'with you' at all. Nursing a delirious child is rather like coping with a night-terror (*see* **Sleep**/Night-terrors).

A delirious child's brain is already receiving too much (inappropriate) stimulation. Apart from necessary disturbances, like your efforts to reduce the fever or a visit from the doctor, it is best if she is not stimulated any more. If she is talking in her sleep, don't try to wake her; try to soothe her into more peaceful sleep instead. If she suddenly talks irrationally in the middle of a conversation, don't ask her what on earth she means, or even let her see you looking taken aback; just pass it off and try to help her doze off. If a baby who does not yet talk suddenly detaches herself and gazes off into space, don't work to get her attention back; just let her rest quietly with you.

● Most people find nursing a delirious or otherwise irrational child decidedly 'spooky'. But children in this state tend to be sensitive to other people's feelings so that if you are frightened or upset they are frightened too. Try not to face this kind of nursing alone. An adult friend or partner, to share the watches with you, can go a long way to helping you hang onto your sane adult self.

● While children who are unwell are no longer automatically put to bed until they are better, a child with high fever, especially fever which is causing this kind of side-effect, is both physically safer and better protected from unwanted extra stimulation if she is in bed. That 'bed' can, of course, be her pram or 'nest' near to you, but until the fever is controlled she will be better off away from the hurly-burly of other children, television, etc.

● Nobody, not even the most sensible adolescent, should be left alone while fever is affecting consciousness. Until she is fully rational again she needs somebody there.

Reducing and controlling fever

When a body begins to get too warm, blood vessels near to the surface of the skin dilate so that they can carry as much blood as possible. This means that as the total volume of blood circulates around the body, an unusually large part of it is exposed to the cooler conditions of the body's surface. You can see this happening. As your child plays vigorously, her face will become flushed and the veins which are visible (on the insides of her wrists, for example) stand out. As body-heat builds up, the sweat glands of the skin produce a thin film of moisture which cools by evaporation. If your hot and sweating child stops playing and stands around, she will rapidly cool off. If there is a breeze blowing and she stands around without a sweater, the cooling effect of rapid evaporation from her skin will be so marked that she will soon feel chilly.

Whether you are trying to reduce a fever which is 'too high', or trying to control one so that it does not rise to your child's own limit of tolerance, the trick is to help her body to carry out its own cooling efficiently and to be ready with artificial aids should it fail to do so.

Whenever a child is feverish

Don't insulate her with warm pyjamas and heavy bedding. The extra blood circulating through those dilated blood vessels under her skin is meant to carry coolness back into the general blood supply. If the skin surface is being kept as warm as her internal organs, it cannot do so. Her lightest nightdress, and the minimum of bedclothes under which she can feel comfortable, will give her body a better chance.

Don't keep room-air too warm or too still. A child in bed always gives off heat so that the air inside the bed is warmer than the air around it. A feverish child gives off extra heat which her skin is trying to shed. As well as avoiding trapping too much heat *in* the bed, you need to ensure that, as she moves around, there is plenty of cooler air into which her fever-heat can be dispersed. Try to get the temperature of the room as a whole down to around 65–68°F and to keep the air circulating. If your windows can be opened, open them at the top so that warm air (which always rises) goes out, bringing cooler air in. If your windows are sealed, try keeping the door open and using the 'cold' setting of a blower-heater to keep the air moving.

Don't leave her snug and still for long at a time. If she snuggles down with even that lightweight bedding pulled well round her and her face half-buried in the pillow, for a good long nap, she will have accumulated a lot of super-warmed air by the time she awakens. Sitting up while you turn those pillows cool side up and shake out the bedclothes will help her to cool down again.

● Watch out for duvets or continental quilts. Their whole point is that they are excellent insulators which swathe the child, leaving no drafty gaps. The quilt which keeps your child snug on a winter's night may keep her far too snug when she has a fever. If she will not accept a sheet or light blanket instead, try at least to persuade her to have the quilt over her rather than rolled all round her . . .

Make sure she drinks plenty: her body needs surplus fluid for efficient sweating/cooling as well as to prevent general dehydration.

When a child's fever is 'too high'

It may not be enough just to give her body easy circumstances in which to keep itself cool, you may have to do the cooling for it. But it is still better to cool the child by the body's own methods than by the cruel and ineffective measures which used to be suggested. Putting her in a cold bath, for example, will not only distress, even shock her, it will also cause all those superficial blood vessels to close up *so as to preserve body heat*. Unless you are actually instructed to do this, by a doctor, don't. Instead:

Provide an artificial sweat layer by sponging the child with water which feels just warm to your own hand. It will still feel cool to her overheated skin but, because it is warm, those blood vessels will stay dilated and, as it evaporates, the blood they carry will cool. Concentrate your sponging on areas where you can actually see a lot of blood vessels, such as her face and neck, the insides of her wrists and arms and, unless it disturbs her too much, her groin and inner thighs.

Leave her skin wet. If you dry the moisture away there will be less evaporation to cool her.

Speed up the rate of evaporation by providing an 'artificial breeze'. If you have an electric fan, place it so that a stream of air passes over her. Failing that, place a fan-heater near to the bed with the setting on 'cold'. Even if the air-current does not play directly on her skin, it will rapidly remove the warm air from around her damp body. Failing any electric gadgetry, fan her for a few minutes with a magazine or book. By the time her skin is dry, her fever should have dropped by at least half a degree.

● A very feverish child may find even this, comparatively gentle, cooling very unpleasant and may feel cold and shivery when you have finished. Don't make the mistake of providing a hot water bottle and three extra blankets or all your work may be undone.

If your child's illness is forcing her fever up against everything you can do to help her body cool itself, she may need the further help of fever-reducing medicines.

Consider aspirin or its equivalent. If you are already consulting a doctor about this illness, ask him what he recommends. If not, give the dose of soluble aspirin which is appropriate to the child's weight, along with the biggest drink you can persuade her to take. She could have this dose again, four hours later, but if her fever continues to run so high that you feel you must go on with regular doses for more than a day, a doctor should be consulted.

Don't give aspirin to a baby without a doctor's advice.

Don't give aspirin to anyone with stomach-pains associated with fever.

Don't persist in trying to give it if it makes her vomit; each time she vomits she is likely to lose more fluid than there was in that medicine glass, and water matters more than aspirin to her feverish body.

Getting back to normal

After most illnesses, most basically healthy children snap rapidly back to normal as soon as fever and other symptoms subside. Unless your doctor advises you otherwise, there is no need to impose any of the old rules like 'twenty-four hours in bed after the fever drops' or 'one full day quietly at home for every day of illness'.

Illnesses do, of course, use energy and may have depleted bodily reserves, but bodies are remarkably good at meeting their own needs so the convalescent child who needs extra food or rest will probably simply eat and sleep more than usual. You can usually assume that a child who has no fever or other symptoms, is eating well, seems full of energy and enthusiasm again and wants to get on with life, is ready to do so. Sometimes, though, you may have more complicated decisions to make in convalescence:

Symptoms which outstay illness

Some illnesses recede leaving symptoms which drag on. Whooping cough, for example, may leave a cough which lasts for weeks after the child is better. Illnesses which have been treated with antibiotics sometimes leave diarrhoea to remind you that even the most useful drugs can have side-effects. Upper respiratory infections can leave catarrh and/or a cough which sounds like active illness but is not. The point is usually that the body has dealt with the original infection but the affected body-parts have not yet returned to their pre-illness state. Sometimes parents keep such a child at home because they are afraid of other people thinking them irresponsible if the child returns to public life. Others reject public opinion and return her to normal, only to regret it later because she picks up a secondary infection and is ill all over again.

A happy medium probably involves having a final check made by the doctor and, if he is happy for her to be out and about, keeping an eye on her activities for a while both to try and avoid situations in which further infection is especially likely and to spot it early should it occur.

Depression after illness

Some illnesses, perhaps especially 'flu (*see* **Influenza**) are notorious for leaving their victims depressed. A child who is uncharacteristically irritable and/or liable to sudden tears, probably is not ready for the hurly-burly of ordinary daily life, but will feel better sooner if she can be busy and interested rather than sitting drearily around thinking how awful she feels. That old-fashioned remedy 'a holiday' often works wonders, even if it only consists of a weekend. Failing that, a couple of days of traditional 'convalescence', complete with tempting food and treats geared to her stage of recovery, usually helps. An older child or adolescent, puzzled and worried by her own feelings, is certainly entitled to reassurance that they are a hangover from the illness. Often knowing that there is a physical reason for misery is cheering in itself (*see* **Depression**).

Difficulty in giving up the 'sick role'

Even when the illness itself was not especially depressing, it can be difficult for a child to make the switch from her ill self to her normal self, especially if being ill has brought her a lot of gratification and her everyday life is less-than-perfect. A small baby, for example, may have lost the recent patterning of her eating and sleeping during even a brief illness; she may go on being 'demanding' and unpredictable for a while. A pre-school child may have enjoyed a few days of your (almost) undivided attention and find herself reluctant to return to her minder or kindergarten. A schoolchild may be sure that she has lost her best friend to a rival, while an adolescent may be worried about catching up on missed assignments or training sessions. Even without special worries of this kind, anyone whose workday routine has been broken by illness, and its attendant freedom from responsibility, may feel that 'getting going again' is a big effort.

If your child seems to feel like this – so that her face falls when the doctor says, 'you're better young lady; back to normal by Monday,' – try to re-introduce the more enjoyable aspects of everyday life *first*, so that by the time she has to face the less desirable bits she can remember the shape and point of it all. If your small child spends her mornings with a minder but usually plays with her friend from next door in the afternoon, make sure the two of them get together the day *before* you go back to work. If your schoolchild has been missing her favourite 'late-night' television programme because of her illness, make sure you hand back that privilege of health as soon as you are calling her fit for school. If a full day plus all her after-school activities is going to be too much for her for a while, don't assume that she should complete the school day but miss her fun. A few days of morning school, an afternoon nap and then those activities may make a transition back to normal life which is both fairer and smoother. Many adolescents who say that they are worrying about what they have missed at school are actually missing the current gossip more than the work-assignments. A few chats on the telephone will help. Having friends to visit the house at the end of the illness may then help them to change easily back into their normal independent gear.

Obesity *see* **Eating**/Eating problems: Obesity: the problem of eating too much; **Growth**.
One-parent families *see* **Divorce, Separation and One-parent Families**.
Operations *see* **Hospital**/Surgery.
'Organically grown' and 'natural' foods *see* **Eating**/Commonsense about family eating.
Overweight *see* **Eating**/Eating problems: Obesity: the problem of eating too much; **Growth**.

Pain and Pain Control *see also* **Abdominal Pain**; **Accidents**/Shock; **Cramp**; **Headaches**; **Hospital**/Procedures: Sedation and Anaesthesia; **Teeth**/Some dental emergencies.

Although pain is an experience which is common to every human being and almost universally detested, it is a complicated phenomenon which is still not fully understood by scientists and is seriously misunderstood by many other people. If you know at least a little about pain and its functions, you will be both better able to cope with a vast variety of childhood mishaps and behaviours, and better able to teach those children to understand and cope with their own pains and to use them properly in learning to look after themselves.

The ability to perceive pain is vitally important; so important that an individual who had no pain-sensitivity would be unlikely to survive. The most primitive, and arguably the most vital, pain mechanism is the 'reflex arc' which makes a child snatch his hand back from the hot stove even before he is aware of being burned. His hand gets dangerously close to the heat and pain-receptors in the skin despatch impulses along special nerve fibres. While most of these will travel to the brain (*see below*) some take a short cut through the spinal cord and stimulate reflex muscular withdrawal of the threatened hand or finger. The speed of the reflex arc prevents or minimizes damage while the automatic muscular response ensures that the correct avoiding action is taken. A newborn baby might not 'know how' to escape the needle which jabs his heel for a blood sample; the reflex arc does it for him. The drunken or unconscious individual might be too confused to respond appropriately to pain, but the reflex arc will continue to function, at least until he is deeply in coma.

The importance of those pain-receptors in the skin in protecting us from injury can most clearly be seen when they are lacking. When a dentist gives a local anaesthetic in the mouth, for example, he warns the patient not to drink hot liquids and to be careful not to bite the numbed parts of his mouth. But despite the warning and despite the short period of insensitivity, some minor damage is very usual. The anaesthetic wears off and the patient finds that he has made a sore patch on the inside of his cheek while chewing the end of that pencil . . . Some accidental injuries leave areas of insensitive skin and, however aware of the risk the patient may be, and however hard he tries *consciously* to protect that area from damage, he is usually unable to do so. The 'dead' area on a hand may be repeatedly burned during cooking, ironing, boiler-stoking or smoking; a dead area on the face may mean that wet-shaving is impossible.

Underneath the skin, almost every area of the body is liberally supplied with special nerve-fibres whose sole function is to carry to the brain impulses which that brain may bring into consciousness as pain. It is important to understand that when pain is felt, it is not the wound itself, nor yet the nerves, which hurt. It is the brain which interprets the impulses it is receiving and, so to speak, tells you 'that hurts'. Sometimes you can prove this for yourself. If you bang your head on a low beam or stub your toe on something, there is often a noticeable delay between the damage and the onset of pain. You may have time to collapse on the floor and rub your head before it starts to hurt. You are not waiting for the knock – that has already happened – nor for the nerve fibres to send their impulses – they start to react almost instantaneously – you are waiting for your brain to sum up the whole incident as painful.

This idea that pain is not a thing-in-itself nor an integral part of injury/disorder but an interpretation by the brain, is an important one. If you accept it, you will not subscribe to the many misconceptions about pain which make sufferers miserable. When no obvious physical cause can be found for a child's pain, for example, many people say scoffingly that it is 'all in the mind'. But of course the pain is in his mind; *all pain is in the mind* because only the mind (brain) can give the individual a pain-message. Pain which is due to a demonstrable physical cause – to appendicitis or a fractured bone for example – is therefore no different from the pain of a tension headache or the recurrent stomachache of a child who is anxious about school (*see* **Abdominal Pain**/Recurrent abdominal pain). If he feels pain, then that pain is real. It is sometimes important to explain to a sufferer that there *is* no physical cause for his pain, but he must never be allowed to think that this message means that he is thought to be lying about being in pain; to be 'making it all up'. Similarly, when someone tells you that an experience you would assume to be painful does *not* hurt, that person too will usually be telling the truth. Most women experience pain in childbirth, for example, but some women, sharing the physical experience, nevertheless do not share the pain-sensations. Their brains interpret similar nerve impulses differently.

Although pain is a vitally important warning system it is by no means an infallible one. The intensity of pain, for example, is not always appropriate to the degree of trouble being experienced by the body; an unimportant bang on the head may be as painful as a bang which has actually damaged the skull (*see* **Accidents**/Head injuries), while trivial and temporary distension of the bowel with gas can be as painful as a serious abdominal condition. Some life-threatening conditions are not painful at all, or at least not until the disease-process is very far-advanced; this is why many forms of cancer, for example, go undetected for so long. In some illnesses pain continues to be perceived long after the disease-process seems clinically over (*see* **Chickenpox and Shingles**, for example) while in other conditions, such as some kinds of low back-pain, pain is not felt during ill-advised activity (when it might serve the useful purpose of restraining the individual) but hours afterwards. Sometimes, too, the site at which pain is felt is misleading because the brain fails to interpret the source of its signals correctly. If you sharply hit the inner side of your elbow, for example, you will probably feel acute pain in your little finger. This is because all your brain 'knows' is that it has received impulses which it perceives as painful from somewhere on the ulnar nerve which runs from that little finger up the inner arm and then via the spinal cord to the brain. Insults to that pathway are always perceived as pain in the finger where it begins. Furthermore, your brain would continue to tell you that it was your little finger which was hurt, rather than your elbow, even if that little finger had been amputated. (This phenomenon is called 'phantom pain'.) Some pathways from internal organs converge in the spinal cord. Since many of these organs begin their development in one part of the embryo and later migrate to another part, trailing their original nerves with them, the confusion of 'referred pain' is very common. The diaphragm, for example, which separates the heart and lungs from the liver and the stomach, first develops in the same part of the embryo as the shoulders. When the diaphragm is inflamed during pleurisy (*see* **Chest Infections**) or liver disease (*see* **Jaundice**) pain tends to be felt in the shoulder and may easily be mistaken for muscular pain.

Clearly, then, while our brains dictate the presence or absence of pain, by telling us or not telling us 'that hurts', we have to interpret for ourselves the significance of perceived pain as well as deciding what, if anything, we should do about it. In the notes which follow it will be clear that 'doing something about pain' is still something which medicine finds difficult. Much research is in progress and many people believe that a breakthrough may come when we understand more of the body's own means of pain control. It has been found, for example, that our brains produce chemicals called endorphins which can be described as nature's own opiate-type painkillers. They appear to be produced and circulated, at a low level, more or less all the time and may be responsible for our *not* receiving pain-messages from our brains more often than we do. The level of these chemicals in the body is raised in circumstances which are only now being described; the known circumstances do, however, make sense of some previously recognized but unexplained phenomena. It is known, for example, that when somebody has chronic pain that is not extremely intense, that pain often ceases to be felt if *another* painful stimulus is applied. We all act on this idea of 'counter-irritants' in our daily lives when we bang our hands on the table to distract ourselves from that stubbed toe . . . The explanation may lie in the fact that the second painful stimulus raises the level of circulating endorphins and thus provides a raised dose of 'natural painkiller' to cope with the original pain. It may even be that this partly explains the mechanism by which acupuncture can sometimes help with chronic pain. Endorphin production has also been found to increase when individuals have been given dummy pain-killers (placebos) and therefore have reason to *believe* that their pain will lessen. It may be that the much discussed 'placebo-effect' (often treated as a phenomenon which suggests that the pain was not 'real' in the first place) results from real biochemical pain relief, but relief provided by the body for itself rather than by active chemicals in tablets.

It is to be hoped that research of this kind will produce a much clearer understanding of both pain and its relief over the next few generations, but in the meantime we can help our children to make the most of the knowledge and relief which is available.

Coping with pain

Every child will experience pain and every parent has to draw a careful line between taking it too seriously and not taking it seriously enough. Pain-sensations are not only unpleasant, they are also frightening. Fear and anxiety increase sensitivity to pain, probably by making the brain likely to interpret more of its received signals as pain than it would do otherwise. If a child hurts himself and at once becomes the focus for anxious adult attention, he is bound to fear for himself and thus increase his own distress. On the other hand, pain *is* a protective signal. If that same child's pain is ignored, he is actually being prevented from learning to take due notice of his own body's signals. If his pain is not only ignored but *denied* ('it doesn't really hurt, don't make such a fuss') he may become very confused about what it is that he is actually feeling. The fine line therefore is the one which keeps him interested and in touch with his body, but confident in it and unafraid of its phenomena.

Attitudes to a child's pain   The secret seems to lie in showing your child, from the beginning of his life, that the first thing which matters is the *cause* of his pain. It is a signal from his brain about his body, to himself – a self for which you stand in when he is very young. If the signal is correctly interpreted the pain can be appropriately dealt with.

When the cause of the pain is obvious and trivial he needs acknowledgement of the unpleasant sensation ('bad luck, that is a nasty scrape') plus confident reassurance that the *damage* is not in any way serious and that the *pain will soon stop*. You can use this set of messages to fit innumerable circumstances and over all age groups. It applies, for example, to routine injections in the immunization programme as well as to dressing boils or removing splinters.

When the cause of the pain is not obvious he needs to see both that you are interested in looking for the meaning of the signal and that failure to find a cause does not lead you to dismiss his discomfort. If he is complaining of pain in a watering eye, you are interested in looking for a foreign body; if it is his ankle which is hurting, you are interested to see if there is swelling or discolouration which might suggest a sprain (*see* **Accidents**). But if you can find nothing, you are still interested in helping him to feel better (*see below* Pain control).

When the cause of pain is discovered, and suggests that the pain will continue, he needs you to separate for him dislike of the sensation from fear of bodily damage. If his tummyache is diagnosed as part of tonsillitis (with inflamed glands around the abdomen) you cannot assure him that now you know the cause you also have a cure. But you can explain that cause, and explain that as the infection recedes so will the pain, and you can emphasize that it will not get worse and does not suggest anything dangerous 'happening inside him'. If a girl has pre-menstrual pain (*see* **Adolescence**/Menstruation) you cannot promise that it will not recur, but you can explain the mechanism and assure her that discomfort does not suggest that her newly grown-up self works less than perfectly.

When pain has no discoverable cause, you can teach him that once its signals have been attended to and found unanswerable, it is legitimate to concentrate on turning them off. This is probably the best approach to take to pains like headaches or recurrent stomachaches, for example. That headache does not mean anything sinister; will go of its own accord eventually, but may be hastened on its way.

Extreme pain   Very acute pain, even when the cause is trivial or probably psychogenic rather than physical, is *a personal emergency*. Not only does the sensation crowd out all competing sensations, it also leads the body to declare crisis, stimulating other physical reactions such as sweating, racing pulse, nausea, pallor and feelings of faintness. A child with this sort of pain needs medical attention because the pain in itself is liable to lead to shock (*see* **Accidents**/Shock). He also needs psychological attention in the sense of needing assurance that nobody expects him to put up with *that*. Parents are likely to be quick to respond to this level of pain because it is usually associated either with an obvious accident or with an acute worsening of a condition (such as appendicitis) which was already being watched. Don't be caught out by occasional causes though. A child who is subject to migraine, and has medication for it, may have a particularly painful attack and require an injected painkiller (*see* **Migraine**). A child with a small burn or scald (which you long to minimize because nobody wants to admit that an avoidable accident was serious) may be suffering 'too much' even if the injury is not dangerous.

Long-continued pain

Very few children are subject to the chronic pain which bedevils so many adults as age makes us liable to degenerative disorders of joints and so forth. There are a few conditions, though, in which pain which is not extreme will nevertheless continue over a long enough period to require special handling. Most such children will be in hospital, but if you have such a child at home, whether with an inflamed and fluid-filled knee which takes several days to settle, or with a pleurisy which does not respond to the first antibiotic, the following points may be useful.

Long-continued pain tends to 'take over' the personality so that although its intensity does not increase (and may even be diminishing) its duration gradually wears down the patient's ability to cope with it. Distress about pain–pain–more distress about pain–more pain becomes a vicious circle.

The pain is easy to *interrupt* even if it cannot be banished; the more it is interrupted the better. Almost everything (*see below* Pain contol) will help for a little while, though no relief will last. The trick is to keep on interrupting that vicious circle of pain–distress with different weapons. If you can do this, the pain will at least be confined to its base level and will never soar to panic-heights.

Since pain is the brain's interpretation of nerve impulses, anything which makes the brain more likely to perceive pain will make that pain worse. Long-continuing pain will almost always be felt more in the solitude of 3 a.m. than the social caring of 3 p.m. It will be worse when the child is tired, bored, uncomfortable in other ways. It will also be worse when – perhaps in an entirely praiseworthy attempt to keep up normal standards of behaviour – you are cross with him.

Pain control

Most people assume that 'pain control' will mean 'painkillers' – that our principal weapons against pain come from the medicine cabinet. In fact our principal weapons are in the kinds of attitude laid out above. Whatever the victim's age and whatever the cause of his pain, each of the following will almost certainly make it worse, by encouraging his brain to force the interpretation 'pain' into his consciousness.

Fear, especially fear about what has happened to him already (perhaps the accident that caused the pain and which he feels might have 'broken' him); fear about what is going to happen to him (perhaps fear of the doctor who is coming or of the hospital to which he is being taken) and fear of the pain itself. Fear of the pain takes many different forms. It may be fear that it will go on forever; fear that it will get worse and worse, or fear that he will 'lose control'.

Other people's anxiety which feeds fear. *Don't* scream for help unless his life is actually in danger. Go and ask for it instead.

Ignorance of what *has* happened and *will* happen. In all but the youngest child in pain, ignorance also feeds fear and fantasy-fears too. An adolescent with severe abdominal pain is far better off knowing that the doctor thinks he does have appendicitis, than left behind closed doors while adults mutter and he secretly imagines that his insides are bursting open.

Other people's ignorance. A person in pain needs to feel that somebody can help. Be careful about announcements like 'you're a real mystery . . .' If a diagnosis is not possible (whether he is to be rushed to hospital for tests or left at home because 'it will pass') he needs to feel that the ignorance is coupled with experience which makes it safe: 'I can't tell you why your legs hurt so much but we do know that lots of children your age get this sort of pain from time to time and that it always passes off in an hour or two . . .'

Other people's disbelief. When a child suffers from pain whose cause is trivial, unknown and/or probably psychogenic, having it implied that he is 'making it up', 'swinging the lead', 'playing for sympathy' or 'just trying to get out of school' will almost always increase the actual pain he feels as well as his general unhappiness. It is almost as if his brain must force into his consciousness additional evidence that he is not cheating. In this sense the sufferers whose regular Monday-morning tummyaches bring pallor and vomiting with them (*see* **Abdominal Pain**/Recurrent abdominal pain) are the lucky ones because however scornfully the illness is labelled 'neurotic' it clearly exists.

In most instances you will be able to do better than just avoiding making the child's pain worse: the following will actually make him feel it less.

Distraction. If people have nothing to think about but their pain, they are more conscious of that pain than they are when other stimuli are competing for conscious attention. This phenomenon is often sadly misunderstood. People will say 'he's laying it on a bit thick; when I try to get on with anything else he just lies there and moans, but he cheers up the minute I pay him attention.' The implication is that he does not *have* to moan when alone if he need not moan when in company. The truth is that he does not *feel like moaning* when distraction dilutes his pain-perception but that the pain overwhelms him when there is nothing else to occupy his mind.

Of course you cannot play with a child in extreme pain with associated shock. But even he will actually suffer less if he can safely be kept in verbal or hand-holding contact with someone and be kept aware of the real world outside the nightmare of his pain. Of course a child with a bad headache may be more comfortable lying down in a quiet room, but the hope is that either the pain will wear off or he will fall asleep. If neither is the case, he too will eventually feel less pain if he is read to or listens to a play on the radio. For any child in pain, appropriate occupation matters (*see* **Nursing**/Passing the time).

Changes of position and other physical stimuli. Some of the measures we take for the comfort of people in pain are really types of distraction and ways of interrupting the pain–distress about pain cycle (*see above*). They are nevertheless powerful weapons in your hands. There may be no single position in which your child's newly sprained ankle or newly set fracture ceases to hurt, but each new position will seem better for the moment. Whatever position (within reason) it is in, the pain he perceives will gradually increase until he changes it, and will then gradually rise again until it is again changed. Fussing with supporting pillows, changes from chair to bed and back again, cold compresses, hot water bottles and so forth are therefore not *only* ways of showing him your loving care, but also of making him hurt less overall, and hurt acutely for shorter periods.

● This is why painful injuries which are treated by immobilizing the child, especially if he must also be isolated, tend to be the most traumatic of all. A child with spinal damage, for example, newly entrapped in traction, will require all your support and a really imaginative use of those stimuli you are free to change: skin sensations from cold sponging, different things to look at and so forth. The newly burned child, with splinted limbs and in an isolation or controlled-humidity room, is exposed to the full and uninterrupted force of his own pain-perception. He will need more painkillers than in any other circumstances.

Non-chemical painkillers

Not all painkillers are drugs. You can sometimes kill pain, whose cause you know, just by removing that cause. Children should learn this kind of painkilling technique from early on. If they do, they will be taking an intelligent interest in their own bodies, they will be able to take sensible care of themselves at a relatively early age and they will be useful to others. Obvious examples are:

The pain of a burn which is relieved by cold water. The pain is due to continuing damage by heat under the burned surface; cold water halts it (*see* **Accidents**/Burns and scalds).

The pain of trapped pus which is relieved by releasing the pressure. The pain is due to pressure on the tissues underneath the skin. If the pus can be released the pain will stop (*see* **Infection**/Types of infection: Localized infection).

The pain of 'cramp' which is relieved by massage. The pain is due to the waste products of muscular activity which have accumulated in the affected muscle because the amount of blood reaching it was not adequate to remove those wastes and re-oxygenate the muscle. Massage hurries the blood supply and dispersal of wastes; the cramp stops (*see* **Cramp**).

The pain of irritation by foreign bodies which is relieved when they are removed. Whether it is dust in the eye or a splinter in the finger, pain will cease when it is gone.

*Chemical
painkillers for
diagnosed
conditions*

If your child is under medical care, relieving his pain will be part of his treatment, not only for humane reasons but also because pain itself may worsen his general condition (*see above* Extreme pain). Sometimes it seems to anxious parents that hospital staff are reluctant to give effective drugs, or effective doses of drugs, for pain. While, of course, every case is different and you should discuss your child with those who are caring for him, it may help to realize that:

Drugs which have sufficient effect on the brain to reduce awareness of pain also have side-effects. Morphine and pethidine, for example, the best-known narcotic pain-relievers, tend to cause vomiting (which may be both agonizing and dangerous following abdominal surgery). Morphine causes constipation which may be similarly unfortunate. Any narcotic drug may depress the cough reflex, or indeed respiration itself, and thus make the patient much less efficient at keeping his chest and upper respiratory tract clear. He may even pay for his pain relief with post-operative pneumonia. Such drugs also tend to make the child sleepy and/or uncooperative. Not only does this make him more difficult to nurse, it may also lead to him feeling more pain and needing more drugs. If a child is half-asleep, non-chemical methods of pain control are far less effective (*see above*).

Drugs which seem puny weapons against severe pain because you yourself use them for minor pain, may have specific effects the child needs. Aspirin, for example, is particularly effective against pain stemming from injury to joints, ligaments and so forth and it also has specific effects against inflammation. The aspirin tablets your child is given following that knee operation may actually relieve his pain far better than morphine.

If you know why your child is in pain but he is not under medical care, any use of painkilling drugs will be up to you. Remember that it is through his experiences of having such drugs used *for* him that your child will learn how later to use them for himself (*see also* **Adolescence**/The long road to independence: Self-care).

You may wish to avoid – and to teach him to avoid – the use of any drug under almost any conditions. On the other hand, you may feel that quick and readily-available pain relief is a legitimate benefit of modern civilization and that a 'pill for everything' is your right. Between these two extremes you may find the following points useful to think about:

Many common pains (headache, muscle strain, menstrual pain) will relieve themselves within a very short period of time. Most headaches of the 'tension' variety will 'go off' if the victim comes out of the crowd/stops trying to learn his French homework/rests and relaxes. Most muscle strains of a minor kind respond almost instantaneously to rest, while most menstrual pain will stop when the flow is fully established and, in the meantime, may be relieved either by a short rest lying down *or* by exercise and a hot bath.

This argues that drugs are unnecessary in such situations and that children should be taught to adopt non-chemical means of responding to these everyday pain-signals. But the argument has another side.

Pain responds better to analgesic drugs when they are taken before it has become severe or has continued for very long. If you 'catch' a headache at the beginning, a single dose of analgesic will probably banish it while if you wait for several hours until the child is miserable with it, the first dose may be ineffective.

There is a conflict here and it is one which has to be resolved in practical terms of the life-demands the child faces. If, for example, the headache starts at lunch-time and he faces a test during afternoon school, with no opportunity to rest or relax, an analgesic is probably sensible. But if he comes home with a headache at the end of the day it may be reasonable to suggest that he do something quiet for a while to give it a chance to go off. If a girl always has menstrual pain, it is a pity if she comes to associate this regular sign of maturity with pain but it is also a pity if she associates it with two days a month of four-hourly analgesics. She should, perhaps, be encouraged to wait and see, each time, how bad the pain is going to be, before she takes anything for it. In this way she at least gives herself a chance to experience pain-and-drug-free menstruation when she can.

Acute pain which you know will end when definitive treatment is carried out, is probably best dealt with energetically from the beginning. The two commonest examples are probably toothache (when the child must get through a night before his dental emergency-appointment) and earache which a doctor has diagnosed as due to middle-ear infection and for which the child is taking antibiotics which will take a day or so to start being effective. In either case, a night of extreme pain will make the child much iller than he need have been. Exhausted, he will tolerate that dental treatment less well. Desperate with the pain in his ear, his fever will be more difficult to control and he will not get the rest which could help his body fight the infection.

● Don't let the effectiveness of a dose of analgesic fool you into putting off the definitive treatment. Getting rid of the toothache or earache does not mean that he does not need the dentist or the doctor.

Chemical pain-relievers for undiagnosed conditions

If a child complains of pain which is outside the ordinary run of headaches and minor aches and pains and neither you nor he has any idea what may be causing that pain, be very cautious about giving analgesics.

If they kill the pain and he then needs a doctor's attention, they may 'mask' the condition so that diagnosis is difficult. This is especially true of babies; they cannot tell the doctor where it was hurting before, and will not give him clues by their behaviour if it is not hurting now. It is also surprisingly true of older people. Pain in the chest, for example, seems unforgettable while it is going on, but relieve it and it becomes difficult to remember *exactly* where it was and *exactly* how deep a breath it took to exacerbate it . . .

Whether or not they kill the pain, just giving the drugs may make you delay in seeking medical advice. A few potentially serious illnesses, such as meningitis, sometimes present with severe headache. If you give the child analgesics, wait four hours, accept that the first dose did not work and give another dose and wait for that to work, you may have delayed most of a day or night before reporting a condition which requires immediate treatment. If your frantic toddler calms down and goes to sleep on a dose of analgesic, he may wake later not just with renewed earache but with a burst ear drum.

Some painful conditions are actually made worse by the very drugs you give to relieve the pain. Aspirin, for example (*see below*) has inflammatory effects on the stomach lining and may even occasionally cause bleeding in the stomach. It may seriously exacerbate many of the disorders that give rise to 'stomachache'.

You may, then, like to develop a rule-of-thumb for yourself along some of the following lines:

If pain is so severe that you are seeking medical advice don't give painkillers meanwhile: wait for a diagnosis and doctor's recommendation/prescription.

Don't give painkillers for undiagnosed abdominal pain. If the child does not (yet) need to see a doctor, he does not (yet) need chemical pain relief.

Don't give painkillers to babies with undiagnosed pain. If a baby is in pain he does need a doctor because he cannot give you any of the information which can safely assure you that the matter is trivial.

Don't give painkillers for unusual pain. If your child is subject to headaches or to menstrual pain or has an old ankle injury which 'plays up' after heavy exercise, home pain relief, on the assumption that this is the picture-as-before, may be fair enough. But if this is a new or different kind of pain from any with which the child and you are familiar, and it cannot be dealt with by non-chemical means, you need a doctor's diagnosis.

Painkillers for home use

There are literally thousands of analgesic tablets available without a doctor's prescription. Most of them are slightly varying combinations of a very few drugs. The drug industry makes enormous profits out of our readiness to believe that this one will be more effective than that. If you want to give your child only the drugs he actually needs, and to do so as cheaply and simply as possible, be wary of:

Advertising. Using the same headache remedy as that prima-ballerina will not make your daughter dance better . . .

Copy-writing. The fact that a package *says* that these tablets are the most effective remedy for a particular kind of pain does not make it so.

Expensive additives. Many of the additives which make you believe that this product will be more effective than another actually have no effect on the pain you are trying to deal with. If you want the additives for their own sake it is usually far cheaper to provide them separately. The many aspirin-containing lemon drinks, marketed for 'the aches and pains of influenza' are a case in point. Three typical British ones work out so that each dose-drink costs about twenty times the real cost of the same dose of aspirin, and about eight times the current cost of a dose of aspirin plus a separate hot lemon drink.

Expensive packaging. Quite apart from the obvious expense of colourful and eye-catching wrappings, some painkillers are promoted on the basis of their convenient-for-your-handbag packs and/or their foil-wrapped safety from exploring children. Remember that small quantities always cost more than large ones, and that if you want to carry a few with you, or give an older child a couple to put in her pocket, you can easily buy a tiny pill-box or bottle (which of course you must label; *see* **Safety**/In the home: Safety with medicines). If you want to keep *any* drug safely away from children, *a foil wrapping will not do*. Drugs need to be locked away.

The actual drugs amongst which you will probably choose are mentioned below. If you consider their various actions and their various side-effects, you will be able to make a sensible choice amongst them for general use and for any more specific purposes. Buy them in the cheapest available form (which, in Britain, will not be under any brand name but under the label 'BP' for which you can ask your chemist).

Before letting yourself be tempted into buying a different – and more expensive – formulation, read the small print which tells you how much of what is in each tablet and compare it with your basic supply.

Aspirin   This is a 'salicylate'. The other very common salicylate is called salicyla-mide. Its effects and side-effects are similar so the two can be considered together, but aspirin is generally the more effective of the two. When you are doing your research, you may also find aspirin referred to as acetyl-salicylic acid; acid acetylsal or acetylsalcylicum.

Aspirin has three principal useful effects: it relieves mild pain, especially in such pains as headache, toothache, painful muscles, ligaments and joints. It is 'anti-pyretic' which means that it brings down fever (*see* **Nursing**/Fever) and it is anti-inflammatory, which is why it is often used in rheumatic/arthritic disorders and why it is doubly effective following sprains and so forth.

Used occasionally and in the recommended doses, aspirin is remarkably safe. Accidents do occur; small children do suffer accidental over-dosage and people do kill themselves with the drug, but this must be set against its wide availability and against the fact that more people take more aspirin, without ill-effects, than any other drug.

Side-effects include: ringing in the ears as a first sign that mild over-dosage has occurred; irritation of the stomach – sometimes with nausea and vomiting, eventually with bleeding.

Contra-indications include: heart disease (aspirin increases the work of the heart); vomiting/diarrhoea/dehydration (aspirin has to be excreted by the kidneys, the patient therefore must have plenty of fluids); inability to eat (aspirin is more likely to irritate an empty stomach and therefore should not be given to a patient who will not eat unless he can drink milk or some other 'food-drink').

Paracetamol   Is a breakdown product of phenacetin – previously a very commonly used pain-reliever but now known to be damaging to the kidneys. Do not buy any product containing phenacetin: all its useful properties, without its dangers, are present in paracetamol. You may find it referred to as acetaminophen or panadol.

Paracetamol relieves mild pain to about the same extent as aspirin; it is therefore a suitable alternative for a child who is sensitive to aspirin. It is anti-pyretic. It has no anti-inflammatory properties and is not therefore useful in rheumatic/arthritic conditions and may be less effective than aspirin in sports injuries, strains and sprains.

Side-effects are less obvious than with aspirin because paracetamol is less irritating to the stomach. Nevertheless, it is probably slightly less safe than aspirin, if taken frequently or over a long period, because it can contribute to anaemia by a direct effect on the red blood cells and it can also cause kidney and/or liver damage.

Codeine   Is obtained from opium and is therefore related to morphine. You may see it referred to as methylmorphine.

Codeine is a somewhat more powerful pain-reliever than aspirin, although far less powerful than morphine. It is not anti-pyretic nor is it anti-inflammatory. You will often find it combined with aspirin to produce a compound with all aspirin's beneficial effects plus an increase in analgesic power.

Side-effects of codeine alone include constipation which, if the drug is taken over a long period, can be severe. It is for its constipating effect that you will find it included in mixtures for the treatment of diarrhoea. Although codeine does not suppress the cough reflex to as great an extent as does morphine, it does have this effect. It is for this reason that you will find it included in cough suppressant cough medicines.

Dosages   Children under five should always be given pediatric ('junior') aspirin or paracetamol. If this is in liquid form, make sure you measure doses with a chemist's 5 ml spoon, not a domestic and variable 'teaspoon' (*see* **Nursing**/Medicines). Follow the recommended doses for your child's weight.

Older children may be given adult aspirin or paracetamol in a suitable dosage which, for a six- to ten-year-old, might be one tablet at intervals of not less than four hours, amounting to not more than four doses in twenty-four hours. (If pain continues, consult a doctor). Once a child is of near-adult weight, he can have adult doses.

● Whatever the age of your child, remember that it is his weight which is relevant to dosage. If yours is a very small six-year-old, he might still be better off with 'junior' aspirin. If in doubt, ask your doctor.

Pets *see also* **Accidents**/Bites and stings. **Rabies**; **Safety**/Safety and pets

Many families find themselves landed with animals which give nobody any pleasure while others keep no creatures but feel a sense of loss as a result. The secret of finding the right 'pet policy' for your family is to think realistically. Who in the family wants a pet? What for? Will the type of creature he or she yearns for actually fill the role envisaged? How will its needs fit in with other family commitments? Would a different kind of animal give the same pleasure for less disruption?

While children are very young – certainly while they are under school age – it is foolish to acquire any animal unless you yourselves positively want it. However much you may believe that a 'house isn't a home without a pet' or that 'children learn responsibility by caring for helpless creatures', *you* are actually the ones who are going to spend money, if not on the animal, then on its housing, food and so forth. And *you* are the ones who are going to do the caring, too. If you will enjoy coping with animals as well as babies, fine. Everybody may benefit. But if you will not, don't give in to your three-year-old's pleas for a rabbit. He may think he wants one and he may mean to look after it himself. But he can neither understand the care that rabbit will need nor the limitations it will have as playmate/toy.

A family pet will probably mean a dog or a cat. Don't acquire a cat because you really want a dog but do not feel you can provide the right environment. Cats are not at all like dogs and are not therefore likely to be very satisfactory as direct replacements. If you can provide decent circumstances and care for a small child you can also provide them for a dog, if you really want to. Do remember, though, that any uncaged animal will restrict the family's freedom to some extent. It is difficult to take a cat out for the day and dogs are not always welcome overnight guests.

Caged pets can usually be taken around to a friend's house for temporary care, but they are not always a suitable mix with small children. Ferrets, for example – exceedingly popular just now in the United States – are often not trustworthy with the very young, while birds, though fun for a child to watch, are too delicate for him to handle.

Children's own pets

School-aged children often genuinely want animals and can certainly learn to take care of them, although the final responsibility will, for a long time, rest with you.

If you are not an animal-loving family, your seven- or eight-year-old probably will not be offered a dog or cat. Rabbits and rodents are cheap to feed and easy to look after but they can be unexpectedly disappointing. Rabbits are misrepresented in children's stories so that new owners often expect a kind of recognition and affection which is not forthcoming. Guinea pigs have some very saddening habits – like fighting each other or eating their young – and they scratch, too. Hamsters are usually so determinedly nocturnal that they will not play, or even eat, when a child is awake. Gerbils and mice are fiendishly difficult to hold onto and do not easily survive being dropped . . . All these creatures breed and die with a relentless speed which may be educational but may be too much either for you or for the young owner (*see* **Death**).

Temporary pets   If you live in a rural area you can sometimes arrange for a child to take temporary charge of an orphaned lamb or calf. Although there is loss implicit in such an undertaking, it is not the tragic loss of a death (often with associated guilt about lack of care or physical carelessness) but simply loss of a baby creature who is a baby no longer. The loss of the creature as a pet and companion may be more than counter-balanced by the joy of having successfully reared it to a point where it can re-join others of its kind. If such an opportunity should present itself to your animal-mad child, do consider it carefully. A couple of months of bottle-feeding a calf, being followed everywhere, called to, butted and played with, can give a child more pleasure and education than years of cleaning out rabbit hutches.

Pets for interest   If your child's desire for animals comes from interest in other species, rather than from a yearning to love and be loved by something warm and cuddly, there are all kinds of creatures he can keep. There is real skill and care in the successful hatching of frog spawn. It is a good thing to do, too, as frogs are becoming horribly scarce in many places. Educational suppliers now sell wormeries and anteries. These viewing houses really do prevent the creatures getting out while enabling a child to feed them and to watch everything they do.

Fish are fun to watch and easy to look after although disease and death can be uncomfortably frequent (*see* **Safety**/Safety and pets).

If you live in a reasonably warm part of the country and have a garden, tortoises are as agreeable as they are undemanding.

Pets to avoid   Obviously a young child should not be allowed to keep dangerous, or potentially dangerous, creatures. But neither should he be encouraged to keep those to whom he is dangerous. Many children rescue a fledgling bird from a cat, or find an injured baby rabbit, and at once long to put it in a cage and keep it. If you let your child do this you are betraying his undoubtedly good intentions. These young creatures will only stand a chance of survival if they are left where their parents can find and retrieve them. Some will actually die of terror (stress) if confined in human hands.

Watching wild creatures   If wild creatures should not be touched or 'kept safe', they can certainly be watched and some can even be sufficiently 'tamed' to give a child enormous pleasure. Bird tables and garden nesting boxes really help species struggling to survive in urban or suburban surroundings, while once you have spotted a hedgehog in your garden, a nightly bowl of milk may turn him into a regular resident.

Phobias *see* **Anxiety, Fears and Phobias**.
Pica (eating dirt) *see* **Habits**.
'Pink eye' *see* **Eyes and Seeing; Eye Disorders and Blindness**/Conjunctivitis.
Plastic surgery *see* **Birthmarks; Hospital**/Surgery. *See also* **Adolescence**/Problems with appearance and body-image.

Play *see also* **Nursing**/Passing the time

Parents need to take children's play seriously enough but not too seriously. If it is regarded as entirely trivial – a matter of keeping children occupied until they are old enough to do something more useful – the wherewithal for satisfactory play probably will not be provided because nobody will bother. But if play is seen as vitally important – the child's work and the principal medium through which she learns – too much self-conscious attention will probably be paid to her activities and she will be deprived of the freedom and spontaneity which is the point of her very best play. It is sometimes helpful to remember that:

Play is enjoyment

A child plays because she wants to play. She goes on playing because she is enjoying herself and she stops when the fun runs out.

Play is therefore self-motivated

Although suggestions for particular kinds of play often come from someone else, the drive to play comes from inside the child. If you make her paddle in the sea she is not playing, until or unless she stops doing it to please you and starts doing it to please herself.

Play is self-directed

No child has to be told how to play. She uses the available ideas, materials and facilities, to develop her games for herself. If there are rules they are her rules. If you make her play your way, she is not playing until or unless she chooses to make your rules her own, in order to share the activity with you. In middle childhood she will eventually choose to adopt group-rules in order to share playground or organized games with others, but this is not at all the same as having rules imposed upon her.

Play and learning

Babies and young children 'learn through play'. This idea is central to pre-school education in the western world, an acknowledgement of the fact that if they are offered appropriate circumstances, opportunities and materials, children will use them, without urging or direction, to find out many of the things adults want them to know. But although it is interesting to think about what your child may be discovering or practising as she plays in various ways, it is important not to let interest tip over into interference. Manipulative play with a construction kit may look more 'useful' than dashing round and round the garden, yelling. But it is just as important for the child to discover what her body feels like when cornering fast, or how much yelling the adults who share her space will stand, as it is for her to learn more 'intellectual' lessons. 'Learning through play' means learning everything about herself, her world and the objects and people in it. Play is the child's work but what she earns from it is her own rounded growth at her own pace, not solutions to a set of problems which adults set for her. Parents who try to provide opportunities for their child to have fun, in any direction she seems to enjoy, will probably facilitate more learning than those whose eyes are always fixed on her 'education'.

Unfortunately, our societies place a high premium on recognizable achievement and the big-business world has not been slow to cash in on parental concern with a vast industry of 'educational' toys, books, records, television programmes and 'early learning schemes'. Salesmen know that many parents will more readily spend money on such products than on toys that are 'just for fun'. If you happen to buy a 'posting box' at just the moment when your child is interested in different colours and shapes *and* enjoying her new ability to drop things accurately from her hand, she may genuinely enjoy it in just the way the manufacturers suggest. But if you buy that same toy at the wrong moment in her development, it may have no play-value for her at all. The lack of play-value will not matter to the child. She will either ignore the toy or use its packaging or component parts to suit herself. But it will matter if, irritated by her apparent inability to perform a 'play task' which the manufacturers maintain is appropriate for her age, you try to make her play with it 'properly'. And it will matter, too, if buying that toy has made it impossible for you to buy some other play material for which she is waiting. If you provide playthings for fun, your child will educate herself. If you buy toys for education she will not always have fun.

Play, teaching and work

Children have an in-built drive to mature, to grow up and to learn to do the things they see older people doing. From her earliest months your child will be watching and listening to you, copying you, picking up ideas and suggestions from you. She will personalize this kind of learning by incorporating it into her play, and, because that play is fun and is under her own control and direction, the learning will be thorough and complete. It is a process, though, which can easily be spoiled or interrupted by too much direct teaching, especially teaching which masquerades as play. If your child is playing in a sandpit, with yoghurt cartons and seaside buckets, you can certainly show her what happens if damp sand is packed into a bucket and the bucket is then gently upturned. She may be delighted. She may instantly set about making her own 'castles' or 'jellies' or 'cakes'. But if you try to *teach* her to make them, insisting on an efficient technique; monitoring the amount of water; helping to upturn the mould and so forth, you will probably distress her and you will certainly spoil whatever sand-play she actually had in mind. This kind of interference, carried into many of her activities over a long period, conveys an extremely confusing message to the child. Is the activity really for her or is it for you? Is it really play or is it a duty? Eventually, the child whose play does not please you because she does not do it 'right' may come to feel that she herself is not pleasing to you; that she does not live up to your expectations and is in general not 'good enough for you'. Teaching skills to very small children is fun and can be fun for them, too, but it is less confusing if you keep it to areas where the motivation and direction clearly *are* yours and where there is no pretence at trying to please her but an open desire to get her to please you. On that basis she may be delighted to learn to put on her own socks . . .

As she grows older she will inevitably learn not only the difference between 'play' and 'work' but the difference in the valuation society puts on them too. At school she will find lessons interspersed with playtimes, and discover that activities like learning to read are compulsory while activities like learning to skip are not. You cannot protect her from this skewed approach to life's activities, but you can at least make sure that every aspect of herself, and of what she does, is equally valued at home. It is sad to hear parents complaining that a three-year-old at nursery 'does nothing but play', making it clear that they already feel there is a better way for her to spend her time. It is sad to find older children being asked to earn the right to play by working, whether at homework or chores, and to see those who are playing constantly interrupted by adults who would respect their peace and privacy if they were at their desks. It is saddest of all to watch schoolchildren discovering that they can only preserve their right to play by turning that play into yet another kind of work; the child who wants to spend a lot of time with a ball must try out for the tennis team; the one who loves music or dancing must accept lessons, practice and examinations . . . We deprive children of growing time by insisting that they have 'something to show for' everything they do. We turn play into work by insisting that 'if it's worth doing it's worth doing well'. It is not surprising that, by puberty, many children have lost the ability to motivate and direct themselves in fun-activities, giving most of their 'leisure time' to the passive relaxations of television and spectator sports. It is a pity, though. Play remains a human need all through life. Everyone manages herself better if she sometimes does things just for fun, when she wants to, as she wants to, for herself and her pleasure alone. We should not have to label our play as a 'hobby' or a 'sport' to get it accepted, nor should we have to apologize for 'just mucking about'. Fun, however 'purposeless', is never a waste of time. The only true waste of time is boredom.

Providing for play

While it is up to your baby or child to choose when, how and with what she plays, offering the widest and most comprehensive possible set of choices is up to you, especially while she is too young to have much experience outside her home. She cannot ask you for paint until she knows of its existence and its potential; she cannot play at being a fireman she has never seen; she cannot discover the thrill of clay or dough if there is none for her to use nor know the thrilling and fearful anticipation of hide-and-seek if nobody draws her into the earliest versions of the game. Your child will play with, and within, the world she sees and experiences. So when you are thinking about providing for many different kinds of play, you have to think about the whole environment and way of life which she shares with you, and try to see it through her eyes. It is not a careful collection of toys which she needs so much as a careful inventory of the kinds of experience and activity which are obviously available to her and of the kinds which she may miss unless you take positive action. Think, for example, about *where* she lives, about the actual house or flat which will be her first environment. Think about the *kind of community* her home is in, and its way of life which she will see and share. And think about the people there are for her to know and love. What will her life be like? What 'play' is built-in to it, and what needs adding on?

Life in a farm-house offers different experiences from life in a city flat

Each may provide a rich and satisfying home for any child, yet each will automatically provide certain play experiences and tend to deprive her of others. In that city flat, for example, she may have other children to play with under the same overall roof; a constantly changing panorama of people and traffic to watch and plenty of interesting places (from playgrounds to big shops or railway stations) to be taken to by adults. But unless you work at it, she may lack experience of her own self in wide-open spaces; of changing seasons; of animals and other living, growing things.

In that farmhouse setting she will have every opportunity to explore the natural world and her own place in it, but unless you make the effort to show her other ways of life, she may have only a very limited view of how most people live, behave and work.

Life in dif-ferent kinds of family-group offers different experiences

The people in your child's household are the most vital factor in her environment; on them hinges the use which she can or cannot make of all the rest. At the beginning of her life they are also her most important playthings and partners. Will your child grow up knowing both sexes and all ages, with brothers and sisters, grandparents and aunts, cousins and relations-of-relations all sharing the interplay of their relationships with each other, and with her? Or will her basic experience be of life-with-mum so that you need to seek out more people for her to know, and know about?

Different amounts and kinds of space offer different experiences

A new baby does not take up as much space as her own equipment, but as soon as she is mobile she needs safe space to explore. As she grows, the amount of space she needs for active play increases, as does her need for different kinds of space for different uses. If you know she is going to be short of space for play, possessions and privacy, you may yearn for a playroom, but if you have one you will probably find it used for anything and everything except children's play. Your child will want to spend her time where you (or whoever looks after her) spend time. The money and effort you might have spent on making a playroom will be better spent on making safe play-space in the kitchen, or on adapting the living-room so that daytime use for play does not make it uninhabitable by adults in the evening.

Gardens are not only rich play-resources in themselves but also accommodate many kinds of play to which the insides of homes may not take kindly. If you have no real garden, you may still have outdoor space which can be made safe and useful with a little money and lots of imaginative work. A basement area, car-port or balcony, for example, can each give her the freedom to play with real mud when she is a year old (yes, you will have to fetch the mud), grow runner beans in pots when she is two and keep guinea pigs when she is three . . .

'Toys'

If people are asked what parents must provide for children's play they usually answer 'toys'. Commercially produced toys certainly have a place in children's play and pleasure, but many of your child's most used playthings will not be purpose-made for children at all but will be pieces of your adult world which you share with, lend to, or adapt for, her. When you do buy things especially for your child's play, you will often find what she needs, at a price you can afford, more easily at a hardware or stationery shop than from a toy counter.

● Remember that while toy manufacturers have to make their products to certain safety standards, stores which are not marketing their goods for children's use do not. Take care (*see* **Safety**/In the home).

Skilful parents can often make playthings which cost much less than the same object bought from a shop and which, designed and decorated specifically for their own children, give more pleasure as well. This book suggests comparatively little do-it-yourself toymaking because, in the author's hands, cardboard boxes and glue turn into sticky cardboard boxes. The playthings-for-making suggested here are either truly easy – requiring more imagination than craft – or items on which you could still save money over toy-shop prices if you employed somebody else to make them for your child.

● If you are skilled and do want to make toys, remember that the fact that your handiwork is on her behalf will not prevent her from resenting the time you spend on it. The most beautiful hand-made Christmas crib will not compensate a four-year-old for many December afternoons spent in lonely boredom while you carved the donkey and stitched Mary's clothes. If the creative process cannot be truly shared (as making the festive cake can be shared) it needs to take place in adult, rather than in family, time.

Playthings for babies

Very young babies have little use for conventional 'toys' despite the millions bought to celebrate their arrival. But most of them love to 'play' if somebody beloved will play with them. Of course your baby will be playing with you every time you pick her up, change her nappy, feed or bath her. But the fun of play does not have to be saved for times when you are doing practical things for her, nor reserved for times when she is distressed and you are trying to comfort her. She can play for pleasure at two months as well as two or twelve years.

Older babies want and need to explore the brand-new world in which they find themselves but they can only explore the pieces of that world which you will offer. If you try to provide enough 'real toys' to satisfy that endless curiosity, you will certainly run out of money and storage space. This is a time when you really need to offer an imaginative range of personal and household objects as well.

Towards the end of this first year, your baby will have explored so many objects, and become so competent at managing her own body and making it manipulate those objects, that she will be ready to *use* toys as well as examining them. This is a stage when you will probably want to buy her quite a lot of 'real' toys, but you can save money and disappointment by making sure that your selection fits her stage and interests. She will also be especially interested in your 'toys' and most interested of all in the ones you use in her care. If you will offer her the hairbrush or the facecloth, richly interesting play for her may actually get one of your jobs done – after a fashion.

Babies can neither ask for, nor go to find, playthings for themselves so they are peculiarly dependent on adults to offer them safe and interesting objects and activities. Remember that the most interesting playthings of all are loved adults and that the very best activities are shared. Whatever else she does or does not have, make sure she gets plenty of *fun with you*. The following chart is designed to suggest the kinds of play and the kinds of plaything which are likely to give pleasure at various stages of development. Because every baby is unique, it contains no *age-guidance* but only *stage-guidance*. Rattles, for example, are superb playthings for babies whose hands are mostly open and who are beginning to use their eyes to look for the source of sounds. But they are useless to babies whose hands are still mostly fisted, because babies at this stage are simply not ready to enjoy deliberate holding on to anything. So if you want to decide whether or not your own baby is likely to enjoy some of the suggestions at a particular point in the right-hand columns, look first in the left-hand column and see where her behaviour has got to. The suggestions which match her very own stage of development are the ones most likely to give pleasure.

The chart is not a prescription. Your baby does not have to do and to have everything it suggests, nor should her play activities be in any way limited by it. It is simply a series of suggestions which may give you an enjoyable jumping-off point in providing for her pleasure (and your own) at various stages. Remember that play is for fun so any activity which your baby does not enjoy is, by definition, wrong for her. She may (or may not) come to it later. Remember, above all, that fear is the enemy of play so any object or activity which upsets or frightens your baby should be abandoned, fast.

Pointers within her development	Some activities she may enjoy and ways of providing for them	
After birth she must settle into an environment which bombards her with stimuli because it is always changing rather than being always the same as was the womb. She may be happiest without much extra stimulation over that which goes with tender loving care.	Sucking, which is, of course, a necessity, but which should quickly become luxurious pleasure. Whether she is fed from breast or bottle try to *offer* rather than force; touch the cheek nearest to you	gently so that she turns towards nipple or teat; let it brush her mouth so that she herself actively takes it, rather than passively accepting.
Her survival depends on the adults who care for her and her first 'developmental task' is to discover human faces and voices and to respond socially to them.	Being held, face to face. Looking at your face; scanning it closely; listening to your voice as you talk to her. She does not need fluffy ducks and plastic rabbits if you will give her your smiling, talking face.	Very soon she will play 'conversations': watching your expression, answering with her own; listening to your voice and making her own sounds.

Pointers within her development	Some activities she may enjoy and ways of providing for them

She is still close to the enclosed world of the womb and likely to be frightened of being exposed in wide-open spaces. Nevertheless she is a highly sensual creature who must discover the pleasures of all five senses and will do so through you.	She will enjoy from the start those which mimic but extend that womb-world which was warm and soft, dark and rhythmical. As she becomes more confident of herself in this outside world, she may enjoy sensual adventures too: movement and touch, her own body in water, sucking for pleasure rather than for food.
	
	Hold her closely, face to face against your shoulder. Support her head carefully and then walk, jiggle gently, dance a little.
	    Hold her cradled on your lap and stroke her bare skin, all over, in a range of rhythms.
	    See if you can hold her in a warm bath so securely that she is not afraid but can discover the joy of moving her limbs freely with the water's support.
	    Choose a time when she is not hungry and help her fist to her mouth and give her your own finger to explore with her mouth and to suck.

As soon as she stays awake for longer periods than you want to hold her she will be ready to start discovering her world by looking at bits of it. She cannot coordinate seeing with doing, eyes with hands, but she can learn about all kinds of things by looking alone. She still looks at your face for preference, but other things – especially complex and moving shapes – will hold her pleased attention. Her best focusing distance is still only about ten inches, so she will see fine detail best from close up.	Looking: at as many new and different objects as you can provide. Hang things at about ten inches above her pram and cot, making sure that they are within her eye-line as she lies in her own preferred position which is probably curled to one side. She can have mobiles and pram toys but the familiar is uninteresting. She will prefer the washing dancing on the line, a balloon tied to the pram handle and moving in the breeze. A foil plate dangling where it catches the light; a shimmery scarf tied to the cot bars . . .
Her first social smile is on the way; it will come in response to your smiling and talking face.	Being held and talked to. Try to make sure that you give her some conversation time which is neither part of her physical care nor interrupted by your talking to her brother. She will concentrate on you if you concentrate on her.
She probably will not be happy alone and awake for long, even with things to look at. She wants to be very close to you.	When you cannot hold and concentrate on her, she will enjoy any 'activity' which keeps her with you. Carry her, sometimes, in a sling as you go about your business. Sit her in a babychair close to where you are working and take time to show her bits of what you are doing.
She will soon find her first 'playthings' which will be her own hands. She will find one with the other, by touch alone, and pull at the fingers without looking. From time to time she will catch sight of one waving in the air and look without touching.	Being awake but alone in her pram or cot *as long as she is content*. If she is awake but 'busy', don't feel you have to get her up immediately. Leave her hands always free of wrappings or mittens so that she can 'find' them as soon as she is able and discover that they are there for her whenever she pleases.

Pointers within her development	Some activities she may enjoy and ways of providing for them

When her hands are open (rather than fisted) most of the time that she is awake and she plays with one with the other, she will be on the verge of making vital discoveries about the connections between seeing and doing, looking and feeling.

Holding onto things which are put into her hands; sometimes glimpsing what she is holding as her waving arms bring it into view. Gradually discovering that those hands are part of her; under her own control; that she can make them bring what they hold to where she can see it and then that she can make them bring what they hold to her mouth for sucking-exploration, too.

Give her lots of *different* things to hold. Rattles are ideal because the sound they make, as she

randomly waves them, attracts her attention and makes it more likely that she will see as well as doing. But novelty is important so home-made 'rattles' are useful. Fill little plastic pots with things which will make different sounds (dried peas, a coin, two marbles, etc. . . .). Put a little water in a small plastic bottle for a different sound and feel. Offer things which are interesting textures even if they do not make sounds: the rubber ring off a kilner jar; a piece of fur fabric; a ball she can hold but not swallow . . .

• Seal home-made 'rattles' carefully and think about the safety of anything she puts in her mouth: soon that will be everything . . .

As her hands open so her body will uncurl so that when she is awake she lies with her back flat on the mattress and both arms and legs free to move.

Learning to kick, smoothly and rhythmically, and experimenting with this new physical freedom which will lead to increasing physical control.

Unwrap her and put her on a rug on the floor, or on the centre of a double bed, so that she can have safe and comfortable freedom of action.

Play physical games with her like gently bicycling her legs or clapping her hands.
Leave time for long baths in which the support of the water will double the power of her kicking and make her feel like a super-person.

By the time her body has uncurled her control over her own head will be much improved.

Activities which allow her to practise holding up her own head rather than always having it supported by your hand.

Hold her against your shoulder with your hand poised to protect her if her head should 'flop' but not interfering with her if it does not. She may rhythmically 'bump'

it against your shoulder as she tenses and relaxes her muscles.
When she can hold it up reliably while you are still, try walking, then jiggling and eventually dancing with her at your shoulder.
Put her sometimes on her tummy, not just for sleep but for floor-play too. She will practise lifting and turning her head.

Once she is confident when her body is free of wrappings on a large surface, she will start to roll over, first from her side to her back, then from her back to her side; then all the way over. Rolling gives her new power: power over herself and power to alter her own position, view and activities . . .

Increasing amounts of physical freedom, until you reach a point where you unwrap her and take blankets, etc. out of her way whenever she is awake.

If you want to leave her to entertain herself in her pram or cot, visit her and take off covers, etc. so that she can choose how she plays. Remember to relieve

her of nappies too, from time to time, so that she can see and feel her whole body. When you can see that she is trying to do something specific, like roll right over, help her to go back and forth so that she experiences some successes.

Pointers within her development	Some activities she may enjoy and ways of providing for them
Once her head is steady and she can control her upper back, she will be ready to be propped up in semi-sitting position.	'Sitting' where she can see you. Find lots of different places where she can be safely propped. Her babychair is fine, but a corner of the sofa or an armchair makes a change, provided you are close by to supervise.
When she has 'found' her hands with her eyes (and learned to explore them with her mouth, too). She will be beginning the vital process of learning to get hold of things. She will not only look at things at different distances, but will actually search for something interesting to look at whenever she is awake.	Looking at things and experimenting with getting her hands to them; especially anything which she can hit, so that she both feels her hand connect and sees it swing. Hang things which she can safely hit at, within arm's reach above cot or pram. Try a woolly ball/soft toy, a softish balloon, a gay paper cup, a chiming ball, paper streamers, a bunch of rattly foil strips . . . Ring the changes so that when she succeeds in her hitting she is rewarded with different feelings, sounds and movements.
Soon she will clearly realize that when she sees something interesting, she can do something about getting hold of it.	Being propped in sitting position with interesting objects on a tray in front of her so that she can try, at her own pace, actually to get hold of them. All those rattles and things she used to have just to look at, will be interesting again for getting hold of. Don't stick to plastic: try a pair of rolled up socks, a soft bread roll and that furry toy rabbit . . . When you must sit still with her in a bus or doctor's waiting-room, wear something interesting around your neck for her to work at reaching.

● Anything she can grasp will now be sucked; is it safe? It may also be wildly waved; will it hurt if she hits herself in the eye?

Once she can reach out for things and get hold of them she will be able to explore her world, object by object.	Getting, holding and exploring the widest possible variety of objects. She will not yet be interested in *doing* anything with them, just in finding out about them. Objects which swing when she gets her hands to them will frustrate her now because she will not be able to grasp them. She needs things which will keep still for her.
	    She will do her best playing with objects when she is properly supported in a babychair.
	
	More and more and *more* objects to handle, look at and mouth. Nobody can afford to buy a new toy every day, so look around and choose what you can offer. Some objects which would not be safe for her to have when she is alone are all right if you are watching. Try for differences of shape, colour, weight, texture, sound . . .
	    Pots, packets, boxes, bottles – empty and full. Little clear plastic bottles can have coloured soapy water for pretty foam when she shakes, or a single marble for a nice thud.
	    Little cloth bags which you make and fill with cornflakes for a light scrunch, lentils for shifting weight, a single potato for a heavy lump . . .
	    Different kinds of paper for different kinds of crumple (not newsprint; the ink may be poisonous). Different kitchen utensils, small saucepans, wooden and plastic spoons and plates . . .
	    Fruits for their shape and a surprise when she sucks them.
	    A few really big things (like an uncut loaf of bread or big soft toy or beach ball) for her to get hold of in both arms.
	    Things for careful looking. Show her a bold picture-book. Make chewable books by sealing bold pictures into plastic wallets.

Pointers within her development	Some activities she may enjoy and ways of providing for them
She will also be exploring her own body-in-that-world; finding out what she can make it do and where it ends and the outside world begins.	Probably all kinds of physical and 'gymnastic' play but with the level adjusted to her enjoyment so that she is never frightened or made to jump. All those nursery games which involve bits of her body: 'This little piggy went to market', 'This is the way the farmer rides'; toe-counting, tummy-tickling. Being held standing so she can 'dance'; being gently pulled to sitting.	'Coming and going' games so that you hide your face and peep out/cover a toy and reveal it; bounce your face towards her and away again . . . A baby bouncer, hung so that as she sits, her toes just touch the floor and as she pushes down, she bounces. (Don't bounce her; let her adjust the activity for herself.)
She will learn to control her limbs and make them do what she wants on purpose, and she will increasingly be able to control her own position, by rolling over; getting into crawling position; sitting forward in her chair so that only the base of her spine is supported.	Any which combine physical freedom with interesting sights, sounds, feelings, objects – especially people. Physical play in lots of different circumstances: being bounced on the middle of your bed; rolling on grass; kicking in the bath, lying on	front or back on a safe floor. Being propped sitting in pram or car seat so she is moving and looking: or near you so she can see (and join) what you are doing.
From the above stage of hand–eye coordination and physical control.? Six months. Having learned a lot about objects by looking at them and a lot more by handling-and-looking, she will become ready to explore not just the objects but what they will do; their behaviour and her own power over them. The direction of this kind of exploration is affected by her deep attachment to you and by her readiness to imitate you.	The beginnings of manipulative play such that she does something (like making a bell ring) by accident and then finds that she can make it happen again on purpose. 'Helping' you and being shown how things work. Play with objects you use in her care. Find her some playthings which give her clear cause-and-effect: toys which squeak when squeezed or rattle when banged (a saucepan and spoon are as good as a drum . . .). Cars that run when pushed, balls and apples that roll, paper which tears. She will be interested, too, in discovering the basic characteristics of objects which do	*not* behave similarly even if she treats them the same. The ball rolls, the brick does not; the biscuit crumbles, the slice of toast does not. Love and imitation will meet in play with her own brush, facecloth and toothbrush, in attempts to feed herself and you, and in a passion for what she sees you use most – whether cooking pots, piano or typewriter. Let her have a go too (whatever the activity) for the best game of all, provided it is safe for her.
She is ready to increase her competence but because she still needs you to arrange experiences for her, its level will depend on what you offer. You probably will not affect her eventual 'intelligence' but you will affect her happiness . . .	Anything which you will do *with* her which she can enjoy *either* at the simple watching level *or* at the more advanced level of discovering how it works and copying. Pull-string music-box, nesting toys, boxes to fill and empty, brick	towers built and knocked down, balls run through cardboard tubes, piano or xylophone banged.

Pointers within her development	Some activities she may enjoy and ways of providing for them

She will now be learning to sit alone and to crawl, and to recognize, match and manipulate objects and soon to name them. These are vital accomplishments and, though she will achieve them all (probably by her first birthday) she may not be able to concentrate on them all at once. If she is a baby whose heart is set on getting mobile, her play with objects may not seem to become much more sophisticated for a while. If objects fascinate her, she may spend so much time and attention on them that she advances less rapidly in the physical areas. Follow her enjoyment-lead. If she is busy and happy most of the time, then the balance of activities you are offering is right for her.

Remember that these are also the months when her attachment to you is likely to reach its peak. There is both a positive and a negative side to this area of development. The positive side is that it is out of her joy in your love and company that she elaborates her communication, until eventually she shares not only your life but also your language (*see* **Language**). The negative side may be that she becomes 'clingy' and shy of strangers so that there are many activities which she enjoys to the full only if you are with her.

If her concentration is on sitting/crawling she will want to practise, again and again, her latest achievement. Unfortunately, this kind of practice usually involves adult help, so although she wants the freedom of the floor whenever she is awake, she also needs a great deal of attention.

Until she can sit absolutely steadily on the floor, her richest play with objects will take place when she is sitting in her chair with objects on its tray in front of her. If objects are her main passion she may want to spend long periods like this; if they are not, 'toys' may only hold her attention for a few minutes while she waits for a meal or her freedom.

Try to arrange times when there is nothing you have to do but be her partner. Sit on the floor with her and pull her into a sitting position or help her turn over to a crawling position as many times as she wants you to. When this is the kind of play she needs, nothing else will give equivalent pleasure and your wholehearted help will be more fun for both of you than attention given only reluctantly and because it is moaned for.

Once she can sit alone, even for moments only, don't expect her to be able to play with her hands: she needs them for balance. Instead, surround her with cushions or rolled quilts and let her practise, with assurance of a soft landing when she topples.

Once she can crawl, or get across the room by some combination of rolling/crawling/wriggling, offer interesting things for her to move towards: a big lorry, a box with things in it, a basket to empty or an animal on wheels which she can push if she can get there. Provide some big objects on which she can vent some of the frustration of her efforts, too: cushions to pummel, big soft toys to 'fight'. Once she really can

crawl she will push and follow a big beach ball or car.

She likes things which she can 'post'. Commercial 'post-boxes' may be too difficult yet awhile but try a shoe-box with big holes cut in the lid and balls and blocks to post in. She needs lots of boxes of every size and shape and lots of things to pile in and empty out. As usual you will hold her interest with novelty: spoons and a biscuit tin? Socks and a shopping bag? Old playing cards and a freezer-box?

She likes (mild) surprises, too, so try her (from a distance at first) with a jack-in-the-box, a pop-up-book, a squeaky toy. If she likes one particular object she will probably enjoy another which is the same-only-different so try a red sausage-shaped balloon to follow success with a round blue one.

She is beginning to enjoy and recognize finely detailed copies of the real world she knows, so she will probably enjoy a doll with removable clothes like her own, picture-books with familiar scenes, the family photograph album and a model car or dog which she can see is like the one the family owns.

Although there is so much of the world for her to explore that she must concentrate on new things and experiences, she is also beginning to remember a repertoire of familiar and enjoyable experiences and to love repeating them. This is the time to take her, again and again, to feed those ducks or visit that cat. It may be boring for you but it is not for her.

Gradually she will build her own kinds of repeated pleasures: she will make a ritual of special bedtime games and stories, and find particular activities which she must always share with particular people.

Pointers within her development	Some activities she may enjoy and ways of providing for them
Her curiosity and her physical abilities develop much faster than the memory or foresight which will one day make her 'sensible'.	Her desire to explore, both physically and by looking and touching, means that (as long as you are there) she will enormously enjoy going to new places. But she will constantly get into danger if they are unsuitable for her.	When home cannot mop up her endless curiosity, find safe places where she will be welcome like a parent-and-baby club, an under-fives playground, parks, gardens and the houses of friends who also have crawlers.
Her increasing passion for you makes her both very ready to imitate you and very keen to do what she sees you doing most often.	Anything that you will demonstrate and then let her try. Play with her, demonstrating building with bricks or scribbling with crayons, and let her do it too *but in her own way*. This is play not teaching. If she wants to knock down the castle she watched you build, do you *really* mind? If you cook, type or play the piano, she will want to, too. Find	a safe way for her to have a go because it will give her not only pleasure but a supreme sense of grandeur, too. Above all, let her share in the things you do as you care for her. Let her have a go at feeding herself, washing her face, brushing her hair and so on. What starts as pure fun will soon be useful, too.
Part of the reason for her extreme attachment to you is her increasing (and sometimes alarming) awareness that you and she are separate people. The more she can control the distance between you and assure herself that you always come together again after separations either in time or space, the more confident she will be of her own ability to manage and to enjoy being what she begins to think of as 'me'.	Games which involve taking turns and swapping over, coming and going, hiding and finding, all enable her to control this sort of separateness and togetherness. Let her feed you bits of what you are feeding her; take turns with anything from an ice-cream to throwing bread to the ducks; play at rolling a ball to each other; invent versions of hide-and-seek from bobbing from behind the curtains to simply covering your face asking 'where've I gone' and uncovering it again to 'here I am' . . .	Recognizable personal possessions will begin to give pleasure, too. This is the time for her special mug, plate and towel. For photos of herself, with and without you. For a safety mirror with holes in the frame so that she can hold it and examine 'me', and for the made-up serial story of her daily life with herself as the main character.
The more she shares with you the more elaborately she will want to communicate with you.	Any verbal activity; not just being talked to and jargoning back, but being read to, recited to, sung to, and joining in. Any game in which you use words with pleasure will please her. If you enjoy reciting Shakespeare, she will listen to the sounds and rhythms and be your best audience ever. If you have a fund of songs and rhymes she will pick them up and store them against the time when she will surprise you by reproducing a snatch. If you are a great one for the telephone she will want to	'talk' too, and perhaps will need a toy one to save the bills. Above all, though, tell her what the two of you are doing; point out to her what other people are doing; help her to tell her father what happened this afternoon. Quite soon now she will be talking, and that is one of the best games of all.

Playthings for near-toddlers and toddlers

By around a year your more-or-less-mobile and almost verbal child will be building a rich and complex play-world out of a combination of the materials you provide and her own rapidly increasing competence. Many of the playthings she already has will not only remain popular but take on a new lease of life as she makes new discoveries about them. That soft toy, which she pummelled in rage two months ago, may now become her dearest companion and bedfellow. That music-box, which you used to set going for her as part of a bedtime ritual, may now become something which she can not only work for herself but through which she can feel the glorious power of having music whenever she pleases. The books you showed her as she sat on your lap will now reveal their secrets without your help, because she can turn the pages for herself, while the stacking beakers, which she never much enjoyed for fitting-play, may prove ideal as doll's cups or sand-toys.

Most parents will nevertheless find themselves buying, making, or otherwise acquiring, a lot of new playthings during this age period because the child is so clearly ready and able to enjoy more and more different things, and because many of the toys available are so attractive to adults' eyes and memories. Choosing from the enormous range available needs some thought. You are the people who know your child best and the only ones who know her in her environment, so trust your own judgement as to what is suitable/desirable/worthwhile for her rather than anyone else's. The following general points may be useful in your thinking not only about toys for now, but also about the organization of her play-life for the next year or two.

Safety   Keeping toddlers safe in a family environment is always difficult (*see* **Safety**/In the home) but ill-chosen or ill-organized playthings can make it impossible. Toxic paints, ill-fixed dolls' eyes and sharp edges are obviously dangerous to a child of any age, but there are particular dangers which are peculiar to this age group:

Watch out for the incompetence of early walking. When she first discovers that she can pull herself up to standing position, she will try to do so using anything within reach. Don't buy, or even have around, a doll's pram, truck or toy intended to be pushed by a child on two feet. If she grabs the handle it will tip over on her. If she should find herself standing up with it, it will run away with her. Push toys should wait until she can both get up without support and walk steadily. Even then, remember that early walking is short on brakes and steering. If you put a toddler in charge of a wheeled vehicle you ask her to control its motion as well as her own. Confine such toys to safe indoor or garden spaces, ban them from pavements and watch out for steps and stairs.

Some children do become very angry when they can get to their feet but cannot actually progress around the room. Don't try to help by buying her the kind of 'walker' which sits her in a canvas sling on wheels and allows her to scoot around. Children have scooted into fires, down flights of stairs and over new babies. If you want to do *something* to help, either arrange the furniture so that she can hand herself from the support of the sofa back to the armchair to the table and round again, or buy her the kind of safety-truck which is usually called a 'baby-walker' or 'toddler-truck'. The special design of this often-magical first birthday present ensures that the vehicle will not tip if she pulls herself up by the handle and will not run away as she lurches forward holding on to it. With years of use ahead as a brick transporter or animal lorry, it may be a real best buy.

Watch out for ride-on toys with wheels rather than castors. Once she can walk well enough to manage the getting on and off, your child will probably much enjoy the kind of vehicle (sometimes animal-shaped, sometimes like a tricycle without pedals) on which she can sit and propel herself with her feet. But she will use those feet to push sideways as well as along; if she does that on a wheeled vehicle it will tip over rather than swivel.

Remember that she has a short memory and little foresight. She will not remember accidents, scoldings or warnings, nor will she foresee difficulties or dangers. That means that whenever danger presents itself as she plays, you have to deal with it once and for all. If she hits her head on the toy cupboard door today, you can be quite sure she will do so again, in something between two minutes and two days, unless you lock, remove or pad it. If she blips her baby brother over the head with her largest block and blacks his eye, nothing you say or do will stop her doing so again next time hand, block, baby and temper happen to meet; it is up to you to make sure they do not. If she finds that she can climb into a high cupboard during a game of hide-and-seek, she will not be stopped by wondering how she will get out again and even getting stuck in that cupboard for a few minutes will not stop her hiding in your chest freezer a day or two later. Stopping her takes a lock and/or supervision.

Supervision is the essence of toddler play which is both safe and free, but although you can (and will) develop eyes in the back of your head and a kind of instinct for the sort of silence which means danger, you cannot watch and attend to her every minute. Sooner or later she will go into a room alone while you are getting dressed, thinking her safely close by, or embark on a new activity while you are engrossed in conversation on the telephone. Supervision needs backing by:

Regular checking of all her playthings as you put them away each evening. The point is to make sure that junk-objects are not deteriorating to reveal sharp rivets and so forth; that vehicle wheels have not come off leaving lethal axles, and that forbidden objects, like sharp scissors, lent for a specific purpose under your eye, have not become mixed in with her things.

Careful organization of her play-storage so that objects which she must not use without your knowledge and attention are out of reach, so that she has to ask you for them (*see below*).

Storage Lack of storage space may limit, even more than lack of money, the playthings you can make available to your child. Poor storage can also make what she does have virtually unusable because she cannot see what is there or find all the bits of anything.

Unless you positively enjoy sorting out cupboards and drawers (probably weekly and certainly monthly) you may find that it is a mistake to try and store the toys of this age group in a way which banishes them from adult sight. A range of open shelves is often more efficient and it can look good, too, if trouble is taken.

You could, for example, accumulate five-litre plastic ice-cream containers and some plastic seed trays and use them for keeping all her small toys, or toys with many separate parts. Large, heavy toys and the ones to which she is allowed to help herself at any time, can go on the lowest shelves; things you want her to have to ask for, plus the ones she uses least, can go higher up. She can be reminded of what is there, even in the boxes she cannot reach, by having one item glued on the outside of the box or a picture of it drawn with felt-tip pen.

You may find that some playthings are best stored hanging up in bags. Drawstring bags are easy to make, either out of a pretty fabric or out of nylon 'string' so that she can see what is in them. Different sizes will take anything from a collection of balls to her favourite dressing-up clothes and accessories.

Dolls and soft toys can be a problem as, if she has many, they will both take up shelf space and keep falling over. You could try the 'hammock' approach. Under one of your existing shelves, fix a simple framework of wooden battens, wide enough to stand proud of the shelf. Tack fabric to the front and back, all along its length, to a depth which fills the space before the next shelf. Her 'people' can now sit in their hammock in a long row. She can see each one; she will feel that they are 'comfortable', and they look friendly, too.

Until she is old enough both to have a lot of books and to be able to find the one she wants by looking only at the spine, visible in a conventional bookshelf, you may find a home-version of the playgroup book-display method useful. All you need is a blank piece of wall or the back of a door or side of a cupboard. You screw pieces of wooden batten across the space at book-sized intervals and then stretch stout elastic between them. The books sit on the battens held flat by the elastic: visible and accessible.

However tidy and efficient your main toy-storage area, you will almost certainly need at least two 'junk' containers, whether they are cardboard boxes (which you could, of course, paint), wicker or plastic laundry baskets or even lovely Victorian blanket chests (watch out for heavy lids which squash fingers). One is for you: a quick and easy place to save for her the hundreds of potentially interesting and useful bits and pieces which come your way from packaging, sewing left-overs and so forth. The other is a place where the child can keep the hundreds of 'treasures' which she finds and cannot bear to throw away – yet.

An added bonus to this kind of toy storage is that for many children it makes the otherwise hateful business of 'clearing up' into a part of play. Sorting toys into the right boxes is (sometimes) fun. Putting books away is like doing a jigsaw puzzle if you can actually see the right-sized spaces; and opening and closing drawstring bags is fun, too. When you first set up a toy-storage or play area, try to allow for the future; for expansion in the collection of playthings and for change in the child.

For the moment she needs her playthings where she plays which is near you but as she overflows that first space she will want/be able to use space which is more separate from you, perhaps in her bedroom. It is usually sensible to *start* in the living-room, and make new storage upstairs later, than to begin with a 'nursery' and then find that although it is never used for playing in, its shelves are overflowing.

She must have floor space now and table space later. If you can arrange for her corner to have suitable wipe-clean flooring, most of her current play will take place on it. Later on you can install a table or counter-top for craft-type play (*see below*).

She will eventually need display space for her current pictures, etc. and probably blackboard space too, so try not to design your first set of storage shelves so that they take up every available piece of wall.

She will probably need lay-out space for farms, zoos, villages, car tracks or railways. If there is nowhere where she can leave an elaborate set-up overnight, she will actually be discouraged from a kind of play which is valuable to many children. If floor space is short, or the room is multi-purpose so that you know you will dislike even the most orderly versions of 'toys on the floor', try to build a wide counter-top or shelf into the storage unit for lay-out purposes.

She will need somewhere that is comfortable for resting, as well as efficient/hygienic for playing. At eighteen months she probably sprawls on your lap for a rest or a story, but at three or four she will need a rug or cushions or somewhere luxurious, to cuddle dolls, look at books or just think.

Choosing toys Bought toys are expensive, so most parents want to be sure that they get good value for the money they spend. Unfortunately, you cannot work out value for money in toys just in terms of whether the object you get is worth the money it cost. Often you will be buying an idea, a name, a patent, rather than an object which is of value in itself. An expensive board game, for example, may consist only of a piece of cardboard and a few pieces of plastic. Clearly the materials and workmanship are not worth the pounds it costs, but if that is the retail price of the game and that game is the one your child wants, it may still be a worthwhile purchase. At the other extreme you may sometimes buy an object whose materials and workmanship clearly are worth the money charged – as with some hand-crafted wooden toys, for example – but if your child does not play with the toy, but leaves it gathering dust on a shelf, it will not have been a worthwhile purchase. The point, of course, is that toys are for play and play is for fun; the true worth of a toy can only be measured in terms of the fun it gives your child.

If you look at some of the toys your child already has, note down their price and divide that by the number of minutes of play in which each has been vital, you will get a range of costs-per-minute's-play. You will probably find that on this basis large, expensive items and small cheap ones both emerge as 'better value' than many medium-priced toys. A climbing frame, for example, may cost £100 but be used by two children for at least an average of one hour per day for half of each of five successive years. That is 1824 play hours for £100 which is less than 1p per *hour*. A little plastic car may cost 50p and be played with for twenty minutes while it is brand new and for another five minutes the next day before it breaks or is forgotten. That is 2p per minute. An educational construction set may cost £5 and be played with for only two hours in total over several months. That is nearly 5p per minute. The point of this frivolous set of calculations is only to help you remember that when you are considering whether or not a toy is 'worthwhile', you have to think in terms of the child's pleasure; of what she wants the toy for. If you are determined never to buy 'junk', or always to buy 'decent educational stuff that will teach her something', you may waste your money while doing her out of a lot of fun.

Sometimes you can get excellent play-value-for-money by making yourself, or having made for you, items on which retailers really do make enormous profits. Blocks are a case in point. Your child needs lots of them and will probably use them in different ways over several years, so if you can afford to buy them they are certainly worthwhile. But if you cannot, you only have to persuade your wood-merchant to cut 2 in. × 2 in. timber (5 cm × 5 cm) into four inch, two inch and one inch lengths and you have your basic blocks for about one third of a toy shop's price. You will have to sandpaper and paint or seal them, but although that is a slow and boring job, there is almost no skill involved. Rather the same applies to the dolls' clothes which most children yearn for at some point. They are usually sold in sets, at absurdly high prices, so that you are forced to buy the handbag and shoes your child will instantly lose in order to obtain the jeans her doll must have. If you can sew, you can make the jeans out of her outgrown ones, for nothing. If you can glue felt, you can make a version for almost nothing. If there is no way you can make the clothes yourself, a dressmaker will probably run them up for you for a quarter the price a shop would charge *and* add the final touches which make them 'just like mine'.

There are a great many large playthings which almost every child yearns for but which are outgrown within a year or two. Your child will almost certainly want a tricycle and, if she has a first one when she is only two or three, she will very likely yearn for a bigger one before she is ready to move on to a first two-wheeler (*see* **Safety**/On wheels). She may want a doll's pram or furniture for 'house-play' (*see below*). You may long for her to have a slide or a garden swing or some other piece of outdoor equipment. Each of these items costs a very great deal of money if you buy it new and it seems ridiculous that, when one child has finished with it, another should not share the pleasure. Buy secondhand if you possibly can. You can usually acquire them through notices in shops, at the baby-clinic or in the local paper, at rock-bottom prices; once a family has outgrown them, their space is usually urgently needed. Of course it is sad for a child who had visualized a shiny new trike for Christmas to be given a battered old one, but even if you pay for professional renovation it will look like new for about half the new cost.

Sometimes you can get the best play-value-for-money of all by *inventing* playthings for your child in the ways suggested in Presents (*see below*). The point here is not that you make a copy of something which is available in the shops, but that you collect, assemble or otherwise put together, small cheap items which, because your idea exactly fits your child's current interests, add up to a major plaything.

When you do buy new from a shop, do check that:

She/you are not being misled by advertising. While every child should sometimes have a particular toy just because it is her heart's desire, many such yearnings will be inspired by television commercials and the disappointment that follows its purchase will often be just as cruel as the disappointment of having that purchase refused.

Always have the box or package opened before you buy. The scenes on the box may show working models, lunar landscapes or whatever, but the contents may be lumpy sterile plastic and pieces of cardboard. Does the toy do what the child thinks it will do? Look as she expects it to look? Is it on the scale she is imagining?

The toy is a practical plaything for her. Will she actually be able to use the toy or does it require more skill than she has, more help than you are prepared to give, more space than is available or weather you cannot expect in the next six months?

It 'fits' with the child's current play. You know how your child plays, the manufacturer does not. She may yearn for that plastic model plane but, if most of her play just now involves trying to make things behave realistically, she will probably throw it through the air to make it fly, which will both break it and turn it into a lethal missile. Can you divert her to a glider which is intended to be 'flown'? She may yearn for that talking doll, but it will not 'talk' for long if all the dolls in your house are bathed every day. Might she settle for a doll which 'wets' instead?

On the other hand, don't refuse items just because your child already has many similar toys. If she is into dolls or soft toys or Lego, her idea of 'enough' will not be the same as yours because she needs new fuel for the same range of play.

She will be free to use it as she pleases. It is usually a mistake to buy toys which are so delicate/expensive/noisy/risky that you have to limit and control their use. If you are going to say 'sshh' every time she bangs that drum or 'careful' every time she touches the doll's house, don't bother to buy them. Don't buy battery-operated toys unless you are prepared to keep on buying batteries, either. The more successful the toy, the more it is going to cost you to keep it running/the child playing.

● When you buy playthings with many small pieces, check the availability of spares and, if possible, buy some extras from the beginning. An expensive marble-run which will only accept its own marbles can be useless in a week if they all get lost. Often the manufacturer will post you this kind of extra if you write at the time of purchase. Check the manufacturer's address with the toy shop: they are often hard to track down from the information given on the packaging.

'Messy' and energetic play for private homes

Some play materials and play experiences are basic to a child's knowledge of the raw materials of her world and of her own self within it. She must, for example, have opportunities to discover how sand and water behave, separately and together, and what she can do with them. She must find out the changing limits of her own physical strength and courage, by climbing, swinging and generally having the opportunity to use herself.

Many parents associate this sort of play with nursery school or play-group and feel that they could not provide it at home. But not every child attends any kind of playgroup and few should attend before they are three. These are play activities which should be available from a much earlier stage and they can be made available under almost any home circumstances as the following notes and suggestions hopefully make clear. The trick is to think what it is that you are trying to offer (let's say 'water'); think what it may mean to the child and then realize that while there are large-scale and grand ways of providing for it, there are also modest and manageable ways. Water-play does not have to mean six chil-dren in matching waterproof aprons pouring the lovely stuff into measur-ing-jugs. It can mean your own child in wellington boots in a puddle.

The basic activity and why she will enjoy it	Ways of providing this kind of fun from the grand to the modest
Water. Playing in, and with, water gives your child all kinds of interesting physical experiences like being extra-buoyant and getting wet. It also gives her the chance to acquire information about the behaviour of her world's most basic element. You know that if you allow water to get out of its container it will splash onto, and spread over, the floor. Your child has to find out for herself. As she plays, scooping up water and letting it go, pouring it from one container into another and so forth, she also makes countless other discoveries which she cannot put into words but we can: she finds out about volume, for example: about how much water will 'fit into' a small cup and how much space that water leaves when she pours it into a bigger one. She finds out a lot of limits, too, like what happens if you go on pouring into a cup which is full. When she has water to use with other materials (sand, mud) there is a whole new range of discoveries to be made about how they behave together.	**Being in water.** If you have garden-space a *paddling pool* is obvious fun when the weather is warm enough. Filling it with warm water helps. Since you cannot leave a full pool in the garden (see **Safety**/In the home) and daily emptying is a nuisance, consider investing in a *splasher pool*. It will be about ten feet across and two feet six inches deep and will cost about the same as five ordinary paddling pools. It is a lot of money, but five paddling pools is a reasonable number for a two-child family to get through (they do eventually puncture beyond repair) so if you have the space it may be a worthwhile one-time investment. A child cannot climb over the high straight sides, so it is safe to leave it full. She can play in it (under supervision) if you put only six inches of water in, but she can actually learn to swim in it if you add more water. At the other extreme, her old *baby-bath*, filled with warm water, will give her almost as much fun as a pool, and is easy to empty and store. If you have no large water-container at all, try a *home-made wallow* on a hot afternoon. All you need is a large plastic sheet with the edges rolled round garden canes or whatever you have. Turn the hose on gently and you have a large expanse of water only about one inch deep. It will leak away, but not before she has had a lot of fun sliding on her bottom and sailing ping-pong balls and leaves. ● It will be slippery. Encourage toddlers to crawl rather than walk and site it so that others cannot hit their heads on anything if they fall. She can go in other kinds of water too. Most *public swimming pools* have toddler-sessions which she *may* enjoy but which do not cater for anything but body-in-water play as they will not allow her to take in containers, etc. She can go in every available *puddle* if you dress her suitably and, above all, *she can play in the bath*. Baths do not always have to be for cleanliness or routine. Provided you have enough hot water and time to supervise, she can get in the bath with all her water toys simply as a pleasure-activity on a boring wet Monday afternoon.

The basic activity and why she will enjoy it	Ways of providing this kind of fun from the grand to the modest
Water . . .	**Playing with water.** Your child need not be submerged in water to enjoy the stuff. If she wants to play with it at all today she will play on the scale which you can provide. If she can safely stand up at the *kitchen sink* you can give her small saucepans, ladles and sieves. If that is impossible try a *washing-up bowl* on newspapers on the floor, but find her small cups and pots (perhaps her own doll's tea-set) to use with it.
Sand. Dry silver sand behaves rather like water but with interesting differences and feelings. Damp sand has a new set of characteristics (like piling up and turning out). Wet sand is different again. As with water, your child will play happily with the basic material on the scale which you can provide.	If you have garden, courtyard or balcony-space, a *sandpit* is an excellent investment. Try for one at least four feet square so that two children can get right in. It can be moulded plastic or wood, but it must be placed where water can drain, and have a cover so that the local cats do not use it as a lavatory. A wooden one is truly easy to make yourself. You need four pieces of timber about four feet long by nine inches wide by one inch thick, plus another piece twelve inches square which you saw in half diagonally to make two corner seats which also brace the structure. Screw the four pieces of timber together at the corners to make a square. Screw the two triangular pieces across the front corners and there you are. On concrete or paving, it will drain itself. On grass or earth, put down a plastic sheet, studded with small drainage holes, first. You can cover with a sheet of hardboard or fold a sheet of heavyduty plastic over the top (as if wrapping a parcel) and staple the corners. You will then be able to slip it on and off.

• Fill with 'washed sand' or 'silver sand' rather than ordinary builder's sand. The latter may contain harsh chemicals and/or stain clothes bright orange.

A *baby-bath or washing-up bowl* full of sand will occupy her almost as happily as a sandpit if you provide ordinary size spoons, pots, etc. rather than spades and buckets. You may feel that sand and water combined is for outside use only, but sand alone is not difficult to sweep up off a hard floor.

If you want to provide this kind of play indoors and cannot cope with real sand, a couple of pounds of flour, or even sugar, is fun, too. Extravagant, perhaps, but you can sweep it up and save it for next time. Once you start on this idea you may want to elaborate it: the cereal which has gone soggy, lentils or porridge oats are all superb and differing materials. She will progress from the dry material to 'play-cooking' and thence to 'real' pastry-making (*see below* Clay, dough, plasticine and mud and *see* Presents). |
| **Clay, dough, plasticine and mud.** Materials of this kind all behave slightly differently but all offer the child the opportunity to explore material which she can mould, pierce, roll, break apart and stick back together again. They all make her 'dirty' too, and let her find out about the way her skin comes clean again under the tap. | Real clay is a difficult material for a small child to use because it is too stiff and hard. There are many easier materials on the market and they have the advantage of being brightly coloured, too, but the disadvantage of being expensive, especially as the colours become mixed to muddy brown and the child wants that lovely red again next time. Home-made play-dough (*see* Presents) is an easy and cheap alternative and she can also have your real pastry scraps whenever any are available.

Not every family will happily dig up a bucket of real mud for a child to dibble in, but 'helping' you to dig the garden, or even fill indoor pots with compost, will give her great pleasure and may lead on to gardening-type activities (*see below* Bringing outdoors indoors).

Whether you live in the country or the town, try to let her take advantage of any opportunities for mud-play, whether they are only the occasional puddle-in-the-park or a regular part of outdoor life. |

The basic activity and why she will enjoy it	Ways of providing this kind of fun from the grand to the modest

Bringing outdoors indoors. Some city and suburban children reach school age so ignorant of the living world that they truly believe that milk comes from bottles; that honey is made like jam and that fresh fruit and vegetables are the ones people forgot to put in cans. While no small child needs biology *lessons*, every child has the right to find out about the real nature of her world and her place in it. If things are not living and growing all around her, import some on which she can exercise her natural curiosity.

If you have a garden and pets (*see* **Pets**) or live in the countryside, your child's interest will lead her to find out all she needs to know. If not, you can easily ensure that some aspect of the natural world is around for her to think about most of the time:

Let her bring natural treasures in and keep them: pebbles, leaves and twigs may be used for sorting-play or just left on her 'display shelf' (*see above*) where she may one day notice how they change as they dry out. A skeleton-leaf is interesting; so is the snap of a dried twig which only bent last week. *Watching things grow is interesting* and, for a small child, growing things to eat is the most fun of all. Try mustard and cress on damp flannel or blotting paper, or mung beans or other sprouts in a screw-top jar of water. She can see daily progress after forty-eight hours and eat them a week later. If she is remotely interested in your house-plants, line an empty jam jar with a cylinder of damp blotting paper and place a bean or pea between the blotting paper and the side of the jar. She will be able to watch both the roots and the shoots, and you will not have to *teach* her that roots go down and shoots go up.

Watching creatures can be fun, too, and even if you have no room or inclination for pets she can have some. Buy a *wormery* or simply fill a glass dish with earth, find some worms to put in it and top with fine wire mesh. She will be able to watch the worms underground and, if she waters the top lightly, they will surface. An *ant farm* is best bought (from a pet shop or educational supplier) as it is difficult to make an ant-proof container yourself. It is not quite as easy to establish a flourishing colony as the instructions suggest, but if you succeed, they are fascinating to watch and the child can feed them herself. Frogs are rare in many parts of the world so if you are going to rear *tadpoles* do it responsibly and make sure that the baby frogs are released back into the pond where you found the frogspawn. Put the spawn and pond water in a large container; add rocks and gravel. Top up with more of the same water whenever possible (going to fetch some more may be a fun expedition in itself) or with rain water when it is not (putting out a rain-water collector is fun, too). Tap water will usually kill tadpoles. Once tadpoles free themselves of the spawn and swim free, let the child feed them with tiny quantities of the fish food sold for baby fish. Raw meat leads to dead tadpoles and stinking water.

Climbing, swinging, jumping and rolling play. The raw materials for this kind of large-scale physical play are only your child's own body-in-space and its own muscles working against a vast range of forces. She will run; she will climb, even if it is only on the furniture; she will swing, even if it is only from her father's hand. A country child with lots of open space and trees and gates to climb, probably needs no extra aids from you. A city child may need, and will certainly enjoy, them. You do not even have to have a garden to provide for active and enormously satisfactory physical play.

The best investment for this type of play is a *climbing frame*. A big one for the garden will cost a lot of money but will give superb play-value and probably hold its re-sale value too. Choose between tubular metal (which is cold and slippery when wet but needs no maintenance) and wood which is kinder but will need checking for loose joints and occasional coats of wood-preservative. Don't try to make one yourself unless you are truly competent. Your child's safety depends on its solidity. If you are going to buy a frame at all, buy the biggest you can: your two-year-old will still be using it when she is ten. Site it in a sunny part of the garden where you can easily supervise it, and preferably on grass rather than concrete or paving. Falls are unusual but a soft landing makes the prospect less alarming.

You can make a wooden climbing frame a wide range of *exciting extras* for very little money.

Platforms. Measure across one of the bays. Buy a rectangle of timber one inch bigger than the space. Sandpaper and wood-preserve it. Mark on the underside exactly where it crosses the frame-bars and screw on stout clips which fit those bars exactly. It can now be clipped safely in place and removed again when the frame is wanted for swinging.

The basic activity and why she will enjoy it	Ways of providing this kind of fun from the grand to the modest
Climbing, swinging, jumping and rolling play. . . .	**Swings.** Buy a rope about 1½ inches in diameter (expensive but it will last forever). Tie it to the top rail of the climbing frame and make a huge knot in the bottom. The child will swing by her arms and eventually discover that she can straddle the knot and sit while she swings. Then you can buy a circle of timber about fifteen inches in diameter, drill a hole through the middle, thread your rope through and knot it underneath to give her a 'monkey-swing'. Try a car-tyre, too.

Balancing planks. If you buy, sand and wood-preserve planks of wood about eight feet long, eight inches wide and one inch thick, you can screw clips on the underside of one end so that they can be securely fastened to the frame as an extension. Your child can eventually walk up them, jump off them and slide down them.

A cover. Some frames have covers as very expensive optional extras but an old double sheet or dustsheet thrown right over the whole frame makes a fantastic house or tent (*see below* 'Houses').

Failing outdoor space, there are indoor climbing frames available which are constructed to stand safely on a hard floor and to fold up when not in use. They take a lot of space even when folded, though, and they are not big and heavy enough for older children. Such a frame may not be a good investment for a single family. If you have no garden, consider instead:

A home-made climbing set. Acquire a couple of big wooden boxes, large enough for the child to get right inside. Tea chests are the easiest to find but check them carefully for sharp metal bits. Buy one or two planks, about six feet long by eight inches by one inch. Sandpaper the lot and paint it, perhaps, with brilliant coloured gloss paint. The child will use this collection, separately and together, for years. She will hide in, climb on, and jump off the boxes; put them together for a train or on top of each other for a ship's bridge. The planks will be walked along on the floor and put across the boxes for a bridge. With one end on the box she has a slide, with the middle over the box she has a see-saw.

● You may help your own storage problems if you find one box which is smaller than the other so that they fit inside each other when not in use. If you cannot store the boxes, it is still worth making the plank alone. Propping one end on the sofa makes a balancing bar or slide and when she is not using it herself she will sit dolls on it or run cars down it.

Indoor swings. If you can screw two heavy-duty hooks into a ceiling joist in a room which has enough clear floor space, your child will have the potential for endless swinging play. The easiest way to provide it is with a 'gym set' which you can buy from large toy-suppliers. The set usually consists of a pair of ropes with special safety-clips either end. You clip one end onto your ceiling hooks and the other onto the interchangeable rope ladder, trapeze bar or swinging rings. Of course you can follow this idea using your own ropes, but those clips do make it easier and safer to ring the changes.

For a brand-new experience for an older pre-school child, hang either the *elasticated rope* from her now-outgrown baby bouncer, or the kind sold by car accessory shops for fastening over roof racks. Holding onto this she can jump and feel that she is defying gravity.

If the floor beneath your hooks is hard, you may be happier if you provide her with a soft landing. A sheet of one and a half inch foam rubber will do a great deal to protect her and can be neatly rolled in an elastic band for storage. Such a 'gym mat' will be a plaything in its own right, encouraging her in all kinds of adventures like turning somersaults and standing on her head.

The basic activity and why she will enjoy it	Ways of providing this kind of fun from the grand to the modest

'Houses' and other secret and private places. Children need 'houses' for many different kinds of play over a number of years. 'Wendy-house' games, involving dolls and domestic equipment, are only a small part of this. A house is also needed as expedition headquarters, clubhouse, camp, hospital or simply as a retreat from adults.

You can buy your child a house, ranging from a wooden one to stand in the garden to an adaptable wooden house/puppet theatre/shop to stand indoors, or a house-shaped tent to be put up anywhere. But they are all expensive and, because they are always the same, a bit limiting. Some or all of the following ideas will probably serve a vast variety of purposes better:

A wigwam is cheap and self-supporting; as useful in the living-room as in the garden and a good pre-school present.

An old-fashioned screen can be used across any corner. If you want to elaborate it you can cut a door and window.

A vast cardboard box of the kind that cookers, fridges and freezers are delivered in, makes a superb house if you can possibly find the space to store it. It will not last forever, but if you enjoy handiwork you can transform it into something a bit more permanent. Seal it all over with size and then with paint and strengthen all the joins and edges with insulating tape. Use simulated-brick wallpaper, stick on flowers, or whatever you please to decorate it, and make a small window (cutting out too much cardboard will weaken the structure). Treated like this it should stand up to months of use.

Curtained bay windows make excellent 'houses' if you hang the curtains so that they draw across rather than around the bay.

Vast tablecloths over tables transform the area under the table into a hideout.

Art and craft play. From the time she first discovers that a crayon can mark a sheet of paper, this kind of play will be important to your child. Through drawing and painting she will not only learn to manage the preliminaries to writing, she will also learn about colour and shape and express some of her views about the world and her own problems. Through cutting and sticking and trying to make things she will acquire manual dexterity as well as the pleasure which can come only through her own efforts. Through dabbling in finger paint or messing around with dough she will get tremendous sensual pleasure and, later on, when she can actually create things which satisfy her, she will discover not only the behaviour of the materials she uses but also that she can control them.

This whole category of play activity can be difficult to cater for if space is very short and cleanliness important. Try to make a corner for her which has an easy-clean table at the right height, shelf-space for her materials and, ideally, at least some space for her to 'display' her afternoon's work.

Remember that when a child first tries out a new activity of this kind she probably does not want to draw, paint or make *anything in particular*. She is exploring the material and its potential, so if you try to make her 'draw mummy' or 'cut out a star' you will be interfering with her play. In the same way, colouring books, painting- by-numbers and many craft-kits can set such rigid limits around the child's activity that they frustrate and bore her. Stick to open-ended activities until or unless she actually asks for something more structured.

On the whole, the younger the child the larger should be her materials – whether these are lumps of dough, sheets of paper or paintbrushes. When she is in a phase of much enjoying this kind of activity, she can easily use twenty very large sheets of paper in an afternoon and perhaps half a pint of paint (some used, the rest inextricably mixed to muddy brown). Few families can afford to cater on this scale if they are buying from an art shop. Your best sources of materials are probably educational suppliers (many of whom produce catalogues for mail-order buying). Sometimes several families can share a bulk-order of a basic supply such as sugar-paper or powder paint. When you have nothing special available for her, your child will be better off with large sheets of shelf paper (or even newspaper) and large quantities of home-made paint, than with a strictly rationed supply of typing paper and 'real' poster-colour. Plasticine and play-dough can become very expensive, too, because a freely playing child mixes the colours as part of the activity but will not happily use the resulting brownish lump for her next session. It is far cheaper to make your own. You will find some recipes under Presents (*see below*).

The basic activity and why she will enjoy it	Ways of providing this kind of fun from the grand to the modest

Imaginative and 'acting' play. In a sense, all play is imaginative but, at certain stages in childhood, much of your child's play will involve *pretending* that she is somebody else or *pretending* that the objects she uses are something else. It is through this kind of play that she tries out other people's roles ('Mummy'; that policeman, etc.) and strives to understand other ways of life ('going to the office', for example). It is also through these games that she may try to sort out, and come to terms with, worries and bad experiences like going to hospital or getting 'lost'. The most important thing you can provide for this whole vital area of activity is a sympathetic, interested but unintrusive ear. But there are a few practical aids she may also enjoy.

There are hundreds of commercially-produced 'props' for imaginative play ranging from tea-sets for dolls to plastic replicas of almost everything adults use from brooms and vacuum cleaners to typewriters and record players. Although your child may enjoy a few possessions of this kind, they are likely to be status symbols rather than uniquely useful playthings because they tend to limit rather than extend the functioning of her own imagination. Take that broom as an example: if she actually wants the floor to be clean, she will probably sweep more efficiently with your handbrush than with that toy broom. If she wants to *be you*, she will certainly feel more like you if she struggles with your own big broom, or pretends that a stick is that broom, than she will with the toy one.

She needs some props for imaginative play but the best ones will be yours which you will let her use and/or old ones which you have finished with. If you can find some junk storage space (if you are lucky enough to have an attic or a cellar, for example, or even a big understairs cupboard) try and save for her your old shopping bag/handbag; discarded cleaning tools and cooking tools; plastic picnicware, slightly broken umbrellas (watch out for sharp bits), old hats, gloves, shoes and any accessories you do not want like hideous scarves or outdated 'jewellery' (watch out for small beads). Anything which you might have sent to a jumble sale may be useful in her play, so when you have a clear-out, put yourself in her shoes before you let anything go.

Imaginative play often involves dressing in the part. Even if you have not the space to store much junk, try to assemble a 'dressing-up box' not of bought costumes for specific characters ('Superman' will not fit her in another six months, anyway) but of cast-off clothes which she can use for many different characters. An old but glamorous nightdress, for example, can serve as ball-gown, queen's robe or fairy dress. Father's discarded pyjamas can clothe a famous cricketer or an overalled workman. Any kind of uniform (even the school gear discarded by an older brother or sister) transforms a very young wearer into a number of official characters from policeman to bus conductor.

When you can see that a particular role is absorbing your child – as a doctor's role may interest her after a stay in hospital, for example – you may be able to help her along with a specific kit, tailored to her particular age, stage and needs. You will find some ideas in Presents (*see below*).

Books. Pleasure in the written word will be almost as important to your child as enjoyable talking (*see* **Language**). She does not have to *learn to read* early, she only has to feel, from her very first months, that books are fun: that they have interesting pictures in them for her to gaze at, then identify, then name . . . that they contain stories and rhymes which you will read to her and which she can relate to those squiggly symbols through their illustrations. If she loves them at two and discovers, at four, that a book will sometimes enable you to answer her 'why?' questions, she will *want* to read. When she is ready, she will do so.

Your child can enjoy books almost from birth. The more she has and the earlier she has them, the more she will take them for granted as a fun-part of her life. She should be a welcome member of your local children's library from the beginning but try to buy her books, too, so that she can turn her favourites into old friends and learn some by heart long before she can read.

She needs some with big, realistic pictures of familiar everyday objects. The two of you can look at them together and, over months of watching you turn the pages for her, she will discover how books 'work' – from front to back and left to right. Cloth, board and home-made books (*see* Playthings for babies) will be valuable; she can hold and chew and 'read' them for herself.

She needs you to read her stories, especially story-books with pictures, so that she can read the illustrations while you read the words. Even when she goes to school (especially if being taught to read is boring her) she needs the pure pleasure of a book she enjoys, read aloud chapter by chapter, night by night. And even before she can read, get her some 'reference books' and let her see you check up on things she wants to know like what Roman soldiers wore . . .

Presents

Buying presents for children is fun if you have enough money. Making presents for children is fun if you have enough time and skill. But *assembling* presents for children, of the kind outlined below, is the most fun of all because with a little money and a lot of loving imagination, the child gets a gift which you can exactly fit to her interests, her age-stage and her very own preferences-of-the-moment.

Don't be prevented from assembling one of these presents by the fact that your child already has and uses one of its component parts: a big part of the point of each is the way the various objects and materials are presented together. She may have been painting for months yet still be enchanted by one of the painting sets. Do take trouble over the presentation, though. One of the sad differences between a 'bought' and a 'home-made' gift is often the presence or absence of a shiny new box to keep everything in . . . if you are going to take this much trouble over your present, it is worth taking the extra trouble to find a box everything will fit into and pretty it up with paint or wallpaper.

The suggestions outlined here are only intended to generate your own ideas: these are all 'kits' which the author's own children enjoyed and used in their play, but that does not mean that they are exactly right for yours. If you are going to do something similar, though, remember that *this kind of present-assembly takes time.* If you are going to do it as cheaply as possible, it may take weeks to assemble all the bits and pieces. Decide well in advance of the child's birthday, or whatever, or you will end up buying a commercial kit after all and losing the whole point.

'Art' presents   Most children love to paint. Very young ones usually enjoy finger painting most of all but seldom have *all* their favourite colours all at the same time, because parents naturally want the only-slightly-muddy green used up before they buy more. These cost very little to make and will keep indefinitely in the refrigerator.

Finger paints. Combine non-toxic wallpaper paste and dry powder paint and mix with water to the consistency of thick cheese sauce.

Use bright and subtle colours (remembering your own child's favourite, however peculiar) and include black and white.

Either buy clear plastic screw-topped jars, or save matching glass jars (instant coffee jars do well if you can save enough in the time you have left yourself) which you cover with sticky-backed plastic so that if they break the glass cannot shatter and splinter free. Leave a clear strip down the jar so that the paint colour can be seen, or paint the screw top to match the contents.

Present with some or all or more of the following:

- A square of white formica-covered board ⎫
- A square of glossy linoleum ⎬ She can paint, wash and re-use all these
- A large 'mirror-tile' from a bathroom centre ⎭

- A comb ⎫
- A plastic fork ⎬ for making patterns in the paint as a change from fingers
- A butter curler ⎭

Folded, drippy and air painting. Even a child who has graduated from finger painting, to a brush and poster paints, may enjoy this kit which is really a set of suggested activities and the wherewithal to carry them out.

Folded paintings require big sheets of paper which you present, already creased down the middle, along with an eye dropper (from the chemist), plastic spoon and drinking straw. She drops paint, from whichever implement she chooses, onto one half of the paper and then closes it for a 'mirror image'.

Drippy paintings require the same tools, but in addition, some large sheets of shiny cardboard. You can buy bright colours from an art shop. The child again drops paint however she pleases, but she then tips the card in different directions to make drip-patterns.

Air paintings can be done either on the same kind of card or on formica board or lino. There are several versions, requiring increasingly expensive equipment and mature skill:

Drop the paint and then blow through a straw.

Apply the paint through a plastic squeezy bottle (you can buy empty ones – intended for cosmetic refills – from Woolworths).

Apply the paint in a fine spray from a garden hand-sprayer (you can buy a half litre size from any garden shop).

These types of 'painting' require rather thin paint but are dull if the colours are not rich. Powder paint mixed to the consistency of milk will do, but liquid paint from a craft shop – which comes in amazing colours and is already exactly the right texture – is better.

Present the paint, the equipment and an example of each result so that she can see the point, all together in a box.

Printing. The process of banging a stamp onto an ink pad and then onto paper, enchants most children, but the standard letter-printing sets are much too fiddly.

You can buy sets of stamps with animal shapes or funny figures, and ink pad sets, but you can give a much more elaborate and imaginative activity for less money if you make your own, or at least add to the bought set.

Make the stamps out of one-inch softwood cubes. Sandpaper them smooth and then glue all kinds of interesting shapes on to one surface of each block. Obvious ones are a curtain ring; a squiggle of string; a cross made of sponge-rubber; a big flat button with holes in it; a random array of matchsticks and a variety of shapes cut out of felt. Make the ink pads by lining flat tins (such as the kind adhesive dressings come in) with quarter-inch sorbo rubber and soaking each in a different brilliant colour of washable ink from an art shop.

If this present catches on, the child can elaborate it for herself by discovering that anything textured which she presses on her ink pads will transfer a pattern onto paper. She can try a make-up sponge, a chunk of bread, a grainy piece of wood . . . one day she will make 'potato cuts'.

To make a grand present out of this idea, take the trouble to paint the stamp-cubes in shiny colours before you glue on their printing ends. You can take the surface off your adhesive-dressing tins with wirewool, too, or paint those with enamel hobby-paints.

Cutting and sticking. However much cutting and sticking your child has done, you can make a present which will thrill her if you give a really large collection and make sure that it includes some items which she has not been offered before. It is getting it all at once, like a treasure-chest, which is the point, so make sure that you present everything in one box and laid out so that she can see tempting corners of this and glimpses of that as she opens it. It might include basics like:

☐ Different colours of sugar-paper (including black)
☐ Shiny gummed papers
☐ A glue pen
☐ Round-ended real scissors

Extras like:

☐ Coloured tissue
☐ Coloured foils
☐ Paper doilies
☐ Stiff coloured cardboard
☐ Gummed paper shapes

Trimmings like:

☐ Sticky stars, labels, pictures and motifs
☐ Pipe cleaners
☐ Paper streamers
☐ Small balls of coloured wool
☐ Scrap book pictures

Making things   Many pre-school children long to make things, things they can really use or keep, but few of them are ready for commercial kits. You can pre-prepare a kit to fit your own child's exact interests and abilities but you will need time, patience and privacy in which to prepare it.

Woodwork. Cut the basic shapes of boats, doll's house furniture, model village houses, or whatever, out of softwood. Balsa wood is much the easiest to work with but also much the most expensive.

Present them with strips of dowelling, sandpaper, glue, scraps of material for sails/cushions, etc. so that the child can finish and decorate them herself.

Dressing up. Cut out masks, crowns, etc. from stiff cardboard and give with paints, sticky papers, elastic, etc. for the child to finish for herself.

Dolls' clothes. Make basic dresses or skirts with elasticated necks/waists so that they will fit a variety of dolls. If you hate sewing, use felt. It needs no hemming and can even be glued.

Give to the child with a collection of pretty buttons, fringing, lace, ribbons, etc. so that she can make them as elaborate as she pleases with a minimum of effort.

Soft toys. The boring part for a child is the sewing of the basic shape. Sew this for her and then present with a bag of foam-crumbs for stuffing and a collection of button eyes, bits of fur fabric for special ears and so forth.

Polystyrene modelling. If your child is old enough to be trusted with orange sticks or cocktail sticks, which are sharp, she can make elaborate people, vehicles, etc. using polystyrene balls, blocks and sheets.

Buy a selection of these polystyrene pieces from a craft shop. Present with cocktail sticks, dowelling, glue, paint, wool and material scraps. She can fasten the polystyrene pieces together simply by pushing a cocktail stick into each. She can then dress or decorate her people or other objects, or paint them to hang as mobiles or Christmas decorations.

Box modelling. Although your child will almost certainly already have 'made' things out of boxes and other junk, a big collection of carefully saved and presented material, perhaps with one model already started to give her the idea, can be bliss. You might want to include:

☐ Stout, pretty boxes – especially shoe and chocolate boxes
☐ Matchboxes
☐ Different cardboard tubes (from lavatory paper, kitchen rolls, etc.)
☐ A good paper glue
☐ Treasury tags
☐ Stamp hinges
☐ Ring reinforcements
☐ Coloured string
☐ Coloured sticky tape

If you want to make a grand present and you can trust the child to take care of her fingers, add a small stapler which is much more effective in box-modelling than yards of sticky tape.

Play-dough and play cooking

If you make dough from equal parts of plain flour and salt, mixed with just enough water to give a 'pastry' texture, it will keep for a long time in the refrigerator and, because it is cheap, you will probably feel able to replace muddy colours with fresh ones.

You can colour the dough either by using food colouring in the water or by mixing powder paint with the flour.

Assemble a basic present by filling matching plastic pots (such as half-litre ice-cream pots) with different colours of dough, sticking a label to match the contents on each pot.

Add extras such as biscuit cutters, rolling pins, etc. and pack in a box with the plastic tablecloth you hope she will use.

Unless the idea of 'playing with food' shocks you (and after all she will one day have to learn to cook) you can assemble a play-cooking set of any degree of elaboration. A really good one might include:

☐ Many small pots and other lidded containers (all with their printing scrubbed off) filled with flour, sugar, various cereals, chocolate vermicelli, hundreds and thousands, alphabet pasta, dried lentils, cocoa powder, etc.
☐ A collection of small plastic spoons, measuring scoops (like the ones which come with baby formula or soap powder), a wooden spoon and one or two plastic mixing bowls.
☐ As many miniatures of jam, ketchup, salad dressing and so forth as you can decently collect.
☐ Any more expensive extras you would like her to have, like patty-tins, an egg whisk or even a battery-operated toy food mixer.

Present the whole lot in a deep plastic tray and make it clear that washing up is part of the fun.

● For her own sake, make one rule for play cooking: 'Always put the things you want to mix into one of your bowls.' If she adds the contents of her chocolate vermicelli pot to her pot of flour, she will have neither next time; if she adds water to her pot of pasta you will have a very smelly collection indeed.

Imaginative play sets   If your child is currently fascinated by doctors, nurses and hospitals, or by shops or offices, you may be able to elaborate on commercial outfits to double their play-value.

Medical kits. Unless you can sew you will probably have to buy a basic uniform, but you can assemble the rest of a realistic kit more cheaply using real items than play ones. For example, your chemist will give (or sell for a few pence):
□ Disposable syringes (without the needles, of course).
□ Pill containers (not child-proof; you do not want her to practise getting those open).
□ Tongue depressors.
  Also:
□ Real adhesive dressings and bandages cost no more than play ones.
□ A pen-torch can be used for inspecting throats, eyes and ears.
□ A thermometer case (when you have broken the contents) can have a play thermometer in it and still seem real.

If you want to assemble a very grand present, or are helping your child to play out a hospital stay which is obviously still haunting her, you can buy even more medical-seeming equipment quite cheaply if you look at the ranges of disposable goods which are intended for families carrying out long-term nursing at home. There are disposable draw-sheets and kidney dishes, for example.

If you want to present all this 'medical equipment' in the equivalent of a doctor's bag, a first aid box intended for schools or offices will be cheaper and look more realistic than a child's 'doctor set'.

Shops. There are plenty of miniature shops on the market but the contents of the little containers are seldom real – which is disappointing – and only the most hideously expensive include the items which are most fun, such as scales.

You can refill commercially produced containers with your own contents and add some extras and some real samples – such as miniature jams and honeys – too. If you want to add bakery, you can either buy doll's house bread and cakes, or bake your own flour and water and then paint them. You can buy or make marzipan fruit and vegetables to add a greengrocery department, too.

For a grand present, add a small set of working scales and a toy till with play-money (or real money if she will not put it in her mouth). Add some tiny paper bags which you can charm out of your sweet shop, and a receipt pad bought from a stationer.

Present the whole lot in a large cardboard box which you have covered in sticky-backed plastic. It will serve as the counter when it is emptied and turned upside down.

Post office or office. Many children are both fascinated and puzzled by the work they see going on behind the counters of post offices, banks and libraries and by the strange activities they hear about 'at the office'. An office set is easy to assemble:

Collect every one of the enormous variety of official-looking forms available to you, free, at the bank, the post office or the building society. Your child will not mind whether this is a television licence application or a paying-in form, as long as she has lots of different ones.

Collect as many trading stamps as you can for her to use as stamps. Ask your post office for 'airmail', 'urgent', 'first class' and 'fragile' stickers.

Supply various kinds of paper, envelopes, etc. from the family supply. So far your kit is more or less free, but the present will become grander if you add some of the following:

☐ Blotting paper and real (washable) ink is a treat these days, for all but the very youngest children.

☐ A telephone is a must for offices (save an old telephone book).

☐ An ink pad and date-stamp will be the pinnacle of grandeur.

Older children and playing at work

By middle childhood, imaginative acting-out play has usually given place to a great desire in the child to try out adult activities for real. Cooking a cake or a meal, digging the garden, cleaning the car or painting the ceiling, doing the shopping or bathing the baby may all be work to you, but to your child they may be amongst the most desirable kinds of play.

Try not to be in too much of a hurry to indict all such chores as 'boring' or to label them as undesirable, by offering the child money for doing them. The more activities she can try out and the more useful activities she can find fun, the better. Sometimes parents are so smitten with guilt at the sight of a twelve-year-old doing the ironing they loathe, that they quite forget that she is only doing it for fun and that in this situation everyone gains. It is, though, important to be sensitive to the moments when novelty wears off, sufficient skill has been acquired and the game is turning into a chore. If she wanted to paint that fence, by all means insist that she finish it, but don't expect her to paint the one at the back as well.

If you can provide enough opportunities for children old enough to acquire the skills but still young enough to lack adolescent self-consciousness, your family may acquire a great many techniques which will benefit them when they are grown up. The child who learns to clean sparking plugs as part of play-tinkering with the car, will not forget how when her own car refuses to start. The one who teaches herself to type or use a computer at ten will have a flying start in that training course later on.

Older children and play

Some children continue to be able to play unselfconsciously with actual toys for far longer than others. The child who can play in this way almost certainly uses her play both to relax herself and to provide a structure for a different kind of thinking-play which is going on inside her head. Don't be in any hurry to get rid of toys and don't ever suggest, or even imply, that any child is 'too old for' anything.

A child who wants to play, but cannot quite let herself, may find a way out in playing with younger children: her own brothers and sisters, neighbours or the children in the local playgroup. Don't open up this harmless piece of self-deception. If she is enjoying herself and the younger ones are having fun, too, why must she be forced to realize that she is really making clay animals for herself rather than them?

Some older children stop playing *games* with their toys but continue to value them – often for years – as friendly familiars and ornaments, who go on inhabiting the shelves in their rooms and a corner of their minds and emotions. Some elaborate collections of dolls or soldiers, model animals, guns or cars, start in this way and a few turn into new kinds of 'game', acceptable to adults, such as a passion for model railways or radio-controlled cars.

Much of the best play of older children does not involve play *objects* at all but either centres around mutual activities like cycling or fishing, or is simply the nameless and varying activity of companions exploring increasing independence. If you ask an eleven-year-old what she is going to do this afternoon, she is likely to answer, 'I'm meeting Jane.' The companionship *is* the activity and they will play in talk always and in action sometimes. They may look totally unoccupied to you yet be absorbed.

Some children's lives become so full of structured activities that spontaneous just-for-fun play almost ceases. Ironically, these include some of the children who seem, to adults, best occupied. They may be children whose parents and community organize for them a ceaseless round of out-of-school activities, so that every evening is taken up with swimming lessons or drama groups or one club or another. Or they may be children who spend almost every moment out of school involved in the organized sports which are so much in vogue. Many sporting activities are referred to as 'playing games', but in truth most are not play at all for the majority of participants. Competition ensures that they are stressful and, to some extent, destructive of social relationships. Training and practice ensures that they are often hard, and sometimes reluctant, work, while the involvement of supporters, coaches and a team ensures that the child is not free to make her own decisions about what she wants to do but is forced to perform, willy-nilly, for the sake of others' opinions.

If your child is singled out for sporting activity by her school or club and wants to participate, you are most unlikely to be able to stop her and therefore you will probably want to support her. But you may at least be able to avoid giving her the feeling that you, like all those others, only love her for her prowess. She needs to be sure that, proud though you may be of her skills, you are even more proud of her as a person, and that her happiness is now, and always will be, more important to you than any of her victories.

Whatever the pattern of your older child's life, whatever its balance between school and home, school friends and home friends, group activities and solitary or paired activities, there does need to be some space left in it for sheer spontaneous, possibly pointless, fun. If we allow our older children to be driven from one achievement to the next, on an ever-tighter schedule, we cannot be surprised if they become as harassed as striving executives and ready, in adolescence, either to break away from all achievement to look for a peace of their own, or to join their ulcer-ridden elders in the nearest bar.

Playgroups *see* **School**/Pre-school and nursery education.
Pleurisy *see* **Chest Infections**.
Pneumonia *see* **Chest Infections**.

Pocket Money *see also* **Adolescence**/The long road to independence: Money

Like it or not, money is important in our society. It does not only *buy* material necessities, comforts, treats and luxuries it also *represents* psychological necessities, like aspects of our self-esteem, status, success and independence.

A child's pocket money will probably be his introduction to financial and economic life. It is worth thinking carefully not just about how much he should have, at what age, but about what you want his pocket money to be for, and to stand for, to him.

Very young children and money

Most pre-school children cannot understand money as anything but 'treasure'; another version of the tokens they put in slot machines, or possibly as mysterious things which can be swapped for things of obvious value like sweets or comics.

There is no real point in money for a child at this stage. If you buy for him the little Saturday treats he may later buy for himself, he will lose nothing by not having pocket money. He is not ready.

● To check on this, try giving your very young child a Saturday coin. You will probably find that:

If circumstances allow he will at once spend it, happily swapping it for that comic but being quite uninterested in either the change or the possibility that he could buy a cheaper comic *and* a lollipop.

If he cannot at once spend it he will abandon it. Although pleased with the friendly gesture of being given the money, even an hour's delay before he can turn it into something 'real' means that you will find that coin dropped on the bathroom floor, forgotten.

First pocket money

However small the weekly sum you can afford, your child's pocket money can be valuable in all senses to him if:

It is money freely, pleasantly and regularly given, as his right. This small sum of money is, so to speak, a non-earning child's equivalent of your wage or salary. You get it because you are you and because you do what you do. Your boss does not withhold your wage because he is angry with you nor threaten to do so, nor forget to give it to you. In the same way, the pocket money must be given to the child because he is himself, and there must be no way whatever (but *see below*) in which that right can be removed.

It is money which is kept entirely separate from any money he earns from 'jobs'. If you want to pay him for mowing the lawn or cleaning the floor or the car, fine, but that should be an entirely separate negotiation. He gets his pocket money anyway, whatever he does or does not do.

It is money which he is genuinely free to spend as he pleases. If you give him a weekly sum but insist that he save half, then you are really only giving him half the pocket money stated between you. If you want him to accumulate money, perhaps in a post office account, for spending on other people's Christmas presents or whatever, give it to him separately. Pocket money is for spending as, when and how he wishes. If he chooses to spend it immediately on sweets, that is his right unless you can educate him out of sweet-eating. If he chooses to buy plastic nonsense which will break before the day is over, that is his right (and his eventual sorrow) too. If he chooses to save up for something specific, fine, and if he chooses just to let the money accumulate in a moneybox for nothing in particular, that's fine too. It is up to him. He may spend it, always, on presents for you. Don't worry; the freedom to give is an important one.

When a child thinks his pocket money is too little

Older children usually feel a great need to be on a financial par with their friends – just as adults like to be paid the same rate for the job as their colleagues. But sometimes your child will completely misunderstand the financial arrangements of other families and will feel hard-done-by when in fact he is not. If he feels that you give him far too little, check on the following:

Are the large sums given to others pocket money or necessity-money? Some parents who cannot be at home at the end of the school day, for example, give their children quite large daily sums to cover the purchase of an afternoon snack and, perhaps, some entertainment. Others give their children lunch-money, rather than paying for a school meal or providing a packed one. In discussion, you should be able to clarify with your child the difference between his pocket money (which is purely for fun) and their 'maintenance money'.

Are these large sums pocket money or an 'allowance'? Some families allocate and give a weekly sum which is not just for pleasure-spending but for *all* occasional spending. Such a child may be expected to pay his own fares, even when he is with his family; to buy his own school supplies; to buy any odd toiletries he needs and so forth. Once again, your child should be able to see the difference between this kind of money and the money he is given which is extra to total provision made for him by you.

● If you and your child want to go onto an 'allowance' system at an early stage, of course you can. Make sure, though, that the child does understand that the allowance is not just *more* money, but money for different purposes. There are also some snags:

It deprives you of the pleasure of buying for him. And the surprise purchase of minor items, like a new drawing block or felt-tip, some new talc and so forth, can be a great pleasure to you both.

It is difficult to stick to the 'rules' when the family is together. If you all go to a movie and want a hot-dog which the child cannot afford today, is he to go without or are you going to buy him one yourself even though he had the money and spent it on something else?

Are these large sums in fact 'wages'? Some families regularly pay their children not just for odd chores but, for example, for Saturday help in the shop (*see* **Adolescence**/The long road to independence: Part-time jobs).

Are these large sums already partly spoken for? Some of the children whom your child considers rich will in fact be forced to put a certain sum in the savings bank, another sum in the church collection box and yet another towards the family's favourite charity. Your child should understand that only the money left over, after all that, can really be compared with his pocket money.

Is your child actually prevented, by his comparative poverty, from taking part in the life of his group? If, for example, a weekend trip to the movies or swimming baths is taken for granted by most of the kids, it is obviously sad for yours if he cannot go because he has no money for a ticket. But if you reckon to give him that kind of money, as and when he needs it and you can afford it, his actual pocket money may not be too little after all.

● Such a child may not be asking for *more money* overall but for the independence of budgeting for himself.

When you think his pocket money is too much

If your child is continually treating others to sweets or chips, buying gimmicks to take to school to show others and generally being generous to a fault, he may be trying to buy attention and popularity. Just cutting down the money he has available will not help, but you might need to ask yourself whether you are giving him money instead of your attention, and whether he might not make more genuine friendships if he was encouraged to offer the warmth and hospitality of his home.

If you think he spends his money stupidly

You cannot control how he spends his money without ruining the point of him having it, but if he does always spend it all on sweets you may like to consider the following:

Is it enough money for him to be able to buy anything other than sweets which he really wants? If you are giving him 20p for example, it may not seem to him worthwhile doing anything with it other than guzzle. He might spend more 'sensibly' if he had rather more – enough, for example, to buy occasional additions to whatever he collects, or items for his current hobby.

Are you sure the items he buys are 'stupid' *in his terms*? While some comics are certainly junk and you may disapprove of them, it can be argued that it is better that he should read comics than that he should not read at all. While small plastic toys do certainly break, they can give a great deal of pleasure in their short lives. Not all 'collections' have to be formalized assemblies of stamps or butterflies; some children informally accumulate balls or dolls or toy guns and get infinite pleasure out of having every one-of-a-type . . . Finally, of course, many of the idiotic items children want/buy are part of mysterious school crazes parents cannot – and probably should not – understand. If yo-yos are 'in' this term, a yo-yo is an essential.

Later on: money to meet commitments

Your schoolchild will eventually need to have some money available to him to meet the self-imposed commitments which are an excellent sign of responsible growing up. How, for example, can he offer to pay for that broken window if he has no money of his own? To have you say 'I shall hold back your pocket money until it is paid for' is to *be punished* rather than to make retribution. How can he buy carefully thought-out and searched-for gifts if he has to ask the recipients for the money? How can he even decide to answer the current UNICEF disaster appeal with real self-sacrifice, if he has nothing to sacrifice?

Somewhere between, say, nine to eleven, every child needs to be helped towards some accumulation of money (however minute) in order to be able to do these things. It still should not be a compulsory segment of that pocket money but it might, for example, be an additional monthly sum to be put in the post office under his own name. The extra can be given instead of an annual pocket money increase, if you prefer.

This money is the part of his 'income' which he may wish to add to, or replace by, money he makes from a Saturday job.

Learning 'the value of money'

Whether you are rich, poor or in-between and whether you reckon that your children's needs and wishes have a high or lower priority in your family budgeting, every child does have to learn those hard lessons about money not growing on trees/having to be earned/not being able to be spent twice, and so forth. Fortunately, most children do absorb this kind of information because they hear you talking, see you shopping around for bargains, and know, almost instinctively, what *sort* of birthday presents it is worth asking for and which are totally out of reach.

Children are far more sensitive to their parents' feelings than many people realize. It is a rare ten-year-old who will ask for a racing bike when you are both out of work.

If you are afraid that your child really does not realize that the money you can earn limits what can be bought, and that what is bought today limits the money left for tomorrow, do him the honour of letting him share your worries and discussions. He may not yet realize:

The difference between salaried, weekly and hourly work. If your child is accustomed to a family in which salaries go on coming in no matter whether the earner is ill, on holiday or what, he may totally fail to understand what a national strike or long period of illness can mean to his friends. If he is accustomed to you being able to organize your working hours around his needs, he may not understand that his best friends' mothers simply cannot afford not to turn up for their evening jobs because attending the school play will cost them three hours' money.

The difference between down-payments and total costs. Many children whose families make all major purchases on extended credit or via credit 'clubs', really believe that the down-payment is the payment. The intricacies of interest may be beyond a seven-year-old, but the idea that if you borrow the money to pay for something you have to pay for the privilege as well as the something and, therefore, that it is cheaper to save up until you can buy outright, will not be.

The difference between what can be afforded and what is worthwhile. Many children, pleading to eat in an expensive restaurant, for example, will ask, 'But haven't you *got* that much money?' They need gradually to learn that just possessing the cash, or having the money in the bank and a cheque book or credit card in your pocket, does not make that meal 'affordable'. Once again, you can put it to quite young children in simple terms: 'There are seven dinners in the week and we usually spend about X on each one. If we spend Y on this one dinner there will only be a very little left for all the others . . .'

'Hidden' expenditure like quarterly bills. While young children are bound to feel that electricity, water and telephone calls are freely 'on tap', older children must learn about service costs. Many of the young adolescents whose parents grumble bitterly about the 'phone bills they run up and the lights they leave on, have actually never been taught about these things. Persuade the child to make one of his 'phone calls from a coin box and let him see how fast he has to put in money; get him to watch the electricity meter while that heater is on; eventually, show him the bills and let him help you to work it out.

Discussions of this kind can be both interesting and educational and, if you start them early enough, you may find your child applying the principles to his own expenditure ('I could buy the car but it uses up batteries so fast I'll never be able to go on affording it') and to yours, too ('shall we go in the cheaper seats and have ice-creams as well?').

Poisoning *see* **Accidents**; **Safety**/In the home: Safety from household poisons; Safety with medicines. *See also* **Pollution**; **Suicide**.

Pollution *see also* **Allergy**; **Eating**/Commonsense about family eating: Food-additives

Human beings have worked to make living environments which are safer, more convenient and more productive/profitable for more and more people. But in doing so we have fouled our own nests. The self-maintaining and self-cleaning processes of our planet are stretched to their limits by the waste and by-products of our mechanized societies and vast populations. Human interference threatens the delicate balance of eco-systems upon which our survival, like that of all living things, depends. Every 'technological fix', which improves some aspect of life for some group of people somewhere, tends to produce a ripple-effect of disaster for another group elsewhere. Many people believe that, unless we can learn to live in cooperative harmony with our natural environment, rather than raping it as the fancy or the invention takes us, we shall eventually poison the whole planet and humanity with it.

Individuals can do a great deal to increase public awareness of environmental issues and to put pressure on governments and industries for specific improvements. But even the most convinced and seasoned campaigner still has to live within the society he is trying to change. Parents, with the particular responsibility which they have for the lives of society's new individuals, have to realize that they cannot completely protect their children from the pollution brought about by earlier generations, nor prepare them to make a better future world by trying to do so. If you allow yourself to be overwhelmed by articles about air pollution, lead poisoning or chemical additives in commercially produced food, you will come to feel that you can keep your children healthy only by dropping right out of society and finding some untouched hillside retreat from which you can scratch a 'natural' existence without technological aid. The truth is that only the very wealthy and eccentric can do that, and that those who do deprive themselves of the best that society can offer, as well as protecting themselves from the worst and offering it nothing.

Most of us are not rich, eccentric or escapist. We want our children to enjoy the best which their world has to offer *and* to be protected from the worst. We have to accept that their overall protection is not in the hands of individual families – except insofar as they are members of pressure groups – but in the hands of governments, industries, public health authorities and all the other giants of bureaucratic life. But if the protection against pollution which parents can give to their own children is limited, it is nevertheless real.

Air pollution   The air we breathe should ideally contain twenty per cent oxygen and seventy-nine per cent nitrogen, with only traces of other gases and no dirt particles. The oxygen balance of the planet as a whole is maintained by the co-existence of plant and animal life. Plants take in carbon dioxide and release oxygen; animals take in oxygen and release carbon dioxide. Urban areas, full of people and denuded of plant life, already strain that balance. Petrol engines – especially the cars which clog city streets – burn oxygen and release carbon dioxide. Furthermore, *unburnt* gases from petrol and diesel engines give off carbon monoxide which is lethal if a high concentration is breathed in. In the streets of Tokyo, traffic policemen carry oxygen equipment so that they can counteract subtle suffocation by carbon monoxide with a quick 'breather' whenever they feel the need. In Britain, the law requires that the flue gases from factory chimneys should not contain more than thirty parts of carbon monoxide per million parts of air. But in a busy street the carbon monoxide level may easily reach three hundred parts per million. In some cities, particular combinations of landscape and climate lead to even greater hazards. In Los Angeles, for example, there are frequent 'temperature inversions' which lead to polluted air being trapped over the city in the form of a smog which, in the presence of sunlight, also contains the even more lethal gas, ozone.

Apart from distortions in the gaseous composition of air, city-dwellers also tend to breathe in minute solid particles of soot and ash; about twenty-five thousand tons fall over London each year despite the major improvement brought about since the mid fifties by the Clean Air legislation. Lung cancer and other lung complaints are commoner amongst city-dwellers – even amongst those who do not smoke.

Family action on air pollution

If a child spends several hours in an atmosphere containing too little oxygen relative to poisonous gases, she may feel ill. It is worth trying to avoid extreme situations, especially for babies and very young children. For example:

Try not to take a baby shopping in a packed high street in still, muggy weather with a cloudy sky; a few hours amidst the trapped fumes and she (like you) may well be headachey and irritable.

● Pushchairs tend to put their occupants at exactly the level of vehicle exhaust pipes. She may be better off if you carry her in a sling.

Try to avoid long periods in a car stuck in crawling traffic jams or queuing to get out of multi-storey car parks. Leave the city or the sports meeting early, if you can, so that you escape before the crowd and its exhaust fumes.

Heed warnings of local 'smog' conditions. If the authorities suggest keeping children inside, or home from school, or out of particular areas, do as they say.

Theoretically, a child who spends all her time in a polluted atmosphere could be liable to mild but chronic ill-effects both from that imbalance of gases and from the inflammatory effect on her lungs of those solid dirt particles. The best that you can do is to ensure that she has the cleanest possible air to breathe for as much of the time as possible. For example:

If you live in a highly polluted part of the city you may be able to enrol her at a school in a suburban area. It is the children who must both live and work in cramped backstreets, packed with traffic and overshadowed by industrial chimneys, who are most at risk.

Within the home you can do at least a little to avoid making dirty air dirtier. Whatever that air is like, living with heavy smokers will certainly make it worse for your child. If you must smoke, try not to do it in her bedroom or to 'share' your cigarettes with her by smoking while she sits on your lap. If your home is on a busy street, try to organize the rooms so that she spends most of her time on the quieter side of the house. If open windows let in the stink of exhaust fumes and a lot of black specks, keep them closed and consider the possibility of air-conditioning.

Try for occasional breaks: country weekends, mountain holidays or trips to the seaside will all help.

Lead poisoning

Lead can accumulate in the bones of young children and it can lead to brain damage. Florid lead poisoning is rare and usually associated with the victim having chewed objects covered with lead-containing paint or picked and eaten old lead-containing plaster (see **Habits**/Pica). Many authorities, however, now believe that lower levels of lead – insufficient to cause obvious illness – may nevertheless be damaging children. Some believe that the 'safe levels' set by governments are too high; others that they are being much exceeded. Although the whole matter is still highly controversial, it may be that young children are being subtly poisoned; their intelligence reduced; their irritability increased . . .

The major additional source of lead in the environment comes from anti-knock additives to petrol which lead to lead-laden exhaust fumes. Some countries already ban such additives. In Britain they are still permitted as I write, although legislation to ban them is about to be passed. It remains to be seen how quickly and how effectively new laws will be enforced. As is so often the case in environmental health arguments, money is the key. A ban on lead in petrol will make British motoring fractionally more expensive and may therefore damage the car industry . . .

Anything you do to give your child clean air to breathe (*see above*) will do something to protect her from lead. In addition:

Family action on lead pollution

If you live in an old house, check for lead-containing paint/plaster. You may believe that no child of yours would be so idiotic as to *eat the inedible*, but some children do.

● If you buy an old cot or painted toy, it is not enough to repaint it with safe paint. If the original covering might be unsafe, you must remove it first. A chewing child will soon get through a top layer.

Check water tanks and piping. Old houses still sometimes have lead-lined plumbing and this can mean running water with dangerously high lead levels, especially if the water is 'soft' and therefore more liable to dissolve that lead.

Water pollution

Rivers and oceans become polluted by industrial wastes from factories which discharge into them, by chemicals used in agriculture which are washed into them, and by human waste from inadequate or overtaxed sewerage systems. In the western world you can be reasonably sure that water described as safe for drinking is safe, although it will usually have been made safe by the addition of chemicals which may, in themselves, be a kind of pollution. You may like to bear the following points in mind, though, especially when you are on holiday:

Family action on water pollution

Don't let children drink from unusual water-sources unless you know that they are pure or purified. The old well at your holiday-cottage may contain ice-cold, delicious-tasting water which generations of families lived on. But it may now be polluted by chemicals running off the nearby factory-farm.

Don't let children swim in lakes, canals or rivers which are in, or downstream of, industrial areas.

Try and check on the state of beaches in your proposed holiday area before booking. Poorly treated sewage, which is not carried far enough out to sea, is not just revolting, it is also dangerous: there are bound to be some disease carriers amongst the tourists in the town (*see* **Infection**).

Pay attention to any warnings you are given about local seafood. Some shellfish, for example, actually concentrate in their bodies the chemicals and metals in polluted sea water.

Projectile vomiting *see* **Pyloric Stenosis.** *See also* **Hospital**/Surgery: Pyloric stenosis
Proteins *see* **Eating**/Types of food. *See also* **Allergy**/What allergy is: Gastro-intestinal allergies.
Puberty *see* **Adolescence**.
Punishment *see* **Discipline, Self-discipline and Learning How to Behave**.
Pus *see* **Infection**/Types of infection: Localized infection. *See also* **Accidents**/Wounds and infection.

Pyloric Stenosis (Projectile Vomiting)

A condition in which the pylorus, the muscular valve controlling the flow of food from the stomach into the intestines, thickens to cause obstruction in early infancy. Over the first week or two of the baby's life milk becomes unable to leave the stomach by the normal route and is forcibly vomited. *See* **Hospital**/Surgery.

Quarantine *see* **Infection**/Preventing the spread of 'infectious' illnesses. *See also* named infectious diseases.

Rabies

Rabies is a virus disease. When a rabid animal bites, viruses are introduced into the victim's bloodstream with the saliva. They then travel along the nerves towards the brain. The incubation period can be as much as a year so that the bite is both healed and completely forgotten long before there are any signs of illness. Once rabies is established, though, it is almost inevitably fatal. The victim suffers many nervous symptoms including the painful spasms of the throat when he tries to drink, or even thinks of water, which led to rabies being termed 'hydrophobia'. He becomes deranged and usually highly aggressive which increases the likelihood of another victim being bitten and infected. Death usually comes during massive convulsions due to the infection having reached the brain.

Rabies mainly affects meat-eating animals and can become established in populations of wild creatures (foxes, skunks and mongooses, for example). Once this happens, any domestic carnivore, such as a dog or cat, which has contact with wild creatures, is at risk of being bitten and contracting the disease which it then brings into contact with its human environment. Humans who work with wild animals are also at direct risk. Blood-sucking (vampire) bats, for example, live off the blood of cattle in the tropics. Rabid ones infect those cattle and also attack the men who care for them.

Britain is still free of rabies, thanks to its island status and to energetic action by public health authorities earlier this century. This freedom is guarded by stringent regulations controlling the import of wild animals and by fierce quarantine requirements for any dog or cat taken abroad and then brought home again. Many people resent these laws. They want to take a pet dog with them to a foreign posting and to bring him home again without the heartbreak and expense of a year's quarantine. They feel that they should be able to take the family cat with them on a boating holiday abroad or they fall in love with a dear little puppy or kitten while they are in a foreign country and do not see why they should not bring him home. Some pet-shop traders even resent the curtailment of their business which the anti-rabies laws impose and may wish to find ways around the regulations. None of these people would intentionally introduce a lethal disease into Britain. When they break the laws they do so because they do not believe that the individual animals with which they are concerned *could* be infected and do not realize that even one animal, incubating rabies, could be enough to establish the disease in Britain, forever. If you are ever tempted to smuggle in a creature, remember:

However healthy it may appear, rabies virus may be working slowly in its nervous system. It may stay healthy for months yet still become a 'killer'.

However convinced you are that it has never been bitten by an animal while abroad you cannot be certain. A tiny nip which only just breaks the skin is enough to introduce the virus.

However carefully you intend to restrain and observe the animal, if it is incubating rabies it will eventually escape your controls as the virus affects its nervous system and alters its habit-patterns, obedience and docility. It will be infectious and dangerous before you are aware that it is ill.

A rabid animal on the loose is not only a danger to the people it may bite but also to any other carnivorous animal – domestic or wild – which it may meet. Your animal may be caught and destroyed before it has infected any person, but it may already have seeded the infection amongst wildlife or started a chain of tragedy amongst the neighbourhood's pets.

Countries which have rabies endemic in their wild animal populations employ a range of controls both to keep down their numbers and to prevent them from having contact with domestic pets and therefore with human beings. In some areas, for example, dogs are not allowed out unmuzzled/off leads/without human escorts. It is vitally important that the public abide by this sort of control.

If you live in, or visit, an area where there is known to be rabies, do make sure that you understand any regulations which may be in force and that you take precautions against the unlikely but disastrous possibility of your child being infected. For example:

Don't let children pet strange dogs or cats especially those which are obviously 'strays'.

Don't encourage them to try to touch any wild creature even if they are passionate naturalists seriously observing wildlife. Remember that a healthy wild animal will seldom allow human handling; the mongoose your child picks up is rather more likely than most to be sick. If there is rabies in the area, it *could* be rabid.

If a child is bitten by an animal which even COULD be rabid

Take the following precautions immediately even if the wound is no more than a pin-prick:

Notice the creature. If it was a dog, you, or other people, may be able to catch it but don't risk getting bitten yourself. Instead, let it go but observe it carefully so that you will recognize it again, and notice where it goes so that you can later bring the authorities to the spot. The point is that doctors must proceed to treat your child as if she had been infected, but the animal must nevertheless be found and caught. They will need to establish whether or not it *was* rabid so as to protect other people and animals in the area if it was, or to relieve you if it was not.

If you are a visitor and the creature is unfamiliar to you (would you recognize a mongoose?), notice it as carefully as you can so that you can describe it to a local expert. If it was not a meat eater, for example, you have nothing to worry about.

Clean the wound as thoroughly as you quickly can. If you can flood away the animal's saliva, you will at least reduce the load of virus introduced into the wound.

Get the child to expert medical attention. Local cleansing of the wound, together with immediate passive immunization against rabies, are vital. Treated immediately, your child's chances are excellent. The disease only becomes unmanageable once the viruses penetrate from the locally infected tissues into the bloodstream and from there into the nervous system.

Immunization against rabies

Both passive and active immunization, for humans and for animals, are rapidly improving. If you live in an area where there is rabies, do find out whether your own pets can be protected. If you work with wild animals or your child plans a trip or a career involving handling them in high-risk areas, enquire about immunization for her.

Ringworm and Athlete's Foot

Ringworm is a generic term for skin diseases which may be caused by any of several groups of fungi. The infecting organisms may be specific to humans, to cats and dogs or to cattle. Although they are not in themselves serious, fungal skin disorders are usually highly contagious so that tiresome epidemics easily occur in schools and other institutions. Laboratory help to identify the exact fungus responsible and therefore the exact treatment to which it will be sensitive is usually needed.

Ringworm of the scalp

Whether acquired from human, pet or cattle sources, the disease is easily passed on by direct contact, either head to head in contact sports or via infected brushes and combs.

First signs of scalp ringworm

A small scaly spot appears on the scalp. It is easily missed because it is still hair-covered, but careful examination shows a few broken hairs on its surface.

Older lesions have greyish scales which may be thicker at the edges so that each patch has a distinct margin. Fungus is growing in the hair shafts, weakening each hair so that it breaks off close to the scalp.

If the infection was acquired from cattle (from rubbing posts, etc.) the patches may be inflamed. The more inflamed the patches, the more likely it is that the body will in fact eradicate the infection for itself. Treatment can, however, shorten the process by preventing the appearance of further lesions.

Treatment of scalp ringworm

Local treatments used to include many ointments and dyes together with plucking out the infected hairs. Now your doctor may prescribe a specific fungicide to be applied locally and a safe and effective antibiotic (griseofulvin) to be taken by mouth.

Most schools will exclude infected children (and may examine others for early signs) until they are clear of active infection. If the school does not exclude your child, you should probably keep her at home anyway. Apart from the risk of her spreading the fungi, she is likely to be extremely self-conscious about her 'bald' patches.

After a widespread infection is over, normal regrowth of the hair takes some weeks. A change in hairstyle may help to camouflage the patches or a bandanna, headscarf or baseball cap may be acceptable 'headgear' in the child's social group.

Preventing the spread of scalp ringworm

Within the home the infection can usually be contained and prevented from spreading to other family members if:

The infected child scrupulously avoids any hairbrush, comb, or towel but her own (and others avoid hers).

She avoids other people's pillows and they avoid hers.

She wears some form of head-covering so as to minimize the likelihood of infected dead hairs and scales falling on other people.

Ringworm of the beard area

This is usually acquired by individuals in close contact with infected cattle. Leaning the face against the flank of an infected dairy cow during milking is the most common cause. This kind of ringworm often produces severe inflammation and swelling and requires medical attention.

Ringworm of the body-skin

This often, though not necessarily, co-exists with scalp ringworm.

First signs of ringworm on the body

As in scalp ringworm, patches of pale scaly discs on the skin may have a raised and defined edge and may, if the fungus is of animal origin, be highly inflamed.

The affected skin is extremely itchy. Scratching can lead to local secondary infection and/or to the eventual appearance of ringworm of the nails (*see below*).

'Dhobie Itch'

Is the name given to ringworm of the groin area which, because of the moist warmth, is often especially active. It was thought to be acquired from native washerwomen (Dhobies) in the tropics who used their feet to pound clothes.

Treatment

Is similar to scalp ringworm: Local fungicide and/or griseofulvin.

Preventing the spread of ringworm of the body-skin

This kind of ringworm can certainly be acquired by contact with scalp ringworm or via shower mats, towels, etc. It may also be acquired from borrowed clothing. The spread of infection within the home (and day institution) can usually be prevented if, as well as avoiding sharing towels, etc. with anyone else, the sufferer takes trouble over the clothing she wears next to her skin and where she removes it.

The easiest system for a day-school child, for example, is to dress and undress in the empty bath or shower stall (which can easily be washed when she has finished). She removes her day clothes and replaces them immediately with freshly laundered nightclothes, the day clothes being put straight for laundering. In the morning she repeats the process, putting on clean day clothes (underclothes at least) and putting her nightclothes for the laundry. In this way shed scales are never left on communal floors and there is no chance of a sister putting on an infected sweater by mistake.

Obviously these precautions require an adequate supply of clothing and excellent laundry facilities. It is for this reason that ringworm of the skin is more common and more difficult to control where social conditions are poor.

Ringworm of the feet (athlete's foot)

The term 'athlete's foot' is used generically to include any fungus infection of the feet. It has nothing to do with athletics but is common in any population which shares communal baths, changing rooms, etc. so that many individuals' bare feet share warm humid conditions. Fungus infection can only be differentiated from numerous other foot afflictions (such as excessive sweating, allergy to chemicals in shoe leather, etc.) by laboratory study.

First signs of athlete's foot

The most typical case begins with sodden, cracking and peeling skin between two toes, often the fourth and fifth. The skin is extremely itchy. Scratching removes the white sodden surface skin to reveal raw red skin underneath.

Bacterial secondary infection of these open sores is quite common and requires medical attention.

Treatment of athlete's foot

Very acute cases can be treated with griseofulvin although this drug may not (for reasons which are ill-understood) totally eradicate minor chronic infection.

There are many local fungicidal applications for the feet. Any one may be effective and, if the first has not proved effective within about ten days an alternative should be tried. Treatment should continue for about four weeks: the time the skin will take to renew itself. If there is no bacterial secondary infection a doctor's advice is seldom needed.

Preventing the spread of athlete's foot

Within the home, people with active infection should not go barefoot and should not share towels, etc. with others. Within schools and other institutions it is usual to exclude sufferers from swimming baths and changing rooms. In a day institution such measures may serve to control infection provided the sufferer does not go barefoot elsewhere (in the gymnasium, for example). In residential institutions infection and re-infection is common.

Ringworm of the nails

Ringworm may infect both toe and fingernails although the latter is more common and probably arises from scratching ringworm infections elsewhere on the body.

Infection in the nails progresses extremely slowly (often over years) gradually producing areas of nail which are dark, crumbly and deformed. Prevention is easier than cure: athlete's foot sufferers should try not to scratch active lesions. Cure is almost certain with griseofulvin but the drug may have to be taken for as much as a year to eradicate the fungus from thoroughly infected nails.

Rituals *see* **Habits**.
Road safety *see* **Safety**/On the road; On wheels.
Rocking *see* **Habits**.

Roseola Infantum

Is a mild, moderately infectious virus disease which almost exclusively affects children under three. Although it is known to occur in small-scale epidemics, little is known about its actual prevalence because it may often pass undiagnosed.

Incubation period. Nine to ten days.

Route of infection. Droplet infection from nose and throat to nose and throat.

First symptoms of roseola infantum

Fever without any other signs. The fever may be high (perhaps as high as 103°–105°F/39.5°–40.5°C) and the child therefore seems extremely unwell. There is nothing to guide the doctor in deciding the cause of the fever.

Diagnostic and final stage of roseola infantum

After three to five days the fever drops and simultaneously a rash of small, flat, separate pink spots appears on the child's chest and back and may spread to the neck and limbs. A doctor who sees the child while the rash is present, and knows of the preceding fever, can now diagnose the disease, but the rash vanishes so rapidly that it is often not seen.

Possible complications

In a susceptible child, the sudden high fever may cause a febrile convulsion (*see* **Convulsions 'Fits' and 'Funny Turns'**).

Rubella *see* **German Measles**.

Safety *see also* Accidents

In the home

Some of the worst accidents to babies and children take place within their own homes. The home-setting can feel safe and comfortable to adults, with all their knowledge, experience, foresight and self-control, yet be a multi-death-trap to a child.

Making your home safe for children involves taking a tour around it, trying to see through their eyes, and then reorganizing any areas or objects which are obviously going to be dangerous. But it also involves taking a critical look at your own living habits. Installing a special cabinet for razors, pills and toiletries is easy; teaching yourself always to use it can be far more difficult. Start during the first pregnancy if you can. After the birth you have about six months before your child has enough physical mobility to match his vital curiosity and lead him into danger. They are unlikely to be the ideal months for installing new cabinets or habits.

Babies and very small children have to be *kept safe* but at the same time they have to learn to *keep themselves safe*. If you are going to have more than one child, they will also have to learn to *keep each other safe* in turn. The keeping safe stage – which applies mostly to babies and toddlers – does involve a lot of physical precautions but, however good those are, it depends above all on supervision. However much foresight and ingenuity you use in child-proofing a room, a toddler will find something dangerous if he is given time. The precautions, then, are to enable you to take your eye off him for long enough to look up a telephone number; they will not allow you to make that call in private. At this stage the precautions are also a contribution to your sanity. If there are no used ashtrays on the coffee table you will not have to spend every other minute preventing the child from eating cigarette ends.

Keeping a first child safe is easier than protecting a later one. Stairgates protect your first child from tumbles. By the time he is three he can manage the stairs perfectly. But what about his little sister who has just started to crawl? She now needs those gates but if you put them up again your son will be stuck and deeply offended if he has to ask for help as 'if he was a baby'. A later arrival in the family makes it even more difficult. The older children are rightly allowed to use knives and scissors but will they remember to put them away in that safe place?

The sooner *all* the children learn to keep themselves safe the sooner you will be able to relax the necessary attitude of 'Go and see what Matthew is doing and stop him'. The very items which you lock away from that baby and toddler must be shown, demonstrated and used under supervision just as soon as the child is capable. It would be madness to leave table forks around a year-old-baby who may put them in her mouth and then fall. But by two she can be shown that they are sharp and shown how to carry them – always pointing away from her – so that if somebody else carelessly leaves a fork around there is at least a chance that she will stick it in the floor rather than in herself. By four or five (when she will certainly be spending some time in houses where people are less safety-conscious than you) she could be quite reliable about either using potentially dangerous things safely or leaving them alone. She could even be beginning to help keep younger children keep safe because there is plenty of pride in being grown up to be milked from 'careful, he's not old enough to be sensible with scissors yet'.

Demonstrations are important to much older children, too. A twelve- or thirteen-year-old sometimes seems so sensible and competent that parents forget that there are still skills which he or she lacks, simply because there has been no learning experience. Keep your electric hedge trimmer locked away, by all means, but make sure your daughter has used it *with* you before you decide that she is old enough to trim the hedges for extra pocket money. Always get a babysitter for your children when you go out in the evening, but make sure your son knows what precautions to take when answering the front door late at night, *before* you decide that he is now old enough to be left in charge.

Life is a risky business. Care, foresight and supervision are important but, if you are human at all, you will have lapses and your children will, from time to time, have accidents. What matters is to try and ensure that you do not lapse over the things which really matter and therefore that those accidents are trivial.

Safety and baby equipment

Design is vital. Your baby could get his head wedged between the too-widely spaced bars of his drop-side cot, or choke on a dummy which comes off its plastic flange.

If you are buying new, stick to items with the BSI Kitemark or those approved by the Consumer Association or the Design Centre. If you are buying secondhand, try to establish the make/model number so that you can check, or consult your local Consumer Association as to what safety points to look for.

Use is vital. If an infant-seat is said to be safe until the child weighs twenty pounds, put it away before he gets there. Remember that a lot of baby equipment is for your convenience, not his, so if you use a changing table it is up to you to make sure he does not roll off. Prams and pushchairs are designed to carry one child unless stated otherwise. Adding a toddler seat to the one or heavy shopping to the other could be a bad mistake.

Maintenance is vital. Pram brakes will not work efficiently if levers are rusty and rubber pads worn. Bouncing cradles and baby bouncers will not be safe once elastic has worn or been replaced with a lighter grade.

Safety harness becomes vital. A child can rock and topple himself out of a highchair, pram or anything else you sit him in, long before he can sit alone. Invest in a harness for each regularly-used item. If the harness is permanently on that chair it will remind you to use it every time. If you use it every time, he will expect it and will neither object nor try to get out.

Safety from burns and scalds   These are usually more traumatic, for victim and parent, than any other injury of comparable severity. A small burn hurts much more than an equivalent cut. A more serious one means more pain, fear, time in hospital and likelihood of permanent scarring, than a fall downstairs with concussion and a fractured arm. Serious burns and scalds can kill. Even if they do not, they commit the victim to weeks of agony and illness and possibly years of plastic surgery; they commit parents to dreadful guilt too, because such accidents are far more preventable than most.

Be careful with fixed fires. Any radiant fire – wood, solid fuel, gas or electric – needs a fixed 'safety-approved' guard: fine mesh to stop things being poked through; far enough from the fire to prevent the guard itself getting too hot and with a top piece to prevent a child 'posting' things behind it.

Do not let children see you mistreat a fire (by poking in paper spills to get a light for a cigarette for example) and do not let young ones watch you undo that guard until you are prepared to let them do so too. If a fire needs regular attention, make a small ceremony of doing it properly so that children learn how before you first ask them to do it for you.

If the fire needs matches, keep them elsewhere.

Try not to keep anything interesting (mirror, ornaments, clock) above the fire. They may tempt the very young to climb up to look.

Choose portable fires carefully. Avoid radiant electric bar fires. The portable ones will not only be unguarded but will turn up in positions the child does not expect and have flex she could trip over. If you need portable electric heat, use a warm air convector or a fan-heater.

Do not use paraffin heaters. Although the heat is still comparatively cheap, these have caused more – and more serious – domestic fires than any other single kind of appliance. Furthermore, the paraffin itself is both a fire risk in your home or garage and a poison. If you need a portable, non-electric, space-heater, bottled gas is far safer.

Your cooker is a hazard. The worst and most frequent kitchen accidents occur when children reach up, grab a pan handle and tip the boiling contents over themselves. Use back burners whenever you can. Keep all pan handles turned to the back so that nothing projects over the edge.

Do not leave young children in the kitchen if anything is frying. Hot fat can spit. Hot oil is the most common cause of kitchen fires.

Check the temperature of the *outside* of the oven when it is up to roasting heat. A poorly insulated model may get hot enough to burn if a child falls against, or even touches, it.

When you open the oven door, watch out for the blast of hot damp air. It may be exactly at face-level for your small companion.

If you should be considering a new cooker, consider a split level, with eye-level oven and burners lined up along the back of the counter. Such an arrangement makes it easier to cook and companion the very young simultaneously.

The sooner children learn to cook safely, the better, but a child who cannot reach to stir a pan while standing on the floor should not use the burners. Ghastly accidents have occurred when children stood on stools to 'help' with the jam-making.

Watch out for matches, cigarettes and lighters. Sudden small flames and unexpected smoke rings are surprising and pretty to babies and very small children so they have a real motive to play with those things if you leave them around. Don't. Smokers need to discipline themselves never to pick up or play with a child while holding a lit cigarette and never to leave one burning in an ashtray. If you often wear clothes without pockets, try a lighter on a thong round your neck.

By school age children should be taught to handle matches safely. Teach them to take out one match and *close the box* before striking it. The match should be struck away from them. Burnt matches should never be put back in the box in case they are still hot.

Some children develop a passion for making fire and, even at seven or eight, find it really difficult to resist striking matches to burn scraps of paper or whatever. If you turn this into an organized, approved and supervised activity, you may speed up the end of the craze and lessen the chance of disaster. He can help with garden bonfires or the barbecue. He can even be given a biscuit tin, a ration of matches and some twigs or dead leaves and be allowed to make mini-fires in the garden, under your eye.

Camping and power cuts can be hazardous. Deprived of electricity, whether by a power cut or because you are camping, you may have to use candles, wax nightlights and various kinds of lamp. Of course children used to survive a life in which these were the sole forms of lighting. But a child who is accustomed to electric light may not.

Don't leave small children alone in a room with any form of un-guarded flame. If they need a light in their sleeping quarters, invest in one of the battery-operated nightlamps.

Don't let even an older child carry candles. Most candlesticks are unsafe, and the candle-in-a-wine-bottle will almost certainly fall out at the wrong moment, or allow a drip of hot wax to fall on his hand so that he drops it. Even a row of candles down the middle of a table can be a hazard to a long-haired child leaning over homework.

Lamps are certainly safer than candles, but paraffin lamps need extremely careful supervision because if dropped or knocked over they may explode. Bottled gas lamps are safer and many are designed to be hung up, out of harm's way.

If you need to provide some general light in a dark house or caravan, try a group of nightlights in the bottom of a pyrex basin with an inch of water. It is unlikely to get knocked over and if a child should try to pick up the whole thing a slosh of water will extinguish them.

Be sure that hot water is not scalding water. Most families have turned down their thermostats for economic reasons but if you have not, check that water from the hot tap is not hot enough to scald, and that central heating pipes and radiators do not get hot enough to burn.

Fixed showers _must_ be thermostatically controlled as water which is not hot enough to scald hands at the basin can still scald the soft skin of a naked child.

Hand showers need watching, too, because a child reaching blindly through a lather of shampoo can easily turn on the hot instead of the cold or get the mixture wrong.

Hot water bottles are a risky luxury. Babies' beds should only be pre-warmed. Older children's bottles should not be filled with boiling water, must have excess air removed before they are closed and must be banned from pillow fights, otherwise they may burst.

Never put an uncovered hot water bottle into the bed of a child or adolescent who is seriously ill or sleeping after a shock or accident. If the sleep is abnormally deep he or she could be burned before being aroused by the pain.

Be careful with hot drinks and foods. Coffee and tea do not have to be boiling to scald; casseroled dishes retain heat long after they reach the table while the fruit in a tart or pie can literally skin the roof of an unwary child's mouth.

While children are very young, try never to use a tablecloth. It can be easily pulled off, complete with scalding meal. Coffee pots and teapots hold the heat of their contents far longer than a mere cup or mug. Ideally they should be left in a safe place in the kitchen rather than being brought to table or living-room.

Highchairs need to be kept well back from family meal-tables and the temperature of a child's portion of food checked, as automatically as the temperature of his bathwater.

Irons can be lethal. Although domestic ironing is a very usual occupation for people companioning playing toddlers, it is a hazardous one if anything distracts your attention. Irons stay hot for a long time after they have been switched off; they sit on ironing boards above head level but have tempting flexes to pull. They are heavy enough to knock out a child while burning her, and those ironing boards themselves are often un-stable and finger-pinching. If you are going to leave your ironing, even for a few moments to answer a doorbell, take the child with you.

Safety from dangerous implements Babies at the sitting and crawling stage will pick up and put in their mouths anything they find lying around. Anything which it would be dangerous for them to suck must therefore count as a dangerous imple-ment, but keeping these things out of their way is comparatively easy. Most parents cast a semi-conscious eye over the room before they release such a baby on the floor.

The toddler stage is far more difficult. A toddler will actively search for interesting things and the forbidden ones are often the most fascinating. While he is less likely to put things in his mouth, he is highly likely to fall down. If he falls while sucking a pencil, it could go through the roof of his mouth. If he falls with sharp scissors in his hand he could stab himself.

Pre-school children rightly want to learn to use (rather than just handle and explore) everything they see adults using. But if such a child is to learn to use knives safely, he needs to do it under supervision. He cannot be trusted to select a table knife rather than a carving knife for private experiments.

The difficulty for families is that of finding storage for potentially dangerous implements which allows members of each age group the right degree of access. How can these things be readily available to busy adults and older children; accessible with permission by pre-schoolers, totally out of the sight, mind and effort of toddlers and *never left around for the baby*? The following are examples of some solutions which have worked for some families:

Knives, scissors and kitchen implements kept on magnetic racks. Placed high on the kitchen wall, these are convenient for adults, unreachable by toddlers, visible, but only accessible via somebody taller, to pre-schoolers. Implements are so easy to find and replace that they are unlikely to be left lying around for the baby. Don't put them on the wall where there is nothing underneath, though. Carelessly placed, a knife can suddenly descend like a dagger. Site racks over work-tops.

Cutlery banished, because although spoons are fun, forks are not. You may need a locked drawer, or cupboard with a child-proof catch.

Special storage for sewing and other hobby materials. A child young enough to be endangered by needles and lino-cutting knives will ruin your creative work if she gets hold of it so it is not much hardship to lock away such things. A Victorian writing box comes with a key and makes a decorative workbox. A blanket chest can serve as an 'adult toybox' while a locked writing bureau, or the 'drinks cabinet' section of a built-in unit, can take everything from knitting to letters you do not want chewed.

Personal pencils, pens and graphics equipment kept out of family-space. Older children need a variety, but will want to protect them from ruination by the very young and so will probably cooperate in keeping them in their own desks or rooms. For general use (and inevitably to be left around, sometimes), large, non-toxic felt-tip pens will do little harm.

Tools and other hardware divided into 'occasionally used' and 'constantly available' categories. Obviously workshops or full-scale toolboxes will have to be locked, but unless there are safe places for potentially lethal oddments such as screwdrivers, fuse wire, cup hooks and drawing pins, nobody will ever be able to find them or be able to put them away safely again. Yet another magnetic rack will take some objects in this category. Sets of plastic oddment drawers, designed to be screwed to the wall and placed high up, will take the rest.

Safety from dangerous machines

Some household machinery can be dangerous to small children even when it is a responsible adult who is using it. Any implement with sharp moving parts which do not stop immediately the 'off' switch is pressed, for example, can do fearful damage even as you watch. Suppose that you are using a hovercraft-type lawnmower and your toddler suddenly rushes towards you. You may switch off even as she stumbles, but you cannot stop the blades and may not catch the child before they do.

Reserve dangerous jobs for times when small children are out of the way or for times when your partner can supervise them while you work.

Real safety from these things will only come with knowledge and understanding of them, so as soon as a child is old enough to listen and be interested, make a point of showing her how each implement works; what it is for and why it is dangerous. Let her, for example, feel the weight of that (switched off) electric drill and then see how fast the sharp bit whirls around and how long it goes on turning after the motor stops . . .

Let primary school children serve as machine-apprentices so that by 'helping' you with varying tasks they become safely familiar, and eventually competent, with this kind of tool. Even a seven-year-old may be able (and delighted) to drill holes in the wall with that drill when you are putting up new shelving. She cannot safely do so without supervision, because young arms tire and attention wanders, but by doing it with you she will learn the safe way to do it without you later on.

Aim to have every child able to use these implements responsibly by adolescence because it is during early adolescence that a sudden desire to 'get it done while they're out as a surprise' or to show off to friends who visit while you are out, may otherwise lead to disaster.

When a child shows that he or she is able to use a particular tool or implement sensibly, it is important to accept that he or she has earned the right to take any risk which may still be involved. If a chisel slips, for example, and there is a lot of blood and perhaps some stitches (*see* **Accidents**/Cuts) it is all too easy to blame the young victim and perhaps to say, 'Since you can't be sensible, you can't use that anymore.' But unless he or she really was being careless, it is not fair. Have you never cut yourself when using a chisel? If attention did wander, won't the accident have taught its own lesson?

Whenever you are trying to decide whether or not a particular child is safe with a particular tool or machine, ask yourself whether he or she is any more likely to come to harm than you would be if you undertook the job yourself.

● Do protect very young children from the early tool-use of these older ones. Your eleven-year-old daughter may be just as safe as you are with that motor mower, and allowed to use it, but she is most unlikely to match your unconscious vigilance for the sudden arrival of that toddler . . . If she is to do the mowing, you concentrate on keeping him well out of her way.

Safe use of electricity   An electric shock can kill a small child and be a serious matter for an older one as well as a nasty experience for an adult. Shocks within the home are best avoided by making sure that you *understand how this vital power source works; prevent anyone from misusing it; keep appliances in good order*.

What you must know about electricity. Current is produced at power stations at extremely high voltages. It is carried by wires to your home's junction box where the voltage is reduced to the domestic standard. It is then carried, by further wires, to each of your electrical outlets.

Wires *into* that junction box, and the junction box itself, are therefore really dangerous to any amateur electrician. They should *never* be fiddled with.

The wires inside the walls of your home have two parts: the 'live' wire which carries the current, and the 'neutral' wire which carries it back to 'earth' at the power station.

It is the nature of all electric current to go back to 'earth'. When you plug an appliance into a wall-socket you complete a circuit, at that point, between the 'live' and the 'neutral' wires, allowing the current to follow its natural path back to earth but tapping it, on the way, to make it power your fire, light or washing machine. Shocks occur when:

Instead of completing the circuit between 'live' and 'earth' wires with an appliance, you tap the 'live' current, offering yourself as the most direct route back to 'earth'. This is what would happen if your child poked a hairpin, or other metal strip, into the 'live' hole of a socket. Current would flow up the wire and go to earth through his body and feet.

Instead of completing the circuit between 'live' and 'earth' with an appliance, you offer the current a 'short-circuit' which you happen to be holding. This is what would happen if a child put one end of a piece of wire into the 'live' hole of a socket and the other end into the 'neutral' and held on to the wire. Current would not flow through his body but would take the shortest route to earth along that wire, not only giving him a shock but probably burning his hand too.

You correctly plug in and switch on an appliance but instead of the circuit remaining complete, with current powering the appliance and running straight back along the neutral wire, the wires inside the appliance are touching its casing. If the casing was metal (a good conductor of electricity) and if the appliance had no third 'earth' wire the casing would become 'live' and anyone touching it would get a shock. If the appliance was made, say, of plastic (a poor conductor of electricity) you would probably get no shock. If the appliance had its own 'earth' wire, any current into the casing would at once flow down the 'earth' wire as the line of least resistance. Instead of the casing becoming 'live' the appliance would simply fuse because the current flowing down this 'earth' wire would have broken the circuit between power-station 'live' and 'neutral'.

You offer electric current an even better line of least resistance back to earth than its own 'neutral' wire: water. Materials which will not conduct electricity when dry will do so when wet. If, for example, your cooker is plugged into a wall-socket which is in the 'on' position although the cooker itself is switched 'off', current is being carried from that plug to the cooker. You can safely touch or dust it with a dry hand or duster, but if you wash it and water seeps behind the plug into the holes of the socket, you may get a shock.

The faulty or broken wires of a live appliance accidentally touch a good conductor of electric current which is permanently embedded in the earth and therefore provides the easiest possible route to earth for the current. The most usual danger here is an electric water heater which, if faulty, may send current down the wet, metal cold-water pipes. If you then touch the pipes you will get a shock.

There are a few useful rules for avoiding shocks:

Have all complicated electrical work carried out by a qualified electrician. Don't even put plugs on new appliances yourself unless you are sure that you can follow a wiring diagram.

Make not touching wall-sockets one of the few rules you insist upon with small children. But holes to poke things into are dangerously tempting, so back discipline with practical action: try to have all wall-sockets with their own switches and keep them switched off, as well as switching off the appliances plugged in to them. If the actual socket is switched off no current will be flowing through it. If some sockets have no switches (or to play doubly safe while children are at the fiddly age or older ones are liable to forget the 'switch off' rule) put dummy plugs into them.

Never leave a light fitment without a bulb. If a bulb needs replacing, leave the dead one in place until you are ready to put in the new one. Left empty, that bulb holder is an easy thing to put a finger into. If the light switch (which may be a long way away or have no 'on/off' indicator) is in the 'on' position, the bulb holder will be carrying current. With no bulb filament to travel around to get back to earth, it will travel through that finger and its attached body, instead.

Try to have all appliances 'earthed'. This means three-core cable and three-pin plugs but it also means harmless fusing instead of harmful shocks if things go wrong. When buying new appliances, avoid those with metal casing (or even metal trims) in favour of plastic wherever possible.

Never touch electric plugs, sockets or appliances with wet hands and teach this rule to everyone else too. Be especially wary in places where people are obviously going to be wet. Bathrooms should only have safety-approved heaters and lights and should have no wall-sockets other than special shaver-sockets. Electrical appliances intended for use in wet or damp conditions are especially insulated. Never use indoor appliances in the garden even if it does suddenly occur to you that you could vacuum the patio . . . If children are helping with wet jobs – such as carpet shampooing or washing down walls – make sure they understand the danger of water carrying current through a wet cloth to a wet hand and that sockets are switched off or avoided.

Play safe over electric blankets and wet beds, too. Although the safety standards for electric blankets are stringent, it is better not to test them either with urine or a glass of water!

Use as few adaptors as possible. If you plug a three-way adaptor into a socket and then plug three separate appliances into the adaptor, the weight of that adaptor plus three plugs can pull the prongs of the adaptor forward just enough to expose some metal. Such over-use of one wall-socket also makes it likely that it will be left switched 'on'. That exposed metal will therefore be 'live' and so will all the adaptor outlets including the one which is empty because you have pulled out the plug of one of those appliances . . .

Minimize the wear on flexes by avoiding excess lengths trailing about or keeping the excess neatly stored in a flex-holder. If you can see that a flex is fraying or losing its insulation, have it replaced.

Don't buy toys which run off the mains (even if they do so via a transformer) until the child concerned is old enough to understand how the electrical system works, rather than just regarding it as magic when those cars whizz about. Transformers can go wrong: unsafe ones occasionally get imported from foreign countries and you cannot expect a child to respect your rule about never touching wall-sockets if it has one exciting exception.

Try to make sure that children learn the principles of electric circuitry and the practices of changing bulbs, plugs, etc. as soon as they are interested, sensible and dextrous enough.

Safety from general household hazards

Homes are designed for people old enough to have understanding and competence. Babies and toddlers have not yet acquired these and therefore cannot safely be left alone and on the loose. For them, the only worthwhile general safety tip is to take them with you as you move around the house.

The following 'hazards' apply most often to children old enough to want to get on with their play while you do your own thing, but not quite mature enough to foresee the results of their own actions. They also apply, often painfully, to a school-age child carried away by a game or a daydream or the victim of bad luck. For all their sakes, give some thought to dangers from:

Glass. Don't keep internal glass doors or french windows so clean that a child can think the glass is open space and try to walk or reach through it. Panes will prevent this as will grubby fingermarks; or have safety glass.

Don't have floor length mirrors in rooms where children play and might fall, unless you use the kind made of plastic rather than glass.

Things that can pinch. Ironing boards, folding chairs, clothes airers, can all pinch, blacken nails or break fingers.

Swing doors or those with automatic closures are difficult for a small child to time his entrance or exit through and dangerous if several are playing together. Hook them open or use a doorstop.

Beware of fingers in the *hinge* side of doors. It is easy to make sure that you are not shutting the door on your child's hand, but much more difficult to be sure that he hasn't got his hand out of your sight but in the hinge. Folding doors, where several leaves move together, are particularly difficult. It is usually best to open them right up, or close them completely, while children are playing.

Unexpected prisons. Pre-school children get into things with no thought of how they are to get out again; schoolchildren, under the stress of 'hide-and-seek', do the same. The most dangerous hiding place in many homes is a chest freezer. Once in, the child is cold, has little air and, because of the insulation, *will not be heard*. Discarded freezers and refrigerators should not be left around in garages either. Make sure walk-in cupboards can be opened from inside as well as outside. Bathrooms and lavatories should have their locks high up out of a very small child's reach, or have the kind of lock which, in emergency, can be opened from outside with a coin. Children who *feel* locked in *are* locked in because panic makes them unable to undo a lock which they can normally manage easily.

Windows. Young children fall out easily because their heads are heavy relative to their bodies and legs. Older children fall trying to rescue cats, inspect birds' nests in the guttering or signal friends below. If you have large, low windows upstairs, 'acorn fasteners' prevent them from being opened more than a few inches. A cheap and invisible alternative to bars.

Steps and stairs. Falls down these are common and seldom serious, but watch out for groups of children pushing past each other; for rugs at the top of flights of stairs and for the open type which a child can fall off or through, rather than simply down.

If you have tempting bannisters, some children will not resist sliding down them, whatever you say. You may need to put uprights at intervals to ruin a really tempting run over a dangerous drop.

Steps in a garden or yard may be a fair hazard for children on foot but dangerous to children on tricycles or bikes. You might need a safety fence or kerbstone until all concerned learn to use their brakes.

All falls will be made less likely if you discourage children from wearing socks without shoes. Bare feet are fine and so are shoes. Socks alone turn many modern plastic floors into skating rinks.

Plastic bags. These constitute the only real danger of suffocation in a modern home. We tend to be aware of the danger to babies and toddlers, but do remember the temptation to older children to use dry cleaners' covers or your freezer bags to make space-helmets, or water bombs to clonk on each other's heads. I have never seen a child killed this way but I have seen eight-year-olds experimenting with putting plastic bags over their heads and then breathing in to make their faces look monstrous and distorted. The more clingy and filmy the plastic, the more likely it is to stick to the nose and mouth for too long . . .

Recent disasters have also made it clear that even non-clingy plastic bags can be dangerous. One child, for example, pulled a child's shopping bag, made of cotton-lined stiff plastic, over her head. Although it did not cling, the size of the bag made it a tight fit and the plastic outside prevented any air getting through to her. She was found unconscious.

Safety from household poisons

Modern products for cleaning, disinfecting and polishing your house, for killing off pests and weeds, for stripping wood, de-rusting metal, glueing one thing to another and for beautifying, deodorizing or depilating yourself, are so many and various, that even in a country which insists on proper content-labelling, you cannot hope to know what is in each product or how dangerous it may be. *Play safe.* Assume that any or all of these products might harm your children and act accordingly.

As with potentially dangerous implements, you have to find ways of storing these things so that different family members can have the right degree of access; ranging from *none* for the toddler to easy for you. Products which might actually kill that toddler must obviously be locked away. But if you try to keep a constantly used shed or garage locked, to protect him from that weedkiller, somebody (maybe you) will be certain to leave it open 'just while I'm gardening' sooner or later. It may be better to have a locked cupboard for the lethal but rarely used products and accept a simple bolt, high on that garage door, to protect him from the undesirable but non-lethal things you need constantly. In the same way, household bleach, ammonia and so forth really must be locked away, but you simply will not keep locking that kitchen cupboard if you try to keep the detergent and the water-softener in there too. Avoid obvious places for infant-exploration (like the cupboard under the sink) but find a workable compromise such as a high shelf. If young children have the run of your bedroom, banish depilatories, hair dyes and so forth to a locked cupboard in the bathroom.

As with other serious hazards, the safety of very young children must really depend on their being supervised by adults. But there are hazards to much older children in this area: even to children who are not being especially silly.

Inadequate and misleading labelling. In Britain and some other countries, manufacturers do not have to put the full contents of products on their packaging if those products are not intended for eating. They do not even have to state if the contents are poisonous, so the words 'for external use only' can cover, in minute print, a multitude of horrors.

To make matters worse, many products are named *as if they might be edible*. I have a jar in front of me instructing me to 'nourish my face with pure heather honey'. Could a child be blamed for having a taste? The bottle of floor-cleaner I am currently using is covered in pictures of real lemons – quite enough to suggest a lemon drink to a child – while the printing does not help much, even for a reader, as after the brand name it simply says 'fill your house with lemon-freshness'. I am not saying that many children would take more than a taste, or that a taste of either of these things would necessarily be a serious matter. But it might be. Teach children about these traps.

As more and more people economize by buying giant, cash-and-carry sizes of household products, the danger from having them decanted into manageable containers that used to hold something else increases. *Never* use old food or drink containers for non-edible products. If labels are wrong (or become blurred and illegible) replace with your own big bold stick-on labels. Some families put scarlet 'POISON' labels on everything dangerous and teach children to steer clear of them. But this is too clever-clever for most of us because there comes that day when you are in a hurry and forget.

Unexpected dangers to skin, eyes and lungs. Even children who are far too mature and sensible to try to eat or drink inedible substances may not realize the dangers of getting certain chemicals on their skin or of spraying them near their eyes or in to the air they are breathing. Many solvents, paint strippers, etc. will irritate the skin if used with bare hands. A pair of rubber gloves taped to the container may remind you to set a good example, as well as reminding independent teenagers to take care. Aerosol sprays can easily be activated while pointing in the wrong direction. Hair lacquer will merely sting, but foaming spot-weedkiller in the eyes could be a disaster. Teach children to check the direction of *any* aerosol spray and avoid buying really dangerous products in this expensive if convenient form. Puffer-packs of insecticidal dusts can be dangerous if they are used in confined spaces so that a child breathes a heavy concentration; many glues and solvents give off dangerous fumes, too. Make sure that children are aware of these dangers and that they are encouraged to use these products in the garden, or with head averted and plenty of ventilation.

Adult pleasures which are child-poisons. Watch out for alcohol and tobacco. Many people do not realize that a good swig of spirits can actually kill a pre-school child, while a whole cigarette, well-chewed, will make a two-year-old extremely ill. While you have very small children around you have to lock away these adult vices, remembering that a drink like cherry brandy will actually taste quite nice to a toddler. You have to go on being careful for quite a long time. That cherry brandy will still taste nice to your eight-year-old who, encouraged by seeing you regard it as a treat, may make himself very ill. Even older children, perhaps dared by friends, may sneak drinks which they really must not have, on medical rather than moral or economic grounds.

Secondary school children often dislike the taste of all alcoholic drinks. If so, don't encourage them to feel that a glass of wine makes them seem 'grown up'. If they don't *want* it they are better off without it, just as we all should be. But some children *do* like it or at least do resent being forbidden it. If so, they will probably have the best chance of adopting a sensible and sociable attitude to alcohol later on if they are allowed a glass of whatever you drink on high days and holidays and are encouraged to take an intelligent interest in the whole business. That intelligent interest can include information about what *is* alcoholic (many children 'don't count' beer for example); knowledge of their country's age-related drinking laws which they should never be encouraged to break by, for example, being bought in an English pub the glass of wine which, at fourteen, they would be allowed at home; some understanding of alcoholism as a growing problem almost everywhere and the immorality of encouraging others to drink (see **Habits**/Habits which easily lead to addiction).

Safety with medicines Considering how difficult it is to persuade many children to take the medicine prescribed for them (see **Nursing**/Medicines) it is extraordinary how readily most children between about one and five years will take medicines meant for other people. But take them they do. Every year, in the western world, thousands of children have to have their stomachs pumped out (see **Hospital**/Procedures: Stomach wash-outs); every year some of them die. Buy, *please* buy, a proper medicine cabinet with a safety lock made to BSI standards. Nowhere else is really safe. If you use a cupboard with an ordinary lock and key, you may one day leave the key in the lock and that will be the day when you do not at once notice your toddler's long sojourn in the bathroom (see **Accidents**/Poisoning).

Use the safety cabinet for *all* medicines. Don't decide that you need not make space for the children's own multivitamins because they are harmless: a whole bottle will not be. Don't keep medicines in current use in the patient's room to remind you of regular doses. Keep a written message to yourself in the room and the medicine in the cabinet.

Iron tablets can be lethal. If you are taking daily iron, perhaps because you are pregnant, keep them locked away.

Remember that contraceptives are medicines. Don't keep your contraceptive pills beside your bed to remind you to take them. A month's supply will do neither sex any good at all. Put a message to yourself on the mirror or your toothbrush or something.

Don't carry medicines in your handbag. If you are prone to sudden headaches or have a chronic condition which means that you must carry tablets with you, ask your chemist for a child-proof container and then play safe by carrying only a very few tablets with you at any time.

Watch out when travelling. It is easy to relax home-vigilance when you are on holiday and may be carrying a variety of remedies against all kinds of eventualities. A lockable vanity case or briefcase is probably the safest solution, provided you do not leave the key in it.

Be careful in other people's houses. If your host's children are much older than yours, these dangers may have been forgotten. Ask and/or check before your children are taken away to play.

Grandparents' houses can be especially dangerous. All too often there are sleeping pills by the bed, laxatives beside the washbasin and 'heart pills' in pockets . . .

Guard against your own mistakes, for example:

Don't give medicines in the dark: you must check the label.

Don't keep medicine from one child or illness to another. Medical prescriptions are personal and immediate, the next child may need something different or the medicine for the first bout may have run out of shelf-life before he has a second.

Don't throw away medicines in waste-bins. Put them down the WC.

Don't rely on breaking adult tablets to arrive at a child's dose. Buy medicines specially formulated for children.

Don't use empty medicine containers for anything else.

Don't ever pretend that a sugar-coated pill is a sweet. It is important to your child's safety that the difference is made absolutely clear; you don't want her eating your iron tablets because she thinks they are Smarties.

Teach adolescents sense about medicines (*see* **Adolescence**/The long road to independence: Self-care). Unless you are morally opposed to taking any but life-saving medicines, you will probably want to teach and demonstrate a commonsense attitude to them from early on. This might include a careful following of doctor's orders over taking any prescribed medicines on time and for the full period, coupled with a restrained attitude to over-the-counter drugs. If children see you buying and using large numbers of patent remedies for everything from headaches and 'stress', to constipation and colds, they are liable to grow up feeling that there ought to be a chemical remedy for everything which ever goes wrong for them.

But by puberty or soon after, children ought to be able to be trusted to take the right dose of a sensible remedy for a bad headache or period pain; to know how much of what to take if they are poor travellers journeying with friends and, of course, to manage any regular medication which has been prescribed for a chronic condition. Don't withdraw your supportive supervision too quickly, though. Many apparently sensible teenagers, going through a headachey time, slip into taking regular doses of paracetamol or aspirin 'just in case' (*see* **Pain and Pain Control**). Many others drift into a laxative habit because they do not realize that a bowel which is over-stimulated one day is likely to remain quiescent for a day or two before it acts naturally again (*see* **Laxatives**).

Safety and pets   Many families feel that pets enrich a home for children (*see* **Pets**). The first choice, if circumstances allow, is usually a dog. Properly cared-for and trained, most dogs will be safe around children, but keep an eye out for the following:

Jealousy. A few dogs – usually long-established pets – are bitterly jealous of a baby. If he is jealous, a dog does not have to be an Alsatian to be dangerous. There have been cases of ordinary small pet dogs seeking out the baby and savaging it to death. It is highly unlikely, but unthinkably horrible, so just be a little wary if the dog always wants attention when you are attending to the baby, tries to push her off your lap and so forth.

Reactions to teasing. Dogs vary in how much mauling they will take from a small child. Some will tolerate almost anything; some treat the child as they would a puppy (and that may mean a few reproving nips) while a few lose their tempers and snap. If you decide to keep a dog of less-than-certain temper while your own children are young, do spare a thought for their visitors. The dog may be even less tolerant of strange children; they will not want to come to the house if he frightens them, while other parents will find any snapping unforgivable.

Puppy-play. If you acquire a pup while your child is a baby, you may have difficulty meeting both their needs safely at the same time. Puppies will chew toys that belong to the baby as well as their own. They will bounce up, even if they knock a toddler down by doing so. They will, especially while they are teething, use their teeth playfully if anyone romps with them; even puppy teeth can hurt.

Diseases. There are various skin complaints and parasites which can be 'caught' from dogs. Keep yours really clean and in tip-top health. Make sure that he is trained not to foul the garden or anywhere where children play. Be scrupulous about keeping any dishes he uses separate from those of the humans in your house and try to ensure that finger-sucking children wash their hands when the dog has been licking them.

Mention the existence of the dog to your doctor if he is ever puzzled by symptoms in the children.

Cats are not usually emotionally concerned with a baby although they are often less tolerant than dogs of inept cuddling and may scratch if bothered. It is wise to use a cat net over the pram to ensure that the cat cannot choose to use it as the ideal bed, with baby as a built-in hot water bottle. If the cat did lie on the baby's face, it is not very likely that the baby would be smothered as his struggles would disturb the cat. But he might be badly scratched as the frightened animal leapt away.

Small mammals, such as rabbits and guinea pigs, can be fun for a small child to watch and help you to care for, but they should not be given to a baby or toddler to hold, for both their sakes. They can inflict scratches which are both painful and unhygienic.

Fish are fun to watch, too, but they are liable to a variety of fungus diseases and therefore their tank water is definitely unsuitable for a small child to dabble in. Keep a top on the tank and don't make cleaning it out one of the jobs children help with, until they can be trusted not to suck their fingers before they have washed.

Safety by, in and on water Babies can and do drown in water no more than a couple of inches deep. If a very small child finds his face submerged in water, he does not hold his breath – as an older person would – instead, he takes a deep breath ready to yell his fear or outrage. That breath does not get him air; it pulls water straight into his lungs.

Baths. A baby needs to be held in the water until he can sit absolutely steadily. But even when he can do this, he cannot safely be allowed to play in the bath unless an adult hovers within quick reach. If he can sit, he can probably crawl and/or pull himself to standing position. If he tries these manoeuvres in the slippery bathtub, he may easily fall face down. Even a two- or three-year-old should have an adult in the room while he bathes. If he slips under water he needs fishing up again, fast.

A baby in the bath must take priority over other calls on your attention. If the telephone rings, let it ring, or take the dripping child with you.

Make sure that older children always let the water out of the bath when they have finished. Toddlers have been known to arrive, find the luke-warm, grubby, fascinating water, lean over to dabble, fall in and drown.

Paddling pools must be treated with just as much respect as baths. One small child will be happy with a small inflatable pool which you religiously empty and deflate after every supervised play-session. If you also have older children who want a larger pool, be careful of a big version of the same because it will certainly be left full and will be a real hazard all summer. If you can find the money for a 'splasher pool' – a miniature version of an above-ground swimming pool – this may keep everybody safe and happy. The rigid sides are too high for a toddler to scramble over without steps (which can easily be removed when there is no adult in the garden) yet it need not be filled to a depth any greater than your children require (*see* **Play**/'Messy' and energetic play for private homes).

Ornamental pools and water butts. These permanent garden fixtures are the worst water-hazard because you cannot keep an absolutely constant eye on a child, for whom the whole point of open space within the home environment is freedom. If you cannot get rid of them, you will really have to work to make them safe. A goldfish pool, for example, can have wire mesh over the surface without bothering the fish. A water butt will need a heavy fitted cover with only a hole for the down-pipe.

Swimming pools. Although still a rare luxury in Britain, these are taken almost for granted in many parts of the United States and, while giving tremendous pleasure, they also claim a lot of young lives.

If you are installing a pool for the first time while your family is very young, consider an above-ground pool rather than an in-ground one. It will not look so glorious but it will be a great deal safer. Four-foot vertical sides will prevent small children slipping in and will foil unauthorized adventures, too, provided the access steps are removed between swimming sessions.

If you already have an in-ground pool you will have to work out how to avoid both accidental and deliberate-but-forbidden dips. Fencing off the whole pool area will deal with the first but it will have to be very securely done if it is to prevent the second. Older children, with free use of the pool, may have to have that privilege made conditional on their behaving responsibly about closing gates, etc. behind them.

Older children
and water   If you live near the sea, a lake or a usable river, water-activities may become central to your child's life. There are clubs catering for almost every imaginable water sport, from canoeing through sailing small boats, to wind-surfing. Highly safety-conscious, such a club will teach your child proper techniques, using well-maintained equipment, and will certainly try to instil responsible good sense and a proper respect for the elements.

But with older boys in particular, competence often brings over-confidence and a growing impatience with club rules. Life-jackets or other flotation devices are abandoned because they hamper movement. Weather warnings are ignored, and the boy may eventually abandon club activities altogether because he wants to do his own thing in his own way. It can be extremely difficult for parents to combat this sort of thing because an element of personal risk is part of the fun of most water sports and your son will probably not be at all cooperative with your attempts to make his chosen pastime as safe as possible.

If he can interest himself in pitting his skill against the skill of others, he may be less inclined to pit himself against the elements. Even quite advanced competitive water sports tend to be less dangerous than, for example, solitary surfing.

If he does not want to compete, you may be able to persuade him that knowledge and skill are more admirable than the more obviously 'macho' qualities of derring-do. If he must sail off that coast, perhaps he would first undertake some serious navigation studies.

If that approach gets you nowhere, he may value the varnish on his own equipment more than he is prepared to value his own skin. Sometimes possession of his own wind-surfer, surf-board or canoe turns an accident-waiting-to-happen into a sensible adult sportsman.

There are a lot of popular and dangerous misconceptions about people and water: teach him to disbelieve the following:

'People float.' Some float better than others, depending on their natural buoyancy, which, in its turn, depends partly on how fat they are. But even the best floaters, lying passively in the water, only float with the tops of their heads above it. That does not enable them to breathe.

'Strong swimmers seldom drown.' In very cold water even the strongest swimmer may collapse and drown within a couple of minutes, so a capsize in winter, even within sight of shore, may be fatal.

'Swimming keeps you warm.' Wrong again. Swimming uses up more energy than it produces in heat. Unless safety is close by and the water is of summer-bathing temperature, the victim will stay in good condition longer if he holds onto something which will keep him afloat and stays still or, if there is nothing to hold onto, if he moves only enough to keep himself afloat.

'Heavy clothing hampers swimming and should be taken off.' With the exception of shoes, this is also bad advice. Swimming is not advisable anyway and heavy clothing, while it does not insulate as well in water as in air, does cut down heat loss and therefore the rate at which the victim becomes dangerously cold (hypothermic). Clothes should be kept on. If an accident on the water is foreseen, as when a small boat finds itself in worsening conditions, for example, all possible protective clothing should be put on.

Make sure that he does believe these:

Alcohol increases the risk of drowning. Even a moderate amount of alcohol makes the body far less able to fight off hypothermia. Many people drown during the midnight swimming parties which round off a good beach barbecue.

Nobody should swim or take part in any water sport, after drinking *or* taking drugs *or* when feverish or ill.

Even the strongest swimmer is more likely to survive with something to hold onto which will keep him afloat. Lifejackets and other flotation devices are *not* 'sissy' and the fact that they hamper swimming does not matter. They are there to save life not to enable the wearer to break the freestyle record.

Any craft, from sailing boat to canoe to pedalo, should have safety lines to hold onto if necessary.

Thin, fit young men and gangly children tend to have least body fat and to succumb to cold most quickly. A wet-suit is a must in cold water. It is not brave and tough to surf off a Cornish beach in April in bathing trunks only. It is simply stupid. Anyone serious enough about such a sport to want to do it outside the warmest season, *must* have such a suit. Any parent with a serious water-sportsperson in the family must, for safety's sake, find a way of making sure he or she has one. Perhaps you could lend the money or provide the wet-suit for a birthday present.

Safety on holiday

Wherever you stay on holiday, your accommodation will be the family's temporary home. All the safety-points which apply in your real home will apply there, too, but you may need to be even more vigilant than usual because you will be without your own safety precautions, and the children will be without the protection of familiarity. While very young children will need constant supervision, freedom may be the point of the holiday for older ones. Parents need to ask themselves whether those older children, whether they are five, ten or fifteen years old, have the knowledge and experience to keep themselves safe in the holiday environment.

Some of the most obvious hazards are noted below. Obvious they may be, but they claim lives (or at least ruin holidays) for some families every year.

Seaside hazards   Children new to the sea cannot be expected to understand the strength of its waves or the likelihood and power of currents or undertow. They cannot know that various states of the tide produce suddenly shelving beaches, wickedly concealed rocks, or a rapidly closing escape route.

If you are in a resort, use a patrolled stretch of beach and make sure children understand the warning symbols. If you have found a deserted place, take local advice.

Be careful with inflatables. A strong on-shore breeze is your best insurance against children being carried out to sea. If in doubt, keep inflatables on a line.

Sand dunes are blissful places to play but don't let children tunnel in them. A cave-in can mean lungs full of sand, however quick the rescue.

Cliff-scrambling is fun, too, but crumbling rock is dangerous and so is getting stuck half-way up.

Water sports – simple swimming, water skiing, sailing or whatever – are all very different in the sea from in a pool or lake. Make children prove their ability to manage these new conditions before you let them venture forth without you or an instructor.

Rural hazards   Even you may not realize the depth of an urban child's ignorance of country hazards. Will he both recognize and avoid a bull? If he has never before met a snake might he try to pick it up? He may be used to finding his way around the city but will he find his way around those woods? If he makes friends with local youngsters, remember that they will be totally familiar with the environment while he is not; they may unwittingly lead him into situations he cannot cope with, especially if, understandably, he is reluctant to admit that it is all new to him.

Foreign hazards   Being in a foreign country emphasizes the risks which are built-in to being in a strange environment. A foreign language, for example, means that a child will not be able to read warning notices or direction signs and will not understand the helpful remarks of local residents.

There may also be specific risks associated with the particular place. For example, African or southern Mediterranean sun is very different from British sun. A warning to be careful may not be enough although a glimpse of the flayed back of another unwary visitor may make the point for you (*see* **Accidents**/Sunburn and heat illness).

If you take children to a country where traffic drives on the 'wrong' side of the road, be very sure that they can reverse the built-in drill of home before you let them wander alone.

Make sure that they understand local laws and conventions, too. In some countries you may only cross the road at a crossing; jay-walking can lead to an instant arrest. A girl in shorts may be spat at in a Middle Eastern country, or find that by crossing a Roman square alone in the evening, she has invited the attentions of every young man in sight. In many eastern bloc countries there are rigid rules about taking photographs. Unwittingly breaking one can mean at best a ruined film, at worst a trip to the nearest police post.

Finally, of course, there may be health hazards which a child simply cannot foresee. It is up to you to make sure she knows if she should avoid drinking water from the hotel taps; eating fruit from local stalls, paddling in nearby streams or putting on her shoes without first checking for scorpions . . .

Safety on the road

In Britain alone more than 500 children under fifteen (twice as many boys as girls) are killed, and around 70,000 are injured, each year, while they are out *walking*. Nearly a quarter of those children are under five years old. Running into the road causes about thirty per cent of those accidents; coming out from behind a parked car accounts for another ten per cent.

While every child and every set of circumstances is different, busy parents, also anxious to encourage their children's independence, may often be too quick to let a child out without an adult. Most of us are city-dwellers. We accept the constant stream of traffic and we forget, until tragedy strikes one of *our* children, just how dangerous it is. If instead of traffic, the streets around your house were surfaced with live high voltage electric wires, lethal at a touch, would you let your three-year-old out and trust him to stay on the pavement? If those wires were broken, for safe crossing of the street, only at controlled crossing points, would you let your six-year-old cross the road alone?

Toddlers and road safety

Toddlers are certainly not safe without an adult anywhere where there is, or might be, moving traffic (watch out in car parks). Even with an adult, most need careful watching lest they dash or stumble off the pavement. Never take a toddler walking where there is traffic without some way to hold onto him. The two of you can hold hands, but that is not very comfortable. He may be happy to hold onto the baby's pram or to help you push his own pushchair. But he will be safest if he wears a harness and reins or is pushed or carried. It may seem restrictive, but the street is not the place for him to have his freedom.

Pre-school children and road safety

By around three, a child can learn that the kerb is a safety line between pedestrians and cars and, by three or four, can often be trusted to stay on the pavement, even to a point where, allowed to run ahead, he can be trusted to stop and wait for you at every crossing.

But traffic is unfair to even the most trustworthy child. Beware of the car which uses that pavement to increase the available space for a U-turn, or of the delivery-lorry which parks with its wheels on the pavement. Beware, too, of places where the pavement is roped off for work on the drains and pedestrians have to go into the road to get around the hole.

Although many pre-school children are allowed, even expected, to cross roads alone, very few are competent to do so safely. Few can distinguish right from left and therefore be sure in which direction they should check for traffic. Few can judge either how far away traffic is or how fast it is moving. *Very* few can begin to anticipate unexpected driving manoeuvres, such as U-turns or turns across the traffic flow. Even those who have grasped (and have available) various kinds of controlled crossing, can easily be caught out by the motorist who anticipates the green light.

If you cannot trust your pre-school child to stay on the pavement, don't let him out alone. If he cannot do your errands without crossing a road, don't ask him to.

Schoolchildren and road safety

Ironically, the children who are most at risk when walking are often the ones who are usually ferried about by car. A child who is old enough for school is ready to learn about traffic behaviour. But he cannot learn what he needs to know from inside a vehicle. He needs to cross hundreds of roads with an adult before he crosses even one by himself.

If you plan to ferry your child to and from school by car 'until he is old enough to walk safely', make sure that you take him out and about on foot at other times, and familiarize him with the route to school, too. If you are going to walk him to school until you feel he is safe alone, use the daily trips for direct teaching.

Whenever and wherever you walk with the child, point out traffic behaviour; let *him* tell *you* where and when it is safe to cross roads; go out of your way to show him various forms of controlled crossing and to point out hazards like failed traffic lights. He will learn road safety by imitation and by doing, just as he best learns other skills.

The Green Cross Code Such heavy reliance is placed on this code that, while entirely sympathetic with its intentions, the author feels it necessary to point out that it has its limitations too.

First find a safe place to cross such as a pedestrian crossing, patrolled crossing, subway or controlled lights. There may be no such place available, especially in a suburban-residential, rural or semi-rural area.

Stand on the pavement near the curb. Look all round for traffic and listen. In a busy area there may be constant streams of traffic.

If traffic is coming, let it pass. Again, there may be continuous traffic so that a child who 'lets it pass' will never be able to cross.

Look all around again. When there is no traffic near, cross. How near is near?

Keep looking and listening for traffic as you cross.

Adapting the code for your child If you live in a quiet area, well-supplied with crossing places, you may be able to teach your child to observe the Code as an absolute set of rules to be obeyed at all times. If so, make sure that you always obey them too and that you do not adopt a 'do what I say, not what I do' approach to rushed Saturday shopping trips.

If you live in a busy city area and your child has regular journeys which he wants to make on foot – to school, to the local shops, to specific friends' houses, club premises and so forth – you can adapt the code *especially for him*.

Walk each route alone and work out:

Where he should cross: is there a pedestrian crossing if he goes on a little further? Is there a School Crossing Patrol at particular times? Are there controlled lights . . . ?

When he should cross. For example, if he must cross a street with no traffic control at all, what markers can he use along the way to tell him that traffic is too close for safety? You need to be able to tell him, 'Don't cross if there is anything closer than that church . . .' If there is some form of control, he must get his timing right. May he cross to a central refuge if the pedestrian light is already on when he arrives, or is it so brief that he should wait for the next round?

How he should cross. For example, if there is a quiet street which has cars parked on both sides, you may have to teach him to hold onto the bumper of one while he edges his way out far enough to peer both ways.

What he is to do if he cannot cross. For example, if the usual Crossing Patrol does not appear, is he to cross all the same? Walk on to a designated alternative? Wait for an adult and ask for help?

Walk each route with the child. Make a game out of teaching and testing him, with increasing independence as the reward and your concern for his safety as motivation. As he learns, he can take you; then go ahead of you (within warning calling range); then do the easiest part of the walk, meeting you half-way and so on.

Don't let him undertake any of these special journeys alone until you are sure that he is no more likely to be knocked down than you are yourself. Be firm, whether he is five or nine. But be tactful, too. If he is meeting you half-way and is with a group of friends, they do not have to know that he is on trial.

Gradually generalize these special journeys to overall road safety. Over months, the things he has learned for these particular walks can be applied more and more generally, until he is safe on other roads of similar difficulty and, eventually, on any road at all.

Road safety for older children in a hurry

Nothing you can do will absolutely ensure that an older child or adolescent will always cross roads sensibly. Can you honestly say that you never take a risk yourself? As with other kinds of safety-teaching, once you are certain that your children have the necessary skills, knowledge and experience to keep themselves safe, you have to trust them to do so.

In the in-between stage, though, perhaps in the nine-to-fourteen age group, watch out for gangs of friends: six running home together tend to move as a mass, each thinking another is giving the signal to cross, and the one who is lagging thinking only of catching up. Be careful also of entrusting very young children to older ones; they may not allow for short legs and lack of concentration. Above all, if you *see* road-idiocy, like games of 'last across is chicken', be as tough as you know how. Maybe your devil-may-care child can be induced to pity the poor motorists . . .

● Whatever your child's age and circumstances, remember that, statistically, three conditions much increase his chances of being involved in a road traffic accident:

□ *Myopia – short-sight* (*see* **Eyes and Seeing, Eye Disorders and Blindness**).
□ *Deafness*, often the temporary result of fluid in the middle ear (*see* **Ears and Hearing; Ear Disorders and Deafness**).
□ *Stress in the family* which may distract him either in the immediate sense of not noticing that car, or in the sense of making him careless of his own safety (*see* **Depression**/In children before puberty).

● Remember, also, that a child who has recently moved house, or even moved from the same house into a new school, has lost the protection of familiarity with local roads and crossings. Such a child may be under some stress as well.

Safety from 'strangers'

Every family has the grim responsibility of trying to protect its children from the remote but hideous possibility of assault. While individual precautions have to be tailored to the home's environment, the family's way of life and each child's age, sex and personality, there are some general points which will apply to most.

First lessons:
NOT 'Don't talk
to strangers'

No child of any age will come to harm just by talking. The child who is forbidden to speak to anyone he does not know is actually at a disadvantage in learning to keep himself safe in his community.

If he takes the message seriously it must make him feel that 'outsiders' are peculiarly dangerous. This is neither true, nor helpful to his eventual social integration.

An intelligent child probably will not take the message seriously for long because he will see it contradicted so often. *You* speak to strangers. You, a stranger, speak to small children if they fall down at your feet, or you find one alone and crying. And you expect him to speak nicely to strange shopkeepers and people known to you but not previously to him.

If he is reluctant to speak, he cannot ask the way when he is lost or even respond civilly when asked the time.

BUT 'Never
go with a
stranger'

Whether approached over the garden gate, on the way home from school, or while playing in the park with friends, a child will almost certainly be safe if nothing a stranger can say will divert her. It is the child who can be tempted into a house by promises of sweets; into the bushes to see a phantom puppy, or into a car for a lift, who is likely to be at risk.

'We must always know where you are' goes with this first lesson and, for a pre-school child, can serve to explain it, too. No two- or three-year-old will think it strange that you want to know where she is, every minute of the day, because she wants to know where you are, too. So the message becomes 'Never go anywhere with a stranger; in fact never go anywhere without telling us first.'

As soon as you take the child to public playgrounds and parks you can start on this. The child is on the swings and you are sitting on a nearby bench. If she wants to move to the sandpit she must come and tell you.

A little later she goes to the local shop, and two doors up the road to her friend's house. If she says she is going to the shop, it must be straight there and back. If she meets the friend and wants to go into her house, she must come and tell somebody first.

When she begins to come home from school alone, the same policy must apply. She must come straight home and tell you her plans before she goes off to play. If you are not going to be there, arrange for her to report to a neighbour.

As the child
gets older,
generalize
and explain

Teach the child that if he should ever get separated from you in a public place like a big shop or the zoo, he should *stay where he last saw you*. He should not accept well-meaning offers from strangers to take him to the manager, home, or to the police. That would be breaking the 'never go with strangers' rule. Equally, he should not try to be clever and get back to the car park alone. That would be breaking the 'We must know where you are' rule. In the same way, teach him that if ever he should get home (from school or play) and find nobody there, he should *stay put* and not go wandering off to look for you.

Gradually introduce the idea that while most people are kind and like children, a few people are not and do not. Explain that kind people will know that children should not go anywhere without their parents knowing, so anyone who tries to persuade him to break this rule cannot be a nice person. Then act upon this the other way around. If the two of you come upon a lost or hurt child, *don't* try to persuade her to come into your house or go with you to the police. Either stay with her, giving what comfort you can, while you wait to see if a frantic adult turns up, or stay with her while another passer-by fetches the nearest policeman or official. If another child chums up with yours in the park and your child asks if she can come home with you to play, insist that she find the adult in charge of her and ask first.

Don't let worries about rape and murder blind you to less mind-boggling but more likely hazards. As children grow up, they will both want and need increasing freedom to come and go as they please, within agreed limits. Children (and adults, too) do get grabbed in the street, dragged into alleys and raped and/or killed, but the chances of such a tragedy striking anyone in your family are truly minute. If you keep on with that early teaching, and extend it so that your children do not walk alone after dark; do not go alone to deserted places of known risk; do not accompany strangers, however friendly they may seem; and do not, *ever*, get into strange vehicles, you are doing all you can to protect them from real disaster.

Sexual molestation of children before puberty

The chances of children being sexually molested in less devastating, but still deeply disturbing, circumstances are much higher. There is a great deal which you can do, both to protect them, and to help them to protect themselves.

The most obvious danger is seldom the real one. A man who gets his kicks from displaying his sex organs to your child may deeply embarrass him or her but is most unlikely to do more. It is probably best to take a single such incident lightly, describing the man as 'silly', 'sad' or 'rude', as your child's reaction suggests. If the man is hanging around next day, he may have fixed on your child's school or route home. Report the matter to the police and to the school, but try to convey irritation rather than danger to the child.

Some people (usually, though not invariably, men) do find children sexually exciting. They are most likely to approach them in stimulating circumstances. In a cinema, for example, a perfectly strange man may try to use your daughter's hand, instead of his own, for masturbation. In a public urinal or changing room, a man may approach your son. The shock of an adult behaving in a way which is incomprehensible, but 'wrong', will probably be less for the child if he or she already knows that some people do these 'peculiar' things. Such contacts can best be avoided by children recognizing that there is safety in numbers and staying together when out without an adult. If your child reports an incident of this kind to you, do try not to over-react. If he or she feels that the information has shattered you, or if it commits him or her to being interviewed by the police and so forth, you may not be told of other, perhaps much more serious, incidents.

Most sexual molestation of children is not by strangers at all but by acquaintances, neighbours and relations. If you are to guard your child, without turning her into a recluse, you must try to keep an easy flow of communication going between you. You want to be sure that she will tell you if that eccentric neighbour, who loves children, wants to show her more than his pet rabbits.

Children do not always object to sexual contact with people they think of as friends. Sometimes the 'odd things' the adult wants to do are accepted as a duty: as part of childishly doing what you are told. Sometimes they are accepted as a price to be paid for other aspects of the friendship, such as sweets. Sometimes a child finds herself drawn into it unwittingly, in a gradual slide from hugs and kisses, and then cannot see how to object without being rude. Sometimes a child sees the power which sex gives her, and uses it with precocious lack of mercy. However it happens, sexual contact with adults is at best inappropriate for a child and, at worst, may distort his or her later development. If you suspect it, put a stop to it, however difficult that may be. If the adult is a relation, it can be very difficult indeed.

How can you guard against this kind of relationship while still allowing your child to be friendly with adults outside the nuclear family? You will have to judge each contact on its merits, but remember:

Your child can probably safely visit a household of two or more adults: a man who is tempted by children *and* a wife who connives at his sexual advances to them, is an unlikely, if possible, combination.

A man living alone may welcome your child because he is genuinely lonely and fond of children's company. But if so, he should welcome your company and that of your child's friends as well. Be a little wary of the entirely private and exclusive friendship. Be wary, here, with relations, too. If that uncle loves to babysit but will never join you for a family meal, ask yourself why.

Don't push your children into visiting people as a duty. If you think that elderly neighbour needs help, give it yourself if the child is reluctant. Don't push him or her into physical contact, even with relations, either. Kissing great aunt Marjorie may make him uneasy for reasons he barely perceives and certainly cannot explain.

Make the child's personal ownership of his or her body, and absolute right to keep it private, part of your everyday attitudes and practice. The use of the term 'private parts' sometimes helps a child to realize that sex organs *are* personal and private and that he or she can therefore expect everyone to keep them to themselves.

Don't indulge in, or permit, sexy teasing of this age group. A nine-year-old is not old enough to have (or want) a boy- or girlfriend, other than as a person-friend. If you encourage even the most lighthearted talk of this kind, you will muddle the child into thinking that perhaps he or she *is* a sexual object. You will make it less likely that assailants will be frozen off by uncomprehending embarrassment.

Non-sexual assaults on children before puberty

Although sexual assault is the kind most parents have nightmares about, non-sexual kinds are much more frequent and, in some cities, a real risk to a child's happiness and health, if not to his life. Attacks are usually carried out by groups of youths or adolescent girls. They seem most often to be caused (and can therefore be largely prevented by attention to) the following:

Solitude. A child alone is an obvious butt/victim.

Conspicuous possessions. That brand new football, vast doll's pram, or shiny bike, is a temptation in direct proportion to its rarity in your neighbourhood. If your child is to be comfortable in his community, keep the possessions he uses in public roughly in line with what others have, or save the flashy ones for use when adults are around.

Conspicuous clothes. A child dressed in the uniform of a 'posh' school often invites the semi-joking wrath of others. In some neighbourhoods a skull-cap or turban has the same effect.

Personal vendettas. A child whose family becomes conspicuous in the neighbourhood, often because it is 'different' along some dimension such as race, colour or social class, may be ceaselessly tormented whenever he or she goes out into the streets where young social life is going on. Do everything you can to help your children blend in to their peer group (*see* **Discipline, Self-discipline and Learning How to Behave**/When other children become important).

While doing all that you can to avoid trouble, teach your children that if they ever are stopped by a gang of older children, they should give up whatever it is the group wants without a struggle. A ten-year-old, however brave, stands no chance against five fifteen-year-olds. He or she could get seriously hurt; they could be in serious trouble and all for ten pence and some false pride.

Before a pre-adolescent demands full independence and starts to resent any 'fussiness' from you, make sure that he or she really knows the home area, can manage him/herself within it and knows how to seek help if it is ever needed. For example:

Make sure she knows where all the local 'phone-booths are; always carries the right change and always knows where to contact a responsible adult. You can give advice or take emergency action, even if you are in an office the other side of town.

She should know where the local police station is and where patrol police can usually be found; at road crossings, for example.

She should know how to get home from anywhere she is likely to go, by public transport as well as on foot and always carry enough money for fares. In cities, buses are usually far safer than the underground.

She should know which strange adults to approach for help in any kind of emergency. Some help or protection can usually be obtained from uniformed officials. Make sure she knows of any park-keepers' offices and bus termini, for example, in the locality.

Help her to make the arrangements which mean she goes around with friends rather than alone. That fishing party, for example, should assemble and disperse at somebody's house rather than on the riverbank. Two or more should go to the cinema together rather than meeting in the foyer.

Try to be kind and generous about lifts and snacks for your child's social group. She is far less likely to walk home alone after dusk if she knows you will willingly pick her up (and drop off the others at their houses too), and she is far less likely to set off alone if her friends are always welcomed when they call at her house . . .

Sexual molestation and assault on adolescents

After puberty, girls are at much greater risk than boys. While only a tiny minority of adult men find young children sexually attractive – those who do being as likely to fancy little boys as little girls – young but sexually mature girls attract a majority of heterosexual men, whether they can admit it or not. It may be that youths are equally attractive to many adult women but, since a forced sexual relationship that way around is physically impossible, boys have in-built protection.

Assault by strangers

The lurking male who drags a girl into the bushes on her way home and rapes her is every parent's horror. Fortunately he is an exceedingly rare hazard even though it is his activities which hit the headlines.

Most such ghastly incidents take place after dark and in lonely places, so it is probably sensible to get your daughter's overall agreement to certain commonsense precautions like not walking alone after dark, and avoiding obviously risky places. But you cannot entirely guard against a hazard which is, by definition, unforeseeable. Violent rapes can and do take place in public places and in daylight. Probably the best that you can do is to teach your daughter to be as cautious for her safety as you are for your own, not forgetting to allow for the fact that you may have a car to get around in and/or a partner to go around with.

Other situations with definite rape-potential include letting men into the house when there is nobody else there, and accepting lifts in cars. Happily, hitch-hiking seems to be going out of fashion and many families will find that their daughters easily accept a complete ban on it. Avoiding letting men into the house is more difficult as refusing entry to somebody claiming to represent the Electricity Board can be embarrassing. In many areas it is sensible to teach girls to put the chain on a door before answering it, and to ask for proof of identity before letting anyone in. Better still, a 'spy hole' lets her see the caller; she need not open to strangers.

Avoiding situations with rape-potential comes hardest on girls with a taste for solitude. It certainly *ought* to be safely possible to sunbathe in a private glade, swim off a gloriously deserted cove or wander alone along a riverbank. But in many places it is not.

Molestation by strangers

If rape is rare, molestation and 'teasing' are not. It must be the unusual adolescent girl who has not been embarrassed and/or frightened by being followed in the street, or joined by uninvited 'guests' at her lunch table, cinema seat or poolside lounger. As long as society treats *any* degree of predatoriness as an acceptable sign of macho-masculinity, this kind of thing will reduce girls' freedom to get on with their own lives in peace. Some girls learn to cope by meeting aggression with aggression, mockery with mockery. Others find that discretion is the better part of valour and abandon their lunch once it is clear that they cannot finish it in peace. They are probably right. Pert answers can misfire; insult the leader of a teasing group and it can turn nasty. Provoke somebody into making a grab, forcing a kiss, having a fumble, and fear of the consequences can quickly provoke the group to violence to 'shut her up'.

Trouble with family and other known adults

Any form of sexual assault or molestation by complete strangers is merely the tip of a much larger iceberg. Many adolescent girls are used sexually, often over a long period, by people they know.

Incestuous relationships are much more common than most people want to realize. Close friends and neighbours, and neighbourhood figures such as shopkeepers, watchmen and so forth, are also common assailants. In all these relationships sexual contact is often minimal at the beginning, but escalates when the assailant finds that he can get away not just with suggestive looks and words but with furtive and then less furtive fumblings . . . Why can such a man get away with it? The key to protecting your daughter is hidden in the complicated answer.

Such men get away with it because girls often do not tell anyone. Girls do not tell because, if and when they do, they seldom get the downright protection they deserve.

At the very beginning of such a relationship, when the thirteen- or fourteen-year-old feels that there is something odd about the way the man looks at her and the frequency with which he collides with her in doorways, it is extremely difficult for her to know *what* to tell. How many girls in this age group are confident enough in their own sexual attractions, *and* in their parents' trust and understanding, to be able to say, 'I think Mr Jones fancies me so I don't want to be around him any more'? If a child did say it many parents would be shocked and angry that their daughter was even able to consider such a thing. Others would simply laugh. Still others would even *tell* Mr Jones (father's friend or the building's janitor), 'Our girl's got a crush on you.' So she apparently acquiesces and the man gets bolder. There is probably no physical violence but there is now the mental violence of blackmail and/or bribery. A kiss for a sweet, or a fuss and I'll tell your Dad you were with that boy from next door.

A girl who does tell, at this kissing, cuddling, fumbling stage, is often not believed. Parents cannot or will not believe that 'a respectable married man' or 'your very own uncle' would 'do such a thing'. Their deep-seated shock at the idea of sexual molestation of a young girl by a much older man does not take the form of fury at *him* but, all too often, of fury at *her*. She may find herself accused of 'making up wicked stories'. Ironically, she may also find herself subject to all kinds of new restrictions in her own life with her peers, as if *she* could no longer be trusted to 'behave decently'.

If proximity makes it impossible for the girl to avoid the man, or if his sexual demands go beyond what she can tolerate, she will eventually bring the matter into the open. But even a girl who has been forcibly assaulted, technically raped, within such a relationship, often finds that she is considered more sinning than sinned against. Forced to believe – often by painful physical evidence – that there has been sexual contact, parents accuse their daughters of 'flaunting themselves' of 'leading him on' or simply of 'bringing shame on the family'. The Catch 22 in which she finds herself is often that if she *really* had not wanted it, she would have told her parents sooner . . .

Such attitudes are even more usual if and when any attempt is made to take legal action against the man.

Even if a girl has clearly suffered physical harm, she will have to prove that she did not consent to being hurt. Sexual congress with a girl under the age of consent is technically rape, whatever the circumstances. Yet consent, or 'reasonable grounds to believe' that she consented, together with evidence that she 'looked older than sixteen', will mitigate the court's attitude and sentence.

In a lesser case of sexual interference, even when parents believe the girl's story, the police will seldom take her word against that of a 'respectable man'. She will be forced to re-live every word and gesture for an audience of police officers whose attitudes seem to stem from a belief (or perhaps a wishful fantasy) that every pubescent girl is really a 'Lolita'. No wonder most such cases are withdrawn before they ever reach a court.

Keep communication channels open. The more you talk, the more likely a child is to feel able to tell you if she is uneasy within any relationship.

Try to accept your daughter's sexuality. She may seem like a child to you, but don't allow your rightful desire to consider her a child blind you to the fact that she is physically mature and, therefore, potentially a victim to anyone who sees her as a sexual object rather than a very young person.

Be sensitive to her feelings. If she is uneasy with somebody, it really does not matter whether she has reason to be suspicious. The simple fact that she is uneasy is sufficient reason to help her avoid the man.

Be very clear in your own mind that in relationships with children, however sexually mature they may appear, responsibility always lies with the adult. Our society pretends to believe in individual freedom. If that freedom is to be meaningful, it must include freedom for young girls to make themselves as attractive as they can and want to be without fear of unwelcome attention being forced upon them. A fourteen-year-old should not have to pay for a provocative new dress by being mauled in corners at the party. Men must keep their hands off the package however prettily it is wrapped. We do not believe in helping them with purdah and veils. If your daughter knows that you are clear about this issue, she is unlikely to be afraid that you will blame *her*, however subtly, if she appeals to you for help.

Try to remain basically on her side whatever storms her adolescence may bring. Mutual trust is vital. She must know that, if the chips finally fell, you would take her word rather than that of another adult, and that you would always put her happiness and her dignity before that of your boss or your brother.

Sexual molestation and assault by peers

Some sexual assaults are dates which go wrong. Some 'rapes' are petting sessions which go too far. Every family has to arrive at its own policy on teenage dating and teenage sex (*see* **Adolescence**/Sex) but as well as deciding what they are going to 'allow' their daughters to do, parents also have to help those daughters to avoid what they do not want to do.

Make sure your daughter understands that if she gets a young man going too fast, his brakes may fail. While it is equally important to bring up boys to understand and control their own sexuality, it is vital that girls realize that theirs is usually less direct and urgent than their partners; if they want to say 'enough' they had better do so while they can still be heard.

Try to ensure that she knows what to expect of any particular occasion or group. If she knows that the midsummer barbecue always ends with a nude midnight swim and she is pleading to go, then whether she goes or not is between you all. But if she is pleading to go to that barbecue without knowing about the midnight swim, she may find herself out of her depth in more ways than one.

Safety on wheels

Cars

With more and more cars on our roads, more and more children are exposed to the dangers of riding in them, as well as the danger of walking near them (*see above* On the road).

Do remember that the difference between 'a little bump' and a serious accident is not measured in scratched paint or buckled metal. What really matters is whether or not anyone is hurt.

In a *majority* of accidents, no-one need be hurt if everyone is using appropriate and well-fitted safety-restraints.

Babies in cars

A baby too young to sit alone travels most safely lying in her carry-cot or pram top on the back seat. But *please* have proper restraining straps fitted so that the bed is held firmly in place. If you do not, an emergency stop may jam bed and baby down between the front and back seats.

If you have more than one child and a station wagon or estate car, you may want to put the baby's travelling bed right in the back. You can have restraining straps fitted in that position too, and you will also need a safety lock on the tailgate.

Don't, please don't, ever have the baby on your lap in the front passenger seat, even if you are belted in. It is illegal now, and rightly so. If there is a crash, it is she who will go through the windscreen; her body which will protect yours. If you want to hold her, go in the back.

An awake baby who can sit must not travel in that car bed, even harnessed in. The first sharp corner will wobble her and she may hit her face on the side. Up to a weight of forty pounds, she needs an approved car safety seat, properly fitted (by a garage) to the back seat of the car. These seats have the tremendous advantage of being raised up so that the baby can see out and, as she gets older, is not, therefore, tempted to try and stand up to look.

Some babies get bolshy about being strapped in their seats but this is one issue on which you have to be firm. The most effective way is often simply to refuse to move the car at all until the child is in and properly strapped.

● Don't use anything but a safety approved car seat. There are plenty of hook-over baby seats around which cost much less. But they are only fit for use as feeding chairs; useful, perhaps, on holiday or on a picnic. They are not strong enough to hold a child in a car crash.

Toddlers and pre-school children in cars

A young toddler can go on using that car safety seat, but when he reaches about forty pounds he should have it replaced by a safety approved child harness. Like adult seat belts these have to be bolted to the frame of the car by a garage, but they include a special cushion which sits the child at a height from which he can see out. Most children, used to seats, appreciate the new freedom of the harness and accept the change as promotion. If yours does not accept it willingly, he too will have to discover that no harness means no travel.

Older children in cars

When a child weighs around eighty pounds, he will be able to wear an adult-type seat belt and that means that he *could* ride in that front passenger seat, properly belted in. But he will still be much safer with a properly fitted belt *in the back*. While a seat belt makes that front seat much safer, it is still the most dangerous place in the car. If you must use it (perhaps because your family fills your vehicle), provide seat belts for all seats and at least save the 'privilege' of riding in front until a child is tall enough to travel with his bottom well back on the seat and his feet flat on the floor.

Friends' cars and friends in your car

Ideally you should not let your children ride in other people's cars unless those cars have appropriate seat belts for them and you know that their use will be insisted upon. By the same token, you should not carry more children than you can belt in. Certainly, if you are going to do so you should point out the deficiency to the other child's parents.

If this is a counsel of impossible perfection, at least avoid the following traps:

Don't put anyone in the front seat without a belt.

● As of 1983 this is illegal as well as irresponsible.

Don't put a small child in the front seat with an *adult* belt. A belt which does not fit can in itself be extremely dangerous, not just because it may not hold the child in a smash, but because it may fit across his neck rather than his shoulder and strangle him.

Don't let anyone have a child on a lap in front.

Don't let anyone hold a baby or toddler on a lap, even in the back, unless he or she is near-adult in size and weight. Even from the back seat, such a baby can be thrown straight through the windscreen if inadequately restrained.

Don't let children stand up on the floor of the back, holding onto the back of the front seats. A smash-somersault can fracture spines.

If you are determined to carry a gaggle of children – on a school round or birthday treat – they will probably be safest in the back section of a station wagon or estate car, facing backwards.

Car windows, doors and locks   Don't have windows open enough for children to put out their heads or their arms. Even if you do not scrape them against another vehicle, high speed dust in the eyes is dangerous and so is the effect of random hand-signals on the cars behind you.

Child-proof locks on all doors are vital, especially at the bored fiddly toddler stage, or with a car-sick child who might try to get out before it is safe to do so. Do get into the habit of waiting until you can see all hands inside the car before you shut children in. Car doors are responsible for thousands of truly agonizing blackened fingers every year (*see* **Accidents/** Bruises: 'Blackened' nails).

Car parking   Try to park so that children can get out, or be lifted out, on the pavement side of the road. In car parks, let everybody out on one side so that you can keep an eye on them; other cars, with drivers who are only thinking about reversing in tight spaces, can be extremely dangerous to those too small to be easily seen.

Never leave the engine running if children stay in the car while you post a letter or whatever. In some cars it is easy to engage 'Drive' and some children would love to try. Likewise, don't leave children in a car parked on a hill with only that handbrake between them and disaster.

It is wiser never to leave the keys in the ignition when you park the car at home. Maybe your own children would not dream of having a go, but there may be others who would.

Bicycles   Almost every school-aged child *wants* a bike; some children actually need bikes to get around on. Only you can decide whether your child should have one and if so, when and for what.

First bikes for fun   Most children can balance a two-wheeler when they are around five. There is fun (and status) to be had even from riding one in the garden.

Small bikes will usually fit in a car and can be taken to parks or out into the country. When your child is safe to walk along the pavement alone, there may be a nearby park to which he can push it.

Falls are inevitable at first so encourage jeans and jackets rather than shorts and tee-shirts.

Don't allow him to ride even a few yards on the road. It is not only his incompetence which may endanger him, but the size of the bike: the driver of a large truck may totally fail to see such a minute vehicle.

Bikes in the country   If you live in a rural area, cycling may be the only way for your children to get to school or to get around in the holidays. Even if they do not actually *need* bikes this urgently, they may desperately want them for the freedom and the vistas they open up.

If traffic is really sparse and the area is not very hilly, a child might manage safely, in daylight, at around eight or nine. You will need to do some advance safety-planning though.

Do make sure that she is consistently safe and sensible on the roads *on foot*, before you consider letting her out on a bike.

Do buy her a bike which fits her, not one she will 'grow into' unless it is the kind designed to change with the child.

Do have her taught properly, under one of the Road Safety Schemes, even if she already rides a bike in your garden.

Do consult with your local police or Road Safety Officer and equip both bike and child with whatever safety gear (reflective strips, etc.) he recommends.

Do have the bike checked over by a professional, even if it is brand new. Many leave the factories with tight chains, slack brakes, etc.

Do have the bike regularly 'serviced' (if you cannot do it yourself).

Do have a proper luggage-carrier fitted. Shoulder bags and parcels on handlebars are dangerous.

Do take her (or find someone else if you do not cycle) on several trial runs before you let her cycle on the roads alone or with her friends. Emphasize safety-points like stopping, as well as signalling, before turning right, and emergency measures like turning into the verge.

Don't let her ride her bike after dusk. Teach her to 'phone if held up at school.

Don't let her ride in really bad weather conditions. When roads are wet and slippery and/or there is a high wind or fog, her riding will be erratic and so will the behaviour of cars.

Bikes in the city The accident rate for adult cyclists in cities is very high; for child cyclists it is devastating. Despite the increasing popularity of the bicycle as a cheap, healthy, non-polluting form of transport, you may feel that it is just too dangerous for a city child unless there are special cycle-routes or it is an area (such as many university towns) where there are so many cyclists that motor traffic is resigned to giving them space. Most city-dwelling nine-year-olds are far safer using public transport than their own bikes.

If your child really needs to get around the city by bicycle, or passionately wants the independence of his personal transport, make sure that he gets as much cycling practice as possible in safer areas, first. That way he will only have to worry about the traffic; control of his own vehicle will already be second nature to him.

Motor bikes and scooters The accident statistics concerning youngsters, especially males, on motor bikes and scooters are truly grim. On a motor bike, your child is as unprotected as he is on a push-bike yet he travels at the speed of a car. Youngsters fall off bikes and later on they make dents in car-fenders, but it is accidents off motor bikes which most often cause serious injury.

If your child yearns for the glamour and open-air speed of motor-cycling and is determined to acquire one the moment he is old enough to take it on the road, you probably will not be able to dissuade him. After all he can back his preference for motor bikes over cars with a whole year's age-difference, cheaper maintenance, cheaper insurance, fuel economy, speed through traffic and easy parking. If he is old enough for a licence he will be old enough to earn the money and too old to forbid.

Use whatever influence you do have to persuade him to *learn to ride that bike*. Tuition really does reduce accident rates. Try to make sure (perhaps with well-timed birthday presents) that he wears not only an approved helmet, but also top-quality protective clothing. That leather may save him from lifelong scars.

See whether you can persuade him that, while he insists on the right to risk his own neck, he does not have the right to risk other people's. He might agree not to carry pillion passengers and you might also be able to ban his sister from riding behind her boyfriend.

Cars instead of motor bikes   If your child is immune to motor-cycle *glamour* and only longs for motor *transport*, you may be able to persuade him to wait until he is old enough to drive a (far safer) car. Your willingness to pay for driving lessons, share the family car with him when he has passed the test, or lend him the down-payment for his own, may all help.

Scalds *see* **Accidents**/Burns and scalds; **Safety**/In the home.

Scarlet Fever and 'Strep' Throats

One child's streptococcal sore throat can be another child's scarlet fever. The two diseases are identical except that in scarlet fever, a particular toxin (erythrogenic toxin) produced by the bacteria, causes a lobster red rash all over the body. People become immune to the effect of that toxin, so that a child can have repeated 'strep' throats but only have scarlet fever once. That child can, of course, pass on his throat infection to another individual who may produce scarlet fever . . .

Although it used to be a killer-disease, scarlet fever is now a very mild one. It is thought that the virulence of the streptococcus has declined. Should more virulent strains re-emerge, they can be efficiently treated with penicillin. The disease is not, therefore, one to be feared and it is not thought worthy of attempts at immunization.

Incubation period. Two to four days.

Route of infection. Often by symptomless carriers who harbour the streptococci in the nose or throat. Infection may be by droplets via the throat but it can be acquired from contaminated food or objects, and infection can also enter the body through wounds. The puerperal fever of past times was in fact a streptococcal infection of the uterus.

First symptoms of scarlet fever   Similar to any 'tonsillitis': a sudden fever, sore throat and perhaps vomiting. The tonsils become enlarged and inflamed and the tongue is furry and white with tiny red dots. The tongue then becomes bright red with the white furry substance peeling back from the tip and edges.

The rash of scarlet fever

If the individual is not immune to the toxin, the rash of scarlet fever appears a day or so after these mouth and tongue changes. The rash usually starts on the neck and spreads, over a day or two, to cover the whole body. From afar the skin looks a uniform bright red. Close examination reveals countless minute red dots. The skin may 'peel' after the rash has faded.

Treatment and complications of scarlet fever

The bacteria can invade the lungs and bloodstream and many scarlet-fever deaths in the past were due to resulting pneumonia or septicemia. Today these side-effects are extremely rare, even in an untreated case, and can always be prevented by treatment with penicillin. An untreated patient today may experience local spread of the streptococci into the sinuses or the middle ear. Penicillin will almost always be given to any patient with a 'strep' throat (with or without scarlet-fever rash) to prevent this.

The 'post-streptococcal' state

Certain diseases, such as rheumatic fever or acute kidney damage (nephritis), can develop one or two weeks after any acute streptococcal infection. They are thought to be due to some unusual reaction in the body to the presence of antigens to streptococci. They are now extremely rare, thanks to antibiotic treatments.

These diseases are infinitely more damaging than the original infection. The chance that an attack of 'tonsillitis' is due to infection with streptococci (rather than more usual and innocent viruses) is one excellent reason why a doctor may prescribe penicillin for such an illness.

● A child with a sore throat accompanied by general signs of illness, such as fever and vomiting, should always be seen by a doctor.

● If antibiotics are prescribed in a situation like this, it is absolutely essential that the full course be given, even if the illness resolves in a couple of days and/or the antibiotic appears to be giving the patient diarrhoea.

Scars *see* **Hospital**/Surgery: Plastic surgery. *See also* **Adolescence**/Problems with appearance and body-image.

School

Pre-school and nursery education

In almost every western country fierce argument flares and dies concerning every aspect of education for children under compulsory school age. Campaigning groups, via the media, simultaneously announce that such education is 'a basic right for every child' and that many children 'do better at home'. They tell us that excellent and universally available pre-school groups are a necessity in societies where women-who-are-mothers expect to work outside their homes and they tell us that pre-school education is irrelevant to the issue of child-care during mothers' working hours . . . One research study tells us that children with experience in a pre-school group acquire basic skills (like reading) more quickly once they start school, but another study tells us that pre-school attendance makes no difference either way. It is all very confusing.

The co-existence of so many conflicting theories and convictions is partly due to the fact that people seldom define their terms. What, for example, *is* pre-school education? Is it a curriculum, an experience or some of each? A sensible answer to that question depends on being able to decide what pre-school education is *for*. Is it intended to give children an academic head-start in formal school, or to broaden their overall experience, or to accelerate their development, or to keep them happy? Or is it primarily intended to take some pressure off their parents? Again, sensible answers to questions of that sort would depend on knowing the actual children, parents, and group-leaders under discussion. What might be appropriate for a four-year-old living alone with a depressed mother in a high-rise flat, may be unnecessary for a three-year-old in jollier circumstances, and downright damaging to many two-year-olds. The truthful answer to questions like 'Is pre-school education a good thing?' has to be 'It depends'. Parents who are trying to decide whether or not to seek admission to a pre-school group for their own child may therefore need to shut their ears to everybody else's theories and convictions and think, in a very down-to-earth way, only about their own child, their own lives and the actual groups which are available to them. Ask yourselves, for example, why you are considering sending the child.

If going to a group is for fun only You need to be sure that the group available is likely to meet the needs you can identify. Does it provide the kinds of activity and the personal relationships which this particular child enjoys? She might, for example:

Enjoy the company of other children. Although toddlers usually play side-by-side rather than actively with each other, many much enjoy watching and copying each other provided that an adult is available to help each one to control her own snatch-and-grab tendencies. Children of, say, three or four are usually very ready to enjoy playing *with* each other, and quickly discover that two together can often manage something that one alone cannot. A child who starts at 'big school' with virtually no experience of other children is likely to find them surprising and rather alarming. She may, for example, always have been given the largest cakes and the winning hands. Pitchforked into school she discovers that she is not a princess but simply one of a crowd. Although she may pick up the new 'rules' at lightning speed, her ignorance of social group life may, quite unfairly, make her unpopular.

Almost any kind of pre-school group will certainly give your child the company of others, but that does not mean that only a group can do so. If yours has brothers and sisters, playmates and neighbours, she may have all the company she needs. The same applies to all the other potential social benefits of group attendance. If a child is isolated with one depressed parent in a high-rise flat, she may indeed benefit from contact with other, interested and interesting adults, of both sexes, as well as from extra space, new things to do, talk, music and fun. But a child can have all those things at home, too. If you and your child have a full and satisfying life, with enough people around so that neither of you is lonely or bored, the group may have little to offer her socially.

Enjoy activities you cannot provide at home. Every child needs a range of activities (*see* **Play**) including some which can seem difficult to find in a small city home. She needs to run and jump and tumble; she needs to climb and swing and balance. She needs to make a noise, too, not just the noise that goes with being physically active but the noise that goes with making rhythm and music and fun. With a lot of ingenuity and a little money, it is usually possible to provide for most of this at, or near, home, especially if you live in an area which has parks and playgrounds, or at least open spaces, nearby. But if you cannot bring yourself to make obstacle-courses out of the living-room furniture on wet days, or tramp to the nearest sandpit on fine ones, she may very much enjoy a group which emphasizes this sort of activity. Do check, though, to be sure of that emphasis. If this is your main reason for sending your child to a group it will be shattering to discover that the garden you were shown is seldom used and that a lot of the children's time is spent sitting down with coloured crayons . . .

If a group is to 'do her good' whether she likes it or not

There are probably aspects of her behaviour or development which are worrying you, even though she is not aware of them. If you feel, for example, that your two- or three-year-old's slowness in learning to talk, or tendency to have tantrums, is your fault, you may also feel that somebody else will be better able to help her than you are. You may be right but you probably will not be. A child who is sent to a group because her parents are dissatisfied with her is rather likely to sense that she is being banished. She is more likely to settle quickly and happily if you can get over the bad patch first and then send her.

Group attendance is not often the right prescription for difficulties of development at this sort of age anyway. That child who is slow in talking, for example, is most unlikely to talk more freely with a teacher whom she does not know than she does with you, and at this stage she will not learn speech directly from other children (*see* **Language**). Tantrums are usually a very direct response to parents: part of the power-struggle which has to take place while a child is asserting her own progress from dependent babyhood to self-possessed childhood. She may not have any tantrums at a group because her relationship with the adults there will probably not be close enough to provoke her need to assert herself. But just being at the group and not having tantrums will not cure her of having them when she is at home. Indeed, if she does not enjoy going to the group and feels that you are making her go, getting rid of her, she may be even more inclined to let rip at home.

The point is that most of a child's important development takes place in the context of her relationship with the person or people she cares about most deeply. Arranging life so that she spends less time with those people, and more with others, is scarcely ever directly helpful to that child's developmental difficulty. But, of course, it may be very helpful to those special adults (*see below*) and if it provides them with renewed stamina it may be indirectly helpful to her.

A four- or five-year-old may be a very different matter. If circumstances have kept your older pre-school child socially isolated, she may, as we have said, truly need some practice in socializing with other people. If she is painfully shy, hates being separated from you, fights any attempts to encourage independence at meals or in the lavatory and so forth, you may be really frightened for her at the prospect of compulsory all-day schooling. Part-time attendance at a small group with sympathetic adults can certainly provide an easier start for such a child, but do make sure that it is the right kind of group. After all, if you are trying to avoid miserable tears when school begins in nine months' time, you are unlikely to do so by provoking them now. If you cannot find a gentle group at which, bit by bit, she can settle happily, it may be better to allow her that nine months for growing up under your very gradually withdrawn wing . . .

If a group is to give her a head-start in education

Try not to let yourselves believe that 'education' is the key to getting on in life and that the more a child has of it, and the earlier she begins, the better. If you do, you will under-estimate the 'education' you have been giving your child since birth. She has learned a fantastic amount already and, provided she is usually busy and interested and has an adult to show her things, talk to her and listen to her ideas and questions, she will go on doing so. The education offered by most pre-school groups is no more formal than the 'lessons' your child gets when you take her to the supermarket and ask her to fetch two red packets of cereal, or when you sit with her to watch a television programme and talk about it afterwards, or when you go for a walk and 'read' the advertisements, count dogs or pretend to fly . . .

Some groups do give four-year-olds formal lessons in reading, writing and number work. While these certainly don't do a child any harm *if she enjoys them*, it is questionable whether they actually speed up her learning of these basic skills, either. Most research suggests that if you start directly teaching a child to read when she is four, she will become proficient two to three years later, but if the formal teaching starts when she is five she will become proficient one to two years later. The point is that that child was going to read at around six to seven anyway. The starting date has more to do with how long drawn-out the process is than with her later competence.

The feeling that education is so important that young children should be pushed ahead, has led to the publication of reading and number schemes designed to be used in teaching babies, as well as to powerful advertising for a vast range of 'educational' toys. Few parents are foolish enough to try to force these activities on a child who is clearly bored or bewildered by them, so they probably do not often do any harm. It is a pity, though, if the rare baby who really does take enthusiastically to the written word at two, makes other parents feel that their children are 'backward' or 'deprived'. And it is a pity if pushy advertising blackmails parents into spending more than they can afford on toys which are 'educational', and less than they otherwise might have done on materials which the child can use as she wishes (*see* **Play**).

If you do decide to send your child to a pre-school group because you want her exposed to as many 'educational' influences as possible, do again make sure that you select the right kind of group. If your child is to settle happily, she will need to feel that you approve of what she is doing and of the people she is doing it with. If you send her to a group which deliberately avoids any formal teaching, preferring to concentrate on free, imaginative and creative activities, and you keep asking her 'didn't you do anything but play?' you may confuse her badly.

Group attendance may be for your sake rather than hers

Some parents find it difficult to admit, even to themselves, that they *could* want to be rid of their child. But many can and do. If she is to be sent to a pre-school group largely for your convenience, do be honest with yourself. If you are not, you may select a group which does not actually meet your needs at all, however much the child comes to like it.

If what you need is some time away from the child, either to be alone to do your own thing or, perhaps, so as to give uninterrupted time to a younger baby, any group at which the child will settle happily may give you what you need. But if you are planning to take a job, or a course, your child's pre-school group will have to be one which offers child-*care* as well as 'education'. It is still quite rare to find the two things provided together with equal weight given to each (*see below* Choosing a pre-school group).

Some parents feel that they and their child have got into a rut, run out of fun or simply reached a point where they are ready for new people and ideas. Others believe that their young child needs to have them around pretty well all the time, but find it boring and lonely being at home with her. You do not necessarily have to choose between being stuck in with her or being without her. You can probably find a group which you will both enjoy. If you can find a pre-school playgroup, or a parent-run community group which really welcomes parents, not just as visitors but as an integral part of the environment of the group, you will eventually have a choice. Once you have been going there for a few weeks or months, you will either find that the child is entirely settled within the group and that you, having broken your isolation, are ready to leave her there and go and do something else, or you will find that whether or not she is fully settled, you have become involved with the group and want to build yourself into its running. As always, though, you will need to choose your group carefully. Names and stated policies can be very misleading. Some playgroups which say that they are run by parents are really run, in the day-to-day sense which matters to you, by a paid and qualified play-leader who wants no more than a fortnightly stint of clearing up from you. Some others are more genuinely run by parents, but have become 'cliquey' so that it is very difficult for a new parent to break into the magic circle as anything more than someone who drops her child off and collects her again. A very great many are still amazed if a father tries to become involved.

Choosing a pre-school group

The provision of pre-school facilities is spotty. In some places there may be a wide range of groups, and spaces in them; in others there will be only two or three and all with waiting lists; if you are unfortunate there may be no group at all within range.

If you do have choice available, you can only pick a group which is likely to be right, for your child and for you, by going to see it. You may need to make several visits because it is important that you see the children getting on with life within it *and* that you talk to the adults who would be in charge of your child *and* that you take her on a visit so that she knows what you are talking about before you expect her to attend. The adults cannot (or certainly should not) give you their attention while they have a group of children in their charge; you cannot (or certainly should not) discuss your own child in front of her. You may need three separate visits.

Names are misleading. A group which calls itself a 'playgroup' may be a nursery school in all but that name; a 'nursery school' may be organized more for the convenience of working parents than the education of children, while a nearby 'day-care centre' offers the very best in child-centred experience . . . Depending what you have decided you want from a group, you may like to look out for (or ask about) some of the following:

Overall size and internal group size

A privately run playgroup may take only six children at a time, offering one, two or three half-day sessions per week to each group. A small group may suit your child, but check that it is always the same children who attend particular sessions, otherwise she may not find it easy to make friends.

A large nursery school or centre may have one hundred or more children. Check how they are split up. It may be by rigid age limits with internal promotion, as in a school, or it may be into groups of all ages. Group size may be dictated by the number of rooms available. Twenty three-year-olds are noisy enough to daunt some children, however high the adult–child ratio.

A big centre may cater for children attending for only a couple of hours per day and for children who are there all day while both parents are at work. Check whether the kind of attendance you want for your child is likely to make her feel 'out of it' or 'abandoned'. A child who must go all day and every day, could find that her eventual 'best friends' are only there in the mornings or even that they only turn up sometimes.

Adult–child ratio in the group

Your child will need a 'special' adult who replaces you in giving her a feeling of being securely cared for. How does the group provide this? Watch out, for instance, for constantly changing 'staff'; for heavy reliance on voluntary and *occasional* help from parents, and for rota-systems which can mean that your child never knows which of several adults will be there.

An ideal ratio of adults to children cannot be stated as it depends on individual personalities, availability of back-up help in emergencies and so forth. But as a general rule even the smallest group must have a minimum of two. One adult (as parents know) cannot properly cope with even three children, because if one requires intensive attention for a while, the others have nobody. Two adults, on the other hand, may be able to cope well with more than twice that number.

If there are too many children for the available adults, your child will not only get rather little 'individual attention', she may also get very bored because every change of activity takes such a long time. It will take a long time, for example, for one adult to get ten children into their outdoor clothes or settled for a snack. Those who are not being seen to (or who need no help) just have to wait.

However good the adult to child ratio, watch a session in progress to ensure that the adults 'on the roll' are actually available to the children. One may be continually involved in discussions with parents, other visitors, or on the telephone. There may be a lot of behind-the-scenes domestic chores going on, or even rather too much gossip between the adults themselves. The ideal, perhaps, is not to have adults constantly calling for children's attention or intervening in their activities, but to have them available, reasonably quickly, to any child who wants to talk or show, weep or cuddle . . .

The group's facilities   Purpose-built and beautifully equipped nursery groups can look very appealing, compared to an old hall or semi-converted slum house. But try to look through your child's eyes. Will she like that long row of identical hand-towels on scarlet pegs or will she feel that she cannot find her own? Will she appreciate the darling little desks or does she prefer to sit on the floor which, here, is cold, hard plastic? Just occasionally you can discover something important about the *feeling* of a group by looking carefully at its facilities. I know a group of twenty, for example, which has fifteen identical pots as well as four lavatories. Why so many pots? Because children are sat upon them all together at pre-arranged intervals, rather than individually when each feels the need. Is the garden impeccably tidy with mown grass and flourishing flowers? It may not be used freely. Is the kitchen or 'utility area' tucked away behind closed doors? Its activities may be a secret from the children and one which takes an adult away. Are the walls covered with tasteful pictures and posters? There may be no space for the children's own work. Within limits, a muddle can be homely and comfortable for children. After all, you cannot keep your own home looking as if no child lived there, can you?

Try to get a careful look at the toys and other equipment, too. Children do not need elaborate 'educational toys' to play and learn, but anything which is provided for them should, if their play-learning is truly respected, be decently kept. Puzzles with missing pieces, trains with broken links, books with missing pages and torn covers, and wheeled vehicles without wheels should all make you wonder. Every group has to economize to some extent, but some things must be freely available to children if they are to be available at all. Exercise-book-sized pieces of paper, for example, are useless to a painting three-year-old; she will be better off with big sheets of the cheapest paper available. The same applies to tiny paintbrushes, minute pieces of clay or dough and demands that she 'use up' the stub ends of crayons or the mud-coloured remains in that paint pot. If, on the other hand, you should find that dressing-up clothes are not only available but clean, mended and occasionally ironed, you can be fairly sure that somebody cares . . .

The group's hours and organization

Short hours (often two and a half hours at a time) may be excellent for children just starting at a group, but they may be tiresome for you. By the time you get home from taking your child you have scarcely time to do anything useful or enjoyable before you must fetch her again.

Short hours every weekday are often easier for a child than longer hours two or three times a week. A three-year-old may find it difficult to keep track of 'group days' and 'home days' and may find it difficult to settle into any satisfactory routine. If this group insists that your child begin in this way, is there any likelihood of daily attendance later on?

All-day attendance may mean anything from a short 'school-day' such as 9.30 to 3.30, to a full adult working day with allowance for travel time: perhaps 8 to 6. Even one meal at the group makes a lot of difference to your child. She will have to face strange food, strange customs and intimate attention from strangers. Providing the meal may take a lot of adult time, too. All-day attendance (with all meals provided) does mean that the group is offering complete day *care* as well as 'education', and you will need to find out how these are balanced. In Britain, for example, old-style 'day nurseries' still sometimes provide what is basically safe-custody rather than any kind of education. The day is seen, by the adults, as being punctuated not by different child-activities but by snacks, toileting, meals and rests. The in-between times are 'just play' and are often used by the staff to 'get cleared up' or 'get ahead with the teas' rather than to interact with the children. Increasingly, in Britain and perhaps more especially in the United States, this is changing, but do find out.

Money and attendance at a group

In some western countries (France, for example) almost all pre-school education is provided by the state and is therefore free or heavily subsidized. In Britain and in America, on the other hand, many groups are provided by voluntary organizations or community funds and some are straight private-enterprise, designed primarily to make money for somebody although they may do a good job by your child on the way. The cost of a place, therefore, ranges from nothing, through a little, to a lot.

One of the troubles about this kind of mixed funding is that free places (as in British nursery classes attached to infant schools) inevitably attract a lot of parents and therefore deprive the groups which must pay for themselves (such as the many playgroups under the umbrella of the Pre-school Playgroups' Association). The further the numbers in a pre-school playgroup fall, the higher the fees which have to be charged to the people remaining. Eventually, groups which have to charge can be put out of business which reduces the choice available to parents.

If you want your child to attend a particular group in your area but cannot afford the fees, do at least talk to the person in charge. Many such groups can find grant-money for a certain number of free, or assisted, places; there is no shame whatsoever in taking up one of these because the very last thing such a group wants is to be left half-empty.

Going to 'big school'

Children have to go to school on every day, on which the school is open, from the moment they reach the legal starting age until they reach the legal leaving age. Unless he or she is ill, the child has no choice in the matter and neither do the vast majority of parents. It is possible to educate your child at home but you need not only qualifications but also a special kind of determination, to win the battle to do so.

Folk-wisdom says that 'school days are the happiest days of your life'. If they prove to be so for your child, you will not need the following pages. But if school days do not prove happy, your child's whole happiness will be at risk. He has got to spend most of the waking hours of 245 days of each year in that school. It is not just a place where he goes to learn while his 'real life' carries on at home. It is the place where he will have (or not have) most of his friends; where he will make (or not make) most of his meaningful relationships with non-family adults; where he will find (or fail to find) most of his sporting and leisure activities. School will be central to his life. If it is not central, then his life may indeed have a vital gap in the middle which home and after-school people and activities will be hard put to it to fill.

Sometimes parents forget how important school is to a child because going to school quickly becomes a routine and what goes on in school is a mixture of mystery and trivia. It is the home-child parents see and know and it is easy for them to forget that the child actually has to *live* those unseen hours. School matters.

It is in school that your child will make relationships and undertake activities which are, by definition, separate from you and from home. You cannot do it for him, but you may be able to help him do it for himself. In all a parent's dealings with a school, whatever the age of the child, there is a fine line to be tactfully drawn between interference and neglect. Sometimes one sees examples of both, when young children have just started school. One parent insists on being told every detail of the child's day, whether he wants to talk about it or not. Furthermore, if he admits that he has been writing his name or learning his colours, the parent at once wants to 'help him at home', settling him down to practise so that he will 'do better' in school. That parent is interfering. Another parent presses for no details and may not even listen to anything the child wants to tell. When an 'open day', parents' evening or end-of-term display comes up, the parent is too busy to go. School is the teacher's business. That parent is being neglectful. The happy medium falls in the wide range in the middle. It has something to do with always being interested enough to listen, and a lot to do with always being eagerly willing to be involved when the child or the school issues any kind of invitation. But perhaps it has most of all to do with sensing when your child wants your help and support, and when he wants to live his school life without any parental involvement at all.

While probably no child can be happy for every day of every term in all the years of compulsory schooling, being happy in the first days of the early terms is a good start. If your child can discover that he can cope with his new independent life, make friends, fit in, meet the expectations of teachers and of his group, he will have a foundation on which to build the rest of his school life. A nine-year-old who has a miserable patch may be mourning a best friend who has left, or reacting against a new teacher whom he dislikes. But if he has already had experience of being happy at school, he will have a much better chance of getting happy again quickly. He knows that children can be friends with him; that teachers can be pleasant. Giving your child a good start is worth a lot of effort.

Starting school   For some children 'school life' really does begin on the first day of their compulsory education. For many others it begins long before, perhaps in a gradual progression from half-days at a playgroup through short days at nursery or kindergarten, to membership of a specially staffed and equipped admissions class. The following suggestions apply to any child past toddlerhood who is first attending regularly at a group without a parent or other known caretaker.

At this first stage, whether your child is three or five, his ability to settle into enjoying school life will probably depend very much on him feeling secure about the link between school and home life. The following are examples common to many children; any parent will be able to add others which are particularly important to a particular child:

He needs to know that by leaving you, he will not lose you. You know he will not, but does he? Sometimes a small child, posted through the door of a big building which seems packed with strangers, feels not just that *he* will never find *you* again but that *you* may not be able to find *him*. It sometimes helps to spell out:

That you know the school; know where it is in relation to everywhere else you ever go; how to telephone it (that nice lady in the office up there . . .) where to find him inside the building; which his classroom is and which his teacher.

That you (or another known and expected caretaker) will always come for him at the right time. Quite apart from the safety aspect (*see* **Safety**/On the road), most children start school more happily if they are collected, at least at the beginning, from the same place at the end of every school day. Muddly arrangements which vary from day to day can put great strain on a young child. He may ruin his afternoon by wondering who he will see at the gate, or whether you have remembered that this is the day when he finishes up at the sports field. With most small children it is worth taking endless trouble to ensure that they are never left standing waiting when others have gone. For some children, even social arrangements which involve them in going home with another child are a bit upsetting. If your familiar figure waiting at the gate is obviously important to your child, yet you want him to deepen his new friendships, it may be worth your while to meet him all the same on these early occasions so that you see him off to his tea-party with assurances that you know where he will be, and that you will be there to collect him at the suggested time . . .

He needs to know that you approve of the school and its people. Some of the things that are said and done, both to him and to other children, will seem strange to the child who is new to group life. The more he feels that you approve of it all and trust the power-figures, the teachers, the more easily he will probably accept his new environment.

Try not to criticize teachers or other children. If he is not allowed to go barefoot at home but has to take off his shoes and socks for PE, for example, you can easily make him feel all right about it by pointing out that it is different at school where the floor of the gymnasium is specially made for bare feet. If he tells you, wistfully, that the other children eat sweets at playtime, try not to say that they will get holes in their teeth. An apple for him to eat at playtime might make a happy compromise.

If the child reports something which makes you angry, do ask his teacher about it. He may have got it wrong (in which case he needs correct information). If he was right and there is a real injustice being done, it is better to explain your feelings about it to the teacher (who can do something about it) than to the child who, without her help, cannot.

He needs to know that you are on his side. While most children are more comfortable knowing that parents like, trust and approve of teachers and school-mates, yours needs to be sure that you will not go overboard and either enter into conspiracies or 'let him down' in the eyes of either.

If a teacher must know of a child's private problem, tell her privately, and don't add unnecessary details about his minor eccentricities. Perhaps she must know that he is having help from a speech therapist, for example, but that does not mean that she also has to know that he still takes a dummy to bed. It is important to be tactful in front of his new friends, too. However glad he is to have you at the school gate, he will not be glad to be greeted by the pet-name he had hoped to keep private.

He needs to know that you trust him to manage and that you will help. There is often a fine line to be drawn here. If the child does not think that you believe he can cope with, and enjoy, his school life he is liable not to believe it himself. On the other hand, lost plimsolls or forgotten messages can loom very large if he has not sorted out the lost property system or got used to being used as a postperson. If he keeps getting into muddles, make it your business to know what he needs on different days so that you can tactfully remind him, and offer to help go through his bag from time to time so that those forgotten pieces of paper are found in time.

Allow for the fact that some schools are really tough on forgetful, inefficient children. Helping him keep himself sorted out is not spoiling. If he is always in a row for having forgotten or lost something, he will not get more efficient, just more confused and miserable.

He needs to know that you are interested in what he does. Sometimes he himself will be bored by what he has to do in school. The fact that you actually want to hear the song, see his somersaults, or read his first bits of writing, may make a real difference both to his feelings and to his performance.

Try to listen properly to everything he volunteers. If he cannot compete with older children (or you are not there), immediately after school, he may like to talk at bedtime. If he volunteers nothing, it is usually better not to push, except in the most general sense of 'was it a good day?' and perhaps 'did anything special happen?' But even if he is a child who gives you almost no information about school:

Try to accept every invitation to go to the school. However offhand he is about it, a young child, at least, will usually be saddened by an open day or end-of-term 'do' at which he has nobody. Teachers also can be saddened if they feel that nobody is interested in what they are doing.

Problems over going to school

Helping your child to take school for granted

Although it may sound brutal, it is helpful to many children to realize, from a very early age, that *school is legally compulsory*. Even at six years old, your child is capable of understanding that if all children have to go, by law, there is little point in him thinking too hard about whether he actually wants to or not. If he is unhappy at school, it will also help him to realize that, while you may be able to do a lot to make school easier for him, even including sending him to a different school if necessary (*see below* Looking for happiness in a different school), you cannot actually let him off altogether.

Occasionally, patchy attendance at a pre-school group gives a child the wrong idea about this. If he has been accustomed to staying at home for the day when he has had a late night, a treat is in store or he just doesn't feel like going to group, it may be a great shock to him to find that he suddenly has to go whatever he is feeling like, unless he is actually ill. A few children quickly decide that illness is the key and learn to say 'I can't go to school today 'cause I've got a stomachache' rather than 'I don't think I'll go today'. If your child goes to a pre-school group at all it is probably a good idea to make sure that he attends absolutely regularly, for whatever hours are expected, at least in the last year before he starts at regular school.

Many schools do in fact allow parents a lot of latitude about sending their children. Your child's school may be prepared to accept vague 'sick-notes', or even more truthful notes saying that the child was 'too tired' for school. But it is often a mistake for parents to accept this casual attitude to attendance. If you allow your child to feel that there is any chance whatsoever of him getting out of going, you force him to make a series of choices about something which it would, in the end, be more comfortable for him to take for granted. And, as we shall see, whatever the reason for the child not wanting to go, it will hardly ever be made better by him staying away.

Helping him want to go to school when going seems an effort

Vague unease about school, or a dispirited reluctance to face it, can often be prevented from getting worse if you spot it early. For example, the child who finds it hard starting again after a weekend, a holiday or an illness has usually got so involved with home that he has, for the moment, forgotten his involvement with school. He feels as if he is going out of a warm life into emptiness. If you can help him to remember that school is warm and full, too, he may cheer up immediately. People are usually the key:

Talking to a friend on the telephone or having one round to the house often works. Some children really need to have contact with school-friends at the end of every break.

A child who has been ill for more than a couple of days will often feel better about going back if he gets a note or a get-well card from his teacher. Most teachers are happy to do this if you let them know that the gesture would be appreciated.

'Getting ready for school' can help the child get ready in his mind as well as his school-bag. The child who starts gloomily on his Sunday night routine may be quite cheerful by the time his clothes are laid out ready for the morning.

The actual business of going to school (especially when he does not like parting from you) is often much easier if he goes with a friend.

Softening the transition between home life and school life can sometimes help children with more serious versions of the Sunday night blues. If your child normally travels both ways alone, you may be able to make Mondays seem more tolerable by arranging to pick him up, just on that day. If he normally comes home well before your working day ends, Monday may be the very best day for you to come home early if you can. In a similar way, a child who really dreads going back to school after a long holiday or illness may feel quite differently about it if he is allowed to come home for his dinner during the first few days. Whatever the particular arrangements that you are able and willing to make (and they will, of course, depend on the school and on your other commitments) the point is to ask the child to make not one hundred per cent of the effort that feels too much, but the ninety-five per cent which, in comparison, feels manageable.

Helping the child who really does NOT want to go to school

A child who is really miserable or frightened about school may be reacting mainly to something in his school life or mainly to leaving his home life. The latter is the fashionable explanation but it is not always the correct one. It can be a mistake to be too 'psychological' too quickly when a child is having trouble going to school. It is possible to get enmeshed in deeply emotional issues when, in fact the problem is a simple one which can easily be dealt with.

All kinds of things about a school can put off a child (especially a young one). Sometimes parents don't ask (because they at once assume that the weeping child is deeply disturbed). Sometimes they ask but do not believe that such distress could be caused by the 'trivial' trouble the child discloses. Sometimes they ask, but the child will not tell. Three recent and genuine examples cover the scope of this kind of problem:

A six-year-old boy's new teacher told him (perhaps a little sharply) that going to the lavatory during lessons was not allowed. Convinced that he would never be able to 'last' from before school until playtime, the child became unable to go to school at all. Once the teacher had explained that she had only meant that children were expected to go in breaks so that they were less likely to need to leave lessons, but that, of course, any child who did need to go could do so at any time, he went back happily to school.

A nine-year-old girl, newly arrived at the school, refused to go on her second Tuesday or Thursday. She had heard that 'everyone has to shower after PE' and had assumed that the only showers she had seen were communal for both sexes. They were not. The child joined the gymnastics club before the end of her first term.

An eleven-year-old girl, newly transferred from a single-sex primary to a mixed-sex secondary school, became upset in her first week and, by the second, was showing every sign of real school phobia. She could only tell her parents that 'there's a boy I don't like'. It turned out that this twelve-year-old had adopted her as his 'girlfriend', to her deep embarrassment. The teacher had noticed them together but had assumed the friendship was mutual. He managed to warn off the boy (gently; he had done nothing wrong) and this cheerful, sociable girl settled in at once.

Some problems which are within the school are much more difficult to deal with. Much the most usual are problems concerning the child's relationships with other people. Sometimes a child really cannot get on with a particular teacher. Although teachers usually have a considerable interest in 'children', no human being, whatever his or her training and experience, can like every other human equally. There will always be some children who irritate some teachers and vice versa. But whatever his or her feelings towards a particular child, it is part of a teacher's job to be able to treat every child fairly and decently. Very often, if a personality clash of this kind is really upsetting your child, the teacher can and will put it right, especially if you can manage to raise the matter without being offensive and therefore putting the teacher on the defensive.

There is less that you can do about problems in the relationships your child has with other children; sometimes trying to do anything is a mistake. Desperate with misery for your deeply unhappy child, you may be tempted to ask the others to 'be nice to Johnny'. Don't. Johnny wants them to like him and only he can make them do that. Your interference will only shame him, embarrass the others, and fuel any dislike which may be smouldering. Try not to encourage him to buy friendship either. Giving him a large bag of sweets to hand round may make you feel you are helping him: it may even pass one lunch break fairly pleasantly for him, but it will not help him to make friends. Children do tend to like others who are generous in sharing whatever they have, but they are very quick to notice the difference between that kind of sharing and the bringing of goodies *to* share.

If your child is friendless

A very young child may be able to use some help in making friends just in the sense of being given plenty of opportunities. At this early stage, when many friendships do still begin with parental ones, it may be helpful if you can be sociable with other parents, willing to chat at the school gate or offer a cup of coffee; able to take the child to the parks or playgrounds others use.

An older child may be trying to break into a group which is already close-knit – he may have changed schools at an unusual age, or moved in from another district. Sports and hobbies can sometimes help: it may be easier for him to make friendly contact in an after-school football practice than in the classroom. You may be able to do some subtle local detective work to discover whether there are classmates whose homes are nearby. Acquaintance made out of school often carries easily into it.

Your child may be behaving in a way which puts off others. If you really want him to be happy, take a hard private look at him, especially at the way he behaves when he is with other children. You may be able to see him in the school playground or walking home; you may pick up clues from what other children (including his brothers and sisters) say about, or to, him. Is he so over-anxious to please that he invites snubbing? Is he extremely bossy and always right? Does he cover up his uncertainty by showing off all the time or boasting about things he owns or has done? Has he characteristics which set him apart from the rest, making it more difficult for him to meld into the group? An early or late growth spurt (*see* **Adolescence**/Worries about puberty), different colour skin, different accent, physical handicap and so forth are not his *fault* and of course *should* not make his life more difficult. But, at certain ages and in certain groups they will, and he will have to find ways of overcoming them while the group learns to find him acceptable. You may have to help at least by allowing your child to adapt. If only goody-goodies go straight home after school, for example, you will either have to change rules or schools, or accept that you are asking your son to survive as a goody-goody.

If your child is actually being bullied adult interference may be necessary both for his sake and for the sake of the bullies and the school. Sometimes parents who would be at the school immediately if a child came home with bruises and torn clothes, do not feel that they can take any action about more subtle bullying. But give the school a chance. Every teacher knows that children can terrorize each other without inflicting physical harm, and that once a reign of terror gets a hold the whole school can be badly affected. In some recent and widely reported instances, where adolescents actually ran away or even killed themselves 'because of bullying at school', the teachers at the schools concerned had had no idea what was going on. They had not even been told that the youngsters concerned were unhappy. Do give your child's school the chance to help him and the others.

School phobia (*see also* **Anxiety, Fears and Phobias**)

If a child continues to be very anxious about going to school, even when any specific worries which he can produce have been dealt with, and even when the teachers seem to like him and there appear to be children who are willing to accept him and be friends, the basic trouble may not be within the school at all but within the child's feelings about leaving home. 'School phobia' is not really an appropriate name because it is not the *school* which makes him anxious but the separation from you which going to school involves.

If this is the case, you will probably find that some of the following suggestions ring true for your child:

That he dislikes other kinds of separation too. You may not have noticed this before (especially if he is very young) because he may be a child who has always lived fairly closely within the family and has not often been expected to be away for hours on end, or nights at a time. But if you consider him anew in the light of his school difficulties, you may realize that he has always preferred to have visitors rather than to go visiting; that he has always liked to know exactly where you were and what you were doing and that he has always tended to get upset if plans went awry so that you were late home and so forth.

That the acute anxiety over school was triggered by something which happened to you, not to him. Sometimes the trigger is an obviously traumatic one, such as parents' separating or one of them being away for a long time in hospital or on business. But sometimes it is something much more trivial. A minor illness, for example, which meant that the child had to leave you in bed when he went to school. A minor depression, perhaps, such that the child was made aware that you were unhappy. An overheard row between the two of you which, rightly or wrongly, made him wonder whether all was well between you or whether his family was going to break up.

The point, usually, is that the child, already sensitive concerning your welfare and already tending to feel it necessary to keep an eye out for it, was made to wonder whether you were 'all right'. Once he has begun to wonder, being away at school all day becomes intolerable as he imagines all the fearful things which may have happened to you while he was gone. Will you be there when he gets home? Will he find you in a crumpled heap/pool of blood/floods of tears? Will you have 'gone mad' so that you no longer know or love him? Once his imagination runs riot in this way, logical probabilities and possibilities cannot comfort him.

That the level of his anxiety varies from day to day being highest after a break from school, or when there is trouble at home, and lowest when he is settled into a school week and everything at home is running smoothly and peacefully.

That at its worst, the anxiety shows up in physical symptoms. The child may be quite unable to eat breakfast; he may be actually sick; he may have stomach pains severe enough to make him a bad colour; he may have headaches or migraines; he may be trembly. If the phobia is severe, some or all of his typical physical symptoms may show up not only when he is actually faced with going to school, but also when he is made to think about, or discuss, going to school.

That fear and fear-of-fear make a vicious circle. The child who finds himself 'in a state' on Monday mornings soon comes to dread those horrible feelings as well as the school which first evoked them.

Coping with school phobia Probably you will be already in close touch with the school as you will have been trying to discover and deal with any practical aspects of school life which might have been causing the child's anxiety. But if you are not, do go and see the child's teacher immediately and enlist help for the child. Between you, it may be possible to help him cope quite quickly. But you may need further help from someone else who can act, for the child, as go-between with both school and home. An older child, in particular, may find it easier to manage if he has someone else to talk to. Through the school you can get help, if you need it, from the school psychological service. Through your doctor, you can get help from him or from someone he recommends. Whether you seek professional help or not, the following brief guidelines may be useful:

Don't take the easy road of allowing the child to stay at home. It is not really making it easier for him because he must, and he knows he must, go to school so that a 'day off' is only a temporary reprieve from something which has to be faced. Furthermore, since going back to school after breaks is usually the most difficult of all for him, having today at home usually only means that tomorrow will seem worse.

Very occasionally a child *has* to be allowed to stay at home because his anxiety when he is taken to school reaches panic levels so that he cannot control himself and will scream, vomit or run away. But if this should be the case (and it is very unusual) the child should certainly be under urgent professional care. A doctor may, for example, make a bargain with the child such that he may stay at home today and tomorrow (Thursday and Friday) but will start again and go *every* day from Monday on.

Don't let milder, but chronic, school phobia lead you into changing schools. The school the child is at may, or may not, be the best available school for him, but if he cannot make himself attend this one at all he certainly will not be able to settle happily in a new one. These are circumstances in which he certainly will take his school difficulties with him. The basic problem has to be at least recognized and partly solved before a change of school can be truly useful (*see below* Looking for happiness in a different school).

Try to offer direct reassurances about your own safety and happiness. Although you will not want to hurt his feelings by stressing how glad you are to be rid of him on school days, you may be able to make it clear that each family member has things of his own to do during the day and is pleased to see the others at the end of it. With a young child in particular, it is often helpful to describe what you do when he is not there in such a way that it sounds both busy and (to him) boring.

If you are not safe and happy without him, don't lie. If his school phobia has flared up while you are mourning your own mother, for example, attempts to put a brave face on things 'for the sake of the children' may be one of the causes of the trouble. He may be relieved if you can manage to admit that you are sad; explain that although elderly people do eventually die, their grown-up children are always sad, but that the sadness does not spoil your basic happiness with your family (*see* **Death**).

If you are ill, it may help to acknowledge this, too, and discuss it with him. However horrible the truth, it is seldom as terrifying to a child as the half-truth upon which his imagination is left to work.

If having him at school does leave you lonely (perhaps because he is your youngest child and you have not yet decided what you are going to do with all the rest of your adult life), it may be that he cannot be happier until you can be. Certainly going to school will be difficult for him if he can sense that you prefer having him around and that you are as relieved as he is if that thermometer records a fever and gives you both an excuse.

An older child sometimes has a much more practical basis for her emotional need to stay at home. Although this can happen to either sex, it is usually a girl who identifies with a mother who is over-stressed by a combination of young children, poor health and difficult circumstances. If your daughter really feels that you cannot manage without her, she may find leaving you very difficult. The more she wants to leave and lead a normal life, the more guilty she is liable to feel about this 'disloyalty' and therefore the more determined she becomes to stay and help you.

Try to demonstrate the safety of going to school by making the pattern of family life as smooth and 'boring' as you can. If the child can go to school at all, he can hopefully discover, as anxious day follows anxious day, that there is actually nothing to be anxious about. You always *are* there, safe and normal when he comes home. The evenings always follow their normal routine. The mornings are always the same kind of rush. Nothing dramatic happens.

Sometimes a change in the usual pattern is the trigger for school phobia and, if you can identify that change and go back to the pattern which preceded it, that is helpful. You may recently have decided that the children are old enough to look after themselves for a couple of hours after school so that you have turned a part-time job into a full-time one, for example. If you can manage to go back to being there when the child comes home, he may settle down again.

Experiment with different ways of getting the child to school remembering that the less anxiety he has to feel today the less frightened of being anxious he will be tomorrow. Some children find it easiest to go to school with a friend, leaving you at home (even if you are waiting to go to work). Some find it easiest to go with another family member. Some do best if you take them and, furthermore, if you take them right into the school and pass them over, so to speak, to the teacher. For some children it is important to get up early enough to have time to face the day in prospect but for others it is easier to get up and go; the greater the rush the better as it leaves less time for dread.

Encourage the child to believe that his anxiety will pass. He sees other children rushing cheerfully into school, apparently able totally to forget their homes and families and to enjoy their own environment. He cannot, and so he feels peculiar. It will help him to know that many children go through patches of anxiety like his; that it will pass and that, as long as he will keep trying, the effort of going to school will get less and less.

School refusal Sometimes the difference between school phobia and school refusal is only one of the child's age. A younger child who is school phobic can, if necessary, be physically forced into school. The older one who is school phobic may refuse to go, knowing full well that if he sticks to his guns there is very little anyone can do to force him. If he is forced to go, he may refuse to stay; school refusal easily turns into truancy (*see below*).

If an adolescent refuses to go to school parents are often wise to seek *medical* help as soon as possible. If a child in this age group comes to the attention of the educational authorities as a 'non-attender' or as a truant, legal proceedings may be started so that the whole issue rapidly comes to be handled as one of delinquency rather than unhappiness. If parents have 'medicalized' the situation right at the beginning, this unfortunate train of events can usually be stopped before it starts.

It must, however, be said that some adolescents who refuse to go to school are not emotionally disturbed at all but simply disillusioned with an institution and an educational system which does not offer them what they feel they need. If nothing can be done through discussions with the school, changes of course and so forth, parents may have to appeal to the child's good sense to keep him on the right side of the law. Sometimes arrangements made out of school can be used as bargaining counters to keep him in school. A boy who loathes the semi-academic courses which he feels to be inappropriate for him and at which he feels a failure, will sometimes agree to maintain a legal minimum of attendance if a part-time apprenticeship, or other forward-looking arrangement, is made for him out of school hours.

Provided that you still have your child's confidence and he still has your goodwill, it is usually possible for home and school together to produce a way of life which he finds acceptable. It is when communication has broken down, between child and family and/or family and school, that things most often go seriously awry.

Truancy   Some children truant without their parents knowing that they are not going to school. Some go to school for long enough for their names to be marked on the register and then leave, appearing home only when the school day ends. Others take the deception further, escaping school altogether with forged notes of excuse and so forth.

Anger is a very natural reaction to this situation. Nobody likes to be deceived and few things can make a parent feel sillier than the appearance of the School Attendance Officer with the bombshell-information that a child has only spent five days in school during the whole term. Be angry if you feel angry, but keep the anger between you and the child. If you tell the authorities that you 'wash your hands of him' or 'can't be responsible', you may find yourself taken at your word and the child being subject to care proceedings as 'beyond parental control'. When you have finished being angry with him, try to make this reality clear to him. He cannot afford to reject your authority and control because other authorities will be substituted.

Some adolescents truant with their parents' connivance. However sympathetic you may be to your child's feeling that he is much too old for school and that the school has nothing to offer him, don't ever imply that you do not care whether he goes or not. Not only is he likely eventually to be pulled up by the educational authorities, he is also extremely likely to be picked up by the police (who are alert for youngsters hanging around in public places during school hours). He is also very likely to break other laws, eventually, out of sheer boredom and the difficulty of finding enough to do all day without much money to do it with. If he cannot and will not live as a school-person any longer, he must be helped to live as something else *which is positive*. Truanting is anti-authority emptiness even when it is fun (*see* **Adolescence**/The long road to independence: Part-time jobs).

But some children – young as well as old – truant, like Tom Sawyer, because blue sky or a town fête beckon and school suddenly feels like a prison. Even as adults, most of us skive, just occasionally, in order to do what we want rather than what we should. One illicit fishing trip does not make a truant.

Looking for happiness in a different school

Chronic unhappiness at school (which may, or may not, sometimes flare up into acute unhappiness), often raises the question of whether a change of school might be helpful. If you are even considering such a step, you will need careful advice from people who know both the child and the present school intimately; his teachers, and perhaps his doctor and any members of the education authority who have been involved. There is no doubt that some parents leave children to be miserable at the same school for years when a change of school *at the right moment* might have changed their whole lives for the better. But there is also little doubt that some parents move their children from school to school (sometimes paying fees that they can ill-afford), always hoping that this time the children will be happier; always disappointed because their child takes his troubles with him.

For most children caution is sensible. 'Better the devil you know' may be a cliché, but it is true for many schoolchildren: starting at a new school is an effort at the best of times. The child may discover, too late, that he managed better within that familiar, if disliked, setting, than he can manage now in a strange one. On the whole, then, *most* children will be better off being helped to battle for a tolerable way of life within their present school than being offered escape to a different one. It is important to remember, too, that if a child *has* to change schools at an unconventional moment (perhaps because the family moves to a new district), he may find settling in far more of a problem than he found starting school in the first place. Children's schools should be considered just as carefully as parents' jobs or the family's housing, when a major move is being discussed. A change of school may be genuinely helpful if:

The child has always felt himself a failure. To be happy at school (as in any other group setting) a child needs to feel himself to be reasonably popular and reasonably successful. If he has always felt himself to be a social or academic failure, liked by no one, good at nothing, his image of himself will be poor and will get poorer as he gets older. Eventually a vicious circle is created: because nobody likes or respects him, he cannot like or respect himself; because he does not like or respect himself, he no longer expects other people to like or respect him. Once he ceases to expect liking and respect he is unlikely to get it. A concerned teacher, or new grouping within a school, can (and often does) break this sort of vicious circle so that the child suddenly 'blossoms' with new confidence and interest. But sometimes the circle can be most easily broken by giving him a 'fresh start'. If such a new beginning is to work for him, he needs to know, in himself, that he can now leave behind the labels which have dogged him so far. He must know that he is not 'a dolt' or 'a bully', a 'fusspot' or a 'crybaby' . . . If his self-confidence allows him, now, to meet with a new school on equal terms, the move may transform his life.

The child has never settled at this particular school. Some children find intolerable certain aspects of school life which are common in some areas. Perhaps the most usual example is size, with its attendant complexity and lack of structure. A child who was content at primary school, for example, sometimes finds a large comprehensive school intolerable. Instead of settling in, gradually, over the first half term, he retreats into himself more and more. He becomes able to find his way around the buildings, but he does not become able to find himself amidst the mass of others. Such a child cannot return to the comparative ease and safety of his first school, but he may do very much better if a far smaller secondary school can be found for him. Sometimes old-fashioned buildings, fewer laboratories and modern teaching aids, and a lesser choice of CSE or O level subjects, are a worthwhile price to pay for happiness. After all, a miserable child will make little use of superb facilities. He may be better off making good use of facilities which are no more than adequate.

The child has 'outgrown' this particular school. Each society or community lays down the stages in a child's life at which he should be 'promoted' from one kind of school to another. Inevitably, there are some children who require promotion either at a different time or of a different type. A child who is bored with school at the age of nine may have *become* bored because he found the demands of school, both social and academic, easy. But that bright child will not stay ahead of the game if he is forced to play by those same rules for another two to three years.

Sometimes a child develops particular interests or skills for which his particular school has no facilities and no respect. An exceptionally musical child, for example, may be happy in a school without particular musical facilities, provided that his interest is appreciated and at least some lee-way allowed to him for making arrangements outside for tuition and practice. But if his school neither provides music nor supports his desire for it, trying only to get him out onto the sports field 'like all the other boys' he may become extremely unhappy, not only with his daily life, but with the institution itself. The same kind of thing sometimes happens where a child develops a strong practical bent within a school which is only equipped for, and interested in, academic subjects. Lack of workshops is bad enough, but scorn for the use of hands as well as head can be intolerable.

In every such case, the danger is that if the child is left in the school which no longer meets his needs, he will come to feel himself at odds with the school as a whole and with all the people in it. He may try to change himself so that he fits better, as an exceptionally bright child will often play the fool or simply stop trying. He may have the strength to fight for his own individuality and come to see himself as a rebel and a cast-out, as so many older children in school do. Or he may retreat from a situation which he can neither fully understand or control. Before any of these things happen, the child needs a change. If things can be changed within the school, well and good. But if they cannot, a change of school may be the only answer.

Discipline in your child's school

If your child is reasonably happy in a school which you trust, its discipline is unlikely to cause you any problems. It is if he is unhappy that you (and he) will naturally tend to feel that punishments and rows are part of the trouble, and it is if you scarcely know the teachers that you are likely to make monsters of them in your mind.

If school is going smoothly for your child it is usually a mistake to over-react if and when he is punished. He may hate being set extra work. You may both feel that writing 'lines' is a complete waste of time and the child may tell you (truthfully or otherwise) that he had done nothing wrong anyway. But after all he is not meant to *enjoy* his punishments. Teachers, being human, can momentarily lose their tempers and be unreasonable. Perfect justice in a large group is not always possible. If a whole class has been rowdy and inattentive and it is your child who was finally punished for talking, it is just his bad luck if he was actually only responding civilly to another child's request to borrow a pencil . . . Sometimes it is important also to remember that the child you know at home may bear only a slight resemblance to the child the maths master knows at school. The child has a right to be whoever he pleases in the different settings of his life, but that teacher can only react to the behaviour he sees. If you cannot imagine your little angel as a hellion remember that the teacher may not be able to imagine him as anything else . . . If clashes are frequent, and *bothering the child*, you may like to arrange for a talk with the school. If clashes are frequent and *bothering the teacher*, he will probably ask to see you.

A few schools may have disciplinary policies of which you disapprove, not only for your own child, but for children in general. Some schools will inevitably contain a few teachers who, even in defiance of school policies, use methods which really upset your child. You may like to find out about policies before you decide on a particular school for him; once he is there you are contracted, so to speak, to accept the school's discipline for him. If an individual teacher uses his authority in ways which you consider wrong, you may need to enlist the confidential help of the school's Head.

Corporal punishment   In the UK many teachers still have the right to beat schoolchildren despite the fact that no other western European country permits this kind of punishment and that we ourselves have long banned it for every other population, including violent adult criminals. Corporal punishment is on the way out, though. In many parts of the UK, local education authorities have already banned it in their areas. Furthermore, many individual head teachers have abandoned it in their schools. A case faced by the British government in the European Court of Human Rights has gone against it and a national ban may follow quite quickly. But in the meantime you may live in an area where schools still beat children and you may therefore want to think about it.

The argument in favour of corporal punishment is one which is put forward by representatives of the teaching profession itself. It is not an argument which says that teachers should be allowed to beat any child they wish, any time they feel like it. Most teachers dislike the idea of hurting children just as much as the rest of us do. The argument is in favour of retaining the *right* for certain designated senior teachers within a school to beat children *as a last resort*. Teachers who fight to retain this right believe that corporal punishment acts as a final sanction underpinning the discipline of a school. They feel that their disciplinary task is increasingly difficult in societies which they see as already lax with the young. Legislation which ties their hands is seen as playing into the hands of disruptive elements within a school, and as possibly contributing to violence, both towards teachers and towards other pupils in the school. As one teacher recently put it: 'Of course we try to persuade them to behave decently. But if they won't be persuaded they have to be forced. Without that final sanction, they can just defy us . . .'

The arguments against retaining even a seldom-used *right* for any teacher to beat any child, rest not so much on the emotional or ethical arguments against it but on the fact that corporal punishment clearly does not work.

Schools which do not retain this right are not less well-disciplined than schools which do keep a cane. Indeed some research shows that such schools are better-disciplined, suffer less from bullying, vandalism, etc. and have fewer truants. Furthermore, schools which have recently abolished corporal punishment often seem to improve in these respects, especially where the Head and other teachers were in favour of abolishing corporal punishment rather than having the change forced upon them.

Within schools which beat children, the 'final sanction' or the ability to 'force them to behave' does not work either. Studies of school punishment books show that the same children are repeatedly beaten. Whatever a beating does or does not do to a child, it certainly does not seem to prevent him from committing further 'offences'.

Children themselves are not always against corporal punishment and much is sometimes made of the results of surveys which show a majority of children stating that they prefer corporal to other forms of punishment. But such children, coming from schools retaining this 'right', can only contrast a beating with other forms of coercion. They cannot know whether they would in fact be happier within schools which rely on getting the cooperation of pupils, rather than on any assertion of direct power by the adults. Many people believe that the mere possibility of physical force being used between a teacher and a child spoils the atmosphere of a school, breeding violence between those who beat and are beaten, and destroying confidence between those who might beat and those who might be (even if they never are) beaten.

At present, in areas where corporal punishment in schools is still officially sanctioned, parents are expected to accept it, just as they are expected to accept the rest of a school's discipline. You may have the right to pick or reject certain schools for your child because of your religious beliefs, for example, but you do not (at least yet) have the same right to pick and choose among schools because of your belief in non-violence.

Parents who try to reject a school for this reason are often told that the teachers stand 'in loco parentis' to their child and that therefore the teachers have the same right to reasonable punishment that they have themselves. Some parents, who do smack their children from time to time, are even convinced by this. But there are very real differences between a smack from someone who loves you and has been irritated beyond bearing and a formal caning from someone with whom you have no loving relationship and to whom you were sent, cold, by somebody else. Parental smacking really has no bearing on the argument over corporal punishment in schools (*see* **Discipline, Self-discipline and Learning How to Behave**).

If you feel strongly against corporal punishment and all that it stands for within a school system, what can you do?

You may be able to find a non-caning school for your child without anyone knowing officially that this is the reason for your choice.

If there is no non-caning school available to you, it may be worth your while to tell the Head (at a preliminary interview) of your feelings in the matter and to ensure that a note of your views is put in the child's file. Such a note does not yet carry any legal weight, although a parent's right to 'opt out' of corporal punishment for his or her child, may be recognized soon. In the meantime it may ensure that your particular child is never faced with that particular punishment. Unfortunately, not being beaten himself does not give him the atmospheric benefits of a non-caning school.

If the school ever does want to cane your child, you will (almost) certainly be informed first. You can, if you think it right, refuse to consent to the punishment on his behalf. A school will not cane a child who refuses to accept the beating. But you must be aware that if you take this line you may be entering a long and painful battle. The school may refuse to re-admit the child unless he accepts the punishment. You may have to face keeping the child at home; wrangling with the educational authorities and, eventually, accepting placement for him at a different school. All this is on the child's behalf but may not be to his benefit. If he himself is happy at the school, and would rather accept the punishment than be the subject of an ethical and legal wrangle, set apart from his fellows and made to look 'cowardly', you may have an extraordinarily difficult decision to make unless you can persuade the school to drop the matter or substitute another punishment.

Competition and shaming

Most modern educationists believe that success in learning breeds success and that the rewards of feeling successful are a better stimulus to effort than the punishment of being shamed. But there are still some schools which encourage cut-throat competition. If your child is one of those who finds it comparatively easy to achieve excellence, he may appear to flourish in such a school, but, even so, it may not be the best one for him. Excellence in mathematics, or in ball-games, may be highly desirable in themselves, but achievement at the expense of kindness, cooperation and the realization of people's different strengths and weaknesses, may be achievement at too high a price.

If you have a choice of schools and want to avoid a highly competitive atmosphere for your child, you may like to enquire about some of the following points:

Marks systems. Every school must assess each pupil's progress from time to time, but the way in which a school does it and, above all, the way in which it communicates results or marks or grades, can usually tell you something about its attitude to competition between pupils.

The most extremely competitive school I know, for example, has a weekly test in all subjects for all classes. On Friday mornings, each pupil's name is posted in a list on the classroom noticeboard, giving his or her mark and position in each subject. On Monday mornings, in assembly, the top and bottom three from each list are read out to the whole school. Anyone who is top in all subjects is called up for public praise. Anyone who is bottom in all subjects is called up to 'explain' to the school how such a disaster could have occurred.

The most deliberately non-competitive, although academically excellent, school I know, has occasional tests in all subjects but these are graded ('A', 'B', etc.) and the children are told their grades within the ordinary class lesson. You can only know that you were top or bottom if yours happens to be the only 'A' or the only 'E' in the group. End-of-term examinations are held in the ordinary way and marked in percentages. The papers are returned to the children in class, so that they see their marks and the teacher's comments, but they can discover other people's marks only if others are willing to tell. Listed positions are not given. A teacher can comment 'well done' if a boy achieves fifty per cent, even if others, who find the subject easier, have achieved higher marks. The termly report includes a 'results card', addressed to the parents, which gives the boy's mark, and position in each subject *plus the average mark attained by the whole class*. From this, parents and child can privately ascertain that his position as top in science was only by three more marks than a close-packed average, or that his position at twentieth was actually only a little below that average. This school keeps a careful eye on academic progress and ensures that pupils and parents know where a child stands, but no public knowledge is ever encouraged nor shaming permitted.

Attitude to cheating. Every child must work at answers without help from books, notes or friends, before he can face a public examination. But too much emphasis on 'cheating' does suggest that marks or positions matter very much, and that the boy or girl who cheats is stealing something from somebody. A healthier attitude may suggest that a child who cheats in a test is cheating *himself* of information concerning his progress. Cheating by getting help with homework can be another indicator. If homework is to contribute to education, it should not always be a test, but a way of acquiring knowledge or putting knowledge into practice. A school which bans all help with homework, and labels the child who gets help as a 'cheat', is likely to be taking a very competitive attitude.

Merits and demerits. Most schools which are trying to run themselves as places of cooperative endeavour, between teachers and children and children and children, prefer to manage without any kind of institutionalized reward or punishment. Children are expected to do their best. Effort is praiseworthy whatever its results. Lack of effort is blameworthy even if it still leaves the child well ahead.

Some schools do find that merits (often little sticky stars) give stimulating pleasure to very young children and therefore use them in early academic work. Others find that demerits, which perhaps accumulate towards an automatic detention for a child who gets, say, six in a term, help to keep down minor nuisances like noisiness in corridors. Such a system does at least have the advantage that the child with four demerits has some control over his eventual punishment or otherwise. If he really does not want to be kept in, he will watch his step for the rest of term. So while any such system can be abused, you really need to know a good deal about how it is used before you can judge it.

Public announcements of success and failure. A school which really cares for individuals, for their feelings as well as their accomplishments, may wish to give public recognition and feelings of success to those who are trying, in any field. But it will not wish to attract public blame and shame to any child. Western societies have long abandoned the stocks. Why then should schools continue to shame children in front of their peers?

You may like to enquire *what is done with* merits and demerits, with examination results, sports results and so forth. A school assembly can be asked to congratulate all the following who passed such-and-such an examination without also being given the list of those who did not pass. Teams can be thanked for playing well for the school without the finger being pointed at teams which did not win. As for merits and demerits: whether these are given for academic work or for other aspects of behaviour, they can fulfil their role as marks of congratulation or disapproval without being made public. What possible business can it be of the whole school assembly, that one particular child has pleased or displeased the adults?

The school's control over your child's personal life

If a family and a school have a cooperative and accepting relationship with each other, the 'right' of the school to dictate matters of behaviour, dress and so forth will seldom be questioned by the one or invoked by the other. Both want the child to be reasonably happy and reasonably behaved. Each accepts the other's basic goodwill and behaves with tact. Nevertheless, there are some issues which regularly cause trouble between some schools and their pupils. Understanding something of the school's rights in these matters may help you to mediate between an adolescent and his teachers. It may also help you to consider carefully before you yourself clash with the school over a younger child. Your daughter's right to wear scarlet tights to school may seem to you to be an issue of principle, but if you get into a real fight over it, your relationship with the Head and, therefore, your child's happiness within the school, is likely to suffer. You do need to be sure that those tights are worth the price.

Schools have, and need, a lot of power to conduct themselves as they think best. In Britain, for example, head teachers have complete control over the internal affairs of their schools, subject only to the advice of the governors (which must include two parent-representatives) and to relevant regulations of the local education authority. In practice, this means that a Head can make any regulations she thinks fit and insist that your child observe them. If you do not like them, you can ask her to make an exception. If she will not, you can try, via the Parent–Teacher Association or the governing body, to put pressure on her. But unless you can show that she is being 'unreasonable', you are most unlikely to be able to *enforce* any change. No regulation which can be shown to contribute (or to be intended to contribute) to the safe, efficient and economical running of the school community, will be considered 'unreasonable'.

If such a lot of power makes you bristle, ask yourself exactly what 'right' you, as a parent, have to insist that your child eats green vegetables or goes to bed at a certain time. Those exact rights are not specified in any law. We cannot legislate for the minutiae of human relationships. Instead they are implicit in your right (and duty) to rear your children as well as you can. Exactly how you do it is left to you. Exactly which issues are important in a 'good upbringing' is left to your judgement. And so it should be. Much the same attitude must be applied to the rights of a head teacher. Some of the issues which most frequently cause trouble are:

Clothes   A Head can insist on 'suitable clothing', taking account of issues such as safety, health, hygiene and the good maintenance of the buildings.

In some schools the Head insists on uniform being worn but there is no legal precedent in Britain which allows her to insist on a particularly distinctive one. Trying to insist that all girls wore pink muslin and all boys maroon velvet, might indeed be considered 'unreasonable'. 'Suitable' grey skirts or trousers with white, blue or grey shirts and jerseys, is the kind of instruction which is usual today. Many heads ban denim clothing, and are on shaky ground in doing so, but a ban on tight skirts and skin-tight trousers can certainly be justified on the grounds that such clothing limits free movement and might lead to accidents on stairs, etc.

Sports clothes. Although the provision of separate sports gear is expensive for rapidly growing children, the Head can insist that shorts or games skirts are necessary to allow children the freedom of movement to benefit from physical education; that special footwear is needed for safety and to protect special sports surfaces; and that a complete change of clothing for active exercise is necessary for hygienic reasons.

Shoes. Restrictions are usually based on safety, noise and the economics of school maintenance. Stiletto heels, for example, cause accidents, are noisy on hard floors and make holes in wood or plastic. Although canvas shoes and 'trainers' are cheap and comfortable the Head may honestly believe that it is bad for a child's feet to wear them all day (*see* **Feet**).

Other aspects   Like other adults, some head teachers have strong prejudices against
of appearance   certain fashions among the young and very much want to persuade pupils against them, or at least to confine them to home. Although a Head may simply categorize certain fashions as 'unsuitable for school', she is usually on stronger ground when she invokes a more objective-seeming reason for any bans.

Hairstyles. Few Heads, today, will try to dictate the length of a boy's hair because as fast as she tells one to get his cut she will find herself demanding that another lets his grow. Both sexes may, however, have to keep long hair tied back for safety (especially in laboratories and workshops) and hygiene (especially in dining-rooms and refectories). Brilliantly dyed hair is often disapproved of, but wise head teachers, realizing that the dye cannot be removed overnight, will seldom comment officially on individuals but will confine themselves to general remarks about what they consider suitable for school.

Jewellery, etc. With the exception of religious symbols, a ban on jewellery is usual and probably reasonable; loss and/or theft can make enormous problems for the school. Some schools make an exception for 'keeper' ear-rings for girls who have recently had their ears pierced. Heads vary in their reactions to similar requests from boys.

Money and possessions at school

Many schools try to limit the amount of money pupils bring and may insist on any money being carried in special purses and so forth. Some try very hard to dissuade pupils from bringing any personal possessions. Once again, the reasoning is that loss and/or theft cause trouble and misery. It is difficult enough to keep track of necessary items, such as watches and calculators, without having other items to worry about.

Younger children often want to take balls or other toys for use at lunch-time. Very young ones may need to take familiar objects from home to give them security. Sometimes a tiny teddy in the pocket will stand in for a large one which the teacher must look after. It is amazing how many lunch-time occupations can fit in a pocket, too.

Behaviour on the way to and from school

In Britain, at least, a head teacher's right to make regulations concerning children's behaviour, does not stop at the school gate but includes his journey. This kind of control is usually very tactfully exercised. Schools do not want to stand accused of 'spying' on pupils, nor to find themselves taking a child to task for being somewhere or doing something of which his family turns out to approve. Your child is only likely to get into trouble in school for behaviour outside it if:

He does, and is known to have done, something illegal. A child who is caught using public transport without paying his fare, for example, will probably be reported to the school and face disciplinary action there, as well as any legal proceedings. The same may apply to a child under age who is seen in a pub drinking alcohol, or who is seen smoking.

Anti-social behaviour is reported to the school or is publicly associated with it. If an elderly lady reports your son's rudeness to the school, it may discipline him for the sake of its own image. Similarly, if a gang of boys erupts out of the school and starts a turmoil on the pavement, the school will take action because passers-by will know where the boys come from.

He is endangering himself or others. A school near a railway bridge, for example, may put it out of bounds and clamp down hard on any child seen playing there. A school may similarly forbid children to take short-cuts through risky places. However inconvenient and unnecessary such a ban may be for your hefty son, it may be important for more vulnerable children and enforceable only if it is applied to all.

Time off for personal reasons

While a head teacher has the legal right to insist that your child attend school whenever schooling is available to him, few Heads will try to prevent a child from attending a family wedding or even from taking part in a family holiday. This is certainly an area where your reputation with the school can make things easier or more difficult. If you seldom take your child out of school and always *ask* (rather than *tell*) when you do intend to do so, you are unlikely to be refused. But if yours is a child who gives the impression that he comes only when he wishes to, and that his life outside the school always takes priority over life within it, the Head may begin to make difficulties.

Homework   Schools, and individual teachers within those schools, vary greatly in the importance which they attach to work which a child does at home. Some schools lay down a 'homework programme' for the year and even expect you to sign it, and play your part in seeing that it is done. At the other extreme, there are schools which set no homework at all or which only do so in the year before public examinations. If you feel strongly about homework you should certainly check on the school's policy before your child ever goes to the school. If homework is expected, there is no way that your child will comfortably keep up with the work of the class without doing it. If it is not expected, you cannot force teachers to set and mark it.

If you really feel that homework is interfering with your child's home life, making it impossible for him to pursue out-of-school activities or making a working day which is too long for him, do go and discuss it with his teacher. Homework can give rise to all kinds of misunderstandings, especially when children are new to a school and unsure what is expected of them. You must check, for example, on whether he is intended to stick to an allotted *time* (such as twenty minutes for maths) or whether he is to complete the set assignment however long it takes him. You may also need to check whether he is expected to ask for help or to battle on alone (and if so for how long) and whether, when truly 'stuck', it is permissible to give in an unfinished piece of work.

Homework should, ideally, be a cooperative effort between the teacher (who will give her time to marking the work), the child, who will do it, and the family who will make it possible for him to do so. If you yourselves resent a homework load which spoils the family's weekends, for example, it must be discussed with the school. Encouraging the child to skimp the work is very unkind however much he would like to go fishing.

School records

A particular teacher or a particular school can have a long-term effect on your child's personal life via the records which he, she or it keeps.

Confidential reports which are about us, but which we are not allowed to see, are a source of anxiety to many people. Patients would often like to see their medical records, for example. Sometimes they do discover that they have been labelled 'neurotic' by medical staff and that the label has delayed the investigation and treatment of a physical complaint. People are increasingly concerned with secret computerized credit ratings and their possible effects on the availability of mortgages and so forth. People seeking references for jobs often wonder and worry about confidential files in the personnel department. Does failure to get the job mean that nasty and untrue things are being secretly written? The confidential records kept by schools are unique in their importance because:

They last for such a very long time. A child who is described as 'disruptive and unpopular with other children' may carry that description from the age of five until he is eighteen. Of course, the teacher who receives his file when he is twelve should realize that remarks made about a small child cannot be applied to an adolescent, but will she stop to think about the dates or will that remark just stick in her memory when she meets her new class?

They are made (and seen) by so many different people of such varying qualifications and degrees of closeness to the child. Your medical file is basically kept by your doctor, whom you presumably trust. He is unlikely to take much notice of an unkind or inaccurate assessment by a consultant you only see once. You may feel the same about your child's current teacher, but what about the school doctor or psychologist, the temporary or specialist teacher or the acting Head? Their written words may carry great weight, yet some may be written on the basis of a bare acquaintance-ship with the child. Some psychological-type assessments are also made by people barely qualified to make them. Yet later teachers who read that long personality-profile of your child aged nine, will have no way of knowing that it was filed by a teacher of three months' experience . . .

They can matter so much. Not only may these confidential records play a major part in decisions affecting every stage of your child's schooling, they may also be used in compiling college references and job references. Even years after his schooling is over, an individual may be asked to provide a reference from his head teacher. She, having completely forgotten him, has only those records on which to base what she now writes.

They are so extremely personal. At least those credit-records are only concerned with money, the medical ones with health and illness. These school records concern themselves with 'personality', likeability, trust-worthiness, intelligence, family background, relationships with parents, even, sometimes, with bodily cleanliness or dirty fingernails.

They are likely to contain actual (and possibly important) inaccuracies because they begin in early childhood and are based, at least in part, on what teachers learn from the child himself. Childish misunderstanding and poor communication are common. One child, for example, only recently discovered that her secondary school 'had her down as from a broken home'. When she had indignantly corrected this mis-apprehension, her new teacher traced it back, in the records, to a statement she herself had made when she was six. Asked about her father she had replied, 'Daddy went away a long time ago.' He had gone away; two weeks previously for a four-week business trip! That father had subsequently attended many primary school functions but had been assumed to be doing so as a divorced husband but devoted father. It had never occurred to anyone to check the accuracy of the information and indeed why should it? More seriously, a boy was recently asked, at his secondary school, about a caution which he had received from the Juvenile Bureau of the police following a rowdy incident when he was nine years old. The note on his file explained that the Juvenile Bureau system had been set up so that youngsters need not appear in court for minor offences and could thus avoid criminal records. But that confidential file had, of course, *given* the boy a 'criminal record' and one which had clearly alerted his new school to the possibility that he would be 'awkward'.

The right of access to school records   Many people believe that some right of access to these confidential records is essential for parents and/or children themselves, so that inaccuracies can be corrected, unfair judgements challenged and outgrown labels shed. In the United States this right has already been given in the Family Educational Rights and Privacy Act (FERPA). Since 1974 American schools have had to allow parents of children under eighteen, or former students over that age, to inspect and review all their own educational records. The parent or student can request corrections and there is an appeals procedure for use if the institution should refuse. Even if the appeal fails to direct the institution to alter the record, the parent or student may then insert a note in the file, explaining the objection. Schools also have to get the written permission of parents or students before showing any but 'directory material' from the file to anyone other than specified teachers, court officials and the like. And they have, by law, to circulate all families with details of these rights every year.

In the UK, attempts to put a similar kind of Bill through Parliament failed even before a second reading. So what can parents (or children themselves) do if they have reason to believe that inaccurate or damaging reports may be on their files?

Try to ensure that teachers have accurate information. If you have rightly shared troubles with a teacher, share also the news of any improvement.

Try, whenever the school schedules confidential conversation between you and the teacher, to give her the chance to tell you what she does think of your child. If she volunteers little, try asking her a few pertinent questions such as 'how do you feel he gets on with the others?' or 'what is he like to teach?' or even 'I hope he isn't a nuisance . . . ?' If you can get her to formulate her thoughts she will tell you the same kind of thing that she might put in the file, and you will be able to argue the matter out.

If your child is ever involved in a school row of any importance, see the Head while it is being sorted out. If there is any confusion about your child's part in it, you can ensure that the Head has your viewpoint even if you cannot insist on her sharing, or recording, it.

At critical points in your child's school life (perhaps especially when he is transferring from one school to another or from school to college or a job) don't hesitate to *ask* the Head whether there is anything on record against your child. Some head teachers will show you reports. Others will certainly be prepared to tell you if a report is going to say that the child is in some way unsuitable for whatever he is applying for. Sometimes she will even welcome contrary evidence, and include information from it in a report. One child, for example, was not going to be heartily recommended for a nursery nurses' course as her records did not suggest that she was especially caring or responsible. Her teacher's view was summed up in the words 'she plays so little part in school life that I cannot see her contributing greatly to a caring institution . . .' The child had been devoting all her spare time over the past two years to helping in a home for the handicapped. The headmistress welcomed a letter from the Matron of that home; heartily recommended the girl for training and expressed her sorrow that the school had known her so little . . .

If your child is unfortunate enough to get on poorly with his last teacher, or the one who is responsible within the school for UCCA (university) applications, ask for an appointment with the Head and express your anxiety honestly. If the present teacher's report *is* unflattering, the Head will certainly take extra trouble to compare her views with those of others who have known your child well.

If your relationship with a school has always been stormy or you have always felt that its view of your child was inaccurate or unfair, consider arming him with reports from other sources. Very occasionally, for example, a young child who is extremely bright dislikes school, will not work, is considered 'below average' and is therefore pitchforked into a vicious circle of under-achievement. A report from a private psychologist might help this school to reconsider its view of him, or another school to place him where he will be better-stretched and therefore happier and better able to work. An adolescent, seeking admission to college, may realize with alarm that she has pigeon-holed her life so that the school knows nothing of her many interests and activities and may therefore describe her as 'narrowly studious'. A letter from a community leader who knows her well may do a great deal to redress the balance.

Choosing a secondary school

In theory it is the legal duty of local education authorities to see to it that children are educated not only according to their own needs, but also according to their parents' wishes. You express your wishes when you fill in your first, second and third choice of school on the official form. Most children, in most districts, are allocated to the first-choice school, but some are not. If an LEA runs three schools, X, Y and Z, and almost every family in a given year wants its children to attend X, many must obviously be disappointed. Not only are there not enough entry-form places at X for everybody, but the entry-forms of Y and Z must also be filled.

You cannot know, in advance, whether your child is or is not going to get the placement you want, or one which you can tolerate. But you can at least make sure, well in advance, that you make the right choices. A few parents, for example, realize that one particular school is very popular and therefore put it down as first choice because 'it must be good'. The child fails to get a place at that school and the parents at once get set for battle because they have not been given what they asked for. Only after weeks of painful struggle do they have enough information about the various local schools to realize that the allocation offered to the child is actually perfectly acceptable.

A few parents, sometimes encouraged by the child's primary school, try to be too clever. They want their child to go to school X but are told that it is so popular they have little chance of a place; they put down Y as first choice thus hopefully avoiding Z which is 'terrible'. The child is allocated to Y, but the parents are dissatisfied: they have got what they said they wanted, but not what they really wanted.

Start, therefore, by collecting information about available local schools, months before transfer-time, with a view to deciding your *genuine* order of preference and entering that order on the form. There is an excellent chance that you will be given the place you say you want, so make sure that you both know, and say, what you want and don't anticipate trouble.

Collecting information about secondary schools

Some schools are locally famous; others notorious. The local grapevine is not always reliable especially as the overall atmosphere, as well as the performance, of a school can change rapidly in response to changes both in staffing and in the intake of pupils.

Under the 1980 Education Act, local education authorities (and the governors of independent schools) must make information about individual schools available to parents. Some schools produce excellent booklets which really do give some idea of what the place would be like to be in, day after day. Others produce only the legally required bare statistical details, of courses offered and examination results achieved. Collect whatever is offered but make sure that you go further:

You must see the school. Most schools welcome prospective parents; many have 'guided tours' going on during the summer terms. Selective schools are sometimes off-putting, though, suggesting that it is for them to decide whether they want your child before there is any point in you seeing whether you would like him to go there. Be wary if you get this reaction when you telephone the school's secretary. The school may have little sense of itself as serving the community.

Talk to families with children already in the school. If you do not know any, your child's primary school may be willing to put you in touch, or at least to tell you the name of one of the parent-governors.

Try to attend one or two events at the new school. A play or a concert will not only tell you something about its drama or music, but enable you to watch the relationship between pupils and teachers, teachers and parents. A jumble sale may tell you something, too: is it run by staff, by pupils or by both in cooperation? Do the pupil-helpers look enthusiastic or dragooned? Is the money going to charity or to the school; if to the school, for what purpose? At a jumble sale you will also be almost certain to find parents and pupils who will be happy to chat to you.

Assessing the school you are thinking of making your first choice

Once you have found a school, or schools, which you think will be right for your child and which he or she feels happy about (probably because friends are also trying to go there) you need to think realistically about it.

Britain is supposed to have a comprehensive education system, but the system in your area may be more apparent than real.

Some areas of the country still have selection procedures, either in the form of the old '11+' examination or in the more subtle form of 'assessments'. Some areas have long-established independent schools and, under the present government's 'Assisted Places Scheme' free, or almost free, places at these may be up for competition at 11+. If selection is 'creaming off' the academically high-flying eleven-year-olds into other schools, your comprehensive school may not be truly comprehensive at all because it may not be being offered a fair share of the top-ability band. Within a 'comprehensive' school the actual organization of pupils may contradict its title. Some are so 'streamed' or 'banded' that children actually enter into, and then stay in, either a 'grammar school within the school' or a 'secondary modern school within the school'. Since children tend to perform at school in a way which conforms to the expectations of that school, a child who goes into a group which is referred to, from the beginning, as a 'CSE form' is rather unlikely to take a batch of O levels. If membership of the sixth form is made conditional upon attaining, say, five O levels, the school may be implicitly denying your child the opportunity of sixth form education even before he reaches puberty.

So whether your child is a high-flyer for whom you want every possible advantage which can be wrung from his academic performance, or a child who seems middle-of-the-road in academic ability, or one whose main strengths are outside the formal classroom, you need to know more about a school than that it is called a 'comprehensive'.

Be prepared to ask questions of the prospective head teacher. He or she should be prepared to tell you anything you want to know about the internal workings of the school.

Check on its suitability for your child by consulting his primary school head teacher. This is both a practical and a political recommendation. In practical terms, he or she may be able to advise you, on the basis of years of experience both of this child and that school, as to whether they are likely to suit each other. In political terms, should you fail to get the placement you finally ask for, the primary school Head's support and help will be extremely valuable to you in any appeal (*see below*).

Making your school choices

When it is time to fill in that vital form, try to decide, with the child, how strongly you all feel about the first, second and third schools. Is the first-choice school not only the first but the only acceptable one? Or is the first only marginally preferable to the second school so that you would happily accept allocation to either? Are there any schools on the list which you really do not feel you could accept? Getting these questions settled in your own mind is important:

If you cannot accept the child's eventual allocation you will have to move fast on the whole business of an appeal (*see below*) so knowing that you are going to appeal, and on what grounds, is a help.

It is infinitely better for the child if you can accept that allocation with pleasure and help him look forward to the move, so it is a pity if your face falls when you see that he has not got his first choice, even though there was little to choose between first and second.

Appealing against an allocated secondary school place

Under that same 1980 Education Act, every local education authority must not only have, but tell you about, an appeals procedure and also make public the grounds for appeal which it takes seriously.

Before you actually start the appeal, another family conference is needed because you have to decide both how far you are all prepared to go in fighting your case (the following notes should help you decide) and exactly what you are appealing for or against. Is the school to which the authority wants your child to go one which you really dislike, or simply not the one you chose? Are you determined to go all out for that one, first-choice school, or would you be prepared to accept the compromise of a place at quite a different one? The point is that the LEA may not be able to give you exactly what you want, but will certainly try not to force you to accept exactly what you don't want. You are more likely to succeed easily if your message is 'any school but that one' than if it is 'no other school but this'.

At the very first meeting after you have objected to the allocation offered, attempts will be made to persuade you to change your mind. If you are determined not to, you must stand (politely) firm from this very beginning. If you sound as if you might change your mind, the authority will not take you seriously.

You will, of course, be asked directly what your objection to the allocated school is. Don't make the mistake of saying that 'X is a better school than Y'. The authority cannot possibly officially admit – and allow parents to act on their admission – that any of its schools is better than any other. The theory is that all children are offered equal educational opportunities through the available local schools. The system depends on that theory even if it clearly untrue in practice.

Working out the grounds for your appeal

The following are the kinds of reason for an appeal which might be considered seriously by most education authorities. Read them along with information from your authority. Then prepare yourself, as well as you can, to make a case on your chosen grounds.

Religion. Preference for a denominational school is always taken seriously. Religious difficulties (such as the impossibility of a Jewish child getting home from this school before sundown on Fridays) may be taken seriously *provided that you can show that religious observance is part of your family life.* You will probably need a letter from your religious leader.

● *Anti*-religious views are unlikely to be taken seriously. If you object to a school because it holds devout assemblies and emphasizes its teaching of religious knowledge, you will simply be reminded of your right to withdraw the child from such teaching.

Medical, psychological, or special educational reasons. Whatever these are, they may be taken seriously *if you can support them with suitable letters from professionals* concerned with your child's welfare. Recent successful appeals of this kind have included a child who was not allowed to cycle because of a tendency to epilepsy and for whom there was no other suitable means of transport from home to the allocated school; a child who had severe asthma, provoked by effort, who had been assigned to a six-storey school; a child who was in five-times-weekly psychotherapy in the town centre and who could only keep her appointments if she went to school nearby, and another whose musical education was important to her but who had been assigned to a school with little musical provision.

Traffic dangers or journey difficulties. These can make good grounds for appeal, but you need to be careful. The simple logic of 'why should she travel six miles, when the school she wants to go to is right next door?' will betray you. You have no clearcut right to send your child to the *nearest* school, or even to the nearest suitable school . . . Furthermore, the authorities do expect children in this age group to travel considerable distances to school. The local authority does not have to offer any assistance with travel (either actual or monetary) if the school is not more than three miles from the child's home. You will probably do better if you can show that to get to the assigned school your child will have to cross a by-pass or ring-road where no safe crossing place is provided within a reasonable distance. If you can *support such an objection with horrifying accident statistics* from your local police station, so much the better. Otherwise you may have to combine journey difficulties with medical or psychological reasons. One appeal was recently allowed, for example, because the journey was a complicated one, involving not only several changes of public transport but a particularly difficult change involving reading indicator boards in order to find the right tube-line. It was successfully argued that this particular child was incapable of carrying out the journey alone, and would remain so, at least for the foreseeable future.

Preference for co-education or for single-sex schooling. Again, you need to be careful. Comprehensive schooling is intended for *all* children (and that means both sexes) and therefore a preference for single-sex education needs to be backed by religious belief or, perhaps, by a preference in the child so strong that it can be (for the purposes of the appeal anyway) described as 'clinical anxiety'.

A preference for mixed-sex schooling should be more sympathetically received, but whether it is regarded as grounds for your appeal is bound to depend upon whether or not the authority is lumbered with a lot of single-sex schools which have to be filled somehow. You can strengthen your case if you can *show that your child has a particular need for contact with the opposite sex*, perhaps because you are a single parent, or because the child is one of four girls . . .

Family associations with the school. Some authorities regard the presence of a brother or sister in the school as a very strong reason for sending the child there, but do not assume that this attitude will be taken. If it was, your child would probably have been assigned to that school in the first place. You may need to support this reason with practicalities, such as the two children needing to travel together, or the fact that you currently assist the school in some way (by helping with out-of-school activities or whatever) and will be unable to do so if they are on different schedules.

However powerful the grounds for your appeal (in the opinion of the authority) it may not *be able* to allocate your child to the school of your choice. You must accept that it cannot arrange the impossible. Indeed, the result of your appeal may be that your rejection of the place offered is accepted, but instead of being offered your first choice you are offered a place at a third . . . On the other hand, an authority may tell you that it 'cannot' give you the allocation you want when in fact it *could*, if it was prepared to try hard enough. You may, for example, be told that your chosen school is full in which case you may like to pursue the matter:

Is your chosen school full?

Although 'the school is full' sounds as if there is a maximum number of desks allowed per classroom and every one of them occupied, it is not quite like that. There are legally laid down standards which allocate the *minimum* space per pupil. But since these are minimums, many authorities rightly try to improve upon them so as to get class sizes down. They may be especially keen to do this if there are other schools (such as the one to which they want your child to go) which really are underfilled. If the authority has decided to limit a first-year class to thirty-four, it may call it full when, legally, it could take thirty-eight.

Because of the low birthrate in the sixties and seventies, quite a lot of schools do have unfilled places all the way up, but education authorities are planning to amalgamate and close schools to cope with this overprovision. They may therefore set an upper-limit of numbers for the whole of a particular school which is known to be well below its maximum. It is 'officially' full even if it is one-third empty.

Talk to the Head. Her view of whether or not the school is full may be different from the authority's view. She cannot allocate your child a place on her own, but her willingness to take him if the authority will make the allocation may be useful in your further discussions.

If, by any chance, she says that there is, *officially*, a place empty, you have probably won your battle. If there is a place available for your child at the school of your choice, the authority must allocate it to him unless it can show that doing so would either be more expensive than the place it has already offered, or in some way unsuitable to your child's 'age, ability and aptitudes'.

If you are trying to persuade the authority that the school it says is full could take your child, do be discreet about it and let the authority know that you are being so. They may be willing to stretch a point for one family *only if they are sure that letting your child in will not provoke a stream of requests from other families.*

Is your chosen school 'unsuitable'?

If your chosen school is not even officially 'full', you may still be refused a place because it is unsuitable for your child's 'age, ability and aptitudes'. This argument should not be used when the schools concerned are 'comprehensive' since such schools are at least intended to cater for everyone (*see above*). If the argument is based on the fact that your child has special needs, you should be pursuing your appeal with the help of experts (*see below* Children with special needs). If the argument is based on your child's failure to achieve particular standards required for admission to a (selective) school, you may, if you are quite sure that the more academic school *is* right for your child, want to argue that the assessment procedure has, in his case, worked unfairly.

Talk to the teachers at his primary school. If the Head, after consulting with her teachers, does not agree with your view of the child's ability or potential, your appeal will almost certainly fail. The fact that you consider him highly intelligent will not sway the authority. You are very likely to be biased and anyway you may not have a realistic view of the educational attainments required for selection. On the other hand, if the primary school expected your child to be selected, and can produce records of consistently high attainment during the past couple of years, you may stand a chance. If selection was by examination, medical evidence of illness at the time may help. So may evidence of acute disturbance at home caused, for example, by your absence in hospital, by a divorce or a death in the family.

But be careful. A selective school does not have to take your child if it does not wish to. There may have been other factors which led to him not being selected. There may even have been an interview at which he did not acquit himself 'well' in the school's terms. Strenuous attempts to persuade a school which has rejected your child to take him after all could lead to real unpleasantness for him. Asking the school whether it will reconsider, in the light of new information brought to the appeal, is one thing. But trying to prove that your Johnny is cleverer than some of the other children who have been accepted is quite another.

If your appeal
fails

You may feel that you have done all you can and that it will be best now to accept either the original allocation or an alternative which the authority has offered. But if you still want to pursue the matter further, you can:

Appeal to the Secretary of State. About one thousand families do this each year so it is not such an extraordinary step as it may sound. The Secretary of State for Education (to whom you write at the Department of Education and Science) can direct your local authority (either formally or informally) to do what you ask. He is only likely to do so if you can show that the local authority is being 'unreasonable' in refusing you the school place you want. Your letter should therefore set out *the reasons they have given for refusing the place* rather than your reasons for wanting it.

Appeal to the Ombudsperson. The Ombudsperson's office is the Commission for Local Administration. Its job is to investigate complaints of maladministration so your letter should concentrate on the *way the matter has been handled* (long delays, incompetence, neglect or prejudice) rather than on the merits of the decision.

The Ombudsperson is intended as a 'last resort' so, while you can write to him or her at the same time as to the Secretary of State, you must be sure that you have first told the local authority that you are going to do so (and given them a reasonable length of time to reply) and that you have consulted your local Councillor.

Unlike the Secretary of State, the Ombudsperson cannot *direct* the local authority to do anything. However, most authorities are anxious to avoid the embarrassment of a critical report from that office, so this kind of intervention (or the prospect of it) can be an effective weapon, especially if the authority has failed in its duty to give you information and to consider your case.

While making these further appeals

You can keep your child at home. This is not a recommendation. Keeping your child away from school until you can get permission to send him to the school of your choice is a very serious, and entirely family, decision. The Department of Education and Science has stated that parents who allow their child to attend his allocated school during appeals procedures will not thereby weaken their position. Officially, then, you can afford to let him go. Experience does, however, suggest that parents who do keep their child out of school altogether tend to get quicker and more satisfactory action than those who do not. A child who is not in school at all once term begins is a major source of embarrassment to the local authority and to the DES. The fact that he is in the school you are saying you cannot accept takes that pressure off them; it may imply that if they stand firm, you will let him stay there. The difficult choice is yours and the child's.

If you keep him at home remember that you have a legal duty to see that he receives full-time education. You may be able to arrange this yourselves; you may have to arrange for private tuition and/or enlist the help of qualified friends. Occasionally a concerned primary school will help, by letting him return there, temporarily, and offering him some extra teaching.

If you send him to school write to the Head, the LEA and the DES making it clear that his attendance is temporary, under protest and pending a decision.

Finally, it must be emphasized that this kind of battle is usually extremely painful for the unwilling child-subject. Often, he himself would be quite willing to accept the original allocation: it is his parents who object. Often, he would have preferred the other school but, while willing to 'have a go' via an appeal to the local authority, would far rather give in when it fails, than face the embarrassment and loneliness of a battle which goes on through what should have been his first term at secondary school. If you find, come September, that you are actually *forbidding* your child to go to school, or refusing to buy him uniform because he is only to go temporarily, do think through the whole matter again. Any advantage which he might have gained from going to the school of your choice could be lost in the disadvantage of starting late, missing lessons and social groupings, and generally being prevented from being an ordinary pupil. Whatever the final outcome, your child is the one who is going to have to live with it, so don't let a campaign which began on his behalf turn into a project in its own right, and one from which he suffers.

Children with special needs

Neighbourhood schools, whether primary or comprehensive secondary schools, are meant to meet the needs of *all* local children. At present many do not do so. Some children go to ordinary schools but fail to meet their full potential because they have special needs for which the school does not provide. Many others are excluded from ordinary schools because they have physical, mental or behavioural problems for which those schools do not cater. These children are sent to 'special schools' which not only segregate them from 'normal' children but also usually segregate them from each other. There are special institutions for the physically handicapped and for those who are blind or deaf, as well as the old-style 'ESN' (educationally subnormal) and 'maladjusted' schools.

'Special' schools are often presented to parents as specialist establishments within which a child can be given very particular attention, teaching and treatment. The parents of a child who is deaf, for example, may be thrilled by a place in a school for the deaf because they believe it to represent her only chance of achieving the adequate speech and skill in lip-reading which will enable her to lead a comparatively normal life. Other parents, less delighted by a special placement, nevertheless accept, without question, that their child 'can't keep up with an ordinary class' or is 'too difficult for an ordinary school'.

There are a few (a *very* few) children for whom separate education probably is appropriate. But almost all of these will be the children for whom there is little hope of an independent adult life. For any child for whom later independence seems possible, there is a very strong argument for education with 'normal' children and within the ordinary community. Whatever a child's particular difficulties, she is still a child. Her difficulties give rise to special needs but in no way lessen all her other needs: the needs of every child. She needs to be a child amongst children, a person amongst people, rather than seeing herself as one in a category labelled 'the blind' or 'the disabled'. The blind child needs Braille in order to learn to read and write, but if Braille teaching and equipment is available within the ordinary school, she can learn to be literate while using almost everything else that school has to offer 'normal' pupils. If she stays in a school for the blind, will she ever discover that, in the eyes of the sighted, she is ravishingly pretty? The child with Down's Syndrome needs academic teaching which is geared to his pace and attention span but, if he has that, he too can use most of the non-academic aspects of school life. If he stays in a school for the educationally subnormal, will he ever get the chance to use his musical talent and singing voice on anything more exhilarating than nursery songs? Even the child with serious physical disabilities which confine her to a wheelchair, will ultimately be better off making the (often considerable) effort to cope in a barely-adapted ordinary school than in the single-storey facilities of a special school. Her adult world is going to be full of ordinarily mobile people and it is going to present her with endless problems of access. In an ordinary school she will learn to cope as she will have to cope later. In return for that effort, she will at least have the opportunity for the best education her community offers to anyone.

Integrated education: the new law

The desirability of integrated education for all children has, at last, been recognized in law. The Education Act of 1981, which came into force in April of 1983, sets out a new system for assessing special educational needs and enjoins local education authorities to provide for these needs in ordinary schools. There seems little prospect of the spirit of the new Act being widely put into practice, but it seems clear that parental pressure on local education authorities will be important.

Some such authorities, with the dedicated work of individual education

officers and schools, already make provision for the needs of many
'handicapped' children within their community schools. The vast majority do not do so and, judging by a recent survey, have no intention of
changing their ways because of this new Act. Inevitably, it contains
several escape-clauses which such authorities can use. The ones you will
hear bandied about state that your local education authority must 'secure'
education in an ordinary school for your child, whatever her special need,
if doing so is compatible with:

☐ Her receiving the special educational provision that she requires.
☐ The provision of efficient education for the children with whom she
   will be educated.
☐ The efficient use of resources.

A local education authority which would rather send your child to a
special school can easily argue that:

☐ It has no ordinary school which can provide for her special needs,
   because it does not have enough teachers, the right facilities or enough
   available expertise.
☐ Her presence would prevent the efficient education of others because,
   for example, she is so disruptive.
☐ Educating her in an ordinary school would not be an efficient use of
   resources because it would mean the purchase of special equipment,
   etc. for her sole use, when that equipment is already available (and
   used by many children) in a special school.

When the new
law might be
important
to you

Your rights and your child's rights under the new Education Act are wide
but complicated. It would be worth your while to investigate them in
detail if:

**Your child is in (or going to be sent to) an ordinary school but you think
she has needs which are not being met.** If, for example, you have a
ten-year-old whom you believe to be dyslexic, but she is being offered no
special help at school, or only help which you consider inappropriate,
such as placement in a class for 'slow-learners', you will obviously talk to
her teachers in the hope that they will recognize and provide for her
special needs (*see* **Learning Difficulties and Disabilities**).

If they will not acknowledge that her difficulties are special, or if they
will not, or cannot, provide appropriate help, you can insist that a full
assessment be made. The new Act gives you the right to a close involvement in the assessment, including attending interviews and psychological assessment if you think this would help your child. If the professionals
agree with your view of the child's difficulties, they will pass it on to the
local education authority. If that authority cannot provide, informally, for
the child, she will be entitled to a 'Statement of special educational need'
which is a detailed formal document setting out exactly what the child
requires, and how and where her needs are to be met. Once a child has
such a Statement, the local education authority is legally obliged to
provide exactly what it says.

**Your child is in, or likely to be sent to, a special school, when you (and
she) would prefer her to be educated in an ordinary school.** Under these
circumstances a full assessment will be made. The authority must have a

Statement for every child for whom it provides special education.

The process of assessment and the provision of the Statement give you new opportunities to put forward your point of view, to consult your own advisers and to have their opinions considered alongside those of the local education authority's experts, to understand exactly why they are recommending one placement rather than another and, eventually, to influence the outcome.

The new law cannot guarantee that you will get the placement that you want, but it does lay down provisions which make it extremely unlikely that you will be forced to accept the direct opposite. It is most unlikely, for example, that your child will be sent to a residential establishment if you want to keep her (and she wants to stay) at home. Professionals in education will not find it possible to argue that enforcing such a placement would be in the best interests of any child.

Exercising your rights under the new law

It is never easy for an individual to force a bureaucracy to act in a way which it finds inconvenient and/or expensive. The Education Act is unusual in that it does openly enlist parents; individuals are intended to use it. If you are going to do so, you will need guidance and help. There are complicated documents to be understood and complicated procedures of appeal to be gone through. You would be well-advised to enlist help either from a teacher or psychologist who knows your child and shares your view of her needs, or from an organization, such as the Advisory Centre for Education, which is concerned that parents should be enabled to use the new Act to best advantage. Whatever happens, remember that:

The Act stresses the need for open frankness between the authority and parents. You have the right to see every single document or piece of professional advice which the authority uses in reaching its decisions and the right to add your own. If you cannot be persuaded to agree to its eventual Statement, the authority has to go on arguing with you.

The Act also gives you the right to attend any interviews or other assessment procedures to which your child is subjected and even, if you wish, to sit in on any conferences held between the involved professionals.

The Act also gives you the right to employ your own professionals and some voluntary organizations are already enlisting people who will provide expert advice to parents in this situation.

Although the Act does not actually give the children and young people involved the right to *decide* their own education and future, it does insist that their feelings be taken into account.

These points are all important because, together, they mean that the local education authority's representatives *must listen* to you, your child and your representatives and that no authoritarian decisions can be taken secretly or without explanation.

Sleep

Our world has a twenty-four-hour cycle of night and day and many of our bodies' biological rhythms are in tune with that timing. Late at night and in the small hours of the morning, normal body temperature, for example, reaches its lowest point whether the individual is asleep or awake: mental agility is at its lowest, whether the individual realizes it or not, and a variety of biochemical functions reach a low ebb only to build again as morning approaches and to reach their peak around the middle of the day.

Sleep is a necessary part of this biological rhythm and the 'natural' time to sleep is during that night-time trough in all activities. People who stay awake through the night (whether to work or to attend an all-night party) are deliberately overriding their body-clocks and, while they can make up the hours of sleep they have missed by napping at another point in the twenty-four hours, they cannot thus put right the timing. This is why people transferred to night work, for example, often find the adaptation very difficult. Even if they manage to sleep for six or seven hours in the daytime (which may be difficult as not only is the world awake and light, but their bodies are awake and alert, too) they still find it difficult to stay awake and efficient through the night because, biologically, their bodies are ready to sleep.

In the modern world, jet-travel has allowed us to turn night and day topsy-turvy by flying across time-zones. 'Jet-lag' can seriously upset every human function from digestion to judgement. Travellers – especially those with difficult decisions to make on arrival or potentially dangerous things to do, like driving cars – have to learn to allow for it. Bodies can and do adapt, but they cannot do so in immediate response to the time stated on the watch you have put forward six hours.

Experiments concerning adaptation to different times have been carried out and have clearly shown that you can, so to speak, *teach your body to believe* that it is any time you care consistently to tell it. Volunteers, living in areas of the world where there is no perceptible night during summer, were given clocks which falsely recorded days twenty-one or twenty-seven hours long. For some days their bodily functions ran increasingly out of step with the clocks, but gradually they adapted to the new lengths of artificial day and night. Nevertheless, weeks after those volunteers thought that their adaptation was complete, certain biochemical functions, such as the release of potassium in their bodies, still clung obstinately to the twenty-four-hour clock. Within normal daily life, the twenty-four-hour clock which is true in nature has also been enshrined in our social behaviour. We 'close down' active life during the hours when our bodies 'close down'. When we want or need to behave to a different time-scale, we have both in-built and learned behaviours to overcome.

Although we still do not know exactly why human bodies need sleep – exactly what scientific function it serves apart from the commonsense function of 'rest' – we do know that sleep is essential. People who are kept awake for long periods (either in traumatic circumstances or during sleep-deprivation experiments) rapidly deteriorate both physically and mentally. Judgement and reasoning suffer; manual dexterity and speed of reaction suffers; eventually the individual begins to suffer from hallucinations, panic, fits of aggression . . . At the end of experiments, many volunteers appear floridly insane. It is the more surprising that a few hours of uninterrupted sleep invariably restores them to normal. Few people living ordinary lives ever experience clinical sleep-deprivation, but a very great many parents have periods in their lives with babies and small children when they come close to it. If your baby awakens you three or four times every night over weeks or months, not only will you lose hours of sleep but also your sleep-pattern will be disrupted. It is easier to make up the hours (by napping in the afternoon or going to bed early) than it is to right the pattern. If you find yourself becoming irritable, tearful, irrational, during one of these phases, try to arrange a full night's uninterrupted sleep for yourself rather than a series of short rests 'while he takes the baby out'.

Two types of sleep

While we sleep our brains continue to give out electrical impulses which can be measured, studied and compared in the form of tracings called electro-encephalograms (EEGs).

Commonsense observation shows that an individual spends some sleeping-time in what looks like 'deep sleep' and some in 'light sleep' during which his closed eyes move rapidly, he makes faces, his muscles twitch, he may be physically restless and he is comparatively easy to awaken. Early scientific study christened this 'lighter' sleep 'Rapid Eye Movement' (or REM) sleep and therefore called the other kind 'Non-Rapid Eye Movement' (NREM, often called Non-Rem) sleep. But the terminology has changed again. In man REM sleep is always associated with rapid movements of the eyes, but a kind of sleep which shows similar brain activity also occurs in animals such as moles, whose rudimentary eyeballs are incapable of rapid eye movements. The two types of sleep are now usually referred to as 'Orthodox sleep' and 'Paradoxical sleep'. Call them what you will, but they are *not* 'deep' and 'light' but qualitatively different.

When a person goes to sleep he almost always passes first into orthodox sleep in which he appears very relaxed and quiet, with only occasional large movements such as rolling over. After a period of about ninety minutes his brain activity changes, rapid eye movements and so forth begin and he enters a phase of paradoxical sleep. For the rest of the night he will alternate between the two although, if he is deliberately awakened every time a period of paradoxical sleep begins, he will, as soon as he is left in peace, spend an unusually large amount of his sleeping time in paradoxical sleep as if he needed to 'catch up'.

Dreaming   Most vivid, active and emotionally laden dreams take place during paradoxical sleep. Some experts believe that it is because of a 'need to dream' (perhaps to discharge emotional tensions or to sort out emotional life) that people 'insist' on their ration of paradoxical sleep. Dreams during this kind of sleep have been shown to occupy realistic spans of time rather than to be concentrated, as many people imagine, into lightning flashes. A person who is awoken after ten minutes of paradoxical sleep may be in the middle of a dream and may actually return to it when allowed to sleep again. These dreams carry with them a full range of emotion and of the physical effects of emotion with which we are familiar in waking life. A sexual dream, for example, may bring all the physical signs of sexual arousal and a full orgasm. An anxious or frightening dream floods the body with adrenalin and sets the heart pounding. Dreaming of competing in an athletics match will put up the heart and breathing rate so that the dreamer may wake to the sound of his own panting. One very common form of nightmare is that in which the victim faces mortal danger but is unable to do anything to save himself because he is 'paralysed with fright'. Even this described feeling has been shown to have some physical reality in paradoxical sleep because nerve impulses to particular muscle groups are selectively blocked for periods of half a minute or so and then surge through. The dreamer's legs may indeed have been 'paralysed' until the dream-tension built to a point where he could escape or awaken.

Most people dream much less during orthodox sleep and when they do the dreams tend to be different. Many of them are everyday and emotion-free: clear replays of the events of the day so that, for example, the dreamer sees herself getting ready for school and walking there, or going shopping, or playing in the garden. These dreams are more like memories of reality than the imaginative roamings of paradoxical sleep. When reality or its memories are painful or frightening, it is orthodox sleep dreams which will reflect the fact as when the victim of an accident will re-live it. It is this kind of sleep which is being affected when a victim dare not let himself sleep 'because I shall dream about that again'. It is also orthodox sleep which is interrupted by night-terrors or by sleep-walking (*see below*). There is no lengthy 'story-dream' but a sudden flash of fear – usually from a single thought or image such as 'something in that corner' – or a sudden urge to go somewhere or search for something.

Varying sleep needs

Although every human being needs to sleep, some need to sleep more than others. The hours of sleep an individual needs tend to be longest when he is a young baby and shortest when he is elderly but, whatever his age, one individual may always need more or less sleep than his peers.

To give the actual number of hours likely to be required by a three-month-old baby, a thirty-year-old or a seventy-year-old is dangerously misleading because of this individual variation. Figures given in books are usually the average number of hours slept (or reported to be slept) by large groups of people of particular ages. Such average figures may be interesting but they should never be applied to individuals. An average figure for three-month-old babies, for example, might be as high as eighteen hours per twenty-four. But if you allowed that information to make you feel that your baby *should* sleep for that long, you might well be worried and he might well become bored with his bed. Your baby may sleep for as little as twelve to thirteen hours each day. Similarly, to believe that you yourself 'ought' only to need seven hours sleep each night might be to deprive yourself of the extra hour or two which meets your personal requirement. It might also deprive you of yet more *time in bed* which you may not need for actual sleep but may, nevertheless, need for physical rest, for privacy from demanding children and for the kind of relaxed and comfortable contemplation which helps you cope with a busy and stress-ful life.

Ideally everyone, baby, child and adult, should be given the opportunity for as much sleep as he or she chooses to take but without anyone even implying that he or she should *try* to sleep. But in this respect, as in many others, family life often falls short of the ideal because it is difficult to mesh a bunch of varied sleep-patterns together so that both each individual and the family-as-a-whole gets what it needs. As an obvious example, take the woman who has a small baby, a young teenage son and her own mother living with her. That baby goes to sleep early in the evening and wakes her rather often in the night while insisting on an early start to his day. To fit with the baby, the mother would probably go to bed rather early herself and accept the early breakfast. But her teenage son has homework and leisure activities and does not want either to go to bed or to get up early, while the grandmother probably needs less sleep than her daughter, is somewhat lonely during the day and would like her to sit up companion-ably late . . . The problem, then, is not so much one of *hours* of sleep but of their timing, and their fitting around companionship and dependency needs. Help yourself to get it right in your family by:

Not allowing yourself to feel guilty at wanting to 'get rid of' a baby or child into bed/sleep. If your day is made easier by your baby taking a midday rest in which he does not sleep but simply plays and talks to himself, what is wrong with that? Of course it would be wrong to imprison him in his cot and leave him there screaming, but if he can be happy away from you, there is no reason to feel that a rest can only be imposed on him if he actually sleeps.

In the same way, many small children are put to bed at night long before they are ready for sleep. Parents often find it necessary to pretend – even to themselves – that a 7 p.m. bedtime is somehow 'right for a four-year-old' when the truth is that to be free of the demands of children in order to have a private evening is 'right for adults' (or for some adults). Provided that child has had a busy and well-companioned day and has sufficient to occupy him in bed, there is nothing the matter with such a plan.

Not allowing yourself to feel that he 'ought' to sleep. This is often the other side of the same coin. Children are sent to bed after an early supper, but instead of being allowed to play and talk until sleep overcomes them, their parents keep urging them to 'go to sleep'. They cannot do so on command any more than you can enforce the command, and simply delivering it, again and again, sets up a sort of anxiety about the whole situation. Unless they are unhappy or actually being destructive or getting into danger, let them be.

Not sticking to conventional routines which do not happen to suit your child/family. Most small children have at least one daytime nap until they are between two and three years old. However long or short their night's sleep, few can stay awake and active right through the day before this age. But some toddlers can. And some, offered a daytime nap, take it at the expense of their night's sleep so that their parents lose either evening peace or some of their own sleeping time. If it suits all of you to keep such a child up all day, or up until an unconventionally late hour in the evening, why not? It will certainly do him no harm because he will sleep when he needs to, and for as long as he needs to, whereas you can only sleep when he lets you.

Making bed a pleasant place from the earliest possible age. In some families, children's beds and bedrooms are places only for sleep. No attempt is made to make them warm, friendly or interesting places in which to *be*, and all enjoyable activities are carried on elsewhere. The trouble with this approach is that it minimizes the time a child of any age will willingly spend in bed when he is not ready to sleep. The opposite approach is far more likely to give you the flexibility to meet everybody's needs:

Make even a baby's cot into a special place with its own playthings and soft toys and its own luxurious comfort. Make sure it is never an isolation cell because if he cries or calls, one of you always goes to him even if it is only for a moment. The more sure he is that you will come, the less often he will need to call and the less likely he is to teach himself to climb out to fetch you.

Make sure that bed is never a punishment cell either. Don't ever let him associate it with anger or punishment, by putting him in that cot to 'cool off' or by sending an older child to his room 'until you can behave'. If you want a cooling off period between you, let it be you who goes away for the necessary minutes.

Make promotion to a 'real bed' a time when his room becomes his castle. Whether you want, and can afford, to spend money on a bunk shaped like a fire engine and all the trimmings of special linen and so forth, or can only give him a corner of the room he must share, you can make it a place which he feels is his personal space. He can gather possessions, keep special books and things he likes to look at, there. He can have a light which he can turn on and off for himself, and permission to do so. He can have friendly stuffed 'people', photographs of the family, baby-things (his old dummy perhaps) which are now for private use only . . . He can also have the feeling of personal ownership which comes from other people respecting his space. His older sister can keep out of 'his bit', even if she shares the room, and keep her hands off 'his things', too. And you can studiously avoid the kind of 'spring cleaning' which makes it feel different and spoils it all for him.

If, instead of being banished to his room as a punishment, a young child voluntarily retires there for comfort, you will know that you are winning and that when you desperately want an extra hour's sleep on a Sunday, it will do him no harm to stay there until later than usual.

Build on the 'castle' idea so that older wakeful children do not need your company. A six-year-old who is woken by a nightmare (*see below*) must have you, but when she wakes at 4 a.m. because she has had enough sleep for the moment, she can manage life for herself in this small private world. Help her to do so by keeping rules about what can go on in the night, to a minimum. If she is forbidden to get out of bed, for example, she will have to call you if she has dropped her teddy bear or needs to go to the toilet. But if she has permission and the necessary light to go by herself, you can be undisturbed.

Gradually separate 'bed' time from sleep time so that even if an older child actually needs less sleep than you do, he is content to spend extra time in the privacy of his room. Ideally, you want to be able to propose an early night to an eleven-year-old without it occurring to him to protest that he is not tired. There is no deprivation for him in going to his room earlier than usual, provided that he can read or play or listen to the radio. Adolescents will usually welcome this kind of 'private time', provided they have a place which feels like home and provided that you do not come barging in saying 'why isn't your light out?' when they had planned to read for half the night. Privacy is two-way. You can have it for yourself by offering it gradually to growing children.

Nightmares

All of us dream for periods of up to several hours each night. We only remember a minute (but widely varying) fraction of our dreams; usually the portion of dream-life which was going on just before we were awakened.

The dreams of paradoxical sleep are imaginative and sometimes fantastic. They can depict, or focus around, anything of which the dreamer has any knowledge or experience. A newborn baby could not, as far as we know, dream the images which richly populate the mental life of older people, because he has not yet seen those things in reality and they are therefore not available to him for thinking or dreaming about. But as he gets older he can certainly build dreams around things he has not actually seen or experienced, provided he has enough information and images (from stories and television, for example) to fuel his imagination.

With such a large amount of rich dreaming going on night after night, it is not surprising that some dreams should be frightening. People who state that they never have nightmares are not necessarily 'better balanced' or 'less anxious' than the rest of us. They may simply be people who do not often remember what they have dreamed.

A baby or child who has had a nightmare usually wakes with a terrified scream or, sometimes, with a gurgling shout. He wakes himself because, in paradoxical sleep, his state is already comparatively aroused and the stimulus of the dream itself eventually penetrates his consciousness. His physical state as he awakens will often reflect the 'story' of his dream, so that if he was crying in that dream he may be soaked in tears; if he was struggling with enemies he may struggle into wakefulness; if he was desperately trying to call out it may be his own, eventually successful, shout which alerts you.

Reach the child who has had a nightmare quickly because whether or not he remembers what he has been dreaming, his own physical state will terrify him. He finds himself crying or shaking, feels his heart pounding, hears his own horrible cry echoing in his head. Unless you arrive instantly to soothe him, that fear will build up upon itself and, if it does, he will remember the horror of the nightmare-experience even if he does not at all remember the actual dream.

Try simply soothing him. Very often he can settle back into peaceful sleep the very moment he hears your familiar voice or feels your stroking hand. Don't feel that you must 'wake him up properly' or 'put on the light, so that he can see there is nothing to be afraid of', unless you see that he cannot drop off again at once.

Don't always try to make him tell you about his dream. If he wants you to know what it was about, he will tell you, but if he does not, forcing him to try and remember may make the whole fantasy more real to him than it need have been.

This kind of 'ordinary' nightmare (*see below*) does not seem to be much influenced by what has been happening to the child before he went to sleep – by scarey television programmes or stories, for example – because it reflects the child's own inner life, his fantasy world, which is only indirectly fed by reality. The frequency of nightmares – or the frequency with which they awaken the child – may, however, be increased by his being in a high overall state of anxiety; less than peaceful in his mind, so to speak. On the whole, though, you can be assured (and should assure the child himself if he is old enough) that everyone does have 'bad dreams' and that for most people they come in patches. He may have a nightmare every night for weeks on end and then not again for months. If you can prevent him from becoming afraid of going to sleep 'in case I have a bad dream', nightmares, quickly soothed by a beloved adult, will do no harm.

Night-terrors

Night-terrors do not occur during paradoxical sleep but during orthodox sleep. Instead of being part of long, complicated story-dreams, as nightmares are, they are usually an extreme response to a single, brief, terrifying thought or image-in-the-mind. The flash of extreme fear cata-pults the dreamer out of sleep and into a state which looks like wakeful-ness but is not truly conscious. Your child suddenly utters an ear-splitting, mind-bending shriek. You rush to his bedside and find him sitting bolt upright, gazing into a corner of the room. He may by now be calling piteously for you, but even when you touch and speak to him he does not seem aware of your presence but only of some other 'Presence' which is lodged in that corner of his mind. As you persist in trying to make contact with him, he may even make you part of the terror, cringing from you, shrieking, 'No no, oh no . . .'

Children never remember night-terrors; parents almost invariably re-member them with horror. A child who seems conscious but is out of touch with the real world is difficult to deal with calmly; his state seems eerie and his fear is infectious. Many a stalwart parent has found herself joining the child in gazing nervously into that corner . . .

Don't insist on your child becoming aware of you. After most night-terrors he will settle back and go to sleep as suddenly as he 'woke'. Give him every chance to do so, but stay quietly beside him in case this occasion is one of the exceptions.

If he tries to get out of bed, try gently to keep him there. It is far better if he does not run, semi-conscious and hysterical, around the house. He might hurt himself and will almost certainly wake himself up and be frightened to discover himself behaving so oddly in the middle of the night.

If he struggles against you, or hysteria seems to be building, offer some reassuring stimulus in the hope that you can wake him up without him ever realizing what has happened. Switching on the room light, changing his pillows around, smoothing back his hair and so forth, are all everyday actions which may gently penetrate to consciousness and 'bring him round'. If he does thus become aware of you, try not to let him see that you have been upset or that there has been any kind of drama. 'You had a nasty dream' is usually the best message to give him to explain your presence and the fact that he is now awake, in the middle of the night, without knowing how he came to be.

If he does awaken completely, you may have to 'put him to bed' all over again because having awoken from orthodox, rather than paradoxical, sleep, he has had a jolting kind of disturbance which it may take him some minutes to overcome. It may be worthwhile to offer a drink, a trip to the bathroom, even a lightning version of his whole bedtime ritual, to get him settled down feeling 'ordinary' again.

Night-terrors do seem to be influenced by things which have happened to the child in reality, although the cue for the terror is not the whole event – the 'story' – but a single feeling from it. A child who is recently home after surgery, for example, may have a succession of night-terrors focused, perhaps, around his own helplessness when 'they' held him for an unpleasant procedure (see **Hospital**/Procedures). Another child may have night-terrors focused around the sight of his mother who had fainted, or around his heart-stopping terror when an older child leapt out at him in the dark. If television or stories are going to cause trouble in sleep it will probably be of this kind, too. He will not dream the horror-story but the horror which he felt as it was told.

Since night-terrors are never remembered and are not, as far as we know, ever about incidents but about raw emotions, directly talking to the child about what has frightened him is seldom useful. It may indeed be damaging because it is scary for him to be told that he was terrified in the night when he himself has no recollection of the incident. A different kind of talking (and of action too) may be needed, though. If you can work out what sort of fear or anxiety your child is likely to be re-living in his terrors, you may be able to open it out and look at it so that it loses its focus. You may also be able to build the child's general confidence, his security that he can manage himself in his world, to a point where his own emotions are easier for him to tolerate. In the meanwhile, don't leave a child who is currently subject to night-terrors with a strange, or very young babysitter. If the stranger awakens him, terror will be added to terror. If a youngster has to cope with a true night-terror, she will be terrified into needing a babysitter for herself.

Sleep-talking

While almost everyone occasionally mutters during paradoxical sleep, some people talk, loudly and fluently, almost every night. A few even carry on conversations with fantasy companions, laugh, scold and make jokes.

Sleep-talking is of no significance to the talker but may make him a very uncomfortable and frightening room-mate. If one of your children is a confirmed sleep-talker, try to arrange for him to have a room to himself.

Whether or not the talker can sleep alone, do try to ensure that nobody teases him about his sleep-talking or tells him even the funniest and most innocent things that he said. Most children find it not only embarrassing, but alarming, to think that they 'communicated' with somebody else without conscious intent. It is as if the child had no power over himself; was 'taken over' by someone else during the night. A slightly older child may worry that he will 'give away his secrets'.

Sleep-walking

Some children sleep-walk frequently throughout childhood; most never do so at all; a few sleep-walk once and never again.

Sleep-walking, like night-terrors, occurs always in orthodox sleep. Contrary to what many people believe, the physical activity of getting out of bed and wandering about is not part of dream-action but rather a response to a sudden and unformulated need to 'do something'. It is, if you like, action for action's sake, just as the night-terror is terror for terror's sake.

If a child is going to sleep-walk he will usually do so early in the night, often towards the end of that initial period of orthodox sleep, perhaps an hour or so after he has fallen asleep. A child who has been asleep for several hours before adults go to bed, will seldom walk in his sleep later on, although you cannot rely on this (*see below*).

A sleep-walking child characteristically gets out of bed and wanders around the house with his eyes open, looking somewhat anxious and distressed but not really frightened. He does not seem to be going anywhere in particular or searching for anybody or anything in particular, although there may be troubled mutterings such as 'must . . . I must . . .' or 'now I got to . . . got to . . . yes got to . . .' There is an old wives' tale which suggests that it is dangerous to awaken a sleep-walking child. This is nonsense. But waking him may be exceedingly difficult; he is deaf and blind to your presence. It may also be tactless because once you have forced him back to consciousness, he has to face the peculiarity of being downstairs in the dining-room in his pyjamas when the last thing he remembers is going to sleep in his bed. Waking a sleep-walking child is hardly ever necessary. If you go to him and gently steer him, by taking his hand or putting yours on his shoulders, he will almost invariably allow himself to be led calmly back to bed. If he sleeps in a high bunk, he will even climb the ladder as soon as you have positioned him at the bottom.

Sleep-walking can put a child in danger. Although sleep-walkers seem to retain some contact with reality, so that they avoid most major obstacles and so forth, children in this state have been known to fall downstairs, to climb out of upstairs windows or to let themselves out of houses . . . If your child sleep-walks more than once, you may need to take some precautions such that he cannot do anything which might endanger him without making enough noise to awaken you.

Sleep-walking does sometimes go with emotional disturbance either in the sense that a child who has never walked in his sleep may do so for the first time when he is very upset or at odds with his life, or in the sense that a sleep-walking child may do so more frequently under these circumstances. You may, therefore, want to use sleep-walking as the cue to a careful consideration of what is happening to the child; what anxieties may be simmering. On the other hand, you may like to comfort yourself with the fact that sleep-walking tends to run in families. If you and other relatives also had this tendency, it may not be that your sleep-walker is *especially* anxious, but that he is a child who is going to sleep-walk whenever he is the *least bit* anxious.

Soiling *see also* **Toilet Training**

For most children, bowel-control is far easier than bladder-control and therefore, once basic 'toilet training' is completed, soiling is a rarity while wetting is not. Of course, any young child can pass an occasional motion in his pants by mistake, especially if he is caught out by the beginning of an episode of diarrhoea. But if a child whom you had thought to be 'reliable' passes faeces in his pants on more than a couple of occasions, don't just dismiss it as 'something he will grow out of'. He may need your help in doing so.

Why young children soil

Soiling seems often to be part of the power-relationship between parents and child, rooted in the kinds of conflict which are common in the toddler years.

Toddlers are still deeply dependent and passionately attached to their parents, yet they have reached an age-stage in which they are also beginning to feel themselves to be separate and independent individuals. The desire to be dependent and protected clashes with the desire to be independent and autonomous. That clash produces the typical emotional lability of the two-year-old who alternates between clinging and cries of 'let me!'

If a toddler feels overpowered, bossed and bullied by his parents, he will tend to look for areas in his life in which he can assert some power of his own. If he is not allowed any such power, feeling himself controlled at every turn, he will seek for ways of asserting power directly over those controlling adults; ways of getting back at them, of wielding some power of his own and thus redressing the balance.

Parents ask toddlers to do, and not to do, a great many things and, when compliance is not forthcoming, they often use their superior size and strength to enforce obedience. The child who will not come in from the garden is carried in, despite his screams and kicks. The child who will not sit up to the table may be forced into his highchair and strapped there. But there are some things which no parent can force an unwilling child to do and among these are some of the things which are most important to them. They can sit him up to table but they cannot make him eat. They can (perhaps) make him stay in bed but they cannot make him sleep. They can sit him on a pot or toilet but they cannot make him pass a stool.

If a toddler is spoiling for a power-fight he may 'choose' any or all of these areas as his arena, but he is most likely to choose one on which his attention has already been focused by obvious parental concern and anxiety. Just as the mother who is anxious about her child's eating is the mother who is most likely to have a toddler with 'eating difficulties' (*see* **Eating**/Eating problems) so the mother who has been over-enthusiastic and/or premature in her efforts to toilet train her child is the one whose child is most likely to choose the lavatory as his battleground.

Most of the toddlers who do put up a fight over the pot, still do not soil. If their objections take the form of refusing to sit on the pot, and their mothers accept the refusal and avoid even trying to force the issue, it usually resolves itself. But if a mother cannot take no for an answer, insisting, so to speak, that the child's stools belong to her and that she will have them, where and when she says and whether he is willing or not, she is inviting him to defy her with his body, and stressing to him the emotional importance of his faeces.

The first steps towards soiling

Quite a lot of two-year-olds go through a phase when they will use the pot or lavatory for urination but not for defecation. The child will sit on the pot, but will either pee or do nothing. As soon as he is allowed up, he will go to some secret place – such as under the table or behind the curtains – and there he will pass his stool, in his nappy or pants.

Sometimes the power-play is even more obvious. When he is first allowed up from the pot, the child knows that his mother is keeping an eye on him, waiting to whisk him back as soon as she can see signs that he needs to pass a motion. So he waits; he waits until she is distracted and doing something else and *then* he slips away and fills his pants before she can catch him.

Coping with early soiling

To an outsider, such transparent defiance, from such a small person, is positively funny. If parents themselves can find it (privately) funny, they will be able to defuse the situation before it progresses any farther. They can choose their own words in which to convey to the child the message: 'You've made it quite clear that you don't want to put your stools where we suggest. So OK. It doesn't matter. Do it in your pants (or wear your nappies) if you prefer. When you're bigger you will probably want to do it in the toilet like older people do, but there's no hurry . . .'

If they *really* don't care, taking off the pressure will drain the emotion out of the whole performance and make it pointless for the child. The lavatory-arena will be closed to him and he will quickly complete his own toilet training while finding something else to fight about with them. But if they really do care, and are furiously angry inside at his defiance, and/or revolted and upset by his dirty pants and bottom, the child will know; assurances to the contrary will only make more of a muddle. So unless the child's parents can truly come to believe that they hurried the whole toileting business, and that perhaps they have been pushy in other ways too and need to let up on him a bit and give him some extra growing-space, it probably will not work.

If it does not work, more and more attention and emotion will inevitably come to be focused on 'The Problem' and, while the child still may turn his attention to other ways of communicating with his parents, he may be unable to let go of what will now have become 'a symptom'.

Some toddlers continue their refusal to defecate in pot or lavatory and go on, through the pre-school years, doing it in their pants. As the child gets older, so this behaviour affects more and more of his life and that of his family. Once he passes an age at which nappies are considered even marginally appropriate, he will be unacceptable in a group and will be an unwelcome guest in many private houses, too. Even his own parents may find the prospect of having to clean him up in public toilet facilities daunting enough to limit the trips on which they are prepared to take him. His own private life with his peers will be affected, too. It is hard to be popular if you are called 'smelly' and hard to feel likeable if your know the name is merited.

Passing stools in inappropriate places

Sometimes such a child gives up passing his stools in his pants but still refuses to pass them in the intended places. He may take down his pants and pass his stool on the floor. Very occasionally parents try to 'normalize' a child's life in this situation, by putting down newspaper for him to use and trying to see that he defecates there first thing every morning so that the matter does not arise to bedevil his day in society. This kind of manoeuvre may indeed enable a child to go to school and so forth without others becoming aware of his peculiarity, so it might, under certain circumstances, be recommended within the context of ongoing psychiatric advice and/or treatment. But it should not replace such advice and treatment. The child who uses newspapers instead of a toilet is insisting on behaving like a dog not a child. His image of himself cannot therefore be a satisfactory one. Furthermore, the child who thus insists on flaunting his stools is offering bits of himself as gifts to the adult world and having those gifts rushed disgustedly out of sight. All concerned need help with their feelings.

Withholding stools and resulting soiling

Most pre-school and later soiling takes a related but importantly different form. Instead of insisting on putting his stools where he pleases, the child passively refuses to give them up to the parents' command, holding onto them instead in his own body.

A child who 'holds on' in this way eventually becomes constipated (*see* **Constipation**). Faeces accumulate in an ever-more distended rectum and eventually become so dry and hard that he could not pass them if he wanted to. But because waste-matter is still accumulating, it will eventually start to leak, in semi-liquid form, from above the now rock-like blockage. Instead of filling his pants occasionally, such a child will soil them, just a little bit, almost constantly.

Unwary parents may be very slow to spot that such a child has a problem. The soiled pants *could* result from inefficient wiping after a normal bowel movement. If they allow themselves to realize that such constant carelessness is unlikely, they may decide, from the liquidity of the leaking faeces, that the child is suffering from diarrhoea. The soiling cannot, therefore, be regarded as his fault or responsibility . . .

Such a child needs medical help first of all. Until his loaded rectum is cleared, normal patterns of elimination cannot be established and, if matters are left too long, the normal sensations, which indicate the need to defecate, may be lost altogether.

Sometimes, especially if the child is very young and the pattern of soiling new, clearance of the blockage will be found to right the whole matter. The withholding may have begun as a response to the pain of an anal fissure (*see* **Constipation**) and once this physical problem is overcome, and the child assured that it will not be allowed to return, it is found that there is no emotional barrier between him and the establishment of ordinary behaviour.

More usually, though, psychological help and guidance will be needed, to prevent the problem recurring, and enable the child to grow through this particular anal phase to find more acceptable ways of coping with, and communicating, his feelings.

Medical treatment of withholding faeces

Some doctors will vigorously clear the lower bowel with enemas, wash-outs and laxatives and then try to 're-educate' the child towards 'normal' habits. While this approach may appear successful, especially in the older child who, consciously at least, wants to be rid of his soiling, it can be psychologically risky. If the child originally began to withhold his faeces in order to keep at least that bit of him under his own control and out of his parents', he is almost certain to see the bowel wash-outs, and other unpleasant procedures, as a punishment, and the successful production of his faeces as yet another naked assertion of his parents' power.

Many pediatricians, especially those with a particular interest in children's psychology, now tend to take a gentler and less direct approach to the necessary clearance of the rectum. They may use dietary adjustments and perhaps mild laxatives, and they will combine these with attempts to modify the difficulties between the child and his parents. The message such a doctor will try to get across to the child might be something like this: 'It is your body and I am entirely confident that it will work perfectly for you as soon as you can feel all right about it doing so. If you want to see whether going to the lavatory the way other people do is nicer for you than all this fuss about dirty pants, this medicine will make the beginning easier for you because it will make the faeces which have got hard because they've been in there so long, a bit softer . . .'

Whatever your doctor's approach, it is important that you yourselves should not undertake *any* procedures which are unpleasant and embarrassing for the child. If he is to have enemas or suppositories, adults looking at and fiddling with his anus and rectum, let doctors, with whom he is not emotionally involved as he is with you, be the ones to inflict these indignities on him.

Soiling and emotional disturbance

Soiling is still a forbidden topic for many people, including many parents of child-victims. When it is mentioned, it is often described as inevitably symptomatic of deep-seated and disastrous emotional disturbance. It is pointed out that, in older children, this symptom tends to go with all kinds of other, obviously emotional, problems, such as difficulty in making friends, failures in school achievement, running away, delinquent behaviours and so forth. No wonder parents find it difficult to admit, even to themselves, that their child soils.

While the *beginning* of soiling does seem usually to be based in conflict between parents and child, and on unrecognized and unmet needs in him, these conflicts are not necessarily more sinister than those of other young children which present, for example, as eating or sleeping difficulties. The later associated difficulties which children who soil experience, are as likely to be the *result* of their soiling as to be part of a seriously disturbed whole. Our society will not tolerate a child who stinks. In that simple statement lies the urgency of facing, and trying to deal with, the soiling the moment it becomes inappropriate to the child's age-stage. If you allow a child to go on soiling after infancy, you are rearing one whom society will not tolerate. What better recipe could there be for the creation of a child who is unhappy, isolated, sure of his own worthlessness and, eventually, anti-social?

Sudden soiling in older children   An older child who suddenly begins to soil *may* be suffering from chronic constipation. He may be as upset as you are by his inability to control leaking faeces. It is certainly worth talking to him, immediately and matter-of-factly, to establish whether this is a purely temporary, physical problem which, perhaps with help from his doctor, he can quickly deal with. If this is the case, a full explanation of what has happened to him, either from the doctor or from you, is essential. Once both his anxiety and his overburdened bowel is relieved, make sure that he understands that he must not allow this to happen again; that he is eating sensibly and drinking enough fluids and that he will ask for help, on another occasion, more quickly.

If the soiling is not caused by long-standing constipation and the doctor finds no sign of any other physical cause, you will have to face the fact that an older child who suddenly begins to soil for emotional reasons is 'choosing' a peculiarly self-damaging symptom. It is likely to reflect a very poor valuation of himself and a very great anger at the world in general, and probably at his parents in particular. It is difficult to imagine a more extreme way for a child to shout, 'I don't care . . .' (*see also* **Depression**/In children before puberty).

The child himself will not, of course, have any idea why he soils; it is no good asking him. You will probably not have any idea, either. If you all knew what each other was feeling, the problem would not have arisen. Seek professional help, via your doctor, as quickly as you can because your child, even more than a younger one, will quickly be ostracised by, or withdraw from, his fellows.

Special education *see* **School**/Children with special needs. *See also* **Hyperactive Children**; **Learning Difficulties and Disabilities**.

Speech *see* **Language**.

Splinters *see* **Accidents**/Cuts and scrapes, grazes and puncture wounds.

Spoiling *see* **Discipline, Self-discipline and Learning How to Behave**. *See also* **Anxiety, Fears and Phobias**; **Tantrums**.

Spoon feeding *see* **Eating**/Eating problems: Babies and eating problems.

Sports injuries *see* **Accidents**. *See also* **Cramp**.

Sprains *see* **Accidents**.

Squints *see* **Eyes and Seeing; Eye Disorders and Blindness**. *See also* **Hospital**/Surgery.

Stammering *see* **Language**.

Stealing *see* **Discipline, Self-discipline and Learning How to Behave**/Some common issues in discipline.

Step-parents *see* **Divorce, Separation and One-parent Families**/Children's relationships with step-parents.

Sterilizing *see* **Infection**/Preventing infection: Sterilants, disinfectants and antiseptics.

Stitch *see* **Cramp**.

Stitches/sutures *see* **Hospital**/Procedures. *See also* **Accidents**/Cuts and scrapes.

Stomachache *see* **Abdominal Pain**. *See also* **Adolescence**/Menstruation.

Stools *see* **Constipation; Diarrhoea, Gastro-enteritis and Food Poisoning; Toilet Training**.

Styes *see* **Eyes and Seeing; Eye Disorders and Blindness**.

Sucking *see* **Eating**/Types of food for babies; **Habits**/Comfort habits. *See also* **Teeth**.

Sudden Infant Death Syndrome *see* **Death**.

Suffocation *see* **Accidents**/Choking; **Safety**/In the home: From general household hazards.

Suicide *see also* **Adolescence; Depression**

Suicide by children and young people

Many people believe (and perhaps choose to believe) that only adults ever kill themselves on purpose. This is a dangerous delusion. Thousands of adolescents, hundreds of twelve- to fourteen-year-olds, and a handful of even younger children, are officially recognized as having died by their own hands each year. Concealed within 'open' verdicts or verdicts of 'death by misadventure', there are probably many times more suicides among the young. Few coroners will burden parents with a verdict of suicide if there is any room at all for uncertainty.

There is no uncertainty about the figures for attempted suicide amongst children and young people. Self-poisoning, for example, accounts for around twenty per cent of all teenage admissions to acute medical wards.

Adult society chooses to believe that most of these attempted suicides are attention-seeking acts rather than 'serious' attempts to die. They are now usually referred to as 'parasuicide' and are often treated with scorn and anger by overworked hospital staff who see these unhappy children as selfishly taking up professional time which could be better spent on 'people who are really ill . . .' Occasionally, necessary treatment, such as washing out the stomach of a girl who has taken 'an overdose' (*see* **Hospital Procedures**), is carried out in such a way that it is seen not as care but as punishment.

Many young people who survive suicide attempts do say that they are glad to be alive after all; some say that even at the time of the act they did not actually want to be dead; they agree that they arranged matters so as to make it likely that they would be discovered in time. But this does not justify taking a suicide threat lightly nor treating a child who takes poison as if she were a spoiled toddler who had thrown an especially embarrassing temper tantrum. Are we only to respond helpfully to those who are beyond help? A person who thinks about killing herself, threatens to kill herself or takes actions which she knows might kill her, is *suffering*. It is up to those around her to see her pain and relieve it.

Many adolescents go through periods of acute unhappiness with, and within, themselves. The vast majority eventually find ways of coming to terms with themselves and making an adult life. But the stories of a few who killed themselves leaving notes behind, or who attempted suicide and later worked out what had led to their attempts at self-destruction, may illustrate the kind of misery for which parents should watch, and in the context of which, any hint that the child is suicidal should be treated as an emergency. It is no coincidence that all these youngsters shared in feeling hopeless, helpless and angry . . .

Suicide by a schoolboy aged fifteen This boy lived with his mother, his father having left the family. He had never enjoyed school and had been treated for school phobia (*see* **School**) at the time of his transfer to secondary school. During the school year which ended in his death he had been continually bullied by other boys and had confided this to his headmaster, his mother, and the truancy officer following enquiries into his frequent absences. His note said: 'Day after day it's the same with no way out. I can't stop them; I ought to be able to stand up for myself but I can't. Nobody will stand up for me because nobody really cares about me and I can see why . . .'

Suicide by a girl aged fourteen

This girl's mother had died of cancer two years previously and her father had recently remarried, making, he and his new wife honestly believed, a secure new home for her. She left a long letter which read, in part: '. . . I know you will be very unhappy and I am truly sorry because I know you tried; but although everybody said I'd feel better one day, that day just never comes. I just want to be with Mum. I can't manage without her. Nobody will do instead so I'm going where she is . . .'

Attempted suicide by a girl aged sixteen

This girl had been at loggerheads with her parents for the past eighteen months, with trouble focusing around her sexuality. She took every pill she could find in the family bathroom after her father had found her in bed with her boyfriend, and told her that he had always known she was a slut. She explained it like this: 'It wasn't exactly that I wanted to be dead; I didn't think about it like that. I didn't really think much at all, I just took them. What else could I do? He was right, wasn't he? I am what he said. But there's nothing *I* can do about it, is there? I mean it's a bit late to call names now. Anyway, I gave him something else to think about, didn't I?'

Attempted suicide by a boy aged seventeen

This boy came from an apparently happy and devoted family and was a highly successful student who excelled at music and art. His suicide bid amazed everyone concerned. Fortunately, a concerned social worker at the hospital outmanoeuvred the family's attempt to treat it as a 'brainstorm' and arranged for him to see a psychiatrist. Over several lengthy conversations, it became clear that the boy was deeply dissatisfied with the self which the adults around him so appreciated. He did not want to be a sensitive musician but a tough sportsman. He did not want to be a beloved son but a sexy lover. He did not want to be the adult world's ideal teenager but his peer-group's hero. His actual suicide attempt was touched off by a particular fantasy during masturbation which had suddenly led him to decide that he was probably homosexual. But he described himself as 'trapped, you see, because they like me as I am and I don't, and they don't seem to see that I'm the one who's got to *be* me . . .'

Probably everyone who is suicidal feels hopeless, helpless and angry, but these feelings are especially likely to overwhelm those who are both vulnerable and very young. An adult who is deeply depressed may be able to remember what she felt like as a person before she entered the illness. She may, therefore, be able to accept assurances that, like other illnesses, the depression will pass and she will feel 'herself' again. A thirteen- or sixteen-year-old has had no time to discover herself as an adult female and, therefore, has no such reassuring memories with which to combat a present which feels swamped in a grey mist. If she is encouraged to look forward, what is she looking forward to? An unknown which, from her present position, can only be grim.

While anyone who is clinically depressed is helpless to 'snap out of it', youngsters are often realistically helpless, too, because every outward aspect of their lives is under someone else's control. An adult who is finding life in her present job or marriage intolerable can, if she can only find the psychic energy, break free and try something else. A child has no room for manoeuvre. She cannot choose to leave school or find herself a new family.

While every suicide is probably at least partly an act of aggression against other people, youngsters, newly emerging from the complete dependency of childhood, are particularly vulnerable to adults failing to understand or help.

Far from refusing to take seriously the threatened or attempted suicide of someone who is 'scarcely more than a child', we should probably take it more seriously. Far from 'punishing' those who 'waste medical time' by taking pills 'just to get attention', we should be grateful that their need was forced on our attention before it was finally too late to meet it.

Suicide by parents and other people important in children's lives

Suicide is not a loving act. It is always a selfish and rejecting one and usually aggressive also. The grandmother who leaves a note saying that she has killed herself because 'you will all be better off without me' may see her self-destruction as loving, even self-sacrificing, but within that open message are the hidden barbs: 'you made me feel a burden/in the way/not worth having'.

A child whose parent commits suicide faces not only the grief which must follow any bereavement but also additional psychological burdens. Perhaps the heaviest is the burden of knowing that that parent did not love him, or at least did not love him enough to stay alive and be with him. Voluntarily to die is to desert a child in the most final way there is. When all the grieving and talking and explaining is over, that agonizing knowledge remains. The dead parent abandoned him.

The death of someone close always causes guilt, but a suicide causes more than most because that message 'he/she did not care enough about me to stay alive for me' inevitably carries with it the message 'if I had loved him/her more/been a better son/daughter/been more helpful, more understanding, more worthy of love, more *something*, perhaps he/she would have felt able to stay alive.'

Anger at being so cruelly deserted, and guilt at having failed the dead parent, tend to interact with each other. The child finds himself angry, yet to be angry with someone so tragically dead is in itself something to be guilty about. If the anger dominates the child's feelings he may come to hate the dead parent for the misery his/her death has caused – and feel guilty for that hate. If guilt dominates his feelings he may actually come to feel that he *caused* the death by his behaviour and/or by his secret aggressive feelings to the parent during life. Then he will feel angry at the injustice of feeling so guilty for something which the rational bit of him knows was not his responsibility.

When someone who is close to a child or young person commits suicide, there are hard decisions to be made which the living parent and other family members may themselves be too involved to make. Should the child (whatever his age) *know* that the death was a suicide if it could be kept from him? Should he be told why it happened, insofar as others understand it? Whatever decisions are taken, their consequences can be far-reaching so it may be wise to take them, if it is possible, with the help of a health professional who can look at the situation with enough objectivity to see beyond the family's present hell and into the child's future. A suicide within the close family is a crisis which merits psychological first aid.

Youngsters are often deeply shocked by the suicide of a friend or schoolmate. There may be personal guilt associated with it, ranging from 'If I'd only known how unhappy she was . . .' to the more direct 'I wouldn't have joined the ragging if I'd known she really minded.' But there is usually also a degree of personal fear: 'could I be unhappy enough to die?' and perhaps of envy, too, because the dead youngster has, in a single act, achieved the kind of concentrated attention from the adult world which many adolescents feel that they lack in life. If your adolescent should meet this experience, make sure that it is discussed and that your carefully tuned ear picks up her subtle messages. You may, for example, need to help her realize:

That she is not all-powerful and that nothing she could have done/left undone would have made any difference because her relationship was not central to the dead girl's life.

That she is not in a position to assign blame to herself, to the dead girl, or to anyone else who might have contributed to that death because, as a friend or acquaintance, she simply does not know those concerned well enough to understand their relationships with each other.

That such a death is always, and above all, a waste because whatever happens to the very young, their lives are always going to change and that change is always worth working and waiting for.

Sunburn *see* **Accidents**.
Suppositories *see* **Nursing**/Medicines which are not to be swallowed: Enemas.
Surgery *see* **Hospital**/Surgery.
Swallowed foreign bodies *see* **Accidents**/Foreign bodies.
Swearing *see* **Language**/Pre-school years: Nonsense and 'naughty nonsense'. *See also* **Discipline, Self-discipline and Learning How to Behave**.
Sweets and snacks *see* **Eating**/Some commonsense 'snack policies'. *See also* **Teeth**.
Talking *see* **Language**.

Tantrums

Temper tantrums have nothing to do with 'naughtiness' and very little to do with 'temper' in the usual derogatory sense. A genuine tantrum is a sort of emotional blown-fuse caused by an overload of frustration. It is not within the child's control at all and, while probably infuriating and embarrassing for you, it will usually be downright terrifying for her.

Drive, frustration and tantrums

Human babies are born very incompetent compared with most mammals, but they pack a truly fantastic amount of learning into their lengthy infancy and childhood. Fortunately, a baby does not rely on you, or anything outside herself, to provide the motivation for all this learning and developing. Every baby seems to be born with an in-built and self-perpetuating drive to learn, to practise and to succeed in every one of the thousands of tiny tasks which contribute to her growing up. When she is a schoolchild, you and her teacher may have to push and tempt her into learning her French verbs, but in infancy nobody has to push her to learn to walk. As soon as she is physiologically ready, she will start trying and she will go on and on trying, no matter how many times she falls and hurts herself, until she succeeds. Any adult who found walking that difficult would give up and send for a wheelchair. But not that baby: the pushchair may be meant to rest her legs, but it will also frustrate her drive to walk; it may well be one tantrum-trigger.

While every baby has this kind of inner drive (and no baby could develop fully without it) children do vary both in how easily they become frustrated, and how violently they react when they do. Where one child will go on patiently trying to unscrew a lid, another will give up much sooner. Where one will eventually admit defeat gracefully and move on calmly to something else, another takes every failure to heart and gives full voice to her despair. Of course, every child's frustration-tolerance varies, both from day to day and from stage to stage, but there is no doubt that some are more phlegmatic, almost, one might say, philosophical, overall, than others. When you are coping several times a day with a tantruming child you may wish for a more placid one, but it helps to remember that the frustrated screaming child is only frustrated because she is trying and that, because she is trying, she will learn.

● Some of the children who have a great many tantrums and/or start them comparatively early – perhaps in their first year rather than the more usual second – turn out to be particularly bright: they frustrate themselves a great deal because they can see how to do, and therefore want to do, a great many things they are not yet physically mature enough to do. But be careful if you are taking comfort from this fact. Some others have a great many tantrums because some unsuspected disability – notably deafness (*see* **Ears and Hearing; Ear Disorders and Deafness**) – is loading them with a basic frustration with which they cannot cope.

Triggers for tantrums

Children frustrate themselves by setting themselves tasks they cannot perform; objects frustrate them by not behaving as they intended them to behave; but, above all, adults frustrate them, usually by trying to exercise the kind of total control which contravenes a toddler's dawning sense of personal autonomy.

Babies start out quite unable to distinguish between themselves and the people who care for them. Your baby does not know where she stops and you begin; indeed you can regain the use of your hand when she is sucking it by giving her her own hand to suck instead. Through the first year or so a baby tends to feel herself still part of you. She has no idea that you have separate feelings and activities; no concept of your adult life.

You-and-she are the centre of her world and she assumes that the same is true of you. But in order to grow into an independent, mature human being, that child has to discover her lonely separateness from everybody else; she has to practise being that self even when her wishes and activities clash with yours. It is during the early part of the second year that this necessary drive for personal autonomy usually becomes clear. Unfortunately, separating off from you is often a painful business for the baby because she still loves you and depends upon you totally. Every time she clashes with you she is caught between the devil of giving in and the deep blue sea of losing your support and approval. Developmentally, she must assert herself, but emotionally, it would be far easier for her to go on being a comparatively biddable baby.

Any situation in which you try directly to control your child's behaviour can become a tantrum-trigger at this stage. The more 'personal' she feels her behaviour to be, the more likely she is to be violently frustrated by your insistence that she do it (or not do it) your way. She is liable to resent, for example, your insistence on her using a pot, eating certain foods at certain times; going to bed when she does not accept that she is tired; wearing 'suitable' clothes; coming when she is called, going out when it suits you and coming home when you say it is time.

If she feels harried, bullied, pressurized and rushed she will resist and, if you use your superior strength and intelligence to defeat her, she is likely to explode into a tantrum. She does not want to wear a sweater; she feels (perhaps) that it is her body and that the clothes put onto it should (for this moment at least) be up to her. She throws the sweater on the floor and runs away. When you catch her, hold her between your knees and force that sweater over her head, she is likely to blow that fuse. She does not want to leave the supermarket and she cannot see why she should come with you just because you are in a hurry. She tries the passive resistance of just going on pottering around the aisles, but when you pick her up and strap her in her pushchair, her furious frustration overwhelms her. She wants to get out her bricks and neither can nor wants to understand that the afternoon's play is over. She tries to get them for herself; finds that they are too heavy; looks to you to help her as you usually do but, when you remain adamant, explodes. The tantrum is triggered by helplessness, by defeat, by feelings of being overpowered by people or circumstances.

Avoiding tantrums With some children you will not be able to avoid tantrums entirely because the degree to which any child is frustrated is not entirely within your control. But whether your child is a placid type or has a very low frustration-tolerance, you can keep tantrums to a minimum by teaching yourself to feel sympathetic to these difficulties in growing from baby to child and by learning to behave tactfully in the danger-areas.

Try to help her feel that she is in control of her own personal life: it is up to you what food you give her, but it can be up to her whether she eats it or not. It is up to you to take her to that pot, but it can be for her to decide whether to sit on it or not. It is your responsibility to see that she dresses adequately, but you can protect her from being cold later on just as effectively by taking the hated sweater with you as by forcing her to wear it, this minute, when she does not feel cold . . .

Cultivate talent as an actress. There will be many occasions when you are in a hurry but when, if you rush her, there will be trouble which will waste more time. If you can conceal your impatience and, instead of dumping her in that pushchair, offer to be a horse and *pull* her home in it, you will get there faster as well as more happily.

Try not to back her into corners. Absolute orders absolutely refused spell nothing but trouble; leave her an escape route and her intact dignity, whenever you can. Often this means offering her an excuse for her own behaviour ('I know you're tired so I'll help you pick it up this time . . .'). Often, too, it means distracting her: 'This quarrel over touching the plugs is getting boring; let's go and . . .' It is 'walking around trouble' but why not? Trouble is trouble for both of you and tantrums teach nothing (*see* **Discipline, Self-discipline and Learning How to Behave**).

Try to treat her as politely as you treat older people. If your partner picked up your knitting and inspected it, would you scream at him while snatching it away and hiding it? Probably you would just say, 'Do you like the colour? You'll watch out that no stitches come off, won't you . . . ?' If your older child was washing his face, very slowly and ineffectually, would you grab the facecloth and his hair and do it for him, rather too hard? I doubt it. If your teenage daughter, trying to be helpful, spilled the dust out of your dustpan, would you shout at her and push her into another room? You would be more likely to say, 'Oh, isn't it maddening when that happens? Never mind, just sweep it up again for me . . .'

Try to cultivate the sense of humour that will let you enjoy your small child. Many quarrels stem from a kind of teasing which is your child's way of testing the water of your mood. It is sad if she *always* finds that water freezing. Running away is a very usual example. She runs away from you partly because she does not want to come home/come to bed/get dressed, but partly to see whether this is one of the days/times when you will join a chase-game or one when you will be furious. The chase-game is usually more enjoyable *for both of you* and quicker, too.

Keep an eye on the other sources of frustration in her daily life. Of course you cannot (and should not) try to protect her from everything she finds difficult because she must learn and she must experience success. But while frustrating objects can be extremely educational, objects which are too frustrating, offering her no chance of victory, contradict their own ends. For example, she may be getting furious because she cannot fit those round pegs into the square holes of that posting toy. It is a fact of solid geometry that round pegs will not fit square holes and, if she is ready for fitting toys at all, it is a fact which she might as well learn. But she need not do so unaided. Help her make the discovery. If posting is her current passion and this toy is really too grown up, you could offer her an easier version such as a cardboard carton with big holes for balls and blocks . . . (*see* **Play**). The point is to distinguish between the kind and degree of frustration which will spur her onto greater efforts and eventual success and pleasure in her own achievement, and the kind which is self-defeating because she just becomes angrier and angrier, less and less competent.

The child is learning to understand objects and their behaviour, so toys whose behaviour she does understand but which she still cannot manage because of her physical immaturity, are an unfair additional source of frustration. She may, for instance, long to push that doll's pram but be unable to reach the handle; long to kick that football but be too unbalanced to manage its weight; long to play the music-box but be unable to turn the tiny, stiff handle. To be faced with a push toy which is too high is as maddening for her as a six-foot cooker would be to you; to try to play ball with a real football is as sad as it would be to try to play tennis with a cricket ball; to have to manipulate that little handle to make music is as frustrating for her as it would be for you to face a violin and bow rather than a piano. Children do not need rooms full of expensive toys either for their development or their pleasure, but any equipment they are to have must be appropriate for them. If she cannot have a little pram or push-truck, a plastic 'football' or a pull-string music-box, she is better off with none at all until she is older.

Form and frequency of tantrums

Tantrums take many forms. Some children rush frantically around, screaming and banging into the furniture. Some throw themselves onto the floor and behave as if they were wrestling with devils. Some use any weapon which comes to hand to bang and wallop things and will hit their own heads against the wall if there is no alternative. A very few 'scream themselves blue in the face' (*see* **Convulsions, 'Fits' and 'Funny Turns'**).

Whatever form your child's tantrums take, do realize that they are a normal phenomenon. If you are tempted to feel that yours is the only affected child, recent British survey figures may comfort you. Two research studies, carried out amongst large and differing samples, showed that parents admitted to frequent tantrums amongst sixty per cent of boys and forty-five per cent of girls aged twenty-one months and to very frequent tantrums in seventy per cent of both sexes at three years. A further sample showed that fourteen per cent of babies were having very frequent tantrums by their first birthday while fifty per cent were already having at least one big one every fortnight.

Coping with tantrums

A child who is having a tantrum is lost to the conscious world. She is not open to exhortations to 'stop that'; scolding will do no good because she cannot hear you. She is overwhelmed by her own flooding internal anger and she is probably terrified by it too. She behaves as if she would like to kill everyone and destroy the world. Can she in fact know that she cannot? Over the years she has got to learn that it is safe to be angry: that feelings and words cannot physically injure people or objects. But at this stage she cannot be sure. Her anger must feel hideously dangerous.

The adult's job is to try and ensure that the child 'comes round' from her tantrum to find no evidence that she is dangerous.

She must not find that she has hurt herself/hurt you/broken anything. If she does she will feel not only that she cannot control herself, but that you cannot control her either: she is truly an all-powerful monster.

If she will let you, hold her securely in your arms, safely on the floor. As her anger subsides she finds herself close to you. As she relaxes, the screams changing into sobs, she finds, often with obvious amazement, that everything is quite unchanged by the storm. The furious monster reverts to a pathetic baby who has frightened herself silly.

Some children are too big and heavy to hold safely and/or are further provoked by being physically restricted. If yours is one of these don't put a shoulder-lock on her arms or keep her still by lying on her. Leave her free, but try to fend her off the walls and to remove objects she will otherwise knock over or smash. Wait for the change in note, from fury to pathos, and then try to gather her to you.

Try not to meet anger with anger. This is much easier said than done because anger is infectious. Many parents lose their tempers with a tantruming child and match her shout for shout. About fifty per cent of the mothers surveyed (*see above*) admitted that they lost their tempers and punished children for having tantrums. It really is better not to. Anger and punishment while the tantrum is on will have no effect. Afterwards, they will only increase the child's feeling that the world is an angry and dangerous place, with herself one of its angriest and most dangerous occupants.

If you feel yourself losing control, it is sometimes best to remove yourself while the storm blows itself out. The risk of the child hurting herself without your protection is probably less than the risk of you hurting her if your temper goes completely.

Never, ever, let a child's tantrums affect your behaviour towards her. If she had the tantrum in the first place because you would not give her something or let her do something, don't allow it afterwards. She needs comfort and the assurance of your love as she recovers, but not sweets or anything she could see as a reward, and certainly not evidence that the tantrum has served to manipulate you. She must see, from her very first outburst, that tantrums are horrible for her and absolutely nothing to do with whether or not she gets her own way.

Unfortunately, many mothers find public tantrums horribly embarrassing and therefore are affected by the mere likelihood of the child throwing one in the street, in the shop or in front of visitors. Try not to treat her with saccharine sweetness whenever there are strangers present, in the hope of averting trouble. She may not notice at two, but she will certainly realize this power by the time she is three and she would not be the intelligent human being she is if she did not then move towards the semi-voluntary tantrums typical of mishandled four-year-olds. Such children work themselves up on purpose, one eye on mother's reactions, until, if the ruse looks like failing, they reach the point of no-return and genuinely lose control.

Older children and tantrums We can all lose our tempers and some of us find it difficult to find a way of releasing the extreme tension of our frustration without resorting to some violent physical action. Some people shout or stamp or bang doors; some marital rows regularly end with broken china and some battered babies are the result of this kind of episode.

If your child works herself up (*see above*) to genuine tantrums when she is of school age, try pointing out to her, very straightforwardly, that more self-control than that is expected from people of her age and that, while you know that she cannot help herself once she has got started, you also know that she could pull herself up at an earlier stage if she tried. If you do not, in fact, believe that she could stop herself, try offering (still entirely openly) some more acceptable ways for her to relieve herself of that intolerable tension. It can help if you actually encourage her to shout as loudly as she can. She may learn, with your help, to erupt out of the house and pelt round the garden three times whenever she feels herself intolerably angry. She may even like to have a special cushion for pounding when she feels like pounding you or her baby brother . . . Whatever particular plans you make, the point is to acknowledge the feelings, but make it clear to her that tantrums will not do and therefore that she must find another way of dealing with them.

Teeth

The formation of teeth

Teeth before birth

A baby's first (or 'milk' or 'baby') teeth begin to form very early in your pregnancy and go on developing until shortly before she is born.

Healthy first teeth need minerals, such as calcium and phosphorus, together with the vitamins which facilitate their proper absorption (*see* **Eating**/Types of food: Vitamins and minerals). But ensuring that the growing foetus gets what she needs is not difficult because:

That growing baby's needs are met first out of the nutrients in your bloodstream. This means that as long as your diet is providing enough of these substances to keep *you* healthy, you can be quite certain that *she* is getting all she needs. If your diet before pregnancy should contain only *just* enough of one of them so that there is not an adequate supply both for you and the foetus, it is your body which will go short, not hers. This is why babies born to women on very inadequate diets – in occupied countries during the Second World War, for example – were often amazingly healthy. Their intra-uterine development was achieved at the expense of increased privation for their mothers' bodies. So if you are healthy yourself, do not worry about 'drinking enough milk for the baby'.

Ignore old wives' tales such as 'you lose a tooth for every baby'. That saying was based on the idea that a foetus somehow 'drained' the calcium from her mother's teeth to form her own. It is nonsense, of course. If your pregnant body was so short of calcium that the baby's needs could only be met by breaking down some part of you to provide it, it would be your bones from which it would come, not your teeth.

Pregnant women do sometimes have dental problems but this is due to hormonal changes. They may cause swelling of the gums which consequently trap more food particles, breed more bacteria and cause extra tooth decay (*see below* Why teeth need cleaning). See your dentist early in each pregnancy and take extra trouble over dental hygiene during it.

If you stay healthy yourself you are doing all you can for her developing teeth. A severe infection during pregnancy *could* upset your body's biochemistry and prevent her teeth (as well as other aspects of her body) from developing perfectly, but there are no positive steps which you can take to produce extra-good infant teeth. Fluoride, for example, will be extremely valuable in strengthening her teeth later, but you cannot get it to her in the womb, by taking extra yourself, because almost no fluoride can pass across the placenta.

After birth: the time to think about fluoride

Even though you cannot yet see them, her first teeth are formed and waiting to emerge. It is her second (permanent) teeth which are now being formed. You can help them to develop well and to be strong and resistant to attack by caries, by feeding her in such a way that her body has adequate supplies of vitamins and minerals and by making sure that, one way or another, she has an adequate intake of fluoride.

Few people any longer doubt that an adequate intake of fluoride helps produce teeth whose enamel is comparatively hard and caries-resistant. The continuing arguments you may hear are not about that basic proposition but about the best way to ensure that every baby gets that fluoride. Some people believe that community water supplies should be fluoridated (except in areas where there is plenty in the water already); others believe that fluoridation is equivalent to 'dosing people without their consent' and is therefore immoral. In between, there are people who do not object to fluoridation on principle, but who are concerned lest it lead to a few children taking in an overdose of fluoride which, far from being good for them, can actually be harmful.

In order to ensure that your own baby gets enough fluoride but not too much, you will need the advice of your own doctor and/or dentist and he will need information on the following points:

How much fluoride occurs naturally in your community's water supply. If it is rich in fluoride your child may never need a supplement and indeed may be far better off without one. Too much fluoride will produce tiny white spots on the surfaces of her teeth.

Exactly how she is fed at various ages. Very little fluoride passes into breast milk so a baby who is *exclusively* breast-fed may benefit from daily fluoride drops from birth.

If she is bottle-fed, or breast-fed with occasional supplementary bottles, her need for fluoride will depend not only on the amount which is in the water with which the bottles are made up, but also on the formula which is used. Some manufacturers add fluoride along with other minerals.

Once she is being weaned and is also drinking ordinary cow's milk, her fluoride needs will have to be re-assessed. In a low fluoride area she will almost certainly benefit from daily drops or tablets; in an area with some natural fluoride in the water a small supplement may still be considered safely desirable while in a high fluoride area she may get plenty.

A time to encourage sucking

Sucking is not only a means of getting nourishment, it is also a baby's greatest pleasure. Fortunately, at this stage of life, it is to be encouraged, from the dental point of view. The more the muscles of her mouth, jaw and face are exercised, the better they will play their proper role in steering those first teeth into their proper places. Breast-feeding makes a baby work ideally hard at sucking, but bottles, fists, thumbs and dummies can all be useful. Do read the notes on malocclusion, though (*see below* Looking after teeth) because while sucking is excellent for teeth which have not yet emerged, it becomes progressively less desirable for teeth which are actually through . . .

Cutting the first teeth

Teeth are usually cut in a certain order but may do so on a widely varying time-scale. There is no advantage or disadvantage in cutting them early or late. The timing has no connection with a baby being generally 'forward' or 'backward' in overall development. At *least* six months on either side of the following 'average ages' counts as entirely within the normal range.

The first tooth: usually a lower central incisor. The incisors are the flat teeth in the front of the mouth and they tend to appear in pairs. The very first tooth will probably be one of the lower pair and the second will probably be the one next to it. Six months is a usual time to see the first one. The second will probably appear before the next pair begin:

The third tooth: an upper central incisor. One of the top central incisors will probably be seen at about seven to eight months and its matching pair will emerge soon after to be closely followed by:

The fifth to eighth teeth: lateral incisors (the lower ones tend to appear first). With a pair of incisors in the front of either jaw the baby will next produce an incisor on either side of each. These four teeth will probably begin to emerge at around nine months.

The ninth to twelfth teeth: first molars (the lower ones tend to appear first). With four teeth along the front of each jaw the baby will now produce the first molars which are not next door to the existing teeth but one space away. You may see the first of these four at around ten months; they will probably all be in at around fourteen months.

The thirteenth to sixteenth teeth: the canines (the lower ones tend to appear first). These are the more pointed teeth which fill in the four spaces left between the lateral incisors and the first molars. They will tend to appear between sixteen and eighteen months.

The seventeenth to twentieth teeth: second molars (the lower ones tend to appear first). These are the final four which appear behind the first molars in each corner of the child's jaw. They usually come through towards the end of the second year.

● If a child does not have a complete set of twenty first teeth by the time she is three (or if she should have an extra one) it is important to show her mouth to a dentist (*see below*). It is important to her later dentition that these first ones should all be present and correctly placed. And it is important to her maturing jaw and face that those permanent teeth take up their proper positions.

Teething   Cutting teeth is probably not nearly as uncomfortable for babies as many people think. The 'crankiness' which is often put down to teething may well be due to other factors in her development, such as an increasing need for company in the second half of the first year. If the fact that you think she is 'teething' makes it easier for you to be sympathetic with such moods and feelings, fine. It often *is* easier to go on being patient with a grumpy baby if she is thought to have a *physical* discomfort. But don't ever let yourself believe that any physical symptoms more important than dribble are due to those teeth:

If your baby has a temperature she is unwell; if she goes off her food she is unwell; if she vomits she is probably unwell; if she keeps crying while rubbing an ear she probably has earache. All these are signs of probable illness, and should be treated as such: of course, she may be teething as well . . .

Aids to teething babies   If your baby really does seem restless and irritable when a tooth is coming through, and she has no symptoms of illness (or has been checked by her doctor), any of the following tricks may help. The chances are that the main effect is to make you feel you are doing something for her and therefore for her to feel your confidence. Still, if it makes you both feel better, where's the harm?

She may like to chew. Chewing is good for babies anyway so she cannot have too much practice. She will chew her own fingers – and yours – but she can have harder, nicer-tasting, things as well. You can offer obvious things like teething rings or other things like scrubbed carrots or hard rusks. If she is too young to hold them, hold them for her and let her really work at them.

● Watch out for choking. A toothless baby may chew a rusk until pieces are soft enough to go down her throat. A baby with one or two brand new teeth may grate a tiny piece off that carrot and choke. Even the earliest chewing is a game for her to play when she is sitting up and has your attention (*see* **Accidents**/Choking).

She may like cool things in her mouth. Some teething rings are filled with a gel which cools and holds its low temperature if it is kept in the refrigerator between sessions. Failing that, those carrots may be more acceptable from the refrigerator.

● Don't give her ice, or even rub unwrapped ice on affected gums. It could damage the covering of the gum.

She may like to have her gums rubbed. Dip your finger in ice-cold water first for maximum effect. Unless your doctor or health visitor advises it, don't rub any of the proprietary 'teething gels' on her gums. Some of them contain local anaesthetic agents which, while they may comfort her, are neither necessary nor desirable. A few contain aspirin-like chemicals which could overdose her. Some, which you may be offered if you are abroad on holiday, even contain alcohol. Others contain sugar: just what you do *not* want to put on an emerging tooth.

Losing first teeth and cutting permanent ones

Your child is going to lose twenty teeth and acquire twenty-eight to thirty-two. Those permanent teeth are not only more numerous than the ones they replace but also much larger and often not so white. Prepare yourself not only for that (often enchanting) gappiness, but also for a child with a decidedly mixed set.

At around six. The first permanent teeth start to emerge. They are the four molars which come in behind the existing baby teeth, without displacing any. Your child's mouth now has four new 'corners'.

At around seven. Those first four front incisors will be shed, one by one, and your child will have various 'gaps' until the permanent ones have completed their replacement at around ten.

Eight to ten. The first and second 'first' molars will gradually be shed, one by one, to be replaced by the eight permanent pre-molars. Your child will now have twenty-four teeth.

Ten to thirteen. The canines loosen, come out and are replaced, while the second permanent molars appear behind those first, six-year-old molars. By the time your child is around fifteen, this stage will be completed and she will have twenty-eight permanent teeth.

Fifteen upwards. The third permanent molars (the 'wisdom teeth') may or may not appear (*see below* Some dental problems of adolescence).

Looking after teeth

The principles of looking after teeth apply as much to the first as to the permanent ones. Your child is going to have to use most of them for many years; furthermore, their presence, position and health can affect the permanent teeth you cannot yet see. Don't bank on that second (and final) set to correct the mistakes or omissions of the early years, such as:

Not cleaning the first few teeth

Of course, two or three single teeth do not need the full suggested routine, but if you read the notes on why teeth need cleaning, you will see that it is a good idea to clean the surfaces of even her very first tooth on a regular basis. Wiping them carefully with a piece of damp gauze each morning and evening will be a help.

Allowing first teeth to spend hours bathed in sweet fluids

A child who has ten teeth with holes in them at the age of four or five has almost always been allowed one of the following:

A bottle with which to suck herself to sleep, filled with milk or juice . . . Often it stays in her mouth for occasional sipping through the night.

A 'dinky feeder' filled with juice or syrup to use instead of a dummy.

A dummy dipped in sugar, honey or some other sweet stickiness.

Do remember that these habits are truly pernicious for teeth *and are in your control.* Your baby may need a dummy; fine. But if you never dip it in anything sweet she is never going to think of demanding it, any more than she can think of the joy of taking her bottle to bed . . . if you let these habits start she really may refuse to go to sleep without (*see below* Sugar, sweets and dental decay).

Conniving with comfort habits (see **Habits***) which may lead to malocclusion*

Many of the kinds of comfort sucking which babies enjoy are good for them on every level *provided that they do not go on, too intensively, for too long*. Some will tend to misplace first teeth, and possibly the teeth which are to follow, if they continue for hours each day until the child is five or six.

If your baby has a dummy that's fine if, as she reaches a year, you can gradually confine its use to the few minutes before she drops off to sleep. If she prefers her own thumb or fingers, that's fine too provided she does not suck for too long, too often. It is the child who sucks on something in a particular way, for long periods of every day, right through pre-school, who may do damage.

Not taking toddlers for dental check-ups

Most dentists prefer to meet a patient for the first time when she is two or three years old. Regular supervision will help to prevent anything from going wrong; early recognition will make any treatment easy and pain-less; practice will make later trips to the dentist an accepted part of life.

Letting young children care for their own teeth too soon

A child will not have the fine coordination to care for her teeth properly until she is at least five, perhaps older. If she cannot yet manage a pencil well enough to begin to write, she will not manage brush and floss. Encourage her to help, but keep the responsibility yourself.

Dentists' knowledge of the causes of decay has increased dramatically in recent years and their recommendations for home care have changed with it. If you understand modern thinking, the time you spend supervising the care of your children's teeth will be used effectively:

Why teeth need cleaning: plaque

Plaque is a thin film of sticky material which forms all over teeth all the time. On this film bacteria breed, feeding on the food we put in our mouths and releasing acid as they break down sugars (*see below*). Left undisturbed, the plaque layer gets thicker and thicker and provides a home for more and more bacteria. As they use up the oxygen in that sticky layer, the environment becomes acceptable to anaerobic bacteria and it is the gases which these release which are most often responsible for bad breath (halitosis). That sticky plaque is not only the breeding ground for all these acid-producing bacteria: it is also the glue which holds them against the tooth enamel. Over time, that acid will eat into the enamel and make the entry point for the bacteria which will then produce caries. Left undisturbed for long enough, some of that plaque will harden into the chalky white deposit called tartar removeable only with special tools.

Obviously that sticky layer of plaque will sometimes be disturbed by things we eat (this is the argument for crisp foods like apples). But unless steps are taken to remove it, it will certainly accumulate down the sides of the teeth, where they butt against each other; in the irregularities in molars and around the bottom where the tooth goes into the gum.

The more efficiently plaque is regularly removed, the fewer bacteria there will be in the mouth to produce acid from food, and the less 'glue' there will be to hold that dangerous combination against the enamel.

How to keep plaque at bay

It takes about twenty-four hours for plaque to build up to a tooth-damaging level if the teeth were adequately cleaned the time before. Once-daily cleaning that was really thorough would be enough. Twice-daily is a better bet for families because somebody is bound to skimp sometimes. But it is certainly better for a child to clean properly once a day than to give her teeth a quick token scrub morning and evening.

It is best to get your dentist to show you how to clean your child's teeth so that you first do it correctly yourself and you then teach her correctly, too. The principles are:

As soon as she has any teeth at all, wipe each one carefully every day, with a piece of damp gauze.

As soon as she has molars and teeth with next-door neighbours, switch to a brush.

Use a softish brush with a small head. Scrub every surface of each tooth, quite gently, but quickly so that you swirl off the film. If you want to use toothpaste make sure it is a fluoride one. This is an excellent way of regularly applying fluoride to the tooth surfaces.

You have now cleaned plaque off all the outer surfaces of the teeth but not off the cracks between them or the margins where they go into the gum. *You cannot do this with a brush.*

Follow brushing by using a length of dental floss which you work gently in between each pair of teeth so that it rubs against every surface. Then bring it round the base of each tooth so that it clears that gum margin. Be gentle (with her or with yourself). Unlike the old hard brushes, dental floss should never hurt or make healthy gums bleed.

When cleaning is most important

It would be ideal for *teeth* to be thoroughly cleaned whenever food was eaten and therefore the resident bacteria were busily making acid. But it would not be ideal for *people*, few of whom are going to carry toothbrushes and dental floss with them to school, to college or to work. The most vital time to remove plaque and bacteria is before the night. If the teeth are cleaned after the last food of the evening there will not be much acid formed to attack them while the child is asleep. Cleaning them again after breakfast will give them a good start to the day, too.

But this regime, even if the cleaning is really thorough, will not prevent all caries in all children. What she eats, and when and how she eats it, will affect her teeth, too.

Sugar, sweets and dental decay

Everyone knows that sweets are 'bad for the teeth' but not everyone understands exactly why this is so. The following points are designed to help you work out a sensible family policy concerning sweets and to help you avoid the waste of effort involved in trying to ban *sweets* while freely allowing all kinds of other highly sweetened foods (*see also* **Eating/Commonsense** about family eating: Commonsense about sweets). Sugar is 'worse' for teeth than any other foodstuff because:

It feeds the acid-producing bacteria in the mouth rapidly and directly so that a sugary mouth is both acid and hospitable to bacteria.

Other foods – such as bread – are broken down much more slowly by the bacteria. That means that the bread particles may be cleansed out of the mouth by the flow of saliva before enamel-attacking acid is produced. If a particle of such a food is caught between two teeth so that saliva cannot sweep it away, it will still take time before it is broken down into the sugars which will produce acid and that is time during which the next brushing–flossing session is approaching.

Sugary foods are often sticky. The more sticky a sweet food, the more likely it is that fragments will be trapped between teeth or in their crevices; that overall stickiness will help the sugar to adhere to the plaque all over the teeth.

These points apply to every kind of sugar and all sugary foods. Bacteria do not produce acid more readily if fed on refined white sugar rather than demerara, or honey rather than an apple. The only differences, in terms of dental health, are the differences in the concentration of sugar and that stickiness. A spoonful of white sugar, for example, produces a rapid burst of acid in the mouth but it is acid which can be washed away comparatively easily. An apple has less concentrated sugar and the flow of saliva caused by chewing will help to wash it away, but it may leave pieces of skin wedged between teeth. Catalogue sweet foods, then, in terms of their sugar-concentration and their texture. If you do this, you will see that while sweets (always concentrated sugar and often sticky, too) are obviously dangerous, so is sticky parkin or gingerbread and so, sadly, are the items some parents often offer instead of sweets. Worst offender here is probably the raisin.

But sweets may still be the worst hazards to your child's teeth for reasons which are to do with her eating habits rather than the sugar-content or texture.

Every time a concentrated dose of sugar is taken into the mouth it takes about twenty minutes for the saliva to neutralize the acid and wash the mouth clean. If there are trapped particles which saliva cannot reach, acid will remain in close contact with the tooth for much longer, but twenty minutes of risk is an educated average guess. If your child eats an apple or a slice of bread and honey or a piece of cake, she is likely to eat it all and then stop. Twenty minutes afterwards her mouth will be back to normal. But if she eats a sweet she is very likely to suck it slowly. All the time she is sucking, sugar is being released and acid is being formed. She is also very likely to follow that sweet with another and then another. Indeed, she may eat several sweets in every half hour for several hours getting slowly through a quarter-pound packet during a journey for example. If she does this her teeth will be in a dangerously acid environment throughout.

Sweet *foods* are usually eaten at mealtimes. This both restricts the number of times per day that acid assaults the tooth enamel, and makes it likely that a teeth-cleaning session will soon follow. Sweets, on the other hand, are most usually eaten between meals and, very usually, in circumstances where teeth-cleaning is most unlikely. Watch commuters eating them in cars and trains; children eating them on their way to and from school and whole families settling with them in cinemas or in front of television sets.

A sensible sugar policy
While every family must decide for itself how seriously it will take the threat to teeth posed by sugar and sweets, and what attitude it will take to sugar on other, perhaps moral, grounds, a plan like the following would allow your child to enjoy sweets and sweet foods without posing any extra threat to her teeth at all. All you have to remember is that the shorter the time sugar remains in her mouth, and the less often it is put there, the less acid will be made and the less likely it is that it will eat into tooth enamel. So:

Give sweets and other sweet sticky foods immediately before teeth-cleaning. If your child is going to clean her teeth after supper, there is no reason why she cannot finish the meal with her favourite dessert and/or some sweets. But watch out for fool-traps like that mug of hot chocolate *after* she has cleaned her teeth and before she goes to sleep. If she likes sweetened cereal and toast and jam for breakfast, they will do no harm if she cleans afterwards.

If she has sweets and other sweet foods at other times of day, keep them to mealtimes. She is going to eat some lunch anyway. If she adds a sweet food to that sandwich and apple, or a sweet to the school's treacle tart, she will not be much increasing the risk to her teeth. It is if she eats the treacle tart, gives her mouth time to neutralize the acid and then starts eating sweets at 3 p.m. that she is really putting her teeth at extra risk.

If she has sweets between meals control the type. If you are being fairly liberal about sweets and sweet foods, you may find that a family ban on the very worst kinds – like toffees – is easily accepted. Smarties will do far less harm.

Encourage her to munch and finish. If she is to be allowed three individual sweets or a tiny packet, or ten pence worth or whatever, encourage her to eat them all immediately. Try never to let her just have sweets *available*, to nibble when she pleases. Again, this is not a difficult rule to enforce: you would not let her keep a large slice of bread in her room to nibble through the day, would you?

● You will obviously have to set an example here. If you nibble sweets you cannot expect her not to. Equally, if you keep a well-stocked sweet tin or a large box of chocolates lying around the house, she is bound to help herself.

Don't offer sweet alternatives to sweets. Those raisins may give you a virtuous feeling that you are avoiding giving your child those nasty commercial sweets, but they will be no less harmful to her teeth.

Try to make readily available snacks out of savoury foods (*see* **Eating**/ Commonsense about family eating: Some commonsense 'snack policies'). Many of the snacks children eat *are* sweet because it is sweet foods which are attractively packaged and heavily advertised for them. But there are a range of these 'high status' snacks in the savoury bracket too (such as all those potato crisps, corn puffs and nuts) and it just as quick and easy to give a child a water biscuit with cheese as a sweet, chocolate-covered one. Older children may enjoy having the week's snack foods left pre-prepared in the refrigerator so that they know there are celery sticks, tiny tomatoes and cubes of cheese readily available.

Remember that a child can 'buy' a sweet-indulgence by cleaning her teeth. If she wants a slice of cake for her mid-morning snack and you don't want her to have it, 'you can eat and then clean or not eat and not clean' will often seem a fair bargain.

Remember that sweet drinks contain sugar. Some families are careful, or even strict, about sweets and sugary foods, yet take a pretty well constant consumption of sweet drinks for granted. Don't. A constant intake of cola or its equivalent certainly will not help your child's teeth. Once again, restricting sweet drinks to mealtimes (and encouraging ad lib water in between) is usually the answer.

Additional protection for teeth

Fluoride While it is important that your child take into her body the optimum amount of fluoride for healthy, decay-resistant enamel (*see above*), fluoride which is applied to the enamel itself (topical fluoride) can also strengthen teeth. This is the only dental reason for using a toothpaste when brushing. Non-flouride toothpaste is nothing but a pleasant taste.

Your dentist may also suggest one of various methods of applying more concentrated fluoride to your child's teeth. There are various fluoride gels and paints available and he will probably have his own favoured one.

Other cleaning aids **Toothpaste** is useful if it contains fluoride, or encourages brushing.

Electric toothbrushes can do an efficient job, provided they substitute only for the ordinary brush, not for the floss. Bought to encourage a reluctant older child, they will probably only be effective while the novelty lasts.

Mouthwashes sweeten the breath by masking the odour which is usually caused by gas-producing bacteria in neglected plaque. If you buy them at all, don't let them be used to put off necessary visits to the dentist or dental hygienist or to substitute for tooth-cleaning. They cannot remove plaque.

Fluoride mouthwashes are another way of bringing fluoride into contact with the teeth but, if your dentist wants your child to have topical fluoride on her teeth, he has more effective ways of putting it there.

Water jets and other irrigating devices. These can be effective in removing *loose* food particles; useful to a child who wears a brace or to someone with extensive bridgework. They do not remove plaque though.

Toothpicks, etc. Many types now exist but none are as good, or as safe for a child to use, as dental floss.

Chewing gum does not clean teeth. Sweetened gum does the opposite.

Rinsing the mouth with water may remove harmful food debris, especially sugar, so it is better than nothing, but rinsing cannot remove plaque.

Eating crisp food might dislodge some food particles and might even break up some of the plaque layer, but it will also leave its own bits and pieces and its own bacteria-feeding sugars in the mouth. Don't rely on it. A rinse with water is certainly better: neither is adequate.

Treatment by a dentist

The more regularly a child visits a dentist the less treatment she will need – now, or in the future. Ideally, you should have a family dentist just as you have a family doctor. Someone who knows you all, and sees each child at every stage of her life, will be far better able to advise you well and treat everyone without upset than someone who sees you for the first (and perhaps the only) time because of an emergency. Unfortunately, it is not always easy to find such a dentist. In Britain, by no means every dentist welcomes time-consuming small children onto his already full lists; in the United States, such visits can be expensive enough to deter parents unless their children have toothache.

If possible, take your child to the dentist for the first time when she is around two (unless, of course, you have had worries about her teeth even earlier). This is a 'get to know you' visit. She may never sit in the chair (or only in your lap), she may not even open her mouth while the dentist is looking, but even if she does not, it will make next time easier.

Try to schedule appointments every six months after that. If you really take your child that often to the dentist, as well as looking after her teeth as outlined above and as he shows you, there is no reason why any major treatment should ever be needed. Good dentistry is almost all preventative. And that applies even to the tiny cavity which appears despite your best efforts and which he can fill so easily at this early stage.

Helping your child to tolerate dentistry

Try to remember that dentistry really has changed since you were a child. If yours becomes frightened, it is as likely to be due to her sensing your tension as to genuine pain. The high-speed drills of today neither vibrate, nor take so long, as the old ones did. First teeth can often have a tiny cavity filled without any need for an injection. If an injection is needed (perhaps because the dentist can see that he is likely to touch a nerve: he will not wait until the child yells to decide), the child can have a local anaesthetic jelly rubbed onto the gum first, after which most injections can be given almost painlessly with the dentist putting the anaesthetic in very slowly so that the tissues are numbed ahead of his advancing needle. It is not all *fun*. Few people, even today, actually enjoy fillings, but it really is not the horror it once was.

As part of his routine treatment your dentist will probably want his hygienist to clean the child's teeth so that every bit of plaque is removed. Do remember that if plaque has been left in peace to form tartar, this has to be 'chipped' off down the cracks between the teeth and along the gum margin and this can be unpleasant. Dental floss can save your child that discomfort.

The dentist will also keep a close eye on the child's emerging teeth and on the ones that are loosening. Occasionally a first tooth needs to be taken out, because it is delaying a permanent tooth or getting in its way. If he knows your child well, the dentist will be able to advise on the kind of anaesthesia she should have for an extraction. Most (especially the extraction of first teeth which have small roots and whose roots may, in any case, have begun to be re-absorbed ready for natural shedding) can be taken out with a local anaesthetic and little trouble. Most dentists believe that no general anaesthetic of any kind should ever be given to a patient unless there is a second professional present, to act as anaesthetist. If a single-handed anaesthetic should ever be suggested for your child, you might prefer to delay until there can be a second person, or to go elsewhere.

With a close eye kept on her teeth, any irregularity or mis-spacing can be rapidly corrected as soon as it begins. Very early orthodontic treatment is now generally accepted as saving both time and money. Your nine-year-old will not mind wearing a brace now, nearly as much as she would mind later, and if it is done now she probably will not have to wear it for nearly as long.

Some dental emergencies

Most dentists do not provide twenty-four-hours a day, seven days a week 'cover'. Unless yours is willing to give you his home telephone number and otherwise encourage you to call on him in time of need, do make sure that you know the address of your nearest dental hospital with outpatient facilities. A weekend can be a long time.

Toothache Sudden excruciating toothache is usually due to a cavity in which bacteria are living and breeding and producing acid. The pain starts at the moment when that acid finally breaks through the base of the cavity and touches the nerve. Often this kind of intense pain starts when the child has been eating something sweet: the sugar produces a burst of acid from the resident bacteria.

Use a really good light and try, with the child, to identify the painful tooth. Use a toothbrush to clean out the cavity (or what look to you like the normal indentations on the tooth) really well. If you can clean it of all food particles and most of the bacteria, the pain will stop in a few minutes because no more acid will be produced to penetrate.

● Don't let the complete relief of the pain deter you from making an immediate appointment with the dentist. It will recur when she next eats.

A second type of toothache sometimes starts off less dramatically with a dull throbbing ache which comes and goes. Neglected, it may suddenly wake the child in the night. The tooth is agony to touch or bite down on. The gum, or even the side of the face, may be swollen. Decay in the tooth has killed its nerve and made an abscess. The memorable pain is the result of pressure from gas and/or pus confined inside. Nothing but opening it up to relieve the pressure will fully cure the pain.

Sometimes the tooth will 'open itself up' by making a gum boil through which to discharge gas and pus. Sometimes the dentist will drill an opening. Sometimes the tooth will have to be removed. Just occasionally, if the infection is dealt with by antibiotics, the whole affair may settle so that the original cavity can be filled.

For the moment, try cleaning out the tooth as above. Pain may be being made worse by foodstuff pressing through the cavity, onto the nerve.

The child may be more comfortable well propped up so that the blood does not feel as if it pounds through her head quite so strongly. Aspirin, or a compound of aspirin with codeine, will help relieve the pain (*see* **Pain and Pain Control**).

If you cannot get her to the dentist within the next few hours – especially if there is visible swelling – take her to your doctor. He will prescribe antibiotics if he thinks them advisable. If she is in a great deal of pain he may even prescribe something to help her through the waiting time. Whether she sees the doctor or not, she needs the first possible appointment with the dentist.

When a tooth is knocked out

Front teeth are vulnerable, especially in toddlers who tumble and in eight- to ten-year-olds playing gang or team games. Apart from obvious safety precautions (*see* **Safety**/On wheels):

Always use a seat belt, as the law requires, if a child travels in the front of the car.

Always use a safety seat or belt for a young child in the back.

Encourage your child to use a mouth guard for contact sports (these are gradually becoming more usual in junior school games. You cannot encourage your child to do what he thinks will make him appear a 'sissy', but if anyone wears protection, encourage him to do likewise).

If you can find the tooth, wipe or rinse it and put it back in its socket, pressing it in as far as it will go. Make for the nearest dentist. If you cannot bear to do this (perhaps because the mouth is also cut) either wrap the tooth in a damp tissue or, if he is old enough and calm enough, get the child to hold it in his cheek or under his tongue while you make for the nearest dentist.

A first tooth which is re-implanted in this way will usually give good service until the child's permanent replacement is almost ready to come through.

A permanent tooth will not usually survive for more than two or three years after being re-implanted. Dentists are trying to find ways of preventing the roots re-absorbing.

When a tooth is broken

Assess whether or not the chip or fracture has exposed or penetrated the nerve. If it has the child will be in pain. Assess whether or not the tooth is now sharp or jagged enough to be dangerous to the child's lip.

If either of these is the case, treat as an emergency and make for the nearest dentist.

If there is no pain and no sharpness, make the first possible appointment with your own dentist (if much delay is suggested make sure his receptionist understands that a tooth is broken). Assure the child that the tooth can be repaired so that the final result is indistinguishable from a whole tooth. With the use of liquid quartz, a perfect result can often be achieved without the extensive drilling (and expense) of a cap.

Some dental problems of adolescence

Wisdom teeth   The third molars, way back in the jaw, do not always emerge. They may stay there, visible only to X-rays, causing no problems. Your dentist may check on their position/progress from time to time during the adolescent years.

Sometimes a wisdom tooth begins to push up but, without emerging through the gum, becomes jammed up against the root system of the second molar. This can be a very painful situation. The dentist should certainly be consulted if there is pressure-pain. Neglected, that pressure may build up and cause swelling of the face and sometimes of the gum, or even the tissues at the very back of the mouth and top of the throat.

Wisdom teeth which will neither emerge nor lie dormant usually have to be removed, surgically. This will be done in hospital with a general anaesthetic and your child should allow for several days' discomfort and recuperation afterwards.

Sometimes a wisdom tooth begins to emerge, cannot find enough space for itself, and causes pain by pressing against the second molar. 'Impacted' wisdom teeth are often removed in the dental surgery under local anaesthesia but the extraction is also often remembered with some horror. If your child is offered overnight admission to hospital and a general anaesthetic, you may like to encourage her to accept. These teeth are large and very deep-rooted. Even once they are visible they cannot just be pulled out. The force needed to prise and lever them is very unpleasant. There will be considerable soreness afterwards.

Bleeding gums   Periodontal (gum) diseases are more usual in adult life than in childhood,
(gingivitis)   but mild episodes of gingivitis sometimes occur in adolescence, especially if new independence breaches old habits of dental hygiene.

In gingivitis, the margins of gum around the teeth become swollen and delicate so that they bleed when the teeth are brushed. While there may be actual infection from the bacteria in plaque which has been allowed to accumulate and work its way into those margins, the condition can be due to that plaque solidifying into deep-seated tartar which is causing inflammation. In either case, especially thorough brushing and flossing, despite the bleeding which this causes, should clear the condition within a few days. Your child should *not* avoid brushing a particular area because it bleeds, as only cleansing will cure. If gingivitis is long-lasting or recurrent, she should see the dentist. It may be that tartar has penetrated deeply and must be professionally removed.

Bad breath   Although bad breath can be caused by digestive upsets and, of course, by
(halitosis)   the lingering smell of garlic and other foods, the most common cause is lack of dental hygiene. If plaque accumulates so that it can provide an oxygen-free environment for anaerobic bacteria, these will join the others which are already resident in the mouth. The gas which is given off by their activity is hydrogen sulphide: the same gas which comes out of sewers. Don't let your child assume the smell is from decaying food particles: it is not, so just brushing out all particles will not deal with halitosis. It is the plaque which has to be attacked.

Television

Modern western societies are notable for their reliance on mass facilities made available by advanced technology. Television is one such facility and the target for much worry and complaint. Is it bad for children? Does it destroy family life/conversation/individuality? Is it depriving us of the habit of reading for pleasure or of providing our own entertainment? Would families be better off if it did not exist at all? Would individual families be better off if they had no sets in their homes? . . . While every family must pose and answer questions of this kind for itself, it is perhaps important to remember that exactly the same issues are raised by other products of high technology which are largely accepted without comment. Would our society be better off without private cars, for example? However bad the influence of television may sometimes be, it certainly does not kill as many people as cars do . . . Would we be better off without advertising and mass marketing? However difficult it may be to escape television culture, it would be even more difficult to get back to home production of all a family needs . . . Would we be better off without computers, without the thousands of facilities made possible by the microchip, without worldwide instant communication networks? Perhaps; but these things are fundamental to our society's organization and inveighing against them is not going to remove them from our lives. We have to learn to live with them and to control them so that they do not control us. The same applies to television.

You can, of course, decide that you will *not* live with television; that you will not have a set in the house. But absence of a set will not mean that you have banished the medium's influence. Other children will tell yours about the programmes they see. If you will not allow them to watch on their friends' sets they will be left out of many games/fantasies/in-group jokes and 'languages'. And they will miss out on some information which even their teachers assume they will have. If they may watch in friends' houses you may find that, far from having more family conversation than other people, you have less because your children are always next door . . . Looking at the main criticisms of television, made by parents during a research project, it does look as though it is better to *regard television as a facility*, and concentrate on *using it well* rather than pretending, or wishing, that it did not exist.

Common worries about children and television

Television takes up so much time that children play/talk/read/study too little. But television takes up just exactly the amount of your child's time as he spends sitting watching it. How much time that is must be up to you.

Figures for the average hours spent viewing, by children of different ages, are alarmingly high. But why do they watch for so long, so often? Could it be that, because television programmes are available and can be counted upon to keep children quiet and out of mischief, other activities (especially those which will involve adults) are not provided? Would he view all Saturday morning if you were keen to take him out or play a game or entertain his friends? Would she insist on viewing right up to bedtime if her father was waiting to read the next instalment of their bedtime story?

Television is all tripe. But television programmes *vary*. Whatever your personal definition of 'tripe' you will certainly find plenty, but you will find plenty else, too.

Selective viewing apart, the sheer volume of information made available to every one of us through this medium must never be ignored. Children who grew up before it was available laboured under an ignorance which now seems incredible. Many, for example, had never seen a person of a different race or colour from themselves; had never seen an environment (large city, high mountain, ocean, snowscape) foreign to their own; had never seen this planet's creatures outside the confines of a zoo or seen down a microscope or inside an operating room. Many simply did not know that there *were* people who talked differently from their neighbours; families who lived differently; people who worked at jobs not locally available. And few people, of course, had actually seen the rich or famous and shared their privileged activities, or seen the lives of the impoverished and shared their pain. If your child knows what a lighthouse is like, he probably saw one on television. If he can tell you the difference between a brown bear and a polar, that will be television, too. And if he has seen a wide range of plays and movies, most of those will have been through television because few families have the money or the facilities to take their children regularly to the cinema or the theatre.

Television takes over children's lives so that they all play 'Batman'. Children have always created sub-cultures for themselves so that they could share imaginative play and hero worship. They use the stimuli which adults make available to them (*see* **Play**) and create for themselves. Batman is not the worst that can be offered. The children of Northern Ireland use playgroup Lego to make guns. Ask them, 'Now shall we make something nicer?' and many will reply, 'When we've finished these we're going to make petrol bombs.'

Television violence makes children behave violently. Nobody knows whether this is literally true or not. The occasional murderous youth maintains that he copied his monstrous methods from television drama, but so do others maintain (without such publicity) that they copied theirs from brutal real-life adults or the sadistic sections of pornographic magazines. The truth is probably that a violent *society* produces violent people *and* screens violent 'entertainment'.

Tips from parents who use television rather than letting it use them

Keep viewing as a positive decision/activity from the beginning. That means that, from toddlerhood onwards, children are encouraged to have particular programmes which they watch, which are planned for and switched on for them, but that the set is *never* switched, or left, on 'to see what's on' or 'because I'm bored' or as background 'company'.

Many families forbid young children to switch on for themselves, pointing out that such a ban is no more authoritarian than forbidding children to help themselves to ice-cream from the freezer.

As children get older, the positive approach to viewing is kept up by buying, and encouraging them to use, the television guides, and, when necessary, to choose between available programmes. These parents seldom recommend rigid rationing of viewing-time; this only increases the likelihood of children seeing television as a constant good of which they cannot get enough. Furthermore, a 'ration' contradicts the central idea of selective viewing: that the family watches television when, but only when, there is a programme people genuinely want to see.

Keep viewing sociable. Very young children can get little benefit from viewing without an adult, because even the most excellent children's programme cannot be geared to each child's attention span, need to play out what he has just seen, and bewilderment when he returns to find that it has moved on without him. Children who habitually watch with parents and/or older brothers and sisters take *talking about programmes* for granted. Many of these families maintain that family viewing creates at least as much conversation as it quashes.

Avoid using television as a babysitter. If a child is encouraged to view because it suits you, rather than because the programme suits him, the positive-viewing attitude will be lost.

Make sure the whole household follows the same line. If he knows that you watch all evening, as soon as he has gone to bed, or he finds you dozing in front of a movie you are clearly not enjoying, he will quickly adopt the same habits.

Remember that extras like video-recorders may assist positive viewing. These families insist that, far from leading to even more viewing, a recorder can help selectivity because it enables the family to escape from the presenters' timetabling and see the programmes they want to see at times which suit them.

Temper *see* **Tantrums.** *See also* **Discipline, Self-discipline and Learning How to Behave:** Violence.
Temperature *see* **Nursing**/Fever. *See also* **Infection**/Infections which cause illness.
Testes *see* **Adolescence**/Puberty. *See also* **Mumps; Undescended Testicle**.

Tetanus ('Lockjaw')

Tetanus is not an infectious disease in the sense of being one which can be passed from victim to victim. But it is an extremely serious illness which still kills thousands in the developing countries and is a potential threat to everyone. Its rarity is due to immunization. Carelessness in following recommended immunization programmes, including later boosters, is often due to misunderstandings about the nature of the infection; this is tragic as the disease is, and is likely to remain, very much easier to prevent than to treat (*see* **Immunization; Infection**). Tetanus is caused by bacteria with two important characteristics:

They are spore-forming bacteria and, while the bacteria themselves are normally sensitive to antibiotics and to a variety of sterilization and disinfection procedures, as well as requiring particular conditions in which to live and multiply, the spores are a different matter. Tetanus spores are highly resistant to heat and to chemicals, to drying, etc. They can remain, in a state one might call 'suspended animation', for long periods in conditions which would provide no sustenance for the living bacteria. When and if circumstances become ideal, the spores produce active bacteria, which, in their turn, produce more spores.

The bacteria themselves are anaerobic, meaning that they flourish and multiply only under conditions where there is no, or very little, oxygen. Their normal habitats include soil and the bowel content of many animals. Living tetanus bacilli can normally be found deep in the earth of a garden or in the droppings of a horse or goat. Spores are frequent inhabitants of road dust or surface soil.

Infection by tetanus

These bacteria and their spores are harmless while they remain outside the body or if they are swallowed and thus taken into the digestive system. Your child will not 'get tetanus' from sucking fingers contaminated with manure-enriched soil. But if these bacteria or their spores are introduced into a wound which happens to provide anaerobic conditions, infection may take place.

A wound which is liable to active infection by tetanus is one where there is tissue without much blood supply and therefore with very little oxygen, contaminated by the kind of 'dirt' which is liable to contain tetanus organisms. Most of the world's deaths from tetanus occur where the umbilical cords of newborn babies are either cut with contaminated instruments or actually 'dressed' with cow-dung. That cut cord, designed to dry up and shrivel, provides both a low-oxygen environment and a route into the baby's bloodstream. While any large or deep wound incurred out of doors (on the battlefield or in road accidents, for example) carries a risk of tetanus infection, much less serious injuries of particular kinds carry the risk too. A small but deep burn, for example, kills tissue and may provide an ideal breeding ground for tetanus organisms if it is contaminated. A deep puncture wound damages tissue to a considerable depth, yet rapidly seals itself at the surface thus cutting off the external oxygen from the interior of the wound. If tetanus organisms were introduced by whatever made the wound (a stableyard nail, for example) and if the wound does not itself have an excellent oxygen-carrying blood supply, the risk is very real.

Tetanus bacilli merely colonize a wound, they do not themselves invade the body. They cause disease by releasing a toxin (infinitely more poisonous than strychnine) which affects the nerves and the central nervous system. Damage to the nerves leads to muscular spasms (often first affecting the jaw, hence the popular name for this disease: Lockjaw). These spasms may increase to generalized convulsions and eventually to death from asphyxia.

Treatment of tetanus

In a modern hospital, a tetanus victim receives intensive nursing and supportive care, combined with muscle-relaxants to banish or reduce the spasms, and, if necessary, assistance with breathing. He will be given antibiotics to halt the multiplication of bacteria in his wound. The wound itself will also be energetically treated, to remove all dead tissue and thus expose any bacteria to oxygen. Tetanus anti-toxin will be given to neutralize the effects of the poison but, while this can effectively prevent *further* nerve damage, it cannot touch toxins which have already invaded nerves.

Prevention of tetanus

Immunization against tetanus is not aimed at producing antibodies against tetanus bacteria but against the toxins they release. Tetanus toxoid is the 'T' in the triple vaccine given to infants. It is highly effective, but *must be 'boosted'*, at five years and about ten-yearly, if high levels of protection are to be maintained (*see* **Immunization**).

In an immunized individual, a booster of tetanus toxoid, given at the time of a risky injury, rapidly increases the level of protection. But in an unimmunized individual tetanus toxoid at the time of injury is useless. One injection cannot produce enough immunity quickly enough to be of any use on this occasion.

Until quite recently, unimmunized individuals (or those whose immunization was years out of date) were given tetanus anti-toxin to confer passive immunity to the infection in a susceptible wound. Although anti-toxin clearly saved many lives during the First World War (when toxoid was not yet available) and was used, as well as immunization with toxoid, for soldiers wounded in the Second World War, it is now discredited in many places. Despite extremely careful refinement, many individuals are hypersensitive to the horse serum from which the anti-toxin is derived.

Hospital treatment of susceptible wounds in unimmunized individuals now tends to consist of measures designed to prevent tetanus bacilli from multiplying and therefore releasing toxin, and simultaneously to prevent tetanus spores finding the right circumstances in which to come alive. Very careful cleaning of wounds to remove all damaged tissue and thus expose tetanus organisms to the oxygen in the circulation and/or the air, or even an artificially oxygenated environment, is combined with the administration of antibiotics.

Commonsense about tetanus and small wounds

If every member of your family receives the full course of primary immunization against tetanus and receives boosters at the recommended intervals, you need not add tetanus into your consideration of everyday wounds. If a wound is serious enough to require medical attention, the doctor will decide whether a tetanus booster is needed. If it does not, in itself, merit medical attention then you can rely on that basic protection while treating the wound sensibly at home.

If an unimmunized member of the family, or one who has not received a booster for more than ten years, receives a susceptible wound, medical attention should certainly be sought and the whole drama should mean that he now receives the first injection of toxoid *and will return for the rest of the series.*

A shallow wound which bleeds freely is not susceptible to tetanus.

A deeper wound which bleeds freely is unlikely to be susceptible if you can see every cut surface and can therefore be sure that oxygen from the air meets with oxygen in the blood which oozes from its deepest points.

A wound which does not meet these criteria is still not likely to be susceptible if it was made by something which is unlikely to have been in contact with soil or animal faeces. Even a deep puncture wound is unlikely to be a tetanus risk if it was made, for example, by a corkscrew. But if that corkscrew was being used on a picnic in a field grazed by animals, it might be a different matter. Did it come straight out of the hamper or had the toddler been digging in the earth with it?

Wounds with dead tissue (tissue which is not being constantly suffused with oxygen-carrying blood) are susceptible to tetanus infection later on, even if there was no risk at the time that they were caused. Burns, etc. should therefore be covered, as should septic wounds in which tissue will have been destroyed by other bacteria. Even in minor wounds (cuts on the fingers, damage from ingrown toenails, etc.) it is best to remove obviously 'dead' flaps of skin, provided they are not acting as complete seals for underlying damage, as does the skin of a blister, for example.

Despite popular belief, there is no particular risk of 'lockjaw' if the web between thumb and first finger sustains a cut. Nor is there any particular danger attached to rust. The rusty nail in the foot is dangerous because of the outdoor circumstances in which the nail is likely to have gone rusty. If a non-stainless steel knife has gone rusty in the steam of your kitchen, its cut is no more likely to carry tetanus organisms than are any of your other kitchen implements.

The kind of everyday wound which might possibly merit medical attention because of the risk of tetanus when, without this risk, you would treat it at home, is a graze, acquired on the road or gravel drive, which has left pockets in the skin. Although such grazes are often very painful, first aid must include the kind of bathing which ensures that every 'pocket' is laid open. If this is done, dirt which might carry spores is washed out and none can heal over to leave a contaminated and airtight breeding ground (*see also* **Accidents**/Cuts and scrapes, grazes and puncture wounds).

Thrush (Candidiasis)

The yeast-like organism candidiasis is a normal and harmless inhabitant of the mouth and bowel. Infection only takes place when there is some local or general reduction in the tissues' resistance to infection. The most usual causes of lowered resistance to candidiasis are:

Wide-spectrum antibiotics   By suppressing the growth of both pathogenic and harmless bacteria, antibiotics, particularly if taken over a long period, can upset the normal balance of micro-organisms in various parts of the body and thus predispose to invasion by candida albicans (*see* **Infection**/Treatment of infections which cause illness: Problems in antibiotic use).

Corticosteroids   Whether these drugs (such as cortisone or prednisolone) are taken by mouth or applied locally, to reduce inflammation in eczema for example, they disturb the body's resistance in many ways and may therefore predispose to invasion by a variety of micro-organisms including candida albicans (*see* **Infection**/Treatment of external infection and inflammation).

Pregnancy, diabetes and the Pill
Yeasts thrive in acid conditions, especially when there is plenty of carbohydrate available. The epithelial cells of the vagina, normally inhospitable to yeasts, may become ideal breeding grounds during pregnancy, diabetes or the taking of oestrogen-containing contraceptive pills.

● Young babies easily become infected, not because their resistance is lowered but because it has not yet been built up.

Recognizing thrush
Infection with candida albicans has a similar appearance whatever part of the body is affected. Clusters of the yeast organisms produce fluffy white patches (like the white down on the breast of a thrush, from which the popular name comes). Under the white growth is raw, inflamed skin or mucous membrane. Thrush may be itchy. Scratching alters the appearance of the lesions and may lead to secondary infection.

Common sites for infection by candida albicans include:

Vagina and external female genitals. Infection produces a whitish discharge together with itching and, perhaps, sore patches on the labia.

Mouth – usually of infants but occasionally of adults following drug treatment. White fluffy patches can be seen inside the cheeks. If they are wiped away, raw patches appear underneath. A baby may be extremely reluctant to feed. The baby born to a mother with vaginal thrush may acquire the infection during the birth process.

Anus and buttocks, usually of infants. Thrush may complicate 'nappy rash', especially if the baby has been receiving antibiotics for another infection. Since the organisms are normal bowel-inhabitants, every soiled napkin introduces more to the area and, once the skin is infected, careful hygienic measures (frequent changing, sterilizing of napkins, etc.) will be needed (*see* **Infection**/Sterilants, disinfectants and antiseptics).

Already inflamed skin being treated with corticosteroids. If anti-inflammatory ointments and creams are being used on skin already damaged by, for example, eczema, especially if the area is covered by an airtight dressing, invasion by candida albicans may follow. Sometimes this leads to the assumption that the treatment is not working, when in fact it has done the anti-inflammatory job for which it was applied, the continuing lesions being due to invasion by these yeasts.

Treatment of thrush
Although a variety of local applications used to be employed and some (gentian violet, for example) were reasonably effective, an antibiotic called nystatin is now usually prescribed. Its absorption from the gut is limited so, except in rare cases of heavy infestation of the bowel, it is seldom given by mouth. Instead, various local applications are manufactured for application to different sites. A vaginal infection may be treated with nystatin pessaries; infection of the napkin area or other part of the skin may be treated with creams or lotions containing the antibiotic, while thrush in the mouth of an infant will often be treated with nystatin liquid, applied in drops to the patches.

Thumb sucking *see* **Habits**/Comfort habits. *See also* **Teeth**/Looking after teeth.
Tics and other habit spasms *see* **Habits**.
Toes and toe injuries *see* **Feet**. *See also* **Accidents**/Bruises: 'Blackened' nails.

Toilet Training *see also* **Bedwetting**; **Soiling**

In recent years most parents have come to realize that a child-paced and child-orientated approach to toilet training saves time, energy and aggro. Parents used to look at it as a matter of *preventing a child from wetting and soiling his nappies or the floor*. This negative aim could (and often did) start from the earliest months, with 'catching' motions and urine in a pot. This may have saved some washing, but had nothing whatsoever to do with 'training'; it usually led to rebellion as soon as the child realized that those were *his* excreta and therefore that what he did with them was, or should be, his business. Hardly surprisingly, toilet training struggles were common and the pot often served as a focus for toddlers' struggles for independence. Now, most parents are able to look at toilet training as a matter of *helping a child to take charge of his own excretion and waste-disposal as do the older members of his society*. This positive aim is with and for the child, rather than at and against him. It cannot begin until the child shows that he is ready for the responsibility and, far from contradicting his dawning desire for autonomy, it can pander to it.

If you should have remaining doubts about taking this positive approach, the following points may help to resolve them:

However hard you try, however tough you are prepared to be, you cannot *make* your child use a pot/toilet. You may be able to force him to sit on it, but only he can decide whether or not to perform. Any battle is one which you cannot win and had therefore better not join.

Your child can only cooperate in toilet training because he wants to cooperate with you, as representatives of the grown-up world. He has no other motive for becoming clean and dry. In this sense, toilet training is different from socializing other natural functions like eating. When you ask him to eat 'nicely', you have going for you the fact that he wants the food. But when you ask him to pee in a pot you have nothing going for you but that desire to please. He was going to pee anyway; only you care where.

Almost every healthy child will be clean and dry before he goes to school. Turn by all means to the entries on **Bedwetting** and **Soiling**. But before you despair of your three-year-old, ask yourself how many school-children you know who still wear nappies.

'Readiness' for toilet training   Your child cannot begin to take charge of his own excretion until he is aware of what he does. At one year, everyone in the household may know (from his scarlet face and happy grunts) when a motion is coming – except him. If he passes a motion, or pees, when he happens to be naked, he will squat, perform, and then go on with his play without so much as a glance at what came out of him. Until he makes this vital connection between the feeling and the product, he is not ready for 'training'.

Somewhere between twelve and eighteen months this awareness usually begins; there is no doubt that summer nakedness speeds it up. Now when he makes a puddle he may turn to inspect it; exclaiming with interest over it. But as long as he is only aware *after the event* he is still not ready.

Bowel training   Bowel training is infinitely easier for a child than urine training:

He probably only passes one or two motions per day while he may pee eight or ten times.

He may be quite regular in his timing whereas his urination is irregular.

Once he connects the sensations of an impending motion with what comes out, he has plenty of time to go to a pot or toilet if he wishes. Early awareness of a coming urination gives him only a couple of seconds before the flood.

The simplest way to bowel train a child is simply to point out to him, once he is aware of the feeling–product connection, that, *if he wanted to,* he could put that motion in a pot or lavatory, like other people do, instead of in his nappy. If it is presented as an interesting new idea, backed by an interesting new pot or toilet seat, he will probably want to give it a try. You can repeat the suggestion next time you can see that he is going to pass a motion, but if he is too busy playing to bother, drop it. The secret is to *avoid any implication that he must.* If and when he does, you can of course comment with pleasure on how grown up he is getting, but it is a mistake to go overboard with the congratulations and an even bigger mistake to be disappointed when he uses his nappy the next time. Using that pot is not the be all and end all of everything. It is just something that you are absolutely confident that he will do, because everyone does eventually.

● If you have no strong preference for pot or lavatory, these are some of the pros and cons of each:

Pots are portable, and can therefore be put where the child will be, and where he can easily get to them himself. This can be a big advantage when urine training begins. Speed becomes important and urination is so frequent that it is irritating for the toddler if he must always be taken upstairs to the toilet.

Well-designed pots (preferably pot-chairs) are safe and comfortable. The child can sit himself down without help, and has his feet firmly on the floor, instead of being perched up on a lavatory where, even with a small seat, he may feel worried.

Lavatories are what older people use and therefore using one may make it clearer to the child that his new behaviour is 'grown up'.

A child who is used to lavatories will not need you to cart his pot around and carrying a pot wherever you go can become tedious.

Whichever you choose (and both is usually the best) remember:

A pot for a boy needs a shield on the front; he will pee sitting down for quite a long time and it will not go in the pot without this aid!

- Don't use a shielded pot for a girl. Sitting down unwarily has led to lacerations of the labia which, in a few children, have actually had to be stitched.

A lavatory a child will use must have a small seat and a footstool. The small seat stops him feeling as if he is going to fall in; the footstool helps him climb up, makes him feel more safely planted when he gets there *and* gives him a physiologically efficient position in which to pass a motion.

Whichever he uses, be tactful about disposing of his motions. Many children are terrified of a toilet's flush; their size-concepts are still so primitive that they may truly believe that they, too, could be flushed away. Furthermore, those faeces are part of them; their body's product. When you flush their faeces away you do, in a way, flush part of them away. So whether you are emptying a pot or flushing a toilet your child has used, wait until he is out of the room. When he expresses unworried interest in what happens to the motions, explain where they go and why; point out that there will always be more tomorrow, and see if he would like to flush the toilet for himself.

Urine training   Although a child's awareness of being about to pee and of producing a puddle, may develop simultaneously with his awareness of bowel movements, taking charge of them is far more difficult. They happen often and unpredictably; sensation only gives him a few seconds' warning, and once he has the warning he cannot run for his pot because the only way he can delay, even that long, is to 'clench his bottom' and stay rooted to the spot. You will not have to suggest to your child that he could pee in the pot instead of in his nappy because he will often do so while passing a motion, but don't take him out of nappies, and thus expose him to endless failures (and your carpets to inevitable disasters), until he can recognize the need to pee while there is still time for him to get to his pot.

Once he can wait a little, you can start in one of two ways. If it is summer and warm, so that you can leave him without pants, playing around in the garden, pot to hand, do. Encourage him to sit on the pot when he feels a pee coming and encourage him, for a change, to 'water' a particular bush, too. It will all help him to bring his urination under voluntary control.

If he cannot be outside, pick a day when he happens to wake up dry from a nap and suggest that he might like to pee on his pot. If he would *not* like to sit there, or if he sits and does not pee, just leave him without nappies, making sure the pot is close by, and suggest he sits down when he feels one coming. The point here is to try and give him a success-experience without too much boring waiting around. If he stayed dry all through that nap he is bound to pee soon . . . If he does pee in the pot be calmly congratulatory but dress him, nappies and all, as usual. If he gets absorbed in play and makes a puddle, don't make a fuss; just dress him. After a few days of occasional casual successes, take him out of nappies *when he is awake and at home*. Don't make too big a thing of this or he will feel sad and demeaned by having them back on again for naps, outings and nights. Just say that he will probably be more comfortable in pants and the pot is right there when he needs it. At this stage you need to be actually sympathetic about puddles ('Bad luck; you left it a bit late, didn't you? Let's mop it up . . .'). It *is* a puddly stage. You may find that plastic coated trainer-pants reduce the flood-damage a bit.

You will now be at a half-way stage where tact, and giving the child as much choice as possible, is vital.

As long as he ever wears nappies in the day-time, he will not finally realize that every full-bladder sensation means a trip to the pot or toilet. You cannot expect him to think to himself, 'I'm going to pee in a minute; now let me see, am I wearing a nappy or not?' so he will not become reliably dry until those nappies become something he wears only at night.

But once half-trained, he will not like wetting himself so it is unfair to take him to the supermarket without nappies when you know there is no toilet you could reach if it were needed.

Sometimes the best compromise is to agree with him that he doesn't need nappies in the day any more *except when you go to particular places*, and to let him choose whether or not he prefers to wear nappies for naps.

Urine training should now proceed smoothly, although not without plenty of 'accidents'. Do bear in mind the following points though:

If you keep reminding him to sit on the pot you ruin the whole process. However it may sometimes feel to you, you are not trying to keep the floor dry but trying to help him recognize and act on his own need to pee. If you keep reminding him, you are doing his thinking for him and you may actually delay the time when he can be fully reliable.

He cannot urinate in advance of feeling the need and will certainly not be able to do so before he is three or four years old. Sending him to the lavatory before you go out 'so you won't need to go later' is useless. Scolding him for a puddle in the car, because 'you should have gone before we came out', is unjust.

Your skill as a lavatory-finder is important. When he does need to go he will still need to go *now*; the best parents have an almost magical ability to find a toilet at almost any time and under almost any circumstances. Learn where your local public facilities are; get into the habit of spotting that important door in any fast-food joint or service-station and be charmingly ruthless about asking shopkeepers for the use of their facilities if no public ones are available. And don't, *ever*, allow a driver to refuse to stop for a child to pee, or a nursery teacher to reprove a child who needs to go during story-time instead of break . . .

Help children learn the art of al fresco peeing. Unless you introduce the idea of peeing outside, at an early stage, a newly trained child may be so shy about it that he or she is actually unable to let go.

Little boys have the edge here; it is easy for them to pee behind a bush or even, in a real emergency, against the back wheel of the car or down a drain. Little girls need a bit more help as mine crossly pointed out when she asked me why I hadn't given her one of those useful things her brother had, to bring on the picnic . . . A girl obviously needs protection from nettles, thistles and ants. She also needs help with keeping her pants out of the way while she squats because the whole performance is ruined for her if her pants get wet all the same. If there is enough privacy, taking the pants off altogether is usually the best solution. Finally, if she finds the squatting difficult, try 'holding her out' by crouching behind her with your hands holding her bent knees and your elbows cradling her hips. She may find the whole thing easier if you do.

• When you start thinking about toilet training your child you have to decide what words you are going to use. Our language is full of euphemisms for lavatories and what we put in them but, while adults usually find it easy to adapt their language to the company they are in, small children will tend to accept your early labels and go on using them for years. An invented baby-name for a bowel movement may seem perfectly appropriate when your child is two, but totally fox a teacher three years later. Correct medical terminology from the beginning may seem the answer, but unfortunately classmates are liable to laugh if your four-year-old announces, 'I need to urinate . . .' Family slang may be automatically picked up by the child, but some teachers will raise an eyebrow if he announces, 'I need a crap. . .'

It may be worth your while to listen carefully both to the words local families use among themselves, and to the words small children use in your local parks and playgrounds. You are looking for that fine (and personal) line between 'acceptable' and 'rude'.

Tonsils

The tonsils are a pair of oval bodies of lymphoid tissue situated at the top of the throat where they are often visible on either side of the uvula.

Like the nearby adenoids, the tonsils play a role in trapping and destroying bacteria and viruses which might otherwise penetrate more deeply into the body. Enlargement and redness of the tonsils (often with fever and sore throat) is called 'tonsillitis'; it is not really a disease in itself but a sign that the tonsils are actively engaged in coping with one of a variety of 'germs'.

It used to be thought that enlarged tonsils were more often a focus and source of infection than a protection from it. Very young children had their tonsils surgically removed, almost as a routine. Now most doctors are reluctant to recommend removal of the tonsils as long as they are active. The operation is rarely carried out before middle childhood, if at all. (*see* **Hospital**/Surgery: Tonsillectomy.)

Tuberculosis (TB)

Although TB is now extremely rare amongst the privileged families of western societies, it is still probably the most important infectious disease in the world. There are more than twenty million active cases today. In the next year one to two million of today's victims will die of the disease and two to three million new victims will be infected.

The full story of man's fight against tuberculosis has no place in this book (it would make it even longer!), but every family should know something of what is done to protect us if only so that each can cooperate, with understanding, in vital public health measures.

Tuberculosis is caused by one of two types of bacteria: the 'human' form or the 'bovine' (cow) form.

The bacteria can be taken into the body either by respiration – breathing air contaminated by bacteria from a coughing TB victim – or by drinking – milk from an infected cow, for example.

Entry of the tubercle bacilli to the body is by no means always followed by open disease. Whether or not an exposed person develops open infection seems to depend both on the size of the dose of bacilli and on the age and health of the infected individual. TB spreads most widely in areas where poverty and malnutrition combine with a large reservoir of infection in the human and cattle population.

● If your healthy child has passing contact with someone later shown to have active tuberculosis, the chances of her getting the disease are still very small. Medical authorities will investigate and take precautions (*see below*) *not* because they think she has, or will have, acquired it, but because the infection is so serious that even the slightest risk merits action.

The bacilli are carried in the bloodstream and can affect virtually any organ of the body, including the central nervous system. Infection of the lung is the most common form (pulmonary tuberculosis). Infection in babies and young children ranges from the widespread, overwhelming attack which so rapidly kills malnourished infants in underdeveloped countries, to the localized attack (often affecting only a small portion of lung tissue and associated glands) which is still occasionally seen in the west.

Control of tuberculosis in the western world

Tuberculosis and poverty walk hand in hand. It is in underdeveloped countries that the disease is still rampant, and in poverty stricken corners of affluent ones that it can still be found. Most of us in the west are primarily protected by the standards of living, and especially of nutrition, which we are fortunate enough to enjoy. Specific effective control measures of the last generation have included:

Control of bovine tuberculosis

Bacilli circulate in the bloodstream of infected cows and pass into the milk. Separation of that milk, so that cream may be sold or made into butter, tends to concentrate the bacilli so that these dairy products may be even more infective than the milk itself. Cow's milk used to be a major source of infection, especially to young children. Now, all dairy cows must, by law, be tested; no cow shown to have (or ever to have had) the infection may be used in milk production. Herds must be tested regularly and, as a further precaution against this and other milk-borne infections, almost all milk sold commercially is further treated by pasteurization or sterilization.

● Wise families will not buy raw, untreated, milk from farmers who are not commercial producers. However attractive you may find the idea of 'milk straight from the cow', it is not worth the minute risk that the cow is less than healthy.

Development of effective drugs

Antibiotics, such as streptomycin or isoniazid, control the disease in the individual patient and, by rendering her non-infective, reduce the reservoir of infection in the community. It is these drugs which have made the safe treatment of tuberculosis possible at home, and thus removed the horrors of long confinement in sanatoria.

Diagnosis of early pulmonary TB by mass X-ray

Mass radiography now detects so few new cases of TB that the service is being brought to an end. However, there is no doubt that, by detecting cases which might have remained infectious but symptom-free for many years, the service made a major contribution to the control of tuberculosis. It has, in the best sense, 'worked itself out of a job'.

● In some communities, institutions and jobs, chest X-rays are still required. They should always be accepted as a measure designed to protect both the individual and the rest of the community. If any member of your family has such a chest X-ray, do make a note of the date so that the doctor or public health official will know whether or not she should be X-rayed again on another occasion.

Development of vaccine (BCG)

BCG stands for bacillus, Calmette and Guérin; Calmette and Guérin being the two French scientists who devoted their lives to developing it. It is an effective vaccine which appears to give almost complete and long-lasting protection against infection. People are often confused, however, by the way it is used:

Use of BCG vaccine

Many people, even in western communities, many people are immune to TB because, even without open and obvious infection, they have had contact with the disease and their bodies have manufactured their own protection against reinfection.

Unlike many infectious diseases, TB does not produce circulating antibodies which can be detected by a blood-test. The body's immunity is at cellular level.

Unlike many vaccines, BCG must not be given to people who *are* immune to TB, whether they are actually suffering from the disease or have simply had sufficient contact with it to produce an immune reaction. Immune individuals react 'allergically' to the attenuated bacilli in the vaccine. They may develop ulcers at the injection site and other unpleasant side-effects.

The Mantoux test

Before any individual is given BCG vaccine, then, she must be tested to see whether or not she already has TB, or immunity to TB. Since it is not possible to tell with a blood test, a special test using the purified products of killed TB bacilli (tuberculin) is carried out. A tiny quantity of tuberculin is smeared on the upper arm and then a Heaf gun is used to make several tiny punctures carrying the tuberculin into the skin.

Individuals without tuberculosis, or immunity to tuberculosis, show no skin reaction to tuberculin.

Individuals who have tuberculosis, or had contact with it in the past and are therefore immune, have a reddened and swollen patch of skin at the site of the punctures.

- A *negative* (no reaction) Mantoux test means that the individual is not immune and will be amongst those to be given BCG.

- A *positive* (skin reaction) Mantoux test means that the individual has either TB or immunity from past contact. She will *not* be given BCG but may be the subject of further investigations.

Different countries use the Mantoux test and BCG vaccination in different ways; usage is changing as infection becomes rarer.

Mass vaccination. In some areas of the world, mass testing and vaccination is carried out and is being extended as rapidly as possible. Vaccination in earliest infancy is used to protect babies who, because the disease is endemic and conditions are poor, would be very likely to acquire active tuberculosis during childhood. A new baby can be protected with BCG without the precaution of a Mantoux test because she has had no time to acquire the infection/immunity which would make immunization dangerous.

United States. In the United States, schoolchildren are tested (often repeatedly), but those with negative tests are not normally given BCG as the risk of contracting the infection is regarded as too small to merit immunization. The Mantoux test is therefore seen not as an indicator for immunization but as an indicator for treatment. Any child with a positive Mantoux test is subjected to a full range of tests in case active infection can be found. But even if all these tests are negative, she is likely to be prescribed anti-tuberculosis antibiotics for a period of around one year, whether or not any signs of active disease ever appear. This is to cover the small risk of a pocket of infection smouldering on within the body to flare up in later life.

Britain. In the UK, all schoolchildren are tested at around the age of twelve or thirteen and all those who are negative on the Mantoux test (which nowadays is the vast majority) are given BCG vaccine a few weeks later.

Those children who have positive reactions to the Mantoux test may be given chest X-rays and other tests to determine whether the positive result is due to present, active infection, or to minor infection long since dealt with by the body.

- Amid these complexities, what parents need to know is that:
- ☐ Children should be given at least one Mantoux test.
- ☐ Those who are negative should accept BCG if it is offered.
- ☐ Those who are positive *may* have contracted TB which may still be active. Any investigations or treatment offered should be accepted. On the other hand, the child may well simply have acquired immunity by having contact with TB which has done no damage and is long past. A positive Mantoux test therefore merits careful discussion with a doctor, but it does not merit panic or despair.

If a child is known to have had contact (however fleeting) with someone who is then shown to have active tuberculosis, a Mantoux test will at once be carried out unless the child has already had BCG vaccine. It sometimes happens, for example, that a member of the staff of a school is found to have the infection. All the pupils will then be tested in order to pick up, as quickly as possible, any who may have been infected. This is why some families will find that Mantoux tests are being carried out on six- or seven-year-olds at school, and why they may also hear rumours about the children 'being exposed to TB'. The precaution is, of course, worthwhile, but the chances of infection are very small indeed.

If your child is given a Mantoux test early (for some reason such as the above) do be sure to check on whether or not those children with negative reactions were then given the BCG vaccine later on. It may be that the school was, at that point, interested only in making sure that no child had been infected and that negative tests were therefore simply greeted with relief and no further action taken. If, when the child moves to a different school in early adolescence, and routine testing is offered, you say only that 'she was done at her old school', it may be assumed that she has had BCG and she may therefore be done out of this protection for adult life.

If you are to travel, or more especially to live for a period, in a community where tuberculosis is endemic, do consult your doctor about protection for your children in advance. Under these circumstances early Mantoux testing and, if appropriate, BCG vaccination, may be given however young the children are.

If you take your child to the doctor because of a persistent cough (*see* **Coughs) do not be surprised if he carries out a Mantoux test** – it is a normal precaution. Do not be too alarmed if the test is positive; it may, but need not, mean that the cough is due to pulmonary tuberculosis.

On the other hand, a long-continuing cough, especially if it is associated with fever (even of low grade) and/or tiredness, loss of weight and night sweating, should certainly lead to a visit to the doctor. Once again, such a complex of symptoms does not necessarily mean that the child has TB but it does mean that you must make sure she has not.

Unconsciousness *see* **Accidents**/Coping with more serious injuries; Head injuries; **Convulsions, 'Fits' and 'Funny Turns'**. *See also* **Fainting**; **Nursing**/Fever. Side-effects of high fever.

Undescended Testicle *see also* Hospital/Surgery

A baby boy's testes descend down the inguinal canal, from the abdomen into the scrotum, shortly before birth. Once they are fully descended, the canal closes behind them. About three to four per cent of boys are born before this descent is complete. Most of these testes will descend spontaneously during the first year, leaving fewer than one per cent of boys with an undescended testicle by their first birthdays.

It is easy for parents to confuse an undescended testicle with one which is 'retractile'. In early infancy the testes can be drawn up out of the scrotal sac and into a superficial 'inguinal pouch', when the scrotal muscle contracts. Contraction of this muscle may take place in reaction to cool air or a cool hand. Whenever you remove your baby's warm clothes or touch his scrotum with a cold hand, his testes may 'vanish', only to reappear when you stop looking for them.

The eventual positioning of the testes in the scrotum is very important to a boy's eventual fertility. A testicle which remains permanently within the abdomen cannot function. A testicle which remains in the abdomen until late in childhood will have been too warm for normal development. Even when it is eventually brought down into the cooler scrotum, it may never produce living sperm.

The doctor who examines your newborn boy will check to make sure that both testes are in the scrotum; he will skilfully persuade one which insists on retracting to descend for his warmed hand to feel. If he can establish that both are descended you can forget the whole matter although it will be checked again at your son's first school 'medical'.

If one testicle does appear to be undescended, the doctor will probably ask you to keep an eye open for its spontaneous descent. One day, perhaps when he is sucking his toes while you try to change his nappy, you will probably see that both testes are in the scrotal sac, clearly outlined, like little eggs, inside the delicate skin.

If you have never seen or felt that testicle by your baby's first birthday, mention it to the doctor, either at the surgery or at the well-baby clinic. If it is truly undescended, rather than still retractile, the baby will probably be referred to a surgeon so that arrangements can be made for it to be brought down into the scrotum and permanently fixed there.

Although this operation used to be deferred until a boy was of school age, many authorities now consider that it should be carried out between the ages of two and four years. The earlier it is done the less chance there is of any reduction in the testicle's later efficiency.

Violence *see* **Discipline, Self-discipline and Learning How to Behave**. *See also* **Tantrums;**
   Television.
Viruses *see* **Infection**. *See also* individual conditions.
Vision *see* **Eyes and Seeing; Eye Disorders and Blindness**.
Vitamins *see* **Eating**/Types of food: Vitamins and minerals.

Vomiting

Vomiting (or 'being sick') is the forcible expulsion of stomach contents.
Nausea (or 'feeling sick') usually warns the victim of what is to happen.
Retching is the name given to the repeated spasms which finally produce
the vomit. If the stomach is fairly full there may be little retching; if it is
more or less empty there may be more. Sometimes violent retching
produces only a little foul-tasting bile. The whole business of vomiting is
unpleasant and exhausting. Although the victim will feel better from her
nausea once she has vomited, she may be covered in cold sweat, limp and
shaky by the time she has finished.

Vomiting which
is not associated
with illness

Some people vomit very easily while others only do so in response to
gastric illness. You will need to know your own child in order to know
how seriously any particular episode should be taken. Some types of
vomiting are due to 'mechanical' causes rather than to infection:

Newborn babies with a fault in the muscular outlet from the stomach
may vomit every feed with great force (*see* **Hospital**/Surgery: Pyloric
stenosis).

Milk-fed babies often bring up milk with air. This is not true vomiting in
the sense that it does not distress the baby or suggest that anything is
wrong. The usual mechanism is that the milk becomes layered, or
intermixed, with air in the stomach so that when that air is burped out,
milk comes up with it. You may be able to lessen the tendency by feeding
the baby in a more upright position. The heavier milk then drops below
the air-level in the stomach and the air can therefore escape without
bringing milk with it. Handling her gently after meals may help, too.

A few children bring up any surplus if they over-eat. While this is much
rarer than all those adult cries of 'you'll make yourself sick . . .' suggest, it
does occasionally happen, especially if a child drinks a great deal of fizzy
liquid along with a large meal. Her uncomfortably distended stomach
may then simply eject what it cannot hold.

Many children suffer from motion sickness. Whether your child gets
sick only on violent fairground rides or rough seas, in cars and coaches
but not in trains or aeroplanes, or in every kind of vehicle, the mechanism
is probably the same: the motion disturbs the balance-mechanism of the
inner ear (*see* **Ears and Hearing; Ear Disorders and Deafness**). For this
reason, the single most effective preventive measure is to persuade her to
keep her head supported and still. If she can actually lie down, so much
the better. If she cannot, being propped with a pillow in a corner of the car
will certainly help. If she insists on looking out, trying to play, walking

around on the boat or going up and down the aisle of the plane or train, she is far more likely to be sick.

Travel-sickness pills help, too, but at least partly because they tend to make her sleepy and therefore more inclined to keep still . . . They do have side-effects, such as an unpleasantly dry mouth.

Some children vomit from excitement/nervous tension and this may be because the excitement keeps the body in a state of action-readiness during which normal digestion cannot take place. Such a child may eat her supper and go to bed where she lies tossing and turning in anticipation of tomorrow's thrilling treat or dread return to school. In the morning she feels sick over her breakfast. She eventually vomits what is clearly last night's almost unaltered food.

A similar type of vomiting may go with frequent bouts of abdominal pain for which no physical cause can be found (*see* **Abdominal Pain/** Recurrent abdominal pain).

With this sort of vomiting (which may, of course, be associated with motion sickness if the excitement is about something which involves travel), care over what the child eats may be worthwhile. A light meal which is easy to digest, given before her excitement builds to a high peak, may make vomiting less likely.

Vomiting and illness

Some children vomit once or twice at the beginning of almost every infection, even if it is not the digestive system which is under attack. Your child may be sick at the beginning of a cold or whenever she has a fever. If this is not your child's usual pattern and/or she vomits several times, the likelihood is that she has some form of gastro-enteritis or food poisoning (*see* **Diarrhoea, Gastro-enteritis and Food Poisoning**). Seek medical advice if:

She vomits repeatedly. Whatever her other symptoms, this kind of vomiting is exhausting; will prevent her from getting much nourishment even if she eats in between, and may eventually lead to dehydration.

She also has diarrhoea. Losing fluid from both ends makes dehydration very likely. In a baby or small child this is a serious threat to life.

She feels ill and nauseated, even immediately after vomiting.

She has stomach pain although you may not be able to distinguish between pain and nausea in a small child who can seldom tell the difference.

She has fever, with or without diarrhoea, etc. Under these circumstances fever or its absence is a valuable guide. If she has fever then there *is* infection and the vomiting is unlikely to be due to simple ejection of food she could not digest.

Vomiting and injury

Very occasionally a child will vomit after an injury. If she does so more than once, a doctor should see her. She may vomit because of the shock, in which case she should be checked over to make sure that her body can now deal with the after-effects of the shock without help. She may also vomit due to head injury (even if you were not aware that the fall or other accident had affected her skull). In that case medical attention is urgent (*see* **Accidents**/Head injury; Shock).

Vomiting and poisoning   If your child eats or drinks something poisonous, it may make her sick. If it does not, it may be necessary to make her vomit, deliberately, in order to rid her body of it (*See* **Accidents**/Poisoning).

Warts and Veruccae

Warts are harmless growths on the skin due to a virus. There are many different kinds, some of which are easily passed from one child to another. The commonest of these is the Plantar wart, or verucca, which develops on the soles of the feet.

The hands, knees and feet are the most usual sites for warts. They may appear in crops and will eventually vanish even without treatment. This is why there are so many old wives' tales about miracle wart cures: swinging that black cat in the churchyard probably coincided with the spontaneous disappearance of the wart it was meant to 'treat' . . .

Veruccae do spread easily wherever children go barefoot together (as in swimming baths and changing rooms) and, because they are on the sole of the foot and therefore get pressed inwards by the child's weight, do also become painful. A child with a verucca should therefore be kept out of public baths, and be forbidden to go barefoot in public places, unless it is covered with a special waterproof covering. Your doctor or clinic may treat the verucca gradually, by daily application of a special ointment or by soaking the area regularly in formalin. Scraping and cutting is quicker, but can be painful enough to matter and usually needs repeating several times; opt for another method if you can.

Weaning *see* **Eating**/Types of food for babies.
Weight *see* **Growth**. *See also* **Eating**; **Adolescence**/Puberty; **Anorexia Nervosa**.
Wet dreams *see* **Adolescence**/Sex.
Wheezing *see* **Allergy**/Asthma; **Chest Infections**; **Croup and Laryngitis**.

Whooping Cough (Pertussis)

Whooping cough has been a serious scourge among children, and a killer disease in the youngest age groups, for at least two hundred years. Although its incidence has been much reduced by immunization, and its mortality even further reduced by antibiotics effective both against the causative bacillus and against other bacteria causing secondary infections, it is still a very serious illness and by no means one which you should allow yourself to believe has vanished.

Vaccination against whooping cough is carried out with a killed vaccine which is not one hundred per cent effective (although it is very nearly so provided that the full course is given). New strains of the causative bacteria do appear from time to time and therefore fully vaccinated children do succumb to infection, even though their illnesses are usually less severe than those of completely unprotected children. Unfortunately, an attack of whooping cough in a vaccinated child is just as infectious as an attack in an unvaccinated one. Small babies, even in families which have been scrupulous in following the vaccination programme, may get whooping cough from an older brother or sister before their own immunization commences or becomes effective.

While scientists work to produce more effective, safe vaccines and to ensure that all the strains active in the community are included in them, parents must do their part by ensuring that all children are immunized unless their doctors advise against the series of injections for a particular child. Recent publicity given to rare side-effects of the vaccine has led to a reduction in the numbers of infants protected. It may therefore lead to a horrifying upsurge in the incidence of whooping cough in years to come. This year's minor epidemic has already killed more than one infant.

The risks from whooping cough immunization

Very occasionally this vaccine causes convulsions. Much more rarely still it can produce permanent brain damage. While even one such tragedy is one too many, and no affected family can possibly be expected to take an objective view, other families have to try to do so.

The numbers of injections which are followed by convulsions is about one in every 110,000. So the risk of this type of reaction to a child having the basic three injections is one in 37,000, except that the real risk is even lower since if he has no ill-effects from the first dose he is even less likely to suffer from the next. The numbers of injections followed by persistent neurological damage one year later is about one in 310,000. Again, the three-injection child therefore has a risk rate rather less than one in 103,000. If you feel that you should avoid even this minute risk by leaving your child unimmunized, do remember that every family which refuses immunization increases the number of children likely to become infected during an epidemic like the present one, and that the more children who catch whooping cough the higher the chances of their friends catching it too. Of those who do suffer a full-blown attack (rather than the milder form which may occur in immunized children) up to forty per cent of those (rare) babies who catch it in the first six months will die. Amongst older babies and young children, one in each several hundred victims will die, and several more will be left with various, but permanent, forms of lung damage. In protecting your child from the risks of immunization, you may expose him to far greater risks from the disease itself.

Now that the risk of ill-effects on the brain and central nervous system are recognized, whooping cough immunization is already much safer. Your doctor will not give these injections to your baby if he has any other illness at the time. He will not give them if the baby has had convulsions for any other reason. Furthermore, if the first injection should produce a convulsion or any nervous system symptoms such as fever or shakiness, he will not complete the course.

The decision whether or not to accept whooping cough immunization for your baby is yours: there is no legal requirement and nobody should pressure you either way. But if you are doubtful, do at least discuss it with your doctor. If you (or he or all of you) do decide that the baby should not have it, it is vital that your doctor realizes his unprotected status. If an epidemic should approach your community, the baby can be given at least a little protection with hyper-immune gamma globulin (*see* **Infection/** Treatment of infections which cause illness: Anti-viral drugs).

Having Pertussis   **Incubation period.** Ten to fourteen days.

Route of infection. Droplet infection spread by coughing. Bacteria invade the bronchi and the bronchioles – the air passages within the lungs.

First symptoms of whooping cough   Similar to a common cold: runny nose, slight fever, cough. This develops into the typical cough in which there are spasms of barking coughs on an outward breath, followed by the characteristic 'whoop' as the child fights to breathe in again through partially closed air passages.

Acute stage of whooping cough   Coughing spasms may occur dozens of times daily and each may end with the child vomiting. Dehydration, loss of weight and exhaustion are real problems. The child may need to be given tiny quantities of food and drink immediately after a coughing fit in the hopes that he will absorb some nourishment and fluid before the next bout leads to more vomiting.

Some babies fail to take in air quickly enough at the end of a coughing fit. Instead of whooping they may turn greyish-blue and lose consciousness and/or have convulsions.

Treatment of whooping cough   Antibiotics (usually erythromycin) may be effective if given in the very early stages. Sedatives are often given to help the child sleep. Careful checks are kept on the state of his lungs and on his general state.

Excellent nursing care is essential. A baby may need to be held upright through every coughing fit and no child should be left to cough alone in the acute stages. The acute stage is usually over in about three weeks.

Convalescence from whooping cough   In an uncomplicated illness, the characteristic cough will last for a further two to four weeks and the child will need this period to rebuild his strength. If there have been complications, such as pneumonia, the whole illness may last much longer. Many children will continue to cough for as long as two to three months after they have stopped 'whooping'.

● Very young babies, in whom the disease is most dangerous, may never develop that characteristic 'whoop'. The definite diagnosis, which in this case is important, may have to be made by laboratory analysis of a swab taken from far back in the throat.

● Whooping cough in an older child, especially a vaccinated one, may be a much milder illness. If your whooping child is up and about within a few days, do remember the small babies in your community and *keep him away from public places*.

● A serious attack of whooping cough is one of the lengthiest and most demanding illnesses from the nursing point of view. As soon as you know the diagnosis, do try to arrange for regular help and relief.

'Word blindness' *see* **Learning Difficulties and Disabilities**.

Working Mothers

Once upon a time, growing up meant marriage and marriage brought babies. Once babies came, men went out to work to earn money while women stayed at home to care for the children. The greater the man's skill and industry, the more money that family would have; the greater the woman's domestic skill and industry, the more comfort that money would buy. No matter how many exceptions there were, that was the generally expected pattern. If you were a rebel, you at least knew what you were rebelling against.

That expected pattern of adult life is now a horror story (or a fairy tale, depending on your point of view). Women have rebelled, with great success, against a division of labour which carried with it a devastating division of responsibility and power between the sexes. Thanks to the Women's Movement, some major battles for equality of opportunity and of reward have already been won. Few political leaders dare speak against 'women's rights' even if they drag their feet on the way to making those rights into realities.

In capitalist societies with a strong work ethic, equality of opportunity and reward has to be fought for first in the job-market. While women are excluded from the man's world of labour and pay, they are also excluded from decision-making and power. While they depend on male productivity for their own subsistence they are deprived of influence. But even in such industrialized societies, jobs and wages are not the whole of a human being's life. Many women, having won the right and the opportunity to work shoulder-to-shoulder with men and to bring home an equal pay-packet, are discovering that in those areas of life which are traditionally unpaid (and often not regarded as 'work' at all), there is another, perhaps subtler, battle still to be fought. Many, for example, find themselves expected to fit what used to be a full-time female role around the edges of what used to be exclusively a male one. They work a full and equal day yet, when it is over, domestic responsibilities are still left to them, together with civic and community responsibilities, the organization of family leisure and most of the social organization which keeps 'home' running smoothly. Worse, perhaps, than the actual labour left to working women, is the responsibility. Many men, for example, will attend that meeting or give that piece of help to a neighbour *if their partners suggest it*. Far fewer make it their business to know when the meeting is coming up or to keep an eye on the neighbour's needs. Many men will wash up the meal their partners cooked, or even cook the food a partner bought. But far fewer reckon it their business to do the thinking and the shopping which ensures that the wherewithal for a meal is in the house. Above all, when some domestic crisis demands that one or the other take a day off work, it is usually women who are expected to do so.

While a couple live together without children, issues of this kind may be mere pin-pricks or only occasional triggers for trouble. The woman still has some choice over the burdens she is prepared to accept. Most domestic chores can be pared to a minimum; couples do not have to be involved with the community or with their neighbours. There does not even *have* to be a meal, and the absence of food may lead to masculine apologies and a quick trip to the nearest 'take-away'. But once there is a baby, the whole issue of two-way equality between partners, at home as well as at work, becomes much more urgent. Child-care is a non-stop imperative. The battle for the rights of women-who-are-mothers has barely begun.

If society had truly recognized men and women as equal persons, all the labour (paid and unpaid, 'productive' and 'personal') which needed to be done would have been pooled for sharing, both according to need and choice, amongst all the available adults. But when it comes to a baby's need for adult attention or instant availability during every moment of each twenty-four hours, it becomes clear that this kind of social organization is still far away. There are many men who would like to take a full share in bringing up their children and who recognize that two adults can meet a child's needs while doing a job outside the home and, hopefully, having fun, too. Some strive to make such a life-pattern work within their families, but strive they must. They are flying against social expectations and can expect little support. There are many forms of communal living designed to aid this kind of whole-life sharing. But against social pressure, few survive from generation to generation. There are nibbles at the conventional 'working day' in the form of 'job-sharing' and 'flexi-time', but vital though these are as possible models for the future, they are far commoner in the media than in real life and more often promulgated as an aid to working mothers than as a more satisfactory or equitable life for us all. There are even some attempts to give men and women equal choice in life-activities. But where these are applied to people-who-are-parents, they are referred to as 'role-swapping'. Could there be a clearer indication of society's view of child-care as still basically a female role? Or of its inability to understand the need for pooled labour? It may suit a particular couple to reverse responsibility for wage-earning and child-care, but it leaves untouched the basic dilemma of being available both to a child and to a paid job. However much a man wants to share children with his partner, society (whether in the form of his friends, his colleagues or his superiors) does not expect the man-who-is-a-father to behave any differently from the man who is not. Whereas a woman who takes a day off work because her child is ill may face disapproval from her boss, a man will face an amazement which may begin in amusement but will quickly lead to worse. Where a woman who is known to have a child to collect from a minder at the end of the working day will usually make a punctual escape, a man may meet real obstruction. He is supposed to put his work first and not dilute that concern with inconvenient family matters. It will often be suggested to him that his refusal of overtime, or of that after-work drink, is a serious barrier to promotion. Even within the world of people who are caring for young children, fathers may find themselves less than welcome. As one put it, after first accompanying his child to playgroup: 'All parents are welcome unless they are male'. That old-style 'woman's world' can be as difficult for a man to break into as was the 'man's world' for women.

Every woman who is (or is going to be) somebody's mother, has to find a personal solution to the dilemma posed by doing, or not doing, a paid job while coping with child-care. Individual circumstances, ranging from partners' attitudes to personal earning-power, make such an overwhelming difference that no general guidance can make sense for all. There are, however, some common problems and problematical social attitudes which you may meet.

Planning in pregnancy   Of course it is sensible to try to plan ahead, but many women regret commitments made in advance once the baby is born. Try to keep some options open, for example:

Think carefully before you accept generous maternity leave and pay in exchange for a guaranteed date on which you will be back at your job. When the time comes you may not want to return. On the other hand, try not to close the door of your work-place finally behind you in your seventh month. If you want to go back later you will have a better chance if your personnel file is still open and if you have discussed possibilities, such as part-time and/or home-based work, with the firm.

Don't rely in your planning on casual offers of day-care, whether from a childminder who can 'always make room' or a neighbour who is 'always at home and pleased to help'. Only a booked place or firm agreement, tied down to the last detail, is worth having.

Build breast-feeding into your thinking. If you want to breast-feed and are doing so happily, you probably will not want to stop. A workplace nursery might enable you to go on, but without it, breast-feeding probably means no outside work . . . (*see* **Eating**/Types of food for babies).

Make sure you get your sums right. Many women who feel they must get back to work as soon as possible for financial reasons discover, over a few stressful months, that the nett gain to the family from their work is almost nil. Make sure you allow for hidden costs like travel to and from a minder as well as to and from work; lunch-hour shopping in comparatively expensive places and uneconomic quantities; convenience foods because you are always in a rush and even placatory treats for other children/partners/minders, because you are always late.

Beware of people who tell you what you should do or what you will do. There are grains of truth in all those contradictory statements like 'every baby needs his mother' and 'women who are content to be "just mothers" are traitors to their sex'. But only you can sift those grains from the over-generalized rhetoric, and put together something that feels true for you. 'You'll never be happy at home, dedicated to your job as you are' and 'of course, you've always longed for the domestic bit . . .' are almost as damaging. Let them all wait and see.

Babies and day-care   Making arrangements for a baby, as opposed to an older child, can be truly agonizing. You may find yourself caught between people who suggest that you will harm your baby if you leave him for a second and people who insist that it is better for babies to be cared for by 'experts'. Both camps will tend to ignore two vital factors: your *own* feelings which may make it quite impossible for you to leave him happily, and the non-existence of those 'experts' which, in many areas, will mean that there is nowhere to leave him.

If you are looking for somewhere to leave him, make your decisions by considering your own relationship with him in terms of his development.

Early learning seems to take place mainly through a baby's interaction with known and loved adults. A lot of recent research has shown that, right from the beginning, a baby does not only *react to* a friendly talking adult but also influences that adult: their interaction is always two-way. You may assume that your baby smiles at you because you are smiling at him, but the truth is just as likely to be that you are smiling because he smiled . . . You may be amazed at yourself for making silly noises at him when you intended never to use 'babytalk', but most of your sounds are copies of his, and that special, high-pitched rhythmical tone you use is not idiocy but the most effective form of verbal communication with a two-month-old human. Adults believe that they provide an environment for a baby, but every baby plays a large part in shaping his environment for himself, and that includes him working to adjust your behaviour to match today's needs, shaped by yesterday's interaction.

This two-way influence is probably the most important contributory factor to a baby's overall development, after the maintenance of health through adequate physical care. You and your behaviour act, so to speak, as a mirror in which he can see himself and his world. He cries; you pick him up and he stops crying and gurgles at you instead. Through your facial expressions, your body-movements, your voice-tones and your readiness to join in the gurgling but not the crying, he learns some important things about crying and about the effects of his behaviour on you. Through the day you bring him little bits of the world to consider, and you shield him from other bits; as you do so you interpret that world for him. Consciously and unconsciously you interpret larger slices of the world which are as yet far beyond his understanding. It is by watching your consistent reaction, for example, that he learns to regard the tele-phone bell as a sound which is alerting but not alarming.

The two-way influence of earliest infancy is the beginning of almost every kind of learning which will be important to the child later on. The early smiles and 'conversations' are the prototypes of later communica-tion and he uses from the beginning the 'rules' which he will use forever (*see* **Language**). He utters and then pauses, waiting for your response, fitting his next utterance to it or ending the interaction, as he will always do, by looking away. Those first games with fingers and toes and toys are prototypes for later cooperation. He 'takes turns', 'shares' and waits, at three months, for the climax of 'this little piggy' as he will wait at three years for the climax of a joke and at thirty-three for the punch-line of a story. Because his behaviour *evokes responses which are consistent*, he learns vital lessons about cause and effect and above all about his own effective-ness. As one British psychologist put it: 'A baby must learn "I see this, I do that and X happens"' (*see* **Play**/Playthings for babies). If your baby is to have the best possible opportunity for this kind of development, he therefore needs:

Consistent care. The mirror in which he sees himself and his own behaviour and the behaviour of his world should always give him the same image, and therefore enable him to build up expectations and cause and effect relationships.

A baby who is cared for within his own family will get this without anybody thinking about it, but a baby who is cared for by a lot of different people (however 'expert') may not, because each new person will react and interact in different ways so that he is presented with different images. He cannot use a stranger until she becomes a familiar.

Continuous care. Babies develop extremely fast but in minute steps, each of which is clear to an adult who sees him constantly, but may be invisible to one who hardly knows him or has not seen him for days, so that the intermediate steps are in the past. Not only does he need to be cared for by the same people all the time, he also needs to see each person who is important in his life, frequently. Every grandmother knows that a month's absence from a baby can make you, for these emotional purposes, into a stranger.

Sufficient care. As well as enough physical care, he needs enough of this consistent and continuous social attention to make the best possible use of his own capacity to signal and receive signals. In a group, for example, he may always be cared for by the same people but, because he must compete with too many other babies, he may simply not get as much attention as he can use.

If your baby is to be cared for by someone outside the family for the whole of every adult day, he may not be best served by group-care, even if there is a purpose-built nursery full of lovely equipment and trained staff available to you. Even a staff–child ratio of one to three does not assure him of this kind of care because it is not only the *numbers* of available staff which matter to him but *who they are* and whether they were there yesterday and will be there tomorrow. He may be better off with a replacement for you, either in his own home (if you have an otherwise unemployed relative or the money to employ someone) or in the home of a member of that much-maligned species: the childminder.

But if he is only to be cared for outside the family for much shorter periods of a few hours at a time, that basic continuous interactive relationship will be rolling along within the family during all the hours at home, and the lack of some part of it during those group hours may not matter. Certainly, whatever the 'babies need their mothers' camp may imply, you will not harm your baby either by sharing his care with someone prepared to act as 'substitute mother' when you are absent, or by sharing it occasionally with someone who cannot be a complete love-object to him. You may like to bear in mind the fact that demands for mothers to care for their babies *alone and constantly* are a recent phenomenon. In our own society in the past, and in many societies today, a baby's care was always shared between mothers, elder sisters, grandmothers, and so forth. It is only we who, by suggesting a twenty-four hour a day, three hundred and sixty-five day a year commitment for mothers, have made 'good mothering' seem impossible.

Job factors which help or hinder   Most working mothers, whatever the ages of their children, walk a continuous tightrope through daily life so that even the minutest slip or alteration of balance spells disaster. These are some of the (often trivial-seeming) factors which seem to make a difference to many:

Distance/travel. The basic problem is that you really need to be in two places at once. The closer together those places are, the more nearly you can achieve this miracle. The two places may be work and home, or work and minder/nursery/school. Close in *time* matters more than distance, but means of transport matters too because a ten-minute train ride exposes you to the vagaries of weather, strikes, etc. So strong is this factor that many women prefer to take a less satisfactory job nearer home. Many of us believe that jobs within local communities should be offered first to local mothers. Perhaps increasing numbers of female *employers* will adopt this attitude. Workplace nurseries can help, too.

Attitudes to you as a mother. Employers and colleagues vary wildly in their attitudes, of course, but ideally you need a job where a certain priority for your children is not just *allowed* but positively *expected*. You will not always find this in obvious places. A child development research unit may be soullessly grudging where the local bank manager positively insists that you attend every sports day 'because she will be sad if you aren't there. . .' A welcome for occasionally visiting children, and helpfulness when they telephone you, usually goes with this.

Possibility of fulfilling work-obligations at home. However nice they may be about it, letting down colleagues is no fun and during a winter full of colds and tonsillitis *you* may feel that you have not earned your wage even if they do not. If you can take work home and do it, if necessary, in the middle of the night, this whole area is much more comfortable. Of course you cannot take a production line home, but many women do manage in a variety of jobs. Typing or telephoning can both be done at home as, of course, can all kinds of work involving reading, writing memos and reports, etc. Teachers can prepare and mark work even when they cannot be in school for lessons. Some women find their lives much improved when they manage to accumulate special work-equipment at home for this reason. If you have a piano, your music pupils can come to you; a drawing board means you need not be late with those designs.

Emergency communications. A job at which you cannot be reached is alarming for you and may be alarming for your child or his caretakers, too. You really do need the number of a telephone which will always be manned and from which somebody will always bring you a message.

Hours and their organization. Few mothers can comfortably hold down absolutely full-time jobs especially if they also involve travel-time and your physical presence.

You may be able to manage full-time *hours* if you are able to have some flexibility (formal or informal) about when you fulfil them. Three long days and two half-days, for example, may make for a much easier pattern of home life than five ordinary-length days.

Part-time work is a usual compromise but can be of dubious value. You may lose a disproportionate amount of money for the amount of time you save, and some part-time workers get passed over for promotion and plum assignments, too. Part-time work in shops and so forth may not fit well with family life because you may be needed at work just at the times when you are most needed at home – on Saturdays, for example.

If an employer really wants you (and sadly, in the present state of the job-market, he may not care very much whether he has you or somebody else), he may be willing to accept a variety of easements. Various women swear by each of the following:

Full-time work for full pay but with acceptance of the principle that while the work must always be completed, when it is finished (or slack/non-existent) they do not have to be there. Work, in other words, with no time-clock to punch. Formalized 'flexi-hours' make this approach possible even where the job involves somebody being there to answer the telephone or deal with the public. One such scheme demands that every employee be 'in' from 11 a.m. to 2 p.m. Beyond that commitment, each sets his/her own hours.

Job-sharing, such that the employer does not care which of two or three of you is there as long as one is. Sometimes two women-who-are-mothers (or two parents if the job pays enough) can work this out very satisfactorily. You might want to do mornings while your pre-school child is at kindergarten; afternoons might suit your friend and colleague because her baby usually sleeps then. Either of you can stand in for the other, at work or at home, during domestic crises.

Shift work, so that however inconvenient and difficult life may be this month, it will be easier (or at least different) next. Some parents work shifts which fit together so that one is always available to the children; but they do not tend to be very available to each other . . . Some women – especially those with older children – do permanent night work and reckon that they can leave home after a pleasant family evening, be home to see everybody off for the day, and then get enough sleep before they come home again . . .

Working at home and/or self-employment

For many women, bringing the demands of work and home together in one place proves a tremendous relief because it not only gets rid of most of the obvious conflict, but it also remoulds life into a coherent whole so that the woman feels like a whole person instead of one who is chopped into little bits. It can improve home life, too, by making it feel like part of life instead of a retirement from it. As jobs get harder to find, more and more people, men and women, are 'setting up on their own', and many believe that the days of the big central organization to which workers flock each day, are numbered. We may all work at, or from, home if the micro-computer people have their way.

But not only is this not possible for everyone, some people find that they dislike it. 'Out-work' has a bad reputation in Britain, as drudgery for peanuts, and you certainly need to be careful before you take on home-knitting or craft assignments, for example. Some find that working at home does them out of the adult company they crave, while others just find it impossible to wear a mother-hat and a worker-hat at the same time.

Work and schoolchildren

It is a myth that working outside the home becomes easier for mothers once their children are at school. In many cases it actually gets more difficult.

However hard they may be to find, day-care facilities for younger children are at least intended to cater for them while you work. Schools do not even pretend to do so, because their stated purpose is the child's education and there is therefore no compulsion on them to concern themselves with any aspect of your convenience.

School hours are short compared to full-time adult work.

School terms are interrupted, not only by half-term breaks and holidays, but also by unforeseeable extras like days when the school building is being used for election booths.

Schools demand greater or lesser participation from parents which may include day-time meetings and so forth. Children whose parents can *never* come may be at a disadvantage (*see* **School**).

Schoolchildren, especially young ones, get ill quite frequently and when they are ill they cannot go to school.

Some people believe that schools should be adapted to fit more closely into the needs of the adult working day and a large number of holiday play-schemes and after-school clubs are being tried in different areas. Other people feel that the school day and year is already quite long enough for many children, and/or that school as a place of education is diluted or disturbed if 'custodial care' is intermingled with it. They would prefer to see the work-world adapted to the school . . . Whatever is available to you, and whatever your own (and your children's) views, do make sure that proper arrangements of some kind are made. Suppose that there is a holiday play-scheme for your child for four weeks of the summer holidays, who will be with him for the other three weeks? If you take your annual leave then, what will happen at Christmas? If you are fortunate enough to live in the kind of neighbourhood where all the children play together and are in and out of each other's houses anyway, you may be able to leave yours with the gang, knowing that some adult will feed them and cope in a crisis. But that kind of life is sadly rare, especially in large cities. Children who are left to fend for themselves all day and every day *do* have more accidents than supervised children; *do* get into trouble with the law more often; *do* suffer from having responsibility for even younger ones imposed on them and *do* get extremely bored and lonely.

Coping with illness   If your holiday arrangements are all right, your child's illnesses may be your main problem. Various women use combinations of the following:

An occasional 'babysitter' (often a retired person) who is happy to be called upon for the occasional day or two to supervise a child in his own home. Some children like some sitters; some tolerate and some detest.

Staying at home and telling employers that they themselves are ill (thought better than allowing bosses any excuse for not employing women-who-are-mothers).

Leaving the child in bed and keeping in touch by telephone (and sometimes by visiting during lunch hours).

Taking the sick child to a relative, neighbour or one-time minder, who does not mind having him as long as she does not have to come out.

Sending the child to school all the same hoping that he will be 'all right' and knowing that if he is not, the school will not send him home if there is nobody there to look after him. (In real illness, though, this only copes with the first day. The child tends to bring a stiff note home with him at the end of it.)

Staying home from work and taking the necessary days as part of annual leave or paid holiday. That may ruin carefully laid plans for coping with the child's next holiday, though.

Staying home from work and asking to have it counted as unpaid or compassionate leave (many find that a decent boss accepts the gesture but does not keep back the money).

Obviously all these measures depend on entirely individual factors like how old/ill/unhappy the child is, and so forth. But, as a bunch, they do serve to illustrate the extreme conflict in which women-who-are-mothers-and-workers often find themselves.

'Latch-key children'   This emotive term is used to describe children who come home from school and let themselves in because there is nobody there to open the door. Is that really so bad?

Again, the only honest answer must be that it depends on your child and your exact circumstances. The emotive term has caught on, especially in Britain, because not having an adult at home after school often *goes with* not having enough adult attention at other times. But, of course, these two things don't have to be linked at all. If your child is at an age and stage where he himself is entirely happy to be first home, and is clearly unlikely to do anything dangerous while he is alone, it will probably be perfectly all right. You may want to try and work out a different plan if:

He is not happy about it, especially if he tends to be frightened of the dark, nervous of noises, etc. It certainly will not be good for him to come home each day to day-mares, in which his imagination fills the house with monsters (*see* **Anxiety, Fears and Phobias**).

He will be expected to look after younger children as well as himself. If those younger children would not be safe alone, it may not be fair to leave them with him, routinely. He might be late; they might refuse to do what he told them, and if anything goes wrong he will feel desperately guilty.

You feel you have to put all kinds of restrictions on him to make it safe. Some children, for example, are forbidden to make themselves a cup of tea or coffee, or to switch on the fire until an adult comes home. In winter that is a pretty miserable prospect for a cold tired child.

He is not, at the moment, happy at school. Not only can a solitary return home be a depressing prospect when a child is facing a depressing day, the fact that you are not there may also mean that he never discusses his miseries with you while they are fresh in his mind (*see* **School**/Problems over going to school).

You would not, under other circumstances, want him to do the journey home alone (*see* **Safety**/On the road).

While a lot of children are, sadly, left to fend for themselves perhaps for several hours after school, the following compromises work well for many families:

The child who is expected to do homework either stays and does it at school (which many schools will allow as there are usually some staff in the building in charge of after-school activities) or goes and does it at the local public library until it is time to meet you on your return.

The child comes and collects you from work (geography permitting) which may have the advantage not only of sociability but of making it clear to your work-mates when it is time for you to go.

The child comes home alone on one or two days of the week but has after-school clubs, or dates with friends, on other days.

He goes and has tea with a friend or neighbour and is either collected from there or leaves in time to meet you at home.

He comes home alone but has an open invitation to visit the house next door if he wishes, and an obligation to do so in any kind of crisis. ('Keeping an eye out for children' is a very valuable skill which the best neighbours develop to a high level and will share.)

He comes home alone and you telephone him as you leave work so that he can walk to meet you.

The child comes home and leaves a note to say where he is going and is then free to play (within agreed limits) with friends, until a specified time after your return.

Miscellaneous additional problems   **Careful planning and arrangements may be ruined for you if your children are at different schools with different holiday dates.** One London mother of three recently enjoyed a spring term in which all the children were at school at the same time *for only two weeks* . . . Everything else being equal, this may be a strong argument for sending your children to the same school whenever the age-gaps make this possible. Otherwise, you can sometimes effectively get together with other parents to put pressure on local schools to cooperate over dates (*see* **School**/Choosing a secondary school).

Sometimes children 'old enough to manage' cannot safely and happily be left to manage together because they quarrel so. You are unlikely to be able to stop them tormenting each other, or even to be sure what is whose fault. Brothers and sisters do not always like each other (or like each other all through childhood) and there may be a real personality clash or problem in the balance of power. Sad and infuriating though it may seem, you will probably have to make separate arrangements for each one. Children change, though. If you do arrange separate after-school 'time-tables', you may suddenly find them saying, 'why can't we just come straight home together?' and this time they may do so companionably.

Worms

Many types of worm can live as more-or-less damaging parasites in human intestines. In the UK, only the harmless threadworm is at all common. Threadworms look like tiny pieces of (lively) white thread and are usually discovered when a child passes a stool in which myriads are moving. It is revulsion rather than physical damage which may give him a stomachache; if he is so young that it is you who wipes his bottom and discovers the worms, *don't show them to him*. He will have to know about them because he will have to be treated, but he need not look. . . An older child who discovers threadworms will probably be horrified. Do explain that the infestation is common, can happen to anyone, is nothing to do with being 'dirty' and can easily be dealt with.

Threadworms'
life-cycle

A child may get threadworm eggs on his fingers when he holds hand with another infested child (*see below*). When he sucks those fingers he swallows some eggs and they hatch in his intestine.

Female worms are fertilized while in his gut, but they like to emerge from the anus and lay their eggs outside the body when it is very warm. The most usual time is when the child is warmly snuggled in bed. The females return through the back passage, but the eggs remain. If the child scratches and then sucks his fingers, he will re-infest himself. If he goes to school with eggs under his fingernails, he may pass them to somebody else.

Coping with
threadworms

Ask your doctor for a prescription for whichever medicine he prefers for threadworms. They are all effective but vary in dosage, taste and any mild side-effects such as diarrhoea.

Every member of the family must take the medicine otherwise it may clear one child of heavy infestation but leave another who is already harbouring a few worms, to re-infest him and all of you.

Dosage is by weight. Your doctor will prescribe enough for all of you but you will have to work out how much each member of the family should have. Your chemist will help if you ask when you collect the medicine.

While the medicine does its job: get the child to cut his fingernails short in case there are eggs trapped there, and suggest that he sleep in close-fitting underpants for a few nights so that if he scratches, he will not pick up more eggs, suck his fingers and re-infest himself.

Wounds *see* **Accidents**.
X-ray *see* **Hospital**/Procedures. *See also* **Growth**/Children who are 'too small'; Children who are 'too tall'.